of the World

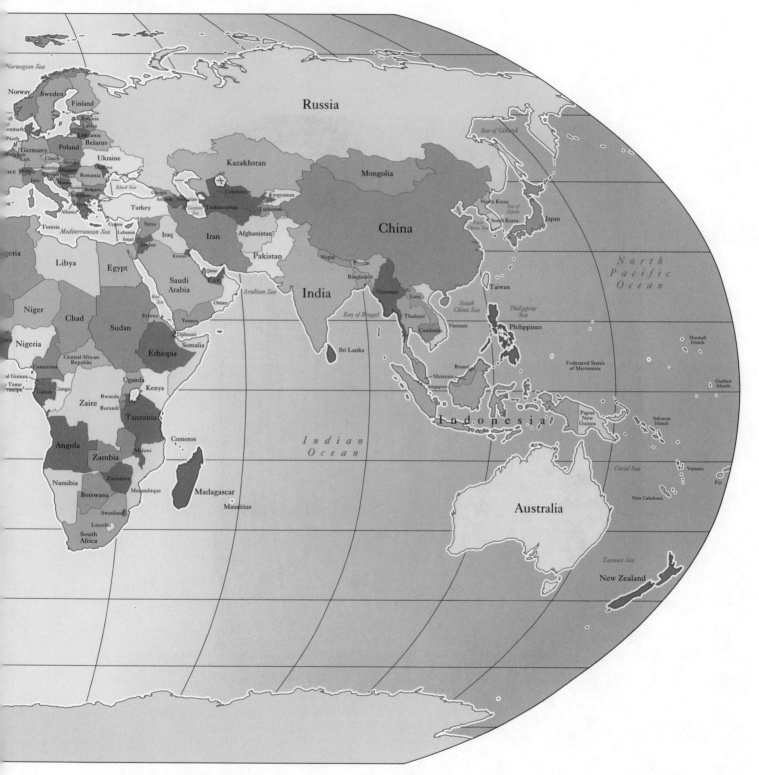

Norwegian Sea

Norway
Sweden
Finland
Estonia
Latvia
Lithuania
Belarus
Germany
Poland
Ukraine
Denmark
Neth.
Lux.
Belgium
Czech
Slovakia
Moldova
Austria
Hungary
Switz.
Slovenia
Romania
Italy
Bosnia
Serbia
Bulgaria
Macedonia
Albania
Greece

Russia

Kazakhstan

Mongolia

Sea of Okhotsk

Turkey
Black Sea
Georgia
Armenia
Azerbaijan
Uzbekistan
Kyrgyzstan
Turkmenistan
Tajikistan
Caspian Sea

North Korea
Sea of Japan
South Korea
Japan
East China Sea

Tunisia
Mediterranean Sea
Cyprus
Lebanon
Israel
Syria
Jordan
Iraq
Iran
Afghanistan
Pakistan
Nepal
Bhutan
China

Libya
Egypt
Kuwait
Qatar
U.A.E.
Saudi Arabia
Red Sea
Oman
Arabian Sea
India
Bangladesh
Myanmar
Taiwan

North Pacific Ocean

Niger
Chad
Sudan
Eritrea
Yemen
Djibouti
Somalia
Laos
Thailand
South China Sea
Philippine Sea

Nigeria
Central African Republic
Ethiopia
Bay of Bengal
Cambodia
Vietnam
Philippines

Marshall Islands

al Guinea
Cameroon
Sao Tome Principe
Gabon
Congo
Uganda
Rwanda
Burundi
Kenya
Zaire
Tanzania
Sri Lanka
Malaysia
Brunei
Singapore
Federated States of Micronesia
Gialbert Islands

Angola
Zambia
Malawi
Comoros
Indonesia
Papua New Guinea
Solomon Islands

Namibia
Zimbabwe
Botswana
Mozambique
Madagascar
Mauritius
Indian Ocean
Coral Sea
Vanuatu
Fiji
New Caledonia

Swaziland
Lesotho
South Africa
Australia

Tasman Sea
New Zealand

ENCYCLOPEDIA OF U.S. FOREIGN RELATIONS

ENCYCLOPEDIA OF
U.S. FOREIGN
RELATIONS

SENIOR EDITORS

Bruce W. Jentleson   Thomas G. Paterson

PREPARED UNDER THE AUSPICES OF THE

Council on Foreign Relations

SENIOR CONSULTING EDITOR

Nicholas X. Rizopoulos

VOLUME 3

Oxford University Press
New York   Oxford
1997

OXFORD UNIVERSITY PRESS

Oxford   New York
Athens   Auckland   Bangkok   Bogotá   Bombay   Buenos Aires
Calcutta   Cape Town   Dar es Salaam   Delhi   Florence   Hong Kong
Istanbul   Karachi   Kuala Lumpur   Madras   Madrid   Melbourne
Mexico City   Nairobi   Paris   Singapore   Taipei   Tokyo   Toronto

and associated companies in
Berlin   Ibadan

Published by Oxford University Press, Inc.,
198 Madison Avenue, New York, New York 10016

Oxford is a registered trademark of Oxford University Press

Library of Congress Cataloging-in-Publication Data
Encyclopedia of U.S. foreign relations / senior editors, Bruce W.
Jentleson, Thomas G. Paterson.
p. cm.
Includes bibliographical references and index.
1. United States—Foreign relations—Encyclopedias. 2. United
States—Relations—Encyclopedias. I. Jentleson, Bruce W., 1951-.
II. Paterson, Thomas G., 1941-.
E183.7.E53   1997   96-8159   327.73—dc20   CIP
ISBN 0-19-511055-2 (4-vol. set)
ISBN 0-19-511058-7 (vol. 3)

Printing (last digit): 9 8 7 6 5 4 3 2 1

Printed in the United States of America
on acid-free paper

K

KAL-007 INCIDENT
(31 August 1983)

The destruction of Korean Air Lines Flight 007 by a Soviet air-to-air missile near Sakhalin Island, in the former Soviet Union. This event became emblematic of the renewed Cold War tension between the United States and the Soviet Union during the first term of President Ronald Reagan. Shrouded in charges and countercharges for years, the mystery of what led the airliner to stray over Soviet air space and why it was destroyed has probably been resolved by Russian president Boris Yeltsin's release in 1993 of the in-flight data recordings found by the Soviets amid the plane's wreckage.

The flight originated in New York on 30 August. The Boeing 747 jet stopped that night in Anchorage, Alaska, for refueling en route to Seoul, South Korea. A series of sloppy navigational errors by the pilot and crew shortly after takeoff caused the plane to fly some 300 miles north of its intended trans-Pacific route. As a result, the airliner flew for more than two hours over Kamchatka and Sakhalin, two particularly sensitive Soviet military centers along the Pacific coast. Throughout this dangerous passage, the Korean flight crew had no idea that it had flown off course into forbidden air space. Soviet air defense tracked the "intruder" for several hours before ordering its destruction. Radar operators initially thought the plane might be a U.S. RC-135 reconnaissance aircraft observed earlier that night just outside Soviet air space. That spy plane sought to monitor a scheduled but later canceled missile test near Kamchatka. Soviet pilots and ground controllers, unsure what they were tracking, made some effort to identify KAL-007. The fighter pilot pursuing the airliner noted that it flew with its navigation lights on, hardly expected of a spy plane. Nonetheless, Soviet rules of engagement specified that air defense forces shoot down any intruder that failed to heed a warning. Pursuit planes attempted to signal the airliner and even fired warning shots, none of which the Korean crew saw or heard. Having made a minimal effort to identify the target, local commanders ordered the Sukhoi-15 fighter pilot to act. He fired two missiles, which struck the 747. The airliner spiraled down for several minutes and crashed in the Pacific, killing 269 passengers and crew, including Representative Larry P. McDonald, a Georgia Democrat.

President Reagan immediately denounced the downing as an "act of barbarism" directed "against the world and the moral precepts which guide human relations among people everywhere." Soviet leaders, he charged, had deliberately and without warning destroyed a civilian airliner that had innocently strayed over their territory, violating every norm of civilized behavior. Although Soviet leader Yuri Andropov and his defense chiefs defended their action by countercharging that KAL-007 had been deliberately sent off course to spy on or provoke the Soviet Union, the Kremlin leadership concluded that navigational error probably accounted for the intrusion. They were reluctant, however, to admit their own errors and their paltry effort to identify the plane. Soon after the incident, U.S. intelligence also concluded that the Soviets had initially believed that the intruder was a military or spy plane and realized their error too late. Although Reagan and his aides soon learned that mistaken identity and bureaucratic rigidity probably accounted for the tragedy, they did not amend their original assertions. As the president later admitted, the incident "gave badly needed impetus in Congress to the rearmament programs and postponed . . . attempts to gut our efforts to restore American military might." For almost a decade Moscow kept secret the fact that it had recovered the KAL-007 flight recorders. Analysis of the data confirmed that the airliner had flown off course through pilot error.

MICHAEL SCHALLER

See also Cold War; Reagan, Ronald Wilson

FURTHER READING

Hersh, Seymour. *The Target Is Destroyed: What Really Happened to Flight 007.* New York, 1987.

Sayle, Murray. "Closing the File on Flight 007." *New Yorker* 69 (13 Dec. 1993): 90–101.

KAMPUCHEA
See Cambodia

KATANGA
See Zaire

KAZAKHSTAN

See Appendix 2

KELLEY, ROBERT

(*b.* 13 February 1894; *d.* 2 June 1976)

State Department official who helped define U.S. policy toward Bolshevik Russia during the 1920s and 1930s. Born in Somerville, Massachusetts, and educated at Harvard University, Kelley's tenure with the government began when he joined the U.S. Army in October 1917. After more than four years in the military, two as assistant military attaché for Denmark and Finland, Kelley entered the foreign service as vice counsel to the U.S. consulate in Calcutta, India. A student and admirer of Czarist Russia, Kelley became alarmed by the Bolshevik government's consolidation of power. Concerned about the possibility of Soviet territorial expansion, he persuaded the State Department in 1924 of the need to train experts to analyze Soviet foreign policy. The following year Kelley was promoted to assistant chief of the division of Eastern European affairs and was entrusted with the training of these analysts. Instead of training them in Soviet politics and ideology, however, Kelley concentrated on traditional subjects, particularly Russian culture, history, and language.

In 1926 Kelley became chief of the Eastern European division of the State Department. He not only established an impressive library on Russian and Soviet affairs, which, according to Soviet foreign minister Maxim Litvinov, possessed better resources than the Soviet Foreign Office, but also trained future foreign policy leaders such as George F. Kennan and Charles Bohlen.

Responding to the possibility of a U.S.-Soviet rapprochement in 1933, Kelley drafted a series of memorandums entitled, "Problems Pertaining to Russian-American Relations," which explained the difficulties facing the reestablishment of diplomatic relations with Russia. The memorandums addressed three issues: Soviet support of Communism in the United States, the protection of legal rights of U.S. nationals in Russia, and the settlement of Russia's debt. To lend credence to his argument, and to delay recognition until these problems were solved, Kelley emphasized the complications that France and Great Britain had encountered in their negotiations with the Soviets. Despite his efforts, Kelley lost the debate over recognition as the United States restored diplomatic ties with Russia in November 1933.

While Kelley's distrust of the Soviets won supporters within the State Department during the 1930s, he alienated influential members of the Roosevelt administration, including the president. In May 1937 the Eastern and Western European divisions of the State Department merged, and Kelley was sent to the embassy in Ankara, Turkey. He remained the embassy's counselor until 1945, when he left the foreign service and returned to private life.

Scott D. Keller

See also Bohlen, Charles Eustis; Kennan, George Frost; Roosevelt, Franklin Delano; Russia and the Soviet Union; Turkey

FURTHER READING

Biship, Donald G. *The Roosevelt-Litvinov Agreements: The American View*. Syracuse, N.Y., 1965.

Browder, Robert Paul. *The Origins of Soviet-American Diplomacy*. Princeton, N.J., 1953.

Harvey, Moses L., and Foy D. Kohler. *The Soviet Union: Yesterday, Today and Tomorrow*. Coral Gables, Fla., 1975.

Kennan, George F. *Memoirs, 1925–1950*. Boston, 1967.

KELLOGG, FRANK BILLINGS

(*b.* 22 December 1856; *d.* 31 December 1937)

Secretary of state (1925–1929). Born in Potsdam, New York, Kellogg moved to Minnesota in 1865 and worked on his parents' farm, from which rugged labors arose his decision to become a lawyer. He passed the bar in 1877. A railroad attorney, he eventually became a special assistant to the U.S. attorney general (1906) and presented the government's antitrust case against Standard Oil. As a progressive Republican U.S. senator (1917–1923), Kellogg supported entry into World War I and became a "mild reservationist" regarding U.S. membership in the League of Nations. A brief stint as ambassador to England (1923–1925) gave him some diplomatic experience prior to his becoming secretary of state in March 1925. White hair, hand tremors, one sightless eye, and a hot temper earned Kellogg the sobriquet "Nervous Nellie." His hyperbolic explanation for U.S. intervention in Nicaragua in early 1927, entitled "Bolshevik Aims and Policies in Mexico and Latin America," persuaded few as he conjured up a communist plot to justify the deployment of U.S. Marines against Augusto César Sandino's rebel forces. Kellogg's legal background influenced him to substitute law for force in international affairs, and he negotiated nineteen arbitration and thirteen conciliation agreements as secretary of state. He won the Nobel Peace Prize for the Kellogg-Briand Pact of 1928, through which Aristide Briand's (France's foreign minister) original proposal for a bilateral security treaty evolved into a multilateral treaty, signed by sixty-two nations, which outlawed war as "an instrument of national policy." The subsequent failure of this agreement to prevent World War II prompted critics to call Kellogg naive, but peace advocates at the time hailed the popular pact as a first step in a long process toward peace. After his retirement from the Department of State, Kellogg served as a judge on the World Court until 1935.

J. GARRY CLIFFORD

See also Arbitration; Kellogg-Briand Pact; Nicaragua; Nobel Peace Prize; Permanent Court of International Justice; Sandino, Augusto César; World War I

FURTHER READING

DiBenedetti, Charles. *Origins of the Modern American Peace Movement, 1915–1929*. Milwood, N.Y., 1978.
Ellis, L. Ethan. *Frank B. Kellogg and American Foreign Relations, 1925–1929*. Brunswick, N.J., 1961.
Ferrell, Robert H. *Peace in Their Time*. New Haven, Conn., 1952.
———. *Frank B. Kellogg and Henry L. Stimson*. New York, 1963.

KELLOGG-BRIAND PACT

The first international agreement ever created with the intention of replacing war with conflict resolution. On 27 August 1928, the leaders of fifteen nations, including the United States, signed the treaty in Paris. Within a few years, sixty-two nations had signed the pact, including the United States, France, Germany, the United Kingdom, Italy, Japan, and the Soviet Union. The U.S. Congress ratified it on 17 January 1929, and President Herbert Hoover signed it into law on 24 July.

The Kellogg-Briand Pact was born out of international disgust with the carnage of World War I. At first, French foreign minister Aristide Briand approached U.S. secretary of state Frank B. Kellogg about a French-U.S. treaty to renounce war between France and the United States. Briand hoped the pact would help France deter a possible German invasion. Kellogg rejected the idea, offering instead a treaty which would ward off war altogether. As the preamble to the pact states, the signees were "persuaded" that the time had come "when a frank renunciation of war as an instrument of national policy should be made." Hoping to encourage other nations to follow their example, the original signees pledged to settle "all disputes or conflicts of whatever nature or of whatever origin…by pacific means." The treaty did not include enforcement powers or prescribe certain responsibilities.

The Kellogg-Briand Pact said nothing about wars of self-defense, yet all the signatories assumed that the agreement did not cover such events. International leaders openly interpreted the pact to be null and void if their nations were invaded. U.S. pacifists, especially those belonging to the American Committee for the Outlawry of War and the Women's Peace Union, termed the pact, "the beginning of the end of war;" and although

critical of its potential pitfalls, worked ceaselessly to educate people about its meaning and to press governmental leaders to put it into practice. Critics dismissed the treaty as ineffectual moralizing. The Senate nonetheless voted 85 to 1 on 15 January 1929 for approval.

During the 1930s, as fascism spread throughout Europe and imperialistic conflict escalated in Asia, the Kellogg-Briand Pact was often cited, but it did nothing to prevent the actual outbreak of war. World War II effectively put the agreement to rest. However, its legacy, that of resolving conflicts through peaceful negotiation, has stood as an ideal in international relations to this day.

HARRIET HYMAN ALONSO

See also France; Kellogg, Frank Billings; Peace Movements and Societies, 1914 to Present

FURTHER READING

Alonso, Harriet Hyman. *The Women's Peace Union and the Outlawry of War, 1921–1942*. Syracuse, N.Y., 1996.
Ferrell, Robert H. *Peace in Their Time: The Origins of the Kellogg-Briand Pact*. New Haven, Conn., 1952.
Morrison, Charles Clayton. *The Outlawry of War: A Constructive Policy for World Peace*. Chicago, 1927; repr., New York, 1972.

KENNAN, GEORGE FROST

(*b*. 16 February 1904)

One of the most brilliant and respected diplomats in U.S. history. In conceptualizing the postwar policy of containment of the Soviet Union and its communist allies, Kennan distinguished himself as one of the principal architects of U.S. foreign policy strategy during the Cold War. After assisting in the formation of the Cold War consensus, he resigned from the U.S. Foreign Service and emerged as a sharp critic of U.S. diplomacy and society. Kennan's dissent, rooted in his profound doubts about U.S. democracy, often left his observers confused as to just where he stood on the central issues of U.S. foreign policy. The collapse of Soviet and Eastern European communism between 1989 and 1991 fulfilled one of his earlier prophecies, however, thus ensuring Kennan's reputation as one of the nation's most eminent statesmen.

Born in Milwaukee, Wisconsin, Kennan attended military school before entering Princeton College. Upon graduating in 1925 he joined the newly professionalized U.S. Foreign Service. Inspired by the career of his famous namesake and distant relation, George Kennan, a journalist and author of the definitive work on the czars' Siberian exile system, he decided to receive specialized training in Russian affairs. After serving in routine consular posts in Geneva and Hamburg, Kennan began his training as a Soviet expert from 1929 to 1931 under the tutelage of anticommunist White Russian émigrés in

Berlin. Kennan then served in posts in the then-independent Baltic republics and helped open the first U.S. embassy in Moscow. Appointed third secretary of the embassy by Ambassador William C. Bullitt, Kennan mastered Russian, traveled widely, and compiled detailed reports. Following the outbreak of the Stalinist purges and the assignment of a new U.S. ambassador, Joseph E. Davies, whom Kennan considered incompetent, the young diplomat returned to Washington in 1937 to occupy the Russian desk of the State Department's European Affairs Division.

As the threat of a second world war loomed in Europe in the 1930s, Kennan proved himself a staunch Germanophile. He mastered the German language and venerated German culture. Even after witnessing Nazi persecution of Jews as second secretary of the U.S. legation in Prague, Czechoslovakia, in 1938, Kennan seemed more concerned about Russia than about Germany as a threat to peace. His desire to see Germany anchor the European balance of power as a check against Stalinism led him to underestimate Adolf Hitler's territorial ambitions and counsel a policy of appeasement.

By the time of U.S. entry into World War II, Kennan's views had changed. Serving in Berlin at the time of Pearl Harbor, Kennan and 130 other U.S. citizens were interned by the Nazis near Frankfurt following Germany's declaration of war on the United States. Kennan supervised the internees and won universal praise for his handling of the group's more than five months of captivity. Upon his release in May 1942, Kennan complained about his assignment as counselor of the legation at Lisbon, Portugal, but took the post seriously enough to gain an audience with President Franklin D. Roosevelt to secure approval of a pledge that he had made to the Portuguese president, Antonio Salazar, that the United States would turn over possession of air bases in the Azores to Portugal after the war. In 1943 Kennan was assigned to the European Advisory Commission, again meeting with Roosevelt and convincing him to change ill-conceived proposed occupation zones in Germany that conflicted with an existing Anglo-Soviet agreement.

Throughout the war, and especially following his return to Moscow as minister-counselor of the U.S. embassy in 1944, Kennan deplored the decision to ally with Joseph Stalin's brutal Soviet regime in the war against Germany, and several times he even threatened to resign over the issue. Kennan advocated instead an open division of Europe into spheres of influence—in effect, an early declaration of Cold War—but Roosevelt was determined to continue the alliance with the USSR until the unconditional surrender of both Germany and Japan. By the end of the war years, however, as the triumphant Soviets moved to reabsorb the Baltic states and established puppet regimes in Poland, Romania, and other border areas, Kennan's drumbeat of anti-Soviet memoranda began to have a pronounced impact on the U.S. ambassador in Moscow, W. Averell Harriman.

The Formulation of Containment

The ascension of Harry S. Truman to the presidency in 1945 led to a decentralization of U.S. diplomatic decision-making, thus empowering the professional diplomats Roosevelt had long ignored. As the Soviet Union carved out its spheres of influence, Harriman and State Department elites paid close attention to Kennan's postwar dispatches. The most notable of these was the February 1946 "long telegram" from Moscow, which warned of Soviet expansionism, subversion, and commitment to spread communist revolution across the globe. The 8,000-word telegram, seconded by Winston Churchill's "Iron Curtain" address less than a month later, galvanized the U.S. foreign policy bureaucracy and helped set the United States on a course toward Cold War with the USSR. Feeling himself vindicated, Kennan returned to Washington in April 1946 to lecture at the National War College and tour the nation to promote containment.

Kennan capped his influential contributions to the formation of the containment consensus through publication of the anonymous "X" article in the journal *Foreign Affairs* in July 1947. The article, commissioned and promoted by James V. Forrestal, the hard-line anticommunist navy secretary and Kennan's benefactor, sharpened the arguments of the Long Telegram. Kennan compared Soviet expansionism to a "fluid stream" and a "persistent toy automobile" that could be stopped only through a "patient but firm and vigilant containment of Russian expansive tendencies…by the adroit application of counterforce at a series of constantly shifting geographical and political points, corresponding to the shifts and maneuvers of Soviet policy." Soon revealed as the author, Kennan was credited as the creator of a blueprint for the policy of global containment that came to dominate U.S. foreign relations for more than forty years. He went even further, predicting that containment would not only halt Soviet expansion but "promote tendencies which must eventually find their outlet in either the breakup or the gradual mellowing of Soviet power."

Publication of the "X" Article catapulted Kennan in 1947 to leadership of the new State Department Policy Planning Staff (PPS), where he served Secretary of State George C. Marshall until 1950. The European Recovery Program, which bore the secretary of state's name as the Marshall Plan, received much of its impetus from Kennan and his staff. The PPS forwarded scores of additional recommendations, most of which the National Security Council approved, allowing for the implementation of containment of communism on a global scale. From the outset, however, Kennan expressed his doubts about U.S.

policy: he criticized the Truman Doctrine for its expansive language and the North Atlantic Treaty Organization (NATO) and the 1950 report NSC-68 for cementing the division of Europe and ensuring the "militarization" of containment. He insisted that his strategy was meant to be "ideological-political" rather than military. He preferred economic to military foreign aid. The nascent nuclear arms race left Kennan profoundly disturbed.

Kennan's critique of U.S. policy led to a falling out with his superiors, notably the new secretary of state in 1949, Dean G. Acheson. Although Acheson respected Kennan's intellect, he judged him impractical. Kennan finally made good on oft-repeated threats to resign. In 1950 he retreated to the Institute for Advanced Study at Princeton at the invitation of his close friend, the noted physicist J. Robert Oppenheimer. There Kennan launched what would become an accomplished career as a historian, beginning with his analysis of U.S. foreign policy in the first half of the twentieth century. The diplomat offered a "realist" critique of U.S. foreign policy, which he set forth in the popular historical primer, *American Diplomacy, 1900–1950* (1951). In this and other works, including *Realities of American Foreign Policy* (1954), Kennan joined Hans J. Morgenthau, Reinhold Niebuhr, and others in emphasizing national interest and power politics while condemning "idealistic" diplomacy.

Kennan returned to the Department of State on an emergency basis after the outbreak of war in Korea. He strongly supported the decision to intervene militarily, although he just as strongly opposed the disastrous decision to cross the 38th parallel to extend the war into northern Korea in the fall of 1950. Kennan somewhat reluctantly accepted Truman's appointment as ambassador of Russia in 1952. The position was one for which he was uniquely qualified, but he could no longer abide life in Moscow. Kennan had served only a few months when, during a visit to Berlin, he compared Stalin's regime to the Nazis, ensuring that he would be declared persona non grata and denied readmission into the USSR. The new secretary of state under President Dwight D. Eisenhower, John Foster Dulles, who had joined the Republican right wing in condemning containment as "immoral" because it supposedly consigned the peoples of Eastern Europe to Soviet domination, sent Kennan into retirement. Kennan criticized Dulles's "liberation" policy, explaining that such an approach risked a wider war, as in Korea, in deference to appeasing the right wing of the Republican party. Actually, the differences between the two were more rhetorical than real, for both advocated containment and measures short of war to undermine Soviet power.

During the 1950s Kennan sharply condemned McCarthyism, advised Adlai Stevenson during his presidential campaigns, and delivered another broadside against U.S. policy in his British Broadcasting Corporation (BBC) Reith Lectures in 1957 and 1958, advocating great-power "disengagement" from Europe. Still hoping to see Germany emerge at the center of an independent Europe, Kennan called on both superpowers to withdraw and negotiate sweeping arms control agreements. Critics in the West—notably Acheson and Dulles—condemned Kennan for appeasement of Russia.

A Brief Return to Diplomacy

Following the return of the Democrats to the White House in 1961, Kennan received President John F. Kennedy's nomination as ambassador to Yugoslavia. Kennan had long viewed the nonaligned communist state as a model that Russia's Eastern Europe satellites might someday emulate. The veteran diplomat studied the Serbo-Croatian language and forged a close personal relationship with the Yugoslav president, Josip Tito. The U.S. Congress, however, undermined trade relations with Yugoslavia, revoking its most-favored-nation (MFN) trade status, which prompted another, and final, resignation from the Foreign Service by Kennan in 1963. From that point on the retired diplomat focused his energies on his finely crafted historical works and advocacy of reduced tensions with the USSR and a deescalation of the nuclear arms race.

The expansion of U.S. military intervention in Vietnam in the mid-1960s profoundly disturbed Kennan. He offered a devastating critique of U.S. policy before the Foreign Relations Committee in 1966 and 1967, once again drawing national attention, although he stopped short of advocating U.S. withdrawal. As in Korea, Kennan feared that any capitulation to communists could result in a "bandwagon" or domino effect that would undermine U.S. credibility and inspire Marxist subversives across the globe. The Korean and Vietnam wars revealed Kennan's struggles to resolve his dual role as both Cold War architect and critic.

Throughout the 1970s Kennan advocated détente with the USSR while sharpening his critique of U.S. society. As he began publication of a multivolume historical work analyzing the origins of World War I, Kennan feared that similar misconceptions on the part of the great powers in his own lifetime could produce an even more devastating global conflict. He aroused the ire of the Cold War establishment with his criticisms of the U.S. military-industrial complex and attempts to explain that defensive motives lay behind many Soviet policies depicted as aggressive in the West. He argued that Washington was overreacting to the 1979 Soviet invasion of Afghanistan, drawing renewed charges of appeasement. On the other hand, he declared that Iran's refusal to release U.S. hostages taken captive in November 1979 should have brought nothing less than a prompt U.S.

declaration of war. Kennan criticized Washington's preoccupation with human rights during the administration of President Jimmy Carter (1977–1981), arguing that such considerations were secondary to securing international stability and arms control accords. Moreover, he asserted that U.S. domestic problems, such as environmental degradation, declining educational standards, race relations, and rampant commercialism, were so profound that the country had no business advising others how to conduct their internal affairs.

In the early 1980s Kennan bitterly condemned President Ronald Reagan's massive arms buildup and reassertion of Cold War orthodoxies as "inexcusably childish." Prone to Cassandra-like assertions, Kennan advised that nuclear war was distinctly possible if not in fact likely. In 1984 he joined Robert McNamara, McGeorge Bundy, and Gerard Smith in advocating "no first use" of nuclear weapons as a means of achieving a breakthrough in the stalled arms negotiations. (NATO doctrine called for responding to a Soviet conventional attack in Europe with nuclear weapons.) Once again, Kennan found himself in the familiar position at the center of a stormy foreign policy debate.

By the late 1980s, critics who had dismissed Kennan as an aging relic of the early Cold War had to confront the fact that his prediction of a "gradual mellowing" of Soviet policy was beginning to come true under the leadership of Mikhail Gorbachev. In August 1991 the complete disintegration of the Soviet state fulfilled the "X" Article's prophecy that the USSR, "like the capitalist world of its conception, bears within it the seeds of its own decay." Although Kennan's timing had been off—he had often suggested during the late 1940s that the mellowing or breakup of Soviet power would occur in less than a generation—the realization of his prophecy was yet another source of vindication. Both President George Bush and congressional representatives called attention to the octogenarian Kennan's remarkable career in ceremonies in 1991.

In addition to his public advocacy on Cold War issues, Kennan continued to produce acclaimed books and articles from his office at the Institute for Advanced Study. He had won a Pulitzer Prize for *Russia Leaves the War* (1950) and another Pulitzer Prize and the National Book Award for the his *Memoirs, 1925–1950* (1967), one of the most eloquent and frequently quoted insider accounts of Cold War issues. In 1993 Kennan published *Around the Cragged Hill: A Personal and Political Philosophy*, explaining the roots of his elitism and the grave doubts, inspired by Alexis de Tocqueville, that he had long nurtured about the efficacy of democratic society. Those doubts, more than anything else, separated Kennan from his more orthodox Cold War colleagues and explain his penchant for inspiring controversy within establishment ranks. Kennan's literary achievements, coupled with his remarkable Foreign Service career, assure his standing as a legendary figure in the history of U.S. diplomacy.

WALTER L. HIXSON

See also Cold War; Containment; Nuclear Weapons and Strategy; Realism; Russia and the Soviet Union

FURTHER READING

Gaddis, John Lewis. *Strategies of Containment: A Critical Appraisal of Postwar American National Security Policy*. New York, 1983.

Hixson, Walter L. *George F. Kennan: Cold War Iconoclast*. New York, 1989.

Kennan, George Frost. *Memoirs, 1925–1950*. Boston, 1967.

———. *Memoirs, 1950–1963*. Boston, 1972.

———. *Sketches from a Life*. New York, 1989.

Mayers, David. *George Kennan and the Dilemmas of U.S. Foreign Policy*. Oxford, 1988.

Miscamble, Wilson D. *George F. Kennan and the Making of American Foreign Policy, 1947–1950*. Princeton, N.J., 1992.

Stephanson, Anders. *Kennan and the Art of Foreign Policy*. Cambridge, Mass., 1989.

KENNEDY, JOHN FITZGERALD

(*b.* 29 May 1917; *d.* 22 November 1963)

Member of the U.S. House of Representatives (1946–1952), U.S. senator (1952–1960), and thirty-fifth president of the United States (1961–1963). Born in Brookline, Massachusetts, Kennedy's education in foreign relations began when, at the age of twenty, he traveled about Europe in the summer of 1937, observing political developments and ruminating in his diary on the relative qualities of fascism, communism, and democracy. The appointment of his father, Joseph P. Kennedy, as ambassador to Great Britain brought him back to Europe for a seven-month period in 1939. With war on the horizon, young Kennedy toured eastern Europe, the Soviet Union, the Balkans, and the Middle East, sending back careful reports to his father.

In 1939–1940, his last year at Harvard College, he wrote an honors essay on the lethargic British rearmament policy and its implications for democracies under pressure. The result, published in 1940 under the title *Why England Slept*, attributed British unpreparedness to the "general weakness of democracy and capitalism." Kennedy called on the U.S. democracy to learn from the British experience and prepare for the worst. Dispassionate in tone, the book was a contrast to the fervent isolationism espoused by his father. In December 1940 the younger Kennedy took further steps. "In your message for America to stay out of the war," he advised his father, "you should not do so at the expense of having people minimize aid to Britain." If Great Britain were defeated, he believed, the United States, "alone in a strained and hostile world," might in a few years itself be defeated by the totalitarian powers.

Serving in the navy during World War II, he returned from the Pacific a hero. ("It was inadvertent," he later said. "They sank my boat.") Appalled by the waste of war, he wrote an article, never published, warning against "a world rearmament race…that can have but one ending—the explosion of war." In 1945 he covered the founding conference of the United Nations at San Francisco for the Hearst newspapers. Soviet hostility to the West, while "understandable in the light of recent history," nevertheless convinced him that "in the next few years it will be prudent to be strong. I am naturally disappointed in this as I haven't changed my views that disarmament is an essential part of any lasting peace." He wrote in his notebook, "War will exist until the distant day when the conscientious objector enjoys the same reputation and prestige that the warrior does today."

He pursued his foreign policy education by covering the British general election and visiting the Potsdam conference. After his election to Congress in 1946, he again disagreed with his isolationist father, who now opposed the Cold War as he had earlier opposed the war against Adolf Hitler. The younger Kennedy on the contrary endorsed the Truman Doctrine, the Marshall Plan, the North Atlantic Treaty Organization (NATO), and the Korean War. At times Kennedy was even more a cold warrior than the administration of President Harry S. Truman, blaming the communist success in China on academic sinologists, the White House, and the Department of State. In 1951 a trip around Asia from Israel through India and Indochina to Japan led him to recast his interpretation of Asian developments. He now saw a continent, as he said in a speech after his return, "in which the fires of nationalism so long dormant have been kindled and are now ablaze…an area of revolution." Western colonialism, he reported, was finished, "communism cannot be met effectively by merely the force of arms," and the United States had appeared "too ready to buttress an inequitable status quo."

Elected to the Senate in 1952, he made revision of Third World policy a major theme. "The sweep of nationalism," he told the Senate, "is the most potent factor in foreign affairs today." Asia, he believed, faced a choice between the communist path of Mao Zedong in China and the democratic path of Jawaharlal Nehru in India. Despite Nehru's neutralism, Kennedy championed increased aid to India. He opposed military intervention in support of the French in Vietnam and hailed Vietnamese independence, believing that Ngo Dinh Diem could turn nationalism against Ho Chi Minh and the communists. In 1957 he shocked the foreign policy establishment by advocating the independence of Algeria from France. As chairman of the African subcommittee of the Foreign Relations Committee, he said in 1959, "Call it nationalism, call it anticolonialism, call it what

you will, Africa is going through a revolution." In Latin America he initially welcomed Fidel Castro's revolution in Cuba as "part of the legacy of Bolívar."

On U.S.-Soviet relations, he sharply criticized the Dwight D. Eisenhower administration for inadequate buildup of U.S. defenses. At the same time, he called for negotiations "with the Russians at the summit or anywhere else," proposed U.S. aid to Poland, opposed the resumption of nuclear testing, and defended George Kennan against Dean Acheson in their 1957 argument over disengagement in central Europe. "We should be ready to take risks," Kennedy wrote in 1960, "to bring about a thaw in the Cold War."

In his successful campaign that year for the presidency, he charged that the Soviet Union had outpaced the United States in attracting Third World nationalists, that the Eisenhower "massive retaliation" strategy would leave the United States helpless in the face of aggression too limited or local to warrant the use of nuclear weapons, and that neglect of U.S. rearmament had created a "missile gap" in the Soviet favor. In debates with the Republican candidate Richard M. Nixon, Kennedy criticized the Eisenhower administration for its commitment to the defense of Jinmen (Quemoy) and Mazu (Matsu), small islands a few miles off the coast of the People's Republic of China, while it tolerated a communist regime in Cuba, ninety miles off the coast of Florida.

The year 1960 was troubling for the United States abroad. A U-2 espionage plane was shot down over the Soviet Union; a U.S.-Soviet summit meeting was canceled; anti-U.S. riots forced Eisenhower to abandon a visit to Japan; and relations with Cuba were broken off. Two weeks before Kennedy's inauguration in January 1961, Soviet leader Nikita Khrushchev in a belligerent speech predicted the inevitable triumph of communism through "national liberation wars" in the Third World. Khrushchev's speech, aimed as much at China as at the United States, was very likely an attempt to show the communist world that nuclear coexistence, which Khrushchev also affirmed, was not incompatible with revolutionary militancy. Kennedy, however, took the speech as a personal test, replying in his inaugural address: "Let every nation know . . . that we shall pay any price, bear any burden, meet any hardship, support any friend, oppose any foe, in order to assure the success and survival of liberty." He went on, however, to declare: "Let us never negotiate out of fear. But let us never fear to negotiate."

The White House Years

Kennedy had an avid and detailed interest in foreign relations, often personally calling desk officers in the Department of State. His foreign policy team covered the spectrum from hard to soft. Secretary of State Dean

Rusk subordinated his personal hard-line views to the more flexible attitudes of the president and of McGeorge Bundy, the White House special assistant for national security affairs. The hard line was also countered within the Department of State by Undersecretary Chester Bowles and his successor George Ball; by Adlai Stevenson, the ambassador to the United Nations; and by the veteran diplomat W. Averell Harriman. Secretary of Defense Robert S. McNamara had no hesitation in disagreeing with and on occasion overriding the addiction of the Joint Chiefs of Staff to military solutions. After the 1961 Bay of Pigs fiasco early in the administration, Kennedy gave his brother Robert, the attorney general, a roving brief in foreign affairs.

If the Soviet Union was on the move, President Kennedy thought it necessary to restore the military balance, which he believed erroneously was tilting in the Soviet favor. To overcome the alleged "missile gap," he called for an increase in the U.S. missile force—a buildup well under way and beyond recall before espionage and reconnaissance satellites conclusively disproved the gap's existence. To increase the capacity to fight nonnuclear wars, he endorsed a shift in strategic doctrine from "massive retaliation" to "flexible response," requiring the diversification of force to meet diverse levels of threat. To counter national liberation wars in the Third World, he utilized covert action by the Central Intelligence Agency (CIA) and ordered the Pentagon to develop counterinsurgency capabilities.

Zealous cold warriors, like Senator Barry Goldwater in his book *Why Not Victory?* (1962) and the Joint Chiefs of Staff, who commanded strong political support in Congress, regarded these steps as inadequate. History judges them an overreaction to Khrushchev's braggadocio. The missile buildup ended any hope of freezing the arms race at lower levels and drove the Soviet Union to accelerate its own missile program. Flexible response, designed to reduce dependence on nuclear weapons, had the fateful side effect of creating forces that could be used in local "brushfire" wars, as in Vietnam.

As for covert action, Kennedy inherited from Eisenhower an expedition of Cuban exiles trained by the CIA to invade Cuba and end Castro's communist dictatorship. Fearing political backlash at home as well as encouragement for Fidelistas in Latin America if he disbanded a military initiative approved by the hero of D-Day, Kennedy permitted the expedition to go ahead, stipulating that under no circumstances would U.S. forces be used. He was subsequently criticized for canceling a second air strike at the beachhead, but a successful strike would not have altered the basic equation—an invading force of 1,200 against 200,000 Cuban militiamen loyal to Castro. The CIA had assured Kennedy that the invasion would set off uprisings behind the line and defections from Castro's militia, but neither occurred.

The failure at the Bay of Pigs disillusioned Kennedy with both the CIA and the Joint Chiefs of Staff and preserved him from following their counsel in subsequent crises. He did, however, urge the CIA to mount Operation Mongoose, a sabotage effort aimed at overthrowing the Castro regime. On its own, the CIA continued attempts, initiated in the Eisenhower administration, to assassinate Castro; there is no evidence that either Eisenhower or Kennedy knew of or authorized these CIA assassination plots. Kennedy's desire to counter national liberation insurgencies in the Third World also led him into an ill-judged fascination with counterinsurgency and the Green Berets, army special forces trained for unconventional war—a misguided enterprise that brought out the worst in the overconfident activism of the New Frontier and strengthened the U.S. belief in the right to intervene in the internal affairs of other countries.

These policies obstructed Kennedy's longer-term objectives. Despite his inaugural rodomontade, he had no illusions about the feasibility of a pax Americana. To play an effective role in the world, Kennedy recognized, the United States would have to strengthen its own economic position. Alerted by the balance of payments deficit to the nation's increasing economic vulnerability, he had mixed success in attempting to liberalize world trade through the Trade Expansion Act of 1962 and the Dillon Round of tariff reductions.

In November 1961 he asked Americans to "face the fact that the United States is neither omnipotent nor omniscient—that we are only 6 percent of the world's population—that we cannot impose our will upon the other 94 percent of mankind—that we cannot right every wrong or reverse each adversity—and that therefore there cannot be American solution to every world problem." He liked to quote Winston Churchill—"We arm to parley"—and his goal was a "world of diversity," a world where "every country can solve its own problems according to its own traditions and ideals." Communism could be one element in this pluralistic world, but diversity, Kennedy argued, was ultimately incompatible with the Marxist commandment that all societies were destined to go through the same stages and arrive at the same destination. In a speech at American University in June 1963 he summed up his policy in a conscious revision of Woodrow Wilson's famous line: "If we cannot now end our differences, at least we can help make the world safe for diversity."

Competition in the Third World

Given the nuclear stalemate, Kennedy agreed with Khrushchev in seeing the Third World as the main battleground of the Cold War. His strategy was to use economic aid and social reform to channel the nationalism of developing countries in democratic directions. "Those who make peaceful revolution impossible," he told the Latin American diplomatic corps in 1962, "will make violent revolution inevitable." As Asia was poised between the Chinese way and the Indian way, so Latin America, he believed, confronted the choice between the Castro way and the democratic way as typified by Rómulo Betancourt of Venezuela. Kennedy organized the ambitious Alliance for Progress to promote economic development and democratic reform. Castro himself called the alliance "a politically wise concept put forth to hold back the time of revolution…a very intelligent strategy."

Kennedy shifted the emphasis of U.S. aid programs from military assistance to economic development. The Food for Peace agency, directed by George McGovern, sought to use the U.S. agricultural surplus to further world economic development. The Peace Corps, an undertaking especially close to Kennedy's heart and directed by his brother-in-law Sargent Shriver, brought the idealism of young Americans into Third World villages. Although the Peace Corps changed the volunteers more than it changed the countries in which they worked, it flourished as a symbol of U.S. idealism. Kennedy invited Third World leaders to Washington—twenty-eight from Africa alone—and backed the United Nations in its successful effort to stop civil war in the Congo.

His hardest Third World problems were guerrilla wars in Laos and Vietnam. Kennedy, who privately thought the United States overcommitted in Southeast Asia, worked out with Khrushchev at their Vienna meeting in June 1961 a plan for the neutralization of Laos. To conciliate hard-liners in the national security establishment, he agreed to help the Diem regime in South Vietnam, where the military odds were more favorable. He increased the number of "advisers"—U.S. military personnel attached to units of the South Vietnamese army—from 685 to 16,732 by the end of 1963 (of whom 120 died in combat). Remembering from his visit to Vietnam a decade earlier the fate of the French army, Kennedy rejected then and later recommendations for the dispatch of U.S. combat units. "It was really the president's personal conviction," General Maxwell Taylor, chairman of the Joint Chiefs of Staff, later recalled, "that U.S. ground troops shouldn't go in." Kennedy also directed the Pentagon to draw up a plan for total U.S. disengagement in 1965. "In the final analysis," he said in September 1963, "it is their war. They are the ones who have to win it or lose it."

He increased economic and military aid to South Vietnam and tried to move the Diem regime toward political and economic reforms. Diem's intransigence and his regime's brutal attacks on the Buddhists precipitated bitter controversy in the fall of 1963 between pro-Diem and anti-Diem factions within the U.S. administration. The anti-Diem group, going farther than Kennedy wished, welcomed and perhaps invited a military coup in November 1963 that resulted in Diem's assassination.

Historians debate as to how Kennedy would have handled Vietnam had he lived. His legacy was contradictory. President Lyndon B. Johnson, inheriting Kennedy's advisers and proceeding on their advice to Americanize the war, unquestionably thought he was doing what Kennedy would have done. Kennedy, however, privately expressed his intention to end U.S. involvement after the 1964 election. While Rusk later said he had never heard Kennedy speak about withdrawal, both Bundy and McNamara later said that they did not believe that Kennedy would ever have committed U.S. ground forces to Vietnam.

The dominating foreign policy issue remained the relationship with the Soviet Union. In his Vienna meeting with Khrushchev, Kennedy proposed a standstill agreement by which each superpower should abstain from actions that might risk miscalculation and compel reaction by the other. Khrushchev brusquely rejected this idea and threatened to conclude the treaty with the German Democratic Republic that would extinguish Western rights in West Berlin. Kennedy responded by requesting a further increase in the defense budget, calling out 150,000 reservists and announcing a program, soon regretted, of fallout shelters for protection against nuclear war. The erection in August of the Berlin Wall stemmed the flow of refugees into West Germany, and the Berlin crisis subsided.

The Cuban Missile Crisis and the Nuclear Arms Race

Khrushchev, determined to repair his own missile gap, embarked in 1962 on the hazardous enterprise of establishing nuclear missile bases in Cuba. Castro, fearing a U.S. invasion, had sought Soviet protection but accepted nuclear weapons only with reluctance. Because the Soviets denied to Kennedy that they were sending offensive weapons and because they had never before placed nuclear weapons in another country, the operation was not suspected until it was discovered in October 1962 by a U-2 overflight. By making short-range missiles effective against U.S. targets, the operation would have increased by half again the Soviet first-strike capacity, and it would have delivered a shattering political blow by proving the Soviet ability to penetrate the U.S. zone of influence in the Western Hemisphere. "Our missiles," Khrushchev later claimed, "would have equalized…'the balance of power.'"

During thirteen days of extreme suspense, Kennedy rejected the proposal of a surprise air attack on the missile sites and instead imposed a naval blockade as a first step to force the withdrawal of the missiles. The situation was more dangerous than was realized at the time. The CIA had estimated 10,000 Soviet troops in Cuba; in fact, there were 42,000. The CIA was never sure that nuclear warheads had arrived; in fact, warheads were there, and for tactical as well as for strategic weapons. Moreover, the Soviet field commanders had authority to use nuclear weapons against a U.S. invasion without further clearance from Moscow.

Kennedy feared that the crisis might spin out of control and believed in providing the antagonists a means of retreat. Khrushchev also sought a negotiated solution. Talks between Robert Kennedy and the Soviet ambassador concluded in a secret deal by which, in return for U.S. assurances that U.S. missiles would be withdrawn from Turkey, Khrushchev would withdraw Soviet missiles from Cuba. A U.S. pledge not to invade Cuba was conditioned on UN inspection of the missile withdrawal; when Castro refused such inspection, the pledge did not go into effect. Kennedy had no intention of mounting an invasion, however, and in the autumn of 1963 he initiated explorations looking toward a normalization of relations with Cuba. These explorations were not pursued after his assassination.

In the aftermath of the Cuban missile crisis, both Kennedy and Khrushchev, having stared together into the nuclear abyss, emerged with new determination to bring the nuclear arms race under control. By now they were changing from enemies to competitors with shared interests. "He would like to prevent a nuclear war," Kennedy told Norman Cousins of the *Saturday Review*, "but is under severe pressure from his hard-line crowd, which interprets every move in that direction as appeasement. I've got similar problems.... The hard-liners in the Soviet Union and the United States feed on each other."

In June 1963 at the American University, Kennedy called on Americans as well as Russians to rethink the Cold War: "No government or social system is so evil that its people must be considered as lacking in virtue." He then sent Harriman to Moscow to negotiate a test-ban treaty. Opposition from the Joint Chiefs of Staff and their congressional backers forced Kennedy to settle for a treaty outlawing nuclear tests only in self-policing environments—in the atmosphere, in outer space, and under water—and underground testing later increased in both countries. The limited test-ban treaty, nonetheless, represented a significant step in the direction of U.S.-Soviet détente. Kennedy also replaced the quest for nuclear superiority with the doctrine of "mutually assured destruction," according to which both superpowers should have sufficient strength to absorb a first strike and retain the capacity to retaliate. Khrushchev wrote in his memoirs: "I had no cause for regret once Kennedy became president. It quickly became evident that he understood better than Eisenhower that an improvement in relations was the only rational course.... He impressed me as a better statesman than Eisenhower."

Although some of his early decisions and his administration's sometimes frenetic activism compounded problems he faced in the world, Kennedy was cautious and careful on U.S.-Soviet issues and showed steady growth in his brief White House years. His lofty rhetoric tended to outstrip his circumspect action, but he was the first Cold War president to promote the cause of détente, the first to understand the power of nationalism in the Third World, and the first to redefine the role of the United States in a world economy it no longer dominated. The explosion of grief around the world at his assassination in November 1963 suggests the extent to which he seemed in other lands to embody U.S. idealism and hope.

ARTHUR M. SCHLESINGER, JR.

See also Acheson, Dean Gooderham; Ball, George Wildman; Bay of Pigs Invasion; Berlin; Bowles, Chester Bliss; Bundy, McGeorge; Cold War; Cuban Missile Crisis; Food for Peace; Harriman, William Averell; Johnson, Lyndon Baines; Kennedy, Robert Francis; Khrushchev, Nikita Sergeyevich; National Security and National Defense; Nehru, Jawaharlal; Peace Corps; Presidency; Rusk, David Dean; Russia and the Soviet Union; Stevenson, Adlai Ewing II; Vietnam War

FURTHER READING

Ball, George W. *The Past Has Another Pattern.* New York, 1982.

Beschloss, Michael. *The Crisis Years: Kennedy and Khrushchev, 1960–1963.* New York, 1991.

Blight, J. G., and D. A. Welch. *On the Brink: Americans and Soviets Reexamine the Cuban Missile Crisis.* New York, 1971.

——— , ——— , and B. J. Allyn. *Cuba on the Brink: Castro, the Missile Crisis, and the Soviet Collapse.* New York, 1993.

Galbraith, John Kenneth. *A Life in Our Times.* Boston, 1981.

Herring, George C. *America's Longest War: The United States and Vietnam, 1950–1975,* 3rd ed. New York, 1996.

Hilsman, Roger. *To Move a Nation.* New York, 1967.

Kennedy, John F. *The Strategy of Peace,* edited by Allan Nevins. New York, 1960.

Kennedy, Robert. *Thirteen Days.* New York, 1969.

Kunz, Diane B., ed. *The Diplomacy of the Crucial Decade: American Foreign Relations During the 1960s.* New York, 1994.

Mahoney, Richard. *JFK: Ordeal in Africa.* New York, 1983.

Martin, Edwin M., *Kennedy and Latin America,* Lanham, Md., 1994.

McNamara, Robert S. *In Retrospect: The Tragedy and Lessons of Vietnam.* New York, 1995.

Newstadt, Richard. *Alliance Politics.* New York, 1970.

Paterson, Thomas G., ed. *Kennedy's Quest for Victory.* New York, 1989.

Rostow, W. W. *The Diffusion of Power.* New York, 1972.

Rusk, Dean. *As I Saw It.* New York, 1990.

Seaborg, Glenn, and B. S. Loeb. *Kennedy, Khrushchev, and the Test Ban.* Berkeley, Calif., 1981.

Schlesinger, Arthur M., Jr. *A Thousand Days.* Boston, 1965.

——— . *Robert Kennedy and His Times.* Boston, 1978.

Sorensen, Theodore C. *Kennedy.* New York, 1965.

Winand, Pascaline. *Eisenhower, Kennedy, and the United States of Europe.* New York, 1993.

KENNEDY, JOSEPH PATRICK

(*b.* 6 September 1888; *d.* 18 November 1969)

Financier, prominent Democrat, and U.S. ambassador to Great Britain (1937–1941). Born in Boston and a 1912 Harvard graduate, the multimillionaire Kennedy temporarily put aside his varied and profitable business ventures during the early 1930s. After backing Franklin D. Roosevelt's presidential candidacy in 1932, Kennedy was appointed head of the Securities and Exchange Commission (SEC). His continued financial support and his book, *I'm for Roosevelt* (1936), helped to sway conservatives, Irish Catholics, and others to vote for Roosevelt's reelection in 1936. Kennedy then served as chairman of the newly created Maritime Commission, which sought to rescue a sagging shipping industry. By skillful self-promotion and some strong action, Kennedy came out of the ordeal with his reputation unscathed.

In December 1937 the aggressive, ambitious Kennedy persuaded Roosevelt to make him the first American of Irish heritage to be appointed ambassador to Great Britain. Kennedy probably sought that post as retribution for all the years the Boston Brahmins had shunned him and his family. He looked forward to the time when the Irish Catholic Kennedys could grace the exclusive clubs of England. The ambassadorship also meant political elevation in Kennedy's quest to become the first Catholic president. He lacked, however, knowledge of international relations, an understanding of European history, and the temperament and judgment to serve effectively at the Court of St. James's. Roosevelt calculated nonetheless that Kennedy had the necessary wealth to survive the ambassadorship, the bargaining skills to negotiate a new Anglo-American trade agreement, and the religion and nationality to appease anti-British Irish Catholics in the United States in the event of U.S. assistance to Great Britain against Nazi Germany. This appointment represented political payment to a dangerous competitor.

The bespectacled, red-haired, and gregarious Kennedy got off to a good start in London. He developed a close relationship with Prime Minister Neville Chamberlain, who shared Kennedy's abhorrence of war and communism. Befriending the British foreign secretary, Lord Halifax, further contributed to Kennedy's detailed Department of State reports. Kennedy also received accolades at home for failing to wear traditional silk stockings and knee breeches in formal presentations at court; he instead appeared in tailcoat and long trousers. He ended, moreover, the inane practice of presenting U.S. debutantes to the king and queen. Under his direction the two countries concluded a new trade agreement largely on British terms.

What most undermined Kennedy's efforts was his violation of a fundamental diplomatic precept: ambassadors are supposed to represent their government's policies. Kennedy confused national well-being with his own and that of his immediate family. The conflict arose over the mounting aggression of Germany and Italy. He played down the moral and strategic danger of Nazism, arguing that differences between European countries were merely economic. He thought it possible to work out an accommodation with Germany's Adolf Hitler. The alternative was the destruction of trade and financial arrangements and, given the collectivist demands of modern war, the ending of capitalism. In the end, Europe would be reduced to rubble, paving the way for communism, an ideology he found much more threatening than Nazism. He also feared for the financial and physical security of his own family: "I have four boys and I don't want them to be killed in a foreign war." As a result, Kennedy reinforced Chamberlain's efforts to appease Hitler and enthusiastically embraced the Munich Agreement of 1938, which cost Czechoslovakia the Sudetenland and ultimately its independence. Soon afterward, in a major address, he pleaded for coexistence with dictatorships, a highly criticized departure from Roosevelt's foreign policy as expressed in the Quarantine Address of October 1937.

Kennedy also committed other indiscretions, including exhibiting an insensitivity to the plight of Jews in Germany. He was also accused of using his position to further his liquor-importing business. More troublesome to Roosevelt were reports of Kennedy's private criticism of the president and his intention to challenge Roosevelt for the presidency in 1940. Kennedy also continued to plead for concessions to Hitler after the latter's violation of the Munich Agreement and invasion of Poland in September 1939. Kennedy's defeatism after the outbreak of World War II—especially the prediction of the collapse of Great Britain and France—proved disconcerting even to Chamberlain. By 1940 Roosevelt and the Department of State were bypassing Kennedy, preferring special envoys to communicate directly with Prime Minister Winston Churchill. At the same time, Roosevelt refused to permit the troublesome Kennedy to return home, until the ambassador threatened to expose the president's handling of the destroyers-for-bases agreement with England. When Kennedy finally saw Roosevelt in October 1940, he agreed to deliver a campaign speech on national radio endorsing his reelection. A probable inducement was Roosevelt's pledge to support Kennedy's son, Joseph, Jr., for governor of Massachusetts in 1942.

The tenuous political rapprochement soon ended after Kennedy's Boston interview on 8 November with reporters in which he predicted the collapse of democracy in Great Britain and its possible demise in the United States. He also made critical comments about Roosevelt's wife, Eleanor, the British cabinet, and the king of England. Even though Kennedy repudiated the interview,

Roosevelt deftly separated himself from the outspoken ambassador, who resigned in February 1941. Despite Kennedy's requests to serve during the war, Roosevelt refused to consider him for any major position.

Only through his second son, John F. Kennedy, would Joseph Kennedy again reach national prominence. From 1946 through 1960, Kennedy, who habitually drove all of his children to win at all costs, expended enormous amounts of money and energy to ensure John Kennedy's election to the U.S. House of Representative (1946), the U.S. Senate (1952), and the U.S. presidency (1960).

JAMES N. GIGLIO

See also Appeasement; Chamberlain, Arthur Neville; Churchill, Winston Leonard Spencer; Communism; Czech Republic; Great Britain; Hitler, Adolf; Kennedy, John Fitzgerald; Kennedy, Robert Francis; Munich Conference; Roosevelt, Franklin Delano; World War II

FURTHER READING

Beschloss, Michael R. *Kennedy and Roosevelt: The Uneasy Alliance.* New York, 1980.
Goodwin, Doris Kearns. *The Fitzgeralds and the Kennedys: An American Saga.* New York, 1987.
Hamilton, Nigel. *JFK: Reckless Youth.* New York, 1992.
Martin, Ralph G. *Seeds of Destruction: Joe Kennedy and His Sons.* New York, 1995.

KENNEDY, ROBERT FRANCIS

(*b.* 20 November 1925; *d.* 5 June 1968)

Attorney general (1961–1964), U.S. senator (1964–1968), and personal adviser to his brother President John F. Kennedy. The third son of Joseph P. Kennedy, a wealthy financier who served as President Franklin Roosevelt's first chairman of the Securities and Exchange Commission (SEC) and as ambassador to Great Britain, Robert Kennedy was born in Brookline, Massachusetts, and graduated from Harvard College in 1948 and the University of Virginia Law School in 1951. A trip to Europe and the Middle East in 1948 began his education in foreign affairs. He covered the Japan peace treaty conference at San Francisco in 1951 for the *Boston Post*, and his conviction of the significance of Asian nationalism was reinforced later that year by a journey across Asia with his brother, Congressman John F. Kennedy.

On the Soviet Union, Robert Kennedy held conventional right-wing views, attacking Roosevelt for allegedly appeasing Joseph Stalin at the Yalta Conference. In 1953 Kennedy joined the staff of Senator Joseph McCarthy's subcommittee on investigations. Concerned after six months by McCarthy's methods, he resigned, later returning as minority counsel and author of the minority report condemning McCarthy's conduct of U.S. Army

hearings. A trip with Supreme Court Justice William O. Douglas through the Soviet Union in 1955 had an impact that Douglas later described as "the final undoing of McCarthyism."

In 1961 President John F. Kennedy appointed him attorney general and, after the Bay of Pigs fiasco in April, valuing his probing intelligence and total loyalty, gave him a roving brief in foreign affairs. Caught up in the activist frenzy of the early years of President Kennedy's administration, Robert Kennedy spurred on Operation Mongoose, a Central Intelligence Agency (CIA) sabotage campaign designed to overthrow the Fidel Castro regime in Cuba, and joined in the enthusiasm for counterinsurgency in the Third World, which he naively thought to be "social reform under pressure." Soon he recognized that "the awakening of peoples in Asia and Africa and Latin America—peoples stirring from centuries of stagnation, suppression and dependency" called for affirmative policies. On visits to the Third World, he advocated political and social change and sought especially to talk to young people. In Indonesia his intervention persuaded President Sukarno to resume talks with the Netherlands, which averted war over West New Guinea. When the Soviet attempt to install nuclear missiles in Cuba in 1962 produced the greatest crisis of the Cold War, Robert Kennedy, in high-level meetings, led the opposition to a surprise attack on the missile sites. In secret negotiations with the Soviet ambassador, he procured the withdrawal of the missiles in exchange for the withdrawal of U.S. missiles from Turkey. In late 1963 he backed the administration's exploration of ways to regularize relations with Castro.

Elected to the Senate from New York in 1964, he broke with President Lyndon B. Johnson's administration in 1965 over what he saw as the transformation of the Alliance for Progress from a program of social reform into one of support for military dictatorships. "If we allow communism to carry the banner of reform," he said, "the ignored and the dispossessed, the insulted and injured, will turn to it as the only way out of their misery"—a theme to which he returned in South Africa and elsewhere.

Although he had initially supported U.S. intervention in Vietnam, he turned against the war in 1965–1966, emphasizing in passionate speeches the "horror" of this "distant and ferocious" conflict and calling for a negotiated settlement. His campaign against the war propelled him into his whirlwind 1968 challenge for the Democratic presidential nomination, and he seemed on the way to winning his party's support when an assassin killed him in Los Angeles shortly after his victory in the California primary. His legacy to the United States was an impressive model of personal growth and of idealism in ends combined with realism in means. He also renewed a sense of an obligation to the desolate and disinherited not only in the United States but around the world.

ARTHUR M. SCHLESINGER, JR.

See also Alliance for Progress; Cuban Missile Crisis; Indonesia; Kennedy, John Fitzgerald; McCarthyism; Third World; Vietnam War

FURTHER READING

Guthman, Edwin O., and Jeffrey Sulman, eds. *Robert Kennedy: In His Own Words*. New York, 1988.
Kennedy, Robert Francis. *Just Friends and Brave Enemies*. New York, 1962.
———. *To Seek a Newer World*. New York, 1967.
———. *Thirteen Days*. New York, 1969.
Schlesinger, Arthur M., Jr., *Robert Kennedy and His Times*. Boston, 1978.

KENNEDY ROUND

See General Agreement on Tariffs and Trade

KENYA

Republic in East Africa and former British colony, bordering the northwestern Indian Ocean between Tanzania and Somalia. Since attaining independence on 12 December 1963, the Republic of Kenya has maintained a pro-West foreign policy orientation that has included strong military and economic ties with the United States. As soon as the country achieved independence, the United States opened an embassy in Nairobi; the first U.S. ambassador to Kenya was appointed 2 March 1964. During Kenya's first decade of independence, however, Great Britain assumed the lead role in helping Kenya address its internal and external security concerns, while the United States supported its client in Ethiopia.

During the mid-1970s the United States began to expand its military role in Kenya. Increasing U.S. concern about Soviet military activities in the Indian Ocean, particularly its construction of port and air facilities at Berbera in Somalia, the loss of access to port facilities in Angola and Mozambique following the April 1974 coup in Portugal, coupled with the Soviet-Cuban interventions in the 1975–1976 Angolan civil war and the 1977–1978 Ogaden war between Ethiopia and Somalia, heightened U.S. fears about the destabilizing effect of Soviet activism in Africa. To secure port-of-call and other military privileges in Kenya, the United States provided Kenya with $90 million in security assistance and sold it $118 million worth of arms, including tanks and F-5 jet fighters, during fiscal years 1975 to 1979.

Military relations between the United States and Kenya were formalized in June 1980 when a ten-year arms-for-access agreement was signed under the aegis of the Carter Doctrine. Along with Oman and Somalia, Kenya became part of the U.S. "over-the-horizon" strategic infrastructure in the Indian Ocean region. The United States initially agreed to provide Kenya with $60 million in security assistance over a two-year period. Massive Soviet arms transfers to Ethiopia during the 1980s, however, prompted the United States to raise the ante in Kenya. Over the course of the next decade Kenya received approximately $350 million in U.S. security assistance and another $150 million worth of foreign military sales (FMS) cash arms transfers.

The strategic partnership with Kenya was of particular importance to the United States, given the uncertainty and controversy surrounding the U.S.-Somali arms-for-access agreement signed in August 1980. Unlike Somalia, Kenya did not pose a threat to its neighbors. Along with Ethiopia and Djibouti, Kenya was one of the targets of Somalia's irredentist policy in the Horn of Africa, which complicated U.S. diplomacy. Before the United States opened formal base access negotiations with Somalia, U.S. officials felt compelled to discuss the situation with representatives of the Kenyan government, who reluctantly gave the green light. Ironically, although aligned on opposite sides of the Cold War in the Horn of Africa, Ethiopia and Kenya both believed that Somalia posed the greatest external threat to their security. In deference to African sensitivities about reopening the question of Africa's colonial borders, Kenya was deemed a more appropriate site than Somalia from which to counter the Soviet position in Ethiopia.

The U.S.-Kenya strategic partnership operated smoothly and largely without controversy throughout the 1980s. By the end of the decade, owing to the collapse of the U.S.-Sudanese and the U.S.-Somali relationships, Kenya stood alone as the leading recipient of U.S. security assistance in sub-Saharan Africa. Besides being a bastion of capitalism in East Africa, Kenya ingratiated itself with the Reagan administration and the congressional conservatives by supporting the RENAMO insurgency in Mozambique.

In the summer of 1990, however, U.S.-Kenyan relations began to sour. No longer constrained by the political-strategic requirements of the Cold War, the U.S. Congress began to focus upon the human rights abuses of the government of President Daniel arap Moi. In fall 1990 Congress forced the Bush administration to impose a partial freeze on U.S. military aid to Kenya; in January 1991, however, President Moi's willingness to accept the Libyan "contras" from Chad and to provide logistical support in the evacuation of U.S. citizens in Sudan and the U.S. embassy in Somalia led to a partial release of U.S. military funds. Moi's refusal to hold multiparty elections until December 1992 and then his suspension of the Kenyan Parliament in early 1993, after the opposition won a voice in Parliament, led the United States, the

European Community, the International Monetary Fund, and the World Bank to threaten to reduce aid to Kenya. That threat worked for a short time. But by the end of 1994 the Moi government had returned to its autocratic and abusive one party ways.

Moi eventually eased restrictions on the political opposition which reopened the door to Western aid in 1994. But in early 1995, confronted by increasingly local political opposition and two insurgences—the Ugandon based February Eighteen Movement (FEM) and the Kenya Patriotic Front (KFP)—Moi once again clamped down on political freedoms and returned Kenya to the pre-1992 style of one party government. As of mid-1996, Western aid donors, including the United States, have raised few objections.

Despite the political problems between the United States and Kenya, Kenya supported the United States against Iraq during the Kuwait crisis, although Kenyan military facilities played only a minor operational role in the Gulf conflict. Like other sub-Saharan African countries, Kenya's perceived strategic value has been greatly diminished by the end of the Cold War and by the high-profile military presence the United States is now able to maintain in the Gulf. Whereas Washington signed a new ten-year base access agreement with Oman in 1990, the United States has preferred to keep its arrangement with Kenya on a one-year notification basis. Because Kenya's port of Mombasa remains a favorite port-of-call for the U.S. Navy in the Indian Ocean and because Pentagon planners believe that Kenyan facilities provide the United States with strategic flexibility to cope with minor military contingencies in East and Central Africa, Washington has maintained a modest security assistance program to Nairobi in order to keep the door open in the event future developments warrant a return to an "over-the-horizon" strategic posture in the region.

For fiscal year 1996 the Clinton administration proposed a total aid package of $41.7 million for Kenya, including $350,000 for military training. This placed Nairobi seventh on U.S. aid list for sub-Saharan Africa, below neighboring states such as Ethiopia, Uganda, and Tanzania.

While Kenya's role in chairing the Intergovernmental Authority on Drought and Development (IGADD) committee negotiating between Khartoum and southern rebels in the Sudanese Civil War is appreciated by Washington, in terms of containing the National Islamic Front (NIF)-backed government in Khartoum, Ethiopia, Uganda, and Eritrea figure more prominently in U.S. plans.

JEFFREY A. LEFEBVRE

See also Africa; Ethiopia; Somalia

FURTHER READING

Farer, Tom. *War Clouds on the Horn of Africa: The Widening Storm,* 2nd ed. New York, 1979.
Lefebvre, Jeffrey A. *Arms for the Horn: U.S. Security Policy in Ethiopia and Somalia, 1953–1991.* Pittsburgh, Pa., 1991.

KHOMEINI, RUHOLLAH

(*b.* 1902; *d.* 3 June 1989)

Cleric and leader of the 1978–1979 Islamic revolution in Iran, which overthrew Shah Mohammed Reza Pahlavi and transformed Iran from a close ally to a major adversary of the United States. The turbulent effects of this revolution have been felt not only in U.S.-Iranian relations but throughout the Middle East and elsewhere. Khomeini was born in the small Iranian town of Khomeini into a family of well-known, well-to-do clerics. He studied theology and gradually established a reputation as an Islamic scholar and teacher, receiving the religious title of honor "ayatollah" by the early 1960s. His first major political activity occurred in 1963, when he publicly denounced the enfranchisement of women and other reforms being implemented by the shah. Khomeini was arrested, sparking huge demonstrations that were brutally suppressed by the shah's security forces. In 1964 Khomeini again publicly criticized the shah's regime, denouncing the close military ties between Iran and the United States and condemning the shah's decision to grant diplomatic immunity to U.S. military advisers. He was arrested again and deported to Turkey but soon made his way to Iraq, Iran's neighbor and rival, where he settled in the holy Shi'ite city of Najaf.

In Najaf, Khomeini began to teach and gradually established a wide circle of students. Many of his students returned to Iran, creating a network that enabled him to keep in touch with events there and to disseminate his speeches and writings. While in Iraq he continued to denounce the shah's regime and its ties with the United States and wrote his seminal work *Islamic Government* (1979), which contains his blueprint for an Islamic political system. As opposition to the shah grew in the 1970s, Khomeini's attacks increased, and he established ties with other Iranian opposition forces.

In 1978 Iraqi President Saddam Hussein expelled Khomeini, in part because of his fears that Khomeini's preachings were also arousing Iraq's Shi'ite population and in part as a result of the Iraqi-Iranian rapprochement in the 1975 Algiers Accord. Khomeini then moved to Paris, where he had closer contacts with other elements of the anti-shah opposition and greater access to communications technologies (from the mass media to cassette tapes on which his recorded messages were smuggled into Iran), which allowed him to have even greater impact. In 1978 he emerged as the preeminent opposition leader, and the revolutionary crowds that swept the shah from power increasingly called for the establishment of an Islamic government under his leadership. After the shah's departure into exile in January 1979, Khomeini returned triumphantly to Iran. He arrived in Tehran on 1 February and appointed a government four days later.

The revolutionary coalition was extremely diverse, ranging from secular moderates to radical Islamists. Khomeini at first remained aloof from the growing confrontation between these factions, naming a government headed by the moderate Mehdi Bazargan but also putting radicals in prominent positions. He frequently denounced the United States but initially took no major actions against U.S. interests. As Islamic radicals gained control over the course of the revolution during 1979, Khomeini began to side with them. When a group of Islamic radical students seized the U.S. embassy compound on 4 November and took some seventy embassy staff members hostage, Khomeini quickly endorsed their actions, leading the Bazargan government to resign. The hostage crisis took on great symbolic importance during the following year, with the radicals—now clearly backed by Khomeini—using it to mobilize popular support for their position and thus further isolate the moderates. It was also a humiliating experience for the United States and President Jimmy Carter's administration, which was made to appear weak and ineffective. By the time the hostages were released in January 1981, the Islamic radicals had consolidated their control over the revolution and Carter had been driven from the presidency, with the hostage crisis one of the key factors in the campaign.

In December 1979 Iranians overwhelmingly endorsed a new constitution based on Islamic law that named Khomeini supreme jurisprudent and gave him extensive powers. From this position Khomeini guided and shaped the revolution during the following decade, purging the few remaining moderates and restructuring Iranian society along Islamic lines. He also sought to mobilize the Islamic world against an international system that he regarded as immoral and exploitative. Under Khomeini, Iran virulently criticized the United States and other Western powers and provided considerable moral and matériel assistance to radical Islamic forces fighting against Israel and pro-Western governments in Saudi Arabia, Kuwait, Lebanon, and other Arab countries. Khomeini was also sharply critical of the Soviet Union, branding it "the other Satan" and providing extensive assistance to Islamic guerrilla forces fighting against the Soviet-backed government in Afghanistan. As the 1980s wore on, Iran became increasingly bogged down in a bloody war with Iraq, which drained its resources and limited its ability to export its Islamic revolution. Khomeini's health deterio-

rated throughout the 1980s, producing growing concern about the succession and the future of the revolution. In the year before his death in June 1989 Khomeini ended the war with Iraq, pronounced a death sentence on the British author Salman Rushdie, and named the relatively hard-line Hojat al-Islam Ali Khamenei as his successor, trying to ensure that the revolution would survive and retain its radical Islamic character.

MARK J. GASIOROWSKI

See also Iran; Iran-Iraq War; Iraq

FURTHER READING

Akhavi, Shahrough. *Religion and Politics in Contemporary Iran.* Albany, N.Y., 1980.

Algar, Hamid. *Islam and Revolution: Writings and Declarations of Imam Khomeini.* Berkeley, Calif., 1981.

Bakhash, Shaul. *The Reign of the Ayatollahs: Iran and the Islamic Revolution.* New York, 1984.

Wright, Robin. *In the Name of God: The Khomeini Decade.* New York, 1989.

KHRUSHCHEV, NIKITA SERGEYEVICH
(*b.* 17 April 1894; *d.* 11 September 1971)

Joseph Stalin's successor as leader of the Soviet Union and the dominant figure in Soviet politics from 1953 until his ouster in 1964. Khrushchev was a contradictory figure who made his career as one of Stalin's most energetic supporters during the 1930s; once in power, however, he delivered the "secret speech" that exposed Stalin's crimes and tried to make the Soviet system somewhat more responsive to its citizens' needs. In foreign policy, he championed peaceful coexistence with the United States but also engaged in nuclear diplomacy in Berlin and Cuba that led to the most dangerous crises of the Cold War.

Born in a small Ukrainian village, Khrushchev left school at the age of fourteen to become a metal-fitter in Yuzovka (now Donetsk). He joined the Bolshevik party in 1918 during the Russian civil war and rose through the ranks during the 1920s and 1930s. Like many party workers of his generation, Khrushchev based his enthusiasm for the socialist system less on his knowledge of Marxist-Leninist theory than on his faith that the regime would create a better society. He also took an active part in Stalin's terror, particularly in Ukraine, where Khrushchev's appointment as party leader in 1938 coincided with purges that decimated the local party apparatus.

As first secretary of the Communist party and later as Soviet premier, Khrushchev took a practical approach to socialism that led him to loosen the reins of Stalinism and to improve Soviet living standards, but he also zealously guarded the party's exclusive claim to power. His foreign policy reflected this approach. In Eastern Europe he accepted Marshall Josip Tito's variant of communism in Yugoslavia but brutally suppressed an uprising that endangered party rule in Hungary in 1956. With respect to the West, he affirmed Communist party doctrine claiming that socialism eventually would triumph over capitalism, but he revised that doctrine to assert that war between the two social systems was no longer inevitable. Soviet nuclear weapons, he argued, would deter any military aggression against the socialist camp and shift the locus of the ideological struggle to an economic and political competition. As part of this strategy, Khrushchev expanded Soviet political interests beyond Eurasia to appeal to nonaligned and nationalist states throughout the world. He also predicted that the Soviet Union would "bury" capitalism, overtaking the United States in productivity by 1980. Finally, although he declared peaceful coexistence to be the guiding principle of Soviet foreign policy, he asserted that this required that the capitalist countries recognize the legitimacy of socialist regimes in East Europe and deal with the Soviet Union as an equal.

Khrushchev's efforts to balance peaceful coexistence and ideological struggle contributed to a series of alternating crises and détentes between 1958 and 1962. After the launch of the Soviet satellite *Sputnik* in 1957, Khrushchev argued that the Soviet Union's superior missile technology allowed the Soviet regime to reduce conventional defense spending to further his ambitious economic program. The growing disparity in strategic weapons between the Soviet Union and the United States challenged this argument, however. Khrushchev also felt pressure from within the socialist camp, particularly from Mao Zedong and East German first secretary Walter Ulbricht, to assert Soviet power more aggressively. These pressures all converged in conflict over the divided Germany. Comparisons between the two German states, it was felt, played a crucial role in the ideological competition, and East Germany, suffering from a lack of legitimacy and economic instability, fared badly in comparison to the booming West. Discussions within the North Atlantic Treaty Organization (NATO) over whether to give West Germany command over nuclear weapons compounded Khrushchev's concerns about East Germany's status. Khrushchev attempted to induce the United States to recognize East Germany by exploiting the image of Soviet nuclear prowess. He proposed an arms control summit that would tacitly recognize the status quo in Europe. When this failed, he resorted to brinkmanship. In November 1958 he threatened to sign a peace treaty with East Germany giving that country control over access routes into West Berlin if the Western powers did not agree to end their occupation of the city within six months. He later lifted the deadline, satisfied that the West would negotiate the question seriously.

In September 1959 Khrushchev met President Dwight D. Eisenhower at Camp David, Maryland. The summit produced no concrete agreements, but recently revealed evidence suggests Khrushchev left the meeting convinced that Eisenhower would accept a transitional agreement on Berlin that later would lead to recognition of East Germany. In early 1960, when it became clear that this would not be the case, the "spirit of Camp David" faded. Then, in May 1960, two weeks before a scheduled summit meeting in Paris, Soviet air defenses shot down an American U-2 spy plane over Soviet territory. When Eisenhower refused to apologize for this violation of Soviet sovereignty, Khrushchev responded with an angry outburst that wrecked the summit.

In 1961 Khrushchev became increasingly concerned about the growing stream of refugees using the open borders in Berlin to leave East Germany. He hoped the election of John F. Kennedy to the presidency would lead to a change in U.S. policy on Germany. When the two leaders met without result in Vienna in June, however, Khrushchev renewed his threat to sign a separate peace treaty with East Germany. When this also failed to produce a favorable response, Khrushchev did not carry out his threat but did order the construction of the Berlin Wall. In the end, Khrushchev's nuclear diplomacy proved counterproductive. Although he abhorred the prospect of nuclear war, he became notorious for his claims that Soviet factories were producing missiles "like sausages" and for threats like the one he issued to former U.S. Ambassador W. Averell Harriman that "if you send tanks [into Berlin] they will burn and make no mistake about it." Such rhetoric exacerbated U.S. fears of communist aggression and encouraged the United States to build up its own defenses even more aggressively.

Khrushchev's nuclear diplomacy reached a climax in 1962, when he ordered the deployment of missiles on Cuba. When in response Kennedy blockaded the island, Khrushchev agreed to remove the missiles in return for U.S. assurance that it would not invade Cuba. Khrushchev, claiming success in the crisis, contended that he had placed the missiles in Cuba to deter such an attack. Many scholars, however, believe he was looking for a quick and inexpensive way to offset U.S. strategic superiority.

After the crisis in the Caribbean subsided, Khrushchev abandoned nuclear diplomacy in favor of détente. In August 1963 he signed the Limited Nuclear Test Ban Treaty with the United States and Great Britain, and the next year he undertook a new initiative to open negotiations with West Germany and again sought to reduce conventional defense spending. His ouster in October 1964 cut these initiatives short. Although most accounts explain the coup by focusing on his domestic reforms and his increasingly arbitrary leadership style, this new foreign policy initiative, combined with perceived failures in Berlin and Cuba, probably played a role as well.

JAMES RICHTER

See also Berlin; Brinkmanship; Cold War; Cuban Missile Crisis; Germany; Limited Nuclear Test Ban Treaty; Nuclear Weapons and Strategy; Russia and the Soviet Union; Stalin, Joseph; U-2 Incident

FURTHER READING

Beschloss, Michael R. *The Crisis Years: Kennedy and Khrushchev, 1960–1963.* New York, 1991.

Khrushchev, Nikita S. *Khrushchev Remembers: The Last Testament.* Introduction by Edward Crankshaw and Jerrold Shecter. Translated and edited by Strobe Talbott. Boston, 1974.

——— . *Khrushchev Remembers: The Glasnost Tapes.* Foreword by Strobe Talbott. Translated and edited by Jerrold Shecter with Vyacheslav V. Luchkov. Boston, 1990.

Linden, Carl. *Khrushchev and the Soviet Leadership, 1957–1964.* Baltimore, 1966.

Richter, James G. K . *Khrushchev's Double Bind: International Pressures and Domestic Coalition Politics.* Baltimore, 1994.

KIM IL SUNG

(*b.* 15 April 1912; *d.* 8 July 1994)

Leader of the Democratic People's Republic of Korea for nearly five decades. He joined the Communist Youth League in 1926 to combat the Japanese occupation of Korea. Kim fought alongside Chinese Communists against Japanese forces in China until traveling to the Soviet Union for training in 1941. Kim returned to Korea in September 1945 with Soviet troops in the north of his divided nation and parlayed his ties with Moscow into leadership of the provisional People's Committee in February 1946. He adroitly maneuvered within a contentious political climate to win election as premier of the Democratic People's Republic of Korea (North Korea) in September 1948. Kim visited Joseph Stalin in March 1949 and again in April 1950. In the latter meeting, Kim and Stalin likely reached a secret military agreement to force the reunification of Korea. Kim's open ties with Mao Zedong's Chinese government also alarmed the Western world at the time. Although years of border clashes with Syngman Rhee's South Korea heightened tensions, Kim deserves a large share of the responsibility for initiating full-scale hostilities in June 1950. Following the Korean War, Kim successfully exploited the growing Sino-Soviet rivalry to maintain a nationalistic and independent regime in North Korea. Kim developed the concept of *chuch'e*, the application of Marxism and Leninism to the specific conditions of Korea. He utilized this principle to espouse a "monolithic ideological system," including an ideology of self reliance, independence in politics, autarkic economic policies, and military self-defense. The United States never established diplomatic relations with North Korea. By 1980 the dictatorial Kim had arranged for his son Kim Jong Il to succeed him as supreme leader of North Korea.

JEFFREY D. BASS

See also Korean War; Rhee, Syngman; Truman, Harry S.

FURTHER READING

Baik Bong. *Kim Il Sung: Biography.* Pyongyang, N. Korea, 1973.

Kim Il Sung. *With the Century: Reminiscences.* Pyongyang, N. Korea, 1993.

Suh, Dae-Sook. *Kim Il Sung: The North Korean Leader.* New York, 1988.

KING, MARTIN LUTHER, JR.

(*b.* 15 January 1929; *d.* 4 April 1968)

Baptist minister, civil rights leader, and opponent of the Vietnam War. Born in Atlanta, Georgia, King received a doctorate in theology from Boston University in 1955. That same year, King rose to national prominence as the leader of the Montgomery Improvement Association, which organized a successful boycott of segregated buses in that Alabama city. In 1957 he helped found the Southern Christian Leadership Conference (SCLC), an organization of black ministers dedicated to ending racial segregation. During his first ten years of civil rights activism, King's statements about international affairs and U.S. foreign policy were limited. He championed decolonization efforts in Africa, opposed U.S. support of all-white regimes in Rhodesia and South Africa, and called for world disarmament and an end to mass violence in international relations. He also contended that the struggle for civil rights in the United States and decolonization in Africa were different aspects of the same battle against white racism.

After receiving the Nobel Peace Prize in 1964, however, King believed that he had a moral obligation to protest all violence and injustice. He criticized U.S. hostility toward the People's Republic of China and protested U.S. intervention in the Vietnam War, urging the United States to invite all parties, including the Vietcong, to peace negotiations. King's early statements questioning the Vietnam War provoked a severe backlash, and in September 1965 he muted his criticism of the war to avoid hampering his civil rights agenda; his references to the war in late 1965 and 1966 were couched in terms of its harmful effects on social reform programs. In early 1967, however, King decided that he could no longer remain silent on the escalating war. On 4 April 1967 he delivered his most famous address on the war, "Beyond Vietnam," in which he charged that the United States, because of its "paranoid anticommunism" and its support of dictators in Vietnam and in other countries, had become the "greatest purveyor of violence in the world." King participated in other Vietnam protests and was rumored to be a peace candidate for president or vice president in 1968, but he was shot and killed by a white assassin in Memphis, Tennessee.

SHANE J. MADDOCK

See also Peace Movements and Societies, 1914 to Present; Vietnam War

FURTHER READING:

Fairclough, Adam. "Martin Luther King, Jr. and the War in Vietnam." *Phylon* 45 (1984): 19–39.

———. *To Redeem the Soul of America: The Southern Christian Leadership Conference and Martin Luther King, Jr.* Athens, Ga., 1987.

Garrow, David J. *Bearing the Cross: Martin Luther King, Jr., and the Southern Christian Leadership Conference.* New York, 1986.

KING, WILLIAM LYON MACKENZIE

(*b.* 17 December 1874; *d.* 22 July 1950)

Prime minister of Canada (1921–1930, 1935–1948), who led his nation into closer diplomatic, economic, and military relations with the United States. Born in Berlin, Ontario, King attended graduate school in the United States (University of Chicago and Harvard University); worked at Chicago's Hull House, a progressive reform settlement house; and during the early years of World War I served as a labor consultant to the Rockefeller family in the troubled Colorado mining industry. King became deputy minister of labor in Ottawa in 1900, a post he held until he won election to Parliament in 1908; soon after he joined the cabinet of Sir Wilfrid Laurier as minister of labor and remained in that post until the government's defeat in 1911. Chosen party leader in 1919, King became the Liberal prime minister in 1921 and for the rest of the decade devoted himself to increasing Canada's autonomy from Great Britain. In 1922, for example, he turned down a British request, made in anticipation of war with Turkey, for Canadian troops. King lost his mandate in Parliament in the election of 1930 but regained his power in 1935. Chosen prime minister once again, he improved economic relations with the United States through reciprocal trade agreements in 1935 and 1938 that substantially lowered tariffs in both countries.

The threat of war also brought King and U.S. President Franklin D. Roosevelt together, beginning in 1937, as they explored options for continental defense. In August 1940, after the fall of France, the two met at Ogdensburg, New York, to create the Permanent Joint Board on Defense. The next year, at Roosevelt's home, they signed the Hyde Park Agreement, which, in addition to resolving Canada's short-term need for U.S. dol-

lars, sped up the long-term process of continental economic integration. After the Japanese attack on Pearl Harbor in December 1941, King acceded to U.S. requests for permission to build a land route through Canada to Alaska; more than 33,000 U.S. military and civilian personnel, at peak strength, worked in the Canadian north. When the war ended, King's government paid full value for all U.S. installations to ensure U.S. withdrawal. During the Cold War, the potential threat posed by the Soviet Union prompted continued U.S.-Canadian cooperation, and in early 1947 King and President Harry S. Truman agreed to expand bilateral military links. A cautious leader but a supremely skilled politician capable of moving ruthlessly in crisis, King was a bundle of contradictions in both personality and policy, at once a nationalist, a British Empire loyalist, and a North American continentalist.

J. L. GRANATSTEIN

See also Canada; Hyde Park Aide-Mémoire Agreement; World War II

FURTHER READING

Granatstein, J. L. *Canada's War: The Politics of the Mackenzie King Government, 1939–1945.* Toronto, 1990.

Pickersgill, J. W. *The Mackenzie King Record*, 4 vols. Toronto, 1960–1970.

Stacey, C. P. *A Very Double Life: The Private World of Mackenzie King.* Toronto, 1976.

KING COTTON DIPLOMACY

See American Civil War; Confederate States of America

KIRKPATRICK, JEANE DUANE

(*b.* 19 November 1926)

U.S. representative to the United Nations (1981–1985). Born in Oklahoma, Kirkpatrick graduated from Barnard College (B.A., 1948) and Columbia University (M.A, 1950). She taught political science at Trinity College (1962–1967) and Georgetown University (1967–1981), both in Washington, D.C. A long-time supporter of Hubert Humphrey, a Minnesota Democrat, Kirkpatrick turned to neoconservative politics in the 1970s, in part because of her anger at the treatment that Humphrey received from leftists in 1968. Kirkpatrick attracted Republican Governor Ronald Reagan's attention with a November 1979 *Commentary* article, "Dictatorships and Double Standards," and, after his election to the presidency the following year, he appointed her to the UN post in appreciation of her argument that the United States should support "authoritarian" rulers, such as the shah of Iran, but oppose "totalitarian" ones, such as the

Nicaraguan Sandinistas. Kirkpatrick advocated funding the Nicaraguan Contras, remaining neutral toward the Argentine military government during the 1982 Falklands War, and defending South Africa and Israel in the UN. Her insistence on scolding or withholding aid from nations and UN agencies that challenged U.S. policies alienated many international officials. Kirkpatrick's reputation as a hard-liner, coupled with her relative inexperience in bureaucratic infighting, limited her influence within the Reagan administration and effectively removed her from serious consideration for appointment to higher positions, such as secretary of state or national security adviser. In 1985 she returned to teaching and devoted much of her time to writing, public lecturing, consulting, and fundraising for conservative organizations.

JUDITH EWELL

See also Reagan, Ronald Wilson; United Nations

FURTHER READING

Ewell, Judith. "Barely in the Inner Circle: Jeane Kirkpatrick." In *Women and American Foreign Policy: Lobbyists, Critics, and Insiders*, 2nd ed., edited by Edward P. Crapol. Wilmington, Del., 1992.
Kirkpatrick, Jeane J. *Dictatorships and Double Standards: Rationalism and Reason in Politics*. New York, 1982.
———. *The Reagan Phenomenon and Other Speeches on Foreign Policy*. Washington, D.C., 1983.

KISSINGER, HENRY ALFRED

(*b.* 27 May 1923)

Political scientist and foreign policy consultant, national security adviser (1969–1975), and secretary of state (1973–1977). A German-born, Jewish refugee from Nazism, Kissinger became a prominent interpreter of U.S. foreign policy during the 1950s, a part-time foreign policy adviser to Presidents John F. Kennedy and Lyndon B. Johnson in the 1960s, and the major architect of U.S. foreign policy in the administrations of Richard M. Nixon and Gerald R. Ford from 1969 to 1977. After leaving government service in January 1977, Kissinger became a highly paid private consultant on foreign affairs, a prolific author, and a frequent commentator on world events in the mass media. Kissinger won praise for his intellectual prowess and his dramatic and unexpected initiatives in foreign affairs, especially toward China and the Soviet Union. At the same time, he often drew criticism for personal shortcomings, notably arrogance and self-promotion, for conducting a secretive foreign policy without appropriate consultation with Congress, and for promoting order abroad with little regard for human rights.

He was born Heinz Alfred Kissinger in Fuerth, Bavaria. After Adolf Hitler became chancellor of Germany in 1933, the virulent anti-Semitism of the Nazi era destroyed the comfortable environment of the Kissingers. Kissinger's boyhood experience as a Jew in Nazi Germany left an indelible mark on him. For the remainder of his career he feared disorder, distrusted intense popular emotions, and felt an intense longing for acceptance in his new land. With his family, he fled Germany in 1938 and settled in New York City, and changed his first name to Henry. Kissinger flourished in high school and entered the City College of New York in 1940. He was drafted into the U.S. Army after Pearl Harbor and became a U.S. citizen in 1943. Kissinger's army service began his professional interest in foreign affairs, and his intellect and ambition caught the eye of superiors. He lectured troops, some many years his senior, about the nature of World War II. After the destruction of the Nazi regime, he served as an intelligence officer for three years in occupied Germany. He left the army in 1947 to enter Harvard University to complete his undergraduate studies.

Kissinger became more Americanized at Harvard. A brilliant undergraduate and graduate career did not diminish his personal insecurities, his desire for acceptance in his adopted country, and his profound sense that social order needed to be preserved. The academic study of realism in international relations (an interpretation that elevated the importance of power in world politics) deeply influenced his studies. He wrote a doctoral dissertation on the aftermath of the Napoleonic Wars, published as *A World Restored: Metternich, Castlereagh and the Problems of Peace, 1812–1822* (1957). In this book Kissinger praised the conservative Austrian statesman Chancellor Klemens von Metternich for preserving world order in a revolutionary period by deft manipulations of the balance of power. Kissinger consciously perceived parallels between the position of the states threatened by the French Revolution and the United States facing the revolutionary Soviet Union in the mid-twentieth century.

After he completed his doctorate (1954), Kissinger remained at Harvard as an instructor and director of the university's International Seminar, a body that invited important politicians and business executives from other countries to the campus. These contacts proved invaluable later, as did the people Kissinger met at the Council on Foreign Relations, where he worked from 1955 to 1957. His principal assignment there was to craft an analysis of the ways in which the development of nuclear weapons had affected modern statecraft. In 1957 he published *Nuclear Weapons and Foreign Policy*, in which he argued that these new, extraordinarily destructive tools of warfare had not made traditional diplomacy obsolete and that the existence of nuclear weapons did not mean the United States could safely rely upon a strategy of massive retaliation, as Secretary of State John Foster Dulles had proposed in 1954. He returned to Harvard as a professor of government and international affairs in 1957.

Kissinger's writings on nuclear weapons brought him to the attention of policymakers and politicians. New York's Republican Governor Nelson A. Rockefeller asked Kissinger for advice on foreign policy to be used in a potential race for the Republican presidential nomination in 1960. After Rockefeller lost the nomination to Richard Nixon, Kissinger offered opinions on nuclear weapons and U.S.-European relations to Democratic candidate John F. Kennedy. Kissinger remained in Cambridge, Massachusetts, during the Kennedy administration, but he served as a part-time foreign policy consultant to the White House, where a number of officials found him vain and pompous, and thus never allowed him in their inner circle. The Lyndon B. Johnson administration used his services more. Kissinger provided information about the policies of French President Charles de Gaulle and West German Chancellor Ludwig Erhard. In 1967 he undertook his most important mission for the Johnson administration when he used contacts developed over years of directing the Harvard seminar to open secret negotiations aimed at ending the war in Vietnam. These talks, code-named "Pennsylvania," did not succeed.

The domestic turmoil created by the Vietnam War represented for Kissinger a dangerous threat to social stability. The tumultuous politics of 1968 provided him an opportunity to influence foreign policy in the administration that succeeded Johnson. He once more worked as foreign policy adviser to Rockefeller. After Rockefeller again lost the nomination to Nixon, Kissinger advised Vice President Hubert Humphrey, the Democratic presidential candidate. Without the knowledge of the Humphrey campaign, Kissinger also provided information to the Nixon camp about the Paris negotiations between the United States and North Vietnam.

The Nixon Years

One month after Nixon won the presidential election, he announced Kissinger's appointment as national security adviser. The two men then began what *Time* magazine characterized as the "improbable partnership" between Nixon, a "secretive, aloof…old-fashioned politician, given to over-simplified rhetoric," and Kissinger, a "Harvard professor of urbane intelligence." Nixon chose Kissinger to gain respect from the foreign policy establishment, which considered the president-elect a crude and untrustworthy anticommunist. Kissinger took the position in the hope of putting his conservative, realist views of foreign policy into practice while enhancing his personal reputation.

From 20 January 1969 until Nixon's resignation in disgrace on 9 August 1974, Nixon and Kissinger worked closely together. Profoundly disturbed at the toll the domestic controversy over the conduct of the war in Vietnam had taken on the bipartisan foreign policy consensus that had existed in the United States since 1947, the two tried to diminish the importance of Vietnam. At the same time, Kissinger, with Nixon's approval, concentrated foreign policy decision-making power within the White House staff of the National Security Council. He used secret, so called back-channel, lines of communications to establish détente between the United States and the Soviet Union and to open relations between the United States and the People's Republic of China, which had been in abeyance since 1949.

Kissinger quickly gained mastery over the foreign affairs bureaucracy and sharply curtailed the authority of Secretary of State William P. Rogers. In Kissinger's numerous private meetings with Nixon, he urged the president to hasten the withdrawal of U.S. ground forces from Vietnam, an initiative designed to reduce domestic concerns over the war. He also counseled an escalation in the air war over Vietnam and neighboring Cambodia and supported the ground invasion of Cambodia, which began on 30 April 1970. During 1969 and 1970 Kissinger met regularly with former academic colleagues and journalists, advising patience with the new administration's Vietnam policy. He falsely intimated to them that his advice moderated Nixon's more aggressive tendencies. In his private meetings with Nixon, he similarly berated his former colleagues and friends in the press for their liberal political views and their unwillingness to use force to achieve foreign policy ends.

Kissinger emerged into the limelight in 1971. His role in creating détente with the Soviet Union and opening a public dialogue with the People's Republic of China overshadowed Vietnam in the public consciousness. In May 1971 his back-channel negotiations with the Soviets bore fruit with the announcement that the United States and the Soviet Union promised to sign a treaty limiting the antiballistic missile systems each would deploy. In July came an even more dramatic revelation: Kissinger had secretly traveled to Beijing to prepare for a 1972 visit by Nixon to China. Kissinger gained a celebrity unlike that accorded any previous U.S. diplomat in the aftermath of his Chinese trip. In 1972 he accompanied Nixon on his February visit to China, where he helped draft the Shanghai communiqué, which provided for the opening of a U.S. diplomatic office in Beijing and a counterpart Chinese representative in Washington.

In March he returned to Moscow to lay the groundwork for a May summit meeting in Moscow between Nixon and Communist Party General Secretary Leonid Brezhnev. At that meeting Nixon and Brezhnev signed the Antiballistic Missile Treaty (limiting each side to two antiballistic missile installations), the Interim Agreement on the Limitations of Strategic Armaments (reducing the rate of growth of each side's strategic arsenal and promised a full Strategic Arms Limitations Treaty by

1976), and the Basic Principles of U.S.-Soviet Relations. These three documents formed the basis of détente between the United States and the Soviet Union.

Kissinger's negotiations with North Vietnamese politburo member Le Duc Tho in Paris also bore fruit in 1972. The two sides agreed to separate the military and political aspects of the war. In late October, two weeks before the presidential election, Kissinger announced that "peace is at hand" in the war in Vietnam. His statement proved premature, because the government of South Vietnam refused to accede to an agreement it considered inimical to its security. Nevertheless, Kissinger's dramatic diplomacy in 1971 and 1972 helped Nixon win a landslide reelection victory. In December, Kissinger advised Nixon to proceed with the heavy bombing of the cities of North Vietnam. The resulting "Christmas bombing" of Hanoi was probably designed more to reassure Saigon of U.S. determination to stand by South Vietnam than to alter North Vietnam's behavior.

Kissinger returned to Paris in January 1973 to resume negotiations with North Vietnam. On 27 January he and Le Duc Tho signed an agreement calling for a cease-fire in place, a return of prisoners of war, the evacuation of the remaining U.S. armed forces, and the continuation in office of the South Vietnamese government with a promise to open talks with the National Liberation Front to create a coalition government. The agreement ending the war in Vietnam created a International Control Commission to monitor compliance. There were no significant differences between the October 1972 terms and the final accord. Most Americans greeted news of the Paris agreement with relief and as further proof of Kissinger's skills as a negotiator. In October 1973 he and Le Duc Tho were awarded the Nobel Peace Prize for their work in ending the war in Vietnam.

Kissinger's reputation continued to grow in 1973, even as Nixon's standing fell because of the growing Watergate scandal. In late summer Nixon nominated him to serve as secretary of state; the president hoped that the public's high regard for Kissinger's conduct of foreign policy might stop further investigations of presidential malfeasance. After his confirmation as secretary of state in September, Kissinger retained his position as national security adviser—an unprecedented consolidation of power.

Secretary of State

Kissinger's diplomatic skills were severely tested almost immediately when war broke out between Israel and Egypt and Syria on 6 October, the Yom Kippur War. The conflict raised the specter of a superpower collision with the Soviet Union, which backed the Arab states. The United States became Israel's principal source of military assistance and political support. Kissinger traveled to Moscow to defuse tensions and arrange a cease-fire. He

succeeded, although not without putting U.S. nuclear forces on alert on 24 October, when it momentarily appeared that the Soviet Union was about to send forces to support Egypt. From late 1973 to the middle of 1975, Kissinger shuttled repeatedly to Cairo, Damascus, and Jerusalem, negotiating disengagement agreements between Israeli and Egyptian armies near the Suez Canal and between Israeli and Syrian forces on the Golan Heights.

The resignation of President Nixon in August 1974 and the succession to the presidency of Gerald R. Ford initially left Kissinger unscathed. The firestorm of criticism directed at Ford for his pardon of Nixon, however, also threatened to engulf Kissinger. In the fall of 1974 the public paid more attention than they had previously to reports that Kissinger had instructed agents of the Federal Bureau of Investigation (FBI) to tap the telephones of his subordinates on the National Security Council staff. His reputation suffered further damage after it became known that he had helped the leaders of Chile's military overthrow that country's democratically elected president, Salvador Allende Gossens, in 1973.

Many Americans, moreover, had grown skeptical about achieving the benefits promised by détente with the Soviet Union. Democratic Senator Henry Jackson, preparing to run for his party's presidential nomination in 1976, assailed Kissinger for negotiating arms control agreements with Moscow that permitted the Soviet Union to maintain more nuclear-tipped intercontinental ballistic missiles than did the United States. Jackson and other critics of détente also complained that Kissinger had ignored the abysmal Soviet record of violation of the human rights of its own citizens in his efforts to foster détente. Liberals and leftists, on the other hand, argued that détente did not go far enough in checking the arms race and went too far in undermining Third World nationalism.

Kissinger's foreign policy suffered more seriously in 1975. The communist victory in Vietnam in April, extinguishing the South Vietnamese government, reversed the earlier public approval of Kissinger and Le Duc Tho's 1973 cease-fire agreement. Kissinger later argued that had Watergate not forced Nixon from office, the United States would have provided sufficient military assistance to South Vietnam to stave off the 1975 communist offensive. That claim is not fully convincing, because Congress and the American public firmly balked at resuming the war after 1973. The U.S. defeat in Vietnam contributed to a further erosion of support for détente with the Soviet Union, a policy more and more Americans came to see as favoring Soviet interests at the expense of the United States. Kissinger and Ford traveled to Helsinki in August to sign the final act of the thirty-five-nation Conference on Security and Cooperation in Europe, an agreement signaling the capstone of détente. The two men claimed that the Helsinki Accords would bring the Soviets and their Eastern European allies closer to conformity with Western standards, because by signing they promised to forswear the use of force to change frontiers, allow more open borders, and monitor human rights. In retrospect, their optimism proved justified, but at the time critics charged that détente had ratified Soviet control over Eastern Europe.

The style and substance of Kissinger's foreign policy became a major issue in the presidential election of 1976. Former California Governor Ronald Reagan challenged Ford in the Republican presidential primaries. Reagan decried Kissinger's handling of relations with the Soviet Union, charging that détente had left the U.S. militarily vulnerable. Reagan also opposed Kissinger's negotiations toward the return of the Panama Canal to Panama. He asserted that Kissinger's opening to the People's Republic of China had betrayed longtime U.S. ally Taiwan. Ford considered Reagan's challenge such a threat that the president forbade his staff to use the term détente. In November 1975 Ford also reduced Kissinger's visibility by replacing him as national security adviser with Brent Scowcroft, Kissinger's deputy. Kissinger remained secretary of state.

Former Georgia Governor Jimmy Carter, the Democratic presidential nominee, also criticized Kissinger's handling of foreign policy. Carter complained that Kissinger's secrecy, his refusal to make appropriate use of the skills of the professional foreign affairs bureaucracy, and his indifference to the promotion of human rights in the communist bloc and in authoritarian regimes allied to the United States had produced a morally deficient foreign policy. Carter advocated arms control with the Soviet Union, but he complained that Kissinger had been so eager to reach an agreement that he had not taken care to reduce the absolute numbers, rather than the rate of growth, of nuclear weapons possessed by each side. Carter also intimated that Kissinger had dominated Ford to such an extent that the president did not exercise the proper control over the nation's international relations. Carter's remarks about Ford's apparent lack of grasp of foreign affairs and excessive dependence on Kissinger struck a responsive chord with the public when Ford blundered badly in a televised debate and suggested that the Soviet Union did not dominate Eastern Europe.

Kissinger left government service when the Jimmy Carter administration came to office in early 1977 but remained an influential and often controversial personality as a private citizen. In 1979 and 1983 he published two long volumes of memoirs of his years working for the Nixon administration; both enjoyed wide distribution. He created Kissinger Associates, an international consulting firm that provided advice on foreign affairs to private clients. He often voiced his opinions on foreign affairs in the mass media, including television. He also participated in public policy debates. He criticized the Carter administration's negotiations with the Soviet Union, and he insisted that Carter authorize the admission of the shah of Iran to the United States for medical treatment in 1979.

At the 1980 Republican National Convention he tried to arrange an unusual "co-presidency" between Reagan and Ford, in which the former would become president and the latter vice president in charge of foreign affairs. This unprecedented scheme did not bear fruit, but Kissinger became a regular adviser to Presidents Reagan and George Bush from 1981 to 1992. In 1983 Reagan appointed him chairman of a Bipartisan Commission on United States Policy toward Central America, which recommended increased U.S. economic aid to the region and a continuation of U.S. military assistance to antileftist regimes and guerrilla fighters. Bush made even greater use of Kissinger, consulting him often about the fall of communism in Eastern Europe and the future of the republics of the former Soviet Union. In 1994 Kissinger published *Diplomacy*, a long book that blended 300 years of diplomatic history with personal observations of leaders he had met. The book was widely praised for its deft characterizations of diplomats and statesmen, but many reviewers severely criticized its old-fashioned approach to the study and practice of international relations.

Throughout his long foreign affairs career, Kissinger sought to bring a European-style realist perspective to the conduct of U.S. foreign relations. Highly intelligent and articulate, a patient and imaginative negotiator, Kissinger enjoyed several significant successes as an informal government adviser and foreign affairs official. He tarnished his achievements, however, by his distrust for democratic institutions, his secrecy, his manipulation of subordinates, his egoism, and his general indifference to the fate of individuals suffering abuse at the hands of government authorities at home and in places as diverse as the Soviet Union, Iran, and Chile. He offered an essentially conservative and often pessimistic view of the world. According to his critics, Kissinger often demonstrated greater ability to resolve problems of the past than to shape the future.

ROBERT D. SCHULZINGER

See also Balance of Power; Carter, James Earl; China; Cold War; Détente; Ford, Gerald Rudolph; Middle East; National Security Council; Nixon, Richard Milhous; Nuclear Weapons and Strategy; Realism; Russia and the Soviet Union; Strategic Arms Limitation Talks and Agreements; Vietnam War; Watergate

FURTHER READING:
Hersh, Seymour. *The Price of Power: Kissinger in the Nixon White House.* New York, 1983.

Issaacson, Walter. *Kissinger: A Biography*. New York, 1992.

Kissinger, Henry. *White House Years*. Boston, 1979.

———. *Years of Upheaval*. Boston, 1983.

———. *Diplomacy*. New York, 1994.

Schulzinger, Robert D. *Henry Kissinger: Doctor of Diplomacy*. New York, 1989.

Starr, Harvey. *Henry Kissinger: Perceptions of World Politics*. Lexington, Ky., 1983.

KNOX, PHILANDER CHASE

(*b.* 6 May 1853; *d.* 12 October 1921)

U.S. attorney general (1901–1904), U.S. senator (1904–1909, 1917–1921), and secretary of state (1909–1913). Born in Brownsville, Pennsylvania, Chase had a notable career as a corporation lawyer in Pittsburgh before serving as attorney general and his appointment to fill the unexpired term of a senator from Pennsylvania. As President William H. Taft's secretary of state, Knox managed the administration's policy of "dollar diplomacy," designed to expand U.S. economic penetration abroad while serving U.S. security needs. Knox used more explicit economic rhetoric than his predecessors at the Department of State, but his commitment to overseas economic expansion was generally consistent with the policies of previous administrations. His desire for stability in Latin America led to repeated threats of military intervention and to the invasion and occupation of Nicaragua beginning in 1912. Knox also supported U.S. financiers who sought concessions in China, but his efforts accomplished little, other than to alienate Russia and Japan. Knox's limited experience and his irascible temperament hindered his effectiveness in Washington. Returning to the Senate in 1917, he supported U.S. entrance into World War I and later became prominent as an opponent of U.S. membership in the League of Nations.

JOHN M. CRAIG

See also Dollar Diplomacy; Taft, William Howard

FURTHER READING

Huntington-Wilson, Francis M. *Memoirs of an Ex-Diplomat*. Boston, 1945.

Scholes, Walter V., and Marie V. Scholes. *The Foreign Policies of the Taft Administration*. Columbia, Mo., 1970.

KOHL, HELMUT

(*b.* 3 April 1930)

Leader of the Christian Democratic Union (CDU), the dominant political party in Germany, and chancellor of West Germany since 1982 and of a united Germany since 1991. Much of the credit for detaching East Germany from Soviet control and for winning acceptance of a united Germany in the face of British and French as well as Russian reservations belongs to him.

Born in Ludwigshafen, the son of a customs official, Kohl was educated at Frankfurt and Heidelberg Universities, graduating from the latter in 1958; for the next eleven years he was an executive in an industrial organization. During these years, he engaged in political activity, first with the youth section of the CDU and then as a member of the Rhineland-Palatinate state legislature in 1959. He achieved national prominence in 1969 when he was elected minister-president of the Rhineland-Palatinate. As head of a German state, he automatically became a member of the Bundesrat, the upper house of the federal government in Bonn. Kohl's transition to party leader was rapid. In November 1969 he was named deputy chairman of the CDU, and in 1973 he became chairman. Defeated for the German chancellorship in 1976, he positioned himself as opposition floor leader in the lower house (Bundestag) to prepare for another challenge to Chancellor Helmut Schmidt in 1982.

An able politician, his forte has been domestic affairs, where he made few errors until the extravagant promises of unification without sacrifice caught up with him in the early 1990s. He barely retained his chancellorship in the election of 1994. Kohl enjoyed close working relations with Presidents Ronald Reagan and George Bush. Under Kohl's leadership, Germany replaced Great Britain in a "special relationship" with the United States after the departure of Margaret Thatcher as British prime minister. Although a devoted champion of European unification, Kohl lost stature abroad through his apparent insensitivity to the danger posted by neo-Nazi outbreaks and by his difficulties in adjusting the federal constitution to the needs of post–Cold War Europe.

LAWRENCE S. KAPLAN

See also Cold War; Germany

FURTHER READING

Bark, Dennis L., and David R. Gress. *A History of West Germany, 1963–1991*. Oxford, 1993.

Ninkovich, Frank. *Germany and the United States*. New York, 1995.

KOREA

Located in eastern Asia, bordering China and across the sea from Japan, it is a peninsula now divided into the two countries of North and South Korea. Contemporary U.S. relations with Korea are influenced by a complex history and by tensions between the two halves of the divided nation. In 1982 the United States and South Korea celebrated the centennial of U.S.-Korean diplomatic relations. Predictably, communist North Korea denounced the celebration as a fraud.

Americans first became involved in Korea as part of an overall effort to expand the U.S. economic presence in East Asia. That effort included Commodore Matthew Perry's opening of Japan (July 1853) and the Open Door Policy in China to limit European imperialism and make way for U.S. trade. Trade was the prime motivating factor for Americans in the region. In 1866 a U.S. merchant ship, the *General Sherman*, attempted unsuccessfully to penetrate Korea. Known in the west as the "Hermit Kingdom," Korea under the Yi (Choson) Dynasty sought to protect itself from the rapid changes being forced upon Japan and—most important—China, Korea's traditional suzerain. The destruction of the *General Sherman* and its crew on the river leading to Pyongyang, along with similar acts against other Westerners trying to open up Korea, precipitated increased efforts to force Korea out into a wider world. In 1871 a small U.S. naval fleet (five vessels) launched an attack that was repulsed at Kanghwa island near Seoul. Ultimately it was Japan that succeeded in breaking down the barriers in Korea. Anxious to join the imperialist conquests, Japan imposed in 1876 the Kanghwa Treaty, a one-sided arrangement that opened up Korea just as the Americans had done to Japan barely a generation earlier.

Koreans initially resisted the Chinese formula for diluting Japan's presence, namely by expanding diplomatic relations with other countries. Seoul considered Western-style relations with one alien country to be bad enough and did not want more foreigners in Korea. Domestic political conditions deteriorated in Korea, however, leading to a failed revolution that caused China to step in to administer Korea directly, including its diplomacy. This temporarily reduced Japanese influence. In the interim, U.S. Commodore Robert W. Shufeldt attempted in 1880 to use Japanese intermediaries to gain access to Korea, but Tokyo was not interested in sharing its hard-won access. When China gained control in Korea, it compelled Seoul to open up to other countries, starting with the United States, which appeared to be relatively benign. In 1882 a U.S.-Korea treaty was signed at Chemulpo (Inchon), and Lucius Foote was dispatched as the first U.S. minister to Korea.

The inauguration of U.S.-Korean diplomatic relations, clearly imposed on Korea by a combination of outside powers' policies, grated on Korean nationalism. Moreover, it unleashed a series of events in Korea that undermined Korean sovereignty. Other countries followed the Western diplomatic precedent set by the United States. Korea became the focus of rival empires. Most devastating were the efforts of imperial Japan and czarist Russia to dislodge the fading Chinese empire. These powers clashed in the Sino-Japanese War of 1894–1895 and Russo-Japanese War of 1904–1905 that produced increasing Japanese control in Korea. During this period, Americans in Korea engaged in business, conducted missionary activities that often benefited Korean society, and generally portrayed themselves as a viable and benign alternative to the more sinister foreign powers intervening in Korea. Americans unintentionally misled Koreans in this regard, arousing hopes that the United States might be able to help Korea fend off these external pressures. The United States' role in mediating the Treaty of Portsmouth that ended the Russo-Japanese War signaled strongly that U.S. interests were not always coincident with Korean interests. That war effectively sealed Korea's fate by removing serious challenges to Japan's interest in Korea, setting the stage for its phased incorporation by Japan in late 1905 and 1910. The United States sanctioned those actions by means of the Taft-Katsura Agreement of July 1905, in which Washington and Tokyo acknowledged each other's rights in the Philippines and Korea, respectively. That episode left a bitter aftertaste in the Korean consciousness—a feeling that Americans should not be trusted. For many Koreans, both North and South, the Taft-Katsura Agreement is a reminder of U.S. "betrayal." From 1905 to 1945 Japan controlled Korea and did so in a manner that initially received U.S. sanction.

During the Japanese occupation, the United States retained some redeeming features in Korean eyes. U.S. missionaries remained in Korea and carried out many useful social programs, and the United States was one of the places where Koreans found safe haven in exile. Korean immigration to U.S. territory (Hawai'i) began in 1903, but did not reach large proportions on the mainland until the 1970s and 1980s. Despite those positive aspects, the failure of the United States to respond in 1919 to pressures of activist exiles in Washington to include Korea under one of President Woodrow Wilson's Fourteen Points—the principle of self-determination—led many Koreans to see another betrayal. Korea launched in March 1919 a concerted campaign for independence, noted in Korea as Sam-Il (March 1) Day, but the campaign was crushed by the Japanese and not supported by the West, including the United States. To Americans, these responses were warranted because Japan had been an ally in World War I.

The interwar period witnessed no formal relationship between the United States and Korea, because Korea did not exist as a separate political entity. Nonetheless, as World War II drew nearer, the small Korean exile group in the United States sought to differentiate itself from ethnic Japanese and make the case for Korea's independence after the war. The exile group had very limited success. Korea was treated by the United States as part of the Japanese Empire. Industries in Korea, some of which were Korean owned, served the Japanese war machine. Moreover, Koreans served in the Japanese armed forces and some of them earned a reputation for particular cruelty during Japanese campaigns in Southeast Asia. When plans were formulated at the Cairo Conference for dealing with that empire after the war, Korea's independence was to be granted in "due course."

Relations 1945–1950

In short, when Korea was liberated from Japan, the United States focused on subduing former enemy territory. From the Korean perspective, however, the United States was unprepared and insufficiently sensitive to Korean aspirations. To the United States, administering Korea was a peripheral event compared to the main situation in Japan. That sense of priorities has, for better or worse, reverberated throughout U.S.-Korean relations since 1945, often to the annoyance of Koreans. In the early postwar years the United States's policy toward Korea, carried out via the U.S. military government, was half-hearted. Washington's main purpose was to shed the responsibilities for Korea it inherited as a consequence of victory over Japan. It started by creating an interim Korean legislature in December of 1946. Unfortunately for Korea, the United States shared jurisdiction with the Soviet Union, which assumed responsibilities in northern Korea and created the informal division of Korea. These arrangements were supposed to be temporary—a fact that reinforced U.S. reluctance to become overly committed. Had Cold War tensions rooted in the U.S.-Soviet confrontation in Europe not erupted, Moscow's role in Korea might have been benign. That was not to be because of the Soviet Union's efforts to extend its control and influence globally. The Cold War quickly contaminated circumstances in Korea, causing North-South frictions as leaders in Seoul and Pyongyang became proxies for their prime backers. As ideological positions hardened, Washington utilized the United Nations as a means to secure free elections in all of Korea but was rebuffed by Moscow. Nonetheless, the UN conducted elections in May 1948 in the southern part of Korea, administered by the United States, that led to the creation on 15 August 1948 of the Republic of Korea (ROK). Washington and many other UN countries recognized the ROK as the only legitimate government in Korea.

Through these occupation and political actions, the United States earned the appreciation of many South Koreans. Nevertheless, some South Koreans often criticized the United States as a party to the division of the Korean nation as much as, or more than, the Soviet Union. U.S. actions also earned the unmitigated animosity of the North Koreans. With Soviet support North Korea created the Democratic People's Republic of Korea (DPRK). Coming into power in September 1948, a month after the ROK, and headed by Moscow's protégé, Kim Il Sung, Pyongyang blamed the formal division on the ROK and the United States. Although it was equally responsible, the Soviet Union received less criticism than the United States from Koreans in both halves of the divided nation.

Despite this U.S. role in shaping postwar Korea, Washington still was intent upon minimizing U.S. responsibilities. Its short-term goal was to make South Korea viable. In meeting that goal the United States resorted to the expediency of installing the most amenable politicians it could identify. This yielded a crop of leaders from the ranks of former exiles and Christian converts who were often not the first choice of South Koreans, but who could communicate with Americans in English and claimed to share an interest in democratic pluralism. Most prominent was Syngman Rhee, who returned from leadership of the small exile group in the United States to become the first president of the fledgling ROK.

On the eve of the Korean War (1950–1953), the U.S. agenda in South Korea was ambiguous. Although Washington helped Seoul organize politically and assisted the South Koreans to start to create a viable economy, Americans admitted the challenges on both fronts were enormous. Korea had virtually no democratic experience and southern Korea had been so overwhelmingly agricultural that the prospects for a more balanced economy were bleak. From a strategic vantage point, Washington was much less engaged prior to the Korean War. The Joint Chiefs of Staff advised President Harry S. Truman that "the U.S. has little strategic interest in maintaining the present troops and bases in Korea." Most U.S. forces were withdrawn in 1949. In that vein, Secretary of State Dean Acheson in January 1950 defined the U.S. defense perimeter in the western Pacific to exclude Korea. Although this is often noted as another example of Americans betraying Korea, Acheson actually recognized Korea's regional importance, but stressed that its security should be addressed in a broad, comprehensive manner. Nevertheless, U.S. actions and policies may have given North Korea and the Soviet Union the impression that the DPRK could take over South Korea with little risk of U.S. intervention. When North Korean forces attacked the ROK on 25 June 1950, and quickly overran much of the country, Washington reevaluated its options and—in recognition of Korea's regional importance and in order to make a statement about rejecting communist aggression—it came to South Korea's rescue by leading a UN-authorized coalition intervention.

The Korean War

The Korean War was a bitter one. Whether it was solely a war of aggression or actually a civil war remains a source of controversy. In many respects it was both. Nonetheless, the United States responded on the basis of communist aggression against a free and independent country, strongly linking the Korean War to the overarching Cold War in Europe. The war risked escalation to a superpower conflict and came very close to escalating to a direct conflict between the United States and the People's Republic of China (PRC). Washington's "police action" in the Korean War created a number of precedents for Cold War concepts: limited war, deterrence, burden-sharing, and—perhaps most important for the rest of Asia—putting U.S. credibility on the line in the region on behalf of global containment. The Korean War also demonstrated some of the tensions in U.S. civil-military relationships when President Truman removed General Douglas MacArthur for not staying within the confines of his orders. In a more limited sense the U.S. public's opposition to the Korean War's pace and Washington's willingness to settle for less than a military victory set the stage for later popular resistance during the Vietnam War.

The Korean War never formally ended, although a truce was signed on 27 July 1953 between the UN forces and North Korea, accompanied by its PRC ally. South Korea was not a signatory because Rhee rejected Washington's readiness to compromise. Those details have complicated the management of the truce relationship ever since and made the adversarial position of the United States vis-à-vis North Korea more central than it might otherwise have been. When the major active hostilities ceased in 1953 (notwithstanding the sporadic flare-ups over the subsequent years), the United States had suffered about 54,000 deaths and a total of 142,000 U.S. casualties. Thousands of the dead were missing in action (MIA), for which most have never been accounted. Korean War MIAs did not become a topic of controversy comparable to those of the Vietnam War.

The Korean War sealed Korea's fate as a divided country for the remainder of the Cold War, and a Korean version of the Cold War persisted long after the U.S.-Soviet version ended. Over the decades since the Korean War, the U.S.-Korean relationship experienced a profound transformation. In the early post–Korean War years South Korea was an impoverished, war-torn country that was dependent upon the United States for material sustenance and its security. While this may seem grim, it was an improvement on the previous U.S.-ROK relationship, because in the late 1950s Washington emphasized a U.S. stake in Korean freedom, stability, and regional importance. Kim Il Sung's attack on South Korea did for the ROK what the prewar Rhee government could not—namely to generate an authentic U.S. commitment to an ally. It also widened the gap between the United States and North Korea, in which each side demonized the other in ways that served South Korea's interests in securing U.S. support. South Korea became for the United States an outpost against global communism and South Korea's enemy became the enemy of the United States. This configuration put a unique spin on the U.S. strategic perspective on Korea that had a lasting impact. In contrast to the U.S. alliance relationship with nearby Japan, which focused directly on the Soviet threat throughout the Cold War years and helped make Japan the cornerstone of U.S. policy in the region, the U.S.-ROK alliance (based on a 1953 treaty) focused explicitly on North Korea rather than on the Soviet Union.

In the post–Korean War 1950s, Washington expended many resources to rebuild South Korea and to help it develop into a country capable of contributing to the U.S.-led network of containment partners. The Rhee government made some progress, but not enough to pull South Korea out of its economic troubles. Furthermore, U.S. largesse contributed to corruption in the Rhee government. There was a sense in the United States that South Korea might be on the U.S. dole indefinitely. This situation, coupled with the relative economic successes being achieved in North Korea at the time, precipitated a political upheaval in Seoul. Rhee was ousted on 27 April 1960 by a combination of student demonstrations and signals from both Washington and the ROK military that they agreed with student complaints about governmental mismanagement.

The Post-Rhee Years

After Rhee fled Korea to Hawaii in 1960 with U.S. assistance, a short-term experiment in democracy occurred. The United States supported the Chang Myun government, but its support proved to be inadequate to forestall a more dramatic intervention by the ROK military in South Korean politics. Elements in the ROK army led by Major General Park Chung Hee staged a coup in May 1961, inaugurating a period in South Korean politics that lasted until 1992 in which the South Korean government was headed by a former general with strong backing of the ROK army. Park's coup was a political setback for the United States, an embarrassment for its Cold War cause. Although the United States initially tried to induce Park to relinquish power, Washington adjusted to his presence as the Park regime began to produce economic successes the Rhee government had not. Furthermore, Park's anticommunism was pronounced and he was far more willing to cooperate with Japan than Rhee was, as evidenced by his normalization of South Korean–Japanese diplomatic relations in 1965 with the blessing of the United States. In short, the 1960s witnessed a new phase in U.S.–South Korean relations, in which South Korea became a more successful client state, led by what some saw as a "friendly tyrant" who was useful for U.S. objectives. This relationship only hardened the U.S.–North Korean relationship, but that too served U.S.–Cold War purposes. Perhaps the most vivid example of the improved utility of South Korea was its willingness to fight in Vietnam as a regional ally.

The U.S.-South Korea alliance was beginning a process of transformation toward a genuine partnership. The Japan and Vietnam War connections facilitated by the United States also bolstered the South Korean economy tremendously, helping to foster the so-called "Miracle on the Han." Ironically this economic transformation created opportunities for more Koreans to immigrate to the United States from the late 1960s, intensifying in the 1970s and 1980s. As their numbers grew, so did their political voice and their ability to reinforce the U.S.–South Korean relationship. South Korea's economic successes since the late 1960s strengthened its value to the United States. For example, per capita gross national product (GNP) rose from $114 in 1965 to over $3,000 in 1990. South Korea became a major trading partner of the United States and helped to foster regional prosperity and stability through economic means.

All was not smooth in the late 1960s and the 1970s, however, because Park's repressive political style generated popular and scholarly criticism in the United States about the wisdom of retaining such an ally. In addition, strains from waging the Vietnam War caused second thoughts about other U.S. commitments in Asia. President Richard Nixon's administration emphasized Asian self-defense, and its removal of one U.S. division from Korea underscored that trend. As the war in Indochina deteriorated, U.S. credibility suffered. The Park government stepped up its lobbying activities in Washington, setting the stage for the "Koreagate" corruption scandal.

During President Jimmy Carter's administration (1977–1981) these themes converged in the form of increased U.S. human rights pressures on South Korea's political conduct; an attempt by Washington to reduce U.S. forces in Korea that was aborted via a controversial reappraisal of the North Korean threat; and the eruption of the Koreagate scandal with congressional investigations into Seoul's influence buying. U.S.–South Korean relations reached a post–Korean War low. Despite superpower détente, this deterioration in alliance relations did not benefit North Korea. After President Park's assassination in October 1979, hopes were raised briefly for improved relations based on a convergence of liberal agendas. The seizure of power by General Chun Doo Hwan during late 1979 and 1980 dimmed those specific hopes because of Chun's hard-line politics.

President Ronald Reagan's administration reversed that temporary course and led to improved relations between Washington and Seoul based on a convergence of conservative values and interests. Despite enormous popular opposition to Chun because of his harsh handling of a May 1980 insurrection in the city of Kwangju with hundreds of casualties, an event that led to allega-

tions of U.S. complicity through the binational military command structure, his government was warmly embraced by Reagan.

The U.S.-South Korean relationship in the 1980s experienced a mixture of close political rapport between the Reagan and George Bush administrations and the roughly concurrent Chun and Roh Tae Woo governments and a gradual evolution of economic and foreign policy interests. Although the period from the 1970s to the 1990s witnessed an expansion of trade between the United States and South Korea, including South Korean textiles, electronics, automobiles, and high technology components, it also experienced growing recognition that the two countries were competitors that would sometimes clash. The United States began to perceive South Korea as part of a significant East Asian challenge.

There also were more foreign policy differences and tensions than when South Korea was more strictly a U.S. client state. Starting in the 1970s, following the OPEC oil shocks, South Korea started to pursue more of an independent foreign policy based on economic interdependence with a range of countries. Although Seoul tried to make its policies complement those of the United States, and treated the U.S. connection as the cornerstone of its foreign policy, Seoul also demonstrated a willingness to assert itself by standing up to the United States. Seoul's pursuit of "Northern politics"—Nordpolitik (modeled on West Germany's Ostpolitik)—caused it to seek relationships with an array of countries, including the Soviet Union, the People's Republic of China, and many Third World states, that Washington had not sanctioned. Although these innovative South Korean policies began under Chun Doo Hwan, they flourished under Roh Tae Woo.

While Chun and Roh possessed similar military backgrounds, Chun seized power but Roh was popularly elected in December 1987. This marked the beginning of a return to democratic civilian rule in South Korea and also underscored the legitimacy of Seoul's international affairs options. Seoul's pre-1988 Olympics-oriented foreign policy (the 1988 Summer Olympics were to be held in Seoul) caused it to expand its diplomatic and economic network well beyond the scope of an erstwhile client state during the Roh years. Pointedly, South Korea was not prepared to cooperate fully with the late Cold War efforts of the United States to step up strategic pressures on the Soviet Union in Korea's backyard.

In these terms South Korea was inadvertently positioning itself to take advantage of the end of the Cold War. Glaringly North Korea was not so farsighted. When events in Europe and the Soviet Union ended the Cold War, there was direct impact on U.S. global strategy with spillover into the Asia-Pacific region. Seoul was prepared to seize the moment and did so by accelerating the normalization of its relations with China and Russia during

1988–1991. Pyongyang found itself without much of the support system provided through Cold War era connections. Consequently, the United States faced a Korean ally that enjoyed more alternatives than it had previously, while the United States also confronted a Korean adversary that increasingly was cornered by circumstances—leading it to explore its nuclear options in ways that heightened tensions.

President Bill Clinton's administration and South Korea's Kim Young Sam both entered office in early 1993 and shared many reformist characteristics. South Korea's reforms enhanced its democratic pluralism, but helped to reveal corruption scandals that produced legal problems for ex-presidents Clon and Rol. These problems complicated the maturation of U.S.-South Korean relations. Both also confronted the near-crisis of North Korean rejection of international monitoring of its nuclear program, its threat to develop nuclear weapons, and the possibility that it might already possess "the bomb." While this crisis was substantially defused in 1994 through an agreement negotiated by the United States and North Korea, and also involving South Korea and Japan through the Korean Energy Development Organization (KEDO), a number of dilemmas remained, including the political uncertainty precipitated by the death of Kim Il Sung in July 1994 and the succession of his son Kim Jong Il, North Korea's proclivity for strategic brinkmanship, as again demonstrated in December 1994 by its shooting down of a U.S. Army helicopter that strayed into the demilitarized zone, its reluctance to get in step with the rest of post–Cold War Asia, and the continued risks of war that its policies fomented. These also pose risks of regional nuclear proliferation and of provoking an undesirable Japanese military response.

Despite those dangers and dilemmas, the United States and South Korea increasingly accepted the likelihood of the eventuality that the two Koreas would reunite either as the result of negotiations, North Korea's economic collapse, or its military defeat. Regardless of the means, Washington had to prepare for the various costs, the emergence of new regional relationships, and the resultant impact on U.S. diplomatic, economic, and military relationships with the prospective unified Korean state and for the contingencies it might face in the Asia-Pacific region. Consequently, the 1990s marked a major transition phase in U.S.-Korean relations as Korea became a far more prominent factor in Asian affairs and as the United States adjusted to a shifting balance of power within a region growing accustomed to post–Cold War multipolarity.

EDWARD A. OLSEN

See also Acheson, Dean Gooderham; Cairo Conference; Cold War; Communism; Kim Il Sung; Korean War; Perry, Matthew Calbraith; Portsmouth, Treaty of; Rhee, Syngman; Russia and the Soviet Union; Russo-Japanese War; Sino-Japanese War

FURTHER READING

Bandow, Doug, and Ted Galen Carpenter, eds. *The U.S.-South Korean Alliance: Time for a Change.* New Brunswick, 1992.
Buss, Claude A. *The United States and the Republic of Korea; Background for Policy.* Stanford, Calif., 1982.
Clough, Ralph N. *Embattled Korea.* Boulder, Colo., 1987.
Cumings, Bruce. *The Origins of the Korean War.* Princeton, N.J., 1981.
Henderson, Gregory. *Korea: The Politics of the Vortex.* Cambridge, Mass., 1968.
Olsen, Edward A. *U.S. Policy and the Two Koreas.* San Francisco and Boulder, 1988.

KOREA, DEMOCRATIC PEOPLE'S REPUBLIC OF

See Appendix 2; Korea

KOREA, REPUBLIC OF

See Appendix 2; Korea

KOREAN AIRLINES FLIGHT 007 INCIDENT

See KAL-007 Incident

KOREAN WAR

The international war of 1950–1953 that engulfed Korea after years of upheaval in that divided nation. The war, which took the lives of millions of Asians and 54,246 Americans, left a significant legacy: it drew U.S. and Chinese forces into battle, poisoning Sino-American relations for nearly three decades; it heightened Cold War antagonisms and contributed to the militarization of the U.S. doctrine of Containment; it perpetuated the division of Korea into two states—with the United States becoming a major ally of the Republic of Korea (ROK or South Korea) based at Seoul, against the Communist regime of the Democratic People's Republic of Korea (DPRK or North Korea), based at Pyongyang. U.S. domestic politics, already beset before the outbreak of war by the anticommunist excesses of McCarthyism, became more unsettled, and the warmaking power of the president increased at the expense of Congress, which was not asked to pass a declaration of war and which did not demand one.

Civil War in a Divided Korea

During World War II, U.S. officials, wary that the Soviets might gain predominant influence in a Korea long dominated by Japan, began to plan for a military occupation of the nation that bordered the Soviet Union and China. President Franklin D. Roosevelt floated the idea of an international trusteeship for Korea, but he never transformed his idea into policy before his death in April 1945. In early August, after Japan's surrender, U.S. diplomats and military officers drew a line in Korea at the thirty-eighth parallel, keeping in the American or southern zone the capital of Seoul. Some 25,000 U.S. troops occupied the south in September. The Soviets, whose forces had entered northern Korea and had begun to move south, accepted the thirty-eighth parallel as a temporary boundary. It became a permanent dividing line, a symbol of Cold War bipolarism. A Soviet-U.S. Joint Commission met in 1946 and 1947 but could not agree on a trusteeship plan or a national election for a provisional government.

In their respective Korean zones, the two occupying powers nurtured political allies. In the north, the Soviets backed their Communist ally Kim Il Sung, a young man in his thirties who coveted his nation's independence from foreign rule. Kim centralized political power, built a formidable army of some 150,000 troops, mobilized the population under the banner of the Korean Labor Party, and sent thousands of Koreans to fight alongside Mao Zedong's Communists in the Chinese civil war, where these Koreans became toughened fighters later able to apply their experience to the 1950–1953 war. Soviet forces left North Korea at the end of 1948, but some 200 military advisers remained. That year, Kim organized the DPRK and vowed to unify his nation.

In the south, the United States endorsed the septuagenarian Syngman Rhee, a U.S.-educated nationalist who had cultivated diplomats and politicians for years in the United States. He, too, ardently pledged reunification. The strong-willed Rhee often rejected U.S. advice, created an authoritarian regime that polarized politics, and threatened war against the north. Washington, which preferred moderate politicians but could not find a leader to counter Rhee, supported him. Rhee worked to stabilize his regime in the face of growing opposition from leftist labor and peasant farmers, many of them organized into "people's committees." Strikes, rebellions, and uprisings bedeviled his government—and U.S. occupation authorities. Kim's north encouraged the protests in the south. Rhee won UN-sponsored elections in May 1948 and created the ROK. An October 1948 rebellion led to sustained guerrilla war in the south.

U.S. officials increasingly worked with Rhee to quell the radical challenge, especially after 1947 when President Harry S. Truman launched the policy of containment. When U.S. policy toward Japan shifted in 1948 toward rebuilding the former enemy, U.S. leaders found another reason for strengthening the southern government: Korea, as a market and raw-materials resource, could help Japan's economic reconstruction. Although U.S. occupation forces left Korea in mid-1949, a military mission remained to train the southern army of some 95,000 troops. U.S. weapons flowed to Rhee's military, although U.S. officials held back heavy armaments out of fear that Rhee would use them to attack the north. Throughout 1949 northern and southern military units crossed into the other's territory, sparking border clashes. In early 1950 UN observers took up positions to monitor both southern and northern military movements. Meanwhile, in February 1950, the U.S. Congress voted $60 million in economic aid for the ROK; a month later Congress authorized $11 million in military aid. By spring 1950 the southern guerrillas had taken a beating from Rhee's U.S.-trained forces, but in May elections Rhee lost control of the South Korean National Assembly. Violence and political turmoil continued to rock South Korea.

Outbreak of War and U.S. Intervention

Kim Il Sung had already decided to reunite the two Koreas by force. He had a large army well supplied with Soviet weapons. He probably hoped to strike before Rhee could utilize U.S. aid, and, with Mao's victory in China in the fall of 1949, Kim had available thousands of returning, battle-tested fighters. In March 1949, as declassified but incomplete Soviet documents suggest, Kim had asked for Soviet Premier Joseph Stalin's help for a northern invasion of the south. Judging Kim's forces ill-prepared and fearing U.S. intervention, Stalin urged caution. In fall 1949, pressed again by Kim, a wary Stalin urged further northern preparedness.

In April 1950, however, Kim met with Stalin in Moscow and they apparently agreed on an invasion with Soviet support. Documents declassified in the mid-1990s suggest that Stalin now believed that a quick northern victory was possible. Perhaps Secretary of State Dean Acheson's January 1950 public statement, reflecting U.S. military opinion, that Korea lay outside the U.S. defense perimeter (even though Acheson qualified his point by saying that the United Nations would resist any assault against South Korea), led Stalin to believe that the United States would not intervene. Perhaps, too, Mao's victory in China prompted Stalin to think that unless he accepted Kim's pleas for an attack, China might gain influence in Korea at Moscow's expense. Or, perhaps Stalin worried that a revived Japan was becoming a U.S. bastion in Asia; an all-communist Korea might serve as a bulwark against a renewed Japanese threat. As for China's Mao, Kim consulted with him in May 1950; Mao apparently backed reunification by military means. But Kim

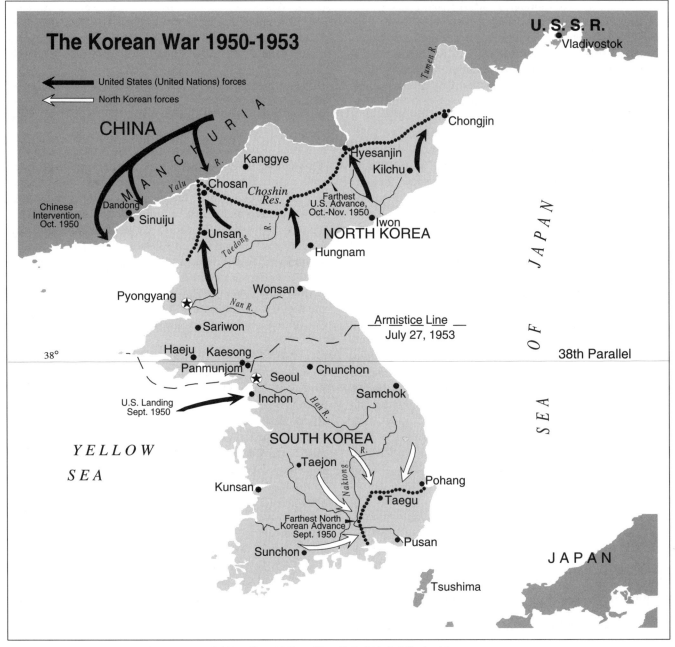

The Korean War 1950-1953

United States (United Nations) forces

North Korean forces

CHINA

MANCHURIA

Chinese Intervention, Oct. 1950

U.S.S.R.

Vladivostok

Chongjin

Kanggye

Hyesanjin

Kilchu

Chosan

Choshin Res.

Farthest U.S. Advance, Oct.-Nov. 1950

Dandong

Sinuiju

Unsan

Iwon

NORTH KOREA

Hungnam

Pyongyang

Wonsan

Sariwon

Nan R.

Armistice Line July 27, 1953

38°

Haeju

Kaesong

Panmunjom

38th Parallel

Seoul

Chunchon

Inchon

Samchok

U.S. Landing Sept. 1950

SOUTH KOREA

YELLOW SEA

Taejon

Kunsan

Pohang

Taegu

Farthest North Korean Advance Sept. 1950

Pusan

Sunchon

SEA   OF   JAPAN

JAPAN

Tsushima

From *American Foreign Relations,* Thomas G. Paterson, Garry J. Clifford, Kenneth J. Hagan, Volume II. © 1995 by D.C. Heath and Company. Reprinted with permission of Houghton Mifflin Company.

apparently did not reveal a timetable for his plans. An insistent Kim had maneuvered two patrons into positions of support. He had persuaded them that his crack troops, assisted by Soviet tanks, could in lightning fashion overrun the south before the United States could mobilize to blunt a DPRK victory. Kim almost succeeded.

In the early morning hours of Sunday, 25 June 1950, some 75,000 DPRK troops struck across the thirty-eighth parallel on a 150-mile front. South Korean forces fell back, unable to halt the advancing army. North Korea

issued a press release charging that the south had provoked the assault. When word of the attack reached Washington, Acheson decided first to notify the United Nations to convene an emergency session of the Security Council. Then he telephoned Truman at his home in Independence, Missouri. Flying to Washington, Truman remembered the 1930s: "Communism was acting in Korea just as Hitler, Mussolini, and the Japanese had acted ten, fifteen, and twenty years earlier." He insisted that there would be no appeasement this time. Meanwhile, the Security Council passed a resolution condemning North Korea for aggression. Except for Yugoslavia's abstention, all members present voted in the affirmative. The Soviet delegation, which could have cast a veto to kill the measure, remained surprisingly absent, still boycotting the United Nations over its refusal to seat the new Communist government in China. (The Soviets returned to the United Nations in August.)

Truman soon met with his key advisers at Blair House near the White House. Giving no attention to the two-part Korean civil war—north versus south and Rhee versus leftists—as a source for the crisis, they instead identified the Soviets as the instigator of the invasion of the south for the purpose of undermining containment. America's Cold War credibility seemed at stake; if the Communists were not stopped in Korea, Truman argued, they would "swallow up one piece of Asia after another." With his own version of the "domino theory," made famous later by President Dwight D. Eisenhower, Truman forecast that unless the communists were halted in Korea "the Near East would collapse and no telling what would happen in Europe." Truman made several decisions in the next couple of days: to send arms to the South Koreans; to use U.S. warplanes and warships to attack the North Korean spearhead; to dispatch the Seventh Fleet to the waters between the Chinese mainland and Formosa to forestall conflict between the two Chinas; and to accelerate military aid to Indochina, where the French were battling an anticolonial rebellion, and to the Philippines, where leftist guerrillas called the Huks challenged the U.S.-backed government. Although Truman met with congressional leaders, he decided against asking Congress for a declaration of war, which some observers judged a constitutional requirement but which the president thought unnecessary because he could act in his capacity as commander in chief. Later, historians marked Truman's bypassing of Congress as a major step toward the development of the "imperial presidency."

Pusan, Inchon, and Chinese Intervention

Seoul fell on 28 June 1950. On 29 June, Truman ordered U.S. pilots to attack North Korea. The next day General Douglas MacArthur urged the president to send U.S. combat troops to South Korea. Truman soon obliged, tagging the undeclared war a "police action." The United Nations urged its members to muster troops for an international force which was put under MacArthur's command. U.S. ground forces (302,483 in mid-1953) made up ninety percent of the UN army (not counting ROK forces of 590,911); Great Britain, Canada, Australia, New Zealand, Turkey, and others also contributed troops and medical personnel. Meanwhile, North Korean forces pushed on, cornering the fast retreating southern units in the Pusan Perimeter at the bottom of the peninsula.

Stoutly defending that territory, U.S. leaders began to think about sending U.S. troops across the thirty-eighth parallel into the north. MacArthur proposed a daring U.S. invasion at Inchon, several hundred miles behind North Korean lines. On 15 September, U.S. Marines staged a successful amphibious landing at Inchon. They shoved North Korean forces back and soon liberated Seoul. Farther to the south, the U.S. Eighth Army broke out of the Pusan bridgehead. MacArthur soon received the momentous orders from Washington to cross the thirty-eighth parallel; his UN forces did so on 8 October. The U.S. war objective of containing the North Koreans had changed to rolling them back and uniting Korea under a noncommunist government. On 15 October, Truman met with MacArthur on Wake Island and asked about the chances of Chinese intervention. The general, touting U.S. air superiority and assuring the president that "We are the best," dismissed the possibility: "If the Chinese tried to go down to Pyongyang there would be the greatest slaughter."

Stalin, always worried about a confrontation with the United States, and Mao, worried about the U.S. advance to China's border, began talking about what to do next. Citing the defense of Chinese security, Mao publicly warned the United States not to push to the North Korea-China border at the Yalu River. But in an 2 October telegram to Stalin, Mao ruled out Chinese intervention because it would provoke "open conflict" with the United States. Such a war would undermine Chinese economic reconstruction and land reform. Moreover, the Chinese people would become "dissatisfied," he said. "The wounds inflicted on the people by the war have not yet healed, we need peace." After further appeals from Stalin to save North Korea and offers of Soviet air cover, and after intense debate in the Chinese government, Mao reversed himself. As declassified but incomplete Chinese records reveal, Mao feared that "the Americans would run more rampant" if China did not stop them. The Chinese Revolution itself might be America's ultimate target.

On 19 October Chinese soldiers called "Volunteers" crossed the Yalu River into North Korea. A week later they battled ROK units and then assumed a defensive posture. MacArthur's troops kept going northward and U.S. bombers kept hitting bridges across the Yalu (the first attack occurred on 8 November). On 26 November, China launched a full-scale intervention; some 200,000 Chinese troops swept down on MacArthur's surprised army, driving it pell-mell southward. General MacArthur called for a massive air strike on China, but Truman rejected his request. The president did hint at a 30 November press conference, however, that U.S. use of atomic bombs was being actively considered. He never did authorize their use in Korea because he feared Soviet retaliation in

Europe and because the U.S. nuclear arsenal remained small. But his suggestion that atomic bombs might be unleashed prompted British Prime Minister Clement Attlee to hasten to Washington to call for negotiations instead.

By March 1951 UN forces had managed to shove communist forces back across the thirty-eighth parallel, where the fighting stabilized. Guerrilla forces in the south, however, continued to cause problems for U.S. troops. As Truman contemplated negotiations, the restless MacArthur demanded war against China proper. Denouncing the concept of limited war (war without nuclear weapons, confined to one place), he hinted that the president was practicing appeasement. On 11 April, fed up with the general's insubordination and backed strongly by the Joint Chiefs of Staff, Truman fired MacArthur. The theatrical general, who had not set foot in the United States for more than a decade, returned home to ticker-tape parades and the lecture circuit, but he soon faded from the American political scene. Truman's popularity sagged because of the MacArthur episode and the stalemated war, but he weathered demands from McCarthyites for his impeachment.

Armistice Talks, POW Question, and Peace

Armistice talks began at Panmunjom in July 1951, but the fighting continued and the negotiations stalled. In the 1952 presidential race, Republican candidate Dwight D. Eisenhower, capitalizing on popular uneasiness with the stalemated war, pledged that, if elected, he would go to Korea to find a way to end the conflict. He did go, but the war raged on. The most contentious point in the negotiations was the fate of prisoners of war (POWs). Defying the Geneva Prisoners of War Convention (1949), U.S. officials announced that only those North Korean and Chinese POWs who wished to go home would be returned. To the U.S. statement that there would be no forced repatriation, the North Koreans denounced what they called forced retention. Both sides undertook "re-education" or "brainwashing" programs to persuade POWs to resist repatriation. Tensions built up in prison camps in South Korea. In early 1952, at the Koje camp, U.S. troops suppressed a Chinese/North Korean POW riot, killing more than 100. In North Korea's camps, murder and illness took the lives of hundreds of POWs.

During the stalemate, U.S. officials made deliberately vague public statements about the possible use of atomic weapons in Korea. U.S. bombers obliterated dams (whose rushing waters then destroyed rice fields and threatened famine for civilians), factories, airfields, and bridges in North Korea. Northern cities took heavy casualties, with hundreds of thousands of civilians dying and countless others forced to live in caves and underground dwellings. Not until 27 July 1953 was an armistice signed, although South Korea refused to accept it. Stalin's death in March and the coming to power of a more conciliatory Soviet government helped ease the way to a settlement that the Chinese especially welcomed. The combatants agreed to hand over the POW question to a special panel of neutral nations, which later gave prisoners their choice of staying or leaving. (In the end, 70,000 of about 100,000 North Korean and 5,600 of 20,700 Chinese POWs elected to return home; twenty-one American and 325 South Korean POWs of some 11,000 decided to stay in North Korea.) The North Korean–South Korean line was set near the thirty-eighth parallel, the prewar boundary, and a demilitarized zone was created between the two Koreas.

Significance of the Korean War

Thus ended a frustrating war—a limited war that Americans, accustomed to victory, had not won but had wisely kept limited. The Korean War carried major domestic and political consequences. The failure to achieve victory and the public's impatience with a limited war undoubtedly helped to elect Eisenhower president in 1952. The powers of the presidency grew as Congress repeatedly deferred to Truman. The president never asked Congress for a declaration of war, believing that as commander in chief he had the authority to send troops wherever he wished. Dissenters such as Senator Robert Taft (Republican of Ohio) disagreed, but Truman saw little need to consult Congress—except when he wanted the $69.5 billion Korean War bill paid.

The implementation of military containment worldwide became entrenched as U.S. policy. The Korean War, Acheson noted, removed "the recommendations of NSC-68 from the realm of theory and made them immediate budget issues." Indeed, the military budget shot up from $14 billion in 1949 to $44 billion in 1953; it remained between $35 billion and $44 billion a year throughout the 1950s. Increased U.S. aid flowed to the French for their die-hard stand in Indochina against nationalist insurgents. Because of heightened Sino-American hostility, South Korea and Formosa became major recipients of U.S. foreign aid. The demilitarized zone in Korea remained into the 1990s a highly fortified, tense area where incidents regularly sparked controversy. The U.S. alliance with Japan strengthened during the war as its economy boomed after filling large U.S. procurement orders worth some $3 billion. Australia and New Zealand joined the United States in a mutual defense agreement, the Anzus Treaty (1951). The U.S. Army sent six divisions to Europe, and the administration initiated plans to rearm West Germany. The Korean

War's "lessons" were measured in another—and cautionary—way in Vietnam in the 1960s: Do not invade North Vietnam. Although some authors have titled their histories of the Korean War the "forgotten" war or the "unknown" war, it ranks among the most significant in U.S. and world history.

THOMAS G. PATERSON

See also Acheson, Dean Gooderham; Anzus Treaty; Cold War; Constitution; Containment; Domino Theory; Eisenhower, Dwight David; Geneva Conventions; Japan; Kim Il Sung; Korea; MacArthur, Douglas; McCarthyism; Nuclear Weapons and Strategy; NSC-68; Rhee, Syngman; Truman Doctrine; Truman, Harry S.; United Nations

FURTHER READING

Blair, Clay. *The Forgotten War: America in Korea, 1950–1953.* New York, 1987.

Chen, Jian. *China's Road to the Korean War: The Making of the Sino-American Confrontation, 1949–1950.* New York, 1995.

Cumings, Bruce. *The Origins of the Korean War, I: Liberation and the Emergence of Separate Regimes, 1945–1947.* Princeton, N.J., 1981.

———. *The Origins of the Korean War, II: The Roaring of the Cataract, 1947–1950.* Princeton, N.J., 1990.

Foot, Rosemary. *A Substitute for Victory: The Politics of Peacemaking at the Korean Armistice Talks.* Ithaca, N.Y., 1985.

———. *The Wrong War: American Policy and the Dimensions of the Korean Conflict.* Ithaca, N.Y., 1985.

Goncharov, Sergei N., John W. Lewis, and Xue Litai. *Uncertain Partners: Stalin, Mao, and the Korean War.* Stanford, Calif., 1993.

Halliday, Jon, and Bruce Cumings. *Korea: The Unknown War.* London and New York, 1988.

Kaufman, Burton I. *The Korean War,* 2nd ed. New York, 1997.

Lowe, Peter. *The Origins of the Korean War.* London, 1986.

MacDonald, Callum A. *Korea.* New York, 1987.

Stueck, William. *The Korean War: An International History.* Princeton, N.J., 1995.

Whiting, Allen. *China Crosses the Yalu.* New York, 1960.

Zhang, She Guang. *Mao's Military Romanticism: China and the Korean War, 1950–1953.* Lawrence, Kans., 1995.

KURDS

Fourth largest ethnic group in the Middle East. The Kurds historically have been a people without a state. There are approximately 20 million Kurds worldwide, living in Turkey (10 million), Iran (6 million), and Iraq (4 million), as well as in Syria and Armenia. The Treaty of Sèvres, signed in August 1920 as part of the post–World War I breakup of the Ottoman Empire, called for the creation of an independent Kurdistan, but no such action has ever been taken, despite insurrections and guerrilla warfare by Kurdish *pesh mergas* ("those who face death") that began in the 1920s.

In the early 1970s the administration of Richard M. Nixon provided covert aid to the Iraqi Kurds in collusion with the shah of Iran, who was seeking to destabilize his traditional rival, Iraq. The United States was seeking to win favor with the shah and to weaken Iraq, which had an alliance with the Soviet Union. In 1975, however, the shah worked out a *modus vivendi* with Iraq, and the United States went along with him in abandoning the Kurds.

During the 1980–1988 Iran-Iraq War, at least one of the major Kurdish factions within Iraq sided with Iran. Iraqi president Saddam Hussein brutally retaliated, using chemical weapons against Kurdish cities and settlements. Despite unanimous support in the U.S. Senate for economic sanctions against Iraq, the Reagan administration refused to impose sanctions against Saddam Hussein's regime.

In February 1991, with Saddam Hussein weakened by his defeat at the hands of the U.S.-led Desert Storm forces in the wake of his calamitous invasion of Kuwait, the Kurds rose again. Some Kurdish leaders claimed that they had been promised assistance by the United States; others felt that they had received at least tacit encouragement; virtually all expected U.S. support. In the event, however, the support did not come until Saddam Hussein had once again suppressed the revolt, and then it took the form of a "safe haven" under Operation Provide Comfort, by which the Kurds were to be secured from further Iraqi attacks by a U.S.-led military presence under UN auspices. Provide Comfort was successful at least as a holding action and in maintaining humanitarian relief, at least until August-September 1996 when factional rivalry among the Kurds led one side to turn to Iran for aid and the other to invite Saddam's froces on its side.

The Turks also have repressed the Kurds. President Mustafa Kemal (Ataturk) refused to go along with the Treaty of Sèvres and in 1925 suppressed a revolt by Kurds seeking their own independent state. In recent years the Kurdish insurgency within Turkey has been led by the Kurdish Workers's Party (PKK), which is Marxist in ideology and terrorist in many of its practices. While the Turkish government has been widely criticized for human rights violations and other repressive measures against the Kurds, the issue has been a difficult one for the United States to deal with, given Turkey's importance as a U.S. ally.

BRUCE W. JENTLESON

See also Gulf War of 1990–1991; Humanitarian Intervention and Relief; Iran; Iran-Iraq War; Iraq; Turkey

FURTHER READING

Gunter, Michael M. *The Kurds of Iraq: Tragedy and Hope.* New York, 1992.

Human Rights Watch: Middle East. *Iraq's Crime of Genocide: The Anfal Campaign Against the Kurds.* New Haven, Conn., 1995.

McDowall, David. *A Modern History of the Kurds.* London, 1996.

KUWAIT

Located in the Middle East at the head of the Persian Gulf between Iraq and Saudi Arabia, an oil-rich state over which the United States and other nations went to war with Iraq in 1990–1991. The relationship between the United States and Kuwait has always had both an economic and a political component. The first contacts between Kuwait and the United States came through the private missions of the Dutch Reformed Church early in the twentieth century. Kuwait's abundant oil reserves, however, made relations with that state an enduring concern to the U.S. government. In 1932 the U.S. corporation Gulf Oil joined with British Petroleum to form the Kuwait Oil Company (KOC), and in 1934 KOC signed an oil concession agreement with Kuwait's ruler. When commercial quantities of oil were discovered in 1938, KOC retained its concession, which it held, with modifications, until 1976, when Kuwait nationalized the company.

Until 1961 Great Britain handled the country's foreign policy, treating Kuwait as a semiprotectorate. In the 1940s the U.S. government requested consular representation in Kuwait, but Great Britain rejected the request, fearing that Kuwait's ruler would play the two powers against each other. As Great Britain's regional and international power faded, however, Kuwait turned increasingly to the United States. In 1961, when Kuwait received independence from Great Britain, the United States recognized the new state, established diplomatic relations, and supported Kuwait against Iraq's attempts to block diplomatic recognition and Kuwaiti membership in the United Nations. (Iraqi opposition ended in 1963, and Kuwait then joined the United Nations.) In the 1960s Kuwait was an early and active member of the Organization of Petroleum Exporting Countries (OPEC). The U.S. Defense Department drafted a major survey of Kuwait's national defense needs, paving the way for arms sales in later years. When oil prices increased during the 1970s, Kuwait also began investing heavily in U.S. property and industry. Despite the growing economic relationship between the two countries, however, their political relationship remained somewhat distant, largely because of the unpopularity within Kuwait and the Middle East of U.S. support for Israel.

Kuwait's ties with the United States strengthened with the onset of the Iran-Iraq War in 1980. Although Kuwait initially had reservations about the U.S. presence in the Persian Gulf and was at times an outspoken critic of military cooperation with the United States, as the war continued, Kuwait's security situation worsened, and its reservations faded. In 1984 Kuwaiti ships in the Persian Gulf became the target of Iranian missile attacks, and the 1986 Iranian occupation of Faw peninsula brought the Iranian threat to Kuwait's borders. In 1986, following a summer of stepped-up Iranian attacks on Kuwaiti vessels, Kuwait approached both the United States and the Soviet Union with a request to reflag its tankers. When the Soviets agreed in February 1987 to protect Kuwaiti vessels, the United States responded with a similar promise, subsequently reflagging eleven Kuwaiti tankers, placing them under U.S. naval protection. This commitment led to a number of attacks and confrontations between the naval forces of the United States and Iran until the August 1988 cease-fire ended the war.

On 2 August 1990 Iraqi troops invaded Kuwait and occupied the country. The invasion followed a summer of escalating tension over economic disputes about oil production and pricing and, less important, about borders. Relations between the two states had improved during the Iran-Iraq War, when Kuwait lent Iraq some $13 billion, but with the war's end, tensions resurfaced. Following the invasion, Kuwait's ruler and members of the ruling family fled to Saudi Arabia and in exile turned to the United States for support. On 2 August President George Bush sought and obtained international backing for Security Council Resolution 660, the first of several resolutions against Iraq, condemning the invasion and calling for immediate and unconditional Iraqi withdrawal. Economic sanctions against Iraq were imposed on 6 August and a naval embargo on 25 August.

The United States also moved militarily to liberate Kuwait. On 7 August the United States opened the first phase of its campaign against Iraq with Operation Desert Shield, deploying air and limited ground forces directly to the region. On 29 November the United States obtained UN authorization for the use of force should Iraqi forces fail to withdraw by 15 January 1991. On 17 January the air war began as Desert Shield gave way to Desert Storm. On 26 February 1991, U.S.-led coalition forces restored sovereignty to Kuwait; on 27 February the last Iraqi troops withdrew from Kuwait.

After the war, the U.S.-Kuwaiti relationship remained close. Kuwait's leaders believed that a large, visible U.S. military presence offered the best protection against the continuing Iraqi threat. In September 1991 the United States and Kuwait signed a ten-year defense agreement under which the United States agreed to position military equipment in Kuwait and to conduct joint military exercises with Kuwaiti forces. Economic relations continued to grow as the Kuwaiti government directed much of the reconstruction work, including contracts to repair the oil wells set afire by retreating Iraqi forces, to U.S. companies. These economic relations deepened in the following years. The U.S. position on domestic political transformations within Kuwait has been more ambiguous. The invasion galvanized Kuwait's existing prodemocracy movement, which succeeded in pressuring the ruler to hold National Assembly elections in October 1992. The years since Kuwait's liberation, however, also brought a new attack by the government on the organizations of civil society that sustained that movement. Both impulses—pro- and anti-democratic—continued to play themselves out in postwar Kuwait.

JILL CRYSTAL

See also Gulf War of 1990–1991; Iran-Iraq War; Iraq; Middle East; Oil and Foreign Policy

FURTHER READING

Assiri, Abdul-Reda. *Kuwait's Foreign Policy: City-State in World Politics.* Boulder, Colo., 1990.

Crystal, Jill. *Oil and Politics in the Gulf: Rulers and Merchants in Kuwait and Qatar.* Cambridge, 1995.

——. *Kuwait: The Transformation of an Oil State.* Boulder, Colo., 1992.

KYRGYZSTAN

See Appendix 2

L

LAFAYETTE, MARIE JOSEPH PAUL YVES ROCH GILBERT DU MOTIER, Marquis de

(*b.* 6 September 1757; *d.* 20 May 1834)

Supporter of the rebellious colonies during the American Revolution and in later years a goodwill ambassador between France and the United States. The scion of a wealthy and aristocratic French family, Lafayette entered the military while still in his teens. He became fascinated with the struggle between Great Britain and its North American colonies, less from a commitment to political liberty than from a desire to see the humiliation of Great Britain following its defeat of France in the Seven Years' War (1756–1763). Dreaming of martial glory, Lafayette sailed for North America in April 1777. On arrival he obtained a commission of major general from the Continental Congress and formed an immediate bond with General George Washington, who as friend and father figure molded the young Frenchman's new devotion to the philosophy of political liberty.

Lafayette's performance in the revolutionary war was honorable if not brilliant. The popular young Frenchman was wounded in the leg at the Battle of Brandywine in September 1777 and recuperated during the desperate winter at Valley Forge (1777–1778). On a return visit to France in 1779, he defended the cause of the colonists and secured a commitment of more French troops. Although the French government put the older and more experienced General Jean-Baptiste-Donatien de Vimeur, Comte de Rochambeau, in command of these new troops, Lafayette, undaunted, returned to the United States. Washington then put him in command of French and colonial troops in the siege of the British garrison at Yorktown, Virginia, where the British were defeated on 19 October 1781. The war ended and the British conceded the independence of the colonies in the Treaty of Paris of 1783.

Lafayette's experience in the United States dominated his actions for the rest of his life. He promoted French-U.S. trade and actively supported the coming of the French Revolution in 1789 as a continuation of the struggle for political liberty. As "the hero of two worlds," he contributed ideas patterned after those of the Virginia Declaration of Rights (1776) to proposals for the French Declaration of the Rights of Man and Citizen (26 August 1789). He supported France's sale of Louisiana to the United States in 1803 and made a final triumphal tour of the United States in 1824–1825. In the twentieth century, his name continued to be synonymous with French-U.S. friendship, and a squadron of U.S. aviators was named for him during World War I.

REBECCA G. GOODMAN

See also American Revolution; France; French Revolution

FURTHER READING

Bernier, Olivier. *Lafayette: Hero of Two Worlds*. New York, 1983.
Gottschalk, Louis R. *Lafayette Joins the American Army*. Chicago, 1965.
——— . *Lafayette in the French Revolution*. Chicago, 1969.
Idzerda, Stanley J., ed. *Lafayette in the Age of the American Revolution: Selected Letters and Papers, 1776–1790*. Ithaca, New York, 1977.
Loveland, Anee C. *Emblem of Liberty: The Image of Lafayette in the American Mind*. Baton Rouge, La., 1971.
Palmer, R. R. *The Age of the Democratic Revolution: A Political History of Europe and America, 1760–1800*, vol. 1. Princeton, N.J., 1959.

LA FOLLETTE, ROBERT MARION

(*b.* 14 June 1855; *d.* 18 June 1925)

Governor of Wisconsin (1901–1906) and U.S. senator (1906–1925). He emerged as an insurgent Republican politician in Wisconsin by the 1890s. After service in the U.S. House of Representatives (1885–1891) and practicing as a lawyer, he won the 1900 Wisconsin gubernatorial election as a progressive. Five years later, after La Follette acquired national fame as a reformer, the state legislature elected him to the U.S. Senate. Seeking to guard the people against increasing corporate influences in both economics and politics, La Follette quickly ascended to leadership among Republican insurgents opposed to President William H. Taft.

La Follette turned his attention from domestic reform to international affairs during World War I. Applying his critique of corporate influences to the foreign policies of Woodrow Wilson, he denounced the new Democratic president's liberal internationalism. La Follette resisted Wilson's efforts to modernize the world using corporate America as the model. In the name of genuine self-determination, abroad as at home, La Follette bitterly criticized Wilson's use of U.S. military force to control other nations. He favored independence for the Philippines, opposed U.S. intervention in Mexico, and denounced U.S. protectorates in Nicaragua, Haiti, and the Dominican Republic. In the name of democracy, La Follette condemned U.S. imperialism. He championed U.S. neutrality during World War I and opposed U.S. military intervention in Europe. He resisted Wilson's preparedness campaign and favored a popular referendum on the question of war and peace. When the president moved toward war against Germany early in 1917, the senator organized a filibuster to prevent the arming of U.S. merchant ships; Wilson armed them by executive order and recommended war against Germany. La Follette was one of six progressive senators who voted against the declaration of war. He continued to resist Wilson's measures to mobilize for war and to silence dissent. Just as La Follette had opposed U.S. military intervention in the Mexican Revolution, he also opposed intervention in the Russian Revolution, believing that the United States should respect the right of revolution in other countries, even for Bolshevism.

After the war La Follette continued denouncing U.S. imperialism and militarism. He opposed the Treaty of Versailles, which included the League of Nations Covenant, and advocated self-government for Soviet Russia, Ireland, India, Egypt, and China. An irreconcilable in the Senate (one opposed to U.S. membership in the League under any conditions), he condemned the treaty for violating the principle of self-determination. Because other Republican senators who did not share his progressivism also rejected the League, the Senate defeated the treaty. La Follette devoted most of his remaining years to domestic reform, including a prominent role in exposing the Teapot Dome scandal of Warren G. Harding's presidency.

LLOYD E. AMBROSIUS

See also League of Nations; Versailles Treaty of 1919

FURTHER READING

Ambrosius, Lloyd E. *Woodrow Wilson and the American Diplomatic Tradition: The Treaty Fight in Perspective.* Cambridge, Mass., 1987.
Cooper, John Milton, Jr. *The Vanity of Power: American Isolationism and the First World War, 1914–1917.* Westport, Conn., 1969.
Thelen, David P. *Robert M. La Follette and the Insurgent Spirit.* Boston, 1976.

LANE, ARTHUR BLISS
(*b.* 16 June 1894; *d.* 12 August 1956)

Career diplomat and political activist who became especially vocal on Cold War issues. Born in Brooklyn, New York, Lane studied at Yale University and at the École de l'Île de France. He joined the Department of State in 1916 and served at various diplomatic postings for thirty-one years. After numerous Foreign Service assignments in Europe and Latin America, he received appointment as U.S. ambassador to Poland in 1944. Alarmed and outraged by the growth of Soviet hegemony over Poland and Eastern Europe, Lane resigned in 1947 to devote himself to combating communism as a global and domestic menace. As the Cold War intensified, he wrote widely on this theme and lent his efforts to various anticommunist pursuits, such as the Committee to Stop World Communism. He set forth his views forcefully in his memoir, *I Saw Poland Betrayed* (1948). Active in the Republican party, Lane was instrumental in committing its 1952 electoral platform to advocacy of liberation of Soviet-dominated countries rather than the containment policy that he considered too defensive. He worked to win support for the Republican ticket from U.S. voters of East European origin.

NEAL PEASE

See also Containment; Poland

FURTHER READING

Lane, Arthur Bliss. *I Saw Poland Betrayed.* Indianapolis, 1948.
Lukas, Richard C. *Bitter Legacy: Polish-American Relations in the Wake of World War II.* Lexington, Ky., 1982.

LANSDALE, EDWARD GEARY
(*b.* 6 February 1908; *d.* 23 February 1987)

Legendary Central Intelligence Agency (CIA) agent who masterminded counterinsurgency programs in the Philippines, Vietnam, and Cuba. Born in Detroit, Michigan, Lansdale became a career U.S. Air Force officer after an early career in advertising. He attended the University of California at Los Angeles (1927–1931), helped organize the Office of Strategic Services (1942–1943), and worked as an army intelligence analyst in the Philippines (1943–1948). As Manila chief of the Office of Policy Coordination (1950–1954), Lansdale launched a successful paramilitary and propaganda campaign to defeat the Hukbalahap insurgency and ensure the presidential victory of pro-U.S. candidate Ramón Magsaysay in 1954. From 1954 through 1957 Lansdale, now a CIA agent, attempted to duplicate his Philippines successes in Vietnam by establishing an anticommunist, anticolonial "third force" in that country. With the help of a small staff, the "Saigon Military Mission," Lansdale trained antiguerrilla forces, conducted paramilitary warfare against numerous Vietnamese sects, attempted to bribe their leaders, and sabotaged Hanoi transportation networks. He also forestalled several coup attempts against South Vietnamese President Ngo Dinh Diem. In 1957 President Dwight D. Eisenhower appointed Lansdale assistant secretary of defense for special operations, and by 1958 his mastery of self-promotion and two fictionalized versions of his Asian exploits, Graham Greene's *The Quiet American* (1955) and William Lederer and Eugene Burdick's *The Ugly American* (1958), had gained him notoriety.

Lansdale believed that the United States could win guerrilla wars by acquiring insights into the enemy's psychology. In 1961 he became chief of operations for President John F. Kennedy's failed Operation Mongoose, a joint military-intelligence scheme to overthrow Cuban President Fidel Castro. Lansdale retired from the air force as a brigadier general in 1963 but continued working for the CIA while advising the administrations of President John F. Kennedy and Lyndon B. Johnson on Vietnam and serving in such government organizations as Food for Peace, the Agency for International Development, and the U.S. Information Agency. He held his last government post, senior liaison officer for the U.S. ambassador to Vietnam, from 1965 to 1968 and spent his final years lecturing at various military institutions.

DEBORAH KISATSKY

See also Central Intelligence Agency; Cuba; Philippines; Vietnam War

FURTHER READING

Callather, Nick. *Illusions of Influence: The Political Economy of United States–Phillipines Relations, 1942–1960.* Stanford, Calif., 1994.
Currey, Cecil B. *Edward Lansdale: The Unquiet American.* Boston, 1988.
Hershberg, James G. "Before 'The Missiles of October': Did Kennedy Plan a Military Strike Against Cuba?" *Diplomatic History* 14 (Spring 1990): 163–198.
Lansdale, Edward Geary. *In the Midst of Wars: An American's Mission to Southeast Asia.* New York, 1972.
Sheehan, Neil. *A Bright Shining Lie: John Paul Vann and America in Vietnam.* New York, 1988.

LANSING, ROBERT

(*b.* 17 October 1864; *d.* 30 October 1928)

Secretary of state (1915–1920), noted international lawyer, founder of the American Society of International Law, and U.S. representative before numerous international tribunals between 1892 and 1911. Lansing was a son-in-law of former Secretary of State John W. Foster and an uncle to future Secretary of State John Foster Dulles. Born in Watertown, New York, Lansing was admitted to the bar in 1889 and practiced law in his hometown. Although appointed counselor for the Department of State in April 1914 and secretary of state after the resignation of William Jennings Bryan in June 1915, Lansing was never in complete sympathy with President Woodrow Wilson's policies. Decidedly pro-British during World War I, Lansing helped shape a U.S. policy of neutrality that benefited the Allies. Indeed, he

deliberately undercut Wilson's last attempt to mediate the war in December 1916 because he thought it might work to the disadvantage of the Allies. Lansing oversaw the purchase of the Danish West Indies (Virgin Islands) in 1917 and negotiated the Lansing-Ishii Agreement of 1917, which recognized Japan's Asian regional interests. A member of the U.S. delegation to the Paris Peace Conference in 1919, Lansing was often ignored by the president (and his intimate adviser, Colonel E.M. House), and he was not a party to most of the major decisions made at the conference. He privately opposed many of the provisions in the Versailles Treaty, such as the Shantung Settlement between China and Japan as well as the concept of collective security in the charter of the League of Nations. Lansing was also skeptical of the Wilsonian principle of self-determination, seeing it as a threat to international stability. He was politically embarrassed when these views became public during the Senate hearings on the treaty in September 1919. Wilson asked for Lansing's resignation in February 1920, ostensibly because Lansing had convened cabinet meetings without the president's approval during Wilson's five-month illness. The real reason, however, was Lansing's long-standing disagreements with Wilsonian foreign policy. Following his resignation, Lansing practiced international law in Washington, D.C.

DIMITRI D. LAZO

See also Danish West Indies, Acquisition of; House, Edward Mandell; Lansing-Ishii Agreement; Paris Peace Conference of 1919; Wilson, Thomas Woodrow; World War I

FURTHER READING

Beers, Burton F. *Vain Endeavor: Robert Lansing's Attempt to End the American-Japanese Rivalry.* Durham, N.C., 1962.
Lansing, Robert. *The Peace Negotiations: A Personal Narrative.* Boston, 1921.
———. *War Memoirs of Robert Lansing.* Indianapolis, Ind., 1935.
Smith, Daniel M. *Robert Lansing and American Neutrality, 1914–1917.* Berkeley, Calif., 1958.

LANSING-ISHII AGREEMENT

(2 November 1917)

An understanding achieved between the United States and Japan concerning their intentions with regard to China. In 1917 a Japanese diplomatic mission headed by Viscount Kikujiro Ishii visited Washington, D.C., to discuss the conflicting interests of Japan and the United States in China. Taking advantage of European preoccupation with World War I, Japan had extended its political and economic position in China through its Twenty-one Demands of 1915. Japan wanted to secure U.S. recognition of these gains. The United States, in turn, sought to restrain the Japanese in China. The United States wanted Japan to publicly endorse the Open Door Policy of equal economic opportunity in China and respect for China's territorial integrity. Secretary of State Robert Lansing and Viscount Ishii ultimately agreed to a vague compromise. The United States admitted that because of Japan's proximity to China, Japan had special interests in that country. In return, the Japanese reiterated their adherence to Open Door principles and pledged not to seek special economic or political advantages in China. This agreement did little to improve U.S.-Japanese relations in the long run because it lacked a precise definition of special interests. It was abrogated in 1923 after the signing of the Nine Power Treaty at the Washington Naval Conference.

DIMITRI D. LAZO

See also China; Japan; Lansing, Robert; Open Door Policy

FURTHER READING

Beers, Burton F. *Vain Endeavor: Robert Lansing's Attempt to End the American-Japanese Rivalry.* Durham, N.C., 1962.
Curry, Roy Watson. *Woodrow Wilson and Far Eastern Policy, 1913–1921.* New York, 1957.
Lansing, Robert. *War Memoirs of Robert Lansing.* Indianapolis, 1935.

LAOS

Landlocked country in Southeastern Asia located between Vietnam and Thailand, now known as the Lao People's Democratic Republic. More so than its neighboring countries, Laos remains an unknown area for most Americans, despite the fact that it was—-and remains— the most bombed country in history, a central area of drug production, and a battleground between U.S. and communist forces. Even during the Vietnam War era, Laotians were represented as a primitive people, led by anticommunist warlords who the United States clandestinely supported, or by Pathet Lao (Lao nation) communists who the United States sought to defeat.

Laos was a French protectorate in the 1880s, a Japanese territory in 1945 and was returned to the French in 1946. In 1949 Laos became a part of the French Union, a league designed by France to give nominal independence to its former colonies but still control their foreign and defense policies. Laotian nationalists objected to this policy and in 1953 Laos received full sovereignty from France. U.S. concerns toward Laos in this period revolved around preserving it as an anticolonial and anticommunist country. After 1954 U.S. policymakers were forced to abide by the Geneva Convention of that year, which prohibited the introduction of military hardware into the country. The joint agreement at this conference and at a second Geneva Conference of 1961–1962, while affirming the neutrality of Laos, limited U.S. options for responding to the communists. The geographic location of Laos, however, continually positioned it between the Cold War interests of the United States, Thailand, Communist China, and North Vietnam. Because of this location, neutrality existed only on paper for the people and government of Laos, a country simply too poor and too small to adequately defend itself.

Americans probably first learned about Laos and its problems in Thomas Dooley's "jungle doctor" exploits, recounted in his best-seller *The Edge of Tomorrow* (1958). Here he gave graphic and at times horrifying renditions of the lives of Laotian peasants—the photographs in the book include lepers, sorcerers practicing their folk rituals, a man mauled by a wild bear, and a little girl in her new (American) dress. Not incidentally, these photographs and the textual vignettes that made up the book were constructed within a framework that celebrated American medicine and commerce and fiercely opposed the tenets of communism. In Dooley's view Laos became a laboratory for the propagation of American modernization theory.

In 1960 President Dwight D. Eisenhower told President-elect John F. Kennedy that the United States might have to send U.S. troops to Laos to prevent the Pathet Lao from attaining power. By 1961, however, Laos became subsumed under the problem of Vietnam. A typical response toward this region was summed up by one U.S. official in Laos: "This is the end of nowhere. We can do anything we want here because Washington doesn't seem to know it exists." Like its neighbor, Cambodia, Laos was a "sideshow" to U.S. efforts to prevent a communist victory in Vietnam.

Throughout the Vietnam War, Vietnamese communist forces used Laotian territory as a staging ground for their attacks on South Vietnam, and the United States responded with massive aerial bombardments and attained effective control over the Laotian military. U.S. bombing campaigns became so extensive that one U.S. official reported after visiting the Plain of Jars: "Nothing was left standing...In the last phase, bombings were aimed at the systematic destruction of the material basis of the civilian society." U.S. actions like these resulted in nearly a million Laotians fleeing their homes and resettling in refugee camps. In addition to the bombing campaigns, the United States recruited Hmong tribesmen of Laos, a preliterate group who actively resisted communist encroachment in Laos. The Hmong paid dearly in loss of life and eventually of country; after the war many fled to Thailand or the United States, where they regrouped in large concentrations in California and the Dakotas. The Hmong's efforts on behalf of the United States have given them a privileged status among foreigners seeking asylum in the United States, notable given that close to 10 percent of the Laotian population has sought refugee status since the communists came to power in 1975.

In February 1971 South Vietnamese forces invaded Laos and were supported by U.S. air power. Known as Operation Lam Son, this mission was described in diplomatic parlance as an incursion rather than an invasion but was designed to destroy North Vietnamese troops and their use of the Ho Chi Minh trail. It was an unmitigated disaster. South Vietnamese forces retreated in March, proving the lie that Vietnamization was working. By the end of the Second Indochina War in 1975, Laotian society was deeply fragmented from the trauma of war and its six hundred year constitutional monarchy was in collapse.

Opium production also figured in the political maneuvers waged within Laos. Taking over from French intelligence agencies in the 1950s, the Central Intelligence Agency (CIA) used the funds generated by opium production to support its own clandestine wars against various communist governments and guerrilla organizations. This policy had tragic results. It not only distorted the local peasant culture within Laotian society into becoming a single cash-crop economy dependent upon the vagaries of organized crime, but it also brought high-grade heroin into U.S. society, through U.S. soldiers who became addicted to it during the Vietnam War.

As the twentieth century drew to a close, Laos remained one of the poorest countries in the world, with a per capita income of $230 in the mid-1990s. The life expectancy for the average citizen was forty-nine years. When the Pathet Lao gained power in 1975, "reeducation camps" were established and flourished for a brief time. In the early 1980s the United States charged this communist regime with using chemical warfare on groups that opposed the communists. Called "yellow rain," it now appears that it was simply bee resin. Interestingly, relations between the United States and Laos were never broken during this time and they continued to maintain diplomatic offices in each others' capitals. While Vietnam continued to exert control over the affairs of Laos, described by Vietnam as a "special relationship," Laos began to chart a more independent path in the 1990s. The Laotian government also cooperated with the United States in finding U.S. soldiers missing in action from the Vietnam War era. These developments have led to an overall improvement of relations between Laos and the United States.

JONATHAN NASHEL

See also Cambodia; Geneva Conventions; Vietnam; Vietnam War

FURTHER READING

Castle, Timothy N. At War in the Shadow of Vietnam: U.S. Military Aid to the Royal Lao Government, 1955–1975. New York, 1993.
McCoy, Alfred W. The Politics of Heroin: CIA Complicity in the Global Drug Trade. Brooklyn, N.Y., 1991.
Steinberg, David Joel. In Search of Southeast Asia: A Modern History, rev. ed. Honolulu, 1987.
Stevenson, Charles. The End of Nowhere: American Policy Toward Laos. Boston, 1973.
Zasloff, Joseph J., and Leonard Unger. Laos: Beyond the Revolution. New York, 1991.

LARKIN, THOMAS OLIVER

(b. 16 September 1802; d. 27 October 1858)

U.S. consul and publicist, notable for increasing U.S. settlement of California while it was a Mexican province and for urging Californians to embrace U.S. annexation. Born in Massachusetts, Larkin migrated to California in 1832 and established himself in the flour-milling business in Monterey. Larkin wrote glowing reports of California for U.S. newspapers in the early 1840s and accepted appointment as the first U.S. consul there in 1843. Two years later, Larkin received a secret dispatch from James Buchanan, secretary of state under President James K. Polk, making him a confidential government agent. As such, Larkin reported on the activities of French and British agents and distributed propaganda to Californians, urging them to separate from Mexico and seek annexation by the United States. Although not affiliated with John C. Frémont's military adventures in California in 1846, Larkin was active in Monterey as Mexico lost control of the province. During the War with Mexico and the U.S. occupation of California, he became a navy agent and naval storekeeper. Having played an influential role in Polk's efforts to acquire California, Larkin went on to serve as a member of the state constitutional convention in 1849. He left public affairs during the final decade of his life and focused on his business interests.

PAUL R. GRASS

See also California; Frémont, John Charles; Mexico; Mexico, War with; Polk, James Knox

FURTHER READING

Hague, Harlan, and David J. Langum. Thomas O. Larkin: A Life of Patriotism and Profit in Old California. Norman, Okla., 1990.
Hawgood, J. A., ed. First and Last Consul: Thomas O. Larkin and the Annexation of California, A Selection of Letters, 2nd ed. Palo Alto, Calif., 1970.

LATIN AMERICA

Countries of Central and South America and the Caribbean, the large majority of whose inhabitants speak either Spanish or Portugese. Since the days of the American war of independence, U.S. policymakers have been torn between realistic calculations of national security and idealistic aspirations for a democratic world community. Toward no region has this tension been more evident than in Latin America, where the United States has wrestled with the contradictions between James Monroe's dictum to exclude foreign rivals and Woodrow Wilson's dream to respect self-determination and celebrate liberty.

This is not meant to imply that the basic choices for U.S. foreign policymakers have remained the same. On the contrary, U.S. policy evolved during the following four periods: (1) securing genuine independence (1783–1822); (2) expansion, division, and national consolidation (1823–1890s); (3) regional projection (1898–1940); and (4) global engagement (1941–present). From one period to the next, U.S. interests and goals changed as the country's wealth and capabilities increased, and the means by which policy is advanced has changed as direct intervention became more costly and economic interdependence became more manifest.

Moreover, almost since independence, but certainly in the twentieth century, U.S. policy toward the Caribbean Basin—the nations in and around the Caribbean—has differed from policy toward South America. The U.S. government has devoted more time, resources, and force in the smaller, nearer nations and less attention and intervention in the larger nations of South America.

Securing Independence: 1783–1822

For nearly four decades after winning its war of independence, the United States concentrated on defending its borders from the three major European powers that retained a presence in North America. Great Britain recognized the independence of the United States in the Treaty of Paris of 1783, but using the excuse of the U.S. failure to pay its debts, the British maintained their garrisons in the Northwest and conspired with Indian tribes to destabilize the young government.

France also probed the young nation for weakness, but Napoleon soon realized that the Louisiana Territories could be expanded only at the cost of his European ambitions. He therefore sold it. The United States doubled its size by the purchase but also gained new problems with Great Britain and Spain because of Louisiana's disputed boundaries. Only after the War of 1812 did the mother country and the young republic come to terms, establishing a nonmilitarized border in the north.

Spain initially tried to extend its influence north from Florida, but the United States resisted and with the impending loss of much of its empire in Latin America, the Spanish sold Florida to the United States in 1819. By that date, the U.S. borders were secure. The major European powers accepted the primacy of the United States in North America, and the United States turned its attention to its first external affairs issue: how to relate to the independence movements in Latin America.

National Expansion, Division, Consolidation: 1823–1890s

During the first three decades of the nineteenth century, Americans were sympathetic to Latin America's revolutions, but the U.S. government did not want to take a position that would provoke the wrath of Europe, so it kept its support covert. When Lord Canning, the British foreign secretary, first proposed to the U.S. ambassador in 1823 that their governments jointly issue a statement warning the rest of Europe not to recolonize Latin America, President James Monroe recognized the significance of the request: the United States had come of age.

Monroe debated the issue in cabinet and with congressional leaders, consulted his predecessors, and decided to answer Britain's question with a unilateral message to Congress on 2 December 1823. Monroe warned Europe not to recolonize Latin America, but instead of basing that warning on British naval power, he concocted the "doctrine of the two spheres," namely, that the Western Hemisphere and Europe should stay out of each other's affairs. The Monroe Doctrine—as it would be called decades later—was the first important foreign policy statement of the United States beyond issues of the security of its own borders, and it symbolized the nation's new confidence, the beginning of a tacit alliance with Great Britain, and the desire to protect Latin America's independence. But it was peculiarly American in the way that it combined the idealistic rationale that this hemisphere was different and better than the Old World with the realistic premise that U.S. security could best be defended by keeping Europe out of the Americas and the United States out of Europe.

Latin America's initial reaction was positive. Simon Bolívar, the liberator of the northern part of South America, called a conference in Panama and invited the United States and the new Latin states to discuss ways to translate Monroe's promise into a collective security agreement. The United States, however, was not ready for such actions, and its delegates reflected that hesitation by arriving late and without instructions.

For most of the nineteenth century, the United States concentrated on continental expansion. Americans who settled in Texas sought and won their independence from Mexico in 1836. The Mexican government warned Washington that annexation of Texas would lead to war. The threat was welcomed by President James Knox Polk, who was an avid expansionist. In the U.S.-Mexican war (1846–1848), the United States seized the northern third of Mexico, from California to Texas and from New Mexico through Colorado. Latin Americans, who had been encouraged by Monroe's pledge to defend their independence, became worried or angered by U.S. expansionism at Mexico's expense.

After the war, the discovery of gold in California led Americans to view the isthmus of Central America as the fastest way to transit between the Atlantic and Pacific coasts. Washington and London negotiated the Clayton-Bulwer Treaty of 1850 in which both countries agreed that any future isthmian railway or canal would be jointly controlled and neutral. The treaty was significant in two ways. First, the most powerful nation in the world recognized a balance of power with the United States in the Caribbean area, and second, no Central American nation signed it or was even consulted. The United States also negotiated a treaty with Colombia to guarantee free and secure transit across its Panamanian province.

By the middle of the nineteenth century, the constraint on U.S. expansionism into Latin America was no longer the power of Europe and not yet the nationalism of Latin America; rather internal divisions or reservations impeded the reach of the United States. Adventurers or "filibusters" like William Walker tried to lure the U.S. government into annexing Nicaragua and other nations, but northerners impeded such efforts for fear that these would enter as slave states. U.S. weakness during its own Civil War was exploited by Spain, which recolonized the Dominican Republic, and by France, which put a puppet leader, Emperor Maximilian, on the throne of Mexico. U.S. threats against these violations of the Monroe Doctrine were empty until the Civil War ended. Soon after, both European governments withdrew.

In an effort to promote trade with Latin America, Secretary of State James G. Blaine invited foreign ministers from Latin America—seventeen attended—to the first International American Conference in 1889–1890. The discussions were wide ranging, but the delegates failed to reach agreement to establish a customs union or an organization to arbitrate disputes. They did, however, set up the International Bureau of American Republics, which later became known as the Pan American Union, the forerunner of the Organization of American States (OAS).

Regional Projection: 1898–1940

At the end of the nineteenth century, Americans were tempted to act like European governments, but until the Spanish-American-Cuban-Filipino War in 1898, the United States largely rejected imperialism. In 1870, for example, Congress debated and subsequently rejected President Ulysses S. Grant's proposal to annex the Dominican Republic. The Spanish-American-Cuban-Filipino War, however, served not only to divide the centuries, but America's role in the hemisphere and the world. In the nineteenth century, the United States was largely unconcerned with chronic instability in Central America and the Caribbean, but in the twentieth century, the United States has often been obsessed with these countries'

internal affairs. The change was due to two related developments. First, expanding trade and investments and the construction of the Panama Canal gave the United States an increasing stake in the region's stability. And second, Americans grew worried that Germany and Japan would take advantage of the region's instability to gain a foothold from which to attack the United States or undermine U.S. interests.

By 1900, the United States was a global power, but until 1941, and except for a brief moment at the end of World War I, the United States viewed itself more as a regional power. To the extent that Washington turned its attention and resources abroad, it concentrated on securing its flank in the Caribbean Basin. During this period, two congressional amendments defined the parameters of U.S. foreign policy toward Latin America. The Teller Amendment to the declaration of war against Spain in 1898 was a unique exercise in self-denial: the United States would not annex Cuba; it would free the island. But in 1901, Congress passed the Platt Amendment which gave the United States the right to intervene in Cuba's affairs. Cuba was obliged to insert the amendment into its constitution. Together, the Teller and Platt Amendments reflected America's distaste for classical imperialism but also its unwillingness to accept equality with small, unstable neighbors. The compromise was an American variation of imperialism, a relationship that acknowledged Cuban independence, but also circumscribed it.

This was a period of dramatic change for the United States. In 1901, when three European governments asked permission from the United States to use force to compel Venezuela to pay its debts, Theodore Roosevelt responded affirmatively: "We do not guarantee any state against punishment if it misconducts itself, provided that punishment does not take the form of acquisition of territory by any non-American power." But the public reaction in the United States to the European bombardment of a Venezuelan port was very negative. Three years later, when Germany was about to undertake similar action in the closer country of the Dominican Republic, Roosevelt changed his mind. On 6 December 1904, he enunciated his famous corollary to the Monroe Doctrine in a message to Congress: "Chronic wrongdoing, or an impotence which results in a general loosening of ties of civilized society, may...ultimately require intervention by some civilized nation, and in the Western Hemisphere, the . . . Monroe Doctrine may force the United States, however reluctantly, in flagrant cases...to the exercise of an international police power."

Between the two statements was the decision to build the Panama Canal, the most expensive and strategic foreign investment undertaken by the United States up to that time. The United States first cajoled Great Britain to revoke the Clayton-Bulwer Treaty. Then, after Colombia rejected a treaty to build the canal, the Panamanians rose up in revolt, as they had done nearly fifty times during the past sixty years. This time, however, instead of helping the Colombians suppress the revolt, as it done before, the United States recognized the new government and prevented Colombia from regaining control of the province. Within three days of its independence, the U.S. secretary of state signed the Hay-Bunau-Varilla Treaty of November 1903, which gave the United States the right to build, operate, administer, and defend the canal and to maintain a zone of land ten miles wide across the isthmus to exercise jurisdiction "as it were sovereign…in perpetuity." The Panamanians resented the treaty, but had a choice of either accepting it or being reincorporated into Colombia.

The canal and Roosevelt's corollary to the Monroe Doctrine provided the reason and the rationale for the "protectorate policy" of the United States during the first three decades of the twentieth century. During this time, Washington intervened militarily in the region nearly twenty times—most often in Nicaragua, the Dominican Republic, Haiti, and Mexico. Historians disagree as to the motives of intervention. Some argue that the purpose was to make the region safe for U.S. business; others write that Washington wanted to maintain stability and preclude European competition. Regardless of the cause, the consequence of these interventions was to engender resentment of the "northern colossus" throughout Latin America.

The United States did *not* intervene in South America. Theodore Roosevelt explained the basis for the different policies: "The great and prosperous civilized commonwealths, such as the Argentine, Brazil, and Chile, in the southern half of South America have advanced so far that they no longer stand in any position of tutelage toward the United States. Their friendship is the friendship of equals for equals. My view was that as regards these nations there was no more necessity for asserting the Monroe Doctrine than there was to assert it for Canada."

European governments had close, if not closer, economic relations with the larger nations of South America than the United States had. Since the turn of the century, Argentina increasingly viewed itself as a rival of the United States and assumed the leadership of its neighbors in trying to get the United States to accept the principle of nonintervention, which it offered regularly at inter-American conferences—much to the irritation of the United States.

After World War I, the United States turned inward, especially away from Europe. Interventions, especially in Nicaragua, had become costly without yielding real benefits. By the late 1920s, the United States began to withdraw its marines from the Caribbean Basin, but its exit strategy included the establishment of national guards to preserve order and the administration of elections to elevate local leaders.

President Franklin D. Roosevelt's Good Neighbor Policy formally dismantled the last vestiges of the protectorate era—withdrawing marines, repealing Platt Amendments (that had been incorporated into treaties with several governments in the region), and accepting the principle of nonintervention. FDR deliberately fashioned new respectful relationships with Latin America based on reciprocal trade agreements, and these paid a handsome dividend in hemispheric solidarity when the United States went to war against Germany and Japan.

Global Engagement: 1941–1981

President Roosevelt had learned from Woodrow Wilson's failure to gain congressional approval of the League of Nations. During World War II, Roosevelt fashioned a strategy that would keep the United States engaged as a global leader after the war ended. The results were important economic institutions—like the World Bank, the International Monetary Fund (IMF), and the General Agreement on Tariffs and Trade (GATT)—and political institutions, led by the United Nations and the OAS. At the San Francisco Conference to establish the UN, Latin American governments insisted on recognizing the role of regional organizations, and in 1948 in Bogotá, they joined with the United States to approve of the Charter of the OAS.

From 1947 until the Soviet Union collapsed in 1991, world politics were largely defined by the Cold War. U.S. resources and attention focused on countering the Soviet/communist threat, first in Europe and next in Asia. When Latin American governments asked Secretary of State George Marshall at the Bogotá Conference for a "Marshall Plan for Latin America" similar to what he had proposed for Europe, Marshall responded that U.S. funds were scarce and the urgency and the threat were greater in Europe. During President Harry S. Truman's administration, the prospects for a communist takeover in the hemisphere were judged to be small, and thus the attention given to Latin American problems was minimal. His administration did experiment with a prodemocracy policy, but when initial efforts were met with resistance in the region and failed to achieve their goals, the policy was abandoned.

President Dwight D. Eisenhower and his Secretary of State John Foster Dulles saw the communist threat more intensely than Truman, and they approved a covert action program to overturn a leftist, democratic regime in Guatemala in 1954. President Jacobo Arbenz's land reform threatened the United Fruit Company, which protested to the U.S. government, but the administration's principal concern was that Arbenz was closely associated with communists at a time when it was even being accused by Republican senators for concealing leftists in the Departments of State and Defense.

Dulles first tried to get OAS action against Guatemala in the foreign ministers meeting in Caracas in March 1954, but only military governments supported him. Dulles then agreed to a Latin proposal for a hemispheric economic conference. That helped him gain majority support for a resolution that declared communism incompatible with the principles of the inter-American system. That resolution was used to justify a coup against Arbenz in June 1954. Organized by the Central Intelligence Agency (CIA), the coup succeeded in June 1954 because the Guatemalan military abandoned Arbenz.

The Inter-American Economic Conference was held in Rio de Janeiro in late November 1954, but Secretary of the Treasury George Humphrey took a rigid position, denying any aid or commodity agreements and insisting that the solution to Latin America's development required self-improvement of their investment climate. Milton Eisenhower, president of the Johns Hopkins University and the U.S. president's brother, had a longstanding interest in Latin America, and his influence on policy began to grow. He encouraged the Eisenhower administration to adopt a positive and helpful approach to the Bolivian Revolution of 1952 as contrasted with the hostile policy toward the Guatemalan Revolution. After Secretary Humphrey was replaced by Robert Anderson in 1957, the administration began to take Latin America's economic proposals seriously. Fidel Castro's takeover in Cuba in 1959 served to accelerate the Eisenhower administration's review and led to new decisions to support commodity agreements and the establishment of the Inter-American Development Bank.

Eisenhower tried to apply the successful strategy he used toward the Bolivian revolution in Cuba, but it failed primarily because the two revolutions and their leaders were different. Fidel Castro was determined to implement a sweeping, socialist revolution under his own rule and to secure Cuba's genuine independence from the United States even at the price of conflict. By February 1960, after the visit to Havana by the Soviet vice premier, Eisenhower adopted a more confrontational approach, which culminated in the abortive Bay of Pigs invasion the next year. To demonstrate that his opposition to Castro was due to Castro's being a dictator, not just anti-American, Eisenhower launched a similar effort to destabilize Dominican dictator Rafael Trujillo. Eisenhower's program was continued by Kennedy and led to Trujillo's assassination in May 1961.

To respond to the Soviet-Cuban threat, President John F. Kennedy launched the Bay of Pigs invasion in Cuba and the $10 billion Alliance for Progress for Latin America. These were the two Janus-faces of the American strategy—a covert, indirect intervention to try to overthrow Castro and a Pan-American initiative to promote economic development. The two sides symbolized the tensions inherent in U.S. policy during the Cold War period. The Bay of Pigs invasion was, of course, an embarrassing failure, while the Alliance for Progress was a modified success that stimulated economic development and planning in the hemisphere. It had, however, little or no effect on helping democracy or social reforms.

The greatest crisis faced by the United States in the hemisphere occurred during the fall of 1962 when the Soviet Union sent nuclear missiles to Cuba. When the Soviets first offered missiles to defend against a possible U.S. invasion, Castro responded that Cuba could defend itself better without the weapons, but if the Soviets wanted to install them to improve the strategic balance with the United States, he would accept them on behalf of "socialist solidarity," and on that basis, he did. For a tense two weeks, the United States and the Soviet Union came as close as they ever did to nuclear war. Soviet Premier Nikita Khrushchev decided to withdraw the missiles in exchange for an agreement by the United States not to invade Cuba. To facilitate the Soviet decision, Kennedy withdrew U.S. missiles from Turkey. Enraged at not having been consulted, Castro refused to allow the international verification of the missile withdrawal, and as a result, the Kennedy administration viewed the agreement as not consummated and continued covert attempts to destabilize Castro.

President Lyndon Johnson maintained Kennedy's policy toward Cuba and also obtained additional funding for the Alliance for Progress. In April 1965, fearful that instability in the Dominican Republic would allow the country there to be captured by Castroite rebels, Johnson ordered U.S. troops there. The OAS endorsed the invasion, shared in peace-keeping efforts, and supervised an election in 1966. Most scholars of the intervention concluded that the prospects for a communist takeover were negligible, but the resentment with U.S. intervention had serious long-term consequences.

As Eisenhower had sent his brother as his envoy to Latin America, President Richard M. Nixon dispatched Nelson Rockefeller in 1969, but Rockefeller had much less influence than Milton Eisenhower. This was mainly because only one Latin American issue seriously engaged President Nixon, the election of a Marxist, Salvador Allende Gossens, as president of Chile in 1970. After failing to prevent his election, Nixon used CIA covert operations to "squeeze the Chilean economy" and try to overthrow him. In 1973, after three years of political polarization, Chilean General Augusto Pinochet Ugarte toppled Allende Gossens in a bloody coup.

Despite the overthrow of a democracy and gross human rights violations by a military regime, Presidents

Nixon and Gerald Ford increased aid to the Pinochet regime. In reaction, Congress insisted that human rights become a U.S. foreign policy priority. When the Ford administration did not modify its support for the regime, Congress reduced and conditioned aid.

However, only after the election of Jimmy Carter as president did human rights become a priority for U.S. foreign policy. The Carter administration conditioned its relations with Latin American governments on the way they treated their citizens. Closest relations were with democracies, and military governments were pressed to democratize. To internationalize the effort, Carter signed the American Convention on Human Rights and increased support for the Inter-American Commission on Human Rights. Progress was made in reducing human rights violations in the most repressive southern cone countries of South America, and the process of democratization began in Peru, Ecuador, Brazil, and the Dominican Republic.

Although the texture of Carter's policy toward Latin America was formed by human rights, the most controversial political issue he faced was the Panama Canal Treaty. Since riots in the Panama Canal Zone in January 1964, every U.S. president understood the logic for new canal treaties. The exclusive control by the United States of a ten-mile wide strip of land through the middle of Panama was an outmoded relic of the protectorate era. The longer the United States refused to correct this wrong, the greater the risk to the canal by nationalistic Panamanians. The American people, however, did not want to give away the canal, and Carter's predecessors avoided the issue. By 1977, however, Panamanian patience had run out, and Carter accepted the political risk. He signed new Panama Canal treaties in September 1977 that would gradually transfer responsibility for the operation and defense of the canal until Panama had full control in 2000. The United States would retain the right to defend the canal. The treaties passed the Senate by a single vote in the spring of 1978.

In 1977, the United States was still exploring the boundaries of détente with the Soviet Union. The Carter administration also began discussions with Cuba that established Interest Sections (less than full diplomatic relations) and permitted thousands of Cuban political prisoners to be released. The Soviet decision to use the Cuban military in Ethiopia and then to intervene in Afghanistan brought an end to both détente and normalization with Cuba. The relationship deteriorated even further when Fidel Castro encouraged the exodus of 125,000 refugees from the port of Mariel to Florida in the summer of 1980.

Leftist revolutions in Nicaragua, Grenada, and El Salvador in 1979–1980 heightened anxiety among conservatives. Overall, Carter's attempt to place U.S. policy on a new multilateral, human rights footing reduced repression and increased the prospects for democracy, but the prevalence of military governments and the resurgence of a new Cold War precluded a reshaping of U.S.–Latin American relations.

The 1980s–1990s

Ronald Reagan was elected president in part because the American people were frustrated by Soviet expansionism, and he promised victory. The center of his policy in Latin America was Central America where he was determined to stop the communists in El Salvador and overthrow the Sandinistas in Nicaragua. His principal instruments were military aid to the Salvadoran government and covert aid to the "Contras"—anti-Sandinista counter-revolutionaries. The Reagan administration often threatened force, but used it directly only in Grenada in October 1983 to replace a leftist government and protect American medical students.

President Reagan was tarred by the brush of the Iran-Contra Affair in which senior officials traded arms to Iran to gain the release of hostages and used the funds to help the Contras, although that was prohibited by law. By the end of Reagan's term, Central America was no more secure, but after hundreds of thousands of deaths, and a sharp economic decline, it was more polarized, as was the debate in the United States. For the rest of Latin America, the 1980s were a "lost decade" due mostly to the debt crisis that left the region in 1989 with a per capita gross national product that was 8 percent below what it had been in 1981.

In the struggle against the Sandinistas, the Reagan administration collaborated with the brutal dictator of Panama, General Manuel Antonio Noriega. When news reports in 1987 connected Noriega to Colombian drug-traffickers, the Reagan administration reversed course and pressured Noriega to resign, to no effect. After Noriega nullified a presidential election in which the opposition won in May 1989, President George Bush stepped up efforts to depose Noriega. On 20 December, Bush dispatched 23,000 troops to capture Noriega and bring him to justice in the United States. It was the first unilateral U.S. intervention in Latin America in more than sixty years.

At the same time, President Bush joined with Congress to depolarize the Contra issue with a bipartisan accord that left Nicaraguans with the political space to negotiate, with outside help, the country's first free election. The end of the Cold War also permitted the United Nations and others to negotiate peace in El Salvador. Treasury Secretary Nicholas Brady's debt plan reduced Latin American debt and put their economies on a sound footing that permitted growth and trade liberalization. The most profound initiative, however, came from Mexican President Carlos Salinas for a North American Free Trade Agreement (NAFTA). Many of the other countries in Latin America were eager to join a hemispheric market, and President Bush promised them the opportunity with his Enterprise of the Americas Initiative. In 1991, the OAS foreign ministers met in Chile and agreed to the "Santiago Commitment" to defend democracy in all of their countries. The first test came in Haiti when the military overthrew the freely elected President Jean-Bertrand Aristide on 30 September 1991.

President Bill Clinton inherited both NAFTA and the crisis in Haiti when he took office in January 1993. Clinton negotiated side agreements on the environment and labor issues to NAFTA, and with a high priority effort, persuaded the U.S. Congress to approve the agreement in November 1993. In December 1994, he hosted a summit meeting in Miami of thirty-four democratically elected presidents and prime ministers from the hemisphere. The summit participants agreed to negotiate and implement a hemispheric free trade agreement by 2005. They also agreed to an elaborate action plan for preserving democracy and the environment.

Although the OAS proved inadequate to the task of restoring democracy to Haiti, multilateral efforts toward other countries proved more effective. When the Peruvian and Guatemalan presidents tried to close their respective congresses, the inter-American community responded with sufficient determination to compel the Peruvian to call new elections and to displace the Guatemalan. The spread of democratization permitted the United States and Latin America to work together more constructively on a wide range of economic, environmental, drug, and political issues than ever before.

Cuba under Fidel Castro remained the main relic of the Cold War in the hemisphere. Despite the implosion of the Soviet Union and the collapse of its military and economic relationship with Cuba, the United States under both Presidents Bush and Clinton chose to intensify its embargo and to demand "irreversible" movement toward democracy as a price of a normal relationship. The rest of Latin America urged Castro to democratize and the United States to lift its embargo—to no effect in either direction.

The United Nations picked up the baton from the OAS on Haiti and tried to negotiate an agreement with the Haitian military in the summer of 1993. When that failed, the UN Security Council moved slowly but deliberately to Resolution 940, approved 31 July 1994. It declared that "the situation in Haiti constituted a threat to peace and security in the region," and asked member states to provide a multinational force to restore the constitutional government.

On September 16, President Clinton asked former President Jimmy Carter, Senator Sam Nunn, and General Colin Powell to try one last time to negotiate an agreement with the Haitian military. They succeeded in reaching an agreement that provided for the peaceful introduction of the multinational force, the departure from power of the Haitian military leaders, and the restoration of President Aristide by 15 October 1994. The precedent of the international community using all means necessary to restore democracy was a very important one for the democratic community of the Americas.

The history of U.S. relations with Latin America can be viewed as a continuous struggle by the region to gain respect and autonomy, with the United States gradually acceding. There is a cyclical, whirlpool-like quality to the relationship, particularly in the twentieth century, when the United States seemed at various times preoccupied to the point of obsession with a small country and then so distracted from the region's affairs so as to almost forget the names of the countries. This cycle between obsession and neglect has been complemented by a political cycle in the region between democracy and dictatorship and an economic cycle between state-intervention and market-oriented approaches.

In the twentieth century, the United States has supported market-oriented and free-trade policies in Latin America and has mostly favored democracy, although some U.S. ambassadors have identified U.S. interests with dictators, and on at least two occasions the U.S. government has contributed to overthrowing democracies because it viewed them as dangerously leftist. U.S. businesses have influenced U.S. policy at certain moments either when Washington was not paying attention or when U.S. business interests overlapped with U.S. strategic interests.

The convergence of economic policies and democratic political systems in the hemisphere coincided with the end of the Cold War. The result has been that domestic, social, and economic concerns have increased in importance in all of the countries. Advances in telecommunications and three decades of very high levels of immigration from Latin America narrowed the cultural distance between the region and the United States. To the extent that democracy and free trade take root in the hemisphere, U. S. relations with Latin America may come to probably resemble the paternalism of past policies less and look more like relations with Europe.

ROBERT A. PASTOR

See also Alliance for Progress; Argentina; Bay of Pigs Invasion; Chile; Cuba; El Salvador; Grenada; Guatemala; Mexico War with; Monroe Doctrine; Nicaragua; North American Free Trade Agreement; Organization of American States; Panama and Panama Canal; Roosevelt Corollary; Spanish-American-Cuban-Filipino War, 1898; Third World Debt; Walker, William

FURTHER READING

Bemis, Samuel Flagg. *The Latin American Policy of the United States.* New York, 1943.

Blasier, Cole. *The Hovering Giant: U.S. Responses to Revolutionary Change in Latin America, 1910–1985.* Pittsburgh, 1985.

Gantenbein, James W., ed., *The Evolution of Our Latin-American Policy.* New York, 1971.

LaFeber, Walter. *Inevitable Revolutions.* 2nd ed. New York, 1993.

Langley, Lester. *Struggle for the American Mediterranean.* Athens, Ga., 1976.

———. *The United States and the Caribbean in the 20th Century.* Athens, Ga., 1985.

May, Ernest R. *The Making of the Monroe Doctrine.* Cambridge, Mass. 1975.

Munro, Dana G. *Intervention and Dollar Diplomacy, 1900–1921.* Princeton, N.J., 1964.

———. *The United States and the Caribbean Republics, 1921–1933.* Princeton, N.J., 1974.

Pastor, Robert A. *Condemned to Repetition: The United States and Nicaragua.* Princeton, 1988.

———. *Whirlpool: U.S. Foreign Policy Toward Latin America and the Caribbean.* Princeton, 1992.

Rabe, Stephen G. *Eisenhower and Latin America.* Chapel Hill, N.C., 1988.

Whitaker, Arthur P. *The United States and the Independence of Latin America, 1800–1830.* New York, 1964.

Wood, Bryce. *The Making of the Good Neighbor Policy.* New York, 1961.

———. *The Dismantling of the Good Neighbor Policy.* Austin, Texas, 1985.

LATVIA

A Baltic republic bordering on Estonia, Lithuania, Belorussia, and Russia. Latvia regained its independence from the Soviet Union in 1991. In 1993, it established a democratic constitution and in June 1993 held parliamentary elections certified by international observers as free and fair. It has close and amicable relations with the United States, and the Clinton administration was of considerable assistance in bringing about the withdrawal of Russian troops from Latvia.

Latvia is a country of 64,600 square kilometers and 2.6 million people. Due to Russian-speaking immigration under Soviet rule, by 1988 barely 52 percent of its population were ethnic Latvians, though this proportion has since increased due to the out-migration of around 100,000 Russians.

Until the thirteenth century, the area of what is now Latvia was inhabited by pagan tribes under Scandinavian and Russian influence. In succeeding centuries, the region was successively conquered by German crusaders, the Swedish and Polish monarchies, and Imperial Russia. During World War I, Latvia was conquered by the German armies. In 1918, after the German collapse, a national government was formed and eventually, with British and Estonian help, prevailed against the Latvian and

Russian communists and the German *freikorps* and secured independence. The United States took a sympathetic attitude to the Latvian national government and put pressure on Germany to withdraw its troops and its support for the forces of the local German minority. However, the United States strongly disapproved of the seizure of the land of the local German landowners, the "Baltic Barons," viewing this as an offense against the rights of private property. Concern about the treatment of the national minorities in Latvia held up Latvia's accession to the League of Nations, but after signing the treaty guaranteeing minority rights, Latvia joined the League. In the 1920s and 1930s, Riga, with its large Russian emigré population, was a major U.S. listening post for events over the border in the Soviet Union. George Kennan served in the U.S. mission in Latvia. In June 1940, with the way prepared by the Molotov-Ribbentrop pact between the Soviet Union and Nazi Germany, Latvia was invaded and subsequently annexed by Stalin's Soviet Union. As with the other two Baltic States, the United States did not recognize the annexation, and made formal statements to this effect at various intervals during and after World War II. The Balts were, however, low on the list of American priorities; and having been forced to abandon the Poles, Czechs, and others to communism, it seemed obvious to U.S. policymakers that there was little the West could do to help the Baltic States. U.S. sympathy for the Balts in the postwar years was also undermined by the prominent part played by Baltic auxiliaries and SS troops recruited by the Germans in the Holocaust of the Jews. Jewish groups in the United States never forgot this, and it was astutely played on by the KGB in their propaganda against the Baltic emigré movements, some of whose members were arrested and deported to the USSR on charges of participating in the Holocaust. During and after the achievement of renewed independence in 1991, accusations of Latvian and Lithuanian anti-Semitism surfaced again in the U.S. media.

In line with U.S. recognition of *de jure* Baltic independence, the official line of the Bush administration toward the Baltic independence movements between 1988 and 1991 was not unsympathetic (as it was toward the Ukrainians) but was heavily colored by a desire not to undermine Mikhail Gorbachev's rule over the Soviet Union as a whole. However, the administration, and still more the U.S. Congress, made it clear that they would penalize the Soviet government for any use of force in the Baltic States. On 24 January 1991 the Senate unanimously passed a resolution to this effect. U.S. interest in the Balts' fates was signalled by the dispatch of U.S. diplomats on visits to the region. On 20 January 1991, two U.S. diplomats from the consulate-general in St. Petersburg narrowly escaped becoming victims of the armed attack by Soviet special police on the Interior Ministry in Riga, in which five people were killed. Congress suspended economic aid to the Soviet Union in retaliation for the Soviet military intervention in the Baltic States, and U.S. pressure was instrumental in bringing that intervention to an end.

After the collapse of the Soviet coup in August 1991, Latvia declared full independence and the U.S. extended de facto recognition—although even then, this was delayed by several days in an effort not to embarrass Gorbachev further. Since then, U.S. aid has played a significant part in helping the Latvian economy, which after that of Estonia is the strongest in the former Soviet Union. The U.S. provided some $15 million in aid to Latvia between 1991 and 1994, most of it for specialized programs, and supported Latvia's application for loans from the International Monetary Fund (IMF). In 1994, President Clinton authorized the Baltic Enterprise Fund to spend $17 million for small business credits in the Baltic States. U.S. diplomatic pressure also helped persuade Russia to withdraw its troops from Latvia, a process completed right on deadline by 31 August 1994. The United States, in company with Scandinavia and the countries of the European Union, attached great importance to this question, seeing the Russian military presence as a significant threat to the stability of the Baltic region. The most important U.S. initiative with regard to Latvia came in early 1994 and was related to troop withdrawal. Russian-Latvian talks on withdrawal were stalled by two issues: Russian desire to retain control for a limited period of time of the space radar station at Skrunda in Latvia; and the determination of the Russian government, and especially the increasingly powerful Russian military, that Latvia should grant permanent residence permits to Russian military pensioners in Latvia. Under a U.S.-brokered compromise, Latvia eventually agreed to allow Russia to use Skrunda for three years, plus one-and-a-half years for dismantlement; the Latvian government, with strong urgings from the Clinton administration, also gave in on the question of the pensioners.

The compromise, however, proved very unpopular with many Latvians, and contributed to the victory of radical nationalist parties in the local elections of May 1994. The bitterly anti-Russian propaganda of these parties has caused concern to U.S. diplomats. On the highly controversial question of citizenship for non-Latvians (mainly Russians) who entered Latvia under Soviet rule, discreet U.S. and European pressure on Latvia to be more generous and abide by Council of Europe standards led to criticism of the West by some radicals.

As with the other Baltic states, Latvia seeks membership in both the European Union (EU) and the North Atlantic Treaty Organization (NATO). Associate membership in the EU is a distinct possibility in the late 1990s. Latvia joined NATO's Partnership for Peace soon after its establishment in January 1994. Thus, while in general Latvia in this period was moving closer to the West, the ethnic situation in this country remained a cause of concern in Washington and a possible sparking-point of confrontation.

ANATOL LIEVEN

See also Estonia; Lithuania; Russia and the Soviet Union; Stalin, Joseph

FURTHER READING

Flint, David. *The Baltic States—Estonia, Latvia and Lithuania.* Brookfield, Conn., 1992.
Hider, John, and Patrick Salmon. *The Baltic Nations and Europe.* London, 1991.
Lieven, Anatol. *The Baltic Revolution: Estonia, Latvia, Lithuania and the Path to Independence.* New Haven, Conn., 1993.

LAW OF THE SEA

A major body of international law regarding the rights and duties of states in the marine environment. U.S. foreign policy for the Law of the Sea reflects a conflict between the status of the United States as a coastal state, with interests in controlling the maritime spaces adjacent to its long coastline, and its status as a global military and commercial power, with interests in unrestricted mobility in the seas and access to distant resources. After World War II the coastal interests of the United States were declared by two Harry S. Truman presidential proclamations in 1945. The first proclaimed U.S. authority over the resources of its adjacent continental shelf. The second asserted U.S. authority to manage the fishery resources of the adjacent ocean waters. At the same time, the United States adhered to the position first adopted in 1793 by Secretary of State Thomas Jefferson that the breadth of the U.S. territorial sea is three nautical miles.

The international community supported Truman's continental-shelf claim that reached well beyond the territorial sea. This endorsement encouraged other states to assert greater jurisdiction in the oceans. The United States strongly opposed those expansive claims. This issue was debated beginning in 1950 during the preparations for the First U.N. Conference on the Law of the Sea (UNCLOS I). The conference was held in 1958 and produced the four 1958 Geneva Conventions on the Law of the Sea: Convention on the Continental Shelf; Convention on the Territorial Sea and the Contiguous Zone; Convention on the High Seas; and Convention on Fishing and Conservation of the Living Resources of the High Seas. These conventions codified the regime of the continental shelf, protected freedoms of navigation and overflight on the high seas, and secured innocent passage for foreign vessels through territorial seas and straits. They failed to establish the maximum breadth of the territorial sea. Nor did they resolve claims of jurisdiction over fisheries seaward of the territorial sea. The United States was a party to all four conventions. In 1960 the Second U.N. Conference on the Law of the Sea (UNCLOS II), held in Geneva, Switzerland, again failed to settle the disputes over the maximum breadth of the territorial sea and resource zones seaward.

In the aftermath, many coastal states claimed extensive zones of jurisdiction beyond a narrow territorial sea. Even the United States claimed by legislation in 1966 a nine-nautical-mile fisheries zone. At the same time, the U.S. interests in the mobility of its military forces, projection of force abroad, and the use of continental shelves and deep oceans for such military purposes as acoustical surveillance was at their height. Extensive coastal state claims of offshore jurisdiction and restrictions on passage through straits threatened these interests. Those coastal state claims were also antagonistic to similar interests of the Soviet Union. This confluence of superpower interests led to their joint effort to convene another Law of the Sea conference. Technological developments coincidentally made it possible to remove from the deep ocean floor manganese nodules containing nickel, copper, cobalt, and manganese. By the time the Third U.N. Conference on the Law of the Sea (UNCLOS III) opened in 1972 at Caracas, Venezuela, the entire Law of the Sea was on the agenda. Issues also included resource scarcity, protection and preservation of the marine environment, and the New International Economic Order. After complex and difficult negotiations lasting ten years, UNCLOS III adopted the 320-article and nine-annex 1982 U.N. Convention on the Law of the Sea (LOS Convention). This document contained virtually the entire international Law of the Sea. The breadth of the territorial sea is fixed by this Convention at 12 nautical miles, and the 200-nautical-mile exclusive economic zone is established. This 200-nautical-mile zone grants the coastal state exclusive jurisdiction over all resources in the zone, as well as rights regarding the marine environment and marine scientific research. Traditional high-seas rights of navigation, overflight, and the laying of submerged cables and pipelines are preserved. Innocent passage through the territorial sea is refined and guaranteed, and the right of transit passage through and over straits used for international navigation is guaranteed. The Convention develops new law with regard to archipelagic waters, marine scientific research, conservation of marine living resources, and protection of the marine environment. The Convention includes a progressive compulsory system for the binding settlement of disputes relating to its interpretation or application.

The United States played a leading role in the negotiation of the Convention. It was opened for signature in December of 1982 at Montego Bay, Jamaica, and attract-ed 159 signatories by the time the period for signature ended in December of 1994. With the notable exception of the controversial regime for the resources of the deep seabed, the United States supported all of the text. For this reason alone the U.S. voted against the adoption of the Convention and did not sign it. President Ronald Reagan declared that the U.S. accepted the non-deep seabed parts of the Convention as binding international law to be followed by the United States. He claimed for the United States a 12-nautical-mile territorial sea and a 200-nautical-mile exclusive economic zone.

After 1982, the Preparatory Commission called for by UNCLOS III made preparations for the entry into force of the Convention. The United States did not participate in those deliberations. In 1990 the U.N. secretary-general began informal consultations with a select group of interested states, including the United States, to resolve the dispute over the deep seabed regime. On 16 November 1993, the sixtieth state's ratification of the Law of the Sea Convention was deposited, triggering the entry into force of the Convention a year later. During 1994 efforts continued with representatives from all sectors of the international community, including the United States, to fashion an agreement modifying the deep seabed regime in order to broaden its acceptability. Negotiations were facilitated by the collapse of the Soviet Union, the increased international acceptability of capitalism and the realization by the international community that deep seabed mining was not economically viable and would not be so for a long time, if ever.

These negotiations were concluded in 1994 and resulted in the Agreement Relating to the Implementation of Part XI of the LOS Convention. It was endorsed by a resolution of the UN General Assembly in July of 1994 with the cosponsorship of the United States and many other states. A broad consensus of the international community supported the resolution which also called for all states to become parties to the LOS Convention and the new agreement (121 states in favor, none opposed, seven abstentions). The United States signed the agreement and bound itself to provisional application of the revised deep seabed regime. In October 1994 President Bill Clinton submitted the LOS Convention and the 1994 Deep Seabed Agreement to the U.S. Senate for its advice and consent to presidential ratification. The Convention entered into force on 16 November 1995, and the Deep Seabed Agreement became provisionally in force on the same date (in July 1996 there were 131 provisional party states and 65 parties). The number of states parties to the LOS Convention grew to 104 by July of 1996. Most of those states are developing countries. Such major states that are parties include: Australia, China, Germany, Greece, France, Italy, Japan, and the Netherlands. In addition, the European Union agreed that all of its members would ratify the Convention and the Deep Seabed Agreement. Many other states, developed and developing, were moving forward with domestic procedures to ratify the Convention. Russia, although it abstained in the 1994 UNGA vote, modified its position and agreed to apply the 1994 Deep Seabed Agreement provisionally.

The LOS Convention provides the framework for the management of other issues of the marine environment. Disputes regarding the delimitation of maritime boundaries between states have been settled on the basis of the Convention through international agreements and litigation before the International Court of Justice or other ad hoc arbitration tribunals. As of 1996 approximately 175 such maritime boundaries were settled.

The 1992 United Nations Conference on Environment and Development endorsed the LOS Convention as the framework for addressing problems related to the marine environment. Specific issues have been addressed by the International Maritime Organization and several multilateral agreements. These include the 1972 London Dumping Convention and the 1989 Basil Convention on the Control of Transboundary Movements of Hazardous Wastes and Their Disposal. Several other agreements address oil pollution of the seas.

A major problem focused upon subsequent to the conclusion of the LOS Convention is the threat to the viability of commercially exploited marine resources of the high seas beyond the 200-nautical-mile exclusive economic zone. In response the UN General Assembly adopted a resolution in 1991 calling for a ban on long-line driftnet fishing on the high seas that effectively ended this practice. Two companion multilateral treaties not yet in force as of 1996 would establish stronger fisheries management agreements in the high seas including coordination with coastal state management in adjacent economic zones and restrictions on the reflagging of vessels to avoid conservation requirements. These agreements are the Agreement for the Implementation of the Provisions of the United Nations Convention on the Law of the Sea of 10 December 1982 Relating to the Conservation and Management of Straddling Fish Stocks and Highly Migratory Fish Stocks (45 signatories as of July 1996) and the Agreement to Promote Compliance with International Conservation and Management Measures by Fishing Vessels on the High Seas (seven parties as of January 1995). Agreements regarding fishing in regional seas have also addressed this problem. One such agreement is the Convention on the Conservation and Management of Pollock Resources in the Bering Sea. The hunting for whales and other cetaceans is increasingly problematic as these stocks have improved as a result of bans established under the 1946 International Convention for the Regulation of Whaling. Such states as Japan and Norway have pressed for lifting some of the hunting bans established under this convention.

JONATHAN I. CHARNEY

See also Antarctica; Clinton, William Jefferson; Environment; Fisheries; Freedom of the Seas; International Law; Neutral Rights; New International Economic Order; Reagan, Ronald Wilson; Truman, Harry S.

FURTHER READING

Balton, David A. "Strengthening the Law of the Sea: The New Agreement on Straddling Fish Stocks and Highly Migratory Fish Stocks." *Ocean Development and International Law*, vol. 27, No. 1-2 (1996): 125-151.

Charney, Jonathan I., and Lewis M. Alexander, eds. *International Maritime Boundaries*. Dordrecht/Boston/London, 1993.

Charney, Jonathan I. "Entry into Force of the 1982 Convention on the Law of the Sea." *Virginia Journal of International Law*, vol. 35, No. 2 (Winter 1995): 381–404.

Hollick, Ann L. *U.S. Foreign Policy and the Law of the Sea*. Princeton, N.J., 1981.

Message from the President of the United States Transmitting United Nations Convention on the Law of the Sea, with Annexes, Done at Montego Bay, December 10, 1982...and the Agreement Relating to the Implementation of Part XI of the United Nations Convention on the Law of the Sea..., with Annex, Treaty Doc. 103-39, 103d Cong., 2d Sess. (Oct. 7, 1994).

Morell, James B. *The Law of the Sea: An Historical Analysis of the 1982 Treaty and Its Rejection by the United States*. Jefferson, N.C., 1992.

The United Nations Convention on the Law of the Sea, U.N. Sales No. E.83.V.5 (1983). Reprinted in *International Legal Materials*. Vol. 21, No. 6. (November 1982): 1261–1354.

LEAGUE OF NATIONS

The first international collective security organization designed to prevent war, it was the predecessor of the United Nations. When the leading allied powers (Great Britain, the United States, France, and Italy) produced the League Covenant at the 1919 Paris Peace Conference the League had the blessing and support of the international community. British and U.S. political theorists had developed the concept as an antidote to the destructive forces of World War I. President Woodrow Wilson became the international spokesman for the League at the peace conference, indicating that the United States would assume a leadership role in the organization. But the U.S. Senate's rejection of the Versailles treaty and League membership weakened the organization during the 1920s and 1930s when it confronted international crises that threatened the postwar world order and contributed to the League's decline.

Shortly after the war began, organizations on both sides of the Atlantic formed to develop and support the league concept. The American League to Enforce Peace (LEP) and its British counterpart, the League of Nations Society, were established independently but contemporaneously, in early 1915. LEP members included Hamilton Holt and William H. Short of the New York Peace Society, ex-minister to Belgium Theodore Marburg, former president William Taft, and professors Theodore Woolsey, and George Grafton Wilson. Although a number of such organizations advocated a league, the League of Nations Society and the LEP were particularly effective pressure groups because they successfully impressed their agenda on their respective governments. Both groups consulted and conferred with one another to coordinate their proposals at critical points. Cambridge classics scholar G. Lowes Dickinson, foremost British publicist of the league, probably coined the term "League of Nations." League of Nations Society members included pacifists Lowes Dickinson, Leonard S. Woolf, J. A. Hobson, Willoughby H. Dickinson, and H.G. Wells, as well as Lord Shaw. Many members were initially associated with the Bryce group, named after the internationally respected statesman Lord James Bryce, who served as group chairman and later (1918) with the League of Nations Union, whose executive committee included Sir Edward Grey and Professor Gilbert Murray.

While the LEP and the League of Nations Society built support for a broadly based movement, the British Fabian Society commissioned Leonard Woolf to write, in collaboration with Sidney Webb, the first detailed wartime proposal for the organization. In 1915, Woolf's report was published in special supplements of *The New Statesman*, which was subsequently transformed into a book entitled *International Government* (1916). The report so impressed Lord Robert Cecil, undersecretary for foreign affairs, that he included much of it in the British draft proposal of the League and then sent it to President Wilson.

Wilson and his special adviser, Colonel Edward M. House, had explored peaceful solutions to international conflict soon after the war broke out and became early advocates of a league. The president was a spokesman for international liberalism and a league of nations, so the British deferred to him, believing the league would be more readily accepted by the leading powers if Wilson introduced the proposal at Versailles. Wilson was the only representative at the peace conference to arrive with an army of advisers, known as The Inquiry, and a detailed peace plan for the postwar world order (the Fourteen Points, the last of which dealt with the League of Nations). Wilson was so committed to the League that he was willing to grant concessions to the other powers to assure inclusion of the League in the Treaty of Versailles. He assumed the League would gain universal support in both Europe and the United States provided it were an integral part of the Versailles treaty. To his amazement, the treaty was more readily accepted by the signatory powers than by his own country.

The League Covenant contained a statement of purpose and outlined the structure of the new organization. League members (treaty signatories and twelve other nations invited to become members) agreed to promote international cooperation, peace, and security through peaceful means. Any self-governing state that agreed to observe its international obligations and League regulations could apply for membership, which was subject to approval by two-thirds of the Assembly. These regulations included Articles 12 and 13, requiring members to resolve disputes through arbitration or judicial settlement. It was left to League representatives to determine how the organs, especially the Secretariat, Council, and Assembly would function in relation to one another. The League had no executive organ. The Secretariat, headed by the secretary-general, served as the chief administrative organ. It prepared and circulated documents and reports and performed other duties assigned by the Assembly.

The two deliberative bodies, the Council and the Assembly, were given similar responsibilities. Either body, for example, could examine any issue under consideration by the League, but neither could overturn or modify a decision entailing the exclusive competence of the other. The Council met at least once a year to consider disputes referred by the secretary-general and the Assembly; it also submitted yearly reports of its activities to the Assembly and formulated plans for the Permanent Court of International Justice. Council members included the "great powers" (Great Britain, France, Italy, and Japan) and four nonpermanent League members (selected by the Assembly), each member having one representative and one vote. The Assembly was the final arbiter of League policy. It met annually to consider issues before the League and to address problems affecting world peace. Article 10 of the Covenant, for example, provided for consultation in cases where a League member was confronted with aggression by another nation state. The Assembly reviewed membership applications subject to two-thirds majority vote for admission. Each League member had one vote and was allowed up to three representatives in the Assembly. Headquartered in Geneva, the League established so-called technical organizations to promote international cooperation in trade, transportation, and health. Because the leading powers were unwilling to grant the League authority to enforce its decisions, it faced serious challenges in the interwar period, challenges that contributed to its demise.

While President Wilson was in Paris, treaty opposition forces, the "irreconcilables" (in cooperation with his bitter rival, the powerful Republican chairman of the Senate Foreign Relations Committee, Henry Cabot Lodge, Sr.), mounted a well-organized movement against the League. Because Wilson (a Democrat) neglected to build bipartisan support for the League and the treaty, he faced the grueling Senate approval process in a weakened position, exacerbated by fatigue from the war and treaty negotiations. The Versailles treaty had widespread popular support but was defeated in 1920 because Wilson was unable to forge a compromise with the Republican-dominated Senate. The Irreconcilables objected to the League as an infringement on U.S. sovereignty and demanded adjustments to other treaty provisions. Lodge seemed willing to accept the treaty with reservations (especially that the United States assume no obligation under Article 10, which provided for consultation in the event that a League member was confronted with aggression by another nation state). Wilson insisted the Versailles treaty be approved without alteration; the treaty and U.S. membership failed because Wilson and the Senate could not come to a consensus. After the Senate defeat, the United States concluded a separate peace with Germany and agreed to send an observer to League meetings. Great Britain, the partner of the United States in creating the League, avoided defeat in Parliament by building support across party lines.

Other U.S. groups besides Congress opposed the League. Critics of various persuasions argued that the League preserved the interests of the leading powers in general and imperial interests in particular. International liberals, who had supported a broadly democratic league, became disillusioned with the League of Nations because its power was concentrated in the Council, assuring dominance by the leading powers. These criticisms were supported, first, by the Soviet Union's publication of the secret 1916 Sykes-Picot Agreement, which divided the Ottoman Empire into French and British spheres of influence, and, second, when the League legitimized this agreement by recognizing French and British authority through the League mandate system.

Although the League dealt successfully with a number of border disputes in the 1920s (in Silesia and Albania, plus a series of Greek-Bulgarian incidents), it failed to resolve conflicts involving the leading powers, as was the case during the Italian occupation of Corfu in 1923 and the Manchurian and Ethiopian crises of the 1930s. The latter two constituted the most serious threats to the League's mission of preserving the status quo, since two member states, Japan and Italy, sought to adjust the world order to suit their own national interests. In both cases, the absence of enforcement powers proved to be the organization's undoing.

Severely crippled by the Great Depression and by the U.S. Smoot-Hawley Tariff (1930), Japan turned to China to expand its economic opportunities in Asia. Junior officers charged with protecting Japanese interests in Manchuria staged the Mukden incident of 1931 in an effort to transform foreign policy under Foreign Minister Kijuro Shidehara into an aggressively imperialistic policy.

The League and the United States initially hoped the Japanese government could resolve the Mukden incident peacefully. When it became obvious that Japan intended to carve out an empire in China, League members realized they had to respond to the first major crisis of the postwar period. At Japan's request, the League appointed a commission headed by Lord Lytton to investigate. On 25 February 1933, the League accepted the commission's report. Although the commission found both Japan and China at fault, Japan was accorded the lion's share of blame. Japan had violated international treaties it had signed, namely, the League Covenant, the Nine Power Pact of the 1922 Washington Conference Treaty affirming the "Open Door," and the 1928 Kellogg-Briand Pact outlawing aggressive war. The League urged Japan to disgorge Manchuria. Japan refused and withdrew from the League in 1933. League architects had assumed that international agreements could ensure world peace through the power of international public opinion alone, but the Manchurian crisis proved otherwise. President Herbert Hoover's policy paralleled that of the League: the United States condemned Japan without taking steps to prevent Tokyo from continued aggression.

Like Japan, Italy was driven to desperate measures because of the Great Depression. Italy suffered heavy war debts, inflation, and unemployment despite premier Benito Mussolini's fascist economic reforms. Mussolini's decision to invade Ethiopia (Abyssinia) on 3 October 1935, was clearly motivated by his desire to divert national attention from insurmountable economic problems and to build a second Roman empire. Since Italy already ruled colonies in East Africa (Eritrea and Italian Somaliland) and planned to annex Ethiopia since the ill-fated Italo-Abyssinian War of 1896, it is not surprising that pre-industrial Ethiopia became the proving ground for the modern Italian army. Italy was dissatisfied with certain territorial settlements in the Versailles treaty (as were Japan and Germany) and correctly assumed that the League would be no more successful in thwarting Italian ambitions than it had been in confronting the Japanese. The 1934 Walwal incident on the border between Ethiopia and Italian Somaliland was a pretext for Italian aggression.

Ethiopia attempted to bring about a peaceful settlement, first under the terms of the Italo-Abyssinian Treaty (1928) and then (as a League member) by appealing to the League for redress. By May 1935, the League Council persuaded both sides to submit the case for arbitration, but this process did not produce satisfactory results. On October 3, Italy invaded Ethiopia. This time, however, the League moved rapidly. A few days after the invasion, the Council denounced Italy for aggressive action in violation of the Covenant. On October 11, 1935, the

Assembly imposed sanctions against Italy—an embargo on arms, credit, and raw materials (except coal and oil) and a prohibition on imports from Italy.

Although the League took swift action, it could not stop Italy because its members were divided over the crisis, and because the world order fashioned at Versailles was disintegrating too rapidly. The League embargo proved ineffective because members failed to observe it. England and France never considered drastic action such as a naval blockade or closure of the Suez Canal, and they were unwilling to go to war over Ethiopia. French Foreign Minister Pierre Laval was more concerned with preserving relations with Italy, which threatened retaliation should oil be embargoed or the Suez Canal closed, than in saving Ethiopia. The United States declared neutrality rather than risk war. In July 1936, the League admitted failure by lifting sanctions against Italy. By that time, Emperor Haile Salassie had fled, and Italy had annexed Ethiopia. Italy left the League in 1937.

Germany, which had been a League member from 1926 to 1933, reoccupied the Rhineland in 1936 (during the Ethiopian crisis) to readjust the terms of the Treaty of Versailles. Perhaps in recognition of the harsh treatment accorded Germany in the treaty, the League did not respond. Although the League remained in existence until its dissolution in 1946, it was rendered impotent by the rise of Japan, Italy, and Germany—nations dissatisfied with the world order represented by the League. The lack of universal membership throughout much of the League's history seriously undermined the organization's effectiveness. The absence of the United States, Germany, Italy, Japan, and the Soviet Union from League membership made it difficult for France and Great Britain to preserve peace through the organization. An early critic of the League, the Soviet Union joined the organization in 1934 to become a staunch supporter of League measures against Germany and Italy during the 1930s. The League expelled the Soviet Union later because of its invasion of Finland in 1939. Nevertheless, faith in the concept of the League continued. The United States and Great Britain joined forces again in World War II when they adopted the Atlantic Charter (1941), which provided for a collective security organization to enforce peace in the postwar world. The League's successor became the United Nations.

JANET M. MANSON

See also Ethiopia; Fourteen Points; Italy; Japan; Kellogg-Briand Pact; League to Enforce Peace; Lodge, Henry Cabot, Sr.; Manchurian Crisis; Mussolini, Benito; Open Door Policy; Paris Peace Conference of 1919; Versailles Treaty of 1919; Washington Conference on the Limitation of Armaments; Wilson, Thomas Woodrow; World War I

FURTHER READING

Bartlett, Ruhl L. *The League to Enforce Peace.* Chapel Hill, N.C., 1944.

Burton, Margaret E. *The Assembly of the League of Nations.* Chicago, 1941.

Dexter, Byron V. *The Years of Opportunity: The League of Nations, 1920–1926.* New York, 1967.

Egerton, George W. *Great Britain and the Creation of the League of Nations: Strategy, Politics, and International Organization, 1914–1919.* Chapel Hill, N.C., 1978.

Knock, Thomas J. *To End All Wars: Woodrow Wilson and the Quest for a New World Order.* New York, 1992.

Kuehl, Warren F. *Seeking World Order: The United States and International Organization to 1920.* Nashville, Tenn., 1969.

Miller, David Hunter. *The Drafting of the Covenant,.* 2 vols. New York, 1928.

Northedge, F. S. *The League of Nations: Its Life and Times 1920–1946.* New York, 1986.

LEAGUE TO ENFORCE PEACE

A nongovernmental U.S. group that advocated the formation of an international collective security organization to settle disputes among nations and to avoid war. The group's ideas contributed to the formation of the League of Nations at the end of World War I. The principal founders of the League to Enforce Peace were Hamilton Holt, a leader in the New York Peace Society and editor of *The Independent*; Abbott Lawrence Lowell, president of Harvard University; and Theodore Marburg, also active in the peace movement. A German U-boat's sinking of the British passenger liner *Lusitania* in May 1915, which resulted in the loss of 128 American lives and the subsequent threat of war, precipitated the founding conference of the League to Enforce Peace held in Philadelphia on 17 June 1915. About 120 conservatives attended, and former President William Howard Taft became the group's president. The participants proposed that the United States join an international organization in which all member nations would agree to allow a judicial tribunal to mediate disputes unsettled by negotiation, use economic and military pressure to prevent aggression, and hold conferences periodically to codify rules of international law. At the National Assembly of the League to Enforce Peace in Washington on 27 May 1916, President Woodrow Wilson announced his first formal commitment to the concept of a league of nations, denounced isolationism, and endorsed most of the organization's platform. By the end of that year, the organization had 4,000 branches in forty-seven states. Taft supported U.S. participation in the League of Nations, yet campaigned against President Wilson's Fourteen Points. Although the group's membership was predominantly Republican, it generally supported President Wilson—a Democrat—during the Paris Peace Conference at the conclusion of World War I. The association initially worked for ratification of the peace treaty, which contained the League of Nations Covenant, but members then clashed over changes proposed by Senate Republicans. The fierce and ultimately losing battle for U.S. membership in the League of Nations destroyed the League to Enforce Peace. The organization accomplished little after the 1920 presidential election, became inactive in 1922, and disbanded the following year.

CAROL A. JACKSON

See also International Law; League of Nations; Paris Peace Conference of 1919; Taft, William Howard; Wilson, Thomas Woodrow

FURTHER READING

Bartlett, Ruhl J. *The League to Enforce Peace.* Chapel Hill, N.C., 1944.

Gelfand, Lawrence Emmerson. *The Inquiry: American Preparations for Peace, 1917–1919.* New Haven, Conn., 1963.

Knock, Thomas J. *To End All Wars: Woodrow Wilson and the Quest for a New World Order.* New York, 1992.

LEAHY, WILLIAM DANIEL

(*b.* 6 May 1875; *d.* 20 July 1959)

Naval officer and diplomat, chief of naval operations (1937–1939), governor of Puerto Rico (1939–1940), ambassador to Vichy France (1940–1942), and chairman of the Joint Chiefs of Staff (1942–1949). Born in Wisconsin, Leahy graduated from the U.S. Naval Academy in 1897, and saw action in the war with Spain, then during the Philippine insurrection, and later in the Boxer rebellion. As commander of the navy secretary's dispatch boat *Dolphin* in 1914, Leahy began a lifelong friendship with Assistant Secretary of the Navy Franklin D. Roosevelt. Appointed chief of naval operations by Roosevelt in 1937, Leahy oversaw a 20 percent increase in naval construction and recast strategic plans in anticipation of a possible two-ocean war. Following a short stint as governor of Puerto Rico, Leahy became ambassador to Vichy France in December 1940 with orders to keep the French fleet out of German hands and to minimize collaboration with the Axis. Despite cordial personal relations with Marshal Philippe Pétain, Leahy could do little to reverse the pro-German course of Vichy policy.

The admiral-ambassador nurtured an enduring suspicion of European politics and politicians when he returned to Washington in July 1942 as chairman of the Joint Chiefs of Staff for President Roosevelt. Because he could talk frankly to the president, Leahy acted effectively for the rest of World War II as liaison between the military and the White House, advocating an early cross-Channel invasion, urging equal support for the Pacific theater, and voicing skepticism about postwar plans for the United Nations. A conservative nationalist who dis-

trusted enemies and allies alike, he described the Yalta agreement on Poland as "so elastic that the Russians can stretch it all the way from Yalta to Washington without ever technically breaking it." As President Harry S. Truman's chief military adviser after Roosevelt's death, Leahy opposed use of the atomic bomb on Japan because "wars cannot be won by destroying women and children." Although he was an early advocate of containing Communist expansion with military force, if necessary, he fought unsuccessfully against unification of the armed forces. After his retirement in 1949, he published his wartime diary and memoir *I Was There* (1950).

J. GARRY CLIFFORD

See also Cold War; Cuba; France; Hiroshima and Nagasaki Bombings of 1945; Puerto Rico; Roosevelt, Franklin Delano; Spanish-American-Cuban-Filipino War, 1898; Truman, Harry S.; World War II; Yalta Conference

FURTHER READING

Adams, Henry H. *Witness to Power: The Life of Fleet Admiral William D. Leahy.* Annapolis, Md., 1985.

Langer, William. *Our Vichy Gamble.* New York, 1947.

Leahy, William. *I Was There.* New York, 1950.

LEBANON

A small but strategically located republic in the Middle East bordered by Israel, Syria, and the Mediterranean Sea, Lebanon has been both an important ally and a problem for U.S. foreign policy. The earliest encounter between the inhabitants of Lebanon and the American people dates back to 1823 when the first American Protestant missionaries reached Beirut. Despite resistance from the local population and the Ottoman authorities who had ruled the region since the early sixteenth century, and the difficulty they faced adapting to this area of the world, the missionaries opened their first school on 23 July 1824. Ten years later, at the initiative of two American women, the first school for girls also was established.

In 1841, Lebanon entered a cycle of violence, originating in the conflict between Muhammad Ali of Egypt and Lebanon's Ottoman rulers and culminating in the massacres of 1860 among the Druze and Christian Maronite communities. Following this bloody episode, during which 12,000 people died, the great powers, namely France, Great Britain, Austria, Prussia, Russia, and Turkey, decided to intervene, with France sending 7,000 troops to Lebanon. In June 1861, the European powers established a semiautonomous entity called Mutasarrifiah, headed by a Christian, non-Lebanese governor-general.

The first Lebanese to emigrate to the United States settled in Boston, Massachusetts, in 1854. The very same year, Daniel Bliss, an American missionary, reached the Levant. Bliss, founder of the Syrian Protestant College in 1866, established one of the most respected institutions of higher learning in the Middle East, renamed the American University of Beirut (A.U.B.) in 1920. The Syrian Protestant College adopted Arabic as the vehicle for learning, and gaining respect and support. The university's graduates would found several newspapers, lead Arab national movements, and play a major role in the future political developments in the Middle East.

The French Mandate and Wilsonianism

In 1908 the Young Turks' military takeover in Constantinople gave the Lebanese and the Syrians hope for a more representative and moderate form of government. They were soon disappointed when Turkey appointed Jamal Pasha as commander in chief of the Fourth Army and as military governor of Syria in October 1914. Pasha abolished Lebanon's semiautonomous status, forced military conscription, and imposed heavy financial burdens on the population. His ruthlessness during World War I brought famine and misery, resulting in the death of approximately 100,000 people. During these difficult days, the private donations of Cleveland H. Dodge, the American Relief Committee, and Americans of Lebanese descent brought badly needed relief to the populations of Lebanon. This gesture of generosity strengthened American-Lebanese relations.

Prior to World War I, U.S. foreign policy in the Middle East had mainly tried to avoid interfering in European power politics. In 1914, Great Britain called upon grand sharif Hussein of Mecca, to lead the Arab revolt against the Ottomans. After a series of letters known as the Hussein-McMahon Correspondence, the sharif agreed to side with the allies and declared war on Turkey. Sir Henry McMahon, British high commissioner in Cairo at the time, had promised Hussein independence for the Arab countries at the end of the war. The Sykes-Picot agreement of May 1917 ignored this promise, dividing the Ottoman empire into British and French spheres of influence. Six months later, British foreign secretary Arthur Balfour issued a declaration supporting the Zionists' quest for a "national home" in Palestine. The Zionist movement, which would play a leading role in colonizing Palestine and creating the state of Israel, had been founded by Leo Pinsker, a Russian physician, and Theodor Herzl, a Viennese journalist. Zionists dreamed of establishing a Jewish state that would offer refuge to persecuted Jews from around the world, especially from Europe. These agreements were the source of growing distrust of the Arabs toward the West.

In March 1919, despite European reluctance and at the initiative of U.S. president Woodrow Wilson, a commission (the King-Crane Commission) was sent to discern the preferences of the local populace. While the Lebanese expressed their preference for a U.S. mandate over a French or British one, due to British, French, and Zionist pressures, and to President Wilson's debilitating illness, the commission's report was never published. In April 1920, at the Conference of San Remo, the Allied Supreme Council declared a British mandate over Palestine, Jordan, and Iraq, while entrusting France with Lebanon and Syria. Although present at San Remo, the U.S. delegation would not attend the meeting. The United States had again decided to return to its political isolationism. That same year, French High Commissioner General Henri Gouraud announced the creation of the "Grand Liban" (Greater Lebanon), present-day Lebanon. On 24 July 1922, under Article 22 of the Covenant of the League of Nations, Lebanon was declared a separate French mandate.

The first constitution promulgated by the French high commissioner on 24 May 1926 gave Lebanon modern parliamentary institutions but preserved French interests and control over the country. It further gave the Maronite Christians the largest share of power, granting them the presidency and other key government positions, which placed the Muslim minority that had recently become part of Greater Lebanon at a disadvantage. In 1932, as a consequence of the global depression and the worsening social unrest, the high commissioner suspended the constitution and appointed a caretaker government.

Nazi Germany's invasion of France in 1940 led High Commissioner Gabriel Puaux to declare his support for the Vichy regime. In June 1941 the combined attack of British troops and Free French Units, reporting to Charles de Gaulle's government in exile, defeated the Vichy forces and occupied Lebanon and Syria. On 26 November, French General George Catroux declared Lebanon an independent and sovereign state. Despite this declaration, the French government continued to seek privileges in Lebanon and Syria.

The United States supported the independence of Lebanon and hoped to see France respect its commitments. On 2 October 1942, in an effort to make U.S. recognition of Lebanon and Syria official, President Franklin D. Roosevelt nominated George Wadsworth as diplomatic agent and consul-general to the governments of Lebanon and Syria. In November 1943, however, the newly elected Lebanese government promulgated the "National Pact," which redefined the confessional distribution of power and attempted to rewrite the constitution. This provoked the anger of the French authorities who arrested the president, the prime minister, and most members of the cabinet, infuriating the Lebanese public. U.S. political pressure was crucial in compelling France to observe its commitments. While the Lebanese view the release of the government officials on 22 November as Independence Day, President Roosevelt recognized Lebanon as independent only on 20 September 1944.

The Cold War Era and the 1958 Eisenhower Doctrine

In the Cold War era U.S. foreign policy toward Lebanon became subject to various regional influences, which often strained U.S.-Lebanese relations. Among these influences were Soviet aspirations in the area; the need to secure access to oil; the Arab-Israeli conflict; and the rise of Arab nationalism. Lebanese constitutional and confessional problems added themselves to this already long list.

President Harry S. Truman's recognition of the state of Israel in May 1948 caused resentment among Arab leaders, which during the 1948 Arab-Israeli conflict led the Lebanese government to detain sixty-nine U.S. citizens, accusing them of cooperation with the Zionists. This incident was soon overlooked by both parties, for in 1951 Lebanon accepted U.S. technical aid through the Point Four Project, an extension of the Truman Doctrine that aimed at strengthening economically and militarily prowestern countries.

On 25 May 1950 President Beshara el-Khouri signed the Tripartite Declaration, in which the United States, France, and Great Britain expressed their willingness to sell arms to the countries of the Middle East. Criticism of the government by the opposition led to the resignation of Prime Minister Riad el-Sulh. Following new parliamentary elections on 15 April 1951, the president asked Hussein el-Owaini to become prime minister and appointed Dr. Charles Malik as foreign minister. Malik, who had been educated in the U.S., would play a major role in strengthening U.S.-Lebanese relations, supporting U.S. involvement in Korea, and promoting U.S.-Lebanese economic and technical cooperation.

Kamil Chamoun was elected president in 1952, after el-Khouri had been forced to resign amid charges of mismanagement and corruption. Chamoun, a proponent of Arab nationalism, was also a strong supporter of the West. During his first years in power, he introduced various reforms to the government. Nevertheless, the 1958 crises, which would involve the U.S. militarily in the Middle East for the first time, would revive old enmities between the Christian and the Muslim communities.

After the nationalization of the Suez Canal by Egyptian president Gamal Abdel Nasser in 1956, Israel attacked Egypt, and France and Great Britain intervened to restore their access to the Red Sea. President Dwight D. Eisenhower, who had tried to prevent this attack, took the case to the United Nations (UN). Egypt, Saudi Arabia, and Syria broke diplomatic relations with France and Great Britain, criticizing President Chamoun for not doing so himself. The Lebanese cabinet resigned, denouncing the president for taking a pro-Western stand.

On 5 January 1957 Eisenhower revealed his plans for a resolution that would authorize him to develop programs of economic and military assistance and "use armed forces to assist any such nation or group of nations requesting assistance against armed aggression from any country controlled by international communism...." The Eisenhower Doctrine, as it was later called, was immediately welcomed by Foreign Minister Malik and officially approved by the Lebanese government. Only a minority of Christians approved of the doctrine, however, and the Muslim community, demanding stronger relations with the Arab world, grew more alienated from the government. Egypt and Syria, backed by the Soviet Union, denounced the Eisenhower Doctrine and launched a media campaign against the Lebanese government. Opposition to President Chamoun unified to form the United National Front. The Front accused Chamoun of enrichment and corruption and proposed a set of reforms threatening to take special measures if the government did not act. Chamoun, like his predecessor, turned a deaf ear and decided to amend the constitution in order to get reelected. As a result, more parties joined the Front.

Following a street demonstration on 30 May 1957, in which five demonstrators were killed and hundreds arrested, the army was called in to restore order and General Fuad Shehab, the head of the army, started mediation between the government and the opposition. An agreement was reached on 2 June and elections were held a week later. The results strongly favored the president, which cast doubts as to their fairness. As a result, the opposition rejected the results and decided to resort to force to remove Chamoun from power.

Meanwhile, Syria claimed to have uncovered a U.S. attempt to topple the government of their prime minister, Shukri Kuwatli. Lebanon, fearful of a possible Syrian invasion backed by the Soviets, urged the United States to send military support, which it did by alerting the Strategic Air Command, stationing the Sixth Fleet close off the Lebanese shores, and airlifting large quantities of arms to the Lebanese government. In February 1958 Syria and Egypt joined to form the United Arab Republic, and pressured Chamoun to join. In refusing to do so he was not alone: moderate Muslims as well as a majority of Christians maintained their attachment to an independent Lebanon. The situation nevertheless continued to degenerate. On 10 May the U.S. Information Library was set on fire.

The White House and Congress discussed the possibility of sending troops to Lebanon. All the while, the Eisenhower administration was trying to avoid a confrontation with the Soviet Union. Following the complaints of President Chamoun to the United Nations and to the Arab League regarding Syrian and Egyptian support to the opposition, the United Nations sent an observation group (UNOGIL) to determine the sources of military infiltration in the country.

When the UN mission was unable to prove the involvement of Syria or Egypt in the smuggling of arms and soldiers, the fighting intensified. As a result, on 27 May the government declared that it would not seek to amend the constitution. The opposition, which wanted the immediate resignation of the president, was not satisfied by this half-solution and fighting resumed. Finally, on 13 June the army, which had until then refused to intervene, was ordered by General Shehab to side with the government.

Meanwhile a military coup engineered by General Abdulkarim Kassem brought down the Hashemite government in Iraq on 14 July 1958. As a consequence, Baghdad moved closer to the Soviet Union. President Chamoun, alarmed by the situation, met with U.S. ambassador to Lebanon Robert McClintock and briefed him on the situation. Following the ambassador's report to Washington, President Eisenhower gave the order to deploy 15,000 U.S. soldiers to Lebanon to restore order. This decision had been prompted by U.S. fears of Soviet expansion in the region and was a clear sign that the U.S. government would not let down its allies and forsake its interests. But the majority of the Lebanese population saw U.S. involvement as an infringement on the country's sovereignty.

General Shehab, who had gained public support for the minimal involvement of the army in Lebanese internal affairs, was elected president on 31 July 1958. He declared Lebanon a nonaligned country, pleasing the opposition and Arab neighbors, but hurting Lebanon's relations with the United States. After the withdrawal of its troops on 25 October 1958, the United States government granted Lebanon $10 million in aid and large quantities of grain and medical equipment. Nevertheless most Arabs regarded U.S. involvement in Lebanon as another example of Western intervention in the Middle East.

The Post–1958 Era

During the years leading to the outbreak of the war in 1975, U.S.-Lebanese relations endured several shocks related to the Arab-Israeli conflict. Tensions escalated as Israeli-Lebanese relations became increasingly belligerent. Palestinians refugees, who had started arriving in Lebanon in 1948, numbered approximately 400,000 by the early seventies. With the support of Syria and other Arab countries, Palestinians organized themselves into military groups and started undertaking military operations against Israel from Lebanese territory. Muslim and Druze communities allied with the Palestinians to bring pressure on the Christian Maronite–led government to implement political reforms.

Following the June 1967 Arab-Israeli war, the U.S. ambassador was asked by the Lebanese government to leave the country and U.S. property was damaged in anti-American riots. In December of the following year, Israel destroyed thirteen aircraft at the Beirut International Airport in retaliation for a machine-gun attack on an Israeli airliner stationed in Athens. The U.S. government condemned the attack by Israel as there was no evidence of the Lebanese government's involvement in this terrorist act.

On 2 November 1969, following continual pressure from Arab countries, the commander in chief of the Lebanese army, General Emil Boustani, and the chairman of the Palestine Liberation Organization (PLO), Yassir Arafat, signed the Cairo Accord, expanding Palestinian territorial right, and legitimizing a Palestinian armed presence in Lebanon. The Israeli invasion of May 1970, which lasted two days, followed serious fighting between the Lebanese army and the Palestinians. Diplomatic intervention by the United States was central in the withdrawal of Israeli troops. The two years that followed were punctuated by Palestinian guerrilla attacks on Israel and by retaliatory air strikes on the refugee camps that had become military training bases.

By 1975 widespread war had broken out. Fighting started between the Phalangists and the Palestinians. Leaders within the government could not agree whether to use the army to stop the fighting. Throughout the rest of the year the Lebanese Front, composed mainly of Maronite militias led by Pierre Gemayel and Kamil Shamun, clashed with the Lebanese National Movement led by Kamal Joumblat and composed of left-wing Druze and Muslim parties and rejectionist Palestinian guerrillas. The Lebanese Front had been opposed to the growing military and political influence of the Palestinians in the country and to the inaction of the government. Arafat's PLO soon joined the Lebanese National Movement in its fight against the Lebanese Front. Attempts at mediation by U.S. ambassador L. Dean Brown in March of 1976 and later in the year by the Arab League were not successful. The June kidnapping and assassination of U.S. ambassador to Lebanon Francis E. Meloy, Jr., and of U.S. counselor for economic affairs Robert O. Waring shocked Americans. A few days later, President Gerald R. Ford announced the evacuation of U.S. citizens from Lebanon. The U.S. government continued to provide emergency food and medical aid to the population while reaffirming its commitment to the "unity" and "integrity" of the country. Throughout 1977 and 1978 confrontations between the Syrians, the Christians, and the Palestinians continued.

In March 1978, following a terrorist attack in Tel-Aviv, Israel retaliated by occupying southern Lebanon. Its withdrawal in June 1978 was followed by the deployment of the UN Interim Force in Lebanon (UNIFIL) sent to maintain the peace between the two countries.

In April 1981, after the Phalangist party, headed by Bashir Gemayel, strengthened its positions in Zahle, a Christian stronghold in the Bekaa valley, the Syrians besieged the city and started an attack aimed at uprooting the Christian militia. During the siege, Syria introduced surface-to-air (SAM) missiles into Lebanon, provoking a strong reaction and threats from Israel. The missile crisis soon took on international dimension, and on 30 June, after extensive mediations by Saudi Arabia, Kuwait, and the United States, the Syrians finally agreed to lift the siege. By 24 July, Philip C. Habib, the U.S. president's special emissary to the Middle East, had facilitated a peace agreement among the belligerent parties.

Following Israeli airstrikes in southern Lebanon and PLO shelling of northern Israel, the Israeli army invaded Lebanon on 6 June 1982. Heavy casualties and loss of property ensued. This massive Israeli attack was aimed at destroying Syrian forces in the Bekaa valley, uprooting the PLO from Lebanon, and bringing Bashir Gemayel and the Phalangists to power. The Reagan administration played an instrumental role in negotiating the withdrawal of the PLO from Beirut and, together with France and Italy, committed to send troops as part of a multinational force (MNF) to oversee the evacuation of Palestinian combatants. The MNF felt it had succeeded on its mission and even went home earlier than planned.

After his election on 23 August but before assuming power, President Gemayel was assassinated. The following day, 15 September 1982, Israel entered Beirut, and on 16 September Phalangist militia carried out the massacres at Sabra and Shatila, killing approximately 600 defenseless Palestinians. A second contingent of U.S. Marines was quickly deployed as part of a second MNF.

MNF II had a much more complex and problematic mandate. The formal mission statement issued by the Joint Chiefs of Staff included "establishing an environment which will permit the Lebanese Armed Forces to carry out their responsibilities in the Beirut area." What this really meant was ensuring that the Israeli withdrawal was completed, getting the Syrians to withdraw, and ending the Lebanese-Christian-Muslim war. On 18 April 1983, a car bomb destroyed the U.S. embassy, killing fifty people. On May 17, following an American initiative by Secretary of State George Shultz, Israel and Lebanon reached an agreement providing for the withdrawal of Israeli troops from Lebanon.

Efforts by the Reagan administration to strengthen the government of President Amine Gemayel, who had succeeded his brother Bashir, were unsuccessful. While the administration took the legalistic position that "we support no faction or religious community, but we are not neutral in our support of the legitimate government of Lebanon," hostilities between the Lebanese army and the pro-Syrian militias continued. Syria, abetted by Iran, started to train and foment Islamic fundamentalist terrorist groups such as the Hizbollah and the Islamic Jihad. In October, the Islamic Jihad bombed the Marine barracks, killing 241 U.S. Marines and other personnel.

In February 1984 the remaining U.S. troops were withdrawn. "Redeployment offshore" was the euphemism used in official Reagan pronouncements, but this could not mask the reality of retreat. The next month, under intense Syrian pressure, President Gemayel abrogated the 17 May agreement with Israel. Israel continued its military withdrawal but kept troops in a self-proclaimed "security zone" in southern Lebanon.

Israel also maintained its alliance with the Christian Southern Lebanese Army (SLA). Meanwhile more Americans were taken hostage by pro-Iranian groups. Whereas not a single American had been taken hostage before July 1982, between 1984 and 1986 eighteen Americans were abducted. Terrorist groups were involved in other incidents including the hijacking of a TWA airliner in 1985.

An attempt initiated by Syria to find an agreement between the three main Lebanese militias was aborted, and in May 1987 the Cairo Agreement of 1969 was abrogated by the parliament, limiting the role of the PLO in Lebanon. Factional strife continued and no agreement could be reached on a successor to President Gemayel when he stepped down in September 1988. Before leaving office, Gemayel had appointed General Michel Aoun as the head of the interim military government. Muslim officers rejected their appointment to this government triggering a constitutional crises. Aoun soon declared a "war of liberation" against the 40,000 Syrian troops. Because of the longstanding rivalry between Syria and Iraq, he received military support from Iraq's President Saddam Hussein.

During these years the United States provided some food aid and other humanitarian assistance, but had little other impact. Also due to the escalating terrorism, on 7 September 1989 the U.S. embassy in Beirut was closed.

After repeated efforts, the Tripartite Arab Committee, composed of the foreign ministers of Algeria, Morocco, and Saudi Arabia, which had been mediating between Syria and Aoun, was able to convince Syrian president Hafiz al-Assad of the need to endorse a cease-fire. The Tripartite committee also convened a meeting of the Lebanese parliament in Taif, Saudi Arabia, on 30 September during which the Taif accords were signed.

On 22 October 1989, the parliament endorsed the National Reconciliation Charter. A redistribution of power was thus agreed upon and a new president was elected on 5 November. However, President-elect Rene Mouawad was assassinated seventeen days later. Next,

Aoun, isolated nationally and internationally, launched a full-scale attack against the Christian Lebanese Forces in an effort to regain total control of the Christian enclave. The attack was a complete failure.

In October 1990, the United States and its allied forces said or did little while Syrian troops crushed General Aoun's forces. This was part of a tacit agreement whereby Syria would support the anti-Iraq coalition that was formed following Saddam's invasion of Kuwait and threat to Saudi Arabia.

The Post–Gulf War Years

Along with Syria and other Arab States, Lebanon agreed to participate in the U.S.-organized Arab-Israeli peace conference at Madrid in October 1991. The Madrid peace process had its up and downs over the next two years, but eventually led to the breakthroughs of the September 1993 Israeli-PLO accord and the October 1994 Israel-Jordan peace treaty. While officially there was an Israel-Lebanon track for the peace talks, it was clear that the Syrians controlled the Lebanese role in the peace process; thus, it is no coincidence that this track was virtually paralyzed until progress could be made on the Israeli-Syrian front.

By 1995 the reconstruction of Beirut and the recovery of the Lebanese economy were sources for some optimism. But U.S.-Lebanese relations have not yet fully normalized and still remain largely subsidiary to Syria.

MAKRAM OUAISS

See also Eisenhower Doctrine; Eisenhower, Dwight David; Gulf War of 1990–1991; Israel; Middle East; Reagan, Ronald Wilson; Syria; Terrorism

FURTHER READING

Bliss, Frederick. *The Reminiscences of Daniel Bliss.* New York, 1920.

DeNovo, John. *American Interests and Politics in the Middle East, 1900–1939.* Minneapolis, 1963.

Eisenhower, Dwight D. *The White House Years, Waging Peace.* New York, 1965.

Hitti, Philip K. *Lebanon in History.* New York, 1957.

Howard, Harry N. "An American Experiment in Peace Making: The King-Crane Commission." *The Moslem World* 32 (1942).

Hudson, Michael C. "The United States Involvement in Lebanon." In *Toward a Viable Lebanon*, edited by Halim Barakat. Washington, D.C., 1988.

Jessup, Henry H. *Fifty-Three Years in Syria.* New York, 1910.

Korbani, Agnes G. *U.S. Intervention in Lebanon, 1958 and 1982.* New York, 1991.

McFarlane, Robert C. *Special Trust.* New York, 1994.

Petran, Tabitha. *The Struggle over Lebanon.* New York, 1987.

Quandt, William B. *Peace Process.* Berkeley, Calif., 1993.

Qubain, Fahim I. *Crisis in Lebanon.* Washington, D.C., 1961.

Tanter, Raymond. *Who's at the Helm? Lessons of Lebanon.* Boulder, Colo., 1990.

Tibawi, Abdul Latif. *American Interests in Syria, 1800–1901.* Oxford, 1965.

LEGISLATIVE VETO

A provision explicitly incorporated by Congress within a broader piece of legislation that allows the Congress the right to stop, to alter, or to endorse the executive branch's actions prior to the policy's actual implementation. The device has been used in legislation involving both the foreign and domestic policy arenas. With the decision in *Immigration and Naturalization Service* v. *Chadha et al.* (1983), however, the constitutionality of most legislative veto provisions has come into serious question. The origins of the legislative veto date back to 1932, when it was introduced as a measure to allow President Herbert Hoover's administration to reform the executive branch without congressional approval of every action. By the end of the 1970s, 274 pieces of legislation contained such as provision. About 30 percent of these provisions were contained in foreign policy, defense, and immigration measures passed by the Congress. Several key legislative reforms aimed at limiting the executive's foreign policy powers contained veto provisions. Among them were the War Powers Resolution of 1973, which allowed Congress the right to withdraw armed forces sent abroad by the president after sixty days; arms sales legislation, which allowed Congress to halt a specific weapons sale abroad; and foreign assistance legislation, which enabled the legislative branch to cut off aid to recipient countries with records of serious human rights violations.

The actual "veto" by the Congress of the executive's action may take a variety of forms. Legislative vetoes can be expressed through a committee's (or combination of committees') disapproval, through a House or Senate (or joint) resolution of disapproval, or through a congressional imposition of a waiting period for the president to implement a particular action. Alternately, the veto may consist of formal congressional consent to an impending executive action. The executive branch, however, is usually not allowed the right to challenge the congressional action under any of these approaches.

A well-known example of the legislative veto provision was included in the War Powers Resolution. Under this legislation, the president was allowed to deploy armed forces abroad for up to sixty days without congressional approval. At the same time, the legislation included a provision that enabled Congress to withdraw those troops prior to the sixty days if a concurrent resolution of disapproval on the deployment was passed in both chambers. The legislation was the basis for the Congress to alter an executive branch action regarding troop deployments years later.

The *Chadha* decision cast doubt on the constitutionality of many legislative veto provisions. The Supreme Court decision held that the one-house veto resolution was unconstitutional because it violated the bicameral provision and the presentment clause provision of the Constitution, that is, legislation must be agreed to by both the Congress and the presidency, and legislation must be presented to the president for his consideration. About two weeks after the *Chadha* decision, the Court held in another case that the two-house veto was unconstitutional as well. As a result, any legislative veto approach that utilized a mechanism that excluded the president from responding to congressional action and that used either a one- or two-house resolution now appears to be unconstitutional.

While specific legislative veto provisions had never been exercised by the Congress to halt foreign policy actions prior to *Chadha*, the possibility of its use had an effect on congressional-legislative relations. Several foreign policy actions proposed by the executive were altered before the use of the legislative veto by the Congress became necessary. Some legislative veto provisions were changed to use a joint resolution to alter executive action. It is clear that the *Chadha* decision significantly weakened the legislative veto mechanism. Instead of a simple majority in one or both houses to stop an executive action, the Congress must obtain a two-thirds majority to overturn an expected presidential veto of its action. As some scholars have noted, however, additional avenues and mechanisms remain available to the Congress to monitor and alter presidential action in the foreign policy arena.

JAMES M. MCCORMICK

See also Chadha Decision; Congress; Presidency

FURTHER READING

Cooper, Joseph, and Patricia A. Hurley. "The Legislative Veto: A Policy Analysis." *Congress and the Presidency* 10 (Spring 1983): 1–24.

Gibson, Martha Liebler. *Weapons of Influence: The Legislative Veto, American Foreign Policy, and the Irony of Reform.* Boulder, Colo., 1992.

Kaiser, Frederick M. "Congressional Control of Executive Actions in the Aftermath of the Chadha Decision." *Administrative Law Review* 36 (Summer 1984): 239–276.

LEND-LEASE

A World War II program to provide U.S. military and economic assistance to nations fighting the Axis powers. Originally designed in 1940–1941 to aid Great Britain in order to keep the United States out of the war, it eventually grew into a program to assist all of America's wartime Allies. Arguing that the United States must become an "arsenal of democracy," President Franklin D. Roosevelt first proposed Lend-Lease in December 1940 as a means of overcoming Great Britain's inability to pay for war supplies. The president sought to lend or lease supplies to any country whose defense he deemed vital to U.S. secu-

LEND LEASE: MAJOR RECIPIENTS (Billions of dollars)	
Country	1941–1951
Great Britain	28.94
Soviet Union	11.04
France	2.99
China	1.61

Source: *Foreign Aid by the U.S. Government.* United States Department of Commerce, Bureau of Foreign and Domestic Commerce. Office of Business Economics.

rity. In a famous analogy, Roosevelt compared such action to lending a garden hose to a neighbor whose house was on fire. By not requiring repayment in dollars, he also sought to avoid a repetition of the acrimony following European failure to repay World War I loans to the United States. Isolationists countered that such a step would pull the United States into the war and extend executive power. Introduced as House Resolution Number 1776, Lend-Lease passed in March 1941; Harry Hopkins and, later, Edward Stettinius administered the program.

In the ensuing months Roosevelt extended Lend-Lease beyond Great Britain to China and the Soviet Union. After official U.S. entry into the war it became one of America's primary contributions to the Allied effort. By war's end approximately $50 billion in assistance had been extended to 38 countries, with Great Britain receiving the largest amount. Lend-Lease did greatly increase executive power as isolationists had warned, and its abrupt termination at war's end caused friction with the Soviet Union, which charged that U.S. economic assistance—and the threat of its withdrawal—was being used to gain diplomatic concessions.

MARK A. STOLER

See also China; Great Britian; Roosevelt, Franklin Delano; Russia and the Soviet Union; World War II

FURTHER READING

Dobson, Alan P. *U.S. Wartime Aid to Britain, 1940–1946.* New York, 1986.

Herring, George C., Jr. *Aid to Russia, 1941–1946: Strategy, Diplomacy, the Origins of the Cold War.* New York, 1973.

Kimball, Warren F. *The Most Unsordid Act: Lend-Lease, 1939–1941.* Baltimore, Md., 1969.

Stettinius, Edward R., Jr. *Lend-Lease: Weapon for Victory.* New York, 1944.

LENIN, VLADIMIR ILYICH

(*b.* 10 April 1870; *d.* 21 January 1924)

Leader of Bolshevik Russia from 1917 to 1924, who sought but failed to gain U.S. recognition of his revolutionary government. Born in Simbirsk (now Ulianovsk),

Russia, young Lenin was successful academically, winning a gold medal for scholastic excellence in 1887. The same year he began studying law at the University of Kazan. His studies were interrupted when his brother Alexander was executed for participating in an abortive assassination attempt on Czar Alexander III. The tragedy caused the family to be socially ostracized and Lenin, after taking part in a political protest, to be expelled from the university. His brother's execution became a driving force behind his interest in the economic, political, and social inequalities of Czarist Russia.

Lenin, who was not allowed to complete his legal studies until 1891, did not embrace Marxism initially. Like many Russian revolutionaries of his era, he responded to the populist ideals of Paul Pestel, Peter Tkachev, and Sergei Nachaev. By 1893, however, he had lost faith in populism, and, after moving to St. Petersburg, became an active Marxist. Two years later he was arrested for participating in a series of labor strikes; he subsequently spent the next four and a half years in prison and in internal exile in Siberia. Upon his release, he left Russia to start a newspaper which sought to unite all Russian Marxists under a common anticapitalist ideology. From this effort came the Russian Social Democratic Labor Party (RSDRP). During this period Lenin made numerous contributions to Marxist organizational theory. Not only did he object to the RSDRP's seeking economic/legal compromises, but he believed that a centralized and disciplined cadre of professional revolutionaries should lead the revolution. At the second congress of the RSDRP in 1903, a disagreement emerged over conditions for membership. Various members, including Leon Trotsky and Julius Martov, walked out, leaving Lenin in command of the party's majority, the Bolsheviks.

With the success of the Bolshevik Revolution in November 1917, Lenin became the leader of not only Soviet Russia but the international Communist movement as well. He approached Europe with caution and contempt while pursuing a cooperative policy toward the United States. The United States, he believed, would be more tolerant of his government than other major powers and hence be the first to extend diplomatic recognition. Therefore, negotiations with the Wilson administration, which began as early as December 1917, took precedence in Soviet foreign policy. Initial discussions between the two nations centered around Russia's ability to continue the war, with U.S. military assistance, against Germany. Negotiations stalled, however, and Lenin, realizing that Russia was too weak to continue the war on its own and that the world revolution was not approaching, was forced to conclude a separate peace agreement with the Germans, the Treaty of Brest-Litovsk, in March 1918.

Because the treaty endangered Allied supply depots in Archangel, Murmansk, and Vladivostok, Allied leaders dispatched troops to Russia within weeks of signing the treaty. The United States initially hesitated to send troops because intervention contradicted President Woodrow Wilson's concept of democracy and self-determination. While Anglo-French diplomatic pressure and his strong anti-Bolshevik stance persuaded him to station U.S. troops in the aforementioned cities, Wilson remained unwilling to commit to further intervention in Russia. When hostilities broke out in May 1918 between the Red Army and a group of Czech-Slovak prisoners of war being transferred to France via Siberia, the Wilson administration began to reevaluate its position toward Russia. Several weeks after the Allied Supreme War Council's decision to broaden intervention and extend support to anti-Bolshevik forces, the United States announced its policy concerning intervention. The policy, which attempted to unite limited military intervention with Russian economic relief, was designed to coordinate Czech-Slovak resistance against the Red Army, assist the Russians in their efforts at self-government, and limit Japanese aggression in Siberia. The Bolsheviks, especially Lenin, reacted harshly toward Allied intervention. Russia's positive attitude toward the United States persisted, however, because Lenin was convinced the Allies had compelled Washington to send troops.

With Russia out of the war, negotiations with the Allies were placed on hold until the end of hostilities. Afterward, the Bolsheviks's primary task was to gain recognition of their government. In December 1918 Lenin sent Maxim Litvinov as ambassador extraordinaire to initiate discussions with Great Britain, the United States, and other nations. The Wilson administration sent a representative, William H. Buckler, to meet with Litvinov in Stockholm. Although the diplomats reached no agreement, their negotiations brought about the Bullitt mission (March 1919).

William C. Bullitt, member of the U.S. delegation to the Paris Peace Conference in 1919, was sent by the Allied leaders to Moscow to augment negotiations with Soviet Russia. His talks with top Bolshevik officials, including Lenin, produced an opportunity for a peace agreement between Russia and the Allies. Both sides made numerous concessions. The Bolsheviks agreed to allow existing governments to maintain de facto control of the territory they occupied, to grant amnesty to the majority of political prisoners, and to assume Russia's prewar foreign debt. In return, the Allies would lift their blockade of Russia and withdraw their troops from Russian territory. The Allied leaders, however, rejected Bullitt's efforts. Despite this refusal, Lenin still hoped for a Soviet-Allied agreement. Because Lenin believed that the reestablishment of trade with the United States would bolster Soviet efforts at diplomatic recognition,

Bolshevik leaders concentrated on restoring U.S.–Soviet cooperation.

Soviet attempts at economic rapprochement were highlighted by the 1919–1920 mission of Ludwig C.A.K. Marten, a representative of the People's Commissariat of Foreign Affairs. Though rebuffed by the State Department, Marten successfully met with U.S. business leaders including those from Ford, International Harvester, and International Paper. He secured many contracts of intent and laid the basis for further U.S.-Soviet trade. Yet, Marten's successes did not last long because his mission encountered obstruction from the U.S. government. He also faced an American public which was becoming increasingly fearful of Bolsheviks. An intense antiradical movement, the Red Scare, ensued, leading to the deportation of Marten and the development of an official U.S. policy toward Soviet Russia.

In August 1920, the United States announced that it would not recognize the Bolshevik government and would maintain a policy of nonintercourse. The Wilson administration cited the undemocratic character of the Bolshevik government, that government's illegitimate existence, and Soviet Russia's continuing support of Communism in the United States as the primary reasons for this decision. Although this policy ended hope of a U.S.-Soviet diplomatic agreement, it allowed for the continuation of economic interaction (by July, the United States had lifted economic restrictions on Soviet Russia). Lenin, however, still hoped to achieve a political understanding after the Republican party victory in the November 1920 presidential elections in the United States. Much to his dismay, the Republicans adopted the official policy of non-recognition developed by the Wilson administration.

While working to improve Russia's economic condition and finalize the party's consolidation of power, Lenin in December 1922 suffered a stroke that partially paralyzed him and forced him to relinquish day-to-day control of the government. Lenin remained a highly influential figure until another stroke in March 1923 incapacitated him. He died the following year.

SCOTT D. KELLER

See also Bullitt, William Christian; Litvinov, Maxsim Maksimovich; Russia and the Soviet Union; Wilson, Thomas Woodrow; World War I

FURTHER READING

Fischer, Louis. *The Soviets in World Affairs: A History of the Relations Between the Soviet Union and the Rest of the World, 1917–1929,*. vol. 1. Princeton, N.J., 1951.
———. *The Life of Lenin*. New York, 1964.
Kennan, George F. *Russia and the West Under Lenin and Stalin*. Boston, 1960.
———. "Soviet-American Relations, 1917–1920." In vol. 2, *The Decision to Intervene*. Princeton, N.J., 1958.
Krupskaya, Nadezhda Konstantinova. *Reminiscences of Lenin*. Moscow, 1959.
Lenin, Vladimir Ilyich. *Collected Works*. Moscow, 1960.
McFadden, David W. *Alternative Paths: Soviets and Americans, 1917–1920*. New York, 1993.
Trotsky, Leon. *The Young Lenin*. Garden City, N.Y., 1972.
Ulam, Adam B. *The Bolsheviks; The Intellectual and Political History of the Triumph of Communism in Russia*. New York, 1965.
———. *Expansion and Coexistence: The History of Soviet Foreign Policy, 1917–1967*. New York, 1968.

LESOTHO

Located in Southern Africa, a kingdom of about 1.2 million people surrounded by the Republic of South Africa. Founded in 1818 by Moshweshwe, the chief of the Mokotedi, the kingdom was originally known as Basutoland. It faced constant military threats from the Orange Free State after the 1840s. Moshweshwe's impending defeat by that country in 1868 led to Great Britain's declaration of a protectorate over Lesotho. Over the next century, Lesotho was governed by either the Cape Colony or Great Britain until achieving independence on 4 October 1966. The United States was the first country to send an ambassador to the capital of Maseru. Lesotho's importance to U.S. policy in southern Africa derived from the kingdom's opposition to South Africa's implementation of apartheid, the separate development of people of color and whites.

The Basotho National Party (BNP) won the general elections held in Lesotho in April 1965. When the BNP was defeated in the elections on 27 January 1970—first held after independence—Prime Minister Leabua Jonathan suspended the constitution, dissolved the parliament, and nullified the elections. He ruled from 1973 to 1986, when a military coup toppled his government. The coup sprang primarily from Jonathan's support of the African National Congress (ANC), a militant anti-apartheid organization. The ANC's presence in Lesotho led South Africa, which took 85 percent of Lesotho's exports, to close the borders and threaten military action against the country. A military council chaired by Major General Justin Lekhanya ruled in conjunction with King Moshoeshoe II, until Moshoeshoe's exile in February 1990. His son Letsie III was installed as king. Lekhanya then aimed at returning Lesotho to democratic civilian rule. Elections held in June 1992 witnessed the victory of the Basutoland Congress Party (BCP), and Ntsu Mokhehle's elevation to prime minister.

In August 1994 a royalist coup, led by Letsie III, briefly dismissed the democratically elected government and brought back the exiled Moshoeshoe. The king wished to step down in favor of his father. Moshoeshoe II was reinstated on 25 January 1995, by Prime Minister

Mokhehle, ushering in a period of stability in Lesotho. Mosheoshoe II championed the role of a full democracy and worked with Mokhehle while trying to maintain the king's position above party politics. Tragically, King Moshoeshoe II died in a car crash on 15 January 1996; Letsie III resumed the throne.

The United States has supported Lesotho's political, economic, and social development, annually supplying approximately $9.6 million through the Agency for International Development (AID); $5.2 million through Food for Peace, and 100 Peace Corps volunteers. AID programs have focused on building roads, strengthening education, and supporting rural development, while Peace Corps volunteers have provided educational assistance in horticulture, animal husbandry, health, and employment-generation projects. The United States has also trained a few Lesotho officers each year in various military specialties through its International Military Education and Training Program. Critics of U.S. policy and AID's role in Lesotho cite the unwillingness of the United States to consider programs suggested by the Lesotho government.

CHRISTOPHER M. PAULIN

See also Agency for International Development; Peace Corps; South Africa

FURTHER READING

Bardill, John E., and James H. Cobbe. *Lesotho: Dilemmas of Dependence in Southern Africa.* London, 1985.
Chan, Stephen. *Exporting Apartheid: Foreign Policies in Southern Africa, 1978–1988.* New York, 1990.

LEWIS AND CLARK EXPEDITION

(14 May 1804 to 23 September 1806)

Mission entrusted by President Thomas Jefferson in 1804 to Meriwether Lewis and William Clark to explore the extent of the region beyond the Mississippi River acquired by the United States in the Louisiana Purchase. Lewis, Jefferson's private secretary, had been chosen by Jefferson because, in the president's estimation, he was endowed by nature with the necessary characteristics— courage, perseverance, discipline, honesty, and knowledge of the frontier—to head such a project. Lewis recommended Clark, with whom he had served in the frontier campaign of General Anthony Wayne in the 1790s, to help him lead the expedition. The mission was also expected to help cultivate the fur trade with the Indians, to map the region, and to seek a convenient route to the Pacific. Moving northward to the Dakotas from St. Louis, the expedition turned westward to the Pacific via the Snake and Columbia Rivers. The expedition not only mapped the territories and meticulously chronicled the explorers' discoveries, it also perpetuated President Jefferson's vision of an expanding Republic, inspired commercial schemes for a Missouri-Columbia river route linking the United States to Asian markets, and substantiated U.S. claims to the western territories. Diplomats in future negotiations would cite the expedition as confirmation of U.S. claims as far west as the Oregon Territory.

DONALD A. RAKESTRAW

See also Continental Expansion; Louisiana Purchase

FURTHER READING

Ambrose, Stephen E. *Undaunted Courage: Meriwether Lewis, Thomas Jefferson and the Opening of the American West.* New York, 1996.
De Voto, Bernard. *The Course of Empire.* Boston, 1952.
Graebner, Norman A. *Empire on the Pacific: A Study in American Continental Expansion.* New York, 1955.
Hawke, David F. *Those Tremendous Mountains: The Story of the Lewis and Clark Expedition.* New York, 1980.
Lavender, David Sievert. *The Way to the Western Sea: Lewis and Clark Across the Continent.* New York, 1988.
Ronda, James P. *Lewis and Clark Among the Indians.* Lincoln, Nebr., 1984.

LIBERIA

The oldest republic located in Africa, bordering the North Atlantic Ocean between Côte d'Ivoire and Sierra Leone. Originally the creation of emigrants from the United States, Liberia has had a unique historical relationship with the United States. Lying within the lower bulge of West Africa bordering on the Atlantic Ocean, it shares boundaries on the northwest with Sierra Leone, on the north with Guinea, and on the east with Ivory Coast. Estimates of its population in the late 1990s, when stable, ranged between two and two-and-a-half million, of whom 4 percent to 5 percent are Americo-Liberians, descendants of African-American emigrants. The vast majority of the remaining population is distributed among sixteen major indigenous African ethnic groups.

Beginning in the 1820s the United States government provided financial and naval assistance to the American Colonization Society, a private organization founded in 1816, in settling on the West Coast of Africa freeborn African Americans, recently freed former slaves, and Africans rescued from vessels engaged in the illegal slave trade. State and local colonization societies soon engaged in similar activities. While the African-American emigrants were inspired by "the love of liberty" to settle in Africa, their sponsors' motives were mixed. As Secretary of State Abel Upshur explained to the British in 1843, their "objects were to introduce Christianity and promote civilization in Africa; to relieve the slave-holding states from the inconvenience of free blacks among them; to improve their condition, and elevate the character of those blacks themselves, by offering asylum in the country of their ancestors, in which they would enjoy political and social equality."

In 1838 several of the settlements merged as the Commonwealth of Liberia and, in 1847, declared themselves to be the independent Republic of Liberia. The settlements established by the Maryland Colonization Society joined the Republic in 1857.

Great Britain and France quickly recognized the Republic, but the United States, constrained by the Southern slavocracy, withheld recognition until 1862.

In subsequent years officials of Liberia and the United States repeatedly proclaimed that ties of history and culture bound their two countries together in a special relationship. Although frequently described in such terms as friendly counselor, near friend, next friend, and foster child, the special relationship has defied a clear, immutable definition immune to changes in the international environment and in the respective interests of the two countries.

Race, however, the principal consideration in Liberia's creation, has provided one element of constancy to the definition of what is special in the U.S.-Liberian connection. In restricting Liberian citizenship to persons of the black race, successive Liberian constitutions have explicitly made race the intrinsic component of Liberian nationality. The United States has expressly acknowledged the saliency of race in its Liberian relations in the tradition of appointing African Americans as U.S. ministers and ambassadors to Liberia, as members of special U.S. commissions to Liberia, as advisers to the Liberian military, and in consulting African-American leaders regarding Liberian affairs, who, while often highly critical of the Liberian ruling elite, nevertheless have tended to rally to the defense of the Liberian state as a concrete symbol of independent black nationhood.

Within Liberia's identity as a black state, however, lay two related paradoxes which raised the principal issues around which the special relationship between the United States and Liberia revolved. Liberia's European neighbors perceived Liberia's very existence as an independent black state on a continent under European dominion as a paradox. The real and ultimately tragic paradox, however, lay in the existence of "two Liberias," the African-American settler community, which never comprised more than 5 percent of Liberia's population, and the indigenous Africans over whom they exercised dominion. The Americo-Liberian elite was never able to resolve the dilemma of how to integrate the two Liberias into a polity of equals while still maintaining its control over the Liberian state.

The most dynamic element influencing U.S.-Liberian relations has been the changing nature of the international political environment. Liberia was founded when slavery and the slave trade were subjects of international discourse. Its territorial integrity and political independence were severely tested in the era of European partitioning of the African Continent. Its status among the community of nations also was affected by the two world wars and international developments between the wars. Finally, the Cold War and the decolonization of Africa collectively provoked challenges to its national identity, its internal stability, and the specialness of its relations with the United States.

During the European scramble for Africa, Great Britain and France exploited the inability of the Americo-Liberian government to exercise authority over the indigenous Africans to successively divest Liberia of over forty percent of the territory that the republic had originally claimed. During the same period, by way of British loans to Liberia in 1870 and again in 1906, Great Britain established a virtual financial protectorate over Liberia.

With its official interest in Africa mainly concerned with promoting an open door for trade, the United States responded rather passively to these developments. It rejected several Liberian requests for loans, gave only moral support to the Liberian government in its efforts to settle its border disputes with its European colonial neighbors as best it could, and refused Liberia's offer of a site for a U.S. coaling station. Its most assertive acts in Liberia's behalf included naval assistance to Liberia in quelling the Grebo rebellion in 1875, a declaration to the French in 1889 and 1892 of its right "as the next friend of Liberia to aid her in preventing any encroachment of a foreign power on her territorial sovereignty...," and a request that the participants in the Brussels Slave Trade Conference in 1890 explicitly recognize Liberia's sovereignty.

During the second decade of the twentieth century the United States played a much more active role in Liberian affairs. Following the visit of a Liberian delegation to the United States, the U.S. government sent a three-man commission, including Emmett J. Scott, personal secretary of Booker T. Washington, to Liberia in 1909. With U.S. "Dollar Diplomacy" in China and Latin America as their conceptual model, U.S. officials subsequently incorporated several of the commission's recommendations into a plan of assistance for Liberia. To retire the British loan and the political constraints on Liberia that it entailed, Liberia secured an international loan from a consortium of U.S., British, and German bankers and appointed a U.S. citizen as head of the Liberian customs receivership.

Liberia also replaced the British supervisors of its frontier force with three African-American officers, who were supervised by Major Charles Young, the military attaché to the U.S. legation in Liberia. In 1915 the frontier force, trained and led by the African-American soldiers and assisted by a U.S. naval vessel, put down an uprising of the Kru.

World War I ushered in an era of even closer relations between the United States and Liberia. After U.S. entry into the war in April 1917, Liberia, too, joined the Allied cause. At the Paris Peace Conference the United States rejected British and French suggestions that Liberia be made a U.S. mandate or protectorate. However, a bill to grant a $5 million governmental loan to Liberia, which the Department of State justified on grounds of the historic ties between the two countries, the interest of African Americans in Liberia, and U.S. national interests, died, in 1922, in the U. S. Senate.

Four years later the Firestone Rubber Company, with the encouragement of the U.S. government, secured a 99-year lease on a million acres of Liberian land for the purpose of producing rubber and, through the agency of a separate corporation under its control, loaned Liberia $5 million.

The Firestone Rubber concession gave the United States its first significant material interest in Liberia. Once productive it relieved the United States of dependence upon European monopolies of raw rubber supplies. During World War II, when access to rubber supplies in Asia was cut off, Liberian-produced rubber became vital to the U.S. war effort.

Meanwhile, criticism of the Firestone concession and loan as economic imperialism increased the U.S. government's sensitivity toward internal developments in Liberia. In response to allegations in 1929 that slavery and forced labor existed in Liberia, the Department of State appointed Charles S. Johnson, an African-American sociologist, to a three-man League of Nations investigatory commission. The commission's report in 1930 describing abuses of the indigenous people analogous to slavery caused President Charles D. B. King to resign. When Edwin Barclay, the secretary of state, succeeded him as president, the United States refused to recognize Barclay and joined with Great Britain and Germany in demanding that Liberia accept supervision by the League of Nations.

Supervision of Liberia by the League of Nations, the institutional expression of the post–World War I world order, portended the loss of Liberia's independence to European colonial powers in the guise of humanitarian internationalism. Nevertheless, the United States preferred temporary League supervision to a U.S. protectorate over Liberia, and, consonant with its 1930s Latin American policy, the United States rejected Firestone's request for U.S. military intervention in Liberia to protect their interests.

However, when Barclay, supported by African Americans in his determination to preserve Liberia's sovereignty as a black nation, resolutely refused to accept external control over Liberia's affairs, the United States finally decided to assist Liberia in implementing a Liberian-approved plan of reform and, in 1935, restored diplomatic relations with the Barclay government.

World War II considerably lessened the disparity between U.S. and Liberian perceptions of the importance of the U.S.-Liberian connection to the interests of each country. Bordered by French and British colonies, Liberia became strategically important to the Allied cause. During the war the United States built an airfield in Liberia, concluded a mutual defense agreement, and stationed 5,000 mostly African-American troops in the country. The United States also provided Liberia Lend-Lease funds, built much of Liberia's physical infrastructure, and replaced the British pound with the U.S. dollar as Liberia's medium of exchange.

World War II was followed, however, by drastic changes in the world order. Europe's colonial empires in Africa and Asia disintegrated and the Cold War enveloped the globe. Liberia lost its distinctiveness as one of two independent black nations in Africa and, like the newly emergent African states, was drawn into the Cold War's vortex. No longer the principal focus of U.S. interests in Africa, Liberia, in turn, was required to develop an Africa policy that would accommodate its relations with the new African states.

The Cold War and decolonization also highlighted Americo-Liberian domination of the Liberian state, contributing to the intensification of the indigenous Liberians's perception of themselves as a colonial people and making Liberia suspect among the leaders of the new African countries as a truly African state.

While affected by these developments, Liberian-U.S. ties remained strong, especially during the long Liberian presidency of William V. S. Tubman (1944–1971). Tubman's related policies of opening Liberia to foreign investments and of integrating the indigenous peoples more fully into the Liberian political and social community and into the Liberian economy were fully compatible with the interests of the United States, which supported both policies financially.

On Cold War issues Tubman sided with the United States. He eschewed diplomatic ties with the Soviet Union and other communist countries and supported U.S. policies on Korea and Vietnam. The Kennedy administration applauded him for his "moderate approach to African problems" as reflected in his "advocacy of a Community of Independent African States to be achieved gradually through cultural, educational, and economic exchanges," and for his opposition to Ghana's Kwame M. Nkrumah's "grandiose schemes for immediate political unity."

During the Tubman era the two countries cemented their relationship through a mutual defense pact and through U.S. aid to Liberia via such instrumentalities of

U.S.–Cold War policy as Point IV, the Agency for International Development (AID), and the Peace Corps.

William R. Tolbert, Tubman's successor, reversed Tubman's policy of nonrecognition of communist states, even establishing diplomatic relations with Cuba. Moreover, in attempting to enhance his status among the new African states, he severed ties with Israel, the United States's close ally, and established diplomatic and economic ties with Libya, a U.S. adversary. Nevertheless, he continued to foster relations with the United States, paying a state visit to the United States in 1976, which President Jimmy Carter reciprocated in a visit to Liberia in 1978. In late September 1979 Tolbert visited President Carter again in Washington.

In February 1980 President Carter appointed a 16-member commission on U.S.-Liberian relations "charged with undertaking a broad-based and general study of U.S.-Liberian relationships in all areas" and with making recommendations to the president based on its findings. Two African Americans, Congressman William H. Gray of Pennsylvania and former Federal Reserve Board member Andrew Brimmer, were appointed chair and vice chair, respectively, of the commission.

On 12 April 1980, a few weeks before the commission was scheduled to travel to Liberia, a group of Liberian soldiers, led by Master Sergeant Samuel K. Doe, a member of the Krahn tribe, ended 133 years of rule by Americo-Liberians over the Liberian state in a bloody coup in which Tolbert, the grandson of a South Carolina emigrant, was killed.

Cold War considerations, U.S. national interests, and the new perception of Liberia as a characteristically unstable African state shaped U.S. policy toward the Doe regime over the next decade. After a period of watchful waiting, the Carter administration decided to provide financial assistance to the Doe government in order to counter the influence of the Soviet Union, Cuba, Ethiopia, and Libya; protect important U.S. interests; and create conditions of stability that would lead to the restoration of civilian rule through democratic elections.

Thereafter, despite Doe's highly questionable claim that he won the 1985 Liberian presidential election, the United States remained "constructive[ly] engage[d]" with his government until its violent overthrow in 1990. By this time U.S. aid to Doe's Liberia amounted to over $500 million, inclusive of $67 million in military assistance.

During the six-year civil war that began with efforts to overthrow the Doe regime, the United States supported, financially and diplomatically, the collective efforts of African states to restore peace. In August 1995, the warring factions signed an African-brokered peace accord, establishing an interim governing council pending elections in September 1996. Renewed fighting in early 1996, however, again dampened hopes for the reconstruction of a Liberia in which race may be less significant in the configuration of elements defining the republic's relationship with the United States.

ARNOLD H. TAYLOR

See also Africa; Slave Trade and Slavery

FURTHER READING

Bixler, Raymond W. *The Foreign Policy of the United States in Liberia.* New York, 1957.

Liebenow, J. Gus. *Liberia: The Quest for Democracy.* Bloomington, Ind., 1987.

Sisay, Hassan B. *Big Powers and Small Nations: A Case Study of United States–Liberian Relations.* Lanham, 1985.

Skinner, Elliot P. *African Americans and U.S. Policy Toward Africa, 1850–1924: In Defense of Black Nationality.* Washington, D.C., 1992.

Sundiata, Ibrahim K. *Black Scandal: America and the Liberia Labor Crisis, 1929–1936.* Philadelphia, 1980.

Taylor, Arnold H. "Afro-Americans and the Liberian Forced Labor Controversy." In *Afro-Americans and Africans: Historical and Political Linkages,* edited by Lorraine A. Williams. Washington, D.C., 1975.

LIBYA

Located in North Africa bordering on the Mediterranean Sea, Egypt, Sudan, Chad, Niger, Algeria, and Tunisia. Libya is an oil-rich Arab country that was a close ally of the United States for most of the first two decades of its independence, but since 1969, under the leadership of Muammar al-Qaddafi, has become an ardent adversary.

The narrowness of the Mediterranean basin, the energy of its peoples, and the allure of its southern coast assured that the modern country of Libya would have a long, complicated, and violent past. Since the Berbers passed westward through Egypt (circa 2700–2200 B.C.E.) on their way to settle in the future Libya, the country's primary sources of wealth have changed from slaves, ivory, and gold traded within empires to oil sold in a global market by a revolutionary Islamic republic; the complexity and combativeness have endured.

Phoenician outposts spread along the western coast of North Africa starting in the twelfth century B.C.E., and eventually comprised a number of Punic cities including three: Tripolis, which became the locus of the present capital; Tripoli; and one of the historic divisions of the eastern part of the country, Tripolitania. Following a practice that would become common in the Arab world the territory's ancient rulers usually pacified only the fertile and coastal areas, leaving the internal desert zones to nomads, areas of today's Libya known historically as Fezzan to the southwest and Cyrenaica to the east. Carthage's control of much of the western Mediterranean coast (fifth to second centuries B.C.E.) included Tripolitania and ended with its conquest by Rome. Greek colonists settled the coast of Cyrenaica, which was named after its most important city, Cyrene, starting in the seventh century B.C.E. A parade of conquerors followed, including Persians, Macedonians, Romans, Vandals, and Byzantines. Arabs brought Islam in the late seventh and eighth centuries of the current era. Rivalries between Berber and Arab dynasties, the assertion of the split in Islam between Shia and Sunni, and even military intervention by the Norman rulers of Sicily in the twelfth century marked the succeeding centuries.

Spain's clashes with the Ottoman Turks in the sixteenth century began the reversal of Islam's expansion, an undoing that gained force for the next four hundred years and ended in the occupation of much of the Arab and Muslim world by the European imperial powers. A latecomer, Italy, invaded Cyrenaica in 1914. Mussolini's Fascist government renewed the military campaign in 1923 and completed the conquest of all the territory between Egypt and Tunisia in 1931. Defeated in World War II, Italy dissolved its African empire, and Libya appeared as a state in 1951, called into existence by the victors in World War II, who for their strategic reasons merged the three dissimilar territories of Tripolitania, Cyrenaica, and Fezzan into a monarchy under the Sanusi Amir, Idris.

Among the poorest countries in the world at independence, Libya exported only a special grass for paper making and scrap metal from the tank battles of World War II. In exchange for badly-needed economic assistance, King Idris granted military bases to Great Britain and the United States. In the 1950s and early 1960s Wheelus Air Base near Tripoli became part of the world-wide network of air bases from which the United States conducted its nuclear deterrence and force projection strategy against the Soviet Union.

The discovery of oil changed Libya's economic future forever. Libya rejected the practice of the Persian Gulf oil-rich countries of making monolithic concessions to the major international petroleum companies, and chose to parcel out its holdings. Some of the major international oil companies, including Esso (later Exxon) and Mobil, won concessions. So did a number of different, sometimes smaller companies, called "independents," such as Armand Hammer's Occidental Petroleum, whose field 103 alone contained half as much oil as the north slope of Alaska. Libya's choice of multiple concessionaires enhanced the government's bargaining power and thus its income. In the long-term it made it easier for revolutionary Libya to play its producers against one another and win control of the country's oil.

The declining importance of Libyan bases, the rise of Arab nationalism, the Cold War, and the unpopularity of intervention because of the war in Vietnam persuaded U.S. policymakers not to oppose Muammar al-Qaddafi and his fellow conspirators when they overthrew King Idris on 1 September 1969 and founded what became formally in 1977 the Socialist Peoples' Libyan Arab Jamahiriya (state of the masses). The U.S. government reasoned that it could get along with nationalist revolutionaries; they could be counted on to keep the country out of the Soviet orbit. The judgment turned out to be half right: Qaddafi and his fellow officers were far too jealous of their power to permit any outsider, communist or capitalist, to dominate them. Unforeseen were Qaddafi's soaring ambition and his hatred of the West.

Qaddafi admired Egypt's Gamal Abdel Nasser and sought to imitate him. Spared Egypt's poverty by his country's great oil wealth, the Libyan dictator shared Nasser's weaknesses raised to the tenth power: a preference for image over reality, a bounding ambition that shies from practicality only to collide with it head-on, a callow philosophizing that claims profundity but ends by only mocking itself, a romantic, apolitical world view that barely shrouds a ponderous but deadly dictatorship that stymies domestic economic and political development.

Nasser failed, but in failure he kept the battered dignity of someone whose grandiose plans to lift his family and neighbors into respectability never quite jelled. Leader of a small country possessed of fabulous oil wealth, Qaddafi's erratic rule showed he was the prodigal son, perpetually out of his depth, squandering his inheritance, endangering himself and his people with foolish schemes.

Under Qaddafi, Libya changed from a loyal ally of the United States to a bitter enemy. Qaddafi moved slowly at first, encouraging the United States to believe that good relations might be established. The lease on Wheelus expired, and U.S. forces withdrew quietly on 11 July 1970. Meanwhile, Qaddafi and his fellow officers established a dictatorship under the Revolutionary Command Council and aimed their energies and the country's great wealth at Israel and the West, particularly the United States. Qaddafi overturned the position of foreign oil companies in Libya first by demanding and winning higher prices and revenues and then by nationalizing their holdings. He joined in the Arab oil embargo of 1973 against the United States, and used oil revenues to purchase huge amounts of military equipment from the Soviet Union and to support terrorist activities against Israel, other Arab states, and governments in Africa, Western Europe, and the United States.

Qaddafi's policies were driven in part by a vision of himself as author of a "third way," an alternative to capitalism, which he explained in his *Green Book*. His rage and attacks against Israel and the West also fed on resentment for what he regarded as crimes against the Arab world and Islam, such as Europe's occupation of Arab lands and the establishment of the state of Israel.

Qaddafi repeatedly tried to cajole, bribe, or intimidate

other Arab rulers into uniting with Libya under his leadership. In this and other ways, he acted out what he believed ought to be the position of the Arab world toward all non-Arab states and especially the West: a stance of defiance and willful self-assertion. Always, the diversity of interests, ambitions, and perceptions in the states from Morocco to Iraq, Qaddafi's flawed judgment, and his country's limited power combined to defeat his schemes.

There is a side to Qaddafi that deserves to be taken seriously, because it touches intimate feelings held by many Arabs. Qaddafi sees himself as the embodiment of Arab defiance of Israel, of the West, and of history itself. In this mode he is all too predictable: he will do whatever he imagines Arabs ought to do to defy their enemies. This explains his many plans to unite Libya with other Arab countries, to buy influence in the Arab world, and to conquer his neighbor Chad. This lies behind his announcement in early 1994 that "We are the mecca of freedom fighters and their natural ally." Typically, his list of freedom fighters included some of the most notorious terrorists in the world. Defiance also lay behind a remarkable speech he gave during Israel's invasion of Lebanon in 1982. Trying to sting his fellow Arab leaders into action Qaddafi raged: "Destruction and unprecedented humiliation now exist. We are defeated...torn apart...expelled. Like the sheep in a boat, the Palestinians were dispersed....They occupied, annihilated, and insulted us. We are the most despicable and contemptible nation on earth."

A few months after seizing power, Qaddafi and Deputy Prime Minister Abdel Salaam Ahmed Jaloud launched a campaign against Western oil companies operating in Libya. Rebuffed at first by the wealthy majors with their diverse suppliers, Jaloud issued an ultimatum to Libyan-dependent Occidental. When Armand Hammer surrendered and agreed to raise Libyan revenues beyond the oil-industry standard of 50-50 profit sharing, the Gulf governments reacted by issuing their own higher demands. Libya then "leapfrogged" the new Iranian prices again at the beginning of 1971. In bitter negotiations in Tehran conducted without the threat of Western military intervention the major oil companies and the Gulf producers finally agreed to 55 percent as the base for profit-sharing and raised oil prices another time, with a promise of stability for five years. Qaddafi promptly jumped over the OPEC price again, this time by 90 cents a barrel. Libya's actions together with the refusal of the West to intervene militarily against their allies in the Gulf ended by revealing a historic shift in power and wealth: the initiative at last belonged to the oil producers.

Successful beyond his wildest dreams in the oil negotiations, Qaddafi afterward chose actions that were often dangerous, usually a nuisance, and seldom successful. Reluctant to polarize the Arab world and turn Qaddafi into a martyr by responding with force, the United States and its allies chose during the 1970s and early 1980s to downplay the significance of state-supported terrorism. In addition, Western oil companies remained in Libya after their nationalization and continued to profit from the sale of Libyan petroleum.

Western patience ran out for a number of reasons: the willingness of Iran's Ayatollah Khomeini and Syria's Hafiz al-Asad to engage in terrorism; the uselessness of restraint in dealing with Qaddafi, apparent after his invasion of Chad in 1980; the assassination of Anwar Sadat; and Libya's involvement in more and more flagrant terrorist acts. The Reagan administration chose one of these, the bombing of the "La Belle" discotheque in West Berlin on 5 April 1986, which killed two U.S. soldiers and wounded 229 people, as the cause for a dramatic air strike against Libya ten days later. Controversial at the time, Libyan complicity in the discotheque bombing was confirmed by disclosures from the newly opened files in the formerly communist countries of Eastern Europe.

Libya was singled out again after the hideous destruction of Pan Am Flight 103 over Lockerbie, Scotland, on 21 December 1988, killing all 259 passengers and crew and eleven residents. In November 1991 the U.S. and British governments sought the extradition of two Libyan citizens accused of taking part in the bombing. When Libya refused, the United States, Great Britain, and France obtained mandatory sanctions from the UN Security Council that blocked all air travel to and from Libya, restricted Libyan diplomatic representation, and imposed an arms embargo, but stopped short of banning imports of Libyan oil.

Through all the confrontations Libya's oil industry thrived, and the Western companies that administered it together with Libya's principal trading partners profited handsomely. Italy takes the largest share of Libya's oil and has the most exports to Libya, followed by Germany and Great Britain. Spain also imports large quantities of Libyan oil. These countries successfully led the opposition to adding mandatory oil sanctions to Libya's punishments for bombing Pan Am Flight 103. Figuratively and literally bound to the earth by the UN sanctions, hampered by falling oil prices, increased opposition to his rule, and his country's near total isolation, stagnation, and irrelevance, Qaddafi has struggled to keep himself and his government alive.

P. EDWARD HALEY

See also Middle East; Oil and World Politics; Organization of Petroleum Exporting Countries; Reagan, Ronald Wilson; Terrorism

FURTHER READING

Cooley, John K. *Libyan Sandstorm*. New York, 1982.

Harris, Lillian Craig. *Libya: Qaddafi's Revolution and the Modern State*. Boulder, Colo., 1986.

Haley, P. Edward. *Qaddafi and the United States since 1969*. New York, 1984.

Lemarchand, Rene, ed. *The Green and the Black: Qaddafi's Policies in Africa*. Bloomington, Ind., 1988.

Pelt, Adrian. *Libyan Independence and the United Nations: A Case of Planned Independence*. New Haven, Conn., 1970.

al-Qaddafi, Mu'ammar. *The Green Book*. London, 1976.

Wright, John. *Libya: A Modern History*. Baltimore, Md., 1982.

Yergin, Daniel. *The Prize: The Epic Quest for Oil, Money, and Power*. New York, 1991.

LIE, TRYGVE

(*b.* 16 July 1896; *d.* 30 December 1968)

Norwegian diplomat and first secretary-general of the United Nations (1946–1953). Lie was born in Oslo and attended the University of Oslo. He rose through the ranks of the Norwegian Labor Party, serving as minister of justice in the 1930s and acting as liaison with the Soviet Union. During World War II, when the Germans occupied Norway, he served as foreign minister for his country's government-in-exile in London. He retained that position in the Socialist government after the liberation of Norway in 1945. After months of negotiations in 1945 among the five permanent members of the Security Council, Lie emerged as a compromise candidate, acceptable to the Soviets because of his socialism and to the United States because of his nationality. Lie's appointment indicated that, during the Cold War, the position of secretary-general would go to a political neutral who lacked a reputation for boldness or innovation.

During Lie's tenure, the emergence of the Cold War overshadowed the United Nations. Throughout the 1940s, Western leaders questioned Lie's motives and competence in dealing with the Soviets. When he entered office, he faced an impasse over the Soviet refusal to withdraw from Iran in a timely manner. Urged by the Western Powers, the Iranian government called on Lie to press the Soviets into fulfilling their treaty obligations. His decision to follow a cautious and legalistic path pleased the Soviet Union and angered the United States. Eventually, Iran and the Soviet Union reached an accommodation that restored Iran's sovereignty.

The outbreak of the Korean War in June 1950 reversed Soviet and U.S. negative perceptions of Lie's performance. The Soviets were boycotting the United Nations in an attempt to have the People's Republic of China take the seat of the Republic of China. Although Lie endeavored to bring the Soviets back to the Security Council, he also supported the U.S. effort to defend South Korea. His actions earned the wrath of Moscow, which refused to

support him for a second term in 1951. Lie remained secretary-general until 1953, when the Security Council chose Dag Hammarskjold to be the second secretary-general. After leaving the United Nations, Lie returned to Norway where he served in a number of government positions. His last official act for the United Nations occurred in 1959, when he unsuccessfully mediated a border dispute between Ethiopia and the Trust Territory of Somaliland.

KURK DORSEY

See also Cold War; Iran; Korean War; Norway; United Nations

FURTHER READING

Barros, James. *Trygve Lie and the Cold War: The UN Secretary-General Pursues Peace, 1946–1953*. DeKalb, Ill., 1989.

Lie, Trygve. *In the Cause of Peace: Seven Years with the United Nations*. New York, 1954.

LIECHTENSTEIN

See Appendix 2

LILIENTHAL, DAVID

(*b.* 8 July 1899; *d.* 15 January 1981)

Attorney, businessman, and prominent New Deal administrator who made numerous contributions to public policy while managing a variety of large state and federal government organizations, including the U.S. Atomic Energy Commission (AEC). Born in Morton, Illinois, educated at DePauw University (1920) and Harvard Law School (1923), Lilienthal began his career as a labor and public utilities lawyer in Chicago. Prominent successes—notably a telephone rate case that resulted in a twenty-million-dollar refund to Chicago subscribers—brought him national attention. In 1931 the governor of Wisconsin appointed him to the state's Public Service Commission where he created a new model for utilities statutes that was quickly adopted by several other states. In 1933 President Franklin D. Roosevelt appointed Lilienthal co-director of the new Tennessee Valley Authority (TVA) and, in 1941, the chairman of its Board of Directors. Throughout his tenure Lilienthal resisted pressure to privatize the TVA, which provided hydroelectric power and initiated flood-control projects. In 1946 he chaired the Department of State's Board of Advisors that wrote the "Report on the International Control of Atomic Energy" (the Acheson-Lilienthal Report). In 1947, after resigning from the TVA, President Harry S. Truman appointed Lilienthal the first chairman of the AEC. During his chairmanship Lilienthal was often embroiled in controversy with conservative members of Congress and Senators who urged a more aggressive nuclear-weapons program, a greater role for private industry, and a ban on the export of radioactive isotopes for medical research. Lilienthal was also criticized by conservatives for not applying sufficiently strict political loyalty tests in awarding AEC fellowships. Nevertheless, as the Cold War developed, he oversaw a significant atomic-weapons buildup that began in 1948 with a series of atomic tests at the Eniwetok Atoll in the South Pacific. However, in 1949, after the first Soviet nuclear test, he unsuccessfully opposed a proposal, popular among conservatives and liberals who had lost any hope of cooperating with the Soviet Union, to initiate a crash program to develop a hydrogen bomb. In 1950, at the end of his appointed term, he resigned as chairman of the AEC. Within a few years he had organized a new type of private business, the Development and Resources Corporation, that helped to direct U.S. foreign assistance to developing countries in Latin America and Asia. A prolific writer, Lilienthal published his journals and other books in the fields of public utilities, business, and atomic energy.

MARTIN J. SHERWIN

See also Acheson-Lilienthal Report; Baruch, Bernard Mannes; Cold War; Hydrogen Bomb; Nuclear Weapons and Strategy

FURTHER READING

Hewlett, Richard G., and Francis Duncan. *A History of the United States Atomic Energy Commission, 1947–1952*, vol. II of *Atomic Shield.* University Park, Pa.
Lilienthal, David E. *Change, Hope, and the Bomb.* 1963.
———. *The Journals of David E. Lilienthal*, 6 vols. New York, 1964–1971.

LILIUOKALANI

See Hawai'i

LIMA, DECLARATION OF

See Pan-Americanism

LIMITED NUCLEAR TEST BAN TREATY

(1963)

Officially known as the Treaty Banning Nuclear Weapons Tests in the Atmosphere, in Outer Space, and Underwater, it was signed in Moscow on 5 August 1963 by representatives of the United States, the United Kingdom, and the Soviet Union. A large majority of the world's states subsequently ratified the treaty. Negotiations for a treaty banning the testing of nuclear weapons had begun in 1958 under the leadership of President Dwight D. Eisenhower and Communist Party Chairman Nikita Khrushchev. The major objective was to take a first step toward ending the arms race. A lesser goal was to end the worldwide radioactive fallout then being generated by nuclear tests, nearly all of which were conducted in the lower atmosphere. After a year of tough negotiations among delegations of scientific experts (political negotiations were to begin only after the experts had agreed on the technical outline of a monitoring system), it became evident that finding common ground was more difficult than anticipated. The most serious difficulties involved the monitoring of underground tests. The West demanded that an extensive system of seismic and other test detectors be in place before any limitations went into effect. The Soviets not only had a more modest detection system in mind but demanded that tests cease before the detection system had been fully designed, much less put in place. Another issue involved the number of so-called on-site inspections that could take place whenever the remote detection systems observed some ambiguous event, such as an earthquake of a certain scale and depth. As a result of the failure to resolve these difficulties, the negotiations continued only sporadically during the Eisenhower administration.

President John F. Kennedy promptly resumed the effort but the difficulties continued. In 1963, he sent Averell Harriman to Moscow for a final try. At almost the last moment the negotiators finessed the problem of monitoring underground tests by exempting such tests from the ban, and the treaty was signed soon after. This limited ban fully met the minor objective, the elimination of worldwide fallout, but failed to achieve the major one, that of ending one dimension of the arms race. After the treaty was signed, the major nuclear powers shifted to underground testing, eventually reaching testing rates that exceeded those experienced before the test ban went into effect.

HERBERT F. YORK

See also Nuclear Nonproliferation; Nuclear Weapons and Strategy

FURTHER READING

Bundy, McGeorge. *Danger and Survival: The Political History of the Nuclear Weapon.* New York, 1988.
U.S. Arms Control and Disarmament Agency. *Arms Control and Disarmament Agreements.* Washington, D.C., 1977.

LINCOLN, ABRAHAM

(*b.* 12 February 1809; *d.* 15 April 1865)

Sixteenth president of the United States (1861–1865). The focus of Lincoln's presidency was domestic; the consequences of his policy decisions were both internal and worldwide. By ending slavery, preserving the Union, and defeating the secessionist attempt of the Confederacy during the Civil War, he established a powerful United States based on free-labor capitalism. By proclaiming in his Gettysburg Address of November 1863 that the ultimate purpose of the war was to ensure "that government of the people, by the people, for the people shall not perish from the earth," Lincoln powerfully reinforced the U.S. belief in the nation's worldwide democratic mission.

Born in Hardin County, Kentucky, Lincoln was largely self-educated and practiced law in Springfield, Illinois, for most of his adult life. As a one-term member of the House of Representatives (1847–1849), he opposed the War with Mexico but otherwise showed little interest in U.S. foreign relations. On assuming the presidency in March 1861, Lincoln told a European diplomat that he knew nothing about diplomacy and would be apt to blunder. He wanted his secretary of state, William H. Seward, a former governor of New York who had traveled extensively abroad and had been an active member of the Senate Foreign Relations Committee, to take the lead in formulating and executing U.S. foreign policy. Historians still debate whether Seward attempted at the start of the Civil War to foment a war against one or more European nations in order to entice the seceding slave states back into the Union. Lincoln supposedly thwarted this scheme by rebuffing an injudicious memorandum written by Seward on 1 April 1861 and then by censoring a diplomatic instruction addressed the following month to the U.S. minister in London. Seward, however, had the president's approval in executing every foreign policy recommendation contained in his "April Fool's" memorandum, while the important portions of his instructions to Charles Francis Adams in England were delivered just as Seward had written them. As the secretary of state later explained: "It has been an earnest and profound solicitude to avert foreign war" that inspired his remonstrances against European intervention in the American Civil War.

The true test of the Lincoln-Seward relationship came during the *Trent* affair, the most dangerous foreign relations crisis of Lincoln's presidency. The chief executive, influenced momentarily by Charles Sumner, chairman of the Senate Foreign Relations Committee, wanted to compromise in the face of a British ultimatum received in December 1861. The ultimatum called for the liberation of four Confederate diplomatic envoys (former U.S. Senators James Mason of Virginia and John Slidell of Louisiana and their two secretaries), who were forcibly abducted from a British mail steamer, the *Trent*, sailing from Havana, Cuba. Lincoln's solution to the imbroglio was to propose arbitration, an expedient that might have led to a severance of diplomatic relations with Great Britain, followed by a transatlantic war. Seward advised

the president to allow him to release the captives and announce that traditional U.S. principles of international law required no less. After deliberating overnight, Lincoln accepted Seward's solution, thus averting a serious conflict.

For the rest of Lincoln's presidency, all foreign relations questions—including blockade-running, foreign construction and supply of southern warships (such as the *Alabama* and the *Florida*, which devastated the northern merchant marine), the desperate desire in Great Britain and France for Confederate cotton, the imprisonment of British subjects thought to be actively assisting the southern cause, and the enlistment of foreign nationals in the federal armies—were all handled by Seward with little or no supervision from Lincoln. The president occasionally submitted matters of foreign policy, such as the *Peterhoff* incident, which involved the seizure of a British vessel carrying cargo intended for transshipment to the Confederacy, to his entire cabinet for discussion, but in determining what action to take he invariably followed the recommendations of his secretary of state.

Lincoln's decision in the summer of 1862 to issue the Emancipation Proclamation freeing southern slaves was based in part upon the pleas of U.S. envoys at European capitals. They argued that such a step would make it difficult for European governments to intervene actively on the side of the southern slaveholders, once the American Civil War also became an antislavery crusade. Seward, whose public opposition to slavery had long antedated Lincoln's, supported emancipation as a war measure, but he quietly obstructed the president's efforts to colonize freed slaves in Africa and Latin America.

Republican radicals in Congress and in the cabinet repeatedly protested Seward's supposedly insidious influence upon Lincoln. On occasion, notably during a White House visit by leaders of the Republican caucus in December 1862, they tried to intimidate the president into ousting Seward. Lincoln steadfastly refused to yield to these high-handed tactics. The result was a Union reunited and a president vindicated, both in his selection of Seward to join his cabinet and in his unyielding support of the foreign policy decisions of his secretary of state. Lincoln won reelection in 1864 but was assassinated by John Wilkes Booth on 15 April 1865, less than six weeks into his second term.

NORMAN B. FERRIS

See also Adams, Charles Francis; American Civil War; Confederate States of America; Presidency; Seward, William Henry; Sumner, Charles; Trent Affair

FURTHER READING

Donald, David H. *Lincoln Reconsidered*. New York, 1956.
Ferris, Norman B. "Lincoln and Seward in Civil War Diplomacy: Their Relationship at the Outset Reexamined." *Journal of the Abraham Lincoln Association* 12 (1991): 21–42.

Oates, Stephen B. *With Malice Toward None: The Life of Abraham Lincoln*. New York, 1977.
Paludan, Phillip Shaw. *The Presidency of Abraham Lincoln*. Lawrence, Kans., 1994.

LINDBERGH, CHARLES AUGUSTUS

(*b.* 4 February 1902; *d.* 26 August 1974)

Internationally known aviator and outspoken opponent of U.S. entry into World War II. Born in Detroit, Michigan, and reared in Minnesota, Lindbergh attended the University of Wisconsin briefly before turning to his love of flying. He barnstormed around the country, graduated at the top of his Army Air Service class as a pursuit pilot, and flew the mails between St. Louis and Chicago. He became the United States' most acclaimed aviator when he piloted his single-engine *Spirit of St. Louis* solo across the Atlantic from New York to Paris on 20–21 May 1927. Tall, lean, bright, and modest, his accomplishment was wildly applauded and improved relations between France and the United States. In subsequent flights to Latin America, Asia, Europe, and Africa, he pioneered routes for international air travel.

Lindbergh's most controversial role derived from his efforts to keep the United States out of World War II. In 1935, after the kidnapping and murder of their eldest son, Lindbergh and his wife, Anne Morrow Lindbergh, sought temporary refuge from harassment by newsmen and crackpots by moving to England. Shortly thereafter the U.S. military attaché in Berlin arranged for Lindbergh to examine aviation developments in Nazi Germany. On three major visits in 1936, 1937, and 1938, he inspected German aircraft factories, conferred with Hermann Göring and other top Nazi military and industrial figures, and piloted German military airplanes. As a consequence, Lindbergh became convinced that Germany had the most powerful air force in Europe, and that a European war would be a terrible tragedy. He urged officials in Great Britain, France, and the United States to speed their air power preparations and to avoid war.

In the spring of 1939 Lindbergh returned to the United States, served for a time in the Army Air Corps, and, when war erupted in Europe, began speaking out against possible U.S. entry into the conflict. In radio broadcasts, articles, public addresses, and testimony before congressional committees, Lindbergh argued that the United States could successfully defend itself in the Western Hemisphere. He feared the destructive consequences, both for the United States and for Western civilization, if the United States were to enter the war. At first Lindbergh spoke as an individual but in 1941 joined the noninterventionist America First Committee and became its most popular speaker. Lindbergh was moved by honest concern for his country, but his opponents, including President Franklin D. Roosevelt, accused him of disloyalty and pro-Nazi sympathies. In his most controversial and criticized speech, given at an America First rally in September 1941, Lindbergh charged that "the three most important groups who have been pressing this country toward war are the British, the Jewish, and the Roosevelt Administration." Lindbergh denied that he was anti-Semitic or pro-Nazi, but his reputation never recovered from those allegations.

After the bombing of Pearl Harbor by the Japanese in 1941, the U.S. government rejected Lindbergh's offer to serve in the Army Air Force. He contributed to the war effort by testing military aircraft manufactured by Ford and United Aircraft. In 1944 he went to the South Pacific as a civilian technical representative for United Aircraft. In that capacity he flew fifty combat missions, shooting down a Japanese airplane in the process. In May 1945, after V-E Day, he went to Europe as a United Aircraft representative with a naval technical mission to study advanced German jet aircraft and rocket propulsion. After World War II Lindbergh quietly channeled his energies into U.S. Air Force affairs and efforts to protect the natural environment. He also worked for Pan American World Airways and wrote his autobiography, *The Spirit of St. Louis*, which won a Pulitzer Prize in 1954. In that same year President Dwight D. Eisenhower and Congress restored his commission in the Air Force Reserve and promoted him to the rank of brigadier general.

Wayne S. Cole

See also America First Committee; Isolationism; World War II

FURTHER READING

Cole, Wayne S. *Charles A. Lindbergh and the Battle Against American Intervention in World War II*. New York, 1974.
Lindbergh, Anne Morrow. *War Within and Without: Diaries and Letters, 1939–1944*. New York, 1980.
Lindbergh, Charles A. *The Spirit of St. Louis*. New York, 1953.
———. *The Wartime Journals of Charles A. Lindbergh*. New York, 1970.

LIPPMANN, WALTER

(*b.* 23 September 1889; *d.* 14 December 1974)

Influential political journalist whose syndicated column was published in the *New York Herald Tribune* and more than 200 newspapers in the United States and abroad from 1931 to 1967. Born in New York City, Lippmann graduated from Harvard University in 1910 and then worked to promote Progressive Era reforms. During World War I he became secretary of "the Inquiry," a group of academics and other experts organized in 1917 that advised President Woodrow Wilson on war aims and peace terms. His reputation rested not only on his column, his unparalleled access to national leaders, and a political independence that resisted allegiances to party, but also on a succession of important books. His first major book, *Public Opinion* (1922), offered a disturbing critique of the theory of democratic government. The *Good Society* (1937) tried to reconcile the sometimes conflicting claims of economic and political democracy. *The Public Philosophy* (1955) sought in the strictures of natural law a standard of political behavior for governments and citizens. Beginning in World War II, Lippmann wrote a series of short books on foreign affairs—most notably *U.S. Foreign Policy* (1943), *U.S. War Aims* (1944), and *The Cold War* (1947)—that powerfully influenced the debate over the role that the United States should play in the post–World War II world.

The newspaper column of serious political opinion was virtually invented by Lippmann. Earlier columnists had been essentially purveyors of gossip and inside information. Lippmann, who had been editorial director of the New York daily *The World* and a founding editor of *The New Republic* magazine in 1914, treated his columns as editorials and his readers as intelligent peers. Lippmann's greatest influence began in the late 1930s when Americans, preoccupied with the Great Depression, realized that they could not ignore the march of aggression in Europe and Asia. Having espoused neutrality during most of the decade, Lippmann became a staunch internationalist after the Czech crisis (1938) and urged resistance to the dictatorships. In an age long before television and op-ed pages, and when informed knowledge of foreign affairs was scarce, Lippmann served newspaper editors as an authoritative commentator and provided newspaper readers with thoughtful analyses of events.

He wrote his most influential book on international issues, *U.S. Foreign Policy*, at the height of World War II. Rejecting the idealism he once shared with President Woodrow Wilson, for whom the Inquiry helped produce the Fourteen Points, he vigorously argued the "realist" position based on military strength, alliances, and great power unity, rather than reliance on international organizations and concepts of world government. Although an early critic of containment doctrine because of its emphasis on ideology and confrontation, by the late 1940s he endorsed the main lines of U.S. Cold War diplomacy. Long a confidant of presidents but often critical of their decisions, he clashed dramatically with President Lyndon Johnson in 1965 over U.S. conduct of the war in Vietnam. From that time until his retirement in 1971 he ardently opposed U.S. intervention in Southeast Asia and allied himself with its most

vociferous critics. Having won renown as a political moderate, Lippmann ended his sixty-year career in journalism as a leading voice of the opposition.

RONALD L. STEEL

See also Cold War; Containment; Fourteen Points; Journalism and Foreign Policy; Public Opinion; Vietnam War; World War I; World War II

FURTHER READING

Blum, D. Stephen. *Walter Lippmann: Cosmopolitanism in the Century of Total War.* Ithaca, N.Y., 1984.
Riccio, Barry D. *Walter Lippmann: Odyssey of a Liberal.* New Brunswick, N.J., 1994.
Steel, Ronald. *Walter Lippmann and the American Century.* Boston, 1980.
Syed, Anwar Hussain. *Walter Lippmann's Philosophy of International Politics.* Philadelphia, Pa., 1963.

LITHUANIA

A Baltic republic bordering on Latvia, Poland, Belorussia, and Russia. Like Latvia and Estonia, Lithuania is now a a state pursuing free market reforms and seeking closer ties with the West. Relations with the United States are amicable, and substantial amounts of U.S. aid were given in the period 1991–1994. Lithuania seeks U.S. support against what it fears may be future Russian expansionism. In 1992 Lithuania established a democratic constitution, it held parliamentary elections, and in February 1993 presidential ones, both of which were assessed as free and fair by Western observer teams.

Lithuania is a country of 65,200 square kilometers and almost four million people. As of 1989 Lithuanians made up nearly eighty percent of the population. Russians constitute nearly ten percent and Poles seven percent.

In the late thirteenth century the Lithuanians, then a pagan people living under a variety of feudal lords and clan chieftains, generated one of the most successful military monarchies of the Middle Ages. This beat off the attacks of the German crusaders, and went on to conquer huge areas of what are now Belarus, Ukraine, and Western Russia, whose Slavic Orthodox princes had been weakened by the incursions of the Tatars. In 1387 Lithuania was united with Poland and converted to Catholic Christianity. At the end of the eighteenth century Lithuania was annexed by Russia. Throughout the nineteenth century Lithuanians kept their national culture alive and supported rebellions against Russian rule in 1831 and 1863. Demands made in 1905 for self government were rejected by the Russians.

During World War I, Lithuania was overrun by the German army. With the German collapse in November

1918 the Lithuanian national council declared independence, and with some help from the West was able to beat off a Bolshevik Russian attempt at reconquest and to establish independence. Diplomatic relations were established with the United States, but the U.S. role in this region between the wars was limited. Despite the wartime alliance with the Soviet Union, Washington continued to extend official diplomatic recognition to the independent Baltic States, and Lithuania retained a consul general in Washington and New York.

Both during and after World War II, the Lithuanian resistance mounted guerrilla warfare against Stalin's forces, but was crushed by the Soviets. An estimated 400,000 Lithuanians were deported under Stalin's repression and some 30,000 were killed. Successive U.S. administrations took a "containment plus" approach to Lithuania and the other Baltics: not quick rollback or liberation, but official diplomatic and rhetorical support for the restoration of the independence of these "captive nations."

During the 1970s and 1980s the Lithuanian dissident movement, mainly concentrated around the Catholic Church and the underground "Chronicle of the Catholic Church in Lithuania," attracted considerable attention in the United States, especially in Catholic circles. When in the late 1980s Gorbachev's new foreign policy stirred hopes of independence, the Bush administration took a cautious stance on supporting the Baltic independence movements, fearing to undermine the Gorbachev reform process. After the declaration of renewed Lithuanian independence on 11 March 1990 Gorbachev responded with economic sanctions against the rebellious republic, and Soviet troops occupied parts of Vilnius.

The U.S. signaled concern and limited support by sending two U.S. diplomats from the consulate general in Leningrad to visit Vilnius, the first such visit since the Soviet annexation. More vocal support for the Lithuanians came from individual U.S. politicians, like Republican Senator Alfonse d'Amato, who made a well-publicized attempt to cross into Lithuania from Poland without a Soviet visa, and was naturally turned back.

Senator d'Amato and others in Congress, with strong support from the Lithuanian-American lobby, proposed that U.S. aid to the Soviet Union should be made conditional on Soviet acceptance of Baltic independence, but the Bush administration resisted this. However, as Mikhail Gorbachev made more and more compromises with Soviet hard-liners in the autumn of 1990 U.S. feeling shifted.

In January 1991 Soviet troops launched a military intervention in Lithuania at least in part timed to coincide with the Gulf War, and fourteen Lithuanians were killed during an attack by Soviet paratroopers and KGB troops on the television station in Vilnius. The U.S. Congress voted to suspend economic aid to the Soviet Union, and in general U.S. pressure seems to have played a key part in Gorbachev's decision not to let the military continue their operation to overthrow the Lithuanian government and parliament.

After the failure of the anti-Gorbachev coup of August 1991, and the collapse of communist and Soviet power, the Russian Federation under Boris Yeltsin recognized the independence of the Baltic States, and the obstacle to U.S. and Western recognition was removed.

U.S. de facto diplomatic recognition of Lithuania occurred on 2 September 1991. Since then, Lithuania and the United States have developed close relations. U.S. pressure on Russia, along with that of the European Union (EU) and Scandinavia, helped to bring about the withdrawal of all Russian troops from Lithuania by 31 August 1993, which greatly reduced tension in Lithuania. The United States, however, has been very cautious about supporting Lithuanian calls, especially from the nationalist opposition, for the demilitarization of Russian Kaliningrad.

Lithuanian leaders have expressed strong interest in membership in the North Atlantic Treaty Organization (NATO), and while preferring full membership, were among the first to join NATO's Partnership for Peace program launched in 1994 as an important step in integrating former Soviet bloc states into a NATO-led European security system. Another long-term goal of Lithuania is membership in the EU, with associate membership as a nearer-term step. However, partly because of the victory of the former communists, confirmed by the presidential elections of March 1993, and partly because of different Lithuanian traditions, economic reform in Lithuania has lagged behind that in Latvia and Estonia. This also has limited somewhat the number of economic contacts between Lithuania and the United States.

The unwillingness of Lithuanian Americans to serve under Brazauskas also has meant that emigrés play a less important part in the Lithuanian government, and one important bridge to the United States is relatively underused. However, Lithuania has introduced a very successful and stable independent currency, the litas, pegged to the U.S. dollar; and in general, the country seems firmly set for progressively greater integration into the West.

ANATOL LIEVEN

See also Estonia; Latvia; Russia and the Soviet Union; Stalin, Joseph

FURTHER READING

Arkadie, Brian van, ed. *Economic Survey of the Baltic States*. New York, 1992.

Crowe, David. *The Baltic States and the Great Powers, 1938–1940*. Boulder, Colo., 1993.

Flint, David. *The Baltic States—Estonia, Latvia and Lithuania*. Brookfield, Conn. 1992.

Gerner, Kristian. *The Baltic States and the End of the Soviet Empire.* London and New York, 1993.

Hider, John, and Patrick Salmon. *The Baltic Nations and Europe.* London, 1991.

Kirby, David. *The Baltic World, 1772–1993: Europe's Northern Periphery in an Age of Change.* London and New York, 1995.

Lieven, Anatol. *The Baltic Revolution: Estonia, Latvia, Lithuania and the Path to Independence.* New Haven, Conn., 1993.

Misiunas, Romualdas, and Rein Taagepera. *The Baltic States: Years of Dependence, 1940-1990.* Berkeley, Calif., 1993.

LITVINOV, MAKSIM MAKSIMOVICH

(*b.* 17 July 1876; *d.* 31 December 1951)

Soviet career diplomat who served as commissar for foreign affairs (1930–1939) and ambassador to the United States (1941–1943), campaigned for collective security against Nazi Germany, and advocated good relations between the Soviet Union and the United States. Born Meir Wallach in the predominantly Jewish city of Belostok, Litvinov served in the Russian army, where he first studied Marxism. He was one of the original members of the Russian Social Democratic Workers' Party and sided with Vladimir Lenin's Bolsheviks in the party split of 1903. He served in the revolutionary underground until 1908, when, disillusioned with the prospects for a successful revolution, he emigrated to Great Britain. He worked for a London publisher, married an Englishwoman, and even became a British subject.

His diplomatic career began in 1918, when Litvinov asked to be appointed Soviet representative to the United States, a request that Lenin approved but the United States rejected because it refused to open diplomatic relations with the Bolshevik regime. In January 1919, at the request of the Soviet government, Litvinov held talks in neutral Sweden with President Woodrow Wilson's envoy, William Buckler. He argued with the American for an end to the foreign intervention in Russia and the establishment of regular diplomatic relations. Litvinov especially tried to downplay the appearance of promoting revolution abroad as a Soviet goal, but this effort failed. In the 1920s Litvinov held several talks with American businessmen in an effort to change U.S. policy toward the Soviet Union, but it was not until 1933 and the administration of President Franklin D. Roosevelt that the United States ended its policy of nonrecognition of the Soviet Union. Litvinov traveled to Washington in late 1933 for direct talks, and during these complicated negotiations, Litvinov agreed to honor, in return for a U.S. loan, Russian debts to Americans that had been repudiated by the communist regime. He also promised religious freedom for any Americans residing in the Soviet Union. Although the central Soviet goal was to obtain U.S. cooperation against Japanese aggression in Asia, the final agreement failed to mention Japan. Litvinov later allowed relations with the United States to sour over the loan issue. Roosevelt insisted that he had meant a "credit" to be spent by the Russians in the United States and under government supervision. Litvinov insisted upon an outright loan to be utilized anywhere. Relations quickly deteriorated. Litvinov later admitted to U.S. journalist Walter Duranty that in fact he had understood Roosevelt intended a credit, not a loan. The whole controversy was an illusion brought on by Litvinov's disappointment with U.S. refusal to help restrain Japan and the Soviet Union's determination not to pay the repudiated debts. In 1939 Joseph Stalin removed Litvinov as foreign commissar, indicating Stalin's readiness to deal with Nazi Germany.

As Soviet ambassador to the United States during World War II, Litvinov pressed hard for a Western front in Europe and for continued and increased U.S. aid to a Russia bearing the brunt of Nazi aggression. In March 1942 Litvinov obtained crucial verbal assurances from Roosevelt that the Soviet Union could retain the territories it had seized between 1939 and 1941, most notably the Baltic states, which possibly bolstered Stalin's belief that after the war he could retain with impunity his country's 1941 borders. In 1943 Litvinov returned to Moscow, holding a powerless sinecure in the government. He quickly became disillusioned with Stalin's rapacious policies in Eastern Europe. Speaking privately with U.S. diplomats and journalists, Litvinov warned that Stalin would continue to absorb territory until the Western powers took a firm line against Soviet expansionism. In a 1946 interview with the U.S. journalist Richard C. Hottelet, Litvinov bluntly compared Stalin to Adolf Hitler and squarely placed the blame for the Cold War on Stalin's rigidly ideological world view. Hottelet prudently did not publish this material until after Litvinov's death.

HUGH D. PHILLIPS

See also Cold War; Roosevelt, Franklin Delano; Russia and the Soviet Union; Stalin, Joseph; World War II

FURTHER READING

Bennett, Edward. *Recognition of Russia: An American Foreign Policy Dilemma.* Waltham, Mass., 1970.

Mastny, Vojtech. *Russia's Road to the Cold War: Diplomacy, Warfare, and the Politics of Communism, 1941–1945.* New York, 1979.

Phillips, Hugh. *Between the Revolution and the West: A Political Biography of Maxim M. Litvinov.* Boulder, Colo., 1992.

———. "Mission to America: Maksim Litvinov in the United States, 1941–1943." *Diplomatic History* 12 (Summer 1988): 261–275.

LIVINGSTON, EDWARD

(*b.* 28 May 1764; *d.* 23 May 1836)

U.S. secretary of state from 1831 to 1833 and minister to France from 1833 to 1835. Livingston, the son of Revolutionary patriot and diplomat Robert R. Livingston, was born in Clermont, New York. He graduated from the College of New Jersey (now Princeton University) in 1781 and on completing law studies, opened a practice in New York City. Largely over matters of patronage, the socially prominent and politically active Livingstons switched from the Federalist to the Jeffersonian cause during the Washington administration. From 1795 to 1801, Edward Livingston served in Congress, where he led the effort against legislation to carry out the terms of Jay's Treaty. He called on the president to provide the House of Representatives all correspondence regarding the treaty. Leaving Congress in 1801, Livingston became U.S. Attorney for the District of New York and, simultaneously, mayor. During this service he suffered devastating financial reverses that led him to leave New York for New Orleans. In 1823 Livingston returned to the U.S. House as a representative from Louisiana. He was defeated in his bid for reelection in 1828 but was chosen to represent Louisiana in the U.S. Senate, serving until his appointment as secretary of state in the spring of 1831.

Livingston's stewardship at the Department of State during Andrew Jackson's presidency was not prodigious. On the longstanding disputed boundary between Maine and Canada, Jackson favored the arbitration award proposed by the king of the Netherlands, but Livingston proved unable to impose the agreement on Maine and a settlement was not reached. Livingston handled claims for French spoliations against U.S. shipping during the Napoleonic wars. In an 1832 treaty, France agreed to pay the United States 25 million francs ($4.6 million) in six yearly installments, but when the first payment came due in February 1833, the Chamber of Deputies refused to appropriate the funds. In May 1833, Louis McLane became secretary of state and Livingston was named minister to France. When the French Chamber demanded an explanation for the language and tone of Jackson's 1834 annual message, in which he threatened reprisals if the claims were not paid, Livingston requested his passport and returned to the United States. Though the spoliation controversy was later settled, this departure from Paris marked the end of Livingston's career in public service.

KENNETH R. STEVENS

See also France; Jackson, Andrew; McLane, Louis; Webster-Ashburton Treaty

FURTHER READING

Belohlavek, John M. *"Let the Eagle Soar." The Foreign Policy of Andrew Jackson.* Lincoln, Nebr., 1985.
Hatcher, William. *Edward Livingston: Jeffersonian Republican and Jacksonian Democrat.* University, La., 1940.
Rawle, Francis. "Edward Livingston: Secretary of State, May 24, 1831, to May 29, 1833." In *The American Secretaries of State and Their Diplomacy*, vol. 4, edited by Samuel Flagg Bemis. (1928):205–263.

LIVINGSTON, ROBERT R.

(*b.* 27 November 1746; *d.* 25 February 1813)

Lawyer; delegate to the second Continental Congress (1775–1776), where he helped draft the Declaration of Independence; and U.S. diplomat who negotiated the purchase of Louisiana from France in 1803. Born in New York City, he graduated in 1765 from King's College (now Columbia University). During the American Revolution, Livingston saw first-hand the problems the nation faced in trying to end the war. In 1781, he became secretary of the newly established Department of Foreign Affairs and took a large part in directing the U.S. diplomats who negotiated the Treaty of Paris in 1783.

Livingston's experiences in making foreign policy led him to become one of the strongest Constitutional advocates from New York. At the New York ratifying convention, he supported the role of the Senate to offer advice and consent on treaties because he expected the Senate to be filled with men who had sufficient acquaintances in foreign countries to be knowledgeable about foreign affairs. He favored strong national government because he thought it best equipped to protect his state, New York, and the northern frontier with Canada.

Notwithstanding his Federalist sympathies, Livingston disagreed with Alexander Hamilton's financial program during Washington's first administration, especially his plan to establish a permanent national debt. In 1798, he ran for governor of the state but lost to John Jay, whose treaty with Great Britain (1794) he opposed. For these reasons, Livingston supported Thomas Jefferson's bid for the presidency in 1796 and 1800.

Livingston realized that western trade on the Mississippi River was important to the young republic. He was therefore not alone in expressing concern when Louisiana was rumored to have been transferred from Spain to France. Jefferson sent Livingston to Paris as minister to France in October 1801, and directed him to prevent New Orleans from changing hands. If he could not prevent the transfer, he was instructed to try to purchase the territory. In France, Livingston threatened a U.S. alliance with Great Britain against France and warned that U.S. residents of the area would wrest control of the province if France did not sell the territory to the United States.

It is doubtful that Livingston's warnings persuaded Napoleon to sell Louisiana to the United States. Rather, the continuing slave rebellion in French-controlled Saint Domingue (Haiti) and the imminent resumption of war in Europe changed Napoleon's mind. For 60 million francs, he agreed to sell New Orleans and French lands west of the Mississippi River. His decision prevented the British from gaining control of the area and financed the renewal and expansion of the Napoleonic wars.

In 1804, Livingston resigned his post in France and returned to New York, where he devoted the remainder of his life to developing his estate (Clermont) and supporting the steamboat enterprises of Robert Fulton, a young inventor he had met in Paris.

RONALD L. HATZENBUEHLER

See also American Revolution; Articles of Confederation; Constitution; France; Hamilton, Alexander; Jay, John; Jay's Treaty; Jefferson, Thomas; Louisiana Purchase; Mississippi River; Napoleonic Wars

FURTHER READING

DeConde, Alexander. *This Affair of Louisiana*. New York, 1976.
Marks, Frederick W., III. *Independence on Trial: Foreign Affairs and the Making of the Constitution*. Wilmington, Del., 1986.

LLOYD GEORGE, DAVID, 1st Earl Lloyd-George of Dwyfor

(*b.* 17 January 1863; *d.* 26 March 1945)

Great Britain's prime minister (1916–1922) and the first self-made man in modern British history to make his way to the apex of political power. Born into a poor family in Manchester, England, Lloyd George grew up in Wales, was educated in the village schoolhouse, and was apprenticed to a law firm at age sixteen. He became a lawyer in his own right, and his brilliant pen and oratorical power enabled him to win a seat in parliament as a radical-liberal in 1890, and he was regularly reelected by the same constituency until his death. He became famous as a bitter, outspoken opponent of Joseph Chamberlain and the Boer War and as a radical reformer and advocate of home rule for Wales. As a dynamic young leader of the Liberal party, he served as president of the Board of Trade (1905–1908) under Sir Henry Campbell-Bannerman, then as chancellor of the exchequer (1908–1915) in Herbert Asquith's ministry. He sought enactment of a radical social reform program, including old age pensions, comprehensive health insurance, and a tax system that particularly raised levies on higher income levels. Although many of his recommendations found favor, he himself suffered a political setback during the Marconi scandal of 1912–1913, which erupted from charges that Liberal cabinet members, including Lloyd George, had profited from the purchase of Marconi Company stock, which, it was alleged, had risen in value because of a government contract.

Nonetheless, a year into World War I, he became minister of munitions (1915) in a coalition government headed by H. H. Asquith. After a brief stint as minister of war (1916), he became prime minister in December 1916 in a coalition government heavily dependent on Conservative support, a position he retained until his fall from power in 1922. The brilliant administrator turned out to be a bold and charismatic war leader who retained his popularity despite constant arguments with generals and admirals, and huge British losses on the Western front. Only by relying heavily on Australians and colonial troops from India and Africa did Great Britain summon the necessary manpower to continue the war. From the time he became war minister, Lloyd George urged the U.S. government to enter the war as an ally. Despite British violations of U.S. neutral rights during the course of the war, resulting from the government's seizure of U.S. cargo ships trading with Germany, there was little doubt in Great Britain that the U.S. Congress and President Woodrow Wilson supported Great Britain's war effort. Official U.S. protests against British violations of U.S. neutral rights on the high seas proved consistently feeble and on 4 April 1917 Congress voted overwhelmingly in favor of war against Germany.

Much as Lloyd George and the other Allied leaders welcomed U.S. participation in the war, the slowness of U.S. mobilization irked them. As late as the spring of 1918, when British and French casualties in one week of fighting amounted to 120,000 men, U.S. reinforcements still were only trickling in. Lloyd George grew skeptical of Wilson's war aims, embodied in the Fourteen Points announced in January 1918. He privately considered Wilson's objectives "vague idealism" and opposed especially Point 2, which called for "freedom of the seas" in war and peace, an unacceptable condition for Great Britain during the war, because it would mean lifting its blockade of Germany; even in peacetime and with a disarmed Germany, Point 2 was unlikely to find favor with the world's predominant maritime power. Nor did Lloyd George or most of his cabinet favor an "association of nations" to keep the peace after the war, as propounded in Point 14, although they opposed it less adamantly than the Italians or the French. The British prime minister nonetheless publicly emphasized the harmony that existed between Allied and U.S. war aims.

In 1919, as a chief British negotiator at the Paris Peace Conference and one of the architects of the Versailles Treaty, Lloyd George openly took issue with President Wilson's League of Nations Covenant and with his demand for freedom of the seas. He privately criticized the president for his "missionary zeal," as he put it, and for the "sermonettes" that Wilson periodically delivered to the Allied leaders. Lloyd George nonetheless took the middle ground between Wilson's visionary hopes and French Premier Georges Clemenceau's insistence that the Allies punish Germany severely. He opposed French demands for the annexation of German territory and ultimately supported the establishment of a League of Nations on condition that Germany be excluded, which it was.

In 1922 Lloyd George resigned as prime minister in the wake of the Chanak crisis with Turkey, but he retained his seat in Parliament and reemerged as leader of the Liberal party (1926–1931). In the 1930s he began to regret the harsh terms of the Versailles Treaty and briefly became an admirer of German leader Adolf Hitler, whom he visited in Berchtesgaden in 1936. Lloyd George supported Neville Chamberlain's appeasement policy. His multivolume memoirs of World War I were published in the 1930s. In 1940 Prime Minister Winston Churchill offered Lloyd George the ambassadorship to the United States, but, on his doctor's advice, Lloyd George turned down the appointment—a rejection that pleased official Washington.

SINA DUBOVOY

See also Great Britain; Hitler, Adolf; Versailles Treaty of 1919; Wilson, Thomas Woodrow; World War I

FURTHER READING

Gilbert, Bentley B. *David Lloyd George: A Political Life*, 2 vols. Columbus, Ohio, 1987.
Lentin, Antony. *Lloyd George, Woodrow Wilson, and the Guilt of Germany*. 1985.
Lloyd George, David. *The Truth About Reparations and War Debts*. London, 1932.
———. *War Memoirs of David Lloyd George*. London, 1938.
———. *Lloyd George Family Letters, 1885–1936*, edited by Kenneth O. Morgan. Cardiff, Wales, 1973.
———. *Memories of the Peace Conference*. New Haven, Conn., 1939.
Pugh, Martin. *Lloyd George*. New York, 1988.

LODGE, HENRY CABOT, JR.

(*b.* 5 July 1902; *d.* 27 February 1985)

Republican senator from Massachusetts (1937–1944, 1946–1952) and vice presidential candidate (1960) who served as the U.S. ambassador to the United Nations (1953–1960) and as ambassador to South Vietnam (1963–1964, 1965–1967) during the escalation of the Vietnam War. Born in Nahant, Massachusetts, Lodge was named for his grandfather, who was the chairman of the U.S. Senate Foreign Relations Committee and majority leader of the U.S. Senate in 1919–1924. After his graduation from Harvard University (1924), he worked in journalism, then served in the Massachusetts legislature (1932–1936). He first won election to the U.S. Senate in 1936. During 1944–1945 he was with the U.S. Army in Europe and was reelected to the Senate in 1946.

Lodge began his senate career as an isolationist but converted to internationalism in 1937. As ambassador to the UN he engaged in propaganda jousts with the Soviet Union and helped negotiate the end of the Anglo-French-Israeli invasion of Egypt in 1956 during the Suez Crisis. During his first tour in South Vietnam he encouraged the coup by Vietnamese generals against the regime of President Ngo Dinh Diem, while steadfastly denying U.S. responsibility for it. He later advocated a bombing campaign against North Vietnam and struggled as ambassador to help South Vietnam build an effective central government. After the Tet Offensive of 1968 he urged President Lyndon B. Johnson to reduce the U.S. military effort in Vietnam, while continuing to build up South Vietnamese armed forces. Lodge subsequently served short stints as an ambassador at large and ambassador to West Germany, before leading the U.S. delegation to the unsuccessful Vietnam peace talks in 1969. He concluded his career as a special envoy to the Vatican from 1970 to 1977.

STEPHEN E. PELZ

See also Diem, Ngo Dinh; Isolationism; Lodge, Henry Cabot, Sr.; Suez Crisis; Tet Offensive; Vietnam War

FURTHER READING

Burke, Lee H. *Ambassador at Large: Diplomat Extraordinary*. New York, 1972.
Ferrell, Robert H., ed. *The American Secretaries of State and Their Diplomacy*, vol. 19. New York, 1980
Lodge, Henry Cabot. *The Storm Has Many Eyes*. New York, 1973.
———. *As It Was*. New York, 1976.

LODGE, HENRY CABOT, SR.

(*b.* 12 May 1850; *d.* 9 November 1924)

Prolific historian, Republican senator from Massachusetts (1893–1924), and chairman of the Senate Foreign Relations Committee (1919–1924). A member of wealthy Brahmin families, the Cabots and the Lodges, he was born in Boston and graduated from Harvard (B.A., 1871; LL.B., 1875; Ph.D., 1876). Lodge had a career as a biographer of George Washington, Alexander Hamilton, and Daniel Webster before becoming one of the most powerful politicians of the late nineteenth and early twentieth centuries. After serving in the Massachusetts legislature, Lodge was elected to the House of Representatives in 1886 and entered the senate in 1893. A lifelong Republican, he was assigned to the Senate Foreign Relations Committee in 1896 and obtained the coveted chairmanship in 1919. By the 1880s he had become an expansionist and an advocate, along with his friend Theodore Roosevelt, of naval power, overseas bases, and a forceful foreign policy. Both men were friends and disciples of naval expansionist Admiral Alfred Thayer Mahan. An early proponent of Cuban independence from Spain, Lodge waited until U.S. public opinion demanded war with Spain in 1898 before supporting that policy. He urged acceptance of the peace treaty providing for the acquisition of the Philippines. Lodge supported President Woodrow Wilson's policies of neutrality in 1914, but he became increasingly pro-British and anti-German and voted enthusiastically for war against Germany in 1917. Mutual personal and political enmity between Lodge and the president contributed to the defeat of Wilson's most cherished accomplishment, the 1919 Versailles treaty. Lodge used his leadership in the Republican-controlled Senate to offer "reservations" and then to ensure defeat of the treaty, and especially U.S. membership in the League of Nations. Questioning Wilson's concept of collective security, Lodge believed in maintaining U.S. freedom of action in foreign affairs and believed, above all, in the primacy of Congress over the president in matters of war and peace. Neither Wilson nor Lodge would compromise on principle or transcend partisan and personal differences. Lodge contributed significantly to the Republican triumph that brought Warren G. Harding into the White House in 1920. Lodge served on the U.S. delegation to the Washington Conference on the Limitation of Armaments in 1921–1922.

JANET M. MANSON

See also Colonialism; Congress; Imperialism; Mahan, Alfred Thayer; Spanish-American-Cuban-Filipino War, 1898; Versailles Treaty of 1919; Washington Conference on Limitation of Armaments; Wilson, Thomas Woodrow; World War I

FURTHER READING

Garraty, John A. *Henry Cabot Lodge*. New York, 1953.
Grenville, John A. S., and George Berkeley Young. *Politics, Strategy, and American Diplomacy*. New Haven, Conn., 1966.
Lodge, Henry Cabot. *Selections from the Correspondence of Theodore Roosevelt and Henry Cabot Lodge*. New York, 1925.
—— *The Senate and the League of Nations*. New York, 1925.
Widenor, William C. *Henry Cabot Lodge and the Search for an American Foreign Policy*. Berkeley, Calif., 1980.

LODGE RESERVATIONS

See League of Nations; Lodge, Henry Cabot, Sr.

LOGAN ACT

Named for but aimed against the Quaker physician and later Republican senator from Pennsylvania (1801–1807), Dr. George Logan, who sought to end the Quasi-War (1798–1800) with France. Convinced that President John Adams and the Federalists wished to bring the United States to war against France to achieve their political goals, which included abrogation of the Franco-American alliance of 1778 and destruction of the Republican party, Logan departed secretly for France in June 1798. Denounced by the Federalists, he was nevertheless received by U.S. expatriates including Joel Barlow, the Connecticut poet and future Republican diplomat.

With diplomatic relations between France and the United States suspended since the XYZ Affair (1797), Logan hoped to resume dialogue. French Foreign Minister Charles Maurice de Talleyrand had become concerned that he and others in the French government might have overestimated pro-French sympathy in the United States and were receptive to overtures from U.S. representatives, even private citizens with no official authority. Although several factors influenced official French actions, the timing was such that Logan came to believe that he had helped influence French policy. He left Paris in August 1798 carrying dispatches to President Adams and the secretary of state from Consul General Napoleon Bonaparte. The letters announced that France was removing its embargo on U.S. ships in French ports, that had been enacted in July 1798, and was freeing U.S. prisoners.

High Federalists in Congress, particularly in the Senate, were angered by Logan's attempts to reconcile differences with France and attacked him for meddling in official Department of State business. Although President Adams probably wanted to mitigate the government's strong position toward France, he succumbed to Federalist pressure and condemned the interference of private individuals in official diplomacy. Increasingly partisan divisions in the country became obvious when Congress began to debate the Logan mission. When the Federalists accused Republicans of being pro-French, Representative Albert Gallatin of Pennsylvania rose to defend his colleagues. In the end, because of a Federalist majority in Congress, Logan was censured and the resulting Logan Act was signed by Adams on 30 January 1799.

Enactment of the Logan Act was an effort to embarrass Republicans. The law stipulated fines and imprisonment for U.S. citizens who, unauthorized and acting independently, corresponded with a foreign government to influence the conduct of that government. Although subsequently modified, the Logan Act is still on the books, and threats have been made to invoke it when individuals generated controversy by engaging in unauthorized diplomatic activities. An example in the twentieth century involved the actress Jane Fonda. During the Vietnam War, the U.S. government considered invoking the law against her for going to Vietnam in a personal attempt to end the fighting.

THOM M. ARMSTRONG

See also Adams, John; France; Gallatin, Albert; Napolean Bonaparte; Talleyrand, Charles Maurice; Vietnam War; XYZ Affair

FURTHER READING

Bowman, Albert Hall. *The Struggle for Neutrality: Franco-American Diplomacy During the Federalist Era*. Knoxville, Tenn., 1974.

DeConde, Alexander. *The Quasi-War: The Politics and Diplomacy of the Undeclared War with France, 1797–1801.* New York, 1966.
Hill, Peter P. *William Vans Murray, Federalist Diplomat: The Shaping of Peace with France, 1797–1801.* Syracuse, N.Y., 1971.
Tolles, Frederick B. *George Logan of Philadelphia.* New York, 1953.

LONDON ECONOMIC CONFERENCE

(1933)

Amid a disastrous global economic and financial situation, sixty-six nations gathered at London from 12 June to 27 July 1933 to secure forceful U.S. intervention to stabilize international currencies and halt protectionism. Some countries hoped the United States would provide up to $500 million in gold to shore up their currencies, while others simply sought reassurance of U.S. commitment to the gold standard and open markets in order to discourage speculation. The administration of Franklin D. Roosevelt, only three months old, was in the throes of securing congressional approval of the pillars of the New Deal and was divided in its support of these international goals. With the dollar recently off the gold standard, world currencies everywhere in flux, and U.S. exports still struggling, Roosevelt was inclined to avoid promises and commitments. On the question of liberalizing trade, Roosevelt decided to wait until after Congress had approved his domestic programs. He tabled an early draft of the Reciprocal Trade Agreement legislation. Early in the conference, U.S. delegates tentatively approved a draft declaration calling for a return to the gold standard and support for currency intervention. It represented the highest hopes of the French, Swiss, and other nations still on the gold standard. U.S. delegates saw in the declaration a statement of goals, while the Europeans felt it represented a firm commitment for immediate action. Perhaps sensing the ambiguity of the resolution, Roosevelt ignored his advisers' recommendations and flatly rejected it. He later rejected a watered-down version as well. This later rejection shocked the conference goers and virtually ended further deliberations on monetary and trade policy. The consequence of the failure of the conference was not the debacle that many feared. By 1934 the United States was again committed to internationalism in economic affairs. Nevertheless, the episode illustrates the difficulties of international cooperation in times of severe economic crisis and domestic economic priorities.

KENDALL W. STILES

See also Gold Standard; Hull, Cordell; Roosevelt, Franklin Delano

FURTHER READING

Feis, Herbert. *1933: Characters in Crisis.* Boston, 1966.

LONDON NAVAL CONFERENCES OF 1930 AND 1935–1936

Opening on 21 January and closing on 22 April 1930, the first of these meetings extended to 1936 the moratorium on battleship construction arranged at the Washington Naval Conference of 1921–1922 and provided for the limitation of lesser ship categories—cruisers, destroyers, and submarines. The conferees hoped that the successful limitation of naval arms, more complicated and requiring more time to build than the tanks, artillery, and small arms employed by armies, would make it possible to hold a general disarmament conference at Geneva in 1932. Through President Herbert Hoover's careful preparations, including a personal meeting with British Prime Minister Ramsay MacDonald, an Anglo-American "yardstick" was devised that roughly balanced the U.S. preference for "heavy" eight-inch gun cruisers of 10,000 tons with the Royal Navy's greater number of "light" cruisers carrying six-inch guns. The able U.S. delegation, headed by Secretary of State Henry L. Stimson and Ambassador Hugh Gibson, also achieved a compromise that extended the Washington Conference ratio of 10:6 to Japan's cruiser tonnage, but required the United States to build cruisers at a slower schedule, thereby giving the Japanese an effective 10:7 ratio for the five-year duration of the treaty. These successful technical arrangements, however, did little to ensure peace during the hectic 1930s. After invading Manchuria in 1931, Japan continued to build to its treaty limits and beyond, while the United States and Britain did not. The Geneva Conference on General Disarmament foundered. In December 1935 the five powers met again London, but by the end of the conference on 25 March 1936, only the United States, Britain, and France seized a naval treaty that set limits on the size of warships and the caliber of their guns. The 1936 treaty terminated in 1938. The structure of naval limitations had collapsed.

J. GARRY CLIFFORD

See also Gibson, Hugh Simons; Hoover, Herbert; National Security and National Defense; Navy, U.S. Department of; Stimson, Henry Lewis; Washington Conference on the Limitation of Armaments

FURTHER READING

Kaufman, Robert G. *Arms Control During the Pre-Nuclear Era.* New York, 1990.
O'Connor, Raymond G. *Perilous Equilibrium.* Lawrence, Kans., 1962.
Pelz, Stephen. *Race to Pearl Harbor: The Failure of the Second London Naval Conference and the Onset of World War II.* 1974.
Tate, Merze. *The United States and Armaments.* Cambridge, Mass., 1948.

LONG, BRECKINRIDGE

(*b.* 16 May 1881; *d.* 26 September 1958)

Assistant secretary of state (1917–1920, 1939–1944) and ambassador to Italy (1933–1936), best remembered for his opposition to large-scale admission to the United States of Jewish refugees from Adolf Hitler's Europe. Long failed to achieve political success in his native Missouri, but his personal fortune and social connections made him an important figure in Democratic party circles. In 1904 he received a B.A. from Princeton University, where Woodrow Wilson was one of his favorite professors. He graduated from St. Louis Law School (now Washington University) in 1906 and was admitted to the Missouri bar. Long had few financial worries after he married wealthy Christine Graham in 1912. Four years later he contributed $100,000 to Wilson's successful presidential campaign, his reward being the office of third assistant secretary of state. Long supervised appointments to the Foreign Service and worked with Colonel Edward House, Wilson's close adviser, especially on foreign affairs.

As assistant secretary of state, Long turned his attention to East Asia, where he championed U.S. business interests in Japan and China. He favored a Western banking consortium to control China's financial structure and to prevent Japanese domination there. With Secretary of State Robert Lansing's support, Long helped persuade a reluctant Wilson that the United States needed to join such a consortium, a move which angered Tokyo. To ensure continued Japanese participation in World War I, Wilson and Lansing in November 1917 gave tacit approval to Japanese penetration of Manchuria and Shantung.

The Bolshevik Revolution in November 1917 forced Long to focus on Russia, and he firmly opposed U.S. participation in the 1918 foreign intervention in Siberia. If Vladimir Lenin's government was to continue the war with Germany, Long favored U.S. recognition of the new Russian regime. When anticommunist pressure mounted and Lansing backed intervention, Long accepted U.S. intervention. Long became frustrated with diplomacy and his failure to be influential and turned to Missouri politics. From 1920 to 1933 he practiced law in St. Louis and ran unsuccessfully in two Senate races.

For his support of Franklin D. Roosevelt's 1932 presidential campaign, Long was appointed ambassador to Italy. Believing the United States could learn from the Italian example, he developed a high regard for Benito Mussolini and the fascist regime. Long refused to criticize the regime's violations of civil rights and liberties. During 1934–1935 Long strongly advocated U.S. isolationism and neutrality, while his superiors at the Department of State tended to oppose these policies. Long wrote in 1935 that a European war was coming because of deep-rooted national, racial, and religious hatreds and argued vigorously that the United States should stay out. Thus, he strenuously resisted British attempts to obtain U.S. support for the efforts of the League of Nations to deter Italian aggression in Ethiopia. When the United States gave limited support to British policy, Long filed a protest. This disagreement contributed to his recall from Rome in 1936, after which he was virtually ignored until 1939, although he remained a loyal Democrat.

From 1936 to 1939, as a confirmed Anglophobe, he continued to uphold neutrality and isolationism, believing the British wanted to drag the United States into European affairs to serve British interests. He also believed that German dominance in southern and eastern Europe was inevitable and even beneficial in bringing order and stability. In Asia he approved of Japanese expansion, believing the alternative was chaos or, worse, communism. With the outbreak of World War II in September 1939, Long returned to the Department of State, but he did not alter his isolationist views until the fall of France in June 1940. For example, he opposed both aid to the Finns during the Russian invasion of Finland and U.S.-British naval cooperation in the early months of the war. By the end of May 1940, however, he realized the danger to the United States if the Allies were defeated. By 1941 he was firmly on the side of the Allies and recognized the need to aid the Soviet Union in their efforts against the Germans.

One of Long's major tasks was the disposition of countless war refugees trying to enter the United States. He unwaveringly opposed lowering immigration barriers, asserting that German and Soviet agents were being smuggled into the country along with legitimate refugees. Long's refusal to compromise earned him a reputation among some critics as an anti-Semite unsympathetic to Jews caught in the Holocaust. There is much evidence to support this contention. Prior to the April 1943 Bermuda Conference on the refugee problem, Long wrote a memorandum to the British, in which he asserted that the United States was already doing everything in its power to help the persecuted peoples of Europe, using the immigration laws in an "utmost liberal and humane spirit." These assertions proved untrue. In November 1943 Congress began consideration of a "rescue resolution," urging the president to take all measures possible to "save the surviving Jewish people of Europe." Long blocked this resolution, reporting to the House Foreign Affairs Committee that the United States had received approximately 580,000 Jews since 1933. The real figure was closer to 250,000. His testimony provoked a storm of criticism both inside and outside the government. At the end of 1943 Secretary of State Cordell Hull released Long from the visa service, effectively ending Long's political career.

HUGH D. PHILLIPS

See also China; Holocaust; House, Edward Mandell; Immigration; Italy; Mussolini, Benito; Russia and the Soviet Union; Wilson, Thomas Woodrow; World War II

FURTHER READING

Israel, Fred, ed. *The War Diary of Breckinridge Long.* Lincoln, Nebr., 1966.

Penkower, Monty Noam. *World Diplomacy and the Holocaust.* Urbana, Ill., 1983.

Wyman, David S. *The Abandonment of the Jews: America and the Holocaust.* New York, 1984.

LOUISIANA PURCHASE

(1803)

Approximately 828,000 square miles of territory acquired from France by the United States in a treaty (and other formal agreements) dated 30 April 1803. Emperor Napoleon Bonaparte had abandoned plans for a new empire in North America and sold the city of New Orleans and the vast territory of Louisiana, comprising the western part of the Mississippi River watershed, to the United States for $15 million. The purchase ended a serious threat to national security and doubled the domain of the young Republic. The roots of the purchase go back to the 1670s, when some people in France were cultivating the idea of linking French interests in Canada with the Gulf of Mexico via the Mississippi River. René-Robert Cavelier, Sieur de La Salle, sailed down the Mississippi to its mouth and in 1682 claimed the Louisiana territory for the king of France. French colonization efforts began in the area around 1700 to block British movement into the region, but lack of money, preoccupation with European affairs, and the greater value of the sugar islands in the West Indies relegated Louisiana to a low priority in French foreign affairs throughout most of the eighteenth century.

During the French and Indian War (1754–1763) in North America, and the Seven Years' War in Europe (1756–1763), French policy on Louisiana changed dramatically. In 1761 France offered Louisiana to Spain in return for a declaration of war against Great Britain. Spain (which had never renounced ownership of the area) agreed, but the two countries were not able to defeat the British and, in fact, found that defeat endangered their control of other territories in North America. In the Treaty of Paris of 1763, France, intent on protecting Guadaloupe, Santo Domingo, and other islands in the West Indies, transferred Canada to Great Britain. Spain retained Louisiana but ceded Florida (including the area between New Orleans and Pensacola, known as West Florida) to Great Britain.

During the American Revolution, Spain again fought with the French against the British and at the end of the war regained control of East and West Florida. With the Treaty of Paris of 1783, which ended the War of the American Revolution, the United States gained territory to the Mississippi River and thereby complicated Spanish control of Louisiana. As U.S. citizens settled in the Ohio River valley, they viewed the Mississippi River and the port of New Orleans as the natural highway for their agricultural products. To control U.S. westward expansion, Spain initially closed trade on the Mississippi to western settlers but in 1795 signed the Treaty of San Lorenzo (also known as Pinckney's Treaty), which allowed westerners to use the Mississippi River and to deposit goods in New Orleans for later shipment. French interest in Louisiana intensified following Pinckney's Treaty. Renewal of warfare with Great Britain threatened the ability of the French to supply the West Indian colonies and rekindled the old dream of a French empire in North America. When Spain appeared willing to transfer Louisiana in the late 1790s, the French moved to reacquire the territory.

The undeclared naval war (Quasi-War) between France and the United States in 1798–1800 complicated these plans. U.S. leaders feared an aggressive France on the western border of the United States, and the Quasi-War itself threatened French interests in Louisiana if the United States launched an attack on New Orleans. In the secret Treaty of San Ildefonso of 1 October 1800 Spain turned over Louisiana to France in return for territory in Italy. Napoleon also achieved peace with Great Britain (the Treaty of Amiens in 1802) in order to be free to occupy the territory and planned an expedition to Louisiana for that purpose. Meanwhile, on 16 October 1802, Spanish officials in the territory canceled the right of deposit at New Orleans that Americans had enjoyed under the Treaty of San Lorenzo. Some citizens in the west talked of war to seize New Orleans before the French could establish control.

As early as March 1801, President Thomas Jefferson had heard rumors from western farmers that New Orleans had changed hands from Spain to France. Long-time champion of the economic interests of settlers on the western frontier, Jefferson saw clearly the disadvantages of replacing a weak Spain with a powerful France that might deny Americans access to the Gulf of Mexico. Ever since the publication of his *Notes on the State of Virginia* in 1787, moreover, Jefferson had expressed a strong interest in transcontinental exploration. The pending transfer of the Louisiana Territory to France revived this interest. He prepared to send expeditions westward to map the area while moving to acquire Louisiana from France.

Writing to the U.S. minister in Paris, Robert Livingston, in April 1802, Jefferson put the transfer in crisis terms: "The day that France takes possession of New Orleans fixes the sentence which is to restrain her forever within her low water mark." If France did not dispose of Louisiana, Jefferson threatened an alliance with Great Britain to fight France, by "marry[ing]...the British fleet and nation." The following March, Jefferson dispatched James Monroe as envoy to Paris to offer as much as 50 million francs ($10 million) for New Orleans and French possessions east of the Mississippi (West Florida, he hoped). Before Monroe could arrive, however, the French government had offered to sell New Orleans and everything France owned west of the Mississippi for 60 million francs ($15 million). Monroe worried about the implications of violating his instructions, but nonetheless agreed.

Given his interest in making Louisiana the base for a French empire in North America, why did Napoleon agree to sell the territory to the United States? Scholars have advanced several explanations. First, the troops Napoleon had planned to send to Louisiana went instead to Saint Domingue (present-day Haiti), where most of them died fighting slaves led by François-Dominique Toussaint-L'Ouverture or from tropical diseases. Until Saint Domingue could be pacified, Napoleon's dream of an empire built on sugar production in the Caribbean could not become reality. Louisiana was supposed to have been a source of supply for Haitian sugar plantations. Second, with a renewal of the wars with Great Britain imminent, Napoleon needed money, which the Americans supplied by purchasing Louisiana. Third, Napoleon never abandoned his dream of a North American empire despite the transfer to the United States and planned to pursue it once again, after Great Britain was defeated.

Had France not sold Louisiana, France most likely could not have held the territory in the nineteenth century in the face of U.S. expansionism. Even if France had acquired Florida, which Napoleon saw as essential to controlling the Gulf of Mexico, U.S. interest in both Florida and Louisiana would have remained intense. In addition, the British would have used their navy to block France's recolonization, as they threatened to do if France acquired former Spanish colonies in the 1820s. The French imperial dream did not die, however, and in the 1860s, Napoleon III tried to resurrect a French empire, this time in Mexico. Like his uncle, however, he found the dream elusive.

RONALD L. HATZENBUEHLER

See also American Revolution; Continental Expansion; France; Great Britain; Haiti; Jefferson, Thomas; Lewis and Clark Expedition; Livingston, Robert R.; Monroe, James; Pinckney's Treaty; Spain; Toussaint-L'Ouverture François-Dominique

FURTHER READING

DeConde, Alexander. *This Affair of Louisiana.* New York, 1976.

Jackson, Donald. *Thomas Jefferson and the Stony Mountains: Exploring the West from Monticello.* Urbana, Ill., 1981.

Kaplan, Lawrence S. *Jefferson and France: An Essay in Politics and Political Ideas.* New Haven, Conn., 1967.

Perkins, Bradford. *The First Rapprochement: England and the United States, 1795–1805.* Berkeley, Calif., 1967.

Tucker, Robert W., and David C. Henrickson. *Empire of Liberty.* 1990.

LOVETT, ROBERT ABERCROMBIE

(*b.* 14 September 1895; *d.* 7 May 1986)

Undersecretary of state (1947–1949) and secretary of defense (1951–1953). After service in World War I and graduation from Yale College (1918), Lovett worked as an investment banker. In 1940 he became a special assistant to Secretary of War Henry L. Stimson. As assistant secretary of war for air from 1941 to 1945, he emerged as a strong proponent of strategic bombing. As undersecretary and de facto chief of staff to Secretary of State George C. Marshall from 1947 to 1949, Lovett worked toward the founding of the North Atlantic Treaty Organization (NATO), strongly supported the Berlin airlift, and urged passage of the Marshall Plan. When Marshall became secretary of defense in 1950, Lovett joined the Department of Defense as deputy secretary; he succeeded Marshall in 1951 and helped guide the buildup of the U.S. military during the Korean War. He also supported President Harry S. Truman's dismissal of General Douglas MacArthur. After 1953 Lovett continued to be a valued adviser to the administrations of Presidents Dwight D. Eisenhower, John F. Kennedy, and Lyndon B. Johnson.

SHANE J. MADDOCK

See also Defense, U.S. Department of; Eisenhower, Dwight David; Johnson, Lyndon Baines; Kennedy, John Fitzgerald; Korean War; Marshall Plan; North Atlantic Treaty Organization

FURTHER READING

Isaacson, Walter, and Evan Thomas. *The Wise Men: Six Friends and the World They Made.* New York, 1986.

Sherry, Michael S. *The Rise of Americans Air Power: The Creation of Armageddon.* New Haven, 1987.

Yergin, Daniel. *Shattered Peace: The Origins of the Cold War and the National Security State.* Boston, 1977.

LOYALISTS

British-Americans who opposed overt resistance to British imperial policy between 1764 and 1776 and remained committed to the British Empire during the American Revolution. Numbering about one-fifth of the total population of 2.5 million, some 19,000 joined British military forces during the conflict. Most loyalists came from New York, Georgia, North Carolina, South Carolina, New Jersey, and Massachusetts. Some were Anglican clergymen, officeholders, affluent landowners, or merchants tied to British commerce. Others were poor farmers who supported royal authority against the colonial aristocracy or wished to be protected against Indian attacks. Thousands of African Americans held in bondage sought freedom behind British lines and were also classified as loyalists. Several state governments punished loyalists with imprisonment, loss of property, or fines. As many as 100,000 loyalists fled to Canada or England. In Canada they formed the United Empire Loyalists, which later fought invading Americans in the War of 1812. The Peace Treaty of 1783 ending the Revolution provided in Articles V and VI that loyalists be allowed to return to the United States and reclaim their confiscated property or be compensated for its loss. Because hatred of the loyalists remained strong in the United States, a number of states refused to carry out this provision, even when challenged in the courts. As a result, a majority of the loyalists remained abroad.

REBECCA G. GOODMAN

See also American Revolution

FURTHER READING

Calhoun, Robert M. *The Loyalists in Revolutionary America, 1760–1781.* New York, 1973.

Calhoun, Robert M., Timothy Barnes, and George A. Rawlyl, eds. *Loyalists and Community in North America.* Westport, Conn., 1994.

Nelson, William H. *The American Tory.* Oxford, 1961.

Norton, Mary Beth. *The British-Americans: The Loyalist Exiles in England, 1774–1789.* Boston, 1972.

LUCE, ANN CLARE BOOTHE

(*b.* 10 March 1903; *d.* 9 October 1987)

Author, member of the U.S. House of Representatives (1943–1947), ambassador to Italy (1953–1957), and foreign policy polemicist. Born in New York City and educated in private schools, from 1930 to 1934 Boothe held prominent editorial positions at Vogue and Vanity Fair magazines. In 1935 she married Henry Robinson Luce, publisher of *Time, Fortune,* and *Life* magazines. She achieved fame as a playwright (*The Women,* 1936), war correspondent (for *Life,* 1940–1942), and author (*Europe in the Spring,* 1940). In 1942 Luce won election to the House of Representatives as a Republican from Connecticut. In 1943 she denounced Vice President Henry A. Wallace's proposal for international cooperation as "globaloney." In 1944 she accused President Franklin D. Roosevelt of having "lied" the United States into World War II. A vehement critic in 1945 of the Soviet Union, an ally of the United States at the time, Luce also became a leader of the anticommunist China Lobby. She served as president of the American China Policy Association in 1947–1948 and denounced the Roosevelt and Harry S. Truman administrations. Making ample use of her vitriolic, sarcastic style, Luce in 1952 effectively campaigned for Dwight D. Eisenhower and the rollback of communism. One of the most admired women in America, she remained highly controversial. In 1952, for example, Luce defended Joseph McCarthy and linked the Democratic ticket to Alger Hiss and other alleged traitors.

President Eisenhower named her ambassador to Italy in 1953, making her the first woman to serve as a U.S. envoy to a major nation. Ambassador Luce had, however, antagonized many prominent liberals, and from 1955 the Democrats controlled both houses of Congress. Democratic Senator Wayne L. Morse of Oregon believed that a woman who had accused President Roosevelt of lying the nation into war was not fit to serve the United States in a public capacity. After a bitter public dispute with Morse in 1959, Luce declined the ambassadorship to Brazil. She became convinced in the 1970s that U.S. military strength was declining, and Republican Presidents Richard M. Nixon (1973), Gerald R. Ford (1975), and Ronald Reagan (1982) named her to the Foreign Intelligence Advisory Board.

ROBERT EDWIN HERZSTEIN

See also China Lobby; Foreign Intelligence Advisory Board; Luce, Henry Robinson

FURTHER READING

Hatch, Alden. *Ambassador Extraordinary Clare Boothe Luce.* New York, 1956.

Herzstein, Robert Edwin. *Henry R. Luce: A Political Portrait of the Man Who Created the American Century.* New York, 1994.

Sheed, Wilfrid. *Clare Boothe Luce.* New York, 1982.

LUCE, HENRY ROBINSON

(*b.* 3 April 1898; *d.* 28 February 1967)

Founder of *Time* (1923), *Fortune* (1930), *Life* (1936), and *Sports Illustrated* (1954) magazines. Born to American missionary parents in China and a graduate of Yale University, Luce was responsible for the "March of Time" radio programs and newsreels of the 1930s and 1940s. Luce built his publishing empire by utilizing innovative techniques such as photojournalism and news synthesis and summary to shape and dispense information to an expanding literate, middle-class audience. He was proud of his access to U.S. and foreign leaders. A conservative Republican, vigorous defender of Nationalist China, and ardent anticommunist, Luce used his popular publications to advocate active U.S. global leadership, including intervention in World War II and in Vietnam, and to promote his vision of U.S. hegemony in what he termed the "American century," the subject of a 1941 essay in *Life*. He was married to Clare Boothe Luce and died in Phoenix, Arizona.

DONNA TULLY CUMMINGS

See also Journalism and Foreign Policy; Luce, Ann Clare Boothe

FURTHER READING

Baughman, James L. *Henry R. Luce and the Rise of the American News Media*. Boston, 1987.

Herzstein, Robert E. *Henry R. Luce: A Political Portrait of the Man Who Created the American Century*. New York, 1994.

LUDLOW AMENDMENT

(1938)

Proposed amendment to the U.S. Constitution, sponsored by Democratic Representative Louis L. Ludlow of Indiana, that would have required that any declaration of war passed by Congress be approved by a majority vote of the people before it could go into effect, except in case of attack or threatened attack. After Japanese bombers sank the U.S. naval gunboat *Panay* on the Yangtze River in China in December 1937, Ludlow obtained the 218 signatures required on a petition to discharge his resolution from the House Judiciary Committee. President Franklin D. Roosevelt strongly opposed the amendment, saying it "would cripple any president in his conduct of our foreign relations." On 10 January 1938 the House voted 209 to 188 against the discharge resolution, and the amendment was thus never voted on in Congress. The vote on the discharge resolution was the first of a succession of defeats for noninterventionists on foreign policy issues before World War II, although the degree of congressional and public support for such a radical transformation of foreign policy practice was evidence that isolationist sentiment remained strong.

WAYNE S. COLE

See also Isolationism; Panay Episode; Peace Movements and Societies, 1914 to Present; Roosevelt, Franklin Delano

FURTHER READING

Bolt, Ernest C., Jr. *Ballots Before Bullets: The War Referendum Approach to Peace in America, 1914–1941*. Charlottesville, Va., 1977.

Griffin, Walter R. "Louis Ludlow and the War Referendum Crusade, 1935–1941." *Indiana Magazine of History* 64 (1968): 267–288.

LUSITANIA

A British passenger liner sunk by a German submarine on 7 May 1915, thereby helping to set Germany and the United States on a course toward war. On 4 February 1915 the German government announced that the seas around the British Isles would become a war zone, where submarines would sink enemy merchant vessels on sight and where neutral vessels might also be in danger. The U.S. Department of State replied on 10 February that the German policy was illegal under international law, which required belligerents to provide for the safety of passengers and the crews of merchant vessels. The U.S. note declared that the German government would be held to "strict accountability" for losses of U.S. lives and property. Secretary of State William Jennings Bryan urged President Woodrow Wilson to prevent Americans from entering the war zone, but Wilson insisted the United States must uphold its rights as a neutral nation. The administration had not settled on a policy when an American was killed in the sinking of the British liner *Falaba* on 28 March or when three Americans died in an attack on the U.S. tanker *Gulflight* on 1 May.

Also on 1 May the German embassy published an advertisement in New York newspapers warning Americans that they traveled on Allied passenger vessels at their own risk. Later that day the *Lusitania* sailed from New York, carrying 1,959 passengers and crew, 197 of them American. On 7 May, as the *Lusitania* neared the Irish coast, Lieutenant Commander Walther Schwieger of the German submarine *U-20* sighted the liner through his periscope. At 3:10 p.m. the submarine fired a single torpedo, which struck the *Lusitania* amidships. A huge explosion followed and the liner sank in eighteen minutes, killing 1,198 people, including 128 Americans.

Many Americans believed the sinking warranted a declaration of war on Germany, but the president believed most people wanted the nation to remain neutral and searched for a diplomatic solution. In a series of notes beginning on 13 May, he demanded that Germany pay reparations for the dead Americans and abide in the future by traditional rules of warfare. The Germans refused to apologize, arguing that because the *Lusitania* carried 4,200 cases of small-arms munitions it was a war vessel. Wilson rejected that argument as irrelevant under international law. Secretary Bryan, sure that Wilson's tough stand would lead to war and having failed to persuade the president that the protest to the Germans should be balanced by a protest to the British for their violations of neutral rights, resigned on 8 June after Wilson rejected the secretary's objections and sent the note unchanged.

In Berlin, the *Lusitania* crisis provoked a behind-the-scenes conflict between civilian leaders, who feared war with the United States and its navy. The civilians won on 6 June, when German Emperor William (Wilhelm) II secretly ordered submarines not to attack any passenger ships at all or any merchant vessels if they were unsure of their nationality. For two months U.S.-German tensions relaxed, but on 19 August, the submarine *U-24* mistakenly sank the

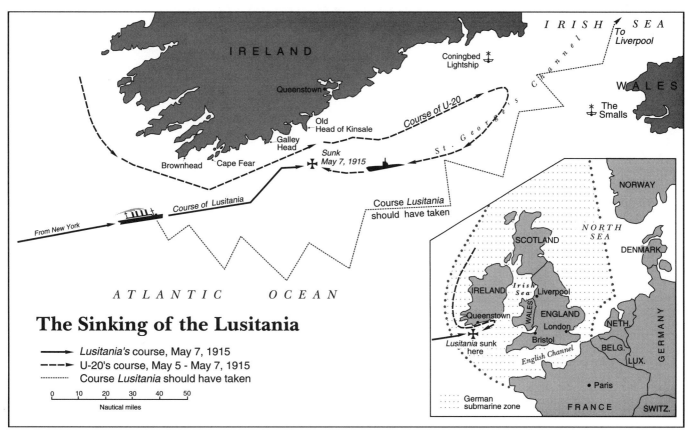

The Sinking of the Lusitania

→ *Lusitania's* course, May 7, 1915

- - -► U-20's course, May 5 - May 7, 1915

.... Course *Lusitania* should have taken

0   10   20   30   40   50
Nautical miles

From *American Foreign Relations*, Thomas G. Paterson, Garry J. Clifford, Kenneth J. Hagan, Volume II. © 1995 by D.C. Heath and Company. Reprinted with permission of Houghton Mifflin Company.

British liner *Arabic*, causing the deaths of two Americans. The German ambassador in Washington, Count Johann Heinrich von Bernstorff, fearing war, pleaded with Berlin to promise publicly that there would be no more unannounced attacks on passenger ships. His issuance of the so-called *Arabic* pledge on 1 September pleased most Americans. In February 1916 the German government promised to pay an indemnity for American lives lost in the *Lusitania* sinking, and the issue was officially closed. When Germany resumed unrestricted submarine warfare early in 1917, however, and discarded its previous pledges, war with the United States followed in April.

KENDRICK A. CLEMENTS

See also Bernstoff, Johann Heinrich; Bryan, William Jennings; Neutral Rights; Submarine Warfare; Wilson, Thomas Woodrow; World War I

FURTHER READING

Bailey, Thomas A., and Paul B. Ryan. *The Lusitania Disaster: An Episode in Modern Warfare and Diplomacy*. New York, 1975.
Simpson, Colin. *The Lusitania*. Boston, 1972.

LUXEMBOURG

See Appendix 2

M

MACARTHUR, DOUGLAS

(b. 26 January 1880; *d.* 5 April 1964)

Commander of the Southwest Pacific Theater during World War II, Allied commander in occupied Japan, and commander of U.S. and UN forces during the first nine months of the Korean War. An officer with a flair for dramatic gestures and political controversy throughout his fifty-two years of military service, MacArthur became the darling of Republican critics of Presidents Franklin D. Roosevelt and Harry S. Truman; he and his supporters accused both presidents of failing to fight the Japanese or the Chinese Communists with sufficient zeal. In 1951 MacArthur's disobedience of the president's order not to express public views on foreign policy without prior approval led Truman to remove him from command. This dramatic confrontation illuminated the clash between an Asian-first (MacArthur) and a Europe-first (Truman) foreign policy. It also contributed to the rise of McCarthyism.

MacArthur was born in Little Rock, Arkansas, and was reared on a series of western army posts where his father was an officer. He graduated from the U.S. Military Academy at West Point, N.Y., in 1903 and served as an engineer officer in the United States, the Philippines, and Panama before joining the general staff of the War Department in 1913. During World War I he fought with the Forty-second Infantry Division and earned numerous decorations for heroism along with promotion to the rank of brigadier general. In 1919 he began a three-year term as superintendent of West Point. He served two tours of duty in the Philippines in the 1920s and was promoted to major general in 1925 and general in 1930. Also in 1930, President Herbert Hoover appointed MacArthur army chief of staff. In that capacity, MacArthur ordered troops to disperse veterans demanding pensions from their encampments in and around Washington, D.C., in 1932. MacArthur's violent handling of the peaceful Bonus Army injured his reputation and led presidential candidate Franklin D. Roosevelt to call him one of the three "most dangerous men in America."

Roosevelt retained MacArthur nonetheless as army chief of staff in his own administration until 1935, when he named him military adviser to the Philippine Commonwealth government. MacArthur spent six frustrating years in Manila trying to organize a modern army capable of defending the archipelago should the United States grant it independence. In July 1941, as tension between the United States and Japan increased, Roosevelt recalled MacArthur to active duty and named him commander of U.S. Army forces in the Philippines. MacArthur underestimated the skill of the Japanese military and overrated the capacity of his own forces to deter or defeat them. On 8 December 1941, the day after the attack on Pearl Harbor, Japanese planes decimated the substantial U.S. air force in the Philippines, and enemy troops soon thereafter swept over the archipelago. For nearly three months MacArthur led a spirited but doomed defense of the Manila Bay region. In March 1942 Roosevelt ordered him to Australia to assume command of the Southwest Pacific Area Theater, one of two commands in the Pacific that fought the Japanese for the next three years.

The high point of MacArthur's achievement during the war in the Pacific came in the fall of 1944 when, despite the opposition of the Joint Chiefs of Staff, he convinced Roosevelt to allow him to liberate the Philippines. In successfully invading Leyte in October, MacArthur fulfilled his dramatic pledge, issued in 1942: "I shall return." Retaking the Philippines did not hasten victory, however, and Japanese troops would continue to fight in Luzon until the end of the war. In December 1944 Roosevelt approved MacArthur's promotion to the rank of general of the army, one of a handful of commanders so honored.

When Japan surrendered in August 1945, President Truman ignored the negative assessment of several advisers and named MacArthur supreme commander, Allied powers (SCAP). For the next six years MacArthur directed the nominally Allied, but almost solely U.S., occupation of Japan. Especially before 1948, MacArthur ran Japan largely as a personal fiefdom, with neither civilian nor military authorities in Washington paying much attention to his actions. He implemented a fairly broad program of economic, social, and political reform in Japan, creating liberal structures and a democratic constitution where none had existed. Still, critics commented, the reforms often proved superficial, leaving entrenched conservative politicians, bureaucrats, and big business in actual control of Japanese society.

MacArthur, who had encouraged a presidential draft for himself in 1944, made no secret of his hope that a successful occupation would strengthen his bid for the Republican presidential nomination in 1948. Many Democrats believed his support for Japanese disarmament and an antimonopoly program—even after the Truman administration concluded that Cold War priorities made them obsolete—represented an effort to appeal to liberal voters at home. MacArthur failed, however, to win a single U.S. primary election in the spring of 1948. After retaining the presidency in the general election that November, Truman reconsidered U.S. policy toward Japan. Leading administration figures such as George Kennan, Dean Acheson, James Forrestal, and William Draper viewed Japan as the "workshop of Asia" that must be rebuilt as an anchor of containment—especially given the Communists' victory in China in 1949—just as Germany was hoped to check Soviet influence in Europe. This required a changed policy toward Japan, sidelining political reform while promoting economic revival. After this shift MacArthur played a diminished role in setting occupation policy and welcomed the outbreak of the Korean War in June 1950 as "Mars' last gift to an old warrior." Even before President Truman decided to commit U.S. forces to the defense of the Republic of Korea, MacArthur began supplying military aid to the embattled South Korean army. His impulsiveness foretold many later conflicts with authorities in Washington.

The Korean War

Citing Republican pressure, Truman named MacArthur commander of both U.S. and UN forces in Korea in July 1950. In this new capacity, MacArthur continually called for a greater commitment of military power. His forceful personality persuaded the wary Joint Chiefs of Staff to authorize the risky amphibious Inchon landing on 15 September 1950, which allowed U.S. forces to break out of their encirclement near the port of Pusan and clear the South of North Korean invaders by early October. MacArthur applauded the administration's subsequent decision to expand the goals of the war to destroy the North Korean regime and unify the peninsula.

Strains had already emerged, however, between the impulsive MacArthur and the Truman administration. In a series of public challenges to Truman during the first months of war, MacArthur visited Taiwan and issued calls to expand the war by utilizing Chinese Nationalist troops to invade the People's Republic of China. Later, as UN forces crossed the 38th parallel into North Korea and approached the border with Manchuria, MacArthur downplayed the danger of Chinese military intervention. At the Wake Island conference of October 1950 he assured Truman that if the Chinese intervened they would be met with "the greatest slaughter" inflicted by American superiority. Privately, MacArthur seemed almost to savor the prospect of Chinese intervention because this might pro-

vide a justification for expanding the Korean War into a more general attack on what he called the communist bloc.

Following China's massive intervention in late November and the subsequent retreat of UN forces south of the 38th parallel, MacArthur clashed frequently with civilian and military superiors. He blamed his problems on restrictions against attacking China and refused to consider seeking an armistice along the prewar boundary. In fact, as the Joint Chiefs of Staff discovered, MacArthur routinely exaggerated the Chinese threat (to make his position seem more desperate) and appeared to fight more vigorously in press releases than on the battlefield. Despite the general's prediction of doom unless the war was expanded, battle lines stabilized in March 1951 as a new field commander, General Matthew B. Ridgway, rallied dispirited U.S.-UN troops. When Truman proposed a cease-fire that month, MacArthur sabotaged the plan by leaking news of it prematurely along with a demand that Chinese forces surrender to him or risk attacks on their homeland. A few days later, the press reported the contents of a letter he had sent to Republican Congressman Joseph Martin condemning Truman's policy in Korea as appeasement. Furious at this partisan challenge to his authority as commander in chief, and fearful that reckless expansion of the war would risk global conflict, the president removed MacArthur from all his commands on 11 April 1951. Two weeks later MacArthur made a dramatic speech to Congress in which he appealed for public support for his strategy. Despite popular appreciation for the general's past service and frustration over the Korean stalemate, neither the average citizen nor most military officers backed his plan to expand the war. Senate hearings into the dismissal of MacArthur revealed that nearly all diplomatic and military experts opposed his strategy. When Korean armistice talks began in July 1951 the public began to lose interest in the subject. In 1952 MacArthur suffered a further disappointment when his former aide and later rival, General Dwight D. Eisenhower, secured the Republican presidential nomination. Eisenhower's election and success in ending the Korean War in July 1953 left MacArthur without a cause. He accepted a job as chairman of the board of Remington Rand Corporation and made occasional public appearances. Shortly before his death he warned Presidents John F. Kennedy and Lyndon B. Johnson against sending ground forces to Vietnam.

MICHAEL SCHALLER

See also Japan; Korean War; McCarthyism; World War II

FURTHER READING

James, D. Clayton. *The Years of MacArthur*, 3 vols. Boston, 1970–1985.

Petillo, Carol Morris. *Douglas MacArthur: The Philippine Years.* Bloomington, Ind., 1981.

Schaller, Michael. *Douglas MacArthur: The Far Eastern General.* New York, 1989.

MACDONALD, JOHN ALEXANDER
(*b.* 11 January 1815; *d.* 6 June 1891)

Key designer of the Dominion of Canada's federal constitution and Conservative prime minister (1867–1873, 1878–1891). When the Dominion of Canada was created in 1867, Great Britain retained ultimate control over Canadian foreign policy, although matters directly involving Canada, such as fisheries, boundaries, trade, and inland navigation, were subject to Canadian approval and/or influence. Thus, when the 1871 Anglo-American High Commission was organized to settle some disputes between the United States and Great Britain, Macdonald was appointed a member to represent Canadian interests. He convinced a reluctant Canadian parliament to ratify those portions of the Treaty of Washington that were of concern to Canadians, including settlement of the water boundary between the state of Washington and New Brunswick and rights of U.S. fishermen in Canadian waters. After winning the 1878 federal election, Macdonald implemented his policy of tariff protection, directed primarily against imports of U.S. goods. Canadian economic continentalists who dominated the Liberal opposition during the late 1880s disputed protection. Macdonald used strident economic nationalism successfully to defend protectionism in his last electoral campaign in 1891, during which he died. Throughout his career Macdonald utilized the traditional anti-Americanism that has flourished in Canada since the loyalists of the American Revolution arrived in the 1780s.

DONALD SWAINSON

See also Canada

FURTHER READING

Creighton, Donald. *John A. Macdonald: The Old Chieftain.* Toronto, 1955.

Smith, Goldwin. *The Treaty of Washington, 1871.* Ithaca, N.Y., 1941.

Swainson, Donald. *Sir John A. Macdonald: The Man and the Politician*, 2nd ed. Kingston, Ont., 1989.

MACEDONIA, FORMER YUGOSLAV REPUBLIC OF

Southernmost of the six constituent republics of the former Federal Socialist Republic of Yugoslavia, Macedonia—as it was known within the federation—declared its independence in September 1991 in the wake of similar moves made by Slovenia and Croatia. It was officially recognized by the United Nations (UN) as the Former Yugoslav Republic of Macedonia (FYROM). A permanent resolution on the FYROM's contested name will depend on the outcome of ongoing negotiations with its southern neighbor, Greece, which claims the (one-word) name "Macedonia," belongs exclusively to its own northern province. This dispute has been a bitter one.

Small in size and landlocked, with a population of approximately two million, FYROM occupies part of an area that has been the flashpoint for numerous local wars since the declining days of the Ottoman Empire and the emergence of various competing strains of Balkan nationalism.

In strictly geographical terms there has never been anything approaching agreement, even among scholars, over the region's formal boundaries. Following local uprisings at the turn of the century and the two Balkan Wars of 1912–1913, most of "ancient" (subsequently Byzantine and Ottoman) Macedonia was divided between Greece, Serbia, and Bulgaria—with today's FYROM emerging as the "South Serbia" of post–World War I Yugoslavia. Greece had inherited the important port of Thessaloníki and its hinterland, while Bulgarian nationalists felt permanently cheated by both of their neighbors. In the event, Yugoslav Macedonia henceforth contained a majority of Serb-affiliated Slavs, with their own language and culture, and a significant minority of disaffected Bulgarians and largely Muslim Albanians. This volatile mix was refashioned by Yugoslav leader Josip Broz Tito in 1945 into the Macedonian Republic. Moreover, Tito—at least in the early postwar years—never let an opportunity go by without taunting both Athens and Sofia with hints of a Belgrade-dominated "Greater Macedonia" still to come.

U.S. involvement in Macedonia was limited in the nineteenth and early twentieth centuries. An 1831 trade agreement with the Ottomans allowed some U.S. commerce in the area, mostly through Thessaloníki. Protestant missionaries from the United States also ventured into the region. The multi-ethnic Macedonian struggle for autonomy from the Turks began with the formation in 1893 of the Internal Macedonian Revolutionary Organization (IMRO), largely Bulgarian-dominated. The bloody but unsuccessful 1903 Ilinden (Saint Elijah's Day) Uprising, led by IMRO against the Ottoman forces, caught Washington's attention if only because of the atrocities committed on all sides. In 1904 President Theodore Roosevelt signed a petition asking the Ottomans to initiate immediate reforms in Macedonia. While unofficial U.S. reaction to the brutality of the Ilinden Uprising was strong, seeing the formation of "Macedonian Committees" in New York and Boston, official U.S. policy still valued friendly relations with Constantinople over purely humanitarian concerns. The rise of the Young Turks in 1908 marked the beginning of the end of the Ottoman Empire, and was the event that added momentum to the Macedonian liberation struggle.

After 1945 and until 1991, official relations between the United States and Macedonia were essentially dictated by those prevailing between Washington and Belgrade. These improved considerably following the 1948 Tito-Stalin rift. With Tito expelled from the Cominform (the Information Bureau of the Communist Parties), Yugoslavia drifted away from the Soviet bloc, and toward freer economic and diplomatic relations with the United States and the West in general. Tito's death in 1980, combined with growing economic problems in all of Yugoslavia, led to a loosening of the ties holding the confederation together and exacerbated long-simmering ethnic animosities in the six republics.

Amidst the general break-up of Yugoslavia, Macedonia elected its first non-communist government in 1990, with Kiro Gligorov emerging as president. In November 1991, a few months after Croatia and Slovenia had declared their independence, Macedonia reluctantly followed suit. However, formal diplomatic recognition by the European Union (EU) and the United States were delayed by the serious dispute that immediately erupted with Greece over the new nation's name and flag. Similar problems ensued in seeking admission to the UN; the new nation was finally admitted in April 1993 and then only under the name Former Yugoslav Republic of Macedonia, or FYROM.

The stability FYROM maintained in its first few years of independence was quite remarkable given both the fate suffered by other ex-Yugoslav republics and the complexity of the threats—external and internal—that the Gligorov government faced. Macedonia has its own ethnic tensions, notably between the majority (Christian) Slavs (about sixty-eight percent of the population in 1991) and a large minority of ethnic (Muslim) Albanians (about twenty-five percent). These internal divisions represent serious disagreements over political power sharing and representation, economic opportunities, and cultural and language issues. While far from "solved," these problems have been relatively well managed by the Gligorov administration, assisted in part through the mediating and oversight efforts of the High Commissioner on Minorities of the Organization on Security and Cooperation in Europe (OSCE), special UN and U.S. diplomatic representatives, and private foundations (the Soros group, in particular).

Slav-Albanian tensions in FYROM also have been influenced by the ongoing Serb-Albanian conflict just over the border in Kosovo—an autonomous region within Serbia, ninety percent Albanian, but also of historic significance to the Serbs as the site of the fabled battle of 1389 in which the Ottoman Turks emerged victorious—as well as by continuing Greek-Albanian tensions. International concern led, in February 1993, to 700 UN peacekeeping troops being deployed on the Macedonia-Kosovo border. These troops originally formed part of the larger UN Protection Force (UNPROFOR), stationed primarily in Croatia and Bosnia; but in April 1995 they were put under their own command and renamed UNPREDEP (UN Preventive Deployment Force). More significantly, they included U.S. troops. Originally, the U.S. contingent was very small—about 325 out of a force of one thousand—and with quite limited duties. But over time they increased in number (520 by April 1994) and began taking on more challenging duties, such as patrolling the tense border with Kosovo. The various efforts of UNPREDEP, the OSCE, and numerous diplomatic missions have been cited as examples of the relative success of preventive diplomacy, in stark contrast to developments in so much of the rest of the former Yugoslavia.

As of mid-1996, tensions with Greece had also begun to subside, following the compromise reached in September 1995 on the flag and a number of other issues, and Greece lifted the embargo it had imposed. But the name issue still remained contentious and unresolved.

JULIA COSENTINO KONMAZ

See also Greece; Serbia; Turkey; Yugoslavia

FURTHER READING

Kofos, Evangelos. *Nationalism and Communism in Macedonia: Civil Conflict, Politics of Mutilation, National Identity*, 2nd ed. New Rochelle, N.Y., 1993.
Perry, Duncan. *The Politics of Terror: The Macedonian Liberation Movements, 1893–1903*. Durham, N.C., 1988.
Pribichevich, Stoyan. *Macedonia: Its People and History*. Philadelphia, 1982.
Vukmanovic, Svetozar. *Struggle for the Balkans*. London, 1990.

MACMILLAN, MAURICE HAROLD
(*b.* 10 February, 1894; *d.* 29 December, 1986)

Prime minister of Great Britain (1957–1963) who repaired and solidified U.S.-British relations, built up Great Britain's nuclear arsenal, oversaw the decolonization of Africa, and helped secure a treaty banning the above-ground testing of nuclear weapons. Educated at Eton and Oxford, Macmillan served as an officer in the British army during World War I and was severely wounded at the Battle of the Somme. After working for Macmillan Publishing Company, the family business, Macmillan gained election to parliament as a Conservative. As Winston Churchill's minister resident at Allied Headquarters in North Africa during World War II, Macmillan established a strong friendship with the Allied commander, General Dwight D. Eisenhower. When the Conservatives returned to power in 1951, Macmillan accepted a series of cabinet appointments. As chancellor of the exchequer in Anthony Eden's government, Macmillan encouraged Eden to recapture by military force the Suez Canal, which Egypt, under Lieutenant Colonel Gamal Abdel Nasser's government, had nationalized. After this venture failed, Macmillan assumed the premiership in January 1957.

Macmillan sought to repair the rift between the United States and Great Britain caused by the Suez Crisis. The long-time friendship with President Eisenhower paid dividends. Macmillan quickly achieved success, measured by Eisenhower's decision to supply Great Britain with sixty Thor intermediate-range missiles, capable of carrying atomic warheads, marking the first time that the United States had traded this technology. When the United States failed to provide Skybolt missiles that it had promised to Great Britain, Macmillan negotiated for the coveted submarine-launched Polaris missiles instead, thus expanding Great Britain's nuclear-weapons capabilities.

Macmillan quickly came to respect President John F. Kennedy, especially after the president's personal acceptance of responsibility for the Bay of Pigs incident in 1961. Macmillan's appointment of Kennedy's long-time friend, David Ormsby-Gore, as British ambassador to the United States further solidified this relationship. At the Nassau talks in December 1961, Macmillan and Kennedy finalized the Polaris sale. Kennedy appreciated Macmillan's advice in Asian affairs, as evidenced in their 1962 agreement for joint support of the neutralist leader Souvanna Phouma in Laos. During the Cuban missile crisis in 1962, Kennedy telephoned Downing Street repeatedly, although Macmillan played little role in the actual decision-making process.

Macmillan's government also saw to the dismantling of Great Britain's African empire. Eight former colonies achieved independence between 1957 and 1963. The Nuclear Test Ban Treaty, ratified 8 October 1963, marked Macmillan's greatest personal triumph. This multilateral agreement banning all atmospheric testing of nuclear weapons had been pursued by Macmillan for more than five years. Shortly thereafter, his government was rocked by the Profumo scandal. This scandal, combined with a faltering economy, forced Macmillan's resignation on 18 October 1963.

CHRISTOPHER M. PAULIN

See also Africa; Eisenhower, Dwight David; Great Britain; Kennedy, John Fitzgerald; Suez Crisis

FURTHER READING

Bartlett, C. J. *The Special Relationship: A Political History of Anglo-American Relations Since 1945*. London, 1992.
Fisher, Sir Nigel. *Harold Macmillan: A Biography*. New York, 1982.
Home, Alistair. *Harold Macmillan*. vols. 1 and 2. New York, 1991.
Macmillan, Harold. *Riding the Storm, 1956–1959*. New York, 1971.
——— . *Pointing the Way, 1959–1961*. New York, 1972.
——— . *At the End of the Day*. New York, 1973.

MACVEAGH, LINCOLN

(*b.* 1 October 1890; *d.* 15 January 1972)

Publisher; U.S. minister to Greece (1933–1941), Iceland (1941–1942), and South Africa (1942–1943); and ambassador to the Greek and Yugoslav governments-in-exile (1943–1944), Greece (1944–1948), Portugal (1948–1952), and Spain (1952). Born in Narragansett Pier, Rhode Island, MacVeagh was the son of Charles MacVeagh, an ambassador to Japan, and grandson of Wayne MacVeagh, a minister to Ottoman Turkey and Italy. He graduated from Harvard in 1913, studied languages at the Sorbonne in Paris (1913–1914), and served with the American Expeditionary Forces during World War I. He worked as an editor for the publisher Henry Holt until 1923, when he founded Dial Press. In 1933, at the recommendation of prominent Democrats in Connecticut, where MacVeagh resided, President Franklin D. Roosevelt named him minister to Greece. His first successful mission was the expulsion from Greece of Chicago financier Samuel Insull, who was under indictment in the United States for fraud. When Nazi Germany occupied Greece in 1941, MacVeagh became minister to Iceland and negotiated the wartime agreement on the important Keflavík Air Base. As minister to South Africa, he helped secure valuable war supplies and facilities for the Allies. As ambassador to the Greek and Yugoslav governments-in-exile (in Cairo), he worked on Allied plans for the liberation of the Balkans.

Before Greece was liberated in the fall of 1944, MacVeagh tried but failed to persuade Roosevelt that the United States had to assume the leading role in postwar southeastern Europe to avert an East-West clash in that region because of competing British and Soviet policies. Despite MacVeagh's eloquent letters, Roosevelt remained unmoved. When civil war broke out in Athens between leftist groups and the newly installed government in December 1944, MacVeagh first attributed the crisis to Greek factionalism and political passions aggravated by British meddling. By August 1946, however, alarmed by the rising level of violence in Greece and the specter of Soviet domination of Eastern and Central Europe, MacVeagh reported that Moscow secretly controlled the Greek communist insurgents. In his testimony before the Senate Foreign Relations Committee in March 1947, he blamed Soviet leader Joseph Stalin for the Greek civil war, an interpretation for which supporting evidence was lacking and one that scholars have largely abandoned. Given the prevailing mood, however, MacVeagh's views offered a powerful endorsement of the Truman Doctrine and the policy of containment.

Ironically, the implementation of the new activist policy he had advocated precipitated his withdrawal from Athens. Although he advocated a strong American role in

Athens, he thought it essential that the appearance of Greece's sovereignty be preserved, and he objected to interference in the work of the local bureaucracy by foreign officials, insisting that his embassy have overall supervision of the American program in Greece. His views clashed with those of the chief of the economic mission, Dwight P. Griswold, a former Republican governor of Nebraska reported to have presidential aspirations. Griswold regarded his personal and frequent intervention in Greek government affairs at all levels as necessary for the success of his mission; he often ignored MacVeagh, whom he considered timid and ineffective. When news accounts of feuding between MacVeagh and Griswold sparked a congressional investigation and Griswold's supporters clamored for MacVeagh's dismissal, President Truman accepted a Department of State recommendation to have MacVeagh recalled (officially for health reasons) and reassigned.

As ambassador to Portugal, MacVeagh facilitated Portugal's adherence to the North Atlantic Treaty in 1949. Unhappy about his forced retirement by President Dwight D. Eisenhower's administration, he made his home in Estoril, Portugal. MacVeagh's clear, precise, and elegant language, his profound knowledge of the history and cultures of Europe and his insights into the policies of the leaders and characters of the people he observed made his dispatches much admired models of diplomatic reporting and analysis.

JOHN O. IATRIDES

See also Greece; Iceland; Portugal; Truman Doctrine

FURTHER READING

Iatrides, John O. *Ambassador MacVeagh Reports: Greece, 1933–1947.* Princeton, N.J., 1980.

MAD

See Mutual Assured Destruction

MADAGASCAR

See Appendix 2; World War II

MADISON, JAMES

(*b.* 16 March 1751; *d.* 28 June 1836)

Architect of the Constitution and the Bill of Rights, author of many of the Federalist Papers, member of Congress from Virginia (1789–1797), secretary of state under Thomas Jefferson (1801–1809), and fourth U.S. president (1809–1817). Born in Orange County, Virginia, Madison

graduated from the College of New Jersey (now Princeton University) in 1771. Madison's contribution to the founding of the United States is unquestioned, but controversies swirled around his belief that economic coercion could force European nations to accept American ideas of free trade and his role in leading the nation to war against Great Britain in 1812.

As a member of the first Congress under the Constitution, Madison wanted the United States to tax British imports more severely than those from other countries to win economic concessions from the British, especially the right to trade with British West Indian colonies. This pursuit of additional markets for U.S. agricultural surpluses has led some scholars to conclude that Madison was a modern-day advocate of mercantilism (a centrally controlled economy to develop colonies for the benefit of the nation) who sought first continental and then global expansion. An alternative view places Madison within a conservative context of Republican ideology, fearful of the worldwide transformation of economic activity from agriculture to commerce to manufacturing. Access to new lands and markets, according to these scholars, would assure the agricultural base of the United States and arrest the nation's development short of the commercial, manufacturing society envisioned by Alexander Hamilton. A third interpretation of Madison downplays the influence of the past on his thinking and emphasizes an interest in establishing a modern society guided by ideas of liberal capitalism instead of Hamilton's economic nationalism. Expanding U.S. commerce, in this view, would stimulate capitalism and individualism, not mercantilism or agrarianism.

Madison also had a pragmatic side, and both as secretary of state and as president he showed a willingness to change course depending on the international situation. When the Embargo Act (1807) and the Non-Intercourse Act (1809) failed to open British and French ports to U.S. trade, Madison devised a plan (Macon's Bill Number 2) in 1810 to trade exclusively with whichever country would repeal its laws regulating U.S. trade. When France's Napoleon Bonaparte appeared to rescind his decrees, Madison opened trade with France and moved toward war with Great Britain. Federalists at the time and numerous historians since have concluded that Napoleon duped Madison into thinking the French would respect U.S. rights to make the United States a partner in France's war against Great Britain.

Other scholars, however, emphasize the fact that during the war Congress (1811–1812), Madison worked closely with Republican party leaders in the House of Representatives to forge a majority consensus for war. Secretary of State James Monroe and Treasury Secretary Albert Gallatin communicated with the key committees (Foreign Relations and Ways and Means) and leaders (especially Speaker of the House Henry Clay) that hammered out the declaration of war against Great Britain.

The war itself severely tested the ability of the young nation to fight against the British, but preoccupation with Napoleon also prevented Great Britain from committing its full strength to the war with the United States. The Treaty of Ghent (1814), which ended the war, said nothing about the causes of the war—impressment, trade restrictions, and threats to national honor and independence—but the British did not insist upon retaining territory along the Great Lakes because the United States had naval superiority on the lakes. Following the war, Madison again proved his resourcefulness by calling for a new national bank (the charter of the First Bank of the United States was not renewed in 1811), a protective tariff for infant manufacturing, and internal improvements to stimulate the development of a national economy.

Historians debate whether Madison's decision for war invalidated his ideas of economic coercion. The Napoleonic Wars limited possibilities for effective U.S. action. Madison might have reached an accommodation with Great Britain short of war, similar to Jay's Treaty (1794), but it is unlikely that the British would have given up their claims to practice impressment, and Madison would certainly have split his Republican party had he moved to appease the British. Such an arrangement would also have meant a rejection of the idea of free trade shared by all of the founders and which succeeding presidents fought to preserve.

After retiring from the presidency, Madison occupied himself with trying to regain control of his Virginia plantation, Montpelier, and devoted most of his public service to local matters. Beginning in 1817 he assisted his friend and neighbor Thomas Jefferson in founding the University of Virginia and succeeded him as chairman of the university's board of visitors when Jefferson died in 1826. In 1829 Madison served as a delegate to the convention that revised Virginia's constitution of 1776. Aside from his association with the American Colonization Society (the group that sought to free American slaves and colonize them in Africa), Madison followed but did not involve himself directly in national concerns until he opposed nullification in the early 1830s and edited his notes on the Constitutional Convention (1787) for publication. Some of his biographers point to these last actions as evidence of Madison's nationalism; others believe they represent his desire to secure Virginia's role as leader of the South.

RONALD L. HATZENBUEHLER

See also Clay, Henry; Economic Sanctions; France; Ghent, Treaty of; Great Britain; Hamilton, Alexander; Impressment; Jefferson, Thomas; Liberia; Napoleonic Wars; Neutral Rights; War of 1812

FURTHER READING

Hatzenbuehler, Ronald L., and Robert L. Ivie. *Congress Declares War: Rhetoric, Leadership, and Partisanship in the Early Republic.* Kent, Ohio, 1983.

McCoy, Drew R. *The Elusive Republic: Political Economy in Jeffersonian America.* Chapel Hill, N.C., 1980.

———. *The Last of the Fathers: James Madison and the Republican Legacy.* New York, 1989.

Rutland, Robert A. *The Presidency of James Madison.* Lawrence, Kans., 1990.

Stagg, J. C. A. *Mr. Madison's War: Politics, Diplomacy, and Warfare in the Early American Republic, 1783–1830.* Princeton, N.J., 1983.

MAHAN, ALFRED THAYER

(*b.* 27 September 1840; *d.* 1 December 1914)

Naval officer, theorist of sea power, and influential commentator on foreign policy. Born in West Point, New York, Mahan attended Columbia University in New York City for two years before graduating from the U.S. Naval Academy in 1859. He spent most of the Civil War on blockade duty off the Confederate coast. His service over the subsequent twenty years was routine, and he was promoted to captain in 1885. That same year, Mahan was selected to lecture on naval tactics and history at the recently established Naval War College in Newport, Rhode Island. In 1886 he became the second president of the college, a position he held until 1889 and again from 1892 to 1893. To his chagrin, Mahan was ordered to sea as commander of the *Chicago* from 1893 to 1895. He retired from the navy in 1896 to devote full attention to his writing, but later served briefly on the Naval War Board in 1898 and as a member of the U.S. delegation to the first International Peace Conference at The Hague in 1899. Despite forty years in the navy and promotion to rear admiral in 1906, Mahan despised and feared the oceans and was a decidedly mediocre seagoing officer.

The admiral's significance derived instead from his work as an author and publicist. Based on his lectures at the Naval War College, he published *The Influence of Sea Power upon History, 1660–1783* in 1890. The two-volume sequel, *The Influence of Sea Power upon the French Revolution and Empire, 1793–1812*, followed in 1892. Mahan directed his arguments even more pointedly to U.S. naval and foreign policies in *The Interest of America in Sea Power: Present and Future* (1897) and through numerous articles in important contemporary periodicals. This corpus of work, together with eight additional books, garnered Mahan international acclaim, substantial royalty income, and extensive influence within the United States.

Mahan argued repeatedly and effectively for U.S. imperialism and for the navy to implement this foreign relations policy. Working within a social Darwinian intellectual framework, he asserted that strategic and economic conflicts among nations inevitably produced wars and that, historically, sea power had determined the victors. More specifically, he contended that U.S. prosperity depended on vigorous commercial expansion to dispose of surplus domestic production. Therefore, both military and economic considerations dictated the construction of a new steam-powered navy and merchant marine. If the United States was to succeed Great Britain as the world's strongest nation economically and militarily, sea power was the essential prerequisite.

Within the navy, Mahan helped seal the strategic transformation from commerce raiding and coastal defense to a blue-water (ocean-going) fleet aimed at battleship engagements. This fleet and strategy embodied U.S. power worldwide after 1890. For policymakers, and the public more generally, he articulated the imperial blueprint that complemented commercial expansion and the new navy. Only by securing insular naval bases, coaling stations, and colonies in the Caribbean, Hawai'i, and the Philippines, by constructing an isthmian canal across Central America, and by exercising hegemony over the Caribbean could the United Stated and its navy effectively protect commerce and national security. In short, Mahan boldly propagated the rationale, the course, and the means for an imperial U.S. foreign policy after 1890.

Although little of this message was original, Mahan deftly synthesized and popularized existing ideas on the interrelations of the U.S. economy, naval power, and international standing. In swaying the general reading public, for whom he consciously wrote, the admiral displayed great skill in isolating central themes and illustrating them with compelling examples. Much of his work combined history and propaganda. His writings and his relentless self-promotion also gave him ongoing access to key policymakers, including Theodore Roosevelt and Henry Cabot Lodge.

JOSEPH A. FRY

See also Colonialism; Imperialism; Navy, U.S. Department of

FURTHER READING

Hagan, Kenneth J. "Alfred Thayer Mahan: Turning America Back to the Sea." In *Makers of American Diplomacy: From Benjamin Franklin to Alfred Thayer Mahan*, edited by Frank J. Merli and Theodore Wilson. New York, 1974.
Seager, Robert II. *Alfred Thayer Mahan: The Man and His Letters*. Annapolis, Md., 1977.
Turk, Richard W. *The Ambiguous Relationship: Theodore Roosevelt and Alfred Thayer Mahan*. Westport, Conn., 1987.

MAINE, USS

The new U.S. Navy battleship destroyed in the harbor of Havana, Cuba, on 15 February 1898, killing 266 U.S. sailors. This tragedy inflamed Spanish-American rela-

tions, which were already strained by the Cuban revolution for independence. A U.S. naval court of inquiry concluded in late March 1898 that an exterior explosion, probably of an underwater mine, caused the disaster. The court, however, did not establish responsibility for the mine explosion. Publication of the naval court's findings provoked a national outcry against Spanish rule in Cuba. The sensational press accused Spanish officials of the crime, and the militant public embraced the vengeful slogan "Remember the *Maine*!" In April 1898 Spain and the United States went to war after diplomacy failed. In 1911 and 1976 U.S. naval investigators reexamined the USS *Maine* disaster. The latter concluded there was no evidence of an external explosion and that an internal bunker fire probably caused the ship's magazines to explode.

JOHN L. OFFNER

See also Spanish-American-Cuban-Filipino War, 1898

FURTHER READING

Rickover, H. G. *How the Battleship Maine Was Destroyed*. Washington, D.C., 1976.
Perez, Louis A., Jr. "The Meaning of the *Maine*: Causation and Historiography of the Spanish-American War." *Pacific Historical Review* 58 (August 1989): 293–322.
Trask, David F. *The War with Spain in 1898*. New York, 1981.

MALAWI

See Appendix 2

MALAYSIA

An independent federation of thirteen states on the Malay Peninsula and the island of Borneo, located in Southeast Asia, bordering the South China Sea between Vietnam and Indonesia. The United States welcomed the independence of Malaya in 1957 and the formation of Malaysia in 1963. The United States and Malaysia have had some disputes since then, but overall U.S.-Malaysian diplomatic relations have remained friendly. The reasons for this amity include Malaysia's contribution to stability in Southeast Asia, the growth of U.S.-Malaysian economic and cultural ties, Malaysia's role in the Association of Southeast Asian Nations, its self-reliant drive to develop its economy and preserve its independence, its strong commitment to the suppression of narcotics trafficking, and its participation in the Five Power Defense Arrangement. The latter involves the United Kingdom, Australia, New Zealand, and Singapore and provides a framework among the parties in the event of an external threat to Malaysia or Singapore.

The United States has cooperated with Malaysia in many areas, including narcotics enforcement, cultural exchanges, and a Fulbright educational exchange program initiated in 1963. For more than twenty years, the Peace Corps maintained an extensive program in Malaysia, and a cumulative total of 3,500 volunteers served there. As Malaysia's economy developed, the Peace Corps program was reduced and then phased out completely in 1983. In the 1980s and 1990s, many Malaysian students came to the United States for tertiary education. Numbering more than 20,000, they formed one of the largest foreign student groups enrolled in American colleges and universities.

U.S.-Malaysian economic and security relations grew during the 1990s. The United States maintained a position as the largest or one of the largest foreign investors, and prospects appeared good for further growth and development of U.S.-Malaysian economic ties. There were few substantial bilateral trade problems. Although Japan used Malaysia as a platform for producing electronic goods for export, and Mitsubishi Motors Corporation coproduced the most popular car in Malaysia, Malaysian officials repeatedly emphasized their desire for U.S. involvement to help the country pursue balanced growth, avoiding excessive dependence on only one outside source of investment and technology.

With regard to their security ties, the United States and Malaysia had increasingly close relations during the 1990s, although officials from both countries chose not to publicize the fact. High level military exchanges, joint exercises, and U.S. military equipment transfers represented important components of the military relationship. Malaysia needed a new fighter aircraft and was offered a MiG 29 aircraft on very attractive terms, but U.S. manufacturers also landed an important sale of F-18 fighter planes in 1993.

U.S.-Malaysian political relations were not as good as economic and security ties during the early 1990s. In part, this reflected a spillover of negative personal feelings between Prime Minister Mahathir Mohammad and leaders in President George Bush's administration, especially Secretary of State James Baker. More basically, it reflected the Malaysian prime minister's continuing tendency to identify Malaysia with Third World or regional positions contrary to U.S. interests. The United States was sometimes suspicious that the prime minister's motives may have had more to do with rallying political support in Malaysia by using the anti-U.S. superpower flag than they had to do with the substance of the issues raised.

Most notable in this regard was the Malaysian prime minister's call for an East Asia Economic Caucus (EAEC). Perceived as a possible trade bloc designed to weaken U.S. influence in Asia, the concept was opposed by the Bush administration, which strongly favored the Asian Pacific Economic Cooperation (APEC) forum, which included the United States. The Malaysians portrayed U.S. opposition in a sometimes sinister light as a superpower force directed at them. Officials in President Bill Clinton's administration adopted a more detached and noncommittal stance on EAEC, while continuing to support APEC. In the minds of some Americans, this modified stance avoided the onus of explicit U.S. opposition, failed to provide a good political target for Malaysian critics, and allowed the EAEC to sink of its own weight because of the reluctance of Japan, China, and other global trading nations to endorse a potential regional trade bloc.

The issue of human rights remained in the forefront of U.S.-Malaysian differences in the mid-1990s. U.S. government officials took a low-key approach to differences over Malaysia's political, economic, and social systems, which they deemed to be prejudicial to Chinese and Indian minorities, who together make up 40 percent of the population. These differences surfaced in the discussion of their respective policies toward the human rights situation in China, Vietnam, and elsewhere. The Malaysians tended to argue strongly that unique Asian cultural factors must be taken into account before applying the Western standards of human rights favored by the United States.

ROBERT G. SUTTER

See also Fulbright Program; Peace Corps

FURTHER READING:

American University. *Area Handbook For Malaysia*. Washington, D.C., 1985.

MALDIVES
See Appendix 2

MALI
See Appendix 2

MALTA CONFERENCE
See World War II

MANCHURIAN CRISIS
(1931–1933)

One of the most important international episodes of Herbert Hoover's presidency, that prompted the promulgation of the Stimson Doctrine. As a prelude to World War II in Asia, the crisis placed a severe strain on U.S.-Japanese relations and tested America's resolve to uphold the Washington Conference on Limitation of Armaments' Nine-Power Treaty of 1922, the Kellogg-Briand Pact of 1928, and the long-standing Open Door Policy. The diplomatic paralysis brought on by the Great Depression best explains the international and U.S. response to this crisis. On 18 September 1931 in Mukden, Manchuria, Japanese and Chinese forces clashed near a Japanese-controlled railroad. This incident marked the culmination of a long series of often violent events surrounding an ongoing power struggle between these two nations. Although it was not known until the war crimes trials after 1945, the Japanese commanders on the spot engineered the confrontation as part of larger plan to make all of Manchuria part of a new Japanese security system.

A major characteristic of the initial crisis was confusion in foreign capitals. Upon learning of the confrontation, U.S. secretary of state Stimson initially suspected that the Sino-Japanese skirmish represented a military mutiny and that moderate, civilian leadership would ultimately prevail. He knew, however, that Japanese leaders considered Manchuria part of imperial Japan's sphere of influence. Japan had maintained a military presence in Manchuria since its defeat of Russia in 1905, and in 1931, 40 percent of Japan's foreign trade and investment were in Manchuria.

The worsening Great Depression complicated Washington's response. One month before the Mukden incident, 158 U.S. banks had closed. Bedeviled by such concerns and with his popularity plunging, Hoover firmly believed from the start that the economic crisis precluded a strong U.S. response in Asia. The president also determined throughout the affair that no vital U.S. interests were at stake. He sought to censure the Japanese for their breach of international law but not to impose strong sanctions that might provoke Tokyo. The majority of Department of State officials supported his caution. Indeed, some U.S. diplomats, such as the ambassador to Japan, Joseph Grew, thought that a Japanese annexation of Manchuria might even benefit the United States. As Japan carried out the economic development of the area, it would need U.S. machinery and other industrial goods, and thus increase U.S. exports in hard economic times. From Geneva, the U.S. consul general, Prentiss Gilbert, informed Hoover that general opinion in the League of Nations firmly opposed any strong measures against Japan. The British government also rejected steps that might antagonize Japan.

As Stimson considered a response to Japanese aggression, he still hoped to preserve good relations because he saw Japan as a buffer for protecting U.S. interests in Asia against Soviet Russia. He decided to try U.S. cooperation with the League of Nations when it took up the issue in October 1931. This effort, however, soon degenerated into a farce of hand-wringing over where the U.S. repre-

sentative should sit at League sessions, because Hoover had instructed that the United States appear as an observer at the League discussions, not a participant. Nonetheless, on 24 October the League of Nations urged the Japanese to withdraw. The U.S. role remained minimal even after Stimson dispatched Hoover's confidant, Charles Dawes, to the League. Dawes sorely and openly lacked any knowledge of Asian affairs. While Dawes attempted to inform himself, Stimson learned on 20 November that the Japanese had proposed a neutral investigatory commission. Secretary Stimson's hopes for an accommodation faded, however, when the Chinese balked at the idea and the Japanese army continued to advance into the south, even though Tokyo had specifically renounced southward expansion.

Livid about this chain of events, Stimson now approached the president about imposing economic sanctions against Japan. Instead, on 9 November, Hoover recommended a policy of nonrecognition of Japanese actions that violated existing treaties. On 10 December, with Japanese and Chinese approval, the League established the Lytton Commission to investigate the incident, but the Japanese southward advance continued. After the fall of the strategic city of Chinchow on 2 January 1932, Stimson decided to act. He drafted what became known as the Stimson Doctrine, which amounted to nonrecognition of the fruits of aggression and violations of the Open Door Policy. On 7 January, following consultations with his advisers and Hoover, Stimson dispatched the brief note to the various powers. Stimson had discussed the policy with the British ambassador, whose reaction seemed favorable, but when the news reached London the Foreign Secretary John Simon refused cooperation. Stimson was not alarmed, realizing that the British faced numerous other international problems, especially in India, not to mention their own economic woes. In any case, as it became clear that Stimson was firm in his position and that the Japanese would ignore this novel form of protest, most of the League of Nations members supported Stimson.

The Japanese response to the new doctrine came quickly. In late January 1932 their forces assaulted Shanghai, carrying the fighting far beyond Manchuria and eventually resorting to aerial bombardment of the civilian population. This attack was much more provocative than the Mukden incident because Shanghai was a major center of Western economic interests. Once again, the United States lodged only diplomatic protests, its leaders believing that the general economic crisis and the reluctance of other powers to act still precluded stronger actions. In February 1932 Tokyo announced the creation of the new "state" of Manchukuo, a puppet regime of the Japanese. Stimson denounced this de facto annexation of Manchuria through a public letter to Senator William

Borah. At the time many diplomats and other observers believed this epistle to be a prelude to strong actions, but Hoover stood firmly against any actions that might lead to war. Yet again, the White House took no positive action; most nations simply refused to recognize Manchukuo. Finally, in October 1932, the League of Nations issued the Lytton Commission's report, which denounced Japan's aggression against China. Tokyo responded by withdrawing from the League in early 1933.

The Manchurian crisis had shown the limits of U.S. power and determination to uphold the Open Door Policy and the Nine-Power Treaty. Few Americans favored war over Manchuria and many feared that economic sanctions against Japan would only strengthen the extremists in Tokyo. Meanwhile, Americans concentrated on their domestic economic crisis.

HUGH D. PHILLIPS

See also China; Grew, Joseph Clark; Hoover, Herbert; Japan; Kellogg-Briand Pact; League of Nations; Open Door Policy; Recognition; Stimson, Henry Lewis; Washington Conference on the Limitation of Armaments

FURTHER READING

Ferrell, Robert. *American Diplomacy in the Great Depression: Hoover-Stimson Foreign Policy, 1929–1933.* Hamden, Conn., 1969.
Iriye, Akira. *After Imperialism: The Search for a New Order in the Far East, 1921–1931.* Cambridge, Mass., 1965.
———. *The Origins of the Second World War in Asia and the Pacific.* New York, 1987.
Ogata, Sadako. *Defiance in Manchuria: The Making of Japanese Foreign Policy.* Berkeley, Calif., 1964.
Thorne, Christopher G. *The Limits of Foreign Policy: The West, the League, and the Far Eastern Crisis of 1931–1933.* New York, 1973.

MANDATES AND TRUSTEESHIPS

Mandates authorized victorious states after World War I to administer under some international supervision the overseas territories of Germany and the Arab territories of Ottoman Turkey. After World War II, trusteeships continued many of the mandates, but transferred Japan's mandate for the Pacific Islands to the United States and put Italian rule of Somalia under international supervision. The mandates system of the League of Nations and the trusteeship system of the United Nations (UN) can be seen as part of two broad international movements: to protect human rights and to promote the end of colonialism. The two systems represented compromises between traditional concepts of Western supremacy and the freedom of imperial powers to do as they would, and progressive ideas. The two systems look much alike, and the trusteeship system was basically an extension, with modest strengthening, of the mandates system. Neither system involved many territories or people. The symbolic significance of the two systems vastly overshadows their immediate effects.

TERRITORIES IN THE MANDATE SYSTEM AND THEIR MANDATORIES

Territory	Mandatory
"A" Mandates	
Lebanon	France
Syria	France
Iraq	France
Palestine	Britain
Transjordan	Britain
"B" Mandates	
Togoland	Britain
Cameroons	Britain
Tanganyika	Britain
Togoland	France
Cameroons	France
Rwanda-Urundi	Belgium
"C" Mandates	
South West Africa	South Africa
The Marianas, Caroline and Marshall Islands	Japan
New Guinea	Australia
Nauru	British Empire exercised through Australia
Western Samoa	New Zealand

The Mandates System

Article 22 of the League of Nations Covenant created the mandates system. Viewed cynically, the article provided a fig leaf for the traditional distribution of the spoils of war. Turkey and Germany had lost the war, and their colonies were divided among the victorious powers exactly according to the division specified in a series of secret treaties negotiated during the war, treaties that were widely criticized when they became public. Reflecting its political sensitivity, the article was written by the Supreme Council at Versailles and not by the League Committee.

To see the article simply as a fig leaf, however, is to ignore the historical background of the article, its provisions, and its effects. The first paragraph of the article declared:

> To those colonies and territories which as a consequence of the late war have ceased to be under the sovereignty of the States which

formerly governed them and which are inhabited by peoples not yet able to stand by themselves under the strenuous conditions of the modern world, there should be applied the principle that the well-being and development of such peoples form a sacred trust of civilization and that securities for the performance of this trust should be embodied in this Covenant.

Control over these territories was not to be transferred outright to the victorious powers; instead they were to be given responsibilities for "tutelage...as Mandatories on behalf of the League" (paragraph 2). The degree of control that could be exercised was to be determined on the basis of the "stage of development of the people, the geographical situation of the territory, its economic conditions and other similar circumstances" (paragraph 3). Mandatories were required to report annually to the League Council (paragraph 7), and a permanent commission was to be established to "receive and examine the annual reports of the Mandatories and to advise the Council on all matters relating to the observance of the mandates" (paragraph 9).

Article 22 reflected a concern for the well-being of peoples in colonies that had been growing throughout the nineteenth century. The antislavery movement was part of this tendering, and at the Brussels conference in 1890 a comprehensive treaty had been signed outlawing the slave trade. The Brussels conference also adopted regulations for the control of liquor and firearms in Africa. Article 22 carried this movement further.

The concept of mandates was first advanced in the United States by George Louis Beer, a distinguished historian who was widely regarded as the most brilliant member of the Inquiry group which, under Colonel Edward M. House, prepared preliminary studies for the guidance of the U.S. delegation at the Paris Peace Conference. The British Labour Party and the Foreign Office also advanced the same suggestion, and it was incorporated in Jan Christian Smuts's *Practical Suggestion*. Both Woodrow Wilson and Lloyd George supported the mandates concept and rejected the arguments of Australia, New Zealand, and South Africa, which preferred outright annexation.

The League Council approved the terms of the mandates. In all, sixteen territories were placed in the mandates system.

Category "A" mandates were those communities that had "reached a stage of development where their existence as independent nations can be provisionally recognized subject to the rendering of administrative advice and assistance by a mandatory until such time as they are able to stand alone" (Article 22, paragraph 4). Category "B" mandates were to be administered as separate territories under conditions prescribed in the agreement establishing the mandate (Article 22, paragraph 5). Category "C" mandates could be administered as an integral part of the mandatory's territory (Article 22, paragraph 6).

The Permanent Mandates Commission was established in 1921, and the system functioned throughout the life of the League. The council nominated members of the commission, and a majority were drawn from states that did not hold mandates. The commission met two times a year, examined reports of the mandatories, questioned the governors and other officials that appeared before it, published the questions and answers, made suggestions, gave commendations and reprimands, and developed a reputation for competence and fairness. F. P. Walters, the deputy secretary general and foremost historian of the League, concluded that "The Mandates Commission left behind a record as satisfactory as that of any of the institutions created by the League."

The mandate for Iraq ended in 1932, when the country became independent and gained admission to the League of Nations. In 1936 France and Syria signed a treaty that specified that the mandate would end in three years and Syria would be admitted to the League. Under this treaty, Lebanon would retain its separate status, and France and Lebanon signed a treaty later in the same year. Lebanon declared its independence in 1941 and Syria in 1944. In a white paper in May 1939, Great Britain proposed that by the end of ten years Palestine might be ready for independence. By the outbreak of World War II, no plans had been made for the independence of the other twelve mandates.

Transformation into the Trusteeship System

Postwar planning in the United States initially focused on extending and strengthening the mandates system. President Franklin D. Roosevelt, Secretary of State Cordell Hull, and others leaned toward establishing a system that would include all colonies and hold imperial powers accountable through international supervision of their colonial rule. There was broad agreement that the powers and authority of the supervisory body should be enhanced. As the war progressed, however, the War Department and the navy became concerned about the application of any supervisory system to Japanese-owned or mandated islands in the Pacific; they preferred outright U.S. control. British prime minister Winston Churchill strongly opposed any weakening of the United Kingdom's authority over the British empire. These conflicts became so severe that the Dumbarton Oaks proposals did not contain any provisions on trusteeship. Decisions taken at the Yalta Conference and in subsequent negotiations filled this gap through compromises.

The United Nations Charter of 1945 reflected the compromises that were made. Chapter XI of the charter

TRUST TERRITORIES WHICH HAVE EXERCISED THE RIGHT TO SELF-DETERMINATION

Togoland under British administration	United with the Gold Coast (Colony and Protectorate), a Non-Self-Governing Territory administered by the United Kingdom, in 1957 to form Ghana
Somaliland under Italian administration	United with British Somaliland Protectorate in 1960 to form Somalia
Togoland under French administration	Became independent as Togo in 1960
Cameroons under French administration	Became independent as Cameroon in 1960
Cameroons under British administration	The northern part of the Trust Territory joined the Federal of Nigeria on 1 June 1961 and the southern part joined the Republic of Cameroon on 1 October 1961
Tanganyika under British administration	Became independent in 1961 (in 1964, Tanganyika and the former Protectorate of Zanzibar, which had become independent in 1963, united as a single State under the name of the United Republic of Tanzania)
Ruanda-Urundi under Belgian administration	Voted to divide into the two sovereign States of Rwanda and Burundi in 1962
Western Samoa under New Zealand administration	Became independent as Samoa in 1962
Nauru, administered by Australia on behalf of Australia, New Zealand and the United Kingdom	Became independent in 1968
New Guinea, administered by Australia	United with the Non-Self-Governing Territory of Papua, also administered by Australia, to become the independent State of Papua New Guinea in 1975
Federated States of Micronesia	Became fully self-governing in free Association with the United States in 1990
Republic of the Marshall Islands	Became fully self-governing in free Association with the United States in 1990
Commonwealth of the Northern Mariana Islands	Became fully self-governing as a Commonwealth of the United States in 1990

From *Basic Facts about the United Nations.* ©1992 by the United Nations

contained a "Declaration Regarding Non-Self-Governing Territories." Article 73 proclaimed that all members of the United Nations that held non-self-governing territories "recognize the principle that the interests of the inhabitants of these territories are paramount, and accept as a sacred trust the obligation to promote to the utmost...the well being of the inhabitants of these territories...." It committed these countries to report regularly to the secretary general "statistical and other technical information of a technical nature relating to the economic, social, and educational conditions in the territories for which they are respectively responsible...."

Chapter XII described the trusteeship system and Chapter XIII the Trusteeship Council. Article 77 of Chapter XII provided that territories under mandate and territories detached from the enemy states would be placed in the trusteeship system and that, in addition, other territories could be voluntarily placed in the system. The terms of the trusteeship would be specified in agreements that would be approved by the General Assembly. Article 76 specified the objectives of the trusteeship, including promoting "the political, economic, social, and educational advancement of the inhabitants of the trust territories and their progressive development toward self-government or independence as may be appropriate to the particular circumstances of each territory and its peoples and the freely expressed wishes of the peoples concerned...." (subparagraph b).

The Trusteeship Council was designated as a principal organ of the United Nations. The council would be comprised of all members administering trust territories, those permanent members of the Security Council that did not administer trust territories, and as many other members of the UN elected by the General Assembly for three-year terms as would ensure that the membership of the council was evenly divided between members that administered trust territories and members that did not. Beyond having the power to consider reports from the administering authorities, the Trusteeship Council could accept petitions from the inhabitants of the territories and conduct periodic visits in the territories.

This enhanced power was counterbalanced by the equality on the council between states that administered trust territories and those that did not, and governments getting the right to appoint representatives to the council, thus departing from the practice of the Permanent Mandates Commission which had a majority of individuals from states that were not mandatories and was comprised exclusively of members appointed in their individual capacity by the League council. The Trusteeship Council was a more political and less technical body than the Mandates Commission.

Article 82 provided that with the agreement of the Security Council part or all of a trust territory could be designated as a strategic area. All functions relating to strategic areas would be exercised by the Security Council, where the permanent members had veto power, rather than the Trusteeship Council.

Ten of the former mandated territories—the two Cameroons, the two Togolands, Tanganyika, Rwanda-Urundi, Nauru, New Guinea, Western Somoa, and the North Pacific Islands (the Marianas, the Carolines, and the Marshalls)—were placed under trusteeship. For the first nine, the former mandatory—Great Britain, France, Australia, or New Zealand, as the case might be—became the administering authority. The United States succeeded Japan as the administering authority for the North Pacific Islands, which were designated as a strategic territory. In addition, Somalia, which had been detached from Italy under the terms of the Italian peace treaty, was also placed under trusteeship with Italy as the administering authority. The terms of the trusteeship agreement for Somalia specified that Somalia should become independent 2 December 1960. No other territories were placed under trusteeship. Great Britain recognized the independence of Transjordan in 1946. The British mandate for Palestine came to an end 14 May 1948, when the state of Israel was proclaimed and war broke out between Israel and the Arab League.

South Africa refused to put South West Africa under trusteeship and argued that it could integrate the territory. The General Assembly, with the backing of the International Court of Justice, insisted that South Africa continued to have international responsibilities with respect to the territory and sought to exercise a form of supervision over South Africa's administration of the territory. In 1966 the General Assembly terminated the mandate agreement, declared South Africa's occupation of the territory illegal, set up a UN Council for Namibia, and changed the territory's name to Namibia. Finally, South Africa changed its position, and after a period that involved considerable UN assistance including electoral supervision, Namibia became independent in March 1990.

The General Assembly also sought to make the modest supervisory mechanisms provided for in Chapter XI function for all non-self-governing territories in ways that were similar to the regimen of the trusteeship system. The Assembly made considerable progress in this direction, especially after the passage, on 14 December 1960, of resolution 1514 (XV), the Declaration on the Granting of Independence to Colonial Countries and Peoples.

Starting in the mid-1950s, the trust territories began to gain independence. After a plebiscite, British Togoland was united with the Gold Coast and formed the new independent state of Ghana on 6 March 1957. The French mandate for Togoland was terminated in 1960, and Togo became an independent state. The French mandate for the Cameroons was also terminated in 1960. Also in 1960, after plebiscites, the Northern British Cameroons joined Nigeria and the Southern British Cameroons joined the newly independent Republic of Cameroon. Somalia gained independence 1 July 1960, five months in advance of the deadline established in the agreement. Tanganyika became independent in December 1961. Western Somoa became independent on 1 January 1962. Rwanda and Burundi became independent on 1 July 1962. Nauru gained independence in 1968 and New Guinea joined Papua and became independent in 1975. Plebiscites or elections were important features of all of these transitions.

The strategic Trust Territory of the Pacific Islands under United States administration was the last territory in the trusteeship system. The Security Council decided in December 1990, that, with the entry into force of the status agreements, the objectives of the trusteeship had been fully attained with respect to the Federated States of Micronesia, the Marshall Islands, and the Northern Mariana Islands. The trusteeship agreement with respect to these three territories was terminated. The agreement with respect to Palau was approved and the trusteeship was terminated in 1994. The Marshall Islands, Micronesia, and Palau became members of the United Nations. The Northern Marianas became a commonwealth of the United States. With the termination of the trusteeships, the Trusteeship Council became an organ with no functions to perform. Given the rules governing its composition, it could not even be constituted and it ceased meeting.

Assessing the Mandates and Trusteeships Systems

Certainly the mandates and trusteeships systems turned out to be more than a fig leaf to cover traditional imperial practices. They symbolized a growing global consensus that outright conquest or transfer of colonial territories could no longer occur without some form of international supervision. In broad historical perspective, the mere existence of the systems probably contributed to the acceleration of decolonization. Declaring that category A mandates were almost ready for independence, stating the aim of the trusteeship system to be preparation for independence, and in the case of Somalia establishing a fixed timetable for independence, all contributed to the international momentum for decolonization. The petitions system, as it developed, gave fighters against colonialism in the territories an international platform that they would not otherwise have had.

The systems probably contributed to improved standards of colonial administration through public accountability and publicity. It would be impossible, however, to argue that those territories placed under mandate or trusteeship were administered more fairly than those that were not. The administration of some of these territories was closely linked with that of other territories (for example, Rwanda and Burundi with the Belgian Congo, Cameroon with neighboring British and French territories, and Tanganyika with Kenya and Uganda). Even where this was not the case, colonial systems tended to have general rather than differential rules. And the United Nations at least partially succeeded in applying the same mechanisms that were developed for the mandates and trusteeships to all non-self-governing territories. The fact that Palestine was a mandated territory did not ensure that its transition to independence would be smooth or peaceful. Nor did the mandates and trusteeships systems ensure that the states that emerged would be democratic and peaceful, or even viable. In the 1990s Iraq and Somalia provided glaring examples to the contrary. The status of the Pacific islands as mandates and trust territories did not prevent Japan from fortifying them and using them in its expansionist efforts, or the United States from conducting nuclear weapon tests in the region.

The mandates and trusteeships systems represented compromises between traditional concepts of Western supremacy and concerns for security on the one hand and broader conceptions of human rights and progressive change on the other, compromises that probably had on balance beneficial consequences for advancing human equality and dignity.

HAROLD K. JACOBSON

See also Colonialism; Dumbarton Oaks Conference; Ghana; Israel; Jordan; League of Nations; Lebanon; Namibia; Pacific Island Nations and U.S. Territories; Palestine (to 1948); Rwanda; Somalia; Syria; United Nations; Versailles of Treaty 1919

FURTHER READING
Castagno, A. A., Jr. "Somalia." *International Conciliation* 522 (March 1959): 339–400.
Chidzero, Bernard T. G. *Tanganyika and International Trusteeship.* London, 1961.
Dugard, John, ed. *The South-West Africa/Namibia Dispute.* Berkeley, Calif., 1973.
Emerson, Rupert. *From Empire to Nation: The Rise to Self-Assertion of Asian and African Peoples.* Cambridge, Mass., 1960.
Haas, Ernst B. "The Reconciliation of Conflicting Colonial Policy Aims: Acceptance of the League of Nations Mandate System." *International Organization* 6 (November 1952): 521-536.
———. "The Attempt to Terminate Colonialism: Acceptance of the United Nations Trusteeship System." *International Organization* 7 (February 1953): 1–21.
Jacobson, Harold K. "Our 'Colonial' Problem in the Pacific." *Foreign Affairs* 39 (October 1960): 56–66.
———. "The United Nations and Colonialism: A Tentative Appraisal." *International Organization* 16 (Winter 1962): 37–56.
McHenry, Donald F. *Trust Betrayed: Altruism vs. Self Interest in American Foreign Policy.* New York, 1975.
Sady, Emil J. "The United Nations and Dependent Peoples." In *The United Nations and the Promotion of the General Welfare.* Washington, D.C., 1957: 815–1017
Wainhouse, David. *Remnants of Empire: The United Nations and the End of Colonialism.* New York, 1964.
Wright, Quincy. *Mandates Under the League.* Chicago, 1930.

MANDELA, NELSON ROLIHLAHLA
(*b.* 1918)

Lawyer, political activist, and president of the Republic of South Africa (1994–). Raised in a prominent African family in rural South Africa, Mandela attended Fort Hare College and the University of Witswatersand and received a law degree in 1942 from the University of South Africa. In Johannesburg, he was one of the founding members of the Youth League of the African National Congress (ANC) in 1944, becoming its president in 1950. Outspoken about its rejection of the new ideology of apartheid, which the National Party had brought to power in 1948, the Youth League became the most influential force within the rejuvenated ANC. Mandela and his colleagues, including Oliver Tambo and Walter Sisulu, moved away from earlier ideas of a racially exclusive African nationalism to a broader ideology of nonracial democracy with socialist leanings.

Mandela was one of the key organizers of the Defiance Campaign of 1952 against the new apartheid laws. Banned by the government from public and political life in 1953, he and Tambo opened a law practice in Johannesburg together. The South African government put Mandela and several other ANC leaders on trial for treason in 1956. Five years later they were finally acquitted, but the slaughter of sixty-nine unarmed black civilians at Sharpeville in March 1960 initiated a further crackdown on all forms of political opposition, including the outlawing of the ANC. Faced with the South African government's utter rejection of peaceful reform, Mandela and his colleagues created an underground military organization in 1961 known as Umkhonto we Sizwe, or Spear of the Nation. Mandela left the country in 1962, seeking international support for the ANC's cause in Africa and Europe and receiving military training in Algeria and Ethiopia. Upon his return later that year, he was arrested and sentenced to life imprisonment (reportedly with the help of the U.S. Central Intelligence Agency).

Faced with the formidable and highly exclusionary system of apartheid orchestrated by the intensely anticommunist National Party government, the ANC created alliances from the 1950s onward with radicals and democrats of all races, including the outlawed South African Communist Party. By contrast, the South African government maintained a very close alliance with the United States and the rest of the anticommunist West. Mandela therefore criticized the United States for supporting apartheid and practicing its own racial segregation, as well as its assistance to the European colonial powers in Africa. Even as he denounced U.S. "imperialism" abroad, however, Mandela continued to express admiration for many of the domestic political institutions and liberties of the United States. In contrast to the United States, the Soviet Union and other communist nations—along with some noncommunist ones—provided political and material support to the ANC throughout its three decades of underground struggle.

By the late 1980s, the South Africa government had become an international pariah, with even the United States undertaking economic sanctions against it. As the Cold War receded, increasing numbers of Americans began to join most of the rest of the world in admiring the long-suffering Mandela and his fellow ANC political prisoners. The new reformist government of President Frederik W. de Klerk released him from prison on 11 February 1990, beginning a halting process of negotiation that culminated in the first nonracial and thus democratic elections in South African history in April 1994. Mandela first visited the United States in June 1990, where he was received with enormous enthusiasm and admiration by both the public and the government. Other visits followed as he sought to raise funds and support for the ANC as it prepared to become the governing party of South Africa. In 1993 Mandela was awarded the Nobel Peace Prize jointly with de Klerk. In May 1994 Mandela became president of South Africa.

THOMAS BORSTELMANN

See also De Klerk, Frederik Willem; South Africa

FURTHER READING

Johns, Sheridan, and R. Hunt Davis, Jr., eds. *Mandela, Tambo, and the African National Congress: The Struggle Against Apartheid, 1948–1990—A Documentary Survey.* New York, 1991.

Meer, Fatima. *Higher Than Hope: The Authorized Biography of Nelson Mandela.* New York, 1990.

Sparks, Allister. *The Past Is Another Country.* N.Y., 1995.

MANHATTAN PROJECT

A research project established by the U.S. Department of War in 1942, during World War II, to develop the world's first atomic bomb. In late 1938 scientists in Germany had discovered the tremendous energy that could be released by splitting the nucleus of a uranium atom. In 1939 several immigrant scientists, led by Leo Szilard and Albert Einstein, who had recently fled the Nazi terror and feared possible development of an atomic bomb by Adolf Hitler, urged the administration of President Franklin D. Roosevelt to launch its own atomic energy research program. For the next two years only basic research on the relevant physical processes ensued. In the fall of 1941, a committee of scientists, chaired by Arthur Compton and including Ernest Lawrence and J. Robert Oppenheimer, urged Vannevar Bush, President Roosevelt's chief science adviser, to initiate a full-scale project to develop an atomic bomb. In 1942, following the Japanese attack on Pearl Harbor and U.S. entry into the wars against both Germany and Japan, the Manhattan Project was established. The project's name came from the official agency in charge—the Army Corps of Engineers Manhattan Engineer District. The official in charge was Major (later Brigadier General) Leslie R. Groves.

A number of university-based research groups—the largest being at Chicago, Berkeley, and Columbia—undertook various elements of the project. A special new laboratory, later known as the Los Alamos National Laboratory, was built in 1943 on a remote mesa in New Mexico to serve as the main Manhattan Project facility. The research was conducted under strict secrecy and in a spirit of great urgency. Some scientists urged that any atomic bomb be tested in unpopulated areas and that international controls be put in place before the bomb was used. By the summer of 1945, when three atomic bombs had been built, their appeals failed to persuade officials in President Harry S. Truman's administration. One was tested successfully in July at the Trinity test site near Alamogordo, New Mexico. On 6 August a B-29 bomber dropped an atomic bomb on Hiroshima, Japan. Three days later the third Manhattan Project bomb was dropped on the Japanese city of Nagasaki. On 14 August Japan surrendered, and World War II was ended.

HERBERT F. YORK

See also Einstein, Albert; Hitler, Adolf; Nuclear Weapons and Strategy; Oppenheimer, Julius Robert; World War II

FURTHER READING

Rhodes, Richard. *The Making of the Atomic Bomb.* New York, 1986.

MANIFEST DESTINY

A phrase used by both contemporaries and, subsequently by, historians to explain the American belief in a natural, if not preordained, advance to national greatness, especially in the course of the nineteenth century. The belief in a national destiny was not peculiarly American; no nation or empire has ever been without it. For Manifest Destiny's proponents in the 1840s, however, it reflected a popular conviction that the United States would rise to political and territorial eminence. They based this belief on the notion that national expansion would occur because of certain unique qualities in the American people—their energy and vigor, their faith in the country's democratic institutions, and their sense of duty to extend the benefits of their civilization to others less fortunate.

John L. O'Sullivan, editor of *United States Magazine and Democratic Review*, reminded the American people in July 1840 that they had been given much and that much would be required from them. He wrote, "We have been placed in the forefront of the battle in the cause of Man against the powers of evil....To no other has been committed the ark of man's hopes....Surely we cannot falter when so much depends upon our perseverance to the end!" The proponents of Manifest Destiny, in the ebullient mood of this era, seldom accepted the possibility of limitations to a universal extension of sound and humane government. They also recognized the significance of the sharp contrast between the United States's dramatic industrial and commercial development and immense agricultural productivity, and the absence of such elements of power and success in the vast regions toward which they believed the hand of Destiny pointed.

The belief in a Manifest Destiny eliminated any U.S. concern for the western Indians or Mexicans. Americans presumed that these people, like the lands they occupied, were destined to be governed by the United States. In fact, proponents of Manifest Destiny anticipated the extension of their civilization over the North American continent. This vision was not lost on Senator James Buchanan of Pennsylvania, who declared in March 1844: "Providence has given to the American people a great and important mission, and that mission they were destined to fulfill—to spread the blessings of Christian liberty and laws from one end to the other of this immense continent." To talk of limiting the American spirit of emigration in any way, he added, "was like talking of limiting the stars in their courses, or bridling the foaming torrent of Niagara." Two years later Congressman John S. Chipman of Michigan predicted with equal assurance that "this continent will be our own; the gentlemen may say it is by Manifest Destiny, or by Adam's will, or by whatever else they will. That destiny was found written in every page of our history."

Because opposition seemed so minimal, contemporaries viewed the prospects of westward expansion as the mere fulfillment of their destiny. Nonetheless, successful expansion across the entire North American continent required something more. This notion of continentalism was detached from reality because it posed no bounds. For O'Sullivan that mattered little. Writing in the New York *Morning News* on 27 December 1845, he declared that it had become "our Manifest Destiny to occupy and to possess the whole of the Continent which Providence has given us."

Expansionists agreed that the country was destined to reach its natural limits, but those natural limits did not coincide at all with the true outer limits of the North American continent. Thomas Hart Benton of Missouri believed the natural limits of the United States ended at the ridge of the Rocky Mountains. Francis Baylies warned the country not to stop at the Rockies. "Our natural boundary," he informed Congress, "is the Pacific Ocean." Expansionists also disagreed on the natural boundary of Texas. Representative C. J. Ingersoll of Pennsylvania found it in the vast deserts between the Rio Grande and the Nueces River. For others it was the Rio Grande itself, but James Gadsden discovered in the Sierra Madre "a natural territorial boundary, imposing in its mountain and desert outlines."

Boundaries proposed by Destiny never seemed to possess any ultimate logic. In January 1846 Robert Winthrop, the conservative Massachusetts Whig, reduced the doctrine of geographical predestination to an absurdity: "It is not a little amusing," he said, "to observe what different views are taken as to the indication of 'the hand of nature' and the pointings of 'the finger of God,' by the same gentlemen, under different circumstances, and upon different subjects." In one direction, Winthrop asserted, they discovered the hand of nature "in a level desert and a second-rate river." But upon turning their gaze toward a different horizon they could find no hand of nature in the loftiest mountains in the universe. The configuration of the continent had lost all significance: "The Rocky Mountains are mere molehills. Our destiny is onward!"

Although Manifest Destiny was a magnificent vision for the ambitious, democratic American people, it had little to do, in fact, with the country's actual expansion. The regions into which the United States ultimately expanded in the 1840s —Texas, California, and Oregon north of the Columbia River—were under the legal jurisdiction of foreign governments that were not motivated by any American notion of Destiny. To acquire these regions required agreements on the specific boundaries desired as well as the necessary money or force.

For U.S. leaders, the burden of policy making lay in defining boundaries in the West that were achievable at a reasonable cost and that would best serve the long-term interests of the country. In Texas the Polk administration decided that the Rio Grande would be an important asset to the country and claimed it as the boundary separating Texas from Mexico. Mexico refused to concede peacefully its claims to the river and only the War with Mexico between 1846 and 1848 enabled the United States to establish it as their own. In the Oregon boundary negotiations of 1818, John Quincy Adams determined that the United States would accept no less than a settlement at the 49th parallel, which would give the United States the great harbor of Puget Sound with access through the Strait of Juan de Fuca. The United States adhered to this maritime objective in subsequent negotiations with Great Britain and included it in the final boundary settlement in 1846.

Like Oregon, the acquisition and setting of boundaries in California were the result of the desire for certain geographical assets. Travelers and hide traders had defined the importance of the marvelous harbors of San Francisco and San Diego. Unable to acquire that frontage on the Pacific through purchase, President James K. Polk incited a war with Mexico by placing an American army in disputed territory along the Rio Grande. The War with Mexico, after May 1846, permitted him to pursue through force what he had failed to acquire through negotiation alone. His specific objective, the California coast as far south as San Diego Bay, was finally achieved through the diplomatic efforts of Nicholas P. Trist, his special agent in Mexico, which ended the War with Mexico. Although the objectives of U.S. territorial policy in the 1840s had nothing to do with the notion of Manifest Destiny, the support for expansionism did help to sustain the costly policies that were required to achieve these territories. Therein lies the contribution of Manifest Destiny to the nation's continental expansion.

Historians have labeled the burst of American expansionism at the end of the nineteenth century as the "new Manifest Destiny." This period of expansionism was largely based on missionary and commercial goals. At the end, it had converted the Caribbean into an American lake; led to the acquisition of the Philippines, Guam, and Puerto Rico; and committed the United States to the Open Door Policy in China.

Thereafter Manifest Destiny left a heritage that continued into the twentieth century in the form of American Exceptionalism—a belief that the country had a superior virtue and obligation to correct the world's ills. Like the earlier idea of Manifest Destiny, Exceptionalism was not accepted by other nations, and it lacked a precise definition of goals and a realistic consideration of how such objectives could be achieved abroad. It is not surprising, then, that American Exceptionalism, despite its perennial appeal, has brought no measurable success to U.S. efforts abroad.

NORMAN A. GRAEBNER

See also Continental Expansion; Mexico, War with; Native Americans; Oregon Question; Polk, James Knox

FURTHER READING

Boime, Albert. *The Magisterial Gaze: Manifest Destiny in the American Landscape Painting.* Washington, D.C., 1991.
Graebner, Norman A. *Manifest Destiny.* Indianapolis, Ind., 1968.
Hietala, Thomas R. *Manifest Design.* Ithaca, N.Y., 1985.
Horsman, Reginald. *Race and Manifest Destiny.* Cambridge, Mass., 1981.
Hunt, Michael. *Ideology and U.S. Foreign Policy.* New Haven, Conn., 1987.
Merk, Frederick. *Manifest Destiny and Mission in American History: A Reinterpretation.* 1963.
Stephenson, Anders. *American Expansionism and the Empire of Right.* New York, 1995.
Weinberg, Albert K. *Manifest Destiny: A Study of Nationalist Expansionism in American History.* Chicago, 1963.

MANN, THOMAS CLIFTON

(*b.* 11 November 1912)

Ambassador to Mexico (1961–1963) and assistant secretary of state for inter-American affairs (1960–1961; 1964). Mann entered the foreign service in 1942, after growing up bilingual in the border town of Laredo, Texas. In December 1963 President Lyndon B. Johnson named Mann, who was the U.S. ambassador to Mexico, to be both assistant secretary and the coordinator of the Alliance for Progress. In March 1964 Mann confidentially informed U.S. diplomats that the Johnson administration's goals in Latin America were the protection of U.S. investments, promotion of economic growth, anticommunism, and nonintervention in internal affairs. By implying that the United States would work with nondemocratic governments and emphasize economic growth more than social change, the Mann Doctrine suggested that the Johnson administration was abandoning the Alliance for Progress's goals of socioeconomic reform within a democratic framework. Claiming fatigue, Mann left the foreign service in 1966. Mann, who had a law degree from Baylor University, settled in Austin, Texas.

STEPHEN G. RABE

See also Alliance for Progress; Johnson, Lyndon Baines; Latin America

FURTHER READING

LaFeber, Walter. "Thomas C. Mann and the Devolution of American Policy: From the Good Neighbor to Military Intervention." In *Behind the Throne: Servants of Power to Imperial Presidents, 1898-1968*, edited by Thomas J. McCormick and Walter LaFeber. Madison, Wis., 1993: 166-203.

Schott, Richard L., and Dagmar S. Hamilton. *People, Positions, and Power: The Political Appointments of Lyndon Johnson*. Chicago, 1983.

Tulchin, Joseph S. "The Promise of Progress: U. S. Relations with Latin America during the Administration of Lyndon B. Johnson." In *Lyndon Johnson Confronts the World: American Foreign Policy, 1963-1968*, edited by Warren I. Cohen and Nancy Bernkopf Tucker. Cambridge, Mass., and New York, 1994: 211-43.

MANSFIELD, MICHAEL JOSEPH

(*b.* 16 March 1903)

Member of U.S. Congress from Montana (1943–1953), U.S. senator from Montana (1953–1977), and U.S. ambassador to Japan (1977–1989). Born in New York City, Mansfield grew up in Montana, served hitches in the U.S. Navy, Army, and Marine Corps; attended the University of Montana (B.A., 1933; M.A., 1937), and taught Asian and Latin American History at that university. As a Democrat, he won election to the U.S. House of Representatives in 1942, where he was appointed to the committee on foreign affairs. In 1944 President Franklin D. Roosevelt dispatched the congressman on a Southeast Asian fact-finding trip, the first of numerous overseas missions Mansfield would undertake for the executive branch over a forty-five year period. These missions complemented Mansfield's life-long commitment to dialogue and exchange as means to international stability; his role as a United Nations delegate for Presidents Harry S. Truman and Dwight D. Eisenhower was a natural extension of this approach to problem solving.

Mansfield's greatest influence came during the Kennedy administration. As Senate majority leader (1961–1977) and member of the Senate Foreign Relations Committee, Mansfield played a significant role in shaping congressional support for the Common Market, the Alliance for Progress, cultural and educational exchange, the Trade Expansion Act, the Peace Corps, and the Nuclear Test Ban Treaty. For Mansfield, a leader of Senate "doves," the Vietnam War represented the repudiation of a world governed by compromise and cooperation.   Mansfield's decision to work against the war's escalation from within, rather than avoid open conflict with Presidents John F. Kennedy, Lyndon B. Johnson, and Richard M. Nixon, failed him badly, and in retrospect the senator viewed his inability to influence the nation's Southeast Asian policy, and to restrain the growing imperial power of the executive branch, as the greatest disappointments of his long congressional career.

Still, no Senate majority leader had ever been as well informed on international issues as Mansfield, and no member of Congress could match his record for overseas fact finding. Recognition of this, coupled with Mansfield's lifelong passion for Asia, won him one of the most significant foreign service positions of the post–World War II period—a 1977 appointment by President Carter as ambassador to Japan. Although Mansfield did not speak Japanese, his composed, low-keyed manner stressing fairness, cooperation, and the necessity for Japanese-American interdependence was instrumental in defusing, but not altogether resolving, trade, militarization, and nuclear weapons policy conflicts between the two countries and in building better working relationships between Washington and Tokyo. Acclaim for Mansfield in Japan was widespread—so much so that in 1981 President Ronald Reagan extended his appointment.

JEFFREY J. SAFFORD

See also Congress; Vietnam War

FURTHER READING

Baldwin, Louis. *Hon. Politician: Mike Mansfield of Montana*. Missoula, Mont., 1979.

Ludwick, Jim. "Mansfield: The senator from Montana." *The Missoulian*, 1988.

MAO ZEDONG

(*b.* 26 December 1893; *d.* 9 September 1976)

The Chinese revolutionary leader who played a pivotal role in shaping Chinese-American relations during the Cold War. In October 1949 he led the Chinese Communist Party (CCP) to nationwide victory in the civil war with the Nationalists and founded the People's Republic of China (PRC), which he ruled until his death. Throughout his life, Mao was motivated by a "revolutionary spirit." He came from Hunan, a seedbed of Chinese nationalism that produced several leaders of the 1911 revolution. As a young farm boy, he rebelled against his father. As a young student, he became a leader of the May Fourth Movement in 1919 against collaborators with foreign imperialists. After helping to found the CCP in July 1921, Mao became one of the greatest revolutionaries in the history of the nation. Receiving no communist indoctrination abroad, he succeeded in seizing power through the creative adaptation of Marxist-Leninist theory to China's realities, leading the CCP in the long war against the Nationalists. He evolved the strategy of organizing the peasantry to encircle the cities and created a successful model of revolution for the Third World. He envisioned the ultimate global application of this strategy, urging the Third World to unite, engulf, and effect the eventual downfall of Western imperialism.

Determined that a "new China" should be totally free of foreign invasion or bullying, however, Mao had mixed feelings about the United States. As an avid student of history, he read a few U.S. history books. Admiring the American Revolution and Abraham Lincoln's Emancipation Proclamation, Mao found some similarities between a "young America" and a "new China." During the anti-Japanese war (1937–1945), he highly valued the United States as China's ally. Immediately after Japan surrendered, Mao hoped that the United States would play an active role in preventing a civil war between the CCP and Sun Yat-sen's Kuomintang (KMT), also known as the Chinese Nationalist party. Late in the summer of 1945, when Major General Albert C. Wedemeyer, Washington's representative to China, guaranteed Mao's "personal safety," Mao met with the Nationalist leader Jiang Jieshi (Chiang Kai-shek). Mao and Jiang, however, did not achieve concrete agreements on how to form a coalition government. In mid-December 1945 President Harry S. Truman sent General George C. Marshall to mediate the CCP-KMT conflict. Mao again welcomed the U.S. effort, but when Marshall's mediation failed, the CCP chairman conceded that "we must completely cast aside illusions about the U.S. government."

As the CCP approached final victory in the civil war in 1949, Mao was increasingly concerned about the possibility of U.S. armed intervention to save Jiang. In Mao's calculation, the United States "would send armed forces to occupy some of China's coastal cities and directly fight against us," or they might "throw in their own forces to blockade China's ports." Even if the United States did not intervene directly, he believed, it would surely try to undermine the CCP's rule through sabotage, espionage, and political infiltration. Mao developed a theoretical concept of the "intermediate zone" which grew out of his understanding of the Cold War. The central argument was that although the United States and the Soviet Union were confronting each other, they were separated by "a vast zone which includes many capitalist, colonial and semicolonial countries in Europe, Asia, and Africa." To Mao, the Cold War period was one in which war between the Soviet Union and the United States would come only after the United States had consolidated its hold on countries within the zone. CCP leaders regarded the Truman Doctrine, the Marshall Plan, the rehabilitation of Germany and Japan, the U.S. occupation of South Korea, and especially U.S. military aid to the KMT and the stationing of U.S. marines along China's coast, as strong evidence of a U.S. struggle for this intermediate zone. As the United States continued to recognize the Nationalists in Taiwan as the government of China and verbally attacked Mao as a puppet of Moscow, the relationship became increasingly hostile.

Expecting the United States to "make trouble," Mao thought the most troublesome spots were the Korean peninsula, the Taiwan Strait, and Indochina. He thus called for military and psychological preparations for possible U.S. intervention. To secure a "strong helping hand," he conceded, his new regime would have to identify itself with the Soviet Union, the chief rival of the United States. After proclaiming in late 1949 that the PRC would lean to the side of the Soviet Union, Mao traveled to Moscow and signed a military alliance treaty with Joseph Stalin in February 1950. As Mao explained: "The basic spirit of the alliance treaty is to prevent the possibility of Japan and its ally [the United States] invading China....With the treaty, we will be able to use it as a big political asset to deal with imperialist countries in the world."

Viewing the United States as China's major threat, Mao was determined to confront the United States in Asia. At the outbreak of the Korean War in June 1950, he wholeheartedly supported North Korea's efforts to "liberate" South Korea. When General Douglas MacArthur's forces pushed the North Koreans north of the 38th parallel and advanced toward the Yalu River, Mao decided to intervene to teach the "arrogant" Americans "a lesson." For more than two and a half years (October 1950–July 1953), as many as 1.2 million Chinese People's Volunteers fought a bloody war in Korea.

Persuaded that the Chinese intervention had forced the United States to a standstill, Mao sought to intensify the conflict in the Taiwan Strait. Proclaiming that China's ultimate goal was to liberate Taiwan, the large island occupied by remnants of the Nationalists and protected by the U.S. Seventh Fleet since June 1950, Mao twice (1954, 1958) ordered military attacks on the offshore islands still defended by the Nationalists, among which Jinmen (Quemoy) and Mazu (Matsu) drew the most attention and sparked Sino-U.S. crises. Meanwhile, Mao committed himself to Ho Chi Minh's "anti-imperialist" movement in Vietnam. Between 1950 and 1955 China had supplied and trained the bulk of Ho Chi Minh's army, and Chinese military and political advisers worked "shoulder to shoulder" with the Vietnamese "comrades" in their attack on the French, including that on the French military post in Dien Bien Phu, a northwestern Vietnamese village. In 1964 Mao promised Ho that China would be North Vietnam's "grand rear area" in its effort to "liberate South Vietnam from the American rule." For eight years China provided North Vietnam with hundreds of thousands of tons of military materiél. A total of 320,000 Chinese regulars, consisting of antiaircraft, naval, railway engineering, transportation, and logistic troops, helped defend North Vietnam.

Mao might have openly intervened in Vietnam had he not been confronted with other external troubles. The Sino-Soviet alliance had been falling apart since 1959. Mao wanted to build a "China Bomb" early in 1955, but

Soviet leader Nikita S. Khrushchev refused to provide nuclear technology. Mao wanted to confront the United States, whereas Khrushchev accused the aggressive Mao of jeopardizing Soviet peaceful-coexistence diplomacy. These former Communist partners wound up in a fierce border war in 1969, causing the Chinese to fear a possible larger-scale attack from Russia. Mao decided to play "the American card" against the Russian "bully." In early 1970 China offered to resume the long disrupted Sino-American ambassadorial talks at Warsaw. Beijing initiated "ping pong diplomacy" by inviting the U.S. table tennis team to visit China in 1971. Shortly thereafter, President Richard Nixon's national security adviser Henry A. Kissinger paid two secret visits to Beijing. Mao explicitly expressed his intention to "normalize" Sino-American relations. As Nixon extended his hand to Premier Zhou Enlai (Chou En-lai) at the Beijing airport on 21 February 1972, Mao relished the advent of a new era of less contentious Sino-American relations, but he died before witnessing the formal establishment of diplomatic relations between China and the United States in 1979.

SHU GUANG ZHANG

See also China; Jiang Jieshi; Jinmen-Mazu Crises; Kissinger, Henry Alfred; Korean War; Nixon, Richard Milhous; Russia and the Soviet Union; Vietnam War; Zhou Enlai

FURTHER READING

Gittings, John. *The World and China, 1922–1972*. New York, 1974.
Goncharov, S. N., John W. Lewis, and Xue Litai. *Uncertain Partners: Stalin, Mao, and the Korean War*. Stanford, Calif., 1993.
Gurtov, Melvin, and Byong Moo Hwang. *China Under Threat: The Politics of Strategy and Diplomacy*. Baltimore, 1980.
Schram, Stuart. *Mao Tse-Tung*. Baltimore, 1972.
Shu Guang Zhang. *Deterrence and Strategic Culture: Chinese–American Confrontations, 1949–1958*. Ithaca, N.Y., 1993.

MARCOS, FERDINAND

(*b.* 11 September 1917; *d.* 28 September 1989)

President of the Philippines from 1965 to 1986. The United States maintained close relations with him until the last days of his rule.

A dynamic member of the Philippine senate, Marcos was elected president in 1965, defeating the incumbent Diosdado Macapagal. Reelected in 1969, he came under attack from student radicals. In September 1972, claiming that the Philippines were threatened by communists, he declared martial law, incarcerated his opponents, and suspended civil liberties.

Marcos received strong support from the U.S. government, which was impressed with his anticommunism, including his support for the United States in the Vietnam War. The United States was interested in retaining control over strategically important military bases in the Philippines. U.S. aid to the Philippines grew steadily, and, thanks to U.S. sponsorship, the World Bank and International Monetary Fund extended large loans to the country. Despite worldwide criticism of human rights violations in the Philippines, Washington placed little pressure on Marcos to reform.

In the early 1980s, as his health declined, the country suffered an economic downturn, and communist insurgence grew. Marcos's hold over the Philippines began to falter. In August 1983, Marcos's chief rival, Benigno Aquino, was assassinated, an event that nearly destroyed Marcos's credibility. Opposition to the Marcos regime grew stronger, and the U.S. government became concerned about the regime's stability. In November 1985, to silence his critics, Marcos decreed presidential elections, held in February 1986. The electorate now clearly favored Corazon Aquino, the widow of Marcos's slain opponent. When Marcos tried to steal the elections by fraud, protest rallies ensued. Defense Minister Juan Ponce Enrile and Fidel Ramos, two longtime Marcos allies, broke with him, and hundreds of thousands of Filipinos flooded Manila's streets in their support. By this time, even U.S. president Ronald Reagan, stalwart supporter of Marcos, recognized that his downfall was near. Marcos fled the Philippines on a U.S. helicopter and died in exile in Honolulu.

GLENN ANTHONY MAY

See also Philippines; Aquino, Benigno S. and Corazon C.

FURTHER READING

Bonner, Raymond. *Waltzing with a Dictator: The Marcoses and the Making of American Policy*. New York, 1987.
Burton, Sandra. *Impossible Dream: The Marcoses, the Aquinos, and the Unfinished Revolution*. New York, 1989.
Rempel, William C. *Delusions of a Dictator: The Mind of Marcos as Revealed in His Secret Diaries*. Boston, 1993.

MARCY, WILLIAM LEARNED

(*b.* 12 December 1786; *d.* 4 July 1857)

Democratic politician and secretary of state from 1853 to 1857. Born in Sturbridge (now Southbridge), Massachusetts, he graduated from Brown University in 1808, studied law in Albany, New York, and served as an officer in the War of 1812. He held various offices in New York: state comptroller from 1823 to 1829; justice of the Supreme Court from 1829 to 1831; U.S. senator from 1831 to 1833; and governor from 1833 to 1838. Marcy served on the Mexican Claims Commission from 1840 to 1842. In 1845 President James K. Polk selected Marcy as secretary of war. Marcy held this post during the War with Mexico.

In 1853 Marcy joined President Franklin Pierce's cabinet as secretary of state. In the four years he held the post he took on dozens of significant foreign policy challenges with skill, intelligence, and a degree of pragmatism not found in other cabinet members of the time. While favoring a more assertive role for the United States in world affairs, he frequently blocked the expansionist dreams of southern cabinet members and filibusters. His handling of a series of conflicts with Great Britain in North America resulted in significantly improved relations. As secretary of State he helped reform international law, directed U.S. diplomats to wear ordinary clothing, improved rights of neutrality among nations, and expanded U.S. trade opportunities. Marcy negotiated two dozen treaties, including the Gadsden Treaty of 1853, which secured U.S. transit rights across Mexico's Isthmus of Tehuantepec; the Marcy-Elgin Reciprocity Treaty of 1854, a treaty with Great Britain which expanded fishing rights in the Atlantic; and a treaty with Denmark to abolish tolls in the Baltic Sea (1857). Though favoring an expansionist policy, he opposed the controversial 1855 Ostend Manifesto to acquire Cuba, which was issued by U.S. diplomats in Europe.

BRUCE D. MACTAVISH

See also Gadsden Purchase; Mexico, War with; Ostend Manifesto; Pierce, Franklin

FURTHER READING

Gara, Larry. *The Presidency of Franklin Pierce.* Lawrence, Kan., 1991.
Learned, H. Barrett. "William Learned Marcy." In *The American Secretaries of State and Their Diplomacy*, edited by Samuel Flagg Bemis. New York, 1928.
Debenham Spender, Ivor. *The Victor and the Spoils: A Life of William L. Marcy.* Providence, R.I., 1959.

MARINE CORPS, U.S.

A component of the Department of the Navy, the Marine Corps was established by resolution of the first Continental Congress on November 10, 1775, and is officially described as being composed of seagoing light infantry. Small marine units were originally carried on Navy ships for purposes of securing hostile ports, harbors and beachheads, repressing pirates operating out of such coastal facilities, serving as boarding parties to capture hostile ships, and similar small-arms and hand-to-hand combat as might be necessary to carry out naval missions.

Quickly building a reputation as fearless professional fighters who could deploy on short notice, marines have served in every U.S. war or warlike action, including China in the nineteenth century; Nicaragua, Haiti, and Mexico in the early twentieth century; World Wars I and II; the Korean and Vietnam wars; the Persian Gulf War; Somalia and Haiti; and almost all other places where the commander in chief in the White House thought a small group of supremely qualified U.S. military personnel could protect U.S. citizens or interests by sudden, hit-and-withdraw commando-style tactics.

The marines' high reputation has worked against them, tempting presidents to order them to help carry out the army's traditional heavy-infantry missions of seizing and holding ground for the long term. For example, because the United States was ill prepared for entry into World War I, marines were thrown into the breach, earning glory in France (almost 12,500 suffering severe casualties from a single brigade) in battles at Chateau Thierry, Belleau Wood, Soissons, St. Mihiel, and Reims. Where the marines carved out whole new ranges of blood-soaked history, however, was in the amphibious assaults of the island-hopping Pacific campaigns of World War II. A bronze version of marines raising the flag at the Battle of Iwo Jima is the centerpiece of the Marine Corps monument in Arlington National Cemetary.

Navy staff units such as the Medical and Dental Corps, Judge Advocate General's Office, Supply Corps, and Chaplains Corps service the marines, as well as the navy. The marines have gained control over basic combat assets including field artillery and tactical aviation. A four-star marine general with the title of Commandant gradually became a fully voting equal member of the Joint Chiefs of Staff after World War II. The marines continue to provide largely ceremonial units on major naval vessels, at embassies, and elsewhere. They are routinely assigned to administrative and teaching staffs of schools such as the Naval Academy and Naval War College (although some marines take umbrage at the fact that no marine has been top officer in charge of either of those elite navy schools), Naval Reserve Officers Training Corp (ROTC) units, and Officers Candidate School (OCS) programs.

The marines are a legendary part of the U.S. armed forces, and they have shrewdly used their status to gain autonomy while remaining part of the navy. They have successfully fought off proposals that they be subsumed by the army.

VINCENT DAVIS

See also Defense, U.S. Department of; Guerrilla Warfare; Haiti; Navy, U.S. Department of; Gulf War of 1990–1991; Somalia; World War I; World War II

FURTHER READING

Millett, Alan R. *Semper Fidelis: The History of the United States Marine Corps.* New York, 1980.
Rottman, Gordon. *U.S. Marine Corps: 1941–1945.* Mechanicsburg, Penn., 1995.

MARSHALL, GEORGE CATLETT, JR.

(*b.* 31 December 1880; *d.* 16 October 1959)

One of the United States's foremost soldiers, secretary of state (1947–1949), and secretary of defense (1950–1951).

Born in Uniontown, Pennsylvania, Marshall graduated from the Virginia Military Institute in 1901; he quickly excelled as a staff officer and student, graduating first in his class at the Fort Leavenworth Infantry and Cavalry School in 1906. For the next thirty years he assumed positions and responsibilities far beyond his rank and consistently impressed his superiors, most notably General John J. Pershing. He won appointment as army chief of staff on 1 September 1939, the day World War II began in Europe. He continued in that post for the duration of the war. After the war he served as special presidential emissary to China (1945–1947) until his appointment as secretary of state. Marshall is generally considered the great organizer of the Allied victory over the Axis powers, and during World War II he became one of the most highly respected and decorated soldiers in U.S. history. He also became one of the most diplomatically knowledgeable and astute, and by the time he became secretary of state he possessed enormous diplomatic experience. Indeed, as one subordinate aptly noted, his entire military career constituted a virtual preparatory course for high-level negotiations.

Marshall's overseas service before 1939 included two tours of duty in the Philippines, one in China, and one in Europe during World War I. In this last assignment he developed an extraordinary reputation for being able to work with allies and organize combined operations. After the war he served as aide to General Pershing, accompanying him throughout Europe as well as in Washington. Marshall also visited Brazil as acting chief of staff in 1939.

The allied, global, and total nature of World War II made Marshall one of the nation's top diplomats as well as soldiers between 1939 and 1945. Winston Churchill noted that it was impossible to divide military from political affairs in a major war, and Marshall's experiences during 1939–1945 clearly verified this generalization. Throughout the war he had dealt with numerous Allied leaders, most notably Churchill and British representatives on the Anglo-American Combined Chiefs of Staff. Marshall participated in numerous wartime strategic conferences with these individuals, including ten summit meetings between Franklin D. Roosevelt and Churchill, and quickly emerged as the "first among equals" within the Combined Chiefs. He also participated in the three tripartite summit conferences with the Soviets (Tehran, Yalta, Potsdam) and one with the Chinese (Cairo). He played a major role in the creation of the Combined Chiefs and the acceptance of the unity of command principle under which all British as well as U.S. air, naval, and ground forces in each theater fought under a single commander. He also championed the Europe-first strategy and the direct, cross-channel approach over British-backed Mediterranean operations. The ensuing strategic arguments were inextricably interwoven with interallied

political issues, and Marshall soon emerged as one of Roosevelt's closest diplomatic as well as military advisers. By 1944–1945 he was drafting many of the president's messages to Allied heads of state and, according to some, serving as a virtual secretary of state.

With Allied victory, Marshall in late 1945 retired as chief of staff, but President Harry S. Truman almost immediately asked him to go to China as his personal emissary with the rank of ambassador to try to settle the civil war between the Nationalists and the Communists. This task proved extremely difficult, and according to many observers was an impossible diplomatic assignment. U.S. willingness to continue to provide the Nationalists with military assistance while Marshall claimed to be an impartial mediator only compounded the difficulties. His enormous prestige and diplomatic ability, nevertheless, led to some notable progress in early 1946. By year's end his mediation effort had collapsed, however, and in his official report he blamed extremists in both camps for the failure. In early 1947 Marshall returned to the United States both to end his failed mission and to replace Secretary of State James F. Byrnes. So great was Marshall's prestige that the Republican-dominated Senate Foreign Relations Committee approved him unanimously and without hearings; the full Senate concurred that same day.

Secretary of State

For the next two years Marshall presided over one of the most significant periods in the history of both the Department of State and U.S. foreign policy. That time witnessed the emergence of Soviet-U.S. conflict, and the U.S. decision to adopt a global, anticommunist foreign policy. As secretary of state Marshall played a major role in defining this internationalist policy, winning public and Republican support for it, and providing the Department of State with the reorganization and prestige needed to implement it successfully. He was assisted by an extraordinary group of subordinates—most notably Dean G. Acheson (who would succeed him in 1949), Robert A. Lovett, Will Clayton, Charles E. Bohlen, and George F. Kennan, whom Marshall selected to head the newly established Policy Planning Staff, and who would soon help author the containment policy.

Marshall strongly supported Truman's 1947 request for aid to Greece and Turkey, but opposed the anticommunist and universalist language of the Truman Doctrine. Furthermore, he was not yet ready to dismiss entirely the possibility of Soviet-U.S. rapprochement. By the end of the Moscow Foreign Ministers Conference in April 1947, however, he had concluded that the Soviets had no interest in cooperation or European recovery, that they were simply waiting for economic chaos and despair to provide them with new opportunities for communist expansion, and that to prevent this result the United States would have to enunciate a clear and specific policy for European reconstruction as soon as possible. He set his subordinates to work on such a policy, and on 5 June at Harvard University publicly enunciated it by inviting the nations of Europe to develop a multilateral plan for economic recovery and integration, and to request assistance from the United States. Once they did, he assumed major responsibility for obtaining public and Republican support for the ensuing multi-billion-dollar appropriation. Officially entitled the European Recovery Program (ERP) and commonly known as the Marshall Plan, it passed Congress in early 1948 and helped initiate the economic revival and integration of Western Europe, including the western occupation zones of Germany.

The Marshall Plan also solidified the growing division of Europe into two camps, however, and was followed by the failed foreign ministers conference in Paris, the Czech coup of early 1948, and the Berlin blockade in June. These events in turn led to the successful Berlin airlift and U.S. counterblockade, accelerated the formation of a federal republic in the western occupation zones of Germany, and led to U.S. agreement to join the North Atlantic Treaty Organization (NATO). Although many of these policies reached fruition in 1949 after Marshall had resigned, he played a pivotal role during 1947–1948 in initiating and obtaining public and congressional support for them. The result was a remarkably successful U.S. participation in the affairs of Europe.

Marshall's efforts proved less successful in other areas of the world. He did attend two inter-American conferences in Rio de Janeiro and Bogotá, which established the Rio Pact and the Organization of American States (OAS), but for the most part Latin American affairs remained a low priority with simmering problems that would explode in the next decade. His efforts to keep China and the Middle East equally low priorities in U.S. foreign policy met with little success. Marshall's World War II and immediate postwar experiences had convinced him that Europe must remain the top priority for the United States, and that China's problems were beyond the power of the United States to resolve. By 1948 he had also concluded that the Nationalist position in the civil war was hopeless. To cease aid to the Nationalists was impossible, however, because of their powerful supporters within the United States— particularly among Republican senators whose votes were needed to pass the European Recovery Program. Marshall consequently agreed to continued but limited aid to the Nationalists, but suppressed the Wedemeyer report which called for greater support. After the Nationalists' 1949 military defeat and retreat to Taiwan, Marshall was fiercely criticized for not providing more support.

In the Middle East, Marshall verbalized Department of State opposition to the partition of Palestine and creation of the separate Jewish State of Israel, and he made brutally clear his belief that domestic politics were interfering with national interests on this issue. Truman nevertheless rejected his advice and supported both partition and early recognition of Israel. Marshall remained completely loyal to Truman and rejected suggestions that he resign over this disagreement.

In late 1948–early 1949 Marshall underwent kidney surgery and retired as secretary of state. After his recovery he agreed to serve as chairman of the Red Cross, but in September 1950 Truman called him out of this semi-retirement to become secretary of defense in the midst of the Korean War. Although his major task was to rebuild the U.S. armed forces for this conflict, he quickly became embroiled in major foreign policy disputes. With McCarthyism in full swing, some Republicans opposed his nomination because of his close association with the Roosevelt and Truman policies, particularly the Europe-first approach. That opposition did not succeed in halting Senate confirmation of his appointment. Criticism continued to build in late 1950 and early 1951, however, as a result of Chinese intervention in the Korean War and the Truman administration's decision to limit the conflict and seek an armistice. When Marshall subsequently recommended and publicly supported the president's decision to relieve General Douglas MacArthur for refusing to accept this limited war and Europe-first policy, Senator Joseph McCarthy and his associates openly accused Marshall of treason. Undaunted by this assault, Marshall nonetheless resigned once the twin crises on the Korean battlefield and in Congress subsided. He went into a long-desired retirement. In 1953 he was awarded the Nobel Peace Prize for the European Recovery Program; he remains the only professional soldier to be so honored.

Most scholars consider Marshall the most notable and important soldier-statesman in U.S. history since George Washington. Marshall's commonly recognized importance for U.S. foreign policy lies primarily in the critical Cold War policies he enunciated, implemented, and won congressional support for during his two-year tenure as secretary of state. These established the foundations for all U.S. Cold War policies over the next forty years. Of perhaps equal importance were the reorganization, prestige, and excellent press relations he gave the Department of State during his tenure and the policies and strategies he championed as World War II army chief and Korean War secretary of defense. These provide a broader perspective on Marshall and his importance in the history of U.S. foreign relations. His record reveals him to have been a strong and important advocate of an internationalist, global role for the United States; of the primacy of Europe over Asia; of the need to make use of economic as well as military tools and limited as well as unlimited war in support of national interests; and of the strict subordination of military to civilian authority.

MARK A. STOLER

See also China; Cold War; Israel; Korean War; McCarthyism; Marshall Plan; Rio Treaty; Truman, Harry S.; Truman Doctrine; World War II

FURTHER READING

Bland, Larry I., ed. *George C. Marshall: Interviews and Reminiscences for Forrest C. Pogue.* Lexington, Va., 1991.
———. *The Papers of George Catlett Marshall*, 3 vols. Baltimore, 1981–1991.
Cray, Ed. *General of the Army: George C. Marshall, Soldier and Statesman.* New York, 1990.
Ferrell, Robert H. *The American Secretaries of State and Their Diplomacy*, vol. 15, *George C. Marshall.* New York, 1966.
Pogue, Forrest C. *George C. Marshall*, 4 vols. New York, 1963–1987.
Stoler, Mark A. *George C. Marshall: Soldier-Statesman of the American Century.* Boston, 1989.

MARSHALL, JOHN

(*b.* 24 September 1755; *d.* 6 July 1835)

Federalist politician and diplomat, secretary of state from 1800 to 1801, and Chief Justice of the U.S. Supreme Court from 1801 to 1835. Raised on the Virginia frontier, Marshall fought in the Continental Army as an infantryman until 1779 and was admitted to the Virginia bar in 1780. He strongly supported ratification of the Constitution and the new government of President George Washington. A leader of the Virginia Federalists, Marshall gained national prominence as a member of the negotiating team sent to settle troubles with France in 1797 and 1798. The mission ended in failure, with Talleyrand's unsavory representatives, known simply as Messrs. X, Y, and Z, insisting on being given money as a prerequisite to negotiations.

On 8 June 1800, Marshall became the country's fourth secretary of state. He was in office for less than nine months but discharged his duties competently and impartially. In contrast to his predecessor, Timothy Pickering, Marshall was a loyal subordinate who had President Adams's complete trust. Adams was away from the nation's capital for extended periods and left Marshall to guide foreign affairs. Marshall despised the French and admired the British, but unlike Pickering, divorced sentiment from the conduct of his office. He sought to protect U.S. interests vis-a-vis France and Great Britain equally as the wars surrounding the French Revolution concluded, and he did everything possible to shepherd the Convention of 1800 through the Senate. The Convention temporarily restored tranquility to U.S.-French relations. In January 1801, Adams named Marshall Chief Justice of the Supreme Court. For the next 34 years, the Virginia-born frontiersman with scarcely any legal training was responsible for a series of landmark, precedent-setting decisions: *Marbury v. Madison* (1803), which established judicial review; *Dartmouth College v. Woodward* and

McCulloch v. Maryland (1819), which safeguarded contractual obligations and expanded federal powers, respectively; and *Gibbons v. Ogden* (1824), which sanctioned the national regulation of interstate commerce.

CLIFFORD L. EGAN

See also Convention of 1800; XYZ Affair

FURTHER READING

Johnson, Herbert A., et al., eds. *The Papers of John Marshall.* Chapel Hill, N.C., 1974–present (in progress).
Montague, A. J. "John Marshall." In *The American Secretaries of State and Their Diplomacy*, edited by Samuel Flagg Bemis. New York, 1928.

MARSHALL ISLANDS
See Appendix 2

MARSHALL PLAN
(1948–1951)

A major U.S. foreign-assistance program officially titled the European Recovery Program (ERP), but popularly named for Secretary of State George C. Marshall. An instrument of early post–World War II U.S. foreign policy, the Marshall Plan also constituted an economic enterprise—a grant of billions of dollars, largely for the purchase of American goods, from the United States to a group of Western European countries for the purpose of aiding the latter to undertake specific economic tasks of reconstruction and reach specific goals within a prescribed period of time. As such, the Marshall Plan occupies a unique place in U.S. foreign aid history. Not only was it the first large-scale U.S. foreign aid program in the postwar period, it was, and still is, the only aid program that stipulated a set of economic objectives and a specific time frame for their fulfillment. The plan's political purpose was to improve Western Europe's capacity to remain noncommunist.

Origins

Following several months of deliberations by administration officials, notably Assistant Secretary of State William Clayton and Undersecretary Dean Acheson, the concept of the Marshall Plan was announced in formal remarks made by Secretary of State Marshall during commencement ceremonies at Harvard University on 5 June 1947. After painting a bleak picture of Europe's economic conditions, he announced that the U.S. government might be prepared to assist the European nations "in a return to normal economic health," through a program designed to provide "a cure rather than a mere palliative." The initiative for drawing up such a program, he added, "must come from Europe," and the program itself "should be a joint one, agreed to by a number, if not all, European nations." Marshall's brief remarks evolved, as intended, into the ERP—a congressionally mandated, four-year program for Western Europe.

The immediate and most pressing consideration behind the U.S. offer to help Europe was the rapid deterioration of the Continent's economies during the severe winter of 1946–1947 and the U.S. perceptions of the consequences of a Western European economic collapse. Several economic and political factors confronted U.S. policymakers during the first half of 1947: the deterioration of U.S.-Soviet relations and the threat—real or imagined—of further communist expansion in Europe; Great Britain's economic and financial difficulties and their political-strategic implications; Germany's economic stagnation and the perceived need to revive its industries and restore productive capacity; internal financial instability in most West European countries; the concern that a continuing dollar shortage and balance-of-payments difficulties in Europe could hinder healthy and unrestricted international trade relationships and thus spell adverse long-term consequences for the U.S. economy; the argument that the key to Europe's economic recovery would be increased European production; the thesis that an improvement in Europe's economic health would, in turn, promote long-run political stability and lasting peace on the continent; and the proposition that Europe's economic as well as political strength must lie in European cooperation and, eventually, unity.

The process of transforming Marshall's statement at Harvard into the legislative act authorizing the ERP stretched over a ten-month period. The process began with the joint drafting by representatives of sixteen European countries (Austria, Belgium, Denmark, France, Greece, Iceland, Ireland, Italy, Luxembourg, the Netherlands, Norway, Portugal, Sweden, Switzerland, Turkey, and the United Kingdom) and the western zones of Germany of a report on European recovery, along lines suggested by U.S. policymakers, and the submission of that document to the U.S. government in late September 1947. A U.S. legislative proposal was then prepared and submitted to Congress on 19 December 1947 and the mobilization of U.S. public support for the Marshall Plan was launched. In their report, the sixteen prospective aid recipients had formally pledged themselves to a series of specific undertakings and presented estimates of required U.S. aid totaling $19.3 billion over a four-year period. The administration of President Harry S. Truman asked Congress to authorize a four-year total of $17 billion, but Congress authorized $5.3 billion for the first twelve months of ERP and insisted that the administration return each year for additional appropriations.

Because Marshall's invitation was extended to all of Europe and was ostensibly a call to improve general human well-being rather than do battle against any specific ideology, the Soviet Union in theory was entitled to participate. The Department of State considered this possibility a "calculated risk." The Soviets sent a delegation to a European preliminary conference in Paris in July 1947 but balked at joining a U.S.-dominated plan. Had the Soviets participated, it is unlikely that Congress would have appropriated the funds. Soviet participation may never have been a credible risk, because Moscow would have been required to provide full information on its economy, cooperate on a basis incompatible with its closed and secret system, and follow U.S. leadership.

Implementation

In April 1948 Congress passed the Economic Cooperation Act, which authorized the ERP and called for the achievement by the countries of Western Europe of "a healthy economy independent of extraordinary outside assistance" by 1952. To that end, the act mandated a recovery plan based on four specific endeavors: a strong production effort; expansion of foreign trade; the creation and maintenance of internal financial stability; and the development of European economic cooperation. The act also provided for the creation of a new U.S. government agency—the Economic Cooperation Administration (ECA)—to administer and disburse ERP funds and to report to Congress, on a quarterly basis, the progress made by the aid recipients. Two weeks after passage of the act, the European countries signed the Convention for European Economic Cooperation, in which they formally bound themselves to work in close cooperation and created a joint organization—the Organization for European Economic Cooperation (OEEC)—to coordinate the implementation of the recovery program and to review the progress achieved by its member countries. The OEEC actually outlasted the Marshall Plan. It continued to function until 1961, when it was transformed into the Organization for Economic Cooperation and Development (OECD), whose members now include the leading economies of the world.

The ERP commenced in April 1948 and terminated on 31 December 1951. During that period, about $12.5 billion, mostly in the form of grants, had been allotted by the ECA to the participating countries. This amount represented approximately 1.2 percent of total U.S. gross national product for 1948–1951, and, on average, about 2.5 percent of the combined national incomes of the recipient countries over the same period. Conventional wisdom has, for the most part, hailed the Marshall Plan as a timely, generous, and extraordinarily successful act of U.S. statesmanship, a foreign policy initiative whose main objective was to help create viable and stable national economies in Western Europe and thereby promote the political strength and stability needed to resist communist subversion and encroachment and secure the survival of a community of free nations in Europe. Indeed, when viewed from a strictly political-strategic perspective, the Marshall Plan can be said to have been highly effective in advancing two major and interrelated U.S. foreign policy goals—the containment of communism in Western Europe and the solidification of a Western alliance under U.S. leadership. To be sure, the ERP was but one of several postwar programs, pacts, and arrangements comprising U.S. containment policy, which had already found expression as early as March 1947 in the Truman Doctrine and aid to Greece and Turkey. During the ERP's official lifetime, two other elements were added: signing of the North Atlantic Treaty in April 1949, soon followed by the formation of the North Atlantic Treaty Organization (NATO); and the congressional enactment of the Mutual Security Act in October 1951, which authorized the Mutual Defense Assistance Program (MDAP). A growing preoccupation with the military defense of the West, further intensified after the outbreak of the Korean War in June 1950, led to an earlier-than-scheduled termination of the Marshall Plan and its replacement by yet another defense-oriented aid program, the Mutual Security Program (MSP). What distinguished the Marshall Plan from the other elements in the overall U.S. policy design was that it was not overtly presented as an anti-Soviet or anticommunist weapon but rather as an economic measure—a measure aimed at promoting economic growth, stability, and political self-confidence. At the same time, however, the Marshall Plan provided a crucial framework for U.S.-European relationships, as well as for inter-European cooperation, a framework within which the other programs could be effectively pursued.

Assessment as an Economic Program

While the Marshall Plan can arguably be considered a highly effective and successful foreign policy measure, its immediate economic accomplishments are less clearcut. That the ERP had a significant and positive impact on Europe's economic growth cannot be doubted. After stagnating throughout much of 1947, European growth accelerated in 1948 and continued at high rates for the next two decades. Some observers in the late twentieth century, however, questioned both the need for the ERP in the first place and its specific contributions to Europe's rapid growth during the 1950s and 1960s. Other observers have argued that although the Marshall Plan did play a needed role in alleviating resource shortages, its main contribution to Europe's economic growth lay primarily in altering the environment for the formation of economic policy. They argued that U.S. aid facilitated the liberalization of production and prices, the restoration of financial stability, and the dismantling of foreign-trade

MARSHALL PLAN AID ALLOTMENTS BY COUNTRY 3 APRIL 1948– 31 DECEMBER 1951 (in millions of dollars)	
RECIPIENT COUNTRY	TOTAL
Austria	634.8
Belgium-Luxembourg	546.6
Denmark	266.4
France	2,576.8
Germany (Federal Republic)	1,317.3
Greece	614.1
Iceland	26.8
Ireland	146.2
Italy	1,315.4
Netherlands	1,000.7
Norway	241.9
Portugal	50.5
Sweden	118.5
Trieste	33.0
Turkey	176.5
United Kingdom	2,865.8
Yugoslavia	61.5[1]
Prepaid freight account	42.5
European Payments Union —capital fund	350.0
Total	12,385.2

[1]Although Yugoslavia received aid, it was not a member of the Organization for European Economic Cooperation and Development.

Source: *First Report to Congress on the Mutual Security Program.* U.S. President. ©1952 by the Government Printing Office, Washington, D.C.

restrictions and controls—all of which accelerated a movement toward market-oriented mixed economies and enabled Europe to return to its underlying growth path more quickly than would otherwise have been possible. Still other scholars suggested that it was the concept of increased productivity, urged by the United States on both European management and labor, that played a key role in promoting Europe's economic growth.

An overall assessment of the Marshall Plan as an economic program must ultimately rest on one central question: To what extent was European economic viability achieved by the time the ERP was terminated? Although Congress, when authorizing the aid program, did not offer precise definitions, the Economic Cooperation Act of 1948 seemed to suggest that economic viability should mean the achievement of a healthy economy independent of extraordinary outside assistance. As mandated by Congress, that goal—a Western European economy sufficiently strong and stable to stand on its own feet without continued U.S. support—was expected to be attained by

1952 through a recovery program based on specific economic undertakings and accomplishments. In other words, the Marshall Plan was designed to provide U.S. financial resources to induce an intensive and speedy economic effort on the part of the European aid recipients. When the short-term results of this effort are tested against the mandated goal and against existing realities at the end of the Marshall Plan, the inescapable conclusion is that Western Europe as a whole did not achieve economic viability by 1952.

That is not to suggest the Marshall Plan failed as an economic program, but rather that, in the short run, it must be judged a qualified success. Of the four specific objectives stipulated in the Economic Cooperation Act, two—a strong production effort and expansion of foreign trade—yielded results far surpassing initial expectations and projections. While industrial production and foreign trade registered spectacular increases, however, agricultural output and overall private consumption levels lagged behind. Moreover, despite the significant expansion of intra-European trade, as well as trade with the rest of the world, Western Europe as a whole had not overcome serious balance-of-payments difficulties. A persistent balance-of-payments disequilibrium and inflation prevailed when the Marshall Plan ended. Although efforts to restore internal financial stability had been somewhat successful by early 1950, the gains made were soon eroded (especially after the outbreak of the Korean War) by expanded government defense budgets, larger imports of high-cost raw materials, and the diversion of domestic resources from civilian to defense production. Renewed inflationary pressures plagued most of the Western European countries from mid-1950 on, and by late 1951 the ground gained in tackling inflation during the first two years of the ERP had largely been lost.

In late 1951 there were also no signs of real progress toward European economic integration. This point is especially worth stressing, because the notion of European integration, or unification, which formally evolved from the initial congressional mandate stipulating economic cooperation, had become a well-established goal of U.S. foreign policy. In the Mutual Security Act of 1951, for example, Congress explicitly declared that one of the purposes of the new aid program, MSP, was to encourage "the economic unification and political federation of Europe." In fact, U.S. policymakers persistently preached the pursuit of European unification throughout the ERP and MSP periods. The most that such proddings accomplished, within the framework of the Marshall Plan itself, was to gain European acquiescence to pursue economic cooperation through intergovernmental machineries (for example, OEEC) for consultation and bargaining. With the exception of the Benelux Customs Union and the newly emerging European Coal and Steel Community, the basic structure of Western Europe's economy and polity remained essentially the same as it had been at the start of the Marshall Plan.

With hindsight, it is possible to suggest that even under the best of circumstances, Western Europe could not have attained economic viability in four years' time, because economic viability required the fulfillment of two conditions: the achievement of a sustainable balance-of-payments equilibrium and the maintenance of adequate per capita real incomes through sufficiently high levels of domestic production. Given Europe's economic posture in 1947–1948, neither one of these conditions could possibly have been achieved by 1952 without drastic, and politically unacceptable, sacrifices of current living standards. Indeed, the congressional stipulation of a particular terminal date for the ERP failed to take into proper account the magnitude of the task facing the European nations in attempting to achieve simultaneously external balance, internal stability, and adequate growth. It also did not allow for the added constraints imposed by the increasing emphasis on military and defense buildups following the Korean War.

Long-Term Impact

Thus, in retrospect, it may be argued that while the Marshall Plan was a one-time, fixed-duration event, its significance lies not so much in its short-term economic results as in its long-term impact. Although the ERP did not enable Western Europe as a whole to achieve economic viability by 1952, it laid a firm basis from which the European nations could generate their own economic momentum. Despite balance-of-payments difficulties and continued dependence on U.S. assistance, most of the Western European economies had reached a point of self-sustaining growth when the ERP ended. This growth continued throughout the 1950s and 1960s and was accompanied by the progressive relaxation of trade and payments restrictions within Europe and the liberalization of trade with the rest of the world—two sought-after goals of U.S. foreign economic policy. By 1960, in fact, Western Europe had become the second most important industrial and trading center in the world. Moreover, the concept of European economic integration, so persistently urged by the United States during the Marshall Plan period, had been translated into concrete terms. In 1957 the six nations (France, Italy, West Germany, and the three Benelux countries) that had earlier formed the European Coal and Steel Community, committed themselves to the establishment of the European Economic Community (EEC) and the European Atomic Energy Community (Euratom). Two years later, in 1959, seven other former ERP participants (Austria, Denmark, Norway, Portugal, Sweden, Switzerland, and the United Kingdom) established the European Free

Trade Association (EFTA). Thus, by 1960 nearly all of the ERP countries had bound themselves in one form of regional economic integration or another. The movement toward closer European integration continued, albeit with many lapses and setbacks, during the 1970s and 1980s, and in late 1991 twelve members of an enlarged European Community signed the Maastricht Treaty for European Unity, providing for the European Economic and Monetary Union. Although the actual contributions of the United States to the cause of European integration cannot and should not be exaggerated, it is nevertheless reasonable to suggest that the cooperative experience and the institutional environment of the Marshall Plan provided a basis for and helped mold Europe's own initiatives in that direction.

As the first large-scale postwar foreign assistance program, the ERP established an organizational-bureaucratic framework and a set of operational guidelines for all subsequent U.S. foreign aid programs. The Marshall Plan and the Economic Cooperation Administration had instituted what has turned out to be a continuous machinery for the administration and implementation of U.S. foreign aid policy. Indeed, in an operational sense, the Marshall Plan can be said to have been preserved to the present day: the ECA became the Mutual Security Agency (MSA) in 1951; the MSA was transformed into the Foreign Operations Administration (FOA) in 1953; the FOA was renamed the International Cooperation Administration (ICA) in 1955; and in 1961 the ICA gave birth to the Agency for International Development (AID), the current foreign aid administration agency. Apart from providing an operational common denominator for subsequent foreign aid programs, the Marshall Plan's real significance was the introduction of the notion of economic assistance as a vital instrument of U.S. foreign policy.

IMANUEL WEXLER

See also Acheson, Dean Gooderham; Clayton, William Lockhart; Cold War; Containment; European Union; Foreign Aid; Marshall, George Catlett, Jr.; Mutual Security Act; Organization for Economic Cooperation and Development; Truman, Harry S.

FURTHER READING

Ellwood, David W. *Rebuilding Europe: Western Europe, America, and Postwar Reconstruction.* New York, 1992.
Gimbel, John. *The Origins of the Marshall Plan.* Stanford, Calif., 1976.
Hogan, Michael J. *The Marshall Plan: America, Britain, and the Reconstruction of Western Europe, 1947–1952.* New York, 1987.
Leffler, Melvyn P. *A Preponderance of Power.* Stanford, Calif., 1992.
Milward, Alan S. *The Reconstruction of Western Europe, 1945–1951.* London, 1984.
Paterson, Thomas G. *Soviet-American Confrontation: Postwar Reconstruction and the Origins of the Cold War.* Baltimore, Md., 1973.
Price, Harry B. *The Marshall Plan and Its Meaning.* Ithaca, N.Y., 1955.
Wexler, Imanuel. *The Marshall Plan Revisited: The European Recovery Program in Economic Perspective.* Westport, Conn., 1983.
Wilson, Theodore A. *The Marshall Plan, 1947–1951.* New York, 1977.

MASSIVE RETALIATION

The first systematic doctrine of deterrence in the Cold War, announced in 1954 during the administration of President Dwight D. Eisenhower. Over the course of the Cold War, the doctrines guiding U.S. nuclear deterrence strategy went through numerous formulations, one of which was massive retaliation. Following the Korean War (1950–1953) the United States enjoyed a substantial superiority in strategic nuclear weapons, and the Eisenhower administration decided to press this advantage as part of its New Look defense policy, which sought to reduce military expenditures by favoring nuclear weapons over conventional forces. In January 1954 Secretary of State John Foster Dulles delivered an address in which he claimed, "The way to deter aggression is for the free community to be willing and able to respond vigorously at places of its own choosing…[and] depend primarily upon a great capacity to retaliate instantly" against any aggressor. Although Dulles did not actually use the phrase, this statement became known as the doctrine of massive retaliation. In essence, Dulles wanted to contain the expansion of the Soviet Union and the People's Republic of China by threatening to use nuclear weapons against them in a confrontation. The doctrine of massive retaliation was criticized by such prominent figures as former army Chief of Staff General Maxwell Taylor, Harvard Professor Henry Kissinger, and Senator John F. Kennedy, who, after his election to the presidency in 1960, replaced this policy with the doctrine of flexible response.

DAN CALDWELL

See also Cold War; Dulles, John Foster; Eisenhower, Dwight David; Flexible Response; Nuclear Weapons and Strategy

FURTHER READING

George, Alexander L., and Richard Smoke. *Deterrence in American Foreign Policy: Theory and Practice.* New York, 1974.
Kissinger, Henry A. *Nuclear Weapons and Foreign Policy.* New York, 1957.
Taylor, Maxwell. *The Uncertain Trumpet.* New York, 1959.

MAURITANIA

See Appendix 2

MAURITIUS

See Appendix 2

MAYAGUEZ INCIDENT
(1975)

A serious diplomatic-cum-military incident with the Cambodian government just as the United States was retreating from Southeast Asia at the end of the Vietnam War. Cambodian gunboats captured the U.S. merchant ship *Mayaguez* and its forty-man crew in the Gulf of Siam off the Cambodian coast on 12 May 1975. President Gerald R. Ford claimed that Cambodia had illegally seized the vessel in international waters and responded with a show of force. A four-day battle ensued between U.S. and Khmer Rouge (communist) forces on the Cambodian mainland and Koh Tang Island, where the crew was mistakenly thought to be detained. U.S. marines secured release of the crew and ship on 15 May, but eighteen servicemen died in the bungled rescue mission on Koh Tang Island. Many Americans commended Ford's expeditious resolution of the crisis because, in the wake of the Watergate scandal and recent communist triumphs in Indochina, the rescue seemed to buoy U.S. credibility as a world power. Critics, however, questioned whether negotiations with Cambodia's new government might have freed the ship and crew without bloodshed.

DEBORAH KISATSKY

See also Cambodia; Ford, Gerald Rudolph; Vietnam War

FURTHER READING

Gabriel, Richard A. *Military Incompetence: Why the American Military Doesn't Win.* New York, 1985.
Guilmartin, John F., Jr. *A Very Short War: The Mayaguez and the Battle of Koh Tang.* College Station, Tex., 1995.
Head, Richard G., Frisco W. Short, and Robert C. McFarlane. *Crisis Resolution: Presidential Decision Making in the Mayaguez and Korean Confrontations.* Boulder, Colo., 1978.
Vandenbroucke, Lucien S. *Perilous Options: Special Operations as an Instrument of U.S. Foreign Policy.* New York, 1993.

MCCARTHY, EUGENE JOSEPH
(*b.* 29 March 1916)

Democratic member of the U.S. House of Representatives (1948–1958) and Senate (1958–1971). Born in Watkins, Minnesota, McCarthy received an M.A. degree from the University of Minnesota in 1939 and taught in both high schools and colleges until he won election to the House of Representatives in 1948. In 1958 he was elected to the Senate, where he gained a seat on the Senate Foreign Relations Committee in 1965. Thoughtful and independent-minded, McCarthy urged greater congressional oversight of U.S. intelligence and opposed arms sales to Third World clients. Skeptical about President Lyndon B. Johnson's bombing policy in Vietnam, the senator denounced the war as "morally unjustifiable"

in 1967 and campaigned for the presidency as a way to end the war. McCarthy's excellent showing in the New Hampshire primary in March 1968, in which he won 42 percent of the vote to President Johnson's 49 percent, contributed to Johnson's withdrawal from the race. McCarthy's bitter barbs at Senator Robert F. Kennedy during the primaries and his endorsement—however reluctant—of Hubert Humphrey after the Democratic National Convention in Chicago disenchanted many of his antiwar followers. His retirement from the Senate in 1971 and his half-hearted runs for the presidency in 1972 and 1976 reinforced, among professional politicians, McCarthy's reputation as a dilettante who preferred poetry to politics. He continued to write and speak on public policy issues.

J. GARRY CLIFFORD

See also Humphrey, Hubert Horatio; Vietnam War

FURTHER READING

McCarthy, Eugene. *The Limits of Power: America's Role in the World.* New York, 1967.
———. *Up 'Til Now: A Memoir.* New York, 1987.

MCCARTHY, JOSEPH RAYMOND
See McCarthyism

MCCARTHYISM

Name given to the era in U.S. domestic political history dominated by Republican Senator Joseph Raymond McCarthy's search for communist subversives in the United States. Speaking in Wheeling, West Virginia, on 9 February 1950, the junior senator from Wisconsin claimed to have a list of 205 "names that were made known to the secretary of state as being members of the Communist party and who nevertheless are still working and shaping policy in the State Department." While not the first public official to raise the issue of communist subversion, McCarthy nonetheless made sensational charges that captured the nation's headlines. In the words of scholars Evan Thomas and Walter Isaacson, McCarthy had "tapped into an old and deep vein of American nativism, a virulent blend of FDR haters, Harvard haters, Wall Street haters, Washington haters, and just plain haters." McCarthy launched a ruthless and often partisan search for communists in the U.S. government, a probe full of lurid accusations and hearsay evidence that uncovered very few subversives but destroyed reputations, demoralized Foreign Service officers (especially Asia specialists), drove the "vital center" of U.S. politics decidedly to the right, and distorted legitimate debate over U.S. foreign policy for decades.

The administration of President Harry S. Truman responded to McCarthy's charges by requesting a Senate investigation. Chaired by Democratic Senator Millard Tydings of Maryland, the special subcommittee held hearings for four months and concluded that McCarthy's accusations were "a fraud and a hoax." Republicans, however, rejected such a conclusion, formally stating that "the pro-Communist policies of the State Department fully justify Joe McCarthy." Republican Senator Robert A. Taft of Ohio told McCarthy, "If one case doesn't work, try another." For the next two years, often in cooperation with Senator Patrick A. McCarran's Internal Security Subcommittee, McCarthy did just that. The senator's accusations became the Republican party's campaign strategy in 1952, summarized in the formula C2K (communism, corruption, and Korea). After the Republican victory in 1952, McCarthy became chair of the Senate Committee on Governmental Operations and used its Permanent Subcommittee on Investigations to continue his crusade against alleged communists in government, targeting the Central Intelligence Agency (CIA) and the U.S. Army as well as the Department of State. Although President Dwight D. Eisenhower privately viewed McCarthy "a pimple on the path of progress," he did little to restrain the senator publicly and refused, as he put it, to get into "a pissing contest with that skunk." McCarthy's own excesses, especially his violations of Senate rules, as demonstrated during the Army-McCarthy Hearings in 1954, led to his censure by the Senate in December 1954. McCarthy died of alcoholism three years later.

U.S. Tradition of Anticommunism

Although in hindsight it is clear that the 40,000 to 50,000 members of the Communist Party in the United States never seriously threatened the security of the United States, the anticommunist paranoia of the McCarthy era had long historical antecedents in what the historian Richard Hofstadter has called the "paranoid style in American politics." The French Revolution stirred fears of foreign radicalism in the United States and led to the Alien and Sedition Acts of 1798; nativism and anti-Masonic movements spawned the Know-Nothing party of the 1850s. The Red Scare of 1919–1920 sprang from the superpatriotic, antiradical, anti-German hysteria of World War I, the victory of Bolshevism in Russia, and widespread labor unrest. At the time, business leaders, nativists, veterans' organizations, professional patriots, and even conservative labor unions backed the short-lived crusade against radicals. In the 1930s conservative opposition to the New Deal, as well as anxieties about foreign-inspired subversives, led to several congressional investigations into "un-American activities," most notably the noisy search by the House Committee on Un-American Activities (HUAC) for subversives in Franklin D. Roosevelt's administration after 1938. A series of antiradical statutes, culminating in the Alien Registration Act (Smith Act) of 1940, required the registration of all aliens and made it illegal to advocate the overthrow of the government by force.

By World War II the anticommunist fervor had expanded beyond its original conservative base. Many new recruits to the cause, including conservative trade unionists and socialists, had themselves been targets of earlier attacks. The Spanish Civil War (1936–1939) intensified the Catholic Church's hostility to "atheistic" communism, as did the Soviet takeover after World War II of traditionally Catholic countries in Eastern Europe. Perhaps the most important converts were former communists and those sympathizers of the Communist party known as fellow travelers, many of whom had broken with Moscow following the Nazi-Soviet Pact of 1939. Fortifying their insiders' knowledge with zealous contrition, such former Communist party members as Whittaker Chambers, Elizabeth Bentley, Louis Budenz, and Herbert Philbrick forged careers for themselves as witnesses and accusers.

Indeed, by the late 1940s there already existed what scholar Ellen Schrecker has called the infrastructure of McCarthyism, namely, a "network of politicians, government officials, businessmen, lobbyists, and others who created and sustained the new politics of anticommunism." Journalists, committee staffers, ex-Communists, and Federal Bureau of Investigation (FBI) agents worked together, shared information, and helped one another find jobs and publishers. FBI director J. Edgar Hoover played a key role. Beginning in 1946 Hoover, a master bureaucrat, carved out a postwar mission for the FBI by mounting a public relations campaign to alert the American public to the need to combat internal communism. Dissatisfied with what he deemed the Truman administration's lax attitude toward subversives, Hoover pressed his superiors in the Justice Department for more vigorous prosecutions. President Truman, even as he worried about an American "Gestapo," deflected partisan criticism by turning over the official campaign against communist subversion to the FBI. Although Hoover pretended to be strictly professional and nonpartisan, he leaked confidential files to right-wing journalists and to politicians on HUAC, which had begun its own hearings and investigations even before McCarthy started his own campaign. When McCarthy needed actual names and evidence to support his lurid charges after his speech in Wheeling, he turned to Hoover, his good friend and fellow racetrack habitué, and Hoover quietly obliged.

Conservative politics alone did not create McCarthyism. The Truman administration's Cold War foreign policy from 1945 to 1950 added its own impetus. Truman's anticommunist rhetoric, which depicted a belated U.S. response to worldwide totalitarian aggression masterminded by Moscow, served to legitimize partisan opposition at home. Ironically, the Truman administration focused on anticommunism abroad partly to persuade fiscally conservative Republicans to appropriate billions for the reconstruction of Western Europe. In nurturing a bipartisan consensus, moreover, Truman heeded the advice of Michigan Republican Senator Arthur H. Vandenberg to "scare the hell" out of the American people and thus created a more conservative political climate that played down reform at home and negotiations overseas. Right-wing critics merely extended the logic of the Truman Doctrine's pledge to "support free peoples" everywhere when they condemned the Yalta "sellout," blamed the Democrats for "losing China," and followed General Douglas MacArthur in demanding full victory in the Korean War. Having argued that communists threatened national security in the international arena, the Truman administration could not deny the threat of internal subversion without puncturing its own anticommunist credentials.

McCarthy thus launched his anticommunist crusade at an opportune time. Some two weeks before his address in Wheeling, a jury had convicted former Department of State official Alger Hiss of perjury for having lied when he denied passing classified documents to a communist agent named Whittaker Chambers. Although scholars still dispute whether Hiss was actually a spy, the Hiss trial and other episodes—the *Amerasia* case (1945), the Igor Gouzenko spy-ring in Canada (1946), the Gubitchev-Coplon atomic spy case (1946)—made espionage a legitimate public concern. Republicans such as California Representative Richard M. Nixon, who had pursued the Hiss case as a member of HUAC, insinuated that Hiss was only the tip of a vast New Deal of State Department plot to surrender secrets and territories to Soviet Russia. When Secretary of State Dean G. Acheson responded to Hiss's conviction by pledging "not to turn my back on Alger Hiss," this intended gesture of charity to a former colleague provoked only anger and vitriol from right-wing Republicans whom Acheson called the "primitives." Taking advantage of the fear and frustration engendered by the recent communist victory in China and the Soviet acquisition of atomic weapons, McCarthy singled out Acheson—"this pompous diplomat in striped pants with the phony British accent"— as the official most responsible for harboring alleged communists within the Department of State. A year later the Wisconsin senator went so far as to designate Acheson's predecessor, George C. Marshall, as the mastermind of "a conspiracy so immense and an infamy so black as to dwarf any previous such venture in the history of man."

McCarthy's charges severely wounded the Department of State. The announcement, some two weeks after the Wheeling speech in February 1950, that ninety-one employees, mostly homosexuals, had been fired as security risks did not placate those intent on rooting out subversives. Departmental morale sank accordingly. Acheson, under attack himself, failed his colleagues. Having squandered his moral capital in defending Hiss, he could no longer protect other Department of State officials who had far less connection to communism than Hiss. President Truman tried to persuade old Republican friends in the Senate to muzzle McCarthy but wound up losing his temper and calling McCarthy "the greatest asset the Kremlin has." McCarthy in turn called the president a "son of a bitch" and later claimed that Truman's firing of General MacArthur in April 1951 had been aided by "bourbon and benedictine." As a result, both the White House and Department of State adopted a siege mentality during the Korean War. The prospect of McCarthyite attacks prompted Truman not to ask Congress for a declaration of war and influenced his decisions to defend Taiwan and to send troops across the 38th parallel in an attempt to liberate North Korea. It became even more difficult to make distinctions between anticommunism at home and abroad in the midst of a "limited" war in Korea.

Department of State morale plummeted even lower during the Eisenhower administration. At his swearing-in ceremony Secretary of State John Foster Dulles greeted his new colleagues with a demand for "positive loyalty." The secretary soon hired former FBI agent Scott McLeod to run the department's new Bureau of Security and Consular Affairs. Dulles's strategy, according to historian David Oshinsky, was "to get the McCarthyites to stop banging on the windows by inviting them in through the front door." McLeod's principal task was to investigate the backgrounds of the Department of State's 11,000 employees. A new Eisenhower directive made it possible to discharge federal workers as security risks for reasons other than disloyalty; such reasons included sexual perversion, immoral conduct, or the suspicion that the employee "may be subjected to coercion, influence, or pressure which may cause him to act contrary to the best interests of national security." Using lie detector tests, steaming open mail, and tapping phones, McLeod and his investigators proceeded to terrorize the department. After seven months, some 193 "security risks" had been discharged, only one of whom was a suspected subversive. The people "don't care whether they were drunks, perverts, or communists," McLeod explained. "They just want us to get rid of them."

Dulles applied the same logic to authors. In early 1953 he ordered books by "Communists, fellow travelers, et cetera" to be banned from the libraries of U.S. overseas information centers. Subordinates interpreted "et cetera" to include such individual authors as Bert Andrews

(Washington bureau chief of the *New York Herald Tribune*), Joseph Davies (former ambassador to the Soviet Union), Walter White (former secretary of the National Association for the Advancement of Colored People), and the historian Foster Rhea Dulles, the secretary of state's own cousin.

Victims of McCarthyism

The most conspicuous victims of McCarthyism were once described by the journalist Eric Sevareid as "the ablest group of American diplomats I have seen in a single American mission abroad." John Paton Davies, Jr., John S. Service, John Carter Vincent, O. Edmund Clubb, and a score of fellow Foreign Service officers who had served in China during World War II became scapegoats for allegedly "losing China" to communism. These diplomats had criticized Jiang Jieshi's Guomindong regime and had urged assistance to Mao Zedong's communists because they believed that Mao would win the Chinese civil war and that U.S. aid and friendship would prevent the communists from seeking close ties with the Soviet Union. When the flamboyant ambassador Patrick J. Hurley resigned in 1945 after failing to mediate an agreement between Mao and Jiang, he accused the China hands of "sabotage" to cover up his own mistakes. John Service, the most brilliant of the China experts, was targeted for having shown classified materials to the left-wing journal *Amerasia*, even though a grand jury later refused to indict him. Senator McCarthy named Service as one of the State Department's 205 Communists in his 1950 Wheeling speech, and eventually the Civil Service Commission's Loyalty Review Board, after reconsidering the *Amerasia* case and relying on faked reports from the Chinese Nationalists on Taiwan, recommended Service's dismissal because of "reasonable doubt as to his loyalty." Acheson reluctantly fired him in December 1951.

In the case of John Carter Vincent, counselor to the U.S. embassy in China during the war, the State Department's loyalty board on three occasions cleared the veteran diplomat of thirty years' service against accusations by Senator McCarthy and ex-communist Budenz that he had been a "known associate and collaborator with communists" and had consorted "with admitted espionage agents." Vincent's real crime, of course, was his hostility to the Guomindong. In December 1952 the Loyalty Review Board finally recommended his dismissal because of "Mr. Vincent's studied praise of Chinese Communists and studied criticism of the Chiang Kai-shek Government" when it had been official U.S. policy to support the Nationalist regime. This time Acheson rejected the board's finding and appointed a special panel, headed by the distinguished judge Learned Hand, to review Vincent's case one more time. Acheson thought he had won agreement from incoming Secretary of State

Dulles to abide by the decision of the special review board. On taking office, however, Dulles dismissed the special panel and said he would follow "established procedures" and make the final decision himself. It is unlikely that Dulles read the six volumes of testimony and dozens of FBI reports that comprised Vincent's case file, but within days Dulles said that he would discharge the diplomat for poor judgment unless Vincent agreed to retire from the Foreign Service. Once Vincent accepted retirement, Dulles announced that Vincent had demonstrated "a failure to meet the standard . . . demanded of a Foreign Service officer of his experience and responsibility at this critical time."

Dulles also ended the career of John Paton Davies, Jr., another capable China hand who had criticized Jiang Jieshi. Davies had been the political adviser to General Joseph W. Stilwell's mission to China during World War II and subsequently served as the East Asia expert on the Department of State policy planning staff. Despite trumped-up charges of perjury from Senator McCarran's Internal Security Subcommittee, the Department of State's Loyalty Review Board, after repeated investigations, decided in December 1952 that it had found "no reasonable doubt" as to Davies's loyalty. Dulles nevertheless transferred Davies in April 1953 from the staff of the U.S. High Commission to Germany to the U.S. embassy in Peru, where Davies served as counselor. When Senator McCarthy cited Davies's continuing employment as proof that the Department of State still coddled communists, Dulles appointed a five-person board to review the charges against Davies for the ninth time. Although none of the board members had any expertise in Sino-American relations, the panel concluded in August 1954 that Davies was guilty of "a definite lack of judgment, discretion, and reliability." Dulles accepted the board's findings and fired Davies. Dulles thereupon astonished Davies by telling him that he would be happy to write a character reference for any future employment opportunity, an offer that Davies declined, opening up a furniture business in Peru instead.

Two more China hands also suffered McCarthy's attacks. O. Edmund Clubb, a Foreign Service officer since 1929 and an early expert on Chinese communism who correctly predicted China's entry into the Korean War, was forced to retire prematurely in 1952 because of Kafkaesque charges by Whittaker Chambers and others that he had known communists in Manchuria in the 1930s. Owen Lattimore, a Johns Hopkins University professor specializing in China and Asia, made headlines in 1950 when Senator McCarthy named him the "top Soviet Spy, the boss of the whole ring of which Hiss was a part." Never a Foreign Service officer, Lattimore had served as a White House consultant to the Guomindong before Pearl Harbor and had accompanied Vice President

Henry A. Wallace to China in 1944. In a four-year ordeal before the Senate Internal Security Subcommittee, Lattimore was indicted for perjury but never convicted. According to Lattimore's biographer, the world's foremost scholar on Outer Mongolia proved that "it is possible for a single individual to prevail over a powerful committee...that was accumulating perhaps the greatest mass of lies and perjuries ever assembled in the halls of Congress." Lattimore ended his distinguished academic career in the 1960s as chair of the Department of Chinese studies at Leeds University in England.

The witch hunt for communists also affected Foreign Service officers who had specialized in Russian affairs. When President Eisenhower appointed the veteran diplomat Charles E. Bohlen as ambassador to the Soviet Union in early 1953, a worried Secretary Dulles asked if there was anything in Bohlen's past record that could be used to embarrass him. When Bohlen answered no, Dulles was relieved, saying he "couldn't stand another Alger Hiss." Bohlen's confirmation, however, did not come easily. Despite unanimous approval by the Senate Foreign Relations Committee, McCarthy claimed to have sixteen "closely typed pages" of dark secrets from Bohlen's personnel file—all amounting to "an ugly record of great betrayal." It was not until Senator Taft personally examined the file and vouched for Bohlen's integrity that the Senate confirmed the nomination by a vote of 74 to 13. Taft, who disliked controversy, later told Dulles, "No more Bohlens." Dulles subsequently told Bohlen's close friend and colleague George F. Kennan that the Department of State had "no niche" for him, thereby forcing the country's foremost Soviet expert to accept mandatory retirement.

One of the more grotesque ironies of McCarthyism was that after the Department of State had been terrorized by McCarthy's exaggerated allegations, it nevertheless sometimes applied the same conspiratorial reasoning to the international arena. Ambassador Richard Patterson, for example, proposed the notorious "duck test" in 1950 to suggest that the reformist government of Guatemala was communist-controlled. "Suppose you see a bird walking around in a farm yard," explained Patterson. "This bird wears no label that says 'duck,' but the bird certainly looks like a duck...[and] he swims like a duck. Then he opens his beak and quacks like a duck. Well, by this time you have probably reached the conclusion that the bird is a duck, whether he's wearing a label or not." Thus, in 1954 the Department of State and CIA overthrew the regime of Jacobo Arbenz Gúzman in Guatemala because, in the words of Ambassador John Peurifoy, he "thought like a Communist and talked like a Communist, and if not actually one, would do until one came along."

Even as the anticommunist hysteria subsided after McCarthy's censure and death, a new wave of rabidly accusatory anticommunism resurfaced after the Cuban revolution in 1959. After blindly supporting the corrupt, pro-U.S. regime of Fulgencio Batista in Havana and having misread the local conditions that spawned Fidel Castro's successful revolution, conservative Republicans in the Department of State sought scapegoats. In particular, Ambassadors William D. Pawley, Earl E. T. Smith, and Arthur Gardner accused Foreign Service officers in the Office of Middle American Affairs of fomenting a pro-Castro conspiracy. Because career officer William Wieland, for example, had argued that Castro was not a communist before he seized power, a view shared throughout the U.S. bureaucracy, including the CIA and FBI, Pawley told the Senate Judiciary Committee in 1960 that Wieland "is either one of the stupidest men living" or he is "intentionally" helping America's "enemies." The committee's reprimand of Wieland as an "active apologist" for Castro effectively ended a promising career.

Similarly, when the administration of President Ronald Reagan backed the Contras in their unsuccessful counterinsurgency against the Sandinista government in Nicaragua in the 1980s, Reagan appointees demanded loyalty, not accuracy, from Department of State officials. When a top expert on Latin America, Francis McNeil, disputed Assistant Secretary of State Elliott Abrams's claims that the Contras were fighting effectively, Abrams had McNeil fired. "The situation reeks of McCarthyism," said McNeil. President Reagan's National Security Adviser Robert C. McFarlane testified after the Iran-Contra scandal that he had never argued against misguided policies because Reagan hard-liners "would have said that I was some kind of commie."

The traumas associated with McCarthyism disappeared all too slowly. "The widespread subpoena of China scholars had the public effect of inhibiting realistic thinking about China," Professor John K. Fairbank later wrote. "The result carried over into unrealistic thinking about Chinese relations with Vietnam and helped to produce our difficulties there." The FBI's secret and illegal counterintelligence program (COINTELPRO) of harassing and infiltrating dissenting political groups continued into the 1960s and 1970s. Within the Department of State itself, the Passport Division, headed by the zealous Ruth B. Shipley and Frances G. Knight, arbitrarily withheld passports from former communists and leftists until the 1970s. "Tailgunner Joe was a good marksman," the historian Bruce Cumings wrote of McCarthy, because "he left a generation of liberals looking over their shoulder to the right, fearing yet another case of mistaken identity." It was not until the Vietnam War that critics began to dissent from official policy. The result was a rigid Cold War consensus that blurred the differences between liberals and conservatives and perpetuated a sterile dialogue on how best to fight the Cold War, not on how to end it.

J. GARRY CLIFFORD

See also Abrams, Elliott; Acheson, Dean Gooderham; Bohlen, Charles Eustis; Central Intelligence Agency; China; China Hands; Cold War; Communism; Contras; Davies, John Paton, Jr.; Dulles, John Foster; Eisenhower, Dwight David; Foreign Service; Hiss, Alger; Hurley, Patrick Jay; Korean War; MacArthur, Douglas; Reagan, Ronald Wilson; Republican Party; Roosevelt, Franklin Delano; State, U.S. Department of; Truman, Harry S.; Vietnam War

FURTHER READING

Broadwater, Jeff. *Eisenhower and the Anti-Communist Crusade.* Chapel Hill, N.C., 1992.
Clubb, O. Edmund. *The Witness and I.* New York, 1975.
Cumings, Bruce. *The Origins of the Korean War.* Princeton, N.J., 1981.
Griffith, Robert K. *The Politics of Fear.* Amherst, Mass., 1987.
Griffith, Robert K., and Athan Theoharis, eds. *The Specter.* New York, 1974.
Kahn, E. J., Jr. *The China Hands.* New York, 1975.
Kutler, Stanley I. *The American Inquisition.* New York, 1982.
May, Gary. *China Scapegoat.* Washington, D.C., 1979.
Newman, David. *Owen Lattimore and the "Loss" of China.* Berkeley, Calif., 1992.
Oshinsky, David M. *A Conspiracy So Immense.* New York, 1983.
Paterson, Thomas G. *Contesting Castro.* New York, 1994.
Powers, Richard Gid. *Not Without Honor: The History of American Anticommunism.* New York, 1995.
Reeves, Thomas C. *The Life and Times of Joe McCarthy.* New York, 1982.
Schrecker, Ellen. *The Age of McCarthyism.* Boston, 1994.

MCCLOY, JOHN JAY

(*b.* 31 March 1895; *d.* 11 March 1989)

Lawyer and diplomat noted for shaping U.S. policy toward Germany after World War II, for participating in negotiations on critical international issues in the 1950s and 1960s, and for being one of the preeminent figures in the U.S. foreign policy establishment during the Cold War years. Born in Philadelphia, McCloy was educated at the Peddie School in New Jersey, Amherst College, and Harvard Law School. He fought with the American Expeditionary Forces in World War I. After the war he became a Wall Street lawyer, achieving prominence in the late 1930s by investigating incidents of German sabotage in the United States during World War I, especially the explosion of a munitions plant on Black Tom Island off New Jersey on 30 July 1916. During World War II, as assistant secretary of war (1941–1945), McCloy supported and helped implement the internment of Japanese Americans and advised against proposals to bomb the Nazi extermination camp at Auschwitz. Along with Sec-

retary of War Henry Stimson, McCloy helped defeat the Morgenthau Plan to deindustrialize Germany after World War II and argued in favor of establishing an international tribunal to prosecute German war criminals. After the war McCloy served as the president of the World Bank (1947–1949) and as high commissioner to Germany (1949–1952). McCloy supported the policies of Chancellor Konrad Adenauer, who favored German integration into the Western alliance through such initiatives as the Schuman Plan and the European Defense Community. McCloy provoked controversy through his leniency toward convicted German war criminals, especially his release of Alfried Krupp, the owner of the infamous munitions works.

Although his position as high commissioner ranks as his most significant public office, McCloy played a continuing role in American foreign policy. He served as a frequent conduit between the German and U.S. governments, conducted negotiations with Egypt after the Suez Crisis of 1956, and advised President John F. Kennedy on disarmament. McCloy also negotiated the terms for the withdrawal of Soviet nuclear weapons from Cuba during the missile crisis of 1962, after Soviet premier Nikita Khrushchev had agreed to withdraw them, and served on the Warren Commission that investigated the Kennedy assassination. In 1966 he was the U.S. representative on the trilateral talks to adjust financial burdens of the North Atlantic Treaty Organization (NATO). McCloy joined Henry Kissinger and David Rockefeller to lobby President Jimmy Carter to allow the deposed shah of Iran to receive medical treatment in the United States in October 1979, a decision that led to the Iranian hostage crisis. An unapologetic advocate of a Pax Americana, McCloy never wavered in his belief in U.S. responsibility for world leadership.

THOMAS A. SCHWARTZ

See also Adenauer, Konrad; Cuban Missile Crisis; Germany; International Bank for Reconstruction and Development; Kennedy, John Fitzgerald

FURTHER READING

Bird, Kai. *The Chairman: John J. McCloy.* New York, 1992.
Schwartz, Thomas A. *America's Germany: John J. McCloy and the Federal Republic of Germany.* Cambridge, Mass., 1991.

MCCONE, JOHN ALEX

(*b.* 4 January 1902; *d.* 14 February 1991)

Director of the Central Intelligence Agency (1961–1965). Born in San Francisco, McCone received an engineering degree from the University of California at Berkeley in 1922, then worked up from the shop floor to executive offices at Llewellyn Iron Works in Los Angeles. In 1937 he joined others in the creation of the engineering firm Bechtel-McCone-Parsons Corporation. During World War II he was president of the California Shipbuilding Company and a board member of the oil shipping firm Panama Pacific Tankers Company, and participated in establishing the Seattle-Tacoma Corporation. After the war he was hired by President Harry S. Truman for service on the Air Policy Commission. A series of government jobs then followed: special assistant to the secretary of defense (1948), undersecretary of the Air Force (1950–1951); and chairman of the Atomic Energy Commission (1958–1960). President John F. Kennedy believed McCone's experience in aircraft, oil, and ship production offered the Central Intelligence Agency (CIA) a new perspective on operations planning and intelligence technologies and appointed McCone director of the CIA in November 1961 after the disastrous Bay of Pigs invasion. McCone brought new approaches to the CIA, including reductions in covert actions and advances in analysis, military intelligence, and scientific applications. He received presidential authority to coordinate and guide the entire intelligence community and strengthened the analytical function at the CIA with several key appointments, including Richard Helms and Ray Cline. Under McCone's direction, the CIA's expanded technical collection capabilities served as vital resources during the critical phases of the Cuban missile crisis in October 1962. McCone stood virtually alone in the presidential policy advisory community in maintaining a position that the Soviets had installed missiles in Cuba. McCone encouraged the establishment of the Defense Intelligence Agency in 1961 and a new science and technology directorate at the CIA in 1963. Frustration with President Lyndon B. Johnson's inattention to intelligence, particularly in connection with the Vietnam War, and with Johnson's rebuffs of the intelligence chief's access to the White House caused McCone to resign in April 1965. His retirement years were spent in relative seclusion.

JAMES D. CALDER

See also Central Intelligence Agency; Covert Action; Cuban Missile Crisis; Intelligence; Johnson, Lyndon Baines; Kennedy, John Fitzgerald

FURTHER READING

Ranelagh, John. *The Agency: The Rise and Decline of the CIA from Wild Bill Donovan to William Casey.* New York, 1986.

MCDONALD, JAMES GROVER

(*b.* 29 November 1886; *d.* 26 September 1964)

First U.S. ambassador to Israel (1948–1951). McDonald was born in Coldwater, Ohio, and educated at Indiana and Harvard universities. As League of Nations high commissioner for German refugees from 1933 to 1935 he became a committed Zionist, believing that the British mandate of Palestine must become a "popular place of refuge" for the Jewish people. When he resigned in protest over the weak position of his office, McDonald warned that Nazi Germany had embarked on a policy of extermination of the Jews. During World War II, McDonald served as chairman of President Franklin D. Roosevelt's committee on political refugees. In 1945 President Harry S. Truman named him a member of the Anglo-American Commission of Inquiry on Palestine, which in April 1946 submitted a unanimous report calling for the admittance of 100,000 Jewish refugees into Palestine and for the establishment of a binational state. Once Truman decided to support the partition of Palestine and to recognize the Jewish state, he selected McDonald as the first U.S. ambassador to Israel in 1948. As ambassador, McDonald retained the respect of Washington while earning the admiration of the Israeli government, in the process setting the highest standard for U.S. diplomats who followed. After returning to the United States in 1951, McDonald served as adviser to the Development Corporation of Israel.

DIANE B. KUNZ

See also Holocaust; Israel; Palestine (to 1948)

FURTHER READING

Louis, Wm. Roger. *The British Empire in the Middle East.* Oxford, 1984.

Spiegel, Steven L. *The Other Arab-Israeli Conflict: Making America's Middle East Policy, from Truman to Reagan.* Chicago, 1985.

MCFARLANE, ROBERT CARL

(*b.* 12 July 1937)

Career military officer, and national security adviser (1983–1985). Born in Washington, D.C., the son of a Texas congressman, McFarlane was raised in Texas and graduated from the U.S. Naval Academy (1958). He later earned an M.S. in strategic studies from the University of Geneva. He served as a marine officer in Vietnam prior to becoming a military aide to National Security Adviser Henry A. Kissinger in 1973. After working on the staff of the Senate Armed Services Committee, in 1981 McFarlane was named counselor to the Department of State under Alexander Haig, then National Security Adviser William Clark's deputy and special envoy to the Middle East in 1982. McFarlane was appointed national security adviser in October 1983. With his aide Lieutenant Colonel Oliver L. North as action officer, McFarlane became embroiled in the illegal Iran-Contra affair by soliciting third-country funds for the Nicaraguan Contras and arranging secret arms shipments to Iran in exchange for U.S. hostages in Lebanon, even going to Tehran secretly in May 1986. He subsequently testified that he did not have "the guts to tell the President" when he was wrong for fear of being called "some kind of commie." In 1989 he pleaded guilty to four counts of withholding information from Congress and was fined $200,000 and placed on probation.

J. GARRY CLIFFORD

See also Iran-Contra Affair; North, Oliver Lawrence

FURTHER READING

Draper, Theodore. *A Very Thin Line: The Iran-Contra Affairs.* New York, 1991.
Walsh, Lawrence E. *Final Report of the Independent Counsel for Iran-Contra Matters.* Washington, D.C., 1993.

MCGHEE, GEORGE CREWS

(*b.* 10 March 1912)

Petroleum business leader and diplomat who helped establish the containment doctrines in the Near East. Born in Texas, McGhee earned degrees at the University of Oklahoma (1933) and Oxford University (1937) and became a successful petroleum scientist and prospector. His interest in world politics stimulated at Oxford, McGhee served on the War Production Board and the British-American Combined Raw Materials Board in 1941–1942, enlisted in the navy in 1943, and joined the Department of State in 1946. As coordinator of aid to Greece and Turkey (1947–1949), assistant secretary for Near East, South Asian, and African affairs (1949–1951), and ambassador to Turkey (1951–1953), McGhee pursued the ambitious objectives of containment of Soviet power, decolonization, economic modernization, Arab-Israeli settlement, and stability in countries historically neglected by Washington. He worked closely with and was highly regarded by Secretary of State Dean Acheson. After devoting the 1950s to private petroleum business, McGhee returned to diplomacy as undersecretary of state for political affairs (1961–1963), ambassador to the Federal Republic of Germany (1963–1968), and ambassador at large (1968–1969). In Bonn he preserved U.S.-West German amity despite deep disagreements over the U.S. balance of payments crisis, nuclear weapons strategy of the North Atlantic Treaty Organization (NATO), the war in Vietnam, and the U.S. pursuit of détente exclusive of German reunification. Never formally a Foreign Service officer, McGhee officially retired from diplomacy in 1968. He continued his work in petroleum enterprises and after 1983 published several books, including his memoirs.

PETER L. HAHN

See also Germany; Turkey

FURTHER READING

McGhee, George C. *Envoy to the Middle World: Adventures in Diplomacy.* New York, 1983.
———. *At the Creation of a New Germany: From Adenauer to Brandt, An Ambassador's Account.* New Haven, Conn., 1989.
———. *International Community: A Goal for a New World Order.* Lanham, Md., 1992.

MCGOVERN, GEORGE STANLEY

(*b.* 19 July 1922)

U.S. senator (1963–1981) and Democratic presidential candidate (1972) who campaigned against the war in Vietnam, lost the election to Richard Nixon, but remained outspoken in his opposition to U.S. intervention abroad. McGovern grew up in Mitchell, South Dakota, where he attended Dakota Wesleyan University. Before going overseas, he married Eleanor Stegeberg, with whom he would have five children. As a bomber pilot in World War II, he flew some thirty-five missions over Germany, Italy, and Austria. In 1953 he earned a Ph.D. from Northwestern University, then taught for a while at Dakota Wesleyan. He entered politics with his election to the U.S. House of Representatives in 1956 and 1958 and lost a close race for the Senate in 1960s. As director of the Food for Peace program (1961–1962) in President John F. Kennedy's administration, McGovern visited many developing countries. By the end of his directorship, Food for Peace had become the single most extensive foreign aid program since the Marshall Plan.

In 1962 McGovern resigned his post and won a seat in the Senate. His first major speech, "Our Castro Fixation Versus the Alliance for Progress," signaled the critical perspective on U.S. foreign policy for which he would become famous. The speech defended Kennedy against right-wing attacks for his refusal to try to overthrow Cuba's Fidel Castro after the missile crisis, but the senator also characterized as a "tragic mistake" the administration's own trespasses against Cuba. The United States, McGovern said, would do better to refrain from ill-advised military intervention undertaken in the name of anticommunism and instead "point the way to a better life for the hemisphere and, indeed, for all mankind."

McGovern was an early critic of U.S. intervention in Vietnam. U.S. resources were being "used to suppress the very liberties we went in to defend," he said on the Senate floor in September 1963. "The trap we have fallen into there will haunt us in every corner of the globe." By 1968 he was considered one of the Senate's leading critics of the war. On 30 April 1970, in the wake of the invasion of Cambodia, he introduced a measure, cosponsored with Republican Senator Mark Hatfield of Oregon, to cut off funds for the war within six months and to withdraw all U.S. combat troops from Southeast Asia by the end of 1971. The defeat of the McGovern-Hatfield

Amendment (by a vote of 55 to 39) did not dissuade him. In January 1971 McGovern announced his candidacy for president. Enthusiastically backed by former supporters of Robert F. Kennedy and Eugene McCarthy, he ran a grass-roots primary campaign and went on to capture the Democratic nomination on the first ballot. He pledged to end the war expeditiously, to pare down the defense budget and curtail military adventurism, and to ensure that every able-bodied citizen had a job. In the face of President Richard M. Nixon's progress in winding down the Vietnam War, McGovern lost the election, one of the most lopsided defeats in U.S. political history, with Nixon winning the electoral votes of forty-nine states.

South Dakota sent him back to the Senate for the third time in 1974. McGovern continued to deplore interventions in the Third World, the nuclear arms race, and the Cold War's depletion of resources that might have been better spent on programs for social reform. In his bid for a fourth term, he was overwhelmed in the Republican Ronald Reagan landslide of 1980, along with several other senior liberal Democrats. Retiring from national political life, McGovern settled permanently in Washington, D.C. Throughout the 1980s he lectured widely on college campuses, appeared on numerous public affairs television programs, and wrote a host of newspaper and magazine articles. His earlier views on foreign policy did not change fundamentally, but they seemed to have gained greater acceptance by the time President Bill Clinton entered the White House in 1993. Advocating a somewhat limited form of Wilsonian internationalism for the 1990s rather than a post–Cold War unilateralist globalism, McGovern, in a sense, continued to beckon, "Come home, America," the theme of his 1972 campaign.

THOMAS J. KNOCK

See also Cambodia; Cold War; Cuba; Cuban Missile Crisis; Democratic Party; Food for Peace; Foreign Aid; Kennedy, Robert Francis; McCarthy, Eugene Joseph; Nixon, Richard Milhous; Reagan, Ronald Wilson; Vietnam War

FURTHER READING

Anson, Robert Sam. *McGovern: A Biography*. New York, 1972.
McGovern, George S. *War Against Want: America's Food for Peace Program*. New York, 1964.
———. *Grassroots: The Autobiography of George McGovern*. New York, 1977.

MCGOVERN-HATFIELD AMENDMENT

See McGovern, George Stanley

MCKINLEY TARIFF ACT

(1890)

Legislation that raised import duties on many items, increased the overall average ad valorem rate to 49 per-

cent, the highest in U.S. history, and approved the negotiation of reciprocal trade agreements. The McKinley Tariff was named after Republican Representative William McKinley, who was elected president in 1896. He superintended the drafting of the tariff legislation that brought consistency and order to customs schedules that had developed in an ad hoc manner. During the late nineteenth century Republicans generally favored high tariffs to protect U.S. producers from foreign competition. The high rates Republicans had imposed beginning in 1861 had generated much-needed revenue for the Civil War, but the high postwar rates created annual surpluses ranging into hundreds of millions of dollars. In 1887 Democratic President Grover Cleveland called for tariff reduction to promote trade and reduce the Treasury surpluses. He lost a close reelection bid to Benjamin Harrison in 1888, and the new president encouraged McKinley to preserve and strengthen the protectionist system favored by the Republicans.

Harrison's secretary of state, James G. Blaine, championed the inclusion of authority for reciprocal trade agreements within the new legislation, and he subsequently negotiated several bilateral treaties with countries eager to lower trade barriers. To reduce the Treasury surplus, McKinley included a provision that canceled the duty on imported sugar, a commodity whose levies sometimes accounted for more than 20 percent of all tariff revenues. Canceling the sugar tariff undermined the Hawai'ian economy, which had benefited from an earlier reciprocity arrangement that gave Hawai'ian sugar a privileged position in the U.S. market, and it helped provoke the unrest that led to a revolution, a key step toward Hawai'i's annexation by the United States. Meanwhile, the Cuban economy experienced a heady prosperity with the expansion of its sugar exports to the United States. After Cleveland's reelection to the presidency in 1892, he approved the Wilson-Gorman Tariff (1894), which canceled all reciprocity arrangements and reimposed a tariff on sugar. Exports from Cuba plummeted, and the Cuban economy tumbled into a depression that helped trigger the 1895 rebellion against Spanish rule and ultimately led to the Spanish-American-Cuban-Filipino War of 1898.

JOHN M. DOBSON

See also Cuba; Hawai'i; McKinley, William; Reciprocal Trade Agreement Act; Tariffs

MCKINLEY, WILLIAM

(*b.* 29 January 1843; *d.* 14 September 1901)

President of the United States from 1897 to 1901, a period during which the United States went to war against Spain, embraced insular colonies, and joined the ranks of the world's great powers. McKinley's early career was typical of his generation of successful Republican politicians. He was born in the small town of Niles, Ohio, fought in the Civil War, and practiced law. He was a member of the House of Representatives (1877–1882, 1885–1891) and was twice elected governor of Ohio (1892–1896). McKinley had no international experience nor apparently much interest in foreign relations before he became president. Indeed, the impact on Cuba and Hawai'i of the McKinley Tariff he had drafted as a member of congress in 1890 was largely unintended. His victory over Democrat William Jennings Bryan in the presidential election of 1896 represented a triumph of business-oriented conservatives over Bryan's agrarian supporters. The Republican platform in 1896 included calls for the annexation of Hawai'i, reassertion of the Monroe Doctrine, and U.S. influence in favor of independence for Cuba, but these issues had only a minor role in the campaign.

The focal point of McKinley's presidency was the Spanish-American-Cuban-Filipino War, a conflict that he tried diligently to avoid. A Cuban rebellion against Spanish colonial control had broken out in 1895. In the year after his inauguration, McKinley urged Spain to institute a cease-fire and allow the United States to mediate a peaceful settlement between the warring parties. The Spanish government was unwilling to do so, recognizing that the president's intervention would ultimately establish an independent Cuba. The fighting and propaganda associated with the Cuban cause attracted increasing sympathy in the United States. Even without the dramatic (and apparently accidental) sinking of the USS *Maine* in February 1898, it is likely that domestic popular opinion would have convinced McKinley to call for U.S. intervention. He sincerely endorsed the Teller Amendment, which promised that the United States would not annex Cuba and which Congress attached to its declaration of war on Spain of 25 April 1898. The president, however, was also concerned that the Cuban rebels would diminish U.S. interests on the island, so his allies in Congress successfully beat back a resolution that would have extended formal recognition to the rebel government. McKinley believed that the Cuban people required a period of U.S. tutelage to prepare them for full independence.

Once committed to intervention, McKinley managed the war effort well, devoting special attention to the War Department, which was suffering under the mismanagement of Secretary of War Russell N. Alger. On 1 May 1898, just a week after the U.S. war declaration, Commodore George Dewey's squadron destroyed Spain's fleet in Manila Bay and with it Spain's effective control of the Philippine Islands. In July the president signed a congressional joint resolution annexing Hawai'i to the United States (an annexation treaty of the previous year had

failed to win the necessary two-thirds support of the Senate). Defeated in military and naval engagements in southeastern Cuba, the Spanish government sought an armistice that took effect on 12 August. Momentum in favor of imperialism was running at full tide in the fall, when the president concluded that the United States should annex the Philippines. The 1898 Treaty of Paris transferred the archipelago to the United States, but U.S. forces had to endure more than two years of guerrilla warfare with Filipino nationalists before they could assert full authority in 1902.

In general, McKinley relied on competent and thoughtful aides to develop the means to achieve his policy goals. Secretaries of State William R. Day and later John Hay, Secretary of War Elihu Root, and General Leonard Wood headed the group that helped the president frame and implement his administration's policies. Attentive to U.S. businesses interested in exploiting the China market, McKinley authorized Hay to circulate his famous Open Door Notes in 1899 and 1900, calling upon other great powers to preserve unlimited international access to trade with all of China. McKinley also approved the Platt Amendment (1901), which had the effect of making Cuba a protectorate of the United States. Anarchist Leon Czolgosz shot the president on 6 September 1901. When he died eight days later, McKinley passed on to Theodore Roosevelt an articulated policy framework for the United States as a great power in the twentieth century.

JOHN M. DOBSON

See also Colonialism; Cuba; Hay, John Milton; Imperialism; McKinley Tariff Act; Open Door Policy; Spain; Spanish-American-Cuban-Filipino War, 1898

FURTHER READING

Dobson, John. *Reticent Expansionism: The Foreign Policy of William McKinley.* Pittsburgh, 1988.
Gould, Lewis L. *The Presidency of William McKinley.* Lawrence, Kans., 1982.

MCLANE, LOUIS

(*b.* 28 May 1786; *d.* 7 October 1857)

Member of the House of Representatives (1817–1827), U.S. senator (1827–1829), minister to Great Britain (1829–1831, 1845–1846), secretary of the treasury (1831–1833), and secretary of state (1833–1834). Born in Delaware, he practiced law and, after serving in both houses of Congress, was appointed minister to Great Britain, where he negotiated a reciprocity agreement granting the United States access to British West Indian ports. As secretary of state, he addressed U.S. disputes with Mexico over the U.S.-Texas boundary and territorial questions with Great Britain over the Maine–New Brunswick boundary; handled a troublesome issue with France concerning that nation's failure to make good on claims to the United States dating from the Napoleonic Wars; and helped reorganize the Department of State. In 1834 he served as president of the Baltimore and Ohio Railroad before returning to London in 1845 to help resolve an Anglo-American dispute over the Oregon Territory. Although the subsequent treaty was negotiated in Washington, McLane's efforts proved vital to the final compromise.

DONALD A. RAKESTRAW

See also France; Great Britain; Oregon Question

FURTHER READING

Munroe, John A. *Louis McLane: Federalist and Jacksonian.* New Brunswick, N.J., 1973.
Pletcher, David M. *The Diplomacy of Annexation: Texas, Oregon, and the Mexican War.* Columbia, Mo., 1973.

MCNAMARA, ROBERT STRANGE

(*b.* 9 June 1916)

Secretary of defense (1961–1968) in the Kennedy and Johnson administrations during the Vietnam War, and president of the World Bank (1968–1981). Born of middle class parents in San Francisco, he became a symbol of U.S. management skills in the postwar era when the United States was at its peak of global influence. His paternal grandfather emigrated from Ireland; his Catholic father never got past eighth grade. His Protestant mother had unlimited ambitions for him. The suffering caused by the Great Depression and the hopes raised by Franklin D. Roosevelt's New Deal impressed young McNamara. In 1937 he graduated in economics from the University of California at Berkeley and entered the Harvard Business School (M.B.A. 1939). There, under the tutelage of Ross Graham Walker, McNamara learned financial control, a management system pioneered by the business executives of the Du Pont family and Alfred P. Sloan, that enabled leaders of giant corporations to oversee far-flung activities through top-down statistical controls. During World War II, the Army Air Forces commissioned McNamara and other business-school instructors at Harvard to apply these controls to the global air war. "Stat control" became a success; one press article concluded that these young men were "putting the bombing on a business basis." A captain in the U.S. Army in 1943, McNamara went to Great Britain to plan the bombing of Germany.

McNamara's talent for statistics made him a star in the precomputer era of U.S. business expansion after the war. He joined the Ford Motor Company in 1946 with nine other "stat control" officers. The story that these "whiz kids" singlehandedly created the ailing company's

subsequent success is exaggerated, however, for several industry veterans and Henry Ford II played pivotal roles. On 9 November 1960, the forty-four-year-old McNamara became the first nonfamily member to become president of Ford. Within the automobile industry, McNamara was an oddly placed liberal. Unlike his fellow executives, he sometimes backed Democrats. He campaigned for auto safety. Through his continued Harvard contacts, he came to the attention of President-elect John Kennedy, who appointed him secretary of defense. McNamara instantly applied management controls to overhaul the Pentagon, becoming an early rising star in the administration. The cool young executive, with slicked-back hair and spectacles, symbolized American youth and drive.

Kennedy's one thousand days in office established McNamara's international reputation. He hired young, mainly civilian "whiz kids" to install program budgeting, which became the new permanent method of Pentagon accounting. He also reshaped the armed services's plans and missions, and sought to reduce interservice rivalries. He was often at odds with the generals. McNamara kept strategic nuclear weapons at the center of the administration's military posture, but he expanded non-nuclear and counterinsurgency forces under the concept of "flexible response," or the ability to meet any kind of threat. Missteps included his approval of the April 1961 Cuban exile invasion at the Bay of Pigs and his snap decision to increase U.S. land-based ICBM missiles to one thousand, which may have triggered the Soviet Union's later buildup of its ICBM force. Despite rocky press relations, McNamara's power grew. His testimony to Congress was brilliant, and the Kennedys opened their doors to him and Margaret, his warm and unpretentious wife. John and Robert Kennedy appreciated McNamara's steadfastness in the 1962 Cuban Missile Crisis. McNamara is often credited with articulating the basic U.S. response: the naval quarantine of Cuba.

A less known achievement was his installation of Permissive Action Links (PALS) devices to prevent an unauthorized launch of NATO nuclear weapons which had proliferated in Europe under the previous administration. Although McNamara's project to build a multipurpose fighter-bomber, called the TFX, faltered because of military opposition and poor aircraft performance, he consolidated the intelligence activities in the Defense Intelligence Agency (DIA) and formed the Nuclear Planning Group to calm the long-standing controversy over nuclear use in NATO. McNamara also made the public case for the doctrine of Mutual Assured Destruction (MAD) and thus against strategic missile defense. In other words, in his view, leaving U.S. and Soviet cities vulnerable to attack would deter nuclear war. This view became U.S. policy and was represented in the SALT II treaty.

When Lyndon Johnson became president, McNamara's influence grew. In 1964, McNamara managed the setbacks to the U.S. advisory effort in Vietnam so the war would not interfere with the whirlwind of Great Society reforms Johnson was pushing through Congress. Years later McNamara would admit that the presidential transition was a chance to disengage from Vietnam, but at the time McNamara obeyed Johnson's admonition to "get along, win the war." McNamara shaped Johnson's 1965 decisions to bomb North Vietnam incrementally and send U.S. troops to South Vietnam while rejecting military pleas to call up reserves. Academics such as Pentagon counsel John McNaughton supplied the war theories under which the enemy was supposed to yield after marginal upward ratchets of force. Though the "body count" of supposed enemy dead was an army invention, McNamara's use of this number to claim progress became a symbol of his business-school approach to the war. The enemy, however, was not deterred by added U.S. bombs and troops; in the fall of 1965 McNamara realized that the war could not be won. He privately told the president about this conclusion and entered a period of personal crisis, but he remained loyal to Johnson, and McNamara refused to share his doubts with the public.

By 1967, McNamara was being criticized by the growing antiwar movement, which held him responsible for the growing number of deaths and devastation in Southeast Asia, and by the political right, which charged that his restraints were losing the war. McNamara was almost alone urging that Johnson stabilize troop levels, curb the bombing of North Vietnam, and press for talks as the only way of resolving the war. In November 1967, Johnson surprised McNamara by naming him to head the World Bank. In retirement ceremonies, McNamara's exhaustion and tears captured the general mood of disillusion. Yet McNamara's arguments influenced Johnson's decision to curtail the bombing and try for negotiations, when the president announced on 31 March 1968 that he would not seek reelection.

As president of the World Bank (International Bank for Reconstruction and Development) after 1 April 1968, McNamara launched his third great institutional makeover. McNamara installed financial controls to expand this development bank devised at the Bretton Woods Conference of 1945. In 1968 the bank committed $735 million (the cost of a few TFXs) and over his first five years it lent $13.4 billion, more than twice the amount loaned in its entire previous history. Echoing the Great Society, McNamara advanced programs in education, health, and housing, but he emphasized rural development to fight malnutrition, overpopulation, and poverty by increasing the farm productivity of the rural poor. At Nairobi in 1973, he announced plans to expand this approach around the world to uplift 700 million "absolute

poor." The oil price shock that winter wrecked the economic basis of his plans, however, as did the second oil price shock of 1979. Thus, by 1981, the "absolute poor" had actually grown more numerous. On the other hand, McNamara's systems approach to spreading the Green Revolution succeeded in meeting the food needs of 300 million to 500 million people who otherwise would have been malnourished. His wife's cancer made McNamara decide to retire midway through his third term in June 1981; she died early that year. McNamara went on to call for curbs on the nuclear arms race in articles and books such as *Blundering Into Disaster* (1986) and *The First Century of the Nuclear Age* (1988).

Throughout his careers, McNamara was praised for his organizational ability, sense of high purpose, and ability to inspire. He surpassed other leaders tainted by Vietnam with his substantial achievements afterwards at the World Bank. But his habit of manipulation and combativeness made him a divisive figure, rather than the Rooseveltean statesman he aspired to be. For example, in 1995, he finally abandoned his reticence on Vietnam by publishing a memoir titled *In Retrospect*. In many passages, McNamara achieved a dignified, regretful review of past errors. But by also insisting fervently that the war was "terribly wrong," and could not have been won because of Vietnamese nationalism, he infuriated millions of veterans and critics who faulted him for a slavish loyalty to the president rather than a commitment to the national interest.

DEBORAH SHAPLEY

See also Cuban Missile Crisis; Defense, U.S. Department of; Flexible Response; Intelligence; International Bank for Reconstruction and Development; Johnson, Lyndon Baines; Kennedy, John Fitzgerald; Mutual Assured Destruction; Nuclear Weapons and Strategy; Vietnam War

FURTHER READING

Art, Robert J. *The TFX Decision: McNamara and the Military.* Boston, 1968.

Maddux, John L. *The Development Philosophy of Robert S. McNamara.* Washington D.C., 1981.

McNamara, Robert S. *The Essence of Security: Reflections in Office.* New York, 1968.

———. *The McNamara Years at the World Bank.* Baltimore, Md., 1981.

———. *Blundering Into Disaster: Surviving the First Century of the Nuclear Age.* New York, 1986

———. *The First Century of the Nuclear Age: Can We Survive It?* Pittsburgh, Pa., 1988.

———. *Out of the Cold: New Thinking for American Foreign and Defense Policy in the 21st Century.* New York, 1989.

———. *In Retrospect: The Tragedy and Lessons of Vietnam.* New York, 1995.

Shapley, Deborah. *Promise and Power: The Life and Times of Robert McNamara.* Boston, 1993.

MEDIA AND FOREIGN POLICY

See Cable News Network; Journalism and Foreign Policy; Television and Foreign Policy

MELLON, ANDREW WILLIAM

(*b.* 24 March 1855; *d.* 26 August 1937)

Multimillionaire financier, diplomat, and patron of the arts who served as secretary of the treasury (1921–1932) for Presidents Warren G. Harding, Calvin Coolidge, and Herbert Hoover and as ambassador to Great Britain (1932–1933). Mellon was born in Pittsburgh and attended the Western University of Pennsylvania (now University of Pittsburgh). In 1874 he joined his father's bank, T. Mellon and Sons, and eight years later became its president. Mellon had a talent for recognizing promising ideas and business opportunities and was a shrewd investor in such industries as coal, petroleum, steel, and coke. One of his most successful investments was in the Aluminum Company of America, of which he became a director in 1891. In 1902 Mellon's bank was incorporated as Mellon National Bank with Mellon as president. A conservative, high-tariff Republican, Mellon joined Henry Clay Frick in 1919 in financing Senator Philander C. Knox's nationwide campaign against the League of Nations.

As secretary of the treasury, Mellon sought to reform the tax system, deal with the national debt accumulated as a result of World War I, solve the problem of Allied war debts, and enforce the new Prohibition amendment. Mellon believed that the success of U.S. business was the key to a growing and dynamic country and that the federal government should encourage business growth. The Mellon Plan, a tax reform package, lowered taxes for wealthy individuals and corporations. Mellon argued that if businesses were profitable, more jobs would be created and add to the country's prosperity, which would trickle down to middle and lower income groups. He also worked to reduce a large national debt (from $24 billion in 1921 to $16.2 billion in 1929) and to refinance loans of the federal government so that interest rates would be lower. As chairman of the World War Debt Commission, he secured agreements with the former Allied countries whereby they began repaying their war debts to the United States. Because high tariffs, supported by Mellon, shut out most foreign goods, European debtor nations were prevented from increasing their production and thereby paying off their debts. The war debt repayments system depended on the collection of German war reparations and U.S. loans to Germany (the Dawes and Young Plans). When the prosperity of the 1920s ended in the Great Depression and U.S. loans to Germany dried up, the repayment system collapsed. In February 1932 Hoover encouraged Mellon to accept the ambassadorship to Great Britain, which he held until Franklin D. Roosevelt took office as president. Returning home, Mellon became heavily involved in philanthropic activities that included the funding for the creation of the National Gallery of Art in Washington, D.C., to which he gave his extensive, prized art collection.

Before the Great Depression undermined his prestige, Mellon was hailed by some as the greatest secretary of the Treasury since Alexander Hamilton. Critics, however, claimed that his huge personal wealth blinded him to problems, such as the disparity between the rich and the poor, that ultimately brought the economy down. They argued that he showed favoritism to big business and that his actions helped encourage the risky stock speculation of the late 1920s.

LOUIS R. SMITH, JR.

See also Coolidge, Calvin; Dawes Plan; Harding, Warren; Hoover, Herbert; League of Nations; Reparations; Treasury, U.S. Department of; War Debt of World War I

FURTHER READING

Ellis, L. Ethan. *Republican Foreign Policy, 1921–1933*. New Brunswick, N.J., 1968.

Hicks, John D. *Republican Ascendancy, 1921–1933*. New York, 1960.

MESSERSMITH, GEORGE STRAUSSER

(*b.* 3 October 1883; *d.* 29 January 1960)

Career diplomat, U.S. minister to Austria from 1934 to 1937, and ambassador to Argentina from 1946 to 1947. Born in Pennsylvania, he served in the U.S. Consulate in Canada during World War I. By 1930 he was consul general in Berlin. Disgusted by the Nazi regime, he firmly defended U.S. businesses and journalists against actions limiting their freedom. As minister to Austria from 1934 to 1937, he remained an opponent of appeasement. He believed the Nazi regime was weak and that it would collapse without outside support. The effectiveness of his diplomatic reporting was limited by a style which earned him the nickname Forty-Page George.

After service in Washington as assistant secretary of state (1937–1940) and ambassador to Cuba (1940–1941) and Mexico (1941–1946), Messersmith was appointed ambassador to Argentina in 1946. A public dispute with assistant secretary of state Spruille Braden over how to bring about Argentine compliance with the Act of Chapultepec, and U.S. participation in the Rio Treaty, contributed to the early retirement of both men in June 1947.

STEVEN SCHWARTZBERG

See also Appeasement; Argentina; Braden, Spruille

FURTHER READING

Stiller, Jesse H. *George S. Messersmith, Diplomat of Democracy.* Chapel Hill, N.C., 1987.

Trask, Roger R. "Spruille Braden versus George Messersmith: World War II, the Cold War, and Argentina Policy, 1945–1947." In *Journal of Inter-American Studies and World Affairs.* vol. 26, No. 1 (February 1984): 69–96.

MEXICAN CESSION

See Mexico, War with

MEXICO

Located in Middle America between Guatemala and the United States, a nation with which the United States has had intense, complex, at times collaborative, but often conflictual relations. In the mid-nineteenth century, mainly through defeat in war, Mexico lost approximately half of its national territory to the United States. The U.S. government intervened militarily in Mexico early in the twentieth century when the Mexican Revolution threatened U.S. interests. The economies of the United States and Mexico have long been intertwined, leading to instances of close collaboration and mutual benefit as well as to moments of sharp conflict and respective losses. U.S. investors played central roles in the development and control of Mexican mining and petroleum resources early in the twentieth century and were among those whose properties were expropriated by Mexican governments after the Mexican Revolution. In January 1994 Mexico, the United States, and Canada enacted the North American Free Trade Agreement (NAFTA) to promote freer trade on the continent. In 1994 Mexico became the second most important U.S. trading partner. In December 1994, Mexico suffered a major financial panic, from which it was rescued in part by a massive international effort led and coordinated by the U.S. government. Over the years, a distinctive culture based on shared experiences developed along the long land border between Mexico and the United States, blurring the distinction between daily life and foreign policy.

Independent Mexico at War with the United States

On 16 September 1810 the Reverend Miguel Hidalgo y Costilla proclaimed the independence of the Viceroyalty of New Spain from Spain. A bitter war ensued. In 1821 Agustín de Iturbide, the commander of Spain's forces in New Spain, rebelled and established an independent Mexican Empire; Iturbide was enthroned. To the south, this empire included all of today's Guatemala, El Salvador, Belize, Honduras, Nicaragua, and Costa Rica. To the north, it included much of what would become the southwestern United States, namely California, Arizona, New Mexico, Texas, and parts of other U.S. states. The United States recognized the Mexican Empire on 27 January 1823. The U.S.-Mexican boundary had been set by the Transcontinental Treaty (the Adams-Onís Treaty) signed by Spain and the United States on 22 February 1819. It began at the Gulf of Mexico outlet of the Sabine River (which today serves as the border between Louisiana and Texas), following its course to the Red and the Arkansas rivers (between which a straight line was drawn as a boundary connector), until reaching the 42nd parallel, which served as the northern border straight to the Pacific Ocean.

In March 1823 Iturbide abdicated. The empire was replaced by a republic and Central America seceded. Mexican domestic politics became highly unstable and would remain so for decades. U.S. policy focused at first on persuading Mexico to permit U.S. immigration into Texas and, then, to sell Texas to the United States. Beginning in 1824 individual Mexican states began to allow U.S. immigration into Texas. With strong U.S. encouragement, in November 1835 Texas (at the time, Texas included only the area marked by the Sabine, Red, and Nueces rivers) proclaimed its independence from Mexico. In 1836 Mexico broke diplomatic relations with the United States (to be restored in 1842). Also in 1836 Mexican armies were defeated in Texas and agreed to withdraw from Texan territory. In 1837 the United States recognized the Republic of Texas, setting off a stormy period in U.S.-Mexican relations.

In the United States the desire for territorial expansion gathered powerful support. Some U.S. citizens believed that it was the Manifest Destiny of the United States to include Texas within the Union, as well as other northern Mexican territories. The United States annexed Texas in 1845 and offered Mexico $40 million for much of its northern territories. Mexico refused. Claiming that the Rio Grande was the proper boundary between the United States and Mexico, in January 1846 President James Polk ordered U.S. troops to cross the Nueces River boundary and march to the Rio Grande. Following a skirmish between Mexican and U.S. patrols, Polk declared that U.S. blood had been spilled on U.S. soil, at best a highly debatable assertion. In April, U.S.-Mexican hostilities commenced, and in May the United States declared war on Mexico. Even in the midst of war with the United States, Mexicans engaged in their own civil war, which weakened Mexican defenses. Despite substantial resistance from many Mexico City residents, in mid-September 1847, U.S. troops led by General Winfield Scott conquered the city.

In February 1848 Mexico and the United States signed the Treaty of Guadalupe-Hidalgo, establishing the Rio Grande and Gila rivers as the new border, and ceding to the United States the region comprising the present states

U.S. MINISTERS AND AMBASSADORS TO MEXICO

MINISTER	PERIOD OF APPOINTMENT	ADMINISTRATION
Andrew Jackson[1]	1823	
Ninian Edwards[2]	1824	
Joel R. Poinsett	1825–1829[3]	J.Q. Adams
		Jackson
Anthony Butler	1830–1835[4]	Jackson
Powhatan Ellis	1836–1842	Van Buren
		W.H. Harrison
		Tyler
Waddy Thompson	1842–1844	Tyler
Wilson Shannon	1844–1845[5]	Tyler
		Polk
John Slidell[6]	1845–1846	Polk
Nathan Clifford	1848–1849	Polk
		Taylor
Robert P. Letcher	1849–1852	Taylor
		Fillmore
Alfred Conkling	1852–1853	Fillmore
		Pierce
James Gadsden	1853–1856	Pierce
John Forsyth	1856–1858[7]	Pierce
		Buchanan
Robert M. McLane	1859–1860	Buchanan
John B. Weller	1860–1861	Buchanan
Thomas Corwin	1861–1864[8]	Lincoln
John A. Logan[9]	1865	Lincoln
Lewis D. Campbell[10]	1866	A. Johnson
Marcus Otterbourg	1867[11]	A. Johnson
John A. McClernand[12]		
William S. Rosencrans	1868–1869	A. Johnson
		Grant
Thomas H. Nelson	1869–1873	Grant
John W. Foster	1873–1880	Hayes
		Garfield
		Arthur
		Cleveland
Philip H. Morgan	1880–1885	
Henry R. Jackson	1885–1886	Cleveland
Thomas C. Manning	1886–1887	Cleveland
Edward S. Bragg	1888–1889	Cleveland
Thomas Ryan	1889–1893	B.Harrison
Issac P. Gray	1893–1894[13]	Cleveland
Matt W. Ransom	1895[14]–1897	Cleveland

AMBASSADOR

Powell Clayton	1897–1905	McKinley
		T. Roosevelt
Edwin H. Conger	1905	T. Roosevelt
David E. Thompson	1906–1909	T. Roosevelt
		Taft

(table continues on next page)

AMBASSADOR	PERIOD OF APPOINTMENT	ADMINISTRATION
Henry Lane Wilson	1909–1913[15]	Taft
Henry P. Fletcher	1916–1919[16]	Wilson
Henry Morganthau[17]		
Charles Beecher Warren	1924	Coolidge
James Rockwell Sheffield	1924–1927	Coolidge
Dwight W. Morrow	1927–1930	Coolidge
		Hoover
J. Reuben Clark, Jr.	1930–1933	Hoover
Josephus Daniels	1933–1941	F.D. Roosevelt
George S. Messersmith	1941–1946	F.D. Roosevelt
		Truman
Walter Thurston	1946–1950	Truman
William O'Dwyer	1950–1952	Truman
Francis White	1953–1957	Eisenhower
Robert C. Hill	1957–1960	Eisenhower
Thomas C. Mann	1961–1963	Kennedy
Fulton Freeman	1964–1969	L.B. Johnson
Robert H. McBride	1969–1973	Nixon
Joseph J. Jova	1973–1977	Nixon
		Ford
Patrick J. Lucey	1977–1979	Carter
Julian Nava	1980–1981	Carter
		Reagan
John A. Gavin	1981–1986	Reagan
Charles J. Pilliod, Jr.	1986–1989	Reagan
		Bush
John N. Negroponte	1989–1993	Bush
		Clinton
James R. Jones	1993–Present	Clinton

[1]Declined appointment.
[2]Did not proceed to post.
[3]Left Post, 3 Jan. 1830.
[4]Butler did not leave post until after his successor had presented credentials.
[5]Shannon left post, 14 May 1845.
[6]Proceeded to post, but did not present credentials; left post about 21 Mar. 1846.
[7]Forsyth left post, 21 Oct. 1858.
[8]During the period 1864–1867 each of the following officers served as Chargé d' Affaires ad interim for more than a year: William H. Corwin, April 1864–April. 1966; Marcus Otterbourg, Apr. 1866–Aug. 1867.
[9]Declined Appointment
[10]Took oath of office and proceeded to Mexico, but did not present credentials.
[11]Otterbourg left post, 21–30 Sept. 1867.
[12]Not commissioned; nomination twice rejected by the Senate.
[13]Returned to post, 14 Feb. 1895, but died the same day without resuming charge of the Legation.
[14]This appointment was characterized as a nullity in an opinion of the Acting Attorney General, 15 Aug. 1895. Sept 1895 new letter of credence filed with the Foreign Minister on this date, and not formally presented.
[15]Nelson O' Shaughnessy was serving as Chargé d' Affaires ad interim when Embassy Mexico was closed at the request of the Mexican authorities, 22 Apr. 1914.
[16]George T. Summerlin served as Chargé d' Affaires ad interim, Jan. 1919–Mar. 1924.
[17]Not commissioned; nomination not confirmed by the Senate.

Source: *The U.S. Government Manual*

of California, Arizona, and New Mexico. The U.S. government paid Mexico $15 million and also assumed the claims of U.S. citizens and firms against Mexico. In 1853 the U.S. minister to Mexico, James Gadsden, negotiated an additional U.S. purchase of Mexican territory for $10 million, which definitively settled the U.S.-Mexican boundary.

Mexico's domestic political instability continued. In the early 1860s France sought to establish a protectorate in Mexico under a puppet emperor, Maximilian. When the American Civil War ended in 1865, the U.S. government sided with Mexican President Benito Juárez's government, which had been waging guerrilla war on the occupying French troops. Pressured also by the threat of war with Prussia, French troops withdrew from Mexico. By mid-1867 the Juárez government reestablished its authority.

The Mexican Revolution
and U.S. Interventions

In 1876 General Porfirio Díaz seized power and held it until 1911. Despite some problems, U.S.-Mexican relations improved steadily during Díaz's rule. The main issues in dispute were the settlement of financial claims incurred since the 1848 treaty, the containment of cross-border raids by indigenous peoples, and rivalries over influence in Guatemala and Nicaragua. The Díaz dictatorship enforced order and embarked on a far-reaching economic development program. It welcomed foreign direct investment, much of it from the United States. By 1911 U.S. investors accounted for almost 40 percent of total foreign investment in Mexico. Trade also boomed. Given the legacy of Mexico's territorial loss to the United States, many Mexicans opposed welcoming foreigners—especially from the United States—to own and benefit from Mexican economic resources. Mexican nationalism was imbued with hostility toward U.S. influence. These strongly felt ideas helped shape conflicts in the decades that followed.

On 20 November 1910 Francisco Madero called for an insurrection against Díaz. Madero claimed that he had been cheated of victory in the 1910 presidential elections. In May 1911 Díaz resigned. The revolution that followed was among the most violent and massive civil wars in the twentieth century, but out of it came the foundations of a new political, economic, and social order in Mexico. The United States exerted considerable influence in Mexico during the revolution. U.S. Ambassador Henry Lane Wilson placed great pressure on President Madero's government and played an active role in fostering General Victoriano Huerta's coup to overthrow Madero in February 1913. Weeks later, Woodrow Wilson was inaugurated as president of the United States. He condemned the Huerta coup and recalled the U.S. ambassador. General Venustiano Carranza formed a new Constitutionalist army, bought weapons in the United States, and opened war on Huerta. The U.S. government organized an arms and financial credit embargo on Mexico.

In April 1914, at the port of Tampico, Mexican officers arrested some U.S. sailors for entering a restricted area but then released them with an apology. The U.S. admiral demanded, however, that Mexican authorities hoist the U.S. flag and give it a twenty-one gun salute. When that was not done and when President Wilson received news that a German ship was scheduled to arrive at the port of Veracruz (Mexico's most important harbor) with an arms shipment for Huerta, Wilson ordered the seizure of Veracruz. This was intended to build up pressure to oust Huerta. The port was also occupied by U.S. forces after a severe bombardment that resulted in hundreds of Mexican casualties and generated violent demonstrations against the United States in several Mexican cities. In July, Huerta resigned, but U.S. troops continued to occupy Veracruz for seven months, while Carranza assumed power in Mexico City. In late 1915 the United States recognized the Carranza government and declared an arms embargo on all of his opponents.

Civil war continued in Mexico, however. From his bases in northern Mexico, General Francisco ("Pancho") Villa fought Carranza. On 9 March 1916 several hundred of Villa's troops attacked the town of Columbus, New Mexico. Days later, President Wilson ordered U.S. troops into Mexico to capture Villa. Commanded by General John Pershing, several thousand U.S. troops roamed through northern Mexico for ten months, but Villa was never captured. As the United States faced the possibility of war with Germany, President Wilson ordered the withdrawal of U.S. troops from Mexico. On 5 February 1917 Mexico proclaimed a new constitution; on that same day, the last U.S. troops left Mexico.

Also in February 1917, German foreign minister Arthur Zimmermann sent a note to the German minister in Mexico, the text of which was intercepted by the British. The telegram recalled the decision announced on 31 January that Germany would start unlimited submarine warfare against the United States. In the event of a U.S.-German war, Zimmermann instructed his minister to offer Mexico an alliance. In return for Mexico's siding with Germany against the United States in World War I, Mexico would recover the territories lost between 1848 and 1853. President Carranza rejected the German offer, but the British government released the text of the Zimmermann telegram in order to intensify anti-German feeling in the United States. On 6 April 1917 the United States declared war on Germany. Mexico remained neutral during the war but it traded actively with the United States and, in that way, indirectly assisted the U.S. war effort.

Major powers also competed for influence in Mexico because the country had become the world's leading exporter of petroleum as a result of increases in its own production and the wartime interruption of oil exports from other areas. Mexico's efforts to control its petroleum resources became a point of friction with the United States and other foreign governments. Revolutionary Mexico's new constitution mandated greater state control and regulation of economic activity. Mexico had also accumulated a substantial foreign debt during the revolutionary years but it had failed to service the debt. In 1923 the Bucareli Agreements established the procedures to settle the financial claims; in August the United States reestablished diplomatic relations with Mexico, which had been interrupted in 1920 when General Álvaro Obregón had overthrown President Carranza. Despite various partial agreements, the dispute over petroleum festered and became acute in the 1930s. On 18 March 1938 President Lázaro Cárdenas expropriated all foreign-owned petroleum firms, which in turn organized a world-wide boycott of Mexican oil. U.S. Ambassador Josephus Daniels recommended, and President Franklin D. Roosevelt agreed, that the U.S. government should not join in this boycott.

From Partnership to New Problems

Following the outbreak of World War II in Europe in September 1939, the United States, mindful of the need to prevent Mexico's being drawn into an anti-U.S. alliance and despite opposition from the oil firms, reached an agreement with Mexico in November 1941 on procedures to settle the oil dispute. When the United States entered the war in December 1941, Mexico broke off diplomatic relations with Germany, Japan, and Italy, and in January 1942 the U.S. and Mexican governments formed a joint defense commission. In April 1942 Mexico agreed to compensate the oil companies for a small fraction of what they claimed the properties had been worth; the U.S. government forced the companies to agree to these terms. After German submarines sank two Mexican tankers, on 30 May 1942 Mexico declared war on the Axis powers. Also in 1942, the United States and Mexico agreed that Mexican workers would work in the United States under an official contract to replace U.S. workers who had become soldiers. Until terminated in 1964, this Bracero Program became an engine for Mexican migration to the United States.

After 1945 the Mexican government focused on fostering economic growth. It attracted as well as regulated foreign direct investment, which overwhelmingly came from the United States. U.S. direct investments in Mexico increased from about $500 million in the early 1950s to nearly $5 billion in 1980. Trade between the two countries also increased, although Mexico stimulated its own industrial production by raising tariff and nontariff barriers against imports, a policy commonly known as import substitution industrialization. Typically, U.S.-Mexican trade accounted for more than 60 percent of Mexico's imports and exports during the 1960s and 1970, proportions that would rise in the late 1980s and early 1990s. The U.S. government opposed the Mexican government's emphasis on state-owned enterprises and economic regulation but on the whole relations remained cordial.

From the 1940s to the late 1960s, Mexico reduced the size of its armed forces and cooperated generally with U.S. foreign policy. Mexico opposed, however, U.S. intervention to overthrow the governments of Guatemala (1954) and Cuba after the 1959 revolution. Mexico was the only Latin American government that did not abide by the collective sanctions that the Organization of American States (OAS) imposed on communist Cuba in 1964 at the urging of the United States. Mexico never broke diplomatic or economic relations with Cuba, in part in response to the wishes of Mexican leftists, but more generally as a continuing symbol of its independence from the United States. Mexico also maintained diplomatic relations with the Soviet Union throughout the Cold War. The large size of the Soviet embassy staff in Mexico City concerned the U.S. government, which feared that Soviet personnel were used to spy on the United States.

From 1970 to 1982 Presidents Luis Echeverría and José López Portillo sought to redefine Mexico's domestic and international policies. The government intervened more to stimulate and to regulate the economy, and the number and size of state enterprises grew markedly. New discoveries of petroleum and natural gas fueled an economic boom in Mexico in the late 1970s. To finance these policies, Mexico incurred large debts. In 1980 López Portillo reaffirmed that Mexico would remain outside the General Agreement on Tariffs and Trade (GATT). The Mexican government sharply criticized aspects of U.S. foreign policy and advocated greater cooperation among Third World countries to enhance their independence from the United States. Mexico supported the Sandinista revolution in Nicaragua and, in the 1980s, strongly opposed U.S. policies toward Central America. Jointly with Venezuela through the San José Agreement, Mexico sold petroleum at discount prices to Central American and Caribbean countries. In the early 1980s the price of oil dropped.

In August 1982 Mexico announced that it could no longer service its foreign debt, and the U.S. government organized a financial rescue, but a long and profound economic crisis hurt Mexico for the remainder of the decade. Beginning in December 1982 President Miguel de la Madrid launched economic adjustment policies, such as deregulating the economy and privatizing state enterprises, policies that after December 1988 would be markedly accelerated by his successor, President Carlos Salinas de Gortari. In 1986 Mexico joined GATT and greatly reduced tariff barriers and eliminated most nontariff barriers. Mexico liberalized rules governing foreign investment; net foreign capital inflows into Mexico amounted to $22 billion in 1991 and $25 billion each in 1992 and 1993.

NAFTA and After

In 1991 President Salinas proposed that the United States and Mexico should negotiate a free trade agreement, and in 1992, Canada, the United States and Mexico signed the North American Free Trade Agreement (NAFTA). After acrimonious debate, the U.S. Senate ratified the agreement in December 1993. When NAFTA went into effect in January 1994, Mexico became the United States' second most important trading partner.

In 1993 and 1994, by virtually fixing the peso-dollar exchange rate the Mexican government permitted the peso's overvaluation in order to lower domestic inflation, increase the prospects that the U.S. government would ratify NAFTA, and lure international investors into Mexico. At the same time, however, the Mexican central bank loosened domestic credit to boost economic growth during a presidential election year. These contradictory policies reached a crisis point in December 1994. A major financial panic broke out; international investors pulled billions of dollars out of Mexico in a matter of days, severely depleting central bank reserves. The peso was allowed to float freely, and it collapsed.

In early 1995 the U.S. government led and coordinated the international financial rescue effort. An international credit facility worth $52.8 billion was created to help Mexico address the crisis. The U.S. Exchange Stabilization Fund (ESF) contributed $20 billion of this sum. The International Monetary Fund (IMF) contributed another $17.8 billion as part of an eighteen-month standby agreement, the largest IMF program ever. The Bank for International Settlements supplied $10 billion, the Government of Canada $1 billion, commercial banks $3 billion, and the governments of Argentina, Brazil, Chile, and Colombia $1 billion. The U.S. funds are contingent on Mexico's observance of the IMF standby program. Under the ESF agreement, the Mexican government allows its oil export revenue to be deposited at the Federal Reserve Bank of New York; the United States can keep these funds if Mexico were to fail to repay the United States.

Political relations between the United States and Mexico improved as well by the early 1990s, thanks to the end of civil wars in Central America and of the Cold War. Mexico and the United States still differed in their policies toward Cuba but had come closer in their advocacy of changes in Cuba. Since the 1960s Mexico has been a leader in seeking to prevent the proliferation of nuclear weapons in Latin America through the Treaty of Tlatelolco, a policy supported by the United States.

Substantial illegal migration from Mexico to the United States remained an occasional cause of friction. Several hundred thousand Mexicans entered the United States without proper documents every year in the 1980s and early 1990s. Such illegal migration, as well as U.S. efforts to block it and to capture and deport those already in the United States, irritated bilateral relations. In November 1994 voters in the state of California approved Proposition 187 which denies health, education, and other public services to illegal immigrants. The Mexican government actively but unsuccessfully sought to prevent passage of this measure, the first time the Mexican government tried to affect the vote in a U.S. state election.

Important conflicts have also developed between the United States and Mexico over the production of marijuana and heroin in Mexico and their shipment to the United States, as well as over the transshipment through Mexico to the United States of South American cocaine. Conflicts between the two governments over the drug traffic were most acute during the mid-1980s, but in the late 1980s and early 1990s, the Mexican government devoted substantial resources to combat drug trafficking, although neither U.S. nor Mexican efforts have been very successful in curbing drug trafficking.

Mexico's domestic political system has remained undemocratic. The ruling Institutional Revolutionary Party (PRI) has received broad support for its long-standing policies of economic growth and public order have received broad support, but the party has also abused its power and used coercion and electoral fraud to win many elections. The PRI has never acknowledged the loss of a presidential election. Although the PRI claimed to have won the 1988 presidential election by nearly a two-to-one margin, Carlos Salinas probably won that election by a whisker. Until 1989 the PRI had never acknowledged the loss of a gubernatorial election, and for decades the PRI has commanded powerful majorities in both chambers of the Mexican congress. In 1994 Ernesto Zedillo was elected president after important electoral reforms had been enacted to make the elections fairer and more transparent, but significant irregularities continued to mar this election as well, although many international observers, including hundreds from the United States, witnessed the elections. The PRI retained control of both chambers of congress. In response to the financial panic and the deep economic recession that developed during 1995, Mexicans began to vote for opposition parties in various state elections, suggesting that the PRI's long hold on the national government may be at risk in the next presidential elections.

For the most part, since the 1940s the U.S. government has refrained from interfering in Mexican domestic politics and has even eschewed public commentary concerning violations of human rights and the undemocratic aspects of Mexico's domestic politics. Since the mid-1980s some members of the U.S. Congress, the mass media, and nongovernmental organizations began to focus their attention on these issues. The NAFTA provisions to oversee labor practices within member countries provide one means for these concerns to be aired. As a result, differences over democracy, human rights, and labor practices may become important sources of conflict between the U.S. and Mexican governments.

Along the long land border that connects the United States and Mexico, a shared culture has emerged. The peoples of both countries mingle regularly as tourists and neighbors and in business. The residents alongside the border are literally joined in their daily lives. They share water and the environment, listen to popular English-language music on similar radio stations, and eat Mexican foods with Spanish-language names; their municipal fire departments assist each other, and their traffic police cooperate to relieve traffic jams near the border. The economy on each side of the border depends on the prosperity of the other side. There is a sharing of quotidian experiences quite independent of the decisions of foreign policy made in Washington or Mexico City.

JORGE I. DOMÍNGUEZ

See also Bucareli Agreements; Cuba; Díaz (José de la Cruz), Porfirio; Gadsden Purchase; Huerta, Victoriano; Immigration; Juárez, Benito Pablo; Mexico, War with; Monroe Doctrine; North American Free Trade Agreement; Oil and Foreign Policy; Pershing, John; Third World Debt; Villa, Pancho; Zimmermann Telegram

FURTHER READING

Cline, Howard F. *The United States and Mexico*. Cambridge, Mass., 1953.
Council on Foreign Relations, *Lessons of the Mexican Peso Crisis*. New York, 1996.
Domínguez, Jorge I., and James A. McCann. *Democratizing Mexico: Public Opinion and Electoral Choices*. Baltimore, 1996.
Green, Rosario, and Peter H. Smith, eds. *Dimensions of United States–Mexican Relations*, 5 vols. La Jolla, Calif., 1989.
Ojeda, Mario. *Alcances y límites de la política exterior de México*. Mexico City, 1976.
Pastor, Robert A., and Jorge G. Castañeda. *Limits to Friendship: The United States and Mexico*. New York, 1988.
Raat, W. Dirk. *Mexico and the United States: Ambivalent Vistas*. Athens, Ga., 1992.
Vázquez, Josefina Zoraida, and Lorenzo Meyer. *The United States and Mexico*. Chicago, 1985.

MEXICO, WAR WITH

(1846–1848)

The U.S-Mexican conflict that ended with Mexico's defeat and an enlarged continental empire for the United States. James K. Polk entered the presidency in March 1845, facing a challenge from Mexico that presaged both trouble and opportunity. He was determined to see, as he advised George Bancroft, his secretary of the navy, that one major objective of his administration was the acquisition of California, a province of Mexico. For Polk, however, the immediate issue in U.S.-Mexican relations was Texas. Repeatedly the Mexican government had warned U.S. officials that it would not tolerate that region's annexation by the United States. Congress voted annexation by joint resolution during John Tyler's final days in the White House. When Polk proceeded to complete the process of annexation, General Juan Almonte, the Mexican minister in Washington, sailed for Vera Cruz to sever his country's relations with the United States.

Issues of Texas and California

Responding to rumors of a possible Mexican invasion of Texas, Polk reinforced the U.S. squadron in the Gulf and ordered General Zachary Taylor to advance from Fort Jessup in Louisiana down the Gulf coast to Corpus Christi on the Nueces River. The president wanted Mexico to accept not only the loss of Texas but also Texas's claim to the Rio Grande. What exacerbated U.S.-Mexican tensions in 1845 was the unpaid claims against Mexico for its failure to protect U.S. citizens in Mexico from robbery, theft, and other illegal actions. Polk knew that Mexico could not pay. If the two countries went to war, it would be for reasons other than the enforcement of claims.

In September William S. Parrott, Polk's special agent in Mexico, assured the president that Mexican officials did not contemplate either a declaration of war or an invasion of Texas. Polk's ready conviction that Mexicans would not attack suggests that his deployment of land and naval forces along Mexico's borders was designed less to defend Texas than to underwrite an aggressive diplomacy that would extract a satisfactory treaty from a weak and disorganized Mexico. He assumed that his limited military measures in Texas would be sufficient to convince the Mexican government that it could not escape the necessity of coming to terms with the United States. Much of the American press lauded the president for his decision to strengthen the country's posture to deal effectively with recalcitrant Mexican officials. Whether the burgeoning pressure that Washington exerted on Mexico would bring a negotiated boundary settlement or war depended on the acceptability of Polk's demands to a distraught and insecure Mexican administration.

Even as Congress, in 1845, prepared to accept Texas into the Union, Polk's attention shifted from the Rio Grande to his major objective, Mexican California. During the summer Thomas O. Larkin, an American merchant and U.S. consul in Monterrey, warned the administration of apparent British and French designs on the Mexican province. Polk appointed Larkin as his secret agent to report British and French activities and encourage the people of California to cast their destiny with the United States. Mexican editors and officials recognized both Polk's ambitions toward California as well as that distant region's vulnerability to U.S. encroachments by land and sea. "California is entirely at the mercy of the North Americans," lamented *El Amigo del Pueblo* (Mexico City) in August 1845. "In regard to the United States," observed *El Patriola Mexicano* (Mexico City) in November, "its designs [on California] are no longer a mystery." For *El Siglo Diez y Nueve* (Mexico City) the strongest evidence of U.S. ambition was the "irritating insolence" that the newspapers of the United States displayed in advocating emigration and the annexation of California.

Mexico reached out to Charles Bankhead, the British minister, for help, even offering his country a protectorate over California, but to no avail. The British government was not prepared to support the Mexican cause. Bankhead advised the Mexicans to avoid a confrontation with the United States.

For both British and Mexican officials, John Slidell's mission to Mexico in November 1845 appeared no less than an American effort to impose an immediate boundary settlement on a chaotic Mexico under the threat of force. In September Parrott informed Washington that Mexico was prepared to resume diplomatic relations. The president responded by appointing Slidell, of Louisiana, as minister to Mexico. The Department of State hurriedly prepared the necessary instructions, troubled by rumors of the impending collapse of the peacefully disposed regime of José Joaquín Herrera. Upon receiving his orders in Pensacola, Slidell departed for Vera Cruz. By early December he had taken up residence in Mexico City. Slidell's presence in Mexico inaugurated a diplomatic crisis; the Polk administration seemed to be offering Mexico the choice between the acceptance of a body of concrete diplomatic demands or eventual war.

Slidell's instructions revealed Polk's territorial designs with considerable clarity. For $40 million and the cancellation of all U.S. claims against Mexico he hoped to acquire a boundary along the Rio Grande to the 32nd parallel and then west to the Pacific. Travelers and sea captains had long agreed that two harbors gave special significance to the California of the 1840s—the bays of San Francisco and San Diego. Polk's pursuit of frontage on the distant ocean especially included the acquisition of San Francisco and Monterey, but included San Diego as well. Never before had the United States asked any country to part with a portion of its home territory, but the president assumed that Mexico, because of its military and financial helplessness, would accept a negotiated settlement, especially one that included a substantial transfer of money. It is true that Polk, in Slidell's instructions, agreed to settle for the Rio Grande boundary alone in exchange for the cancellation of claims, but that arrangement would merely have postponed an inescapable confrontation over California. Herrera, predictably, refused to respond. His government fell to General Mariano Paredes in January 1846. The new regime's equally uncompromising mood eliminated for Washington the possibility of any immediate, satisfactory boundary settlement.

Throughout the crisis months of 1845 and early 1846 writers and officials who shared the president's impatience were prepared to deny Mexico the luxury of further procrastination. Parrott informed Secretary of State James Buchanan in October that he wished "to see this people well flogged by Uncle Sam's boys, ere we enter upon negotiations.... I know [the Mexicans] better, perhaps, than any other U.S. citizen and I am fully persuaded, they can never love and respect us, as we should be loved and respected by them, until we shall have given them a positive proof of our superiority." Mexico's pretensions would continue, wrote Slidell in late December, "until the Mexican people shall be convinced by hostile demonstrations, that our differences must be settled promptly, either by negotiation or the sword." In January 1846 the *Washington Union* publicly threatened Mexico with war if it rejected the just demands of the United States: "The result of such a course on her part may compel us to resort to more decisive measures...to obtain the settlement of our legitimate claims." As Slidell prepared to leave Mexico in March, he reminded the administration: "Depend upon it, we can never get along well with them, until we have given them a good drubbing." Members of the Democratic press, steeped in the rhetoric of Manifest Destiny, had already begun to clamor for war.

Such sentiment, widespread and threatening, placed Mexico under intense diplomatic pressure to negotiate away its territories; it created no moral obligation for Mexico to do so. For Mexican editors and officials the U.S. offer of money for California was, in reality, a demand for capitulation. In their denunciations of American aggressiveness they were undiplomatic and even insulting, but scarcely provocative. Herrera and Paredes had the right to protect their regimes from anti-American extremists by avoiding formal recognition of Slidell and rejecting U.S. boundary proposals, provided that they did not, in the process, endanger any legitimate interests of the U.S. people. Mexico had not invaded the United States or Texas and did not contemplate doing so. Settlers, in time, would have forced a boundary settlement, probably at the Rio Grande, but in 1846 the region between the Nueces and the Rio Grande remained largely an uninhabited wilderness. Except for the president's ambitions, there was nothing to prevent the United States from reducing its demands on Mexico, in quest of a mutual accord, or withdrawing them altogether and permitting U.S.-Mexican relations to drift unattended until some more propitious occasion. But the president sent Slidell to Mexico less to normalize relations than to gain an immediate boundary settlement favorable to the United States.

Polk's Pressures on Mexico

Backed by the country's vast superiority in military power, and by its pervading anti-Mexican mood fed by racist notions of Mexican inferiority, Polk adopted the third course that Mexican resistance offered. He proceeded to escalate the pressures on Mexico in pursuit of an eventual settlement on his own terms. He denounced Mexico in his annual message of December 1845. Then in January 1846 he instructed General Taylor to advance from the Nueces through contested territory to the Rio Grande. That decision revealed his contempt for Mexico. Under no national obligation to expose the country's armed forces, he would not have advanced Taylor in the face of a superior military force. Colonel Atocha, the exiled Mexican, assured Polk that additional military pressure would expose Mexico's financial and military weakness and compel it to accept the American boundary proposal. Thereafter the president never questioned the efficacy of coercion. He reminded his cabinet on 17 February that strong measures alone would bring the Mexican government to terms. A week later he informed the cabinet, as he noted in his diary, that the United States "had attempted to conciliate Mexico in vain, and had forborne until forbearance was no longer either a virtue or patriotic." What drove the president's escalation to the point of war was his determination to gain objectives that lay outside the possibilities of successful negotiations. Senator Thomas Hart Benton of Missouri wrote perceptively: "It is impossible to conceive of an administration less warlike, or more intriguing, than that of Mr. Polk. They were men of peace, with objectives to be accomplished by means of war; so that war was a necessity and an indispensability to their purpose."

During March, Taylor established his headquarters on the northern bank of the Rio Grande opposite the Mexican village of Matamoros, assuring its citizens that the United States harbored no hostility toward Mexico. Mexican officials protested another U.S. assault on the Law of Nations. On 11 April General Pedro Ampudia, backed by 3,000 Mexican troops, arrived at Matamoros and immediately ordered Taylor to return to Corpus Christi. Taylor, proclaiming that he had encamped at the Rio Grande on presidential orders, refused to move. In Mexico City Paredes approached Bankhead with another plea for help. Bankhead advised the Mexicans to avoid any show of force along the Rio Grande frontier, suspecting correctly that the Mexican government, facing a massive threat to its entire diplomatic and military position, would in time reveal the impatience of those who find their defenses disintegrating. Polk faced the certainty of a clash along the Rio Grande and did nothing to avoid it. The cabinet in Washington repeatedly discussed the possibility of a brush with Mexican forces. On 6 May the president received dispatches from Taylor, dated 15 April. He noted in his diary: "No actual collision has taken place, though the probabilities are that hostilities might take place soon." On 9 May the cabinet agreed that any Mexican attack on Taylor's forces would require an immediate message to Congress requesting a declaration of war.

As the crisis mounted, Mexican patience wore thin. On 23 April, Paredes issued a proclamation declaring a defensive war against the United States. Predictably, Mexican soldiers, one day later, fired on a detachment of U.S. dragoons. Taylor's report reached Washington on the evening of Saturday, 9 May. On Sunday Polk drafted his war message and sent it to Congress on the following day. With American forces directly engaged with the enemy on a distant frontier, Polk's assertion that American blood had been shed on American soil was sufficient to assure an immediate and overwhelming congressional acceptance of the War with Mexico. Still, the president's Whig, Abolitionist, and Democratic critics were troubled by his decisions that had placed U.S. forces where they surely would draw Mexican fire. Alexander H. Stephens of Georgia attributed the war to the president's "imprudence, indiscretion, and mismanagement." Joshua Giddings, the Ohio Whig, declared that no sophistry could disguise the fact that "the president obviously intended to involve us in a war with Mexico." John C. Calhoun, the noted South Carolina Democrat, complained that Polk, by placing U.S. troops on the Rio Grande, had "stripped Congress of the power of making war, and what is more and worse, it gave that power to every officer, nay, to every subaltern commanding a corporal's guard." When Congress adjourned in August, Robert Winthrop of Massachusetts boasted that the Whigs in Washington were unanimous in their opposition to the administration.

The War

During the weeks that followed the declaration of war on 13 May, the cabinet addressed the question of war aims. At the outset Polk determined to secure the Rio Grande boundary as well as San Francisco and Monterey on the California coast. In mid-June Secretary of the Navy Bancroft assured Samuel Hooper, Marblehead merchant, that the American flag soon would be flying over these two ports. With this promise Hooper would not rest. He prodded the administration to look southward along the coast. A settlement at the 32nd parallel, he informed Bancroft, would include Los Angeles and the magnificent bay of San Diego. Such a settlement would enable the United States to command all the trade along the California coast. It would, moreover, encompass the entire American population of California and leave a huge, barren wilderness between American California and the large Mexican cities to the south. Acceding to New England's wishes, the administration now looked to San Diego. "If Mexico makes peace this month," Bancroft informed Hooper on 22 June, "the Rio Del Norte and the parallel of 35 degrees may do as a boundary; after that 32 degrees which will include San Diego."

Supported by a national commitment to a victorious war, Polk set out to achieve through force precisely what he had failed to gain through purchase and the assumption of claims against Mexico. Before the end of May he

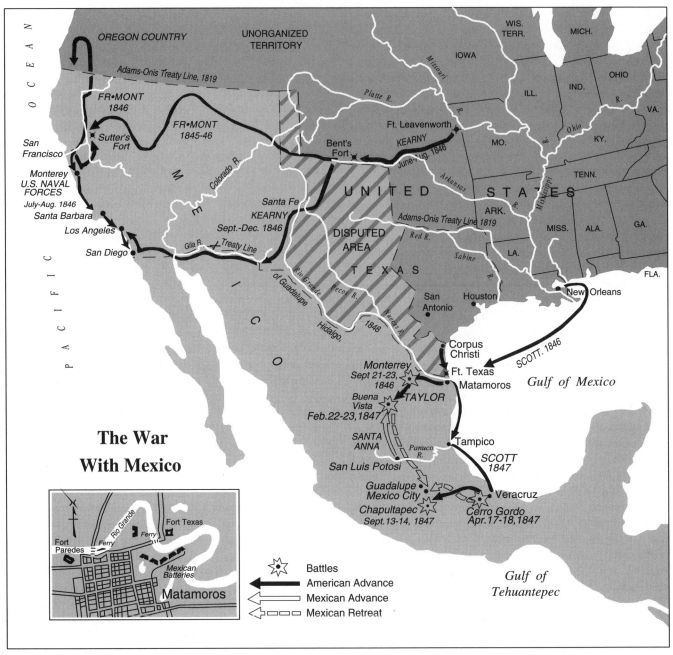

The War With Mexico

From *American Foreign Relations*, Thomas G. Paterson, J. Garry Clifford, and Kenneth J. Hagan, Volume I. ©1995 by D.C. Heath and Company.
Reprinted with permission of Houghton Mifflin Company.

mounted expeditions by land and sea to guarantee U.S. control of California and New Mexico at the end of the war. He ordered Stephen W. Kearny, Colonel of Dragoons at Fort Leavenworth, to occupy Santa Fe and proceed overland to California. That month John C. Frémont, on his third expedition to the West, was encamped at Marysville Buttes on the Sacramento when American pioneers suddenly congregated at his camp and declared the Bear Flag revolt. They captured Sonoma and raised their new flag. Frémont and his men joined the revolt,

raising the possibility that American emigrants would soon convert California into another Texas, but the American fleet quickly took command of the American conquest of California.

Commodore John D. Sloat, commander of the Pacific Fleet, was anchored off Mazatlán when he received news from Mexico City that Congress had declared war against Mexico. On 2 July his frigate, the *Savannah*, reached Monterey where he found two U.S. sloops of war. Sloat took possession of Monterey on 7 July; two days later

U.S. forces occupied San Francisco and Sonoma. Commodore Robert F. Stockton, who received the command from Sloat in mid-July, enlisted the Bear Flag Pioneers and dispatched Frémont by ship to San Diego to gain possession of that port. Stockton followed in the *Congress*, raised the flag at Santa Barbara and took possession of San Pedro. Believing the region secure, both men returned to northern California. But During September the Californians revolted and regained possession of Los Angeles. Kearny learned of the revolt while still in the desert. He fought his way into California and met Stockton at San Diego. Stockton, now reinforced, recaptured Los Angeles in January 1847. All of California was now under U.S. control.

To strengthen his powers of coercion against the Mexican government, Polk required a successful invasion of Mexico itself. Taylor, without specific instructions, followed minor engagements north of the Rio Grande with an advance into Mexican territory, occupying Matamoros on 18 May. During June he moved slowly toward Monterrey, the major trading and transportation center of northeast Mexico. As Taylor approached the city in September, his engineers reported that the city's terrain gave an overwhelming strategic advantage to the defenders. Taylor decided to assault Monterrey directly while General William Jenkins Worth, with 2,000 men, flanked the defenses, gained control of the Saltillo Road, and cut off the supply route into the city. Several days of intense fighting gave Worth control of the Saltillo Road and permitted him to enter Monterrey from the west. Taylor, using his artillery effectively, assaulted the city from the northeast. As the two U.S. forces converged on the heart of the city, General Ampudia surrendered. Taylor permitted the Mexican army to evacuate. In November the U.S. invasion forces occupied Saltillo. Shortly thereafter General John E. Wool reached Saltillo, having completed a rapid march from San Antonio. Thus reinforced, Taylor prepared for a showdown with the Mexican army.

Polk was scarcely overjoyed with Taylor's successes. In the pages of his diary he dealt harshly with the general, accusing him of incompetence and political ambition. Such a view was not without reason, for Whig managers were openly grooming Taylor for the party's nomination in 1848. Polk had no intention of directing a victorious war against Mexico only to hand the presidency to a popular general of his own creation. During the autumn of 1846 the president decided to transfer the main thrust of the U.S. offensive to a direct assault on Mexico City through Vera Cruz. For this expedition he selected, reluctantly, another Whig, General Winfield Scott. At the same time the administration, in an effort to concentrate the country's limited resources and manpower on the Mexico City campaign, ordered Taylor to establish a defense line and hold it. But General Antonio López de Santa Anna, having recently returned to Mexico from exile and taken command of the Mexican army, was convinced that Taylor's army was vulnerable. He moved northward with 20,000 men to capture or annihilate the American forces headquartered at Saltillo. During February 1847 he struck Taylor's defenses at Buena Vista near Saltillo. After some colorful maneuvering and one fierce day of battle, Santa Anna withdrew to San Luis Potosí. His retreat brought the northern Mexican campaign to a close.

The easy U.S. successes in California and northern Mexico against weakened and disorganized resistance presaged brilliant victories for Scott's expedition into central Mexico. During March 1847 Scott's invasion forces invaded the coastal city of Vera Cruz and captured it on 27 March. To avoid yellow fever in the lowlands, Scott set out immediately against little opposition along the main road to Mexico City. Santa Anna, having reconstituted his forces following his defeat at Buena Vista, rushed southward to meet Scott's advance at Cerro Gordo Pass. The U.S. Army reached the pass in mid-April only to find Santa Anna in complete command of the highway. American engineers discovered a route leading off to the left of Mexican positions; over this Scott sent a division under David Twiggs. Placed under fire by direct and flanking attacks, the Mexicans retreated, Santa Anna narrowly escaping capture. Scott pushed on to Jalapa and, on 6 May, occupied Puebla. Here he and his officers, free from guerrilla assault and enjoying the hospitality of the local Mexican aristocracy, prepared slowly for the final advance to Mexico City, 75 miles to the west.

Meanwhile the administration was trapped in the dilemma of conducting a victorious war in pursuit of precise and uncompromisable objectives while it dared not declare those objectives publicly. The principle of territorial indemnity, clearly recognized by the law of nations, was acceptable only to those Americans who placed responsibility for the war on Mexico. For the legions who opposed the war, the acquisition of California would comprise conquest, not indemnity. Even as he intensified the American assault on Mexico, the president informed Congress, in late 1846, that his objective was to obtain "an honorable peace and thereby secure ample indemnity for the expenses of the war." He avoided any precise definition of such indemnification. No longer was there any assurance that a victorious war would guarantee a satisfactory peace. Daniel Webster observed with considerable accuracy that the real barrier to a successful termination of the war was the Mexican government, not the Mexican army. He wrote to his son as early as August, "Mexico is an ugly enemy. She will not fight—and will not retreat." The president himself acknowledged in December: "Such is the distracted state of things in that unfortunate country, that I fear no party in power, will feel secure in making such a treaty as ought to be satisfactory to the United States." But even in his January 1847 request to Congress for a special appropriation to aid him in negotiating a peace, he admitted no purpose other than the defrayment of "any extraordinary expenses which may be incurred in order to bring the existing War with Mexico to a speedy and honorable conclusion."

For Polk the only hope for a satisfactory peace lay in a more ruthless prosecution of the war against Mexico. In Washington, however, he faced a recalcitrant Congress that refused to act on the necessary war measures. Whigs accused him of attempting to wrench California from Mexico by force. Thomas Corwin of Ohio, in typical fashion, belabored the doctrine of territorial indemnity: "You want 'more room'! This has been the plea of every robber from Nimrod to the present day." Those who favored the acquisition of Mexican territory demanded that the president acquire it through purchase or negotiation, not conquest. By early 1847 Polk found himself in the unenviable position of conducting a bitterly assailed and burdensome war whose objectives, demanding victory, he could not reveal. His repeated efforts to contact the Mexican government through friendly Mexican intermediaries ended in failure. Without a promising strategy for peace, the president harangued the cabinet on the need to discard the cumbersome baggage trains and the technical rules of warfare and, instead, move forward with lightning strokes to destroy the enemy wherever he might be found. But congressional trifling and the more and more strident condemnation of the war drove the administration to seek a new solution.

Trist Mission and the Peace Treaty

Despite Mexico's demonstrated reluctance to negotiate, Polk, in his determination to escape the endless congressional condemnation of the war and embarrassing Whig demands that he declare his war aims, grasped at the hope that the U.S. victories of February and March 1847 might compel the Mexican government to acknowledge defeat and accept his peace terms. To maintain secrecy and protect his goals from public scrutiny, the President entrusted his new peace effort to the special mission of Nicholas P. Trist, chief clerk in the Department of State and onetime private secretary of president Andrew Jackson. Trist departed quietly from Washington in mid-April, carrying detailed instructions to join Scott's army and seek some occasion to open negotiations with Mexican officials. His instructions demanded, as territorial indemnity, a boundary along the Rio Grande to New Mexico, west along the Gila, and down the Colorado "to a point directly opposite the division line between Upper and Lower California; thence due west, along said line, which runs north of the parallel of 32 degrees and south of San Miguel to the Pacific Ocean." This boundary

would assure the acquisition of San Diego. Polk agreed to compensate Mexico as much as $25 million for New Mexico and Upper California. Trist, traveling incognito, kept his secret well, but the news of his mission, as well as his instructions, soon appeared in the national press, much to the administration's embarrassment.

Trist reached Vera Cruz in early May and joined Scott's forces at Puebla a month later. He immediately addressed a letter to Charles Bankhead in Mexico City, requesting him to inform Mexican officials of his presence in the country. Bankhead dispatched Edward Thornton of the British legation to Puebla to enlighten Trist on the status of Mexican affairs. Late in June, Thornton returned to Puebla to suggest the possibility of negotiations, adding that the process might be encouraged with the artful application of gold. Meanwhile, to Washington's consternation, a verbal feud had broken out between Trist and Scott. When the general, deeply distrustful of the president, refused to comply with his instructions, Trist chose to absorb Scott's abuse of the administration. He read a lengthy lecture to the general, confiding to his wife, "If I have not demolished him, then I give up." The letter almost drove Scott to derangement. His first impulse, he answered Trist, was to return the "farrago of insolence, conceit, and arrogance to the author," but decided instead to preserve it "as a choice specimen of diplomatic literature and manners."

This vituperative exchange had continued for several weeks when Trist realized that any negotiation required Scott's cooperation; the general alone could delay the army at Puebla and make funds available to secure Santa Anna's cooperation. Scott's response was cordial and soon the two men became fast friends. With no Mexican overtures forthcoming, Scott, in August, moved his army into the beautiful Valley of Mexico. Not until the American victories at Contreras and Churubusco, around 20 August, did Santa Anna agree to an armistice. He balked at Trist's terms, but offered a counterproposal that included the two California ports of San Francisco and Monterey. Trist, in the interest of peace, forwarded the Mexican proposal to Washington. Meanwhile Santa Anna broke the armistice. Scott now made his final assault on the Mexican capital, taking Molino del Rey in a hard-fought battle on 8 September. Five days later his forces stormed the fortress of Chapultepec. Rather than subject Mexico City to bombardment, Mexican officials gave up the capital. Against sporadic resistance the victorious American Army occupied the city on 17 September.

Before the end of September news of the August armistice filtered across the nation through the New Orleans press. The Mexican rejection of Trist's terms convinced editors and political leaders alike that the armistice was a hoax, designed to grant the Mexican forces time to strengthen their defenses before Mexico

City. Trist, moreover, in submitting the Mexican proposal to Washington, seemed to be ignoring his instructions. A brief diary notation explained the president's decision to recall him: "Mr. Trist is recalled because his remaining any longer with the army could not, probably, accomplish the objects of his mission, and because his remaining longer might, & probably would, impress the Mexican government with the belief that the United States were so anxious for peace that they would ultimate[ly] conclude one upon the Mexican terms." In his letter of recall, Buchanan reminded Trist that San Diego was "for every commercial purpose of nearly equal importance to the United States with that of San Francisco." His instructions, Buchanan continued, directed him "to secure to us the port & harbor of San Diego beyond all question." With the rejection of Trist, the administration had no plan remaining to convert the country's military triumphs into an acceptable peace. Polk's initial purpose of exerting vigorous, if limited, pressure on the Mexican government—just enough to gain his precise territorial objectives—ended in miscalculation simply because he possessed no power to compel a Mexican government to accept his terms.

The still-elusive peace, with an ephemeral Mexican government threatening to prolong the costly and troublesome war indefinitely, convinced members of the expansionist press that the United States had no choice but to meet its destiny and annex the entire Mexican Republic. Following the American occupation of Mexico City, the all-Mexico movement gathered momentum as it brushed aside all scruples about annexing millions of Mexican citizens. In October the *New York Globe* called attention to a new spirit in the land, "a spirit of progress, which will compel us, for the good of both nations and the world at large, TO DESTROY THE NATIONALITY of that besotted people. It would almost seem that they, like the Israelites of old, had brought upon themselves the vengeance of the Almighty, and we ourselves had been raised up to overthrow AND UTTERLY DESTROY THEM as a separate and distinct nation." In December the *New York Evening Post* charged that the Mexican people did not possess the elements to exist independently alongside the United States. "Providence has so ordained it," the *Post* continued, "and it is folly not to recognize the fact. The Mexicans are Aboriginal Indians, and they must share the destiny of their race." During December and January, with Congress in session, Democratic orators seized control of the all-Mexico movement and carried this new burst of expansionism to unprecedented heights of extravagance.

In his annual message of December 1847 Polk rejected the demands for all of Mexico and, for the first time, acknowledged publicly his long-established designs on New Mexico and California. He reminded Congress that "the doctrine of no territory is the doctrine of no indemnity; and, if sanctioned, would be a public acknowledgment that our country was wrong, and that the war declared by Congress…was unjust, and should be abandoned." Unable to discover any Mexican government willing to cede California, Polk asked Congress for additional troops so that he might escalate the military pressures against Mexico. The president's limited goals, devoid of any long-range obligations to Mexico's political reform, satisfied the important segment of editors, politicians, and public that wanted a satisfactory end to the American intervention in Mexican affairs and agreed that the surest guarantee of peace lay in greater coercion of the Mexican populace. Meanwhile the antiwar sentiment became more embittered and the president's embarrassment more profound. Week after week the so-called Ten Regiment Bill furnished the vehicle for Whig invectives against the administration and its unending war against Mexico, a war already won by all civilized standards. The *Haverhill (Massachusetts) Gazette* proclaimed, "TO VOLUNTEER OR VOTE A DOLLAR TO CARRY ON THE WAR IS MORAL TREASON AGAINST THE GOD OF HEAVEN, AND THE RIGHTS OF MANKIND." Whig critics termed the war a crime and an outrage upon Mexico. No less than abolitionists and peace advocates, many Whigs demanded that the president abandon his wartime goals and terminate the occupation by withdrawing all U.S. forces from Mexico.

Unknown to Washington, Mexican officials had approached Trist in late November with what appeared to be a serious overture. During subsequent days they pleaded with him to remain in Mexico and negotiate a settlement. Encouraged by Scott and assured that any treaty he negotiated would convey San Diego to the United States, Trist ignored his instructions to leave Mexico. During January 1848 he negotiated the Treaty of Guadalupe Hidalgo, signed on 2 February 1848. Mexico accepted the Rio Grande as the division between Texas and Mexico and ceded New Mexico and California. Trist's line of demarcation across California joined the mouth of the Gila River at the Colorado with a point on the Pacific one league south of San Diego Bay. For the Mexican cession the United States agreed to pay $15 million and to assume the claims of U.S. citizens against Mexico. Polk rejected Trist totally, refusing to see him or to defray his expenses in Mexico. He acknowledged that Trist's recall perhaps rendered the treaty inadmissible, but he quickly accepted it. It not only relieved him of an ongoing crisis for which he had no solution but it also achieved the boundary settlement that he desired.

On 23 February the president forwarded the treaty to the Senate, which approved it on 10 March by a vote of 38 to 14. The treaty's opponents comprised those who wanted more territory from Mexico and those who wanted none. The Mexican Congress ratified the treaty on 25 May. Polk emerged from the war so triumphantly that historians have seldom recognized the dilemma that he faced in Mexico. Peace followed the war so satisfactorily that the process of coming to terms with the Mexican government seemed to pose no problem at all. Yet the president had lost control of U.S.-Mexican relations so completely that he had nowhere to turn. It was only by the narrowest of good fortune that he was permitted to rid himself and the country of the burdensome Mexican intervention before he retired from office.

NORMAN A. GRAEBNER

See also California; Frémont, John Charles; Larkin, Thomas Oliver; Manifest Destiny; Polk, James Knox; Slidell, John; Taylor, Zachary

FURTHER READING

Bauer, K. Jack. *The Mexican War, 1846–1848.* New York, 1974.
Bill, Alfred Hoyt. *Rehearsal for Conflict: The War with Mexico, 1846–1848.* New York, 1947.
Eisenhower, John S.D. *So Far From God: The U.S. War with Mexico, 1846–1848.* New York, 1989.
Fuller, John Douglas Pitts. *The Movement for the Acquisition of all Mexico, 1846–1848.* Baltimore, Md., 1938.
Graebner, Norman A. *Foundations of American Foreign Policy: A Realist Appraisal from Franklin to McKinley.* Wilmington, 1985.
———. *Empire on the Pacific: A Study in American Continental Expansion.* re-issued Claremont, Calif., 1989.
Merk, Frederick. *Manifest Destiny and Mission in American History: A Reinterpretation.* New York, 1966.
Pletcher, David M. *The Diplomacy of Annexation: Texas, Oregon, and the Mexican War.* Columbia, Missouri, 1973.
Singletary, Otis A. *The Mexican War.* Chicago, 1960.

MFN

See Most-Favored Nation Principle

MICRONESIA, FEDERATED STATES OF

See Appendix 2

MIDDLE EAST

The region encompassing part of North Africa and part of Southwestern Asia traditionally thought to include the lands stretching from Libya in the west to Iran in the east, and from Turkey in the north to the southern end of the Arabian Peninsula. Sustained U.S. foreign policy interest in the Middle East and North Africa dates only from World War II. Since that time U.S. foreign policy in the area has had three major goals: to limit Soviet influence, to safeguard U.S. interests in Middle Eastern oil,

and to foster a special relationship with Israel. These aims occasionally came into conflict, and U.S. administrations adopted different tactical approaches toward achieving them, but they provided the conceptual basis for Washington's approach to the area for more than four decades. The end of the Cold War brought little change in U.S. policy toward the Middle East, because involvement there is driven by concerns that were largely independent of the rivalry with Moscow. The fact that the United States fought its first post–Cold War conflict in the oil-rich Persian Gulf indicates that the intensity of Washington's interest in the area did not flag with the end of the Cold War.

Among the first countries to recognize the United States of America was the Sultanate (now Kingdom) of Morocco, with which the United States signed a commercial treaty in 1787. That treaty, updated, was still in force in the late 1990s. During the first two decades of the nineteenth century, U.S. naval forces fought local rulers on the North African coast (often called the Barbary States) to end depredations against U.S. shipping and the payment of tribute. The United States subsequently signed commercial treaties with the Ottoman Empire in 1830, the Sultanate of Muscat (now Oman) in 1833, and Persia (now Iran) in 1856.

Commerce, and not very much of it at that, defined the scope of official U.S. interests in the Middle East during the nineteenth century, but private U.S. citizens and institutions were during that time establishing important cultural presences throughout the region. Protestant missions were founded in Istanbul, in Beirut, and in Azerbaijan in Persia during the first decades of the nineteenth century. These missions concentrated their efforts on building educational and medical institutions. By 1860 more than 1,500 Iranian students were enrolled in U.S. mission schools. In 1863 Robert College, later to become Bosporus University, opened in Istanbul. In 1866 the Syrian Protestant College, later to become the American University in Beirut, opened. Protestant educational and medical missions also operated in Egypt and in the upper Persian Gulf (Basra, Kuwait, and Bahrain). The inevitable frictions caused by their presence in the local societies became, aside from commerce, the major cause of diplomatic contact between the United States and Middle Eastern governments during the nineteenth century.

By the turn of the twentieth century, the search for oil had replaced the search for souls as the major concern of private U.S. interests in the region. Diplomatic pressure from Washington in the 1920s on Great Britain and France led to a consortium of U.S. companies obtaining a one-quarter share in the Iraqi Petroleum Company. Standard Oil of California obtained a concession in Bahrain in 1928. Gulf Oil in 1933 formed the Kuwait Oil Company in a fifty-fifty part-

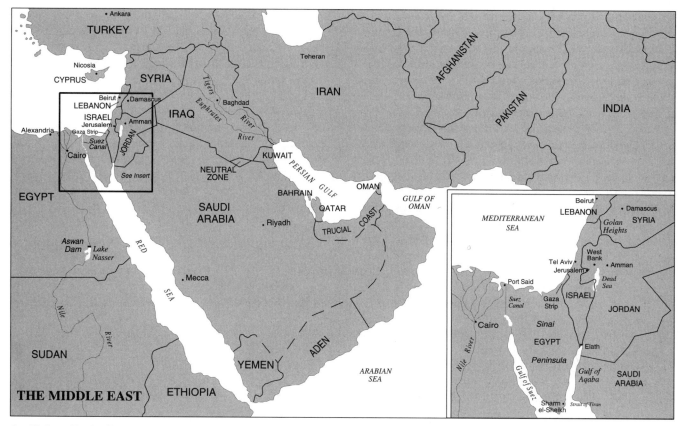

THE MIDDLE EAST

nership with the Anglo-Persian Oil Company (later British Petroleum). In 1933 Standard Oil of California received what would become the richest oil concession of all, Saudi Arabia. It brought in other U.S. companies—Texaco in 1936 and both Standard Oil of New Jersey (later Exxon) and Standard Oil of New York (later Mobil) in 1947—to help develop and market Saudi oil, forming the Arabian American Oil Company (Aramco). Washington waived antitrust regulations to promote the new partnership.

While the U.S. government grew keenly interested in helping U.S. oil companies establish a foothold in the region, it remained largely aloof from political issues prior to World War II, with one brief exception. During the Paris Peace Conference of 1919, President Woodrow Wilson insisted that the territories of the former Ottoman Empire be allocated as mandates under the League of Nations, not as colonies to European powers. He succeeded in imposing his view on France and Great Britain. While the conference was in session, Wilson sent Dr. Henry King, president of Oberlin College, and industrialist Charles Crane to the Middle East to conduct an independent inquiry into the views of the local populations regarding their political future. The King-Crane Commission reported back that the local inhabitants

desired independence for a Syrian state that included Lebanon and Palestine, under a U.S. mandate if necessary. Both the Kurdish and Armenian states mentioned in the Treaty of Versailles settlement also made known their desire that the United States be their mandatory. With the defeat of the Versailles Treaty in the Senate, however, the United States rejected a mandate role.

The interwar period was the height of European dominance in the Middle East and North Africa. France assumed the mandate for Syria and Lebanon; Great Britain for Palestine, Transjordan and Iraq. Great Britain maintained its control over Egypt, its protectorate role on the southern and eastern coasts of the Arabian Peninsula, and its predominant influence in Iran. France continued to control Morocco and Tunisia indirectly and governed Algeria as a part of metropolitan France. Russia and Turkey divided the territory of the proposed Armenian state; Turkey and Iraq did likewise with the territory of the proposed Kurdish state.

World War II and the Beginnings of the Cold War

During World War II the United States began to play a sustained and direct role in the Middle East. U.S. forces fought in the North African theater, and thousands of U.S. noncombatant troops were stationed in Iran, the primary land bridge for Allied supply of the Soviet Union. The Iranian government, fearing the designs of both the Soviets and the British, encouraged this U.S. presence. With the war highlighting the strategic importance of oil, President Franklin D. Roosevelt's administration floated proposals for a direct government role in developing the oil resources of Saudi Arabia. Opposition in Congress and from the oil industry blocked these ideas, but Washington moved during the war to cement its relations with the Saudi regime. The United States declared Saudi Arabia eligible for Lend-Lease aid and built an air base in Dhahran, in the oil-rich Eastern Province of the kingdom.

In the immediate aftermath of World War II, with Great Britain unable to sustain its former strategic dominance and the Soviet Union displaying interest in extending its influence into the area, the United States decided to assume an unprecedented political role in the Middle East. This new U.S. activism was first manifested in the "Northern Tier" states bordering the Soviet Union—Iran and Turkey. In 1946 Washington strongly opposed the Soviet-supported separatist regimes in Iranian Azerbaijan and Kurdistan, helping the Iranian government to weather these challenges to its territorial integrity. Subsequently, the United States expanded its army and air missions in Iran. In March 1947 President Harry S. Truman declared the Truman Doctrine, asking Congress for $400 million in aid for Greece and Turkey to help them resist Soviet pressures; both joined the North American Treaty Organization (NATO) in 1952.

The emergence of the Arab-Israeli issue, however, complicated U.S. efforts to apply the containment policy in the rest of the Middle East. The combatants did not fall into easily identifiable East-versus-West categories. Most of the Arab states confronting Israel remained clients of Great Britain, while the socialist orientation of Israel's governing Labor party attracted support from Soviet allies. Domestic politics, moreover, became an important consideration for U.S. policymakers on Arab-Israeli issues. In the period before World War II, the Zionist movement attracted a few high-profile sympathizers in the U.S. Jewish community, such as Supreme Court Justice Louis Brandeis, but Zionist sentiment was limited to a minority of U.S. Jews. With the revelations of the horrors inflicted on European Jewry by the Nazis, the great majority of U.S. Jews came to sympathize strongly with the Zionist movement and the new state of Israel. General public opinion in the United States, reacting to the same revelations, also shifted toward sympathy for Israel. During the 1948 presidential elections, both the Republican and Democratic party platforms strongly supported the creation of the new state of Israel in the British mandate of Palestine.

Strategic concerns—oil and the prevention of Soviet influence in the area—seemed to dictate a cautious U.S. position toward Israel, while domestic and humanitarian concerns militated for strong support. U.S. policymakers tried to find a middle way between these impulses, supporting the United Nations General Assembly resolution in 1947 to partition Palestine into Jewish and Arab states and encouraging negotiations. In May 1948 Israel declared its independence and its Arab neighbors declared war on the new state. Against the advice of his secretaries of state and defense, President Truman immediately recognized Israel, as did the Soviet Union. While the United States offered no official support to Israel during its first war, it did not impede efforts by private U.S. citizens to assist Israel financially and militarily.

Despite Washington's sympathies for Israel, from the point of view of the global U.S. containment policy the Arab-Israeli conflict was an irritating local problem distracting attention from the Soviet threat and yet inviting Soviet meddling in a significant region. The Tripartite Declaration of 1950, issued with Great Britain and France, aimed at freezing the conflict by guaranteeing the existing cease-fire lines and preventing new outbreaks of fighting by limiting arms exports to the combatants. In 1951 the United States, with Great Britain, France, and Turkey, issued an invitation to all Middle Eastern states to join a proposed Middle East Command, which would help them coordinate their defense against the Soviet Union. The proposal, seen by many Arabs as a way for the British to maintain their colonial influence, also ran afoul of Arab-Israeli tensions, because Israel was invited to join. When Egypt rejected the invitation, the proposal died.

The failure of the Middle East Command did not deter the United States from continuing its efforts to organize a Middle East defense grouping. To avoid the complications of the Arab-Israeli dispute, U.S. diplomacy began to focus on a Northern Tier alliance that would link NATO's easternmost member, Turkey, with Pakistan, the westernmost member of the Southeast Asia Treaty Organization (SEATO). Iraq was eager to join such a grouping, and Great Britain encouraged its inclusion. Washington was hesitant about Iraq's membership, given its recent experience with the Middle East Command, but acquiesced. No other Arab country joined what came to be called the Baghdad Pact, consisting of Turkey, Iraq, Iran, Pakistan, and Great Britain. The new Egyptian president, Gamal Abdel Nasser, subjected it to withering criticism. The United States, measuring the opposition that the pact had generated in the Arab world, limited its participation to involvement only in the grouping's military committee.

The inability to separate Arab-Israeli issues from a containment strategy in the area continued in 1955, when Egypt signed an arms-sale agreement with Soviet-allied Czechoslovakia. The subsequent deterioration of U.S.-Egyptian relations culminated in the withdrawal of the U.S. aid promised to Cairo for building the Aswan Dam. President Nasser retaliated by nationalizing the Suez Canal, initiating a series of events that culminated in a coordinated Israeli-British-French attack on Egypt in October 1956.

For President Dwight D. Eisenhower's administration, the Suez War could not have come at a worse time. The Soviet Union had just invaded Hungary to put down the anticommunist revolt there, giving the United States an excellent opportunity to solidify its ties with neutral countries appalled by Soviet imperialism. Then two of the United States' closest NATO allies invaded a leader of the Nonaligned Movement. The attack, moreover, came just days before the U.S. presidential elections. Washington moved swiftly to condemn the attack and pressed all three attackers to withdraw from Egyptian territory. This episode raised the prestige of Egypt's Nasser, a Pan-Arabist, to new heights in the Arab world, and U.S. officials quickly became worried that his appeal, and his continuing relationship with the Soviets, posed a threat to friendly states in the area. Less than three months after the Suez attack, Washington adopted what came to be known as the Eisenhower Doctrine, pledging support to any friendly government in the Middle East finding itself threatened by international communism. Eisenhower invoked the doctrine in 1958, when U.S. marines were sent to Lebanon. The Egyptian-Syrian union of January 1958 and the violent coup that overthrew the British client regime in Iraq in July 1958 had emboldened the Lebanese opposition to challenge the pro-Western government, although by no stretch of the imagination was the Lebanese opposition communist.

The Lebanese episode of 1958 was not the only example of U.S. intervention in the domestic politics of regional states. Immediately after World War II, Washington was concerned about the stability of the Saudi regime, sitting on enormous reserves of oil but with little ready cash. President Harry S. Truman's administration encouraged the U.S. oil companies working in Saudi Arabia to renegotiate their agreements with the Saudi government, giving the latter 50 percent of the profits accruing from the sale of Saudi oil, in what became known as the "50-50 agreement." In exchange, Washington allowed the companies to write off this new expense against their U.S. tax liability. In effect, the 50-50 agreement was an indirect transfer from the U.S. Treasury to the Saudi government.

Other U.S. interventions, however, were not so welcome to local rulers. In Iran in the early 1950s, Prime Minister Mohammad Mosaddeq nationalized British oil interests and faced down the young shah of Iran (Mohammad Reza Pahlavi) to establish himself as the arbiter of Iranian politics. The support he received from the Iranian Communist party (Tudeh) unnerved U.S. officials, who supported British efforts to maintain a global boycott of Iranian oil. As Iran's economic fortunes worsened, the United States joined Great Britain in 1953 to mastermind a coup against Mosaddeq that returned the shah to power and cemented the U.S.-Iranian relationship. In the aftermath of the coup, U.S. companies received 25 percent of the formerly all-British oil concession in Iran. The United States sponsored a number of failed coup attempts in Syria in 1957 when it appeared that Soviet influence in the country's chaotic politics was increasing, but these served only to drive Syria into the arms of President Nasser, in the Egyptian-Syrian union of 1958.

Upon taking office in 1961, President John F. Kennedy sought to repair relations with President Nasser, the leading figure in the Arab world. The fact that Nasser was then feuding with his Soviet allies over the latter's support for Iraqi President Abdul Karim Qassim, a rival for Pan-Arab leadership, assisted the effort. Washington sought to draw Nasser into the U.S. orbit with promises of development aid and a new understanding of Arab nationalism as a progressive, noncommunist force in the region. At the same time Washington pressed two of its closest Middle East allies, Iran and Saudi Arabia, to implement domestic reforms. After a promising beginning, the effort to woo Nasser foundered on Washington's inability to broker an Egyptian-Israeli dialogue and on the growing confrontation between Nasser and Saudi Arabia over the civil war in Yemen. In 1962 Nasser sent thousands of Egyptian troops to support the republican government of Yemen that had just overthrown the centuries-old monarchy. The Saudis actively supported the royalist opposition in a war that would last until 1970. With the fall of Qassim in 1963, moreover, Soviet-Egyptian relations again began to improve. Once again, isolating Arab-Israeli and inter-Arab dynamics from the U.S. Cold War strategy of containing Soviet influence in the Middle East proved an impossible task.

During President Lyndon B. Johnson's administration, the United States in effect abandoned efforts to court Nasser and began to view Israel as a strategic asset against powerful, Soviet-supported Egypt. At the same time U.S. Jewish groups, taken aback by the ease with which the Eisenhower administration had pressed Israel to withdraw from Sinai in 1956–1957, began to organize more effectively to pressure U.S. politicians to take pro-Israeli stances. These changes in domestic politics and strategic perception led to marked improvement in U.S.-Israeli relations, which during the 1950s had been characterized by some coolness and one major confrontation over the 1956 war. The first major U.S. arms sale to Israel occurred during the Kennedy administration, with the sale of Hawk antiaircraft missiles. The Johnson administration went further, selling Israel offensive weapons such as tanks and Skyhawk fighter-bombers. When Israel occupied the Sinai Peninsula (along with the Golan Heights, the West Bank, and the Gaza Strip) during the 1967 Six-Day War, the Johnson administration did not demand that the Israelis withdraw. Rather, the United States sponsored UN Security Council Resolution 242, calling for the exchange of land for peace. The "land for peace" formula has been the basis of all subsequent U.S. mediations of Arab-Israeli disputes.

Foreign aid was a major instrument of U.S. foreign policy in the 1950s and 1960s, and the distribution of such aid is an indicator of U.S. interests in the region. The two largest recipients by far of U.S. aid, both military and economic, were Turkey and Iran, the two regional states that shared a border with the Soviet Union. Turkey received a total of approximately $5.4 billion from 1953 to 1969; Iran received approximately $2 billion. Next in line were Israel ($1.1 billion) and Egypt ($900 million), although aid to Egypt was drastically reduced after 1965. Other significant recipients included Jordan (approximately $600 million), mostly after the British ended financial support for the regime in the mid-1950s; Morocco (approximately $700 million); and Tunisia (approximately $600 million)—all states that sided with the United States in the Cold War competition. Saudi Arabia received little formal U.S. aid, but the tax laws adopted in 1950 provided an indirect U.S. subsidy for the Saudis, through the Aramco partners, of hundreds of millions of dollars.

Oil and Arab-Israeli Diplomacy: The 1970s

Organizing the Middle East into an anti-Soviet alignment was the dominant theme of U.S. policy in the 1950s; the 1960s saw a growing U.S.-Israeli strategic alignment against Soviet allies in the area. The theme of U.S. policy in the 1970s was active mediation to encourage Arab-Israeli peace on terms that both preserved the special U.S.-Israeli relationship and offered incentives for Soviet-allied Arab regimes to realign with Washington. Two factors accounted for this shift in U.S. tactics in the region. The first was oil. The 1970s saw meteoric increases in the price of oil and the concomitant rise in importance of members of the Organization of Petroleum Exporting Countries (OPEC), particularly Saudi Arabia, the largest oil producer in OPEC. The link established during the 1973 Arab-Israeli war between that conflict and oil convinced U.S. policymakers that a solution to, or at minimum the neutralization of, the Arab-Israeli problem was an important element in safeguarding U.S. oil interests.

The second factor was the extended period of U.S.-Soviet détente ushered in by President Richard M. Nixon's administration. Détente had two superficially paradoxical results in the Middle East. Egypt, long the most important Soviet ally in the region, came to be convinced that Moscow would not risk a confrontation with the United States to help it achieve its military goals vis-à-vis Israel. Therefore, to regain the Sinai and improve the Egyptian economy, Cairo had to turn to the United States for help. With the risk of superpower confrontation in the Middle East reduced by détente, the United States could pursue a more aggressive policy aimed at courting Soviet clients and isolating Moscow.

The Nixon administration, upon taking office in 1969, faced a potential crisis in the Arab-Israeli arena. Egypt and Israel had begun a war of attrition, with artillery and air attacks along the Suez Canal battle line. Cairo had called on its Soviet ally for assistance, which included the deployment of thousands of Soviet soldiers and technicians, new Soviet arms, and Soviet ground-to-ground missiles in Egypt. The United States brokered a cease-fire in the war of attrition in 1970, with the promise of a new round of Arab-Israeli negotiations to follow. That prospect helped to spark a civil war in Jordan in September 1970, as forces of the Palestine Liberation Organization (PLO, formed in 1964) challenged King Hussein, who had expressed an interest in joining the proposed negotiations. Syrian military intervention on the side of the PLO threatened to draw in the superpowers. The United States cooperated closely with Israel during the crisis, helping to neutralize potential Soviet support for Syria and allowing the Jordanian forces to repel the Syrian intervention. This new level of strategic cooperation between Israel and the United States had the unfortunate consequence of blinding Washington to the signals sent by the new Egyptian president, Anwar El-Sadat, of his desire to begin a negotiating process with Washington and, indirectly, Israel. Even his expulsion in 1972 of the Soviet military advisers from Egypt elicited no response from the United States.

Pressed by mounting domestic unrest and economic crisis, Sadat boldly gambled in October 1973 on war with Israel to break the diplomatic logjam. He and the new president of Syria, Hafiz al-Assad (both had come to power in 1970), eschewed the confrontational style and aggressive rhetoric that had characterized inter-Arab politics, allowing them to cooperate with one another and with Saudi Arabia. The Saudis, overjoyed no longer to be the target of Egyptian and Syrian propaganda, pledged to support the war effort through use of the "oil weapon." The declaration by Arab oil producers (except Iraq) during the war of an embargo on oil shipments to the United States and of production cuts, both actual and threatened, created a panic in world oil markets. Prices increased 400 percent, from a base price that had already doubled between 1970 and 1973. U.S. consumers faced rationing schemes and long lines at gas stations. The economies of all the industrialized countries were thrown into a deep recession. For the first time, events in the Middle East had a major impact on the entire U.S. society.

Why was the "oil weapon" effective in 1973 when in the past, even as recently as 1967, similar efforts to cut production and embargo shipments had no effect on world markets? The answer lies in the changing structure of the world oil market. U.S. oil production reached its peak in 1970. For decades the United States had excess production capacity that could be brought onto the market in a crisis. Now this was no longer true. After years of being a net exporter of oil, by 1973 the United States became the world's largest oil importer. Meanwhile, global demand for oil had increased remarkably in the 1960s. Free world petroleum demand went from 19 million barrels per day (b/d) in 1960 to more than 44 million b/d in 1972. More than two-thirds of the new production to meet this rising demand came from the Middle East and North Africa. This change in the world supply/demand balance gave new power to the oil-producing countries. Between 1970 and 1973, led by Libya and Iran, the members of OPEC had successfully pushed for greater control over production decisions, in some cases through outright nationalization and in others through negotiations with the oil companies, and for higher prices. Less than twenty years earlier, British Petroleum had been able to organize a worldwide boycott of Iranian oil to foil the nationalization ordered by Prime Minister Mohammad Mosaddeq. Now, the producer countries could dictate to the oil companies. With demand at an all-time high and little if any surplus production capacity elsewhere, the power of the Arab oil producers to disrupt the world oil market was clear.

During the 1973 Arab-Israeli war, U.S. policy was aimed toward preventing an Israeli defeat and then facing down Soviet pressure for superpower intervention. When it became clear that Israel was doing poorly in the early stages of the battle, the United States launched a massive military airlift to resupply the Israeli armed forces. As the tide of the battle shifted, U.S. diplomacy sought to give the Israelis extra time to improve their military position before the cease-fire ordered by the UN Security Council would take effect. As Israeli forces surrounded and cut off an entire Egyptian army in Sinai, the Soviet Union threatened to intervene directly in the fighting to enforce the cease-fire. In response, the Nixon administration ordered U.S. nuclear forces on a heightened state of alert. The crisis passed as Israel, having achieved its military goals, accepted the cease-fire.

After the 1973 war, U.S. diplomacy concentrated on encouraging Arab-Israeli negotiations, both to prevent a recurrence of the 1973 oil crisis and to woo Egypt away from the Soviet camp. Secretary of State Henry Kissinger

negotiated through shuttle diplomacy two disengagement agreements between Israel and Egypt in 1974 and 1975, and one Syrian-Israeli disengagement agreement in 1974. After the United States committed itself to negotiating the latter agreement, Saudi Arabia lifted the oil embargo. President Jimmy Carter, who took office in 1977, sought at first to pursue a comprehensive settlement of all aspects of the Arab-Israeli problem, including the Palestinian issue. The comprehensive approach, however, ran afoul of divisions in the Arab world over tactics (with Sadat wanting to move faster than others) and over the refusal of the new Israeli government of Prime Minister Menachem Begin, leader of the nationalist Likud party, to consider any proposals that included a role for the PLO or any Palestinian representatives. Faced with this impasse, Sadat undertook another gamble, traveling to Jerusalem in November 1977. With the other Arab states unwilling to follow Sadat's lead, U.S. policy quickly shifted toward brokering a separate peace between Egypt and Israel. That goal was accomplished during the Camp David summit of September 1978, where President Carter spent two weeks in virtual seclusion with Begin and Sadat to hammer out an accord. Egypt and Israel signed a formal peace treaty, in a ceremony on the lawn of the White House, in March 1979.

The Camp David Accords were a brilliant success for U.S. diplomacy, solidifying Egypt's switch from the Soviet to the U.S. side in the Cold War and effectively removing the war option from the Arab side in the Arab-Israeli conflict—but it was not cost-free. Since 1979 Egypt has received approximately $2.3 billion per year in U.S. economic and military aid, and Israel has received approximately $3.5 billion per year, in both cases significant increases over their aid levels before 1979. Israel and Egypt became the major recipients of U.S. foreign aid in the region, far outpacing Turkey and Iran (which, with the oil price increases of the 1970s, no longer received any direct U.S. assistance). Containment of the Soviet Union gave way to solidifying Arab-Israeli peace as the major goal of U.S. aid policy in the region. While the Camp David Accords contained provisions for Palestinian autonomy in the West Bank and Gaza Strip, neither the Israelis nor the PLO were willing to follow up on them, and U.S. policymakers quickly lost interest in pursuing the autonomy issue. Matters in the Persian Gulf had captured Washington's attention.

Islamic Revolution and Gulf Security: 1979–1990

The Iranian Islamic revolution of 1979 was the most serious blow to U.S. interests in the Middle East since World War II. By virtue of its size and geographic position, Iran plays the dominant strategic role in the geopolitics of the Persian Gulf. It has been the second largest oil producer, after Saudi Arabia, in the Persian Gulf. Bordering on the Soviet Union, it was an important link in the global U.S. containment strategy. Its regional power more than overshadowed that of Iraq, the major Soviet ally in the Persian Gulf in the 1970s, providing indirect protection to Saudi Arabia and the smaller gulf states from Iraqi ambitions. After the British withdrawal from the Persian Gulf in 1971, the United States had promoted Iran, with arms sales and diplomatic support, as the region's "policeman." With the overthrow of the shah, Iran overnight became a serious threat to U.S. interests.

The long history of U.S. support for the shah, including direct interference in the domestic politics of Iran, along with the particular political interpretation of Islam put forward by Ayatollah Ruhollah Khomeini, disposed the new regime to be extremely hostile toward and fearful of the United States. Khomeini emerged in the early 1960s as a major critic of the shah's regime and of the U.S. role in Iran. He was deported by the shah to Iraq, where he spent the next fifteen years espousing an Islamic alternative to the shah's rule and encouraging Islamic political opposition in Iran. Exiled from Iraq to Paris in 1978, he returned to Tehran in triumph in February 1979 as the leader of the Iranian revolutionary forces.

When the United States admitted the deposed shah into the country for medical treatment in November 1979, radical factions within the revolution seized the U.S. embassy in Tehran in protest and held the diplomats there hostage. While the ostensible pretext of the hostage-takers was to protest an alleged U.S. plot to return the shah to power, they actually aimed to discredit moderate elements in the new government who sought to put Iran's international relations back on a more normal course. Khomeini supported the radicals, helping to push the revolution in a more extreme direction. The case of the hostages consumed the energies of the Carter administration and the U.S. public for more than a year. Carter used threats, economic boycotts, UN resolutions, secret negotiations, and a military raid (ending in spectacular, abortive failure) to try to resolve the hostage issue. Only in January 1981, on the day that Ronald Reagan was sworn in as president, did Iran release the hostages. The suspicion and bitterness toward Iran engendered in the United States during the hostage crisis lingered well into the 1990s.

The ramifications of the Iranian revolution extended beyond bilateral U.S.-Iranian relations. Saudi Arabia, fearful of the new Iranian regime on both geopolitical and ideological levels, sought to repair the rift in its relations with the United States occasioned by the Camp David Accords, which the Saudis opposed. The Reagan administration reiterated the U.S. commitment to Saudi security with verbal guarantees and new arms sales. The disruption of Iranian oil production caused by the revolu-

tion led to a doubling of oil prices between 1979 and 1981, damaging the economies of the industrialized world and reinforcing the geopolitical importance of the Persian Gulf. Iraq saw the revolution as both a threat and an opportunity: a threat because of the appeal of Iran's revolutionary ideology to Iraqis and Iran's support for Iraqi Islamic opposition groups; an opportunity because the revolution had thrown the Iranian military into chaos. This combination of threat and opportunity led Iraq's new president, Saddam Hussein, to launch a full-scale war on Iran in September 1980. After early Iraqi advances, Iran regrouped and in the summer of 1982 drove the Iraqi forces out of Iran, following them over into Iraq. From there the conflict became a war of attrition.

Given the importance of the Persian Gulf, U.S. foreign policy toward the Iran-Iraq War was remarkably passive. Aside from reinforcing the commitment to Saudi Arabia, Washington took little action until near the end of the conflict, when both Iraq and Iran began to attack international shipping in the Persian Gulf. In 1987 Kuwait requested the protection of foreign navies for its shipping. The United States evidenced little interest in the request until the Soviet Union made clear that it would provide naval support to Kuwait. In response, the Reagan administration sent a large naval flotilla to protect both Kuwaiti and Saudi shipping. The U.S. forces skirmished with Iranian naval vessels, sinking a number of them and destroying some Iranian offshore oil facilities. In July 1988 the USS *Vincennes* accidentally downed an Iranian civilian airliner over the Persian Gulf, killing all 290 people on board. Just days later Iran accepted UN Security Council Resolution 598, calling for a cease-fire, thus ending the war.

The United States could be relatively cavalier about the course of the Iran-Iraq War for two reasons. One was the fact that neither side could achieve a decisive victory over the other and redraw the geopolitical map of the area. The other was that, contrary to expectations, the war did not lead to a third oil crisis. During the war oil prices plunged to their lowest level since 1973, dipping below $10 per barrel in 1986. The price shocks of the 1970s had led both to conservation measures in the industrialized economies and to recessions, which cut demand for oil. The high prices of the 1970s and early 1980s brought new sources of oil, such as Alaska and the North Sea, onto the market. Saudi Arabia also used its spare capacity to exert a downward pressure on prices. With no compelling geopolitical or oil crisis emerging from the Iran-Iraq War, Washington took a low-key approach, until it appeared that the Soviets would get involved. The United States tilted toward Iraq in the war, providing it with intelligence information, diplomatic support, and agricultural credits, but it also conducted secret negotiations with Iran, trading arms and military intelligence for cash and the release of hostages held in Lebanon, in what became known as the Iran-Contra affair.

Very little official attention in Washington was paid to Arab-Israeli issues during the 1980s. The Reagan administration, rejecting the premises of the détente policy of the 1970s, saw Israel as a strategic ally in confronting Soviet influence in the Middle East. Thus, Washington did not discourage the Israelis from invading Lebanon in 1982 and seeking out a military confrontation with Soviet-allied Syria. As part of the international effort to end the war in Lebanon, the United States sent a contingent of marines into Beirut. They had been there more than a year on a vague peacekeeping mission when, in October 1983, a suicide bomber blew up their barracks, killing 241 marines. In February 1984 the marines were withdrawn from Beirut, with little progress having been made in putting the Lebanese political system back together. While there were occasional U.S. initiatives in the 1980s on Arab-Israeli issues, none came to fruition. The most important change in U.S. policy was the decision in December 1988 to open a "diplomatic dialogue" with the PLO after the organization's chairman, Yassir Arafat, publicly accepted UN Security Council Resolutions 242 and 338, recognized Israel's "right to exist," and renounced terrorism.

The Gulf War and the Post–Cold War Period

Iraq's invasion of Kuwait in August 1990 came at a critical juncture in U.S. foreign policy. The Cold War had ended; great power cooperation on previously contentious strategic issues was in vogue; and calls to reconsider the wide-ranging U.S. military and political commitments built up over the previous decades were being heard in Washington. The decision of President George Bush's administration to confront Iraq militarily was evidence that U.S. interests in the Middle East, at least in the eyes of Washington policymakers, extended beyond the Cold War competition with the Soviet Union. President Bush immediately dispatched U.S. forces to Saudi Arabia, at first to protect the Saudis from a potential Iraqi invasion (Operation Desert Shield), and then to eject the Iraqis from Kuwait (Operation Desert Storm). U.S. diplomacy assembled a broad international coalition to fight the war and engineered unprecedented UN support for the war. The bulk of the fighting was done by the more than 500,000 U.S. military forces sent to the region. Air attacks on Iraq began on 16 January 1991; the ground offensive into Kuwait and Iraq began on 24 February 1991 and concluded on 27 February 1991 with a unilateral U.S. cease-fire at midnight. The ground offensive lasted 100 hours. Although there was subsequent criticism that President Bush declared the cease-fire too early, before many of Iraqi president Saddam Hussein's elite units could be destroyed, there was no question that the

stated mission of the forces, the liberation of Kuwait, had been accomplished.

Upon the conclusion of the Gulf War, U.S. diplomatic attention turned back to the Arab-Israeli conflict. Saddam Hussein had linked his withdrawal from Kuwait to an Israeli withdrawal from the occupied West Bank and Gaza Strip, in an effort to rally popular support in the Arab world. That linkage between oil and Arab-Israeli issues, first apparent to U.S. policymakers in 1973, remained troublesome. The Bush administration thus concentrated its energies on restarting the Arab-Israeli peace process. In October 1991 it convened all the parties in Madrid, including in the Jordanian delegation Palestinian representatives who were not formally affiliated with the PLO. The Madrid Conference initiated a series of bilateral and multilateral negotiations aimed at a comprehensive settlement of the Arab-Israeli conflict.

The decision in September 1993 of the new Labor party government in Israel and the PLO to recognize each other and negotiate directly for an autonomous regime in the West Bank and Gaza gave new impetus to the peace process. In May 1994 Israel and the PLO signed a detailed agreement on Palestinian autonomy in the Gaza Strip and Jericho. In October 1994, Jordan and Israel signed a full and ambitious peace treaty, and established formal diplomatic relations. Israel and the PLO hammered out a further accord in late 1995 such that by the end of the year the Israeli military had withdrawn from most West Bank villages and towns, turning them over to the Palestinian Authority, while maintaining ultimate control over security issues in the West Bank. January 1996 saw the first Palestinian national elections, with Yassir Arafat chosen as president of the Palestinian Authority and his allies dominating the 88-seat legislative body. New uncertainties were raised by the Israeli electoral process when Likud leader Benjamin Netanyahu was elected prime minister in June 1996. Nevertheless, negotiations to determine the future of Jerusalem, the role of Israeli settlements in the West Bank and Gaza, and the ultimate political relationship between Israel and the Palestinian Authority are scheduled to be completed during 1998. Washington continued to be directly involved in pushing the negotiations forward on all fronts, including the bilateral talks between Syria and Israel, through mediation, political pressure, and coordination of international aid efforts for all the parties.

With the Cold War over, the Arab-Israeli conflict potentially on the way to a diplomatic solution, and U.S. relations with the oil-rich monarchies in the Persian Gulf solidified by the Gulf War, U.S. interests in the Middle East by the mid-1990s had become more secure than at any time since World War II, but troubling issues remained. The United States had diplomatic relations with neither of the two major regional powers in the Gulf, Iran and Iraq. Saddam

Hussein clung stubbornly to power in Baghdad as UN sanctions strangled his country's economy and as the United States and other Western powers sought to continue to protect an autonomous Kurdish zone in the northern part of the country. The growing challenge of Islamic opposition movements to regimes friendly to the United States and to the U.S. military presence, as demonstrated by the June 1996 terrorist bombing of U.S. troops barracks in Saudi Arabia, caused increasing concern in Washington. The role in U.S. Middle East policy of the promotion of democracy and human rights remained a matter of controversy, as many U.S. allies used repression to combat domestic Islamic opposition groups. Given the continuing importance of oil to the world economy and the sustained U.S. commitment to a special relationship with Israel, the Middle East remained an area of high-priority concern for U.S. foreign policy.

F. GREGORY GAUSE III

See also Arafat, Yassir; Azerbaijan; Bahrain; Begin, Menachem; Camp David Accords; Carter, James Earl; Carter Doctrine; Central Treaty Organization; Cold War; Containment; Egypt; Eisenhower Doctrine; Foreign Aid; Gulf War of 1990–1991; Hussein, Saddam; Iran; Iran-Contra Affair; Iran-Iraq War; Iraq; Israel; Jordan; Khomeini, Ruhollah; Kissinger, Henry Alfred; Kurds; Kuwait; Lebanon; Morocco; Mosaddeq, Mohammad; Nasser, Gamal Abdel; Nonaligned Movement; Oil and Foreign Policy; Oil and World Politics; Oil Companies; Oman; Organization of Petroleum Exporting Countries; Palestine to 1948; Palestine Liberation Organization; Refugees; Sadat, Anwar El-; Saudi Arabia; Shah of Iran; Sudan; Suez Crisis; Syria; Terrorism; Truman Doctrine; Turkey; United Arab Emirates; Yemen

FURTHER READING
Bill, James A. *The Eagle and the Lion: The Tragedy of American-Iranian Relations.* New Haven, Conn., 1988.
Brown, L. Carl. *International Politics and the Middle East: Old Rules, Dangerous Game.* Princeton, N.J., 1984.
Freedman, Lawrence, and Efraim Karsh. *The Gulf Conflict, 1990–1991.* Princeton, N.J., 1993.
Hurewitz, J. C. *The Middle East and North Africa in World Politics,* vols. 1 and 2. New Haven, Conn., 1975, 1979.
Kaufman, Burton I. *The Arab Middle East and the United States: Inter-Arab Rivalry and Superpower Diplomacy.* New York, 1995.
Kuniholm, Bruce R. *The Origins of the Cold War in the Near East.* Princeton, N.J., 1980.
Lenczowski, George. *American Presidents and the Middle East.* Durham, N.C, 1990.
Little, Douglas. "Gideon's Band: America and the Middle East Since 1945." *Diplomatic History* 18 (Fall 1994): 513–540.
Quandt, William B. *Peace Process: American Diplomacy and the Arab-Israeli Conflict Since 1967.* Berkeley, Calif., 1993.
Ramazani, R. K. *Revolutionary Iran: Challenge and Response in the Middle East.* Baltimore, 1988.
Rustow, Dankwart A. *Oil and Turmoil: American Faces OPEC and the Middle East.* New York, 1982.
Safran, Nadav. *Israel: The Embattled Ally.* Cambridge, Mass., 1981.
———. *Saudi Arabia: The Ceaseless Quest for Security.* Cambridge, Mass., 1985.
Spiegel, Steven L. *The Other Arab-Israeli Conflict: Making America's Middle East Policy from Truman to Reagan.* Chicago, 1985.
Stookey, Robert W. *America and the Arab States: An Uneasy Encounter.* New York, 1975.
Yergin, Daniel. *The Prize: The Epic Quest for Oil, Money and Power.* New York, 1991.

MIDWAY ISLANDS

See Pacific Island Nations and U.S. Territories

MILITARY-INDUSTRIAL COMPLEX

Popularized by President Dwight D. Eisenhower during his farewell address on 17 January 1961, the term "military-industrial complex" refers to the massive, complex network of mutually dependent relationships between private and governmental bureaucratic institutions developed during the 1940s and 1950s. This military establishment operates within the executive branch, private industry and business, Congress, and the scientific community. Each of these organized groups wanted more weaponry and equipment to contain the Soviet Union. Industry wanted contracts, with which it could profit; members of Congress wanted military bases and defense industries in their districts to provide jobs and votes; and scientists wanted the prestige and prominence that came with large grants and direct participation in government. Together industry, government, and science advanced in the name of national security and became entrenched as a source of employment and prosperity.

The military-industrial complex originated in World War I, but profound impetus for the rise of a permanent military-industrial complex in U.S. society came with World War II. Almost overnight, the U.S. government redirected itself to wage a global war in which the military expanded enormously, placing the economy and society in position to provide personnel and equipment needed to win. The military-industrial complex continued to grow in size and importance throughout the 1950s as the United States expanded its ability to use force to combat the Soviet Union during the Cold War.

Though President Eisenhower attempted to direct public attention to the dramatic growth of the military-industrial complex and to caution Americans to become an "alert and knowledgeable citizenry" to overcome the dangers it posed for the workings of democracy, little dialogue took place during the 1960s about its implications for U.S. democracy and foreign policy. The public denied the existence of the military-industrial complex and equated it with simplistic conspiratorial notions. Members of the political left, however, were quick to condemn it. Following the Vietnam War and Watergate a massive "military-industrial-scientific infrastructure" has become pervasive in U.S. government and society since World War II, as foretold by President Eisenhower.

From the 1940s to the 1960s, the military-industrial complex contributed to the growth of an anticommunist consensus and a permanent infrastructure supporting containment of the Soviet Union. It also contributed to waste, corruption, the flourishing of vested interests, and resistance to change in the politics of national defense. Since the 1970s the institutions and activities of the military-industrial complex have been challenged, a development that began following the Vietnam War and that has intensified with the collapse of the Soviet Union and the end of the Cold War. In the 1990s the military-industrial complex became subject to downsizing and limitations in defense spending. The consequences of such cutbacks were felt by the government, the economy, hundreds of local communities, and thousands of individuals.

JEREL A. ROSATI

See also Cold War; Defense, U.S. Department of; Eisenhower, Dwight David

FURTHER READING
Kaplan, Fred. *The Wizards of Armageddon.* New York, 1983.
Kotz, Nick. *Wild Blue Yonder and the B-1 Bomber.* Princeton, N.J., 1988.
Yarmolinsky, Adam. *The Military Establishment: Its Impact on American Society.* New York, 1971.

MIRVS
See Nuclear Weapons and Strategy

MISSILE GAP
See Kennedy, John Fitzgerald; Nuclear Weapons and Strategy

MISSIONARIES

Men and women who promote the Christian gospel abroad. Often, they also convey U.S. values, introduce U.S. products, and function as a symbol of the U.S. sense of mission in the world.

U.S. foreign missionary activity began in the early nineteenth century and was entirely Protestant until the first Catholic missionaries from the United States ventured abroad in 1911. The American Board of Commissioners for Foreign Missions, founded in 1810 by Congregationalists and influenced by the Second Great Awakening, a religious revival that swept the country in the early nineteenth century, sent most early missionaries. The first arrived in India in 1812. In the 1830s, missionaries reached Hawaii, Asia Minor, Greece, Southeast Asia, Africa, and China. Before the Civil War most missionaries were white men, although many blacks served in Africa. Missionaries' wives were designated "assistant missionaries," and despite their important contributions, few single women were accepted for service.

In the 1870s and 1880s, the revivals of Chicago businessman-turned-evangelist Dwight L. Moody reinvigorated the movement. Thousands joined the crusade to spread the gospel abroad. Several organizations, including forty-one women's missionary boards, challenged the predominance of the American Board. Soon women missionaries outnumbered men. The new enthusiasm for missionary work reflected and contributed to the expansive mood pervading the United States in an era of imperialism. By 1900, one thousand U.S. missionaries worked in China; by 1905, 583 worked in Japan.

The missionaries' impact in host countries varied. In China, missionaries were often despised. Their work resulted in few converts, but their educational institutions such as Shanghai St. Johns College founded by the Episcopalians in the 1870s, Yenching University formed between 1915 and 1920 when four Methodist and American Board institutions merged, and Syrian Protestant College (which later became American University in Beirut) founded by American Board missionaries in 1866, actually fostered anti-foriegn nationalism. Many early Chinese revolutionary leaders attended mission schools. In the Middle East and North Africa, missionary activities contributed to the cultural revival of Arabs, Armenians, Turks, and Egyptians.

Missionaries provided much of the information and perceptions about foreign lands available to the U.S. public, and they molded attitudes toward much of Asia and Africa. The images they presented to the United States were usually negative. Missionaries in India, for example, reported popular Hindu practices to be unreasonable and barbaric. The Chinese were described as lustful and deceitful. From Japan when the first missionaries arrived in 1869, came accounts of excessive drinking, carousing, and scandalous treatment of girls and women.

Missionaries at times influenced U.S. foreign policy. They had the sympathetic ear of cabinet officers and presidents, and because they enjoyed widespread popular support, the Department of State took their views into account. Missionaries requested and received U.S. government protection, most dramatically during the Boxer Rebellion in China in 1900, when they became the target of widespread antiforeign violence. In 1898 missionary interests favored annexing the Philippines, from which they had hitherto been excluded.

Missionaries formulated and implemented policy that extended beyond their immediate concerns. For much of the century they advised both the government of Siam and U.S. diplomats assigned there. The first U.S. treaty with China, the Treaty of Wangxia of 1844, was largely the work of missionaries. A missionary served as first U.S. consul in Liberia. In Korea, missionary Horace M. Allen was the U.S. diplomatic representative. Missionary protests in the Philippines stopped a government plan to sanction the sale of opium, and Episcopalian missionary Bishop Charles Henry Brent subsequently served as U.S. representative at international opium conferences.

By the early twentieth century missionaries had in many instances begun repudiating negative representations of foreign cultures. Missionaries in India now expressed appreciation for the spirituality of Hinduism, and later reports from Japan emphasized the country's progressiveness. Missionaries in China wrote favorably about Confucianism. By the 1920s the entire missionary enterprise was challenged by theological liberals who questioned whether foreign missionary activity was justifiable. Some missionaries, fearful they might be perceived as imperialist collaborators, rejected protection from their government, and some wished to discard the name "missionary." The appalling slaughter of World War I undermined the missionaries' confidence in Western moral leadership.

Although the missionary movement has declined as a political force in the late twentieth century, it has continued to influence foreign relations. For example, missionaries organized relief efforts for Armenia during World War I, lobbied at the Paris Peace Conference for the creation of League of Nations mandates in the Middle East, and urged the Franklin Roosevelt administration to pressure Great Britain into making concessions to Indian nationalists. The missionaries' sympathetic views of Chinese victims of Japanese aggression helped shape U.S. attitudes toward Japan in the 1930s. During World War II some missionaries worked with the U.S. Office of Strategic Services, the predecessor of the Central Intelligence Agency. John Leighton Stuart, a missionary to China, later served as U.S. ambassador to that country during the crucial years 1946 to 1949. Many children of missionaries, such as John Paton Davies and John Stuart Service, became area specialists in the Department of State.

In the 1990s the mainline Protestant churches have sent few missionaries abroad, particularly in traditional evangelical roles. On the other hand, the Fundamentalist, Pentecostal, and the Mormon churches have increased their foreign missionary activity substantially.

KENTON J. CLYMER

See also Allen, Horace Newton; Armenia; Boxer Rebellion; China; China Hands; Davies, John Paton, Jr.; India; Korea; League of Nations; Thailand; Wangxia, Treaty of

FURTHER READING

Clymer, Kenton J. *Protestant Missionaries in the Philippines, 1898–1916: An Inquiry into the American Colonial Mentality.* Urbana, Ill., 1986.

Fairbank, John K., ed. *The Missionary Enterprise in China and America.* Cambridge, Mass., 1974.

Grabill, Joseph L. *Protestant Diplomacy and the Near East: Missionary Influence on American Policy, 1810–1927.* Minneapolis, Minn., 1971.

Hunt, Michael H. *The Making of a Special Relationship: The United States and China to 1914.* New York, 1983.

Hunter, Jane. *The Gospel of Gentility: American Women Missionaries in Turn-of-the-Century China.* New Haven, Conn., 1984.

Hutchison, William R. *Errand to the World: American Protestant Thought and Foreign Missions.* Chicago, 1987.

Varg, Paul A. *Missionaries, Chinese, and Diplomats: The American Protestant Missionary Movement in China.* Princeton, N.J., 1958.

MISSISSIPPI RIVER

North America's central waterway, running 2348 miles from Lake Itasca in Minnesota to the Gulf of Mexico below New Orleans, Louisiana. Combined with the Missouri River, the Mississippi system expands to 3741 miles in length and comprises the world's third longest river system, after the Nile and the Amazon. Drawing from its other major tributaries, which include the Ohio, Arkansas, and Red Rivers, the Mississippi's triangular drainage area covers approximately 1,250,000 square miles. The Mississippi River, a primary feature of U.S. geography, has figured prominently in the nation's economy, history, and literature.

Securing free navigation on the river was a principal objective of early U.S. foreign policy. The prosperity of the trans-Appalachian West, national unity, and future expansion all depended on U.S. control of the river. That goal came to the young United States in stages. In negotiations that concluded the Seven Years' War in 1763, Great Britain secured France's departure from North America and received Florida from Spain, triumphs that left the British masters of the eastern half of the continent. French Louisiana west of the Mississippi River went to Spain, so the river became the border between British and Spanish territories. Since the West Florida province included the Mississippi's eastern bank at its mouth and for a substantial distance north, the power that possessed the Floridas could influence river traffic as effectively as the one commanding Louisiana. After the Seven Years' War, Great Britain and Spain agreed to share navigation rights on the river.

As part of the Treaty of Paris ending the Revolutionary War in 1783, Great Britain acknowledged the river's source as lying in U.S. territory and granted free and open use of the river to U.S. citizens. Spanish neighbors of the United States in Louisiana, also once again in control of the Floridas after the 1783 treaty, did not agree to this provision and would periodically resist unimpeded U.S. access until 1803.

In 1794 Jay's Treaty included a provision sustaining British rights on the river, but Americans achieved a major concession from Spain in Pinckney's Treaty the following year. Suspicious that Jay's Treaty signaled an impending bond between the English-speaking nations, Spanish officials sought to placate the United States with concessions. As part of Pinckney's Treaty, Spain agreed to the U.S. right to free navigation on the Mississippi. In addition, the United States was granted the right of deposit, or storage for transfer to seagoing vessels, at New Orleans for three years. The treaty thus opened up western farmers' best access to ocean transport for their goods. Gone was the oft-threatened Spanish closure of the Mississippi.

The right of deposit, taken for granted by U.S. traders, whose trade volume through New Orleans had doubled by 1802, became a contentious issue that year. In violation of Pinckney's Treaty, Spain suspended the right as rumors circulated that France had secretly acquired both Louisiana and the Floridas. The prospect of a hostile power closing the river loomed once again. Napoleon's gains in the secret treaty of San Ildefonso with Spain in 1802 included Louisiana and New Orleans. However, his loss of the essential Santo Domingo colony to slave rebellion persuaded Napoleon to dispose of Louisiana just at the time President Thomas Jefferson's emissaries were pressing the emperor to sell New Orleans. The subsequent Louisiana Purchase of 1803 sealed U.S. control of the Mississippi River. Spain lost West Florida to overt U.S. annexation in 1810 and officially acceded to U.S. possession when it ceded all Florida territory in the Adams-Onís Treaty of 1819.

PAUL R. GRASS

See also Adams-Onís Treaty; Florida; Louisiana Purchase; Pinckney's Treaty

FURTHER READING

Bemis, Samuel Flagg. *Pinckney's Treaty: America's Advantage from Europe's Distress, 1783–1800.* Rev. ed. New Haven, 1960.
DeConde, Alexander. *This Affair of Louisiana.* Baton Rouge, 1976.
Horsman, Reginald. *Diplomacy of the New Republic, 1776–1815.* 1985.
Whitaker, Arthur P. *The Mississippi Question, 1795–1803: A Study in Trade, Politics, and Diplomacy.* New York, 1934.

MITTERRAND, FRANÇOIS

(*b.* 26 October 1916; *d.* 8 January 1996)

President of France (1981–1995), and a highly visible figure in French politics for half a century. Educated in law and political science at the University of Paris, his rise to the presidency began after service in World War II when he escaped from German imprisonment to join the resistance movement. Although he was to represent the moderate leftist Democratic Socialist Resistance Union after the war as a deputy in the Fourth Republic's National Assembly, he had served briefly as an official with the Nazi collaborationist Vichy regime. From 1947 to 1958 he was minister in eleven different cabinets under the Fourth Republic. His long-standing opposition to Gaullism was reflected both in his rejection of France's Indochina policy and in his support of the North Atlantic Treaty Organization.

In the 1960s, the decade when French politics was dominated by Charles de Gaulle, Mitterrand became the leading antagonist, opposing in particular the constitution of the Fifth Republic because of the extraordinary powers it bestowed on the president. In 1965, as head of a newly formed Federation of Democratic and Socialist Parties, Mitterrand became the choice of left-of-center factions to challenge de Gaulle's bid for reelection in that year. Although Mitterrand lost the race he was able to bring together in alliance a sufficient number of splinter groups, along with the communists, to force a run-off with the Gaullists. Labor and student unrest in de Gaulle's second term left its mark on Mitterrand as well. The socialist alliance suffered severe losses in the wake of student riots in 1968, which caused Mitterrand to resign as party chairman. But three years later the Socialist Party elected him secretary-general.

After losing a close race with Giscard d'Estaing in 1974, he defeated Giscard in 1981 for the first of two terms as president of the Fifth Republic. His party's loss of the premiership in 1988 and again in 1993 forced Mitterand to modify some of his socialist objectives, such as educational reform, but it did not alter an imperial style that was modeled on de Gaulle's. In effect, the election of a socialist president solidified de Gaulle's Fifth Republic even as is. Despite periodic efforts to ease frictions with the United States, Mitterrand's France retained many of the reservations about the U.S. presence in Europe, including an aversion to the influence of U.S. culture and U.S. entreaties to become more interventionist in the crisis in Bosnia, that were displayed by his predecessors in the Fourth and Fifth Republics. He died on 8 January 1996 from the effects of the cancer which had been diagnosed at the beginning of his fourteen years in the presidency.

LAWRENCE S. KAPLAN

See also Bosnia-Herzegovina; de Gaulle, Charles André Joseph Marie; France; French Indochina; North Atlantic Treaty Organization

FURTHER READING

Costigliola, Frank. *France and the United States: The Cold Alliance Since World War II.* New York, 1992.
MacShane, Matthew. *François Mitterrand: A Political Odyssey.* New York, 1983.
Péan, Pierre. *La Jeunesse de François Mitterrand.* Paris, 1994.

MOBUTU, SESE SEKO
(*b.* 14 October 1930)

President of Zaire (1965–). After stints in the Belgian Congolese army and as a journalist, Mobutu spent a year in Belgium in 1959–1960, where he developed ties with Belgian leaders and the Central Intelligence Agency (CIA). The Congolese prime minister Patrice Lumumba named him chief-of-staff of the army upon declaring his country's independence from Belgium in June 1960. Increasingly skeptical of Lumumba's pro-Soviet policies and aided by CIA funding and guidance, Mobutu became commander of the army on 13 September 1960 and removed Lumumba from office the next day. Mobutu's troops arrested Lumumba on 2 December and transported him to the secessionist Katanga Province on 17 January 1961, where Lumumba was killed by the forces of his bitter enemy, Moise Tshombe.

Mobutu remained a power behind the throne until his second U.S.-supported coup of 24 November 1965, when he named himself president. Through co-option as well as repression, he built a one-party dictatorship notable for its cult of personality and its corruption; Mobutu's personal fortune alone allegedly reached some $5 billion.

While preserving close ties to the United States, Mobutu began a largely unsuccessful cultural and diplomatic offensive in the late 1960s to establish himself as a prominent African and Third World leader. He gave African names to the major cities of the Congo, which he renamed Zaire in 1971. In 1972 he changed his given name from Joseph to Sese Seko and banned the use of European first names by Zairians.

Mobutu remained on the CIA payroll until the late 1960s and worked closely with the United States in supporting first the National Front for the Liberation of Angola (FNLA) and then the National Union for the Total Independence of Angola (UNITA) in the Angolan civil war. This support also aligned him with South Africa. He continued to be militarily dependent on the West and was one of the strongest African supporters of the United States during the Cold War.

In the 1990s, however, Mobutu's presidential power diminished as he faced loss of foreign support, an economy ravaged by mismanagement, and mounting domestic political opposition.

THOMAS BORSTELMANN

See also Angola, Zaire

FURTHER READING
Kalb, Madeleine G. *The Congo Cables: The Cold War in Africa From Eisenhower to Kennedy.* New York, 1982.
Schatzberg, Michael G. *Mobutu or Chaos? The United States and Zaire, 1960–1990.* Lanham, Md., 1991.
Young, Crawford, and Thomas Turner. *The Rise and Decline of the Zairian State.* Madison, Wis., 1985.

MOLDOVA, REPUBLIC OF
See Appendix 2

MOLOTOV, VYACHESLAV MIKHAILOVICH
(*b.* 9 March 1890; *d.* 8 November 1986)

Soviet communist leader and prominent statesman, Molotov served as a Politburo member (1926–1957), chairman of the Council of People's Commissaries (CPC; 1930–1941), first deputy of the CPC (Council of Ministers since 1946) in 1941–1957, and foreign minister of the Soviet Union (1939–1949, 1953–1956). Born near Vyatka in Kukarka, Russia, into a middle-class, educated family, Molotov was involved in clandestine revolutionary activities of the Bolshevik Party by the time he was sixteen (1906). He supported Joseph Stalin in the power struggles after the Russian Revolution, and, although he was never a trained diplomat, he became Stalin's principal foreign policy adviser beginning with the negotiations over the Russo-German nonaggression pact in August 1939. After Germany invaded the Soviet Union in June 1941, bringing that country into World War II, Molotov negotiated a mutual assistance pact with Great Britain in July and with the United States for lend-lease aid, which was granted in November. He also pressed for the opening of a second front in Europe and recognition of Soviet territorial gains in Eastern Europe in 1944–1945. He attended several international conferences during the war, including those at Tehran (1943), Dumbarton Oaks (1944), Yalta (February 1945), and Potsdam (July 1945), and he led the Soviet delegation at the opening session of the United Nations in San Francisco (April 1945). After the war he represented the USSR at the Council of Foreign Ministers meetings and the Paris Peace Conference (1946) to negotiate peace treaties with Germany's former satellites. In July 1947 he walked out of a conference in Paris concerning aid for the economic recovery for Europe (the Marshall Plan), charging that the plan was an "imperialist" plan to enslave Europe. In 1947–1948, in addition to his other positions, he served as head of the Committee of Information, the clearinghouse of Soviet intelligence services.

Molotov's foreign policy was a blend of Bolshevik messianism, ruthless realpolitik, and great Russian expansionism. Relations with the United States and Great Britain were most important. The rest of Europe and Asia, including France, India, and China, played little role in his calculations. By fall 1946 he regarded "U.S. imperialism" as a major threat to the Soviet Union. His belief in Vladimir Lenin's theory of imperialism made him think that world wars could not be prevented but could be postponed by shrewd exploitation of contradictions among capitalist powers. In Molotov's dogmatic vision there was little room for peaceful coexistence and autonomous actions of small countries. In the spring of 1948 he supported Stalin's attack on Josip Broz Tito, which led to the Soviet-Yugoslav split.

In 1949 Molotov lost Stalin's trust when his wife, Polina Zhemchuzhina, was arrested allegedly for sympathies toward Israel, and Molotov was succeeded as foreign minister by Andrei Y. Vyshinsky. After Stalin's death in 1953, Molotov regained his influence in the making of Soviet foreign policy. His priority was the preservation of the integrity of the Soviet sphere of influence in Eastern Europe. Molotov supported the transformation of the Soviet zone of occupation in Germany into the socialist German Democratic Republic and resisted any compromise that threatened reintegration of East Germany into a Western sphere of influence. In the spring of 1955, Molotov, under pressure from Communist party leader Nikita Khrushchev, negotiated a treaty restoring Austria's sovereignty, simultaneously conceding Khrushchev's primacy in international affairs. In July 1956 Molotov lost the position of foreign minister to Dimitry Shepilov. A year later, after an unsuccessful attempt to depose Khrushchev, Molotov was evicted from the Politburo and appointed ambassador to Mongolia. In 1960–1962 he served as Soviet representative on the International Atomic Energy Commission in Vienna. In 1962 he was expelled from the party and retired to a dacha near Moscow, but his party membership was restored in 1984. U.S. and British statesmen and diplomats regarded Molotov as a tenacious advocate of Soviet interests and a dogmatic disciple of Comintern doctrines. Molotov's unflagging, monotonous resistance to Western negotiating positions earned him the nickname "Mr. Nyet."

VLADISLAV M. ZUBOK

See also Austria; Cold War; Germany; Khrushchev, Nikita Sergeyevich; Lend-Lease; Russia and the Soviet Union; Stalin, Joseph; Tito; World War II

FURTHER READING

Resis, Albert, ed. *Molotov Remembers: Inside Kremlin Politics: Conversations with Felix Chuev.* Chicago, 1993.

MONACO
See Appendix 2

MONGOLIA

Located in northern Asia, landlocked between China and Russia and covering an area of 1,565,000 square kilo-

meters. The land is mineral rich and in physical appearance resembles Idaho, Wyoming, and Utah. Only one percent of the land is arable; nine percent is forested; and ninety percent of the land consists of steppe pasture land, semi desert, and desert. It has an extreme continental climate with cold winters and short summers, during which most rain falls. Slight variation in precipitation can cause severe hardship on livelihood, which also can explain traditional patterns of tribal migration and conquest. Present day Mongolia lies within the heartland of the thirteenth-century Mongol Empire, which under the leadership of Genghis Khan and his successors conquered nearly all of Asia and European Russia (1203–1368).

Mongolia's population was estimated at 2,250,000 in 1994. Ethnic Mongols make up about eighty-five percent of the population with the Khalkha group in the majority (ninety percent); Turkic speakers compose seven percent; and the remaining groups are Tunguisic, Chinese, and Russian (eight percent). Directly north of Mongolia lies the Autonomous Region of Buryatia with a Mongol Buriat and Mongol Kalmyk population of 500,000. About three and one-half million Mongols live in China in the Inner Mongolia Autonomous Region.

For over three millennia the geopolitics of this region have had a profound effect on local affairs and at times on world history. Russian influence did not penetrate into Siberia until the seventeenth century, when Buryat Mongols became part of the Russian Empire. In the late seventeenth century Mongolia came under Chinese domination after the Manchus, a tribal group from northeast Asia, conquered China and established the Qing Dynasty. The Manchu regime divided the nation into two units, Inner and Outer Mongolia. When the Qing Dynasty dissolved in 1911, Outer Mongolia sought Russian protection, and by 1924 became the second socialist republic in the world. Since the disintegration of the former USSR, Mongolia has pursued an independent and non-aligned policy, which marks a new course in its foreign policy pattern.

The United States established diplomatic relations with Mongolia 27 January 1987, after unsuccessful post-World War II and Vietnam-era negotiations failed. An embassy opened in the capital Ulan Bator in April 1988.

The *perestroika* movement in the former USSR, the democracy movement in Eastern Europe, and improved Sino-Soviet relations contributed to renewed Mongol nationalism culminating in a peaceful political and economic reform movement in December 1989. In 1992 a new constitution was adopted and the country's name was changed from the Mongolian People's Republic to Mongolia. The first direct presidential elections were held 6 June 1993.

Recent U.S. policy towards Mongolia has aimed at encouraging democratic and economic reform, while specifically supporting expanded economic and cultural relations. The United States has granted Mongolia most-favored-nation status and signed Peace Corps and cultural accords. In 1991 the U.S. Agency for International Development began a technical assistance and training program in Mongolia. During 1991 Mongolia joined the International Monetary Fund, the World Bank, and the Asian Development Bank. In 1992 and 1993 food shortages in Mongolia prompted American relief efforts. In 1993, $10.3 million in infrastructure and developmental assistance was given.

Mongolia has signed international agreements on biodiversity, climate change, environmental modification, law of the sea, and the Nuclear Test Ban Treaty, which is signed but, as of 1995, not ratified.

JOCELYN M. NASH MARINESCU

See also China; Russia and the Soviet Union

FURTHER READING

Akiner, Shirin, ed. *Mongolia Today*. London, 1992.
Allsen, Thomas T. *Mongol Imperialism*. Berkeley, Calif., 1987.
Bawden, C.R. *The Modern History of Mongolia*. 2nd ed., with afterward by A.J.K. Sanders. London, 1989.
Waldron, Arthur. *The Great Wall of China From History to Myth*. Cambridge, 1990.

MONGOOSE, OPERATION

See Covert Action; Cuba; Intelligence

MONNET, JEAN

(*b.* 9 November 1888; *d.* 16 March 1979)

French economist and statesman who played a seminal role in helping to create a united Europe. The European Union of the 1990s owed its inspiration to Jean Monnet. His service to this ideal overshadowed his considerable service to France in two world wars. He was a close political and intellectual partner of the U.S. leaders who, during the early years of the Cold War, were devoted to the reconstruction of a prosperous, anticommunist Western Europe.

Son of a prosperous brandy merchant, Monnet was fittingly born in Cognac, and entered the family business at a young age. His financial acumen, ability as an economic planner, and talent for administration brought him to the attention of the French government before he reached age thirty. Observing the inefficiency of supply shipments from Great Britain during World War I, he proposed new methods for the Allies and helped set up agencies to administer the program. In 1916 France named him permanent representative to the Inter-Allied Maritime Commission.

After the war he served as deputy secretary-general of the League of Nations from 1919 to 1923. His familiarity with the international scene expanded when he became European partner of a New York investment bank in 1925. Throughout the interwar period he made lasting friends in Great Britain and the United States.

At the beginning of World War II France and Great Britain jointly appointed Monnet chairman of a committee to coordinate logistical plans. After France fell to the Germans, Monnet moved to Washington, where he served on the British Supply Council in support of the Lend-Lease program. He joined the Free French in 1943 and used his influence to counteract the reservations of U.S. leaders about General Charles de Gaulle's provisional government.

After serving as president of the French Committee for Supplies, he was charged by General de Gaulle with planning the reconstruction and modernization of the French economy. Monnet used this assignment as a foundation for reconstructing Europe, a goal with which de Gaulle was not in agreement. Monnet's strong connections to Great Britain and the United States divided him and the French leader.

With the support of French foreign minister Robert Schuman, Monnet produced the Schuman Plan, which created the European Coal and Steel Community. The Community was a union of six European countries centered on breaking down national barriers in the coal and steel industries, and was Monnet's model for the gradual unification of Europe. Monnet was principal author of the Pleven Plan of 1950 for the European Defense Community. The Plan was overly ambitious and was not implemented. Monnet favored a gradual approach to European unity, beginning with economic integration.

The Treaty of Rome, which established the European Economic Community in 1957, was a direct result of Monnet's vision. He chaired an Action Committee for a United States of Europe from 1956 to 1975, and lived to observe steady growth of the Common Market after 1971. Monnet's reputation flourished in the United States through his friendship with such influential diplomatic and political figures as George Ball and John McCloy.

LAWRENCE S. KAPLAN

See also Ball, George Wildman; Cold War; European Defense Community; European Union; France; McCloy, John Jay; Schuman, Robert; World War I; World War II

FURTHER READING

Brinkley, D., and C. Hackett, eds. *Jean Monnet: The Path to European Unity*. New York, 1991.
Bromberger, Merry, and Serge Bromberger. *John Monnet and the United States of Europe*. Translated by Elaine B. Halperin. New York, 1968.
Monnet, Jean. *Memoirs*. New York, 1978.

MONROE, JAMES

(b. 28 April 1758; *d.* 4 July 1831)

Secretary of state (1811–1817) and fifth president of the United States (1817–1825). Born in Westmoreland County, Virginia, he served as a young army officer in the American Revolution and went on to devote his life to politics and diplomacy. A protégé of Thomas Jefferson and James Madison, Monroe supported democratic principles and national territorial expansion. After rising rapidly in Virginia politics and serving in the U.S. Senate from 1790 to 1794, he first ventured abroad as minister to France (1794–1796). His sympathy for the French Revolution and for France over Great Britain was out of step with the policies of the Washington administration and caused Monroe to be the target of partisan attack in the United States.

Monroe returned from France, served a term as governor of Virginia, and became President Thomas Jefferson's roving diplomat in Europe from 1803 to 1807. His special mission in the spring of 1803—to help the U.S. minister in Paris, Robert Livingston, acquire the city of New Orleans and secure navigation of the Mississippi River from France—was crowned with success because Napoleon Bonaparte, before Monroe's arrival in Paris, had decided to sell the entire Louisiana territory to the United States. As U.S. minister in London from 1803 to 1807, Monroe plunged into complicated but futile negotiations over U.S. neutrality and British maritime practice. The treaty he and special commissioner William Pinkney negotiated in 1806 with Great Britain likely would have prevented the war of 1812, but President Jefferson would not submit it to the Senate because Great Britain refused to abandon the impressment of seamen from U.S. ships. Monroe's brief mission to Spain in 1805 failed to win U.S. title to West Florida, claimed by the United States as part of the Louisiana Purchase.

Monroe became President James Madison's secretary of state in 1811 and served until inaugurated president in 1817. Proud of his military experience, Monroe exercised force in international affairs more than Jefferson or Madison did. He believed "the respect which one power has for another is in exact proportion of the means which they respectively have of injuring each other" and that diplomacy was "an affair of calculation, dependent upon the physical forces which each has at its command." He argued for U.S. military preparedness as U.S.-British relations deteriorated toward war in 1812. During the ensuing conflict he served as acting secretary of war.

Elected president in 1816 without much opposition, Monroe presided over the so-called "era of good feelings." He hoped to abolish political parties, and worked closely with Secretary of State John Quincy Adams to improve relations with Great Britain. They acquired the Floridas and land in the Pacific from Spain in the Transcontinental, or Adams-Onís, Treaty of 1819, maneuvering through the turbulence of the Latin American wars of independence against Spain. In 1823 he set forth in his annual message to Congress the policy governing U.S. relations with Europe and the Western Hemisphere known as the Monroe Doctrine. The United States, he said, opposed the extension of European colonial territory into the Americas and would view European political interference with the new Latin American republics as a threat to U.S. security. The United States, he said, would not become involved in European politics.

Jefferson, Madison, and Monroe—the Virginia dynasty—occupied the U.S. presidency from 1801 to 1825. Monroe lacked the intellectual brilliance of his two friends and predecessors. He was a hardworking, pragmatic politician and diplomat, not an original thinker. He reached decisions after slow, careful deliberation. He was an unimpressive speaker and his writings, almost all on political subjects, lack color. He worked steadily toward clear goals, however, which were key themes of early U.S. foreign relations.

GADDIS SMITH

See also Adams, John Quincy; Adams-Onís Treaty; Continental Expansion; French Revolution; Impressment; Jefferson, Thomas; Louisiana Purchase; Madison, James; Monroe Doctrine; Monroe-Pinkney Treaty; War of 1812

FURTHER READING

Ammon, Harry. *James Monroe: The Quest for National Identity.* New York, 1971.

Bemis, Samuel Flagg. *John Quincy Adams and the Foundations of American Foreign Policy.* New York, 1949.

Cresson, W. P. *James Monroe.* Chapel Hill, N.C., 1946.

May, Ernest R. *The Making of the Monroe Doctrine.* Cambridge, Mass., 1975.

MONROE DOCTRINE

Three propositions contained in the annual message of President James Monroe to Congress, 2 December 1823, and more broadly a fundamental U.S. tenet, persisting into the late 20th century, that national security required the exclusion of outside political influence from the Western Hemisphere. For a century and a half the doctrine was hailed by presidents, secretaries of state, and editorial writers as a permanent, indispensable first principle of foreign policy. It was invoked emphatically under a great variety of circumstances.

The doctrine, like scripture, meant many things to different people at different times. Always it had a subjective, emotional content. "I believe strictly in the Monroe doctrine, our Constitution and in the laws of God," said the religious leader Mary Baker Eddy in expressing the reverence many Americans felt for the doctrine in the early twentieth century. The liturgical power of the two words inspired feelings of pride and helped Americans define their attitudes toward the rest of the world and the U.S. role in international affairs. Celebrants in the United States saw it as an expression of moral purity compared to European selfishness. But many in Latin America condemned and feared the doctrine as a self-righteous cloak for intervention by the colossus of the North in their affairs.

The Propositions and Their Reception

The three relevant propositions in President Monroe's original message were: 1) the "American continents, by the free and independent condition which they have assumed and maintain, are henceforth not to be considered as subjects for future colonization by European powers; 2) in "wars of European powers in matters relating to themselves we have never taken part, nor does it comport with our policy to do so;" and 3) given the fundamental differences between European political absolutism and American democracy, we "owe it, therefore, to candor...to declare that we should consider any attempt on their part to extend their system to any portion of this hemisphere as dangerous to our peace and safety."

Each proposition was response to a particular perceived international threat. The noncolonization proposition expressed a determination to resist Russian expansion southward from Alaska along the Pacific coast. The words and policy were fashioned primarily by Secretary of State John Quincy Adams. He had already stoutly rebutted Russian pretensions in a diplomatic message. The Russians, faced also with British opposition, backed away. But Monroe deemed it prudent to assert noncolonization as a national security principle.

The second proposition, against involvement in European wars was a restatement of traditional nonentanglement going back to Tom Paine's 1776 pamphlet *Common Sense*, George Washington's Farewell Address of 1796, and Thomas Jefferson's first inaugural address in 1801. By including this principle, Monroe was siding with Adams in a hot debate within the cabinet over whether the United States should actively champion the cause of the Greeks, then fighting for independence from Turkey. While some advocated recognition of Greek independence and even naval assistance, Adams called for sympathy only—and his view prevailed.

The third proposition, declaring that the European political system must be excluded from the American continents, was the heart of the doctrine as it evolved over the succeeding two centuries. In 1823 it was a response to the possibility that the reactionary powers of Europe, banded together as the Holy Alliance and eager to stamp out liberalism in the wake of Napoleonic wars,

might try to impose monarchical governments over the fragile new republics of Latin America. In two previous decades, most of Spain's vast colonial empire stretching from Mexico to Cape Horn had risen in revolt, defeated Spain's feeble military attempt to hold control, and proclaimed independence as separate nations. Spain alone could do nothing to reverse her loss, but conceivably France's military and naval power could be enough to repress republicanism and reestablish European control under a system of puppet monarchies.

The British did not belong to the Holy Alliance and they saw the possibility of French intervention in Latin America as a threat to their growing commercial interests. On 20 August 1823 British Foreign Secretary George Canning made the unprecedented proposal to Richard Rush, the U.S. minister in London, that Great Britain and the United States should issue a joint warning to France. Rush's report of the proposal caused high excitement in Washington. President Monroe consulted former Presidents James Madison and Thomas Jefferson. Both advised acceptance of the British proposal, uniting with Great Britain in opposition to European intervention in Latin America. Jefferson called the question "the most momentous which has ever been offered to my contemplation since that of Independence." The United States would be detaching Great Britain from "the boils of Europe...with her on our side we need not fear the whole world. With her then, we should most sedulously cherish a cordial friendship; and nothing would tend more to knit our affections than to be fighting once more, side by side, in the same cause."

But Secretary of State Adams was skeptical, especially of the idea that Great Britain could be detached form Europe. Furthermore, Great Britain had made no commitment to recognize the independence of the Latin American republics and was quite capable of making a separate deal with European powers which would leave the United States in the lurch. Better, he said, for the United States to state its own position directly and independently and not proceed like a "cockboat in the wake of the British man-of-war." Again Adams prevailed. Common action with the British was not pursued. Monroe's message to Congress was issued instead.

Meanwhile, although unknown to President Monroe and his cabinet, what little chance there had been of actual French intervention had been eliminated by a direct warning from Canning to Prince de Polignac, the French ambassador. In the "Polignac memorandum" of 12 October 1823 Canning said he viewed the restoration of Spanish control over the former colonies as hopeless and implied that Great Britain would be prepared to go to war to prevent French meddling in Latin America. Polignac replied that France would never act against the colonies "by force of arms." Thus, it has been argued that the doctrine was issued to meet a crises that did not exist and that had there been a crisis, Latin America would have been protected by British seapower and not brave American words. Also Professor Ernest R. May has argued that Monroe's message was as much a part of the maneuvering among aspirants for the 1824 presidential nomination as it was a response to international affairs. Domestic politics were involved, just as they are involved in everything an administration does, but in this case they do not seem to have been of critical importance.

The response to the doctrine in Europe was dismissive; the response in Latin America was hopeful. Colombia, Mexico, and Brazil each proposed that the doctrine be transformed into a binding inter-American alliance. Adams refused. He emphasized that the doctrine was a unilateral American statement and that any action taken under it would be for the United States alone to decide. His enthusiasm for alliances with Latin America was even less than for a partnership with Great Britain.

The Doctrine to 1913

For nearly a quarter century after Monroe's address in 1823 the doctrine received little attention. But in December 1845 the fervently expansionist President James K. Polk explicitly revived the noncolonization principle in his annual message. The occasion was the fear, quite exaggerated, that Great Britain might acquire Texas and/or California. "Existing rights of every European nation should be respected, but it is due alike to our safety and our interests that the efficient protection of our laws should be extended over our whole territorial limits, and that it should be distinctly announced to the world as our settled policy that no future European colony of dominion shall with our consent be planted or established on any part of the North American Continent." Polk's concept of "territorial limits" included the continent straight through to the Pacific. His aim, soon to be achieved, was the annexation of Texas and California to the United Sates. By the mid-nineteenth century Monroe's propositions, linked with the exuberant expansionism expressed in the slogan "Manifest Destiny," had acquired the designation of "doctrine." Monroe's words had ascended to the heights of political theology.

The first serious challenge to the Monroe Doctrine was launched by Napoleon III of France while the United States was convulsed by the Civil War. Napoleon sent a French army to Mexico to turn the tide of a Mexican conflict against republican forces led by Benito Juárez. The French concocted an invitation from Mexican monarchists to have Archduke Ferdinand Maximilian, brother of the Emperor of Austria, installed as emperor of Mexico. At the same time Spain also took advantage of U.S. preoccupation with internal conflict to reassert control over Santo Domingo. The fears inspiring Monroe's

original message in 1823 appeared at last to have some substance, but the Union's victory over the Confederacy in 1865 restored U.S. capacity to deal with these incursions. Troops were mobilized on the Mexican border and Washington forcefully condemned the European presence. But even without U.S. threats, the French and Spanish adventures were failing. Bowing to the inevitable, Spain pulled out of Santo Domingo in 1865 and France out of Mexico in 1866. Maximilan chose to stay. He died before a Mexican firing squad in 1867.

The most strident assertion of the Monroe Doctrine came from the pen of Secretary of State Richard Olney in the administration of President Glover Cleveland in 1895. The occasion was the reappearance of an old dispute between Great Britain and Venezuela over the boundary of British Guiana. Gold had been discovered in the contested region, and the Venezuelan government had engaged a well-connected lobbyist and former U.S. minister in Caracas, William L. Scruggs, to publicize its claims. Scruggs's pamphlet, *British Aggression in Venezuela, or the Monroe Doctrine on Trial*, appeared in October 1894 and caused a sensation. By May 1895 the U.S. Congress and much of the U.S. press was in a fever of agitation against what was depicted as British imperialistic bullying of poor, weak Venezuela. "The American people," wrote young Senator Henry Cabot Lodge, "are not ready to abandon the Monroe Doctrine, or give up their rightful supremacy in the Western Hemisphere. On the contrary, they are ready to fight to maintain both." Theodore Roosevelt, Lodge's friend and then commissioner of police in New York City, welcomed the possibility of a war with Great Britain. He believed it would revive the flagging U.S. martial spirit.

President Cleveland, needing to confound critics who depicted him as weak in foreign affairs, instructed Olney to challenge the British. In a public dispatch invoking the Monroe Doctrine, Olney demanded that the British submit the dispute to arbitration and asserted that, "today the United States is practically sovereign on this continent, and its fiat is law upon the subjects to which it confines its interposition." Lord Salisbury, the British foreign secretary, ridiculed Olney's argument and said the Monroe Doctrine had no relation to the present controversy. Nevertheless, the British did submit the dispute to arbitration. They were beset by serious problems in Europe and wanted to ensure a friendly United States in the event of a crisis or war.

The next important expansion of the doctrine was made by President Theodore Roosevelt in 1904. At the time great powers were in the habit of using force and even military occupation to punish "wrongdoing" by small countries—such as default on debt or a break down in law and order leading to the death or injury of citizens of the great power. British occupation of Egypt in 1882 and the German seizure of a sphere of influence over the Shantung Peninsula of China in 1898 were examples. And in 1902 Germany had used force against Venezuela in a matter of unpaid debts. Roosevelt's fear was that "wrongdoing" in Latin America might lead to intervention by a European power, thus violating the Monroe Doctrine and endangering U.S. security. His particular concern was over the chronic instability in the Dominican Republic. For example the thought of a German naval base in the Dominican Republic astride the sea lanes of the Caribbean was intolerable.

The President's solution was to announce what immediately became known as the Roosevelt Corollary to the Monroe Doctrine. In his annual message to Congress, 6 December 1904, he wrote: "Chronic wrongdoing, or an impotence which results in a general loosening of the ties of a civilized nation, and in the Western Hemisphere, the adherence of the United States to the Monroe Doctrine may force the United States, however reluctantly, in flagrant cases of wrongdoing or impotence, to the exercise of an international police power." Acting pursuant to the Roosevelt Corollary, the United States took over the collection and disbursement of the Dominican Republic's customs revenues and between 1916 and 1924 governed the country under military occupation. Haiti, occupying the other half of the island of Hispaniola, was also occupied and governed by the United States at the same time and for similar reasons—to curb "chronic wrongdoing" and deter all possibility of European intervention.

The first concern over a possible Asian threat to the Monroe Doctrine occurred at the turn of the twentieth century. U.S. annexation of the Hawaiian islands in 1898 was motivated in part by a determination to head off acquisition of the islands by Japan, a fanciful fear of a highly unlikely event. Tension between the two countries mounted after 1905 over discrimination in California against Japanese immigrants. Thus, when rumors circulated in 1912 of a possible purchase by a Japanese company, fronting for the government, of a fishing port in Mexico, Senator Henry Cabot Lodge introduced, and the Senate passed, a resolution embodying what immediately became known as the Lodge Corollary to the Monroe Doctrine. It stated the opposition of the United States to the acquisition, "by any corporation or association which has such a relation to another government, not American, as to give that government practical power of control" of any land "in the American continents" with the potential of threatening American security.

Woodrow Wilson and the Monroe Doctrine

Woodrow Wilson, the president whose rhetoric was most idealistic in condemning intervention by powerful states in the affairs of small ones, ordered more U.S. intervention in Latin America than any other. But he also tried to elevate the Monroe Doctrine from a unilateral statement of the self-interest of the United States to a multilateral policy of the American republics and ultimately a policy for the entire world. First, in 1914 he approached the ABC powers—Argentina, Brazil, and Chile—with a proposal for a multilateral Pan-American treaty under which all members would guarantee one another's political independence and territorial integrity, settle disputes by peaceful means, curb the trade in munitions, and prevent their territory from being used by revolutionaries to attack other states. The overriding crises of the European war and the reluctance of Chile doomed this proposal, although Wilson later applied some of its concepts to the League of Nations.

From 1914 through 1916 President Woodrow Wilson and the United States struggled to remain neutral in the European war, but by 1917 the immensity of the war and probability that Germany would challenge the United States by resuming unrestricted submarine warfare led Wilson to believe that the United States would have to intervene. He was aware, however, that intervention would violate the sacred injunction of the Monroe Doctrine to stay out of Europe's quarrels. He resolved the contradiction in his own mind by elevating the doctrine to a universal principle for all mankind. In a major speech, 22 January 1917, he declared: "I am proposing, as it were, that the nations should with one accord adopt the doctrine of President Monroe as the doctrine of the world: that no nation should seek to extend its policy over any other nation, but that every people should be free to determine its own policy, its own way of development, unhindered, unthreatened, unafraid, the little along with the great and powerful."

Germany did resume submarine attacks on merchant, including U.S., shipping. In April 1917 Wilson asked Congress to declare war in order to "make the world safe for democracy." Congress obliged. A year and a half later U.S. military and economic power tipped the balance. Germany in defeat asked for an armistice. The fighting stopped 11 November 1918 and early in 1919 Wilson joined the leaders of the other winning powers in Paris to write a peace treaty including a program for collective security under a new creation: the League of Nations. Article X, the heart of the League Covenant, repeated language from the abortive Pan-American pact of 1914 in requiring all members "to respect and preserve as against external aggression the territorial integrity and political independence" of all other members.

Some U.S. Senators feared that the League might destroy U.S. freedom of action under the Monroe Doctrine. Would the League be free to intervene in the affairs of the American continents, and conversely could the League require the United States against its will to go to war anywhere in the world? In order to answer these questions Wilson secured the addition of a new article, XXI, to the draft Covenant declaring: "Nothing in this Covenant shall be deemed to affect the validity of international agreements, such as treaties of arbitration or regional understandings like the Monroe Doctrine, for securing the maintenance of peace." Article XXI was an invitation to confusion. The Monroe Doctrine had always been a unilateral U.S. statement, never a regional understanding. Some Latin Americans feared Article XXI condoned U.S. hegemony and would leave them powerless to run to the League of Nations, especially if they were ever in conflict with the United States. And how and by whom would the meaning of the Doctrine, and hence its "validity," be determined? Senate critics were not satisfied and demanded that among the reservations accompanying U.S. membership in the League be included the statement that the United States would not accept the jurisdiction of the League over "any questions which...depend upon or relate to its long-established policy, commonly known as the Monroe Doctrine; said doctrine is to be interpreted by the United States alone and is hereby declared to be wholly outside the jurisdiction of said League of Nations." Wilson would not accept this or other reservations and the Senate failed to approve the treaty. The United States never became a member of the League of Nations.

Between the World Wars

During the two decades between World War I and World War II the Senate zealously protected the Monroe Doctrine from any conceivable infringement. For example, the United States ratified the General Pact for the Renunciation of War, more commonly known as the Kellogg-Briand Pact, with the understanding that the "United States regards the Monroe Doctrine as part of its national security and defense. Under the right of self-defense allowed by the treaty must necessarily be included the right to maintain the Monroe Doctrine which is a part of our system of national defense." The doctrine was safe.

In the 1920s there was no perceptible European threat to the Western Hemisphere. But several U.S. administrations grew concerned that Latin American resentment of pretensions under the doctrine, especially under the Roosevelt Corollary, were an obstacle to good relations and trade. Secretary of State Frank B. Kellogg sought to detoxify the doctrine. Following a memorandum prepared by Under Secretary of State J. Reuben Clark, Kellogg declared "the Monroe Doctrine has nothing whatever to do with the domestic concerns or policies or the form of government or the international conduct of the peoples of this hemisphere among themselves" but dealt only with real or potential threats from beyond the hemisphere. "The doctrine is not a lance; it is a shield." This

repudiation of the Roosevelt Corollary and the "Good Neighbor Policy" President Franklin D. Roosevelt proclaimed in 1933 were well received in Latin America.

By 1940 the rising tide of Japanese aggression in Asia and German aggression in Europe led to revived discussion of the Monroe Doctrine. The Japanese replied to U.S. criticism of its effort to dominate China by claiming a "Monroe Doctrine" for themselves. Secretary of State Cordell Hull was infuriated by the comparison. "There is no more resemblance between our Monroe Doctrine," he told the Japanese ambassador in April 1940, "and the so-called Monroe Doctrine of Japan than there is between black and white."

Meanwhile, Germany's conquest of France and the Netherlands in June 1940 led the U.S. government to worry over the fate of French and Dutch colonies in the Caribbean. Invoking the Monroe Doctrine, the United States informed Germany that it would not permit the transfer of any territory in the Western Hemisphere "from one non-American power to another non-American power," from France or the Netherlands to Germany. Nazi Foreign Minister Joachim von Ribbentrop piously denied that Germany had any intention of acquiring American territory and then presumed to instruct Secretary of State Hull on the Monroe Doctrine: "the nonintervention in the affairs of the American continent which is demanded by the Monroe Doctrine can in principle be legally valid only on condition that the American states do not intervene in the affairs of the European continent." The Japanese and German arguments struck Hull as preposterous, but they did illuminate an issue that would plague the disciples of the Monroe Doctrine for another half century. How could the United States under the Monroe Doctrine exclude foreign influence from an entire hemisphere and deny other great powers similar rights in their regions? Was sauce for the goose sauce for the gander?

The German threat enabled the United States to secure the support of Latin American governments, except for Argentina, for the establishment of a hemispheric security zone under the Monroe Doctrine. A 1939 declaration, issued at a conference in Panama, barred belligerent operations from American waters. The 1940 Act of Havana provided for preemptive occupation of any islands or regions whose sovereignty was in danger of being transferred from one European power to another. As the United States moved closer to active intervention against Germany, President Roosevelt defined the limits of the Western Hemisphere protected under the Monroe Doctrine with spacious daring. Greenland, Iceland, and the Galapagos in the Pacific all were brought under the doctrine's protective umbrella.

During World War II a team of planners in the Department of State, led by Leo Pasvolsky, prepared a draft charter for the United Nations, the entity that was intended to replace the failed League of Nations. Pasvolsky's focus was on Europe and on the creation of an organization with universal jurisdiction, not one hampered by spheres of influence or regional arrangements. When the conference to negotiate the final draft of the charter convened in San Francisco in May 1945, the universalist approach was attacked within the U.S. government and by Latin American governments as leaving the Western Hemisphere vulnerable to political maneuverings initiated by non-American great powers, especially the Soviet Union. There must be no outside veto on American regional action. The hemispheric regionalism prevailed at San Francisco and secured the addition of Articles 51 and 52 to the UN Charter. The articles allowed for individual and collective self-defense and permitted the formation of regional security pacts and organizations.

The Cold War Era

After World War II the Monroe Doctrine was applied as a regional part of the general policy of containing the expansion of Soviet influence and specifically "international communism." Initially no one in the U.S. government saw an immediate Soviet military threat to the Western Hemisphere. The threat was seen as primarily political and psychological, with communists exploiting local discontent and weak governments to insinuate themselves gradually in positions of power. In March 1950 George F. Kennan, famous as principal author of the doctrine of containment and founder of the Department of State's Policy Planning Staff, argued that defense of the Monroe Doctrine, the exclusion of a dangerous political system from the hemisphere, required that the United States support regimes capable of dealing ruthlessly with the local communist problem. In a long memorandum for Secretary of State Dean Acheson he advanced what could be called the Kennan Corollary to the Monroe Doctrine: "We cannot be too dogmatic about the methods by which local communists can be dealt with...where the concepts and traditions of popular government are too weak to absorb successfully the intensity of communist attack, then we must concede that harsh measures of government repression may be...the only alternatives to further communist success."

Although the Kennan memorandum was classified as secret and not widely circulated within the government, its assumptions were widely shared and were frequently applied to specific situations as late as the 1980s. The first application came in Guatemala in 1954. For a decade that country had been democratically governed by regimes mildly on the left. President Jacobo Arbenz, elected in 1950, increased the rights of labor and imposed limitations on the economic power of the United Fruit Company, an U.S. corporation with huge banana plantations. Arbenz also was on friendly terms with a handful of Guatemalan communists and resented U.S. advice on how he should root out subversive influences. By 1954 Secretary of State John Foster Dulles saw the continuation of the Arbenz regime as a threat to the Monroe Doctrine and American security. When the U.S. effort to remove Arbenz through political and economic pressure failed, President Dwight D. Eisenhower ordered a covert attack organized by the Central Intelligence Agency using anti-Arbenz Guatemalans as well as a few Americans. The United States also pressured the British and French into preventing a Guatemalan complaint, backed by the Soviet Union, from reaching the agenda of the United Nations Security Council. The Soviet Union, Dulles told British Foreign Secretary Anthony Eden, is "trying...to destroy the Monroe Doctrine which was the first assumption of international responsibility by the United States."

The covert attack succeeded. Arbenz fled to Mexico. The United States installed the leader of the attacking forces, Colonel Castillo Armas, as the new president. He and his successors maintained the kind of regime envisioned in the Kennan Corollary. John Peurifoy, the U.S. ambassador to Guatemala and key figure in the operation, declared afterwards that "In proving that communism can be defeated, we relied on the traditional American principle of honesty in the conduct of foreign affairs and the American doctrine of continental liberty from despotic intervention, first enunciated by President Monroe 131 years ago." Of course, the United States had relied on the very opposite of honesty.

Five years later, 1 January 1959, the Monroe Doctrine seemed to many U.S. diplomats and commentators to be threatened again when Cuban rebel Fidel Castro overthrew the anticommunist dictator Fulgencio Batista. Once in power, Castro moved steadily to the left, nationalizing foreign (mostly U.S.) properties, denouncing U.S. imperialism, and courting the support of the Soviet Union. The Eisenhower administration applied escalating economic sanctions, inflicted some minor covert harassment, and began planning Castro's overthrow by CIA-trained exiles, an operation inspired by happy memories of the success against Arbenz in Guatemala. As tension increased, Soviet premier Nikita Khrushchev in July 1960 caught U.S. attention and banner headlines in the world press by publicly declaring the Monroe Doctrine dead. "Now the remains of this doctrine should best be buried as every dead body is so that it should not poison the air by its decay." Khrushchev praised the doctrine of 1823 as a noble expression of democratic ideals and anticolonialism. But today it belongs, he said, "to the imperialists of the United States of America, the colonialists, who, like vultures, snatch the last crumb out of the mouths of the dying children and old just to wax fat and rich. And it is through the Monroe Doctrine that they want to assure themselves the right to go on with this robbery forever." An indignant Department of State replied that the doctrine was as valid in 1960 as in 1823, and that its principles were now embodied in the Rio Treaty.

By 1961 John F. Kennedy was president and Castro seemed more firmly entrenched than ever and completely dependent on Soviet aid. Professor Samuel Flagg Bemis, an authority on U.S. relations with Latin America, wrote Senator Prescott Bush of "this ominous hour" and predicted that the Soviets soon would have submarine bases and missile launching pads in Cuba.

"We have suffered nothing less than a staggering defeat of the Monroe Doctrine," wrote Bemis. Matters rapidly grew worse from the U.S. point of view. In April 1961 the invasion of CIA-organized anti-Castro exiles failed at the Bay of Pigs. In May 1962 Khrushchev made the decision to place intermediate-range nuclear missiles in Cuba.

In response to the undisguised flow of Soviet conventional weapons to Cuba and rumors of nuclear missiles, a great outcry arose in the United States Congress. President Kennedy was attacked for failing to oust Castro and the Soviet presence. He admitted, charged Senator Strom Thurmond, "that the clear historical meaning of the Monroe Doctrine has been abandoned as a cornerstone of United States foreign policy and that here has been substituted therefore, in desecration of the name of the Monroe Doctrine, a policy of expediency, hesitation, and indecision." James Monroe, 139 years after delivering his original message, made the cover of *Time* magazine. On 3 October 1962 Congress passed and Kennedy signed a resolution declaring in the name of the Monroe Doctrine that the United States would use all necessary measures to prevent a threat to its security in Cuba. Kennedy himself, a pragmatist with an aversion to sweeping doctrines of any sort, was annoyed by the congressional invocation of the doctrine and ordered the words not be used to explain whatever proved necessary. The outcome of the crisis was a mixed victory. The Soviets removed the nuclear missiles, but the United States pledged not to invade Cuba. The island became and remained until 1991 a Soviet protectorate "90 miles from the American shore." A large, semipermanent exception to the doctrine had been granted. Many U.S. politicians and writers of right-wing bent never forgot or forgave.

The specific phrase "Monroe Doctrine" was seldom used during the administrations of Presidents Lyndon B. Johnson and Richard M. Nixon, but both acted in the spirit of the doctrine in their determination to prevent "another Cuba" in the hemisphere. Johnson was prepared, if necessary, to send U.S. forces to assure the success of a military coup in Brazil against the leftist regime

of President Joao Goulart, a regime believed to be lurching erratically toward communism. The coup succeeded with American encouragement, but direct military assistance proved unnecessary. Johnson also sent 20,000 U.S. Marines to the Dominican Republic during an uprising against the country's military government. The United States feared that the uprising had been planned or would fall under the control of communists. Chile was President Nixon's potential "another Cuba." He and Secretary of State Henry Kissinger involved the United States in the machinations which led to the overthrow and death in 1973 of democratically elected but far-left President Salvador Allende in a bloody coup led by General Augusto Pinochet. "I don't see," said Kissinger in an oft-quoted remark, "why we have to let a country go Marxist just because its people are irresponsible."

President Jimmy Carter, taking office in January 1977, tried to repudiate, and even apologize for, previous coercive and covert American actions in Latin America. He was particularly opposed to support by the United States for totalitarian regimes and violators of human rights. In a major speech at Notre Dame University in May 1977 he in effect renounced the Kennan Corollary to the Monroe Doctrine by declaring: "We are now free of that inordinate fear of Communism which once led us to embrace any dictator in that fear....For too many years, we've been willing to adopt the flawed and erroneous principles and tactics against treating Latin America countries paternalistically in terms of a special hemisphere policy." He noted that most Americans saw the Monroe Doctrine as "a selfless U.S. contribution to hemispheric security; but to most of our neighbors to the south it was an expression of presumptuous U.S. imperialism." The Carter administration's main achievement in Latin America was the negotiation of treaties with Panama by which the United States turned over ownership and operation of the Panama Canal by the year 1999. These treaties barely won the necessary assent of the Senate and stirred emotional opposition from Ronald Reagan and others for whom an American-owned canal was, like the Monroe Doctrine, a sacred principle. Reagan exploited the canal issue effectively in his successful presidential campaign against Carter in 1980.

President Ronald Reagan considered himself the heir and true protector of the Monroe Doctrine. He preferred, however, to speak in terms of a broader proposition, called the Reagan Doctrine: the assertion of an American intention to assist insurgent movements seeking to overthrow communist regimes wherever they existed. In the Western Hemisphere this meant the creation and support of guerrilla forces, the so-called "Contras," fighting to overthrow the Sandinista regime in Nicaragua. The Reagan administration's support of the military forces of El Salvador—while pretending to be unaware of murderous brutality—was designed, in the spirit of the Kennan Corollary, to protect that county from "international communism."

The Reagan administration emphasized not only the direct threat to U.S. security from the incursion of communist influence originating in the Soviet Union and acting through Cuba, but also how this threat would force the United States to use resources for hemispheric defense which then would not be available for action around the world. The original Monroe Doctrine had been designed to keep the United States detached from trouble beyond the hemisphere. The Reagan version argued that an exclusive American sphere in the one hemisphere was necessary in order to facilitate intervention in the other. The concept was well expressed in the 1984 report of the Bi-Partisan Commission on Central America appointed by Reagan and chaired by Henry A. Kissinger 1984: "To the extent that a further Marxist-Leninist in Central America...required us to defend against security threats near our borders, we would face a difficult choice between unpalatable alternatives. We would either have to assume a permanently increased defense burden, or see our capacity to defend distant trouble spots reduced, and as a result have to reduce important commitments elsewhere in the world."

The majority of Congress did not share the Reagan administration's perception of an overpowering Soviet threat in Central America justifying covert action. Congressional restrictions frustrated the administration and tempted action in direct defiance of law. Deputy Director of Central Intelligence Robert Gates expressed the administration's impatience with congressional unwillingness to permit whatever was necessary to prevent "a second Cuba." In an October 1984 memorandum to Director of Central Intelligence William Casey, Gates wrote: "The fact is that the Western Hemisphere is the sphere of influence of the United States. If we have decided totally to abandon the Monroe Doctrine, if in the 1980s taking strong actions to protect our interests...is too difficult, then we ought to save political capital in Washington, acknowledge our helplessness and stop wasting everybody's time."

The Monroe Doctrine came into play on two other occasions during the Reagan presidency. In the spring of 1982 the only war of the twentieth century occurred in the Western Hemisphere between a European and Latin American nation: the seizure by Argentina of the British-occupied Falkland Islands (Malvinas) and their recapture by the British. Supporters of the Argentine position argued that the British presence, dating from 1833, had always been a violation of the noncolonization principle of the Monroe Doctrine and that in 1982 the United States should atone for a long failure to uphold the Doctrine by pressuring the British to withdraw. But President

Reagan and the majority of his advisers said the issue was Argentine's unprovoked aggression. In a conflict between theoretical adherence to the Monroe Doctrine and support for a close NATO ally, the Monroe Doctrine had no chance. The United States provided logistical, moral, and intelligence support to the British and applauded their victory.

But the Monroe Doctrine was very much alive in October 1983—although not invoked by name by U.S. officials—when President Reagan ordered the invasion of the tiny island of Grenada after a coup had yanked the government further to the left. By defeating the defending forces and expelling a Cuban construction group working a new, large airfield, the United States—in the eyes of the Reagan administration—protected itself from a strategic threat and vindicated the Monroe Doctrine.

For more than a century and a half, from 1823 until the late 1980s, the indispensable life support for the Monroe Doctrine had been the perception and often the reality of a sinister, calculating great power in Europe or Asia determined to extend hostile political and military influence over the American continents and thereby undermine the security of the United States. But with the end of the Cold War in 1989 and even more with the collapse of the Soviet Union in 1991, not even the most perfervid imagination could conceive an external threat. The important issues of U.S. security involving Latin America no longer had anything to do with outside great powers. They involved the illegal trade in narcotics, the flow of immigrants, and rules of trade. The words "Monroe Doctrine" in the 1990s disappeared from contemporary discourse.

GADDIS SMITH

See also Bay of Pigs Invasion; Carter, James Earl; Chile; Clark Memorandum; Cuba; Cuban Missile Crisis; Dominican Republic; Falkland Islands; Good Neighbor Policy; Grenada Invasion; Guatemala; Kennedy, John Fitzgerald; Latin America; Mexico; Monroe, James; Olney, Richard; Panama and Panama Canal; Polk, James Knox; Roosevelt, Franklin Delano; Roosevelt, Theodore; Reagan, Ronald Wilson; Roosevelt Corollary; Wilson, Thomas Woodrow

FURTHER READING

Bemis, Samuel Flagg. *The Latin American Policy of the United States.* New York, 1943.

Blasier, Cole. *The Giant's Rival: The USSR and Latin America.* Pittsburgh, Pa., 1983.

LaFeber, Walter. "The Evolution of the Monroe Doctrine from Monroe to Reagan." *Redefining the Past: Essays in Diplomatic History in Honor of William Appleman Williams,* edited by Lloyd Gardner. Corvallis, Ore., 1986.

Logan, John S., Jr. *No Transfer: An American Security Principle.* New Haven, Conn., 1961.

May, Ernest R. *The Making of the Monroe Doctrine.* Cambridge, Mass., 1927.

Perkins, Dexter. *The Monroe Doctrine, 1867–1907*. Baltimore, Md., 1937.
———. *A History of the Monroe Doctrine*. Boston, 1955.
Smith, Gaddis. *The Last Years of the Monroe Doctrine, 1945–1994*. New York, 1994.

MONROE-PINKNEY TREATY

An 1806 Anglo-American agreement that defined neutral and belligerent rights and established the terms of trade between the United States and Great Britain during the Napoleonic Wars. Designed as a successor to Jay's Treaty (1794), the agreement was never ratified by the United States.

President Thomas Jefferson, who had no love for Jay's Treaty, also showed no interest in entering into a new pact with the British, but events in 1806 forced his hand. In the wake of the *Essex* decision (1805), a British admiralty case that struck at American trade in the West Indies, the British Navy seized several hundred U.S. vessels in the Caribbean. American merchants appealed to Congress for relief, and that body urged the president to send a special mission to England to resolve outstanding differences. Bowing to congressional pressure, Jefferson appointed a commission consisting of William Pinkney, a Baltimore Federalist, and James Monroe, the resident minister in London.

Secretary of State James Madison's instructions to the envoys called for extensive British concessions on neutral rights, but only two demands were deemed essential: the British had to give up impressment, and they had to stop interfering with the West Indian trade. Although the British refused to surrender impressment, they agreed to the other major demand and showed a disposition to make additional concessions as well; hence Monroe and Pinkney decided to sign a treaty that fell short of their instructions.

Besides securing the United States's Caribbean trade, the Monroe-Pinkney Treaty recognized an extension of U.S. territorial waters from three to five miles, established a narrow definition of contraband, promised better notice of naval blockades, presaged a reduction of duties for U.S. merchants trading in British ports, and provided for compensation of U.S. merchants who suffered from British violations of the treaty. In exchange for these concessions, the United States promised to employ no commercial sanctions against Great Britain, to give up the doctrine of free ships-free goods (thus sanctioning the seizure of French property carried on U.S. ships), and to accede to greater restrictions on U.S. trade to the British East Indies. In effect, the United States secured a relatively broad definition of neutral rights in exchange for a promise of benevolent neutrality toward Great Britain. In a note appended to the treaty, the British reserved the

right to retaliate against France for the recently issued Berlin Decree, which proclaimed an illegal blockade.

In the realm of trade and neutral rights, the Monroe-Pinkney Treaty was more favorable to the United States than Jay's Treaty had been. Jefferson, however, refused to send the agreement to the Senate because it did not end impressment. This was an important turning point in the period, for the United States missed a chance to reestablish the Anglo-American accord of the 1790s. Instead, the nation pursued a policy of confrontation with Great Britain that led to trade restrictions and culminated in the War of 1812.

DONALD R. HICKEY

See also Great Britain; Impressment; Jay's Treaty; Jefferson, Thomas; Napoleonic Wars; Neutral Rights; War of 1812

FURTHER READING
Hickey, Donald R. "The Monroe-Pinkney Treaty of 1806: A Reappraisal." *William and Mary Quarterly* 44 (January 1987): 65–88.
Perkins, Bradford. *Prologue to War: England and the United States, 1805–1812*. Berkeley, Calif., 1961.

MONTREAL PROTOCOL
(1989)

A November 1987 international agreement that went into effect in 1989 to limit the production of chlorofluorocarbons hazardous to chemical balances in the stratosphere. The publication of a seminal scientific paper in 1974 putting forth a hypothesis on ozone depletion in the stratosphere sensitized both the scientific and the policy communities to a hitherto unrecognized environmental problem. The stratospheric ozone layer generates a natural protective barrier against the effects of the sun's ultraviolet radiation ultraviolet (UV-B) reaching the surface of the earth. Excessive levels of radiation produce adverse health effects in humans (notably skin cancer) and harm many forms of plant and animal life. The subsequent discovery in the early 1980s of the ozone hole in the Antarctic stratosphere, based on empirical measurement, galvanized the international community into action. The protocol requires governments to regulate consumption and production of chlorofluorocarbons (CFC-11, -12, -113, -114), to be frozen at 1986 levels in 1990 and reduced by 20 percent in 1993 and by 50 percent in 2000; and the protocol requires the regulation of Halons (1211, 1301, 2402), to be frozen at 1986 levels by 2005. The protocol also stipulates that developing countries could have a ten-year period of grace prior to enforcement. As amended in London in 1990, the protocol was broadened, covering a significantly larger number of critical chemicals. In 1991 the Interim Multilateral

Fund for financial assistance to developing countries was established to facilitate and accelerate compliance. In 1992 the amendment entered into force, thereby binding signatory nations to the most stringent statutes ever formulated by national or international bodies. The United States assumed a lead role in the diplomacy that led to the protocol. The Montreal Protocol is widely regarded as a crucial precedent for formation of institutional responses to environmental degradation buttressed by financial resources to facilitate implementation.

NAZLI CHOUCRI

See also Environment; United Nations Environment Program

FURTHER READING

Benedick, Richard Elliott. "Ozone Diplomacy," *Issues in Science and Technology.* IV (1) (Fall 1989): 43–50.

Molina, Mario J., and F. S. Rowland. "Stratospheric Sink for Chlorofluoromethanes: Chlorine Atom Catalyzed Destruction of Ozone." *Nature,* Vol. 249 (1974): 810–814.

United Nations Environment Programme. *Montreal Protocol on Substances that Deplete the Ozone Layer.* Nairobi, 1987.

MORGENTHAU, HANS

(*b.* 17 February 1904; *d.* 19 July 1980)

German-born political scientist and historian whose writings on international relations and U.S. foreign policy had a lasting influence throughout the post-World War II period. Born in Coburg, Morgenthau was educated at the Universities of Berlin, Frankfurt, and Munich and did postgraduate work at the Graduate Institute for International Studies in Geneva. He taught in Geneva and Madrid in the mid-1930s, came to the United States in 1937, and was naturalized in 1943. After teaching at Brooklyn College in New York (1937–1939) and the University of Kansas City, Missouri (1939–1943), he went to the University of Chicago (1943–1971) and published during his tenure there his most widely acclaimed works. Morgenthau's first book in English, *Scientific Man vs. Power Politics* (1946), was a sharp though brief critique of liberal illusions and "utopianism" in foreign policy. His second, *Politics Among Nations* (1948), was an ambitious survey of the theory and practice of international politics that became the leading exemplar of the newly emerging school of U.S. realism (and a widely used text in college courses). A third book, *In Defense of the National Interest* (1951), made the case that states had an ethically sanctioned right to pursue their own interests; a fourth, *The Purpose of American Politics* (1960), insisted that "in order to be worthy of our lasting sympathy, a nation must pursue its interests for the sake of a transcendent purpose that gives meaning to the day-by-day operations of its for-

eign policy." The U.S. purpose he identified was the pursuit of "equality in freedom" and he probed the "contemporary crisis" in relation to animating that vision.

Morgenthau was a highly visible participant in the ideological battles of his adopted country and a stout defender of both the intellectual's independence and his duty to "tell truth to power." He became a bitter opponent of the war in Vietnam, and deemed Lyndon Johnson's policies to be "morally dubious, militarily hopeless and risky, [and] politically aimless and counterproductive"; the risks the United States took in pursuit of victory were "out of all proportion to the interests at stake." Vietnam was primarily a civil war, not a war of aggression by the North; its global significance was "remote." Far from containing China and communism, it would aid both "by destroying the social fabric of Vietnamese nationalism, which is implacably hostile to China." Though acknowledging that U.S. prestige was undeniably engaged in Vietnam, Morgenthau doubted that it was "really a boon to the prestige of the most powerful nation on earth to be bogged down in a war that it neither is able to win nor can afford to lose."

Morgenthau's volumes of collected essays (*Dilemmas of Politics* [1958], *Politics in the Twentieth Century* [3 vols., 1962], and *Truth and Power,* [1970]) are, like his other books, distinguished by philosophic depth, wide range, and the inventive use of historical parallels. In the last decade of his life, he was affiliated with the City College of the City University of New York (1968–1974) and, from 1974, the New School for Social Research.

DAVID C. HENDRICKSON

See also Realism; Vietnam War

FURTHER READING

Russell, Greg. *Hans J. Morgenthau and the Ethics of American Statecraft.* Baton Rouge, La., 1990.

Smith, Michael J. *Realist Thought From Weber to Kissinger.* Baton Rouge, La., 1987.

MORGENTHAU, HENRY, JR.

(*b.* 11 May 1891; *d.* 6 February 1967)

Secretary of the treasury from 1933 to 1945, who significantly influenced U.S. foreign relations because of his friendship with President Franklin D. Roosevelt. Son of a wealthy Democratic Party activist who served as ambassador to Turkey under Woodrow Wilson, young Morgenthau rejected offers to participate in his father's business and took up farming in Dutchess County, New York, where he met Roosevelt in 1915. The two became lifelong friends, which provided Morgenthau the base from which he made numerous contributions to foreign policy.

Morgenthau readily admitted that Roosevelt used him as his "whipping boy" to test public reactions to new measures, particularly tax proposals. Morgenthau was a willing participant in Roosevelt's famous bureaucratic juggling acts in which he turned to the Treasury Department to draft policies or to undertake actions which the Departments of State and War opposed, as was the case with diplomatic recognition of the Soviet Union in 1933 and drafting of the Lend-Lease Act in 1941. Often Morgenthau acted as a policy entrepreneur. A talented bureaucratic in-fighter, he assembled a skilled and devoted staff at the Treasury Department. Morgenthau was to the right of the New Deal consensus on domestic economic policy.

Morgenthau was an early, indefatigable opponent of fascism. He urged the deployment of U.S. financial resources to aid victims of aggression and punish perpetrators. He successfully urged the president to aid China in 1937, proposed seizing Japanese assets in retaliation for the *Panay* incident, and in 1941 advocated U.S. embargo of oil and scrap iron shipments to Japan. In these and other instances, Morgenthau regarded the policies of the Department of State under Cordell Hull as "timorous" and warned the president to avoid becoming the Neville Chamberlain of the Far East, that is, an appeaser. In Europe, he urged the president to consider economic sanctions and even a "defensive war" against Germany after the Munich crisis of 1938. Morgenthau predicted the fate of Europe for the next hundred years would be sealed if Hitler were not stopped.

During the war, Morgenthau was devoted primarily to financing the Allied effort. In early 1944, he complained to the president of "gross procrastination" on the part of the U.S. Department of State in responding to genocide of European Jews in the Holocaust. Roosevelt then created the War Refugee Board. Morgenthau also prepared a harsh proposal aimed at demilitarizing and deindustrializing Germany and to dividing it into two states. Roosevelt supported the Morgenthau Plan sporadically; but antagonism with the Soviets, as well as practical and humanitarian considerations and opposition from the Departments of State and War eventually led Roosevelt away from the plan. When Harry S. Truman became president, Morgenthau knew his policy, which he thought necessary to prevent a third world war led by a resurgent Germany, had been abandoned. Realizing that the basis of his influence had rested on his personal relationship with Roosevelt, he resigned as secretary of the Treasury and returned to his farm in New York. During the late 1940s and early 1950s he helped Jewish philanthropic organizations raise money for Israel.

PHILIP ABBOTT

See also China; Germany; Holocaust; Hull, Cordell; Israel; Lend-Lease; Morgenthau Plan; Munich Confer-

ence; Panay Episode; Roosevelt, Franklin Delano; Russia and the Soviet Union; Treasury, U.S. Department of

FURTHER READING

Blum, John Morton. *From the Morgenthau Diaries*, 3 vols. Boston, 1959, 1965, 1967.
Kimball, Warren F. *Swords or Plowshares? The Morgenthau Plan for Defeated Nazi Germany, 1943–1946*. Philadelphia, 1976.
Morgenthau, Henry, Jr. *Germany Is Our Problem*. New York, 1945.

MORGENTHAU PLAN

A harsh proposal for the treatment of postwar Germany. In August 1944 Secretary of the Treasury Henry Morgenthau, Jr., grew alarmed by reports of Nazi atrocities and was angered by State Department proposals for a postwar policy of lenient occupation. He prepared a plan which called for the complete demilitarization and deindustrialization of Germany. Armaments and heavy industrial plants would be destroyed and dismantled, and key territories such as East Prussia, the Saar, and Silesia would be ceded to neighboring states. The remainder of Germany would be divided into a northern and southern state. The plan recommended that the Ruhr industrial region, "the cauldron of wars," would not only "be stripped of all presently existing industries but so weakened that it can never again become an industrial area." Morgenthau argued that the Plan would encourage U.S. cooperation with the Soviet Union in controlling Germany, and benefit Great Britain by removing an economic competitor. With the approval of President Franklin D. Roosevelt, who wished it "driven home to the German people" that their "nation has been engaged in a lawless conspiracy against the decencies of modern civilization," Morgenthau proposed his plan to the British at the Quebec Conference in September 1944 and gained their approval.

There remained strong opposition to Morgenthau's ideas within the U.S. government, led by Secretary of War Henry Stimson and Secretary of State Cordell Hull. Stimson argued that the destruction of the Ruhr would lead to starvation and unrest in Germany and in Europe as a whole. He also feared an expansion of the Soviet Union into the vacuum of power in Central Europe. When the Morgenthau Plan was leaked to the press after the Quebec Conference, it occasioned widespread public criticism. Although Roosevelt distanced himself from the proposal, its basic ideas and concerns influenced U.S. policy, especially in the early months of the occupation. As the Cold War unfolded, the Morgenthau Plan was scrapped in favor of rebuilding the western zones of Germany.

THOMAS A. SCHWARTZ

See also Germany; Morgenthau, Henry, Jr.; Roosevelt, Franklin Delano; Stimson, Henry Lewis; World War II

FURTHER READING

Eisenberg, Carolyn Woods. *Drawing the Line: The American Decision to Divide Germany, 1944–1949.* New York, 1996.

Kimball, Warren F. *Swords or Ploughshares? The Morgenthau Plan for Defeated Nazi Germany, 1943–1946.* Philadelphia, Pa., 1976.

Hammond, Paul Y. "Directives for the Occupation of Germany: The Washington Controversy." In *American Civil-Military Decisions: A Book of Case Studies*, edited by Harold Stein. Birmingham, Ala., 1963.

MOROCCO

An Arab kingdom located in the Maghreb region of Northern Africa, bordering the Atlantic Ocean and the Mediterranean Sea between Algeria and Western Sahara, that has had a fairly close relationship with the United States since gaining its independence in 1956. During World War II, while still a French colony, it was the scene of numerous battles and the host (at Casablanca) to one of the wartime summits between U.S. President Franklin D. Roosevelt and British Prime Minister Winston Churchill. During the 1990–1991 Gulf War it was a member of the U.S.-led multinational coalition against Saddam Hussein. It also has been among the more moderate Arab countries towards Israel, as demonstrated by the meeting between Israeli Prime Minister Yitzhak Rabin and Moroccan King Hassan II on 14 September 1993, the day after the signing in Washington, D.C., of the Declaration of Principles between Israel and the Palestine Liberation Organization.

One of the key bilateral issues in U.S.-Morocco relations has been the Western Sahara, where Morocco has been enmeshed since the early-1970s in disputes and wars with the Polisario Front Independence Movement. The United States provided some military aid for the Moroccans during the war in the Western Sahara. One reason was Libya's support for the Polisario Front. Another was U.S. interest in closer military cooperation with Morocco, which was achieved in a 1982 accord granting the United States rights to establish air bases in Morocco in case of crisis.

A second key issue has been human rights. Morocco is a constitutional monarchy, ruled since 1962 by King Hassan II. Allegations of human rights abuses in Morocco over the years have generated some U.S. protests, but never a major break in relations. Overall, Morocco's foreign policy moderation on most issues has been more important to U.S. administrations interested in building closer relations with non-radical Arab states, first to contain the Soviet Union and more recently to broaden and strengthen the Arab-Israeli peace process.

CATHERINE ELKINS

See also Israel; Libya; Middle East; World War II

FURTHER READING

Entelis, John P. *Culture and Counterculture in Moroccan Politics.* Boulder, Colo., 1989.

Lacroix-Riz, Annie. *Les protectorats d'Afrique du Nord, entre la France et Washington, Maroc et Tunisie.* Paris, 1988.

Zartman, I.W. *Morocco: Problems of New Power.* New York, 1964.

MORRIS, GOUVERNEUR

(*b.* 31 January 1752; *d.* November 1816)

New York political leader, businessman, and diplomat best known for writing the final version of the U.S. Constitution. Morris played a small role in U.S. diplomacy in the early 1790s. While on a business trip to France in 1789 President Washington entrusted Morris, an old friend, with an unofficial diplomatic mission to London in 1790–1791 to negotiate a commercial treaty and secure British withdrawal from fur-trading posts on U.S. soil near the Great Lakes. The British demanded the United States pay its pre-Revolutionary War debts and restore property to Americans who had remained loyal to Great Britain. The British were antagonized by Morris's abrupt and aggressive manner, and the mission failed.

The archconservative Morris returned to France in January 1791 and witnessed the development of the French Revolution with dismay. Although he was pro-Royalist and openly contemptuous of the revolutionary government, President Washington appointed him minister to France in December 1791. Even after beginning his official duties in May 1792, Morris ignored the president's advice to be more discreet. He gave asylum in his home to French aristocrats and was involved in a failed plot to secure Louis XVI's escape from France. Still, he was the only foreign diplomat to remain in Paris during the Terror (the most violent phase of the French Revolution from late summer 1793 to July 1794). He reported its horrors and recorded the times in his diplomatic dispatches. Morris's diplomatic efforts were ineffective. While the U.S. debt to France continued to be paid on schedule, the French government ignored his protests over French seizure of U.S. merchant ships in violation of the Treaty of Commerce of 1778, and continued seizing American vessels.

After embittering U.S.-French relations, Morris was recalled in 1794. He traveled in Europe before returning to the United States in 1798. He won election to the U.S. Senate as a Federalist in 1800, serving for three years. He helped administer the construction of the Erie Canal and was critical of President James Madison's policies leading to the War of 1812. A supporter of the anti-war Hartford Convention from 1814 to 1815, Morris defended states' rights in his audacious style.

REBECCA G. GOODMAN

See also France; Hartford Convention

FURTHER READING

Bowman, Albert H. *The Struggle for Neutrality: Franco-American Diplomacy During the Federalist Era.* Knoxville, Tenn., 1974.

Davenport, Beatrix Cary, ed. *Gouverneur Morris: Diary of the French Revolution.* Westport, Conn., 1972.

DeConde, Alexander. *Entangling Alliance: Politics and Diplomacy Under George Washington.* Durham, N.C., 1958.

Elkins, Stanley, and Eric McKitrick. *The Age of Federalism: The Early American Republic, 1788–1800.* New York, 1993.

Kline, Mary-Jo. *Gouverneur Morris and the New Nation, 1775–1788.* New York, 1978.

Ritcheson, Charles R. *Aftermath of Revolution: British Policy Toward the United States, 1783–1795.* Dallas, Tex., 1969.

MORRIS, ROBERT

(*b.* 20 January 1734; *d.* 8 May 1806)

Known as the financier of the American Revolution because of his position as U.S. superintendent of finance from 1781 to 1784 and his role in raising money and supplies for the Continental government. Born in Liverpool, England, he went to the North American colonies in 1747 and rose from apprentice to active partner in the import-export firm of Willing, Morris and Company of Philadelphia. Morris opposed the Stamp Act in 1765 and signed the nonimportation agreement not to purchase or sell British goods until the Stamp Act was repealed. When fighting between Great Britain and its colonies erupted in 1774, he expanded his commercial network in Europe and the West Indies and involved it in the war effort.

A bold and shrewd entrepreneur and forceful, energetic organizer and administrator, Morris became vice president of the Pennsylvania Council of Safety in 1775, where he headed the committee organizing the state's defense measures. On 3 November 1775, he was elected to the second Continental Congress. In August 1776 he signed the Declaration of Independence after initially disapproving of the measure as being premature. As chairman of the Secret Committee of Trade and an active member of other committees, he managed international procurement and financial and naval affairs in Congress. He shared in government contracts and often disguised public ventures as private to facilitate secrecy and reduce costs. His complex engagement in public and private affairs both assisted the war effort and augmented his personal wealth. Potential conflicts of interest brought him under frequent investigation.

Morris retired from Congress in 1778 and prospered as an agent supplying French forces in the United States and the West Indies. Congress, faced with financial and military collapse in 1781, elected Morris superintendent of finance, and in 1782, agent of marine in addition. After raising money and supplies for the Yorktown campaign, Morris struggled to reestablish public credit both home and abroad. He scrutinized and controlled the budget; founded the nation's first bank with the help of French funds; and solicited and administered foreign loans. Morris kept the nation afloat financially until the peace treaty was signed in 1783, but his program for strengthening the confederation was not entirely successful. His campaign for state ratification of Continental taxes to pay off the national debt failed. Nevertheless, his policies established precedents for the adoption of the U.S. Constitution in 1787 and Alexander Hamilton's funding plan in 1790. After participating in the Constitutional Convention, Morris served in the U.S. Senate from 1789 to 1795. There he helped enact national commercial and tariff legislation, backed Hamilton's financial program, and supported Washington's policy of neutrality during the European wars of the French Revolution.

As a private merchant Morris attained international prominence. He sponsored the first U.S. commercial vessel sent to China in 1784 and in 1785 signed a controversial tobacco contract with the Farmers General, holders of the monopoly on the French tobacco trade. In the 1790s he engaged in vast land speculation and schemes to refinance the U.S. foreign debt. Acting through his son Thomas, in 1797 Morris concluded a treaty with the Seneca Indians for title to lands in western New York. During the wars of the French Revolution, Morris could not obtain sufficient foreign capital and credit for his ventures. He was imprisoned for debt from 1798 to 1800 and died penniless in 1806.

ELIZABETH NUXOLL

See also American Revolution; China; Constitution; Declaration of Independence; Hamilton, Alexander; Washington, George

FURTHER READING

Ferguson, E. James, et al, eds. *The Papers of Robert Morris, 1781–1784.* 9 vols. (7 published to date). Pittsburgh, Pa., 1973–.

Ferguson, E. James. *The Power of the Purse: A History of American Public Finance.* Chapel Hill, N.C., 1961.

Ver Steeg, Clarence L. *Robert Morris, Revolutionary Financier, with an Analysis of His Earlier Career.* Philadelphia, Pa., 1954; reprinted in New York, 1972 and 1976.

MORROW, DWIGHT WHITNEY

(*b.* 11 January 1873; *d.* 5 October 1931)

Prominent corporate lawyer and Wall Street banker who served as U.S. ambassador to Mexico from 1927 to 1930. Born in Huntington, West Virginia, Morrow was educated at Amherst College and Columbia Law School. After graduating in 1899 he became a specialist in foreign loans and corporate financing at the law firm of Reed, Simpson, Thacker, and Bartlett in New York.

In December 1913, he joined J.P. Morgan and Company, and rose to partner within months. Following U.S. entry into World War I, Morrow became engaged in war bond financing and international finance. He served as adviser to the Allied Maritime Transport Council during the Versailles Conference and later represented J.P. Morgan and Company in negotiations involving loans to the government of Cuba.

Morrow's college classmate Calvin Coolidge named him U.S. ambassador to Mexico in September 1927, at a time of renewed crisis regarding U.S.-owned oil operations there. Morrow surprised Mexicans by demonstrating an interest in their culture and by advocating conciliation. He developed a personal relationship with Mexican president Plutarco Elias Calles, and accompanied him on inspection trips into the interior. Morrow's informal contacts with Calles and other key Mexican government officials enabled confidential and unofficial discussions and afforded Morrow a thorough understanding of Mexican sentiments and sensibilities.

The principal issue in U.S.-Mexican relations was the legality of oil concessions granted to the United States before the enactment of the Mexican Constitution of 1917. Calles rejected the Bucareli Agreements of 1923, contending they constituted a personal agreement by his predecessor, Àlvaro Obregón, not a formal and binding commitment by the Mexican government. This stand raised the issue of retroactive enforcement of Article 27 of the Mexican Constitution, reserving ownership of subsoil mineral rights to the Mexican government, which was to act for the nation at large regardless of who owned the surface. Under Hispanic legal interpretation, purchases of land gained no mineral rights, an interpretation that contravened the basis of sales and concessions granted by Porfirio Díaz. The United States contended that terms of the original concessions remained valid, and cited the Anglo-Saxon legal principle, which grants subsoil rights to the owner of the land.

A Mexican decree requiring foreign oil corporations to apply for new concessions raised the specter of the Mexican government's denying the legality of the previous contracts. Appreciating Mexican interpretations and the prevailing Mexican nationalism, Morrow departed from the practice of earlier envoys who demanded a formal agreement with the United States and suggested to Calles that he arrange for the Mexican Supreme Court to issue a ruling supporting the "doctrine of positive acts" contained in the Bucareli Agreements. In this manner, the Mexican government could legalize the concessions in cases in which drilling had been initiated without violating the Constitution or yielding to U.S. pressure, while continuing to act according to the Bucareli Agreements. This approach provided a face-saving way to make a concession that resolved the basic issue and defused the crisis while respecting Mexican sovereignty. The arrangements and the new cordiality changed the tone of U.S.-Mexican relations and were Morrow's principal contribution to U.S. foreign policy.

Morrow left Mexico to participate in the London Naval Conference of 1930, then resigned later that year to run for election as a Republican senator from New Jersey, an election he won. He died in office.

KENNETH J. GRIEB

See also Bucareli Agreements; Coolidge, Calvin; Díaz (José de la Cruz), Porfirio; Mexico

FURTHER READING

Nicolson, Harold. *Dwight Morrow*. New York, 1935.
Cline, Howard F. *The United States and Mexico*. New York, 1963.
Vázquez, Josefina Zoraida, and Lorenzo Meyer. *The United States and Mexico*. Chicago, 1985.

MORTEFONTAINE, TREATY OF
See Convention of 1800

MOSADDEQ, MOHAMMAD
(*b.* 1880; *d.* 5 March 1967)

Prime minister of Iran (1951–1953). The combination of a confrontation between Iran and Great Britain (provoked by Iran's nationalization of the country's British-owned oil industry) and U.S. concerns about growing Soviet influence precipitated a coup against Mosaddeq led by the Central Intelligence Agency (CIA). The U.S. role in overthrowing Mosaddeq and subsequently installing an authoritarian regime in Iran led many Iranians to become very resentful of the United States, fueling the anti-Americanism of the 1978–1979 Iranian revolution and the ensuing hostage crisis.

Mosaddeq was born into a wealthy Iranian landowning family. He participated in the 1905–1906 constitutional movement and was then exiled to Europe, where he studied law. He returned to Iran in 1914 and held several government positions but was forced into internal exile after opposing the 1925 coronation of Reza Shah Pahlavi. After Reza Shah was deposed in 1941, Mosaddeq was elected to parliament and became associated with a movement to nationalize the British-controlled oil industry. In 1949 he founded the National Front, a coalition of organizations and individuals that sought to nationalize the oil industry and democratize Iran's political system.

The National Front quickly became popular, and Mohammad Reza Shah Pahlavi—successor to and son of Reza Shah—was forced to appoint Mosaddeq prime minister in April 1951. Mosaddeq immediately nationalized the oil industry, leading the British to organize a global boycott of Iranian oil and make repeated efforts to overthrow him. The United States was initially favorably disposed toward Mosaddeq and tried to resolve the oil dispute, sending W. Averell Harriman to Iran on a mediation mission and hosting Mosaddeq in Washington in October 1951. U.S. officials pressured the British to resolve the dispute and blocked a September 1951 British plan to invade Iran. Mosaddeq, in turn, was friendly toward the United States, welcoming U.S. mediation efforts and praising the U.S. commitment to democracy and freedom.

As the oil dispute continued, U.S. officials became increasingly concerned that Mosaddeq's stubbornness would produce growing turmoil in Iran that would benefit the Soviet Union. Nevertheless, under President Harry S. Truman's administration the United States tried to mediate the dispute and rejected British requests for a joint effort to oust Mosaddeq. President Dwight D. Eisenhower was much more alarmed about the situation, however, and directed the CIA to undertake a coup. Mosaddeq initially resisted the August 1953 coup but eventually surrendered, realizing that resistance was futile and would only create further turmoil. Mosaddeq was imprisoned for three years and then kept under house arrest until he died in 1967. Although he had failed to achieve most of his goals, he was considered a heroic martyr by many Iranians, and the 1953 coup remained a potent symbol of U.S. imperialism in Iran.

Mark J. Gasiorowski

See also Iran; Shah of Iran

FURTHER READING

Bill, James A., and William Roger Louis, eds. *Mussadiq, Iranian Nationalism, and Oil.* Austin, 1988.
Elm, Mostafa. *Oil, Power, and Principle: Iran's Oil Nationalization and Its Aftermath.* Syracuse, N.Y., 1992.
Katouzian, Homa, ed. *Musaddiq's Memoirs.* London, 1988.

MOST-FAVORED-NATION PRINCIPLE

A policy that seeks to promote nondiscriminatory international trade relations by mandating that countries apply the identical import restrictions to the goods of all countries. Applied unconditionally, the Most-Favored-Nation Principle (MFN) entails no favoritism; a country automatically extends to every other country the same trade treatment on specific products as that granted to the country receiving the most favorable trade treatment. For example, if the United States reached a trade agreement with Australia to reduce to 3 percent the U.S. tariff rate imposed on widgets, the new duty would be applicable to identical products imported from all other countries with MFN status, even if no specific agreement had been reached with these countries. The economic rationale of MFN treatment is to maximize the reduction of official trade barriers and to minimize the distortions in the patterns of trade and in the costs of traded goods that would occur if countries maintained multiple schedules of import barriers. There is also a foreign relations rationale: to reduce international political frictions by divorcing the business of trade from a system of favoritism that awards better treatment to the goods of an importing country's closest allies.

The MFN concept can be traced back to the treaties of commerce and navigation negotiated in the seventeenth century. It became an integral part of modern U.S. trade policy when the Reciprocal Trade Agreements Act of 1934 declared that bilateral tariff reductions negotiated under the terms of the act would be extended on an MFN basis. The principle became an integral part of the multilateral trading system following World War II, when Article 1 of the General Agreement on Tariffs and Trade (GATT) enshrined it as a priority duty of all contracting parties to the agreement. MFN is still revered in principle but is being eroded increasingly in practice. Beginning in the 1970s discriminatory import treatment in favor of less developed countries, the so-called Generalized System of Preferences, became an accepted and encouraged international trade policy. The rise of trade blocs, such as the European Community and the North American Free Trade Agreement (NAFTA), expanded the practice of providing internal free trade to members while imposing tariffs and nontariff barriers on nonmembers.

During the Cold War the United States denied MFN treatment to most communist countries as part of a larger effort to impose trade-retarding economic sanctions on unfriendly countries. Any country excluded by the United States was subject to the duties of the 1930 tariff act, which are ten times greater, on average, than MFN tariff rates. In the early 1970s Congress, despite opposition by the administrations of Presidents Richard M. Nixon and Gerald Ford, sought to use MFN as political leverage against the Soviet Union on the issue of emigration by Soviet Jews. The linkage was embodied in the Jackson-Vanik Amendment of 1974 and was made applicable to all communist ("nonmarket") economies. Indeed, this was the same legislation that was the basis for the controversy, following the 1989 Tiananmen Square massacre, over linking MFN status for China to mandated improvements in China's human rights record.

Stephen D. Cohen

See also General Agreement on Tariffs and Trade; North American Free Trade Agreement; Tariffs

FURTHER READING

Jackson, John. *The World Trading System: Law and Policy of International Economic Relations.* Cambridge, Mass., 1992.

Snyder, Richard C. *The Most-Favored-Nation Clause: An Analysis with Particular Reference to Recent Treaty Practice and Tariffs.* New York, 1948.

MOYNIHAN, DANIEL PATRICK

(*b.* 16 March 1927)

Analyst of social issues, diplomat, and senator from New York (1977–). A diversity of interests, depth of intellect, and recurrent controversy have distinguished Moynihan's career. Born in Oklahoma but raised in the Hell's Kitchen section of New York City, Moynihan received his B.A. and M.A. degrees from Tufts University (1948, 1949) and his Ph.D. from the Fletcher School of Law and Diplomacy (1961). Moynihan rose to prominence as an outspoken analyst of the problems of poverty and the domestic policies of Franklin D. Roosevelt's New Deal and Lyndon B. Johnson's Great Society. A member of the Department of Labor (1961–1965) during the administrations of Presidents John F. Kennedy and Johnson, by the late 1960s Moynihan began expressing an increasing interest in international affairs, largely in response to what he called the "incredible experience" of the war in Vietnam. In his speeches and articles criticizing the war, Moynihan stressed the importance of international law and human rights. This emphasis persisted as a structuring principle for his views on international relations and his service as a senator from New York.

After teaching at Harvard University from 1965 to 1971, Moynihan commenced his foreign affairs career under President Richard M. Nixon with his 1971 appointment as a special adviser to Nixon. Moynihan's defense of the movement in East Pakistan that culminated in the creation of Bangladesh won Nixon's confidence in his acumen and secured Moynihan's appointment as ambassador to India (1973–1975). Frustrated by the radical positions of the Third World nations of the Nonaligned Movement, Moynihan railed against the anti-Americanism expressed in many international institutions in the 1970s. He said, "It is time for the United States to go into the United Nations and every other international forum and start raising hell." Persuaded that few U.S. diplomats could raise hell as effectively as Moynihan, Secretary of State Henry Kissinger appointed him U.S. ambassador to the United Nations in June 1975. During his controversial six-month tenure at the United Nations, Moynihan denounced Uganda's "Zionism is racism" resolution and exchanged fierce words with his Soviet counterpart on issues of Arab-Israeli relations. He briefly served as president of the UN Security Council (February 1976). Elected to the Senate in 1976, Moynihan served on the Select Committee on Intelligence and the Finance Committee, among others. Opposed to the U.S. invasions of Grenada (1983) and Panama (1989), the funding of the Nicaraguan Contras, and U.S. participation in the Gulf War of 1990–1991, Senator Moynihan publicized his views on foreign affairs as the author of several books and articles on international relations, including *Loyalties* (1984), *On the Law of Nations* (1990), and *Pandemonium: Ethnicity in International Politics* (1993).

LeeAnna Y. Keith

See also Bangladesh; Contras; Grenada; Gulf War of 1990–1991; India; Middle East; Nonaligned Movement; Panama and Panama Canal; Uganda; United Nations; Vietnam War

FURTHER READING

Schoen, Douglas. *Pat: A Biography of Daniel Patrick Moynihan.* New York, 1971.

Traub, James. "Liberal, Conservative, or Just Pat?" *New York Times Magazine* (Sept. 16, 1990).

MOZAMBIQUE

Located in southern Africa, bordering the Mozambique Channel between South Africa and Tanzania opposite the island of Madagascar, and a former Portuguese colony that declared its independence on 25 June 1975. Nine months before this declaration, the Front for the Liberation of Mozambique (FRELIMO), which for ten years had waged a war of national liberation against Portugal, took power in Maputo, Mozambique's largest city. Shortly after independence, the United States recognized Mozambique, established diplomatic relations, and opened an embassy in Maputo. Over the next seven years, however, relations between Washington and Maputo deteriorated. Prior to Mozambique's independence, the United States was ambivalent about whether or not to support FRELIMO. When FRELIMO was founded in June 1962 the United States viewed it as a strongly nationalist, anticommunist liberation movement. The Ford Foundation openly gave aid to educate FRELIMO youth and the Central Intelligence Agency (CIA) provided covert assistance. The administration of President John F. Kennedy also imposed a boycott on the sale of arms for use in Africa, which was aimed at French military actions in Algeria and Portuguese repression in Mozambique and Angola. Washington's fear of antagonizing a North Atlantic Treaty Organization (NATO) ally and losing access to military facilities in the Azores (islands in the Atlantic Ocean owned by Portugal) caused President Kennedy to reduce U.S. support for FRELIMO.

For the United States, the economic and strategic stakes in Mozambique were minimal and did not justify antagonizing a NATO ally. In 1969 President Richard M. Nixon's administration conducted a review of U.S. policy options in southern Africa, which resulted in the adoption of NSSM-39. Department of State opponents of this policy—referring to the Uncle Remus story about Brer Rabbit getting himself stuck in Brer Fox's Tar Baby—named it the "Tar-Baby option." This option provided the operating directives for U.S. policy toward southern Africa until the spring of 1976. It assumed that the white minority regimes in South Africa and Rhodesia (Zimbabwe), as well as those of the Portuguese, were in Africa to stay. The United States accommodated itself to Portuguese colonialism in Africa. The U.S. Navy, for example, used port facilities in Mozambique and Angola. The policy of Nixon and his secretary of state, Henry Kissinger, toward southern Africa collapsed, however, when a military-led coup occurred in Portugal in April 1974 that brought to power a government committed to abandoning Portugal's costly overseas African empire.

Following independence, the leftist orientation of the new government in Maputo was not of particular concern to the United States because FRELIMO did not appear to be beholden to the Soviet Union. Seeking to gain a position of influence in Mozambique, the administration of President Gerald R. Ford began providing aid. In 1977, however, Congress prohibited funding to Maputo because of allegations that FRELIMO was committing gross human rights violations arising, in particular, from its military campaign to defeat the Rhodesia-South Africa–backed Mozambique National Resistance Movement (MNR or RENAMO), which itself committed many war atrocities. Moreover, Mozambique's expression of ideological solidarity with Moscow and acceptance of Soviet military aid did not sit well with the United States. In March 1981 Maputo expelled four U.S. envoys from the country after charging them with participating in a CIA plot against the government. The United States retaliated by not filling the ambassadorial post, which had been vacant since July 1980, and leaving it unfilled until November 1983. During this period of estrangement, Mozambique became one of Moscow's leading arms recipients in sub-Saharan Africa, behind Ethiopia and Angola. Mozambique maintained the Soviet arms connection until the end of the 1980s, by which time several billion dollars worth of Soviet weaponry had flowed into the country.

Washington's concern about increasing Soviet military involvement in Mozambique and Maputo's resentment over indirect U.S. support for the MNR insurgency did little to relax tensions between the two countries. Diplomatic relations between the United States and Mozambique were further strained by the civil war in Angola between the Popular Movement for the Liberation of Angola (MPLA) government in Luanda, which Maputo supported and which was backed by the Soviet Union and Cuba, and Jonas Savimbi's National Union for the Total Independence of Angola (UNITA) forces, backed by South Africa and the CIA. Of more direct consequence was the struggle in South Africa between the white minority government, with whom the administration of President Ronald Reagan was involved through a policy of constructive engagement, and the African National Congress (ANC), for which Maputo provided political sanctuary. Following the repeal of the Clark Amendment in 1985, which had been passed by the U.S. Congress in 1976 and explicitly prohibited covert aid to UNITA, Angola became one of the primary targets of the Reagan Doctrine. Some leading conservatives in Congress, such as Jesse Helms, favored adding Mozambique to the target list. Despite such sentiments, U.S.-Mozambique relations began to improve in 1983, as both sides saw the possibility of a quid pro quo involving South Africa and Angola that could help stabilize the region and, at the same time, serve Washington's Cold War agenda and bolster FRELIMO's campaign against the MNR. Several meetings between high-ranking U.S. and Mozambique officials conducted during 1983 produced an understanding whereby the United States would press South Africa to ease its destabilization campaign in Mozambique by reducing support for the MNR, and Maputo would use its influence to get Cuban troops out of Angola. On 16 March 1984 the governments of Mozambique and South Africa signed the Nkomati Accord. Both sides agreed not to interfere in the internal affairs of the other country and to prevent the use of their territory for bases or the training of insurgents. In other words, South Africa would terminate military support for the MNR and Maputo would not aid the ANC.

In the post-Nkomati period the United States further encouraged Mozambique's tilt to the West through economic incentives. In April 1984 Congress lifted the ban on U.S. aid to Mozambique. Three months later Maputo signed an agreement with the U.S. Overseas Private Investment Council to provide bilateral investment guarantees for U.S. investors doing business in Mozambique. That same year the United States authorized an $8 million aid program to Mozambique, increasing the amount to $66 million in 1985. In 1985 and again in 1986 the Pentagon and the Department of State lobbied in favor of establishing a small U.S. security assistance program in Mozambique. Congress rejected this request, however, and made it contingent upon the holding of free elections in Mozambique.

High-level visits by U.S. officials to Mozambique in late 1986 and early 1987 and Reagan's White House meeting with President Joaquim Chissano in October 1987 cemented this new era of good and steadily improving relations between Mozambique and the United States. Chissano subsequently placated Washington by officially abandoning Marxism-Leninism in July 1989. The following year Maputo opened talks with the MNR, which led to the signing of a cease-fire agreement on 16 October 1992, and pledged to adopt a multiparty political system. During this time Mozambique supported U.S. initiatives on Angola and Namibia and acted as a moderating influence among the frontline states (Angola, Botswana, Tanzania, Zambia, Zimbabwe, and Mozambique itself), that through the years had aided the ANC's struggle in South Africa. Maputo also supported United Nations resolutions condemning Baghdad following Iraq's August 1990 invasion of Kuwait. The United States responded with increased aid and support for UN peacekeeping operations in Mozambique. U.S. Development Aid and PL-480 funds for Maputo steadily rose in the early 1990s. The $57.6 million worth of economic assistance authorized for fiscal year (FY) 1992 made Mozambique the leading recipient of U.S. foreign aid in sub-Saharan Africa. Then, with multiparty elections scheduled to be held (which took place in October 1994), Congress authorized funding for FY 1994 for the establishment of a small international military education training (IMET) program for Mozambique. For FY 1996 the Clinton administration proposed an aid package of $55.5 million, including $125,000 to continue the IMET program, the fourth largest U.S. aid program in sub-Saharan Africa.

JEFFREY A. LEFEBVRE

See also Africa; Angola; Kissinger, Henry Alfred; Nixon, Richard Milhous; Portugal; Reagan Doctrine; South Africa

FURTHER READING

Gunn, Gillian. "Learning from Adversity: The Mozambican Experience." In *Regional Conflict and U.S. Policy: Angola and Mozambique*, edited by Richard Bloomfield. Algonac, Mich., 1988.

McCormick, Shawn. "Mozambique's Cautious Steps Toward Lasting Peace." *Current History* 92 (May 1993): 224–228.

Noer, Thomas. *Cold War and Black Liberation: The United States and White Rule in Africa, 1948–1968*. Columbia, Mo., 1985.

MULTINATIONAL CORPORATIONS

Corporations that operate in more than one country at a time, variously termed "multinational enterprises" (MNEs), "transnational corporations" (TNCs), and "global corporations." Of the major events that have transformed the world political and economic environment since the mid-1970s, few have been so profound as the global spread of multinational corporations (MNCs). According to figures from the United Nations Conference on Trade and Development (UNCTAD), in 1990 there were approximately 37,000 MNCs with total worldwide sales of about $5.5 trillion. The 100 largest MNCs had combined worldwide sales of slightly more than $3.1 trillion and held total worldwide assets of almost $3.2 trillion, of which slightly more than $1.2 trillion were located outside their home countries. Indeed, MNCs accounted for a significant percentage of all global economic activity in the early 1990s, although calculation of a precise measure of the role of the MNC in the world economy is frustrated by data limitations.

Precisely defining a multinational corporation is somewhat problematic. In most general terms, an MNC is a business organization with activities under its managerial control (as opposed to passive investments) that cross national boundaries, so that a significant percentage of the organization's net revenue and income derive from operations located outside its home country. Conceptually, managerial control implies that different organizational subentities respond to a common overall business strategy set by a centralized headquarters. Exactly how to measure control, however, is difficult and subject to differing standards.

A term closely linked to multinational corporation is "foreign direct investment" (FDI). As with the MNC, there are some definitional problems with FDI but these reflect differing national balance-of-payments accounting standards rather than conceptual problems per se. In principle, FDI is a balance-of-payments line item representing the net flow of equity funds between an investor (usually an MNC) and an investment (usually a subsidiary organization) located outside the home nation of the investor and over which the investor holds managerial control. Different nations have differing standards with respect to what constitutes control; the U.S. Department of Commerce, which keeps the relevant data for the United States, considers a holding of 10 percent or more of voting equity to constitute control, but some nations use higher thresholds. There are also differing standards as to what is constitutes equity. The Department of Commerce considers retained earnings and intrafirm loans as well as new equity funds components of FDI, whereas the Japanese Ministry of Finance considers only equity funds as FDI. One result is that FDI flows are not measured on a completely consistent basis worldwide, as reflected in the fact that in any given year, the measured inflows of FDI, based on data collected from recipient (host) countries, tend not to match measured outflows, based on data collected from investor (home) nations. Some of the discrepancy reflects measurement error, but most of it results from definitional differences.

Some scholars of business organization would exclude from the definition of an MNC those business firms whose sole international activity is to handle imports and/or exports. The distinctions, however, between export-import activities and activities associated with FDI are becoming increasingly blurred, especially in the services industries. For example, if a U.S. subsidiary of a European-based insurance company were to sell a policy to a U.S. client, but payoff of this policy were to be guaranteed by the European parent, would this be sales of a service by the subsidiary (a transaction attributable to direct investment) or sales of a service by the parent (an export)? Conceptually, the distinction is a fine one. Moreover, MNCs handle an increasingly large percentage of the world's trade in merchandise. For example, DeAnne S. Julius estimated in 1990 that perhaps half the merchandise trade of both the United States and Japan is conducted by MNCs. Much of this trade is generated by the cross-hauling of intermediate goods (components and subassemblies destined to become part of a final product), such that the distinction between export-import activities and activity generated by FDI has become blurred even in the manufacturing sector.

Definitional and measurement problems aside, FDI is the primary, but not the exclusive, mode by which MNCs establish control over overseas affiliates and is the most easily measured. UNCTAD has attempted to measure the world's stock of FDI (the net sum of all annual flows), adjusting these to establish a consistent basis for analysis, and has arrived at a figure of slightly less than $1.95 trillion for the year 1992. Twelve years earlier this figure stood at slightly over $0.5 trillion, evidence that the activities of MNCs expanded enormously during the 1980s. In 1994 foreign direct investment was among those issues that policymakers identified as likely candidates for inclusion in the World Trade Organization (WTO) agenda now that the Uruguay Round (1986–1994) of the General Agreement on Tariffs and Trade (GATT) had ended.

The MNC in Historical Perspective

Although the term "multinational corporation" entered parlance only after 1960, neither the MNC nor its global spread are new phenomena. There were numerous MNCs in existence during the late nineteenth century, and examples can be found in earlier eras, such as the East India Company, chartered in London in 1600. The MNC first became firmly established on the world scene in the period roughly from the end of the U.S. Civil War to the outbreak of World War I. Because no official statistics on either FDI or any other aspect of the operations of MNCs were kept by any nation during these years, it is difficult to quantify with any precision the role of MNCs in the world economy during this period. Business historians agree, however, that this role was substantial, and late twentieth-century research suggests that it was quite likely greater than previously estimated by most historians.

What is certain is that during the late nineteenth and early twentieth centuries enormous sums of long-term capital investment flowed across national boundaries. It is unclear, however, how much of this was direct investment. In the pioneering study *America's Stake in International Investment* (1938), Cleona Lewis estimated that as much as 90 percent of this flow represented portfolio rather than direct investment. Economic historians held to this estimate for about forty years, yet reexamination of the evidence has cast doubt on the figure, which now appears to have been too low. For example, Tom Houston and John H. Dunning estimated in *U.K. Industry Abroad* (1976) that in 1913 the total stock of United Kingdom direct investment abroad was almost 35 percent of the long-term foreign assets held by the United Kingdom. At that time, it is commonly agreed, the United Kingdom was the world's largest international investor nation. Again, later research suggests that even this figure might be too low.

The United States became both a substantial outward direct investor nation and host to inward direct investment during this period. According to Mira Wilkins, the first highly international U.S. business firm was the Singer Manufacturing Company, whose operations in Europe date from the 1860s and which by the 1880s had sales offices in dozens of countries and manufacturing operations in at least four. During the last two decades of the nineteenth century, the Standard Oil Company established operations in numerous countries, and when the Standard Oil trust was broken up under court order in 1911, nine of the thirty-four successor firms were multinational in their own right. In *The Emergence of Multinational Enterprise* (1970), Wilkins lists thirty-seven U.S. firms that built or purchased manufacturing operations between 1890 and 1914; most of these firms held operations in at least three foreign nations. By the 1880s several large U.S. insurance companies, such as the Equitable Life Assurance Society, New York Life Insurance Company, and Mutual of America, also were active abroad.

Not all U.S. firms that attempted to establish themselves overseas during the late nineteenth century were successful. Joint efforts by Alexander Graham Bell and Thomas Alva Edison to establish telephone operations in Europe floundered, largely because European governments chose to establish and operate their own companies. However, Western Electric initially in partnership with the ill-fated International Bell Telephone Company, did succeed in establishing the manufacture of telephone equipment (as opposed to the provision of telephone services) in Europe and elsewhere.

The extent of foreign-controlled business activity in the United States prior to World War II was also very significant. Most foreign-controlled business in the United States was held by British or continental European firms, including some that are still flourishing, such as Rolls-

Royce and Daimler-Benz. Substantial numbers of these operations ceased to be under foreign control during the interwar years because of the nationalization of German properties during and after World War I, the closing or selling of businesses during the Great Depression, or the selling of British-controlled firms to U.S. investors under the terms of the Lend-Lease Act of 1941 after the outbreak of World War II in Europe.

Despite the early twentieth-century presence of MNCs in the manufacturing and financial services sectors based in Europe with operations in the United States (and vice versa), the bulk of the activity of MNCs at that time was concentrated in resource-based (extractive and agricultural) industries and in the utilities and transportation services (mostly railroad) sectors. Direct investment in these industries was, by and large, north-south in nature, representing the investments of European, North American, and Japanese firms in the developing countries. Scholars have estimated that in 1914 more than 53 percent of British FDI was in the resource-based industries and 31 percent in utilities and transportation and that at least 59 percent of British FDI was in developing countries. Wilkins estimates that 68 percent of the stock of U.S. FDI in the same year was in resource-based industries, utilities, and transportation, while only slightly more than 18 percent was in manufacturing industries, and more than 54 percent of this stock was in developing countries.

By 1929 the share of total U.S. FDI in resources, utilities, and transportation had shrunk slightly, to about 61 percent. The reason was that, after a six-year lull occasioned by World War I, numerous overseas manufacturing affiliates of U.S. firms were established or expanded during the 1920s, especially in Canada, Europe, and South America. As a result, the share of the manufacturing sector in the total stock of U.S. FDI grew to slightly more than 24 percent in 1929. This was the period when, for example, Ford Motor Company established extensive operations in the United Kingdom, which it used as a base for entering the rest of Europe. General Motors responded by acquiring firms in Germany (Adam Opel AG) and the United Kingdom (Vauxhall Motors Limited). The bulk of U.S. FDI remained in developing countries. Indeed, the share of these countries in the total stock of U.S. FDI had risen to 59 percent, the result of an enormous expansion of the overseas holdings of U.S. petroleum firms in Latin America, Asia, and Oceania, as well as expansion of U.S.-controlled manufacturing holdings in Latin America.

The Great Depression, however, reduced or stopped the international expansion of most MNCs, with the major exception of the international oil companies. During the 1930s the world economic landscape came to be dominated by international cartel arrangements in many

industries, often formed with government encouragement. The cartel agreements often featured territory-splitting provisions whereby firms agreed not to operate in certain geographic areas, reserving these for competing firms. In some cases, firms sold or closed their international operations to comply with these agreements. The outbreak of World War II in 1939 further curtailed the international activities of business firms, with the result that by 1949 MNCs accounted for a substantially smaller fraction of world economic activity than in 1929. The end of almost two decades of depression and war especially affected the operations of U.S. firms in Europe in the manufacturing sector. Between 1929 and 1950 the share of the total stock of U.S. direct manufacturing investment that was in Europe fell from more than one-third to less than one-quarter.

Beginning in the early 1950s, however, international business activity began again to expand rapidly and continued to do so for about twenty years. The leading foreign direct investors of this period were predominantly U.S.-based firms in the manufacturing sector, although the petroleum industry also witnessed substantial expansion of international activity, including that of firms not based in the United States. Many firms new to international activity entered the ranks of the MNCs during this period. By 1967 three-fourths of those on *Fortune* magazine's list of the 500 largest U.S. industrial firms had manufacturing operations in at least one country other than the United States, and 187 had manufacturing operations in six or more foreign countries. The majority of the overseas investments of U.S. manufacturing firms went to other developed countries, especially the European nations and, to a lesser extent, Canada. Between 1950 and 1970 the stock of U.S. manufacturing direct investment increased almost fifteen times in Europe and five times in Canada. As a consequence, the share of U.S. FDI in developing countries declined dramatically. By 1970 less than 40 percent of the stock of U.S. FDI was located in these countries. In addition, the share of resource-based industries, utilities, and transportation in the U.S. stock of outward FDI had fallen to less than 40 percent, the bulk of which was in the petroleum sector, while the share of manufacturing had grown to 41 percent.

Despite the declining share of U.S. direct investment in developing nations, the operations of U.S. multinationals in such nations had more bearing on U.S. foreign policy during the period from 1950 through the 1970s than operations in the advanced nations. At root were conflicts created by rising nationalism in developing countries on one hand and control of indigenous natural resources by MNCs on the other. At the extreme, the United States backed coups in a number of countries where local governments nationalized or attempted to nationalize U.S.- or European-controlled enterprises. For example, U.S. MNCs have been cited as instigators of coups in Iran and Guatemala in the early 1950s and Chile in the early 1970s. All of these coups were against what were perceived as Marxist governments sympathetic to the Soviet Union.

However, in other countries where nationalization occurred, such as Peru in 1968 and in several member nations of the Organization of Petroleum Exporting Countries (OPEC) during the mid-1970s, U.S. government support for the MNC position was equivocable. In 1962 Congress passed the Hickenlooper Amendment, which requires the president to cut off foreign aid to any country that expropriates a U.S.-owned property without adequate compensation. The Hickenlooper Amendment has been applied only in one case (the expropriation of International Telephone and Telegraph property in Brazil); rather than actually invoke this law, the United States has typically used a threat of invocation to obtain leverage in cases of nationalization. Nationalization as a major issue largely faded after the early 1980s.

Evaluating MNCs

The spread of MNCs after World War II triggered many studies that attempted to explain why firms engage in FDI and to evaluate the consequences of the MNC. In his pioneering study *American Investment in British Manufacturing Industry* (1958), John H. Dunning compared the operations of British affiliates of U.S.-headquartered firms to their British-owned rivals. By a number of measures, the U.S.-owned operations were more successful than their local rivals. Dunning attributed this to the abilities of the former to transfer superior technologies and other intangible assets (for example, marketing and other managerial skills) from the United States to the United Kingdom and effectively adapt these to the British environment. Dunning also demonstrated that over time the British firms caught up with their U.S.-owned rivals. He concluded that the overall effect of U.S. FDI served to raise British levels of productivity in all firms, generating net benefits for the British economy. He also noted the dual personality of U.S.-owned subsidiaries—their strengths came from strategic links with their U.S. parents. These links gave them a status that was not that of just another British firm.

In another study, *The International Operations of National Firms* (1959), Stephen H. Hymer proposed that in order to operate internationally, a firm must possess special advantages over its noninternational rivals. These advantages were identified as "economies of scale" and "special management skills." These advantages created benefits for society, because firms holding such special advantages were likely to be more efficient than their rivals. There were also costs, because the advantaged

firms would gain market power over rivals and the benefits of competition would be lost. Hymer believed that the costs dominated the benefits. Hymer also articulated certain issues that dominated the debate on multinational firms during the 1960s and 1970s. During the 1970s a host of writings critical of multinational firms were published, and they tended to view MNCs as powerful, monopolistic institutions that could corrupt governments and, in various ways, exploit host economies to the detriment of local welfare. These studies provided a rationale for governments in host countries to restrict inward FDI and regulate closely the activities of multinational firms. In the 1970s such policies proliferated in developing nations as well as in some advanced nations, such as Canada, and led to efforts to impose international controls on the activities of these firms.

A number of analysts came to different conclusions. Raymond Vernon, for example, emphasized the importance of new product technology as a determinant both of international trade and investment. He also stressed the role of factors specific to the home markets of firms as a determinant of how this technology gets created and diffused. Peter J. Buckley and Mark C. Casson noted that it is not necessary that a firm actually own and manage international operations in order to exploit firm-specific advantages. For example, a firm could exploit many of these advantages via licensing agreements with firms based in nations outside the home market. To explain the existence of operations in one nation actually owned and managed by a firm in another nation, Buckley and Casson turned to the organizational theory of the firm as originally developed by Ronald H. Coase (1937) to suggest that there are economies to be gained by internalizing within one organization production and marketing functions, even if this means crossing national boundaries.

Buckley and Casson triggered a number of subsequent studies that applied the organizational theory of the firm to multinational corporations. For example, John Cantwell argued that because there is much rivalry between multinational firms, FDI would lead to more rapid development and diffusion of desirable new technologies than would occur in a world where there were no economies of internalization and where technology was transferred by licensing. Most of the studies have suggested that the spread of multinational enterprises has a very positive effect on economic efficiency and growth. These studies have provided a basis for reexamination of the restrictive policies adopted by many countries during the 1970s and partly account for the considerable liberalization that has occurred since then.

International Policy Toward MNCs

Appropriate policy towards MNCs has been hotly debated both within nations and in various international forums since the 1960s. International debate on the issue assumes that nations behave as "unitary rational actors," but this assumption is, of course, essentially untrue. Thus, while the United States has largely espoused the view that international policy towards MNCs should be open, there are major constituencies in the United States, such as the organized labor movement, that have long advocated that some sort of restrictive measures be placed upon these firms.

Whether or not international law should explicitly cover issues pertaining to MNCs and FDI has in fact long been at issue. The stillborn International Trade Organization (ITO) would, for instance, have embodied provisions pertaining to international capital flows and to restrictive business practices by large international business firms. Ratification of the Treaty of Havana of 1947, which would have brought the ITO into existence, foundered in the U.S. Senate over whether such provisions were warranted. Issues pertaining to international investment and the MNC did not reappear on the agenda of any round of GATT negotiations until the onset of the Uruguay Round in 1986. Such issues, however, were taken up in other international forums during the 1960s and the 1970s.

Since the early 1970s the tensions first brought out in Hymer's work have marked international discussions of multinational corporations. On one hand, some nations have seen the MNC as essentially an extension of the power and influence of industrial nations, especially the United States. At the extreme, the MNC has been seen as an agent of neocolonialist powers, to be treated as a fifth column of a foreign enemy. A milder version holds that while the MNC might be a rapacious monopolist seeking only to maximize the interests of its home nation shareholders, the MNC nonetheless holds technology and other resources potentially beneficial to the local economy. It is argued that because no single host nation has the power to control the MNC, policies must be pursued at an international level to enable transfer of these assets to the local economies while preventing transfer of monopoly rents back to the home nation. Nations subscribing to these points of view have sought some sort of international code that would act to restrict the power of MNCs and promote (or even force) resource transfer by them to poorer nations. Such views have mostly been held by leaders of developing nations, who have occasionally been joined by certain of the more advanced nations, especially during periods when these nations have themselves been the site of new MNC activity.

Acting as a bloc with the United Nations, those developing nations, known as the Group of 77, holding this range of views forced onto the UN agenda during the 1970s, over the objections of the United States and other advanced nations, the negotiation of two codes, one meant to be a binding code of conduct for MNCs and the other a code on restrictive business practices. The negotiations quickly became deadlocked and stayed so for more than a decade. In 1976, in what amounted to an effort to placate at least some countries of the Group of 77, the member nations of the Organization for Economic Cooperation and Development (OECD) adopted a set of nonbinding guidelines on the conduct of MNCs. Efforts were made to revive the by-then moribund negotiations on the code of conduct in the early 1990s, but support for the code had waned among many of the countries, especially those in Latin America, that had initiated the exercise in the first place, and the negotiations were terminated.

During the 1970s the United States, joined by most other advanced nations, was opposed to the Group of 77 position, although the U.S. position started from some of the same premises, notably that MNCs hold technology and other resources that, when transferred across national boundaries, promote economic growth and development. The United States and other advanced nations have, however, rejected the doctrine that this transfer must be closely regulated. Instead, they have advocated an international regime that would liberalize governmentally imposed restraints on capital movements and would guarantee "national treatment" standards for local subsidiaries of MNCs in host nations. National treatment for international investors implies that their investments (e.g., subsidiaries) in any nation will receive treatment under national and local law that is no less favorable than the treatment accorded domestically owned enterprises engaged in the same or similar lines of business activity. (National treatment in this context differs from the GATT Article 3 concept of national treatment, which deals with imports.)

In accordance with this position, the advanced nations have created a number of limited international instruments to liberalize capital movements and provide for national treatment for MNCs. Until 1993 these instruments were all negotiated under the aegis of the OECD and applied only to OECD member nations. In particular, the OECD nations developed two codes during the 1960s and 1970s, each of which has since undergone revision. These are the Code of Liberalization of Capital Movements and the Code of Liberalization of Current Invisible Operations. Under these, member nations pledge to remove barriers to international investment, to allow free transfer of capital following liquidation of assets or obtaining long-term loans, and to allow current transactions to proceed freely. These codes are meant to be binding on all OECD nations. Upon subscribing to the codes, a member country must publicly announce any exception to its obligations under the two codes as a long-term "reservation" or a temporary "derogation" and to bind itself to a "standstill" on new reservations and derogations. The codes also commit each member nation over time to "roll back" its exceptions, that is, to reduce these in number or scope. There has, however, been very little such reduction since the 1980s.

The OECD has also drafted a nonbinding national treatment instrument (NTI). Member nations choosing to adhere to the NTI must grant national treatment to enterprises that are controlled by investors from another member country, again subject to reservations and derogations. Efforts mounted over the years to make the NTI binding have foundered over a number of issues. Regular reviews are designed to ensure that member nations are meeting their code and NTI obligations.

In December 1993 the North American Free Trade Agreement (NAFTA) came into effect, containing what easily are the most far-reaching international provisions affecting MNCs and FDI. These provisions are, of course, binding upon only the three NAFTA member nations (the United States, Canada, and Mexico), but they could provide a model for a future multilateral accord. NAFTA's Chapter 11 contains a strong national treatment article plus articles bearing upon the issues of the two OECD codes. These articles are subject to numerous exceptions, treated in three appendices, as well as to overriding provisions contained in other NAFTA chapters. More important, Chapter 11 sets up dispute settlement procedures under which investors (that is, MNCs) can seek arbitrated settlement of violations of Chapter 11 obligations by the three signatories. Arbitral awards made under these procedures are limited to compensatory damages.

The Uruguay Round of multilateral trade negotiations, which included the Agreement on Trade Related Investment Measures (TRIMs), concluded in 1994. The TRIM agreement is rather narrow and limited and does little more than reaffirm an earlier GATT-panel ruling that certain types of performance requirements placed on MNCs, such as requirements to employ local content or to balance imports and exports, are inconsistent with GATT obligations. Nations are given varying lengths of time, depending upon state of development, to bring laws and policies inconsistent with the agreement into compliance. The United States, joined by most advanced nations, had sought a wider agreement than the one that emerged, but in the mid-1980s the developing countries were not amenable to measures then being proposed. Over the next nine years the policy landscape changed, and there was much talk about FDI and MNCs being included in the future GATT (or, by then, WTO) agenda.

The New Agenda

The 1980s, and especially the second half of that decade, witnessed a large surge in foreign direct investment and the activities of multinational corporations. This surge abated after 1990, but by that time the scope of MNCs had been enlarged considerably. There were some indications of a new surge of FDI beginning in 1994. All of this led many observers to predict that FDI would be one of the major issues on the multilateral trade agenda following implementation of the Uruguay Round.

Unlike the surge of the late 1950s to mid-1960s, the 1980s surge was not dominated by FDI from the United States, but by FDI from Europe and Japan. Indeed, for the first time since early in the twentieth century, FDI flowed into the United States in massive amounts. As a result, in 1991 the United States had become both the world's largest host and home to FDI. Long the leading advocate of open policies towards FDI and the MNC, the United States, beginning in the late 1980s, witnessed considerable debate over whether the incursion of foreign-based enterprise was in the best interests of the nation. One outcome was the Exon-Florio Amendment to the Omnibus Trade and Competitiveness Act of 1988, which gave the president new authority to block foreign takeovers of U.S. firms if these threatened to impair national security. Other legislation that would put foreign investment in the United States under greater scrutiny or regulation has been proposed but not enacted. For example, the Manton amendment would have imposed conditional national treatment standards on the participation of foreign-controlled firms in the U.S.-sponsored technology consortia. Simply, the United States has backed away somewhat from its consistent post–World War II position of unqualified advocacy of open FDI policies.

The NAFTA debate in the fall of 1993 also reopened examination of the effects of outward direct investment on the U.S. economy. H. Ross Perot scored political points in this debate by playing upon the fears of U.S. workers, as long articulated by the organized labor movement, that this investment would reduce job opportunities in the domestic economy. Although Perot and other anti-NAFTA elements did not prevail, they did reignite old fears about possible malign effects of the international operations of MNCs on the home economy. Similar fears surfaced within the European Community, in what became known there as the delocalization issue.

By the mid-1990s, policy in much of the rest of the world had swung in the other direction. Across the globe, developing nations, impressed by the experiences of Singapore and other nations that have been quite open to FDI and have witnessed high economic performances, have liberalized their policies toward FDI and the MNC. Nations, such as Mexico, that only a decade earlier viewed the MNC with great suspicion (and even China, which had shunned FDI altogether) openly welcomed international investors with few strings attached. Other major developing nations that once subjected MNCs to considerable regulation, such as Indonesia, Brazil, and even India, were reforming or reevaluating their policies. Also, but thus far without great success, Russia and most other former Council for Mutual Economic Assistance nations were actively courting MNCs.

Thus, at a time when FDI and the MNC were likely candidates for inclusion in whatever multilateral trade negotiations would follow the implementation of the Uruguay Round, the global policy landscape was greatly changed from that which existed when the Uruguay Round was launched. In late 1994 the announcement of a set of nonbinding investment principles was one of the major elements of the Asia Pacific Economic Cooperation meeting. Although these were nonbinding in nature and somewhat ambiguous in wording, they represented the first international economic agreement ever signed by China. Also, at the Ministerial meeting of the OECD in May, 1995, authorization was granted for negotiation within the Organization of a "Multilateral Agreement on Investment" that would update and supersede the two OECD codes and the National Treatment Instrument. If successfully negotiated and implemented, this agreement could be the model for a future agreement within the WTO.

EDWARD M. GRAHAM

See also Colonialism; Foreign Direct Investment; Free Trade; General Agreement on Tariffs and Trade; Imperialism; International Trade and Commerce; International Trade Organization; North American Free Trade Agreement; Oil and Foreign Policy; Oil Companies; Organization for Economic Cooperation and Development; Organization of Petroleum Exporting Countries; United Nations Conference on Trade and Development; World Trade Organization

FURTHER READING
Barnet, Richard J., and Ronald E. Mueller. *Global Reach: The Multinational Spread of U.S. Enterprises*. New York, 1974.
Buckley, Peter J., and Mark C. Casson. *The Future of the Multinational Enterprise*. London, 1976.
Cantwell, John A. *Technological Innovation and Multinational Corporations*. Oxford, 1989.
Graham, Edward M., and Christopher Wilkie. "Multinationals and the Investment Provisions of the NAFTA." *International Trade Journal* 8 (1994): 9–38.
Hexner, Ervin P., and Adelaide Walters. *International Cartels*. Chapel Hill, N.C., 1945.
Julius, DeAnne S. *Global Companies and Public Policy*. New York, 1990.
Vernon, Raymond. *Sovereignty at Bay*. New York, 1971.
Wilkins, Mira. *The Emergence of Multinational Enterprise: American Business Abroad from the Colonial Era to 1914*. Cambridge, Mass., 1970.
———. *The History of Foreign Investment in the United States to 1914*. Cambridge, Mass., 1989.

MUNICH CONFERENCE
(29–30 September 1938)

Meeting of the heads of the German, French, British, and Italian governments in Munich, Germany, at which time part of Czechoslovakia was severed and given to Germany. This famous episode was considered to have been the high point of Western appeasement of Hitlerite Germany.

After World War I, Czechoslovakia had been created out of the former Austro-Hungarian Empire. More than 3 million Germans lived in a region of Czechoslovakia called the Sudetenland, and these Germans demanded union with their homeland. Nazi leader Adolf Hitler inflamed these demands, invoking the principle of self-determination, which the victorious powers had used in 1918 to create the new nations of Central and Eastern Europe. War appeared imminent in Spetember 1938 because Czech independence had been guaranteed in treaties with both France and the Soviet Union. British Prime Minister Neville Chamberlain traveled to Germany twice to meet with Hitler in an effort to avoid war. President Franklin D. Roosevelt praised Chamberlain for his mission, although the United States did not play a significant role in the crisis. Hitler demanded the Sudetenland and promised that he would seek no further territorial gains. Meanwhile, the Soviets were committed to intervene only if France moved first, and France had signaled that it would not go to war for Czech independence. Italian leader Benito Mussolini asked Hitler to postpone the German invasion of the Sudetenland. Hitler then invited Chamberlain, Mussolini, and Edouard Daladier of France to meet with him in Munich. Neither the Czechs nor the Soviets were invited. At the Munich Conference the four heads of state agreed to the dismemberment of Czechoslovakia in order to avert war. In the United States and throughout Europe people seemed relieved but, despite Hitler's promises, only six months later Germany annexed all of Czechoslovakia. The appeasement of Hitler at Munich became a symbol of defeatist policy. The "lesson of history" drawn was that it is dangerous to appease dictators; instead, they must be confronted, by force if necessary. This "Munich syndrome" was invoked by President Harry S. Truman during the Korean War, by President John F. Kennedy during the Cuban missile crisis, and by President Lyndon B. Johnson during the Vietnam War.

BERNARD V. BURKE

See also Appeasement; Chamberlain, Arthur Neville; Czech Republic; Germany; Hitler, Adolf

FURTHER READING
Rock, William R. *Chamberlain and Roosevelt: British Foreign Policy and the United States, 1937–1940*. Columbus, Ohio, 1988.

Taylor, Telford. *Munich: The Price of Peace.* Garden City, N.Y., 1979.

Weinberg, Gerhard L., William R. Rock, and Anna M. Cienciala. "Essay and Reflection: The Munich Crisis Revisited." *International History Review* 11 (November 1989): 668–688.

MURPHY, ROBERT DANIEL

(*b.* 28 October 1894; *d.* 9 January 1978)

Career diplomat, who entered the Foreign Service in 1917 and held numerous diplomatic posts over the next forty-two years. His most notable activity occurred during World War II, when he played a key role as U.S. consul-general in planning the Allied invasion of French North Africa. He negotiated with French High Commissioner Jean-Louis-Xavier-François Darlan the end of Vichy French resistance to U.S. and British forces invading Algeria and Morocco. Murphy also served as political adviser to General Dwight D. Eisenhower and, after the war, to the U.S. military governor in Germany. From 1949 to 1952 Murphy was ambassador to Belgium and then became the first postwar ambassador to Japan (1952). Between 1953 and his retirement in 1959 he served in a succession of important State Department posts, including undersecretary of state for political affairs. A staunch cold warrior, he worked well with Secretary of State John Foster Dulles during those years. He was influential in 1956 in shaping the prudent U.S. response to Soviet intervention in Hungary: the United States would not risk war to help liberate Hungary from Soviet domination. A diplomatic troubleshooter, Murphy prided himself on his appreciation of power as an ingredient in diplomacy, as his memoir, *Diplomat Among Warriors* (1964), attests.

MARK A. STOLER

See also Belgium; Germany; Hungary; Japan; World War II

FURTHER READING

Funk, Arthur Layton. *The Politics of TORCH: The Allied Landings and the Algiers Putsch*, 1942. Lawrence, Kans., 1974.

Murphy, Robert D. *Diplomat Among Warriors.* Garden City, N.Y., 1964.

MURROW, EDWARD (EGBERT) ROSCOE

(*b.* 25 April 1908; *d.* 27 April 1965)

Broadcast news correspondent whose career reflected the rising importance of radio and television in international affairs. Murrow's coverage of World War II for the Columbia Broadcasting System (CBS), notably the Battle of Britain, established his reputation as the nation's foremost radio foreign correspondent. He was instrumental in making radio a source of information. Although Murrow presented himself as an objective observer, his sup-

port of Great Britain and advocacy of U.S. intervention in the war was unmistakable. After the war he delivered nightly news summaries and commentaries and generally supported U.S. policies in the Cold War. In 1951 Murrow began appearing on television as the host of *See It Now*, which occasionally dealt with foreign policy. Several of the programs proved memorable, including a 1954 telecast that criticized Senator Joseph R. McCarthy's extremist anticommunist campaign. When Murrow became director of the U.S. Information Agency (USIA) in February 1961, President John F. Kennedy pledged to involve him in policymaking deliberations, but Murrow never belonged to the administration's inner circle. Murrow, however, loyally shifted the USIA's primary mission from publicizing American culture and institutions abroad to promoting specific administration policies, notably in Cuba and Vietnam. Afflicted with lung cancer, he resigned from the USIA in January 1964.

JAMES L. BAUGHMAN

See also Broadcast and Film Companies; McCarthyism; United States Information Agency; World War II

FURTHER READING

Culbert, David H. *News for Everyman: Radio and Foreign Affairs in Thirties America.* Westport, Conn., 1976.

Kendrick, Alexander. *Prime Time: The Life of Edward R. Murrow.* Boston, 1969.

Persico, Joseph E. *Edward R. Murrow: An American Original.* New York, 1988.

Sperber, A. M. *Murrow: His Life and Times.* New York, 1986.

MUSKIE, EDMUND SIXTUS

(*b.* 28 March 1914; *d* 26 March 1996)

Senator (1959–1980) and secretary of state (1980–1981). After service in World War II, Muskie practiced law and entered politics, serving first as a member of the Maine House of Representatives (1946–1951) and governor of Maine (1955-58) and then as a U.S. senator. He became the Democratic vice-presidential candidate in 1968 and a candidate for the presidential nomination in 1972. In 1980 President Jimmy Carter selected Muskie as secretary of state to succeed Cyrus Vance, who had resigned in protest over the failed Iranian hostage rescue mission. Muskie was easily confirmed by his Senate colleagues, but his tenure of less than a year was too brief for him to have much impact. He focused on the crisis with Iran and eventually helped secure the release of the American hostages held by Tehran, but only after Carter was defeated for reelection. In 1986 Muskie served on the Tower Commission that investigated the Iran-Contra affair. Muskie died from a heart attack suffered 21 March 1996 in Washington, D.C.

MARK A. STOLER

See also Carter, James Earl; Iran

FURTHER READING

Carter, Jimmy. *Keeping Faith: Memoirs of a President.* New York, 1982.

Smith, Gaddis. *Morality, Reason, and Power: American Diplomacy in the Carter Years.* New York, 1986.

MUSSOLINI, BENITO

(*b.* 29 July 1883; *d.* 28 April 1945)

Founder of the Italian Fascist party (1919), who became prime minister and then dictator of Italy (1922–1943) and an ally of Germany's Adolf Hitler. Mussolini was born in Predappio, a village in Romagna, the son of a blacksmith with socialist sympathies, who named his son for Benito Juárez, the Mexican liberator. In 1902, in order to evade military service, Mussolini settled in Switzerland where he associated with revolutionaries and became a socialist. Expelled from that country, he returned to Italy and, while living in Trentino in 1908–1909, became an ardent Italian nationalist. At the outbreak of World War I in 1914, Mussolini was the editor of the Italian Socialist party newspaper, *Avanti.* Later that year he lost his editorship and was expelled from the party for his espousal of the cause of the Entente allies. He then founded his own right radical newspaper in Milan, *Il Popolo d'Italia.*

Favoring Italy's participation in the war on the Entente side, Mussolini volunteered for the army and was wounded fighting against the Austro-Hungarians. He returned to his paper, having abandoned his association with socialism. Exploiting the general fear of communism and taking advantage of patriotic discontent, he formed the *Fasci di combattimento,* which he used to attack strikers, communists, and socialists. By 1921 he had organized the Fascist party on a national scale and helped break a general strike. While Mussolini remained in Milan, he arranged a carefully staged march on Rome by his Black Shirts, a name derived from the uniform of the party's militia, on 28 October 1922. King Victor Emmanuel III, fearful of a communist revolution, called upon Mussolini to form a coalition government. At first his government tolerated opposition, but by 1928 he had established a one-party fascist state. His major accomplishments were an impressive public works program and the ending of friction between the Vatican and Italy through the Concordat of 1929.

An adept mythmaker and propagandist, Mussolini sought and won popular support abroad. Many Americans admired his stance against communism, his encouragement of individualism and private enterprise, and his creation of what they saw as an efficient and competent government. They compared favorably his charismatic leadership with that of President Theodore Roosevelt. Mussolini reached the peak of his popularity in the United States in 1934, when he intervened to prevent Hitler's first attempt to annex Austria. The repressive nature of Mussolini's government was largely overlooked until the Italian invasion of Ethiopia in 1935. His standing in the United States continued to decline when, in 1936, in cooperation with the Germans, tens of thousands of Italian troops and aircraft intervened in the Spanish civil war on the side of General Francisco Franco. In the same year Mussolini joined forces with Germany, and a year later with Japan, in the Axis alliance.

At first a role model for Hitler, Mussolini had, by the outbreak of World War II, been reduced to a figurehead under Hitler's domination and was widely regarded as ineffectual. His reputation in the United States plummeted even further following Italy's lack of support for France, which Hitler invaded in May 1940, and Italy's invasion of Greece later that fall. Dismissed by Victor Emmanuel in July 1943, Mussolini was arrested and interned by his successor, Pietro Badoglio, who concluded peace terms with the United States and its allies that September. Mussolini was rescued by the Germans, who briefly maintained him as a meaningless puppet in northern Italy. Captured in German uniform by Italian partisans as he attempted to escape at war's end, Mussolini was executed along with his long-time mistress, Clara Petacci.

Bernard V. Burke

See also Ethiopia; Hitler, Adolf; Italy; Spain; World War II

FURTHER READING

Deakin, F. W. *The Brutal Friendship.* New York, 1962.

Diggins, John P. *Mussolini and Fascism: The View from America.* Princeton, N.J., 1972.

Smith, Denis Mack. *Mussolini.* New York, 1982.

MUTUAL ASSURED DESTRUCTION

One of the doctrines guiding U.S. nuclear deterrence strategy during the Cold War. As a presidential candidate in 1960, John F. Kennedy criticized the Dwight D. Eisenhower administration's policy of massive retaliation. Upon entering office, President Kennedy ordered Secretary of Defense Robert McNamara to determine how many nuclear weapons would be needed to inflict "unacceptable damage" (defined as the destruction of 20 to 25 percent of the Soviet population and 50 percent of its industrial capacity), even in the event of a Soviet first strike against the United States. By the mid-1960s U.S. policymakers had determined that approximately 1,054 intercontinental ballistic missiles (ICBMs) and 656 submarine-launched ballistic missiles (SLBMs) were sufficient to ensure that the United States could deliver unacceptable damage on the USSR. In light of this decision, the

United States maintained the same number of ICBMs and SLBMs from 1967 until the end of the Cold War.

Essentially, the doctrine of mutual assured destruction (MAD) was a recognition that neither the United States nor the Soviet Union could hope to achieve meaningful objectives by attacking one another. It was, in short, a recognition of the mutual vulnerability of each side to a devastating attack from the other side, and the belief that in a world of imperfect options, this was the optimal strategy for avoiding a superpower nuclear war. Although this doctrine was first announced by the Kennedy administration, Presidents Lyndon B. Johnson, Richard M. Nixon, Gerald R. Ford, and Jimmy Carter continued to base their policies on this foundation. Although the U.S. government throughout the 1960s and 1970s accepted assured destruction, some strategists questioned its assumptions. It was, in fact, these opponents who added the word "mutual," making the acronym MAD reflect their opinion of the doctrine. Supporters of assured destruction contended that plans to actually use nuclear weapons in war, which they called nuclear utilization theory, were, like the theory's acronym, "nuts." The stability of deterrence could be threatened by any situation that promised significant advantages to one side and not the other. If such advantages were great enough, leaders of one country could be induced to attack the other. Because such a destabilizing development was possible, some strategists advocated an alternative strategy to assured destruction known as damage limitation. The proponents of this strategy were particularly influential in the first administration of President Ronald Reagan (1981–1985).

DAN CALDWELL

See also Cold War; Flexible Response; Kennedy, John Fitzgerald; McNamara, Robert Strange; Massive Retaliation; Nuclear Weapons and Strategy

FURTHER READING

Enthoven, Alain C., and K. Wayne Smith. *How Much Is Enough? Shaping the Defense Program, 1961–1969.* New York, 1971.

Smoke, Richard. *National Security and the Nuclear Dilemma: An Introduction to the American Experience in the Cold War*, 3rd ed. New York, 1993.

MUTUAL SECURITY ACT

(1951)

Legislation that reorganized U.S. military- and economic-aid programs, placing most of them under the control of the new Mutual Security Administration, created in October 1951. The law reflected the overall militarization of foreign policy during the Korean War. The reorganization also expressed the desire of President Harry S. Truman's administration to combine military and economic aid into a single package that would be more appealing to conservative members of Congress. Although willing to support military aid when it was tied to the security interests of the United States, these congressmen were reluctant to support economic aid for European countries establishing social-welfare programs that they themselves opposed in the United States. Some members of Congress also alleged at the time that the Department of State was harboring communist sympathizers, and these legislators were therefore especially eager to place the supervision of these programs under an independent body. Because the Mutual Security Act eliminated the Economic Cooperation Administration (ECA), which had administered Marshall Plan aid, the 1951 law spelled the end of the Marshall Plan; however, many Marshall Plan programs were continued under the auspices of the new Mutual Security Administration. The Mutual Security Administration was superseded by other foreign-aid agencies and abolished in 1955.

BENJAMIN FORDHAM

See also Agency for International Development; Foreign Aid; Marshall Plan

FURTHER READING

Block, Fred. *The Origins of International Economic Disorder.* Berkeley, Calif., 1977.

Hogan, Michael J. *The Marshall Plan: America, Britain, and the Reconstruction of Western Europe, 1947–1952.* New York, 1987.

MX

See Nuclear Weapons and Strategy

MYANMAR

Nation formerly known as Burma, located in Southeast Asia, bordering the Bay of Bengal between Bangladesh and Thailand. The United States greeted the independence of the Union of Burma on 4 January 1948 as the proper outcome after British colonial rule was weakened by Japan's invasion of the region during World War II. The governance of Burma has been plagued however, by unending insurgency conducted by separatist ethnic groups, and a military-dominated ruling party since 1962. In its foreign relations Burma has adhered strictly to assertions of independence and nonalignment, and the "Burmese Way to Socialism," while accepting assistance from international economic organizations such as the World Bank, IMF, and the Asian Development Bank, but only in 1996 did it approach the Association of Southeast Asian States as a possible new member. During the U.S. war in Vietnam the Burmese had remained aloof.

The United States maintained friendly relations with Burma and provided limited economic aid, until rejected by the Burmeses Government in the mid-1960s. In 1974 the U.S. provided $65 million in military equipment to track down drug traffickers in the ethnic enclaves near the Thai border, the largest heroin producing area in the world. In 1980, health care and agricultural aid, and token cultural exchange were added to the aid program. In September 1988 a brutal military crack down on pro-democracy students spoiled relations with the U.S. and other democratic states. The UN Human Rights Commission and the European Community expressed their particular dismay at the prolonged house arrest of Aung San Suu Kyi, the leader of the National League for Democracy which decisively won a multiparty election permitted in 1990 and was then denied the authority to govern. She meantime was awarded the Nobel Peace Prize in 1991, and her arrest was lifted in 1995. The oppressive military ruling council, the restrictive managers of a stagnant economy, were testing the price in human rights concessions for attracting badly needed outside investment.

MacAlister Brown

See also Colonialism; Human Rights

FURTHER READING

Bunge, Frederica M., ed. *Burma: A Country Study*. Washington, D.C., 1988.
Cady, John F. *The United States and Burma*. Cambridge, Mass., 1976.

MY LAI INCIDENT

(14–16 March 1968)

The most publicized massacre of the Vietnam War, which took place in the small village of My Lai, south of Hue. During the height of the Tet offensive, soldiers from the U.S. Army Americal Division killed several hundred unarmed villagers (the official army count was 347). Although the massacre occurred when Americans were in a combat setting and 5,000 Vietnamese civilians in Hue had been shot by communist execution squads, this context was less important than the fact that the incident was not revealed to the American public until a year and a half later, following a cover-up by army officials. The freelance journalist Seymour Hersh broke the story. The public debate that ensued put the war policies of newly elected President Richard M. Nixon on the defensive. The army's investigation of My Lai was thorough. The division was found guilty of a cover-up and recommendations for courts-martial were handed out to two dozen officers, including the division commander, General Samuel H. Koster. Only one officer, Lieutenant William L. Calley, Jr., was convicted. His crime: the premeditated murder of 102 civilians. President Nixon ordered Calley released from jail; army juries and army officials dismissed murder and cover-up charges against all other personnel connected with the My Lai masscare.

Timothy J. Lomperis

See also Tet Offensive; Vietnam War

FURTHER READING

Goldstein, Joseph, Burke Marshall, and Jack Schwartz. *The My Lai Massacre and Its Cover-Up*. New York, 1976.
Hersh, Seymour M. *My Lai 4: A Report of the Massacre and Its Aftermath*. New York, 1970.
Sim, Kevin, and Michael Bilton. *Four Hours in My Lai*. New York, 1992.

N

NAMIBIA

Located in Southern Africa, bordering the South Atlantic Ocean between Angola and South Africa, a state formerly known as Southwest Africa. Twice the size of California in area, its population is only 1.5 million (1994 census). Namibian independence was proclaimed on 21 March 1990, following more than a century of colonial domination and only after an armed campaign for self-determination and a dozen years of intensive negotiations. For the first time in its history, the United Nations directly sponsored and supervised a transition to independence. Namibia's first years as a democratic member of the family of nations were peaceful, which may account for the absence of attention it was given by Western media.

With its 824,000 square kilometers (319,000 square miles) Namibia is the eleventh largest country in Africa. Thanks to its large land area and small population, its population density of 1.8 per square kilometer is one of the lowest in the world. The country's geography explains its sparse population. Within its borders is the world's oldest desert, the Namib, which occupies 15 percent of the territory. The rest of the country is arid or semi-arid, with the exception of about 12 percent of river-fed areas in the north. Two-thirds of the population lives in the north as farmers and herders. While 70 percent of the population still depends on agriculture, this occupation contributes only some 10 percent to the country's gross domestic product (GDP). By comparison, mining accounts for almost half of the country's GDP, of which 20 percent is from diamonds. Uranium, copper, gold, lead, silver, and zinc mining make up the rest. Mining is the leading source of export revenue. Namibia's per capita GDP in 1994 was $1,420; its growth rate is 5 percent. One of Namibia's greatest natural assets is its 1,100-mile coastline on the south Atlantic, which includes the port of Walvis Bay. The port returned to Namibian sovereignty in February 1994. The offshore waters contain fishing grounds reputed to be among the richest in the world. An asset of great undeveloped potential is tourism. Indeed, Namibia's game parks are world renowned.

Namibia's population and political life are dominated by the Ovambo, numbering some 600,000. In addition, there are 40,000 Caprivi. The Kavango and the Caprivi live in the northern strip of that name; it extends 500 miles east to Zambia. Since independence, Namibia's population growth has remained between 3 percent and 3.3 percent.

The Pursuit of Self-Determination

The contemporary era in the history of Southwest Africa began with Germany's seizure of the territory in 1884. The Germans exercised thirty years of harsh colonial administration, but the outbreak of World War I forced them to abandon the area. South Africa assumed administrative control of its neighbor in 1915; five years later, it was given a League of Nations mandate over the territory of Southwest Africa. From the outset, colonial authorities—German and South African—encountered indigenous resistance. The demand for self-determination grew more insistent after World War II. By the mid-1960s it took the form of an armed liberation movement, the South West African People's Organization (SWAPO). The movement began among the Ovambo peoples of the north and soon gained majority support throughout the country. As pressures for self-determination grew, the movement was polarized and complicated by the Cold War confrontation between the United States and the Soviet Union. Specifically, in 1971 a dispirited SWAPO, having found little Western support for its cause, turned to the Soviet Union for funds and arms.

The 1974 leftist "coup of the colonels" in Portugal intensified East-West competition for control of Angola, Southwest Africa's northern neighbor. Both Cuba and South Africa intervened militarily in Angola. Cuba sent troops, and South Africa used its bases in Southwest Africa. Neither the United States nor the Soviet Union sent troops. However, both engaged in covert action and other assistance. In short, outside interventions in other parts of the region combined to raise the issue of Southwest Africa's independence to an important place on the agenda of East-West negotiations. As a consequence, South Africa portrayed its continued administration of Southwest Africa—and its resistance to Namibian self-determination—as contributions to anticommunism. South Africa thus forced the United States to waver between its espousal of self-determination and its opposition to communism. Independence for Namibia became hostage to multiparty negotiations across the global ideological divide.

Negotiations dragged on for twelve years. Only in

December 1988 were U.S.-brokered agreements concluded. Preconditions to their success included departure of all South African military forces from Namibia and withdrawal of Cuban troops from Angola in stages. The respective troop withdrawals, tacitly but never formally linked, became preconditions for implementation of Security Council Resolution 435 of 1978. Another precondition was "free and fair elections" administered by a United Nations "Transition Assistance Group" (UNTAG). UNTAG's role was to assure law and order and to monitor elections for a constitution-writing assembly. Namibian independence was celebrated at last on 21 March 1990 in the capital, Windhoek. The U.S. delegation was headed by Secretary of State James Baker. The prestigious U.S. representation reflected the central U.S. role in Namibia's independence, first as a leader of the so-called "Contact Group" of western countries (the others were the United Kingdom, the Federal Republic of Germany, France, and Canada) in drafting Security Council Resolution 435; and second, as the moving force in the prolonged negotiations.

U.S. diplomatic initiatives since 1977 have overcome the early distrust of SWAPO and the slow pace of independence negotiations. U.S.-Namibian relations are marked by a high degree of mutual understanding and respect. One important reason is that many Namibians in exile attended American universities. Indeed, eight members of the nineteen-member Namibian government, which was elected in March 1995, had received some of their education in the United States. Another indication of Namibia's high standing is evidenced by the March 1993 visit of President Sam Nujoma to the United States. President Nujoma was the first foreign chief of state to be received by President Clinton. U.S.-Namibian citizen exchanges are modest. As of early 1995, 212 Namibians were registered as living in the United States. Not included are Namibian students estimated at perhaps twice that number. By contrast, only a half-dozen Americans are believed to have studied at the University of Namibia. The spirit of friendly U.S.-Namibian relations extends across the political and economic spectrum. U.S. development assistance has remained at between $6 and $8 million per year. U.S. help has focused principally on basic education, teacher training, and democratization. With unemployment at more than 30 percent, Namibia's overarching economic concern is job creation. The social consequences of joblessness are especially evident in urban centers such as the capital, Windhoek, which has doubled in population since 1990. Increased crime is the nation's single most pressing social issue.

Despite years of Namibian frustration stemming from the "globalization" of its independence negotiations, relations between the United States and Namibia are friendly and cooperative. From the U.S. perspective, Namibia's record of respect for political and economic freedom, democracy, and human rights has earned the respect of the United States.

DONALD R. NORLAND

See also Africa; Angola; South Africa

FURTHER READING

Kahn, Owen E., ed. *Disengagement from Southwest Africa: Prospects for Peace in Angola and Namibia.* (East-South Relations Ser.). New Brunswick, N.J., 1990.

Katjavivi, Peter H. *A History of Resistance in Namibia.* (UNESCO Apartheid and Society Ser.). Lawrenceville, N.J., 1990.

NAPOLEON BONAPARTE
(*b.* 15 August 1769; *d.* 5 May 1821)

Ruler of France, initially as first consul (1799), then as consul for life (1802), finally as emperor (1804)—until his forced exile on the island of Saint Helena in June 1815, following his defeat at the Battle of Waterloo. Born in Corsica, which had only recently become part of France, the young Napoleon Bonaparte (the family name was also spelled Buonaparte) was educated in military schools and was commissioned as an artillery officer in 1785. Following the outbreak of the French Revolution, Louis XVI's execution in 1793, and France's declaration of war against Prussia, Austria, and their allies, Napoleon advanced rapidly in the army, becoming brigadier general at age 24. After immensely successful campaigns in Italy in 1796 and 1797 and more inconclusive ones in Egypt and the Near East in 1798 and 1799, he returned to France to take control of the country through the coup of the Eighteenth Brumaire and the establishment of the Consulate.

As first consul, Napoleon instituted important fiscal and tax reforms and concentrated on improving the French judicial system. The brilliant second Italian campaign against the Austrians, the Concordat with Rome, and the short-lived Peace of Amiens in 1802 with England followed. Napoleon toyed with the idea of invading the British Isles, but after assuming the title of hereditary emperor and following the disastrous naval engagement at Trafalgar in 1805, he concentrated on defeating the Austrian, Russian, and Prussian Armies. In 1807 Napoleon became arbiter of Europe according to the peace terms of the Treaty of Tilsit.

To deprive his primary adversary, Great Britain, of European markets, Napoleon designed the Continental System, which forced European states under his control to boycott English goods. He confiscated ships and cargoes of countries that insisted on trading with the British. By 1810, Russia was chafing at the costly importation of French goods and was emboldened by Great Britain's challenge to Napoleon's European hegemony by the military successes in Portugal and Spain of General Sir Arthur Wellesley (later, the duke of Wellington). In June 1812, Napoleon led an army of 600,000 into Russia to force Russian compliance with his plan for Europe. The Russians retreated without engaging the superior French force, resorted to scorched-earth tactics, and allowed Napoleon to capture Moscow in September, after his Pyrrhic victory at Borodino. When Czar Alexander refused to discuss terms of surrender, Napoleon decided to bring his Russian invasion to an end rather than spend the winter in Russia, and returned hurriedly and ignominiously to Paris. His army suffered massive losses in retreat, which fatally compromised his ability to avoid defeat by the British and their allies.

Napoleon's first abdication occurred in April 1814, and he was then exiled to the island of Elba during the initial restoration of Louis XVIII. He escaped in March 1815, returned to Paris, ruled as emperor again during the "Hundred Days," and was finally defeated by Wellington and Prussian Field Marshal Gebhard Leberecht von Blücher at the Battle of Waterloo in June. His second abdication was followed by permanent banishment to Saint Helena.

Throughout his tenure as ruler of France, Napoleon treated the United States as an inconsequential, second-rank nation. His decision to sell Louisiana to the United States in 1803 hinged more on his failure to quell the slave rebellion in Santo Domingo (Haiti) and his determination to keep Louisiana out of the hands of the British than on sympathy for U.S. expansionism.

In the United States, Federalists accused President Thomas Jefferson and his successor, James Madison, of being Napoleon's dupes and making the United States a willful supporter of French ambitions during the period of the Napoleonic Wars (1799–1815). This charge permeates scholarly accounts of Madison's decision under Macon's Bill No. 2 (1810) to trade openly with France despite Napoleon's attempts to control trade. To the contrary, Madison and his advisers distrusted Napoleon.

Jefferson and Madison hoped to use Napoleon to U.S. advantage. When he invaded Russia in 1812, they hoped the United States would be aided in the war against the British by hampering British efforts to control Canada and by keeping British forces involved in Europe. In the end, neither Napoleon nor the United States gained much from the actions of the other.

RONALD L. HATZENBUEHLER

See also France; Great Britain; Haiti; Jefferson, Thomas; Louisiana Purchase; Madison, James; Napoleonic Wars; War of 1812

FURTHER READING

Connelly, Owen. *The Epoch of Napoleon*. Huntington, N.Y., 1978.
———. *The French Revolution and Napoleonic Era*. 2nd ed., Fort Worth, Tex., 1991.
Kaplan, Lawrence S. *Entangling Alliances with None: American Foreign Policy in the Age of Jefferson*. Kent, Ohio, 1987.
Lefebvre, Georges. *Napoleon*. 2 vols. Translated by Henry F. Stockhold. New York, 1969.

NAPOLEONIC WARS

The wars between France and Great Britain (the main belligerents) and their allies, 1799–1815, that continued and expanded upon the wars of the French Revolution (1793–1799). A brief lull in the wars took place from March 1802 until March 1803 (the Treaty of Amiens period). The wars grew after 1803 to involve almost all of the nations of Europe, and they ended in 1815 with the Battle of Waterloo. Throughout the Napoleonic wars, the United States tried to continue its policy of neutrality outlined by President George Washington in 1793, aimed at safeguarding the rights of neutral nations. But under Presidents John Adams and Thomas Jefferson, the nation became less and less able to avoid conflicts with either the French or the British, especially over interruptions of U.S. commerce. In 1812, under President James Madison, the United States declared war on Great Britain and in British eyes, became a participant in the wars on France's side. European monarchs found the foreign policies of Napoleon Bonaparte, who became first consul in 1799, no more acceptable than those of the succession of governments that had ruled France since the fall of Louis XVI's absolutist monarchy. They also discovered, however, that Napoleon was better able to coordinate the wartime capabilities of the French nation than had been his predecessors. Under Napoleon, national conscription replaced professional armies; two million men (7 percent of the French population) swelled the size of Napoleon's armies between 1800 and 1814.

In the United States, President Thomas Jefferson promised in his first inaugural address (March 1801) that his administration would pursue "peace, commerce, and honest friendship with all nations—entangling alliances with none." Because the United States was "kindly separated by nature and a wide ocean from the exterminating havoc of one quarter of the globe," the president saw no reason for standing armies and expensive navies. Once the pro-British policies that Treasury Secretary Alexander Hamilton had implemented were replaced by an even-handed approach toward Great Britain and France, Jefferson believed that American trade could continue to grow and secure the nation's commercial interests, despite Europe's wars. During the uneasy peace between the two European belligerents under the Treaty of

Amiens, Jefferson's policies seemed to be working. He used threats of an alliance with Great Britain to pressure Napoleon (and this, in part, induced him to sell Louisiana). He thereupon reduced taxes and the size of the navy and the army. As warfare between the British and the French resumed, however, the same problems U.S. citizens had faced in the 1790s resurfaced. The French attempted to increase trade by opening their West Indian ports to U.S. ships. In response, the British evoked their "Rule of 1756," which declared that ports closed to trade in peacetime were also closed in war. In mid-1805, without warning, the British began seizing American ships carrying French goods.

In the fall of 1805, the international crisis deepened. First, British Admiral Horatio Nelson defeated the combined French and Spanish fleets at the Battle of Trafalgar. From then on, Great Britain ruled the seas. In November, Napoleon became master of the continent when he defeated the combined Russian and Austrian armies at the Battle of Austerlitz. In the meantime, both the British Parliament and Napoleon sought to gain control over the trade of all countries, especially that of the United States. The British Orders in Council regulated trade with the continent by forcing ships of neutral nations to go first to England to be searched for contraband before completing their voyages. In France, the Berlin (1805) and Milan decrees (1807) provided that all ships that had docked in Great Britain became British ships and hence were subject to capture without compensation. Because the British controlled the seas, they were better able to enforce their restrictions on American trade. As they had done before Jay's Treaty (1794), the British began stopping American ships, searching holds for contraband, and seizing provisions. In addition, because the British needed more and more able-bodied seamen for their frigates, they repeatedly forced American citizens whom they wrongly accused of being British deserters to serve in the Royal Navy—a practice known as "impressment."

Following the humiliating attack on USS *Chesapeake* by HMS *Leopard* in June 1807, Jefferson tried to implement his long-standing idea of forbidding U.S. trade with either belligerent to coerce respect for the nation's neutral rights. This policy proved impossible to implement, as U.S. commercial interests were anxious to expand their markets. The Embargo Act (1807–1809) and later the Non-Intercourse Act (1809–1810) damaged the U.S. economy far more than they hindered either the British or the French. Other developments also compromised the nation's ability to implement restrictive commercial policies against the British. When Napoleon closed British trade in lumber and naval supplies with the Baltic countries in 1808, Secretary of State James Madison believed that the French emporer was inadvertently advancing

U.S. interests by increasing British need for American resources. But the British instead turned to Canada to acquire the goods no longer available in Europe; and as the Canadian economy prospered, Madison feared that Washington would lose whatever influence it still had over London. In late 1810, Madison and key members of Congress (from the Republican party) worked out a policy ostensibly designed to force the belligerents to lift their punitive decrees and show respect for U.S. commercial rights or in effect, to see the United States drop its neutral posture and choose sides (Macon's Bill No. 2). In October, Napoleon issued an ambiguous repeal of his decrees, and Madison responded with the announcement that trade with Great Britain would cease. When the British declared that they would not repeal their orders-in-council, Congress passed additional legislation to cease importation of British goods and pursue trade only with France. Madison and Congress soon discovered that Napoleon had no real intention of abandoning his economic warfare, but the president and Republican party leaders had at least achieved one aim: exposing Britain as the nation's main enemy. When war with Great Britain eventually came in 1812, Republicans justified the battle by claiming that the British were carrying out a diabolical plot to destroy American independence. Opponents of the war pointed out that the nation's problems with France were quite similar to those with Britain. The war strained the young nation's military and economic capacity to the limit. In sum, far from taking advantage of Europe's distress, the United States found that the Napoleonic wars threatened the nation's very survival. Ironically, the British military victory over Napoleon—far more than the British diplomatic "defeat" in the peace treaty signed with the Americans at Ghent—allowed the United States the opportunity, after 1815, to concentrate on domestic problems as well as to pursue continental expansion.

RONALD L. HATZENBUEHLER

See also Adams, John; Canada; Chesapeake-Leopard Affair; Convention of 1800; Economic Sanctions; France; Ghent, Treaty of; Great Britain; Impressment; Jay's Treaty; Jefferson, Thomas; Madison, James; Napoleon Bonaparte; Neutral Rights; Orders in Council; War of 1812; Washington, George

FURTHER READING

Glover, Michael. *The Napoleonic Wars: An Illustrated History 1792-1815.* New York, 1978.

Hatzenbuehler, Ronald L., and Robert L. Ivie, *Congress Declares War: Rhetoric, Leadership, and Partisanship in the Early Republic.* Kent, Ohio, 1983.

Kaplan, Lawrence S. *Entangling Alliances with None: American Foreign Policy in the Age of Jefferson.* Kent, Ohio, 1987.

McCoy, Drew R. *The Elusive Republic: Political Economy in Jeffersonian America.* Chapel Hill, N.C., 1980.

Perkins, Bradford. *The Creation of a Republican Empire, 1776-1865.* Vol. I. The Cambridge History of American Foreign Relations. Cambridge, England, 1993.

Sutherland, Donald M. G. *France 1789–1815: Revolution and Counterrevolution.* New York, 1986.

NARCOTICS, INTERNATIONAL

Nations have fashioned common policies to restrict the global flow of illegal narcotics such as opiates, cocaine, and marijuana since early in the twentieth century. The United States traditionally has taken the lead in this international control effort.

U.S. official recognition of narcotics trafficking as a foreign policy issue dates from the Spanish-American War, as a result of which the United States acquired imperial responsibilities in the Philippines—a country then afflicted by rampant opium addiction. Also, early U.S. narcotics policy was shaped by the perception that the opium scourge in China threatened the survival of the Ching (Manchu) dynasty and hence jeopardized U.S. economic and political interests in East Asia. For most of the twentieth century, though, U.S. efforts to create a global anti-drug regime relied on diplomatic pressures and moral suasion rather than on concrete federally funded programs to combat the drug trade across national borders. Antinarcotics programs are largely a phenomenon of the past quarter century, taking shape initially during the Nixon administration, and expanding rapidly thereafter. Between 1972 (the first year for which U.S. data for foreign drug assistance are recorded) and 1993, U.S. spending on international programs increased twenty-five fold from slightly more than $20 million to $523 million. By the late 1980s, drug control had emerged as a significant issue in the formulation and implementation of U.S. foreign policy. This is especially true with respect to Latin America, which supplies most of the marijuana, at least one-fifth of the heroin, and virtually all the cocaine consumed in U.S. markets. Likewise, the drugs–foreign policy nexus is firmly established in U.S. legislation: the antidrug abuse acts of 1986 and 1988 contain an explicit threat of sanctions (cut-offs of foreign aid and trade benefits) that demonstrate insufficient resolve in combating narcotics trafficking, drug money laundering, and drug-related corruption.

U.S. Antidrug Programs Overseas

A host of U.S. government departments and agencies in the mid-1990s administered different aspects of the overseas counternarcotics effort; among them, the State Department's Bureau of International Narcotics Matters (INM), the Drug Enforcement Administration (DEA), the Pentagon's Service Branches (the Army, Navy, and Marines), the Customs, the Coast Guard, the Federal Bureau of Investigation (FBI), the Agriculture and Treasury departments, the Central Intelligence Agency (CIA), the U.S. Information Agency (USIA), the Agency for International Development (USAID), the National Security Council (NSC) and the White House Office of National Drug Control Policy. Primary operational responsibility for combating drugs beyond U.S. borders, however, is assigned to INM and the DEA. INM, which stands at the forefront of policy planning and implementation efforts, directly administers programs in fourteen key drug-producing and trafficking countries, and funds counternarcotics activities in fifty-six other states. Such programs focus on training, building, and equipping antidrug and criminal justice institutions; also, INM provides technical, logistical, and financial support for initiatives to control drug crops in foreign lands—subject, of course, to host governments' willingness to implement such increases. The DEA with some 300 agents operating in fifty countries has a mandate to collect foreign narcotics intelligence and to support investigations of major traffickers abroad; the DEA also designs, participates in, and sometimes leads operations against drug laboratories and narcotics trafficking infrastructures, especially in the Andes.

The main policy objective of U.S. antidrug programs overseas has been criminal enforcement—attacking and disabling the infrastructures for narcotics trafficking by supporting (and occasionally conducting) frontline operations to eradicate drug crops, dismantle laboratories, constrict transport options, and generally impede the export of illegal drugs by narcotraffickers. A secondary thrust of U.S. policy has been to curb production by offering rural populations positive economic inducements to abandon narcotics-related activities. This effort, administered mainly by USAID and the State Department, emphasizes assistance in cultivating legal crops, as well as various rural "alternative development" schemes. (United Nations (UN) agencies and various European states also fund such programs.) In addition, Washington has not shrunk from also using narcotics assistance programs to promote certain political objectives—not only limiting the intrusion of drug dealers into the political systems and economies of drug-source countries, but helping such countries cope with narcoterrorist threats and strengthening the influence of established, more legitimate ruling elites. As world supplies of heroin and cocaine inexorably expand, such "collateral" objectives as promoting stability and fighting corruption are increasingly cited by U.S. policy makers as justifications for maintaining narcotics assistance programs overseas.

Major Obstacles

Combating the global narcotics trade has proved to be a Sisyphean task. Major production and trafficking complexes in the Andes, Southwest Asia, and the Golden Triangle of Southeast Asia persistently thrive, impervious to international enforcement programs. Indeed, between 1985 and 1995 world opium and world output of coca leaves roughly tripled. Opium cultivation has expanded rapidly in several communist or former communist states: China, Vietnam, Uzbekistan, Tajikistan, and Turkmenistan. In China, where a revolutionary government could claim four decades ago to have all but obliterated a once-pervasive problem of opium addiction, poppy plantings have now been reported in seventeen of the nation's thirty provinces and drug use is rising rapidly. Colombia, which produces an estimated 70 to 80 percent of the world's refined cocaine, is now the world's third- or fourth-largest opium producer as well, with an estimated 6,540 hectares under poppy cultivation; moreover, Colombian-refined heroin with its own distinct signature now accounts for at least one-third of the heroin sold in U.S. retail markets. A similar trend toward diversification is also evident in Peru, currently the world's largest producer of coca leaf, where small amounts of poppy cultivation are now being recorded.

The results of international drug control efforts have been discouraging, to say the least. Once again, the U.S. experience is particularly illuminating. Over much of the past decade and a half, increases in U.S. funding for anti-drug programs in South America have had a direct and demonstrable positive correlation with increases in Andean cocaine output. During the Bush administration, expenditures on such antidrug programs doubled, from approximately $70 million to almost $350 million, while the imputed production of coca leaves and cocaine expanded by more than ten percent from 1989 to 1992. By 1995, cocaine on U.S. streets was fifteen percent cheaper, almost as pure and at least as plentiful as it was when the Bush administration took office. Furthermore, during the 1980s and early 1990s—while Washington's attention and resources were focused on stopping South American cocaine—international traffickers, especially from Southeast Asia, apparently increased shipments of heroin to the United States. According to the U.S. DEA, average street prices of heroin plummeted sixty-four percent from 1981 to 1995, while average purity increased 700 percent, and heroin-related hospital admissions (1981 to 1993) more than tripled—probable indications that U.S. supplies of the drug were expanding rapidly.

Why has international drug policy aimed at stanching the supply "at the source"—especially policy promoted by Washington—been so ineffective? One set of reasons has to do with the fractured political cultures of the main states that produce and export illicit drugs. Typically, their governments are weak, power is diffused, and instability and lawlessness are rife, severely limiting opportunities for counternarcotics operations. Indeed, the drug trade itself has contributed in no small measure to problems of governability. In Colombia, for example, the government in Bogotá shares de facto control over broad swathes of its territory with drug kingpins, who own at least ten percent of the agriculturally productive land in the country, and with Marxist guerrilla groups that earn a majority of their income from taxing the coca or opium trade. In Pakistan, the opium and heroin businesses are intertwined with the political ambitions of tribal separatist groups—and, indeed, of elements in the political mainstream: according to a recent CIA report, reputed drug lords and narcotics traffickers sit in the National Assembly and in the provincial assemblies of the Northwest Frontier Provinces, Punjab, and other regions. In Burma (renamed Myanmar by its military rulers), Khun Sa's Shan United Army controls significant enclaves along the Thai-Burmese border, financing its activities—declaredly aimed at preserving an "Independent Shan State"—almost entirely from opium and heroin sales.

In addition, throughout the world's major narcotics producing regions, narcotics money buys protection for drug dealers at the highest political levels, underwrites party organizations and election campaigns, and creates coteries of compliant officials in all important government institutions. In Colombia, President Ernesto Samper and his closest advisers stand accused of illegal enrichment and electoral fraud in connection with a Cali cartel donation of approximately $6 million to Samper's 1994 election campaign. Traffickers are in a position to influence directly legislation or government policy decisions that affect their interests; in the Andean region, for instance, narcotics lobbies have successfully blocked or watered down enforcement initiatives ranging from the spraying of illicit crops, asset forfeiture, and money laundering laws to arrangements for the extradition of drug criminals. In Colombia, the government jailed several Cali cartel leaders in 1995; yet as a 1996 State Department report notes, "these criminals have continued to manage their crime empires while in jail and their trafficking organizations have not been dismantled."

A related point is that, in most of the developing nations that produce illegal drugs, no strong political consensus to combat drugs has emerged. Part of the reason is that large constituencies have developed around narcotics industries, which provide jobs, income, and foreign exchange where all are in short supply. Colombia's criminal narcotic earnings (from cocaine and heroin) are estimated at $8 to $9 billion or ninety-two to 103 percent of 1994 legal exports. An estimated 450,000 to 500,000 are employed in cultivating coca bushes or in cocaine trafficking and money laundering operations. This does not count those who are indirectly employed in selling goods and services to traffickers or in providing favors in return for bribes. In Peru and Bolivia, the cocaine industry employs an estimated eight to ten percent of the work force. Narcotics constituencies have tended to expand over time as drug lords launder their profits and legitimize themselves by acquiring landed estates or by buying into banks, service enterprises, and industrial conglomerates. To be sure, the drug economy has negative effects—overvaluing local currencies and depressing legal exports, for example—yet such effects are subtle and are partly compensated by increased availability of cheap imports of goods paid for with narcodollars. Hence, intense public indignation against narcotics industries is difficult to arouse.

It is true, of course, that factors other than direct or indirect economic dependence on narcotics businesses determine national attitudes and policies, but not always in favor of suppressing the trade. In the Western Hemisphere, some drug control initiatives—such as extradition of nationals to the United States, or the deployment of U.S. military advisors—clearly irritate Latin American sensibilities and sometimes play into the hands of the narcotics industries. Moreover, viewed strictly in domestic terms, many governments see fighting drugs as a low priority compared to other national objectives, and sometimes undercutting them. Peruvian leaders, for example, believe that destroying farmers' coca crops creates reservoirs of peasant support for Peru's Shining Path guerrillas, thus complicating the nation's rural counterinsurgency efforts; Peru terminated a U.S.-funded crop eradication program after 1989. In Colombia, successive governments have shown more resolve in combatting narcoterrorism and its perpetrators, particularly the leaders of the infamous Medellín cartel, than in attacking the cocaine trafficking infrastructure per se. In Colombia and other Latin American countries the cocaine business is viewed as an "international problem"—a product of the voracious demand for the drug in the United States and other industrialized countries. Furthermore, in Latin America—most notably (but not exclusively) in Colombia—the costs of confrontation with narcotics industries are prompting top government officials and political figures increasingly to express support for nonrepressive solutions to the drug trade. Several times during the past decade, the Colombian government has conducted negotiations with drug kingpins in an effort to obtain their voluntary withdrawal from narcotics businesses. (Strong opposition from the United States, however, has prevented full implementation of the negotiation strategy.) In the 1990s, leaders such as Colombia's Prosecutor General Gustavo De Grieff have favored both reaching an accommodation with drug lords and—eventually—legalizing production and sale of narcotics. The Colombian Constitutional Court's recent decision to legalize possession of small doses of drugs further highlights the changing shape of Colombia's national consensus on drug-fighting issues.

Other factors have to do with the intrinsic characteristics and dynamics of narcotics industries. One is that such industries tend to be highly profitable. Farmers typically earn higher, or at least more secure, returns from planting coca, marijuana, or opium poppy than they can earn from planting legal crops. Moreover, infrastructures necessary for successfully marketing legitimate agricultural products are rarely found in drug-source countries. And the income advantage runs down the entire stream of narcotics operations: participants in the industry—ranging from chemists, engineers, and pilots to accountants and security guards—enjoy far higher incomes than they would working in their professions on legal activities. Policemen, government officials, and military commanders can greatly enhance their meager official salaries by providing traffickers with advance warning of government raids or by renting aircraft and equipment to drug dealers. At the top, of course, a few kingpin entrepreneurs, such as Khun Sa in Southeast Asia and the late Pablo Escobar and Gilberto Rodríguez in Colombia, have become fabulously rich from drugs.

The lure of narcotics profits is partly a function of depressed economic conditions in countries that grow and refine illicit narcotics. Of eleven important producing states identified by the U.S. State Department's Bureau of International Narcotics Matters in 1995, eight could be defined as relatively poor in 1992 or 1993 with per capita incomes ranging from $250 to $1500 (the exceptions, Mexico, Iran and Thailand had per capita incomes of $3750, $2230, and $2040, respectively). The economies of many producer countries, moreover, suffered from severe inflation, high unemployment, regional inequalities, and other debilitating problems.

A second factor is that the number of potential suppliers of drugs is virtually unlimited; there are few geographical, organizational, or technological barriers to entry into narcotics industries. Drug crops such as opium and coca can be grown in most tropical regions of the world. Heroin and cocaine are not difficult to manufacture and laboratories can be set up anywhere. Laboratories, drug shipments, planes, money, chemicals, and other trafficking assets can be easily replaced, once destroyed. Damaging a major trafficking network can temporarily constrict drug supplies, but ultimately competitors pick up the slack. For example, a bloody three-year crackdown on the Medellín cartel in Colombia, supported by $160 million in U.S. military and police aid, has had no lasting effect in the world cocaine market: a rival coalition based in Cali and other small trafficking groups simply expanded their supply and distribution networks to meet demand.

This is not to say that there have not been some apparent successes in controlling drug crop cultivation in

ESTIMATED WORLDWIDE POTENTIAL
ILLICIT DRUG NET PRODUCTION 1987-1995
(metric tons)

Drug and Country	1995	1994	1993	1992	1991	1990	1989	1988	1987
Opium									
Afghanistan	1,250	950	685	640	570	415	585	750	600
India	71	82	66	-	-	-	-	-	-
Iran	-	-	-	-	-	-	-	-	300
Pakistan	155	160	140	175	180	165	130	205	205
Total SW Asia	1,476	1,192	891	815	750	580	715	955	1,105
Burma (Myanmar)	2,340	2,030	2,575	2,280	2,350	2,255	2,430	1,280	835
China	16	25	-	-	-	-	-	-	-
Laos	180	85	180	230	265	275	380	255	225
Thailand	25	17	42	24	35	40	50	25	24
Total SE Asia	2,561	2,157	2,797	2,534	2,650	2,570	2,860	1,560	1,084
Colombia	65	-	-	-	-	-	-	-	-
Lebanon	2	-	4	-	34	32	45	-	-
Guatemala	-	-	4	-	17	13	12	8	3
Mexico	53	60	49	40	41	62	66	67	50
Total Above	120	60	57	40	92	107	123	75	53
Total Opium Gum	4,157	3,409	3,745	3,389	3,492	3,257	3,698	2,590	2,242
Coca Leaf									
Bolivia	85,000	89,800	84,400	80,300	78,000	77,000	77,600	78,400	79,200
Colombia	40,800	35,800	31,700	29,600	30,000	32,100	33,900	27,200	20,500
Peru	183,600	165,300	155,500	155,500	222,700	196,900	186,300	187,700	191,000
Ecuador	-	-	100	100	40	170	270	400	400
Total Coca Leaf	309,400	290,900	271,700	265,500	330,740	306,170	298,070	293,700	291,100
Cannabis									
Mexico	3,650	5,540	6,280	7,795	7,775	19,715	30,200	5,655	5,933
Colombia	4,133	4,138	4,125	1,650	1,650	1,500	2,800	7,775	5,600
Jamaica	206	208	502	263	641	825	190	405	460
Belize	0	0	0	0	49	60	65	120	200
Others	3,500	3,500	3,500	3,500	3,500	3,500	3,500	3,500	1,500
Total Cannabis	11,489	13,386	14,407	13,208	13,615	25,600	36,755	17,455	13,693

Source: *International Narcotics Control Strategy Report*, March 1996. U.S. Department of State

a few countries. In fact, cultivation has declined dramatically in Thailand (by eighty percent or more) since the mid-1970s. But this reduction was more than offset by dramatic increases in cultivation in Burma. Indeed, Burmese opium production—2,300 tons in 1995—is now more than ninety times that of Thailand. In Colombia a massive aerial eradication effort eliminated 8,750 hectares of coca in 1995; yet because of new planting, the area of coca under cultivation actually increased twelve percent between 1994 and 1995. If by some chance a superlative international enforcement effort could entirely shut down South America's cocaine production, street prices for consumers would rise in the face of restricted supply—temporarily. Enterprising drug dealers would undoubtedly set up shop in other countries with amenable climatic and social conditions—and, in the meantime (and perhaps worse), switch to peddling alternative drugs such as heroin, amphetamines, or synthetic opiates.

A third factor is that narcotics industries are dynamic, evolving, and increasingly efficient. As law enforcement pressure has increased, production techniques, storage technologies, and smuggling strategies have improved commensurately. For instance, some Colombian and Bolivian cocaine laboratories now are equipped with chemical recycling and recovery plants as well as with vacuum-packing facilities and microwave drying ovens (removing moisture lengthens the shelf life of the product). Also, traffickers have shown considerable ingenuity in finding alternatives to common essential chemicals used in cocaine processing; in Colombia, chemists have increased extraction rates for cocaine base by ten to fifteen percent by substituting alcohol for gasoline or kerosene in the initial processing phase. Also in Colombia, farmers and traffickers reportedly are pulverizing coca leaves instead of macerating them (the traditional first step in processing) in an effort to increase base yields.

Agricultural technology is improving: in Bolivia, for example, declines in acreage devoted to drug crops since the mid-1980s has coincided with significant increases in yields. in Bolivia, yields increased more than twenty-five percent from 1989 to 1994 and total coca leaf output reached a record level in the latter year—a phenomenon at least partly attributable to increasingly efficient and capable farmers. Yet in Colombia, entreprenurial farmers cultivating large coca farms (of 3 to 30 hectares) reportedly have been able to obtain leaf yields of at least four metric tons per hectare annually, using intensive applications of fertilizer and other techniques. Finally, ordinary farmers all over the Andes are acquiring expertise in the production of semiprocessed cocaine, spurred by the prospect of relatively extraordinary economic returns; also, the

threat of economic ruin from volatile leaf prices had encouraged such "forward integration."

In addition, smuggling methods continue to advance and to proliferate. Colombian traffickers have extended their smuggling reach by buying or leasing cargo planes, including jets and turboprop aircraft; smuggling aircraft today may carry one to six tons of cocaine compared to 400 or 500 kilograms in the 1980s. The sheer variety of vehicles that modern smugglers use to move bulk cocaine shipments—airplanes, maritime containerized cargo, tractor trailers, camouflaged small boats, and even (in Colombia) specially produced semisubmersible vessels—represents a daunting challenge to law enforcement officials. Also, traffickers' reliance on state-of-the-art communications methods—encryption devices, faxes, express courier mail, and the like—tends to defeat traditional law enforcement surveillance tactics.

Also, the apparently increasing saturation of the U.S. market for cocaine (most data suggest that U.S. consumption of that drug peaked in the mid- or late 1980s) has forced Colombian traffickers to diversify into new products and new markets. Colombians today earn at least $1 billion annually from refining and exporting heroin. Also, at least one-quarter of Colombian cocaine exports is directed to Western and Eastern Europe, where wholesale prices for cocaine are two to three times those prevailing in the United States.

Finally, the expansion of global narcotics trafficking has spawned new patterns of domestic and international cooperation among criminal empires that deal in illicit drugs. Such cooperation encompasses such criminal groupings as the Colombian cartels, Mexican smuggling organizations, the Japanese *yakuza*, Hong Kong Chinese syndicates, the Sicilian Mafia, and Russian organized crime formations; it centers on such issues as organization of markets, trade deals (such as drugs-for-weapons, drugs-for-cash, and drugs-for-drugs exchanges), smuggling logistics, and laundering or repatriation of trafficking proceeds. Exchanges of criminal expertise and joint business planning may also characterize certain of those arrangements. Cooperation between Colombian traffickers and Italian organized crime groups to sell cocaine in Italy and Europe appears to have reached a particularly advanced stage. The effects of international narco-cooperation are to open new markets for narcotics and other illegal products, to exploit economies of scale in selling to those markets, to increase organized crime's penetration of legal economical and financial systems, and generally to augment the power of criminal formations relative to national governments.

Such discouraging realities suggest that, in the face of continuing strong demand, substantially restricting supplies of drugs is not an attainable objective for international narcotics policy, at least in the near term.

Political and Security Goals of Narcotics Control

Of course, international narcotics control is not just about controlling narcotics. The "war" on narcotrafficking may be justified as a moral imperative even if it is a practical failure. Also, the United States has its national prestige and has predicated its diplomatic relations with several countries on combating the drug scourge. More important, overseas antidrug efforts often also involve larger goals than the evidently unattainable one of reducing the volume of illicit drugs flowing to those tempted to use them. As one former U.S. ambassador to Bolivia, Edwin Corr, notes, "The reason for an effective international narcotics control program goes beyond the goal of reducing the supply of illicit drugs to the lucrative American market. The United States needs to help selected besieged governments defend their societies against the corrupting, disintegrating effects of the illicit drug business." Or, viewed in these terms, international narcotics assistance programs are extensions of diplomacy, and thus may serve important political or security interests. Resources allocated to supporting governments against real or perceived threats from narcotics dealers have, in fact, produced some solid achievements.

For example, U.S. military and technical aid to Colombia during the Medellín cartel's "war against the state" in 1989–1991 proved instrumental in blocking the Medellín traffickers' pretensions to power and in containing narco-terrorist violence in Colombia. The leadership of the Medellín cartel, which at one time accounted for more than seventy percent of Colombian cocaine exports, is in disarray—indeed, all the coalition's founding fathers today are either dead or in jail—and the political ambitions and agendas of powerful Colombian drug lords such as Pablo Escobar and Carlos Lehder (and Roberto Suárez in Bolivia) have been thwarted. (Unfortunately the cocaine trade continues to flourish under the Cali cartel's leadership.) U.S. pressure or intervention resulted in the ouster of narcotics-linked military regimes in Bolivia in 1980–1981 and in Panama in 1989—two countries where narcotics trafficking interests had established cozy relationships with the military, giving them de facto control of the national government apparatus "controlling" drug crime. In Bolivia, a combination of U.S. diplomatic and economic sanctions brought about the downfall of the Luis García Meza regime and the eventual restoration of civilian rule in the early 1980s; in Panama, the United States sought to disrupt the relationship by an unprecedented invasion and the seizure of narcotics-linked military strongman Manuel Noriega in January 1990. In Colombia a U.S. threat of sanctions prompted a govern-

ment crackdown on the Cali cartel hierarchy in 1995; yet, in 1996, the United states, citing the "corrosive impact of drug-related corruption," cut off most foreign aid to Colombia. Apparently, Washington is seeking the ouster of President Ernesto Samper, although as of this writing the president remains in office.

In addition, since the mid-1980s a well-designed U.S. economic assistance program in Bolivia has diminished the relative economic clout of the Bolivian cocaine industry, even if there is little evidence of any decline in absolute levels of cocaine production. According to the USAID, the value added from coca and cocaine declined from eight and a half percent of Bolivia's gross domestic product in 1988 to four percent in 1994. Bolivia's legal economy has grown an average of 3.8 percent since 1988. Such encouraging trends provide at least a foundation for positive economic and political development in Bolivia, and could strengthen the resolve of Bolivia's ruling elite vis-à-vis the cocaine traffic. In Thailand, rapid economic growth (averaging seven percent since World War II) and infusions of some $120 to $130 million into highland development projects since the early 1970s have greatly expanded poppy growers' income opportunities in legal commerce. This, in turn, has enabled Thailand to reduce poppy cultivation by an estimated sixty to eighty percent in the past quarter century. Opium and heroin today are economically marginal industries in Thailand, although the country remains an important conduit for and consumer of Burmese heroin.

Such political victories admittedly have done little or nothing to halt the flow of drugs into the lucrative markets of the industrialized world, in particular the United States. In Colombia, the epicenter of the international cocaine trade has merely shifted from Medellín to Cali. Arrests of top Cali leaders have had little impact on the functioning of these cocaine trafficking empires. In Bolivia, for whatever salutary political goal was realized by the demise of the García Meza regime, the cocaine business still expanded enormously following its ouster and the return to civilian rule in the early 1980s. Cocaine trafficking and money laundering were at least as rampant in Panama in the years following Noriega as they had been during General Noriega's regime. The Thai "success story" of a real and enduring reduction in opium production had little impact on world heroin supplies because it was dwarfed by the massive and uncontrolled expansion of Burmese production.

The Former Soviet Union

The former Soviet bloc countries represent an increasingly large part of the world's dismal drug panorama, and the problems there suggest the need for a central player—presumably the United States or the United Nations—to develop an "early warning" capability for compelling international attention to the emergence of dangerous new patterns of drug production or abuse and initiating action to deal with the problem before it spins out of control. The growing drug problems in the postcommunist region have been all but overlooked by the international community, even though the unrestrained growth of criminal narcotics enterprises threatens the integrity of Eastern economic and governmental institutions, saps the economic vitality and potential recovery of the region, magnifies the potential for new forms of East-West tension, and complicates the building of a stable postcommunist order in Eurasia. Police, public health officials, and financial authorities in formerly communist countries not only lack the training to deal with drug abusers, but are hopelessly unprepared to cope with an unfettered drug trade. Critical shortages of basic equipment like vehicles, typewriters, computers, herbicides, and bulletproof vests are common. As drug crops are increasingly sown in Central Asia's inaccessible mountain or desert regions, police forces stand by, virtually helpless. Northeastern Europe is also evolving into a source region for amphetamines. Poland ranks as the most important producer and exporter, with the highest-quality drugs in Europe; yet Russia and Latvia also have shipped large quantities of amphetamines to Scandinavia and Western Europe in the 1990s.

Ominously, international trafficking organizations are seeking to co-opt more East European nationals into smuggling. Their strategic objectives are easily discernible: to widen avenues of penetration into West European markets and to reduce the visibility and exposure of the parent organization. The authorities associate Colombians, Nigerians, and Turks with organized drug trafficking, making them targets for customs officials at national borders; East European nationals do not yet suffer that stigma. Heroin and cocaine are increasingly prevalent in northeastern Europe and even in Russia en route to markets in the West. In February 1993 almost 1.1 tons of cocaine was seized by Russian customs officials in Vyborg near the Russian-Finnish border.

Confronting increasingly out-of-control drug traffic, police and public health officials from Warsaw to Bishkek desperately need outside anti-drug assistance. But the region receives miserly antinarcotics assistance, and both Washington—mired in an expensive and unproductive cocaine war in the Andes—and in Vienna, where United Nations Drug Control Programs (UNDCP) is located, have viewed drugs in postcommunist societies as an exotic and essentially tangential problem. Of $213 million requested by the State Department for international narcotics control in fiscal year (FY) 1996, only $4 million was estimated for Eastern Europe and the former Soviet Union. This is precisely where an early warning function should sound an alarm, while the problem appears relatively manageable (certainly when compared with other areas of the world—Southeast Asia, South America, Mexico). The marginal impact of sending drug-fighting assistance to the Central American countries—where opium cultivation still covers only a few Thailand hectares—could be much greater than that of sending the same resources to the Andean countries, where coca extends over more than 200,000 hectares and where approximately $1 billion in U.S. funding since 1989 has failed to make a dent in cocaine production.

Conclusion

Nations now have an opportunity to explore new approaches in international narcotics policy, assessing the successes, partial successes, and outright failures of the various measures with which they have experimented over the past quarter century. Past failure and general budget constraints will require a redefinition of priorities. Total U.S. foreign assistance for all narcotics-related programs dropped forty percent between FY 1993 and FY 1995. The test to determine whether to undertake antinarcotics measures should not simply be whether overall drug flows are reduced; truncating the economic and political reach of drug dealers and their criminal cohorts is in itself a worthwhile objective. The question remains what combination of measures produces the maximum range of impacts within the limits of resources that U.S. taxpayers are willing to provide. Even if reducing domestic demand—rather than the chimera of reducing foreign supply—constitutes the long-term solution to the drug problem in consuming countries, a notion to which even the United States now pays lip service, Washington and other Western capitals can still apply their resources internationally to good effect, destabilizing the malevolent drug lords that threaten the stability of nations in Latin America and elsewhere.

A pragmatic international policy—both by the United States on a bilateral basis and by the UNDCP—would expend fewer resources on the traditional, strategies of interdiction, eradication, and (unless viable markets exist for replacement crops) crop substitution, including less emphasis on a U.S. military presence in the front lines in guerrilla-torn countries such as Columbia and Peru, and focus more on dismantling the leadership structures of multinational trafficking organizations and bolstering the criminal justice institutions, the political will, and legal economies of drug-source countries. Outside law enforcement personnel—either in a UN capacity or, as in many U.S. anti-drug assistance programs, as agents deputed directly by their governments—can help host countries probe traffickers' political linkages and expose instances of high-level corruption (assuming top government officials want such corruption exposed and suppressed). U.S. guidance and intelligence support could undergird negotiating or plea-bargaining strategies that allow drug kingpins the possibility of eventually reentering society in return for dismantling their illegal businesses. Well-designed foreign aid packages also can help foster sustained economic growth, eventually diminishing drug kingpins' relative economic influence and their access to governing elites. Much also would need to be done to shape popular attitudes against drugs in the Andes, Southeast Asia, and elsewhere, convincing leaders and relevant publics that narcodollars are not worth the damage they cause to national institutions and to the society at large.

In addition, some resources might be better spent on developing a more effective antinarcotics presence in the increasingly important but politically troubled former Soviet states, as well as in China and Vietnam. Perhaps international drug policy cannot substantially curtail drug trafficking where it has entrenched itself, but supply-side efforts can be reconfigured to promote stability and growth in the victimized countries, strengthen the social fabric, and expand U.S. influence in beneficent ways.

Finally, a word about the oft-debated subject of legalization. Advocates, of course, argue that legalization—by removing the enormous profits now associated with drug smuggling, wholesaling, and distribution—would undercut the economic power of the narcotics mafias; at the same time governments could earn significant revenues by taxing legal narcotics businesses. Expectations about the positive benefits of legalization, though, possibly are misplaced—particularly where drug-source countries are concerned. In an international regime of legalization, the United States—having access to the most advanced plant genetics, agricultural technology, and processing methods—probably would emerge as the world's most efficient producer of illicit drugs. That is, Third World producers would have a difficult time competing with the United States. A country such as Colombia, which has a strong "comparative advantage" in drug refining and smuggling, would be especially unlikely to benefit under such a regime.

A second caveat concerns the effects of legalization on the organized criminal formations that now produce and sell illicit drugs. While the illegality of drugs was instrumental in the development of these formations (as legalization supporters correctly argue), it does not follow that legalization will result in their demise. Consider the example of Prohibition: American organized crime clearly received a major boost from Prohibition; when alcohol was again made legal and the mafia lost effective monopoly over liquor sales, though, criminals simply expanded into other illegal activities—such as gambling, loan sharking, extortion, murder-for-hire and, of course, drugs. Similarly, in Colombia and Pakistan—countries that have powerful criminal coalitions engaged in refining and

smuggling drugs—legalization would not stop crime (criminals, after all, have developed new lifestyles and expectations from their illegal occupations) but would shift the locus of criminality to other, possibly equally dangerous areas. Legalization then is not necessarily an antidote to organized crime (although street crime and burglaries by addicts seeking the wherewithal to pay for their habit undoubtedly would diminish). At the same time, narcotics policymakers in both developing and developed countries must recognize the potential costs of such a step, calculated in terms of increased addiction, a worsening public health picture, diminished work performance, and a general human degradation.

RENSSELAER W. LEE III

See also Bolivia; Colombia; Drug Enforcement Agency; Noriega, Manuel Antonio; Peru

FURTHER READING

Clawson, Patrick, and Rensselaer Lee. *The Andean Cocaine Industry.* New York, 1996.
Congressional Budget Office. *The Andean Initiative, Objectives and Support.* Washington, D.C., 1994.
Corr, Edwin. "Rubik's Cube, Manwaring's Paradigm for the Gray Area Phenomenon and a New Strategy for International Narcotics Control." In *Gray Area Phenomena: Confronting the New World Disorder.* Boulder, Colo., 1993.
Levitsky, Melvin. "U.S. Foreign Policy and International Narcotics Control: Challenges and Opportunities in the 1990s and Beyond." In *Drugs and Foreign Policy, A Critical Review*, edited by Raphael. Boulder, Colo., 1994.
U.S. Department of State. *International Narcotics Control Strategy Report.* Washington, D.C., 1996.
Walker, William W. "U.S. Narcotics Foreign Policy in the 20th Century, An Analytical Overview." In *Drugs and Foreign Policy, A Critical Review*, edited by Raphael. Boulder, Colo., 1994.

NASA

See National Aeronautics and Space Administration

NASSER, GAMAL ABDEL

(*b.* 15 January 1918; *d.* 28 September 1970)

Egyptian army officer and president from 1952 to 1970, who was a prominent nationalist and international statesman. Gamal Abdel Nasser became a major figure in Middle Eastern politics and contested the interests sought by the United States in the region. His relationship with Washington evolved from friendship in the early 1950s to rivalry and mutual mistrust. An army officer by training, Nasser turned to politics to address what he considered his country's three principal enemies: the British Empire, the monarchy under King Farouk, and the Zionist movement that led to the creation of Israel. A devoted nationalist all his life, Nasser participated in a series of anti-British demonstrations as a schoolboy. In 1936 British gunfire wounded him during a rally against the Anglo-Egyptian treaty of that year. Later, he deplored the Farouk regime for its corruption, incompetence, and subservience to London. In the Palestine War, Nasser distinguished himself as the commander of the Egyptian garrison besieged at Falluja from October 1948 to January 1949. Egypt's bitter defeat in that war convinced him that the army had to act to overthrow the king and modernize the country. Through the Free Officers group, a secret society of army malcontents, Nasser conspired against Farouk and staged a successful coup d'etat in July 1952. In 1954, he wrested power from General Mohammed Naguib, a rival within the Free Officers clique, and emerged as president and prime minister of Egypt. A true son of the people, beholden to no foreign interests, Nasser attracted widespread public adulation in his country.

Initially, U.S. officials eagerly embraced the rebels after they overthrew the monarchy. The United States deterred Great Britain from reversing the revolution, sustained the new government with moral and material aid, and encouraged Nasser's domestic reform programs as well as the suppression of the Communists and the reactionary Muslim Brotherhood. The Dwight D. Eisenhower administration helped negotiate the 1954 Anglo-Egyptian base treaty, which provided for the gradual departure of British military forces from Egypt. Nasser cultivated personal friendships with U.S. officials, such as Kermit Roosevelt of the Central Intelligence Agency (CIA). In the middle 1950s, however, Nasser's relations with Washington soured. Eisenhower refused to provide Nasser with arms, as implicitly promised, after he had signed the Anglo-Egyptian treaty, because supplying weapons would, it was felt, spark a regional arms race and undermine Western efforts to negotiate an Arab-Israeli peace treaty. Nasser in turn adopted a foreign policy opposing western imperialism and promoting the spread of Egyptian influence in the Middle East and Africa. He resisted U.S. pressure to join a Western-oriented regional defense pact and emerged as a leading critic of the Baghdad Pact (signed 24 February 1955), because it sustained British influence and enhanced the position of his political rival, Iraqi Premier Nuri al-Said. Nasser also attended the Conference of Non-Aligned Peoples at Bandung in April 1955. U.S. relations with Nasser turned bitter in 1955–1956 over issues pertaining to Egyptian security. On 28 February 1955, only four days after the signing of the Baghdad Pact, Israeli forces conducted a devastating and humiliating raid on the Egyptian army outpost at Gaza. Nasser desperately sought U.S. weapons to defend his forces and his political reputation. Repeatedly denied arms by the United States, he instead purchased Soviet

weapons in September 1955. Eisenhower administration officials urged him to repudiate the deal. Nasser refused, and Soviet weapons began to reach Cairo in late 1955.

To deter Nasser from making additional deals with Moscow, the United States offered to arrange Western financing of a substantial portion of the projected Aswan High Dam. But Nasser refused to submit to the conditions that the United States and Great Britain attached, and he continued to goad Washington by accepting additional Soviet weapons and recognizing the People's Republic of China. In July 1956 Washington and London abruptly withdrew their offers to fund the dam; whereupon Nasser nationalized the Suez Canal Company and announced that its revenues would finance the dam. That move provoked the Suez Crisis, during which Eisenhower's relationship with Nasser languished, even though Washington rescued Nasser from Anglo-French-Israeli aggression. From 1957 to 1958, Eisenhower's relations with Nasser remained cool. Nasser sought to generate a Pan-Arab political movement by merging Egypt and Syria in the United Arab Republic (UAR). He accepted additional arms and aid for the Aswan High Dam from Moscow. He broadcast propaganda through the Voice of the Arabs radio network to disparage Western interests in the region and to undermine the pro-Western regimes of Iraq, Jordan, and Lebanon. In return, the United States backed Jordan's King Hussein, and after radicals overthrew the Hashemite dynasty in Baghdad in July 1958 U.S. and British forces occupied Lebanon and Jordan.

Eisenhower and Nasser repaired their strained relationship somewhat during 1959–1960. Nasser quarreled with the Soviets over the spread of communism in the Arab world and grew particularly enraged by Moscow's encouragement of communist activity in the Iraqi revolution. As U.S. forces departed Lebanon in late 1958, Nasser also grew suspicious of Iraqi leader Abdul Karim Qassim. He became receptive to Eisenhower's suggestions that Cairo accept U.S. food aid and that the two states place questions pertaining to Israel "in the icebox." President John F. Kennedy tried, but ultimately failed, to strengthen the rapprochement begun by Eisenhower. Kennedy expanded the food aid program and extended the "icebox" agreement, and the two presidents exchanged many personal letters. Each seemed to identify with the other's youthful zest, machismo, and idealism. But U.S. efforts to arm Israel angered Nasser. He accused the United States of complicity in the murder of Patrice Lumumba in the Congo in January 1961, and he suspected the CIA of encouraging the withdrawal of Syria from the UAR later the same year. Recurrent congressional appeals for an end to food aid annoyed the Egyptian president. Kennedy's opposition to Nasser's deployment of tens of thousands of Egyptian troops to Yemen in 1962 signaled a sharp downturn in their relationship. The situation worsened during the presidency of Lyndon B. Johnson. Nasser criticized additional U.S. arms exports to Israel and condemned Johnson's policies in the Congo and Vietnam. Johnson criticized Nasser's continuing military involvement in Yemen and protested a series of incidents harmful to U.S. citizens in Egypt, most notably a mob torching of the United States Information Agency office in Cairo in November 1964. When Nasser insulted Johnson, the U.S. president suspended food aid shipments. Johnson had tried to woo Nasser through personal diplomacy, but Nasser had reacted with contempt.

The Arab-Israeli War of June 1967 deepened the animosity between Nasser and the United States. The enormity of the Egyptian defeat—and the Israeli occupation of the Sinai—embarrassed Nasser, and he doubted that Israel by itself had the capability to inflict the casualties Egypt suffered. The legacy of Anglo-French collusion with Israel in the 1956 Suez Crisis led Nasser to charge that the United States had secretly participated in the most recent Israeli attack, most notably that U.S. aircraft carriers in the Mediterranean launched the Israeli warplanes that devastated his armed forces early in the war. On 6 June 1967 Nasser severed diplomatic relations with Washington and expelled thousands of U.S. citizens from Egypt after the war. Nasser continued to loathe Washington for supporting Israel during his "war of attrition" against Israeli emplacements along the Suez Canal (1967–1970). He once again eagerly accepted Soviet weapons, and by 1968 had replenished the armaments lost in the 1967 war and welcomed 3,000 Soviet military advisers. Nasser visited Moscow in 1970 and secured antiaircraft rockets and military jets operated by Soviet servicemen.

In mid-1970, however, Nasser's and President Richard M. Nixon's aims converged. Nixon eagerly sought to end the Arab-Israeli war of attrition in order to stabilize the region. Stymied by the Arab-Israeli war, Nasser in turn hoped to use Nixon to persuade Israel to return the Sinai without additional fighting. Nasser endorsed a U.S. plan that included a cease-fire and a compromise peace agreement. When fighting erupted between the Palestine Liberation Organization (PLO) and Jordan in September 1970, Nasser served as an arbiter. But by now the physical stress was taking a serious toll on Nasser's health, a situation compounded by earlier medical problems. In the fall of 1970, immediately following a meeting with King Hussein, Nasser suffered a fatal heart attack. His death closed a tumultous era in Egyptian history and U.S.-Egyptian relations.

PETER L. HAHN

See also Central Treaty Organization; Egypt; Eisenhower, Dwight David; Eisenhower Doctrine; Israel; Johnson, Lydon Baines; Kennedy, John Fitzgerald; Middle East; Nonaligned Movement; Palestine Liberation Organization; Palestine (to 1948); Suez Crisis

FURTHER READING

Heikal, Mohamed Hassanein. *The Cairo Documents: The Inside Story of Nasser and His Relationship with World Leaders, Rebels, and Statesmen.* Garden City, N.J., 1973.
Lacouture, Jean. *Nasser: A Biography.* New York, 1973.
Woodward, Peter. *Nasser.* London, 1992.

NATIONAL AERONAUTICS AND SPACE ADMINISTRATION

Created by the 1958 Space Act, which was signed 29 July 1958. In the aftermath of the Soviet launch of the first artificial satellite, *Sputnik I*, on 4 October 1957, the Eisenhower administration chose to separate civilian and national security space activities and to create the National Aeronautics and Space Administration (NASA) as a new agency to manage the civilian space program. President John F. Kennedy decided in 1961, after the Soviet launch of the first spaceship with a human crew, to commit the United States to sending people to the moon before 1970. NASA became the focus of an almost warlike mobilization of human and financial resources; at its peak in the mid-1960s, the NASA budget of $5.2 million was nearly 4 percent of the U.S. gross domestic product (GDP). Competition between the United States and the Soviet Union continued to provide the major political underpinning for NASA's programs after the *Apollo* program was successfully completed; *Apollo* spacecraft made six trips to the moon between July 1969 and December 1972. However, no single goal gave focus to the civilian space effort, and its overall priority declined over the next two decades. In the mid-1990s, the NASA budget was less than 0.25 percent of the U.S. GDP; even so, the agency's budget remained substantial, with a 1996 level of $13.6 billion. With the end of the Cold War and the space race, NASA had to find a new rationale for its activities. The agency has a Washington, D.C., headquarters and eight "field centers," each specializing in a particular aspect of the aeronautics and space efforts. Over 90 percent of the NASA budget is spent outside the organization: in industry and at universities. NASA employed approximately 20,500 persons in 1996, down from 36,000 at the peak of the *Apollo* program.

JOHN M. LOGSDON

See also Cold War; Eisenhower, Dwight David; Kennedy, John Fitzgerald; Space Policy; Sputnik I; Strategic Defense Initiative

FURTHER READING

Report of the Committee on the Future of the U.S. Space Program (Norman Augustine, Chair). Washington: Government Printing Office, December 1990.
McCurdy, Howard E. *Inside NASA: High Technology and Organizational Change in the U.S. Space Program.* Baltimore, 1993.

NATIONAL ASSOCIATION OF MANUFACTURERS

Founded in 1895 in Cincinnati, Ohio, by small business owners that, since the 1920s, has represented and promoted the views of large manufacturers on domestic economic and international trade issues. The National Association of Manufacturers (NAM) is headquartered in Washington, D.C., and its membership consists of more than 12,000 large industries, accounting for 85 percent of U.S. manufacturing output. NAM is also affiliated with 150 state and local trade associations of manufacturers. With a staff of 180 operating under a $14 million dollar budget, NAM reviews and attempts to influence governmental legislation, administrative rulings, and judicial decisions affecting the manufacturing industry. It also maintains public affairs and public relations programs for communicating its views throughout the government and society. NAM usually takes conservative positions, championing free enterprise with little or no regulation by government—opposing, for example, most of the New Deal legislation of the 1930s and the Clean Air Act of 1970. NAM has also supported more aggressive export policies by the U.S. government, including the North American Free Trade Agreement (NAFTA) between Canada, Mexico, and the United States.

JEREL A. ROSATI

See also International Trade and Commerce

FURTHER READING

Burch, Philip H., Jr. "The NAM as an Interest Group." *Politics and Society* (Fall 1973): 97–130.

Steigerwalt, Albert K. *The National Association of Manufacturers, 1895–1914*. Ann Arbor, Mich., 1964.

NATIONAL DEFENSE EDUCATION ACT

(1958)

Signed into law in 1958, the National Defense Education Act (NDEA) focused on swift improvement of the U.S. school system, after the Soviet Union's launch of *Sputnik I*. In the years immediately following World War II, the United States held an unchallenged position of technological superiority over other nations. The successful development of the atomic bomb was fresh in citizens' minds, and most assumed that, despite the uncertainties of the new Cold War era of brinksmanship and confrontation, U.S. society remained strong and capable of meeting any external threat. A prevalent (if unvoiced) assumption was the complete adequacy of the educational system to prepare the scientists and technicians who were essential to maintaining a necessary strategic and scientific edge over the Soviet bloc. This assumption was rudely dispelled on 4 October 1957, with the Soviet Union's launch of *Sputnik*, the first artificial satellite. National response to this publicly visible and audible sign of advanced space technology where none had been assumed ranged from paranoia regarding future attack to close evaluation of contributing factors not previously assessed. Particular attention focused on improving the school system at all levels, which took legislative form as the NDEA. This emphasis on better education was grounded in a misperception: The surprise of advanced Soviet technology presupposed a system of general education superior to that of the United States. The Act contains ten titles, each promoting skills seen as essential to the national defense. Topics addressed include financial assistance for strengthening instruction in science, mathematics, and foreign languages (including establishing research centers specializing in specific regions); the creation of National Defense fellowships to more widely distribute graduate programs; effective use of all forms of media in education; expansion of vocational education in science and technology; establishment of a Science Information Service; and improvement in testing and guidance counseling. Title X also contains provision for adequate statistical reporting and a loyalty oath required of all fund recipients. The specific categories of aid to be provided to local schools sharply depart from previous government legislation relating to education; such legislation dealt only with broad subject fields such as the social sciences. The NDEA is part of a historical concern with the quality of U.S. education, a concern that reaches back to the earliest years of the republic. The NDEA closely defines those skills seen as vital to the maintenance of national security. While successful in stimulating a resurgence in technological and scientific education, the NDEA formed the basis for charges by 1960s campus radicals that higher education in the United States was merely a source for workers for the military-industrial complex that supported the Defense Department.

ROBERT B. MARKS RIDINGER

See also Cold War; Russia and the Soviet Union; Space Policy; Sputnick I

FURTHER READING

Clowse, Barbara Barksdale. *Brainpower for the Cold War: The Sputnik Crisis and National Defense Education Act of 1958*. Westport, Conn., 1981.

Kaestle, Carl F., and Marshall S. Smith. "The Federal Role in Elementary and Secondary Education, 1940–1980." *Harvard Educational Review*, 52 (November, 1982):384–408.

Sufrin, Sidney C. *Administering the National Defense Education Act*. Syracuse, N.Y., 1963.

NATIONAL ENDOWMENT FOR DEMOCRACY

A private, Washington-based organization, primarily funded by the U.S. government, dedicated to promoting democracy abroad. The Endowment funds programs in Eastern Europe, the former Soviet Union, Latin America, Asia, Africa, and the Middle East related to the fostering or strengthening of democratic institutions and values, including efforts to support constitutional reform, free and fair elections, political party development, independent trade unions, human rights advocacy, civic education, and legislative strengthening.

The idea for a U.S. democracy endowment was developed in the 1970s by a small group in Washington, including Congressman Dante Fascell, Lane Kirkland of the AFL-CIO, William Brock of the Republican Party, Charles Manatt of the Democratic Party, and George Agree, a social scientist. Promoting democracy, they believed, was an essential means of fighting communism abroad, and a publicly funded, nongovernmental organization (loosely modeled on the German political party foundations) could do the task more effectively than a governmental one, given foreign sensitivities about U.S. government interventionism.

The plan this group developed was positively received by President Ronald Reagan and his foreign policy aides in the early 1980s; it fit well with the Reagan administration's interest in fighting more actively the "war of ideas" with the Soviet Union. In 1983, after some deliberation, Congress approved the Reagan administration's proposal for the establishment of the National Endowment for Democracy, giving it an initial annual budget of $18 million. The NED has operated continuously since 1984 with annual budgets generally ranging between $25 million and $35 million.

The Endowment has a complex, multipartisan structure, reflecting the diverse roots of its founders as well as their intention of crafting an organization that would attract wide support in Congress. The Endowment has four core grantees: the Free Trade Union Institute (FTUI), the Center for International Private Enterprise (CIPE), the National Democratic Institute for International Affairs (NDI), and the International Republican Institute (IRI)—affiliated respectively with the AFL-CIO, the U.S. Chamber of Commerce, the Democratic Party, and the Republican Party.

These grantees receive the bulk of NED's funds. For many years, FTUI received a larger share of NED funds; in recent years the core grantees have all received approximately the same funding from NED. They also receive funding from the U.S. Agency for International Development (USAID), funding that in recent years has often exceeded the monies they receive from the NED.

Each of the core grantees specializes in a particular area of democracy promotion. FTUI works with the AFL-CIO's other international outreach organizations to support the development or strengthening of independent trade unions in other countries. Its work is a continuation of the union-building work that the AFL-CIO has pursued abroad for many decades. During the Cold War, the AFL-CIO's international work had a strong anticommunist orientation. Since 1989, it has functioned under the general rationale that independent trade unions are an essential part of a democratic society.

CIPE promotes private enterprise and free market economic policies in other countries through a variety of programs. CIPE advises on economic law reform, trains business journalists, strengthens business associations, and promotes the teaching of private entrepreneurship. Its local partners are usually economic policy institutes devoted to research and advocacy favoring free market economic reforms. CIPE's work is based on the dual proposition that free market economic policies are a universal good and that the pursuit of such policies reinforces prodemocratic transitions.

The two political party institutes concentrate on fostering democratic political processes. The main emphases of their work are promoting free and fair elections, bolstering political party development, strengthening civic education, and assisting parliaments. Although the programs that the two institutes carry out are similar in type, they do differ with respect to their approach to political party development. NDI generally follows a multipartisan approach in which all parties in a country are invited to take part. IRI sometimes takes this approach but in some cases, as in many Latin American countries and in parts of Eastern Europe and the former Soviet Union, follows or has followed a partisan approach of backing one particular party or group of parties whose ideology it believes is compatible with its own.

In addition to its payments to the four core grantees, NED also has a category of what it refers to as "discretionary funding," which goes to other organizations. The discretionary share of NED's funding has increased in the past several years and now represents approximately 30 percent of NED's funding. NED's discretionary funding generally consists of small (under $50,000) direct grants to foreign organizations, usually nongovernmental organizations working in the areas of human rights, independent media, or democratic education. Unlike the core grantees's programs, NED's discretionary funding is often aimed at nondemocratic countries, such as China, Cuba, and Iraq.

The National Endowment's work is one part of the striking growth of U.S.-funded assistance programs oriented toward promoting democracy abroad that has occurred since the early 1980s. Although USAID is a much larger actor in this field, with the total amount of its democracy programming generally exceeding the NED's by a factor of between five and ten, the NED has often attracted more attention from Congress, the media, and the policy community. Congress, in particular, has frequently debated the NED's work and has held several close votes over the years on the question of whether to continue funding for it.

Debates over the NED tend to center around several issues. The first is NED's status as an international affairs organization that on the one hand is private, with an independent board of directors and staff, and yet on the other hand, is almost entirely funded by the U.S. government. Critics call this a constitutional anomaly representing a dangerous "privatization" of U.S. foreign policy. Supporters reply that the U.S. government underwrites many private organizations involved in economic and political assistance abroad, and that the NED arrangement is neither exceptional nor dangerous. They also point out that NED operates in an entirely transparent fashion and that the Department of State can stop any NED programs it thinks are inconsistent with U.S. policy.

A second issue concerns possible redundancy between the NED's work and USAID's democracy-related programming. Critics charge that there is substantial duplication in the activities of the two organizations and that in a period of declining governmental budgets, the NED should be streamlined out of existence. Supporters counter that the NED differs in important ways from USAID, arguing that as a nongovernmental organization, the NED has greater flexibility to pursue democracy promotion activities in politically sensitive areas, such as China. They also assert that the NED is less bureaucratic than USAID, and that its leaner structure results in more innovative programs and a better ability to respond to fast-breaking situations.

A third point of contention is the question of whether the NED is, in the words of its critics, a "Cold War relic." NED's detractors dismiss the organization as an anachronistic holdover from the Reagan years that lives on only because of its close ties to powerful interests in Congress, especially the Democratic and Republican parties and the AFL-CIO. Proponents of NED highlight the fact that both the Bush and Clinton administrations have made democracy promotion a major element of their foreign policies and argue that the NED is an important tool in furthering this post–Cold War U.S. policy objective.

THOMAS CAROTHERS

See also Agency for International Development; Cold War

FURTHER READING

Carothers, Thomas. "The NED at 10." *Foreign Policy* 95 (Summer 1994): 123–138.
———. *Assessing Democracy Assistance: The Case of Romania.* Washington D.C., 1996.
Diamond, Larry. *Promoting Democracy in the 1990s.* Washington D.C., 1995.
Muravchik, Joshua. "U.S. Political Parties Abroad." *The Washington Quarterly* 12 (Summer 1989): 91–100.
National Endowment for Democracy. *Annual Report.* Washington D.C., 1995.
Pinto-Duschinsky, Michael. "Foreign Political Aid: The German Political Foundations and their U.S. Counterparts." *International Affairs* 67 (January 1991): 33–63.

NATIONAL SECURITY ACT

Passed by Congress in July 1947, the National Security Act was the most sweeping postwar reorganization of the U.S. national security bureaucracy. The act emerged from debates over the possible unification of the armed services and from concerns about the ability of foreign policymakers and the military to cope with the problems of the Cold War. In particular, the military services' command structure had been coordinated only through informal arrangements during World War II, and after the war ended a more secure and permanent arrangement was necessary. The National Security Act created several new agencies to coordinate the efforts of such existing bodies as the National Security Council (NSC), which was to improve interdepartmental coordination on defense and foreign policy matters; and the National Security Resources Board, which was to develop plans for economic mobilization in the event of war. The National Security Act also created the Central Intelligence Agency (CIA). The CIA, which succeeded the informally organized Central Intelligence Group created immediately after World War II, was to serve as the principal civilian source of foreign intelligence for the president and other executive branch decision-makers.

The act also reorganized military departments and provided for greater coordination between them. The National Security Act merged the War Department and the Navy Department into a new National Military Establishment (NME), headed by a secretary of defense. President Harry S. Truman appointed James Forrestal as the first to fill this position. The NME included the Department of the Army and the Department of the Navy, as well as the new Department of the Air Force, now officially designated as an independent military service. A number of other defense-related agencies created during World War II, such as the Munitions Board and the Research and Development Board, were also placed under the authority of the secretary of defense. The NME proved to be unworkable, however, because the secretary of defense did not have clear authority over the secretaries of the army, navy, and air force and could do little more than encourage them to cooperate. The National Security Act was amended in 1949 to correct this problem, replacing the NME with the Department of Defense and establishing the secretary of defense's authority over the secretaries of the three services.

The National Security Act also established the NSC to coordinate the activities of all executive branch departments concerned with national security. NSC members are the president, the vice president, the secretary of state, and the secretary of defense. Other major foreign policy officials, such as the CIA director and the chair of the joint chiefs of staff, are not statutory members but do frequently participate in NSC meetings. The NSC has a staff and an assistant to the president for national security affairs. The latter is referred to as the national security adviser. The position was not created by the 1947 act, but rather was added in 1953.

BENJAMIN FORDHAM

See also National Security Agency; National Security Council

FURTHER READING

Caraley, Demetrios. *The Politics of Military Unification: A Study of Conflict and the Policy Process.* New York, 1966.
Leffler, Melvyn. *A Preponderance of Power: National Security, the Truman Administration, and the Cold War.* Stamford, Conn., 1992.
Rearden, Stephen L. *History of the Office of the Secretary of Defense: The Formative Years, 1947-1950.* Washington, D.C., 1984.

NATIONAL SECURITY AGENCY

Established in 1952, primarily to decode and analyze foreign signals and communications and to protect U.S. secret communications systems from similar action by other countries. The National Security Agency's (NSA's) formation reflects national security managers' determination that there never be another intelligence failure like the one that enabled Japan to attack Pearl Harbor in 1941. The NSA's mandate is quite broad and includes the interception and analysis of all signals and communications intelligence. The agency employs cryptographers, linguists, scientists, and engineers who have the technical skills to acquire, decode, and translate information from all over the world. The NSA operates an extensive network of spy satellites in conjunction with the Central Intelligence Agency (CIA) through the National Reconnaissance Office and maintains electronic listening posts in the United States and elsewhere. Although it is believed to have the most employees and the largest budget of all intelligence agencies, the NSA is among the least open of all U.S. government entities and relatively little is known about its activities. In 1959, Congress granted the NSA a special exemption from all requirements that it reveal any information concerning its mission, activities, or employees. The NSA is headquartered in a thousand acre complex in Fort Meade, Maryland. Its director is traditionally a high-ranking military officer. The agency has organizations and several smaller units

providing support, staff, and training facilities. The operational units are in the Office of Signals Intelligence, which carries out the agency's primary functions the Office of Communications Security, which develops codes for U.S. use; the Office of Research and Engineering, which develops eavesdropping and signals interception equipment; and the Office of Telecommunications and Computer Services, which manages the agency's computer facilities, some of the fastest and most sophisticated machines available, used primarily for decoding intercepted information. The 1975 Church Committee Hearings on domestic spying revealed that the NSA maintained files on American citizens thought to be subversive, ostensibly in case they sought federal employment. Many of these files, collected under the Federal Employee Loyalty Program, contained personal information gained through the agency's signals and communications collection apparatus, especially through intercepted telephone conversations. This information was passed along to the Federal Bureau of Investigation (FBI) and other interested government agencies. Surveillance was also directed against prominent Americans opposed to the Vietnam War who were placed on "watch lists" submitted to the NSA by other government agencies. Unlike the CIA, the NSA has no statutory prohibition against operating within the United States. However, following the Church Committee Hearings, these activities were ordered stopped.

BENJAMIN FORDHAM

See also Central Intelligence Agency; National Security Act; National Security Council

FURTHER READING

Bamford, James. *The Puzzle Palace: A Report on America's Most Secret Agency.* Boston, 1982.
Volkman, Ernest, and Blaine Baggett. *Secret Intelligence.* New York, 1989.
U.S. Senate, Select Committee to Study Government Operations with respect to Intelligence Activities. *Hearings on Intelligence Activities*, vol. 5. The National Security Agency and Fourth Amendment Rights. 94th Congress, 1st Session, 1975.

NATIONAL SECURITY AND NATIONAL DEFENSE

National security is the business of defending core national interests from external threats, chiefly threats of a coercive nature and reflecting a predatory intent. National security draws its distinct character from the international context within which it is pursued. From the perspective of any country's security, the international system's most notable feature is the absence of commonly accepted norms of conduct and of a political authority capable of preventing aggression or, at least, of ensuring that it will not go unpunished. In other words, what distinguishes "national" security from the security of individuals and groups is that the former must be sought in conditions of quasi-anarchy, principally via reliance on a nation's own actions and power. National insecurity is tempered by the military deterrence of potential enemies, by networks of international commercial and financial interdependence, by a rudimentary body of international law, and by certain widely accepted cultural norms. Still, the fact of quasi-anarchy, stemming from principles of autonomous national decisions, is a defining feature of the international system. The primacy of national security in a quasi-anarchic world springs from the fact that so much of what societies value is contingent upon its attainment, and, while some nations feel far more secure than others, objective external threats tend to generate similar responses.

Definitions

Like public interest and national welfare, national security both defines an objective and provides a standard against which policy can be judged. Much like the other two concepts, the murkiness of its content has made it more suited to purposes of rhetoric than analysis; it must be given firmer meaning if it is to provide a useful guide to policy evaluation.

Definitions vary greatly. Political scientist Gabriel Almond defines national security as the business of "the allocation of resources for the production, deployment, and employment of what we may call the coercive facilities which a nation uses in pursuing its interests." In this view, then, national security is an *enterprise* essentially related to coercive capabilities; it is a process, not a state of affairs.

A much broader definition is offered by former Secretary of Defense Harold Brown, who describes national security as: "the ability to preserve the nation's physical integrity and territory; to maintain its economic relations with the rest of the world on reasonable terms; to protect its nature, institutions, and governance from disruption from outside, and to control its borders." Here, national security is an attribute, the ability to fend off external threats to interests central to the nation's well-being, although the boundaries of these interests are quite vaguely defined (for instance, maintaining "economic relations with the rest of the world on reasonable terms.")

Even more expansive is the definition offered by Richard Allen, former White House national security adviser, who maintains that the concept "must include virtually every facet of international activity, including (but not limited to) foreign affairs, defense, intelligence, research, and development policy, and reaching even into the domains of the Departments of Commerce and Agriculture. In a word, 'national security' must reflect the presidential perspective, of which diplomacy is but a single component." There is little that could not be squeezed into Allen's definition; by extending it too far, the concept is made virtually meaningless.

Despite the variety of definitions, a common core of meaning seems to run through most references to national security. Whether viewed as a process, an objective, or a state of affairs, most uses of the term refer to the protection of core national interests from external threats. The concept is thus defined by the interests whose security may be threatened and by the sorts of threats to which they are subjected.

Three broad categories of core interests are generally encompassed by national security, each of which can, in principle, be threatened from abroad. First and most obvious is the *physical security* of the nation's citizens and of their private and collective possessions. This is what we think of most often when the threats in question are of a military nature, and this is what the military capacity of most nations is designed to protect against. The *rules and institutions* that the nation has chosen to live by, especially its constitutional and legal order, represent the second type of interest encompassed by national security. While these rules and institutions may well be subject to military threats, they can be undermined from the outside by subversive means as well. The third interest includes the sources of the nation's *prosperity*—capital resources, raw materials, financial system, and so forth. While a nation's prosperity can be menaced by military or subversive methods, external economic blows or pressures, such as trade sanctions, are the main dangers to which it is generally exposed.

It has been suggested that the health of the environment be included among the core interests encompassed by national security, but this does not seem appropriate. Although the integrity of the national environment is central to the national *interest*, and although it can be threatened from abroad, such threats are usually the by-product of the economic activity of other nations—not the expression of a coercive threat or of predatory intent.

Applied to national security, the term "threat" has a two-dimensional meaning. On the one hand, it refers to the *likelihood* that the interests in question would be assaulted. On the other hand, it refers to the damage or *costs* to these interests that would result from the assault, should it occur. If either were extremely low, the threat to national security could not be very serious. No matter how high the likelihood of an assault, national security is not seriously imperilled if the anticipated costs are minute. By the same token, if the probability of an assault approaches zero, the threat to national security becomes increasingly trivial, no matter how high the theoretical damage could be.

Accordingly, national security is a state of affairs characterized either, and preferably both, by a very low *likeli-*

hood of external assaults on the nation's physical security, the rules and institutions it has chosen to live by, and the sources of its prosperity, and by the very low *costs* to the nation of such an assault, should it occur. National security policy is policy designed to achieve this objective; its success is measured by this standard.

A concept closely associated with national security is the concept of "national defense." Because national defense is directly related to military force, it is most usefully examined from this perspective. A helpful and fourfold characterization of the functions of military force is provided by political scientist Robert Art. In his view, a first purpose of military force is *defense*—protecting national security by fending off foreign military aggression and mitigating its consequences by countering the aggressor's armed force with one's own. The second function is *deterrence*—preventing an assault from occurring in the first place, typically by threatening retaliatory punishment. The third possible purpose is *compellence*—the actual or threatened application of military force to prevent another nation from pursuing some objective of its own (military or otherwise) or to force it do something it would not otherwise choose to do. The fourth function is *swaggering*, the acquisition of military capability for purposes of national prestige.

There are consequently three functions of military force that are logically distinct from national defense, although they may have practical implications for it. While swaggering is presumably irrelevant to defense (although, exceptionally, it might affect deterrence by impressing an adversary with one's power), compellence can, under very specific circumstances, contribute to defense (for example, by coercively removing from power a government sympathetic to one's aggressor, thus improving the prospects for a successful defense against that aggressor). Deterrence and defense, however, have natural points of intersection. Deterrence need not always operate via retaliatory threats, for it is also possible to discourage aggression by making its costs appear too high to the adversary, or by making the probability of successful aggression unacceptably low. Either objective can be achieved with a strong defensive capability (especially in the realm of conventional armaments). At the same time, defense may be rendered more effective by threatening retaliation for an extension of the aggression (by deterring it). Both defense and deterrence are directly related to the broader notion of national security. The relevance of national defense is, on the one hand, that it stands to minimize the costs of aggression should it occur; on the other hand, by increasing the adversary's estimate of the difficulty of aggression, a capacity for defense, like a capacity for deterrence through retaliation, decreases the likelihood that an assault would occur in the first place.

National Security and Military Capability

Because a capacity for both defense and deterrence tends to improve a nation's security, and since both require certain military capabilities, one might conclude that military power is directly related to national security; but the relation between the two is surprisingly indeterminate for several reasons.

Threats to the interests involved in national security need not be of a military nature. Where they are not (because the threats are economic or, perhaps, subversive), military power may be irrelevant to the peril, and other instruments of national security policy may be required. But increased military capacity may not enhance national security even with regard to military threats to key national interests. This is so because, assuming an initially hostile relationship between two countries, it is sometimes not possible to decrease both the likelihood of an external assault *and* its potential costs via military means.

The likelihood of external assaults by one nation on the key national interests of another depends substantially on the overall state of relations between the two. These relations, in turn, are shaped by an interactive process in which, very often, increases in one nation's security seem to imply an approximately equivalent decrease in the security of the other (a phenomenon often witnessed during the years of the U.S.-Soviet rivalry, or in the relations between Israel and the "front line" Arab nations). This conundrum, termed the "security dilemma," has several further implications. The tension that often accompanies arms races may count among its consequences an increased likelihood of preemptive strikes—as one nation contemplates the consequences for its own security of a more powerful adversary. At the same time, the associated mutual distrust may make it more difficult to resolve any objective conflicts of interest standing at the origin of the rivalry. In this way, the probability of conflict may be greater than had the initial addition to military capability not been sought. Improving one's ability to fight an aggressor may therefore either deter the aggression or, via its impact on mutual perceptions, make it more likely.

There is yet another reason why national security may not always be directly related to military capability: the greater a nation's power, the higher its level of aspiration in international politics—a tendency with two important implications. First, as power and aspirations increase, the range of issues that the country comes to identify with vital national interests expands—a tendency that has been termed the "Parkinson's Law" of national security. For example, a country capable of shaping the domestic political arrangements of other nations may, to a larger extent than a country incapable of doing so, come to identify the security of its own normative order with the maintenance of as many like-minded regimes as possible. Because of this, the greater the national power, as measured by military capacity, the greater the *sources* of possible insecurity. Second, as the range of a nation's interests expands in tandem with its power, there is a corresponding increase in the possibility of clashes occurring with regard to the interests of other countries on which this expansion impinges—increasing the probability of objective conflicts of interest between the contending nations and, by implication, increasing the threat they pose to one another. Finally, to the extent that the range of interests which must be protected are partly determined by the means available to defend them, a fluctuating and unstable conception of national security interests is more likely than when these interests are firmly rooted in an objective conception of the nation's well-being.

Thus, there is no simple and direct relation between military capacity and national security. On the one hand, armed might is associated with an expanding range of national interests that may be deemed vulnerable while, at the same time, increasing international tension and distrust (via the "security dilemma"). On the other hand, military strength stands to reduce the costs of any attempted assault on key national interests (by bolstering defensive capabilities) while, at the same time, making it less likely that such assaults would occur (by providing for credible deterrence).

Nor is there a set formula for determining what combination of military and non-military tools of national security policy are optimal. To a large extent, this depends on a given nation's geopolitical circumstances and historical traditions, and, in any case, the most confident answers to such questions are generally provided only with the benefit of hindsight.

Despite the military emphasis of national security policies during the Cold War decades, traditionally the United States has sought the protection of crucial national interests in a quasi-anarchic world through a policy of restrictive and selective involvements beyond its borders. This policy, often referred to as "isolationism," was advocated in Thomas Paine's injunction in *Common Sense* (1776) against ensnarement in the affairs of other nations (so that the new country could better protect its own interests, which were, in many ways, deemed purer than those of the European powers). It is also rooted in President George Washington's farewell address (1796), in which he argued against external commitments by which the United States would be tied to the fortunes of "foreign influence."

Despite the concept's connotations, isolationism as a U.S. foreign policy doctrine has not implied a withdrawal from the affairs of the world, but a very selective engagement in foreign affairs, driven exclusively by an assessment of U.S. interests—not by international obligations. The policy assumed a lack of international structure and predictability, for it implied that a stable coalition bound by a common purpose and consistent with U.S. interests could not be expected. By the same token, this policy implied that few nations could be considered total and permanent foes of the United States.

Diplomatic flexibility based on a pragmatic assessment of external challenges was thus the strategy on which U.S. national security rested during much of the nation's history. While foreign policy goals were occasionally pursued through armed coercion—as, for example, in Jefferson's naval expeditions against the Barbary States in the Mediterranean or the Spanish-American-Cuban-Filipino War in 1898, the emphasis on military power was traditionally far less than during the post-World War II decades. Most importantly, the nation's quasi-insular position and its militarily weak neighbors provided the geopolitical foundation for security at a time when no nation had substantial force projection capabilities and, with the exception of the skirmishes surrounding the War of 1812 (and, perhaps, the 1835 War with Mexico), the United States has been spared the threat of direct aggression from abroad.

As the United States attained the status of a major power in the late-nineteenth century, the world began to impinge on its interests more persistently than before. By the first half of this century the policy of isolationism was shaken by several major international tremors. Despite President Woodrow Wilson's hope that the United States could remain neutral in World War I, German U-boat attacks on U.S. merchant ships, as well as the growing conviction that the United States could play a role in shaping the postwar international order only if it participated as an active belligerent in support of the Triple Entente, led the United States, in April 1917, to join the war. Yet this embroilment in the affairs of the world was of limited duration. The Senate's refusal to adhere to the Versailles Treaty system, and the country's unwillingness to get involved in major efforts at creating a new world order, led to a foreign policy characterized, once again, by what has been termed "independent internationalism" during the Hoover administration—a policy of flexible disentanglement and selective engagement permitting a wide latitude for independence in foreign policy.

There is no doubt that the United States recognized the stakes involved in World War II, and its naval and air power played a decisive role in its outcome. But not many Americans initially regarded wartime involvement as portending a leading *postwar* role in the affairs of the world. Still, by the time of the Yalta summit, the notion of renewed isolationism, or even of an "independent internationalism," seemed increasingly chimeral. As the Cold War congealed in the early postwar years, as atomic weapons were introduced into the superpowers' arsenals, and as the image of a powerful and implacable foreign foe etched itself into U.S. political thinking, an entirely new conception of the threats to U.S. security, and of the proper way of addressing them, took root.

The Cold War and the New Culture of National Security

By 1947, the entrenchment of Soviet-style regimes in Poland, Romania, Yugoslavia, and Albania, and communism's imminence in Czechoslovakia and Hungary, settled, from the U.S. point of view, the question of whether the Soviet Union was an ineluctably expansionist nation. It became generally accepted that a historic struggle of indeterminate duration was under way.

The United States emerged from World War II as the world's strongest military power and with approximately half of the world's economic product. Nevertheless a powerful adversary, armed with atomic weapons, espousing an ideology antithetical to core U.S. beliefs and values, and claiming to have historical determinism on its side, made the United States feel more vulnerable than it had probably ever felt before. The U.S. response was its first explicit and open-ended rejection of isolationism and the acceptance of an approach to national security based predominantly on the acquisition and judicious exercise of military power.

The governmental structure needed to conduct an all-encompassing national-security policy was created. The National Security Act of 1947 reorganized the government's national security bureaucracy, creating: an integrated Department of Defense (previously each service was represented by its own Department), the Central Intelligence Agency (a successor to the wartime Office of Strategic Services and the first peacetime intelligence-gathering agency in U.S. history), and the National Security Council, whose function is to "advise the President with respect to the integration of domestic, foreign, and military policies relating to national security."

The Truman Doctrine, enunciated in March 1947, pledged U.S. support for "free peoples who are resisting attempted subjugation by armed minorities or by outside pressure." The Brussels Treaty in 1948, and the establishment of the North Atlantic Treaty Organization in the following year, provided the framework for Western military cooperation. By 1950, U.S. national security policy received its first articulated statement in a position paper drafted for use within the National Security Council and entitled *NSC-68*. Its most apparent feature was an apocalyptic description of the Soviet threat and an emphasis on a response of a military character. It predicted: "An indefinite period of tension and danger...for the United States and for the West—a period that should

be deemed less a short-term crisis than as a permanent and fundamental alteration in the shape of international relations."

According to the authors of *NSC-68*: "This means a virtual abandonment by the United States of trying to distinguish between national and global security....Security must henceforth become the dominant element in the national budget, and other elements must be accommodated to it."

The defining feature of U.S. national security policy during most of the Cold War years was, on the one hand, its tendency to equate security with the instruments of military force, and, on the other hand, the vast geographic range of the interests identified with national security ("a virtual abandonment by the United States of trying to distinguish between national and global security.)"

Two major issues provided much of the focus for national security policies during the Cold War: the first was the matter of strategic weapons, the second was the policy of containment, primarily through conventional force, of the Soviet Union's international influence. Both facets of U.S. national security policy marked a more total and protracted involvement in the affairs of the world than the nation had ever before experienced; at the same time, this engagement illustrated some of the dilemmas of a national security policy predominantly based on military tools.

Nuclear Weapons and Strategic Doctrine

Nothing has had so profound an effect on the course of U.S. national security policy as the development of nuclear weapons of an intercontinental range—strategic weapons. The strategic arms race began with the detonation of the first U.S. fission bomb in 1945, followed, four years later, by the Soviet Union's acquisition of a nuclear device of its own. Fusion (thermonuclear) bombs were developed by the United States in 1952, followed by the Soviet Union in 1953. The strategic rivalry thereafter was characterized by improvements in the design of nuclear bombs and, even more significantly, by the development of more efficient and more accurate ways of delivering warheads to their targets (accuracy benefiting enormously from the development of integrated circuitry and breakthroughs in computer software).

Nuclear bombs were initially carried by intercontinental bombers and, in the U.S. case, by shorter-range aircraft stationed on allied bases within reach of the Soviet Union. While the Kremlin enjoyed neither sort of capability at first, the U.S. lead in delivery vehicles was, nevertheless, of short duration. The launching of *Sputnik* in 1957 marked Soviet acquisition of an ability to deploy long-range rockets, moving both superpowers to focus very energetically on the acquisition of an intercontinental missile capability.

The first U.S. deployments in this area were the Titan I and Titan II intercontinental ballistic missiles (ICBMs); these missiles were followed by the Minuteman I, II, and III. The Minuteman II was the first U.S. missile to be armed with multiple, independently targetable, reentry vehicles (MIRVs). During the 1960s, intercontinental missiles were deployed on submarines as well (the Polaris and Poseidon missile). Further developments included the MX missile, carrying ten warheads capable of extreme accuracy, and the cruise missile—a small self-propelled rocket travelling very close to the earth's surface at subsonic speeds and carrying a single, conventional or nuclear warhead.

At the same time, short-range (tactical) nuclear weapons were developed and deployed in Germany and a variety of other locations. Their use was threatened in Korea, and it was made clear that a Soviet conventional assault on Western Europe would encounter a tactical-nuclear response.

Nuclear doctrines accompanied the new military technologies. Providing a rationale for the acquisition of nuclear weapons and an explanation of the use to which they would be put, these doctrines illustrate several paradoxes of national security. The initial effort to develop nuclear weapons during World War II was prompted by fear that Germany might soon develop them, as well as by a desire to expedite Japan's surrender. But the early years of the Cold War were not guided by a clearly articulated set of principles concerning the circumstances under which the U.S. nuclear arsenal might be used. Although tactical nuclear weapons were to function, under certain circumstances, as an extension of conventional U.S. forces, the purpose of strategic nuclear forces remained more nebulous.

The possibility of a U.S. strategic assault against the Soviet Union had been part of operational war plans since 1946, but the conditions that would warrant and govern such action were not fully articulated by the civilian leadership until several years later. In January 1954, Secretary of State John Foster Dulles explained that nuclear arms would henceforth be given a major emphasis in U.S. security strategy. To deter Soviet aggression, the "free community" should be "willing and able to respond vigorously and with means of our choosing." Specifically, Dulles called for a "deterrent of massive retaliatory power"—in other words, the nuclear bomb.

This approach, which came to be referred to as "Massive Retaliation," was generally interpreted to mean that, if the Soviet Union launched a foray into some part of the world that the United States considered essential to its own interests, even if this was limited to conventional weapons, a large-scale U.S. nuclear attack against Soviet cities and industrial facilities might follow (although other forms of retaliation were not excluded).

Massive Retaliation was made credible by the fact that, at the time, the Soviet Union was in no position to respond with a comparable counter-retaliation. Although it had both fission and fusion weapons by the early fifties, it could not deliver them effectively enough to actually attack the United States. Long-range missiles had not yet been developed and the Soviet Union possessed neither an adequate fleet of long-range bombers nor military bases near the United States from which nuclear warheads could be delivered by shorter-range aircraft. From the U.S. point of view, then, massive retaliation was meant to decrease the likelihood of Soviet incursions into areas deemed vital to the U.S. national interest by making the costs of such action to Moscow unacceptably high.

The doctrine lost its attractiveness by the late fifties for two major reasons. First, the threat of massive nuclear retaliation for a conventional provocation was not wholly credible to most minds, given the gap between the provocation and the magnitude of the response. Second, the Soviet Union soon acquired the ability to deliver nuclear weapons to U.S. territory; as counter-retaliation became feasible, the credibility of an initial U.S. use of nuclear weapons waned even further. The *Bear* and *Bison* bombers, with a range of more than 8,000 miles, entered the Soviet inventory in 1956 and 1957 and, with *Sputnik*, Moscow also acquired a long-range missile capability. This implied not only that the Soviets could counterattack with equal force but also that, if a U.S. nuclear attack was expected, they might be tempted to launch a preemptive attack—heightening the risk of nuclear war at times of particularly acute international crises.

A major rethinking of nuclear strategy coincided with President John F. Kennedy's assumption of office in 1961 and a desire to expand the range of strategic options beyond that of an all-out nuclear attack. The result was the policy of "flexible response," according to which nuclear weapons, probably of a tactical sort, would only be used on military targets at first, keeping a portion of the nuclear inventory back as a reserve for bargaining and leverage. Cities would be attacked only on the last rung of the escalatory ladder, which, it was hoped, would never be reached.

As with massive retaliation, however, enthusiasm for flexible response did not last very long. On the one hand, it was feared that it would make nuclear war more probable by increasing the range of contingencies under which nuclear weapons would be used. By decreasing the expected costs of an altercation, it could increase the likelihood of its occurrence. On the other hand, by focusing on military targets, it set no apparent upper limit on the number of nuclear weapons that might eventually be needed—thus creating the prospect of an endless arms race. Faced with these problems, the administration discarded this policy in 1963, shifting the emphasis from nuclear war fighting to deterrence, and from military to civilian targets.

The major purpose of the U.S. strategic arsenal was now to deter a Soviet nuclear attack on the United States itself. This would be based on the expectation that a U.S. retaliatory strike would follow a Soviet assault, and that the expected devastation would outweigh any advantage the Soviet Union could hope to gain through a first strike. This implied a U.S. ability to weather a first-strike well enough to counter with a level of destruction unacceptable to the attacker. The doctrine came to be known as that of Mutual Assured Destruction (MAD). Extended deterrence, especially involving Europe, would continue to rest on the principle of flexible response and the possibility that tactical nuclear weapons would be used to deal with Soviet conventional force. The idea, then, was to increase national security by decreasing the likelihood of a nuclear assault, and this, in turn, required that its costs be made unacceptably high.

But this doctrine too soon came under attack. As with massive retaliation, critics argued that MAD did not provide enough options in a confrontation with the Soviet Union. Because in cases short of an all-out first strike the costs of a nuclear exchange were too high, the range of provocations that could be deterred with nuclear weapons was unduly restricted. At the same time, military technology yielded the prospect of new sorts of strategic weapons, whose acquisition could not easily be justified by the tenets of MAD. For instance, MIRVs implied far greater numbers of warheads than were needed for the destruction of major Soviet cities, while advances in missile guidance technologies allowed levels of accuracy that were not required for the sprawling targets involved in MAD.

By the late 1970s, the apparent need to justify deployment of the new technologies had combined with a search for a greater range of strategic options. At the time of the Carter administration in 1979, and in a more pronounced manner as President Ronald Reagan came to office in 1981, the doctrinal pendulum swung in the direction of nuclear war fighting. The new doctrine, generally termed the "Counterforce Doctrine," extended the range of contingencies that could be addressed with nuclear weapons and articulated, for the first time, an explicit willingness to consider the possibility of fighting, and attempting to win a nuclear war—while maintaining, if possible, the level of fighting below that of total destruction. In other words, the doctrine stressed the very kinds of attributes that the newly developed weapons possessed—abundant warheads, extreme accuracy, survivability (in the case of mobile systems, such as the ground-launched cruise missiles), and penetrability and radar evasion capabilities (the cruise missile and

stealth bomber). At the same time, in the eyes of critics, the number of roads that could lead to nuclear war were multiplied, and the nature of the new weapons, and of the doctrine with which they were associated, seemed to increase the likelihood of a preemptive strike in the case of an acute U.S.-Soviet crisis.

The history of U.S. strategic doctrine, therefore, demonstrated the frequent incompatibility between goals of increasing security by reducing the costs of potential destruction and attempts to do so by reducing the probability of war. Attempts to control the former (as in flexible response and counterforce) seemed ineluctably to increase the latter, while decreases in likelihood (massive retaliation and MAD) were purchased at the expense of far greater damage, should deterrence fail. A choice between the two, when made, generally seemed to have as much to do with the current state of weapons technology as with a logically-rooted conception of the requisites of security, implying considerable ambiguity about the impact of the new weapons on national security.

The only apparent attempt to decrease both costs and likelihood simultaneously was linked to President Ronald Reagan's notion of an impenetrable shield against a nuclear attack, articulated in his initial vision of the Strategic Defense Initiative (SDI). But, as it was quickly determined that such a shield could do little more than protect a limited portion of one's strategic arsenal, its rationale in terms of national security was rapidly undermined.

Developments in U.S. and Soviet strategic weaponry also highlighted the operation of the security dilemma. For example, the initial Soviet attempt, in the late 1960s, to develop an anti-ballistic missile system was, from Moscow's viewpoint, no more than a defensive program. From the U.S. perspective, however, it seemed designed to acquire the ability to launch a first strike while escaping the full consequences of U.S. retaliation. Similarly, the SDI program was presented in purely defensive terms; in Soviet eyes, it seemed part of a U.S. program to acquire the ability to use strategic nuclear weapons against the Soviet Union with considerable impunity.

The history of strategic weapons and nuclear deterrence thus illustrated several of the paradoxes associated with national security policies molded around the instruments of military force. And although deterrence is often credited with maintaining the peace between the superpowers, it is precisely as a deterrent that its successful operation can neither be proven nor disproved.

Containment and Conventional Force

While a major focus of U.S. national security policy during the Cold War was on deterring a Soviet nuclear attack, as well as on adapting the doctrinal justification for nuclear weapons to the current state of their technology, a second major emphasis was on the goal of containment—an objective that, while relying on a broad gamut of foreign policy instruments, also stressed the role of conventional force. Containment, in turn, applied rather differently to Western Europe and to the developing regions of the world.

A number of reasons accounted for the conviction that threats to West European security were coextensive with assaults on America's vital interests. Some of these reasons transcended simple power politics, others were of a directly geostrategic nature.

Europe's centrality to the global balance of power was amply appreciated by both superpowers, an appreciation that coincided with geopolitical conceptions prevailing at the time of the Cold War's onset. Geopoliticians had divided the Eurasian landmass into two strategically distinct parts. Its center, loosely speaking, was the area occupied by the Soviet Union and denominated the "heartland." Although European and Asian history had witnessed numerous struggles within this area, the key to global power had been identified more recently with the control of the Eurasian "rimland:" the tier of states—from maritime Europe, to the Middle East, to southern Asia, to eastern Asia—encircling the heartland. In the opinion of Nicholas Spykman, an influential political geographer writing in 1944, the countries of the rimland—because of their substantial population and relatively developed societies, abundant natural resources, and valuable geostrategic position—should be considered the key to world power. In Spykman's view, "who controls the rimland rules Eurasia; who rules Eurasia controls the destinies of the world."

U.S. containment doctrine reflected this geopolitical credo. According to this doctrine Soviet efforts to alter the international balance of power to its advantage, particularly within areas associated with the "rimland," would be met with measured yet adequate counterpressure. From the U.S. viewpoint, no parts of the rimland had quite as a great a significance as those parts associated with Western Europe; its defense ranked at the top of the nation's containment priorities.

Apart from the fact that Western Europe was perceived as being geostrategically and economically central to U.S. interests, U.S. commitment to its defense was also rooted in less tangible causes. Much of U.S. history since independence had been entangled with the nations of maritime Europe, and a crucial link in this relationship was provided by the political culture and values that had become a symbol of what was endangered. As political democracy represented a system to which only a minority of nations adhered during the Cold War decades, it seemed imperative that it be preserved there where it had the longest roots; other-

wise, belief in its viability on both sides of the Cold War might be questioned.

Although nothing in its initial design implied that containment was to rely primarily on military rather than, say, economic or diplomatic, tools, the dominant emphasis was in fact on military force. The U.S. military commitment's institutional structure was provided by the North Atlantic Treaty Organization (NATO)—the first peacetime military alliance in U.S. history and the nation's first military alliance with Europe since the American Revolution. The commitment was also expressed in the deployment of several hundred thousand U.S. troops in western Germany and in the link established between conventional forces and nuclear weapons—as the most fundamental task of U.S. deployments in the area was to provide a credible coupling between U.S. conventional and nuclear forces devoted to the security of Western Europe.

The most plausible form of Soviet military threat was generally deemed to be an attack, spearheaded by armored vehicles, across the border between the two Germanies—an attack benefiting from the substantial conventional forces that the Soviets and their allies could mobilize for this purpose. To offset the Soviet advantage in conventional power, the United States began deploying tactical nuclear weapons in West Germany as early as 1953. The troops themselves would provide a "tripwire," their probable destruction making it likely that the United States would escalate at least to the level of tactical nuclear weapons. Because the psychological and military "firebreak" between conventional and nuclear weapons would have been breached at that point, escalation to the central strategic level could not be dismissed—providing a powerful deterrent to any Soviet plans for conventional aggression.

Although the history of U.S. contribution to the common defense had numerous facets, some of the most distinct issues have concerned the link between conventional and nuclear forces. Beyond the fact that some reliance on weapons of mass destruction was necessary, at least for deterrent purposes, and beyond the general Western acceptance that a doctrine of nuclear "no first use" was incompatible with the needs of Europe's defense, the specific extent and nature of the necessary nuclear arsenal remained controversial. Thus, the ultimate value of such weapons as the neutron bomb and theater nuclear forces (such as the ground-launched cruises missile) was inevitably nebulous.

Conclusions regarding military containment in Europe, like the issue of strategic deterrence, are necessarily ambiguous. As with most sorts of deterrence, beliefs concerning its effectiveness must rest on counterfactual assumptions. Nevertheless, there is a widespread conviction among politicians, scholars, and informed observers that the U.S. military commitment provided the physical security that allowed political democracy and market economics to flourish in Western Europe, and that the successful performance of both strengthened the invidious comparisons that undermined communism's legitimacy within the Soviet bloc itself. At the same time, it may be argued that the security dilemma thus provided a justification, that might not otherwise have existed, for the perpetuation of the rigidity and security-consciousness of Soviet rule.

Because of the extent to which the structure of rival alliances had hardened by the end of the 1940s, Cold War advantage within Europe could only be pursued by military adjustments, not by political realignments, implying, in turn, too great a danger of nuclear destruction. Within much of the developing world, however, the political situation was less settled, both with regard to the internal politics of nations and their Cold War affiliations, and this state of affairs multiplied the levels and methods of superpower competition. Since political loyalties need not necessarily have been taken as given, a large part of the contest was devoted to molding regional politics and this, along with the more direct forms of military competition, defined the pursuit of U.S. containment policy. Since containment was a core component of national security policy, national security was viewed as being closely linked to developments in the Third World, as illustrated by the fact that one of the early clashes between the two superpowers occurred over Iran in 1946.

The link established between political developments in various parts of the Third World and vital U.S. interests varied across the course of the Cold War. With Stalin's death, and Khrushchev's increasing conviction that the Third World might ultimately hold the key to the Cold War's outcome, U.S. concerns with the less-developed areas increased—reaching an apogee during the Kennedy and Johnson administrations. They declined with Nixon and Kissinger, increased during the Carter years, reached a new zenith with Ronald Reagan, and faded somewhat with the Bush administration.

U.S. concern with containment in the Third World also varied depending on the military, economic, or psychological significance of particular regions. Some areas (such as the Middle East) received a fairly consistent degree of U.S. attention; others (for example Africa) had a bearing on U.S. security concerns that varied substantially across administrations and with the nation's ability to project military power to the region involved. Regions characterized simultaneously by political instability and the ability to serve some geostrategic purpose were prime candidates for Soviet-U.S. competition (as witnessed by the Middle East or, because of its importance with regard to sea-lanes of communication, the Horn of Africa). Although nations that were part of the Eurasian rimland (most notably the Koreas) have always had an identifiable geostrategic significance from the perspective of the Soviet-U.S. competition, other developing regions were less obviously relevant to either superpower's Cold War calculations (although their importance could be magnified by invoking the "domino" theory of communist expansion).

The tools of U.S. containment in the Third World were often found somewhere along the continuum between simple diplomacy and armed coercion. Covert activities directed against hostile, or potentially hostile, foreign governments and leaders represented one such tool. These were generally administered by the Central Intelligence Agency and often involved efforts to remove or undermine foreign leaders, such as Patrice Lumumba in the Congo, Mohammad Mosaddeq in Iran, or Achmed Sukarno in Indonesia. Economic instruments of foreign policy were also dictated largely by security and diplomatic objectives. As Khrushchev initiated the first significant Soviet foreign assistance programs in the early 1950s, the United States placed increasing emphasis on economic inducements to cooperative behavior in the developing world. Finally, "public" diplomacy, in the form of propaganda (as, for example, via Voice of America), was used in efforts to sway the sympathies of the population of adversary nations away from their governments and toward the United States.

Although numerous foreign policy instruments were applied to containment within the Third World, military force played a visible part in the overall enterprise. According to one study, 215 instances of U.S. use of military power in developing areas were recorded between 1946 and 1975, ranging in form from mere shows of force to large-scale warfare. U.S. military intervention in these regions served three categories of functions. One purpose was to force the removal of governments deemed too sympathetic to Soviet interests, or to maintain in power politically loyal, but domestically beleaguered, governments whose continued incumbency seemed doubtful without U.S. military help. The 1983 intervention in Grenada was an example of intervention of the former kind, the 1958 intervention in Lebanon was an instance of the latter sort.

A second purpose served by military intervention was to restrain a hostile Third World government's external behavior, or to reverse certain of its external gains where that behavior or those gains appeared prejudicial to U.S. geopolitical interests and, by extension, to U.S. national security. The most dramatic instances of the sort were the U.S. interventions in the Korean peninsula and in Vietnam. In both cases, the justification for the commitment of substantial U.S. military force was to protect the southern, pro-Western, part of a divided country against aggression from its northern, pro-Soviet or pro-Chinese part. In the case of Korea, this initial purpose was subsequently supplemented by the goal of destroying Communism in North Korea and achieving Korea's reunification on U.S. terms.

The use of force in the Third World was also often linked as much to goals of deterrence as compellence. Because the policy of containment was conducted globally, the very large number of points at which it could be threatened vastly outnumbered the number of points at which U.S. military capacity could actively promote it. Under the circumstances, it became necessary to limit as much as possible the *likely* number of threats, which, in turn, required that U.S. willingness to use force should be firmly established. Thus, ensuring *credibility* may at times have seemed as pressing, or even more so, to U.S. decision-makers as the proximate objective by which the specific use of force was justified. For example, the need to maintain the credibility of U.S. armed force in the wake of Vietnam lent particular urgency to the Reagan administration's military action in Grenada.

Since it is logically very difficult to prove either the success or the failure of deterrence, we cannot confidently judge its contribution to U.S. containment policy in the Third World. Nevertheless, the geographically inconsistent and historically fluctuating nature of U.S. security interests in the developing regions suggest that the signals regarding U.S. intentions may have made it rather difficult for potential adversaries to establish a connection between their behavior and likely U.S. responses—an obvious condition for effective deterrence in many developing regions (for example, the Soviet Union's increasing level of activity in Africa in the late seventies was, it seems, attributable to uncertainty in Moscow as to how important these regions were to the United States).

The ambiguity and shifting nature of U.S. security concerns in the Third World, moreover, indicate that the perceived salience of Third World developments to U.S. national security interests depended on U.S. belief in the effectiveness of its own military force. If so, the outer limits of U.S. security concerns may depend significantly on the perceived utility of military tools of foreign policy (lessened, for example, after Vietnam, much increased following the Persian Gulf war). This perception, in turn, is largely shaped by current historical memory, the options that the current state of military technology seems to allow, as well as by the influence, within the councils of government, of those whose personal and organizational interests are linked to the role of armed force in U.S. national security policy.

More important still, the extent of desired containment determined the number of points at which superpower interests could collide—highlighting the paradoxical ultimate effect of containment on U.S. national security. On the one hand, security may be undermined by allowing an extension of an adversary's power; on the other hand, security may be threatened by increasing the points of potential conflict with that adversary—both by exacerbating security dilemmas and expanding the area of conflicting interests.

In the Cold War's aftermath, it is difficult to gauge whether containment's dominant effect was to extend the superpower conflict or to decrease the likely scope of Soviet power; therefore, the policy's net effect on U.S. national security cannot be confidently assessed. It has, however, underscored some of the dilemmas attendant upon militarily assertive national security policies.

National Security After the Cold War

The end of the Cold War thoroughly altered the foundation of U.S. national security thinking. The prior clarity of objectives, summed up in the dual imperative of deterring Soviet expansion while averting a nuclear war, yielded to confused perceptions of external challenges and threats, as well as to tentative and largely inchoate visions of appropriate U.S. responses. The years initially following the collapse of the Soviet Empire in 1989 were accompanied by U.S. efforts to devise appropriate responses to a restructured international order, a learning process that has proceeded by trial and error.

The circumstances confronting the United States in the 1990s were new to the nation's experience. On the one hand, it no longer faced a significant and identifiable enemy—a nation, or cohesive group of nations, whose vital interests were opposed to America's and whose power made it capable of threatening U.S. interests. On the other hand, the United States continued to have unchallenged military power and, therefore, a considerable capacity to influence the course of global developments. The mid-1990s thus combined a lack of a clear national security imperative with unparalleled military power. While both conditions were encountered separately in the past, they were never present simultaneously. During earlier phases of U.S. history, when the country's military power compared less favorably to that of many other nations, national security policy focused largely on decisions to avoid entanglements in the affairs of the world. With the power it enjoyed after the Cold War, the temptation was much stronger to mold international conditions according to U.S. interests—even if it was not always clear what must be molded or in what manner.

Ultimately, then, a major post-Cold War challenge has been to identify how, if at all, fundamental national interests can be externally threatened in the absence of a clear and present danger, and how effective approaches to national security can be devised to deal with largely hypothetical threats. A scrutiny of the three sorts of core interests that could, in principle, be involved highlights the uncertainties involved.

First, there are not many plausible ways, in the post-Cold War world, that the physical security of the country's citizens and of their private and collective possessions may be threatened externally. Even during the decades of superpower rivalry, the most salient peril—a Soviet nuclear attack—was rarely more than a very distant contingency. Threats of external assault against the United States are even more remote in the post-Cold War world. The most plausible related threat may be provided by terrorist organizations, for whom U.S. citizens and property may represent visible targets, as well as, potentially, by new members of the club of nuclear nations. Addressing these dangers is a legitimate concern of national security policy, but the peril did not seem very imminent in the 1990s.

The second sort of interest involves the nation's prosperity. From several points of view the U.S. position of global economic dominance has been challenged, and it is feared that economic rivals are lapping at the foundations of U.S. prosperity. The point, however, is that these threats are of an economic rather than coercive nature, and that they are a matter of economic rather than national security policy (threats to prosperity require a response via national security policy when the threats are of a coercive nature). To the extent that limp economic foundations undermine the basis for military power, the issue may be one of national security concern, but that is a different matter.

External threats to fundamental U.S. values in the mid–1990s were even more difficult to identify. U.S. political beliefs and institutions are not threatened by external subversion, as they were sometimes thought to be during the Cold War. Moreover, the international spread of democracy in the 1980s and early 1990s indicated that these sorts of values had become the dominant source of political legitimacy in the world. This is not to say that democracy is not occasionally threatened abroad, or that very basic humanitarian values are not violated on a large scale, but that such violation can be linked to U.S. security only by a very indirect and intricate causal path.

Accordingly, the three core interests involved in national security face few identifiable and plausible foreign threats in the post-Cold War period. There are certainly international developments that concern U.S. foreign policy interests and preferences, such as the war in Bosnia, or democratization in Russia, but U.S. national security is not directly involved (additional developments would be required in both examples for this to be the case).

This does not mean that national security policy should slide to a much lower level of priority, even if it loses its sense of urgency, since international circumstances can change abruptly. In a quasi-anarchic world based on the principle of national sovereignty, the absence of security threats does not preclude their emergence, especially since the initial post-Cold War hopes for a New World Order, defined by the end of aggression, the rule of law, and the dominance of the United Nations, largely yielded to a more sober realism.

In such a world, the challenges of national security policy are of two sorts: (a) anticipating threatening future contingencies, and, (b) molding the overall structure of international relations so that hypothetical threats to national security are minimized. By focusing on specific hypothetical contingencies, the expected benefits to U.S. security are directly identifiable; at the same time, the scope for security dilemmas and other conundra associated with national security policies is correspondingly greater. With policies targeting the structure of international relations, the assumption is that conditions that affect the security of other nations also affect that of the United States, and that, by creating a global order emphasizing international security, the security of the United States will benefit as well. While a structural approach benefits U.S. interests only in an indirect way, it has the attraction of not creating counterproductive security dilemmas. Obviously, the two emphases are complementary.

The problem with planning for threatening contingencies lies in their hypothetical and foggy nature. As Colin Powell, former chairman of the Joint Chiefs of Staff, observed after the collapse of the Soviet Union, "We no longer have the luxury of having a threat to plan for." In the absence of an identifiable enemy with known military capabilities, the criteria for U.S. force planning became murkier than at any time during the previous half-century. In turn, this has engendered a debate over broad approaches to force planning.

According to one approach, in the absence of specific threats, a more general goal should be pursued, defined as assuring a militarily dominant U.S. position with regard to most or all other nations, implying, in turn, that virtually *any* contingency could be dealt with successfully. In one national security planning document of 1991, the stated goal, since abandoned, of the nation's military power was to assure a one-superpower world, in which the United States would strive to prevent the rise of any competitors to its primacy in Europe and East Asia. In a somewhat related vein, former Secretary of Defense James Schlesinger suggested that the basis for future U.S. forces should "not simply be the response to individual threats, but rather that which is needed to maintain the overall aura of U.S. power." Obviously, this sort of approach provides no clear upper ceiling to U.S. military needs, nor any explicit link between military power and security imperatives.

Another, less open-ended, approach is to think of hypothetical, yet fairly concrete, future security contingencies, and to plan accordingly. Some contingencies could involve the emergence of specific hostile powers. Scenarios include a Russia ruled by right-wing, totalitarian nationalists, wielding nuclear weapons in support of expansionary designs. Other hypothetical contingencies include a hostile, economically and militarily very powerful, and anti-Western China. Regional threats, such as that presented by Iraq in the very early nineties, may be included as possible contingencies. Moreover, the threat of nuclear-armed terrorists is frequently included in the list of possible national security threats of the future.

In March 1993, then-Secretary of Defense Les Aspin initiated a comprehensive review, termed the Bottom-Up Review, of U.S. force structure and defense strategy in the wake of the Cold War's end and the Soviet Union's dissolution. According to the *Report on the Bottom-Up Review*, the major post-Cold War threat to the United States was that of aggression by regional powers against U.S. interests. Under these circumstances, the armed forces of the United States had to maintain the ability to fight and win two regional wars simultaneously. This capacity was deemed important because it would dissuade a potential aggressor in one region from taking advantage of the fact that the United States was already militarily engaged in another region. In addition, a two-war capacity would hedge against the eventuality that a future adversary might confront the United States with a larger-than-expected threat. The exact nature of the regional interests, however, was not specified in the report.

The challenge, then, is not only to identify correctly the most plausible (or least implausible) future threats but to devise, on this basis, a sensible force posture. Of course, a contingency-based approach to the acquisition of military capabilities runs the risk of encouraging a process wherein, at some stage, challenges to national security come to be defined largely by the types of capabilities acquired, or by those capabilities that, for purely organizational as well as geostrategic reasons, the defense establishment would like to acquire. It is also a process that is intrinsically associated with the creation of security dilemmas.

From the perspective of U.S. security, an insecurity-driven international system has two implications. In the first place, the sorts of behavior by which any nation can threaten the interests of another may eventually be directed against the United States—particularly given the continuing wide international range of U.S. interests. An instance of the sort was the threat to U.S. oil supplies stemming from Iraq's invasion and occupation of Kuwait that sparked the Gulf War. Second, because of the extent of U.S. power, nations that are each other's adversaries will continue to seek to enlist U.S. support on their own behalf, implying a continual danger that the United States could be drawn into the clashes of others, as long as the international system allows considerable scope for conflict.

One facet of post-Cold War U.S. national security policy has therefore been directed at the structure of the international system, usually at some aspect of the distribution of coercive capacity within it. A modest amount of effort has been aimed at establishing a collectively managed system of international peacekeeping—one that would not have the fully automatic and unambiguously legitimate nature of a pure form of collective security, but one that would, nevertheless, mitigate reliance on self-help and balance of power to deal with international aggression. The U.S.-led international action in Somalia in the early 1990s was an example.

Even in a very tentative form, such a system requires both a method of identifying international aggression and of mustering the means to confront it. The first task has generally been relegated to the United Nations, which determines the occurrence of aggression and decides on the appropriate nature of the response via a resolution of the Security Council (as in the example of the Gulf War). The actual provision of force may occur in the context of U.N. peacekeeping missions or, exceptionally, through regional security organizations (for example NATO). However, furnishing military force for a combat role is a politically difficult decision for the participating nations, for it involves tangible costs and risks. From the perspective of the United States, statements of relatively unreserved support for international peacekeeping missions in the early phases of the post-Cold War period have yielded to increasingly restrictive conditions on U.S. participation in such ventures. An illustration was the National Security Revitalization Act of February 1995, which placed new financial and legal restrictions on the president's ability to commit U.S. forces and resources to collective security undertakings.

Attempts to establish an internationally managed system of peacekeeping seem likely to succeed only in those instances where the United States and other permanent members of the UN Security Council perceive that their own national interest is directly involved, as, for example, in the case of the Gulf War. Accordingly, collective security is unlikely to approach universal reach.

Another strand of U.S.-supported policies to mitigate some of the more threatening facets of international society seeks to curb the proliferation of weapons of mass destruction. A special focus concerns the efforts of the International Atomic Energy Agency and of the Nuclear Suppliers Group to halt the spread of fissionable material and of various types of nuclear technology. This general policy also seeks a regime to control the spread of chemical and biological weapons, and to check the proliferation of ballistic missile technologies by which all such weapons could be delivered to their targets.

U.S. activities directed at the structure of the international system have thus focused preferentially on its coercive capabilities; less has been done to devise alternative methods of conflict resolution (for example, via an expanded role of the International Court of Justice).

MIROSLAV NINCIC

See also Cold War; Containment; Covert Action; Deterrence; Flexible Response; Gulf War of 1990–1991; Isolationism; Jefferson, Thomas; Massive Retaliation; North Atlantic Treaty Organization; NSC-68; Nuclear Weapons and Strategy; Sputnik I; Strategic Defense Initiative; Truman Doctrine; Versailles Treaty of 1919; War of 1812; Washington, George; Wilson, Thomas Woodrow

FURTHER READING

Art, Robert J. "To What Ends Military Power?" *International Security* 8 (Spring 1980): 3–35.

Aspin, Les. *Report on the Bottom-Up Review*, Washington, D.C., 1993.

Butterfield, Herbert. "The Tragic Element in Modern Human Conflict." In *History and Human Relations*, edited by Herbert Butterfield. New York, 1951.

Buzan, Barry, Charles Jones, and Richard Little. *The Logic of Anarchy: Neorealism to Structural Realism*. New York, 1993.

Carpenter, Ted G. *A Search for Enemies: America's Alliances After the Cold War*. Washington D.C., 1992.

Gaddis, John Lewis. *Strategies of Containment: A Critical Appraisal of Postwar American National Security Policy*. New York, 1982.

Glaser, Charles L. *Analyzing Strategic Nuclear Policy*. Princeton, N.J., 1990.

Kennedy, Paul M. *The Rise and Fall of the Great Powers: Economic Change and Military Conflict from 1500 to 2000*. New York, 1992.

Leffler, Melvyn P. *A Preponderance of Power: National Security in the Truman Administration and the Cold War*. Stanford, Calif., 1992.

Nincic, Miroslav. *Anatomy of Hostility: The U.S.-Soviet Rivalry in Perspective*. San Diego, Calif., 1989.

Russett, Bruce M. *Grasping the Democratic Peace: Principles for a Post-Cold War World*. Princeton, N.J., 1993.

NATIONAL SECURITY COUNCIL

Established by the National Security Act of 1947 to coordinate the activities of all executive branch departments concerned with national security. The official members of the National Security Council (NSC) are the president, the vice president, the secretary of defense, and the secretary of state, but other government officials are invited to participate in an advisory capacity. Historically, NSC meetings have often been attended by the chair of the joint chiefs of staff, the director of the Central Intelligence Agency (CIA), and representatives from agencies concerned with issues to be discussed at that meeting. The NSC also has a staff and an adviser to the president for national security affairs. This office was not originally

---

NATIONAL SECURITY COUNCIL

Members:

The President
The Vice President
The Secretary of State
The Secretary of Defense

Statutory Advisers:

Director of Central Intelligence
Chairmen, Joint Chief of Staff

Standing Participants:

The Secretary of the Treasury
U.S. Representative to the United Nations
Chief of Staff to the President
Assistant to the President for National Security Affairs
Assistant to the President for Economic Policy

Source: *The U.S. Government Manual*

---

part of the NSC staff but was added in 1953 by the Eisenhower administration and subsequently grew in importance. The NSC meets when the president requires it to do so. It met 366 times during the Eisenhower administration, more frequently than under any other president. Aside from managing immediate crises, the NSC plans coordinated national security policies, usually in cooperation with relevant cabinet departments, and submits them to the council members for consideration. The president is the final authority on enacting official policy. Documents that have passed through the NSC have helped launch some of the best known and most important policy initiatives of the postwar era. For example, NSC-68, a 1950 general statement of national security policy that called for a much larger military establishment in response to the Soviet threat, is often considered the most important policy statement of the Cold War era. Although it was originally intended to serve as a coordinating body, the decision-making role of the NSC staff and especially the role of the national security adviser have grown over the years, sometimes eclipsing that of the secretary of state and the secretary of defense. Because of the overlapping functions of the NSC and these executive departments, as well as serious personality and power struggles, conflict has sometimes arisen between the national security adviser and the secretaries. Such conflict was especially severe during the Nixon administration, ending only when Henry Kissinger assumed both offices in 1973. During the Carter administration, conflict between National Security Adviser Zbigniew Brzezinski and Secretary of State Cyrus Vance eventually led Vance to resign, commenting

NATIONAL SECURITY COUNCIL ADVISERS

ADMINISTRATION	ADVISER	PERIOD OF APPOINTMENT
Truman	Sidney W. Souers	1947–1950
	James S. Lay, Jr.	1950–1953
Eisenhower	Robert Cutler	1953–1955
	Dillon Anderson	1955–1956
	William A. Jackson	1956
	Robert Cutler	1957–1958
	Gordon Gray	1958–1961
Kennedy	McGeorge Bundy	1961–1966
L. Johnson		
	Walt W. Rostow	1966–1969
Nixon	Henry A. Kissinger	1969–1975
Ford		
	Brent Scowcroft	1975–1977
Carter	Zbigniew Brzezinski	1977–1981
Reagan	Richard V. Allen	1981
	William P. Clark, Jr.	1981–1983
	Robert C. McFarlane	1983–1985
	John M. Poindexter	1985–1986
	Frank C. Carlucci	1986–1987
	Colin L. Powell	1987–1989
Bush	Brent Scowcroft	1989–1993
Clinton	Anthony Lake	1993–Present

Source: U.S. National Security Council

that he was "tired of losing to Zbigniew Brzezinski." During the Reagan administration, NSC staff became involved in illegal covert actions that ultimately resulted in the 1986 Iran-Contra scandal.

President Bill Clinton's national security adviser, Anthony Lake, has written that the NSC should return to the coordinating role it originally played during the Truman administration and that it should move away from the involvement in policymaking that its staff has increasingly played during the past twenty-five years. However, criticism of Lake for allegedly failing to articulate a compelling vision for U.S. national security policy illustrates the pressures to become involved in policymaking that the NSC staff, and especially the national security adviser, now face.

BENJAMIN FORDHAM

See also Brzezinski, Zbigniew; Kissinger, Henry Alfred; National Security Act; National Security Agency

FURTHER READING

Andrianopoulos, Gerry Argyris. *Kissinger and Brzezinski: The NSC and the Struggle for Control of US National Security Policy.* New York, 1991.

Barnet, Richard J. *Roots of War.* New York, 1972.

Destler, I. M., Leslie H. Gelb, and Anthony Lake. *Our Own Worst Enemy: The Unmaking of American Foreign Policy.* New York, 1984.

Lord, Carnes. *The Presidency and the Management of National Security.* New York, 1988.

Shawcross, William. *Sideshow: Kissinger, Nixon and the Destruction of Cambodia.* New York, 1979.

NATIVE AMERICANS

Sometime referred to as American Indians, the term refers to the aboriginal peoples of North America, South America, and the Caribbean.

From its inception, the United States, determined to increase territorially and resolved to safeguard its citizens and frontiers, placed relations with the American Indians at the forefront of the foreign affairs agenda. Scientific and linguistic analysis suggests that the first people came to America some 15,000 to 25,000 years ago. During the Ice Age, northeastern Asia and northwestern North America were joined where the Bering Strait is today. Hunter-gatherers, in small nomadic bands and over thousands of years, migrated across the Bering Strait land bridge and began filling in the Americas. Humans reached the southernmost part of the Western Hemisphere by 8000 B.C.

From the diffusion of people came the diffusion of languages and cultures. The first Europeans to arrive in North America (A.D. 1500) found two continents where some 2,000 native languages (not dialects) existed. The Indians residing north of the Rio Grande spoke as many as 350 separate languages. The Indian societies of what is now the United States also varied greatly in culture and way of life. Many were farmers who grew a wide variety of crops. Others engaged in fishing. Some hunted to obtain food. Still others combined hunting, gathering, and farming. The forms of Indian political organization varied widely, too. The Plains Indians, for example, were divided into small tribal groups, while the Indians of the Southeast often organized themselves into confederacies.

The Europeans also found a substantial Native American population. About seven to twelve million Indians lived north of Mexico. About twenty-five million lived in Mexico and Central America. The rest, some thirty to forty million people, lived in South America and on the islands in the Caribbean Sea. The Indian population declined catastrophically, perhaps 30 to 50 percent, within 100 years of colonial settlement due to exposure to European diseases, especially smallpox.

During the colonial period, three European powers came to control the lands that would become the contiguous United States. By 1600, Spain held California and much of the trans-Mississippi West. East of the Mississippi River Valley a contest raged, by 1700, between England and France for mastery of that substantial region. English and French relations with Native Americans exhibited marked differences. The Indians's strained, suspicious, and frequently violent relationship with the English and American colonists stemmed primarily from a white colonial population determined to acquire tribal land, hold it, then expand it for farming and non-agricultural enterprises. On the other hand, natives served French imperial interests well as soldiers and as partners in the lucrative fur trade business. As a result, the French developed and retained a friendship with Indians that their European rivals never earned or enjoyed.

To the distress of many Canadian and Great Lakes tribes, the Anglo-French wars for empire ended with an absolute British victory in 1763: France ceded Canada, plus virtually all its North American territory, to Great Britain. England's rule over tribes living west of the Appalachians and in the Great Lakes region was tenuous and brief, lasting less than three decades. The American Revolution (1775–1783) swept away the British and placed these tribes under U.S. dominion.

England had accepted the nationhood of Indian groups and throughout the colonial period concluded treaties with them based on this principle. The United States government concurred, grounded its national policy on this principle, and, for almost 100 years, dealt with Indian tribes as sovereign nations. This changed in March 1871 when Congress passed legislation declaring that: "No Indian nation or tribe within the territory of the United States shall be acknowledged or recognized as an independent nation, tribe, or power with whom the United States may contract by treaty." Thereafter, the federal government primarily dealt with the American Indians by means of acts of Congress or executive orders.

The "Indian Question"

Americans, once securing their independence, surged outward from the Atlantic seaboard and across the Appalachian chain, moving with intense determination to acquire and settle a vast domain, first in the trans-Appalachian West, then in the trans-Mississippi West. By 1850 the United States had realized its "Manifest Destiny" in stretching its holdings from the Atlantic to the Pacific Coast. Many dreamed still of adding Canada, more of Mexico, and various Caribbean islands to the Republic. Each decade of the nineteenth century witnessed Americans moving into the frontier areas until finally, in 1890, the U.S. superintendent of the census declared that the American frontier had ceased to exist.

This staggering movement of a people and acquisition of territory made up one of the greatest shaping forces in the nation's history. The settlement of the frontier also proved to be the foremost source of a constant state of friction, and often hostility, between the United States, its citizenry, and the Native Americans. The vast areas acquired by the Republic and settled by Americans were homelands to native groups, and they did not long forbear the newcomers who moved to displace them, regulate them, and occupy their patrimony. In the face of aggressive westward expansion, the pattern most representative of U.S.-Indian relations became clear early. Through it ran a strain of unremitting determination to dislodge the inhabitants of the western lands. Government from time to time relented. Americans wanting land never did.

The Indians's resistance to westward expansion, combined with the response of Americans, produced extended periods of violence. Because most whites considered Indians a dangerous impediment to their and the Republic's territorial, cultural, and economic aspirations, the U.S. government could not easily temporize in addressing the "Indian question." Suggestions ranging in scope from prudent to foolish and from mean-spirited to generous came in abundance because most Americans acknowledged the desperate need for a solution to the Indian question. Some sought to erect a geographic barrier, much as the British had done in 1763 when they created a permanent frontier line along the Appalachians. Indians, this group argued, might maintain their accustomed way of life free from white encroachment. Others believed that acculturating the Indians, then assimilating them into the dominant society, was the wisest course. Still others applauded extermination. Generations of federal officials struggled to fashion a policy to solve the Indian question, even though the permanent resolution they sought remained elusive.

As soon as the American Revolution came to an end, white settlers began to penetrate the Ohio country and other western lands in search of homes. Although Great Britain granted these lands to the United States in the Treaty of Paris of 1783, the native peoples who had thought for centuries that the land beyond the Appalachian Mountains was their own were determined to resist. In the early 1790s, three U.S. expeditions went up the Miami River to the Auglaize and the Maumee to subdue Shawnees, Miamis, Ottowas, Chippewas, Potowatomies, and others who held the Ohio country with the support of, and with guns from, the British in Canada. The first two expeditions, commanded respectively by General Josiah Harmar and Ohio Territorial Governor Arthur St. Clair, were unmitigated disasters. For the third, President George Washington called on General "Mad Anthony" Wayne. At the Battle of Fallen Timbers near Maumee, Ohio, in 1794, he routed these Ohio tribes. A year later they came to Greenville and signed a treaty highly unfavorable to their claims to the Ohio Territory.

Among the defeated warriors was a Shawnee named Tecumseh, who knew there could be no peace if whites continued to push farther west. He wanted white and red people to live together in peace by mutually respecting a boundary line between them. Whether the boundary was in western Ohio or farther west on the Wabash in Indiana was less important than the resolve of both sides to respect it. Tecumseh found strong backing from his brother Lalawethika, a drunken braggart who had experienced a Christian religious conversion to become Tenskwatawa, known to the whites as the Shawnee Prophet. He claimed divine revelations, and to Indians he preached a rejection of the white man's ways and a return to traditional native values. In time the brothers moved their village from Ohio to Tippecanoe Creek in western Indiana.

Tecumseh knew what his aim was as he journeyed tirelessly during the first decade of the nineteenth century from tribe to tribe, from Wisconsin to Florida, from Indiana to Mississippi, trying to rally support to block U.S. settlement. Everywhere he was listened to with respect—but no real support. Some whites were sympathetic: Thomas Jefferson for one. But the president's solution, like that of most other Assimilationists, was conversion of the Indians's hunting and gathering society into an agricultural society. Indians could live happily in

the United States, these whites contended, by virtually converting into white men. They had only to learn the white man's ways, seek his education, herd cattle and plough fields like him, wear his clothes, speak his language, and practice his faith.

In one of the most significant episodes in Indian-United States relations, the Cherokees not only tried such assimilation during the early-nineteenth century, but did it with phenomenal success. Yet even when they did it, the state of Georgia and the United States government insisted that they abandon their homes in the southern highlands to settle beyond the Mississippi. Tecumseh's strategy met with no greater success. He and his followers had vowed to block further white expansion into the Old Northwest, but Indiana Territorial Governor William Henry Harrison's victory at the Battle of Tippecanoe in November 1811 effectively ended that pledge.

Other Americans, the Removalists, during these same years argued the opposite side of the issue about how to solve the Indian question. They too sought peaceful relations between Americans and Indians, but they were never sufficiently persuaded that the Assimilationists's plan held much likelihood of success. The Removalists contended that most Indians were little interested in becoming "civilized." Perhaps the actual problem, they speculated, really was not one of disinclination, but of incapacity. Most Americans, concluded one commissioner of Indian Affairs, regarded Indians as "irreclaimable, terrible savages." The scientific community seemed to validate this assertion. "Do what we will," wrote one of the South's leading surgeons, Dr. Josiah C. Nott, in 1847, "the Indian remains the Indian still. He is not a creature susceptible of civilization....He can no more be civilized than the leopard can change his spots....He is now gradually disappearing, to give place to a higher order of beings."

The Removalists concluded that the Indians, incapable of being civilized, were doomed to extinction and thus any effort to civilize them would prove futile. They also argued that the unrelenting westward thrust of white settlement would occur too rapidly to permit peaceful coexistence on the frontier. Everyone knew that taking too much tribal land at one time led to warfare. To avoid further bloodshed and depravation on the frontier, and, equally as important, to throw open more Indian land for white settlement and enterprise, the Removalists offered their own solution: Indians must exchange their lands east of the Mississippi for territory west of that river. If some tribes proved recalcitrant, as might be anticipated, the Removalists suggested forced removal as an appropriate option for the U.S. government.

Forces stimulating U.S. expansion were never long dormant, and during the early-nineteenth century the frontier pushed relentlessly into Indian country. It

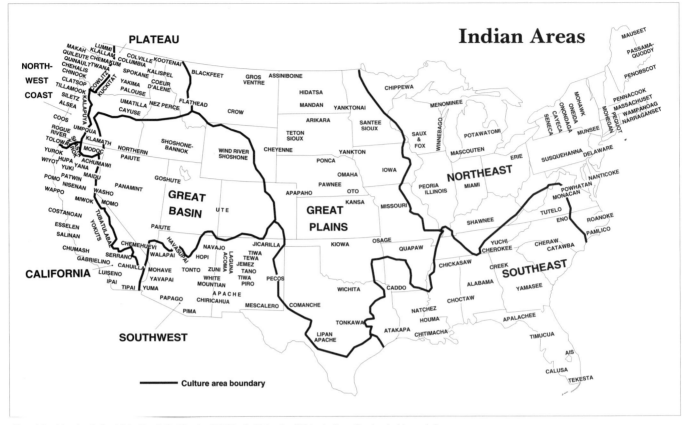

Indian Areas

Culture area boundary

From *Atlas of American Indian Affairs*, Francis Paul Prucha. ©1990 by the University of Nebraska Press. Reprinted with permission of the University of Nebraska Press.

pressed deeper into the Old Northwest with the collapse of significant Indian resistance under the leadership of Tecumseh. It spread across the Old Southwest, especially with the rapid expansion of the cotton belt. By 1820 settlers had pushed as far west as the valley of the Mississippi River. The census of that year indicated that almost a fourth of the American people lived in the trans-Appalachian West, and there was no hint that the human flow would diminish. This activity fanned interracial conflict, and for a growing number of Americans solidified their conviction that only removal would solve the Indian question. Removalists stepped up calls for the federal authority to initiate a comprehensive plan to colonize Eastern Indians on lands west of the Mississippi River.

President James Monroe, like his mentor Thomas Jefferson before him, supported the assimilation program. But he also concluded that removal, to be followed by government-assisted educational and training programs in the West, offered the best solution. Monroe took action in 1824, proposing a plan for the voluntary relocation of Eastern tribes westward. The government's plan for the Indians did not rule out persuasion, but at this juncture it did not yet contemplate a policy of force.

This changed following the election of 1828. President Andrew Jackson gave personal attention to passage of federal legislation authorizing forced removal, stressing the need for Congress to endorse a policy of separation to resolve the Indian question. Like Monroe and earlier nineteenth-century presidents, Jackson believed that Indians were capable of acculturating, and could be assimilated. But considering the desperation with which whites coveted Indian lands and the virulence directed against them by many Americans, achieving these results was impossible so long as the Indians remained east of the Mississippi. Unlike his recent predecessors in the White House, Jackson would not leave the choice up to the Indians. Indians would be required to sign treaties in which they would exchange their lands for western territory. This would separate them from the American people, so that they could not impede white settlement and enterprise, and so that Assimilationists would have the necessary time to implement successfully their civilization measures. When far in the future the thrust of white settlement again reached the Indians, thought Jackson, they would be culturally, religiously, politically, and eco-

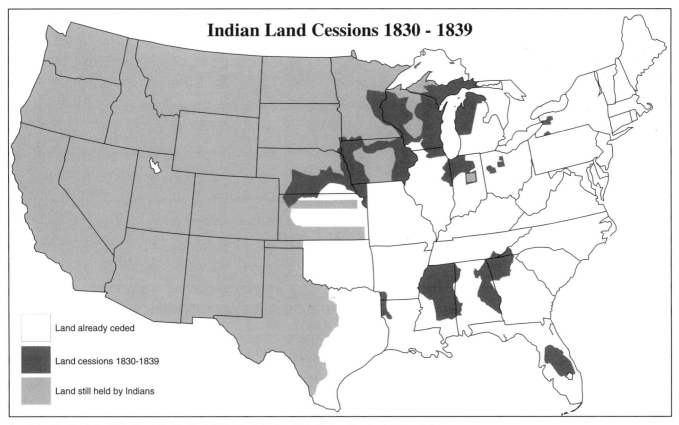

Indian Land Cessions 1830 - 1839

Land already ceded

Land cessions 1830-1839

Land still held by Indians

From *Atlas of American Indian Affairs*, Francis Paul Prucha. ©1990 by the University of Nebraska Press. Reprinted with permission of the University of Nebraska Press.

nomically ready to take their place in U.S. society. For these reasons, the president stressed, a policy of separation was the only solution to the Indian question.

The debates in Congress over proposed legislation to enact the policy of separation sparked rancorous debate, but in the end Congress passed the Indian Removal Act. Jackson signed it into law on 28 May 1830. The government of the United States was empowered to appropriate tribal lands by negotiating new treaties and to exile the Indians of the South and the Old Northwest to the trans-Mississippi West. During the 1830s it executed the policy. Tribes of the Old Northwest, such as the Shawnee, Miami, Wyandot, Wea and Piankasha, agreed to removal treaties and quietly withdrew to lands that later became Kansas. Many factors compelled them. Harried by settlers, many corrupted by alcohol, and void of strong leadership such as Tecumseh's, the Indians acknowledged continued resistance as futile.

In the South, three of the five major southern tribes forfeited their lands within two years of the passage of the Indian Removal Act. The Choctaws in 1830 and then the Chickasaws and the Creeks in 1832 concluded treaties with the federal government mandating their resettlement in lands that later became Oklahoma. Only the Cherokees and the Seminoles remained. While each selected different tactics, both tenaciously resisted removal. The Seminoles rejected their removal treaty and withdrew into the depths of the Florida swamps where, from 1835 to 1842, they fought courageously but unsuccessfully against the U.S. Army. When military operations finally halted, the government had removed most of the tribe to the Indian Territory (present-day Oklahoma), although several hundred were never apprehended and remained in Florida. The Cherokees were equally determined to resist removal. They appealed their case in the federal courts, in two decisions—*Cherokee Nation v. the State of Georgia* (1831) and *Samuel A. Worcester v. the State of Georgia* (1832). The U.S. Supreme Court upheld the rights of the Cherokee Nation. But Georgia ignored the court's decisions, and President Jackson refused to use his influence to enforce them. The Cherokees continued to resist the move, but they knew that sooner or later they would have to forfeit their homeland. Criminals from Georgia began to raid their property, driving the Cherokees from their homes. The state of Georgia began selling off the Cherokees's land while they still lived on it. A malleable faction signed the New Echota Treaty exchanging its people's land in the East for land in the Indian Territory. Then in April 1838, General Winfield Scott brought an army into the Cherokee homeland to remove them. The troops rounded up more than 16,000 Cherokees. The trek westward, a trying one even under the best of conditions, was handicapped by a lack of sufficient provisions. In addition, a terrible drought blasted the Southeast through the early fall of 1838. More than 4,000 people, or roughly one quarter of the Cherokees, died during the journey. The missionary Elizur Butler, witness to a portion of the odyssey, confessed, "I have felt I have been in the midst of death itself." The *New York Observer* lamented: "When I [the reporter] passed the last...of those suffering exiles and thought that my countrymen had expelled them from their native soil and much beloved homes,...I turned from the sight with feelings language cannot express."

By 1840, the lands east of the Mississippi had been lost by those people who had lived there for centuries. Federal officials and the American public overwhelmingly agreed with Jackson's judgment. He exuded confidence that the policy of separation had successfully dealt with the Indian question: It provided safety for Americans and the United States, and prevented the annihilation of the Indians. "The states which had so long been retarded in their improvement by the Indian tribes residing in the midst of them are at length relieved from the evil," Jackson assured a grateful nation, "and this unhappy race—the original dwellers in our land—are now placed in a situation where we may well hope that they will share in the blessings of civilization and be saved from degradation and destruction."

"Concentration"

The solution of separation was not, however, the panacea Americans expected and predicted it to be. The rationale undergirding that policy was destroyed in the 1840s by two factors: massive American migration across the trans-Mississippi West and over the Indians's land to Oregon and California, and vast territorial acquisition resulting from the War with Mexico (1846–1848). These factors dramatically altered the nation's perception of the Indian sanctuary on the prairies and plains. In the 1830s Americans viewed it as advantageous to the United States because it provided part of the answer to the nation's Indian question. But a decade later, that sanctuary had become an impediment to unifying a transcontinental nation, an open space that some day had to be filled and exploited.

U.S. policy toward the Native Americans took a significant turn during the 1850s. The government abandoned the policy of separation and in 1851, by means of the Indian Appropriation Act, adopted a new policy, that of concentration, which called for the drastic reduction of Indian landholdings in the West and the compulsory relocation of tribes to federal reservations where permanent residency, under strict governmental, judicial, and cultural control, would be enforced. The federal Indian Bureau rapidly concluded more than fifty concentration treaties with the Plains tribes and other western Indians whereby they forfeited more than fifteen million acres to the United States. Their new reservations provided them with less than 1.5 million acres.

Most tribes realized they could not resist the demands of the U.S. government and so settled on their assigned lands. Except for efforts to avoid conversion into farmers and to resist government programs aimed at transforming their culture, they generally caused the government in Washington few problems. The nomadic buffalo-hunting societies of the plains, such as Sioux, Cheyennes, Comanches, and Arapahoes, and certain other western tribes, such as the Apaches, proved to be a markedly different case for one principal reason: still controlling vast domains, they possessed the strength of their convictions in combination with superb martial skills to defend their land against the United States. Their resistance to the concentration policy and Washington's absolute determination to impose it on them resulted in a titanic struggle during the 1860s and 1870s called the Plains Wars.

The struggle had three phases. In the first, between 1865 and 1869, the army cleared the Central Plains of free-roaming Indians and forced the tribes onto reservations. The Medicine Lodge Creek Treaty established reserves south of Kansas in the Indian Territory (present-day Oklahoma), while treaties like that concluded at Fort Laramie in 1868 created reserves north of Nebraska. The United States demanded the confinement of tribes on their new reservations, where white missionaries and educators could then labor at transforming the Indians (after 1871, no longer officially dealt with as members of sovereign nations, but as wards of the United States) into "Americans." The United States also bluntly pledged that it was fully prepared to employ the military to ensure that tribes obeyed its dictum. The occasion arose twice, as the Plains Wars erupted again in the 1870s.

The second phase witnessed the final military destruction of the Plains Indians and their concentration on reservations. The Medicine Lodge Creek Treaty granted the Kiowas, Comanches, Southern Cheyennes and Arapahoes the right to supplement food allotments by hunting those buffalo grazing on the lands to the south of the Arkansas River, off their Indian Territory reservations, so long as the "buffalo may range thereon in such numbers as to justify the chase." Contained in this seemingly benevolent clause was the legal justification for restraining the southern plains tribes from all activity on the white settlers's lands and ultimately for permanently restricting them to their reservations. White buffalo hunters, in the late 1860s, killed off the remaining herds on the Central Plains and then, in the early 1870s, moved their operations farther south. Realizing what was at stake, warriors burst from their reservations and in June 1874 assaulted the white hunters. The ensuing conflict, known as the Red River War, represented the last significant armed encounter between the United States and the Southern Plains tribes. During this conflict, General Philip Sheridan chose a tactic approximating a war of attrition: a total war against the entire population, combatants and noncombatants, residing off the reservations. Sheridan brought the Red River War to a conclusion by the spring of 1875.

In 1874, the army discovered gold in the Black Hills on the Sioux reservation. Soon, thousands of whites tramped across Indian lands which the Fort Laramie Treaty protected. Many Indians, resentful of the invasion of their territory, left the reservation. The U.S. government ordered them all to return. Any found off the reservation after 1 February 1876 would be brought back by force. When the Indians refused, the army attacked them. Although Sioux and Cheyenne warriors destroyed Colonel George A. Custer and his command at the Battle of the Little Bighorn in June 1876, the victory did the Indians little good. By early 1877 most had been forced back onto their reservation. Only a small band under Sitting Bull remained at large. Five years later, even they, faced with starvation, returned to the reservation. The Great Sioux War closed belligerencies on the northern plains.

The 1880s made up the third phase, characterized by smaller, futile scuffles with the military. This phase culminated in the battle at Wounded Knee in 1890. Many Indians were discouraged and unhappy with life on their reservation. In Nevada, a Paiute named Wovoka had a vision that gave new hope to Indians. All Indians, he preached, must adopt a pacific life-style. They must put violence behind them, purge themselves of enmity toward whites, dance in a great circle and sing special songs. If they obeyed, Wovoka's dream would come true: the earth would be returned to the Indians with buffalo herds again filling the land.

The Ghost Dance became especially popular among the Sioux. Army and government officials became worried and ordered it halted. Most Sioux stopped. Some of the believers in the Ghost Dance left the reservation and tried to flee to the Dakota Badlands. Troops intercepted them and took them as prisoners to the small settlement of Wounded Knee, South Dakota. On the morning following their capture, the soldiers moved to disarm the Sioux. A shaman harangued the men to resist. One pulled a rifle and fired into the massed soldiers, who responded with a volley of rifle, pistol, and artillery fire.

Hand-to-hand combat followed. Of the 350 Sioux in the camp, as many as 300 died. The army returned the survivors to the reservation. Wounded Knee was the last battle between the Indians and the U.S. Army.

"Americanization"

Once the U.S. Army broke the military power of the western Indians, their existence meant life on a federal reservation. For people who had exalted freedom of movement, confinement was galling. It was rendered even worse by the deplorable conditions in which they lived. A few continued to leave the reservation in an attempt to regain freedom. But once shedding confinement, they collided with a world increasingly different from the one they had known. The buffalo, which once covered the land from horizon to horizon, could not be found. Railroads crisscrossed the West, dissecting their old lands. They saw settlers, cowboys, towns, farms, ranches, fences, cows, sheep, longhorns, telegraph lines—in short, everything that told of a burgeoning and alien way of life. The new and repellent cultural environment on the outside eventually served to keep most Indians on the inside, in the end effectively stifling any inclination to escape.

Beginning in the mid-1870s, the federal government modified its Indian policy to reflect the belief that its principal responsibility was to "Americanize" the Indians. Washington now sought the means to bring Indians into the American family, eventually hoping to eliminate the necessity for the government to maintain land reserves for Indians. Officials believed that only when Indians were fully integrated into the U.S. mainstream would their physical safety, material well-being, legal, and property rights be protected.

Thus, Washington turned to education and land reform to accomplish this "Americanizing" process. The government erected an elaborate three-tier system of Indian education, comprised of reservation day schools, reservation boarding schools, and off-reservation boarding schools. The schools's function, beyond the simple education of the children, was to remove them from the influence of their elders and to break the bonds of family, neighborhood, cultural heritage, and ethnic identity. Officials hoped too that adults on the reservations would be more inclined to remain peaceful and give up their traditional ways if their children were attending government schools, often many miles away. The curriculum in the schools sought to teach reading, writing, arithmetic, spelling, U.S. culture, patriotic citizenship, and vocational skills. Educators of the late-nineteenth and early-twentieth centuries believed that all Indians were good with their hands; hence boys learned skills and girls received instruction in home economics. There was no college preparatory curriculum for Indians since it was assumed that no "savage" could possess the innate intelligence to master college course work.

The schools accomplished half of their intended aim: they destroyed much of the social coherency and traditional identification of the Native Americans. However, they did not produce many "white Indians." On the contrary, they bred even deeper resentment toward the dominant white society. They also produced in their wards a keener awareness of the plight of their people and, at least in some, a determination to resist.

The policy of Americanization also rested on land reform, in particular allotment in severalty. This would teach the Indians self-reliance by the holding and working of private property, direct them toward economic self-sufficiency, and provide for the ultimate elimination of the reservation system. Congress in 1875 passed general legislation that extended the land benefits of the 1862 Homestead Act to Indians willing to surrender tribal status. Few Indians availed themselves, however. In 1887 President Grover Cleveland signed the Dawes General Allotment Act into law—legislation that President Theodore Roosevelt would later characterize to Congress as "a mighty pulverizing engine to break up the tribal mass." The Dawes Act authorized the president to subdivide the Indians's land into private plots without the consent of the tribes affected. The measure awarded a quarter section, or a 160-acre lot (the traditional plot of a white homestead), to the head of a family and smaller plots to individual family members. The government offered for sale to whites the communal tribal lands that it designated as surplus (that is, unallocated). The allotment system proved an unqualified failure. Not only did it violate the Native Americans's deepest feelings about the place of people in nature, but it at the same time robbed them of 70 percent of the land left them after the Plains Wars.

The trend of federal Indian policy following the defeat of the Plains Indians can be divided into four periods. The first, from the mid-1870s until roughly 1933, witnessed confinement within a reservation under careful scrutiny and rigid supervision. Indians were not actually imprisoned, but there were disturbing similarities to prison camps. The entrance of the United States into World War I in 1917 may be seen as a major turning point for the Native Americans. Eight thousand of them volunteered for and served in the armed forces. Seven years later, in 1924, the United States granted national citizenship to all Indians.

During the second period, which flowered briefly in the 1930s, the government initiated a reorganization and reconstruction of Indian policy, which was chiefly the result of the dedication and imagination of John Collier. As commissioner of Indian Affairs, Collier officially terminated the federal program of Americanization. He not only defended the Indians's right to their own cultural practices, but he believed there was much of value in those ways, value which could add a new depth to American society. Collier's policy of self-determination also envisaged the creation of new Indian governments free to forge their own societies within the United States. President Franklin D. Roosevelt liked what his commissioner was trying to do. He wrote of the status of the Indians in 1934: "The continuance of the autocratic rule by a federal department over the lives of more than 200,000 citizens of this nation is incompatible with American ideals of liberty. It is also destructive of the character and self-respect of a great race." Congress in 1934 approved the Indian Reorganization Act, which recognized the Indians's rights to traditional religion and religious practices, as well as a life-style free from federal interference and federally mandated norms. The U.S. government also ended allotment in severalty and tried to compensate tribes for lost lands.

The promise of the 1930s faded with the outbreak of World War II in 1939, followed by the entry of the United States in 1941. Many Indians welcomed military service as a traditional and honorable activity in which manhood could triumph over the degradation of reservation life. More than 25,000 men and women entered military service. (The Indian population numbered 345,252 in 1940.) Many served at the front and earned awards for distinguished service. In addition, some 50,000 left their homes to work in defense industries. Although legislation for Indians came to a virtual standstill during the war years, the experiences of those who departed the reservation produced greater acculturation than all the legislation which had acculturation as its aim. The war provided the first opportunity for a large number of Indians to observe the non-Indian world closely and over a prolonged period of time. The war years benefited Indians in another way too: they provided leadership and the training needed for dealing with the white world. Following World War II, many decided to remain living, working, and raising their families in the non-Indian world.

In the third period, from the late 1940s to the early 1960s, the federal government opted for a new implementation of an old policy: a speeded-up assimilation to be brought about by the termination of the federal trust and the integration of Indians into the mainstream of American society. Under one phase of the policy of Termination and Relocation, those Indians still residing on the reservation would be gradually placed in the non-Indian world. In typical fashion, federal agents transferred Indian families to large U.S. cities where they would receive housing and employment assistance and vocational training. But when these Indians found little work in the cities, they clustered in ghettos as African Americans had done a generation earlier. Indians strenuously opposed the government's newest policy, charging that it caused tribes extreme hardship and social disorganization. In the end, the United States did not terminate the federal trust with tribes, and many Indians never left the reservation.

The 1950s also saw the questioning of educational standards for all Americans, in large part because of the Soviet success in putting *Sputnik* into orbit. The value of learning, which had seemingly slipped in priority in an affluent and self-confident post-war U.S. society, became important again. The Native American young people joined the trend toward more serious study. Their college registration rose dramatically in the late 1950s. Many went on to graduate or professional school.

This development carried with it two important consequences. It exposed these students to the rapidly growing civil rights movement, which was particularly active on the nation's campuses. They inevitably perceived the relation of civil-rights grievances to the plight of their own people, both on and off the reservation. Further, the education they acquired made it possible for them, for the first time in the twentieth century, to look to their own community for trained and qualified professionals to provide leadership, rather than that of the whites.

The fourth period originated in the 1960s. Stimulated by the turbulent events of that decade, activism accelerated among the Native Americans as it did among other disadvantaged groups in the United States. Indian activists increasingly urged the federal government to become more concerned about the difficulties of Indian life. They bitterly pointed out that of all minority groups in the United States, the American Indians were the poorest: three out of five lived below the federally established poverty line. They demanded that something be done, and quickly, to address the blighted existence of their people, which was attributable in large measure to federal Indian policy as it developed in the nineteenth and continued into the twentieth century. Indians pressed for long-buried rights and demanded that white America fulfill its many unkept promises. The non-Indian world's consciousness was jolted into recognition of these demands by three events: the nineteen-month occupation of Alcatraz Island in San Francisco Bay beginning in the fall of 1969; the takeover of the Bureau of Indian Affairs office in Washington, D.C., in 1972; and the occupation of Wounded Knee, South Dakota, by members of the activist American Indian Movement (A.I.M.) in early 1973. However, as the U.S. war in Vietnam steadily decreased in the early 1970s, so too did most manifestations of 1960s radicalism, including Indian activism and any white support for it. Still, one legacy of the Indian rights movement is an increased pride among native peoples in being a Native American and in their people's traditional ways and beliefs. Another legacy

is that today there is somewhat more attention paid at national parks and museums, and in textbooks and school curriculums, to the history of the Native Americans and the Indian role in, and perspective on, the past.

The issue of what means could solve the Indian question, and the ensuing search for an answer shaped, reshaped, and to this day continues to affect the relationship of the federal government with the Native Americans. The search for "solutions" to the Indian question lies at the heart of understanding the relationship between the United States and the American Indians.

PHILIP WEEKS

See also American Revolution; Cleveland, Stephen Grover; Continental Expansion; Harrison, William Henry; Jackson, Andrew; Jefferson, Thomas; Monroe, James; Roosevelt, Franklin Delano; Roosevelt, Theodore; Washington, George

FURTHER READING
Debo, Angie. *A History of the Indians in the United States.* Normal, Okla., 1970.
Fixico, Donald L. *Termination and Relocation.* Albuquerque, N.M., 1986.
Gibson, Arrell Morgan. *The American Indians: Prehistory to the Present.* Lexington, Mass., 1980.
Goetzmann, William H. *When the Eagle Screamed.* New York, 1966.
Hoxie, Frederick E. *A Final Promise.* Lincoln, Nebr., 1984.
McConnell, Michael N. *A Country Between.* Lincoln, Nebr., 1992.
Prucha, Francis Paul. *American Indian Policy in the Formative Years.* Lincoln, Nebr., 1970.
——— . *The Great Father.* 2 vols. Lincoln, Nebr., 1984.
Weeks, Philip. *The American Indian Experience: A Profile, 1524 to the Present.* Arlington Heights, Ill., 1988.
——— . *Farewell, My Nation.* Arlington Heights, Ill., 1990.
Wooster, Robert. *The Military and the United States Indian Policy, 1865–1903.* New Haven, Conn., 1988.

NATO

See North Atlantic Treaty Organization

NAVY, U.S. DEPARTMENT OF

Established by the U.S. Congress in 1798 in response to the XYZ affair and deteriorating Franco-American relations. Actual construction of a small U.S. navy, under the auspices of the Department of War, had begun four years earlier in response to attacks by Barbary pirates on U.S. ships in the Mediterranean and its approaches. Already by 1798, however, it was apparent that the complexities of managing a naval establishment and the pressures of directing overseas naval operations in support of the young republic's emerging foreign policy would exhaust the limited institutional resources of the War Depart-

SECRETARIES OF THE NAVY

ADMINISTRATION	SECRETARY	PERIOD OF APPOINTMENT
J. Adams	Benjamin Stoddert	1798–1801
Jefferson	Robert Smith	1801–1809
Madison	Paul Hamilton	1809–1812
	William Jones	1813–1814
	Benjamin W. Crowninshield	1815–1818
Monroe		
	Smith Thompson	1819–1823
	Samuel L. Southard	1823–1829
J. Q. Adams		
Jackson	John Branch	1829–1831
	Levi Woodbury	1831–1834
	Mahlon Dickerson	1834–1838
Van Buren		
	James K. Paulding	1838–1841
W. H. Harrison	George E. Badger	1841
Tyler	Abel P. Upshur	1841–1843
	David Henshaw	1843–1844
	Thomas W. Gilmer	1844
	John Y. Mason	1844–1845
Polk	George Bancroft	1845–1846
	John Y. Mason	1846–1849
Taylor	William B. Preston	1849–1850
Fillmore	William A. Graham	1850–1852
	John P. Kennedy	1852–1853
Pierce	James C. Dobbin	1853–1857
Buchanan	Isaac Toucey	1857–1861
Lincoln	Gideon Welles	1861–1869
A. Johnson		
Grant	Adolph E. Borie	1869
	George M. Robeson	1869–1877
Hayes	Richard W. Thompson	1877–1880
	Nathan Goff, Jr.	1881
Arthur	William H. Hunt	1881–1882
Garfield		
Arthur	William E. Chandler	1882–1885
Cleveland	William C. Whitney	1885–1889
B. Harrison	Benjamin F. Tracy	1889–1893
Cleveland	Hilary A. Herbert	1893–1897
McKinley	John D. Long	1897–1902
T. Roosevelt		
	William H. Moody	1902–1904
	Paul Morton	1904–1905
	Charles J. Bonaparte	1905–1906
	Victor H. Metcalf	1906–1908
Taft	George von L. Meyer	1909–1913
Wilson	Josephus Daniels	1913–1921
Harding	Edwin Denby	1921–1924
Coolidge		
	Curtis D. Wilbur	1924–1929

(table continues on next page)

ADMINISTRATION	SECRETARY	PERIOD OF APPOINTMENT
Hoover	Charles F. Adams	1929–1933
F. Roosevelt	Claude A. Swanson	1933–1939
	Charles Edison	1939–1940
	Frank Knox	1940–1944
	James V. Forrestal	1944–1947
Truman		
	John L. Sullivan	1947–1949
	Francis P. Matthews	1949–1951
	Dan A. Kimball	1951–1953
Eisenhower	Robert B. Anderson	1953–1954
	Charles S. Thomas	1954–1957
	Thomas S. Gates, Jr.	1957–1959
	William B. Franke	1959–1961
Kennedy	John B. Connally	1961
	Fred H. Korth	1962–1963
L. Johnson	Paul H. Nitze	1963–1967
	Paul R. Ignatius	1967–1969
Nixon	John H. Chafee	1969–1972
	John Warner	1972–1974
	J. Wm. Middendorf II	1974–1977
Ford		
Carter	W. Graham Claytor, Jr.	1977–1979
	Edward Hidalgo	1979–1981
Reagan	John Lehman	1981–1987
	James H. Webb, Jr.	1987–1988
	William L. Ball III	1988–1989
Bush		
	H. Lawrence Garrett III	1989–1993
Clinton	John H. Dalton	1993–Present

Source: U.S. Department of the Navy

ment. In building a navy and establishing a Navy Department in the 1790s, the United States was able to draw upon the American nation's earlier experiences with naval power, particularly the Continental Congress's construction and operation of the makeshift Continental Navy during the Revolution, a force which was disbanded and sold off during the period of the Confederation.

The Department of the Navy exercises responsibility for both the U.S. Navy and the U.S. Marine Corps and is headed by a civilian secretary appointed by the president subject to Senate confirmation. From 1798 until 1947, the Department of the Navy was an independent executive agency, and the secretary of the navy was a cabinet member. Expansion of U.S. military forces during World War II and increased U.S. involvement in world political-military affairs following the war led to public and political pressure for military service reorganization to ensure effective coordination and to avoid duplication of effort.

Largely as a consequence of vigorous navy opposition, the National Security Act of 1947 stopped well short of complete merger of the military services. Nonetheless, the 1947 act greatly reduced the navy's autonomy: the Department of the Navy and its secretary were subordinated to a newly established cabinet-rank secretary of defense. In 1949, amendments to the 1947 act further reduced the Department of the Navy's independence; these amendments strengthened the secretary of defense, created a Department of Defense, and removed the secretary of the navy from the National Security Council (NSC). Navy resentment over unification and concern about the possible transfer of naval aviation to the air force and of the Marine Corps to the army came to a head during the 1949 congressional hearings on the B-36 bomber and led to the so-called "revolt of the admirals," when top naval officers testified against the Truman administration defense policy. The Defense

Reorganization Act of 1958 shifted yet more authority to the Office of the Secretary of Defense (OSD) and to the Joint Chiefs of Staff (JCS). In the 1960s, during the tenure of Secretary of Defense Robert S. McNamara, development of institutional and analytic capabilities and consolidation of power in the OSD reached new heights, resulting in considerable tension between the military services and the OSD.

Within the navy, the highest-ranking officer is the chief of naval operations (CNO), whom the president selects on the advice of the secretary of the navy and the secretary of defense. Though subordinate to the civilian secretary of the navy, the CNO possesses expertise, service loyalty, and staff support not generally available to the secretary. Consequently, the CNO's actual power and influence often dwarf those of the secretary. As a practical matter, a "bilateral system" of administration, which reflects the special competencies of the secretary and the CNO, has developed. While the secretary retains direct responsibility for business and political matters, in military matters he typically delegates authority to the CNO. The CNO is thus responsible for equipping, training, and administering the fleet and for maintaining overall discipline, morale, and military effectiveness. In the Marine Corps, the position of the commandant is analogous to that of the CNO. In addition to their duties within the Department of the Navy, however, the CNO and (since 1978) the commandant are also members of the JCS. As members of the JCS, these officers are not subordinate to the secretary of the navy but directly advise the president and the secretary of defense.

Under the system established in 1958 and that, with modification, continues today, the actual command of naval combatant forces operates through channels outside the Department of the Navy. Combatant forces are assigned to "unified" commands (composed of units from several services) or to "specified" commands (composed of units from a single service). Unified and specified commanders answer directly to the JCS, the secretary of defense, and the president. Historically, internal navy management and operations have been largely decentralized. The navy has relied on relatively autonomous bureaus or functional commands to handle research, development, and procurement. Operationally, the navy is divided into Pacific and Atlantic commands and, since early in the Cold War, into four fleets: two home fleets (the Third in the eastern Pacific and the Second in the Atlantic) and two forward fleets (the Seventh in the western Pacific and the Sixth in the Mediterranean). Since the late 1970s, the U.S. Navy has also maintained a significant regular presence in the Indian Ocean.

For most of the first century of its existence, the U.S. Navy was a relatively modest force with relatively modest duties. In peacetime, navy vessels typically operated individually and were stationed far from the United States, where they represented U.S. commercial and diplomatic interests. In wartime, the Navy was expected to protect U.S. coastal cities, to harass enemy commerce, and if possible, to protect U.S. commerce. During the Civil War, the U.S. Navy underwent major expansion, which permitted it to blockade the Confederacy and to assist the army in riverine campaigns and amphibious operations. In the quarter century following the Civil War, however, the navy was allowed to slip into technological and material obsolescence. The emergence of the modern U.S. Navy dates from the 1890s when, under the influence of the writings of Alfred Thayer Mahan (who argued the critical role of sea power in world history), the United States undertook a major naval buildup aimed at creating a fleet of battleships that operated as a unit and that destroyed an adversary's fleet in a decisive engagement. In the disillusionment following World War I, U.S. pursuit of naval power was temporarily put on hold: the Washington Naval Treaties of 1922 and the subsequent London Naval Treaty of 1930 severely limited the great powers' naval construction. The treaties prevented a looming Anglo-American naval arms race, but they assured Japanese predominance in Northeast Asia. Japanese abrogation of the treaties in 1936 resulted in a belated U.S. resumption of naval construction.

The development of naval aviation and its successful application during World War II led to the replacement of the battleship by the aircraft carrier. With the defeat of Japan and the decline of Britain, the United States emerged as the world's greatest naval power. In response to deteriorating U.S.-Soviet relations after World War II, the United States developed a policy of continuous forward naval presence, effectively establishing a U.S. protectorate over the world's seas and using this command to facilitate both alliance arrangements and overseas intervention. The U.S. Navy also fought successfully for a share in the nuclear deterrence mission: first U.S. aircraft carriers and later specially designed ballistic missile submarines were incorporated into U.S. nuclear war planes. To maintain sufficient naval and marine forces for these duties, the United States typically devoted roughly 2 percent of the gross national product (GNP) to the Department of the Navy during the Cold War. With the dissolution of the Soviet Union and the decay of the Russian Navy, the U.S. Navy emerged in effectively unchallenged command of the high seas; however, increasing dispersion of high-technology weapons continued to make coastal and narrow-seas operations potentially hazardous. In the 1991 Desert Storm campaign against Iraq, the U.S. Navy provided carrier-based airpower and cruise-missile strikes; although Iraqi-laid minefields proved an obstacle to close-in operations and no amphibious assault on the Iraqi or Kuwaiti coast was conducted, the threat of amphibious assault served to tie down significant numbers of Iraqi troops in coastal defense positions.

The end of the Cold War and the Desert Storm experience combined to encourage a rethinking of the role of naval power, and U.S. naval strategy underwent substantial revision in the early 1990s. Beginning in the late 1960s, in response to the détente process and to disillusionment with containment policies in Vietnam, U.S. naval strategy had focused on the politico-military task identified as central in Mahan's writings: maintaining command of the seas and control of the world's oceanic commons by decisively defeating the adversary's fleet. In the 1970s and 1980s this vision of naval power led to the development of the Navy's "Maritime Strategy," which stressed aggressively pursuing the Soviet fleet and threatening to alter the nuclear balance by destroying Soviet ballistic missile submarines. In the early 1990s, the U.S. Navy and government moved away from this fleet-versus-fleet and high-seas emphasis: the new Navy strategy, "From the Sea," emphasized the importance of projecting force ashore, against terrestrial political and military targets, and dominating littoral regions of the globe.

Although the navy and the Marine Corps experienced substantial cuts in the aftermath of the Cold War, both continue to deploy globally. In 1993, the U.S. Navy had approximately 510,000 men and women in active duty; the U.S. Marine Corps had about 183,000. The navy operated roughly twenty ballistic missile submarines, twelve aircraft carriers, ninety attack submarines, ninety cruisers and destroyers, fifty frigates, and fifty amphibious warfare ships. The Marine Corps had three active divisions and one reserve division.

EDWARD RHODES

See also Barbary States; Defense, U.S. Department of; London Naval Conferences of 1930 and 1935–1936; Mahan, Alfred Thayer; National Security Act; War, U.S. Department of; XYZ Affair

FURTHER READING

Albion, Robert Greenhalgh. *Makers of Naval Policy, 1798–1947.* Annapolis, Md., 1980.

Baer, George W. *One Hundred Years of Sea Power: The U.S. Navy, 1890–1990.* Stamford, Conn., 1994.

Coletta, Paolo E., ed. *American Secretaries of the Navy,* 2 vols. Annapolis, Md., 1980.

Hagan, Kenneth J. *This People's Navy: The Making of American Sea Power.* New York, 1991.

Love, Robert William, Jr., ed. *The Chiefs of Naval Operations.* Annapolis, Md., 1980.

Paullin, Charles Oscar. *Paullin's History of Naval Administration, 1775-1911.* Annapolis, Md., 1968.

NAVY LEAGUE

An organization founded in New York in 1902 by industrialists and naval enthusiasts to "acquire and spread before the citizens of the United States…information as to the condition of the naval forces and equipment of the United States, and to awaken public interest and co-operation in all matters tending to aid, improve and develop their efficiency." The league has consistently supported stated budgetary goals of a growing navy through publications (including at different times *The Navy,* *Sea Power,* and *Now Hear This*); rallies; congressional lobbying; and the development of the long-popular "Navy Day," which is held on Theodore Roosevelt's birthday. Despite its efforts, the league never became a major force in promoting the navalist agenda. With the 1947 consolidation of the armed services into the Department of Defense, navalism as a political movement lost most of its momentum. The league is based in Arlington, Virginia, from which it lobbies Congress and the public for expansion of the fleet. The league's message resounds less forcefully in a climate of interservice or joint operations.

MARK RUSSELL SHULMAN

See also Navy, U.S. Department of; Roosevelt, Theodore

FURTHER READING

Baer, George W. *One Hundred Years of Sea Power: The U.S. Navy, 1890-1990.* Stamford, Conn., 1994.

Rappaport, Armin. *The Navy League of the United States.* Detroit, 1962.

NEHRU, JAWAHARLAL

(*b.* 14 November 1889; *d.* 27 May 1964)

The first prime minister of India (1947–1964). Born in the city of Allahabad in the state of Uttar Pradesh in northern India and schooled in Great Britain, at Harrow and Cambridge, Nehru returned home on the eve of World War I and gradually rose to a leadership position in India's struggle for independence from British colonial rule. From his earliest days in politics, Nehru admired America's anticolonial heritage, but also disapproved of what he viewed as U.S. imperialism in Asia and Latin America. Following the bitter but ultimately successful struggle for independence from Great Britain in August 1947, Nehru crafted a foreign policy of nonalignment in the Cold War designed to steer India clear of military conflict and to assert India's independent role in international politics. He criticized Washington's nonrecognition of the People's Republic of China, the nuclear arms race, and U.S. support of France in Indochina. To Washington officials, nonalignment often seemed like thinly veiled procommunism, and Nehru's tone appeared increasingly abrasive. Tensions also arose over the subcontinent. Nehru had reluctantly accepted the

British partition of India along religious lines, into India and Pakistan; but the two nations went to war in October 1947 when the independent northern state of Kashmir, Muslim populated but led by a Hindu maharaja, aligned with India. Officially neutral in the dispute, Washington nonetheless worried about its destabilizing effects, helped broker a cease-fire in January 1948, and criticized Nehru's refusal to agree to a U.N.-sponsored plebiscite to determine the state's permanent status. In 1949, Kashmir was partitioned between Pakistan and India, but fighting over the disputed territory continued. On a different front, Nehru's domestic policies, especially his Congress Party's commitment to a mixed economy and heavy regulation of foreign investment, also contributed to friction in Indo-U.S. relations. These deteriorated badly in 1954 when the Eisenhower administration agreed to provide staunchly anticommunist Pakistan with military assistance.

Nehru's impact on world affairs reached its zenith after the Bandung Conference of nonaligned nations, held in April 1955 in Bandung, Indonesia, where he emerged as one of the best-known leaders of the so-called Third World. Both the United States and the Soviet Union wooed Nehru's India with economic aid. Praising India as the world's largest democracy, the Eisenhower administration had by 1960 made that nation its top candidate for development assistance. President John F. Kennedy further increased U.S. aid and tried nurturing warmer relations with New Delhi. Nonetheless, Nehru continued to criticize Washington's Cold War policies and especially U.S. military ties with Pakistan. Nehru's own prestige diminished dramatically after October 1962, when the People's Republic of China overwhelmed Indian troops in a brief border war. During that crisis, Nehru abandoned nonalignment and asked for Washington's help. The United States provided only modest levels of assistance. Nehru's popularity—at its height in 1961 after India had seized Goa from the Portugese—never recovered from the Chinese debacle. He died in office two years later.

DENNIS MERRILL

See also Cold War; India; Nonaligned Movement; Pakistan

FURTHER READING

Brands, H. W. *The Specter of Neutralism: The United States and the Emergence of the Third World.* New York, 1989.
Clymer, Kenton J. *Quest for Freedom: The United States and India's Independence.* New York, 1995.
Gopal, Sarvepalli. *Jawaharlal Nehru: A Biography*, 3 vols., New Delhi, 1975, 1979, 1984.
Hess, Gary R. "Accommodation Amid Discord: The United States, India, and the Third World." *Diplomatic History* 16 (Winter 1992): 1–22.
McMahon, Robert J. *The Cold War on the Periphery: The United States, India, and Pakistan.* New York, 1994.
Merrill, Dennis. *Bread and the Ballot: The United States and India's Economic Development.* Chapel Hill, N.C., 1990.

NEO-ISOLATIONISM

See Isolationism

NEPÂL

See Appendix 2

NETHERLANDS

Located in Western Europe, a nation bordering the North Sea between Belgium and Germany, with which the United States has had long and largely friendly relations. In January 1781, John Adams was formally appointed the U.S. minister to the Netherlands and was dispatched to negotiate a treaty and to secure loans for the fledgling nation. On 19 April 1782, after a period of customary Dutch caution, the States General of the United Provinces accepted Adam's credentials, making the Dutch government the first, after France, to recognize the United States. In October of the same year, a treaty of amity and commerce was signed, consistent with both Dutch pragmatic economic considerations and an affinity for the U.S. experiment in representative government and republican style of government.

Loans extended by the Dutch during 1782–1788 prevented national bankruptcy by allowing the United States to pay the interest on its debts to France. Of the $10 million U.S. debt in 1788, half was owed to Dutch creditors. Dutch loans allowed for U.S. capital investment and improvements in infrastructure.

In 1828 the United States asked Dutch King William to arbitrate a boundary dispute between the United States and Canada over the border between Canada and the state of Maine. This role was consistent with the evolving position of the Netherlands, which, aware of the vulnerability of small and middle powers, officially declared in 1837 a policy of noninvolvement and neutrality in world affairs. Although the king's judgment subsequently was rejected by the U.S. Senate in a vote of twenty-one to twenty, and the United States was accused by the king of attempting unduly to influence his decision, the dispute was insufficient to damage relations between the two countries.

The rest of the nineteenth century and the early part of the twentieth saw little cause for conflict between the foreign policies of the United States and the Netherlands. Dutch colonies in the East Indies were far removed from U.S. areas of concern and the Dutch policy of neutrality prevented an intersection of their national policies. Even at the onset of World War I, both the United States and the Netherlands were neutral. The United States later became a belligerent, however, and when the

Netherlands accorded sanctuary to the German kaiser, just prior to the armistice when U.S. troops were still committed, U.S. public opinion turned against the Netherlands.

With the advent of World War II, both the United States and the Netherlands again attempted to pursue neutralism. However, Hitler's invasion of the Netherlands in the Spring of 1940 and subsequent occupation until 1945 forced Queen Wilhelmina to move her government to London in exile. Before the invasion and U.S. entrance into the war, President Franklin Roosevelt, motivated in part by his family's Dutch ancestry, offered the royal family safe haven in the United States. The subsequent intimate cooperation between the free Dutch and the U.S. armed forces created a bond between the two nations and people that had never been stronger. U.S. participation in the liberation of the Netherlands and the establishment of the Marshall Plan in 1947 to aid in postwar reconstruction ushered in a new era of close U.S.-Dutch relations.

Under the Marshall Plan, the Netherlands received more than $1.1 billion in aid, the fifth largest recipient after Great Britain, France, Italy and West Germany, and the largest recipient in terms of aid per capita. The United States, however, did use Marshall Plan aid as leverage to dissuade the Netherlands from reestablishing control over its former East Indies possessions. When the Dutch took military action in Indonesia in 1948, they were denounced before the United Nations by the U.S. representative, and the termination of Marshall Plan aid was threatened. The Dutch ultimately acquiesced to U.S. pressure despite regarding it as undue interference. From the U.S. perspective, the pressure seemed appropriate given the onset of the Cold War and U.S. fears of antagonizing nationalist forces in Asia and the Middle East and driving them into the Soviet sphere of influence. U.S. anticolonial sentiments and widespread sympathies in Congress for the cause of Indonesian nationalism also drove policy. Later, President Kennedy also pressured the Dutch to cede Dutch New Guinea to Indonesia in an effort to lure the Indonesian leader, Sukarno, away from Moscow. Again, the Netherlands grudgingly relented.

The United States and the Netherlands proved to be strong military allies within the NATO alliance and political allies within the United Nations. The Netherlands sent a combat unit of volunteers to join fourteen other countries as part of the UN-sanctioned forces during the Korean War. U.S. military aid accounted for half the military equipment the Dutch acquired during the 1950s. During that decade—and in the 1960s—the Dutch were willing to leave matters of NATO strategy to the United States, trusting in the reliability of U.S. strategic guarantees to Europe and firmly rejecting the formation of an independent European nuclear force. In 1957 the Netherlands was the first NATO country to react positively to the U.S. offer for deployment of tactical nuclear weapons on European soil and for placing them under NATO command. The Netherlands also consistently supported the U.S. position of excluding the People's Republic of China from UN membership and even defended early U.S. involvement in Vietnam.

Starting in the 1970s, however, the Netherlands began to demonstrate a desire for some distancing from the superpower rivalry, despite its continuing commitment to NATO membership and military cooperation with the United States. In 1972, for example, the Dutch criticized the Christmas bombings of North Vietnam and they provided development aid to Cuba and North Vietnam from 1973 to 1977. In 1977, the Netherlands led the drive against President Carter's intention to produce the neutron bomb and deploy it in Western Europe and in 1979, the Dutch also resisted NATO deployment of new generation intermediate-range nuclear missiles on their territory.

With the end of the Cold War, containment and nuclear issues are no longer points of disagreement between the United States and the Netherlands. Dutch leaders in 1991 reaffirmed their commitment to a strong NATO, demonstrating that military and diplomatic links remain strong. Economic relations also are close as Dutch foreign direct investment in the United States continues to rank third, exceeded only by British and Japanese foreign direct investment in the United States.

REBECCA BRITTON

See also Indonesia; Marshall Plan; North Atlantic Treaty Organization; World War II

FURTHER READING

Flynn, Gregory, ed. *NATO's Northern Allies: The National Security Policies of Belgium, Denmark, the Netherlands, and Norway.* Totowa, N.J, 1985.

Reichenbach-Consten, Gertrude, and Abraham Noordergraaf, eds. *Two Hundred Years of Netherlands-American Interaction.* Bryn Mawr, Pa., 1985.

Schulte-Nordholt, J.W., and Robert P. Swierenga, eds. *A Bilateral Bicentennial: A History of Dutch-American Relations, 1782–1982.* Toronto, 1982.

NEUTRALITY ACTS OF THE 1930S

Legislation designed to keep the United States out of future wars, passed by Congress and signed by the president in 1935, 1936, 1937, and 1939. Endlessly debated and frequently revised, these acts became the central element of U.S. foreign policy from 1935 to 1941.

The legislation had its origins in three sometimes-conflicting streams of thought, all of which can be seen as interpretations of the U.S. experience in World War I. The first held that in the face of the massive changes in warfare in the twentieth century, some traditional neutral rights had to be relinquished to maintain the neutrality of the United States in future international conflicts. This concept, which was advanced by Secretary of State Henry L. Stimson in the waning days of the Hoover administration, was widely promoted by experts in international law and was substantially adopted by the Department of State in 1935. A second element was the idea that, to maintain peace and thereby promote its own security, the United States should cooperate with international collective security efforts that promoted disarmament and the cutting off of arms shipments to nations at war; Stimson had tried unsuccessfully to move in that direction, and the new administration of President Franklin D. Roosevelt pursued it in 1933 and 1934. The final, and ultimately the determining, element in neutrality legislation was the isolationist impulse, which sought to insulate the United States against war by prohibiting activities that were deemed to have brought the country into World War I. A majority of the members of Congress, and almost certainly a majority of the American people, shared that impulse for most of the decade of the 1930s.

In 1935, the Roosevelt administration sought authorization from Congress for a discretionary embargo on the sale of arms to belligerents, hoping to bring an end to the Chaco War between Bolivia and Paraguay and, if possible, to avert an impending Italian attack on Ethiopia. Under the influence of revelations produced by the investigation of the munitions industry by the Senate committee headed by Gerald P. Nye, and with pressure provided by powerful isolationists who feared that the discretionary application of embargoes might involve the United States in war, Congress instead passed the Neutrality Act of 1935. This act required the president, in the event of war anywhere, to bar the shipment of arms and ammunition to all participants, regardless of which ones had been the aggressors. Arms shipments to the Allies during World War I, it was argued, had been a major cause of U.S. entry into the war, and banning such shipments would do much to keep the country out of future wars. The bill passed both the Senate and the House by an overwhelming vote of 79 to 2 in the Senate and was signed by Roosevelt on 31 August. The Neutrality Act of 1935, however, left the president some discretion both in the definition of what constituted arms and ammunition and in the application of the law to new belligerents entering an existing conflict. While it set up a National Munitions Board to license and supervise all arms shipments and forbade munitions destined for belligerents to be carried on U.S. ships, it allowed the president to choose whether to bar the shipment of supplies from U.S. ports on vessels of a belligerent power, to keep such a country's submarines out of U.S. ports, and to proclaim that American citizens traveling on belligerent ships did so at their own risk.

Even this partial compromise between Congress and the president had been difficult to achieve, and the law was to expire in six months. The presumed lessons of World War I were to be found in its every clause. Roosevelt invoked the new law in the Italian-Ethiopian War on 5 October, but he noted its unneutral effects: Ethiopia was denied access to American arms it desperately needed (but had no realistic possibility of acquiring), while well-armed Italy ran its tanks and planes on increasing quantities of U.S. oil. Still eager to use neutrality laws as a foreign policy tool, Roosevelt now sought to gain discretionary embargo powers for war material other than arms. A large majority of Congress remained suspicious of presidential discretion and of two minds on the trade issue. In February, the Neutrality Act of 1936 was approved by a vote of 353-27 in the House of Representatives and without a record vote in the Senate. It extended the mandatory arms embargo for a year and, drawing another ostensible lesson from World War I, added a ban on loans to belligerents. The next armed conflict to break out in Europe was not in war between nations but an internal conflict in Spain: in 1936, General Francisco Franco, supported by Italy and Germany, sought to overthrow the government of the Spanish Republic, which was, in its turn, aided by the Soviet Union. U.S. neutrality legislation did not apply to civil wars, but Roosevelt undertook to extend it. He was motivated in part by the wish to cooperate with the Nonintervention Committee established by Great Britain and France in hopes of limiting the Spanish conflict, and he acted in the mistaken belief that extending the embargo to Spain would hurt Franco's rebel forces more than the elected government. Congress, primarily interested in keeping the United States out of war, approved the necessary legislation with only a single dissenting vote on 6 January 1937.

By that time, discussion of the "permanent" Neutrality Act of 1937 was already under way. Once again Congress tried to insulate the United States against future conflicts while the Roosevelt administration sought to retain some flexibility that would allow cooperation with collective security efforts. The House agreed to a compromise measure by a vote of 376-12, but in the Senate, whose isolationists made a strong stand, the conference report which agreed with the House bill was accepted by a vote of only 41 to 15, with 39 abstentions. Signed by Roosevelt on 1 May, the measure applied to all wars and required the president to embargo arms and implements of war, to ban loans and American travel on belligerent ships, and to forbid the arming of American merchant ships trading with warring states. Its new "cash-and-carry" clause allowed the president to limit trade with belligerents in war material other than arms by requiring that such goods be paid for before they left the country and not be carried on American ships. This legislation did not insulate the United States against wars elsewhere in the world any more than its predecessors had. It was marginally helpful to Great Britain and France, which would have greater access to money and ships than their potential adversaries in any foreseeable future war, and, had it been invoked, would have helped Japan in its war against China. It may have given encouragement to Adolf Hitler's moves toward building a greater German Reich, since he might now virtually take for granted that the United States would do nothing to stop him.

The rationale for neutrality legislation came increasingly into question as Germany's annexation of Austria in 1938 and its territorial demands on Czechoslovakia in 1938 and early 1939 appeared to be threats not only to world peace, but to American security as well. In the spring of 1939, Roosevelt proposed scrapping the arms embargo and putting all trade with belligerents on a cash-and-carry basis, thereby making military aid to Great Britain and France possible. But the "selling arms means war" mood in Congress remained strong enough to prevent passage. When the House voted to restore an only slightly modified arms embargo to the administration proposal and, by a vote of 217 to 173, refused to delete it, the measure was effectively dead. Only after World War II broke out on 1 September 1939 and Hitler's forces overran Poland in less than a month was Congress persuaded that attempts to insulate the United States from foreign conflict no longer served the nation's needs. Still, the Neutrality Act of 1939 which Roosevelt signed on 4 November retained all the provisions of the earlier law except for the arms embargo.

Over the next two years the 1939 act was circumvented in various ways, most spectacularly by the president's September 1940 agreement with Great Britain to swap fifty American destroyers for the right to establish U.S. naval and air bases on British territory in the Western Hemisphere, thus giving Great Britain the use of ships of the officially neutral U.S. Navy; and by the passage of the Lend-Lease Act in March 1941, which negated the "cash" portion of the cash-and-carry provision of the Neutrality Act. Not until October 1941, however, did Roosevelt request formal revision of that law. Congress responded in November by voting, by margins of 50 to 37 in the Senate but only 212 to 194 in the House, to permit the arming of American merchantmen and their entry into war zones and belligerent ports. Though the United States had by this time moved far away from anything that might be properly described as neutrality, remnants of the neutrality acts were still in place when the Japanese attacked Pearl Harbor.

MANFRED JONAS

See also America First Committee; Austria; Bolivia; Collective Security; Czech Republic; Ethiopia; Franco, Francisco; Germany; Hitler, Adolf; Isolationism; Italy; Neutral Rights; Nye, General Prentice; Paraguay; Roosevelt, Franklin Delano; Spain; Stimson, Henry Lewis; World War II

FURTHER READING
Cole, Wayne C. *Roosevelt and the Isolationists, 1932–1945*. Lincoln, Neb., 1983.
Divine, Robert A. *The Illusion of Neutrality*. Chicago, 1968.
Ginsburg, Thomas N. *The Pursuit of Isolationism in the United States Senate from Versailles to Pearl Harbor*. New York, 1982.
Jonas, Manfred. *Isolationism in America, 1935–1941*. Ithaca, N.Y., 1966 and Chicago, 1990.

NEUTRALITY PROCLAMATION OF 1793

See Washington, George

NEUTRALITY PROCLAMATION OF 1914

See World War I

NEUTRAL RIGHTS

The trading rights of neutral states in time of war. The assertion and defense of neutral rights were important elements in American foreign policy from the nation's earliest days, and on two occasions, in 1812 and 1917, played a major role in bringing the United States into war. The concept of neutral rights developed during the seventeenth and eighteenth centuries, as the world's oceans became major commercial highways and sea power acquired a decisive role in European wars. Belligerents sought to prevent all nations from trading with their enemies. Neutrals, caught in the middle and dependent on trade for their prosperity, sought to trade as freely as possible and claimed "neutral rights." Maintaining the right of neutrals to trade in wartime (even with belligerents) required laying down rules of blockade and definitions of contraband as well as developing a set of ground rules that defined the rights and duties of neutral states. Although belligerents were rarely inclined to recognize the rights of neutrals, they were frequently compelled to do so in order to prevent retaliation or a wider war, and over the course of time these rights were incorporated into treaties, domestic legislation, and the rulings of prize courts, where they became part of international law.

The concept of neutral rights was firmly established by the time of the founding of the United States. A central concern of the American colonists who declared their independence from Great Britain in 1776 was to escape the effects of British mercantilism and Great Britain's wars. The economy of the colonies, they believed, could flourish as never before if it were relieved of restrictions imposed from London and could trade with the entire world, both in peace and war. Accordingly, the Continental Congress opened trade with all nations in April 1776, nearly two months before delegate Richard Henry Lee introduced his motion for independence. In response to Lee's resolve of 7 June, Congress simultaneously appointed three committees to develop plans for the future. The first of these was to draft a declaration of independence, the second a plan of government, and the third a model treaty to regulate relations with foreign nations, beginning with France.

The model treaty, drafted under the chairmanship of John Adams, contained a broad definition of neutral rights. It called for the list of contraband goods to be both limited and short, for freedom to trade between the ports of a country at war, and for acceptance of the principle that free ships make free goods, that is, neutral ships (free from belligerent status) made the cargo free from capture. Contraband was defined as instruments of war, such as swords or guns, which even neutrals accepted could be captured by a belligerent to prevent delivery to an enemy. The treaty of amity and commerce with France, a companion to the 1778 alliance, actually contained these provisions, as did a commercial treaty with the Netherlands two years later. After the end of the American War for Independence, the Americans concluded similar treaties of amity and commerce with Sweden (1783), Prussia (1785), and Morocco (1787).

The United States did not, however, succeed in making such arrangements with Great Britain or Spain, two of the major maritime powers. The British did not even fully respect the commercial rights they had acknowledged in the Treaty of Paris (1783), which had recognized U.S. independence. The inability of the government under the Articles of Confederation to command acceptance of its views was a key factor leading to their replacement by the Constitution of 1787. Major problems concerning neutral rights arose with the outbreak of war between Great Britain and France in 1793. These problems plagued the new nation until the end of the Napoleonic Wars more than twenty years later.

To steer clear of these wars, in which the alliance with France might have involved the United States, and to protect its commerce, now severely threatened, President George Washington issued a proclamation of neutrality on 22 April 1793. Congress passed a Neutrality Act in June 1794, and Washington sent Chief Justice John Jay to London to negotiate a treaty of commerce and navigation that might reduce tension between the countries and secure U.S. trading rights. Jay's Treaty (19 November 1794) almost failed to win approval in the Senate, largely because of its shortcomings on the trade issue. It accepted Great Britain's notorious Rule of 1756, which had seriously limited neutral rights during the Seven Years' War and specifically granted the British the right to capture enemy goods on American ships in clear violation of the principle that free ships make free goods. The treaty failed to mention the rancorous issue of impressment, the practice of removing seamen from U.S. ships on the high seas and forcing them into British service, or the more recent British seizure of U.S. merchant ships bound for France. Americans sympathetic to the French Revolution and ideologically antipathetic to Great Britain denounced Jay's Treaty as a betrayal of the French ally, the nation whose assistance had made American independence possible. The seeming breach of the alliance with France and approach to Great Britain that the treaty represented allowed the United States to reach a new agreement with Spain, which incorporated the U.S. conception of neutral rights. Pinckney's Treaty (27 October 1795) provided for a narrow list of contraband, the right to trade with belligerents except in the case of fully enforced blockades, and for the general principle that free ships make free goods. The Senate approved that treaty unanimously.

France retaliated against Jay's Treaty with a series of decrees in the summer of 1796, stipulating that henceforth neutral shipping would be treated as it allowed itself to be treated by Great Britain and specifically authorized the seizure of neutral vessels laden in whole or in part with property bound for the British Isles. On 15 November 1796 France also announced the suspension of diplomatic relations with the United States. Attempts to settle matters between the countries led first to the notorious XYZ affair, when officials of France's Directory demanded a bribe from the U.S. delegation that had been sent to Paris but received "not a sixpence," and then to more assertive action. During June and July of 1798 Congress declared all treaties with France abrogated and suspended all trade. It then provided for the construction of naval vessels and an increase in the size of the army and authorized President John Adams to use the navy to protect U.S. merchant ships from seizure by the French—even by capturing armed French vessels if necessary. Congress also permitted the arming of U.S. merchant ships, and, by an act of 2 March 1799, created a separate Navy Department.

The Nineteenth Century

The Quasi-War with France that resulted from these countermeasures to the French decrees continued for nearly three years. A brief respite occurred in the battle over neutral rights when the Convention of 1800 abrogated the French Alliance of 1778 and replaced it with a commercial treaty that retained the liberal definition of neutral rights, and the Treaty of Amiens (1802) temporarily ended the European war. When war resumed between France and Great Britain in 1803, and especially after Austria, Russia, and Prussia also entered the war against Napoleon in 1805, each side took steps to shut off the other's trade, neutral rights went unrecognized, and U.S. commerce with Europe and its colonies was threatened once more.

A British admiralty court ruled in the case of the *Essex* (1805) that the U.S. practice of carrying goods from France's American colonies to France, with only a brief stop at a U.S. port (such goods made up more than half of U.S. "exports" in that year), did not legally constitute a broken voyage and did not exempt U.S. vessels from seizure. A series of Orders in Council set up a blockade of all ports controlled by France, thus forcing neutrals to trade with the Continent through Great Britain. With the Berlin and Milan Decrees, Napoleon in turn placed an embargo on trade with Great Britain and on all British merchandise and ordered the seizure of all ships paying a tax to the British government or otherwise obeying the Orders in Council. In subsequent decrees, he sequestered U.S. ships in French ports and confiscated their cargoes.

The competing orders and decrees did not destroy the carrying trade of the United States, but it was seriously injured. Because the nation lacked the military means to protect its shipping, Presidents Thomas Jefferson and James Madison tried negotiation, chiefly with Great Britain, and peaceful coercion of both Great Britain and France in an effort to win respect for U.S. rights as a neutral. Negotiations made little progress. What James Monroe and William Pinkney were able to secure in London provided even less protection for neutral rights than had Jay's Treaty. Jefferson did not even submit the proposed arrangements to the Senate for consideration. The Erskine Agreement (1809), negotiated by the British minister in Washington who had exceeded his authority, was promptly repudiated in London. The Americans tried various schemes of coercion, beginning with the Nonintercourse Act of 1806, which excluded important British manufacturers from the United States, continuing most drastically with the Embargo Act of 1807, which forbade all foreign commerce of the United States from 1807 to 1809, and culminating in Macon's Bill No. 2 (1810), which reopened trade with everyone, including Great Britain and France, but stated that if either of these countries ceased "to violate the neutral commerce of the United States," nonintercourse would be resumed against the other. All attempts had unsatisfactory results.

The apparent failure to persuade the British to retreat on the issue of neutral rights helped sway public sentiment for war against Great Britain in 1812. The belief that Great Britain denied U.S. rights as a neutral, together with its practice of impressment, struck at American independence and became the major impetus for the War of 1812. "A violation of our neutral rights," Secretary of State James Monroe told the U.S. peace commissioners, "was among the principal causes of the War with England." The war did not settle that issue, although, ironically, Great Britain had revoked the Orders in Council so far as they applied to U.S. commerce on 23 June 1812, five days after the U.S. declaration of war, but before that declaration had been received in London. The Treaty of Ghent, which ended the war in December 1814, and the final defeat of Napoleon the following year, which ended more than two decades of warfare in Europe, effectively removed neutral rights from the center of U.S. policy concerns. The commercial treaty concluded by the United States with Great Britain in 1815 did not go beyond Jay's Treaty in the recognition of neutral rights, and impressment ended only in practice, but the absence of major maritime wars for the remainder of the century effectively removed the threat to U.S. trade.

The United States officially maintained a neutral position in the Texas War for Independence (1835–1836) and the Canadian Uprising of 1837, and although it failed to live up to its own neutrality laws, in neither case did it face a challenge to its rights as a neutral. During the War with Mexico (1846–1848), the United States was able to establish an effective, and therefore legal, blockade of Mexican ports and encountered no difficulties with neutral nations. When the Crimean War broke out in 1854, Great Britain and France independently agreed to the principle that free ships make free goods, accepted the notion that blockades must be effective to be legal, and, for good measure, stipulated that privateers could not be commissioned. Subscribed to by all other major European powers, this agreement formally became the Declaration of Paris of 1856. Ironically, the United States, which had long championed these ideas, failed to endorse the declaration, primarily because it was unwilling to surrender the right to commission privateers. The irony was compounded when, after the outbreak of the American Civil War in 1861, the United States offered to adhere to the declaration if its provisions were applied to the Confederacy.

The Civil War, in fact, placed the United States on the opposite side of the neutral-rights controversy from the one to which it had become accustomed. President Abraham Lincoln's administration never recognized the Confederacy, did not declare war against it, and officially regarded all military operations as a police action against rebellious citizens. When the Union declared a blockade of Confederate ports on 19 April 1861, however, Great

Britain declared its neutrality on 13 May, thus in effect granting the Confederacy belligerent status and bringing the U.S. blockade within the scope of traditional neutral rights. Because the United States lacked the means to make the blockade effective until late in the war, the possibility grew of a confrontation with Great Britain. The Confederacy, which sought diplomatic recognition, repeatedly urged all European nations to challenge the blockade, but Great Britain thought it more prudent not to do so.

Only in the *Trent* affair did the British seriously assert their rights as neutrals. On 8 November 1861, a U.S. warship intercepted the British mail steamer *Trent* on the high seas in the West Indies, took off two Confederate commissioners, and sent them as prisoners to Boston in clear violation of Great Britain's rights as a neutral. London's reaction was electric. It demanded the return of the commissioners with suitable apology, threatened to close its legation in Washington, and made preparations for war. In finally yielding to the British ultimatum, Secretary of State William H. Seward wryly expressed satisfaction that the British had accepted a principle concerning neutral rights that the United States had long asserted.

Seward expressed no satisfaction, however, with the building of warships in Great Britain for the Confederacy. These vessels, the most notorious of which was the *Alabama*, were designed as commerce raiders and posed a serious threat to U.S. trade. The United States argued that Great Britain had failed to perform its duty as a neutral in permitting the ships to leave British waters, but satisfaction came only after the war was over. In 1871 an international arbitration tribunal awarded the United States $15.5 million for the damage inflicted by the Confederate cruisers, and the principles established in these proceedings found their way into a convention on the rights and duties of neutrals at the Second Hague Conference (1907).

The Twentieth Century

The promotion of neutral rights was a major cause for the United States both at the First Hague Conference (1899) and at the second. When the convention adopted at The Hague in 1907 left loopholes with respect to rules of contraband and of blockade, the United States participated in a subsequent conference that produced the Declaration of London (1909), which finally included the expansive concept of neutral rights long championed by the United States. This declaration remained unratified, however, when war broke out in Europe in 1914.

On 4 August 1914 President Woodrow Wilson issued the first of his ten separate declarations of neutrality, and two days later the Department of State asked all belligerents to adhere to the terms of the Declaration of London. Germany promptly signified its agreement, but Great Britain, which planned to use its superior navy to blockade Germany, responded at once with an Order in Council that made major modifications in the rules laid down in 1909. Among other things, the order greatly expanded the contraband list and virtually wiped out the distinction between absolute and conditional contraband. France and Russia soon followed the British example. Secretary of State Robert Lansing at first called the modifications unacceptable, but by 24 August the United States had withdrawn its insistence on the Declaration of London and retreated from its protests against Allied practices to the vague terrain of international law. These practices soon included the bringing of neutral vessels into British ports to be searched, the condemning of cargoes on neutral ships bound for Scandinavia on the suspicion that their ultimate destination was Germany, and the sowing of underwater mines to help enforce the blockade.

Such measures constituted a massive interference with U.S. trade and drew repeated protests from the Department of State. The British generally sent conciliatory replies to the U.S. notes but changed their policies only for the worse. Unlike during the Napoleonic Wars, however, the United States did not seek to protect what it deemed to be its rights as a neutral against Great Britain and its allies, either through economic retaliation or the threat of force. Wilson, to be sure, wrote to Colonel Edward M. House in London on 23 July 1916 that he was about at the end of his patience with Great Britain and was "seriously considering asking Congress to authorize me to prohibit loans and restrict exportations to the allies." Action along these lines did not take place at first because of basic sympathy and understanding for the allies, and then because of violations of neutral rights stemming from Germany's use of the submarine. These violations involved the loss of lives as well as property and therefore overshadowed those hardships caused by Great Britain.

The effectiveness of the British blockade and the growing stream of supplies reaching England from beyond the Atlantic persuaded the Germans on 4 February 1915 to declare a war zone around the British Isles in which all merchant vessels would be sunk without warning. The United States protested at once, calling any possible sinking of U.S. vessels "an indefensible violation of neutral rights" and promising to hold the German government "to a strict accountability for such acts of their naval authorities." Germany thereupon offered to reconsider its policy if the United States could persuade Great Britain to allow passage of food and other nonmilitary supplies. When Washington agreed to try, the German Admiralty Order of 18 February 1915, calling for "commercial warfare with U-boats" was amended to instruct submarine commanders to exercise extraordinary care "to avoid the unintentional sinking of [American] vessels."

The United States did try, to no avail, but it also accepted the British response to Germany's declaration of submarine warfare without serious protest. When the Order in Council of 11 March put a stop to all neutral trade with Germany, the United States merely reserved its right to trade with European neutrals and to seek future compensation for any damage done by the new British policy. Nor did it protest strongly to Germany when the first U.S. ships were attacked by U-boats, or even when one American was killed in the torpedoing of the British passenger ship *Falaba*. On 7 May, however, a German submarine sank the British liner *Lusitania* outward bound from New York, with a loss of 1,198 lives, including 128 U.S. citizens.

In its first response to the sinking on 13 May, the United States insisted that Germany halt its submarine war on merchant shipping. A second *Lusitania* note was even sterner in tone and threatened direct action if German trepidations did not cease. Berlin made a conciliatory reply and offered compensation, but when the British liner *Arabic* was sent to the bottom on 19 August with two Americans aboard, the United States approached the brink of action. Germany retreated by reiterating its naval order of 18 February and offering the so-called *Arabic* Pledge: submarines would no longer attack passenger ships without giving adequate warning and rescuing passengers and crew. By 18 September full U-boat warfare had effectively been halted in the English Channel and along Great Britain's west coast. In countering the protest registered against this decision by his admirals, Germany's William II (Kaiser Wilhelm) offered the classic reason for recognizing neutral rights. "America," he asserted, "had to be prevented from participating in the war against us as an active enemy." When an errant U-boat commander nonetheless torpedoed the French passenger ship *Sussex* in March 1916, injuring several Americans, the German government responded to the strong U.S. protest by reaffirming the *Arabic* Pledge.

On 1 February 1917, however, Germany resumed unrestricted submarine warfare in a wide zone around Great Britain and France and in the eastern and central Mediterranean. Two days later the United States broke diplomatic relations, as it had threatened to do after the *Sussex* incident in 1916. Between 16 and 18 March, three U.S. ships were sunk by German submarines. On 6 April the United States declared war. As in 1812, the defense of neutral rights was a major factor leading to that declaration.

In the aftermath of World War I, the definition of neutral rights underwent major changes. For the world at large that was due primarily to the U.S.-sponsored Covenant of the League of Nations, which stipulated that if a member state made war in violation of its obligations, the league would prohibit trade and financial relations with that state and require even nonmembers to abide by these sanctions. The traditional right of neutrals to trade with belligerents was thus virtually eliminated, at least in theory. For the United States, the retreat from neutral rights was carried even farther by the growing belief that the assertion of these rights had led this country into war, a decision whose wisdom many of the events of the 1920s seemed to call into question.

As the world headed for a new war in the early 1930s, the idea that traditional neutral rights would have to be relinquished to keep the United States out of war was advanced by Secretary of State Henry L. Stimson in the waning days of President Herbert Hoover's administration. Promoted by experts in international law, both public and private, the idea was substantially adopted by President Franklin D. Roosevelt's Department of State in 1934. Bolstered by the priority given by Congress to the avoidance of war, it found its way into U.S. neutrality legislation. By the Neutrality Acts of 1935, 1936, and 1937, the United States prohibited all trade in arms and ammunition with belligerents, even through neutrals, and trade in war materials other than arms and ammunition in U.S. ships. It also banned loans to belligerents, barred U.S. citizens from traveling on belligerent ships, and forbade the arming of U.S. vessels trading with warring states. In practice, the United States actually surrendered few neutral rights. It did not invoke the laws in the Sino-Japanese conflict, and it progressively amended them as soon as war broke out in Europe in September 1939. Mindful of the events of 1917, Germany did not challenge neutral rights even as the United States moved into a state of "dynamic nonbelligerency" in support of the Allies.

The defense of neutral rights ceased, in any event, to be a major concern of U.S. foreign policy after World War II. In the aftermath of that war, the United Nations became the successor to the League of Nations and carried even further that body's limitations on neutral rights. The United States became so powerful and so deeply involved in world affairs that in subsequent conflicts it was never really a neutral and, in any event, was unlikely to be seriously challenged. For other nations who wished to remain neutral, nonalignment replaced neutrality for a time, but the rights of the nonaligned were never defined or recognized. The defense of neutral rights, a centerpiece of U.S. foreign policy since the Republic's earliest days, had been overtaken by events.

MANFRED JONAS

See also Adams, John; Alabama Claims; American Civil War; American Revolution; Articles of Confederation; Blockade; Economic Sanctions; Germany; Great Britain; Hague Peace Conferences; Impressment; International Law; Jay, John; Lusitania; Mexico, War with; Monroe-Pinckney Treaty; Napoleonic Wars; Navy, U.S. Department of; Neutrality Acts of the 1930s; Nonaligned Movement; Orders in Council; Pinckney's Treaty; Trent Affair; War of 1812; Wilson, Thomas Woodrow; World War I; XYZ Affair

FURTHER READING

Bowman, Albert Hall. *Diplomacy During the Federalist Era.* Knoxville, Tenn., 1974.

Divine, Robert A. *The Illusion of Neutrality*, 2nd ed. Chicago, 1968.

Gabriel, Jurg Martin. *The American Conception of Neutrality After 1945.* New York, 1988.

Horsman, Reginald. *The Causes of the War of 1812.* Philadelphia, Pa., 1962.

Jessup, Philip C., et al. *Neutrality, Its History, Economics, and Law,* 4 vols. New York, 1936.

May, Ernest R. *The World War and American Isolation, 1914–1917,* 2nd ed. Chicago, 1966.

Orvik, Nils. *The Decline of Neutrality, 1914–1941.* Oslo, 1953.

Trefousse, Hans L. *Germany and American Neutrality, 1939–1941.* New York, 1951.

NEWFOUNDLAND

The easternmost province of the Dominion of Canada, consisting of the Isle of Newfoundland and the Labrador coast. From the fifteenth century, North Atlantic fishermen have been drawn to the great cod fisheries at the Grand Banks southeast of the island. For centuries, cod has dominated Newfoundland, shaped its economy, and embroiled it in international conflicts, including several with the United States. Fishermen from the New England colonies actively pursued the cod and sought to continue the practice after the American Revolution. Beginning with the Treaty of Paris of 1783, which granted Americans the right to fish within Canada's territorial waters but did not allow them to cure fish on Newfoundland, Great Britain and the United States engaged in a long-running battle over access to the fishing grounds. In the Convention of 1818, which restricted U.S. fishermen to certain areas but granted them the right to come on shore, and treaties signed in 1854 and 1871, which offered expanded U.S. rights in exchange for reciprocal trade and a financial indemnity, respectively, the two nations attempted to resolve the fishing rights question, but changing diplomatic and domestic circumstances undermined each agreement.

Newfoundland, which was granted self-government by Great Britain in 1855, refused to join the rest of British North America in the Canadian Confederation in 1867, which complicated the fishing matters until 1949, when Newfoundlanders voted to join the Dominion of Canada. Not only did the Newfoundland government struggle to limit the rights of American fishermen, but it also tried to maintain its freedom of action with regard to the govern-

ments in Ottawa and London. This trend was never more clear than in 1905, when the government at St. John's ruled that Americans could no longer fish the inshore waters. Facing a diplomatic impasse, all parties agreed in 1909 to arbitrate the case before the Permanent Court of Arbitration at The Hague. The arbitrators engineered a compromise the following year that basically upheld Newfoundland's right to regulate its fisheries, with ultimate authority residing in London. With the outbreak of World War II, the four governments moved quickly to use Newfoundland as a base for antisubmarine activities. In September 1940, as part of the destroyers-for-bases deal with the British, the United States leased military facilities in Newfoundland. In August 1941 President Franklin D. Roosevelt met with Prime Minister Winston Churchill in Argentia Bay off Newfoundland, where the two agreed to the Atlantic Charter. In 1994 the last U.S. military base in Newfoundland, at Argentia, closed, leaving behind uncertainty about who would pay for its cleanup. In the 1990s, Canada has aggressively moved to conserve the dwindling fisheries of Newfoundland. Canada has generally found the United States to be cooperative in this endeavor; but in April 1995, Ottawa took the unprecedented step of extending the fisheries laws beyond the 200-mile limit, targeting Spanish fisherman.

KURK DORSEY

See also Canada; Destroyers-for-Bases Deal; Fisheries

FURTHER READING

Chadwick, Gerald St. John. *Newfoundland: Island into Province.* Cambridge, England, 1967.

Gilmore, William C. *Newfoundland and Dominion Status: The External Affairs Competence and International Law Status of Newfoundland.* Toronto, 1988.

NEW INTERNATIONAL ECONOMIC ORDER

Program adopted in 1974 at the Sixth Special Session of the United Nations General Assembly, which has a majority of Third World nations, together with a charter of Economic Rights and Duties of States. This was the apex of the North-South conflict, a fissure in international politics that, unlike the political-military East-West conflict, was defined primarily in economic terms and between the developed (North) and developing (South) worlds. The agenda of the New International Economic Order (NIEO) program was nothing short of a sweeping revision of the rules of international trade, investment, and development.

The basic concept of the NIEO emerged primarily from Marxist and other radical analyses of the international political economy that posited the inherent unfavorability to the South of international economic relations as structured. Dependency theory derived from one of the most prominent of these analyses. The central thesis of dependency theory was a view of capitalism as potentially exploitative at the global level because of the transfer of raw materials, labor, and skills from the South to the North. Such Latin American authors as Fernando Enrique Cardoso (who was elected president of Brazil in 1994) and Raul Prebisch argued that if trends were left unchecked, Third World economies would find themselves progressively depleted. The resulting "deteriorating terms of trade" refers to the tendency of Third World exports, in relation to Third World imports, to decline in price over time. Such a condition stems from the relatively low added value of many Third World exports (commodities, tourism) and the high added value of developed countries exports (manufactured goods, specialized services). Developing nations saw themselves as locked in a vicious cycle of exporting more and more in order to import less and less. Another key problem, as diagnosed by Third World policymakers, was the loss of economic autonomy by virtue of the predominance of foreign investment in the local economy. These investments, while they were important sources of hard currency and industrial expertise, were blamed by many in the Third World for resource depletion, depressed wages, and the tendency to create separate enclaves of developments, while the majority of the country remained impoverished.

Prior to the 1970s the principal strategies pursued by Third World countries for dealing with these problems were domestic. Going back a number of decades in some cases, many developing nations implemented some form of import substitution industrialization, which involved state promotion and protection of local industry with the goal of replacing expensive imports with local manufactures. This was typically done through direct state control of whole sectors of the economy or, at least, aggressive promotion of private firms through subsidies, favorable social policies, and protectionism in trade policy. Another strategy, used less frequently but often more controversially, was the coercive seizure of foreign assets through nationalization or expropriation, particularly in the area of raw materials. Thus, Mexicanization (Mexico), Zairianization (Zaire), and other nationalization policies were typical of the 1960s and 1970s. Another, more radical, approach to dependency was autarky, or the severance of ties with the West. The People's Republic of China set the pattern for this approach in the 1950s, which was later imitated by Cuba, Tanzania, and other radical regimes for a time. The autarkic approach proved short-lived for most nations whose resources and industry base were too limited to provide for the needs of their populaces.

NIEO was not wholly motivated by economic concerns. A political concern of developing nations in the 1960s was the issue of power in the international commodity markets and in international economic policy organs generally. Shut out during the Bretton Woods negotiations, 1–22 July 1944, which created the basic structures for the international economic system, most governments of less developed countries (LDCs) felt the rules of the game were tilted against them since the end of World War II and sought opportunities not only to reform the rules but also to gain more control over their drafting and revision. Thus, the NIEO platform was shaped in various UN bodies, but the principal one was the UN Conference on Trade and Development (UNCTAD), established by the General Assembly in 1964. UNCTAD was an unusual body in that it was clearly structured along coalitional lines into four groups. Group B was made up of Western nations, and Groups C and D consisted of socialist bloc countries. It was Group A, however, made up originally of seventy-seven African, Asian, and Latin American nations, that dominated UNCTAD. These seventy-seven developing nations consistently voted as a bloc (hence the origin of another name, the G-77). The extraordinary success of the Organization of Petroleum Exporting Countries (OPEC) during the Arab-Israeli Yom Kippur War of 1973 was a major inspiration for NIEO. OPEC demonstrated the capacity of a Third World producer cartel to dictate world commodity prices in certain circumstances.

As far as the North was concerned, however, OPEC was to be the exception and not the new rule. The responses of the developed nations, and the U.S. response in particular, were ambivalent at best. They were willing to accommodate the more modest elements of the program, those not considered a direct or deep threat to the Bretton Woods system. They agreed to provide some infant industry export advantages for developing states through the tariff and other competitiveness-enhancing measures of the Generalized System of Preferences. They also agreed to expand multilateral official lending through the International Monetary Fund (IMF) and the World Bank, particularly with concessional development-oriented lending through such new institutions as the International Development Authority (IDA). A number of developing countries were assisted in acceding to the General Agreement on Tariffs and Trade (GATT), and the 1979 GATT Tokyo Round Agreement allowed for numerous exceptions favorable to Third World interests. The broader goal of establishing a new international economic order, however, fundamentally geared to the redistribution of wealth, was not something the United States or most other developed states shared or were prepared to foster, concede, or allow.

One of the issues on which the North-South conflict was joined most intensively was the Integrated Program for Commodities (IPC). The goal of the IPC, as the South saw it, was to deal with both the persistent instability and decline of commodity prices for all commodities, from bananas to tin to bauxite to coffee, and so on. From the North's perspective, the IPC would be a whole series of cartels that would violate the principles of free trade, would be inflationary, and was largely politically inspired. UNCTAD was the principal forum for this debate. The IPC plan was approved by UNCTAD, an approval owing in part to coalitional alignments. By the time the General Assembly approved the formal NIEO declaration, many of the less controversial proposals had already been incorporated in some fashion. The IPC provided for buffer stocks for commodities and a common fund to pay for their creation and maintenance. Buffer stocks were intended to remedy the problem of price instability by creating a large-scale stockpile of a particular product to be expanded during years of high output and depleted during leaner years. The expectation was that, through judicious manipulation of the world supply of certain commodities, prices could be stabilized. Most developing country governments also sought to use the buffer stocks to increase global prices gradually. Whereas buffer stocks for a few commodities, including copper and bauxite, did, in fact, come into existence, the increasingly political character of commodity pricing undermined their legitimacy and continuity. Another key factor was the low levels of funding actually provided by the developed states for the common fund.

As the UNCTAD-NIEO debate wore on in the late 1970s, several developments undermined the effectiveness of the dialogue. The Third World's solidarity began progressively to collapse as more and more significant differences emerged among G-77 members. A few developing nations experienced dramatic growth, either through industrialization or because of increases in global oil prices. Brazil saw annual gross domestic product growth rates of 10 percent during the 1970s, as did South Korea, Mexico, and a few other so-called newly industrializing countries (NICs). At the same time, the per capita incomes of Saudi Arabia, Kuwait, Qatar, and other oil exporters rose to levels that surpassed the most advanced nations of Europe. These nations found their interests more and more compatible with those of the industrialized West rather than the South. Saudi investments in Western securities markets and U.S. Treasury bills caused it to pull back from supporting policies that could precipitate recession in the United States. Likewise, Latin American NICs began borrowing heavily from Western banks to diversify their industrial base and hoped to avoid antagonizing their newfound sponsors with any return to combative rhetoric at UNCTAD.

On the other extreme, a number of developing nations found themselves unable to sustain even subsistence. The nations of sub-Saharan Africa, Southeast Asia, and Central America—beset by war, famine, imperialism, and natural disasters and often governed by venal dictators uninterested in bettering the living conditions of their people—found poverty an almost constant condition without hope of remedy. These nations became known as the Fourth World, and the depth of their plight robbed them of the bargaining power to extract anything more than charity from the West. The plodding debates of UNCTAD lacked the promise of emergency relief they so desperately needed. Thus, the solidarity of developing nations was essentially broken by the late 1970s.

In addition to the end of Third World solidarity, many developing nations were preoccupied with problems that required a different kind of international bargain. As early as 1974, several developing nations had incurred significant hard currency debts that they were unable to service. With high interest rates and the explosion of the "debt bomb" in the period from 1979 to 1982, the long-term goals of global reform melted away in significance relative to the crisis of debt rescheduling. Much like the problems of the Fourth World, the debt crisis forced many NICs into a relatively weak position, which a few manipulated into temporary strength, vis-à-vis the West. The NIEO would have to wait.

Most important, however, was the departure by 1981 of what had been a relatively sympathetic group of Western leaders in the late 1970s. President Jimmy Carter of the United States, Helmut Schmidt of West Germany, and various Labour party leaders in Great Britain had given the NIEO advocates a fair hearing. The publication of *North-South: A Programme for Survival by the Brandt Commission* (named for Willy Brandt, former West German chancellor and leader of Socialist International) in 1980 represented the culmination of Western attention to the NIEO. It called for acknowledgment of NIEO demands: the need to provide greater access to developing nations to the centers of economic power, greater transfers of wealth and technology with fewer strings attached, and tolerance for new rules and standards of conduct in economic matters to the benefit of developing nations.

With the election in 1979 of Margaret Thatcher as prime minister of Great Britain, soon followed by the elections of President Ronald Reagan in the United States and Helmut Kohl as chancellor of West Germany, these sympathetic voices were essentially silenced. The Cancun Summit of 1981, intended to serve as the capstone of NIEO achievements, was a nonstarter. President Reagan took the occasion to dismiss the redistributive policies of the NIEO and call instead for developing nations to rely on the "magic of the marketplace." For all intents and purposes, the NIEO was a dead letter. By the end of the 1980s, the UN General Assembly passed resolutions that included warm words for entrepreneurship and liberalized markets. A new model for development emerged in Asia, characterized by technological advance and aggressive exporting. A wave of privatization and liberalization swept the developing world, and manufactured goods, rather than commodities, became the leading edge of developing country advance. There was little if any talk of a new international economic order.

KENDALL W. STILES

See also Brazil; Bretton Woods System; Carter, James Earl; China; Cuba; General Agreement on Tariffs and Trade; Generalized System of Preferences; International Monetary Fund; Kohl, Helmut; Kuwait; Mexico; Organization of Petroleum Exporting Countries; Reagan, Ronald Wilson; Saudi Arabia; Schmidt, Helmut; Tanzania, United Republic of; Thatcher, Margaret; Third World; United Nations Conference on Trade and Development; Zaire

FURTHER READING

Krasner, Stephen D. *Structural Conflict: The Third World Against Global Liberalism.* Berkeley, Calif., 1985.
Rothstein, Robert L. *Global Bargaining: UNCTAD and the Quest for a New International Economic Order.* Princeton, N.J., 1979.

NEW LOOK

See Eisenhower, Dwight David; Nuclear Weapons and Strategy

NEW ZEALAND

An island nation located 1,000 miles southeast of Australia in the South Pacific Ocean. Formerly a British colony, it became independent in 1931 but is still a member of the British Commonwealth. In 1839 the United States established a consular office in New Zealand to represent American shipping interests. More than a century later, in 1942, the two countries raised their representation to the diplomatic level. After World War II and throughout much of the Cold War period, New Zealand was closely associated with the United States through the tripartite ANZUS (Australia-New Zealand-United States) security treaty signed in 1951. New Zealand sent forces to fight in the Korean and Vietnam Wars, has actively participated in UN peacekeeping operations, and has been an active supporter of Western interests among the small South Pacific Island countries.

Until 1987, access to New Zealand ports by U.S. naval vessels contributed significantly to the flexibility and

effectiveness of U.S. forces in the Pacific. In 1984 a Labor Party government that was strongly opposed to the presence of nuclear weapons in Oceania took power in New Zealand. In 1987, it pushed through legislation banning all nuclear weapons and nuclear-powered warships from New Zealand. It was U.S. policy not to identify which of its naval vessels were nuclear-powered; the ban therefore effectively closed New Zealand ports to the U.S. Navy. The United States responded by suspending military alliance relations with New Zealand and reduced other government contacts to a low level. In 1990–1991, President George Bush and Secretary of State James A. Baker resumed a few high-level contacts. The president's decision in late 1991 to remove nuclear weapons from all U.S. Navy ships except ballistic missile submarines helped to narrow some differences between the two countries.

On 17 December 1992, a report commissioned by the New Zealand government found that nuclear-powered ships posed no threat and should be allowed to visit the country. On 18 February 1994, the U.S. Department of State announced the resumption of high-level official contacts with New Zealand, although the U.S.-New Zealand leg of the ANZUS military alliance was not reactivated.

ROBERT G. SUTTER

See also Anzus Treaty; Australia; Pacific Island Nations and U.S. Territories; World War II

FURTHER READING

McIntyre, W. David. *Background Into the Anzus Pact: Strategy and Diplomacy, 1945–55.* New York, 1995.
Young, Thomas-Durell. *Australian, New Zealand, and United States Security Relations, 1951–1986.* New York, 1992.

NGOS

See Nongovernmental Organizations

NICARAGUA

Located in Central America between Costa Rica and Honduras, a nation that has witnessed considerable U.S. intervention since the nineteenth century. Nicaragua achieved its independence incrementally during the first half of the nineteenth century, having broken away from Spain in 1821 as part of Agustin de Iturbide's Mexican Empire, then seceded from Mexico in 1823 to form the United Provinces of Central America. After the collapse of this union in 1838, the sovereign Republic of Nicaragua addressed the growing intrusion of the United States into its politics and economy.

The experience of North American adventurer William Walker in Nicaragua during the 1850s foreshadowed the long and troubled relationship between the United States and its Central American neighbor. Exploiting the factionalism of rivals for power in Grenada and Léon, Walker briefly occupied the Nicaraguan presidency between 1855 and 1857. The quintessential filibuster, Walker attempted to reintroduce legal slavery on the isthmus and declared English the nation's official language. The administration of Franklin Pierce in the United States extended diplomatic recognition to Walker's government, which enjoyed the avid support of nervous slavery advocates in the U.S. South. Walker erred fatefully when he challenged shipping magnate Cornelius Vanderbilt's exclusive rights to passage on Nicaragua's transoceanic waterway. Supported by Vanderbilt, the British navy, and Costa Rica, Walker's opponents overthrew his government in 1857.

Walker's fall did not put an end to U.S. intervention in Nicaragua. North Americans cherished the idea of building a transoceanic canal on the Nicaraguan isthmus. The terms of the 1850 Clayton-Bulwer Treaty stipulated that any Nicaraguan canal must be a joint U.S. and British project, reflecting Great Britain's longstanding presence on the Mosquito (Atlantic) Coast. Attempting to displace the British, U.S. investors orchestrated an uprising among the Mosquito Indians. In support of this rebellion, U.S. Marines landed on Nicaraguan soil for the first time in 1894. U.S. ambition to control the Nicaraguan canal route survived the construction of the Panama Canal. In a move that antagonized the United States, Nicaraguan President José Santos Zelaya, a Liberal party leader, actively solicited European investment in a Nicaraguan canal that would compete with the U.S. project.

A brutal dictator but fervent nationalist, Zelaya continued to provoke the United States throughout his tenure (1893–1909), welcoming German and French investment and urging a new Central American union. In 1910 U.S. Marines landed at Bluefields on the Mosquito Coast to assist a Conservative party rebellion against Zelaya's successor, José Madriz (1909–1910). Adolfo Díaz won the presidency in 1911, and U.S. banks insisted on a $1.5 million U.S. loan to replace European capital. In 1912 when Díaz's presidency was threatened by Liberal rebels, he requested and received U.S. forces, which put down the rebellion after a two-month skirmish. During the subsequent fourteen-year occupation, the United States obtained exclusive rights to canal construction in Nicaragua with the 1916 Bryan-Chamorro Treaty.

Following U.S.-sponsored elections in 1925, U.S. Marines withdrew from Nicaragua, but political turmoil provoked another invasion in 1926. Citing the interference of "Bolshevist" Mexico in Nicaragua's civil war, the United States engaged in its most direct and violent confrontation with Nicaraguans. The Marines succeeded in their effort to silence the rebel armies, but could not convince a lone holdout—Augusto César Sandino—to meet Washington's terms and support a provisional government under the pro-American Adolfo Díaz. Refusing to lay down his arms, Sandino launched a campaign against U.S. domination in Nicaragua that would reverberate through the twentieth century. Unprecedented bloodshed, troop commitments, and frustration characterized the U.S. attack on the "bandit" forces of Sandino. Despite aerial bombardment by seventy U.S. planes, the Marines failed to bring to heel Sandino's Defending Army of National Sovereignty, which continued to harass U.S. and government troops and to capture U.S.-owned businesses. Embarassed by the failure to curb Sandino and pressed by the desire to control government spending in the depression-ravaged United States, President Herbert Hoover withdrew the Marines in 1933. Elections, and the creation of a new national guard in Nicaragua, shifted responsibility for terminating Sandino's rebellion to local forces.

The Somozas

The United States looked to the Nicaraguan Guardia Nacional and its counterparts in other Latin American countries as the solution to the dilemma of maintaining political order in the hemisphere during the era of the Good Neighbor nonintervention policy. The employment of U.S.-trained and -equipped troops, Washington hoped, would obviate the need for U.S. intervention. Under the command of Anastasio "Tacho" Somoza García, the Guardia Nacional initially offered an impressive confirmation of U.S. goals. Allying with Nicaraguan conservatives and the hierarchy of the Catholic church, Somoza's troops brought Sandino's tired army to the negotiating table in 1934. Policymakers in the United States conceived the national guard as an instrument for keeping order in Nicaragua but miscalculated the political implications of independent armed forces in the region. Somoza's army assassinated Sandino after the surrender of 1934, overthrew the government in 1936, and installed Somoza at the apex of political power in Nicaragua.

As Nicaragua's strongman until his assassination in 1956, Tacho Somoza devoted himself to the accumulation of personal wealth, the distribution of power and perquisites to the National Guard, and a fawning obedience to the dictates of U.S. foreign policy. Confiscating coffee plantations and cattle ranches, monopolizing Nicaragua's choice investments, and putting the full financial and legislative resources of the Nicaraguan government at his disposal, Somoza amassed a personal fortune even as Nicaragua's economy stagnated. The maintenance of good relations with the United States secured

Somoza's standing within Nicaragua. Policymakers in Washington valued his demonstration of solidarity with the Allied cause in World War II, his efforts to counter progressive social movements in neighboring Central American republics, and his eagerness to prove his loyalty to the United States. Generous allocations of military and economic assistance flowed to his regime.

During the Cold War, Somoza's vigilance for U.S. priorities in the region grew in importance. While Washington refused Somoza's offers to send support troops to the U.S. war effort in Korea, policymakers relied on Nicaragua's unflagging support in the United Nations and the Organization of American States (OAS). Somoza's support provided a critical link in the 1954 Central Intelligence Agency (CIA) operation to unseat the reformer Jacobo Arbenz in Guatemala. The CIA trained anti-Arbenz guerillas under Carlos Castillo Armas at Somoza's estates in Nicaragua, and launched air strikes on Guatemala City from Managua's municipal airport. The U.S. government rewarded Somoza with more aid, much of which found its way into the pockets of his family and their cronies.

When an assassin's bullet felled Somoza in 1956, President Dwight D. Eisenhower sent his personal physicians to Nicaragua. They could not save Somoza, but his death did not interrupt the pattern of overweening U.S. influence in Nicaraguan political life. Luís and Anastasio "Tachito" Somoza Debayle, who assumed the offices of president and chief of the national guard, respectively, had graduated from colleges in the United States. The younger Anastasio, a graduate of the U.S. Military Academy at West Point, claimed to prefer speaking English to Spanish. Both sons continued their father's domestic policy of looting the treasury and securing the most lucrative businesses in Nicaragua. Their foreign policy, like their father's, followed Washington's course unswervingly.

Following the success of Fidel Castro's revolution in Cuba in 1959, U.S. attention to the potential for nationalist challenges in the Caribbean basin assumed obsessive proportions. The value of Somoza loyalty to U.S. interests increased accordingly. The CIA launched the disastrous Bay of Pigs operation against Castro's Cuba from Nicaragua's Puerto Cabezas in 1961. Citing their personal relationship with President Lyndon Johnson, the Somozas rushed to commit troops to the U.S. occupation of the Dominican Republic in 1965. Infusions of U.S. aid, now expanded exponentially by the Alliance for Progress and the Military Assistance Program, continued to sustain the Somozas' financial empire and political mandate in Nicaragua. Assuming absolute power after Luís Somoza's death in 1967, Tachito contributed $1 million to Richard Nixon's presidential election campaign, perpetuating a family traditon of cultivating powerful friends in Washington.

Sandinistas and Contras

As the U.S.-Somoza relationship grew cozier, the foundations of dynastic authority in Nicaragua began to crack. The Sandinista National Liberation Front (FSLN), founded in 1961 by Carlos Fonseca, Tomás Borge, and Silvio Mayorga, combined guerrilla warfare tactics with ideological mobilization of workers' and students' organizations in the cities. The latter-day Sandinistas also relied upon peasant support, mobility, and knowledge of the mountain terrain in their efforts to unseat the heirs of Sandino's assassin. Despite early defeats at the hands of the Guardia Nacional, natural and international disasters undermined Somoza's authority and broadened the FSLN's base of support. When an earthquake destroyed Managua in 1972, Somoza's Guardia failed to keep order, resulting in the dispatch of U.S. Marines to prevent chaos in the shattered city. In the aftermath of the earthquake, wholesale expropriation of international relief funds and supplies by Somoza and his henchmen alienated a mourning urban population. The global oil crisis of 1973 compounded Nicaragua's already-spiraling rate of inflation and imposed new barriers between Somoza and Nicaragua's propertied classes.

In 1974 a coalition of middle-class opposition to Somoza's regime led by newspaper editor Pedro Joaquín Chamorro organized a boycott of Somoza's staged reelection. After Somoza's openly fraudulent victory, officials of the Catholic church refused to participate in inaugural ceremonies. Even the United States appeared to be closing ranks with Somoza's opponents; President Jimmy Carter's emphasis on human rights in world politics threatened to end the warm relationship between the United States and Somoza's repressive regime.

Somoza responded badly to mounting pressures on his government. He increased political violence in Nicaragua, employing the Guardia Nacional in a campaign against villagers suspected of supporting FSLN guerrillas. Somoza ordered the assassination of Chamorro in 1978, lending to the journalist's cause the unifying force of martyrdom. The FSLN emerged as a broad opposition coalition, bringing together peasants and oligarchs, countryside and city. By 1978 Somoza had resorted to bombing Nicaraguan cities as the FSLN extended its control of the country. In July 1978 he fled to Paraguay, a country he had once called "the last place on earth for the worst people in the world." He was assassinated there in 1980.

Somoza's overthrow did not put an end to Nicaragua's social and economic problems, or curtail U.S. interference in its internal affairs. The left-leaning Sandinista government under Daniel Ortega Saavedra met with the opposition of the United States. Carter's administration looked dubiously on Nicaragua's experiment, and the U.S. Congress labelled the Sandinista government socialist. U.S. military and economic assistance terminated abruptly. Estranged from its traditional sources of aid, and ideologically inclined to seek the support of Marxist-Leninist governments, the FSLN turned to the Soviet Union and Castro's Cuba, accepting hundreds of Cuban advisors and technicians, and hundreds of millions of dollars in Soviet assistance.

The inauguration of Ronald Reagan as president in 1981 signalled serious complications for U.S.-Nicaragaun relations. Alarmed by radicalism in Nicaragua and neighboring El Salvador, Reagan and his right-wing supporters in the United States determined to rid the hemisphere of the communist menace, starting with the Sandinistas. At the same time, splits developed within the Nicaraguan government, and key non-Sandinista members cited dogmatic and authoritarian tendencies in the Sandinista coalition as they declared their opposition. Covert assistance to counterrevolutionary insurgent groups—the Nicaraguan Democratic Forces, or "Contras"—provided the centerpiece of Reagan's Nicaraguan strategy. These armies, which brought together former national guardsmen and other opponents of the Sandinista regime, began harassing the Nicaraguan government with CIA assistance after 1981. Other efforts to dislodge the FSLN from Managua included the mining of Nicaraguan harbors by the CIA in 1984 and the imposition of economic sanctions in 1983 and 1984.

Reagan's increasingly overt campaign against Nicaragua's government drew mounting criticism as the Nicaraguan civil war continued. By 1984, opponents of Reagan's Central American policy in Congress challenged the administration's military strategy. The Boland Amendments cut off aid to the Contras. Other bills attempted to distinguish military from humanitarian aid to the Contras, choking off critical arms supplies. Seeking to keep the Nicaraguan rebellion alive, the Reagan administration turned to extralegal sources of support for the Contras, resulting in the Iran-Contra scandal of 1986.

Derailed from its military track, the Reagan administration disdained negotiation as a means of ending the civil war in Nicaragua. Sandinistas, distracted by mounting internal dissent among middle-class and Indian groups, responded slowly to appeals for talks. The Contadora process, initiated by several Latin American countries in the mid-1980s, was ineffective. The Central American peace plan championed by Costa Rican President Oscar Arias brought warring factions to the table, but failed to defuse completely armed tensions in Nicaragua.

The surprising defeat of the FSLN's Ortega in the internationally supervised presidential election of 1990 ended Nicaragua's socialist experiment and Sandinista rule. Under Violeta Barrios de Chamorro, leader of the United Nicaraguan Opposition (UNO) party and widow

of the martyred newspaper editor, Nicaraguans turned their attentions to healing the wounds of two decades of civil war. Keen political disputes persisted in Nicaragua, reflected in UNO's break with President Chamorro in 1993, the agitations of former Contras, and the complications arising from FSLN's continuing control of the Nicaraguan army, police, and unions. Despite the restoration of U.S. aid ($731 million for 1994–1995), Nicaragua's economic performance continued to lag behind that of its Central American neighbors, reflecting the ravages of recent history.

LeeAnna Y. Keith

See also Alliance for Progress; Contadora Group; Contras; Filibusters; Good Neighbor Policy; Iran-Contra Affair; Latin America; North, Oliver Lawrence; Panama and Panama Canal; Reagan, Ronald Wilson; Sandino, Augusto César; Walker, William

FURTHER READING

Burns, Bradford E. *At War in Nicaragua: The Reagan Doctrine and the Politics of Nostalgia.* New York, 1987.

Kagan, Robert. *A Twilight Struggle: American Power and Nicaragua, 1977–1990.* New York, 1996.

LaFeber, Walter. *Inevitable Revolutions: The United States in Central America.* 2nd edition. New York, 1993.

Pastor, Robert A. *Condemned to Repetition: The United States and Nicaragua.* Princeton, 1987.

Tulchin, Joseph S., and Knut Walter. "Nicaragua: The Limits of Intervention." In *Exporting Democracy: The United States and Latin America: Case Studies,* edited by Abraham F. Lowenthal. Baltimore, 1991.

Walker, Thomas W., ed. *Revolution and Counterrevolution in Nicaragua.* Boulder, Colo., 1991.

NIGER

See Appendix 2

NIGERIA

Located in Western Africa, bordering the North Atlantic Ocean between Benin and Cameroon, formerly a British colony that gained its independence in 1960. The United States and Nigeria did not develop a serious relationship until the latter's independence. This was partly attributable, as the American Africanist Sanford Ungar contends, to the fact that "prejudice toward Africa was just as strong in the United States as in Europe, and was related to the virulent racism in the United States' society toward its own black citizens." Such attributes, however, began to change during the administration of President Dwight D. Eisenhower, as the United States made progress in and took a more positive approach to domestic civil rights. The 1960 International Year of Africa

Movement accelerated U.S. policy concerns toward Africa and consequently toward Nigeria. The United States recognized Nigeria one month before it formally became independent on 1 October 1960, and New York's Governor Nelson Rockefeller represented President Eisenhower at the independence ceremonies in the capital of Lagos. Rockefeller assured Nigerian leaders that the United States did not expect Nigeria to be "an active and committed ally" but warned them to "guard this place against all threats from without or perils within," a less than oblique reference to the Soviet Union and local leftists. Full diplomatic relations began with President Eisenhower's appointment of Joseph Palmer II as the first U.S. ambassador to Nigeria.

Nigeria's physical size, population (the largest in Africa), and a well-educated leadership led President John F. Kennedy's administration to conclude that Nigeria would quickly emerge as Africa's principal leader. Thus, Kennedy and his successor, President Lyndon B. Johnson, made Nigeria the largest African recipient of U.S. foreign aid, hoping that Nigeria would become a model of liberal, capitalist, democratic development, and a moderate voice in pan-African affairs. Relations suffered a major setback during the Nigerian civil war of 1967–1970 between the Nigerian government and the secessionist province of Biafra. The United States refused to provide arms to the Nigerian military government that had come to power in 1966, although it continued to recognize that government during the Nigerian civil war. The huge private relief shipments from the United States to Biafra, where famine raged, were regarded in Lagos as defying Nigeria's sovereignty and contributing to the prolongation of the insurrection.

Discord in U.S.-Nigerian relations increased between 1970 and 1976, although relations never became completely polarized and hostile. Lagos blamed the discord on frequent frictions over policy objectives and their own assertion of regional leadership independent of U.S. support. The Nixon and Ford administrations pointed to the continued repressiveness of the military regime, and what they considered unwarranted anti-Americanism. The main issues of dispute sprang from U.S. support for the white minority regimes in Rhodesia and South Africa and for continued Portuguese colonial control in Angola and Mozambique. Nevertheless, Nigeria and the United States showed some pragmatism on oil trade amidst the 1973 world oil crisis. As a member of the Organization of Petroleum Exporting Countries (OPEC), Nigeria benefitted handsomely from the major increases in world oil prices. But since the Arab-Israeli war was not Nigeria's issue, it did not participate in the anti-U.S. embargo, instead becoming one of the United States' major sources of oil at the time.

Relations improved between 1977 and 1979, largely as a result of President Jimmy Carter's 1977 visit to Nigeria, the first by any U.S. president, which was seen as a direct recognition of Nigeria's growing role in Africa and the world. Washington conceded to Nigeria the position of preeminence in African affairs, and Nigerian leaders in turn endowed the U.S. claim to Western leadership in Africa with moral legitimacy.

When Alhaji Shehu Shagari became president of Nigeria, however, relations seemed to return to the lopsided dependency in bilateral and regional ties characteristic of the period before Nigeria's civil war. The African policies of President Ronald Reagan's administration undermined Nigeria's capacity to resolve regional problems and tended to heighten conflicts in southern Africa and Chad, while encouraging fragmentation in the ranks of the Organization of African Unity, which did not please Lagos. President George Bush did not give Nigeria priority in Africa, and the periodic shifts between despotism and democracy in Nigeria did not help. The political and economic instability that had long been prevalent in Nigeria contributed significantly to Washington's lukewarm attitude. Occasionally, the United States called on Nigeria to help solve some thorny African problems, such as the civil war in Liberia, where the Nigerian military featured prominently, and the crisis in Somalia.

Relations during the Clinton administration have been dominated by human rights issues. The military regime of General Ibrahim Babangida annulled the presidential elections of 1993 after it became apparent that Chief Moshood Abiola was going to be the winner. Over the next few years political conditions in Nigeria worsened, most notably with the government's killing of the leading human rights activist Ken Saro-wiwa in late 1995. The United States led efforts to impose economic sanctions against Nigeria. But these efforts encountered opposition at the United Nations as well as from major oil companies such as Royal Dutch Shell, which held extensive investments in Nigeria.

Ogwo Jombo Umeh
Victor Aikhionbare

See also Africa; Colonialism; Oil and Foreign Policy

FURTHER READING

Ate, Bassey E. *Decolonization and Dependence: The Development of Nigerian-U.S. Relations, 1960-1984.* Boulder, Colo., 1987.
Shepard, Robert B. *Nigeria, Africa, and the United States: From Kennedy to Reagan.* Indianapolis, Ind., 1991.
Unger, Sanford J. *Africa: The People and Politics of an Emerging Continent, 3rd Ed.* New York, 1989.

NINE POWER TREATY

See Washington Conference on the Limitation of Armaments

NITZE, PAUL HENRY

(*b.* 16 January 1907)

Longtime government official, author of NSC-68 (the blueprint for the Truman administration's Cold War strategy), and one of the chief arms control negotiators of the 1970s and 1980s. Born in Amherst, Massachusetts, he graduated from Harvard in 1928 and joined the investment banking firm of Dillon, Reed that same year. During World War II Nitze held several government positions, including that of vice chairman of the Strategic Bombing Survey. After the war, Nitze initially focused on international economic affairs, serving as deputy director of the Office of International Trade Policy and deputy to the assistant secretary of state for economic affairs (1946–1950). He replaced George F. Kennan as director of the Policy Planning Staff in 1950, the year he developed NSC-68 at the request of Secretary of State Dean Acheson. Nitze's influence reflected Acheson's disillusionment with Kennan's waning faith in the military instruments of foreign policy.

Nitze left government in 1953, but in 1957 he saw a new opportunity to influence policy when he worked with a presidential study committee, headed by Rowan Gaither, investigating U.S. national security programs and policies. Nitze helped write the committee's report, which was critical of President Dwight D. Eisenhower's strategic policies. The report warned of a "missile gap" and recommended a large increase in military spending. Throughout the Kennedy and Johnson administrations, Nitze held numerous posts in the Pentagon, including secretary of the Navy and deputy secretary of defense. In 1969, President Richard M. Nixon named him head of the negotiating team for the Strategic Arms Limitation Talks (SALT). Nitze helped negotiate the SALT I agreement and began work on the SALT II treaty before resigning in 1974. When President Nixon refused to accept his resignation immediately, Nitze took the unusual step of terminating his own appointment; he then issued a press release lambasting Nixon and Secretary of State Henry A. Kissinger for compromising U.S. security in their eagerness to obtain an agreement. During the Carter administration, Nitze helped found the Committee on the Present Danger, a lobbying group that criticized President Jimmy Carter's national security policy, including the SALT II Treaty, and called for a large military buildup.

In 1981, Nitze joined the Reagan administration as an arms-control adviser and negotiator. He helped formulate U.S. strategy for the Intermediate Nuclear Forces Talks (INF) and the Strategic Arms Reduction Talks (START), but he diverged from enthusiastic supporters of President Ronald Reagan's Strategic Defense Initiative, seeing SDI less as an end in itself than as a diplomatic tool to pry concessions from the Soviet Union. He resigned from government in 1989 and subsequently published his memoirs. Despite his long and distinguished career, Nitze's confrontational personality and sometimes shrill criticism of his superiors served to block his ascendance to the cabinet-level position he always desired. In 1989 the School of Advanced International Studies of the Johns Hopkins University, a degree-granting institution he helped found in 1944, added Nitze's name to its own.

SHANE J. MADDOCK

See also Carter, James Earl; Cold War; Committee on the Present Danger; Intermediate-Range Nuclear Forces Treaty; NSC-68; Reagan, Ronald Wilson; Strategic Arms Limitation Talks and Agreements; Strategic Arms Reduction Treaties; Strategic Defense Initiative

FURTHER READING

Callahan, David. *Dangerous Capabilities: Paul Nitze and the Cold War.* New York, 1990
Nitze, Paul H., Ann M. Smith, and Steven L. Rearden. *From Hiroshima to Glasnost: At the Center of Decision—A Memoir.* New York, 1989

NIXON, RICHARD MILHOUS

(*b.* 9 January 1913; *d.* 22 April 1994)

Thirty-seventh president of the United States (1969–1974) who pursued détente with the Soviet Union and rapproachment with China and resigned the presidency over his role in the Watergate scandal. Born in Yorba Linda, California, Richard Nixon grew up in the nearby town of Whittier. Excelling scholastically at Whittier High School and Whittier College, he was graduated from Duke University Law School in 1937 and returned to Whittier to practice law until 1942. He married Thelma Catherine (Pat) Ryan in 1940 and after working briefly in Washington, D.C., served in the South Pacific from 1942 to 1946, rising to the rank of lieutenant commander in the U.S. Navy.

Nothing distinguished either his civilian or military activities until he was elected to Congress in 1946, but his political career prior to assuming the presidency proved meteoric and controversial. Elected to the 80th Congress in 1946 at the age of thirty-three, he served two terms, then ran successfully in 1950 for the California seat in the U.S. Senate. Controversy marked both of these successful anti-communist campaigns against five-term liberal Democratic Congressman Jerry Voorhis and equally liberal Helen Gahagan Douglas. Nixon received national attention for his role in the Alger Hiss spy case as a member of the House Un-American Activities Committee. By 1952 he was elected vice president of the United States at age thirty-nine. During that year he gave his famous "Checkers" speech, in which he overcame charges of having created a slush fund. Nixon only narrowly missed being elected president in 1960 at age forty-seven, and eight years later he won the presidency in an almost equally close contest. Having been re-elected by a landslide in 1972, he was forced to resign on 9 August 1974 or face impeachment proceedings for obstructing justice in a national constitutional scandal known as Watergate. His resignation culminated a political career plagued by contention, largely stemming from his combative personality and aggressive campaign tactics, but due as well to an already ferocious political atmosphere in the country with regard to the war in Vietnam—a conflict Nixon inherited from the administration of his beleaguered predecessor, Lyndon Johnson. Nixon's formalistic, top-down, management style while in the White House also became the subject of criticism and ultimately contributed to his downfall.

Foreign policy is the area in which Richard Nixon's unprecedented resignation as president over Watergate has least obscured his achievements. Praise for his foreign policies, with the exception of the war in Vietnam, dominated the eulogies at his funeral in 1994. As a Republican president from 1969 to 1974 he sought accommodation with the two major communist nations—the People's Republic of China and the Soviet Union—much to the surprise of those who considered him an inveterate Cold Warrior. He brought broad geopolitical and structural approaches to U.S. diplomacy during a transition period marked by the end of the bipartisan Cold War consensus in Congress. Nixon took advantage of this opportunity to fight the Cold War other than by traditional containment policies.

To aid him in bringing about his "grand design" for the world, Nixon chose Henry A. Kissinger, a Harvard professor whom he scarcely knew, to be his special assistant for national security affairs. At first glance Nixon and Kissinger appeared to be an odd couple—an American Quaker and a German Jew—to collaborate in the formulation of U.S. foreign policy. In fact, however, by the time they met in 1968 they shared many similar viewpoints and operational styles. Both of them thrived on covert activity and decisions reached in private; both distrusted the federal bureaucracy; both resented any attempts by Congress to interfere with their diplomatic initiatives; and both agreed that the United States could impose order and stability in foreign affairs if the White House controlled policy by appearing conciliatory but acting tough.

Little wonder then that the president and his national security adviser developed a "special relationship." However, their partnership went beyond the collaboration on foreign policy that existed between Woodrow Wilson and Colonel Edward M. House or between Franklin D. Roo-

sevelt and Harry Hopkins. Characterized by extensive meetings and telephone calls, it became a relationship that often brought out the worst characteristics of both men, including the paranoid and dark sides of each. It was a relationship that also appeared capable of significantly changing the conduct of U.S. foreign policy in a time of transition. But despite structural reforms and their combined personal determination and expertise, Nixon and Kissinger were never able to institutionalize their "grand design" approach to foreign affairs.

As a result of this close relationship, conflicts between Secretary of State William Rogers and Kissinger usually ended in favor of the latter until Rogers finally resigned in September 1973 and Kissinger replaced him while remaining special assistant for national security affairs—the only time one person has held both positions.

Reorganizing the National Security Council

Shortly after Nixon and Kissinger joined forces, they put into place a White House-centered organization model of foreign-policymaking by restructuring the National Security Council (NSC). They turned the NSC into a series of interdepartmental groups all subjected to review committees headed by Kissinger. This design undercut the preeminence of the Department of State in the formulation of foreign policy. In theory the Department of State was to implement NSC policy, but often in practice, Nixon's and Kissinger's personal management of policy merged policy formulation and operational functions inside the NSC system. Yet when a decision could be carried out that did not depend on the civilian or military bureaucracy for implementation, even the NSC was ignored, whether the action was covert or not. The NSC was utilized, however, whenever the covert or overt policy required large-scale bureaucratic support.

Consequently, the National Security Council, as a debating forum for presenting options to the president, was not seriously utilized, for example, in formulating the policy of Vietnamization, the Nixon Doctrine, the secret Kissinger negotiations with North Vietnam, Nixon's New Economic Policy (NEP), the intervention in Chile that culminated in the overthrow of President Salvador Allende, or the planning of Nixon's trip to China. It was used, during Nixon's first year as president, in deciding to begin the secret bombing of Cambodia and to respond to the EC-121 incident, involving the shooting down of a U.S. Navy plane by North Korea. Later in his administration, Nixon did consult the NSC on the attempt to keep Taiwan in the United Nations with a "two China" policy; the decision to conduct incursions into Cambodia and Laos; the détente agreements with the Soviet Union; Middle Eastern policy *before* the 1973 October War; and U.S. policy in Angola and southern Africa in general.

Rapprochement with China and Détente with the USSR

Improved relations with the People's Republic of China and the Soviet Union are often cited as the most successful diplomatic achievements of Nixon's presidency. Both were important components of his grand geopolitical design. Since 1949 the United States had refused to recognize communist China. In the early 1970s Nixon began to reverse this standard Cold War policy of non-recognition by ordering a number of unilateral gestures of reconciliation. Normalization of U.S. relations with China was designed to bring this communist giant into the ranks of "civilized" nations.

The opening of relations with China appears to have been on Nixon's mind from the beginning of his presidency: it was, indeed, an idea whose time was ripe for implementation. By the mid-1960s, U.S.-China specialists had openly begun to question the continuing isolation of the People's Republic, and even though anti-Chinese sentiments loomed large in public opinion because of the PRC's support for the North Vietnamese, China had been gaining international credibility for more than twenty years. As leader of the group of nonaligned nations, China challenged both superpowers's right to dictate to the Third World. China's ties with the Soviet Union had been severely strained, if not actually broken, by 1969. By the early 1970s the Cultural Revolution inside China had subsided. Thus, conditions seemed propitious for rethinking Chinese-U.S. relations—a fact not lost on Nixon.

It has often been said that only a conservative Republican president could alter U.S. relations with the People's Republic of China at the height of the Cold War. Yet Nixon knew that even with his reputation as a Cold Warrior he would face conservative criticism for opening up China to the West, especially if his "two China" policy failed (as it did). Kissinger, for his part, worried more about how to sell the historic change in policy on China to "liberals." At a meeting recorded by Nixon's aide H.R. Haldeman, between Ron Ziegler, Nixon's press secretary, and Kissinger, the two men worried that liberals would simply claim that the rapprochement was simply another "Tricky Dick" initiative that came about without proper consultation with Congress. Kissinger, convinced that the "libs will try to piss on it as an election year gimmick," said that "if [liberals] do [charge this] we say they've unmasked [them]selves: you're not against *what* we're doing; you're against the fact *we* are doing it."

Despite the obvious importance and overall success of the rapprochement with the People's Republic of China (symbolized by the president's globally televised trip in February 1972 and its attendant joint "Shanghai Communiqué"), Nixon never believed that the media gave it as much credit as it deserved. As late as 1988, he was saying: "We changed the world. If it had not been for the China initiative, which only I could do at that point, we would be in a terrible situation today, with China aligned with the Soviet Union and with the Soviet Union's power."

Like the opening to China, détente toward the Soviet Union proved more controversial at the time than in retrospect. Détente represented a political process for avoiding nuclear war, building mutually advantageous relationships, and modifying Soviet behavior by gaining its *de facto* acceptance of both international cooperation and competition (sometimes referred to as "competitive coexistence") in order to preserve international stability by according the Soviet Union a greater stake in the global status quo. To a lesser degree détente was a response to the domestic and international economic problems the United States faced as a result of the Vietnam War. The one thing détente did not represent was a continuation of the traditional Cold War policy of containment.

Détente was highly dependent on the personal interactions among such individual leaders as Nixon, Kissinger, and Soviet Premier Leonid Brezhnev, as well as on their changing perceptions of their nations's relative strength and possible benefits accruing from a "relaxation of tensions." For example, the Soviet Union never viewed détente as a static condition, or status quo concept, in the way that the United States did. Inside the USSR the perceptual factors promoting détente by the beginning of the 1970s were: the idea that history was on the Soviets's side; improving Sino-U.S. relations; U.S. unilateral troop withdrawals from Vietnam; Nixon's acceptance of strategic parity; and such domestic economic considerations as the Soviet need for U.S. wheat.

There is still no concrete evidence that because of Soviet concern over the success of Nixon's trip to China in February 1972, rapprochement became indirectly "linked" to negotiations leading to the ten formal agreements signed in Moscow between the United States and the USSR in May 1972. These agreements provided for: prevention of military incidents at sea and in the air; scholarly cooperation and exchange in the fields of science and technology; cooperation in health research; cooperation in environmental matters; cooperation in the exploration of outer space; and facilitation of commercial and economic relations. Also, and most controversially, the Antiballistic Missile Treaty; the Interim Agreement on the Limitations on Strategic Arms (SALT I); and the Basic Principles of U.S.-Soviet Relations.

The Strategic Arms Limitation Talks (SALT I) conducted in Helsinki in 1969 and Vienna in 1970 led to the two arms control documents signed at the 1972 Moscow summit. These included a treaty limiting the deployment of antiballistic missile systems (ABMs) to two for each country, and an agreement freezing the number of offensive intercontinental ballistic missiles (ICBMs) at the level of those then under production or already deployed. Unlike SALT I, the ABM Treaty was of "unlimited duration. . .and not open to material unilateral revision," regardless of attempts by the Reagan administration to do just this beginning in 1985. Until the SDI efforts in the second half of the 1980s, however, the ABM Treaty essentially succeeded in relegating deployment of conventional ballistic missile defense systems to minor strategic significance.

SALT I, on other hand, was an agreement of limited, five-year duration that attempted to establish a rough balance or parity, between the offensive nuclear arsenals of the two superpowers, despite the "missiles gap" which continued to exist between them in specific weapon systems. For example, when Nixon signed SALT I the United States had a total of 1,710 missiles; 1,054 land-based ICBMs and 656 on submarines. The USSR had a total of 2,350 missiles; 1,6l8 land-based ICBMs and 740 on submarines (SLBMs). SALT I not only recognized the strategic parity of the USSR but gave it a numerical edge in missiles and a slight throw-weight advantage. The U.S. retained a numerical advantage in warheads and a superiority in strategic bombers—460 in 1972 to 120 for the Soviets. SALT I by no means stopped the nuclear arms race, but it recognized that unregulated weapons competition between the two superpowers could no longer be rationally condoned. By freezing further missile buildup, SALT I meant that by the time SALT II was signed in 1979 total U.S.-Soviet missile strength remained essentially unchanged: 2,283 to 2,504, respectively. From 1972 until the mid-1980s, SALT talks were regarded as a barometer of relations between the two countries. The development of Multiple Independently-targeted Re-entry Vehicles (MIRVs) by both sides has tended to obscure the generally parallel missile buildup between the United States and the Soviet Union from 1972 to the end of the Cold War.

While it is relatively easy to generalize about the meaning of SALT I now that the Cold War is over, at the time there was much controversy and confusion over its specific terms. The controversy was largely partisan, but the confusion was legitimate because in terms of sheer complexity and scope this summit meeting between Nixon and Brezhnev was unprecedented by contrast to the previous five summits following World War II. Complicating matters, we now know—from those who participated in the multilevel negotiations and in the drafting of the various technical provisions—that Nixon and Kissinger did not fully understand all the terms, let alone their implications, especially the SLBMs sections of the Interim Agreement.

Also, until the collapse of communism in Central and Eastern Europe and in the Soviet Union almost thirty years later, Nixon's and Kissinger's immediate successors proved unable (or unwilling) to build upon the delicate distinction between containment and détente which they left behind. In part this also was due to the fact that there were no radical leadership changes in the USSR (or the former Soviet bloc countries) to reinforce the concept of détente during the last half of the 1970s—as there began to appear at the end of the 1980s. Thus, the Nixon-Brezhnev détente remained essentially a "tactical" development because the Cold War had not yet significantly begun to recede. Hence, there was no basic change in conflicting Cold War strategies under détente—only a temporary blurring of hostilities that President Ronald Reagan revived to a fever pitch in the early 1980s.

The Vietnam War and the POW/MIA Issue

It was clearly in Nixon's political self-interest to end the war in Vietnam as soon as possible. Although he came to office committed to negotiate a quick settlement, he ended by expanding and prolonging the conflict in the name of "peace and honor." As he unilaterally withdrew U.S. combat troops in Vietnam under a policy known as Vietnamization, Nixon allowed Kissinger to carry on largely nonproductive, secret negotiations with the North Vietnamese from 4 August 1969 to 25 January 1972 (when they were made public over Kissinger's protestations).

Only marginally better terms were finally reached in 1973 that had not already been agreed to in 1969. The trade-off of Hanoi's agreement that President Nguyen Van Thieu could remain in power in return for allowing its troops to remain in place in South Vietnam pales when compared to the additional 20,552 American lives lost during this three-year negotiation period—especially when the inherent weaknesses of the Saigon government, circa 1973, are taken into consideration. The most embarrassing evidence of this weakness occurred when President Gerald Ford was forced to order an emergency evacuation of the last remaining U.S. troops from Saigon in April 1975. Neither Nixon nor Kissinger ever conceded that their policies destabilized most of Indochina, let alone—as some critics still argue—that they led to the horrific Khmer Rouge rampage in Cambodia in which hundreds of thousands lost their lives.

With the exception of ending the draft, creating an all-volunteer army, and finally publicly endorsing the return of U.S. POWs as a major condition of peace, practically every action taken by Nixon with respect to Vietnam created resentment, suspicion, and outright hostility at home amongst those many millions who gradually grew to oppose the war. The only area in which the administration consciously and successfully courted public opinion turned out to be the prisoner of war (POW) issue. Nixon did not consider the POWs or those missing in action (MIAs) a major public relations possibility when he entered office. He had pledged to bring "an honorable end to the war in Vietnam" when accepting the Republican nomination in 1968, but the POWs/MIAs had not figured prominently in his calculations for a negotiated peace. Return of POWs had always been a condition in negotiations with the North Vietnamese under President Lyndon Johnson, as it was in any previous peace settlement in which the United States had participated.

For the public, the POW/MIA issue remained the most urgent aspect of the war when it ended. A Harris poll for May 1973 showed that bringing home the POWs ranked first among all foreign-policy issues, above relations with the USSR and China, with eighty-one percent approving Nixon's handling of this issue with the announcement of the Paris Peace Accords ending the war.

In March 1973, in the same speech in which Nixon said that "all of our American POWs are on the way home," he also indicated some "problem areas" such as inadequate accounting for MIAs in Indochina, but he did not specifically mention the possibility of any more being held in North Vietnam. The POWs/MIAs became a popular culture phenomenon in the 1970s and 1980s, despite Pentagon and Congressional investigations indicating that there are no more than 200 unresolved MIA cases, out of the 2,266 the Department of Defense still lists as missing, and around a dozen POWs unaccounted for. Approximately 300,000 North and South Vietnamese are still considered MIAs.

The question resurfaced in the 1990s whether Nixon and Kissinger did all they could to free servicemen "knowingly" left behind, or whether they were so desperate to get out of Vietnam that they sacrificed POWs. Both Nixon and Kissinger have maintained that it was the doves in Congress who prevented any effective military action to find out the truth about POWs when it was still possible to do so in the spring and summer of 1973. Not until President Bill Clinton removed the nineteen-year-old embargo against Vietnam in February 1994 did the Vietnamese government begin cooperating with veterans groups in locating the remains of U.S. soldiers.

The Middle East and Third World

In the Middle East, and especially in regard to the persistent Arab-Israeli confrontation, Nixon and Kissinger at first followed a policy of stalemate—at least up to the outbreak of the 1973 October War. While Secretary William Rogers and Joseph Sisco, the assistant secretary of state for Near Eastern and South Asian affairs, hammered out an even-handed Middle Eastern peace plan in 1969 to present to the Soviets, Kissinger met separately with Ambassador Anatoly Dobrynin telling him that the White House had no interest in the Rogers Plan, which called for a more neutral stance toward Israel and the Arabs and substantial Israeli withdrawal from occupied territories in return for a contractual peace brokered by the United States and the USSR.

In October 1969 the Soviet Union officially rejected the Rogers Plan, leaving the new Republican administration with no apparent constructive alternative—until the Yom Kippur War in 1973, when Kissinger's shuttle diplomacy helped prevent an escalation of the conflict in ways totally inconsistent with U.S. interests. Still, relations with the Organization of Petroleum Exporting Countries (OPEC) worsened under Nixon, when OPEC embargoed exports to the United States in October 1973 in retaliation for U.S. support of Israel during the October War, thus producing the first oil crisis of the seventies and the attendant global economic dislocations. By 1975 only minimal progress toward reconciliation among Egypt, Israel, and Syria had taken place—through a series of temporary interim agreements signed in January 1974, May 1974, and September 1975. There was to be no further breakthrough in the Middle East peace process until the 1978 Camp David Accords.

The diminished Cold War views of the Nixon administration did not usually extend to the Third World, where relative U.S. indifference to endemic local social and economic problems and excessive attention to larger geopolitical calculations led to American actions that too often disregarded fundamental issues of political freedom, human rights, and international laws. Thus, the "tilt" toward Pakistan in 1971 in its war with India led to Pakistan's attempt to suppress the independence of newly founded Bangladesh; the "tar baby" policy adopted for all of Africa in 1970 favored white-minority regimes at the expense of the black majorities; the use of the Central Intelligence Agency to destabilize the democratically elected socialist regime of Allende in Chile, beginning in 1971, contributed to his downfall in 1973; the indecisive policy towards Biafra during the Nigerian civil war of 1969–1970 led to mass starvation; and tactics favoring the rightist military junta in Athens helped pave the way to the overthrow of Archbishop Makarios, the president of Cyprus, in 1974 while also not discouraging the subsequent Turkish invasion of the island.

Also with regard to the Third World, the Nixon Doctrine, announced on 25 July 1969, declared that the United States would supply military and economic assistance, but not soldiers to help nations defend themselves.

Economic Foreign Policy

In his economic foreign policy Nixon employed less debatable tactics and followed the advice of a much broader-gauged group of advisers. U.S. foreign economic policy took on new importance not only because of the energy crisis, following the October 1973 War, but also because of the international dimensions of Nixon's 1971 New Economic Policy (NEP). Faced with a dangerous drain on U. S. gold reserves and a trade deficit, the Nixon administration initiated the NEP, which, in addition to wage and price controls, closed the "gold window" and allowed the dollar "to float" on international markets in order to increase markets abroad and stop any more speculative pressures against the dollar. The NEP effectively killed the post–World War II Bretton Woods system, which had been designed to stabilize currency exchange rates. What followed was an international rivalry based on three competing currencies—the dollar, the yen, and the mark.

Although John Connally dominated the economic views of the Nixon administration largely through the formulation and implementation of the NEP during his short service in the administration as secretary of the treasury from February 1971 to May 1972, the president ultimately found more sustained support and advice in the person of George Shultz. Shultz succeeded Connally in 1972 and also became head of the new cabinet-level Council on Economic Policy (CEP).

Next to Connally, Nixon was most impressed with the economic views of Peter G. Peterson, who, after starting out in 1971 as assistant to the president for international economic affairs, became secretary of commerce in January 1972. In January 1971, Nixon persuaded Congress to establish an entirely new cabinet-level Council on International Economic Policy (CIEP), with Peterson as executive director. The CIEP's mission was to fill an existing void in the federal structure by coordinating domestic and foreign policy. Nixon thought the CIEP so important that he initially chaired its meetings, as it attempted to "deal with international economic policies (including trade investment, balance of payments, and finance) as a coherent whole." For a variety of reasons, not the least of which was Kissinger's general disinterest in the complicated and unglamorous aspects of international economics, in 1975 the Murphy Commission on the Organization of Government for the Conduct of Foreign Policy recommended (with Kissinger's whole-hearted support) that the CIEP be abolished.

Despite the CIEP's ultimate failure to centralize U.S. economic foreign policy, the Nixon administration dealt successfully with a number of international economic issues, including the Trade Reform Act of 1973, the president's Expropriation Policy Statement of 1972, preparation and follow up on economic issues for the 1972 summit meeting with the Soviets, the on-going Lend-Lease settlements, all commercial and maritime agreements, international investment policy, and the expropriation of U.S. property by foreign countries on a case-by-case basis. Jurisdictional problems involving the CIEP, the

Commission on International Trade and Investment Policy, and the National Advisory Council of the Department of the Treasury prevented any systematic centralization of economic foreign policy issues.

In the eyes of his critics, Nixon's diplomatic achievements left much to be desired. For example, the pursuit of "peace and honor" in Vietnam basically failed; his—and Kissinger's—Middle Eastern policy lacked real substance; Nixon pursued no systematic or constructive Third World policies, except to use certain countries as pawns in the ongoing geopolitical and ideological battle with the USSR. His so-called "tar baby" policy toward Africa is thought to have reinforced apartheid in South Africa. Détente with the USSR soon floundered in the hands of his successors; likewise the Nixon Doctrine led to unprecedented arms sales by the United States, and has not prevented use of U.S. troops abroad. Only the policy of rapprochement with China remains intact because it laid the foundation for formal recognition in 1979 under the Carter administration.

Nixon continued to write on foreign policy issues after his resignation. His books, particularly *1999: Victory without War* (1985), *In the Arena* (1990), *Seize the Moment* (1992), and *Beyond Peace* (1994) partially rehabilitated his reputation as an internationally respected foreign policy expert by the time of his death in 1994.

JOAN HOFF

See also Angola; Antiballistic Missile Treaty; Bangladesh; Chile; China; Cold War; Containment; Cyprus; Détente; Kissinger, Henry Alfred; Middle East; National Security Council; Nigeria; Nixon Doctrine; Nuclear Weapons and Strategy; Rogers, William Pierce; Russia and the Soviet Union; Shultz, George Pratt; South Africa; Strategic Arms Limitation Talks and Agreements

FURTHER READING

Ambrose, Stephen E. *Nixon*, 3 vols. 1987–1991.
Garthoff, Raymond L. *Détente and Confrontation: American-Soviet Relations from Nixon to Reagan.* Washington D.C., 1985.
Hersh, Seymour M. *The Price of Power: Kissinger in the Nixon White House.* 1983.
Hoff, Joan. *Nixon Reconsidered.* New York, 1994.
Isaacs, Arnold. *Without Honor: Defeat in Vietnam and Cambodia.* Baltimore, Md., 1983.
Litwak, Robert S. *Détente and the Nixon Doctrine: Foreign Policy and the Pursuit of Stability.* Cambridge, Mass., 1984.
Nixon, Richard M. *Six Crises.* Garden City, N.Y., 1962.
———. *RN: The Memoirs of Richard Nixon.* New York, 1978.
Osgood, Robert, et al. *Retreat of Empire? The First Nixon Administration.* Baltimore, Md., 1973.
Parmet, Herbert S. *Richard Nixon and His America.* 1990.
Schurmann, Franz. *The Foreign Policies of Richard Nixon: The Grand Design.* Berkeley, Calif., 1987.
Thornton, Richard C. *The Nixon-Kissinger Years: Reshaping America's Foreign Policy.* 1989.
Wicker, Tom. *One of Us: Richard Nixon and the American Dream.* 1991.

NIXON DOCTRINE

A statement made by President Richard M. Nixon before a group of reporters on 3 November 1969, in an off-the-record press briefing in Guam, his first stop on an around-the-world trip, in which he declared that the United States would help "free nations of the world" defend themselves, but that they must provide for their own defense before the United States committed troops. While the Nixon Doctrine was initially aimed at "southern tier" developing countries in East Asia as a rationale for unilateral withdrawal of U.S. troops from Vietnam, it came to represent Vietnamization, a policy whereby the United States would support regional security and local self-sufficiency in Asia without direct military involvement. The doctrine had important implications for the Atlantic Alliance because, like détente, it embodied U.S. acceptance of a five-power, "northern tier" strategy to replace bipolar confrontational aspects of the Cold War. Instead of continuing to deal bilaterally with the Soviet Union, Nixon wanted to bring the five great economic regions of the world—the United States, USSR, China, Japan, and the European Economic Union—into multilateral negotiations for mutual military and economic benefit.

The Nixon Doctrine represented the corollary to détente between the United States and the USSR and rapprochement with China. It allowed the United States to begin to resolve the contradiction that had plagued its foreign policy throughout the Cold War: how to maintain regional commitments abroad while reducing direct military involvement in a pentagonal world. The Nixon Doctrine repudiated the domino theory rationale under which the United States had first intervened in Vietnam. The doctrine transformed that conflict from a geopolitical struggle between two great powers, the United States and China, into a local war that could be lost or settled without grave damage to U.S. interests or increased threats.

In his 25 February 1971, foreign policy report to Congress, Nixon elaborated upon his original Guam press statement by indicating that his doctrine had evolved into the internationalization of Vietnamization or, at least, its blanket application to Asia. "In cases involving other [non-nuclear] types of aggression we shall furnish military and economic assistance when requested in accordance with our treaty commitments. But we shall look to the nation directly threatened to assume the primary responsibility for the manpower for its defense." Nixon wanted "to ensure that there were no more Vietnams in the future."

Subsequent invasions of Cambodia and Laos violated the intent, if not the letter, of the Nixon Doctrine. The doctrine led to unprecedented amounts of U.S. weapons sales to such Asian and Middle Eastern powers that acted as U.S. surrogates during the Cold War—Indonesia, South Korea, the Philippines, Pakistan, Israel, Saudi Arabia, and especially Iran before the fall of the shah. The Nixon Doctrine did not prevent deployment of U.S. troops abroad by other presidents.

JOAN HOFF

See also China; Détente; Nixon, Richard Milhous; Russia and the Soviet Union; Vietnam War

FURTHER READING

Hoff, Joan. *Nixon Reconsidered*. New York, 1994.
Litwak, Robert. *Détente and the Nixon Doctrine: Foreign Policy and the Pursuit of Stability*. Cambridge, England, 1984.
Osgood, Robert, et al. *Retreat of Empire? The First Nixon Administration*. Baltimore, Md., 1973.

NOBEL PEACE PRIZE

An award established under the will of Swedish dynamite magnate Alfred Bernhard Nobel, a scientist and inventor who died in 1896. In his will, Nobel left most of his fortune to establish annual prizes in five fields—physics, chemistry, medicine, literature, and peace—for those "who, during the preceding year, shall have conferred the greatest benefit on mankind." The first four prizes were to be granted by Swedish institutions, but Nobel directed that the peace prize be awarded by a committee of five people elected by the parliament of Norway, which was then in a monarchic union with Sweden. The peace prize was to be awarded "to the person who shall have done the most or the best work for fraternity between nations, for the abolition or reduction of standing armies, and for the holding and promotion of peace congresses." Since 1901 the award ceremonies have been held on 10 December, the day of Nobel's death, in the capital cities of both Sweden and Norway.

The special statutes governing the peace prize allow it to be awarded to institutions as well as to individuals. Those authorized to make nominations for each year's prize include current and former members of the Norwegian committee and their advisers; former winners; members of national ministries and parliaments; members of the international court at The Hague; members of the board of the International Peace Bureau (Geneva); members of the Institute of International Law; and university professors from any country of political science, jurisprudence, political science, and history.

The Norwegian Nobel committees have interpreted their mandate very broadly, and the Nobel Peace Prize is the most prestigious award in the world for service to humanity. Political leaders and diplomats have coveted the prize, and they had won about one-third of the 96

NOBEL PEACE PRIZE WINNERS

Date	Winner	Country	Reason
1901	Dunant, Jean Henri	Switzerland	Founded the International Committee of the Red Cross; Originator of the Geneva Convention
	Passy, Frédéric	France	Founded the first French peace society
1902	Ducommun, Élie	Switzerland	Honorary Secretary, Permanent International Peace Bureau, Berne
	Gobat, Charles Albert	Switzerland	Secretary General, Inter-Parliamentary Union, Berne
1903	Cremer, Sir William Randal	Great Britain	Member of British Parliament; Secretary, International Arbitration League
1904	Institute of International Law		
1905	von Suttner, Baroness Bertha	Austria	Author, *Lay Down Your Arms*
1906	Roosevelt, Theodore	United States	Mediated Russo-Japanese War
1907	Moneta, Ernesto Teodoro	Italy	President, Lombard League of Peace
	Renault, Louis	France	Professor of International Law
1908	Arnoldson, Klas Pontus	Sweden	Founded the Swedish Peace and Arbitration League
	Bajer, Fredrik	Denmark	Honorary President, Permanent International Peace Bureau, Berne
1909	Beernaert, Auguste Marie François	Belgium	Ex-Prime Minister; Member Belgian Parliament
	D'estournelles de Constant, Baron Paul	France	Member of French Parliament; Founded the Committee for the Defense of National Interests and International Conciliation
1910	Permanent International Peace Bureau		
1911	Asser, Tobias Michael Carel	Netherlands	Prime Minister; Originator, International Conferences of Private Law at The Hague
	Fried, Alfred Hermann	Austria	Journalist
1912	Root, Elihu	United States	Negotiated treaties of Arbitration
1913	La Fontaine, Henri	Belgium	President, Permanent International Peace Bureau, Berne
1917	International Committee of the Red Cross		
1919	Wilson, Thomas Woodrow	United States	Founded the League of Nations
1920	Bourgeois, Léon Victor Auguste	France	President, Council of the League of Nations
1921	Branting, Karl Hjalmar	Sweden	Prime Minister; Swedish Delegate, Council of the League of Nations
	Lange, Christian Lous	Norway	Secretary General, Inter-Parliamentary Union, Brussels
1922	Nansen, Fridtjof	Norway	Originator, Nansen passports for refugees
1925	Chamberlain, Sir Austen	Great Britain	Part-originator, Locarno Pact
	Dawes, Charles Gates	United States	Chaired Allied Reparation Commission (originator, Dawes Plan)
1926	Briand, Aristide	France	Part-originator, Locarno Pact, Kellogg-Briand Pact
	Stresemann, Gustav	Germany	Part-originator, Locarno Pact

(table continues on next page)

Date	Winner	Country	Reason
1927	Buisson, Ferdinand	France	President, League for Human Rights
	Quidde, Ludwig	Germany	Member, German Parliament
1929	Kellogg, Frank Billings	United States	Part-originator of Kellogg-Briand Pact
1930	Söderblom, Lars Olof Nathan	Sweden	Leader, ecumenical movement
1931	Addams, Jane	United States	Co-founder, Women's International League for Peace and Freedom
	Butler, Nicholas Murray	United States	Promoter, Kellogg-Briand Pact
1933	Angell, Sir Norman (Ralph Lane)	Great Britain	Member, Executive Committee of the League of Nations; member, National Peace Coucil; author, *The Great Illusion*
1934	Henderson, Arthur	Great Britain	President, Disarmament Conference
1935	von Ossietzky, Carl	Germany	Journalist; pacifist
1936	Saavedra Lamas, Carlos	Argentina	President, League of Nations; mediated a conflict between Paraguay and Bolivia
1937	Cecil of Chelwood, Viscount	Great Britain	Founder, International Peace Campaign
1938	Nansen International Office for Refugees	Switzerland	
1944	International Committee of the Red Cross		
1945	Hull, Cordell	Untied States	Co-founder of the United Nations
1946	Balch, Emily Greene	United States	Co-founder of Women's International League for Peace and Freedom
	Mott, John Raleigh	United States	Chairman, International Missionary Council; President, World Alliance of YMCAs
1947	The Friends Service Council	England	The Quakers
	The American Friends Service Committee	United States	
1949	Boyd Orr of Brechin, Lord John	Great Britain	President, National Peace Council and World Union of Peace Organizations
1950	Bunche, Ralph	United States	Acting mediator in Palestine, 1948
1951	Jouhaux, Léon	France	Trade union activist
1952	Schweitzer, Albert	France	Missionary Surgeon; Founder, Lambaréné Hospital
1953	Marshall, George Catlett	United States	General, President, American Red Cross; ex-Secretary of State and of Defense; author of the Marshall Plan
1954	Office of the United Nations High Commissioner for Refugees	Switzerland	
1957	Pearson, Lester Bowles	Canada	Former Secretary of State for External Affairs, Canada; President, 7th Session of the UN General Assembly
1958	Pire, Georges Henri	Belgium	Leader of refugee relief agency
1959	Noel-Baker, Philip J.	Great Britain	Member of Parliament; worker for international peace and co-operation
1960	Lutuli, Albert John	South Africa	President, African National Congress
1961	Hammarskjöld, Dag Hjalmar Agne Carl	Sweden	Secretary General, United Nations
1962	Pauling, Linus Carl	United States	Helped achieve partial Test Ban Treaty
1963	International Committee of the Red Cross	Switzerland	
	League of Red Cross Societies	Switzerland	
1964	King, Martin Luther, Jr.	United States	Leader, Southern Christian Leadership Conference

(table continues on next page)

Date	Winner	Country	Reason
1965	United Nations Children's Fund (UNICEF)	United States	
1968	Cassin, René	France	President, the European Court for Human Rights
1969	International Labour Organization	Switzerland	
1970	Borlaug, Norman	United States	Father of "the Green Revolution"
1971	Brandt, Willy	Germany	Chancellor; orchestrated the WestGerman détente policy of Ostpolitik
1973	Kissinger, Henry Alfred	United States	Secretary of State
	Le Duc Tho	Vietnam	Declined the Prize
1974	Mac Bride, Seán	Ireland	President, the International Peace Bureau, Geneva; President, the Commission of Namibia, United Nations
	Sato, Eisaku	Japan	Prime Minister, Japan
1975	Sakharov, Andrei Dmitrievich	USSR	Soviet Nuclear Physicist
1976	Williams, Betty	Northern Ireland	Founders of the Northern Ireland Peace Movement
	Corrigan, Mairead		
1977	Amnesty International	Great Britain	
1978	Sadat, Mohamed Anwar El	Egypt	President, the Arab Republic of Egypt
	Begin, Menachem	Israel	Prime Minister, Israel
1979	Mother Teresa	India	Leader of Missionaries of Charities
1980	Perez Esquivel, Adolfo	Argentina	Human rights leader
1981	Office of the United Nations High Commissioner for Refugees	Switzerland	
1982	Myrdal, Alva	Sweden	Diplomat; writer
	García Robles, Alfonso	Mexico	Delegate to the United Nations General Assembly on Disarmament; former Secretary for Foreign Affairs
1983	Walesa, Lech	Poland	Trade union leader
1984	Tutu, Desmond Mpilo	South Africa	Political activist against apartheid
1985	International Physicians for the Prevention of Nuclear War, Inc.	United States	
1986	Wiesel, Elie	United States	Holocaust survivor; Chairman, The President's Commission on the Holocaust
1987	Arias Sanchez, Oscar	Costa Rica	President, Costa Rica
1988	The United Nations Peace-Keeping Forces		
1989	The 14th Dalai Lama (Tenzin Gyatso)	Tibet	Exiled leader
1990	Gorbachev, Mikhail Sergeevich	USSR	President, USSR
1991	Daw Aung San Suu Kyi	Burma	Opponent of military regime
1992	Menchu Tum, Rigoberta	Guatemala	Human rights activist
1993	Mandela, Nelson Rolihlahla	South Africa	Political activist against apartheid
	De Klerk, Frederik Willem	South Africa	Prime Minister, South Africa
1994	Arafat, Yassir	Palestine	Chairman, Executive Committee of the Palestine Liberation Organization
	Peres, Shimon	Israel	Foreign Minister of Israel
	Rabin, Yitzhak	Israel	Prime Minister of Israel
1995	Joseph Rotblat and The Pugwash Conferences on Science and World Affairs	United Kingdom	For their efforts to diminish the part played by nuclear arms in international politics

prizes granted as of 1995. The U.S. recipients, who have won the lion's share of these, have included two presidents, five secretaries of state, and the chairman of an international reparations committee. Other pathfinders to peace recognized by the committees in their awards have included peace activists, humanitarians, international lawyers, religious leaders, and champions of human rights. U.S. laureates in these fields have included Jane Addams (1931) and Emily Greene Balch (1946), leaders of the Women's International League for Peace and Freedom; John R. Mott of the International Young Men's Christian Association (YMCA, 1946); the American Friends Service Committee (Quakers, 1947); Linus Pauling, who mobilized other world scientists in behalf of the cessation of atomic bomb testing (1962); Martin Luther King, Jr., for his nonviolent leadership for civil rights (1964); Norman Borlaug, father of the Green Revolution (1970); and Elie Wiesel, the Holocaust survivor who has spoken forcefully for human rights (1986).

The very first statesman prize was awarded to President Theodore Roosevelt (1906) for his mediation in ending the Russo-Japanese War. Like many statesmen prizes to follow, the award sparked controversy. Roosevelt was known as the wielder of the "big stick," who had himself enjoyed soldiering and had sent troops into the Caribbean. In his memoirs he declared that his greatest contribution to peace was sending the Great White Fleet of U.S. warships around the world. Roosevelt's skillful personal diplomacy, however, did produce the Treaty of Portsmouth (1905), and he strongly supported the Hague Conferences and arbitration treaties. Elihu Root, Roosevelt's secretary of state (1905–1909), also supported arbitration. In the 1912 award ceremony, the Norwegian committee spokesman specified Root's "work in bringing about better understanding between the countries of North and South America" and noted how after leaving office he had given "himself heart and soul to the cause of peace" as senator from New York and president of the Carnegie Endowment for International Peace.

In 1920 President Woodrow Wilson was honored with the postponed prize of 1919 for his role in establishing the League of Nations. While Nobel committee discussions are secret, it is known that the vote was 3 to 2, with Wilson's opponents on the committee considering the Versailles Treaty punitive. Charles G. Dawes, a general in World War I, businessman, and vice president of the United States, won half of the 1925 prize for chairing the committee of experts that resolved the problem of German reparation payments. The Dawes Plan began the policy of postwar reconciliation that later led to the Locarno Agreements. The three coauthors were granted Nobel Peace Prizes; Sir Austen Chamberlain, British foreign secretary, shared the 1935 prize with Dawes, and the foreign ministers of France and Germany, Aristide Briand and Gustav Stresemann, jointly won the 1926 prize. Briand later negotiated the Pact for the Outlawry of War (1928) with U.S. Secretary of State Frank B. Kellogg, for which Kellogg was honored with the 1929 prize. Nicholas Murray Butler, president of Columbia University and of the Carnegie Endowment for International Peace after Root, was recognized as a major promoter of the pact (1931). The breakdown of peace in the following years minimized the diplomatic accomplishments of the 1920s.

After the end of World War II, Cordell Hull, who had earlier been considered by the Norwegian committee for his Good Neighbor Policy toward Latin America as Franklin D. Roosevelt's secretary of state, was granted the 1945 prize for helping found the United Nations. Roosevelt, who would have had strong claim himself, supported Hull's candidacy. In 1953 the role of the United States in rebuilding the war-shattered economies of Europe was recognized by the committee with the award going to General and Secretary of State George C. Marshall, author of the European Recovery Program or Marshall Plan.

Of all peace prizes, the 1973 award to presidential assistant Henry A. Kissinger and North Vietnamese diplomat Le Duc Tho for their attempts to negotiate an end to the Vietnam War has been the most criticized by world public opinion, Kissinger being perceived as a warmaker. Two dissenting committee members later resigned, the armistice failed, Le Duc Tho declined his prize, and Kissinger unsuccessfully tried to return his award after North Vietnam defeated South Vietnam in 1975. Kissinger himself declared in his memoirs that he deserved the prize more for his shuttle diplomacy in the Middle East, where other U.S. diplomats have also sought to promote peace. The first American to receive the prize for his achievement in this area was Ralph Bunche (1950). As United Nations mediator in the conflict between Arab states and the new state of Israel, he succeeded in negotiating an armistice. President Jimmy Carter brokered peace negotiations between Egypt's President Anwar El-Sadat and Israel's Prime Minister Menachem Begin, for which these two Middle East leaders—but not Carter—shared the 1978 prize. While the Swedish committees often divided their prizes into three parts, the Norwegian committees never went beyond two recipients until the 1994 prize for Israel's Prime Minister Yitzhak Rabin, Foreign Minister Shimon Peres of Israel, and Yasir Arafat, chairman of the Palestine Liberation Organization (PLO).

As the United States became a superpower with global interests, the work of many laureates intersected with U.S. foreign policy, including Dag Hammarskjöld, UN secretary-general (1960); Chancellor Willy Brandt of the Federal Republic of Germany (1971); President Oscar

Arias Sánchez of Costa Rica, architect of the Central American peace agreement (1987); and President Mikhail Gorbachev of the Soviet Union, honored for ending the Cold War (1990). The United States has supported several winners of human-rights prizes, including the Soviet dissident Andrei Sakharov (1975); Poland's Solidarity leader, Lech Walesa (1983); the fourteenth Dalai Lama of Tibet (1989); and Aung San Suu Kyi of Burma (Myanmar, 1991), freed after six years of detention by the military government as a result of pressure from the United States and others. The United States also supported opponents of apartheid in South Africa such as Archbishop Desmond Tutu (1984) and Nelson Mandela (1993). The United States has also played an important role in international agencies that have won the peace prize, including UNICEF (United Nations Children's Fund; 1965), the International Labor Organization (1969), and the UN Peacekeeping Forces (1988).

IRWIN ABRAMS

See also Addams, Jane; Arbitration; Begin, Menachem; Bunche, Ralph Johnson; Carnegie Endowment for International Peace; Carter, James Earl; Gorbachev, Mikhail Sergeevich; Hague Peace Conferences; Hull, Cordell; Human Rights; Kellogg, Frank Billings; Kellogg-Briand Pact; King, Martin Luther, Jr.; Kissinger, Henry Alfred; League of Nations; Mandela, Nelson Rolihlahla; Marshall, George Catlett, Jr.; Marshall Plan; Middle East; Peace Movements and Societies to 1914; Peace Movements and Societies 1914 to Present; Roosevelt, Theodore; Root, Elihu; Sadat, Anwar El-; United Nations; Vietnam War; Wilson, Thomas Woodrow

FURTHER READING

Abrams, Irwin. *The Nobel Peace Prize and the Laureates. An Illustrated Biographical History, 1901–1987*. Boston, 1988.

Abrams, Irwin, ed. *Nobel Lectures Including Presentation Speeches and Laureates' Biographies. Peace. 1971–1990*, 2 vols. Singapore, 1995
——— . *The Words of Peace: Selections from the Speeches of the Winners of the Nobel Peace Prize*. Revised. New York, 1995.

Falnes, Oscar J. *Norway and the Nobel Peace Prize*. New York, 1938.

Hoberman, Frederick W., ed. *Nobel Lectures (Including Presentation Speeches and Laureate's Biographies) in Peace. 1901–1970*, 3 vols. New York, 1972.

NONALIGNED MOVEMENT

The origins of the Nonaligned Movement (NAM) can be traced to the increasingly regular contact among the independent countries and emerging developing areas of the Third World after World War II. Key among these meetings was one at Bandung in 1955, in which twenty-nine delegations, the majority of which were from Asia (six were from Africa), came together to discuss colonialism, economic development, and the maintenance of peace. Because many of the participants at the conference were aligned with either the Soviet or U.S. Cold War blocs (for example, China with the Soviet Union, and Southeast Asia Treaty Organization members like Thailand with the United States), Bandung was critical for the sense of community it fostered among emerging states, rather than for an emphasis on nonalignment. The leaders of three countries (India's Jawaharlal Nehru, Yugoslavia's Marshal Josip Broz Tito, and Egypt's Gamal Abdel Nasser) banded together to play a leading role in organizing the NAM. Regionally isolated to some extent, each had reasons for creating a form of collective resistance to the two Cold War powers. These three leaders, together with those of twenty-two other states, met in Belgrade in 1961. This meeting, which was later recognized as the first official NAM conference, ranked issues of peace and war ahead of decolonization. One product of the meeting was a letter from the nonaligned countries to President John F. Kennedy and Soviet Premier Nikita Khrushchev, asking them to enter into dialogue to reduce tensions and to avoid conflict. The Belgrade Conference also addressed economic cooperation among Third World countries. This emphasis was indirectly responsible for the establishment of the 1964 United Nations Conference on Trade and Development (UNCTAD). Many of these themes continued to dominate the NAM agenda during the years between the Belgrade meeting and the 1970 Lusaka Conference. During the 1960s, Tito was a leader for the as yet inchoate movement. Because of tense East-West relations and heightened levels of conflict within many of the Third World member countries, the movement was somewhat adrift during these years, although it expanded to include approximately seventy member countries. The Lusaka Summit not only institutionalized the movement but also reaffirmed its commitment to the principles of nonalignment. These factors, in conjunction with deteriorating economic conditions in much of the Third World during the 1970s, caused the radicalization of the NAM during that decade. Examples of this radical stance include the key role the NAM played in proposing a New International Economic Order (NIEO), which was based on the economic platform of the 1973 Algiers NAM Summit. The NAM also began to act as a voting bloc within the United Nations (UN); it pressured members to vote in accordance with nonaligned positions. As a result, not only was the United States condemned in the various NAM conference declarations and resolutions for its policies in countries such as South Africa, Vietnam, and Cuba, but the United States found it increasingly more difficult to muster support from Third World delegations on key votes in the UN General Assembly.

NAM criticism of the United States and its policies reached a high point during the 1979 Havana Summit.

Competition for the movement's leadership by heads of state such as Fidel Castro nearly led to a split in the NAM between its radical and more moderate members, particularly with respect to Castro's failed efforts to position the movement as a "natural ally" of the socialist bloc. Because of these divisions and the Soviet Union's subsequent invasion of Afghanistan, the movement entered a period of temporary paralysis and drift. Although the NAM subsequently was able to regroup, mainly because of India's leadership role, the events in Havana highlighted some of the problems of nonalignment. These were intensified by the movement's continued reliance on consensual decision-making, its lack of enforcement mechanisms, and the addition of new members (as of mid-1996, more than 100 countries). The latter factor produced not only a growing diversity in the NAM's interests and views but also a certain loss of programmatic coherence. In turn, the end of the Cold War has made nonalignment irrelevant. Nevertheless, the NAM reaffirmed its existence as an organization at the 1992 Jakarta Summit. Although the end of the Cold War may remove an important source of conflict between the United States and the NAM, some tension between the two is likely to remain as they continue to diverge on issues centered in the economic realm.

CAROLINE A. HARTZELL

See also Bipolarity; Cold War; New International Economic Order; Third World; United Nations

FURTHER READING

Jackson, Richard L. *The Nonaligned, the UN, and the Superpowers.* New York, 1983.

Misra, K. P., ed. *Nonalignment: Frontiers and Dynamics.* New Delhi, 1982.

Murthy, P. A. N., and B. K. Shirvastava, eds. *Neutrality and Nonalignment in the 1990s.* London, 1991.

Singham, A. W., and Shirley Hune. *Nonalignment in an Age of Alignments.* London, 1986.

NONGOVERNMENTAL ORGANIZATIONS

Nongovernmental organizations (NGOs) are the sinews of civil society. They are as vital to the well-being of the United States as the structures of democratic government and free enterprise, and their behavior inevitably affects the content and conduct of U.S. foreign relations. NGOs provide a vast array of human services, unmet by either government or the market, and they are the self-designated advocates for action on virtually all matters of public concern. Abetted by the revolution in communications and information technology, NGOs are weaving their own worldwide networks that operate largely beyond the reach of governments, while generating political and social forces that few governments, least of all a democracy, can ignore.

NGOs cannot be easily defined or categorized. There is even disagreement over what they should be called: private voluntary organizations (PVOs), the independent sector, nonprofit organizations, peoples' organizations, the third sector. By the mid–1990s there were an estimated 1.4 million nonprofit organizations in communities across the United States with a combined income of over $400 billion and some eight million employees. In addition, nearly half of the country's adults provide some form of voluntary service each year. Whatever label one attaches to the diverse array of civic, cultural, ethnic, religious, public policy, educational, professional, labor, welfare, or other groups, NGOs reflect a broad popular belief in the value of citizens doing what governments appear unwilling or unable to do. The proportion of U.S. nonprofit organizations and resources devoted to service abroad, or to advocating public policies that bear on U.S. foreign relations, is still very small. But the size and influence of these NGOs have increased substantially since World War II. There are currently about 600 U.S. NGOs with annual budgets in excess of $1 million that either operate internationally or focus on international policy issues. Reporting on this activity is incomplete and it is difficult to differentiate between purely domestic and international programs, but the combined expenditures of these NGOs probably exceeded $11 billion in 1996.

Types, Funding, and Activities

NGOs whose primary interests are international can be grouped in three broad categories. Public policy advocacy organizations, which typically have small staffs, very little presence overseas, and devote their energies to encouraging, informing, and influencing national and international debate about such issues as human-rights abuses, hunger, refugee protection, the environment, population, and many other concerns. These include not only activist groups, such as Human Rights Watch, the Sierra Club, or the Population Council, but also public-education NGOs, such as the United Nations Association, the Council on Foreign Relations, or The Americas Society, and influential thinktanks, such as the Brookings Institution, Resources for the Future, or the Heritage Foundation. Humanitarian and development organizations have grown enormously since World War II and now include some of the largest NGOs, such as CARE, Save the Children, and World Vision, with annual budgets in the hundreds of millions of dollars with thousands of staff around the world. In 1994–1995, 434 humanitarian and development NGOs worked with the U.S. Agency for International Development (USAID), a 240-percent increase since 1982 when only 126 were registered. Practitioners of conflict resolution, or what is increasingly called "Track II" diplomacy, comprise the newest and smallest category of NGOs involved in foreign relations. The work of the Carter Center, Search for Common Ground, and the Kettering Foundation, among others, have sought with some success to clarify differences and reach nonbinding agreements among parties to various disputes in Africa, Latin America, the Balkans, and Central Asia that have facilitated or supplemented official bilateral and multilateral mediation.

Most NGO activity, whether at home or abroad, is financed privately by contributions from individuals, corporations, and independent foundations. While U.S. tax laws are favorable to NGOs and the philanthropic giving that supports them, direct government contributions to NGOs have been declining, relative to private support, for more than a decade. For example, among the 434 humanitarian and development NGOs registered with USAID, private contributions rose 160 percent between 1982 and 1992, while federal funding fluctuated upward some 41 percent. Of the $7.3 billion in total resources raised by these same NGOs in 1994–1995, $4.9 billion or 67 percent came from private sources, with the remaining 33 percent from USAID ($1.4 billion) and other U.S. government agencies and international organizations. As overall U.S. development assistance levels have declined, the proportion that is administered by NGOs has gone up, from barely 20 percent of $2 billion in 1990 to nearly 40 percent of $1.5 billion in 1995. At the 1995 United Nations (UN) Social Summit in Copenhagen, Vice President Al Gore announced that the percent of development aid channeled through NGOs would grow to 50 percent by the end of the century.

The huge growth in private support for internationally active NGOs largely reflects individual giving, through religious organizations, mass membership public interest groups, and emergency appeals, rather than an increase in resources provided by foundations. Of the $11.1 billion donated by the United States' 37,500 private foundations in 1993, barely 10 percent went for international purposes, and the proportion of $6 billion in annual corporate giving that supported international activities is much smaller. If new public-private partnerships are to be forged to meet the foreign relations challenges of the post–Cold War world, these will most likely involve NGOs that enjoy broad-based domestic support. Interaction, the national coalition of over 150 NGOs with interests in international development and humanitarian action, estimates that as many as 40 million citizens donate money by mail, at work, or through their place of worship to the overseas operations of these groups.

Most large humanitarian and development NGOs have become significant international actors only since the 1960s. Their current rate of expansion is largely a response to the exploding needs of the world's most desperate people, a population that in 1996 was estimated to include more than fifteen million refugees plus another twenty-two to twenty-four million internally displaced people. Most of these people were uprooted by the proliferation of complex emergencies since the end of the Cold War.

Internationally minded NGOs concerned with public policy normally do not have large operations abroad, but their role in influencing the United States' standing and role in the world dates back to the founding of the country. The impact of advocacy NGOs has varied widely across issues and over time, as these NGOs represent the full range of ethnic, ideological, religious, professional, labor, and other "special interests" that reflect U.S. pluralism. NGO advocacy in the area of political and human rights, for example, dates back to the antiroyalist movement prior to the American Revolution. In the nineteenth century powerful abolitionist NGOs that opposed current policy on slavery were themselves influenced by the British and Foreign Anti-Slavery Society, which was founded in 1838 and is considered to be the first modern transnational NGO. By helping to precipitate the Civil War and a subsequent restructuring of the political foundation of the U.S.—from a nation defined by states' rights to one based on individual rights—abolitionist NGOs also contributed to altering the domestic underpinnings of U.S. foreign policy. The same universal values espoused by nineteenth-century abolitionists have resurfaced repeatedly among NGOs active in promoting civil rights at home and human rights abroad. These interest groups supported Eleanor Roosevelt in the successful campaign to infuse the United Nations Charter with human rights themes and to promote passage of the Universal Declaration of Human Rights. The changes forced in U.S. policy toward South Africa in the 1980s were part of a worldwide NGO campaign to end apartheid.

NGOs and the Cold War

To some degree, Cold War politics tended to marginalize NGO efforts to promote human rights, especially in countries where the U.S. government deemed maintenance of the status quo to be essential in containing the spread of communism. Some NGOs did assist in the reconstruction of Europe and then in the broader U.S. campaign to help poor countries in Africa, Asia, and Latin America. And the government was generally supportive of NGO human rights campaigns directed at the Soviet Union and its allies. Cold War foreign policy also ignited the biggest NGO-led popular protest movement since the Civil War, opposition to U.S. involvement in Vietnam. That experience also caused many NGOs to become much less willing to cooperate with U.S. government programs and policies abroad. Among those affected were the large and growing number of NGOs involved in promoting economic development in the Third World. These NGOs have roots in early twentieth-century famine relief, Red Cross operations, overseas missionary work, and the international labor movement.

Deep divisions over whether and how the United States should become involved in the affairs of other nations, first in Vietnam and then elsewhere in the Third World, persisted during the 1980s. These were manifest in two opposing camps: 1) the "international development community" was largely composed of liberal internationalist NGOs and that part of the federal bureaucracy engaged in foreign assistance; and 2) a smaller group of conservative NGOs who were allied with those in government who emphasized the need for a strong defense. This ideological and policy battleground extended not only to the regional conflicts in Central America, Southern Africa, and elsewhere. It also included a growing number of issues involving many other countries and that resonated with domestic opinion: how should the United States respond to population growth, changes in the global environment, resource scarcities, threats to bio-diversity, the role of women, narcotics, immigration, rising unemployment, and other matters. With the end of the Cold War, however, the core issues that divided the foreign affairs community into the liberal "international development" and conservative "national security" camps have lost salience. It is too early to say whether the mutual suspicions and antagonisms that inhibited greater cooperation between NGOs and the government in foreign relations, at least since the height of the Vietnam War, will give way to new partnerships of the type now prevalent in several smaller established democracies such as Norway, Sweden, and the Netherlands. NGOs in the United States have a longer and stronger tradition of opposing government than is the case in most other democracies. At some level, U.S. NGOs will remain independent and individualistic, protect their prerogatives, and resist assuming greater accountability to anyone other than their own members. Meanwhile, many Washington officials no doubt will continue to view NGOs as often reckless, irresponsible, intolerant, and capable of sowing dangerous uncertainty about U.S. intentions that comforts our adversaries and confuses our allies.

Despite these persistent tensions, the foreign relations of the United States in the coming decades are likely to be profoundly influenced by a significant convergence of interests between a growing number of NGOs involved in international affairs and those in government responsible for foreign and national security policy. Since the end of the Cold War the two sectors have become highly interdependent, perhaps to a degree that neither would yet concede. Cynics may explain this interdependence by pointing to Washington's need to offload development assistance and other international programs to privately funded NGOs in order to meet congressionally mandated cutbacks to balance the budget, and NGOs' reliance on the U.S. military and UN peacekeepers for the safety and logistical support required to undertake major humanitarian operations in complex emergencies.

NGO-Government Cooperation

Beyond the immediate budget and security imperatives for greater NGO–U.S. government cooperation, there are at least five fundamental and positive dimensions to these emerging partnerships, with far-reaching implications for U.S. foreign relations. First, NGOs seek—and are readily acknowledged by Washington to have—vital roles to play in helping transitions to democracy and market economics in Russia and the other newly independent states of the former Soviet Union, in post-authoritarian East and Central Europe, and elsewhere. Ensuring that these positive but still fragile trends become irreversible will remain of the highest longterm national interest. Thus far the level of public and private funds for this purpose has been largely inadequate, and neither political leaders nor NGO advocacy groups have been willing or able to mobilize the necessary congressional and public support. Yet many community-based organizations and international NGOs are providing invaluable technical and other forms of assistance. Successful collaboration between NGOs and publicly funded facilitating agencies such as the National Endowment for Democracy and the Eurasia Foundation, the extensive network among Sister Cities and Sister States, the Citizens Democracy Corps, educational consortia, government and private environmental initiatives, and other activities reflect a new consensus about the importance of assisting development of civil society as the foundation for post-Cold War foreign relations.

Second, NGOs have assumed major burdens in responding to the growing number of complex emergencies, also with strong backing from the U.S. government. For the large humanitarian organizations, accustomed to dealing with natural disasters at the behest of local governments and with little fear of physical security, the manmade political disasters of failed states pose new and daunting challenges. In Bosnia, Somalia, Rwanda, and Liberia, and elsewhere, NGOs have had to improvise security arrangements, deal with internally displaced people who are not covered by the international agreements that apply to refugees, try to restore some degree of local law and order, and seek an end to impunity of human rights abuse. Many NGOs long opposed to U.S. intervention in the Third World are now lobbying hard for greater engagement and working directly with peacekeeping and other armed forces as never before. Meanwhile, the U.S. government is discovering that the traditional diplomatic, military, and economic means to prevent interstate conflict are inadequate for dealing with the outbreak, escalation, and recurrence of mass violence and complex emergencies within states. And it is beginning to register that proliferating domestic violence will not only create huge humanitarian costs, but cumulative effects that threaten to undermine the foundations of international order and vital U.S. longterm interests in sustaining a stable and prosperous international environment. Washington also has begun to recognize that, while it has the military capability to maintain the balance of power among states, it must increasingly rely on NGOs and other nontraditional instruments to help prevent and overcome dangerous imbalances of power within states. Early and sustained preventive action requires deepening engagement in the internal affairs of other states. Transnational NGOs, working with local counterpart groups, may be better able to receive and act on early warnings of human rights abuse, economic dislocations, land and water issues, or other signs that a state may be sliding toward failure and mass violence. And their unofficial status may be more acceptable to local authorities and to foreign governments reluctant to incur the political and economic costs of early intervention. But effective preventive action cannot be left to NGOs. It usually requires the added weight of official diplomacy, threats of sanctions or more forceful measures, and a mix of economic and political incentives that only governments can provide. Harmonizing and strengthening such efforts at all stages of crisis management will require major changes in how the United States organizes and funds the conduct of foreign relations and deals with NGOs. A significant experiment in this regard has been the Burundi Policy Forum, a coalition of U.S. government, NGOs, and international organizations that convened in January 1995 and by June 1996 had met fifteen times to promote concerted efforts aimed at preventing a new round of ethnic warfare in Burundi. Such partnerships are proving especially important, not only in working with local factions to prevent state failure in Burundi, but also during the reconstruction phase in Bosnia, when rebuilding civil society is essential if peace processes are to be sustained.

Third, emerging NGO-government partnerships reflect a shared interest in deepening cooperation among the established democracies. Among NGOs in the United States, Europe, and Japan there is a growing "transnational civil society" that could become as important to the strength and resilience of relations among democracies as local variants of civil society for the domestic health of these democracies. NGO activity, which first accelerated in the United States during the 1960s, has in the past decade grown rapidly in Western Europe, Japan, and most recently across Latin America, Asia, Africa, and the new states of the former Soviet Union.

Meanwhile, a small number of large NGOs that originated in Europe and the United States, for example, Amnesty International, the World Wildlife Fund, CARE, Greenpeace, Oxfam, and Save the Children, have become significant multinational actors. U.S. leadership in the international NGO movement is a function of both the size and the number of U.S.-based organizations and their financial base of support. Private sources of income in the U.S. for humanitarian and development NGOs exceed, by some 34 percent, the combined private contributions to internationally active NGOs by the citizens of all the other twenty leading Western donor nations. The Union of International Associations lists about 14,500 NGOs that operate in more than one country, with over a third of them having multinational membership and governing structures. Helping to strengthen this incipient transnational civil society is one way for the United States and its main allies in Europe and Japan to pursue their shared goal of deepening and enlarging the community of democratic nations. As India, South Korea, Brazil, South Africa, and other developing countries gain affluence and political freedom, they are spawning literally thousands of local NGOs, many of whom are already connecting electronically to counterpart groups in the United States and elsewhere.

Fourth, closer cooperation between NGOs and government is essential if the major problems that will bedevil world politics in the twenty-first century are to be addressed: environmental threats, economic development, public health, narcotics and crime, and other issues that are of increasing concern to the public in the established democracies. Traditionally, NGOs have played modest supporting roles as part of official U.S. delegations to major international gatherings. President Woodrow Wilson's inclusion of labor leader Samuel Gompers in the conference that led to the Peace of Paris is an early example. And beginning with the 1932 World Disarmament Conference, NGOs have sought to influence the proceedings of major conferences by holding parallel "advisory" meetings. More recently, NGOs have been in much greater evidence at intergovernmental gatherings, especially the series of UN conferences on global issues. At the 1992 UN Conference on the Environment and Development in Rio, for example, 4,000 individuals representing over 1,400 NGOs were officially accredited while another 25,000 private individuals from 167 countries participated in a nearby Global Forum. Similar NGO efforts were mounted during UN conferences on human rights (Vienna, 1993), population (Cairo, 1994), and social development (Copenhagen, 1995). At the UN's Fourth World Conference on Women (Beijing, 1995) the number of NGO delegates officially accredited was 4,035, almost as many as the 4,095 government representatives and more than ten times the 400 NGO delegates to the First World Conference on Women (Nairobi, 1985).

Fifth, NGO and U.S. government interests converge around a shared need for broad-based bipartisan congressional and public support for greater U.S. engagement abroad. Such political support gives U.S. foreign policy its real authority and legitimacy and will generate the necessary resources to fund expanding and effective NGO-government partnerships to meet the many humanitarian, development, and longterm national security challenges that will drive U.S. foreign relations well into the twenty-first century.

Traditionally, the public has entrusted the formulation and conduct of U.S. foreign relations to a small, exclusive, mostly white male foreign policy elite. While the rest of U.S. society and government became more pluralistic, the foreign affairs establishment did not. During the Cold War this was partially due to the nature of the Soviet challenge. Preventing nuclear war required highly centralized, secretive, and technologically advanced national security structures and personnel, about which the public knew very little. All this has changed, beginning with the Vietnam failure and accelerating with the collapse of the Soviet Union. Public judgments about the priorities and direction of U.S. engagement abroad can be volatile and contradictory; but they also reflect a growing popular belief that foreign policy is too important to be left to the experts. The politics of foreign and domestic policy—for better or worse—are becoming increasingly indistinguishable. And as NGOs claim new stakes in this process, they slow consensus building in some cases and facilitate it in others.

Advocacy NGOs will still influence the give-and-take of political debate about issues bearing on the U.S. role in the world. In the decade ahead, however, the larger service NGOs with expanding international programs that draw financial and volunteer support from mass member U.S. religious, professional, environmental, and other national groups will likely have an increasingly important influence on the underpinnings of U.S. foreign relations. As these NGOs extend their operations abroad through more robust national and transnational networks, their overall role in foreign affairs—reducing public dependence on government policies and market forces—begins to resemble their domestic role. U.S. officials may still view the international behavior of NGOs as sometimes unhelpful or even hostile to U.S. interests and foreign policy. But there is also a growing recognition that NGOs are a major asset to world affairs that enhance the United States' influence and leadership. NGOs contribute to an international environment conducive to U.S. values and longterm interests in ways similar to the broad role they play in U.S. business. Moreover, those NGOs that either draw on a mass membership or otherwise have close ties to local communities in the U.S. also serve as transmission lines for the lessons and experiences acquired through work abroad that are then brought home and invigorate civil society and internationalism in the United States.

The growing capacity and special advantages that NGOs demonstrate in dealing with such difficult issues as complex emergencies, conflict prevention, and development have prompted some U.S. officials to call for delegating to them even greater responsibilities in foreign relations. If this transfer policy is only undertaken as a government cost-saving measure, however, the national interest will not be well served. International challenges facing the United States on the eve of the twenty-first century require a robust partnership between NGOs and the government that will produce benefits substantially greater than either could accomplish separately. Mobilizing public support for such partnerships, and sufficient public and private funding to sustain them, is a burden that leaders in government and NGOs must bear together. Without such cooperation there is a danger that the United States will fail to seize the opportunities to consolidate the gains of the Cold War and broaden the foundations for an international order based upon shared commitments to democracy, market economics, and civil society.

JOHN J. STREMLAU

See also Foreign Aid; Humanitarian Intervention and Relief; International Red Cross and Red Crescent Movement; National Endowment for Democracy; Preventive Diplomacy; United Nations

FURTHER READING

Bolling, Landrum R. *Private Foreign Aid.* Boulder, Colo., 1992.
Salamon, Lester M. "The Rise of the Nonprofit Sector." *Foreign Affairs* (July/August 1994): 109–122.
Smillie, Ian. *The Arms Bazaar.* Ottawa, 1995.
Smillie, Ian, and Henny Helmich, eds. *Non-Governmental Organizations and Governments: Stakeholders for Development.* Paris, 1994.
Spiro, Peter J. "New Global Communities: Nongovernmental Organizations in International Decision-Making Institutions." In *Order and Disorder After the Cold War,* edited by Brad Roberts. Cambridge, Mass., 1995.
Weiss, Thomas G., and Leon Gordenker, eds. *NGOs, the UN, and Global Governance.* Boulder, Colo., 1996.

NONPROLIFERATION

See Nuclear Nonproliferaton

NOOTKA SOUND AFFAIR
(1789–1790)

An Anglo-Spanish dispute over Nootka Sound, a small body of water on the west coast of Vancouver Island, in present-day British Columbia, Canada. It was here that the newly formed U.S. government under President George Washington faced its first diplomatic crisis. During the summer of 1789, Spanish authorities seized several British trading ships attempting to establish a trading post, claiming the territory for Spain and placing it off-limits to foreigners. Both sides prepared for war, spurred on by their conflicting imperial claims in North America.

The United States found itself in a difficult position. Should war break out, Great Britain might attempt to cross U.S. soil from Canada and strike at Spanish territories in Louisiana, Florida, and New Orleans. If called upon to grant permission to do this and it agreed, the United States could find itself at war with Spain. Should permission be denied, it could go to war with England. Given this dilemma, the president sought advice from his two most important department heads, Secretary of the Treasury Alexander Hamilton and Secretary of State Thomas Jefferson. Hamilton harbored pro-British sentiments and recommended that they be allowed to cross U.S. soil, whereas Jefferson distrusted the British and cautioned against it. War did not occur between Spain and Great Britain, and the president did not have to decide between his advisers' conflicting counsel. Spain had counted on assistance from its French ally and was forced to back down when that assistance was not forthcoming because of France's internal upheaval during the French Revolution. In the Nootka Sound Convention of 1790, Spain agreed to return British property, and conceded to the British the right to trade and settle in the area it had once claimed as its own.

Politically and diplomatically, the Nootka Sound crisis proved significant to the fledgling Republic. The crisis prompted the British to view the United States with more respect as a nation under the Constitution, which was considerably different from the way it had acted toward the United States while it operated under the weak Articles of Confederation. Fear of U.S. reaction produced alarm in England, where the prospect of economic reprisal, along with U.S. seizure of British trading forts in the north, forced an official reexamination of policies toward the United States. The result was the first duly accredited British minister to the United States, George Hammond, who arrived in Philadelphia in October 1791.

THOM M. ARMSTRONG

See also Canada; Great Britain; Hamilton, Alexander; Jefferson, Thomas; Spain; Washington, George

FURTHER READING

Cook, Warren L. *Flood Tide of Empire: Spain and the Pacific Northwest, 1543–1819*. New Haven, Conn., 1973.
DeConde, Alexander. *Entangling Alliances: Politics and Diplomacy Under George Washington*. Durham, N.C., 1958.
Weber, David J. *The Spanish Frontier in North America*. New Haven, Conn., 1992.
Wright, J. Leitch, Jr. *Britain and the North American Frontier, 1783–1815*. Athens, Ga., 1975.

NORIEGA, MANUEL

(*b.* 11 February 1940)

Military officer who ruled Panama from 1983 to 1989. Born and raised on the streets of Panama City, Noriega rose from poverty by winning a scholarship to a Peruvian military academy in 1958. After spying on Peruvians for the U.S. Central Intelligence Agency (CIA), he joined the Panamanian National Guard in 1962 and became an intelligence officer. He became Panama's ruler after the death of his predecessor, Omar Torrijos, in a mysterious plane crash. Because Noriega continued to cooperate with the CIA, infiltrated labor unions, permitted the anti-Sandinista Nicaraguan Contras to train in Panama, and did not disrupt the transitional status of the Panama Canal, the administrations of Presidents Ronald Reagan (1981–1989) and George Bush (1989–1993) blocked investigations into Noriega's drug trafficking activities. When Noriega became defiant of U.S. authorities, endorsing the Contadora peace process for Central America (which the United States opposed), while brutally overturning the results of democratically held elections, the Bush administration decided to remove him from power. A Florida grand jury indicted Noriega on charges of racketeering, money laundering, and violation of drug laws in 1988, and in December 1989 U.S. troops invaded Panama. Noriega surrendered to the United States after taking refuge in the residence of the papal nuncio, and in April 1992 was convicted and sentenced to a total of forty years in prison in the United States.

STEPHEN M. STREETER

See also Central Intelligence Agency; Contras; Panama and Panama Canal

FURTHER READING

Albert, Steve. *The Case Against the General: Manuel Noriega and the Politics of American Justice*. New York, 1995.
Buckley, Kevin. *Panama: The Whole Story*. New York, 1991.
Kempe, Frederick. *Divorcing the Dictator: America's Bungled Affair with Noriega*. New York, 1990.
Scranton, Margaret E. *The Noriega Years: U.S.-Panamanian Relations, 1981–1990*. Boulder, Colo., 1991.

NORTH, OLIVER LAWRENCE

(*b.* 7 October 1943)

Member of the National Security Council staff (1981–1986) and central figure in the Iran-Contra affair. A graduate of the U.S. Naval Academy in 1968, he joined the Marine Corps and was decorated for service in the Vietnam War. A colorful, can-do self-promoter without patience for bureaucratic or constitutional obstacles, he helped execute U.S. policy in the 1982 Falklands War, the 1983 invasion of Grenada, and antiterrorism activities—notably the 1985 midair capture of the *Achille Lauro* cruise-ship hijackers. In 1987 North admitted he helped engineer sales of missiles to Iran, had laundered the money in Switzerland, and had dispatched the funds to help the Nicaraguan Contras, contrary to U.S. law. He was a principal U.S. official in operational charge of the unsuccessful U.S. clandestine attempt to use the Contras to overthrow the Nicaraguan Sandinista government. North destroyed evidence and lied to Congress about these acts. His claims of a close relationship with President Ronald Reagan were later denied by Reagan himself. In 1989 North was found guilty on three counts (aiding and abetting the obstruction of Congress; altering, concealing, and destroying NSC documents; and receiving an illegal gratuity). His convictions were subsequently reversed on technicalities. In 1994 North, strongly supported by evangelical Christian conservatives, won the Republican nomination for senator from Virginia but was narrowly defeated in November by incumbent Democrat Charles Robb.

WALTER LaFEBER

See also Contras; Iran-Contra Affair; Nicaragua; Reagan, Ronald Wilson

FURTHER READING

Bradlee, Ben, Jr. *Guts and Glory: The Oliver North Story.* New York, 1988.

Draper, Theodore. *A Very Thin Line: The Iran-Contra Affairs.* New York, 1991.

North, Oliver Lawrence. *Under Fire: An American Story.* New York, 1992.

NORTH AMERICAN FREE TRADE AGREEMENT

(1992)

An agreement between the United States, Canada, and Mexico to gradually eliminate most barriers to the flow of goods and services among the three countries. A new era in the relationship of the United States with its two closest neighbors began with the signing of NAFTA in December 1992. All tariffs between the three countries were to be removed within fifteen years, as were most restrictions on and discriminatory actions against foreign direct investment. The agreement, which took effect on 1 January 1994, consists of more than 2,000 pages of detailed text on the operational aspects of trade liberalization, plus three supplemental side agreements dealing with protection of workers' rights, protection of the environment through better enforcement of national laws, and arrangements to contain import surges in a specific product sector. When measured in terms of total output, the free trade area in North America was the world's largest trading bloc as of 1994.

In many respects, NAFTA merely formalizes among the three countries the process of economic integration that had been intensifying steadily for many years through private sector initiatives. Canada is traditionally the United States' biggest trading partner; Mexico was its third largest export market and third largest source of imports in 1992. A significant percentage of two-way U.S. trade with Canada and Mexico entered the country duty-free even before the agreement, and subsidiaries of U.S. corporations were numerous in both countries. NAFTA is a deviation from the long-standing U.S. preference for reduction of trade barriers on a nondiscriminatory global basis under the General Agreement on Tariffs and Trade (GATT). Nevertheless, GATT allows preferential trading agreements that reduce internal tariffs to zero and do not increase average levels of external tariffs. Thus, NAFTA remains consistent with one of the central goals of U.S. trade policy—pursuit of a trading system with a minimum of official barriers and a maximum of global production based on relative national efficiency.

NAFTA provoked considerable political controversy, and the process leading up to congressional approval of the implementing legislation in 1993 was marked by a debate whose intensity was unprecedented in the history of modern U.S. trade policy. Proponents argued that the relatively higher Mexican trade barriers would decline more than those of the United States, that NAFTA would reinforce the market-oriented economic reforms introduced in the 1980s that had strengthened the Mexican economy, and that most economic models projected positive, albeit modest, overall benefits to the U.S. economy. Opponents argued that free trade areas were traditionally formed between countries at similar stages of economic development and with comparable forms of government, that U.S. factory wages would be depressed because of accelerated U.S. foreign direct investment in Mexico and threats to workers to accept management wage offers or face transfers of production south of the border, and that the agreement would intensify the already high level of environmental pollution in the border region resulting from Mexico's allegedly lax enforcement of its environmental protection laws.

STEPHEN D. COHEN

See also Canada; General Agreement on Tariffs and Trade; Mexico

FURTHER READING

Congressional Budget Office. *A Budgetary and Economic Analysis of the North American Free Trade Agreement.* Washington, D.C., 1993.

Greenspun, Ricardo, and Maxwell Cameron, eds. *The Political Economy of North American Free Trade*. New York, 1993.

Hufbauer, Gary Clyde, and Jeffrey J. Schott. *NAFTA—An Assessment*. Washington, D.C., 1992.

NORTH ATLANTIC TREATY ORGANIZATION

The North Atlantic Treaty Organization (NATO), under which the United States and the countries of Western Europe have pledged mutual defense against armed attack since 1949, has been the United States' largest alliance commitment since World War II and has consumed a greater share of its defense budget than any other foreign obligation. Aside from the scope of the mutual commitment that it represents, NATO is unusual in two ways. It is one of the most formally institutionalized peacetime alliances in history, if not the most so, with elaborate military and diplomatic bureaucracies at its Brussels headquarters in addition to the many national-level officials involved in its work. It was also the United States' first peacetime mutual defense treaty outside the Western Hemisphere, one that set a precedent for many others. Today, NATO's role is changing significantly with the end of the Cold War, and there is much uncertainty as to its eventual destination.

NATO emerged from the strategic vacuum in Central Europe created by the defeat of Nazi Germany and the fear in the West that the Soviet Union under Josef Stalin would fill it. After World War II, Stalin set out to fortify his Western frontier against what he saw as an implacably hostile capitalist world. He sought to recreate a sphere of influence at least as extensive as that enjoyed by the Russian czars. In doing so, he put pressure on Iran and Turkey, tightened the Soviet grip on Eastern Europe, tried to force the occupying Western powers out of Berlin through a land blockade, encouraged civil unrest in France and Italy, and generally seemed in the West to be seeking a Eurasian hegemony.

Two underlying problems split post–World War II Europe into sharply antagonistic blocs, one dominated by the United States, the other by the USSR. One was desperate economic conditions and the U.S. belief that this might lead to communist subversion. This fear produced the European Recovery Program (the Marshall Plan) to subsidize economic rehabilitation in Western Europe, an offer Stalin forced his satellites to refuse. The other major problem was failure among the World War II victors to agree on the reconstruction of Germany. The United States and Britain insisted on integrating western Germany into the West economically, and resisted what they saw as Soviet inducements to unify and neutralize the defeated country. When Washington, London, and Paris tried to stimulate economic recovery in the three

German zones they occupied, Stalin responded with a land blockade of Berlin. The blockade failed, due to a U.S.-engineered airlift of supplies into Berlin, but it convinced Western leaders that European economic recovery was futile without shared confidence that Soviet intimidation and potential aggression could be resisted. The result was a Western mutual defense treaty.

NATO was built in several stages. The British-French Dunkirk Treaty of 1947 was the first peacetime defense pact between these erstwhile rivals. Their concern at that point was at least as much the future prospect of a resurgent Germany as the immediate threat of the Soviet Union. But by 1948, growing concern about possible Soviet aggression or subversion led Britain, France, and the Benelux group (Belgium, the Netherlands, and Luxembourg) to conclude the Brussels Treaty. It bound its members to mutual defense for fifty years, and was signed the same day that President Harry S. Truman asked the U.S. Congress to reinstate military conscription (that is, the peacetime draft). Just as Western Europe was beginning to coalesce militarily and the Truman administration was moving slowly to shed the United States' peacetime habit of military isolationism, the opposition Republicans in the U.S. Congress, who had a strong isolationist tradition, began to accept the emerging alliance with Western Europe, thus removing the last politically serious obstacle to U.S. participation in NATO. Republican Senator Arthur Vandenberg, soon to become chair of the Senate Foreign Relations Committee, sponsored a resolution that supported "regional and other collective self-defense" consistent with the relevant clauses of the United Nations Charter. The Senate approved the Vandenberg Resolution in June 1948. With these domestic and international foundations in place, the United States, Canada, and ten European governments—Belgium, Denmark, France, Iceland, Italy, Luxembourg, the Netherlands, Norway, Portugal, and the United Kingdom—signed the North Atlantic Treaty in April 1949.

Key Treaty Provisions

The treaty had three key provisions, the most important of which was Article 5. While the United States insisted that Article 5 did not automatically require signatories to go to war, since this would have nullified Congress's prerogatives, Article 5 did clearly define an attack on any member as an attack on them all, and it bound all members to take any action "deemed necessary" to repel it. Article 4 allows any signatory to consult with other members if it feels threatened. Article 6, which has caused repeated controversy over the years, carefully limits NATO's area of responsibility to an attack on the territories of one or more members in Europe or North America. The United States sought this provision

U.S. AMBASSADORS TO NATO		
AMBASSADOR	PERIOD OF APPOINTMENT	ADMINISTRATION
William H. Draper, Jr.	1952–1953	Truman
		Eisenhower
John C. Hughes	1953–1955	Eisenhower
George W. Perkins	1955–1957	Eisenhower
W. Randolph Burgess	1957–1961	Eisenhower
		Kennedy
Thomas K. Finletter	1961–1965	Kennedy
		L. B. Johnson
Harlan Cleveland	1965–1969	L. B. Johnson
		Nixon
Robert Ellsworth	1969–1971	Nixon
David M. Kennedy	1972–1973	Nixon
Donald H. Rumsfeld	1973–1974	Nixon
		Ford
David K. E. Bruce	1974–1976	Ford
Robert Strausz-Hupé	1976–1977	Ford
		Carter
W. Tapley Bennett, Jr.	1977–1983	Carter
		Reagan
David M. Abshire	1983–1987	Reagan
Alton G. Keel, Jr.	1987–1989	Reagan
		Bush
William H. Taft IV	1989–1992	Bush
Reginald Bartholomew	1992–1993	Bush
Robert Hunter	1993–Present	Clinton

Sources: *Principal Officers of the Department of State and United States Chiefs of Missions.* ©1991 by Office of the Historian, Bureau of Public Affairs, Washington, D.C.; *The U.S. Government Manual,* Annual. Washington, D.C.

as a way to stay out of conflicts involving European colonial possessions.

Initially, U.S. leaders favored a temporary and fairly loose security pledge. Europeans, by contrast, sought a tight military link. Beginning in the early 1950s, in large part precipitated by the half-a-world away Korean War, the United States deepened its troop commitment to NATO and the alliance became much more institutionalized. Even though few historians now believe that Stalin intended to attack Western Europe, the invasion of South Korea seemed to confirm some U.S. officials' dire warnings about worldwide communist intentions. In particular, the attack seemed to validate the reasoning of NSC-68, the U.S. policy paper written in early 1950 that urged massive rearmament in the wake of Moscow's successful test of an atomic bomb. Accordingly, after the Korean invasion, U.S. containment policy became globally militarized, especially in Europe.

NATO's present organizational structure took shape at this time. Because the sudden Korean attack suggested that improvised military planning could be costly, NATO members' defense preparations became integrated after 1950. The alliance soon acquired a headquarters and secretariat, an integrated Supreme Command headed by an American, and four extra U.S. divisions deployed to Europe. Politically, the North Atlantic Council (NAC) was established to guide NATO at the highest collective level. The NAC convenes periodically at the level of heads of government, foreign ministers, or the ambassadors each member sends to Brussels. Defense Ministers meet apart from the NAC, in a Defense Planning Committee and Nuclear Planning Group. A separate committee composed of senior uniformed officers is in overall charge of operational military planning. Under its direction, the Supreme Allied Commander for Europe (SACEUR) is charged with training troops to implement agreed alliance plans and supervising the major subordinate commands. This command structure is "integrated" because it mixes different national forces during peacetime for planning and exercises. Until recently, however, this mixing took place only at the level of headquarters; most formations have consisted of only a single nationali-

THE NORTH ATLANTIC TREATY ORGANIZATION
(number in thousands as of mid–year 1994)

MEMBER	YEAR OF ACCESSION	POPULATION	ARMED FORCES
Belgium	1949	10,071	47.2
Canada	1949	28,130	70.5
Denmark	1949	5,214	33.1
France	1949	58,125	409
Germany, Federal Republic of	1955	81,109	339.9
Greece	1952	10,455	171.3
Iceland	1949	270	no forces
Italy	1949	57,867	328.7
Luxembourg	1949	406	0.8
Netherlands	1949	15,446	74.4
Norway	1949	4,353	30
Portugal	1949	9,869	54.2
Spain	1982	39,144	206
Turkey	1952	61,284	507.8
United Kingdom	1949	58,288	236.9
United States	1949	263,119	1,547.3

Source: *The Military Balance 1995–96.* The U.S. Committee of the International Institute for Strategic Studies

ty. The extra divisions sent to Europe in 1950 (as well as increased U.S. support for France's efforts to hold on to Indochina as a colony) helped France accept West German rearmament, though that process was quite bumpy. The Brussels Treaty of Western Union was eventually revised into a new Western European Union that integrated West German forces under NATO's SACEUR. In joining NATO in 1955, West Germany made a number of far-reaching commitments. It accepted multinational command of all of its forces not used exclusively for territorial defense, and pledged neither to recreate a general staff nor to deploy nuclear, chemical, or biological weapons. In doing so, it decisively cast its lot with the West, a decision that would be reiterated in 1990 when a reunited Germany, backed by the United States, bargained hard with the Soviets to stay firmly in NATO. In 1952 NATO also set a force goal of ninety-six divisions, though a partial thaw in the Cold War after Stalin's death the next year and the U.S. "extended deterrence" guarantee to respond to a conventional attack on Western Europe with nuclear weaponry produced a political climate in which that goal was never taken seriously.

Major Issues During the Cold War

By the mid-1950s, NATO'S political and organizational structure had taken shape. Despite rhetoric from figures in the incoming Eisenhower administration suggesting that Soviet-bloc nations would be liberated from Moscow, NATO was never intended or equipped for an offensive mission. Nevertheless, West German accession to the North Atlantic Treaty gave Soviet leaders a reason or excuse to announce formation of their own alliance, the Warsaw Treaty Organization. This completed Europe's division into two military blocs. As a result, Western Europe became tightly linked militarily to the United States, and NATO's European members had to adjust to a kind of military dependence they had never experienced. Their safety was seen ultimately to depend on the credibility of the United States' extended nuclear deterrence guarantee. France after a time refused to accept this condition, and left NATO's integrated command in 1966, but no other member acted likewise. Four major issues preoccupied NATO from the early 1950s to the early 1990s: credible nuclear deterrence, balancing firmness toward the Soviet bloc with conciliation, how NATO should manage disputes that originated outside the Article 5 Treaty area, and how the costs of containment should be allocated among NATO's members.

NATO's nuclear dilemma had two related roots. First, all of its members wanted a low-cost, credible military deterrent that would serve as a counterweight against the numerically superior Warsaw Pact conventional forces. Yet no NATO country would fully face the risks associated with an overreliance on nuclear weapons. Second, given this basic strategic choice, the United States came to differ with its allies, especially West Germany, as to how quickly nuclear escalation should occur if deterrence failed. The differences stemmed from geography:

North America might be a sanctuary during a European war, as it had been twice before, but Europe could not be. NATO's first military doctrine, the threat of early nuclear use known as "massive retaliation," was originally controversial. Massive retaliation meant the threat of a large-scale nuclear strike against a wide range of provocations. This policy had support in the United States, since it was fairly inexpensive—nuclear weapons cost less than the salaries and equipment of a militarily comparable conventional force—and also seemed to be more potent in dissuading attack than a nonnuclear deterrent. The steady deployment of U.S. tactical nuclear weapons in Western Europe reinforced the credibility of the threat to use nuclear weapons. NATO formally adopted massive retaliation in 1957, three years after Secretary of State John Foster Dulles had first articulated it, and did so despite fairly serious opposition within Germany and scattered critiques elsewhere in Europe. Germans feared that they would suffer most casualties in a nuclear war and that overreliance on nuclear weapons would obviate the need for a large U.S. presence on the ground, which they wanted for symbolic reasons. A number of factors, however, began to strip massive retaliation of its credibility. As with any threat, if too often made but not carried out, believability corrodes. Moreover, following the Soviets' successful launch of the space capsule *Sputnik* in 1957 and ensuing testing of intercontinental ballistic missiles, the United States found itself potentially vulnerable to a Soviet nuclear attack. This added to doubts about the credibility of the U.S. commitment to retaliate with nuclear weapons for a conventional attack on Europe—whether, as it was often put, Washington in fact would sacrifice New York for Paris in a war.

The Kennedy administration tried to address this problem with the doctrine of "flexible response," adopted in 1962 through a series of speeches and changes in the nuclear targeting plan. This new doctrine held that a conventional attack by the Warsaw Pact would no longer automatically result in escalation to nuclear use, which had been how massive retaliation was publicly perceived, and that any such use would be carefully controlled. In general, flexible response meant that the West's military reaction would be calibrated much more closely to the military provocation. This new doctrine required a compensating increase in conventional forces and readiness, which the United States largely wanted the European allies to supply. But while flexible response sought to increase the credibility of some U.S. nuclear response to major aggression from the East, French President Charles DeGaulle was openly skeptical of the U.S. nuclear commitment to Europe, and others shared his suspicions. Yet no European NATO country wanted to increase military spending significantly in order to provide insurance against the risk that the United States

might not be reliable in a crisis. Robert McNamara, secretary of defense at this time, later admitted that he wanted to defend Europe by conventional forces only, whereby the threshold at which nuclear weapons would be used would ascend out of sight. But this could not be admitted at the time, for it could have confirmed European fears that a major war might be confined to European territory. This would have raised major questions about whether the United States was living up to its Article 5 commitments. U.S. allies thus demanded and got repeated pledges that U.S. intercontinental nuclear weapons would not be held back in event of a large-scale war; for their part, U.S. officials tried not to explicitly break the nuclear link between their territory and Europe, although they did hedge the vulnerability this created for them. A notable example was the "limited nuclear options" strategy that would try to keep the use of nuclear weapons carefully controlled even in wartime and spare U.S. territory. NATO members debated the U.S. policy of flexible response for six acrimonious years before reluctantly accepting it in 1967. Even then, the key issues of how the costs and risks of deterrence would be shared were fudged. Left unresolved were the roles of tactical nuclear weapons in battlefield defense and how long NATO's Supreme Allied Commander for Europe (SACEUR) would have to wait before nuclear use would be authorized, if at all. But NATO's conditional policy of first-nuclear use persisted for the duration of the Cold War despite recommendations during the 1980s from several prominent former U.S. officials that it be abrogated.

In 1962, amid the controversy over flexible response, the Kennedy administration proposed a Multilateral Nuclear Force (MLF), in which ships manned by troops of various NATO members would carry nuclear weapons and authority for their use would be shared. The plan, supported mainly by U.S. enthusiasts for European unity, had two purposes: it tried to assuage doubts about U.S. willingness to cross the nuclear threshold, and it encouraged the Europeans to integrate further their own defenses. It died when only West Germany showed much interest, the other allies remaining skeptical on a mix of political and practical grounds, and Moscow indicated that its support for a general nuclear nonproliferation treaty, a key U.S. goal, would vanish if NATO took such a step. By late 1964, NATO quietly let the idea die. If the MLF episode indicated how hard nuclear policy-making had become in NATO, the deployment fifteen years later of the so-called Eurostrategic missiles showed that cohesion was possible on this issue, though only barely so. The problem arose in the mid-1970s when the Soviets began to deploy a new group of medium-range missiles, the SS-20s, which eventually were aimed at targets all over Western Europe. At one point, Moscow added one SS-20 a week. NATO at that time had no weapon of similar range on European territory, so only U.S. long-range weapons could hit comparable targets in the USSR. Under some interpretations of flexible response, retaliatory options at that intermediate level in Europe were deemed necessary to show Soviet leaders that they could not intimidate Europe or isolate it strategically from the United States. In a 1977 speech, German Chancellor Helmut Schmidt argued that the European theater nuclear imbalance risked decoupling the European theater from the bipolar superpower nuclear balance. This implied that some countervailing NATO deployment in Europe was needed to emphasize the link between North America and European territory. Schmidt's advocacy was complicated by German politics: his Social Democratic Party had a pacifist wing that strongly opposed new missiles on German territory. But Schmidt insisted that the European nuclear balance be rectified, and a number of U.S. strategic analysts and political leaders agreed. In 1979 NATO decided to deploy a group of U.S. Pershing II ballistic missiles and ground-launched cruise missiles in Europe unless negotiations with the Soviets led to withdrawal of the SS-20s. This was labeled the "two-track" decision to highlight that NATO was combining firmness and a willingness to negotiate. Schmidt also insisted that other NATO members deploy some of the weapons lest Germany be singled out as more anti-Soviet than the rest of the alliance.

Over the next four years, while the two-track decision held, the debate over NATO's nuclear policy both in Europe and in the United States was extremely intense. Belgium and the Netherlands opposed the decision; opinion in West Germany, where the Pershings were to be deployed, was deeply divided; and even Britain, a close U.S. partner on most issues, was split over accepting its share of the cruise missiles. A strong transnational antinuclear movement developed in the early 1980s, energized by a feeling that the Ronald Reagan administration was not serious about the arms-control negotiating track and was not genuinely trying to avoid actually deploying the missiles. The United States proposed to forgo the NATO deployment if Moscow would scrap the SS-20s; in the eyes of the Reagan administration, this "double-zero" option would simply restore the status quo as of the early 1970s. Moscow refused the offer. In the end—in part because of U.S. pressure, in part because of evident Soviet efforts to foment the antinuclear movements, and in part because of the persistent logic of the original deterrence rationale for deployment—Britain, Germany, and Italy accepted the missiles on schedule in late 1983. Moscow responded by walking out of strategic and intermediate-range nuclear negotiations. Beginning in 1985, when Mikhail Gorbachev became Soviet leader, Moscow moved gradually toward accepting the double-zero position. This was part of a larger reorientation of Soviet for-

eign policy. Gorbachev believed that the East-West military competition had become counterproductive. In particular, he and his advisers felt that improvements in the Soviet standard of living and productive potential would require much better political relations with the West and large investments in the domestic economy at the expense of military programs. As a result, he made a major concession in abandoning the SS-20s. In December 1987 the Intermediate Nuclear Forces (INF) Agreement provided for removal of all Eurostrategic weapons. As the first treaty that reduced existing weapons, it was a landmark in winding down the Cold War.

NATO's final major nuclear decisions came at the end of the Cold War and, in relative terms, were much easier. During much of 1989, the Bush administration asserted that it was necessary to replace the aging U.S. LANCE short-range nuclear missiles on West German territory with a newer model. German leaders resisted. They increasingly resented what they called "singularization"—the expectation that Germany would assume disproportionate military deployments or risks due to its central location. The fall of the Berlin Wall in November 1989 and the demise of the Warsaw Pact obviated the issue, and by May 1990 the Bush administration had come around to proposing that NATO cancel the modernization. Finally, at the October 1991 meeting of NATO's Nuclear Planning Group, alliance defense ministers decided that nuclear weapons for ground-launched short-range ballistic missiles and artillery could be eliminated from NATO territory, and that the number of air-delivered nuclear weapons outfitted for NATO's dual-capable (nuclear and conventional) aircraft would be cut by more than half. This reinforced Bush's earlier decision to destroy nuclear warheads for ground-launched systems worldwide, to withdraw all tactical nuclear weapons from surface vessels, attack submarines, and land-based naval aircraft, and to destroy many of these weapons. Gorbachev soon announced reciprocal steps. These measures dramatically reduced NATO's reliance on nuclear weapons. It should also be noted that some U.S. nuclear-weapons decisions that affected Europe during the Cold War were taken outside of NATO. Bilateral arms control negotiations with the Soviet Union such as SALT and START were not vetted by any NATO body, nor was the U.S. decision in 1983 to actively pursue space-based ballistic-missile defenses. The Strategic Defense Initiative, announced by President Reagan in 1983, raised especially thorny issues. As Reagan envisioned it, the program had the potential to eventually replace mutual assured nuclear destruction with the ability to defend against incoming missiles. In that sense, if the project had succeeded, it would have dramatically affected relations with Europe by removing the element of shared nuclear risk that gave political meaning to extended deterrence.

In the view of many Europeans, this would have been the ultimate strategic decoupling. On the other hand, many experts viewed a limited program to defend only nuclear silos—not the civilian population—as a way to reinforce rather than replace deterrence. The end of the Cold War effectively wiped out the more ambitious program and the problem it created within NATO.

Political Relations with the Soviet Union, the New Russia, and Eastern Europe

The same separation from Eurasia that made the United States see nuclear escalation differently from Europeans has also helped to shape different relationships with the Soviet Union and, to a lesser extent, Russia after the USSR dissolved. U.S. culture played a role as well. Americans tend to see other states as either friends or enemies. Europeans, sensitized by long experience in a less ideological, multipolar international system, tend to resist such dichotomies. To the continental Europeans (and to a lesser extent the British), the Soviet Union was a military adversary but not necessarily a political enemy. As David Calleo wrote in *NATO's Middle Course*, Western Europeans repeatedly were inclined to try to "coax" the USSR into a mutually interdependent relationship that would obviate war and promote internal reform. These sentiments had led Winston Churchill and some other European leaders to propose a summit meeting to settle the Cold War with the new Soviet leaders just after Stalin's death. But Dulles refused, believing that a more conciliatory Western policy would only tempt Moscow to act more aggressively. In 1967, NATO moved toward the European view. At the same NATO Council meeting that ratified flexible response, the Harmel Report was adopted. It specified two equally important functions for NATO: deterrence and détente. Several key NATO members during this period had reasons to want to relax the competition with Moscow. Gaullist nationalism in France required relative calmness in the East-West relationship to succeed; West German leaders saw détente as a way to begin normalizing relations with East Germany; Britain was turning toward a closer relationship with Europe, which suggested a policy less closely tied to Washington's; and the United States was focusing more on Vietnam and less on Europe. Yet important differences separated the U.S. position on détente at this time from any of its European allies. Détente enhanced the political side of the alliance and the role of its smaller members at the expense of the United States, whose position as nuclear guarantor was strongest when the East-West relationship was militarily and politically tense. For all these reasons, the Europeans embraced détente earlier and with fewer reservations than did the United States. This was most evident in the West German policy of *Ostpolitik*, championed by Foreign Minister

and then Chancellor Willy Brandt. *Ostpolitik* was based on the assumption that the eastern policy of Konrad Adenauer, West Germany's first post–World War II chancellor, had been unproductive in political and human terms. Adenauer had refused to recognize the legitimacy of the East German regime or deal with it. Brandt's Social Democratic party, by contrast, was willing to accept the reality of Europe's and Germany's Cold War division. As Chancellor, Brandt also made it clear that he accepted the loss of German territories that had been incorporated into Poland after World War II and that he would accommodate himself to a separate East Germany. His policy emphasized human and economic contacts with the East, as a way to soften the political separation. U.S. leaders were ambivalent at best about warmer ties between Bonn and the Warsaw Pact, but they ultimately reconciled themselves to *Ostpolitik*. They were haunted by the memory of the 1922 German-Soviet Rapallo Treaty, in which the two nations, then outcasts in Europe, agreed to repudiate debts and reparations and codified bilateral trade arrangements. U.S. Secretary of State Henry Kissinger feared that Germany would tilt toward neutrality, at least outside Europe, in an attempt to buy better relations with its Eastern neighbors. This might even affect NATO directly if the balance of power in Europe itself shifted as a result. Kissinger eventually saw that Brandt's policy was also premised on a strong NATO and a continued, if politically looser, connection to the United States. The U.S. willingness to swallow these doubts, at least publicly, seemed to fulfill President Richard Nixon's implicit promise to give U.S. allies more responsibility as they pursued their own particular interests. This broadened emphasis on political coexistence in the late 1960s and early 1970s led to two major coordinated East-West initiatives: the conventional force reduction talks (at that time known as the Mutual and Balance Force Reduction talks, or MBFR), and the beginning of the Conference on Security and Cooperation in Europe (CSCE), which facilitated the Helsinki Final Act of 1975. Both had been inspired by the Harmel Report. Although the Helsinki Final Act sanctioned international scrutiny of the signatories' human rights practices, it also ratified the World War II territorial boundaries in Europe. The Soviets were happy to make this compromise, since the human rights guarantees were clearly unenforceable, and might in practice be sacrificed by the West to the benefits of détente. As the visible high point of détente, Helsinki thereby became politically controversial in the United States by the mid-1970s, when the original promise of better East-West relations failed to materialize in a way that most Americans favored. The Helsinki negotiations had been held under the auspices of the CSCE, which acquired a permanent institutional identity. After the Cold War a significant number of Europeans wanted the CSCE, which was renamed in 1994 as the Organization for Security and Cooperation in Europe (OSCE), to form the core of a new European security structure. This was seen as a way to diminish NATO's and America's political leverage. Predictably, few Americans agreed with this.

Events such as the Soviet invasion of Afghanistan dimmed the appeal of détente in the United States. Most Europeans, on the other hand, were reluctant to let détente go. As noted, they supported the two-track intermediate-range nuclear strategy as necessary for strengthening deterrence, but they also wanted to to continue to seek cooperation with the Soviets in other ways. An example of this was the Europeans' insistence on continuing with a major natural gas deal involving both substantial increases in European imports of Soviet natural gas and European exports of equipment and technology for building the new Soviet natural gas pipeline. The Reagan administration opposed the project from the start, and then used the imposition of martial law in Poland in December 1981 as an opportunity to impose sanctions against it. The Europeans, however, resisted going along with these sanctions, prompting a situation in which the Reagan administration sought to force them to comply by imposing secondary sanctions against the European companies whose exports for the pipeline included U.S. parts, equipment, or technology. The Reagan administration was forced to retreat, lifting the counterembargo, albeit with some face-saving compromises. And while NATO survived yet another round of ruminations over the possibility that it would split apart, the battle of "pipeline politics" stood as one of the the more bitter intra-alliance political conflicts. With the demise of the Warsaw Pact and the unification of East and West Germany, the massive, short-warning military challenge from the East shrank considerably. As a result, NATO's self-proclaimed role vis-à-vis Russia changed considerably. More emphasis was now placed on integrating Russia politically into the new Europe and cooperating politically where possible with Moscow. If Russia were to again pose a military threat to Western Europe, it was now assumed that NATO would have months or more of warning. Consequently, NATO's planning for Article 5 contingencies faded in prominence, while out-of-area issues came to center stage.

The Out-of-Area Issue

Interests never coincide completely in an alliance. Disputes over action in areas outside NATO's Article 6 treaty area were common during the Cold War; as the political scientist Gregory Treverton put it in 1985, "the minimum lesson of postwar history is that neither Europeans nor Americans will automatically accept the other's view of issues beyond Europe *"Making the*

Alliance Work." At U.S. insistence, aside from what in 1949 were France's Algerian Departments, none of the Europeans' colonial holdings was included under the Article 5 guarantee. Roughly speaking, some Europeans sought alliance support (meaning mainly that of the United States) for their individual actions out of area in the 1950s and 1960s, when the United States was particularly strong globally and they were declining colonial powers. The British-French attack on Suez in 1956 and France's efforts to put down rebellion in Algeria were key examples. This situation reversed from the 1960s on, when the United States at times acted alone out of NATO's area with little European support. Some of these disputes—especially Suez, Vietnam, and at times the Persian Gulf—were acrimonious. Suez in particular was a blow to alliance solidarity. When Egyptian President Gamal Nasser nationalized the canal in July 1956, which was within his legal rights but which upset the regime which had governed its use for a century, Britain, France, and Israel conspired to use force to retake it. Israel would go to war against Egypt, which would provide Britain and France a pretext to occupy the canal area. What none counted on was determined U.S. opposition: Eisenhower ordered that Britain be given no U.S. help in defending the pound, and even acted to freeze British accounts in the International Monetary Fund (IMF). The episode produced bitterness on all sides, with France in particular concluding that it needed to loosen its military and political ties to NATO and the United States. Yet overall, NATO's strict geographic perimeter probably served it well during the Cold War by emphasizing the major source of threat and the primary theater of contention in Europe. In effect, its members agreed to disagree about other matters.

For three reasons, however, out-of-area issues will be difficult for the alliance to handle after the Cold War. First, for any action outside the treaty area, NATO relies on ad hoc, informal procedures for deciding what to do, in sharp contrast to the well-worked-out procedures for dealing with Article 5 contingencies. Second, the military forces that members are capable of actually projecting outside Europe are fairly small, not integrated, and lack the sophisticated command and control, logistics, and intelligence assets needed to fight wars against capable modern opponents. This could change if NATO's European members augment their individual and collective capability to act out of area, but that outcome is highly uncertain. Third, as discussed more fully below, the political will for members to act together out of area cannot be assumed. This makes out-of-area operations quite different from Article 5 missions. As discussed in greater detail below, NATO was especially hobbled by this in responding to the breakup of Yugoslavia.

Burden Sharing

Allocating military and financial burdens among NATO's members has caused discord since the beginning. Not surprisingly in a consensual alliance of democracies, burden sharing has often been domestically divisive. Analysts expect small states to try to "ride free" on the efforts of their larger partners, who see more of a stake than their less powerful allies in providing the collective goods of deterrence and theater defense. Yet little makes U.S. legislators angrier than a perception that others are doing this very thing. The problem has worsened when it has been conflated with out-of-area issues. While U.S. officials often said beginning in the 1960s that U.S. global responsibilities implied more contributions by the Europeans to their own defense, Europeans took issue on the grounds that U.S. out-of-area commitments, with which they often disagreed, would not affect their own defense efforts. Burden sharing was most divisive within NATO from 1966 to 1974. At the beginning of this period, congressional desires for scaled-back U.S. military commitments spilled over from Vietnam to Europe, where many felt that the Europeans could do more for themselves. Foreign-based troops were also a major source of the dollar outflow that was squeezing U.S. official gold reserves, all redeemable for dollars to foreign governments under U.S. Bretton Woods obligations. In this context, Senate Majority Leader Mike Mansfield introduced periodic resolutions to pare drastically U.S. troops in Europe. Although one of Mansfield's amendments came close to passing, none did pass. Nevertheless, one congressional burden-sharing initiative that was successful was introduced by Senators Henry Jackson and Sam Nunn in 1974. It required the NATO allies to offset the part of the U.S. balance-of-payments deficit associated with forward-based U.S. troops. These congressional pressures declined after the U.S. left Vietnam and Bretton Woods, though it was sometimes pointed out that Washington spent more in absolute terms to defend Europe than the Europeans themselves did. A key burden-sharing success was NATO's adoption of the Long-Term Defense Program in 1978. The Jimmy Carter administration took office with an ambitious response to the large growth in Soviet military strength since the mid-1960s. It included more standardization of weapons within NATO, augmented capabilities for mobilization and reinforcement in wartime, and modernized air defenses. Partly to gain leverage in each country's legislature for the required funds, NATO members agreed to raise real annual military spending by 3 percent between 1979–1983. Though compliance by some members was suspect, an annual report mandated by Congress in the early 1980s showed that overall most members kept their pledge. This coincided with the last phase of the Cold War and served to put more pressure on the Soviet Union.

NATO's Role After the Cold War

The question of NATO's role after the Cold War has sparked considerable discussion. Some analysts doubt that NATO ultimately has much relevance for the future. From a balance-of-power perspective, they claim, it ought to weaken and eventually dissolve now that its main rationale—deterring the Soviet Union—no longer exists. Although NATO could assume other missions in and around Europe, a power-balancing view oriented to the security conditions of the 1990s, and the foreseeable future beyond that, suggests that these may be ill-suited to an alliance without a clear military purpose. Jonathan Clarke summed up this view: "if NATO did not already exist, it is doubtful that Washington would now invent it." Others, however, contend that Russian expansionism is still possible, and that the best way to extend security guarantees to Ukraine or other members of the former Warsaw Pact is through NATO. In this view, NATO retains a deterrent military role even though the Russian threat has diminished. They further believe that NATO provides a continuing forum through which the United States can cooperate militarily with Europe on other joint missions, or through which the Europeans allies can work together if they wish, and that NATO provides the continuing efficiencies of interoperable forces and combined training. Finally, those who believe that the security dilemma in Western Europe could reappear wonder whether national militaries would go their own ways if NATO dissolved or the United States left it. This could make the Western part of Europe unstable once again. These analysts feel that NATO's integrated planning system provides useful insurance against this possibility. None of NATO's members, in any case, wants it to disappear. By the mid-1990s, they seemed to agree that NATO has a post–Cold War role to play, if only because it alone has the collective military means to act in and around Europe. Other institutions, such as the OSCE or the Western European Union (WEU), the defense arm of the European Union (EU), either lack any collective means of enforcement or are presently too underdeveloped to take on a major conflict management role. In seeking to define what its new role will be, NATO has encountered three major issues: how it can act out of area if it chooses, the form that a more autonomous Western European defense entity might take, and how it can help organize East-Central European security.

The out-of-area issue was transformed dramatically by the demise of the Soviet threat, since areas of insecurity and instability in Europe were now almost exclusively outside the Article 5 perimeter. In the words of U.S. Senator Richard Lugar, NATO either had to "go out of area or out of business." In the summer and fall of 1992, NATO responded by agreeing to enforce CSCE and UN

Security Council resolutions on an ad hoc basis. That represented an effort to define a post–Cold War mission and to acquire broader political legitimacy for acting out of area. Almost immediately, the disintegration of Yugoslavia loomed as a test of this mission. Although UN Secretary-General Boutros Boutros-Ghali threatened Serbian forces in Bosnia in August 1993 with NATO retaliation if they did not heed Security Council resolutions, NATO did nothing all that fall despite continued violations of cease-fires and a succession of vague threats. Nevertheless, by early 1994 NATO was acting to enforce UN resolutions with respect to the Balkan War. In February it issued an ultimatum to the warring parties in Bosnia to remove their heavy guns from the area surrounding Sarajevo, and force was finally used a month later after a horrific attack on civilians in the Bosnian capital of Sarajevo. This created two precedents: NATO had never threatened compellent military action and had never set out to enforce the authority of the Security Council. Further ground was broken several weeks later, when NATO warplanes shot down Serb aircraft that had been pounding the Bosnian Moslem enclave of Gorazde. NATO's role in Bosnia before the Dayton Peace Accords was very controversial. Nevertheless, the actions of individual members there should be distinguished from that of the alliance as an organized entity. The positioning of British and French peacekeeping and humanitarian forces in Bosnia hampered further collective or individual actions to stop the fighting because these countries feared Serbian retaliation against their troops. This same concern made Paris and London reluctant to push for enforcement of the no-fly zone by NATO planes. In effect, the peacekeepers had a different mission from that of the enforcement arm—NATO—and that conflict of objectives limited what either could do. Despite this, NATO might have made more of an effort to define for itself somewhat earlier than it did an independent role in Bosnia that did not depend on cumbersome coordination with UN personnel. Even though the alliance agreed to monitor the maritime embargo against Serbia and Montenegro, undertook operation Deny Flight at the behest of the Security Council, and pledged to help implement any agreed peace plan, none of this stopped Serbian forces from carving up Bosnia and committing near-genocide in the process. In fact, NATO officials admitted this. In a tough speech by NATO Secretary General Manfred Worner in November 1993, NATO members were chastised for irresolution in deciding how far to act under the umbrella of the UN.

In December 1995 NATO undertook its first sustained post–Cold War mission: implementation of the Dayton Peace Accords that ended the Bosnian War. Under the terms of that accord, 60,000 NATO troops were responsible for a variety of functions that skirted the once-traditional distinction between peacekeeping and multinational enforcement. These tasks included monitoring cease-fire lines, verifying that weapons are stored in proper depots, and—in what would have once been considered unacceptable partiality by a conflict-management body—supervision of the Bosnian Moslems' military training. The mission, while considered a limited success by many observers, was not without controversy. The political emphasis on the need for an "exit strategy" led some to wonder if NATO would leave Bosnia after a year whether its job was finished or not. And while there was political pressure on NATO to apprehend war criminals, there was resistance within the U.S. military to taking on such tasks rather than continuing to focus on identifiably "military" tasks.

Two other developments during 1994 seemed to justify more optimism about out-of-area operations. One program, sponsored by the United States and adopted at the January 1994 NAC meeting, tried to make NATO more politically and militarily flexible in dealing with these issues. Called the "Combined Joint Task Forces" (CJTFs) plan, it will take military contingents from various NATO members and different branches of their armed services and assemble packages of forces that can be fitted to specific military intervention tasks. A typical CJTF might involve the WEU borrowing NATO assets such as intelligence and airlift and acting by itself, without the United States. As U.S. officials see it, this will allow the Europeans to take more responsibility for their security without encouraging them to set up a separate defense organization that would threaten NATO and the U.S. security link to Europe. CJTFs may well represent NATO's future. There is widespread sentiment in the U.S. Congress for Europeans to take care of more of their local security, without U.S. ground participation. At the same time, as Karl Kaiser put it, the United States could revive its enthusiasm in working with its European allies if it finds that it can do so flexibly, according to the nature of problems that arise. Since no one expects an armed attack on NATO territory, CJTFs could become the standard way of running NATO missions for all but the most dire emergencies. A second reason for optimism is that Germany is now constitutionally able to join NATO out-of-area operations. In a landmark ruling, Germany's Constitutional Court held that there is no legal bar to such action, provided that it is organized multilaterally and is explicitly endorsed by the Bundestag. Since 1945, strong pacifist sentiment, concentrated in the Social Democratic Party but not confined to it, has tried to shield Germany from any defense role other than protecting national territory, and many have interpreted language in the 1949 Basic Law (Constitution) to require such a constraint. Germany may now act out of area through NATO or the WEU in a CJTF, though German politicians will likely act cautiously in probing the political limits of this new-found flexibility. More generally, of course, NATO can only do what its members have the will to do. Rapidly falling national defense expenditures during the early 1990s and a strong aversion to casualties in virtually every member country make extensive out-of-area NATO operations fairly unlikely, especially if they demand large contingents of ground troops. In particular, NATO has been very cautious about including the resolution of ethnic conflicts among its new mandates. Out-of-area operations will also depend critically on effective, politically consensual ways to share military and financial burdens. The burden-sharing issue was transformed when the USSR dissolved. Without the glue provided by a sharp, common threat, according to several U.S. legislators, finger-pointing about relative national efforts could kill NATO. For a while, the issue receded due to the dramatic drawdown in U.S. troops from Europe—from a high of over 300,000 in the early 1960s to a projected floor of 100,000 or fewer by the late 1990s. Yet the risk is always there that this issue will resurface when U.S. legislators tire of foreign expenditures, or some key alliance members feel that others are not bearing a fair share of the risks or financial burdens of NATO's new peacekeeping role.

NATO and a Stronger Western European Defense Pillar

The end of the Cold War has intensified long-standing debates about whether and how Western Europe might take more responsibility for its own defense. This has been a long-standing U.S. goal, and the drawdown of U.S. forces permanently stationed in Europe gives it an immediacy it lacked before 1989. If the Europeans do achieve a more independent defense policy and capability, often called a European Defense Identity (EDI), it could be used to organize joint military action in which the United States and Canada would not necessarily participate. Such a capability would almost certainly be organized through a strengthened WEU. Yet if WEU becomes too autonomous of NATO, that could threaten the U.S. defense link to Europe and ultimately the existence of NATO. During the Bill Clinton administration, U.S. policymakers changed their thinking in several ways that made them more comfortable with an EDI. Before 1993, U.S. officials tended to worry that any distinctly European defense capability could split Europe from North America. This fear is still present, but is now less severe. As Robert Hunter, President Clinton's ambassador to NATO, has put it, the argument that NATO military planning and action must be centralized no longer invariably applies. With no massive and potentially immediate military threat in sight, NATO members can organize what are called "coalitions of the willing" to

take on specific missions that will probably not involve defense of members' territory. The CJTFs, as discussed above, are a way to implement this. Further, as Hunter also emphasizes, the more the Europeans are seen to be bearing the burden of security in their immediate region, the more Congress will continue to support a strong military connection to Europe for trans-Atlantic tasks. This points toward more enthusiastic if still qualified U.S. support for an EDI.

For some time to come, most military coalitions of European countries will need NATO assets such as satellite intelligence, transport planes, and command-and-control capabilities. Most of these assets are of the United States, but U.S. officials have stated that this assistance would usually be made available to the WEU or a European CJTF. Nevertheless, France argues that this could give the United States a veto over WEU operations, and that in the long run an EDI, to be truly autonomous, must be able to act without consulting NATO. France's long-term preference, fueled in part by the expectation that the United States will eventually leave Europe entirely, is for the EDI to eventually come under the authority of the EU. This appears unlikely to happen any time soon. By the end of 1993 it was understood that the WEU would be considered the defense arm of the EU, but that it would not be allowed to duplicate or politically undercut NATO. Likewise, the French-German Eurocorps would come under NATO command in an emergency, even though in peacetime it would be solely subject to the jurisdiction of those who contributed to its forces. In other words, NATO's role as Europe's primary security organization was assured for the foreseeable future. The consequences would be profound if a truly autonomous EDI were some day to emerge. Domestic support in the United States for NATO would probably wither, since Americans would wonder what role they had left to play in European defense. But such an outcome, if it occurs at all, is at least several decades away. Many defense analysts believe that the logistical, intelligence, and communications capabilities necessary for Europeans to act militarily without U.S. help would would take a decade or more of substantially greater defense spending. No European country (with the partial exception of France) seems willing to commit these resources now, and none may for some time to come. The likeliest outcome is an EDI still linked closely to NATO, but one with a somewhat greater capacity to act independently on a case-by-case basis.

Organizing East-Central European Security

Other than peacekeeping and enforcement operations, NATO's major task after 1989 was twofold: to project security and stability to East-Central Europe while coming to terms with a postcommunist Russia. Neither would be easy, and the two objectives at times are in conflict. The demise of the Warsaw Pact, which had been Moscow's "outer empire" during the Cold War, left a security vacuum between the Oder River on the west and Russia's Western border on the east. Historically, this area, consisting of Poland, the Czech Republic, Slovakia, and Hungary, has been an object of great-power contention and an invasion corridor between Russia and Central Europe. It also contains the seeds of many potentially violent ethnic disputes, some of which cross national boundaries. Russia strongly opposes NATO expansion closer to its borders. At the same time, Central Europeans mistrust Moscow and ardently seek NATO's protection. Czech President Havel and Polish President Walesa made impassioned pleas to join NATO around the time of the 1994 Summit. Led by the United States, NATO members faced difficult tradeoffs in deciding how to proceed. Absorbing the Central Europeans too quickly, not to mention Ukraine or the Baltics, could reignite serious rivalry with Russia. On the other hand, acting too slowly might make these countries more insecure and threaten reform. In late 1991, the North Atlantic Cooperation Council (NAAC) was instituted to address some of these problems. This is a wide-ranging program of consultation between NATO and the former Warsaw Pact countries; it includes seminars on defense-related topics, military officer and staff visits, and various other cooperative projects. It was designed to ease the transition between the Cold War and post–Cold War systems. Yet no former Pact country was satisfied with this, as it offered no direct enhancement to their defenses.

NATO took another step at the 1994 Summit in establishing the Partnership for Peace (PFP). PFP grew from a U.S. attempt to walk the line between NATO membership and nonmembership, while taking some practical steps to prepare for possible expansion later. The program allows former Pact members to consult with NATO under Article 4 of the North Atlantic Treaty if the country feels threatened, a right they did not have within the NACC. It also provides an opportunity for countries to join NATO in peacekeeping and military planning projects, and to prepare their forces to operate interchangeably with those of NATO members. The program is partially individualized: after committing itself to civilian control of the military, nonuse of force for aggressive purposes, and internal reform, each PFP country can stipulate its specific objectives in associating itself with NATO and the resources it will contribute to joint projects. But none of this is an automatic ticket to membership, and PFP members are not covered by NATO's Article 5 guarantee. As a half-way measure, PFP had some weaknesses. While the United States and other NATO governments were divided in the fall of 1993 about how quickly to absorb new members, pleas to join the alliance from Eastern Europe grew, especially after the national-ist Right did well in the December 1993 Russian Duma elections. Among others, Zbigniew Brzezinski, Henry Kissinger, and Senator Lugar critiqued this indecision.

The critics made five main arguments. First, by including every former Warsaw Pact country but not extending membership, PFP risked diluting NATO to the point of meaninglessness. Second, Russian intimidation of some countries on its periphery made it inopportune to waver on extending NATO's security guarantee. Third, avoiding a decision on expanded membership now, for fear of heightening tensions within and with Russia, would not make it any easier to admit new members later. Fourth, since Russia was seen as relentlessly expansionist, she had to be firmly contained, but PFP did nothing concrete about this. Fifth, by lumping the former Pact countries together, PFP did not sufficiently distinguish those that needed security guarantees from those that did not. Yet strong arguments were also made for a tentative approach to expanded membership. Some U.S. officials argued that to admit some former Pact countries but not others would draw a new line through Europe, something that had supposedly ended with the Cold War. (Some such line was seen as inevitable if members were added quickly, since the four Central European countries and perhaps the Baltic states were much closer to qualifying for membership than Ukraine, Belarus, or Russia itself.) This in turn would heighten Russian anxieties about encirclement and strengthen the nationalists there. U.S. defense officials argued that no prospective member had a military establishment ready to operate interchangeably with those in NATO's integrated command; it was better to move slowly to bring new members up to that standard than to erode what had been achieved. By January 1994, the issue was largely settled. At that time, President Clinton pledged that NATO expansion was a question of "when, not if," and U.S. officials began a long-term effort to reassure Moscow and explain the policy to her. By mid-1994, the PFP program had gotten off to a quick start as twenty-two former Pact countries had joined it. PFP states were invited to send a military officer to a special planning cell at NATO military headquarters and to send a civilian official to NATO's political headquarters in Belgium. The officer might, for example, help draw up scenarios indicating how his country would participate in CJTFs operations. Many of these countries, however, are emphasizing economic privatization and development rather than military modernization, and the major NATO governments are not encouraging them to do otherwise. Major reshaping of their armed forces to conform to NATO's will clearly take time. Nevertheless, it is almost certain that a number of them will join NATO by the end of the century. This could accelerate or widen to include more countries if Russia reverts to more overt expansionism or internal authoritarianism. When Russia joined the PFP in June 1994, some analysts noted a sharp split between her view of NATO's future and that of the major NATO governments. Where the latter see association with NATO as a way to ease Russia's insecurity and tame her tendency to expand, Russians want to use PFP to blur NATO's identity. Not surprisingly, they continue to prefer a blocless Europe. Who will change whom more is the major question. If Russia acts for the most part in a benign way and continues to democratize, its leaders might get what they want: over time, the political rationale for a distinct NATO could fade. Such an outcome is not likely at this point, but it is conceivable.

At present, NATO remains poised between a mutual defense pact, in which membership is selective, and a more inclusive body that treats all or most of Europe as a potential zone of peace to be guaranteed collectively. That ambivalence could ease if NATO admits a half dozen or more new members, which would eventually effectively carry NATO up to the borders of Ukraine. But genuinely continent-wide security may be impossible without some form of Russian participation, and that may be precluded by continued instability in Moscow or a belief that Russia's security interests conflict too significantly with NATO's. In the meantime, NATO will experiment with new roles, military and political decision procedures to implement them, and a search for the political rationale to support them.

JOSEPH LEPGOLD

See also Cold War; Containment; McNamara, Robert Strange; National Security and National Defense; Nuclear Weapons and Strategy; Russia and the Soviet Union; Stalin, Joseph; Warsaw Pact; World War II

FURTHER READING

Art, Robert. "A Defensible Defense: America's Grand Strategy After the Cold War." *International Security* 15 (Spring 1991): 5–53.
———. "Why Western Europe Needs the United States and NATO." *Political Science Quarterly* 3 (Spring 1996):1–39.
Asmus, Ronald D., Richard L. Kugler, and F. Stephen Larrabee. "Building a New NATO." *Foreign Affairs* 72 (September/October 1993):135–147.
Barnet, Richard J. *The Alliance: America, Europe, Japan, Makers of the Postwar World.* New York, 1983.
Calleo, David. "NATO's Middle Course." *Foreign Policy* 69 (Winter 1987–1988):135–147.
Clarke, Jonathan. "Replacing NATO." *Foreign Policy* 83 (Winter 1993–1994):22–40.
Glaser, Charles L. "Why NATO is Still Best: Future Security Arrangements for Europe." *International Security* 18 (Summer 1993):5–50.
Halperin, Morton H. *Nuclear Fallacy: Dispelling the Myth of Nuclear Strategy.* Cambridge, Mass., 1987.
Joffe, Josef. *The Limited Partnership: Europe, the United States, and the Burdens of Alliance.* Cambridge, Mass., 1987.
Kaplan, Lawrence S. *NATO and the United States: The Enduring Alliance.* Updated edition. New York, 1994.
Kaiser, Karl. "Reforming NATO." *Foreign Policy* 103 (Summer 1996):128–143.
Kugler, Richard L. *U.S.–West European Cooperation in Out-of-Area Military Operations: Problems and Prospects.* Santa Monica, Calif., 1994.
Lepgold, Joseph. *The Declining Hegemon: The United States and European Defense, 1960–1990.* Westport, Conn., 1990.
Stuart, Douglas, and William Tow. *The Limits of Alliance: NATO Out-of-Area Problems Since 1949.* Baltimore, 1990.
Treverton, Gregory F. *Making the Alliance Work: The United States and Western Europe.* Ithaca, N.Y., 1985.

NORTHERN IRELAND

Part of the United Kingdom occupying the northeastern section of the island of Ireland. Northern Ireland has emerged as an issue in U.S. foreign relations because of the large number of Irish-American immigrants committed to Irish independence from Great Britain. When Ireland achieved independence within the British Commonwealth in 1922, it was partitioned, with six of Ulster's nine counties remaining part of the United Kingdom. In 1969 the politics of Northern Ireland erupted into a maelstrom of civil conflict. The Protestant Unionist Party dominated the government of the province and represented two-thirds of the population. The Protestant majority viewed the one-third Catholic Nationalist minority as irredentist seeking a united Ireland. Thus, the government of Northern Ireland discriminated against Catholics in the areas of voting, services, employment, and law enforcement. When a 1968 middle-class, nonviolent civil rights movement demanded the removal of discrimination, the government cracked down with traditional forms of police violence that had been used since 1922. This provoked a civil insurrection in 1969 that led to widespread clashes and, finally, British troops being placed in Ulster. The Irish Republican Army (IRA) and its political wing, Sinn Fein, were revitalized in 1970 by this conflict and transformed the civil rights demands into a struggle for the elimination of British rule over Ulster.

In the United States, organizations emerged that developed grass-roots support for the Catholic Nationalist minority. The first militant organization was the Northern Aid Committee (NORAID), formed in 1970, which supported the IRA explicitly and was forced by the Justice Department in 1984 to register as an agent of the IRA. NORAID came under surveillance by the Federal Bureau of Investigation (FBI) not only for its fundraising (it raised millions between 1970 and 1975) but for illegally smuggling arms to Ulster. The Irish National Caucus was created in 1974 with the goal of lobbying Congress and mobilizing public opinion in support of Sinn Fein and the IRA.

Irish-American politicians responded in the early 1970s with condemnation of British policy and calls for a united Ireland. Senator Edward M. Kennedy of Massachusetts sponsored a Senate resolution that called for a withdrawal of all British forces from Ulster and a united Ireland. Calls for violence, however, did not draw support from U.S. politicians, business leaders, journalists, academics, doctors, and lawyers. Sean Donlon, Irish ambassador to the United States, and other Irish leaders condemned support for groups that funded the IRA and thus extended IRA violence. The message was that traditional Irish-American nationalism was out of date and that the British and Irish governments shared, despite their differences, an opposition to the IRA and sought a peaceful solution based upon negotiations.

In 1975 the Department of State refused visas to members of Sinn Fein on grounds that they were supporters of terrorism. Irish Prime Minister Liam Cosgrave in 1976 asked the administration of President Gerald R. Ford to monitor and prevent the sale of arms to the IRA. In 1982 the Justice Department brought gun smuggling charges against the most effective of the arms smugglers, George Harrison, and a well-known founder of NORAID, Michael Flannery. These charges did not prevail, however, as the defense brought up alleged Central Intelligence Agency (CIA) ties to the gunrunners.

In 1977 U.S. House Speaker Thomas P. O'Neill, Jr., Senator Kennedy, New York Senator Patrick Moynihan, and New York Governor Hugh L. Carey issued the first of annual statements released on each Saint Patrick's Day. They condemned Irish-American support for the violence in Northern Ireland and criticized the British for their excesses and lack of political initiatives in the north. That same year President Jimmy Carter made the first official statement of U.S. government policy specifically on Northern Ireland. (The United States government had heretofore treated Northern Ireland as a matter of British politics.) The United States pledged to prosecute those who transferred money or guns to groups in Ulster, called for a form of government acceptable to both communities and promised job-creating investment to benefit all people of Northern Ireland. New York Congressman Mario Biaggi,a supporter of the NORAID and Irish National Caucus view, had formed the Ad Hoc Congressional Committee for Irish Affairs in 1977 with 100 members. Biaggi pressed for hearings on Ulster, which Speaker O'Neill prevented. O'Neill was unwilling to grant a U.S. forum to Sinn Fein because he deplored their campaign of bullets and bombs and condemned their politics as undemocratic. In 1979 O'Neill pressured the State Department not to license the export of 3,500 weapons from a U.S. company by the Ulster police. President Carter, in fact, embarrassed the British government by including it, based upon their policies in Northern Ireland, on the annual list of states that had violated human rights.

Ireland's ambassador to the United States, Sean Donlon, mounted intense attacks on Irish-Americans groups that supported the IRA. In doing so he alienated groups that felt their views on Sinn Fein and the British record in Ulster were being minimized. Donlon was called back to Dublin in 1980 and transferred to a post at the United Nations. The Irish-American politicians who had worked with Donlon became angry and demanded his return to the embassy. The real issue was which Irish-American groups should prevail. When Donlon was restored, it was clear the NORAID and Irish National Caucus view had been marginalized. Congressmen and senators who shared the O'Neill-Kennedy approach to Northern Ireland were organized as the Friends of Ireland in 1981 with Speaker O'Neill as leader.

President Ronald Reagan, at the request of O'Neill, brought up Northern Ireland with British Prime Minister Margaret Thatcher in 1984 and 1985 and urged her to be flexible on possible solutions. In late 1985 the Anglo-Irish Agreement was signed, in which Dublin and London pledged to cooperate on the governing of Northern Ireland. Shortly thereafter Congress approved an aid bill for Northern Ireland for $50 million the first year and two more years at $35 million each. President Reagan also sought to limit the political exemption in extradition cases to limit the claims of terrorists, especially the IRA, for in a number of celebrated cases the British requests for extradition were refused. The administration submitted an extradition treaty with the United Kingdom in 1985, approved in 1986, which significantly redefined political exceptions. During the 1980s a grassroots campaign was quite successful in getting states, cities, and labor unions to adopt the McBride Principles, which state that no investment should take place in companies in Northern Ireland which discriminate against Catholics.

President Bill Clinton in 1994, reversing an earlier policy, allowed a visa to be issued to Gerry Adams, the head of Sinn Fein, on the grounds that it would advance the peace process to bring Adams into the dialogue. Initiated by the Prime Ministers of Ireland and the United Kingdom in December 1993, the peace effort was encouraged and supported by the Clinton administration and led to an IRA cease-fire in August of 1994. A prolonged period of discussion followed in which the optimism of people in Ireland, the United Kingdom, and the United States was not matched by movement toward talks. The government of John Major at first sought assurances that the cessation of violence was permanent, and then that the IRA decommission its arms before all party talks could begin. President Clinton sought to move the talks forward by visiting Northern Ireland in November 1995, the first American president to do so. An International Commission chaired by former Senator John Mitchell was agreed upon by Dublin and London to resolve the arms issue. The Commission's recommendation in January 1996 that the talks go forward without decommissioning arms was rejected by the Northern Unionists and Prime Minister Major. Major sought to have elections in Northern Ireland prior to any talks that would include Sinn Fein. In February 1996 the IRA placed three bombs in London, one of which killed two people and injured twenty-six. The peace process was of course stalled, and the Clinton administration supported new talks that were agreed upon for the spring of 1996.

RICHARD B. FINNEGAN

See also Great Britain; Ireland

FURTHER READING

Cronin, Sean. *Washington's Irish Policy, 1916–1986: Independence, Partition, Neutrality.* Dublin, 1987.
Holland, Jack. *The American Connection: U.S. Guns, Money, and Influence in Northern Ireland.* New York, 1989.
Wilson, Andrew J. *Irish America and the Ulster Conflict.* Wash., D.C., 1995.

NORTH-SOUTH DIALOGUE

See Third World

NORTHWEST ORDINANCE

(1787)

The mechanism through which five new states were incorporated into the United States from an undemarcated frontier. The peace treaty signed by Great Britain and the United States in 1783 after the American Revolution not only recognized the independence of the United States but also brought into U.S. possession a vast area of land between the Appalachian Mountains and the Mississippi River. The domain between the Great Lakes and the Ohio River was designated the Northwest Territory. The U.S. government, with limited power under the Articles of Confederation, had the unenviable challenge of organizing this enormous area, into which many U.S. citizens were already moving. Fears that Native Americans would attack the settlers in the region and anxiety that frontier dwellers would be difficult to govern led to congressional passage of the Northwest Ordinance in 1787. This document replaced the Ordinance of 1784, written by Thomas Jefferson, and provided for a division of the West into districts, each eligible for statehood when the district population reached 20,000. It omitted his call for self-government. Instead providing for a three-stage system of territorial expansion under strong congressional control, in the first stage, Congress would name a governor, a secretary, and three judges. When 5,000 adult free males had settled in a territory, inhabitants who owned at least fifty acres of land could elect a legislative assembly that would govern with a council of five persons appointed by the governor and Congress. The governor had the right to veto any bills passed. When the territory's population reached 60,000 inhabitants, the assembly could write a constitution and apply for admission to the Union on the basis of equal status with the original states. The territory was to be divided into no fewer than three and no more than five states. Reflecting the ideology of the American Revolution, slavery was forbidden and settlers were to enjoy all the civil liberties and other rights guaranteed to citizens of states already in the Union.

The Northwest Ordinance ranks as an outstanding achievement of the peacetime Confederation Congress. Reenacted in 1789 under the Constitution, the ordinance formed the basis for the settlement and admission of the states of Ohio, Indiana, Illinois, Michigan, and Wisconsin. With the exception of the omission of a ban on slavery, most other American territories thereafter also were admitted to the Union under this general plan. The ordinance laid the groundwork for a single continental nation created out of temporary internal colonies, thereby solving the problem on which the first British Empire had foundered: how to tie imperial control and expansion to private commercial development, local self-government, and individual liberty.

REBECCA G. GOODMAN

See also Continental Expansion

FURTHER READING

Jensen, Merrill. *The New Nation.* New York, 1950.
Onuf, Peter S. *Statehood and Union: A History of the Northwest Ordinance.* Bloomington, Ind., 1987.
Rakove, Jack N. *The Beginnings of National Politics.* New York, 1982.

NORTHWEST TERRITORY

See Continental Expansion

NORWAY

A Scandinavian country bordered by the North Atlantic Ocean, Russia, Finland, and Sweden, that has been a key U.S. ally in the post–World War II era. The United States established diplomatic relations with Norway in 1905, after that country gained independence from Sweden; full relations were established a year later. The United States had consular representation in Norway since 1809, but under the aegis of the foreign ministries of first Denmark and then Sweden. Both countries proclaimed their neutrality at the onset of World War I and worked jointly to maintain their shipping rights to all the belligerent nations of Europe. When the United States entered the war, Washington embargoed exports to Norway because of Norway's continued trade with Germany, instigating the first diplomatic crisis between the two generally cooperative countries. The dispute was settled in an executive agreement in 1918, whereby the United States banned Norwegian exports to the Central Powers only on any products imported from the United States or its Allies. After the conclusion of the agreement the United States resumed sending supplies to Norway, and the Norwegian government allowed U.S. government representatives in Norway to implement trade controls. German submarine activity in World War I exacted a toll on Norwegian shipping, and at Washington's behest Oslo agreed to mine its territorial waters. In return, the United States promised to protect the neutrality of Norwegian waters. Cooperation progressed further after the Bolshevik coup in Russia, when Oslo agreed to look after U.S. interests in Moscow.

The peace of the interwar period allowed the two countries to expand their relationship, chiefly through trade. The 1928 Treaty of Friendship, Commerce, and Consular Rights replaced the 1827 Treaty of Commerce and Navigation initially signed between the United States and Sweden. World War II brought the two countries together as allies. Although the German invasion of Norway in 1940 sent the Norwegian king and government into exile, Washington refused to recognize the Nazi puppet government in Oslo and continued to conduct relations with the exiled government in London, allowing it to draw upon Norwegian gold reserves held in the United States. In May 1942 the United States elevated the U.S. minister to the Norwegian government in London to the post of ambassador. Concurrently, the Norwegian legation in Washington was upgraded to an embassy. In July of that year, the United States used the Lend-Lease Act to arm Norway's dispersed merchant fleet, which still provided vital supply services to the Allies across the Atlantic.

The trauma of the war convinced the Norwegian government in London that neutrality had merely encouraged German aggression, but in the immediate years after the war, Norway still wished to maintain neutrality and an "on the fence" policy regarding the Western powers and the USSR. With its sense of the Soviet threat intensified by the forced neutrality treaty imposed by the USSR on its neighbor Finland, the Soviet-inspired coup in Czechoslovakia, and other events, Norway reassessed its security interests. In July 1948 the Norwegian parliament authorized participation in the U.S.-sponsored European Recovery Program (Marshall Plan). The United States offered diplomatic assistance to Norway as well by supporting Norwegian claims over those of the Soviet Union to the Spitsbergen Islands. After negotiations

between Norway, Sweden, and Denmark over a neutral defensive Nordic alliance broke down, Norway turned to its allies in the West, becoming a founding member of the North Atlantic Treaty Organization (NATO) in 1949.

Norway's decision to join NATO prompted Denmark and Iceland to follow suit. Norway was considered a steadfast U.S. ally during the Cold War, and Washington repeatedly praised Norway's willingness to uphold its commitments to the security alliance. Norway was strategically important to the U.S. early warning system because of its proximity to the Soviet Union, and its command of the Barents Sea provided a line of defense against the Soviet Northern Fleet. Despite disputes over the Strategic Defense Initiative (SDI), U.S. policy in Nicaragua, and U.S. allegations that Norwegian companies sold sensitive technology to the Warsaw Pact, the United States and Norway have maintained a friendly relationship and a close alliance since formal relations were inaugurated in 1905. Norway further upheld its commitment to NATO when Norwegian troops were assigned in December 1995 to the U.S. sector in Bosnia-Hercegovina as part of NATO's Implementation Force (IFOR).

DAVID P. AUGUSTYN

See also North Atlantic Treaty Organization

FURTHER READING

Cole, Wayne S. *Norway and the United States, 1905–1955: Two Democracies in Peace and War.* Ames, Iowa, 1989.
Dorfman, Gerald A., and Peter J. Duignan, eds. *Politics in Western Europe,* 2nd ed. Stanford, Calif., 1991.
Scott, Franklin D. *Scandinavia.* Cambridge, Mass., 1975.
Solheim, Bruce O. *The Nordic Nexus: A Lesson in Peaceful Security.* Westport, Conn., 1994.

NO-TRANSFER PRINCIPLE

This maxim dates from the 1800s and maintains that the United States will regard the transfer of any territory in the Western Hemisphere from one European power to another as a threat to U.S. security. The security threat implicit in a transfer was especially acute when territory fell from the hands of a weak, harmless power into those of a powerful, potentially hostile state. An early example was the transfer of the territory of Louisiana and the city of New Orleans from Spain to France by secret treaty in 1800. Powerful France, ruled by Napoleon Bonaparte, could have shut off U.S. navigation of the Mississippi River and blocked westward expansion. The French threat evaporated in 1803 when Napoleon changed his mind about reestablishing an empire in North America and sold Louisiana to the United States. In 1811 President James Madison declared that the transfer of Spanish Florida to another European power posed a security threat to the United States.

The No-Transfer Principle antedates and is a variant of the non-colonization principle of the Monroe Doctrine of 1823, which declared the opposition of the United States to the acquisition of any new territory in the Americas by a European state. The principle was invoked repeatedly throughout the nineteenth century regarding Spanish Cuba and became linked to the idea of independence for European colonies. For example, in 1869, President Ulysses S. Grant reiterated that colonies in the Americas were not to be transferred from one European colony to another and said "when the present relationship of colonies ceases, they are to become independent powers." A related concept, the so-called Henry Cabot Lodge corollary to the Monroe Doctrine (1912), stated U.S. opposition to the commercial purchase of strategically valuable places, such as a harbor in Mexico, by interests under the control of a foreign government.

The No-Transfer Principle was elevated into a multilateral assertion in the Act of Havana in 1940, which was adopted at the second meeting of American Foreign Ministries in July. Directed against the possibility that Nazi Germany, having conquered much of Europe, might gain control of European colonies, especially French and Dutch colonies, in the Western Hemisphere, the act called for preemptive occupation of those colonies by American states. The colonies would become independent in the future or the will of the inhabitants would be executed by other means. Since Nazi Germany lacked the naval power necessary to control territory in the Western Hemisphere, the Act of Havana was not implemented. A variant of No-Transfer Principle applied during the Cuban missile crisis of 1962, when the United States declared firm opposition to the use of land in the hemisphere for an "offensive" Soviet military base.

GADDIS SMITH

See also Continental Expansion; Cuban Missile Crisis; Louisiana Purchase; Mississippi River; Monroe Doctrine; Pan Americanism

FURTHER READING

Bemis, Samuel Flagg. *The Latin American Policy of the United States.* New York, 1943.
Logan, John A. *No Transfer: An American Security Principle.* New Haven, Conn., 1961.

NSA

See National Security Agency

NSC

See National Security Council

NSC-68

National Security Council Memorandum Number 68, a lengthy U.S. document produced by an interagency working group in the winter and spring of 1950 that set much of the broad policy pursued by the United States toward the Soviet Union during the most intense period of the Cold War. Headed by Paul H. Nitze, director of the Policy Planning Staff at the Department of State, the working group included five officials from the State Department, four from the Defense Department, and two from the National Security Council. The secretary of state and the secretary of defense forwarded this study, begun at the end of January 1950, to the president on 11 April. After further examination and the preparation of cost estimates, the National Security Council approved the report as "a statement of policy" on 29 September 1950.

NSC-68 emerged from a general review of national security policy ordered by President Harry S. Truman when he made the decision in January 1950 to proceed with the development of the hydrogen bomb. NSC-68 identified a major Soviet threat to U.S. interests and to Western values and specified that a peak year of danger would occur in 1954, when Soviet conventional rearmament and nuclear buildup would reach a sufficiently high level to pose great danger to the United States. In response to this magnified threat, the authors called for a large sustained defense buildup on the part of the United States and its allies. NSC-68 is especially important because it reflected the attitudes and policies that dominated U.S. policy in the Cold War after the outbreak of war in Korea in June 1950. Had the North Koreans not attacked in mid-1950, when NSC-68 was still under review, the study might never have won Truman's approval or come to shape so much of U.S. diplomatic and military policy.

Background and Drafting

Through the autumn of 1949, U.S. leaders felt an increasing sense of danger as a succession of new challenges came from the Soviet Union and its communist allies. On 23 September President Truman announced that the United States had detected evidence of an atomic explosion in the Soviet Union. This news, coupled with the prospect, well understood within the government, that the Soviets were developing an intercontinental bomber, meant that the basic security of the United States would be threatened in new and fundamental ways for the first time in well over a century. New evidence also surfaced that a communist bloc was solidifying as its military capabilities increased. On 7 October, in response to the Western powers' establishing from their three occupation zones a unified government in West Germany, the Soviets created the German Democratic

Republic from their zone. In the same week, having defeated Jiang Jieshi's regime, Mao Zedong announced the establishment of a communist government in the new People's Republic of China. The following January the Soviet delegate to the United Nations, Jacob A. Malik, walked out of the Security Council in protest over the council's refusal to give the seat of China to the government of the People's Republic. On 14 February the Soviet Union signed a treaty of friendship, alliance, and mutual assistance with the new Chinese regime. Meanwhile, on 3 February, British authorities had arrested for espionage Klaus Fuchs, a British scientist who had worked on the Manhattan Project and had remained active in atomic energy research. On 9 February, Senator Joseph R. McCarthy launched his first wave of charges that communists held high positions in the Truman administration in a speech in Wheeling, West Virginia.

Many Americans viewed these events as threatening, and in response they wanted to strengthen military capability and adopt a nuclear strategy to exploit U.S. technological advantages. A significant debate arose among the scientific and foreign policy elite over whether the administration should proceed with the rapid development of a hydrogen bomb; many who believed that the Soviet Union would soon have thermonuclear capability as well wanted to limit development and try to establish international control of atomic energy. Those in favor of international control soon lost out to the group that believed the Soviet Union would not honor agreements for international control and might be inclined to take advantage of any technological edge that it might gain. President Truman dealt with this debate by ordering a special committee of the National Security Council to study the question. On 31 January 1950 he approved recommendations that an urgent feasibility study of the technical prospects of building a thermonuclear weapon be launched, and that the administration simultaneously undertake a major review of strategic policy. The prospects for increased defense spending and for adoption of a primarily nuclear strategy increased even further when leading opponents of that course, such as Atomic Energy Commission (AEC) Chairman David E. Lilienthal and State Department Counselor George F. Kennan, decided to leave government in February and June 1950, respectively.

Another obstacle to the defense buildup was the president's idea that military spending was a detriment to the development of a sound economy. The president and many of his principal advisers in the White House and the Bureau of the Budget believed that national security depended on a strong economy and a powerful air force, and in his 1948 campaign, the president had argued that the economy could not afford defense spending greater than $15 billion per year. This firm ceiling remained his attitude, and those who understood his thinking realized that it would take significant new evidence to convince him to change his mind and to authorize expenditures for a massive military buildup.

The group drafting NSC-68 worked quickly to complete their task. Officially known as the State-Defense Policy Review Group, they worked under the active leadership of Nitze, who set the tone, shaped the argument, and wrote much of the paper while others drafted some of the sections. The basic writing of the paper was done within Nitze's Policy Planning Staff at the Department of State. Working with him from that staff were Deputy Director George H. Butler, Executive Secretary Harry H. Schwartz, and two additional members, Carlton Savage and Robert Tufts. Other members of the planning staff, such as John Paton Davies and Robert Hooker, played an occasional role in the study. Also from the Department of State was Gordon Arneson, special assistant to the undersecretary of state. Department of Defense members were retired Major General James H. Burns, assistant to the secretary of defense for foreign military affairs; Major General Truman H. Landon, the air force member of the Joint Strategic Survey Committee of the Joint Chiefs of Staff; Robert LeBaron, adviser to the secretary of defense on atomic energy affairs and liaison with the Atomic Energy Agency; and Najeeb Halaby, director of the Office of Foreign Military Affairs. Two officials from the National Security Council rounded out the committee—James S. Lay, Jr., the executive secretary, and his deputy, Dr. S. Everett Gleason. The members of this group had developed an outline of their report by 27 February and had completed the final version by the end of March.

As the working group assembled information and prepared its report, a strong body of opinion developed inside the government and among senior advisers for a vigorous new effort to resist Soviet challenges. Nitze did a study on "Recent Soviet Moves," in which he concluded that the leadership in the Kremlin was taking more aggressive action in local areas and raising the chances for an accidental war. On 12 January 1950 Secretary of State Dean Acheson made a speech at the National Press Club in Washington, D.C., outlining U.S. policy in Asia. Strongly critical of Soviet expansionism, he drew a defensive perimeter for the United States that notably excluded South Korea. While drawing such a precise line of defense later appeared ill-advised to many inside the administration, the secretary was attempting to emphasize how much the United States had done to protect its interests in the Pacific, not to forecast how the United States would act in future contingencies. A month later, in addressing advertising executives at the White House, Acheson asserted that the United States had learned that the only way to deal with the Soviet Union was from a position of strength. At roughly the same time, the Central Intelligence Agency (CIA) produced an estimate that by 1953 the Soviet Union would have 100 Nagasaki-type bombs. Within several days Department of Defense specialists contended they had evidence that the Soviet capability would be even greater.

In building support for its recommendations, the working group consulted several senior officials, including Robert A. Lovett, an investment banker and widely respected Democratic leader who within six months would be appointed deputy secretary of defense. After reviewing the arguments and recommendations of the committee, Lovett provided a strong endorsement and said, "We must realize that we are now in a mortal conflict; that we are now in a war worse than any we have ever experienced.... It is not a cold war; it is a hot war. The only difference between this and previous wars is that death comes more slowly and in a different fashion." The draft of NSC-68 was completed on 30 March 1950 and circulated to the secretaries of state and defense. Secretary Acheson approved it quickly, and the secretary of defense forwarded it to the president on 11 April with his endorsement. The study was ready for discussion by the National Security Council on 20 April.

The Study's Contentions and Reception

NSC-68 began by saying that the traditional balance of power system was challenged by a new type of aggressive state. "The Soviet Union, unlike previous aspirants to hegemony, is animated by a new fanatic faith, antithetical to our own, and seeks to impose its absolute authority over the rest of the world." The study contended that the United States was the principal opponent to the Soviet Union and that the Kremlin's basic objective was to undermine the integrity and vitality of the leader of the West. In its opening sections the study posed a conflict between freedom and slavery and asserted: "The assault on free institutions is world-wide now."

The basic objective of the United States remained the policy of containment as had been set forth in earlier NSC documents dating from November 1948. NSC-68 contended, however, that the new Soviet nuclear capability meant that "we can expect no lasting abatement of the crisis unless and until a change occurs in the nature of the Soviet system." The means proposed to meet this new definition of the threat were more extensive and more open-ended than those previously adopted. The argument of NSC-68 was that the United States must take whatever action was necessary to protect its basic values and turn back the Soviet challenge. Within this rhetoric lay the justification for many subsequent actions, some of which very likely stimulated the Soviet Union to do more than it would have done had the United States continued its existing policies.

The study placed special emphasis on the new atomic threat emanating from the Soviet Union. It named the year 1954 as a year of peak danger, when the Soviet Union would have, according to intelligence estimates, 200 fission weapons and a delivery capability to hit targets in the continental United States with at least 100 of these bombs. The authors contended that this new and expanded Soviet capability would increase both the danger of surprise attack and the prospects of limited aggression in regions where the United States would not want to use nuclear weapons in response.

In their concluding analytical section, the authors examined four proposed courses of action for the United States: isolation, preventive war, continuing current policies, and a rapid buildup of political, economic, and military strength. In a fairly superficial analysis, the authors rejected the first three and advocated a broad and rapid buildup, insisting that significant new military programs would be necessary, but not specifying the type or the costs. They called for new programs in internal security and civilian defense as well as "intensification of affirmative and timely measures and operations by covert means in the fields of economic warfare and political and psychological warfare with a view to fomenting and supporting unrest and revolt in selected strategic satellite countries." The study concluded that the government needed to launch a large campaign for the education of Congress and the public in order to win their support for these significant new commitments.

Most officials in the Departments of State and Defense approved the report, but some important senior policymakers opposed it, and serious criticism came from top Soviet specialists, such as Charles E. Bohlen, and economic specialists, such as Willard L. Thorp, who argued that the Soviet Union was neither as aggressive in intent nor as strong economically as the study contended. The critics did not attempt to organize opposition to NSC-68, because Nitze had been very shrewd in building a strong base of support by showing drafts to highly respected outside advisers, such as Robert Lovett and James B. Conant, and in winning the approval of the secretary of defense and the secretary of state.

President Truman himself was skeptical about the need for a new military buildup. When the National Security Council discussed the report on 20 April, it expressed reservations about the lack of specific recommendations and established an ad hoc committee to respond to the president's desire for more detail on the recommended military and civilian programs and their costs. Prior to the outbreak of war in Korea, this ad hoc committee had met eight times. It had not completed the cost estimates, but from the work it had done it became obvious that the programs being recommended would require substantial increases in spending for both the Department of Defense and the CIA. After war broke out in Korea, many programs expanded rapidly and new ones were initiated. On 29 September the National Security Council adopted NSC-68 as U.S. policy with the implementing programs to be put into effect "as rapidly as feasible."

Assessment

NSC-68 was a warning that a new type of threat existed in the Soviet Union and an exhortation for the United States to do more to defeat this challenge. It contained bold, open-ended recommendations for using any means to protect the "free world" and called for programs to change the Soviet system through new economic, propaganda, psychological, and covert activities. The study had a more urgent tone than previous policy documents and dramatically increased the estimate of the threat for which the West needed to be prepared.

As a call to action, the study was strikingly incomplete and subjective. It sharply overdrew the monolithic nature and military capability of the communist world. It ignored evidence of Sino-Soviet rivalry and tensions, and its assumptions about Soviet military strength and technological progress were exaggerated. The rhetoric was alarmist and overblown. The final analysis posed four broad policy options, including two obviously unacceptable choices (isolation and war), one that the whole document labors to destroy (continuing current policies), and the preferred solution (rapid buildup across the board).

Recent evidence indicates that many of the assumptions and arguments of the study were misleading or completely erroneous. The Chinese communists were considerably more involved in North Korean war preparations than U.S. policymakers believed at the time. Between the summer of 1949 and the spring of 1950, the Chinese communist leadership had ordered 60,000 Korean troops that had been serving with the People's Liberation Army to assist in preparations for the unification of Korea. Chinese officials almost certainly had participated in talks with the North Korean leader Kim Il Sung about his plan to reunify Korea by force in the near future. After the war began, the Chinese provided staff support for the North Korean command and moved more than 250,000 troops to the Chinese-Korean border.

The Soviet Union was both more involved in the Korean conflict than it claimed and more cautious than the United States believed. Evidence revealed in the 1990s indicated that a hesitant Joseph Stalin approved the invasion only after repeated requests by Kim Il Sung and with the North Korean leader's assurance that the United States would not intervene. The Soviet Union provided supplies and staff support in planning the invasion but was so concerned to avoid direct conflict with the United States that it reneged on a promise to provide air support for the Chinese when their troops intervened as "volunteers" in the fighting. The Soviets did as much as they reluctantly did because of their suspicion of Mao Zedong

and the fear that he might try to seize the leadership of the world communist movement if they did not act.

NSC-68 gave warning to U.S. leaders of great challenges ahead. Officials in the United States were more prepared to act when war came in Korea than they would have been had they not been through the exercise of preparing this interagency study. The report's assumptions, however, about Soviet aggressive intent and its domination of the communist movement led the United States to conclude that Moscow initiated the North Korean attack with the purpose of probing U.S. will and ability to defend its allies. The United States reacted by a massive buildup in Korea as well as the dispatch of four additional army divisions to Europe, by rearming West Germany and creating an integrated NATO force, by expanding the overall budget for defense and international affairs from $17.7 billion in fiscal year 1950 to $52.6 billion in fiscal year 1953, by building air bases around the Soviet Union, and by significantly expanding covert activity. The extent and nature of this buildup almost certainly caused the initiation of some new Soviet military programs that would not otherwise have been funded and provided arguments for those hard-line proponents in the Soviet leadership who supported aggressive policies toward the West. The study was a timely warning, but it proved to be excessive in its recommendations for programmatic action.

Samuel F. Wells, Jr.

See also Bohlen, Charles Eustis; China; Cold War; Containment; Hydrogen Bomb; Korean War; National Security Council; Nitze, Paul Henry; Russia and the Soviet Union; Truman, Harry S.

FURTHER READING:

Gaddis, John Lewis. *Strategies of Containment: A Critical Appraisal of Postwar American National Security Policy.* New York, 1982.

Hershberg, James G., ed. "New Evidence on the Korean War" in *Bulletin of the Cold War International History Project* 6–7 (Winter 1995–1996):30–125.

Leffler, Melvyn P. *A Preponderance of Power: National Security, the Truman Administration, and the Cold War.* Stanford, Calif., 1992.

May, Ernest R., ed. *American Cold War Strategy: Interpreting NSC-68.* Boston, 1993.

Nitze, Paul H., Ann M. Smith, and Steven L. Rearden. *From Hiroshima to Glasnost: At the Center of Decision, A Memoir.* New York, 1989.

Weathersby, Kathryn. "The Soviet Role in the Early Phase of the Korean War: New Documentary Evidence." *Journal of American-East Asian Relations* 2 (Winter 1993): 425–458.

Wells, Samuel F., Jr. "Sounding the Tocsin: NSC-68 and the Soviet Threat." *International Security* 4 (Fall 1979): 116–158.

NUCLEAR NONPROLIFERATION

Strategy developed to prevent the spread of nuclear weapons beyond those nations already possessing them.

Since covertly developing the first nuclear weapons under the Manhattan Project (1942–1945), U.S. leaders have recognized the dangers in the spread of these unprecedented instruments of destruction to other nations. The Atomic Energy Act (AEA) of 1946 attempted to clamp a hermetic lid of secrecy on the technology that could produce such weapons. Only three years later, through both espionage and a herculean national effort, the Soviet Union exploded its own atomic device. In 1952, Great Britain (benefiting from wartime nuclear cooperation with the United States) tested its first device. In the same year, the United States demonstrated the first thermonuclear (fusion) device, potentially thousands of times more potent than fission weapons.

Although the United States sought to limit the spread of nuclear weapons from the start, it frequently found that pursuing this objective conflicted with other of its policies, such as support for Israel or maintaining the cooperation of Pakistan in assisting Afghan resistance against Soviet occupation. American leaders subordinated the non-proliferation goal accordingly. With the end of the Cold War (and with the revelations after the 1991 Gulf War of how close Iraq had come to building a nuclear weapon), non-proliferation commanded heightened attention from both the executive branch and Congress. The problem of conflicting objectives, however, persisted.

From Atoms for Peace to the NPT

Early in 1946 Secretary of State James F. Byrnes instructed undersecretary Dean Acheson to form a committee to develop a proposal for controlling nuclear weapons, to be presented to the newly established UN Atomic Energy Commission (UNAEC). Acheson's committee and its panel of consultants (which included Manhattan Project director Robert Oppenheimer) produced what became known as the Acheson-Lillienthal Report. The report proposed turning over atomic energy activities to an international authority that would both control all uses of the atom and carry out inspections to assure that no nation was building atomic weapons. Byrnes then selected financier Bernard Baruch to present the plan, with alterations, to the UNAEC. The Baruch Plan would have given the control organization (under authority of the UN Security Council, but without the usual veto rule) the power not only to inspect member nations' territories, but to punish accused violators. Since the plan allowed the United States to retain its nuclear monopoly until the international inspection and enforcement mechanisms were fully operational, it is not surprising that the Soviet Union rejected it.

By 1953, U.S. secrecy had failed to prevent proliferation of nuclear weapon technology to either the USSR or Great Britain, and a U.S.-Soviet arms race in both fission and fusion weapons was underway. The new president, Dwight D. Eisenhower, worried about where the arms race would lead and hoped to bring it under control; on the other hand, U.S. government military policy, with its money-saving "new look," was shifting to ever greater reliance on nuclear weapons as central guarantors of U.S. and Allied security. These conflicting concerns led Eisenhower to offer his Atoms for Peace plan.

Speaking before the United Nations General Assembly (UNGA) on 8 December 1953, Eisenhower acknowledged that, although the U.S. nuclear head start had given it a quantitative edge, its monopoly had been transient: more nations would learn to make the bomb, and even a vast superiority in numbers of weapons for retaliation would not prevent the fearful harm that a surprise nuclear attack would inflict. The President offered private negotiations with other nuclear states to bring nuclear armaments under control. But the centerpiece of his modest proposal was a provision for the nuclear powers to contribute natural uranium as well as fissionable materials to an International Atomic Energy Agency (IAEA), which would guard them and devise methods for their peaceful allocation to the "peaceful pursuits of mankind." In September 1954, Congress modified the Atomic Energy Act to permit transfer of peaceful applications of atomic energy on the condition that they not be diverted to military use.

Eisenhower apparently hoped that his plan would (a) induce the Soviet Union to divert its limited quantities of fissionable materials away from weapons that could threaten the United States, (b) begin a process of nuclear arms control, and (c) offer other nations the opportunity to reap the promised benefits of atomic energy while avoiding weapon programs entirely (and, not incidentally, give the U.S. nuclear industry a chance to sell its technology abroad). The Soviets were not ready to yield their fissionable materials while the United States held a much larger supply. The leaders on each side sought military security by further developing their own nuclear arsenals rather than trying to restrain build-up of the other side.

Despite Eisenhower's hopes, arms control and disarmament negotiations during the 1950s—and beyond—remained largely games of propaganda advantage rather than searches for agreement. By the time the IAEA opened for business in October 1957, only the third goal remained a realistic prospect: the Agency did not acquire a stockpile of fissionable materials, but it did become an instrument for the transfer, under safeguards, of nuclear technology, equipment, and materials to many nations.

Beyond their inability to contain the nuclear arms race, the United States and the USSR had not yet agreed in the late 1950s on the priority to be attached to keeping the nuclear club to three. The Soviets supplied China with nuclear technology that would help its fledgling

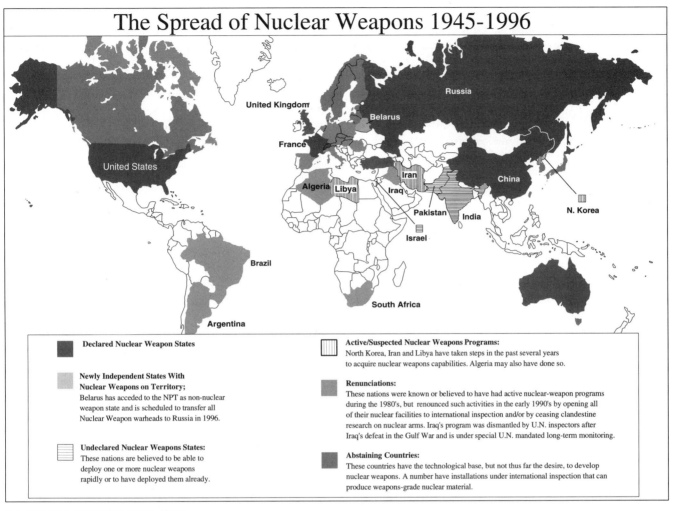

The Spread of Nuclear Weapons 1945-1996

Declared Nuclear Weapon States

Newly Independent States With Nuclear Weapons on Territory;
Belarus has acceded to the NPT as non-nuclear weapon state and is scheduled to transfer all Nuclear Weapon warheads to Russia in 1996.

Undeclared Nuclear Weapons States:
These nations are believed to be able to deploy one or more nuclear weapons rapidly or to have deployed them already.

Active/Suspected Nuclear Weapons Programs:
North Korea, Iran and Libya have taken steps in the past several years to acquire nuclear weapons capabilities. Algeria may also have done so.

Renunciations:
These nations were known or believed to have had active nuclear-weapon programs during the 1980's, but renounced such activities in the early 1990's by opening all of their nuclear facilities to international inspection and/or by ceasing clandestine research on nuclear arms. Iraq's program was dismantled by U.N. inspectors after Iraq's defeat in the Gulf War and is under special U.N. mandated long-term monitoring.

Abstaining Countries:
These countries have the technological base, but not thus far the desire, to develop nuclear weapons. A number have installations under international inspection that can produce weapons-grade nuclear material.

Source: Carnegie Endowment for International Peace

nuclear weapon program. In 1958, the United States revised the Atomic Energy Act so as to again permit U.S. assistance to the British weapon program (which had achieved a fusion weapon in 1957). Observing the "special relationship" between the United States and Great Britain, France sought to assure its national independence by moving forward toward its own nuclear arsenal (it tested a fission weapon in 1960 and a fusion weapon in 1968). Fearing that the Federal Republic of Germany would soon come to distrust the U.S. nuclear "shield" and seek weapons of its own, the United States attempted to institute a NATO multilateral nuclear force (MLF) intended to give the Germans a sense of being a nuclear player without actually giving them a finger on the button. The very thought of a nuclear-armed Germany evoked a strong interest in nonproliferation from the Soviet Union.

In December 1961, the UNGA passed an Irish-brokered resolution calling for international agreement to stop the further proliferation of nuclear weapons. In 1963, the Assembly also endorsed an effort (begun in the wake of the Cuban missile crisis in 1962) by several Latin American countries to make their area a nuclear weapon free zone. The Treaty for the Prohibition of Nuclear Weapons in Latin America and the Caribbean was signed at Tlatelolco, Mexico in 1967 and entered into force in 1968.

In the meantime, however, the United States and the USSR, while agreeing that they had a common interest in global nonproliferation, failed to agree on the terms of a treaty for that purpose. The United States insisted on maintaining a legal option for "nuclear sharing" with its allies; the Soviets insisted on blocking every conceivable avenue to German nuclear weapon ownership.

China exploded its first atomic device in October 1964, spurring U.S. and Soviet concern about proliferation. President Lyndon B. Johnson appointed the Task Force on Preventing the Spread of Nuclear Weapons, a panel of eminent citizens chaired by former Deputy Secretary of Defense Roswell L. Gilpatric. The Gilpatric Committee, as it became known, reported in January 1965 that the United States must urgently increase its nonproliferation efforts if it was to have any hope for success. The committee argued for three kinds of effort: (a) negotiation of formal multilateral agreements, (b) the application of U.S. and other nations' influence on individual nations considering nuclear weapons acquisition, and (c) the example of U.S. policies and actions.

Even thirty years later, such efforts appeared to be prerequisites to an effective nonproliferation policy. But they presumed a commitment which the U.S. government was unprepared to make. The Gilpatric Committee Report was classified, and Johnson attempted to suppress even the fact that it had been submitted in writing.

Elements of the report's recommendations nevertheless emerged in U.S. policy initiatives. In 1965 the Johnson administration began to pull the plug on the MLF, whose long-lingering but finally complete demise permitted U.S.-Soviet agreement in December 1966 to what were to become the cardinal articles of the Treaty on the Non-proliferation of Nuclear Weapons (NPT).

In the NPT as finally recommended by the UNGA for signature in June 1968, each nuclear-weapon state party (initially, the United States, the USSR, and Great Britain, joined in 1991 by France and China) to the treaty undertook not to transfer nuclear weapons or control over them to anyone, nor to in any way assist any nonnuclear weapon state to manufacture or otherwise acquire nuclear weapons. For their part, the nuclear weapon parties agreed not to receive nuclear weapons, not to make or otherwise acquire them, and not to seek or receive any help in making them.

To verify that fissionable materials for them were not being diverted from nominally peaceful nuclear energy programs into weapons, the nonnuclear weapon states agreed to conclude safeguard agreements with the IAEA to maintain accountancy of those materials. As advanced as this arrangement was for its time, it did not constitute a complete verification regime, but only addressed one possible proliferation route. Each party also agreed not to transfer either source or fissionable material, or the means of producing them, to any nonnuclear weapon state unless the materials were subject to IAEA safeguards.

The NPT Bargain

As negotiations on the NPT had proceeded, several of the nonnuclear weapon states had protested its inherently discriminatory nature: those who already had the weapons (as of 1 January 1967) could keep them; all others must renounce any right to them. In exchange for surrendering their nuclear-weapon options in this way, the treaty offered the non-nuclear weapon states several incentives. The safeguards would be carried out so as to avoid hampering peaceful national and international nuclear activities. All the parties retained an "inalienable right" to acquire and use nuclear energy for peaceful purposes. All the parties would have the right to share in international exchanges of peaceful nuclear materials, equipment, and information; those who could do so would also cooperate in contributing to the further development of peaceful applications of nuclear energy in nonnuclear weapon states, especially in the developing world. Nuclear-weapon states would make the benefits of peaceful nuclear explosions available to nonnuclear-weapon states. Each party would undertake "to pursue negotiations in good faith on effective measures relating to cessation of the nuclear arms race at an early date and to nuclear disarmament, and on a treaty on general and complete disarmament under strict and effective international control." To assure that the purposes of the treaty were being realized, a review conference would be held every five years after its entry into force after 25 years (in 1995), a conference would meet to decide whether the treaty should be renewed indefinitely or for some fixed period.

The NPT, which the United States signed in July 1969 and ratified in March 1970, embodied two of the Gilpatric Committee measures: multilateral agreement to stop proliferation, and nuclear-weapon state behavior meant to reduce the security incentives for nonnuclear-weapon states to acquire the weapons. It also attempted to establish an international norm against acquisition. The Treaty entered into force in 1970 with ratification by forty-three signatories. Notable hold-outs included India, Pakistan, Israel, and South Africa, all of whom later acquired some degree of nuclear-weapon capability.

In the following years, the nuclear powers and other advanced industrial nations capable of supplying nuclear technology moved to strengthen the supply-side restraints on proliferation. In 1971 a group of seven nuclear suppliers, following through on the NPT commitment, formed the Zangger Committee to develop a "trigger list" of nuclear export items for which IAEA safeguards would be required. An expanded Nuclear Suppliers Group (NSG) of 15 (including France, which had abstained from the Zangger Committee), known as the "London Club," announced early in 1978 an additional set of Nuclear Suppliers' Guidelines calling for further controls on nuclear technology transfers.

The U.S. Nuclear Nonproliferation Act of 1978 tightened export controls, requiring recipients of U.S.-supplied nuclear materials and technology to accept IAEA safeguards on all their peaceful nuclear activities, not just those directly utilizing the transferred items (so-called "full-scope safeguards"). Besides tightening and formalizing U.S. export controls in various ways, the Act directed the president to seek agreement from other exporters to require full-scope safeguards. It also formally established the U.S. system of controlling exports of "dual-use" items which, while having legitimate civil applications, also could be used to make nuclear explosives. It was not until fourteen years later, in the wake of revelations about Iraqi progress on nuclear weapon development, that the United States succeeded in persuading the NSG (with twenty-seven members in 1992) to agree on a list of dual-use materials and equipment to be uniformly controlled.

On the whole, safeguards on exported nuclear materials and equipment seem to have prevented their diversion from peaceful to military programs. At the same time, countries determined to develop nuclear weapons despite the NPT regime have been able to acquire the knowledge, technology, and materials they needed. Countries that have, by hook or by crook, successfully worked around supplier controls on nuclear-related trade to make appreciable progress towards (or, in some cases, actually build) nuclear weapons include Argentina, Brazil, India, Iraq, Israel, North Korea, Pakistan, and South Africa.

Supplier controls also have proven imperfect. Buyers and unscrupulous companies have become adept at fraud and smuggling to obtain wanted items. The governments of supplier countries have varied in the motivations, zeal, efficiency, and thoroughness of their export-control regulations and enforcement (the U.S. record is better than most). Sometimes the weakness of enforcement has been due to lack of resources or attention devoted to the problem; in other cases, commercial opportunism has reigned; in still others, other political priorities have led governments to turn a blind eye to suspicious purchases by states they prefer at the moment not to offend.

The spread of nuclear power technology also has meant the spread to numerous other countries of knowledge and facilities that would be useful if they ever decided to become nuclear powers. In the late 1970s, the administration of President Jimmy Carter attempted to move the global nuclear power industry away from using plutonium fuel, which was usable in nuclear weapons (the uranium used in power reactors, on the other hand, is not). This effort met with international resistance but, in the longer run the economics of breeder reactors and reprocessing of the plutonium they produce has placed some limits on the spread of the technology. By the 1990s, the only nonnuclear state definitely planning to reprocess plutonium for commercial use was Japan. Nevertheless, possession of other nuclear fuel and reactor technologies made dozens of nations technically capable of producing weapons within a few months or years of a decision to do so. At least two states, Iraq and North Korea, tried to develop weapons despite their NPT pledges to remain nonnuclear.

At successive NPT review conferences, non-weapon states continued to scold the nuclear powers, the United States and the USSR in particular, for their failure to uphold their end of the bargain by moving on to genuine nuclear disarmament, or, at least, concluding a comprehensive nuclear test ban. Only with the deep mutual reductions in nuclear forces that accompanied the collapse of the Soviet Union could the nuclear superpowers begin to argue credibly that they were on the path envisaged in the NPT. Nevertheless, they and the other nuclear states were still far from renouncing nuclear weapons as central instruments of international security and status.

The Recent Record

Many nations have come to the conclusion that the possession of nuclear weapons would decrease, rather than increase, their security. Some, however, have bridled at the notion that a select group of nations should be entrusted to use nuclear weapons as an instrument of foreign policy, while they were considered too irresponsible to do the same. Moreover, the process of discrimination appeared to extend beyond the declared nuclear-weapon states of 1967. The United States seemed to accept that Israel could become an undeclared nuclear power, but that no Muslim state should. It legislated sanctions against Pakistan for its nuclear program (the 1985 Pressler Amendment to the Foreign Assistance Act), but not against India or Israel.

For the long run, it seemed unlikely that the international community would continue to accept nuclear diplomacy as illegitimate for some countries but legitimate for others. This observation led some to conclude that nuclear nonproliferation is ultimately a losing fight, and therefore not worth the effort. It led others to conclude (with the Gilpatric Committee) that nonproliferation had a chance of success if the international role of nuclear weapons could be significantly downgraded and dissociated from military security. A third view held that "counterproliferation," possibly involving U.S. unilateral actions to halt nuclear weapon programs, might be both necessary and workable.

Dire predictions of the early 1960s placed the number of potential nuclear-weapon states in the twenties or thirties within twenty years. By that measure, nonproliferation policy up to the mid-1990s had been more successful than most people expected. By mid-1995, 178 countries had joined the NPT. The intention to make nuclear weapons had spread more slowly than the technical and financial capability. It is even possible to point to several cases in which states abandoned initial intentions. Other cases, however, illustrate that the nonproliferation struggle was only partly successful and is far from over.

Several countries have begun nuclear weapon programs and then reversed course. Sweden apparently maintained a low-level, covert nuclear weapon program (in parallel to its nuclear power program) as late as 1968. In Latin America, most nations had signed the Treaty of Tlatelolco banning nuclear weapons in that region, but Argentina and Brazil maintained covert weapon programs until 1992. (Brazil had ratified, but declined to waive the provision delaying compliance with the treaty until all Latin American nations had signed and ratified; Argentina had not ratified.) Then they agreed to open their nuclear facilities to international safeguards. South Africa, according to its leaders, went so far as to assemble six nuclear weapons before destroying them in 1990, joining the NPT in 1991, and opening its facilities for inspection.

Another nuclear reversal was wholly involuntary: that of Iraq. Following that nation's expulsion from Kuwait in Operation Desert Storm in 1991, UN-IAEA inspectors in Iraq found evidence of a more substantial nuclear weapon program than most observers had suspected. The UN Security Council had made dismantlement of Iraqi nuclear, chemical, biological, and ballistic missile programs a condition of the cease-fire. In the wake of the exposure of the Iraqi program, the Council also identified proliferation as one of the potential threats to peace which could justify Security Council action. Iraq also became the first nation in which IAEA inspectors (under Security Council aegis) visited not just declared peaceful nuclear program facilities, but suspected nuclear weapon facilities as well.

North Korea's nuclear weapon program for a while seemed to be in reversal. North Korea had ratified the NPT in 1985, finally allowing initial IAEA inspections in 1992. In 1993, inspections found evidence of undeclared plutonium reprocessing; foreign analysts estimated that North Korea might have acquired enough plutonium to build at least a single nuclear weapon. The IAEA asked to inspect two undeclared sites to address the question (invoking authority impicit in its statute, but not previously exercised). North Korea threatened to withdraw from the NPT, then rescinded the threat but continued to refuse inspections. The United States attempted to mobilize international pressure for full North Korean compliance with its NPT obligations. Many feared that, should North Korea acquire nuclear weapons, South Korea would be tempted to do likewise; ultimately, Japan (possessing many tons of plutonium and planning to acquire more) might counter Korean weapons with its own.

In the fall of 1994, the United States negotiated an agreement with North Korea exchanging abandonment of its current nuclear reactor program for two externally supplied power reactors whose fuel would be more difficult to convert to weapon purposes. Eventually, before the new reactors received fuel, North Korea would pemit further inspections that would help clarify whether it had previously extracted weapon materials from its old reactors. Shortly after agreeing to the bargain, the North Korean government began to cast doubts on its commitment by saying it would refuse new reactors coming from South Korea, the only plausible source. The United States continued to hope that the deal would succeed, with the only apparent alternatives appearing to be acquiescing in North Korean possession of nuclear weapons or risking armed conflict over the issue.

Another NPT country of concern in the mid-1990s was Iran, which the United States accused of building a nuclear technology infrastructure that might produce weapons sometime after the end of the century. The United States was taking the lead in trying, with little success, to persuade other nations to withhold any help from Iran's ostensibly civilian nuclear power program.

Three nations remaining outside the NPT were widely believed to have become de facto nuclear-weapon states: Israel, India, and Pakistan. India claims only to have demonstrated a single "peaceful" nuclear device and not to have built an arsenal. U.S. legislation cut off aid to Pakistan after the U.S. president failed to certify to Congress that Pakistan did not possess a nuclear explosive device; President George Bush stopped supplying such certifications in 1990. Israel is widely reported to have deployed an arsenal of at least some tens of nuclear weapons. These undeclared nuclear powers posed a major enigma for the nonproliferation regime: inducing them to surrender their weapons had not been feasible, but recognizing them as nuclear-weapon states would appear to legitimize proliferation.

In May 1995, the NPT conference adopted without a vote a resolution indefinitely extending the treaty. The treaty conference closed without reaching a consensus on a final declaration, but it did approve resolutions strengthening the review conference process (review conferences would continue every five years) and affirming a set of principles and objectives for the further pursuit of nuclear nonproliferation, nuclear disarmament, and international cooperation in the peaceful uses of nuclear energy. In the area of disarmament, the resolution called for: conclusion of a comprehensive nuclear test-ban in 1996, commencement and conclusions on a convention banning the production of fissile material for nuclear weapons, and "determined pursuit" by the nuclear-weapon states of efforts to reduce and ultimately eliminate nuclear weapons.

In the wake of the 1995 NPT renewal conference, the prerequisites for an effective nonproliferation policy remained much the same as those identified thirty years earlier in the Gilpatric Report: increasing multilateral cooperation, bringing U.S. and other national influence to bear on specific proliferation problems (Iran, North Korea), and altering the conditions of international security to reduce incentives to acquire weapons of mass destruction. As analysts at the beginning of the nuclear age had predicted, the technical and financial ability to produce nuclear weapons had spread to many nations, making control by denial increasingly difficult, and thus increasing the requirement for international consensus.

The collapse of the Soviet Union in the early 1990s further complicated the nonproliferation problem: four nuclear powers (Russia, Ukraine, Belarus, and Kazakhstan) now replaced one. By the end of 1994, the latter three had joined the NPT as non-nuclear-weapon states and promised to dismantle their weapons. Still, in all the former Soviet republics, desperate economic conditions, coupled with weak enforcement of such export controls as existed, threatened to foster the dissemination of nuclear expertise and materials, and perhaps even weapons, to foreign nuclear weapon aspirants.

The Soviet collapse made the notion of a new, cooperative, international security order seem more plausible—and more essential, as well. In the structured, bipolar world of U.S.-Soviet nuclear deterrence, the existence of a handful of established nuclear powers paradoxically made the task of nonproliferation easier: potential nuclear states could feel relatively assured that superpower nuclear weapons would deter overwhelming conventional or nuclear attack from the other side. Thus the United States's promises of protection to Germany, Italy, Belgium, Australia, Japan, South Korea (and perhaps even Taiwan) made it that much easier for them to accept nuclear abstention for themselves. With the end of the Cold War, security guarantees no longer involving the guarantor's life-and-death struggle with the other superpower, but only more ambiguous regional interests, would seem less credible. Therefore, persuading nations that they need not try to assure their security unilaterally by acquiring nuclear weapons will require new cooperative international arrangements.

THOMAS H. KARAS

See also Cold War; India; Indonesia; International Atomic Energy Agency; Iran; Iraq; Israel; Korea; Nuclear Weapons and Strategy; Pakistan

FURTHER READING

Beker, Avi. *Disarmament without Order: The Politics of Disarmament at the United Nations.* Westport, Conn., 1985.

Dunn, Lewis A. *Containing Nuclear Proliferation.* Adelphi Paper, no. 263, Winter 1991. London.

Molander, Roger C., and Peter A. Wilson. *The Nuclear Asymptote: On Containing Nuclear Proliferation.* Santa Monica, Calif.,1993.

Pilat, Joseph F., Robert E. Pendley, and Charles K. Ebinger, eds. *Atoms for Peace: An Analysis After Thirty Years.* Boulder, Colo., 1985.

Reiss, Mitchell. *Without the Bomb: The Politics of Nuclear Nonproliferation.* New York, 1988.

Seaborg, Glenn T., and Benjamin S. Loeb. *Stemming the Tide: Arms Control in the Johnson Years.* Lexington, Mass., 1987.

Shaker, Mohamed Ibrahim. *The Nuclear Nonproliferation Treaty: Origin and Implementation, 1959–1979.* New York, 1980.

Spector, Leonard S., and Jacqueline R. Smith. *Nuclear Ambitions: The Spread of Nuclear Weapons, 1989–1990.* Boulder, Colo., 1990.

U.S. Congress, Office of Technology Assessment. *Nuclear Proliferation and Safeguards.* New York, 1977.

U.S. Congress, Office of Technology Assessment. *Proliferation of Weapons of Mass Destruction: Assessing the Risks.* Washington, D.C., 1993.

NUCLEAR TEST BAN TREATY

See Limited Nuclear Test Ban Treaty

NUCLEAR WEAPONS AND STRATEGY

Nuclear weapons have played a major role in U.S. military strategy since the end of World War II and have had a significant impact on the conduct of the nation's foreign policy. During this period, a symbiotic relationship developed between U.S. nuclear weapons doctrine and U.S. arms control strategy. Indeed, the two have become so intertwined that it is sometimes difficult to determine which one is more important in driving the other, but the question of how to employ nuclear weapons, without destroying the area their use is intended to defend, has been a major problem for U.S. policymakers. It is a problem that persisted even as the twentieth century drew to a close, and one that is likely to endure into the twenty-first century.

The first U.S. president to address the nuclear weapons issue was Franklin D. Roosevelt. On 2 August 1939 the renowned physicist Albert Einstein sent Roosevelt a letter in which he warned the president about the possibility of a German atomic bomb. In December 1938 two German physicists, Otto Hahn and Fritz Strassmann, had bombarded uranium with neutrons and, in the process, split the uranium atom, producing energy as one of the by-products, a process called nuclear fission. Einstein cautioned that uranium, if present in sufficient quantity (called its critical mass), could generate enough neutrons to produce a chain reaction—and a nuclear explosion.

President Roosevelt responded by appointing a study committee that concluded in the summer of 1941 that a controlled chain reaction could be produced in twelve months and a bomb in four years, predictions that proved to be uncannily accurate. In the meantime, British scientists had discovered that, in addition to uranium, plutonium was an effective fission material. After the Japanese attack on Pearl Harbor, on 7 December 1941, Roosevelt authorized a crash, top-secret program (code-named the Manhattan Project) to build an atomic bomb. Roosevelt and British Prime Minister Winston Churchill agreed that British scientists would participate in the Manhattan Project and that both countries would share the benefits of its results. Although Roosevelt was willing to share atomic information with the British, he was unwilling to do so with his other ally, the Soviet Union. Prompted by fear of Soviet expansion after the war, on 18 September 1944 Roosevelt and Churchill agreed that the bomb project would be kept secret from the Soviets and that, if successfully developed, it would be used against the Axis.

President Roosevelt's successor, Harry S. Truman, did not challenge the assumption that the atomic bomb would be used if it were developed, but after Germany surrendered on 8 May 1945, the only remaining enemy was Japan—never seriously considered an atomic threat—and thus the question of why the United States used the bomb against Japan has generated considerable controversy. One reason for using the bomb was a desire on the part of Truman and his advisers to end the war with Japan as rapidly as possible in order to save U.S. lives. Evidence also supports the argument that the Truman administration believed that use of the bomb would not only preclude a costly invasion of Japan, but might also end the Pacific conflict before the Soviet Union could enter it, thereby precluding a Soviet role in the postwar occupation of Japan. The first combat use of the atomic bomb occurred at Hiroshima, Japan, on 6 August 1945. A U.S. B-29 bomber, the *Enola Gay*, dropped an atomic bomb, employing uranium and nicknamed "Little Boy," on the city. Of Hiroshima's 340,000 population, 130,000 were dead by November 1945, and an additional 70,000 died by 1950. But still the Japanese did not surrender. Three days later, on 9 August (one day after the Soviet Union entered the war against Japan), a second atomic bomb, employing plutonium and nicknamed "Fat Man," was dropped on another Japanese city, Nagasaki. Over the continued opposition of the militarists, who wanted to prolong the war, the Japanese emperor decisively intervened to bring the conflict to an end on 14 August 1945.

The Early Cold War

Despite the advantages that some of President Truman's advisers believed the atomic bomb would give the United States in dealing with the Soviet Union after the war, the U.S. atomic monopoly did not enable the administration to end the Soviet occupation of Eastern Europe. Nor did it deter the Soviets from demanding naval bases and territory from Turkey. On 5 March 1946, in a speech at Fulton, Missouri, Winston Churchill accused the Soviet Union of building an "iron curtain" across Central Europe. By 1946 the wartime Grand Alliance with the Soviet Union was over. The outbreak of the Cold War, in turn, made the United States even more unwilling to share atomic information with the Soviet Union. On 27 October 1945 Truman announced that the U.S. atomic monopoly was "a sacred trust," which, he implied, the United States would retain indefinitely. Although Bernard Baruch submitted a U.S. plan for international control of atomic energy to the United Nations in 1946, it seems obvious that the plan was designed to be rejected. The Baruch Plan called for an intrusive inspection system that would be implemented before the United States agreed to turn over its nuclear weapons to an international agency. The Soviet counterproposal, the so-called Gromyko Plan, reversed the stages of the Baruch Plan by calling for nuclear disarmament and the sharing of atomic secrets before an international control system was established. As expected, the United States rejected the Gromyko Plan and the Soviet Union turned down the Baruch Plan. The demise of the Baruch Plan strengthened the impression of the U.S. people that the Soviet Union was the primary obstacle to international peace. In 1947 Truman responded by adopting a policy designed to contain the Soviet Union's expansive tendencies. It included the Truman Doctrine, which provided military and economic assistance to Greece and Turkey, and the Marshall Plan, a massive economic aid program to rebuild war-torn Europe. The Soviets refused to participate in the Marshall Plan and successfully blocked the participation of their satellite states as well. By the spring of 1948, with a communist coup that brought Czechoslovakia firmly into the Soviet camp, the last vestiges of democracy vanished in Eastern Europe. In 1949 the West responded by signing the North Atlantic Treaty, which bound the United States to the defense of Western Europe. Six years later, after West Germany joined the North Atlantic Treaty Organization (NATO), the Soviet Union bound its satellites to a military alliance, the Warsaw Pact, thereby cementing the division of Europe into two rival blocs.

During the Soviet blockade of West Berlin in 1948, the Truman administration sent sixty B-29s to Great Britain. Although they carried no atomic weapons, the B-29s were called "atomic bombers." For the first time the previously tacit threat of U.S. nuclear action against the Soviet Union was made explicit. The Truman administration followed with steps designed to make nuclear "deterrence" of the Soviet Union the major component of U.S. military strategy. A 1949 war plan, codenamed "Dropshot," called for the U.S. Air Force to drop 300 atomic bombs on the 100 largest Soviet cities. In July 1950, one month after the outbreak of the Korean War, President Truman approved the stockpiling of nonnuclear components of nuclear weapons at forward U.S. bases in Great Britain and on aircraft carriers stationed in the Mediterranean and the western Pacific. By the end of

NUCLEAR WEAPONS AND STRATEGY GLOSSARY

Antiballistic missile (ABM): A defensive missile designed to destroy an incoming enemy ballistic missile before its warhead reaches its target.

Anti-satellite weapon (ASAT): A weapon system designed to destroy or incapacitate enemy satellites.

Anti-tactical ballistic missile (ATBM): A system designed to destroy or incapacitate tactical ballistic missiles.

Ballistic missile: A rocket-propelled missile that leaves the atmosphere and returns to earth in a free fall.

Ballistic missile defense (BMD): A system for defending against an attack by ballistic missiles.

Comprehensive Test Ban Treaty (CTBT): An agreement that would prohibit all nuclear testing.

Cruise missile: A guided missile that flies to its target within the earth's atmosphere, close to the surface. The cruise missile can carry a nuclear warhead and can be launched from the air, land, or sea.

Delivery vehicle: A missile or strategic bomber that delivers a warhead to its target.

Deployment: Installing weapons, making them ready for action.

First strike: An initial nuclear attack by one country intended to destroy an adversary's strategic nuclear forces.

International Atomic Energy Agency (IAEA): An organization created in 1957 to establish and monitor a system of international atomic energy controls.

Intercontinental ballistic missile (ICBM): A land-based missile capable of traveling more than 3,000 nautical miles to deliver one or more warheads.

Intermediate-range nuclear forces (INF): Sometimes called theater nuclear forces, these weapons have a range of about 3,000 miles.

Medium-range ballistic missile (MRBM): A ballistic missile with a range between 500 and 1,500 nautical miles.

Missile experimental (MX): An American ICBM capable of carrying as many as ten MIRVs.

Multiple independently targetable reentry vehicle (MIRV): A vehicle loaded with a warhead and mounted, along with similar vehicles, on one ballistic missile. Once separated from the missile, each MIRV can be directed against a different target.

Multiple reentry vehicle (MRV): A multiple-warhead vehicle in which the warheads cannot be guided to separate targets.

Mutual assured destruction (MAD): The ability of both the United States and the Soviet Union to inflict damage so severe that neither is willing to initiate a nuclear attack.

Neutron bomb: An "enhanced radiation weapon," this nuclear bomb is designed primarily to kill people and inflict less damage on buildings than other bombs.

North Atlantic Treaty Organization (NATO): An alliance initiated in 1949 which today binds the United States to the defense of Canada and fourteen European nations.

Nuclear freeze: The immediate halt to the development, production, transfer, and deployment of nuclear weapons.

Nuclear Nonproliferation Treaty (NPT): An international agreement designed to check the proliferation of nuclear weapons.

Second strike: A retaliatory nuclear attack launched after being hit by an opponent's first strike.

(table continues on next page)

Short-range, intermediate nuclear forces (SRINF): Land-based missiles with a 300-600 mile range.

Single Integrated Operational Plan (SIOP): The U.S. strategic nuclear war plan.

Strategic Arms Limitation Talks (SALT): Negotiations initiated by the administration of Richard Nixon in 1969 which were designed to limit the number of strategic offensive and defensive nuclear weapons.

Strategic Arms Reduction Talks (START): Negotiations initiated by the Reagan administration in 1982 which were designed to reduce the number of strategic offensive nuclear weapons.

Strategic Defense Initiative (SDI): Popularly know as "Star Wars," SDI was President Ronald Reagan's 1983 proposal to build a space-based, defensive system that could establish a protective shield over the United States and its allies with the capability to shoot down incoming ballistic missiles.

Strategic weapon or arms: A long-range weapon capable of hitting an adversary's territory. ICBMs, SLBMs, and strategic bombers are so classified.

Submarine-launched ballistic missile (SBLM): A ballistic missile carried in and launched from a submarine.

Surface-to-air missile (SAM): A missile launched from the earth's surface for the purpose of knocking down an adversary's airplanes.

Tactical nuclear weapons: Short-to medium-range, low-yield nuclear weapons for battlefield use.

Theater High Altitude Area Defense (THAAD): the Clinton administration's anti-tactical ballistic missile program.

Triad: The three-part structure of American strategic forces (ICBMs, SLBMs, and strategic bombers).

Warhead: That part of a missile which contains the nuclear explosive intended to inflict damage.

Sources: *American Foreign Relations,* Thomas G. Paterson, J. Garry Clifford, and Kenneth J. Hagan, Volume II. ©1995 by D.C. Heath and Company. Reprinted with permission of Houghton Mifflin Company; Ronald E. Powaski

1951, as the U.S. nuclear arsenal approached 1,000 atomic bombs, nuclear weapons were targeted on Soviet military installations as well as cities.

The U.S. reliance on a nuclear deterrent strategy added a sense of urgency to the Soviet atomic bomb effort. On 29 August 1949 that effort was finally successful; the Soviets detonated an atomic device in Siberia. The Soviet atomic bomb, as well as the fear that the Soviets could soon develop a thermonuclear (hydrogen) bomb, prompted Truman's decision on 31 January 1950 to proceed with a U.S. thermonuclear weapons program. The U.S. hydrogen bomb, which was designed by the physicist Edward Teller, was based on the fission-fusion-implosion principle. Teller's design called for a core of the hydrogen isotopes deuterium and tritium, surrounded by a shell of fissionable material encased in a conventional explosive. When detonated, the conventional explosive would drive the fissionable material inward, compressing it into a critical mass and creating an atomic explosion. The heat and compression generated by the atomic explosion would fuse the hydrogen isotopes into helium, liberating enormous energy in the process The first fusion test, called "Mike," occurred in the Marshall Islands on 31 October 1952. The explosion yielded an energy equivalent of ten megatons (ten million tons of TNT), an amount roughly one thousand times greater than the energy released by the bomb dropped on Hiroshima (some thirteen kilotons). The following year, in August 1953, the Soviets exploded their first thermonuclear device.

The nuclear strategy of Truman's successor, President Dwight D. Eisenhower, was greatly influenced by his perception of the Korean War. The use of nuclear weapons in a localized war, Eisenhower believed, would enable the United States to avoid a repetition of the enormous casualties (50,000 dead) it had suffered in Korea. Moreover, emphasizing the nuclear deterrent, he believed, would preclude the necessity of maintaining costly conventional forces, and would thereby enable him to cut the defense budget. Accordingly, in 1954 Defense Secretary John Foster Dulles announced that it would be the intention of the United States to react massively, with nuclear weapons, in the event of communist aggression at any level. To back up the administration's new massive retaliation strategy, the nation's armed forces were given a New Look. It called for a major cut in conventional forces and a massive buildup of nuclear forces. In June 1953 the air force ordered the nation's first intercontinental jet bomber, the B-52. The administration also emphasized the development of the nation's first intercontinental ballistic missile (ICBM), the Atlas, which was designed to deliver a one-megaton warhead 5,500 nautical miles. In 1957 the administration approved the development of the first solid-fueled ICBM, the Minuteman, which, when it became operational in 1962, replaced the manned bomber as the primary component of the nation's strategic forces. The Eisenhower administration also initiated the development of the nation's first intermediate-range ballistic missile (IRBM), the Thor. It could carry a nuclear warhead 1,500 miles.

Not to be excluded from a nuclear role, the U.S. Army developed the Jupiter IRBM, an almost identical version of the Air Force's Thor. The U.S. Navy concentrated on developing a submarine-launched ballistic missile (SLBM), the Polaris. Each Polaris was a solid-fueled missile designed to deliver a one-megaton warhead more than 1,000 miles. Both the army and the navy also began to nuclearize their nonstrategic arsenals. Ground and naval forces were equipped with relatively low-yield (less than 100 kilotons of TNT equivalent) tactical nuclear weapons, which were seen as a relatively inexpensive way to offset the perceived Soviet superiority in conventional forces. For this reason primarily, in December 1954 NATO decided to integrate some 7,000 tactical nuclear weapons, including atomic cannons, missiles, and even land mines, into its defense system. Under Eisenhower, NATO's ground forces would serve primarily as a tripwire for triggering the use of nuclear weapons, rather than the primary means of defending Western Europe. By the end of the Eisenhower administration, the U.S. nuclear arsenal grew to 18,000 fission and fusion weapons. In the summer of 1960 the Eisenhower administration established a permanent system for preparing a nuclear target list and an integrated plan for general nuclear war—the Single Integrated Operational Plan (SIOP). It called for launching 3,500 nuclear weapons at 1,042 military and civilian targets in the Soviet Union and the Sino-Soviet bloc.

The U.S. nuclear buildup only spurred the Soviets to press ahead with their own nuclear weapons program. By 1955, however, they had amassed a nuclear arsenal of only some 300 to 400 atomic and thermonuclear weapons, with fewer than 100 long-range bombers capable of delivering them. Rather than building expensive long-range bombers in large numbers, the new Soviet leader, Nikita Khrushchev, decided to concentrate his country's economic resources on the development of ballistic missiles. Emphasis was placed initially on intermediate-range missiles, with which Khrushchev hoped to hold Western Europe hostage in order to prevent a U.S. first strike against the Soviet homeland. Much less emphasis was placed on the development of Soviet ICBMs. Nevertheless, when the Soviets launched the first orbiting satellites, *Sputnik I* and *II*, in the fall of 1957, many U.S. citizens concluded that the Soviets had an enormous lead in ICBMs, a fear Khrushchev exploited in an attempt to conceal the Soviet Union's relative nuclear inferiority. Eisenhower, however, was not fooled. U-2 photo-reconnaissance aircraft flights over Soviet territory, which began in mid-1956, revealed no widespread deployment of Soviet ICBMs. Consequently, the president assured the U.S. population that the nation's strategic forces were more than adequate to deter a Soviet attack, but Eisenhower withheld from the public the evidence that supported this assessment in order to preserve the secrecy of the U-2 program. His assurances did not satisfy the Congress, and ultimately he was compelled to increase the production of bombers and missiles far beyond what he believed was necessary.

To reassure European allies that their defense was intimately bound to the defense of the United States, Thor IRBMs were deployed in Great Britain and the army's Jupiter IRBMs were stationed in Turkey. France, however, refused to accept any U.S. missiles until the United States agreed to assist the French nuclear weapon program, an action that was blocked by Congress, which did not want to see more countries develop nuclear weapons. Turned down by the United States, the French developed their own nuclear weapons, successfully testing their first atomic bomb in 1960 and their first hydrogen bomb in 1968. The Chinese, in turn, were encouraged to develop nuclear weapons by atomic threats made against them by the United States during two Taiwan Straits crises (in 1955 and 1958). In addition, Khrushchev's 1959 decision to halt Soviet assistance to the Chinese nuclear program spurred their determination to do it alone. When China successfully tested a nuclear device in 1964, the number of states with nuclear weapons grew to five. Three years later, China exploded its first thermonuclear device. By 1973 the Chinese had developed a missile with a 5,600-kilometer range, giving them the ability to target a large part of the Soviet Union.

In an effort to restrict the horizontal proliferation of nuclear weapons (the acquisition of nuclear weapons by nonweapon states), President Eisenhower announced the Atoms for Peace Plan in 1954. It offered to provide nuclear technology and materials to nations that promised to use them only for peaceful, nonmilitary activities. In an attempt to ensure that this nuclear assistance would not be diverted to military projects, in 1957 the United States helped to create the International Atomic Energy Agency (IAEA). Its primary function was to establish and monitor a system of international atomic energy controls. The nuclear activities of the nuclear weapon states (the United States, Britain, and the Soviet Union) were excluded from the IAEA controls, an omission considered discriminatory by the nonweapon states.

The continued testing of nuclear weapons in the atmosphere by the United States and the Soviet Union during the 1950s contributed to growing public concern about radioactive contamination of the environment. As a result, the Eisenhower administration reluctantly accepted a Soviet invitation to participate in negotiations for a comprehensive test ban treaty (CTBT). In 1958 a Geneva conference of experts from the Soviet Union, the United States, and Great Britain concluded that, by various means, including seismology to detect underground tests, a comprehensive test ban was verifiable. In the autumn of 1958 the Soviet Union announced that it would unilaterally cease testing, an action that compelled Great Britain and the United States to follow suit. The test moratorium would be in effect for three years, until the Soviets resumed testing in September 1961. In the spring of 1960, however, the general anticipation was that a test ban treaty could be concluded at a forthcoming Paris summit meeting, but the summit was wrecked after the Soviets shot down a U-2 spy plane over their territory on 7 May. The consequent collapse of the Paris summit doomed the comprehensive test ban talks during the remainder of Eisenhower's term.

The Cuban Missile Crisis

Eisenhower's successor, John F. Kennedy, was determined to revise his predecessor's massive retaliation strategy. Nuclear weapons, Kennedy insisted, were not usable without destroying the area one intended to defend. Kennedy introduced a "flexible response" strategy, one that would enable the U.S. military to meet the full spectrum of communist challenges, from nuclear war to guerrilla infiltration. Ironically, the new strategy not only required a major expansion of U.S. conventional forces but its nuclear forces as well. By mid-1964 the number of nuclear warheads in the U.S. arsenal reached 30,000. The Kennedy administration wanted more nuclear weapons partly because it wanted greater flexibility in using them. A new "damage limitation" strategy would attempt to avoid the destruction of U.S. cities by retaliating initially only against Soviet military installations (a counterforce attack), rather than against Soviet

cities (a countervalue attack). The administration also wanted more nuclear weapons in order to give the United States an "assured destruction" capability, that is, sufficient forces, even after a Soviet first strike, to retaliate effectively against Soviet military installations and, if necessary, Soviet cities as well. The Kennedy administration also attempted to reassure Europeans about the credibility of the U.S. nuclear deterrent, which was called into question by the launch of the *Sputnik* satellites. The number of U.S. tactical nuclear missiles deployed on the continent was increased by more than 60 percent. In addition, the administration agreed to sell Polaris SLBMs to the British and, partly to ward off the development of an independent NATO nuclear force, agreed to an interallied nuclear force consisting of British Vulcan bombers and five U.S. Polaris submarines. Simultaneously, the administration began negotiations with the allies to create a NATO mixed-manned fleet of ships armed with Polaris missiles. The creation of this so-called multilateral nuclear force, however, proved to be unworkable, primarily because neither the British nor the French were willing to give up their own independent nuclear forces. Not everyone, however, believed that more nuclear weapons were either necessary or wise. Joint Chiefs of Staff Chairman General Maxwell Taylor, an advocate of the so-called finite deterrence school, believed that only a few hundred reliable and accurate missiles would be sufficient to deter a Soviet attack on the United States. The air force, however, insisted that the nation needed at least 3,000 ICBMs. Kennedy's defense secretary, Robert McNamara, settled for 1,054, not because he believed that many missiles were needed for effective deterrence, but because he thought that it was the smallest number Congress would accept.

The Soviet military was undoubtedly alarmed by the new U.S. nuclear strategies and buildup. Partly to counter U.S. nuclear superiority, as well as to defend Cuba from a U.S. invasion, in early 1962 Khrushchev decided to deploy on that island-nation forty-eight medium-range ballistic missiles (MRBMs), with a range of 1,000 nautical miles, and twenty-four IRBMs, with a range of 2,200 nautical miles. Kennedy, however, refused to allow Khrushchev to redress an imbalance of strategic power that favored the United States. He initiated a naval blockade of Cuba, prepared forces for an invasion, and placed U.S. strategic nuclear forces on a war-ready level of alert. The U.S. reaction touched off a crisis that represented the closest approach to nuclear war during the entire Cold War. The crisis ended on 28 October 1962, when Khrushchev agreed to withdraw the Soviet missiles. In return, Kennedy pledged to refrain from invading Cuba and promised to withdraw the U.S. Jupiter IRBMs stationed in Turkey. The U.S. concessions enabled the Soviet leader to salvage some meager semblance of face, but it did not prevent his removal from power in October 1964.

In the wake of the Cuban missile crisis, both Kennedy and Khrushchev agreed to resume negotiations on a nuclear test ban. Shortly after the talks convened, however, in Moscow on 15 July 1963, it became apparent that there was no chance of negotiating a comprehensive test ban agreement (CTBT). Khrushchev rejected on-site inspections, which Kennedy insisted were necessary to verify a CTBT. Instead of a comprehensive ban, on 25 July, Great Britain, the Soviet Union, and the United States signed an agreement that prohibited the testing of nuclear weapons in the atmosphere, in outer space, and beneath the surface of the seas. The Limited Test Ban Treaty went into effect on 11 October 1963. While it ended the atmospheric testing of nuclear weapons by the superpowers and Great Britain, it in no way ended the nuclear arms race. It simply drove it, quite literally, underground, where U.S. nuclear testing continued for the next three decades.

Nuclear Buildups, Arms Control, and SALT

During the presidency of Lyndon B. Johnson, the objectives of U.S. nuclear strategy remained essentially the same as they had been under Kennedy: assured destruction and damage limitation. By 1967, however, the foundation on which they were based, continued overwhelming U.S. nuclear superiority, was beginning to erode. As a result of the expansion of the Soviet strategic nuclear arsenal, the number of Soviet ICBMs reached 1,060 by the end of 1969, giving the Soviet Union, for the first time, a slightly larger ICBM force than the United States. As a consequence, the assured destruction capability that once was a U.S. monopoly had become a mutual assured destruction (MAD) capability. No matter which side struck first, the other would be able to launch a devastating retaliatory attack. While the Johnson administration accepted the idea of parity with the Soviet Union in numbers of strategic launch vehicles, it nevertheless intended to maintain a U.S. lead in numbers of warheads. In 1964 the administration began equipping Polaris SLBMs with multiple reentry vehicles (MRVs), that is, multiple warheads (three warheads on each missile), all of which could be delivered in a close pattern to the same target. Even more sophisticated were two additional weapons, the Minuteman III ICBM and the Poseidon SLBM. Each would be equipped with multiple, independently targeted reentry vehicles (MIRVs)—multiple warheads each of which could be internally guided to a different target. As a result of MIRV deployments, more than 3,000 warheads were added to the U.S. strategic arsenal by the mid-1970s. One reason for the expansion of the U.S. nuclear warhead arsenal was a desire to

have the capability to overwhelm an embryonic Soviet antiballistic missile (ABM) system, which the Soviets began deploying in 1962. MIRVs also gave the United States the ability to destroy more Soviet targets without adding launch vehicles or relying as heavily as it did on strategic bombers. As a consequence, the Johnson administration retired 345 older B-52s and two squadrons of B-58s and canceled plans to build the B-70. The Johnson administration also was prepared to forgo deployment of a U.S. ABM system, called Sentinel, if the Soviets dismantled theirs. The Soviets, however, insisted that their ABM system was purely defensive. As a result, in January 1968 Johnson requested Congress to appropriate $1.2 billion for the Sentinel system.

While the superpowers were taking the first steps in an ABM race, in 1967 they ratified the Outer Space Treaty, which prohibited the placement into orbit around the earth, or the stationing in outer space or on celestial bodies, of weapons of mass destruction. In 1968 the superpowers and other interested parties concluded the Nuclear Nonproliferation Treaty (NPT), which prohibited nonweapon states from manufacturing or procuring nuclear weapons. In return, the treaty obliged the nuclear powers to provide nonmilitary nuclear assistance to nonweapon states that ratified the treaty. The nuclear weapon states also promised to engage in a serious effort to reduce the size of their respective nuclear arsenals, as a step toward eventual nuclear disarmament. Johnson, however, was unable to conclude a strategic arms limitation treaty (SALT) before he left office in 1969. The Soviets were reluctant to negotiate with the United States at a time when the United States was trying to bomb North Vietnam into submission, and the Johnson administration was unwilling to engage in SALT in the immediate wake of the Soviet invasion of Czechoslovakia in August 1968.

For a variety of reasons, Johnson's successor, Richard M. Nixon, embraced SALT. For one, Nixon realized that SALT was the only feasible way to restrain the Soviet offensive strategic buildup as well as the expansion of the Soviet ABM system. In addition, Nixon's national security adviser (and later secretary of state), Henry Kissinger, impressed upon the president that, without nuclear arms control, détente with the Soviet Union was neither possible nor desirable. Both Nixon and Kissinger believed, however, that the United States had to develop additional nuclear weapons in order to provide the Soviets with incentive to conclude a SALT agreement on U.S. terms. Accordingly, in late 1971 the administration accelerated the development of the Trident submarine, which was capable of carrying twenty-four SLBMs, each with up to fourteen warheads; a new long-range bomber, eventually dubbed the B-1; and a new ICBM, the MX, which would have the capability of carrying ten MIRVs. Predictably, the Soviets reacted with new nuclear weapons programs of their own. In January 1974 the Soviets tested four new ICBMs, three of them (the SS-17, the SS-18, and the SS-19) with multiple warheads.

The Nixon administration also decided to proceed with a U.S. ABM, renamed "Safeguard," not only to protect Minuteman silos against a preemptive Soviet attack, but also to give the nation a means of defending itself against an accidental launch or an attack by a future nuclear power; but instead of the twelve sites initially planned, only one site was built, and that one was shut down in 1975. The demise of Safeguard was due not only to declining support in Congress, which argued that the system could be easily overwhelmed by Soviet MIRVs, but by the ratification of the ABM Treaty in 1972. The ABM Treaty permitted each side to build only two ABM sites, one around the national capital, the other around an ICBM field. (In 1974 both sides agreed to permit only one ABM site in each nation.) The treaty also limited each ABM site to 100 interceptor missiles and prohibited the construction of ABM-related radars outside the two permissible sites. It also prohibited the development and deployment of space-based ABM components. The treaty would be monitored by national means of verification, primarily reconnaissance satellites, thereby bypassing the old obstacle of on-site inspection. To facilitate verification, the treaty provided for a joint U.S.-Soviet Standing Consultative Commission to monitor compliance with the treaty. While the ABM Treaty was of unlimited duration, each party could withdraw from the treaty with six months' notice. The other major SALT agreement concluded by the Nixon administration was the Interim Offensive Arms Agreement. For a five-year period, beginning on 1 July 1972, both sides were prohibited from constructing additional fixed, land-based ICBM launchers, in effect limiting the United States to 1,054 ICBMs and the Soviet Union to 1,618. A protocol attached to the Interim Agreement limited the United States to a total of 710 SLBMs and forty-four ballistic missile submarines, and the Soviet Union to 950 SLBMs and sixty-two submarines. The Interim Agreement, however, placed no limitations on MIRVs, bombers, or land-mobile ICBMs, which both sides agreed to discuss in SALT II.

Neither Nixon nor his successor, Gerald Ford, was able to conclude a SALT II agreement. In November 1974 Ford and Soviet leader Leonid Brezhnev met in Vladivostok, Russia, and agreed that a SALT II accord would be based on the principle of equality. Each side would be limited to an overall ceiling of 2,400 delivery vehicles, with a subceiling of 1,320 MIRVed missiles. In addition, bomber-launched and land-mobile missiles would be included in the overall total, and Soviet "heavy" missiles would be limited to 313 deployments. In addition to the growing hostility to détente that occurred during Ford's

presidency, two major unresolved issues prevented the superpowers from concluding a SALT II treaty before he left the White House in 1977. One was the Soviet Backfire bomber. The U.S. side considered it a long-range bomber and therefore insisted that it should be included in the limitations, a position the Soviets refused to accept. The other obstacle was the cruise missile, a pilotless, jet-powered missile that the Soviets wanted restricted by the new treaty, a demand the United States refused to accept.

Ford's successor, Jimmy Carter, was determined to end the nuclear arms race when he entered the White House. He canceled production of the B-1 bomber and refused to deploy in Europe enhanced radiation weapons (the so-called neutron bomb). In 1978 Carter also signed the Nuclear Nonproliferation Act, which prohibited U.S. nuclear assistance to nations that refused to accept full-scope IAEA safeguards. He also supported a comprehensive test ban treaty. Paradoxically, considering his goal of ending the nuclear arms race, Carter permitted the continued development of the Trident SLBM as well as air-and-ground-launched cruise missiles. He also approved a plan to deploy 200 mobile MX ICBMs in the deserts of New Mexico and Utah. Carter also obtained the acquiescence of NATO to the stationing in Western Europe of 108 Pershing II (IRBMs) and 464 ground-launched Tomahawk cruise missiles (GLCMs). These missiles were designed to counter the deployment in Eastern Europe of Soviet intermediate-range SS-20 ballistic missiles.

In 1979 President Carter did succeed in completing the SALT II Treaty. It placed both qualitative and quantitative restrictions on strategic nuclear weapons. The treaty limited each party to an equal aggregate ceiling of 2,400 strategic nuclear launchers, with subceilings of 1,320 MIRVed ICBMs and aircraft armed with cruise missiles, another allowing a maximum of 1,200 MIRVed ICBMs and SLBMs, and still another permitting only 820 MIRVed ICBMs. Among the qualitative restrictions imposed by the treaty was a ban (until December 1981) on the deployment of mobile launchers, ground-and sea-launched cruise missiles with ranges greater than 600 kilometers, and the flight-testing and deployment of air-launched cruise missiles. Carter, however, felt compelled to withdraw the SALT II Treaty from the Senate's consideration after the Soviet Union's invasion of Afghanistan in December 1979. Because of conservative opposition to the treaty, many believed it would not have gained the required two-thirds affirmative vote of the Senate even had the Soviets refrained from invading Afghanistan. Conservatives argued that the treaty was inequitable, primarily because it permitted the Soviets to retain their heavy missiles while allowing the United States to build none, and was unverifiable, primarily because it did not ban all encryption of missile telemetry, that is, the encoding of communications between missiles being tested and their ground-based command centers.

The Reagan Era

President Carter's successor, Ronald Reagan, had vigorously opposed the SALT II Treaty. He charged that it had enabled the Soviets to augment their strategic forces to a point where the United States was vulnerable to a Soviet first strike. Instead of SALT, which placed only ceilings on strategic weapons, Reagan favored talks that would produce deep cuts in the warhead as well as launcher arsenals of the two sides. Ironically, however, the Reagan administration observed the unratified SALT II Treaty until 1986, primarily because it halted the deployment of Soviet strategic weapons more than those of the United States. Before engaging the Soviets in strategic nuclear arms reduction talks (START), Reagan believed that the United States would have to build up and modernize its nuclear arsenal, not only to close the so-called window of vulnerability, but also to gain leverage in bargaining with the Soviets. As a result, U.S. defense spending nearly doubled during Reagan's first administration. Major strategic nuclear weapon systems that had been shelved by Carter, like the B-1 bomber, were revived. The deployment of the MX ICBM and the Trident submarine was accelerated. The development of new systems, like the B-2 bomber and the Strategic Defense Initiative (SDI, or "Star Wars"), a space-based, ballistic missile defense system (BMD), and antisatellite weapons (ASAT) were begun. Plans also were made to modernize and upgrade the nation's tactical nuclear weapons, including accelerating the production of the enhanced radiation (neutron) weapon, whose deployment Carter had rejected in 1978.

The nuclear strategy of the Reagan administration was based on an ardent refutation of the MAD doctrine, which, Reagan's advisers argued, made no provision for the failure of deterrence short of suicide by retaliation. The only way for the United States to deter a Soviet attack, they insisted, was to acquire the ability to wage and "prevail" in a "protracted" nuclear war. The Reagan Single Integrated Operational Plan (SIOP-6) identified some 40,000 targets in the Soviet Union and its allied nations, including sixty "military" targets within the city of Moscow alone. To implement this strategy, the administration planned to increase the size of the U.S. nuclear arsenal from the level to which it had declined during the 1970s (25,000 warheads) to 28,000 by the end of the 1980s. Not surprisingly, considering the new nuclear weapons the Reagan administration was developing, it abandoned the long effort to negotiate a comprehensive ban on nuclear testing.

Despite the administration's deep-seated dislike for arms control, pressure from NATO allies, Congress, and a burgeoning antinuclear movement compelled the United States to engage in nuclear arms negotiations with the Soviets. In 1981 the administration offered the so-called zero option plan as its Intermediate-Range Nuclear Forces (INF) proposal. It called for the United States to cancel plans to deploy its Pershing IIs and Tomahawks in return for the dismantling of all the Soviet intermediate-range missiles, particularly the SS-20s. At first, the Soviets rejected the zero option, and when the deployment of the U.S. missiles began in December 1983, the Soviets walked out of the INF talks. The START process also languished during Reagan's first term in office. The administration's initial (1982) START proposal called for deep cuts in Soviet missiles and warheads, an approach the Soviet leadership had rejected when Carter had first proposed it in 1977. For a variety of reasons, however, during his second term, Reagan displayed a much more flexible attitude toward nuclear arms talks. One was the continued pressure of the Democratically controlled Congress, which tied funding for Reagan's military buildup to his willingness to engage in meaningful arms reduction talks. In addition, by 1984 Reagan's military buildup was well underway and consequently the president was more receptive to the idea that nuclear arms reductions could be advantageous to the United States.

Another factor that facilitated progress in the arms reductions talks during Reagan's second term was the rise to power of a much more flexible Soviet leader, Mikhail Gorbachev. At a summit meeting with Reagan in Reykjavík, Iceland, in October 1986, Gorbachev agreed to a START proposal calling for the reduction of warheads carried by ballistic missiles and air-launched cruise missiles (ALCMs) to 6,000 and the number of long-range missiles and bombers to 1,600. Gorbachev, however, insisted that this concession was contingent on continued U.S. adherence to a strict definition of the ABM Treaty, which required that BMD research be confined to the laboratory. Reagan expressed his willingness to abide by the ABM Treaty, but only for an additional ten years. Moreover, he favored a much looser interpretation of the ABM Treaty, one that would have permitted extensive testing and development of BMD outside the laboratory. As a result of the superpowers' inability to reach an agreement on this issue, a START agreement proved impossible to conclude before Reagan left office in 1989. The superpowers did agree to an INF treaty in 1987. It required the United States and the Soviet Union to eliminate all land-based missiles with a range of 1,000-5,500 kilometers as well as short-range, intermediate nuclear forces (SRINF), that is, land-based missiles with a 500–1,000 kilometer range. A decisive factor in the U.S. decision to sign the INF Treaty was the willingness of the Soviets to permit a comprehensive verification program, including—for the first time in the history of nuclear arms agreements—on-site inspection.

The End of the Cold War

President Reagan's successor, George Bush, witnessed the end of the Cold War, the overthrow of communism in Eastern Europe and the collapse of the Soviet Union. In July 1990 the NATO countries responded to the demise of the Cold War by adopting a new strategy making nuclear forces the weapons of last resort. On 27 September 1991 Bush announced that the United States would remove or destroy all ground-based, tactical nuclear weapons, including artillery shells and short-range missiles, that were deployed in Europe. With the Soviets withdrawing their forces from Eastern Europe, the only targets that remained for NATO's tactical nuclear missiles were located in the newly democratic states of that region.

President Bush's initiative was motivated by a desire to persuade Gorbachev to do away with Soviet tactical nuclear missiles, or at least concentrate them in the Russian republic, where they would be easier to control in the event the Soviet Union broke up. While Gorbachev announced his willingness to reciprocate the U.S. initiative, he was unable to implement it. In December 1991, following an unsuccessful attempt to overthrow the Soviet leader the preceding August, the Soviet Union did disintegrate into its constituent republics. As a result, the task of accounting for—let alone reducing—the tactical nuclear weapons of the former Soviet Union fell to Boris Yeltsin, the president of the Russian republic. Yeltsin also assumed the Russian responsibility for implementing the START I Treaty, which Gorbachev and Bush had signed on 31 July 1991. The treaty required each party to reduce the number of their deployed strategic warheads to no more than 6,000 and their launchers (missiles and bombers) to a maximum of 1,600. (At the end of 1990 the United States had slightly fewer than 12,778 strategic warheads on 1,876 launchers and the Soviet Union had 10,880 warheads on 2,354 launchers.) In a major concession to the United States, the Soviet Union agreed to cut in half (to 154) the number of their "heavy" SS-18 ICBMs, carrying no more than 1,540 warheads.

With the demise of the Soviet Union, it was necessary to make START I a multilateral agreement. This was accomplished on 23 May 1992, when the four former Soviet republics with nuclear weapons—Russia, Ukraine, Belarus, and Kazakhstan—signed the Lisbon Protocol, by which they assumed the obligations of the former Soviet Union under START I. In so doing, Ukraine, Kazakhstan, and Belarus agreed to remove to Russia for dismantling the approximately 3,000 strategic nuclear warheads that remained in their territories. In addition, the three non-Russian states agreed to accede to the NPT, a condition Russia made a prerequisite to the completion of the START I ratification process. While Belarus and Kazakhstan joined the NPT in 1993, the Ukrainian parliament did not vote to do so until 16 November 1994, and only after the United States, Russia, and Great Britain provided separate security guarantees to the three non-Russian nuclear states. On 5 December 1994 the START I Treaty entered into force.

The ratification of the START I Treaty made possible the implementation of another strategic arms reduction treaty, START II, which the United States and Russia signed on 3 January 1993, shortly before Bush left office. The START II Treaty committed both sides to reduce the number of their deployed strategic warheads to 3,500 for the United States and 3,000 for Russia—roughly two-thirds of their 1990 totals—by 1 January 2003. The treaty also required both sides to eliminate land-based, multiple-warhead missiles and "heavy" ICBMs (including all the Soviet SS-18s and the U.S. MX ICBMs), thereby virtually eliminating the possibility that either side could launch a successful first-strike nuclear attack. To facilitate the implementation of the START treaties, in November 1991 Congress passed the Nunn-Lugar Act. It authorized the United States to spend up to $400 million in fiscal year 1992 to help the Soviet Union destroy nuclear, chemical, and other weapons, as well as to establish verifiable safeguards against the proliferation of such weapons. After the breakup of the Soviet Union, Nunn-Lugar assistance was granted to Russia, Ukraine, Belarus, and Kazakhstan. While Bush agreed to make major reductions in the size of the U.S. nuclear arsenal, he refused to abandon Reagan's quest for an effective ballistic missile defense. The Bush version was a massive, space-based system called "Brilliant Pebbles," which would employ kinetic-kill weapons to destroy enemy ICBMs after they were launched. The administration was unsuccessful in getting either the Soviets or their Russian successors to accept modifications in the ABM Treaty, which would have permitted a spaced-based BMD. President Bush also refused to endorse a CTBT, which he argued would have prevented the United States from maintaining the credibility of its remaining nuclear weapons. To encourage the successful negotiation of a CTBT, Congress passed a law in 1992 reducing the number of permitted U.S. nuclear weapon tests and halting them completely after September 1996 unless other countries continued their test programs.

The Clinton administration helped to make possible the implementation of the START I and II treaties that his predecessor had successfully negotiated. In a January 1994 Moscow summit with Yeltsin and Ukrainian President Leonid Kravchuk, Clinton was able to persuade Ukraine to join the NPT (one of the conditions Russia required before it ratified the treaties) in exchange for U.S. economic aid and security guarantees. At the same Moscow summit, Clinton and Yeltsin also announced that the United States and Russia would "detarget" their strategic missiles by 30 May 1994. While this initiative was largely symbolic, because the missiles can be re-aimed at specific targets in a matter of minutes, the gesture nevertheless contributed to the further winding down of the Cold War.

As the U.S.-Ukrainian aid package demonstrated, the Clinton administration is very concerned about the threat of nuclear proliferation. Favoring indefinite extension of the Nuclear Nonproliferation Treaty, which was due to expire in 1995, the administration argued that the major nuclear powers had lived up to their end of the nonproliferation bargain by making substantial reductions in the size of their nuclear arsenals. In addition, the United States and Russia agreed to begin negotiations on a treaty requiring both countries to end the production of fissile material for nuclear weapons. In the spring of 1995, an international conference voted to renew the NPT for an indefinite period. As another way of encouraging indefinite extension of the NPT, the Clinton administration also gave strong support to a Comprehensive Test Ban Treaty (TBT). On 30 January 1995, Clinton extended the moratorium on U.S. nuclear testing, which he initiated in 1993, through at least September 1996, when the nuclear powers were expected to sign a CTBT. Partly because of these efforts, and fear of the consequences if the NPT were allowed to expire, a NPT Review and Extension Conference (held in New York from 17 April to 12 May 1995) voted overwhelmingly to extend the treaty indefinitely. However, delegates from a number of nonnuclear states expressed regret that the conference established no deadlines or target dates for the complete elimination of nuclear weapons, which is called for in Article 6 of the treaty. Instead, the conference's statement of principles merely described nuclear disarmament as an "ultimate goal."

Despite the major reductions in their strategic arsenals brought about by START, for the foreseeable future both Russia and the United States will retain more than enough nuclear power to devastate the planet. On 22 September 1994, Defense Secretary William J. Perry announced the results of the Nuclear Posture Review, which established the missions and levels for U.S. strategic nuclear forces through 2003. The 3,500 "accountable" warheads permitted the United States under START II would be deployed on 500 single-warhead equipped Minuteman III ICBMs; fourteen Trident submarines, carrying 336 SLBMs, each with four warheads; and a bomber force comprised of twenty B-2s and sixty-four B-52-H bombers (ninety-five B-1 bombers are being converted to conventional warfare roles). Moreover, the START treaties do not require the destruction of existing nuclear warheads. As a result, the Clinton administration is planning to retain a reserve stockpile of warheads for "uploading" onto ICBMs, SLBMs, and bombers, if relations with Russia change for the worse. It has been estimated that the size of the U.S. nuclear stockpile in 2003 will be 8,500

warheads: 3,500 in active strategic forces, 3,500 in reserve, 1,000 nonstrategic warheads, and 500 spares.

The United States did not renounce the option to use nuclear weapons first, even if only as a last resort. In November 1993 Russia announced that it was abandoning the "no-first-use" of nuclear weapons policy which the Soviet Union had followed. In the minds of representatives from the nonweapon states, the refusal of the major nuclear countries to accept a no-first-use policy brings into doubt the sincerity of their promises to end the nuclear arms race. The continued reliance on nuclear deterrence by the major weapon states is an important reason why some nonweapon states may withdraw from the NPT (after giving the requisite three months' notice) and acquire nuclear weapons of their own.

Equally ominous for the prospects of checking the spread of nuclear weapons is the delay in the ratification of the START II Treaty. The U.S. Senate approved the treaty on 26 January 1996. But for a variety of reasons, the Russian parliament has not yet ratified the treaty. For one, many of its members believe asymmetrical cuts required by the treaty give the United States an unfair advantage. The START II ban on MIRVed ICBMs, and particularly heavy (SS-18) missiles, would eliminate Russia's land-based ten-warhead ICBMs. By contrast, the treaty permits the United States to retain not only 500 of the formerly-MIRVed Minuteman III ICBMs (downloaded to single warhead missiles) but also all 336 planned Trident II submarine-launched ballistic missiles (each downloaded from eight to five warheads). In addition, START II permits the United States to keep up to 100 heavy bombers by reorienting them to conventional missions. The Russians fear that the bombers could quickly be reconverted to a nuclear role if the United States chose to breach the treaty. Russian analysts also are bothered that START II does not limit long-range nuclear sea-launched cruise missiles (SLCMs). While both sides have withdrawn SLCMs from service in subsequent unilateral initiatives, the United States would have a definite advantage over Russia if the Americans decided to redeploy SLCMs.

The Russians are also concerned about the asymmetrical costs they will have to incur to implement the START agreements. By retaining existing systems, except the banned multiple-warhead MX missile, the United States can achieve START II reductions with relatively small implementation costs. Russia, on the other hand, must bear sizable dismantlement costs. The Russians will have to physically destroy the silo and railmobile launchers for nearly 200 MIRVed ICBMs. They must also convert up to 90 SS-18 silos to enable them to house smaller, single-warhead missiles. In addition, the Russians will be required to eliminate missile submarines and their nuclear power plants and spent nuclear fuel, all at a formidable cost. Another obstacle standing in the way of the treaty's ratification is the revival of the ABM issue. While the Clinton administration proclaimed the death of Reagan's SDI, funding for ballistic missile defense research has continued to the extent of about $3 billion per year. However, rather than spending the money on the development of space-based, anti-ICBM weapons, as Reagan did, the Clinton administration's Ballistic Missile Defense Organization (BMDO) is concentrating its efforts on developing anti-tactical ballistic missiles (ATBMs). Designated the Theater High Altitude Area Defense (THAAD) system, Clinton's ATBM program would have the capability to intercept tactical missiles with a range of up to 3,500 kilometers and traveling up to five kilometers per second. Clinton has argued that such defenses are needed to shield U.S. troops deployed overseas, as well as the soldiers and cities of U.S. allies and friends. Some Russian defense officials would like their country to have an ATBM capability, and have been negotiating with the United States since 1993 on a "demarcation" agreement that would distinguish between ABMs and ATBMs in order to permit ATBM testing and eventual deployment without violating the ABM Treaty. However, other Russian defense experts and some parliament members are worried that the deployment of theater missile defenses would eviscerate the ABM Treaty, whose basic purpose is to bar deployment of nationwide ABM defenses against strategic missiles. They want a strict demarcation "line" to separate theater from strategic ABMs. The Russians generally are reluctant to reduce their country's offensive missile forces further if the ABM Treaty's ability to limit defensive missile deployment is eroded. And they are linking Russia's ratification of the START II Treaty to the preservation of the ABM Treaty.

Still another issue complicating the ratification of the START II Treaty is NATO's plan to expand its membership to include some of the former Warsaw Pact countries, specifically Poland, Hungary, and the Czech Republic. NATO's expansion plans are regarded by Moscow as a potential threat to Russian security. If this highly emotional and potentially explosive issue is not defused, it may poison the atmosphere in which START II will be voted on in the Russian parliament, perhaps in 1996, if—and it is a big if—Boris Yeltsin gets his way.

While some Russian parliamentarians favor reopening the START II negotiations, it is more likely that both sides will accept adjustments during the implementation phase of the treaty. Such adjustments probably would reduce and delay Russian dismantling costs and deadlines. Additional U.S. Nunn-Lugar financial assistance would facilitate the Russian dismantlement process. Some have also suggested that the total number of warheads should be reduced to 2,000 for each side, which would relieve both the Russians and the Americans of the expense of maintaining the 3,000-warhead ceiling. However, this probably will have to wait for START III.

Many feel it is also vital to maintain the integrity of the ABM Treaty, since the Russians are unlikely to ratify START II, let alone reduce the size of their nuclear arsenal further in START III, if the United States pursues an ABM defense system with strategic capabilities. It would also help the ratification process considerably if the problem of NATO expansion were resolved without totally alienating Russia. An isolated Russia is unlikely to be a cooperative partner of the United States in the effort to eliminate the nuclear weapons menace.

Thus, while the prospect of a major nuclear war has abated considerably, and will continue to do so if START II is ratified, the threat posed by the continued existence of nuclear weapons in the possession of the nuclear powers, and the prospect that they will be acquired by current nonweapon states as well, is likely to persist for the foreseeable future.

RONALD E. POWASKI

See also Antiballistic Missile Treaty; Atoms for Peace, Baruch, Bernard Mannes; Cuban Missile Crisis; Détente; Deterrence; Einstein, Albert; Flexible Response; Gorbachev, Mikhail Sergeevich; Gromyko, Andrei Andreyevich; Hiroshima and Nakasaki Bombings of 1945; Hydrogen Bomb; Intermediate-Range Nuclear Forces Treaty; Kissinger, Henry Alfred; Limited Nuclear Test Ban Treaty; Manhattan Project; Massive Retaliation; Mutual Assured Destruction; North Atlantic Treaty Organization; Nuclear Nonproliferation; Science and Technology; Strategic Arms Limitation Talks and Agreements; Strategic Arms Reduction Treaties; Strategic Defense Initiative; Teller, Edward; Verification

FURTHER READING

Arkin, William M., Thomas B. Cochran, and Milton M. Hoenig. *Nuclear Weapons Databook*, vols. 1 and 2. New York, 1984, 1985.

Bundy, McGeorge. *Danger and Survival*. New York, 1988.

Campbell, Christopher. *Nuclear Weapons Fact Book*. New York, 1984.

Cantelon, Philip L., Richard G. Hewlett, and Robert C. Williams, and eds. *The American Atom: A Documentary History of Nuclear Policies from the Discovery of Fission to the Present*, 2nd ed. Philadelphia, 1991.

Craig, Paul P., and John A. Jungerman. *Nuclear Arms Race: Technology and Society*. New York, 1990.

Dennis, Jack, ed. *The Nuclear Almanac: Confronting the Atom in War and Peace*. Reading, Mass., 1982.

Freedman, Lawrence. *The Evolution of Nuclear Strategy*. New York, 1983.

Gay, William. *The Nuclear Arms Race: A Digest with Bibliographies*. New York, 1987.

Green, William C. *Soviet Nuclear Weapons Policy: A Research and Bibliographic Guide*. Boulder, Colo., 1987.

Holloway, David. *The Soviet Union and the Arms Race*. New Haven, Conn., 1983.

Labrie, Roger P., ed. *SALT Hand Book: Key Documents and Issues, 1972-1979*. Washington, D.C.: 1979.

Newhouse, John. *War and Peace in the Nuclear Age*. New York, 1989.

Powaski, Ronald E. *March to Armageddon: The United States and the Nuclear Arms Race, 1939-1987*. New York, 1987.

NUNN, SAMUEL

(*b.* 8 September 1938)

Democratic senator from Georgia (1972–1996), recognized as a leading spokesman on military and national security issues. Nunn was first elected to the Senate in a special election after the death of Senator Richard Russell, long-time chairman of the Senate Armed Services Committee, and was reelected in 1978, 1984, and 1990. Nunn immediately became a member of the Senate Armed Services Committee and was chairman from 1986 to 1995. He also chaired the Permanent Subcommittee on Investigations. Both committee assignments provided him with important venues for examining a wide array of foreign policy issues. A moderate to conservative southerner, Nunn proved to be a loyal supporter of the military throughout his career in Congress. He has been a leader in the effort to maintain a strong defense as the United States entered the post–Cold War era but also sought to reexamine U.S. domestic and foreign priorities through his work on the Commission for Strengthening of America. Much of his legislative efforts focused upon strengthening the military by improving efficiency within the Pentagon and improving conditions for the personnel who serve in the armed forces. At the same time, he had an interest in effective arms control and arms reduction. In 1987, for example, Nunn engaged in a marathon three-day discussion on the Senate floor to thwart the efforts of President Ronald Reagan's administration to reinterpret the Antiballistic Missile Treaty (ABM) and to proceed with the development of the Strategic Defense Initiative (SDI, or Star Wars). He cosponsored and enacted legislation offering substantial economic assistance to the former republics of the Soviet Union for the safe dismantlement of nuclear weapons under the Strategic Arms Reduction Treaties (START).

Nunn's senatorial influence derived primarily from his position as chairman of the Armed Services Committee. Under his leadership, the committee was quite structured, with all the majority staff assigned to him and no staff assigned to the various subcommittees. As a result, Nunn had considerable control over information within the committee and could more easily develop and shape defense policy recommendations constant with his views. Nunn's reputation began to suffer in the early 1990s, over his opposition to President George Bush's policy of moving quickly from the economic sanctions imposed against Iraq following its August 1990 invasion of Kuwait to a military attack. Nunn held extensive hearings in late 1990 seeking to build support for at least giving the sanctions more time to work and then voted in the Senate against the resolution approving immediate military action by the Bush administration. Even when fellow Democrat Bill Clinton was elected president, Nunn continued to demonstrate independence and often disagreement. He immediately clashed with the presi-

dent over the issue of gays in the military. Despite his opposition to Clinton's policy over Haiti, however, Nunn agreed to be a member of the diplomatic mission, led by former President Jimmy Carter and including retired General Colin Powell, that went to Haiti on 17 September 1994 in what proved to be a successful effort to avert a forcible U.S. invasion.

JAMES M. McCORMICK

FURTHER READING

Deering, Christopher J. "Decision Making in the Armed Services Committee." In *Congress Resurgent: Foreign and Domestic Policy on Capitol Hill,* edited by Randall B. Ripley and James M. Lindsay. Ann Arbor, Mich., 1993.

Morrison, David C. "Sam Nunn, Inc." *National Journal* (15 June 1991): 1483–1486.

Nunn, Sam, and Pete Domenici. *The CSIS Strengthening of America Commission First Report.* Washington, D.C., 1992.

Thompson, Kenneth W., ed. *Sam Nunn on Arms Control.* Lanham, Md., 1988.

NUREMBERG, INTERNATIONAL MILITARY TRIBUNAL AT

A special tribunal which presided over the trials of German Nazi leaders held after World War II. Shortly after the surrender of Japan, the United States, Great Britain, France, and the Soviet Union agreed on the London Charter, which defined the jurisdictions and powers of the International Military Tribunal. The tribunal consisted of four judges and four alternates from each of the four powers. From November 29, 1945, until 1 October 1946, the International Military Tribunal was located in Nuremberg, Germany, site of the Nazi party's largest rallies. Twenty-four Nazi leaders were indicted, including such prominent figures as Hermann Göring and Rudolf Hess. One of these, Robert Ley, committed suicide before the trial, and proceedings against another, Gustav Krupp, were suspended because he was senile.

The intent to punish Axis war criminals was promised as early as the Tehran Conference in 1943 and was deepened by the unprecedented nature of Nazi and Japanese atrocities. The United States and Great Britain disagreed over the best method of punishing top Nazi leaders, the British favoring summary execution. The United States hoped to use the trials not only to punish Nazi atrocities such as the mistreatment of prisoners and the extermination of millions of Jews, but to establish a new standard of international law. They argued that a trial before the United Nations would "give a serious precedent that might operate as an added deterrent to waging aggressive war in the future."

Led by U.S. prosecutors Robert A. Jackson and Telford Taylor, the Nuremberg trials involved hundreds of witnesses and thousands of documents. The records of the proceedings, including documentation of Nazi atrocities, were published in forty-two volumes. Although there were isolated protests about "victor's justice," the fairness of the trials impressed impartial observers. In all, nineteen of the twenty-two defendants were convicted, twelve of whom were executed. An international tribunal conducted trials against Japanese war criminals also, and subsequent trials of less prominent Nazi leaders were held by individual powers that discovered the criminals in their countries. The United States was active in this effort, indicting 185 defendants in twelve trials involving industrialists, government officials, and doctors.

Critics of the Nuremberg trials, among them the diplomat George F. Kennan, condemned inclusion of the Soviet Union among the judges, noting the Hitler-Stalin Pact and such Soviet atrocities as the Katyn massacre. Others criticized the creation of *ex post facto* law in the tribunal's pronouncement that initiating a war of aggression was a crime under international law. Contemporary international law largely endorses this position of the International Military Tribunal, as well as its rejection of the defense that offenders were merely following orders.

By establishing an undeniable record of Nazi atrocities, the Nuremberg trials played a crucial role in preventing the resurgence of any "stab in the back" or "war guilt" myths in postwar Germany. Nuremberg remained a powerful symbol of international law throughout the Cold War, sometimes with troubling implications for the United States. During the Vietnam War, Nuremberg was invoked by some civilian and military personnel who refused to serve in Indochina. Like defendants at Nuremberg, Lieutenant William Calley, perpetrator of the massacre at My Lai, argued that he was following orders. Although Calley was convicted, none of the other participants in the massacre, some of whom used the same defense, were punished.

THOMAS A. SCHWARTZ

See also Germany; Holocaust; Kennan, George Frost; World War II

FURTHER READING

Taylor, Telford. *The Anatomy of the Nuremberg Trials*. New York, 1992.
————. *Nuremberg and Vietnam: An American Tragedy*. Chicago, 1970.
Smith, Bradley F. *Reaching Judgment at Nuremberg*. New York, 1977.

NYE, GERALD PRENTICE

(*b.* 19 December 1892; *d.* 18 July 1971)

Republican senator from North Dakota from 1925 to 1945, known for his isolationist views and investigation of munitions manufacturers. Nye helped popularize the idea that greed of the "merchants of death" had pushed the United States into World War I.

Born in Hortonville, Wisconsin, Nye joined the family newspaper business first as publisher of *The Hortonville Review*, then as manager and editor of newspapers in Iowa and in North Dakota. Young Nye's activism in the agrarian radical Nonpartisan League of North Dakota, which was antagonistic toward eastern business interests, shaped his views on domestic and foreign policy.

In 1925, Nye was appointed to the U.S. Senate after the death of North Dakota Senator Edwin Ladd. A Republican with radical agrarian views, Nye was elected in 1926 and served until defeat in 1944. Nye's vigilant opposition to foreign policies which he believed advanced business interests at the expense of farmers laid the groundwork for his crusade against big business, international banking, and Wall Street. The Senate Committee Investigating the Munitions Industry, which he chaired from 1934 to 1936, was part of this crusade, a crusade that garnered widespread support for isolationism in the 1930s. Nye joined other isolationist senators, especially Bennett Champ Clark, Arthur H. Vandenberg, and Homer T. Bone, in passing neutrality legislation from 1935 to 1937. The legislation, designed to keep the United States out of a second world war, restricted presidential powers and trade with belligerents. Nye became a frequent spokesman for the America First Committee, which opposed U.S. participation in World War II. He used his position on the Senate Foreign Relations Committee from 1940 until his last term expired in 1945, to become one of President Franklin D. Roosevelt's most powerful opponents over aid to Great Britain and the Soviet Union. Although he supported Roosevelt's decision to declare war on Japan after the attack on Pearl Harbor, Nye's failure to recognize increasing public support for the war caused him to lose his Senate seat in 1944. From 1945 to 1966 he served as president of Record Engineering, Inc., as a special assistant in the Federal Housing Administration, and as a staff member of the Senate Committee on Aging.

JANET M. MANSON

See also America First Committee; Isolationism; Neutrality Acts of the 1930s; Vandenberg, Arthur Hendrick; World War I

FURTHER READING

Cole, Wayne S. *Senator Gerald P. Nye and American Foreign Relations*. Minneapolis, Minn., 1962.

NYE COMMITTEE

See Nye, Gerald Prentice

O

OAS

See Organization of American States

OECD

See Organization for Economic Cooperation and Development

OFFICE OF STRATEGIC SERVICES

The Office of Strategic Services (OSS) was created by executive order of President Franklin D. Roosevelt in June 1942. The OSS gathered secret intelligence and conducted commando operations during World War II. OSS director William Donovan, a distinguished veteran of World War I, lobbied extensively to garner support for the nascent intelligence agency. Though Donovan founded the OSS on the erroneous assumption that German fifth-column activities posed a grave threat to the Allied war effort, he proved adept at reorienting the agency to meet changing intelligence requirements. The OSS made its greatest contribution to Allied victory by contacting and providing aid to resistance movements in France, Yugoslavia, and other countries in Europe and Asia. A gregarious and dynamic leader, Donovan experimented with a variety of intelligence-related activities. He recruited university professors to provide research and analysis, deployed operational groups behind enemy lines, and ordered OSS agents to collect battlefield intelligence. Donovan's only consistent goal remained his desire to establish the OSS as a permanent U.S. agency. Attainment of that goal eluded Donovan because the effectiveness of his organization was limited by inexperience. Internecine disputes with more established U.S. bureaucratic and military departments further undermined OSS operations. Donovan's personal style attracted the ire of such influential leaders as J. Edgar Hoover and General Douglas MacArthur. President Harry S. Truman disbanded the OSS in September 1945, and Donovan was removed from active service shortly thereafter. The permanent impact of the OSS on the conduct of U.S. foreign policy became apparent after the Central Intelligence Agency was established in 1947. Future CIA directors Allen Dulles, Richard Helms, and William Colby began their careers in intelligence as OSS operatives. Intelligence strategies employed during World War II contributed to the CIA's subsequent reliance on covert actions in performing less-controversial intelligence activities such as research and analysis.

CHARLES D. McGRAW

See also Central Intelligence Agency; Covert Action; Intelligence; World War II

FURTHER READING

Dunlop, Richard. *Donovan: America's Master Spy.* New York, 1982.
Smith, Bradley F. *The Shadow Warriors: O.S.S. and the Origins of the C.I.A.* New York, 1983.
Troy, Thomas F. *Donovan and the CIA: A History of the Establishment of the Central Intelligence Agency.* Frederick, Md., 1981.

OIL AND FOREIGN POLICY

No commodity has been more closely associated with U.S. foreign relations than petroleum. United States foreign policy has at various times been concerned with petroleum because of its association with national defense, the security of domestic energy supplies, and with the protection of American-owned foreign property. United States petroleum policy has been governed by four basic principles: (1) U.S. firms should have equal access to oil concessions in foreign countries; (2) U.S. firms should be supported in conflicts with governments that violate contracts with U.S. investors; (3) the U.S. economy should have a high degree of self-sufficiency in petroleum; and (4) the major foreign sources of petroleum should not fall into the hands of unfriendly powers, including combinations of oil producing countries using oil as a political or economic weapon.

The United States was self-sufficient in petroleum during the first two decades of the twentieth century and, therefore, neither the U.S. government nor the U.S. oil industry aggressively pursued the development of oil resources outside the Western Hemisphere until after World War I.

The Open Door Policy

By the late nineteenth century oil had become a primary weapon of war as well as a rapidly growing source of ener-

U.S. DEPENDENCE ON PETROLEUM NET IMPORTS[a], BY SOURCE
(Net Imports as Share of US Petroleum Products Supplied)

Year (Average)	From Arab OPEC[b]	From OPEC[c]	From all Countries
	%	%	%
1973	5.3	17.3	34.8
1975	8.5	22.0	35.8
1977	17.3	33.6	46.5
1979	16.5	30.4	43.1
1981	11.5	20.6	33.6
1983	4.1	12.1	28.3
1985	3.0	11.6	27.3
1987	7.6	18.3	35.5
1989	12.3	23.8	41.6
1991	12.3	24.3	39.6
1993	11.6	24.7	44.2

[a]"Net Imports" are imports minus exports. Imports from members of the Organization of Petroleum Exporting Countries (OPEC) exclude indirect imports, which are petroleum products primarily from Caribbean and West European areas and refined from crude oil produced by OPEC.
[b]The Arab members of OPEC are Algeria, Iraq, Kuwait, Libya, Qatar, Saudi Arabia, and the Untied Arab Emirates. Net imports from the Neutral Zone between Kuwait and Saudi Arabia are included in net imports from Arab OPEC.
[c]OPEC currently consists of Gabon, Indonesia, Iran, Nigeria, and Venezuela, as well as the Arab members. Ecuador was a member of OPEC from 1973-1992; for this period, net imports from Ecuador are included in net imports from OPEC.

Sources: *Mineral Industry Surveys*. U.S. Department of Interior, Bureau of Mines. *"Petroleum Statement, Annual."* In *Energy Data Reports*, by the Energy Information Administration; *Petroleum Supply Annual*; and *Petroleum Supply Monthly*.

gy for domestic economies. Before and immediately after World War I, Great Britain, France, and the Netherlands acquired stakes in newly discovered oil fields in the Middle East and the Dutch East Indies, and sought to restrict access to these areas to their own nationals. Although the U.S. Department of State supported U.S. petroleum firms following the 1917 action of the Mexican government to restrict foreign ownership of Mexican oil, the first major United States diplomatic initiative in petroleum took place in 1922. The U.S. Embassy in London sent a letter to the British government insisting that U.S. nationals not be excluded from a reasonable share in developing the resources of territories under the mandate. The Treaty of Versailles, which ended World War I, gave Great Britain a mandate over Iraq, whose petroleum reserves were entirely under the British-dominated Turkish Petroleum Company (TPC). The U.S. government accused Great Britain of violating the treaty, which provided that territories acquired under the treaty must be governed in a way that would assure equal treatment to nationals of all countries. This policy came to be known as the "open door policy."

Negotiations for the participation of U.S. companies in the TPC began in July 1922 and continued until July 1928 when an agreement was reached giving twenty-four percent of the shares in TPC to five U.S. oil companies: Standard of New Jersey, Standard Oil of New York, Gulf Refining Company, Atlantic Refining Company, and the Pan American Petroleum and Transport Company. United States diplomatic efforts were motivated not simply by a desire to support U.S. oil companies, but also by a concern that domestic self-sufficiency in petroleum would soon end.

The U.S. Congress provided an effective weapon in passing the Minerals Leasing Act of 1920, which accorded foreign-owned affiliates the right to minerals exploitation in the United States, provided U.S. firms had the right to operate without discrimination in the home country of the affiliate. When the Dutch government ignored this reciprocity principle by discriminating against U.S. firms in the Dutch East Indies, the U.S. government refused to grant a concession on American public land to the Royal Dutch Shell Oil Company. After long negotiations, the Dutch government accepted the principle of reciprocity and granted Standard Oil of New Jersey additional oil concessions.

In 1928 the participants in the TPC, later changed to the Iraq Petroleum Company (IPC), negotiated the Red

Line Agreement. The participants agreed not to compete with each other for concessions within the Red Line, an area that encompassed the former Ottoman Empire, including Turkey, Syria, Jordan, Iraq, Palestine, and the Arabian Peninsula, excluding Kuwait, or to hold any individual concessions there without the permission of the other partners. This meant that a small number of companies controlled a substantial portion of world oil reserves, since the British government allowed only British Commonwealth members access to oil concessions within the Red Line area. However, in 1929 Standard Oil of California (SOCAL) obtained a concession on Bahrain in the Persian Gulf via a Canadian subsidiary, the Bahrain Petroleum Company (BPC). SOCAL sold half its stock in BPC to Texaco, and later SOCAL and Texaco formed a joint venture, the Arabian-American Oil Company (ARAMCO), to operate in Saudi Arabia. With the help of the U.S. Department of State, Gulf Exploration Company was able to overcome British efforts to prevent it from securing a concession in Kuwait, and the concession came to be held jointly by Gulf Exploration and the Anglo-Iranian Oil Company. By the end of the 1930s, U.S. companies had obtained concessions in Bahrain, Iraq, Kuwait, and Saudi Arabia. This was achieved with considerable assistance from the U.S. government in overcoming Great Britain's efforts to keep the Middle East for British Commonwealth companies. Nevertheless, the U.S. Department of State acquiesced to the Red Line Agreement, which was anything but "open door" for U.S. companies not associated with the IPC.

United States diplomatic efforts in Latin America were largely directed at supporting U.S. companies against actions by governments to control or nationalize their operations. Although Latin America was recognized as a sphere of U.S. influence, in accordance with the Monroe Doctrine of 1823, the U.S. government did not attempt to prevent European companies from obtaining concessions. United States diplomatic action was used against the Mexican government when it nationalized certain mineral rights held by U.S. citizens during the 1920s, and the U.S. government launched a trade boycott against Mexican oil and other commodities in 1938 when President Lázaro Cárdenas nationalized all oil companies owned by foreigners. Subsequently, nationalization of U.S. oil companies occurred in Argentina, Bolivia, Brazil, and Venezuela. By 1980, nearly all Latin American petroleum production was government-owned, despite U.S. government efforts opposing the trend.

Oil Policy During World War II

During World War II, petroleum came a paramount concern of President Franklin Roosevelt's administration. In July 1943, the Petroleum Reserves Corporation (PRC) was created by an executive order, with broad powers to acquire reserves of petroleum from sources outside the United States and to construct and operate refineries, pipelines, and other facilities abroad. From the events that followed, it became evident that the immediate purpose of the PRC was to acquire privately held American oil concessions in the Middle East (Feis, 1946, pp. 276–279). In July 1943, President Roosevelt authorized the PRC to negotiate for the purchase of the stock of ARAMCO and BPC. The proposal was later amended to provide for the purchase of only minority interest in these concessions, but SOCAL and Texas Gulf announced their refusal to sell. (The government probably would not have paid the companies much more than the costs they had incurred in developing the concessions.)

Following the breakdown of these negotiations—which had little support from the Department of State—Harold Ickes, the president of PRC and secretary of the interior, announced a tentative agreement with ARAMCO and Gulf Exploration whereby the PRC would construct a pipeline to transport oil from Saudi Arabian and Kuwaiti fields to a port on the eastern Mediterranean Sea. In addition, the tentative agreement gave an option to the U.S. government to purchase oil at a discount of twenty-five percent below the market price, and the companies were to give prior notice to the Department of State of any negotiations with foreign governments relating to the sale of products from these concessions. No sales of petroleum were to be made to any government or its nationals if, in the opinion of the Department of State, such sales were contrary to U.S. interests. Because of protests from the oil industry and a cool reception in Congress, the agreement was never consummated. The reason given for both proposals was the protection of U.S. ownership of the concessions. However, either proposal would have led the U.S. government into direct conflict with Middle Eastern governments. Also, the Roosevelt Administration was undermining its own principles of international competition and free entry into the oil business.

The U.S. stake in Middle East oil has influenced U.S. government policies in the region in various ways. One policy was Palestine, which until 1948 was under British mandate. Both the Arabs and the Jews in Palestine engaged in violence against the mandate and against one another as well. The British government requested help from President Harry S. Truman's administration in formulating and implementing a long-range plan for Palestine that would satisfy the U.S. and British commitments to the 1917 Balfour Declaration for a Jewish homeland, and that would be acceptable to the Arabs. The British government favored the proposal of the Anglo-American Cabinet Committee (1946) creating semi-autonomous Jewish and Arab states, but with Jerusalem and certain other areas remaining under the control of a British or United Nations mandate. The Truman administration was split between those who favored a single Jewish state and those who favor an Arab state on the grounds that a Jewish state and massive immigration of Jews could lead the Middle East oil countries to interrupt American oil operations. The strong influence of the U.S.-Jewish community led the Truman administration to reject the Cabinet Committee proposal. As a result of continuing violence, the British withdrew from Palestine in 1948 and the State of Israel was founded. In the following years U.S. policy toward Israel was frequently influenced by a concern over United States relationships with the Arabian oil countries. The almost continual diplomatic efforts of the Department of State to diffuse, if not settle, the Israeli-Arab disputes have been motivated in part by United States concern for is Middle East oil interest.

Following the nationalization of the Suez Canal by President Gamal Abdel Nassar in July 1956, there was a joint attack on Egypt by Israel, Great Britain, and France. This led to the closure of the Canal, and the disruption of the pipeline transporting Saudi Arabian oil. A substantial portion of Saudi, Kuwaiti and Iranian oil was transported through the Canal and pipeline, most of which was destined for Western Europe. The United Nations demanded a cease-fire and the United States made strong protests to Great Britain, France, and Israel, which were ignored. The United States responded by making delivery of petroleum from the Western Hemisphere conditional on British and French withdrawal from Egypt, and a cease-fire was agreed to in November 1956.

Saudi Arabia was in great need of financial assistance following the outbreak of World War II, largely because the war interfered with the annual pilgrimage to Mecca by Muslims from all over the world. The U.S. Minister to Saudi Arabia, Alexander Kirk, urged direct financial aid as early as 1941, and in 1943 Roosevelt declared Saudi Arabia eligible for Lend-Lease aid. Saudi Arabia's great oil potential brought the country into the United States defense perimeter, where it remains to the present time. Some aid took the form of cereals, but a larger portion was silver and gold for domestic currency circulation, which consisted of silver Ryals and British gold sovereigns. In 1948 the U.S. government sent a two-person mission, George Eddy of the Treasury Department, and Raymond F. Mikesell, professor of economics at the University of Virginia and consultant to the Department of State, to advise Saudi officials on the establishment of a single currency system. Other advisers sent later included Arthur N. Young, who played an important role in the establishment of the Saudi Arabian Monetary Agency. With expansion of Saudi oil production, the country became the largest source of imported petroleum for the

United States. Therefore, the security of Saudi Arabia, the pipelines, and the Persian Gulf became a primary military objective of the United States. This led the U.S. government to provide sophisticated equipment for Saudi defense and close military cooperation which culminated in the joint defense against the Iraqi invasion in 1990.

U.S. Intervention in Iranian Oil Dispute

Although U.S. companies had no oil concessions in Iran, the U.S. government played an important role in the conflict between the Iranian government and the Anglo-Iran Oil Company (AIOC) following the former's decision to nationalize AIOC's concession in 1951. The major international oil companies refused to purchase and market Iranian oil, with the result that an important source of oil was lost to Western Europe. In addition, the U.S. government feared that Iran and its oil might fall into Soviet hands. The British government denied Iran's right to nationalize its oil industry and set up a naval blockade in the Persian Gulf to prevent oil shipments. The U.S. Department of State took the lead in negotiating a settlement whereby Iranian oil would be marketed by an international consortium of British, Dutch, French, and U.S. companies. It may be noted, however, that the U.S. position acknowledged the sovereign right of the Iranian government to nationalize its petroleum industry.

The increased dependence of the domestic economy on oil imports after World War II directed United States policy toward protecting the market for domestic oil. Low-cost Middle East oil reduced the incentive of international companies for U.S. domestic oil exploration and development. There was a demand for import quotas as a security measure, but there was also a strong domestic political interest by members of Congress from western states in promoting the economic welfare of independent oil producers. After attempts to implement a voluntary import restriction program failed, in March 1959 President Dwight Eisenhower announced mandatory import quotas with preference given to Western Hemisphere sources, especially Canada and Mexico, from which imports could be transported over land. The mandatory program was in effect until April 1973, but was replaced by other attempts to promote oil self-sufficiency.

The import quota program was costly to consumers and U.S. industrial firms competing with producers in Western Europe who paid less for oil. It also transferred income to international oil companies. The existing high degree of self-sufficiency in energy (eighty-five to ninety percent from domestic or overland foreign sources) meant that the United States did not require import quotas for security in the short run, while the resulting increase in domestic production depleted domestic reserves faster than otherwise would have been the case. United States long-term security would have been better promoted by leaving our oil in the ground and importing more from abroad.

OPEC

During the 1960s and 1970s, the major oil producing countries greatly increased their control over production and export prices, and over their share of oil revenue. In September 1960, the five largest oil exporting countries representing eighty percent of world oil exports, formed the Organization of Petroleum Exporting Countries (OPEC) and achieved considerable policy coordination in negotiating with international oil companies. Following the Six-Day War of June 1967 between Israel and Egypt, Jordan, and Syria, the Suez Canal was again closed. The Arab members of OPEC, except Algeria and Libya, stopped shipping oil to Britain and the United States in retaliation for their support of Israel. The boycott failed because oil shipments could be rerouted. A series of negotiations between the oil companies, which organized the London Policy Group, and OPEC over tax and pricing policies followed, but the producing countries gradually increased their control over prices and their participation in the ownership and control of the assets of the oil companies. The growing world demand for crude in the 1970s and the decline in excess capacity resulted in sharp price increases. Yet during this period the U.S. government maintained a largely noninterventionalist policy, a policy that continued until the inauguration of the administration under Richard Nixon in 1971. Both the oil companies and prominent oil economists, including M.A. Adelman and Walter J. Levy, criticized the lack of action by the Department of State and the failure of the Organization for Economic Cooperation and Development (OECD) to actively oppose the growing power of OPEC.

With the advent of the Yom Kippur War between Israel, Egypt, and Syria in October 1973, the Arab oil producing countries shut off shipments to the United States and cut production by twenty-five percent. The price of crude rose to $11.65 per barrel as compared with $2.18 three years before. The Arab countries demanded that the United States force Israel to withdraw from the Arab occupied territories it had conquered, and respect the legitimate rights of the Palestinians in Israeli territory. President Nixon's response to the oil embargo was an announcement in November 1973 of Project Independence, which was aimed at making the United States self-sufficient in oil by 1985. The SOAL was to be achieved by subsidizing investments in domestic production, imposing fees on imported oil, and developing alternative sources of energy.

U.S. policy toward OPEC vacillated between threats of military intervention, mutual accommodation, and international cooperation. Henry Kissinger, secretary of state under Nixon, sought to arouse both the nation and the world to combat, by military action if necessary, a "monstrous cartel" that threatened Western civilization. The Europeans, who were almost completely dependent on Middle Eastern oil, were more interested in conciliation than in actions that might cut off the oil supply entirely. Also, they were not directly affected by the oil embargo against the United States. As a result of Kissinger's efforts, the International Energy Agency (IEA) was organized by the OECD in November 1974 for the purpose of reducing dependence on Middle East oil, developing alternative energy sources, and oil sharing among the OECD countries in the event of another embargo. This effort did not weaken the resolve of OPEC members to maintain a high price for oil. Kissinger's military threat was a paper tiger, not only because Europe would not have joined in a military action which would have been disastrous for their economies, but also because after the U.S. defeat and withdrawal from Vietnam, the U.S. public would have had no appetite for another overseas adventure. Kissinger turned his attention to reducing United States dependence on oil imports and to various forms of cooperation with the members of the eighteen-nation IEA. President Jimmy Carter's energy plan also was designed to reduce United States dependence on imports, but placed greater emphasis on conserving and stimulating alternative sources by means of tax incentives. President Ronald Reagan's oil policy emphasized stimulating domestic production and building a strategic petroleum reserve.

Petroleum Policy in the Future

It is highly unlikely that the U.S. government would have sent a large army to the Persian Gulf to liberate Kuwait and defend Saudi Arabia against Iraq if the world were not heavily dependent on petroleum supplies from the region. The United States remains fully involved in defending the Persian Gulf from actions by regional or external governments that would threaten oil supplies to the world. Yet serious problems remain that may call for diplomatic or even military action in the future. These include continued threats from both Iran and Iraq, and the potential for an internal revolution in Saudi Arabia.

Some of the issues that faced U.S. policy makers in the past will continue to influence the future: the Israeli-Arab conflict, increasing American dependence on oil imports, and the potential power of OPEC or an Arab oil cartel. European domination of developing countries' oil reserves has been replaced by petroleum nationalization in the producing countries, with the international oil companies serving as contractors and marketers. The economic power of OPEC has been weakened by excess oil capacity and competition among oil-producing countries for market share. The termination of the Cold War has removed the fear of Soviet domination in the Middle

East, and shattered Arab unity caused by the Persian Gulf War has made another oil embargo highly unlikely during the next decade. In addition, OPEC's ability to maintain oil prices during the early 1990s has been waning. These developments have made increasing American dependence on oil imports much less of a security threat. However, conditions could change and U.S. foreign petroleum policy might again become paramount.

RAYMOND F. MIKESELL

See also Egypt; Gulf War of 1990–1991; Iran; Libya; Mexico; Middle East; Oil and World Politics; Oil Companies; Organization of Petroleum Exporting Countries; Russia and the Soviet Union; Saudi Arabia

FURTHER READING

Adelman, M. A. "Is the Oil Shortage Real?" *Foreign Policy* (Winter 1972): 59–107.
Bohi, Douglas R. and Milton Russell. *Limiting Oil Imports: An Economic History and Analysis.* Baltimore, Md., 1978.
Feis, Herbert. *Scene from E.A.* New York, 1947.
Div. of Federal Register. *Federal Register.* Washington, DC: National Archives, vol. 8. 1943.
Ghosh, Arabinda. *OPEC, the Petroleum Industry and United States Energy Policy.* Westport, Conn., 1983.
Karlsson, Svante. *Oil and the World Order: American Foreign Oil Policy.* Totowa, N.J., 1986.
Levy, Walter J. "World Oil Cooperation or International Chaos?" *Foreign Affairs* (July 1974): 690–713.
Mikesell, Raymond F. and Hollis B. Chenery. *Arabian Oil: America's Stake in the Middle East.* Chapel Hill, N.C., 1949.
U.S.G.P.O. *A History of the Petroleum Administration for War.* Washington, D.C.: U.S. Government Printing Office (1946) 276–279.
U.S. Senate, Special Committee Investigating Petroleum Resources. *American Petroleum Interests in Foreign Countries.* 79th Cong., 1st sess., 1946, p. 317.
U.S. Senate, Committee on Foreign Relations. *Multinational Corporations and United States Foreign Policy.* Hearings before the Subcommittee on Multinational Corporations. 93rd Cong., 1st sess., Washington, D.C., January 2, 1975, p. 34.
Young, Arthur M. *Saudi Arabia: The Making of a Financial Giant.* New York, 1983.

OIL AND WORLD POLITICS

Oil or petroleum refers chemically to a number of complex compounds of hydrogen and carbon, the remains of plants and animals from hundreds of millions of years ago, that are found under the ground and are flammable; the precise mixture varies from place to place. Oil is a nonrenewable resource; when it is used, there is no more. Thus, there has always been concern about it running out. We do not know how much more oil is left in the world; it is hard to tell what is under the earth. New technologies increase extraction capabilities, and if the price of oil goes up, more expensive recovery techniques will be used. As a result, projections about future oil supplies

historically have been both wildly divergent and comically inaccurate. We know that the overall supply is limited, but not what the limits are.

The value of oil has varied greatly over time. In the Middle East, one form called bitumen was used from about 3000 B.C. for mortar in walls, waterproofing, drugs, and the basis for "Greek fire," a devastating weapon rather like modern napalm. Throughout most of history, however, oil was little more than a curiosity. It became a resource only recently, when people developed important uses for oil. This resulted in the development of technologies to extract it, refine it into products, and use those products. As technologies changed, the value of oil shifted accordingly. Technological innovation continues, and it is entirely possible that oil may someday again be viewed as worthless.

The price of oil has been the source of great controversy. Should it be priced in terms of the cost of production, cost of substitutes, cost of repairing the environmental damage caused by its extraction and use, cost to future generations of not having the present supply of oil available, or some other criterion? In practice, the price of oil for many years usually was set by oligopolistic pricing, by the major oil companies until 1973 and then by Organization of Petroleum Exporting Countries until 1985. Since then the price has been set in international commodity markets with governments influencing supply and demand.

Aside from price, much of the economic conflict over oil has centered on who should receive the profit. Producer governments own it, oil companies find and market it, and consumer governments provide the market; all claim the profits. In practice, a series of political battles determined the distribution of oil profits, with dominance shifting among these contenders. The value of oil for governments stems from its role in a modern economy and its particular importance for a modern mechanized military force, but this does not by itself ensure its importance in world politics. For example, water is more valuable but less significant internationally because water is more evenly distributed than oil; most countries get adequate supplies domestically. In the case of oil, however, the major known sources of oil are generally outside the boundaries of the consumer countries (with some interesting partial exceptions, such as the United States, Russia, and the North Sea deposits controlled by Great Britain and Norway). This combination of value and distribution has made oil central to international affairs for decades.

1850–1911

The first important modern use of oil was as a source of artificial illumination. For many centuries light within buildings had been provided by candles made of animal fats or sperm whale oil. In the 1850s, however, techniques to refine kerosene from oil or coal, produce kerosene lamps, and drill for oil were developed and applied in Pennsylvania, which soon became the world production center of kerosene. Kerosene very quickly became the standard source of artificial illumination worldwide (roughly half of U.S. kerosene production was exported as early as 1870). The oil business was easy to enter and was composed of many small companies until John D. Rockefeller, Sr., created the Standard Oil Company in 1870, the first great oil company in the United States and one of the first major multinational corporations to own all stages of drilling, transporting, refining, and selling oil through vertical integration. Its dominance of the industry seemed complete, but it proved to be temporary. New discoveries in California, Texas, Russia, the Dutch East Indies, and Mexico created corporate competition, and political opposition to monopolies within the United States resulted in the dissolution of the Standard Oil Company in 1909. Through the first decade of the twentieth century the oil companies dominated the industry; governments were primarily concerned with oil's economic aspects, and it was treated like any other commodity. That was about to change.

1911–1939

The development of the electric light by Thomas A. Edison about 1880 completely undercut the basic market for kerosene, but at just about the same time, a new use for oil appeared—fuel for ships and vehicles. Naval vessels powered by fuel oil were faster and had greater range while using fewer personnel than those driven by coal. The British and U.S. fleets began to convert to oil in 1911. The development of the automobile, propelled by the internal combustion engine powered by gasoline, created another new market. During World War I oil was critical for land and sea warfare: propelling cars, trucks, and ships for transportation and fighting machines like the airplane, the tank, and warships. Germany had no oil of its own, and oil shortages were one reason it sued for an armistice in 1918. Guaranteed access to oil was clearly essential for a major power, and government attitudes toward oil changed fundamentally.

As oil became a strategic resource for consumer governments, reliable supplies became essential. The usual response was to ensure that companies owned by their own nationals controlled supplies and distribution. In fact, this strategy did not always guarantee privileged access to oil, as later demonstrated during the Arab oil embargo of 1973–1974. Nonetheless, this logic escalated the competition among oil companies into competitions among governments. Thus, the U.S. government tried to obtain oil concessions after the war for its companies by competing with Great Britain and France in Iraq, with the Dutch in the Dutch East Indies (now Indonesia), and with Great Britain in Saudi Arabia, Bahrain, and Kuwait. The result was a series of consortiums in which U.S. oil companies cooperated with those from other countries.

Such agreements guaranteed access to oil for U.S. corporations but also reduced competition between the major oil companies. Oil production increased late in the 1920s with new discoveries. In the 1928 Achnacarry Agreement the major companies agreed to not compete with one another and to set the world price of oil in terms of U.S. production costs, which guaranteed high profits because other sources were much cheaper. State governments, particularly Texas, limited production, also keeping prices up. The U.S. government was divided on the issue but usually preferred foreign access for U.S. firms, even at high prices, to competition.

During the interwar period, producer governments became important players. Previously, the producer governments, many of which were remote and undeveloped countries unable to develop their resources themselves, simply gave out oil concessions to various corporations and hoped to make money on them. Typically, foreign investment for natural resources in poor countries can get good terms initially but, after discovery and capital investment, the government of the producing country becomes more concerned about where the profits are going and conflict with the developer company becomes much more likely. The consumer government sometimes winds up caught in the middle, wanting "its" company to have the oil but unwilling to totally alienate the government for foreign policy reasons. In such situations the U.S. government was often unwilling to support its companies too forcefully.

After the Bolshevik Revolution of 1917, the new Soviet government nationalized its oil industry, refused to compensate its former owners, and withstood severe pressures to reverse these steps, including limited military intervention as well as extensive diplomatic and economic pressure from consumer governments and the oil companies. The Soviet experience demonstrated the potential power of producer governments, and the Soviet Union soon became a major oil exporter.

For the United States the most intense conflict over the nationalization issue took place in Mexico. The first large strikes of Mexican oil were made by U.S. and British companies before World War I, just as the Mexican Revolution (1911–1927) was beginning. In 1917 Mexico declared that oil in the ground belonged to the state, not the land owner. A tentative compromise allowed foreign companies to establish an oil industry there, but the dispute inflamed relations between the U.S. and Mexican governments over the next two decades, and war seemed a possibility at times. During World War I the U.S. government was worried about dri-

TOP 10 PRODUCERS OF PRIMARY ENERGY, BY SOURCE, 1993

Crude Oil[1]

(thousand barrels/day)	1993	mid-1996
Saudi Arabia	1. 8,198	1. 8,295
Russia and the Soviet Union	2. 6,730	2. 5,838
United States	3. 6,847	3. 6,401
Iran	4. 3,540	4. 3,685
Norway	5. 3,201	
Venezuela	6. 3,040	
China	5. 2,890	7. 3,160
Mexico	6. 2,673	8. 2,870
Venezuela	7. 2,450	
Norway	8. 2,350	
United Arab Emirates	9. 2,159	9. 2,260
Nigeria	10. 1,960	10. 2,170

Natural gas plant liquids

(thousand barrels/day)	1993
United States	1. 1,736
Saudi Arabia	2. 704
Canada	3. 506
Mexico	4. 459
Russia and the Soviet Union	5. 380
United Kingdom	6. 169
United Arab Emirates	7. 160
Algeria	8. 145
Venezuela	9. 113
Norway	10. 100

Dry natural gas

(trillion cubic feet)	1993
Russia and the Soviet Union	1. 21.80
United States	2. 18.24
Canada	3. 4.96
Netherlands	4. 3.11
United Kingdom	5. 2.31
Turkmenistan	6. 2.13
Algeria	7. 1.98
Indonesia	8. 1.85
Uzbekistan	9. 1.58
Saudi Arabia	10. 1.27

Coal[2]

(million short tons)	1993
China	1. 1,293
United States	2. 945
Russia and the Soviet Union	3. 336
Germany	4. 315
India	5. 291
Australia	6. 246
Poland	7. 214
South Africa	8. 201
Kazakhstan	9. 123
Czech Republic	10. 88

Hydroelectric power[3]

(billion kWh)	1993
Canada	1. 319.1
United States	2. 258.2
Russia and the Soviet Union	3. 220.0
Brazil	4. 225.0
China	5. 143.1
Norway	6. 117.8
Japan	7. 90.4
India	8. 68.0
Sweden	9. 75.5
France	10. 63.4

Nuclear electric power[4]

(billion kWh)	1993
United States	1. 610.3
France	2. 350.2
Japan	3. 234.0
Germany	4. 145.8
Russia and the Soviet Union	5. 116.9
Canada	6. 88.6
United Kingdom	7. 81.0
Ukraine	8. 75.2
Sweden	9. 58.7
Korea, South	10. 55.2

Geothermal, Solar, and Wind Electric Power Generation[5]

(billion kWh)	1993
United States	9.6
Brazil	7.5
Phillipines	5.4
Mexico	5.0
Italy	3.5
New Zealand	2.0
Japan	1.6
United Kingdom	1.5
Australia	1.0
Denmark	1.0

[1] Includes lease condensate.
[2] Includes anthracite, subanthracite, bituminous, subbituminous, lignite, and brown coal.
[3] Includes both utility and nonutility sources. Data are reported as net generation as opposed to gross. Net generation excludes the energy consumed by the generating unit and excludes generation from pumped storage.
[4] Includes both utility and nonutility sources. Data are reported as net generation as opposed to gross. Net generation excludes the energy consumed by the generating unit.
[5] Includes both utility and nonutility sources. Data are reported as net generation as opposed to gross. Net generation excludes the energy consumed by the generating unit.

Sources: *International Energy Annual 1993*. ©1993 by the Energy Information Agency; *International Petroleum Statistics Report September 1996*. ©1996 by the Energy Information Agency.

ving Mexico toward Germany and was later pressured by its investors in Mexico who feared reprisals. Eventually, Washington proved unwilling to go beyond diplomatic and economic pressure to support its oil corporations, so the oil companies agreed to Mexico's terms. In 1938 the dispute escalated when Mexico nationalized the oil companies after a wage dispute, politically an immensely popular decision in Mexico. The oil companies embargoed Mexican oil; Mexico sold some oil to Nazi Germany, Fascist Italy, and Imperial Japan. The British government supported it own company, Shell, so strongly that Mexico broke diplomatic relations. The U.S. government, under President Franklin D. Roosevelt, was again concerned about German influence in Latin America and was reluctant to alienate the Mexican government. It applied diplomatic and economic pressures rather unevenly and attempted to resolve the dispute. Eventually the oil companies received some compensation, but the expropriations remained and an important precedent had been set.

World War II

Oil played a central part in the outbreak, development, and outcome of World War II. Neither Germany nor Japan had a reliable supply of oil, and both governments resolved to remedy the situation; some of their actions led to war. Germany developed an impressive synthetic oil capability, making oil from coal by a complex chemical process that by 1939 produced about half of its oil and almost all of its aviation gasoline. In addition, in 1940 Germany gained access to Romania's major oil resources and facilities through a political alliance. Germany invaded the Soviet Union in 1941 in part to gain control of the oilfields in the Caucasus region, and Adolf Hitler refused to abandon this objective and concentrate on Moscow as his generals wanted. One of Germany's objectives in North Africa was to reach the oil fields in Iraq and Iran. Hitler's last great offensive in Europe, the attack in the Ardennes in 1944 known as the Battle of the Bulge, was motivated in part by a desire to capture Allied oil supplies. None of these objectives were reached, in part because oil shortages plagued the German military throughout the war, especially after the Allies bombed the synthetic fuel plants and Soviet troops captured the Romanian oil fields. By the end of the war, the German war machine was unable to function because of a lack of oil.

The Japanese situation was even worse; they had less success with synthetic fuel and no allies with oil. Indeed, before the war they imported oil primarily from the United States. Their remedy was to control the oil fields in the Dutch East Indies. The U.S. government was deeply divided on the issue, with some members advocating strong resistance to Japanese conquests and others con-

tending that the United States simply could not fight Germany and Japan at the same time. As Japan became more aggressive, domestic pressure increased in the United States to embargo oil shipments to Japan, which was done in July 1941. The Japanese government decided to attack the Dutch East Indies; unwilling to leave the U.S. naval threat on its flank, it first attacked the U.S. Pacific fleet at Pearl Harbor in Hawai'i on 7 December 1941. Ironically, although the attack destroyed many U.S. ships in the harbor, the oil supplies for the entire Pacific Fleet, in surface tanks near the harbor, were untouched. Japan conquered much of Southeast Asia, including the oil fields, but U.S. submarines made it very difficult for the Japanese to transport the oil. The Japanese navy and air force eventually had insufficient fuel for training purposes, and the kamikaze system of suicide attacks was developed in part to save gasoline.

Great Britain faced similar problems of oil transportation when German submarines devastated U.S. and British tankers during 1942 and 1943, but the Allies eventually developed new techniques to attack the submarines. While British survival was not again threatened directly, oil remained a central part of the Allied strategy. By 1940 the United States was responsible for nearly two-thirds of the world's oil exports. Increased domestic production during the war supplied its civilian population, its armed forces, and its allies, in particular Great Britain. However, this was the high point of oil export by the United States.

1945–1970

After World War II oil use increased dramatically everywhere, but new discoveries in the United States did not keep pace. Europe could no longer be supplied from the United States alone. The Middle East was clearly the major production area of the future, even though it was far from the consumer countries, vulnerable to attack from the Soviet Union, and internally unstable. U.S. foreign policy therefore faced a whole new set of political issues.

The question of Palestine was a major dilemma for the U.S. government. There was strong domestic pressure to support the establishment of a Jewish state, Israel, both from Jewish interest groups and from many other Americans reacting to the horrors of the Holocaust. Such support, however, would clearly risk access to Arab oil because those governments were bitterly hostile to a Jewish state. President Harry S. Truman decided to support Israel. The immediate consequences were not severe, but the issue would become more difficult later on.

While the demand for oil increased greatly in the two decades after World War II, the supply increased even more, as new, mammoth oil discoveries were made all

WORLD CRUDE OIL PRODUCTION, 1960–1995
(million barrels per day)

	1960	1970	1975	1980	1985	1990	1993[a]
OPEC							
Indonesia	0.41	0.85	1.31	1.58	1.33	1.46	1.52
Iran	1.07	3.83	5.35	1.66	2.25	3.09	3.64
Iraq	0.97	1.55	2.26	2.51	1.43	2.04	0.56
Nigeria	0.02	1.08	1.78	2.06	1.50	1.81	2.03
Saudi Arabia[b]	1.31	3.80	7.08	9.90	3.39	6.41	8.23
Venezuela	2.85	3.71	2.35	2.17	1.68	2.14	2.75
Other OPEC[c]	2.06	8.59	6.87	6.91	4.79	6.52	7.75
Total OPEC	8.69	23.41	26.99	26.78	16.35	23.47	23.48
Non-OPEC							
Canada	0.52	1.26	1.43	1.44	1.47	1.55	1.81
China	0.10	0.60	1.49	2.11	2.51	2.77	3.02
Mexico	0.27	0.49	0.71	1.94	2.75	2.55	2.62
United Kingdom	d	d	0.01	1.62	2.53	1.82	2.49
United States	7.04	9.64	8.37	8.60	8.97	7.36	6.53
Russia and the Soviet Union	2.91	6.99	9.52	11.71	11.59	10.98	2.49
Other Non-OPEC[e]	1.43	3.50	4.30	5.41	7.82	10.07	13.51
Total World	20.96	45.89	52.83	59.60	53.98	60.57	62.23

[a]Preliminary.
[b]Includes about one-half of the production in the Neutral Zone between Kuwait and Saudi Arabia.
[c]Includes Algeria, Ecuador, Gabon, Kuwait, Libya, Qatar, and United Arab Emirates.
[d]Less than 5,000 barrels per day.
[e]Ecuador; which withdrew from OPEC on 31 December 1992, is included in "Non-OPEC" for all years shown in this table.

Sources: *International Petroleum Statistics Report, September 1996*. ©1996 by the Energy Information Agency; *Annual Energy Review 1991*. ©1991 by the Energy Information Agency.

over the world. Between 1945 and 1972, U.S. oil production almost doubled, but its share of total world production fell from two-thirds to one-quarter. Production in the Middle East increased fifteen times during the same period. As the Soviet Union recovered from World War II, it once again became a major oil exporter. Moreover, Middle Eastern oil was incredibly cheap to produce, often pennies a barrel. All these factors kept oil prices low. In the consumer countries, cheap oil both drove economic expansion and encouraged the displacement of coal by oil as an energy source, increasing dependence on oil. The producer governments, however, found their revenues dropping even as their production rose, which increased nationalist pressures on foreign oil companies. Cheap oil posed problems for the consumer governments as well. In the United States, it threatened the domestic oil industry, whose production costs were much higher than those in areas like the Middle East. The resulting pressure for limits on oil imports was resisted by the major oil companies and by President Dwight D. Eisen-

hower. Nonetheless, a system of oil import quotas was established in 1959.

Not surprisingly, the producer governments asked for a larger share of the profits. The principle of dividing profits evenly between the oil company and the producer government was established in Venezuela during World War II and spread to the Middle East. The U.S. government did not support the oil companies in opposing these changes. No one wanted to repeat the trauma of Mexican nationalization in Venezuela, and the Department of State was concerned about regional stability and oil supplies in Middle Eastern countries, especially in Saudi Arabia.

In Iran, however, British Petroleum (BP) was reluctant to move to equal sharing and was very unpopular locally. In 1951 Iran, under Mohammad Mosaddeq, nationalized the BP holdings. The U.S. government wanted BP to negotiate a new agreement because it feared communist influence if Mosaddeq failed; the British government wanted to remove him. The major oil companies refused to buy Iranian oil, and their embargo undermined the Iranian economy. After two years of failed negotiations, and Mosaddeq's ouster of the pro-Western shah, the new administration of President Dwight D. Eisenhower launched a successful covert operation, in cooperation with Great Britain, to overthrow Mosaddeq and restore the shah. This time nationalization had been reversed. The oil concession was given to a new consortium of the major British, U.S., and French oil companies, and the challenge of the producer governments seemed to have been met. This turned out to be an illusion.

The next challenge came from a transit government, Egypt. The largest Arab country had no oil, but the Suez Canal, through which much Middle Eastern oil flowed, was within its territory, although controlled by a British-French company. The new Egyptian leader Gamal Abdel Nasser, who came to power in 1954, wanted to unite the Arab people under his leadership. When Western governments refused to sell him weapons, he turned to the Soviet bloc. In retaliation, the United States cut off aid for the Aswan High Dam, which was to be the center-piece of Egyptian development. Nasser, in turn, nationalized the Suez Canal in 1956. The canal was important both as a symbol and as the artery for roughly two-thirds of oil going from the Middle East to Europe. The British, French, and Israeli governments attacked Egypt on 31 October 1956, assuming that the U.S. government would acquiesce and would supply oil if the canal was closed. Both assumptions were wrong; President Eisenhower was furious and, when the Egyptians closed the canal by sinking ships in it, the United States refused to help its allies with oil. Saudi Arabia embargoed Great Britain and France, and Syria shut down the pipeline from Iraq to the Mediterranean. Great Britain, France, and Israel were forced to withdraw their forces from the canal. Since the canal was still closed, governments and corporations in Europe and the United States cooperated to supply Europe from the Western Hemisphere again temporarily. By April 1957 the Suez Canal had opened again, firmly under Egyptian control; Egypt was getting the revenue and, more important, had demonstrated that it could defy the consumer governments.

After the Six-Day War of 1967 between Israel, Egypt, Syria, and Jordan, in which Israel reached the Suez Canal and gained control of the neighboring Sinai Peninsula, several Arab governments embargoed oil shipments to the United States and Great Britain. Saudi Arabia and Libya stopped production entirely, and the pipelines and the Suez Canal were closed. This time the oil companies changed shipping methods, using new supertankers to ship oil around Africa instead of through the Suez Canal, and drew on the stockpiles and oil reserves in the ground in the United States. The Arab states lost revenue and had no real impact on policy; the oil weapon had not worked.

Meanwhile, the troublesome issue of money would not go away—who should benefit from the sale of oil? As the market prices were driven down by new supplies of oil, the revenues of the producer governments declined. In response they created the Organization of Petroleum Exporting Countries (OPEC) in 1960. It had relatively little impact for some years because of even more oil discoveries and internal disputes and seemed ineffective, but it was a portent of things to come.

1970–1980

As long as supply exceeded demand, prices continued to drop and producers had little leverage, but by the end of the 1960s the situation was changing. Demand continued to increase; the number of automobiles continued to grow; oil was cheaper and cleaner than coal; and prices had been low for a long time. Oil supplied about one-quarter of the energy used in Western Europe in 1955 and about two-thirds by 1972. Increases in supply started to lag, however, and low prices discouraged exploration. New discoveries like those in Alaska and the North Sea were slow to come on line because they were physically inaccessible, although they were politically secure. Moreover, a major new political movement called "environmentalism" questioned the whole idea of basing an economy on burning nonrenewable resources.

Another major change was that oil production within the United States peaked in 1970 and declined thereafter. The United States began to relax its quotas to allow more imported oil to enter the country; by 1973 one-third of the oil consumed by the United States was imported. The U.S. surplus capability, which had defeated Arab sanctions in 1956 and 1967, was gone. The producer governments thus were able to obtain more of the profits from the consumer oil companies and governments.

The revolutionary government of Libya that seized power in 1969 applied pressure to Occidental Petroleum, which got most of its crude oil from Libya. When Occidental agreed to a new contract in 1970, Iran and other producer governments demanded more concessions from other companies. This whipsaw technique drove oil prices from $1.80 a barrel in 1970 to $3.01 in early 1973. As the producer governments strengthened their position on price, they raised the issue of ownership again. Nationalization of the local oil was immensely popular in the producer countries. In 1970 OPEC declared that producers should take twenty percent equity in the oil operations of companies, rising to fifty-one percent over time. A number of countries (including Venezuela, Algeria, Iraq, and Libya) moved faster, and the general direction was clear.

The U.S. government did not strongly oppose nationalization. Oil prices did not seem very important, and higher prices would encourage conservation. More important, Great Britain in 1971 had ended its military commitments "east of Suez," in particular in the Persian Gulf, where it had been the guarantor of security for the many weak oil states and principalities. The United States, in the midst of the Vietnam War, was in no position to replace the British by making military commitments in the Persian Gulf. Instead, it decided on a "twin pillars" policy, to support Iran and Saudi Arabia as friendly regional powers. Thus, the United States did not want to fight Iran and Saudi Arabia on behalf of the oil companies. It also understood that oil nationalization was an important domestic issue for the producer governments and much preferred conservative, pro-Western governments in power, even with higher oil prices and the nationalization of holdings of U.S. oil corporations, to more radical regimes.

On 6 October 1973 Egypt and Syria attacked Israel. Within a week, Israel needed massive weapons shipments in order to continue fighting. The Soviet Union was supplying Egypt and Syria, and the United States did the same for Israel. In retaliation, most of the Arab oil states invoked the oil weapon: they restricted oil shipments (embargoing the United States and the Netherlands entirely and reducing shipments to other states, depending on their position in the Arab-Israeli dispute) and reduced production so the embargoed states could not simply buy their oil on the world market. Unlike 1967, supplies were very tight, and there were no U.S. reserves. The shock to the consumer countries was enormous; the very basis of their economies and societies seemed threatened. Long lines appeared at gasoline stations in the United States, the center of the automobile culture. The chief of police in Tokyo warned of possible rioting. The Organization for Economic Cooperation and Development (OECD) had earlier agreed on an oil-sharing plan, but when the Netherlands asked that it be put into effect, its European partners refused.

The oil companies shifted deliveries and schedules so that Arab oil went to appropriate customers and oil from other sources went to embargoed countries. The effect was to share the pain; all customers had their deliveries reduced by about fifteen percent. Thus, while the companies abided by the embargo requirements, they effectively undercut it, because customers could not get more oil by adopting the Arab position on the Arab-Israeli dispute.

The Arab governments allowed all this to go on. It is interesting to speculate how the companies would have responded to a demand from the Arab governments that they not shift non-Arab oil deliveries on pain of having their concessions nationalized. It is also intriguing that the Arab governments never issued such an ultimatum.

This first oil shock had a major economic impact. The Arab OPEC members raised the barrel price of oil to $5.11 in October, a seventy percent increase. Moreover, they did it unilaterally, without consulting the oil companies, symbolizing a power shift. Iran and other non-Arab OPEC states did not join the embargo and the production cutbacks, but they took advantage of them to maintain the October price increase and then boost the price to $11.65 in December. The price of oil had increased four times in a few months. The resulting shock waves in Western economies caused a worldwide recession and inflation. The countries that suffered most, ironically, were not the ostensible targets of the oil weapon but the underdeveloped countries that had to pay higher prices for oil and for industrial products made with oil.

The impact of the oil weapon on U.S. foreign policy is less clear. The Arab oil weapon had been tied to a set of political demands, although their precise nature varied depending on who claimed to be speaking for the Arabs, primarily to force Israel to return territories captured in 1967, to establish a Palestinian state, and to alter the status of Jerusalem. (Qadaffi reportedly suggested that Europe be required to convert to Islam.) Clearly the United States was the only country that could possibly accomplish any of this, but in fact it is hard to find any major changes in U.S. foreign policy as a result of the oil weapon.

Before the oil weapon, the United States had advocated negotiations leading to a "land for peace" settlement, in which Israel would withdraw to its 1967 borders, with some possible adjustments, in exchange for a peace agreement with the Arabs. Secretary of State Henry Kissinger negotiated the Sinai disengagement agreements between Egypt, Syria, and Israel, and the oil weapon was lifted. President Jimmy Carter pursued the same goals through the Camp David meetings that resulted in the Egyptian-Israeli treaty of 1979. The treaty met only the first of the three Arab demands of 1973 and was in fact roundly condemned by them. On balance, then, the oil weapon may have made the issue more important for the United States, but it does not seem to have changed U.S. foreign policy, nor that of other industrial countries, even Japan, which seemed the perfect target.

The balance between producer governments and major oil companies, however, shifted fundamentally. Producer governments now produced the oil (often by hiring the companies on service contracts) and sold it to the major oil companies, which could transport and either market it directly in the consumer countries or sell it through third party agreements to independent or state-owned oil companies. OPEC, not the major oil companies, set oil prices. In response, the companies developed production areas that, although more expensive, seemed more politically reliable, such as Alaska, the North Sea, and Mexico.

As the producers became dominant, however, divisions among the producer governments became clearer. One group (Iran, Iraq, Nigeria, Venezuela, and Indonesia, joined by Libya for noneconomic reasons) had substantial populations (and therefore substantial economic needs) and relatively small reserves. Its members wanted high prices to meet their pressing domestic needs. Other countries with small populations and large reserves (Saudi Arabia, Kuwait, and the United Arab Emirates) did not need much revenue immediately and wanted prices kept relatively low to discourage the development of substitutes for oil that would undercut their long-term markets. The immediate effect of these differences was to hold oil prices roughly stable after the leap of the first oil shock.

Just when things seemed to be stabilizing, the shah of Iran was overthrown by a revolution in 1979. Iranian oil production stopped without warning, producing the second oil shock. While the actual shortfall was only about five percent of world production, panic gripped the industry. Instead of a few major oil companies that could juggle oil between themselves, many buyers competed for a smaller supply. As prices rose, the majors canceled their long-term third party contracts, adding new and urgent buyers to the ranks. The competition drove prices up from about $12 a barrel to about $34. Gasoline lines returned. Then Iranian militants took the personnel of the U.S. Embassy in Tehran as hostages, and the panic intensified; oil was quoted at $50 a barrel.

The Price Collapse of the 1980s

The astronomical prices did not last. Instead, they reduced demand by triggering inflation, which led to a worldwide recession, reducing energy consumption. As oil became expensive, the consuming countries suddenly discovered that they did not need as much of it. In the period following World War II, one percent growth in economic output required roughly one percent growth in energy consumption in the Western countries. Conservation changed the ratio to 0.6 or 0.7. High prices also encouraged the substitution of other fuels, such as coal, natural gas, and nuclear power, although synthetic fuels turned out not yet to be economically competitive; world oil consumption actually declined from 1979 to 1984. The prices also drove up oil exploration, discoveries, and production in non-OPEC areas, such as Alaska, Mexico, the North Sea, and Angola, and old oilfields could suddenly be profitable again. Even the outbreak of the Iran-Iraq War in 1980, which removed Iraqi oil from the world market, did not cause a third oil shock. By 1982 OPEC found it necessary to limit production to try to raise the price of oil, but it ran into the usual problem that besets cartels—each member profits more by increasing its production, which drives down the price. When Israel invaded Lebanon in 1982, Arab states did not attempt to use the oil weapon because there was an oil glut.

The ultimate result was a price collapse, the third oil shock; in 1985–1986 the price of oil fell from $31 a barrel to $10. This revealed an ambivalence in the United States about oil prices, because the country is both the world's largest importer of oil (thus benefiting from low prices) and one of the world's largest producers of oil (thus benefiting from high prices). One immediate result of the third oil shock was the virtual collapse of domestic U.S. oil production. The U.S. government, also concerned that low prices would undercut conservation efforts, was therefore not unhappy when OPEC finally was able to limit production enough to push the price up toward the target of $18 per barrel.

The price collapse had several important and nonobvious consequences. It ended the control of oil prices by OPEC. The increased number of oil producers and buyers and the explosive price changes led to the development of a massive commodity market for oil. OPEC countries could influence that market by manipulating production, but they could no longer dictate price. By 1988 approximately two-thirds of all foreign transactions in crude oil went through commodity markets. The profit centers within the oil industry shifted from production to distribution and marketing. The major oil companies, which were vertically integrated, made the change fairly easily. Independents concentrated in production had a harder time. Some producer governments, led by Venezuela, Libya, Kuwait, and Saudi Arabia, bought marketing networks in the consuming countries to vertically integrate themselves.

The third oil shock also undercut the Soviet economy. Economically, the Soviet Union was a Third World country; it imported finished goods and exported raw materials, primarily oil (it was the world's second leading exporter, behind Saudi Arabia). The oil price collapse thus deepened the economic crisis, which led to the eventual collapse of the Soviet Union and the end of the Cold War, marking the end of an era.

The price collapse also contributed significantly to the international debt crisis. When oil prices soared, bankers and governments loaned money freely to producer countries like Mexico and Nigeria. When the price collapsed, these countries simply could not repay the loans. If the countries defaulted, the world's largest banks would be devastated, threatening a worldwide financial collapse, but if the banks simply wrote off the loans, they might collapse anyway, and who would ever repay debts in the future? The U.S. government worked with banks and the debtor countries to get payments stretched out and some of the debt forgiven.

Meanwhile, the Iran-Iraq war escalated to involve attacks on tankers in the Persian Gulf by both belligerents. In 1987 Kuwait asked for protection against Iranian attacks on tankers going to and from its ports. The U.S. government in response "reflagged" Kuwaiti tankers, making them U.S. vessels eligible for naval escorts and thus committed itself militarily in the Gulf because of the threat of disruption of oil supplies. A series of skirmishes followed, including the U.S. shooting down an Iranian airliner by mistake, until the war ended in August 1988. This war was followed by Iraq's invasion of Kuwait, in part because of low oil prices, in what some have called the "First Oil War." Kuwait itself was a major producer, but influence over Saudi Arabia was the real prize. The United States organized an international coalition through the United Nations to first support Saudi Arabia and then to drive Iraq out of Kuwait. This military activity was justified domestically in terms of access to oil, an argument that eventually was key in overcoming great uneasiness about involvement in the war. The war doubled oil prices briefly when commodity markets proved as vulnerable to panic buying as the former oligopoly, but the underlying glut soon reasserted itself, depressing prices again. Many experts predicted another oil shortage in the 1990s because the low prices halted exploration and increased demand.

Throughout its existence, the Soviet Union held the only major source of oil outside the Western economic system. Because the Soviet Union had its own oil supply it was able to compromise and back down in confrontations with the U.S. over the Middle East, making nuclear war much less likely. Moreover, subsidized oil exports were one of the few economic tools the Soviet government had, and their termination after the Cold War produced considerable trauma in Eastern Europe, Cuba, and parts of Africa.

After the Soviet collapse, oil exports became central to the economies of the successor states, especially Russia. Western oil companies were invited in to undo decades of mismanagement, raising the possibility of a major new world export center to compete with the Middle East. However most authorities thought this unlikely, in the short run because of fierce technical problems and uncertainty about the political and legal environment, and in the longer term because of rapidly increasing domestic demand if economic reforms succeed.

The importance of oil is determined by its value and its distribution, and neither of these had changed much by the mid-1990s. Acceptable energy substitutes had not yet been developed, and the new discoveries that kept the price low were still concentrated in the unstable Middle East. The U.S. continued to import almost half of its oil. In 1995 it appeared that petroleum would remain a central issue in its foreign policy until one or more of these factors changed radically.

ROY LICKLIDER

See also Egypt; Gulf War of 1990–1991; Iran; Libya; Mexico; Middle East; Oil and Foreign Policy; Oil Companies; Organization of Petroleum Exporting Countries; Russia and the Soviet Union; Saudi Arabia

FURTHER READING

Blair, John M. *The Control of Oil.* New York, 1976.
Engler, Robert. *The Brotherhood of Oil: Energy Policy and the Public Interest.* Chicago, 1985.
Kohl, Wilfrid. *After the Oil Price Collapse: OPEC, the United States, and the World Oil Market.* Baltimore, Md., 1991.
Krasner, Stephen D. *Defending the National Interest: Raw Material Investment and U.S. Foreign Policy.* Princeton, N.J., 1978.
Licklider, Roy. *Political Power and the Arab Oil Weapon: The Experience of Five Industrial Nations.* Berkeley, Calif., 1988.
Lieber, Robert J. *The Oil Decade: Conflict and Cooperation in the West.* New York, 1983.
Quandt, William B. *Decade of Decisions: American Policy Toward the Arab-Israeli Conflict, 1967–1976.* Berkeley, Calif., 1977.
Rustow, Dankwart. *Oil and Turmoil: American Faces OPEC and the Middle East.* New York, 1982.
Sampson, Anthony. *The Seven Sisters: The Great Oil Companies and the World They Created,* 4th rev. ed. New York, 1991.
Schneider, Steven A. *The Oil Price Revolution.* Baltimore, Md., 1983.
Spiegel, Steven L. *The Other Arab-Israeli Conflict: Making America's Middle East Policy, from Truman to Reagan.* Chicago, 1985.
Vernon, Raymond A. *The Oil Crisis.* New York, 1976.
Wildavksy, Aaron, and Ellen Tenenbaum. *The Politics of Mistrust: Estimating American Oil and Gas Resources.* Beverly Hills, Calif., 1981.
Venn, Fiona. *Oil Diplomacy in the Twentieth Century.* New York, 1986.
Yergin, Daniel. *The Prize: The Epic Quest for Oil, Money, and Power.* New York, 1991.

OIL COMPANIES

The production of petroleum and petroleum products is dominated by a relatively limited number of companies that are among the largest corporations in the world. A significant number of these are U.S. corporations, and in 1990, for example, they included seven of the top twenty U.S. corporations on the Fortune 500 list. Opinions differ as to why oil companies are such massive operations. One view is that the industry requires it, with immense capital requirements for investment, refining, and marketing, along with enormous costs and risks in exploration. Others contend that monopoly profits have allowed large corporations to ruthlessly drive out smaller competitors. Whatever the reason, the oil companies have always been large, but their roles in the industry and in foreign policy have drastically changed over time.

Monopoly and Standard Oil: 1850–1909

The first modern large-scale extraction of oil occurred in the United States in the late nineteenth century. Corporations were independent and fiercely competitive, while government was relatively weak. The industry was initially composed of many small, competitive companies until John D. Rockefeller, Sr., created the Standard Oil Company by applying several principles, the first of which was vertical integration—the control by a single company of drilling, transporting, refining, and selling oil—in order to control costs and become the lowest cost producer. Rockefeller's other principles included self-financed expansion rather than bank loans, tolerating short-term losses to undercut his competition and survive the vagaries of the business cycle, negotiating lower transportation rates with the railroads, and bringing former rivals into his corporation and using their talents. By 1890 Standard Oil's dominance of the industry worldwide seemed complete, but in fact it was about to end as a result of new oil discoveries and changes in the American political system.

New production centers appeared in Russia, the Dutch East Indies (now Indonesia), Mexico, Venezuela, and Romania, as well as California, Texas, Oklahoma, and Louisiana. These discoveries created new oil companies that Standard Oil was unable to drive out of business or take over, including the precursors of Shell, Texaco, and Gulf. Moreover, in the climate of general concern over the role of monopolies (then known as "trusts") in the United States at the end of the nineteenth century, Standard Oil became a popular target for journalists and politicians. Under President Theodore Roosevelt, who made "trust-busting" one of his major domestic policies, the federal government sued Standard Oil for violating the Sherman Antitrust Act of 1890. In 1909 the Supreme Court dissolved the corporation, breaking it up into corporations that were still central to the oil business as the twentieth century drew to a close: Exxon (formerly Standard Oil of New Jersey), Mobil (Standard Oil of New York), Chevron (Standard Oil of California), Conoco (Continental Oil), Amoco (Standard Oil of Indiana), and Sohio (Standard Oil of Ohio), now part of British Petroleum.

From Monopoly to Oligopoly: The Seven Sisters 1909–1973

Early in the twentieth century, the rapidly expanding use of the internal combustion engine—in automobiles, airplanes, and other new technologies that were of major economic and, eventually, military importance—suddenly made oil a vital strategic material. The U.S. government had dissolved Standard Oil with no concern for its national security implications; in 1909 oil simply was not that important. Within a few years, however, the U.S. government was much less comfortable with simply assuming that oil companies, many of which were foreign, would automatically deliver oil as needed. Some consumer governments created their own "national champion" oil companies (Compaigne Française des

Pétroles (CFP) and later Enterprise de Recherches et d'Activités Pétrolières CEIF-ERAP or ELF by France, for example), or took over existing companies (British Petroleum, BP, by Great Britain) to guarantee their own national oil supplies. Such control was often rather tenuous, but it escalated disputes between oil companies from different countries into disputes between the governments of the consumer countries.

After World War I the United States became convinced it was running out of oil and encouraged existing U.S. oil companies to form consortiums to compete for foreign oil, backing them with its influence. Washington successfully pressured Great Britain and France in Iraq, the Dutch in the Dutch East Indies, and Great Britain in Saudi Arabia, Bahrain, and Kuwait to give U.S. companies access. As a result of these arrangements, the oil industry split into two levels—the major companies and the independents. The major oil companies monopolized Middle East oil, where the concessions were exclusive and no new companies were admitted, and dominated transportation, marketing, and refining in the United States and in other countries. The seven largest companies became known as the "Seven Sisters." (The French CFP also had Middle East concessions but could not match the size of the others.) Each of the Seven Sisters developed a somewhat different personality. Exxon, the largest U.S. company, was perhaps the most diversified, with marketing and production widely spread all over the world, weaker in exploration and often a little short of crude oil. Shell (now sixty percent Dutch-owned, forty percent British-owned) was the only company of the same magnitude as Standard Oil; its divided control and its chronic need for crude oil made it the most international, decentralized, and diplomatically sensitive of the majors. BP (formerly Anglo-Persian, British Petroleum) produced more oil than it could market until it purchased Standard Oil Company of Ohio in the 1960s. The remaining four firms were all based in the United States. Mobil was the smallest of the seven, the best marketer but weaker in production—self-described as "long on brains, short on crude." Standard Oil of California (Chevron) was the discovery company, in particular opening Saudi Arabia and producing a surplus of crude oil. Texaco was the most profitable, as well as the stingiest, most autocratic, and most independent. Gulf specialized in production and shipping and was the least international in terms of marketing, reflecting the preferences of the Mellon family which long dominated it; in 1984 Gulf merged with Chevron and became the first of the majors to disappear.

The new U.S. interest in foreign oil has fundamentally complicated the domestic political situation ever since World War I. Antimonopoly attacks on the majors were very popular politically in the United States, but in organizing U.S. companies for foreign exploration, bigger was better; the large companies had the capital, expertise, and marketing apparatus to compete effectively with companies like BP and Shell. The result was a fundamental conflict within the U.S. government that dominated oil politics for decades. Each side was represented by coalitions between some oil companies and some government organizations. The independent oil companies, which produced oil within the United States, allied with the antitrust division of the Department of Justice and Congress, where their deep involvement in local politics usually offset the greater resources of the bigger companies. The majors, on the other hand, were supported by the Departments of State and Defense, which were more concerned with access to foreign oil. This permanent tension was temporarily resolved by ad hoc decisions by the current president; the resulting policy was often erratic at best.

Immediately after World War I there was no conflict because the United States seemed to be running out of oil, so domestic production and foreign access could both be pursued without driving down prices. By the late 1920s, however, the world was awash in oil. The Soviet Union was selling large amounts and undercutting the oil companies on price. New production in Mexico and Venezuela was accompanied by major new discoveries in Iraq and Iran. Moreover, much of this oil was much cheaper to produce than comparable U.S. deposits, and the independents found themselves at a disadvantage.

The majors responded to the oil glut by agreeing to limit production and restrict competition in two agreements in 1928. In the Red Line Agreement they agreed to develop Middle East oil jointly, restricting production and excluding the independents. At Achnacarry Castle in Scotland they agreed to limit production worldwide to keep the price up, to not compete in marketing, and to set the world price of oil in terms of production costs in Texas, with higher profits from cheaper oil accruing to the companies. They had established a cartel to control world oil supplies and prices, in direct opposition to the desires of consumers and governments. Independents would not be undercut in price by cheap foreign oil, although they were excluded from the Middle East, and the majors would make enormous profits, solidifying the distinctions between these two different groups of oil companies.

For the agreement to work, the world supply of oil had to be held roughly constant with world demand. The Seven Sisters controlled production in much of the world, but not in the Soviet Union or the United States. In 1930 the discovery of the mammoth East Texas oilfields triggered a classic U.S. oil rush. Eventually, the independents encouraged the state governments of Texas and Oklahoma to limit production and push prices back up. Cartels were illegal in the United States, but the

production limitations achieved much the same results. The U.S. government accepted the situation, which was often justified in terms of conserving oil.

Over time the producer governments became increasingly important. At first, they often just gave out oil concessions to various corporations and hoped to make money. This is a fairly typical pattern of foreign investment in natural resources. Initially, investors can get good terms; the producer government has nothing to lose and a good deal to gain. If a discovery is made, the foreign concessionaire must make major capital investments in drilling, transportation, infrastructure, and equipment. Once this investment is made, however, the producer government has a stronger bargaining position, because the investment is not portable, other investors may be willing to compete, and nationals acquire new skills and knowledge. Moreover, the foreign dominance of the economy becomes a domestic political issue, encouraging the government to exercise its bargaining position. Thus, conflict is much more likely at this stage. The consumer government may find this a difficult period. On the one hand, it presumably wants its country's corporations to have access to the resources. On the other hand, it may not want to strain relations with the producer government for foreign policy reasons of its own. In such situations the U.S. government has been increasingly restrained in supporting its companies.

The most intense such conflict involving the United States occurred in Mexico. U.S. and British companies had secured concessions and discovered oil before World War I. The Mexican Revolution (1911–1927) began at about the same time, and it was not surprising that oil and revolutionary politics became intermingled. Originally foreign companies got control of land under which they found oil. But the revolutionary constitution of 1917 said oil was owned by the state, not the land owner. The companies saw this as a damaging precedent and refused to agree. After a prolonged dispute the companies agreed to develop Mexican oil in an uneasy compromise; in 1938 the Mexican government nationalized their investments. The U.S. government, under President Franklin D. Roosevelt, applied diplomatic and economic pressures, but the expropriation stood.

The majors periodically came into conflict with different parts of the U.S. government, although they usually managed to come off fairly well. During World War II, for example, they headed off proposals for the government to purchase the concessions in Saudi Arabia or build and own pipelines in the Middle East. After World War II, the U.S. and British navies protested the policy of setting the world price of oil in terms of U.S. production costs, which raised the price of Middle Eastern oil shipped to Europe to that of Texas oil, even though the former was much cheaper to produce. The issue escalated when the

Marshall Plan spent large sums on oil. Congressional investigations brought calls for antimonopoly suits. The majors eventually agreed to price Persian Gulf oil separately (and lower).

The government itself was often deeply divided on issues. Projects like building the TAPLINE pipeline from Saudi Arabia to the Mediterranean by the majors after World War II were supported by the State and Defense Departments, but were strongly opposed by independent producers in the United States who saw inexpensive Middle Eastern oil as undercutting them. The majors were given priority export licenses for steel and pipe and government support in getting transit agreements with the countries involved. Similarly, the U.S. government agreed to the decision by Chevron and Texaco to invite Exxon and Mobil to participate in the Arabian-American Oil Company, better known as Aramco, in 1947 to produce oil in Saudi Arabia, despite the obvious antitrust implications.

The most fundamental conflict, however, concerned the U.S. position toward the new state of Israel at the time of its founding in 1948 and thereafter. The majors and the foreign policy branches of the government (State and Defense Departments) opposed recognition for Israel because it would anger the Arabs and threaten U.S. access to Middle Eastern oil. They were completely unsuccessful. Domestic political pressure and strong feelings of many decision makers, including President Harry S. Truman, resulted in early and strong support for Israel in 1948 and over the next four decades. The total inability of the world's largest corporations to alter a policy that they see as dangerous and misguided illustrates the limits of their political power in the United States. When the U.S. government is divided on an issue, as it is on this one, policy is often poorly coordinated. Diplomatic decisions (speeches, negotiations) are made by the executive branch, where the opinions of the Departments of State and Defense carry great weight. Economic initiatives, on the other hand, must be approved by Congress, where there is much support for Israel and little for the majors.

The interests of oil companies and the government often conflicted. In 1951 the new, militantly nationalist prime minister of Iran, Mohammad Mosaddeq, with Iranian communist support, nationalized the BP concession in 1951. Although the company involved was British, U.S. oil companies strongly opposed nationalization, cooperated in a boycott of Iranian oil and increased production in Kuwait and Saudi Arabia to make up for lost Iranian oil, undermining the Iranian economy. The U.S. government worried that Mosaddeq might be replaced by a communist ruler and was willing to sacrifice British oil interests to avoid that; thus, it took two years of negotiation among all the parties (and a new president,

Dwight D. Eisenhower) for the U.S. and British governments to decide to overthrow the Iranian government.

After Mosaddeq's ouster the U.S. government wanted to get oil flowing again quickly to strengthen the new regime and encouraged the U.S. majors to join a consortium with BP in Iran. But the U.S. companies did not need Iranian oil, and the political risks of internal revolution and Soviet pressure were clear. At the same time, a major antitrust suit against the majors was developing in the Justice Department. Eventually, the majors agreed to participate in the new consortium, and the suit was reduced from a criminal to a civil action dealing only with marketing rather than production. The Department of Justice had been forced to alter its antitrust policy because of pressures from the government's foreign policy organizations to get the majors to cooperate.

As producer governments gained increased leverage, they pressured the majors for more revenues. During World War II Venezuela had reached an agreement with the majors to share oil profits equally, fifty-fifty, by levying an income tax on the companies, which, under U.S. law, would offset taxes owed to the U.S. government. The effect was to transfer money from the U.S. government to the producer government, allowing the oil companies to make bigger payments without spending any money. Both the policy and the strategy spread to the Middle East after World War II, and the U.S. government acquiesced, despite the considerable loss of income.

The OPEC Era: 1973–1985

Nationalism increased throughout the Third World as former colonial territories became independent states. The major oil companies were seen as foreigners exploiting a local resource and doing little for the countries other than paying off some people in the government. One sign of this was the formation of the Organization of Petroleum Exporting Companies (OPEC) in 1960, the first successful attempt by the producer governments to band together. Its initial impact was minimal, but it foreshadowed major changes.

At the same time, the independent oil companies were increasingly restive at being frozen out of inexpensive Middle Eastern oil. The combination of the producer governments and the independent oil companies created a revolution in the oil industry worldwide. The major oil companies were trying to limit production to keep the prices up and not to compete too much with one another. In order to break into their monopoly on low-cost resources, independent oil companies gave individual Middle Eastern governments a larger share for new concessions, up to seventy-five percent. None of this, however, really changed the situation as long as the terms of the concessions already given to the major oil companies remained intact.

Libya changed all that. It had deliberately given out concessions to many different oil companies, including several independent companies, among them Occidental Petroleum, which had no other major sources of crude oil. In 1970 Muammar al-Qaddafi, who had seized power the year before, demanded that Occidental pay more than fifty percent of is profits to the Libyan government. After Exxon refused Occidental's request to guarantee a supply of crude oil to compensate for Libyan cutbacks, Occidental agreed. Libya then used this to force the other companies, including Exxon, to do the same or lose their concessions. Iran in turn used these gains to get fifty-five percent from the majors in its consortium. Venezuela specified sixty percent. Then Libya reopened negotiations to increase its share again. The oil companies banded together to fight the changes but were not supported by their governments. The price of oil rose more than fifty percent between 1970 and 1973.

Then, in October 1973, war broke out between Israel and its Arab neighbors and the Arab nations imposed an oil embargo on the United States and other supporters of Israel. These events, combined with production cutbacks by the Arab members of OPEC, allowed OPEC to drive the price of oil up explosively and, more important, to set the prices without consulting the oil companies.

The U.S. government had assumed that U.S. corporations would act in the American national interest, but when Arab states applied the oil weapon in 1973–1974, U.S. oil companies enforced the embargo on the United States and made enormous profits from the price increases, mostly because of increases in the value of oil in storage and reserves at the time. The image of the oil companies in the West, never positive to begin with, plummeted. As the oil companies pointed out, however, they found themselves responsible for distributing oil all over the world, in part because no group of governments was prepared to make the decisions. They sent non-Arab oil to the embargoed countries and distributed the cutbacks roughly equally among their customers. While they thus ostensibly enforced the embargo, they also undercut its basic political purpose, because governments that the Arabs classified as "friendly" (Great Britain and France) suffered the same fifteen percent cutbacks as the embargoed ones (the United States and the Netherlands). Even oil companies owned by consumer governments did the same thing; when British Prime Minister Edward Heath tried to pressure Shell and BP into giving Great Britain preference, they refused, and reportedly the same thing happened with French oil companies.

The embargo only lasted a few months but the severe rise in prices and the impact of the oil weapon confirmed a total change in role of the major oil companies. They had lost control of oil production. In 1987 the Seven Sisters controlled only about one-third of their 1973 oil pro-

duction because the OPEC countries had effectively nationalized their oil. From being producers of crude oil, the companies became buyers from the producer governments. In response to this decline, they sold off much of their refining capacity, going from forty-seven percent of world capacity in 1973 to thirty percent in 1987. They had lost the ability to set oil prices, which now was done by the OPEC governments. Their marketing dominance was shaken by increased competition from independent and state-owned oil companies.

As a result of these changes, the major oil companies were no longer major independent actors in international affairs. They could not embargo countries by refusing to buy their oil as in Iran and they could not reallocate oil supplies around the world as in 1973. The majors did not disappear, but they became more like ordinary companies, despite their size and profitability.

From Oligopoly to Market: 1973–Present

Much of this change was not immediately apparent in 1974. After the embargo the majors wound up buying oil from producer governments and selling it to consumers through long-term third-party contracts. Such contracts assumed price and supply stability, as in the past, but OPEC could not maintain stability in the same way that the major oil companies had done. During the second oil shock that followed the Iranian revolution in 1979, the majors were unable to purchase enough crude oil and canceled their contracts. Their buyers, now desperate for oil and inexperienced in the market, drove up the price even more. The experience also contributed to the development of commodity markets in the 1980s, which further undercut the position of the majors in the international marketplace.

The third oil shock—the price collapse of 1985–1986—weakened the oil companies economically; more important, it confirmed the fact that the majors were important for economic rather than political or security reasons. As profits and stock prices dropped, they became attractive targets for corporate raiders, on the theory that their oil reserves were worth more than their stock prices. One such foray by T. Boone Pickens drove Gulf to merge with Chevron in 1984. Even more bizarre was Texaco's purchase of Getty Oil, one of the major independents. Pennzoil, another independent, sued, saying Getty had agreed to accept its offer first, and won a $10 billion judgment. Texaco went into bankruptcy and emerged as a much smaller company. In 1987 the British Conservative government sold the last of its BP stock. After the collapse of the Soviet Union, the successor governments generally invited the oil companies to revive the local oil industries.

National security issues were irrelevant to these transactions. The major oil companies had survived and (mostly) thrived as major economic institutions. They remained powerhouses of technical and marketing expertise. Their political impact, however, had vastly diminished. They were now ordinary corporations, not important independent actors in the international system.

ROY LICKLIDER

See also Iran; Iraq; Libya; Mexico; Middle East; Oil and Foreign Policy; Oil and World Politics; Organization of Petroleum Exporting Countries; Saudi Arabia; Venezuela

FURTHER READING

Blair, John M. *The Control of Oil*. New York, 1976.
Engler, Robert. *The Brotherhood of Oil: Energy Policy and the Public Interest*. Chicago, 1977.
Greene, William N. *Strategies of the Major Oil Companies*. Ann Arbor, Mich., 1985.
Kohl, Wilfrid. *After the Oil Price Collapse: OPEC, the United States, and the World Oil Market*. Baltimore, Md., 1991.
Krasner, Stephen D. *Defending the National Interest: Raw Material Investment and U.S. Foreign Policy*. Princeton, N.J., 1978.
Sampson, Anthony. *The Seven Sisters: The Great Oil Companies and the World They Created*, 4th rev. ed. New York, 1991.
Turner, Louis. *Oil Companies in the International System*. London, 1978.
U.S. Senate Committee on Foreign Relations, Subcommittee on Multinational Corporations. *Multinational Oil Corporations and U.S. Foreign Policy*. Washington, D.C., 1975.
Vernon, Raymond A. *The Oil Crisis*. New York, 1976.
Yergin, Daniel. *The Prize: The Epic Quest for Oil, Money & Power*. New York, 1991.

OKINAWA

One of the Ryukyu Islands in the Pacific Ocean and the site of some of the bloodiest fighting during World War II. Okinawa was occupied by U.S. forces after World War II and developed as a major strategic base for U.S. forces in Asia. Okinawa had been a prefecture (district) of Japan since 1879. Although the U.S. military occupation of Japan ended with the signing of the formal peace treaty in 1952, Okinawa remained under U.S. military administration for an indefinite period. It was a key base for U.S. presence in Asia, especially against the People's Republic of China in the 1950s and 1960s. Within Japan, however, popular pressure increased to see Okinawa returned to Japanese rule. In the 1960s both countries worked closely to fulfill the U.S. peace treaty promise to return all Japanese territories acquired by the United States in war. In June 1968 Iwo Jima and other Bonin Islands were returned to Japan. Partisan political pressure on Japan's pro-U.S. government to obtain reversion of Okinawa grew until November 1969. At that time, Japanese Prime Minister Sato Eisaku and U.S. President Richard Nixon announced the agreement to return Okinawa to Japan in 1972. An agreement was formally signed in June 1971 and carried out the following year. The United States retained the right, however, to station forces there. In the 1990s, about 30,000 U.S. troops occupied twenty percent of Okinawa's land, which was a major source of friction with the local population.

ROBERT G. SUTTER

See also China; Japan; World War II

FURTHER READING

Dolan, Ronald and Robert Worden. *Japan: A Country Study*. Department of the Army. Washington, D.C., 1992.

OLNEY, RICHARD
(*b.* 15 September 1835; *d.* 9 April 1917)

Attorney general (1893–1895) and secretary of state (1895–1897) who declared the United States the hegemonic power in the Western Hemisphere. A graduate of Brown University (1856) and Harvard Law School (1858), Olney became a lawyer in Boston (1859–1874), specializing in corporate law, and served as Massachusetts state representative in 1874. As U.S. attorney general, Olney helped persuade President Grover Cleveland in October 1893 not to send troops to Hawai'i, where the native queen had been deposed by conspirators who sought Hawai'i's annexation to the United States. Olney feared that the new planter regime could be displaced only by actual force, loss of life, and destruction of property. The United States, he declared, had "no right to redeem the original wrong by the commission of another still greater wrong, to wit, the imposition upon Hawaii of a Government not wanted by its people." If the United States failed to restore Queen Liliuokalani by "peaceful methods and without force," he continued, the matter should be referred to Congress, which alone had the authority to declare war. Even then, Olney advised, the White House should undertake no military effort without a royal Hawai'ian commitment to full pardon for the entire provisional regime.

Olney's major crisis as secretary of state centered on the Venezuelan boundary dispute. On 20 July 1895, after Great Britain had rejected arbitration with Venezuela, the secretary of state issued the Olney Corollary to the Monroe Doctrine. In a letter of instruction to Thomas F. Bayard, U.S. ambassador to Great Britain, Olney accused the British of putting Venezuela "under virtual duress," thereby creating a condition that the United States, whose own honor and interests were involved, could not regard with indifference. Owing to its isolation and resources, Olney stated, "the United States is practically sovereign on this continent, and its fiat is law upon the subjects to which it confines its interposition." He continued that 3,000 miles of ocean "make any permanent political union between an European and an American state unnatural and inexpedient." By such a move, Olney sought to remind Great Britain of continued U.S. opposition to any European territorial expansion in the New World.

Cleveland's bold message to Great Britain of 17 December 1896, threatening U.S. intervention in the dispute and the subsequent war scare, renewed calls for a long-considered Anglo-American arbitration treaty. After much jockeying between Olney and the British, such an agreement—the Olney-Pauncefote Convention—was negotiated on 11 January 1897. By its terms, such questions as territorial claims and national rights could go before a tribunal of six arbiters, three from each side, with five needed to declare an award binding. Minor issues would be decided by majority vote. At the same time, each country could cast vetoes on important matters. The British Parliament ratified the convention, but the treaty failed to pass the U.S. Senate by just three votes. The vote was taken on 5 May 1897, just two months after the inauguration of William McKinley as president, and the Republican-dominated Senate contained enough Cleveland foes to defeat the agreement.

When the Cuban insurrection broke out on 24 February 1895, Olney first sided with Spain, but soon doubted that Spain could quell the revolution. On 4 April 1896 he tendered the good offices of the United States to create Cuban autonomy, that is, the island's dominion status within the Spanish Empire. He sought a pacification that would "leave Spain her rights of sovereignty." At the same time, the Cubans must be secure in "such rights and powers of local self-government as they can reasonably ask." Spain declined his offer, finding it a violation of its sovereignty. Madrid, however, did promise reforms as soon as the insurgents laid down their arms.

After he left the secretaryship, Olney returned to the practice of law. Remaining a prominent figure in the Democratic party, he turned down offers from President Woodrow Wilson to serve as U.S. ambassador to Great Britain and governor of the Federal Reserve Board. He did, however, serve from 1915 to 1917 on the Permanent International Commission created in 1914 by the Bryan-Jusserand Treaty with France. Somewhat unfairly, Olney has been remembered more for his Olney Corollary than for his efforts to pursue peace with Hawai'i and Spain.

JUSTUS D. DOENECKE

See also Cleveland, Grover Stephen; Cuba; Hawai'i; Venezuelan Boundary Dispute

FURTHER READING

Eggert, Gerald G. *Richard Olney: Evolution of a Statesman.* University Park, Pa., 1974.
Grenville, John A. S., and George Berkeley Young. *Politics, Strategy, and American Diplomacy: Studies in Foreign Policy, 1873–1917.* New Haven, Conn., 1966.
Welch, Richard E. *The Presidencies of Grover Cleveland.* Lawrence, Kans., 1988.

OLYMPIC GAMES

The world's most important international sports festival, with athletic contests held both in summer and winter. The Olympics have occurred at four-year intervals since 1896, except 1916, 1940, and 1944 when the two World Wars forced their cancellation. The United States has sent athletes to every Olympics, except for the 1980 summer games in Moscow.

Baron Pierre de Coubertin, the founder of the modern Olympic Games, publicly justified the event as a means to build international understanding among the young athletes of the world. Privately, however, the baron hoped that international athletic competition would help reinvigorate his native France physically and spiritually after its defeat in the Franco-Prussian War of 1870. With this nationalist goal at the root of the games, the Olympics quickly became an arena for international confrontation rather than cooperation. Host countries used the games to celebrate their accomplishments and cultures, most markedly in 1936 when Nazi Germany hosted the games. Officiating controversies also revealed the intensity of nationalist feelings surrounding success in the games.

The Soviet Union joined the Olympic movement after World War II, and Soviet athletes first competed in the games in 1952. Western and Soviet journalists immediately cast the games into a Cold War context, using a complicated point system to measure whether the Soviet or U.S. teams had greater success. At the request of the International Olympic Committee (IOC), both countries replaced the point system with a simple medal count in 1960. The games also faced Cold War controversies over allowing teams from West and East Germany, North and South Korea, and Taiwan and the People's Republic of China to compete. The IOC constructed compromises that enabled both Germanies and Koreas to send athletes to the games, but the People's Republic of China did not send a full contingent of athletes to any Olympics until 1984.

Throughout the postwar period, international conflicts threatened to damage the games both through boycotts and by acrimony resulting from questionable officiating. The greatest tragedy occurred in 1972 when a Palestinian terrorist attack led to the death of nine Israeli athletes in Munich.

The reintensification of the Cold War in the 1980s posed one of the most serious threats to the Olympics's future. In February 1980, the U.S. Olympic Committee voted to heed President Jimmy Carter's request that no U.S. athletes attend the Moscow summer games in protest of the Soviet invasion of Afghanistan the previous year. Because of U.S. efforts, over sixty teams declined to send teams to the 1980 Summer Olympics. In retaliation, the Soviet Union and its allies refused to participate in the 1984 Los Angeles games. The successive boycotts led many commentators and officials to question whether

SITES OF SUMMER OLYMPIC GAMES

1896	Athens, Greece	1932	Los Angeles, U.S.	1968	Mexico City, Mexico
1900	Paris, France	1936	Berlin, Germany	1972	Munich, W. Germany
1904	St. Louis, U.S.	1940	Tokyo, Japan*	1976	Montreal, Canada
1908	London, England	1944	London, England*	1980	Moscow, USSR
1912	Stockholm, Sweden	1948	London, England	1984	Los Angeles, U.S.
1916	Berlin, Germany	1952	Helsinki, Finland	1988	Seoul, S. Korea
1920	Antwerp, Belgium	1956	Melbourne, Australia	1992	Barcelona, Spain
1924	Paris, France	1960	Rome, Italy	1996	Atlanta, U.S.
1928	Amsterdam, Netherlands	1964	Toyko, Japan	2000	Sydney, Australia

SITES OF WINTER OLYMPIC GAMES

1924	Chamonix, France	1956	Cortina d'Ampezzo, Italy	1984	Sarajevo, Yugoslavia
1928	St. Moritz, Switzerland	1960	Squaw Valley, U.S.	1988	Calgary, Canada
1932	Lake Placid, U.S.	1964	Innsbruck, Austria	1992	Albertville, France
1936	Garmisch-Partenkirchen, Germany	1968	Grenoble, France	1994	Lillehammer, Norway
		1972	Sapporo, Japan	1998	Nagano, Japan
1948	St. Moritz, Switzerland	1976	Innsbruck, Austria	2002	Salt Lake City, U.S.
1952	Oslo, Norway	1980	Lake Placid, U.S.		

* indicates games not celebrated

Source: ©1996 by the International Olympic Committee. Reprinted with permission of the International Olympic Committee.

the Olympics could survive. The Seoul Olympics, however, saw a record number of participants, with only North Korea and Cuba absent in protest. With the end of the Cold War, the intensity of nationalist feelings surrounding the Olympics seems to have subsided, but has not disappeared.

SHANE J. MADDOCK

See also Afghanistan; Carter, James Earl; Cold War

FURTHER READING
Espy, Richard. *The Politics of the Olympic Games.* Los Angeles, 1981.
Hill, Christopher R. *Olympic Politics.* New York, 1992.

OMAN

A sultanate that lies on the southeast corner of the Arabian Peninsula along the Gulf of Oman and the Arabian Sea. Oman controls a small peninsula at the strategic Strait of Hormuz and dates its independence from the mid-seventeenth century. Since the mid-1740s Oman has been ruled by the Al-Bu Said family. During the first half of the nineteenth century, what was then known as the Sultanate of Muscat and Oman emerged as the strongest regional power in the Indian Ocean (the name was changed to Oman following a palace coup in July 1970 against Sultan Faisal bin Ali al-Said by his son Qaboos

Bin Said, the current ruler of Oman). By the end of the nineteenth century, however, Oman had come under British influence, although the sultanate still retained its independent status. British military assistance proved crucial in helping Oman reclaim the Buraimi Oasis from Saudi Arabia in the early 1950s and to suppress a tribal rebellion, supported by Saudi Arabia, at the end of the decade. British military advisers and Iranian forces helped Sultan Qaboos claim victory in 1976 over a Marxist-oriented rebellion in the Dhofar province, which was supported by the People's Democratic Republic of Yemen (South Yemen).

Since the British military withdrawal from the Persian Gulf region in 1971, Oman's foreign policy orientation has been moderate and pro-West. Although formal diplomatic relations between the United States and Oman were established in 1833 with the signing of a treaty of friendship and commerce, it was not until 4 July 1972 that the United States opened an embassy in Oman and appointed a resident ambassador. Oman is of economic interest to the United States, which is one of the sultanate's major trading partners, because it does possess oil, but Oman is not oil-rich and is the least wealthy of the Persian Gulf states. Washington's primary interest in Oman has been strategic.

Oman has earned a reputation as the most reliable U.S. ally in the Persian Gulf. In 1977 Oman granted the

United States limited air and naval military rights at Masirah Island in the Arabian Sea—just 500 miles from the Strait of Hormuz. Oman was the only Persian Gulf state to endorse the Camp David peace process and not sever diplomatic relations with Cairo after Egypt signed the peace treaty with Israel in 1979. Masirah Island was reportedly used in the failed U.S. hostage rescue attempt directed against Iran in April 1980. In June 1980 Oman formally became a part of the U.S. strategic network in the Indian Ocean region, developed under the aegis of the Carter Doctrine, when Washington and Muscat signed a ten-year base access agreement. Under the original terms of this agreement, Oman received $100 million in U.S. security assistance over a two-year period. By 1990, when the agreement came up for renewal, the United States had provided approximately $1 billion worth of security assistance to Oman. In December 1990 the United States and Oman agreed to renew this arms-for-access arrangement for an additional ten years.

Since the early 1980s Oman has been a key factor in U.S. Central Command (CENTCOM) planning for the Persian Gulf region. Throughout the 1980s the country conducted annual military exercises with the United States. Despite Oman's open strategic partnership with the United States and membership in the Gulf Cooperation Council (GCC), the sultanate maintained a strict neutrality during the Iran-Iraq War (1980–1988). Following Iraq's invasion of Kuwait in August 1990, however, Oman voted in favor of anti-Iraq resolutions at the Arab League, provided military access to U.S. forces, and contributed troops to the frontline GCC force. Given Oman's strategic location at the entrance to the Persian Gulf and its need for foreign assistance and protection, Washington and Muscat have continued to nurture a close military relationship that includes arms sales, joint military exercises, and military access and prepositioning arrangements.

JEFFREY A. LeFEBVRE

See also Camp David Accords; Carter Doctrine; Gulf War of 1990–1991; Middle East; Oil and Foreign Policy

FURTHER READING

Cordesman, Anthony. *The Gulf and the West: Strategic Relations and Military Realities.* Boulder, Colo., 1988.
Gause, F. Gregory. *Oil Monarchies: Domestic and Security Challenges in the Arab Gulf States.* New York, 1994.
Graz, Liesl. *The Turbulent Gulf.* London, 1990.
Kechichian, Joseph A. *Oman and the World: The Emergence of an Independent Foreign Policy.* Santa Monica, Calif., 1995.
Kelly, J. B. *Arabia, the Gulf, and the West.* New York, 1980.
Twinam, Joseph Wright. *The Gulf, Cooperation, and the Council: An American Perspective.* Washington, D.C., 1992.

OPEC

See Organization of Petroleum Exporting Countries

OPEN DOOR POLICY

A policy promulgated by the United States in 1899 and 1900, demanding equal access for American and other foreign nationals to markets in an undivided China. Articulated in two unilateral declarations by a U.S. government struggling to be recognized as one of the major powers in East Asia, the Open Door Policy had long historical roots. The principle of equal trade opportunity rested at the core of U.S. foreign policy from the beginning of the Republic. On several occasions throughout the nineteenth century, European governments had forced the Chinese Empire to make trade concessions. Partly to diffuse the impact of these concessions, China invoked the most-favored-nation principle and accorded concessions to the United States as well. Japan's defeat of China in their 1894–1895 war had repercussions that threatened to limit or even eliminate U.S. trade. Japan annexed the island of Formosa and assumed colonial control over Korea, while Great Britain, France, Russia, and Germany established or strengthened spheres of influence fanning out from key Chinese ports. Meanwhile, the United States, having won the Philippines from Spain in 1898, was aggressively extending its control over the archipelago, which some Americans hailed as a major entrepôt for trade with China.

Urged on by Americans interested in expanding Chinese-American trade, President William McKinley and Secretary of State John Hay decided to take a stand in the summer of 1899. Hay drafted a set of notes asking each nation occupying a sphere of influence to pledge that it would not interfere with the free port within its sphere; that it would allow the Chinese government to continue collecting customs duties at that port; and that all parties would be assessed identical fees and no foreign trader would suffer discrimination within its sphere. Correctly concluding that no single power would acquiesce alone, Hay delivered the first three notes in September 1899 to the British, Russian, and German governments, each of which had recently issued declarations that appeared consistent with Hay's objective. They more or less grudgingly agreed to support free trade access, provided that all the other sphere holders did so as well. Hay then dispatched identical notes to Japan, France, and Italy. In the early spring of 1900, he ignored what he chose to consider minor quibbles in several responses and announced that all the major powers had agreed to maintain an "open door."

Some Chinese were determined to slam it shut. Tacitly supported by the Chinese government, the antiforeigner Boxer Rebellion swept through northern China and engulfed the capital. As several nations, including the United States, mounted a major military expedition to relieve the besieged legation district in Beijing, Hay worried that the foreign troops might not stop until they had established full-scale colonies in China. He therefore dispatched a second Open Door note to the major powers on 3 July 1900, calling on them to "preserve Chinese territorial and administrative entity…and safeguard for the world the principle of equal and impartial trade with all parts of the Chinese Empire." Although the various nations pursued their own interests after the rebellion had ended, the international balance of power prevented any of them from establishing a colony in China.

In subsequent years, the Open Door Policy's twin elements—free access to markets and preservation of China's territorial integrity—remained the cornerstone of U.S. policy in Asia. Other nations formally acknowledged the Open Door tenets in the Nine-Power Treaty that emerged from the Washington Naval Conference in 1922. Secretary of State Henry L. Stimson invoked the Open Door principles as a rationalization for applying his nonrecognition policy to the Japanese conquest of Manchuria in 1932. As a general policy, nonspecific as to region, the Open Door Policy has remained a fundamental tenet of U.S. trade policy.

JOHN M. DOBSON

See also Boxer Rebellion; China; Hay, John Milton; McKinley, William; Manchurian Crisis; Most-Favored-Nation Principle; Opium Wars; Philippines; Stimson, Henry Lewis; Washington Conference on the Limitation of Armaments

FURTHER READING
Cohen, Warren I. *America's Response to China.* 3rd ed. New York, 1990.
Hunt, Michael H. *The Making of a Relationship.* New York, 1983.

OPEN SKIES

President Dwight D. Eisenhower advanced the Open Skies Proposal of July 1955 to enhance security in a world shadowed by nuclear weapons. At a conference in Geneva attended by the leaders of the United States, the Soviet Union, Great Britain, and France, Eisenhower called for reciprocal overflights of military installations by unarmed aircraft to reduce Cold War tensions, lessen the threat of surprise attack, and test the utility of intrusive inspection measures for effective arms control. The proposal promised to deliver a positive political and psychological victory to the United States while penetrating the closed society of the USSR to reveal the momentum of the Soviet nuclear program. Equating national security with total secrecy, the Kremlin rejected the proposal. On 12 May 1989, President George Bush revived Open Skies with a broader, more intrusive version embracing all North Atlantic Treaty Organization (NATO) and Warsaw Pact states. After three years of negotiations, the Open Skies Treaty was signed in Helsinki on 24 March 1992,

opening territory from Vancouver to Vladivostok to aerial inspections for the first time.

EMILY O. GOLDMAN

See also Arms Control and Disarmament Agency; Cold War; Eisenhower, Dwight David

FURTHER READING
Michael Krepon and Amy E. Smithson, eds. *Open Skies, Arms Control, and Cooperative Security.* New York, 1992.
W. W. Rostow. *Open Skies: Eisenhower's Proposal of July 21, 1955.* Austin, Tx., 1982.

OPERATION DESERT SHIELD
See Gulf War of 1990–1991

OPERATION DESERT STORM
See Gulf War of 1990–1991

OPERATION JUST CAUSE
See Panama and Panama Canal

OPERATION MONGOOSE
See Covert Action; Cuba; Intelligence

OPERATION RESTORE HOPE
See Somalia

OPIUM WARS
(1839–1842, 1856–1860)

Conflicts between Great Britain and China that ended in diminished Chinese sovereignty and a stronger British presence, from which U.S. citizens, missionaries, and merchants gained benefits. In 1839 the British went to war with China, using as a pretext the Chinese prohibition of the import of opium; in reality they were seeking to end China's major restrictions on foreign trade and the activities of British merchants. In 1842 British military successes forced the Manchu emperor to accept the Treaty of Nanjing (Nanking), which opened the ports of Guangzhou (Canton), Xiamen (Amoy), Fuzhou (Foochow), Ningbuo (Ningpo), and Shanghai to trade and residence, and ceded Hong Kong to Great Britain. The following year President John Tyler commissioned Caleb Cushing to negotiate a formal treaty with China that would give similar conces-

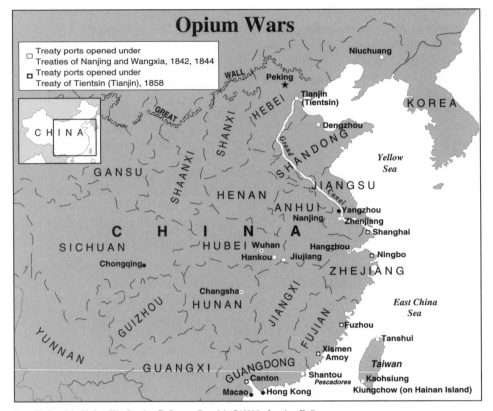

Opium Wars

- ☐ Treaty ports opened under
  Treaties of Nanjing and Wangxia, 1842, 1844
- ◻ Treaty ports opened under
  Treaty of Tientsin (Tianjin), 1858

From *The Search for Modern China* Jonathan D. Spence. Copyright ©1990 by Jonathan D. Spence.
Reprinted with permission of W. W. Norton & Company, Inc.

sions to American citizens. In 1844 Cushing signed the Treaty of Wangxia (Wanghia), which gave the United States the same trade and residence privileges as the British in the five ports and, in addition, a most-favored-nation provision and the right to maintain hospitals and churches in the port cities. Just as significantly, Cushing secured an extraterritoriality guarantee that went further than the one the British had obtained, extending U. S. extraterritorial jurisdiction not only to civil but also to criminal matters.

The Treaty of Wangxia served as the standard for other international treaties until 1858, when it was superseded by the Sino-British Treaty of Tianjin (Tientsin), signed in the midst of the Second Opium War. This treaty provided for the opening of ten additional ports to trade and residency, gave Protestant and Catholic missionaries freedom of movement throughout China, and granted foreigners the right to diplomatic representation at Beijing (Peking). Fighting was renewed when the Manchu court balked at implementing the provision allowing diplomats to take up residence in Beijing, but the Chinese capitulated after an Anglo-French military expedition occupied Beijing and burned the Summer Palace. This resulted in the Conventions of 1860, which reaffirmed the provisions of the Tianjin treaty and grant-

ed additional concessions to Great Britain and France. On the basis of its most-favored-nation status, the United States participated in the negotiations and in 1858 obtained a similar Treaty of Tianjin for the benefit of U.S. merchants and missionaries. Overall, the two Opium Wars and the unequal treaties that resulted from them eased the United States's mid-nineteenth century entry into the international politics of the Asian arena and, without formal U.S. resort to arms, enabled American citizens to obtain the privileges wrested from China by Great Britain and France. The treaties also undercut Chinese sovereignty, weakening China in the face of the rising tide of accelerating imperialism.

EDWARD P. CRAPOL

See also China; Cushing, Caleb; Extraterritoriality; Great Britain; Gunboat Diplomacy; Missionaries; Most-Favored-Nation Principle; Tyler, John; Wangxia, Treaty of

FURTHER READING

Chang, Hsin-pao. *Commissioner Lin and the Opium War*. Cambridge, Mass., 1964.

Fairbank, John K. *The United States and China*. 4th ed. Cambridge, Mass., 1983.

Fay, Peter Ward. *The Opium War, 1840-1842*. Chapel Hill, N.C., 1975.

Hunt, Michael H. *The Making of a Special Relationship: The United*

States and China to 1914. New York, 1983.

Polachek, James M. *The Inner Opium War*. Cambridge, Mass., 1992.

Wakeman, Frederic, Jr. *Strangers at the Gate: Social Disorder in South China, 1839-1861*. Berkeley, Calif., 1966.

OPPENHEIMER, JULIUS ROBERT

(*b.* 22 April 1904; *d.* 18 February 1967)

Physicist, director of the Manhattan Project, adviser to President Harry S. Truman's administration on nuclear and defense matters, director of the Institute for Advanced Studies, and a prominent victim of the McCarthy era. Born in New York City and raised in comfortable circumstances, Oppenheimer was educated at the Ethical Culture School, Harvard University, and the University of Göttingen, where he earned a Ph.D. in theoretical physics in 1927. In 1929 he accepted a unique joint appointment as an assistant professor at the University of California at Berkeley and the California Institute of Technology. In less than a decade he had established Berkeley's reputation as a major center for the study of quantum physics in the United States. In the mid-1930s Oppenheimer became a political activist and a contributor to some of the causes also supported by the Communist party of the United States, including desegregation, better working conditions for migratory farm workers, and the Loyalists in the Spanish Civil War.

In 1942 Oppenheimer joined the top-secret Manhattan Project in Los Alamos, New Mexico, as director of the laboratory responsible for the design and construction of the atomic bomb. On 16 July 1945 the first atomic device was successfully tested in the Alamagordo desert in New Mexico. Less than a month later, the first atomic bomb was dropped on the Japanese cities of Hiroshima and Nagasaki, ending World War II and ushering in the atomic age. Oppenheimer emerged from academic obscurity as "the father of the atomic bomb." Appointed director of the prestigious Institute for Advanced Study in Princeton, N.J., in 1947, he frequently served on government advisory committees, the most important of which was the General Advisory Committee (GAC) to the Atomic Energy Commission (AEC), which he chaired from 1947 to 1952. In the autumn of 1949 the Soviet Union unexpectedly tested an atomic bomb. As a result, physicist Edward Teller, Admiral Lewis L. Strauss, Senator Brian McMahon, and others called for a crash program for the development of a hydrogen bomb. The GAC members unanimously concluded that such a commitment was unnecessary, unwise, and immoral. Although President Harry S. Truman rejected the GAC's advice and authorized work on the hydrogen bomb, resentment of Oppenheimer's continuing influence spread among the U.S. Air Force high command and conservative members of Congress.

After President Dwight D. Eisenhower's election in 1952, Oppenheimer's former communist associations and his opposition to the hydrogen bomb were cited by his enemies as evidence of his unreconstructed sympathy for the Soviet Union. In 1954 a grueling AEC security hearing, distorted by illegal telephone tapes obtained by the Federal Bureau of Investigation and a biased hearing board, led to the removal of Oppenheimer's security clearance. Oppenheimer continued to direct the Institute for Advanced Study and lectured throughout the world on science and education. With respect to the most important issue of the day, the nuclear arms race, he had been silenced by his enemies. In 1963 he received the AEC's Fermi Award for contributions to theoretical physics.

MARTIN J. SHERWIN

See also Atomic Energy Commission; Cold War; Hydrogen Bomb; Manhattan Project; Nuclear Weapons and Strategy; Strauss, Lewis; Teller, Edward

FURTHER READING

Goodchild, Peter. *J. Robert Oppenheimer: Shatterer of Worlds*. New York, 1985.

Stern, Phillip M. *The Oppenheimer Case: Security on Trial*. New York, 1969.

Smith, Alice Kimball and Charles Weiner, eds. *Robert Oppenheimer: Letters and Recollections*. Palo Alto, Calif., 1995.

ORDERS IN COUNCIL

A series of executive decrees issued by the British government between 1807 and 1809, during the Napoleonic Wars, regulating neutral trade with the European continent. The orders were issued in response to France's Continental Decrees, particularly the Berlin Decree (1806) and Milan Decree (1807), which sought to crush Great Britain by ending its trade with Europe. The United States was caught in the middle of this trade war, and the repeal of the European belligerents's restrictions on trade became the paramount objective of U.S. foreign policy in the years before the War of 1812.

Napolean's Berlin Decree proclaimed a blockade of the British Isles, but the blockade—illegal because France did not have the naval power to enforce it—was simply a pretext for excluding from the Continent goods transshipped or produced in Great Britain. Great Britain retaliated with the Orders in Council of 1807, which prohibited neutrals from engaging in the coastal trade of the Continent, proclaimed a blockade of all ports from which goods from Great Britain were excluded, and required neutrals who wished to trade with those ports to stop in England and pay transit duties first. France countered in late 1807 with the Milan Decree, which announced that any neutral vessel submitting to the British Orders in Council or even allowing a British search party to board was subject to seizure. The British issued a new Order in Council in 1809 that reduced the scope of their blockade and eliminated the transit duties. They also issued thousands of licenses that authorized trade with ports that were nominally under blockade. Even so, U.S. merchants found it difficult to trade with Europe without risking seizure by one side or the other. Both Great Britain and France conceded that their restrictions on neutral trade violated international law, but each claimed that it was merely retaliating for the illegal acts of the other. Both belligerents used the trade war as a pretext for looting U.S. commerce. The British seized U.S. vessels on the high seas, while the French confiscated U.S. property in continental ports. Between 1807 and 1812 the two warring nations and their allies seized some 900 U.S. vessels.

At first the United States resorted to trade restrictions in an effort to force the belligerents to give up their war on neutral trade. France responded in 1810 by promising to rescind the Continental Decrees, but Great Britain, rightly suspecting that the French promise was spurious, refused to follow suit by repealing the Orders in Council. The United States responded by imposing new restrictions on British trade in early 1811 and then by declaring war against Great Britain in June 1812. Just as the young Republic was declaring war, the British were rescinding the Orders in Council. Republican leaders later conceded that if they had known that the repeal of the Orders was imminent, they probably would not have insisted on war, but at that time it took weeks for European news to reach the United States, and by then the die was cast.

DONALD R. HICKEY

See also Clay, Henry; France; Great Britain; Impressment; Madison, James; Napoleonic Wars; Neutral Rights; War Hawks; War of 1812

FURTHER READING

Horsman, Reginald. *The Causes of the War of 1812*. Philadelphia, Pa., 1962.
Perkins, Bradford. *Prologue to War: England and the United States, 1805–1812*. Berkeley, Calif., 1961.
Watson, Steven J. *The Reign of George III, 1790-1815*. Oxford, 1960.

OREGON QUESTION

An early nineteenth-century Anglo-American dispute over trade, settlement, and ultimately the possession of Oregon—the vast territory extending from Spanish California to Russian Alaska, and from the Rocky Mountains to the Pacific Ocean. By the end of the 1820s Spain and Russia had relinquished their claims to the territory leaving the status of an area delineated by the 42nd parallel on the South and 54-40° on the North to the wrangling of U. S. and British diplomats. In both the Conventions of 1818 and 1827 those diplomats were unable to settle the dispute and determine to grant open access to the entire ter-

ritory to the citizens and subjects of both nations. There was little need for urgency at the time since the only U.S. post, Astoria (Fort George) was manned exclusively by the British Hudson's Bay Company. After American missionaries, merchants, and others propelled by "Oregon fever," moved in increasing numbers to the territory in the 1830s and early 1840s, however, resolution became critical.

In 1842 a British special commissioner, Lord Ashburton (Alexander Baring), and Secretary of State Daniel Webster met in Washington to resolve this and other issues, but failed to reach a compromise that would ensure both sides essential access to the Columbia River and the harbors of the Juan de Fuca Strait. Their inability to remedy the Oregon problem unfortunately relegated it to the growing American zeal for expansionism generally referred to as "manifest destiny." In 1844 Democratic presidential candidate James K. Polk promised the entire territory to 54-40° if elected and precipitated a diplomatic crisis with Great Britain by proclaiming the United States's "clear and unquestionable" rights to Oregon in his inaugural address in 1845. Although the slogan attributed to Ohio Senator William Allen that threatened "Fifty-Four Forty or Fight!" was not a part of the 1844 Democratic campaign, expansionists in the party helped to force the Oregon issue. After a botched effort at settlement that would have divided the territory at the 49th parallel, both nations talked of war. Polk, however, had no desire for war with Great Britain and so maneuvered the issue into Congress for a face-saving compromise. The astute diplomacy of the British Foreign Secretary Lord Aberdeen, who saw more value in Anglo-American rapprochement than in the Oregon Territory, joined with the political finesse of Senator John C. Calhoun to provide an opening for a negotiated settlement in early 1846. That spring the British minister to Washington, Richard Pakenham, joined with Secretary of State James Buchanan to draft a treaty partitioning the territory. The Oregon Treaty of 1846 established a boundary along the 49th parallel from the Rocky Mountains to the Pacific Ocean preserving to Great Britain all of Vancouver Island and navigational rights for the Hudson's Bay Company on the Columbia River. The United States received the area that now forms the states of Washington, Oregon, and Idaho and portions of Montana and Wyoming.

DONALD A. RAKESTRAW

See also Astor, John Jacob; Buchanan, James; Calhoun, John Caldwell; Canada; Fur Trade; Great Britain; Polk, James Knox; Webster, Daniel

FURTHER READING

Merk, Frederick. *The Oregon Question: Essays in Anglo-American Diplomacy and Politics*. Cambridge, Mass., 1967.
Pletcher, David M. *The Diplomacy of Annexation: Texas, Oregon, and the Mexican War*. Columbia, Mo., 1973.
Ronda, James P. *Astoria and Empire*. Lincoln, Nebr., 1990.

ORGANIZATION FOR ECONOMIC COOPERATION AND DEVELOPMENT

Formed in 1961 as the successor to the Organization for European Economic Cooperation (OEEC), which administered Marshall Plan aid following World War II. The United States played a major role in creating the OECD to foster global economic cooperation, world trade expansion, and the coordination of aid to developing countries. By 1961 Western Europe had recovered from the devastation of World War II and both the European Economic Community and rival European Free Trade Area had been established. The United States foresaw the need to establish mechanisms of Atlantic cooperation to deal with increasing economic interdependence. The United States was also eager to have other industrialized nations share the burden of providing aid to growing numbers of new, developing nations. By 1995 the OECD had expanded to twenty-four members; in addition to the Western European countries, Australia, Canada, Japan, New Zealand, Turkey, the United States and Mexico, the latter after the North American Free Trade Agreement (NAFTA) was approved. As of 1995 OECD members accounted for sixty percent of world economic output and seventy percent of world trade.

The OECD has no operational activities or decision-making powers, but it provides extensive statistical analysis and economic forecasts. The annual conference of the Council of Ministers provides the forum for discussion of those forecasts and of policies to achieve its goals of economic growth and financial stability. The central objective is coordination and collaboration by means of awareness of each country's general approach, combined with the formulation of common or parallel actions where indicated. By directly involving governmental ministers, the OECD aims to influence national policymaking in its formative stage.

The OECD also has a number of subsidiary organs that deal with specific issues. The Development Assistance Committee coordinates the aid programs of major donor countries. The Trade Committee deals with commercial policies and specific trade issues. The Payments Committee deals with matters of invisible transactions and multilateral settlements. The International Energy Agency (IEA), Nuclear Energy Agency, Development Center, and Center for Educational Research and Innovation have evolved into autonomous and semiautonomous organs within the organization's orbit. The IEA played a role in coordinating the policies of the major oil-consuming countries (except for France) in the energy crises of the 1970s and formulated strategies for dealing with future fluctuations in oil supplies. The OECD has also become involved in efforts to assist European countries in transition from socialism, including the Czech Republic, Slovakia, Poland, and Hungary. The Center for Cooperation with the European Economies in Transition acts as a focal point of contact between the OECD and Central and Eastern European countries.

Since the mid-1970s the OECD has successfully harnessed the voluntary cooperation of its members and coordinated action in a number of areas of crucial importance—international trade rules, global capital movements, export credits, and aid to developing countries. By the 1990s, however, major conflicts of interest have emerged among Western European countries, the United States, Japan, and the developing world with protracted low growth in the latter, as well as widespread inflation, rising interest rates, and systemic unemployment. This often resulted in protectionist trade and industrial policies, involving substantial reductions in the levels of official development aid the OECD was able to put together from among its members' financial resources.

U.S. foreign policymakers often refer to the OECD as one of those institutions that would have to be created if it did not already exist. Although the Group of Seven (G-7) summit meetings have emerged as rival settings for economic policy coordination, the OECD remains an important forum for exchanging views, discussing policy choices, and negotiating agreements among the principal developed countries, often in preparation for other international meetings, including the G-7 summits.

Margaret P. Karns

See also European Union

FURTHER READING
Aubrey, Henry G. *Atlantic Economic Cooperation: The Case of the OECD.* New York, 1967.
Camps, Miriam. *First World Relationships: The Role of the OECD.* New York, 1975.
Snowden, P. N. *International Institutions in Trade and Finance.* London, 1981.

ORGANIZATION OF AMERICAN STATES

The successor to the Pan American Union established in 1890, continuing a long tradition of regional cooperation. The Organization of American States (OAS) grew out of the Ninth International Conference of American States in 1948 in Bogotá, Colombia, with the purpose of fostering a commitment to peace, justice, solidarity, collaboration, national sovereignty, territorial integrity, and independence among the nations of the Americas. It is one of the oldest regional organizations in the world. The OAS serves as a forum for consultation and inter-American cooperation on a wide range of issues, including human rights, peacekeeping, and economic, social, and technological development. On an operational level, it provides technical assistance to member states for national and regional research institutes and educational centers as well as fellowships for students and professors. The organizational structure includes the General Assembly, the Meeting of Consultation of Ministers of Foreign Affairs, three councils, the Inter-American Juridical Committee, the Inter-American Commission on Human Rights, and the General Secretariat.

In its early years the OAS focused heavily on matters of peace and security—issues of primary concern to the United States. As the collective defense alliance of the Western Hemisphere, it provided support to the Cold War effort to contain communism. It also lent support to U.S. intervention in Guatemala (1954) and the Dominican Republic (1965) designed to forestall left-wing revolutions and regimes. Cuba was expelled from the OAS in 1962, following the 1959 revolution and evidence of Cuban support for revolutions elsewhere in the hemisphere as well as Cuban ties to the Soviet Union. The United States sought OAS support in isolating Cuba, but no common policy toward the Cuban regime ever emerged; many of the countries that joined the U.S.-led embargo against Cuba reestablished ties with Cuba in the 1970s and 1980s. Nonetheless, Cuba remained outside OAS membership.

In the 1980s and 1990s economic and social development, as well as human rights issues and the development of democratic institutions, came to the fore as Latin American countries sought to make the OAS serve their interests more effectively. The organization's Inter-American Economic and Social Council and its Special Committee for Consultation and Negotiation (CECON) deal with protectionist trade practices and restrictions that are frequently used by the United States and other industrialized countries against many Latin American countries. These agencies also have developed programs to deal with the problems related to unemployment, food shortages, inflationary pressures, and energy crises.

Through the Inter-American Commission on Human Rights the OAS has become closely involved with issues of human rights throughout Latin America. On its recommendation, the United Nations General Assembly created the Inter-American Court of Human Rights, formally established in September 1979 in San Jose, Costa Rica.

In 1991 the twenty-first session of the OAS General Assembly adopted the "Santiago Commitment to Democracy and the Renewal of the Inter-American System," in which signatories affirmed their "inescapable commitment to the defense and promotion of representative democracy and human rights in the region." This clause was invoked after the coup d'état in Haiti and the expulsion of President Bertrand Aristide in 1991. The OAS continually called for the full restoration of law and constitutional order in Haiti, as well as Aristide's reinstatement, while also calling for diplomatic isolation of the Haitian military regime and the suspension of all economic, financial, commercial, and technical ties with Haiti. The OAS, however, was unwilling to authorize intervention in Haiti; it was superseded by the United Nations, which authorized U.S. intervention in Haiti in the fall of 1994.

The OAS also issued in that same session the "Resolution of Representative Democracy," instructing the secretary-general to call a meeting of the Permanent Council in the event of "any occurrence interrupting the democratic, political, and institutional process or legitimate exercise of power by a democratically elected government in any member state." This was invoked in 1992, when President Alberto Fujimori of Peru disbanded Peru's congress and proceeded to rule by presidential decree. Fujimori defied the OAS successfully, and with his program of economic stabilization and privatization, as well as his electoral victory in 1993, was gradually accepted.

The continuation of the OAS's broad range of activities is likely to be affected by domestic economic problems in many countries. In addition, the United States reduced its contribution to the regular budget from sixty-six to forty-nine percent in the early 1990s. Like many other international organizations, the OAS finds itself in the 1990s streamlining administrative operations, decreasing the size of staff, and working to improve its overall efficiency in meeting increased demands.

MARGARET P. KARNS

See also Cuba; Dominican Republic; Grenada Invasion; Guatemala; Haiti; Latin America; Pan-Americanism

FURTHER READING

Ball, Margaret. *The OAS in Transition.* Durham, N.C., 1969.
Farer, Thomas. *The Future of the Inter-American System.* New York, 1979.
Sheman, Ronald L. *The Inter-American Dilemma: The Search for Inter-American Cooperation at the Centennial of the Inter-American System.* New York, 1988.
Slater, Jerome. *The OAS and United States Foreign Policy.* Columbus, Ohio, 1967.

ORGANIZATION OF PETROLEUM EXPORTING COUNTRIES

Organization concerned with coordinating and harmonizing the petroleum policies of its member states, established in Baghdad in September 1960. The Organization of Petroleum Exporting Countries (OPEC) has been a key instrument for less developed oil-producing countries seeking structural change in global energy markets.

Its thirteen members (as of 1995) were Algeria, Ecuador, Gabon, Indonesia, Iran, Iraq, Kuwait, Libya, Nigeria, Qatar, Saudi Arabia, the United Arab Emirates, and Venezuela. Through coordinated actions and policies, OPEC nations have sought to control world oil supplies and prices. By acting together as a producer cartel, OPEC countries gained control over the world's oil markets in the 1970s, increasing their economic rewards and also their political power.

From the end of World War II until 1973, world oil prices continually decreased in both monetary and real terms, and oil importers worldwide became accustomed to low-cost energy sources. The price of oil was set by a cartel of the seven major international oil companies that controlled supply, transportation, refining, marketing, and technology. For some years after OPEC was formed in 1960, neither the oil companies nor Western governments (including the United States) took the new organization very seriously. Between the 1971 Tehran Conference, at which the Persian Gulf oil-producing states met with the major oil companies, and the 1973 Arab-Israeli war, however, the oil supply situation was radically altered. Between 1971 and 1973, the oil-producing countries negotiated the nationalization of production, shifting ownership from the oil companies to governments. The OPEC members then came together to unilaterally increase prices. By December 1973 the price of crude oil had risen from $2 per barrel to $11.65 per barrel, and the Arab oil-producing countries had imposed an embargo against the United States and the Netherlands for their support of Israel in the Arab-Israeli War.

In March 1975, with its "Solemn Declaration," OPEC members affirmed the necessity of creating a new economic order, which they defined as one based on justice, mutual understanding, and genuine concern for the well-being of humanity. OPEC thereby indicated support for the demands of other developing countries for a New International Economic Order (NIEO) and fueled the confrontation in the 1970s between North and South (industrialized nations versus developing nations) over the structure of international economic relations. As part of this commitment to the South, in 1976 OPEC instituted a special fund (eventually converted into the OPEC Fund for International Development) to provide loans for financing balance of payments deficits and development projects in non-oil producing, developing countries that were adversely affected by the rising price of oil, but it proved insufficient for their needs.

OPEC's control over the world's oil markets was to prove relatively short-lived. Its early success was aided by the rapid increases in oil consumption in industrialized countries, and particularly by the increase in U.S. oil imports. Two additional factors in OPEC's success were the industrialized countries' heavy reliance on Middle East and North African supplies and the accumulation of large official foreign exchange reserves by Libya and Saudi Arabia. The latter enabled Saudi Arabia to reduce its own production to maintain overall OPEC quotas, thus controlling supplies. That early success was also aided by the inability of the consuming countries, especially the Europeans and Japanese, to agree on a common policy toward the OPEC producers. OPEC's success in wresting control of oil supplies and prices from the international oil companies inspired other commodity producers to attempt to form cartels, but the OPEC model proved difficult to reproduce and none of them enjoyed OPEC's success. OPEC itself encountered the chief problem of cartels—the difficulty of maintaining unity.

Throughout its history, however, OPEC itself has witnessed frequent disagreement between its more moderate members, led by Saudi Arabia, and its radical members, including Algeria, Libya, Iran, and Iraq. In 1976, OPEC instituted a special fund eventually converted into the OPEC Fund for International Development to provide loans for financing balance of payments deficits and development projects in non-oil producing, developing countries that were adversely affected by the increasing price of oil. It proved insufficient for their needs.

Throughout its history, OPEC has witnessed frequent disagreements between more "moderate" members led by Saudi Arabia and its "radicals"— Algeria, Libya, and Iraq. Rifts emerged over policies to be implemented on oil pricing, production, export capacity, and royalties. OPEC displayed a remarkable degree of cohesion throughout the 1970s, particularly in dealing with Western Europe and Japan, but after that unity has proved more elusive. With the 1979 revolution in Iran, the Iran-Iraq War (1980–1988), the conflicting economic and political interests, and Saudi Arabia's growing reluctance to absorb some of the costs associated with the functioning of the cartel, it became increasingly difficult for the OPEC members to reach agreements on long-term pricing and production strategies. The second oil crisis in 1979 resulted from a combination of rising demand, reduced supplies (triggered in part by the halt in Iranian oil exports), and Saudi Arabia's inability to offset these production losses. Prices rose rapidly and the system spun out of control. The Iran-Iraq War dashed hopes for stability in world oil markets by halting exports from both Iran and Iraq, which led to further price increases.

Moreover, OPEC's success in increasing oil prices in the 1970s eventually transformed the world oil market. As a result of conservation efforts, greater energy efficiency in automobiles and housing, slow rates of economic growth, and worldwide recession, demand fell after 1980. Non-OPEC producers, such as Norway and Great Britain, emerged, and a long-term surplus developed, pushing prices down and making it difficult for OPEC to manage prices. Between 1980 and 1989 total industrial-country oil fell by ten percent. The collapse of the oil market in 1986, combined with the depreciation of the dollar, rising interest rates, and a declining share of the world oil market exacerbated OPEC's difficulties.

In the face of OPEC's oil price hikes, the United States pursued a policy of seeking stable oil prices; in particular, the United States feared that further price rises would fuel inflation, prove recessionary, and have an adverse effect on the international trade system. Internationally, the United States sought to pursue policies that would bring stability back into the price of oil while letting inflation erode its real price. Domestically, consensus never developed in the United States on what to do about oil prices and energy conservation despite the fact that these were central political issues of the mid-1970s.

OPEC's collective success, especially in the 1970s, in directing the forces of the world energy market, demonstrated that power shifts are possible even in industries that are controlled by major multinational companies. Since the early 1980s, however, price management has required the cooperation of the non-OPEC producers, including Mexico, the Soviet Union, China, Malaysia, the United Kingdom, and Norway.

MARGARET P. KARNS

See also Kuwait; Middle East; New International Economic Order; Oil Companies; Oil and Foreign Policy; Oil and World Politics; Saudi Arabia; Libya; Venezuela

FURTHER READING

Amuzegar, Jahangir. "Oil and Changing OPEC," *Finance and Development* 27 (September 1990): 43–5.

Ghanem, Shurki. *OPEC: The Rise and Fall of an Exclusive Club.* London: KPI, Ltd., 1986.

Mikdashi, Zuhayr. *The Community of Oil Exporting Countries: A Study in Governmental Cooperation.* Ithaca, N.Y., 1972.

Skeet, Ian. *OPEC: Twenty-five Years of Prices and Politics.* Cambridge: Cambridge University Press, 1988.

Spero, Joan Edelman. *The Politics of International Economic Relations,* 4th ed. New York, 1990.

ORGANIZATION ON SECURITY AND COOPERATION IN EUROPE

The Organization on Security and Cooperation in Europe (OSCE), known until January 1995 as the Conference on Security and Cooperation in Europe (CSCE), has been a principal part of the political and diplomatic "security architecture" of Europe. The only body in Europe with comprehensive membership, the OSCE's 54/55 members include the United States, Canada, and virtually all of Europe and the former Soviet Union (Ser-

bia's membership was suspended in 1992). Members of the OSCE signed the Final Act in Helsinki in 1975, which established norms and principles on key issues of both internal and external affairs of signatories at the height of détente in East-West relations. Since then the OSCE has pursued a broad concept of security based on promoting human rights, the rule of law, democratic and market precepts, and non-use or threat of force. The OSCE was formally acknowledged as a regional organization under Chapter VIII of the United Nations Charter in 1992.

The CSCE began as a loose series of periodic international conferences and evolved into a multilateral organization with a permanently sitting body and operational capabilities. The organization operates offices in Vienna, Warsaw, the Hague, and Prague—an indication of its importance in the post-Cold War period. Despite changes instituted in the 1990s, however, with few exceptions, the OSCE has remained reluctant to depart from its origins as a consensus based process, often its critics charge, restricting its ability to act.

In its first twenty years, the most striking CSCE achievement was to encourage human rights groups in the Soviet Union and Eastern Europe by enabling them to hold their governments accountable to agreed CSCE norms. It served as an impetus for human rights activity in the East, sparking the formation of Helsinki monitoring groups in the Soviet Union and the Baltic states, Charter '77 in Czechoslovakia, and the Committee for the Defense of Workers (KOR) in Poland, among others. At its 1980–1983 Madrid and 1986–1989 Vienna follow-up conferences as well as at other meetings, the CSCE provided an ongoing international forum where Western countries could voice human rights concerns about victims of communist repression. Later CSCE standards provided parameters for peaceful German unification, Baltic independence, and the emergence of the new states of the former Soviet Union. The OSCE sees itself as protecting human rights and fundamental freedoms of "all individuals, regardless of race, color, sex, language, religion, social origin or of belonging to a minority...." (Budapest Summit Declaration of 1994).

In the 1984–1986 Stockholm Conference and other meetings, the CSCE pursued confidence- and security-building measures designed to reduce the danger of surprise attack, miscalculation and misunderstanding, and laid the foundation for the 1990 Vienna Document of expanded confidence- and security-building measures and the Conventional Armed Forces in Europe (CFE) agreement on levels of force and structures to be instituted from the Atlantic to the Urals.

A response to the end of the Cold War, the Charter of Paris for a New Europe (concluded in 1990) underscored the desire of CSCE members to overcome the ideological divide and unify Europe within a framework of common values and democracy based on human rights and fundamental freedoms, the rule of law and minority rights (Copenhagen, 1990), market economies, and equal security. In the 1990s, the OSCE enhanced the security, as well as humanitarian and economic dimensions of its activities, including increased conflict prevention and conflict management, a comprehensive framework for conventional arms control and confidence- and security-building, a comprehensive security model study, increased attention to human rights and humanitarian issues, and improved economic cooperation through the Economic Forum.

The OSCE mandate has broadened to include a Permanent Council of heads of OSCE delegations for political consultation and decision-making, a Chair-in-Office for executive action, and a Senior Council, which meets periodically. Summits are held every two years and ministerials at least once a year. The wide range of OSCE activities is reflected in the permanent office of High Commissioner on National Minorities (the Hague), a Conflict Prevention Center (Vienna), and the Office for Democratic Institutions and Human Rights (Warsaw), along with missions to areas of conflict or potential conflict such as Chechnya, Moldavia, South Ossetia, Macedonia, and Tajikistan as well as other election monitoring and conflict prevention activities. An OSCE Minsk Group sought to resolve the conflict in Nagorno-Karabakh, and in 1994 at the Budapest summit the OSCE authorized the creation of a peacekeeping force to support a settlement in Nagorno-Karabakh. The OSC has contributed to the Bosnian settlement under the Dayton Peace Accords with the design of confidence- and security-building measures (restrictions on military deployments, heavy weapons, and specified activities) as well as measures to reduce the risk of continued conflict in the region, including subregional arms control. It also will monitor and report on the human rights situation and set up the necessary framework for elections.

GALE A. MATTOX

See also Cold War, Helsinki Accords

FURTHER READING

Bloed, Arie. *The Conference on Security and Cooperation in Europe: Analysis and Basic Documents, 1972–1993.* Boston, 1994.
Dean, Jonathan. "The CSCE: Can It Do the Job?" In *Ending Europe's Wars.* New York, 1994.
Fry, John. *The Helsinki Process: Negotiating Security and Cooperation in Europe.* Washington, D.C., 1993.
Lucas, Michael R., ed. *The CSCE in the 1990s: Constructing European Security and Cooperation.* Baden-Baden, 1993.

OSS

See Office of Strategic Services

OSTEND MANIFESTO

A secret diplomatic dispatch, dated 15 October 1854, recommending that the United States purchase Cuba or take it by force if necessary. Written by James Buchanan, U.S. minister to Great Britain, John Y. Mason, U.S. minister to France, and Pierre Soulé, U.S. minister to Spain, after they had met in Ostend, Belgium, and Aix-la-Chapelle, Prussia, the dispatch was sent to Secretary of State William L. Marcy, who received it in November.

In February 1854 Spanish officials in Havana, Cuba, had seized the cargo of the U.S. merchant ship *Black Warrior* for violating a custom regulation. The ensuing crisis rekindled interest in acquiring Cuba among proslavery interests and expansionists in the United States. Spanish officials resolved the problem by writing President Franklin Pierce a justification for the seizure and agreeing to pay reparations to the ship's owners.

In April 1854, Marcy, a Southerner who wanted to protect the institution of slavery and acquire new slave territory, instructed Soulé to offer Spain up to $130 million for the island. If the Madrid government declined the offer, then Marcy told Soulé to consider other methods the United States could use to assist Cuba in gaining its independence. When Soulé's efforts proved nonproductive, Marcy ordered Buchanan, Mason, and Soulé to meet and consider options regarding Cuba and to report their ideas by confidential messenger. In October the three ministers met in Ostend, later moving to Aix-la-Chapelle, and secretly forwarded their report to Marcy on 15 October.

Soulé provided the main ideas for the document although Buchanan wrote and edited the final version. The dispatch advised that the United States offer no more than $120 million for Cuba. If Spain refused to sell and conditions in Cuba endangered "our internal peace," the United States would be "justified in wresting it from Spain if we possess the power." The ministers feared that if the United States did not take Cuba it might be "Africanized and become a second Saint Domingo," where slaves had revolted and established their own republic.

Before Marcy received the document European and U.S. newspapers had leaked much of it, calling it the "Ostend Manifesto." As reported in the press, Marcy and Pierce were ready to fight in order to obtain Cuba as a slave state to balance newly admitted California. The resulting outcry from anti-expansionist and antislavery forces hurt supporters of Pierce in the congressional elections of 1854. Following this negative publicity and the success of antislavery forces in the congressional elections that year, Marcy rejected the report. Soulé soon resigned as minister to Spain, but the interest of the United States in Cuba did not diminish through the rest of the nineteenth century, as the Spanish-American-Cuban-Filipino War of 1898 demonstrates.

LOUIS R. SMITH, JR.

See also Buchanan, James; Cuba; Marcy, William Learned; Pierce, Franklin; Slave Trade and Slavery; Spain; Spanish-American-Cuban-Filipino War, 1898

FURTHER READING

Ettinger, Amos A. *The Mission to Spain of Pierre Soule, 1853-1855.* New Haven, Conn., 1932.

May, Robert E. *The Southern Dream of a Caribbean Empire, 1854-1861.* Baton Rouge, La., 1973.

Pérez, Louis A. *Cuba and the United States.* Athens, Ga., 1990.

OVERSEAS MILITARY BASES

The term is generally used to denote defense arrangements between the United States and a foreign nation to allow for a large U.S. military presence involving long-term military installations, the ongoing stationing of troops and support personnel, and the granting by the host state of extensive latitude to stage military operations.

The United States has maintained overseas military bases for almost a century, going back to the naval outposts won in Cuba and the Philippines in the Spanish-American-Cuban-Filipino War. Questions involving the scope and purposes of these bases have been central issues in U.S. foreign policy, especially with the vast expansion of U.S. bases during the Cold War to the post–Vietnam War retrenchment that entailed conflicts with key allies over renewal of long-standing base agreements. With the scaling back and consolidation of the post–Cold War era, the role of overseas military bases within the broader contours of U.S. foreign policy again commanded national debate.

Acquisition

As a result of the Spanish-American-Cuban-Filipino War, the United States obtained control over the former Spanish possessions of Guam, the Philippines, Cuba, and Puerto Rico, along with the attending rights for access and military use of their territory. In 1900, the Philippines, for instance, served as a staging area for the deployment of U.S. troops to China to assist in the fight against the Boxer Rebellion; and by 1905, the U.S. naval station at Subic Bay was in full operation. Similarly, U.S. Navy installations were established in Cuba, at Guantánamo Bay and Bahía Honda. An agreement concluded with the Republic of Cuba in 1903 placed both these sites under the "complete jurisdiction and control" of the United States for the duration of their occupation.

Based on the Hay-Herránn Treaty of 1903, the United States also was granted in perpetuity sovereignty over the lands and waters of the Panama Canal Zone "to the entire exclusion of the exercise by the Republic of Pana-ma of any such sovereign rights, power and authority," as Charles Bevans states in his book *Treaties and Other International Agreements of the United States of America, 1776-1949.* This amounted to a purchase of the right to build and annex the canal and surrounding zone in exchange for an initial payment plus an annual fee. Designed to subdue the natural impediments posed by geography, the construction of the canal constituted an unquestionable engineering feat as well as what was to become the most controversial U.S. basing commitment overseas.

Guided by the strategic vision of historian and navy officer Alfred T. Mahan, the principal function of these outlying naval bases was to serve as commercial and military strongholds in the quest for command of the seas and for world markets. More narrowly defined, these "coaling stations," as they were characteristically called, provided valuable repair, refueling, and support services to the big battleships that served to ensure open trade routes.

The initial foray into military basing was nonetheless a tentative one. For nearly four decades the country remained deeply suspicious of permanent military commitments. During this entire time the United States reined in its capabilities to project power beyond its borders for fear that it would invite rather than deter aggression. Even the demonstrable utility of overseas bases in World War I did not temper in a lasting way the strength of the opposition. At the conclusion of hostilities the impulse to isolate the country from the outside world prevailed. U.S. military installations established abroad during the war were promptly dismantled and the sites returned to the host governments; for example, the United States transferred back to Portugal the naval base at Ponta Delgada in the Azores.

Throughout the interwar years, the United States maintained a low profile in the establishment of overseas military bases. With the sole exception of the heavily fortified Panama Canal Zone, overseas installations were underutilized and lacking in strong defenses. A flotilla was kept at Shanghai and small naval deployments were placed in Cuba, Puerto Rico, and the Virgin Islands. Fortification of the Philippines was minimal, for the prevailing view held that anything more might antagonize the Japanese. Even when the winds of war started gathering in Europe and the Pacific, very little was done to strengthen the U.S. network of military bases.

In 1940–1941 the United States finally moved to strengthen the existing infrastructure and to add new base sites. In the Caribbean and the Atlantic, Lend-Lease arrangements with Great Britain afforded control over several air and naval facilities. U.S. forces were deployed to Bermuda, the Bahamas, Jamaica, Antigua, Saint Lucia, Trinidad, British Guiana, Newfoundland,

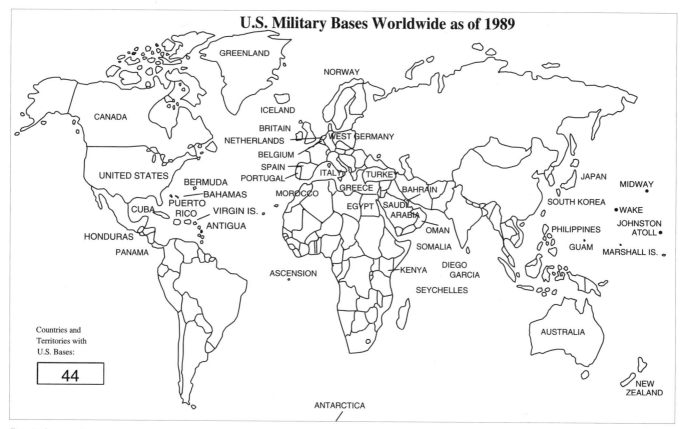

U.S. Military Bases Worldwide as of 1989

Countries and
Territories with
U.S. Bases:

44

From the Center for Defense Information, Washington, D.C.

and Labrador. A strong diplomatic effort to preempt the Axis powers from gaining military access in Latin America proved successful. By the end of 1941 numerous agreements were concluded granting the United States overflight and basing rights in almost every Latin American nation. An upgrading of U.S. forces in the Pacific also took place in 1941. Military facilities were built at Palmyra Island, south of Hawaii, and U.S. garrisons in Hawa'ii and in the Philippines were bolstered.

Once the United States formally joined the ranks of belligerents following the Japanese attack on Pearl Harbor, the acquisition of overseas bases and facilities grew at an unprecedented rate. According to one count, the number of U.S. overseas military sites increased from fewer than 100 sites at the beginning of World War II to well over 2,000 at its end.

The 1942 decision to make Australia the operational hub of the campaign in the Southwest Pacific led to the improvement as well as new construction of numerous bases in Australia itself, New Caledonia, Fiji, and New Hebrides, among other Pacific locations. In 1944–1945 an additional string of bases, such as Saipan, Palau, Iwo Jima, and Okinawa, was captured from the retreating Japanese and added to the U.S. inventory.

The Cold War Global Network

By the end of World War II, a modest number of bases had been transformed into thousands, making up a vast global network. Several installations were obtained with the help of friends and allies; others were captured from defeated enemies. Many were also contructed from the ground up as warranted by the exigencies of the war.

Even more significant than the increase in the number of overseas bases was a turnabout in the foreign policy assumptions regarding their use. With the onset of the Cold War the case for a permanent foreign military presence became compelling, marking the end of historic isolationism. The United States, like other great powers before, came to recognize the projection of its military beyond the home shores as a symbol of power and as a valuable instrument with which to shape the world. Thus, where the United States had once used its bases primarily to facilitate commerce, it now conceived of them as a means to advance world stability, to promote free trade, and to influence geopolitics.

On 12 March 1947 the Truman Doctrine, enunciated in response to the ongoing crisis in Greece, occasioned by the communist-instigated war there, offered a formal declaration of the U.S. intention "to support free people who are resisting attempted subjugation by armed minorities or by outside pressures." The policy of containment, as it came to be known, gave meaning and direction to overseas basing for more than four decades. The presence of U.S. military bases in a given nation or territory constituted tangible proof that the United States held vital interests in that part of the world and was prepared to defend them by whatever means necessary. By the same token, U.S. bases helped ensure the host country's military preparedness, lending credibility to its political commitments.

Once the policy lines were drawn, a process of base consolidation and expansion began in earnest, first in Europe and then on a worldwide scale, following the eruption of the Korean War. A profusion of formal alliances and informal agreements provided the legal foundation on which to build a network of overseas military bases. Between the end of World War II and 1960 the United States concluded four multilateral treaties: the Inter-American Treaty of Reciprocal Assistance, or Rio Treaty (1947) and (joined the related Organization of American States (1948) under the UN Charter); the North Atlantic Treaty (1949), establishing the North Atlantic Treaty Organization (NATO); the Security Treaty with Australia and New Zealand or ANZUS pact (1951); and the Southeast Asia Collective Defense Treaty (1954), establishing the South-East Asia Treaty Organization (SEATO). It became, in addition, an associate member of the Central Treaty Organization (CENTO) in 1958.

At the bilateral level, the United States signed a base agreement (1947) and a defense treaty (1951) with the Philippines, as well as mutual cooperation and security treaties with Japan (1951, 1952, 1960), the Republic of China (Taiwan) (1954), and South Korea (1954). Also, a number of bilateral base agreements were concluded at the executive level, most notably with Iceland (1951), Denmark (1951), Greece (1953), and Spain (1953). Lastly, the earlier treaties with Cuba (1934) and Panama (1903) remained in effect, allowing the United States bases in Guantánamo Bay and the Panama Canal Zone.

Through multilateral and bilateral defense agreements, U.S. military bases providing various types of facilities were established throughout the world in the 1950–1960 period. In addition to army, naval, and air force bases, types of facilities included those for communications and intelligence; various training, support, and technical facilities; airfields; ammunitions depots, and nuclear weapons storage facilities. With the sole exception of Norway, all NATO members provided base sites, including France until its partial withdrawal in 1967. The Rio Treaty did not develop a corresponding base network, save for preexisting installations in the Panama Canal Zone, and at a much later stage, U.S. access to Honduras under a separate bilateral defense treaty (1985).

In many respects the 1950s marked the golden age of the U.S. military presence overseas. The United States was able to further establish bases obtained or constructed during World War II, and to add new ones with little difficulty. Framed in terms of shared values and conditioned by a heightened perception of a common threat, the accompanying defense agreements were expeditious, amicable, and for the most part, favorable to U.S. positions. At the apex of its economic and military strength, the United States offered its allies protection as well as generous military and economic assistance to help them build up their defenses. The host countries, in return, were prepared to renounce absolute sovereignty in order to allow military access and base privileges to a foreign power. This exchange was cushioned by the shared anticommunist ideology. In the unique circumstances of the Cold War, and perhaps for the briefest of moments in history, mutual security interests and a sense of common purpose nearly converged.

Stark differences characterized Soviet and U.S. base structures in the 1950s. With strong alliances and bases around the world, the United States could rightfully claim to have attained a global reach. During the same period the Soviet Union retained a comparatively smaller number of foreign bases with a much more limited geographic scope. The highest concentration and the largest of Soviet installations closely followed the postwar advances of the Red Army in Eastern Europe. The Warsaw Treaty Organization (1955) and the subsequent status-of-forces agreements with Hungary, Romania, the German Democratic Republic, and Poland were employed to lend legitimacy to an already militarily and politically entrenched situation. Between 1958 and the 1961 Soviet-Albanian split Soviets were allowed some access to submarine bases in Albania. On its frontier to the south and east, Soviet forces originally deployed in Mongolia in 1936 persisted until 1956 (and were again deployed in 1966).

The relatively modest Soviet foreign military presence was further constrained by the lack of a strong navy, and a dearth of access to international ports. Despite its rise to superpower status, the USSR remained essentially landlocked, possessing only coastal naval defenses and a small submarine fleet. It was not until after the 1962 Cuban Missile Crisis that the Soviet leadership strove to break its military out of Eurasia, devoting considerable energies and resources to building up naval strength, as well as soliciting allies and facilities in the Third World.

As early as 1967 the Soviet Mediterranean Fleet, *Fifth Eskadra*, was deployed. Within a year a smaller squadron was placed in the Indian Ocean. In 1970 a naval patrol was established in Africa, and by the late 1970s the Soviet Pacific Fleet was introduced. Increases in merchant marines and in fishing fleets further added to the Soviet Union's maritime prowess. Commercial vessels comprised a key component of naval strategy, as they were called upon systematically to perform a variety of military operations. Merchant tankers, for instance, provided support services meeting up to fifty percent of the refueling needs of the Soviet Navy. Meanwhile, special equipment on board fishing vessels allowed them to fulfill critical intelligence and communications functions.

Soviet naval successes were complemented by significant gains in establishing overseas bases and facilities. A barrage of diplomatic activities, including security and economic assistance, arms sales, training of foreign military personnel, and military support to leftist regimes, were used to secure basing access in many Third World countries. By the late 1970s, the Soviet Union had achieved status as a global contender with a widely dispersed foreign military presence in more than thirty different countries. But the practical significance of Soviet gains in military-basing needs to be qualified.

First, a closer look at the mode of basing arrangements reveals most of them to have been concluded on an ad hoc and restricted basis. By and large, the USSR received limited privileges for refueling, repairs, and anchorage but was denied much-desired, permanent onshore installations.

Second, Soviet initiatives to set up bases often met with failure. The dissolution of the military partnership with Egypt in 1976 and the attendant loss of access to the Mediterranean was one such setback, especially in light of almost two decades (1955–1972) of uninterrupted Soviet military and economic assistance. Similarly, the defection of Somalia in 1978 deprived the Soviet Union of its most important naval and air facilities on the Indian Ocean; to add insult to injury, these same facilities were transferred within two years to the United States. The failure of the protracted Soviet military engagement in Afghanistan (1979–1989) proved costlier yet in terms of lives lost, resources expended, political capital squandered, and, within the East Asian context, greatly diminished military access.

Third, the Soviet Union followed a general strategy of self-sufficiency and as a result was less reliant than the United States on overseas bases. Intelligence and communications functions, traditionally performed from land-based installations, were carried out aboard ships. In addition, shortfalls in overseas naval bases led Soviet military planners to rely on alternatives such as deepwater anchorages, offshore repair facilities, and mooring buoys.

Limitations in the Soviet base structure, clear in retrospect, were difficult to put in perspective while in the midst of the U.S.-Soviet competitive struggle. The overwhelming perception in the 1970s was that the global advantage was shifting away from the United States and its allies. The USSR had in one decade developed the capability to project an international military presence. As the challenger, the Soviet Union seemed to hold an added advantage. A degree of alarm was understandable in any circumstances. But with the overseas gains of the Soviet military coming into full view on the heels of the Vietnam War, the psychological impact was far greater than it would have been otherwise.

Retrenchment and Reconstruction

Following its disengagement from Southeast Asia, the United States underwent a period of retrenchment and base constriction. As early as 1964, the United States and Great Britain started negotiating with Libya over gradual withdrawal from the Whellus Air Force Base. Within a year of the 1969 military overthrow of King Idris and the establishment of the Libyan Arab Republic, the last of the U.S. and British contingents were removed from Libyan soil. By the late 1970s the United States had also voluntarily abandoned its facilities in the Republic of China. Meanwhile the 1979 Iranian Revolution brought an abrupt and involuntary end to all U.S. military access to that country.

The downward trend generated sufficient alarm to force a backlash, making strategic reconstitution the hallmark of the 1980s. Existing bases were expanded and new ones added. Among the gains were the development of facilities on the British island of Diego Garcia; expansion of access to Omani bases and to Kenya; acquisition of the naval base at Berbera, Somalia (previously operated by the Soviet Union); and staging access to two airfields in Morocco.

Starting in the late 1970s and gaining momentum under President Ronald Reagan, new emphasis was placed on national conflicts. Strategy was still driven by Cold War considerations, and regional threats were interpreted along the East-West axis, but overseas bases became more attuned to meeting contingencies most likely to arise within the Third World. The development of new military capabilities reflected these changes in strategy. Large units of Special Operations Forces, such as navy SEALS and Green Berets, were deployed to bases in Germany, Great Britain, Panama, the Philippines, and Puerto Rico. In addition, a new Rapid Deployment Force was created for quick and effective response to crises in the Middle East. To carry out its military missions, the Rapid Deployment Force relied heavily on access to overseas bases in the Philippines and

Greece. In 1983 the U.S. Central Command (CENT-COM) was introduced to take over the regional and operational responsibilities of the Rapid Deployment Force. CENTCOM fully incorporated the strategic concepts of out-of-area operations, as it was designed to draw exclusively upon existing forces and to depend on links with overseas facilities for its logistical support and material.

Conflict with Allies

The success achieved in revamping the structure of U.S. military bases during the 1980s was unfortunately not duplicated in addressing intra-alliance problems. The collapse in the 1970s of the consensus on respective rights and responsibilities marked a true turning point in allied relations and in the historical evolution of U.S. bases overseas. The readiness of allies and friends of the United States to compromise their territorial integrity was supplanted by a resurgent nationalist determination to reassert the principle of sovereignty and right to autonomous action.

The relaxation of East-West tensions displaced the security threat just long enough for the U.S. allies to reappraise their interests. Security considerations, previously insulated from the rough-and-tumble of politics, were now becoming caught up in a maelstrom of rival concerns, ranging from economic development and world trade to nuclear fears and environmental issues. Old issues and new priorities, moreover, were heavily influenced by pent-up resentments against past U.S. policies.

The long years of coexistence with a U.S. military presence engendered a polemical brand of nationalism, almost analogous to anticolonialism. The most vehement critics of the U.S. bases, whether in the Philippines or Germany, often zeroed in on the "Americanization" of their societies. For instance, the drinking and nightlife of U.S. servicemen stationed in Greece, and particularly in the environs of Athens, had proved a constant irritant. One of the chief reasons for Spain's demands for the removal of the U.S. F-16 wing from the Torrejon Air Base had been its proximity to population centers.

The common conclusion among citizens of host countries that U.S. actions (or inaction) were motivated by a desire to safeguard its military privileges at all costs contributed to the resurgent nationalism. For example, the willingness of the United States to conclude the 1953 base agreement with Generalissimo Francisco Franco in Spain and its unwillingness to condemn the dictatorships of George Papadopoulos in Greece and Ferdinand Marcos in the Philippines rendered U.S. motives suspect and embittered the people of those countries. In the 1970s and early 1980s the return of democracy brought these issues out into the open. An abatement in the U.S.-Soviet ideological conflict and the perceived security threat

allowed for an overall scrutiny of the defense relationship with the United States.

Some allies used negotiations for the renewal or extension of base accords to channel their grievances and to restructure the goals of the alliance. Negotiating demands usually have involved a combination of greater host control and higher quid pro quos for the use of facilities. Host nations have negotiated, and on occasion have imposed, restrictions on specific U.S. operations as well as the right of consultation and approval of certain others. For example, Spain demanded the removal of Poseidon submarines in 1979. New Zealand banned all visits by nuclear and nuclear-powered submarines (leading the United States to terminate the defense alliance in 1986). Greece, on the other hand, included the right of preapproval of all U.S. missions to the Middle East as one of the terms of the 1983 defense and economic agreement with the United States. Demands for quid pro quos have entailed increases in economic and military aid as well as U.S. contributions in the form of assisting in the development of indigenous defense industries, sharing of those industries, and intelligence. Greece, for example, in the 1983 negotiations obtained a U.S. promise for assistance to modernize and expand its weapons production. Spain received $50 million from the United States for the modernization of its aircraft patrol and warning network.

On a more narrow monetary basis, the issue of compensation or "rent" in return for basing access has proved increasingly costly as well as controversial. The yearly compensation paid by the United States for access to overseas facilities has climbed from $200 million in 1975 to $2 billion in 1987. The demands for higher "rent" have not been due to simple avarice. Instead, they almost invariably have had a strong political dimension. Under Premier Andreas Papandreou, Greece, for instance, used its demands for increased compensation as a means to make an appeal to Greek nationalists that the transaction was purely an economic one and that the bases served exclusively U.S. security interests. This argument turned the original intent of security assistance on its head. The United States had premised helping its allies to build up their defenses on the logic of mutual contributions to alliance strength. As the irate Congressional Panel on Burdensharing admonished in 1988, "the existence of a U.S. base overseas in a particular area either is necessary for defense purposes or it is not. Whether or how much security assistance a country receives from the United States has no bearing on the military necessity of a base."

After the Cold War

The collapse of the Soviet Union and the breakup of its satellite empire have formally ended the Cold War. But wars rage and threats still abound to one degree or another, and in one form or another, in virtually every region of the world. As if these dangers were not enough, a Pandora's box of transnational threats has also sprung open, allowing terrorism, drug trafficking, and international crime to come to the fore with enhanced intensity. Most of the challenges are difficult to assess or plan for, and what is worse, to foresee. As General Colin Powell, chairman of the Joint Chiefs of Staff, warned in a 1993 address to the Senate, "it may very well be that in the post–Cold War era, the primary threat to our security is instability and being unprepared to handle a crisis or a war that no one expected or predicted."

Iraq's invasion of Kuwait, as important as it was and as successful as was the U.S.-led response, already is moving to be at most only partially a post–Cold War model. Thankfully, in this particular circumstance, the United States was able to rely on previous planning and preexisting capabilities as a basis for launching the appropriate response. Although there were no U.S. forces geared specifically for the Iraqi-Kuwaiti theater of war, the structure of CENTCOM was able to buttress Operation Desert Shield and, during the final offensive, Operation Desert Storm. Demonstrating another pattern for the future, overseas bases played a pivotal role in transport operations as well as in the actual conduct of the Gulf War of 1990–1991. Massive, and by all accounts indispensable, logistical support was provided by bases in Germany, Spain, Greece, and Turkey, among others.

To cope with the changed security requirements, especially as they pertain to the unpredictability of the future, the administration of President Bill Clinton has focused strategy away from a single global scenario to several regional ones. The central concept has been to structure a general-purpose Base Force which would deter, and failing that defend against, a wide array of military contingencies. The general forces would continue at a level of preparedness and flexibility that would permit rapid and militarily appropriate response to crises emerging anywhere in the world.

Overseas bases thus remain vitally important to the evolving U.S. military posture, providing a building block on which the Base Force has been founded. The bases are, much as before, relied upon to bestow credibility to U.S. commitments, to reassure friends and allies, and to deter or defend against enemies. The one notable difference is that these roles are cast more in terms of distinct, albeit interlinked, regional strategies than as parts of a singular global strategy. Furthermore, the number of overseas bases and troop deployment has decreased in conjunction with the decline in the Soviet threat. The greatest cutbacks are slated for Europe, which throughout the Cold War was the area with the highest force con-

centration and the highest risk of superpower confrontation. Of the 490 bases marked for closure worldwide in 1993, 350 were in Germany.

In juxtaposition to this trend, there has been an effort to supplant some of the military activities performed by overseas bases with alternative arrangements. Two such arrangements have been prominent: the repositioning of supplies and material, mostly on container ships, but also on land; and the temporary access to the facilities or territory of friendly regimes on the basis of contingency agreements. Neither practice is new. Repositioning was introduced in the 1960s, and contingency access has been systematically used since the 1980s, in Egypt and Israel, among other places. However, as critical elements for reducing the response time to regional crises, both practices have now received a new impetus.

When fully achieved, overall size reduction combined with alternative basing provisions will significantly alter the U.S. overseas base structure as we know it. It is too early for us to predict its final configuration. Nonetheless, the past history of U.S. overseas military bases can help us discern some of the challenges that lie ahead.

Greater reliance on contingency access recommends itself on the grounds of lowered political costs. Since it does not rely on permanent placement of military personnel and large installations, it is perceived to be less intrusive to the host's sovereignty and less likely to spark widespread criticism and nationalistic resentment. These advantages, however, need to weighed against the restrictions on operating rights that invariably accompany access agreements. Oman, for instance, has insisted on a treaty stipulation requiring the United States to report all materials routinely flown in and out of Omani territory and to obtain approval prior to the use of Omani bases in the case of a military emergency.

A mixed picture also emerges in regard to monetary costs. In a general sense, contingency access allows the United States to perform valuable technical, intelligence, staging, and overflight activities without the financial burden of having to maintain a continuous military presence on the actual site. But even temporary use of another nation's territory is not altogether free. To obtain access agreements, the United States usually extends economic and security assistance. In addition, the lack of supporting infrastructure and military facilities capable of meeting the needs of U.S. forces often necessitate additional funding in order to bring the host nation's bases up to par.

As part of U.S. operations in support of the Nicaraguan Contras, $40 million was expended in the mid-1980s on improvements of the Honduran Air Force base at Palmerola and on the establishment of temporary quarters for U.S. troops. In Kenya, it has cost the U.S. Navy $58 million to improve the Mombasa airfield and to dredge the harbor. In Egypt, the United States spent $55 million between 1980 and 1985 on improving the military bases at Ras Banas, Qena, and Cairo West, even though no formal access agreement existed between the two countries.

The issue of compensation or "rent" will continue to complicate U.S. efforts in base negotiations. As the United States finds itself dependent on increasingly fewer bases than before, the leverage of certain host nations may very well increase. Contingency access agreements for the use of bases owned and operated by our friends and allies can offer only a partial solution to the problem because both security assistance and indirect expenditures are associated with them. In addition, there are no assurances that as access relationships take root and mature, demands for payments, especially from impoverished Third World countries, will not intensify.

Efforts by host governments to constrain U.S. basing rights in the interest of reasserting sovereignty poses another potential difficulty. The shift in U.S. strategy from a global to a regional focus has renewed the threat of U.S. military and political interests clashing with the hosts' own local priorities.

The imposition of contraints on the use of bases becomes particularly frustrating when spending limits are taken into account. Critics charge that operational constraints compounded by cost increases for compensation and maintenance tend to diminish the benefits of certain overseas bases. A more fundamental argument is that the U.S. budgetary crisis may necessitate lowering the levels of the U.S. military presence around the world. This argument was, in fact, advanced by the U.S. Congressional Panel on Burdensharing in 1988. Since then, the withdrawal from some bases, as in the Philippines, and the partial closure of other facilities, as in Europe, have helped bring overall base expenditures down. But the need for continuous assessment of overseas bases and monetary costs clearly has not been eliminated.

It would appear that tendencies for base constriction will persist in the post–Cold War environment, as will the political and economic motives that sustain them. Maintaining alliance strength and cohesion will require considerable adjustment of mutual expectations and contributions. One promising course of action would be for the United States to relinquish some control and leadership responsibilities, and for the allies to assume a greater share of the defense burden in recompense. The idea for this kind of compromise solution is not novel, having been proposed in 1988 by the Congressional Burdensharing Panel. Indeed, a precedent was established in 1990 when Spain negotiated the removal of the U.S. F-16 fighter wing from the Torrejon Air Base at the compensating value of renouncing any future security assistance from the United States for the use of Spanish bases.

The Clinton administration has set down the principal guidelines for an overseas military base policy that does not merely follow the mandates of military concerns. Rather, it emanates from a deeper conception of our national goals and aspirations. It is, in the words of Powell, an expression of how we view our role as "the sole remaining superpower." He says, "We seek no territory. We desire no hegemony in any region. But we cannot ignore our responsibility to help lead the world community along the path of peace and prosperity. And such leadership means we must remain engaged."

There will be difficulties in forming a consensus on the meaning and upper limits of such an engagement. How much in outlays is this country willing to devote in order to keep its overseas bases? How much dissention are we willing to tolerate from our allies and friends? And, last but not least, how are we to uphold continuity and persistence in our security commitments and military posture in the face of shrinking budgets and a rapidly changing strategic environment? These questions are crucial to the future of U.S. foreign policy.

MARIA COURTIS

See also Cold War; Containment; Greece; North Atlantic Treaty Organization; Philippines

FURTHER READING

Blaker, James R. *United States Overseas Basing.* New York, 1990.
Courtis, Maria. *Asymmetrical Bargaining: A Framework for Small Power-Great Power Cooperation.* Ph.D. diss., University of California, Davis, 1995.
Gerson, Joseph, and Bruce Birchard, eds. *The Sun Never Sets…Confronting the Network of Foreign U.S. Military Bases.* Boston, 1991.
Harkavy, Robert E. *Great Power Competition for Overseas Bases: The Geopolitics of Access Diplomacy.* New York, 1982.
———. *Bases Abroad.* New York, 1989.

OVERSEAS PRIVATE INVESTMENT CORPORATION

U.S. government agency whose function is to encourage profitable private investment in developing countries and countries in economic transition. The Overseas Private Investment Corporation (OPIC) began operations in 1971 to promote economic reforms in less-developed countries, and, more recently, in formerly communist countries. Its operations are based on the belief that private investment is a vital ingredient in promoting economic growth in those countries, but that private investors will not invest sufficiently without U.S. government assistance. OPIC thus supports, finances, and insures foreign investment projects of U.S. corporations. OPIC-supported projects in some 140 eligible countries seek to increase overall U.S. corporate competitiveness, U.S. exports, and repatriation of foreign profits.

OPIC's operations seek to reduce or eliminate certain perceived political risks in investing in nonindustrialized countries and to provide financial services not otherwise available. The three principal services provided are medium- and long-term financing, insurance, and investor servies.

OPIC provides direct loans to projects sponsored by small businesses in the United States, and loan guarantees to larger projects developed by major corporations. Because it is chartered to support only financially viable projects, OPIC does not offer concessional terms usually associated with governmental lending programs. The agency also sponsors several investment funds that provide equity (ownership) funding for projects in sub-Saharan Africa, East Asia, Israel, Poland, and Russia.

OPIC mitigates the political risk of investing in developing countries by providing insurance to U.S. investors, contractors, and financial institutions for protection against political violence (loss of assets or income due to war, revolution, or civil strife), expropriation of an investment, or currency inconvertibility (inability to convert profits, and other remittances from local currency, into U.S. dollars).

As a provider of investor services, OPIC offers fee-based consultations to U.S. companies on such topics as feasibility studies and investment missions.

From 1971 through 1993, OPIC claims credit for having supported investment in projects worth nearly $60 billion and generating $26 billion in exports—all at no cost to taxpayers because appropriations provided by Congress are repaid from the fees generated. It is now issuing more than $3 billion annually in insurance coverage and more than $400 million annually in loans and loan guarantees.

Whereas OPIC originally was created in response to the broader U.S. foreign policy objective of promoting market-based economies overseas, with the end of the Cold War, OPIC now finds itself focusing much of its new programming on the former Soviet Union and other formerly communist countries. Following the September 1993 signing of the Israeli-Palestinian Declaration of Principles, OPIC programs were authorized for the West Bank and Gaza. After the end of apartheid and the election of President Nelson R. Mandela, OPIC also expanded its activities in South Africa. In sum, while the geographic focal points have shifted, and may continue to shift, OPIC's means supporting broader U.S. foreign policy objectives remains the same.

STEPHEN D. COHEN

See also Foreign Aid; Foreign Direct Investment

FURTHER READING

Breenglass, Alan. *The Overseas Private Investment Corporation*. New York, 1983.
Overseas Private Investment Corporation. *Annual Report*. Washington, D.C.
U. S. Congress, House Committee on Foreign Affairs. *The Overseas Private Investment Corporation*. 1973.

P

PACIFIC ISLAND NATIONS AND U.S. TERRITORIES

Located in the central and south Pacific Ocean that includes the Federated States of Micronesia, the Marshall Islands, Guam, American Samoa, Palau, the Northern Mariana Islands, Western Samoa, Papua New Guinea, Fiji, the Solomon Islands, Vanuatu, and other smaller islands.

U.S. commercial and missionary interests in the Pacific islands were active throughout much of the nineteenth century, most notably with the whaling industry deploying hundreds of ships to the region in the mid-1800s. U.S. political interests grew markedly with the 1898 acquisition of the formerly Spanish territories in Guam and the Philippines, and the concurrent U.S. annexation of Hawaii. Midway Island was annexed in 1867, and is administered by the Department of Defense, United States Department of the Navy. Midway Island is part of a Naval Defense Sea Area that is restricted to military use only. Subsequently, Great Britain, Germany, and the United States arrived at a settlement of the disputed Samoa Islands. Great Britain renounced its claims in 1899, and the following year Germany and the United States divided the archipelago. Germany acquired the larger share, which became Western Samoa. The smaller eastern portion and its harbor, Pago Pago, went to the United States, becoming American Samoa.

During World War I, Japan occupied Germany's Micronesian possessions north of the equator and ruled them as a mandate of the League of Nations after the war. The islands became a major World War II battleground. At the end of World War II the United States replaced Japan in much of Micronesia, and in 1947 the area became the U.S.-administered UN Trust Territory of the Pacific Islands (TTPI).

Postwar attention to the region remained low as developments there appeared favorable to U.S. interests. For the most part, democratically elected governments controlled the region, encouraged free-market economic development, and were friendly toward the United States. These governments allowed U.S. warships and aircraft to be based in, stop at, and pass through their territory, and rebuffed Soviet efforts to gain influence in the region. As a result, the United States enjoyed secure lines of communication through Oceania (a collective name for the islands scattered throughout most of the Pacific Ocean), to Asia, the Indian Ocean, and the Persian Gulf.

The United States has maintained military bases on the U.S. territory of Guam. Through agreements that took effect in 1986, the United States has leased an important missile test site at Kwajalein, in the Marshall Islands, and has leased territory for possible future military use in the Northern Mariana Islands.

To secure its strategic interests, the United States has carried out extensive government spending programs in Guam, American Samoa, and the trust territories in Micronesia. To represent its interests elsewhere in the Pacific, the United States has relied considerably on the diplomatic and aid efforts of Australia, New Zealand, and Great Britain.

U.S. trade with Oceania has represented only a small fraction of its overall foreign trade. The region's economic significance for the United States has derived partly from its extensive fishing resources. U.S. tuna fishing fleets used regional fishing grounds, including those large maritime areas claimed by some island states as Exclusive Economic Zones (EEZs).

In the 1980s the growing crisis in the Philippines called into question the ability of the United States to maintain large air and naval bases there, underlining the importance of secure lines of communication for U.S. warships through the Pacific, and prompting planners to give more attention to alternative U.S. basing arrangements in the Pacific Islands. The ability, however, to secure those interests became complicated as a result of several developments. New Zealand refused to allow U.S. warships to visit her ports unless the United States declared (contrary to its stated policy) that they had no nuclear weapons aboard. Calls for a treaty making the Pacific a nuclear-free zone, among other antinuclear measures, received popular and government support in Australia and several Pacific Island states, curbing U.S. ability to expand the use of military facilities in the region. The Soviet Union and some Pacific Island states made agreements giving the Soviet fishing fleet greater access to Oceania. Criticism of the United States in the region grew as a result of the U.S. refusal to condemn its ally, France, whose nuclear testing in French Polynesia and colonial administration in New Caledonia had become a point of antipathy in the region. Criticism continued in

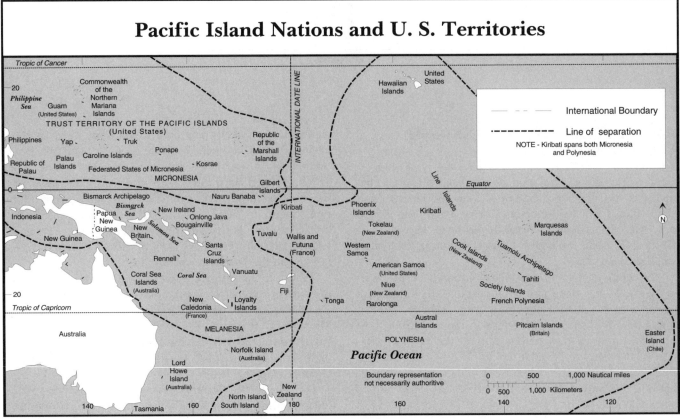

Pacific Island Nations and U. S. Territories

From *Oceania: A Regional Study*, Robert Sutter. ©1984 by American University. Reprinted with permission of American University

the region against U.S. policies on fishing, economic aid, and trusteeship administration.

The United States moved forward with plans for autonomy and self-government for the four parts of the TTPI: the Northern Mariana Islands, the Federated States of Micronesia, the Marshall Islands, and Palau. A 1976 accord made the Northern Mariana Islands a Commonwealth of the United States. A compact was reached with the other three territories in the mid-1980s which gave them the status of "freely associated states," with self-government under their own constitutions and authority to conduct their own foreign policy in consultation with the United States. At the same time, the compact committed the United States to defend and assist the freely associated states for at least fifteen years, guaranteed U.S. access to the Kwajalein Missile Range in the Marshall Islands for at least thirty years, and gave the United States the right in perpetuity to deny other nations any military presence in the freely associated states. The arrangements with the Marshall Islands and the Federated States of Micronesia were in effect by 1990, having been approved by Congress and the United Nations.

The terms of a draft compact with Palau allowed U.S. nuclear-capable warships to transit Palau and allowed the use of military facilities for fifty years. Although it was

supported by a majority of Palau voters in each of seven referenda, the compact failed to be approved. Palau's constitution required that the compact be approved by a seventy-five percent majority because the agreement would grant the United States nuclear rights that would conflict with provisions of Palau's constitution. In a November 1992 vote, Palau voters approved a constitutional amendment to reduce the seventy-five percent majority to a simple majority to amend antinuclear provisions of the constitution. A November 1993 referendum on the compact passed by sixty-eight to thirty-two percent.

Many of the small Pacific Island states have depended heavily on income derived from fishing, claiming rights to the fishing resources in and around their territory, zones most countries have recognized as off-limits. Until the 1990s the United States took the position that the zones, extending 200 miles from the land area of an island state, did not apply to tuna, a highly migratory fish species. As a result, U.S. tuna fishing fleets were seen as repeatedly violating the rights claimed by several Pacific Island governments, and some boats were seized and fined.

The U.S. government attempted to ease the problem by negotiating a regional fisheries agreement with the Pacific states that would be acceptable to their governments and the U.S. tuna fishing interests. Talks began in

1983 and ended in late October 1986 with a five-year, $60 million agreement. The accord, in the form of a treaty, was signed on 2 April 1987. Under its terms, the United States agreed to a $12 million annual financial package, made up of $2 million from the U.S. tuna fishing industry ($1.75 million in license fees for thirty-five boats in the first year, plus $250,000 in technical assistance). A U.S. government assistance package was divided between $9 million in aid grants and $1 million in project assistance. The treaty was ratified by the senate on 6 November 1987 and went into effect on 15 June 1988. The administration of President George Bush and Congress followed through with the $10 million in annual aid required under the treaty. Negotiations to extend the treaty were completed in May 1992. The accord involved a ten-year extension of the previous five-year agreement, including annual payments of $14 million and $4 million by the U.S. government and U.S. fishing industry, respectively.

In October 1990, President Bush became the first U.S. president to hold a summit meeting with eleven Pacific Island leaders, resulting in a number of diplomatic, economic, and public information programs and initiatives between the Pacific Islands and the United States. A senior U.S. delegation headed by the assistant secretary of state for East Asian and Pacific affairs participated actively in the August 1991 South Pacific Forum's Post-Forum Dialogue. The U.S. diplomatic presence in the Pacific Islands doubled in the early 1990s by the addition of six embassies, for Papua New Guinea, Fiji, the Federated States of Micronesia, Marshall Islands, Solomon Islands, and Western Samoa. (Funding shortages forced the post in the Solomon Islands to close in September 1993.) On 12 January 1993 the United States and officials from thirteen Pacific Island countries signed a memorandum of understanding establishing the U.S.-Pacific Island Nations Joint Commercial Commission.

On the whole, Pacific Island countries welcomed the U.S. initiatives and increased attention. The collapse of the Soviet Union and end of the Cold War reduced the strong strategic imperative behind U.S. policy initiatives of the 1980s. U.S. government funding shortages also prompted the administration of President Bill Clinton to consolidate aid and information programs, and to close diplomatic posts. U.S. support for the multiyear fishing agreement continued, however.

ROBERT G. SUTTER

See also Mandates and Trusteeships; United Nations

FURTHER READING

Bunge, Frederica M., and Melinda W. Cooke, eds. *Oceania: A Regional Study.* Washington, D.C., 1985.
Dorrance, John C. *The United-States and the Pacific Islands.* Westport, Conn., 1992.

PACIFIC MAIL STEAMSHIP COMPANY

The company that provided the best mail delivery service between the Atlantic and Pacific coasts of the United States until the opening of the transcontinental railroad in 1869. The mail was carried by steamship to the Isthmus of Panama, where it was carried overland to another steamship for delivery to the coast of destination. Established in 1848 with substantial U.S. government subsidies, the company helped cultivate and maintain U.S. interests in Central America and Asia. Instrumental in opening Japanese ports to the United States in the 1850s, the company initiated steamship service for mail delivery between San Francisco and Asia in the 1860s. Despite the scandal resulting from the exposure of corruption on the part of the company president, the company continued to play a role in the advancing overseas influence of the United States during the 1870s. In the following decade the threat to company life and property by Panamanian revolutionaries offered a pretext for U.S. intervention in Panama. In the early 1890s the company opened passenger service connecting New York to Panama and San Francisco to Yokohama and Hong Kong. In 1917 an arrangement negotiated by Pacific Mail with Chinese authorities provided the United States leverage in a diplomatic tangle among the United States, Japan, and Great Britain over control of the stategic Kiangnan Naval Dockyard near Shanghai. In cooperation with the company, the United States succeeded in preserving Chinese authority over the port. The company, which offered around-the-world service after 1920, was absorbed by W. R. Grace & Company in 1931 and renamed the Panama Mail Service.

DONALD A. RAKESTRAW

See also Communications Policy; Japan; Panama and Panama Canal

FURTHER READING

Hagan, Kenneth J. *American Gunboat Diplomacy and the Old Navy, 1877–1889.* Westport, Conn., 1973.
Kemble, J. H. *The Panama Route, 1848–1869.* New York, 1970.
Schroeder, John H. *Shaping a Maritime Empire.* Westport, Conn., 1985.

PACIFISM

See Peace Movements and Societies to 1914; Peace Movements and Societies, 1914 to Present

PAINE, THOMAS

(*b.* 29 January 1737; *d.* 8 June 1809)

Political commentator who ardently endorsed the American and French Revolutions, and whose stirring pamphlet *Common Sense* (1776) became a popular statement of the case for American independence from Great Britain. Born in Thetford, England, Thomas Paine was the son of a Quaker corset maker. He left school at the age of thirteen to work for his father. For the next twenty years he held a variety of jobs that included work as a teacher, shopkeeper, grocer, and tax collector.

Paine wrote a pamphlet advocating an increase in the salaries of tax collectors, *The Case of the Officers of Excise* (1772), which had far reaching consequences. It led to contact with Benjamin Franklin, then a colonial agent in England. Franklin advised Paine to go to the American colonies and gave him a favorable letter of recommendation. After arriving in Philadelphia in November 1774, he began writing for local newspapers and the *Pennsylvania Magazine*. His essays identified him as an advocate of the revolutionary cause, and in 1775, Benjamin Rush, a supporter of independence, encouraged him to write a pamphlet supporting the rebellion.

On 10 January 1776, Paine published *Common Sense,* which established him as the Revolution's leading public advocate. The tract was a mirror of his own articulate, passionate, imaginative and completely opinionated personality. Paine described the long colonial connection with England as a violation of the laws of nature and human reason, repugnant to "the universal order of things." He challenged the long-held belief that colonial rights were rooted in the ancient British constitution and protected by their connection with the mother country. Arguing that American rights were based on natural law, he attacked the British constitution as founded on two hereditary tyrannies, monarchy and aristocracy, both of which violated the natural rights of man. He contended that it was absurd for a continent, like North America, to be governed by an island. In an early assertion of American isolationism Paine believed England was a part of the European power system while the American colonies were part of the Western Hemisphere: "The true interest of America is to steer clear of European contention." Since the Revolutionary War already had begun, he argued that, "The blood of the slain, the weeping voice of nature cries 'Tis time to part.'" *Common Sense* became popular immediately, with possibly 500,000 copies sold. It produced a decisive change in sentiment in the colonies in favor of independence, causing George Washington to write, "the sound doctrine and unanswerable reasoning contained in the pamphlet *Common Sense* will not leave members at a loss to decide upon the propriety of a separation."

Between 1776 and 1783 Paine published a series of articles in the *Pennsylvania Journal* entitled "The American Crisis" that exhorted the colonials to see the conflict through to its end. "These are the times that try men's souls," he wrote. "The summer soldier and the sunshine patriot will…shrink from the service of their country; but he that stands it now deserves the love and thanks of man and woman." These articles helped revive the spirit of the Continental Army. During the remainder of the war years Paine served first as secretary to the Committee for Foreign Affairs in the Continental Congress (1777–1779) and as clerk of the Pennsylvania Assembly (1779–1781).

After the war Paine's restless imagination sought new challenges. He first worked successfully on a project to build an iron bridge in New Jersey and then went to Paris to investigate the French Revolution. He became its ardent supporter and between 1789 and 1792 made several trips to England to popularize the ideals of the Revolution. Responding to Edmund Burke's critical *Reflections on the Revolution in France* (1790), Paine wrote a strong defense of the revolutionaries in *Rights of Man* (1791–1792). In this essay Paine supported the French government's commitment to defend every human being's natural right to liberty, property, security, and resistance to oppression.

Although made a French citizen in 1792, Paine was imprisoned during 1793–1794 in an outbreak of xenophobic hysteria. The American minister to France, James Monroe, helped obtain his release. While in prison Paine wrote *The Age of Reason* (1794–1795) in which he argued for a view of reality based on science. He condemned Christianity as a myth.

After living in Paris from 1794 to 1802, he returned to the United States and became a supporter of Thomas Jefferson. Many Americans, however, had become antagonized by Paine's attack on Christianity and his *Letter to George Washington* (1796), which alleged that the president had not tried to secure Paine's freedom from a French prison. Paine died in poverty.

REBECCA G. GOODMAN

See also American Revolution; Franklin, Benjamin; French Revolution

FURTHER READING:

Dyck, Ian. *Citizen of the World: Essays on Thomas Paine.* New York, 1988.

Foner, Eric. *Tom Paine and Revolutionary America.* New York, 1976.

Foot, Michael, and Isaac Kramnick, eds. *The Thomas Paine Reader.* New York, 1987.

Ford, Worthington C., ed. *The Writings of George Washington.* vol. III, 1775–1776, p. 396. New York, 1889.

Hawke, David F. *Paine.* New York, 1974.

Keane, John. *Thomas Paine: A Political Life.* Boston, 1995.

Paine, Thomas. *Political Writings.* Edited by Bruce Kuklick. New York, 1989.

PAKISTAN

Located in the northwestern corner of the Indian subcontinent, bordered by China, Iran, India, and Afghanistan. Throughout most of the U.S. relationship with Pakistan—one of the major powers of south Asia—an underlying tension between limited common interests, and sharply different priorities on the Indian subcontinent, resulted in mutual disappointments and recrimination. In recent years, however, reduced expectations have resulted in a more realistic interaction and have facilitated understanding.

Pakistan seemed a distant dream when in 1940 the All-Indian Muslim League demanded a homeland for India's large Muslim population. The movement, however, gathered strength during and immediately after World War II. At the time most U.S. officials, generally sympathetic to India's aspirations for independence, agreed with the leadership of the Indian National Congress that a single Indian state would bring greater stability. Hence, when the British government in 1947 decided to partition the subcontinent into the independent states of India and Pakistan, there were some misgivings in Washington.

While considering south Asia as a secondary concern in the emerging Cold War, the United States also saw both new states as important beyond south Asia. Pakistan was a potential bridge to Islamic peoples of the Middle East. India, as the world's largest democracy, symbolized the realization of Western values among emerging peoples. From the outset, Pakistan's leaders stressed a militant anticommunism, courting U.S. favor. As India and Pakistan clashed militarily and diplomatically over several issues, most notably the disputed state of Kashmir, U.S. policy generally seemed more sympathetic to Pakistan's interests.

The definitive event in Pakistani-U.S. relations came in 1954 when the administration of Dwight D. Eisenhower, as part of its development of an alliance system directed against the Soviet Union and its allies, entered into a Mutual Defense Assistance Agreement with Pakistan. From Pakistan's perspective, U.S. military assistance was valued principally as a means of enhancing its security on the subcontinent. India strongly denounced the pact. Later in 1954, Pakistan was one of three Asian countries to join the U.S.-sponsored South East Asia Treaty Organization. In that instance, the United States, trying to avoid further antagonizing India, which rejected entreaties to join, reluctantly accepted Pakistan's request for membership.

From the outset, Pakistanis were disappointed by the limitations of the alliance with the United States. They resented the large scale U.S. economic assistance to India, which seemed a scheme to underwrite the Indian economy in ways that facilitated India's military buildup. The dispatch of U.S. military assistance to India when it was attacked by China in 1962 and the subsequent discussions—although futile—of an ongoing Indo-U.S. military arrangement struck Pakistanis as a betrayal, and encouraged their gravitation toward a closer relationship with the People's Republic of China.

The troubled relationship unraveled during the crises which transformed the political balance on the subcontinent between 1965 and 1971. A territorial dispute over the Rann of Kutch (along the western-most portion of the Indo-Pakistani frontier, near the Arabian Sea) led to a brief clash of Indian and Pakistani forces in 1965. Both sides condemned the United States: India for arming the Pakistani Army for a decade; Pakistan for adopting a stance of neutrality in the conflict which, by imposing an arms embargo on both sides, worked to India's benefit. As the Soviet Union played a key role in mediating the 1965 conflict, Pakistan found it expedient to adopt a more balanced approach toward the major powers.

Having earned the antipathy of both India and Pakistan, the United States reduced its aspirations and programs in south Asia. With the election of Richard Nixon, who had developed an affinity for Pakistan when visiting the country as Eisenhower's vice president and had always been critical of Indian nonalignment, U.S. policy was reoriented in ways that seemingly worked to Pakistan's benefit. Nixon visited India and Pakistan in 1969 and received—as in 1953—a more enthusiastic reception in Pakistan. Shortly afterward he authorized a "one-time exception" of the embargo by authorizing arms sales to Pakistan. Seeing Sino-U.S. cooperation as potentially beneficial to its interests, Pakistan played an intermediary role and stopover point in national security adviser Henry Kissinger's secret visit to the People's Republic of China in 1971.

That same year the Pakistani government faced a challenge to the nation's fragile integrity as Bengalis in the more populous East Pakistan—separated from the larger and politically dominant West Pakistan by 1,000 miles of Indian territory—demanded autonomy. As the government of Yahya Khan tried to suppress the Bengalis militarily, they demanded independence and gained much international support, including wide sympathy in the United States. The Nixon administration, however, refused to join in the international criticism of Pakistan's actions and as warfare erupted between India and Pakistan in December 1971, it "tilted" in Pakistan's favor. In a show of strength, Nixon dispatched a U.S. naval task force headed by the carrier *Enterprise* to the Bay of Bengal. Yet from Pakistan's perspective, U.S. rhetoric and gestures were meaningless. They saw an ally essentially standing by as Indian armies dismembered Pakistan, and Bangladesh emerged as an independent nation. Nixon and Kissinger defended their actions, in part, on the grounds that the "tilt" demonstrated to China that the United States stood by its allies; the irony of that justification is that the "tilt" ended whatever remained of Pakistani good will toward the United States.

U.S.-Pakistani relations further deteriorated as the pursuit of human rights became an increasingly important objective of U.S. foreign policy. Pressed initially in Congress and then championed by President Jimmy Carter, the issue of human rights abuses in Pakistan attracted considerable attention in the United States and U.S. pressures to address such concerns were resented by Pakistani authorities.

By the end of the 1970s, regional strategic interests again pulled the United States toward Pakistan militarily. The weakening of the U.S. position in the Middle East, notably the outcome of the Iranian Revolution, and the Soviet Union's invasion of Afghanistan led to a renewal of military assistance. After Pakistan rejected as "peanuts" the military assistance offered by Carter, it found his successor more generous.

The administration of Ronald Reagan in 1981 provided a military assistance program—capped by forty F-16 fighters, America's most advanced aircraft—and a program of economic assistance. While that large-scale assistance seemed reminiscent of the 1954 military agreement, there were substantial differences between the two acts. In the 1950s, Pakistan had viewed arms as beneficial in terms of its competition with India, while its principal objective in 1981 paralleled that of the United States: concern over the consequences of the warfare in Afghanistan. Pakistan also coupled the military assistance of 1954 with membership in the U.S. alliance system, but in 1981 remained nonaligned.

Pakistan's reported secret development of nuclear capability was a major challenge to U.S. nonproliferation policy. As one of the principal non-adherents (along with India) to the Nuclear Nonproliferation Treaty, Pakistan evidently was determined to counter India's nuclear program. To pressure Pakistan, Congress in 1985 passed the Pressler Amendment which stipulated that economic and military assistance to Pakistan depended upon the Pakistani president's annual certification that his country did not have a nuclear device. Assurances from Pakistani authorities notwithstanding, the considerable evidence of Pakistan's secret nuclear program has plagued the relationship with the United States for the past decade.

Critics of U.S. policy toward Pakistan, both in America and south Asia, have contended that the history of U.S. weapons sales upset the regional balance by enabling Pakistan to wage war in 1965 and to suppress the Bengalis prior to Indian intervention in 1971. These arms also have perpetuated the military's dominance of Pakistani politics, in turn retarding the development of democratic institutions and practices and leading to widespread human rights abuses. Altogether, critics see much of the U.S. policy as undermining genuine Indo-Pakistani accord.

GARY R. HESS

See also Afghanistan; Bangladesh; China; India; Southeast Asia Treaty Organization

FURTHER READING

Choudhury, G. W. *India, Pakistan, Bangladesh, and the Major Powers: Politics of a Divided Subcontinent.* New York, 1975.

Malik, Iftikhar M. *U.S.–South Asian Relations, 1940–1947: American Attitudes toward the Pakistani Movement.* New York, 1990.

McMahon, Robert J. *Cold War on the Periphery: The United States, India, Pakistan.* New York, 1994.

Venkataramani, M.S. *The American Role in Pakistan, 1947–1958.* New Delhi, 1982.

PALAU
See Appendix 2

PALESTINE
TO 1948

The name the Romans gave to a territory in the Middle East bounded by the Mediterranean Sea on the west, the Arabian Desert on the east, the Litani River on the north, and the Gaza Valley on the south. Although Palestine's boundaries have changed over time, Jerusalem has remained its center. Basically coextensive with present-day Israel and the territories of the West Bank and Gaza Strip, Palestine has been known as the Holy Land of Judaism, Christianity, and Islam. Arabs and Jews have lived in the territory, often in conflict, for tens of centuries. Jews began to move to what they viewed in their biblical tradition as the "promised land" during the thirteenth century before the Christian Era (B.C.E.) and ruled there from the twelfth century to the sixth century B.C.E., before being conquered by the Assyrians and Babylonians. The name "Palestinian," as used in the twentieth century, refers to the Palestinian Arabs who fled or were driven out of the territory after the creation of the Jewish state of Israel in part of Palestine in 1948. For many of these Arabs, now numbering some five million people around the world, Palestine stands as a symbol of their quest for a "homeland."

Governed by the Romans (63 B.C.E.–614 C.E.), who expelled most Jews in a diaspora, Palestine fell to the Arabs in 634 and was overrun by the Crusades from 1098 to 1197. From 1516 to 1917, Palestine was incorporated in the Ottoman Empire. Zionism, the movement for the establishment of a Jewish homeland in Palestine, grew in strength among diaspora Jews during the nineteenth century. The first Zionist settlement in Palestine, comprising Jews escaping the pogroms of Russia and Eastern Europe, occurred in the 1880s in a Palestine largely inhabited by Christian and Muslim Arabs. Under the Sykes-Picot Agreement of 1916, Great Britain, France, and Russia carved up the Ottoman Empire; the British received Palestine, which they seized from the Turks in 1917. Eager to gain the support of Zionist leaders for British control of the territory, London issued the Balfour Declaration (November 1917), which designated "Palestine" as a "national home for the Jewish people," provided that the rights of the Arabs were not sacrificed. At the time, some 650,000 Arabs and 60,000 Jews lived there. The United States endorsed the Balfour Declaration.

At the Paris Peace Conference of 1919, some Arab leaders appealed for the establishment of a unified and independent Arab nation that included Palestine. President Woodrow Wilson, known for his endorsement of the principle of self-determination, urged sending an international commission to the region to ascertain local sentiment. He appointed Henry Churchill King, president of Oberlin College, and Charles R. Crane, an industrialist-philanthropist, to the commission, but when British and French support for the mission cooled, Wilson sent King and Crane on their own. The King-Crane report recommended abandonment of a Jewish homeland because of the overwhelming Arab majority in the territory. Although King and Crane proposed a U.S. mandate, their report made little impact on Wilson, who became preoccupied in 1919 with trying to persuade the U.S. Senate to accept the Versailles Treaty and the League of Nations. The Allied Supreme Council, in the 1920 San Remo agreement, assigned Palestine as a mandate to Great Britain. In 1922 the League of Nations formally named Palestine a British mandate, which lasted until 1948.

Washington seemed content to let the British handle Palestine and the growing Arab-Jewish violence stemming from increased Jewish immigration to the area. Jews in the United States, meanwhile, divided over Zionism and whether Palestine should be the site for a Jewish national home. But the conversion of Supreme Court Justice Louis D. Brandeis to Zionism and his description of Palestine as a sort of second United States won followers. Beginning in the 1920s both major political parties in the United States regularly endorsed Zionism. Both houses of Congress in 1922 passed resolutions favoring Palestine as a national home for the Jewish people. In December 1924, a U.S.-British agreement provided for the protection of U.S. economic and cultural interests in Palestine, particularly Protestant philanthropies, Standard Oil Company of New York claims, and development projects sponsored by Jews in the United States. In the interwar years, moreover, U.S. archaeologists excavated ancient sites and U.S. philanthropists helped fund museums, building on the activities of U.S. scholars, religious missionaries, and explorers who had visited Palestine in the nineteenth century. In August 1929, Arabs and Jews clashed in Jerusalem; hun-

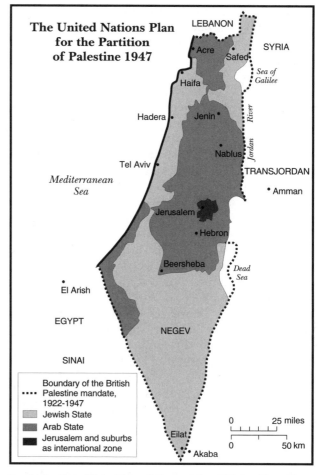

From *American Foreign Relations*, Thomas G. Paterson, J. Garry Clifford, and Kenneth J. Hagan, Volume II. ©1995 by D. C. Heath and Company. Reprinted with permission of Houghton Mifflin Company

dreds died, including eight Jewish Americans attending a religious college in Hebron.

During the Nazi German persecution of the Jews, beginning in the 1930s and continuing through World War II, the Jewish population of Palestine grew markedly, although the British in 1939 began to limit Jewish immigration to the territory (by 1948, 1.38 million Arabs and 700,000 Jews lived in the British mandate). In May 1942, Zionists met at the Biltmore Hotel in New York City and called for unlimited Jewish immigration into Palestine. Lobbying groups such as the American Palestine Committee, the Zionist Organization of America, and the Christian Council on Palestine pressed Washington to take action on their behalf. State legislatures passed resolutions of support for a Jewish homeland; in 1944 the Republican and Democratic parties wrote platforms that included calls for a Jewish state. President Franklin D. Roosevelt expressed mild support for Zionism, but he also assured Arab leaders that he would make no decisions on Palestine without consulting them. By the end of World War II, Roosevelt had not formed a Palestine policy. At one point, he had toyed with the idea of a Palestine governed by three trustees—a Jew, a Christian, and a Muslim.

Roosevelt's successor, Harry S. Truman, could not ignore Palestine because the plight of Jewish refugees from war-ravaged Europe had become an issue of widespread concern. He urged London to ease its restrictions on immigration to Palestine, while the United Jewish Appeal in the United States sent millions of private dollars to Palestine for relief. An official U.S.-British Committee of Inquiry recommended in April 1946 that 100,000 victims of European fascism be admitted and that Palestine be made a United Nations trusteeship, with eventual independence as a nation comprising both Arabs and Jews. Arab leaders denounced the plan as a violation of Palestinian Arab rights, and Zionists intent upon a Jewish state also rejected the committee's proposal. Another 1946 U.S.-British plan (Morrison-Grady) soon emerged with the suggestion of partition into Jewish and Arab sectors under British trusteeship, with U.S. economic assistance to help settle Jewish immigrants. This scheme, too, met resistance. Committed to reducing its expensive overseas commitments, the British decided in early 1947 to send the issue of Palestine to the United Nations. In November the United Nations partitioned Palestine into a Jewish area (5,600 square miles or about fifty-four percent) and an Arab area (4,800 square miles).

The Truman administration endorsed the partition, calculating that the United States would not seriously alienate oil-rich Arab states. Arab-Jewish violence in Palestine sabotaged the UN plan. On 15 May 1948 the British mandate over Palestine ended, and Jews in Palestine declared the new state of Israel, which Truman quickly recognized, despite the opposition of U.S. oil companies and some "Arabist" segments of the Department of State. In the Palestine War of 1948–1949, Israeli forces defeated the Palestinian Arabs and beat back attacks from neighboring Arab nations, which vowed to eliminate Israel. Feuding Arab nations also sought to take advantage of the instability to advance their different territorial ambitions in the area. In early 1949, Israel signed armistice agreements with Egypt, Lebanon, Transjordan, and Syria. In the agreements, Israel received territory it had taken militarily—another 2,500 square miles, for a total of 77 percent of Palestine. Transjordan acquired 2,200 square miles (the West Bank), and Egypt took control of 135 square miles (Gaza Strip). Hundreds of thousands of Palestinians became refugees. In the 1990s the Middle East peace process produced several agreements that may lead to the creation of an independent Palestinian state.

THOMAS G. PATERSON

See also Balfour Declaration; Great Britain; Israel; Jordan; Mandates and Trusteeships; Middle East; Palestine Liberation Organization; Refugees; Roosevelt, Franklin Delano; Self-Determination; Truman, Harry S.; Turkey; United Nations; Wilson, Thomas Woodrow

FURTHER READING

Kimmerling, Baruch, and Joel S. Migdal. *Palestinians: The Making of a People*. New York, 1993.
Schoenbaum, David. *The United States and the State of Israel*. New York, 1993.
Shadid, Mohammed K. *The United States and the Palestinians*. New York, 1981.
Smith, Charles D. *Palestine and the Arab-Israeli Conflict*, 2nd ed. New York, 1992.
Suleiman, Michael W., ed. *U.S. Policy on Palestine: From Wilson to Clinton*. Normal, Ind., 1995.
Tessler, Mark. *A History of the Israeli-Palestinian Conflict*. Bloomington, Ind., 1994.

PALESTINE LIBERATION ORGANIZATION

Under Egyptian President Gamal Abdel Nasser's influence, the Arab League created the Palestine Liberation Organization (PLO) in 1964 to help Palestinian Arabs regain lands lost in Israel's 1948 War of Independence. The PLO's first chairman was Ahmed Shukairy, a pro-Egyptian Palestinian diplomat. The PLO's National Charter, adopted in 1964 and amended in 1968, rejected Israel's sovereignty and stipulated that "armed struggle is the only way to liberate Palestine." In 1969, two years after Israel captured the West Bank and Gaza Strip in the Six Day War, Yasir Arafat, leader of Fatah, the largest Palestinian guerrilla group, won control of the PLO and made it more independent of Arab governments.

Widely supported by Palestinians, the PLO was designated by the Arab League in 1974 as the "sole, legitimate representative of the Palestinian people." Recognition and support were also forthcoming from the Soviet Union, China, and members of the nonaligned movement. All U.S. administrations from Johnson to Bush, in line with both U.S. geopolitical and strategic interests and Israeli government policy, rejected PLO demands for a Palestinian state. The U.S. also opposed the PLO for its involvement in civil wars in Jordan in 1970 ("Black September"), and in Lebanon in the late-1970s and early-1980s, as well as for its role in Mideast and international terrorism.

These actions led the United States to question the PLO's commitment to a diplomatic resolution of the conflict, despite the organization's Ten Point Plan adopted in 1974 indicating a readiness to accept a state based in only part of historic Palestine—namely the West Bank and Gaza Strip. Jewish-American domestic political pressure also was a key factor in isolating the PLO. Andrew Young, the Carter administration's ambassador to the United Nations, was forced to resign for violating the prohibition on diplomatic contact with the PLO.

Forced out of Beirut in 1982 after the Israeli invasion of Lebanon, under terms of a truce brokered in part by the Reagan administration, the PLO set up headquarters in Tunis, the capital of Tunisia. The ensuing diplomatic stalemate was broken in 1987 when frustrated Palestinians began an uprising (*intifadah*) in the Israeli-occupied territories. In 1988, the Palestine National Council, the PLO's legislative body, issued a declaration of Palestinian independence. Arafat announced the PLO's recognition of Israel's right to exist. The moves were intended to signify Palestinian acceptance of a "two-state solution" and, as such, superseded the National Charter.

The United States reciprocated by lifting the conditional ban on U.S. dialogue with the PLO imposed in 1975 by Secretary of State Henry Kissinger. The U.S. ambassador to Tunisia began initial official talks with the PLO. These talks did not amount to official recognition, nor were they free of tension and disagreements. When the PLO refused to denounce a terrorist attack on Israel in June 1990, the talks were suspended. Later that year, the PLO supported Saddam Hussein's invasion of Kuwait, doing still more damage to its relationship with the United States.

After leading the military campaign to dislodge Iraqi forces from Kuwait in the 1991 Gulf War, the United States renewed its efforts to negotiate a comprehensive peace in the Mideast. U.S. policy always preferred King Hussein of Jordan as a negotiator for the Palestinians, but starting with the Madrid Conference in 1991, the PLO indirectly took part in peace talks involving Israel and several Arab states. When progress in the U.S.-brokered talks stalled in 1993, a back channel of secret and direct discussions with Norwegian mediation opened between the PLO and the Israeli government. Both parties had grown concerned by the rise of Hamas, a militant Islamic movement challenging the PLO's claim to represent Palestinians. The PLO-Israeli talks in Oslo led to the Declaration of Principles, signed at a historic White House ceremony on 13 September 1993 by Arafat, Israeli Prime Minister Yitzhak Rabin, and President Bill Clinton.

Strategically weakened by the collapse of the Soviet Union and loss of support from key Arab allies such as Iraq and Saudi Arabia, the PLO accepted a substantial compromise: Palestinian self-rule in the West Bank and Gaza Strip to be developed gradually over a five-year interim period. Negotiations during that five-year period were to deal with the specific terms and timetable for autonomy, as well as resolve issues such as the final status of the territories, the return of refugees, Jewish settlements, and the status of Jerusalem.

SCOTT MACLEOD

See also Arafat, Yassir; Israel; Jordan; Lebanon; Middle East; Palestine; Terrorism

FURTHER READING

Cobban, Helena. *The Palestinian Liberation Organization: People, Power and Politics.* Cambridge, Mass., 1984.

Gresh, Alain. *The P.L.O.: The Struggle Within.* London, 1988.

Quandt, William B., Fuad Jabber, and Ann Mosely Lesch. *The Politics of Palestinian Nationalism.* Berkeley, Calif., 1973.

PALMERSTON, THIRD VISCOUNT
Henry John Temple
(*b.* 20 October 1784; *d.* 18 October 1865)

British Whig politician who served as foreign secretary (1830–1834, 1835–1841, 1846–1851) and prime minister (1855–1858, 1859–1865). A tough, acerbic defender of British interests and honor, he threatened war with the United States over the 1841 trial of a British subject, Alexander McLeod, for his alleged participation in the *Caroline* affair, a dispute along the U.S.-Canadian border that led to the death of an American. Although Palmerston often railed against compromise solutions with the United States, he was enough of a pragmatist to recognize its increasing power and thus acquiesced to the Oregon Treaty (1846), in which Great Britain gave up its claim to territory in the Northwest, and the Clayton-Bulwer Treaty (1850), which provided for joint U.S.-British control of a projected canal through Central America. As prime minister during the American Civil War, Palmerston strove to maintain a policy of neutrality toward the belligerents while assessing developments on the battlefield. But when U.S. Navy personnel forcibly removed Confederate envoys from the British packet *Trent*, he demanded their release as well as reparations. Palmerston punctuated his insistence by sending troops to Canada. The controversy over British construction of ships meant for use by the Confederacy also strained relations. Palmerston began his political career supporting the slave trade, but by the 1840s he had become one of its most determined opponents, negotiating in 1841 the Five Power treaty which set in motion the series of international agreements, later in the century, that were to quell the practice.

DONALD A. RAKESTRAW

See also Adams, Charles Francis; American Civil War; Caroline Affair; Great Britain; Trent Affair

FURTHER READING

Bell, Herbert C. F. *Lord Palmerston,* 2 vols. London, 1936.

Bourne, Kenneth. *The Foreign Policy of Victorian England, 1830–1902.* Oxford, 1970.

———. *Palmerston, the Early Years, 1784–1841.* New York, 1982.

Campbell, Charles S. *From Revolution to Rapprochement: The United States and Great Britain, 1783–1900.* New York, 1974.

Webster, Charles K. *The Foreign Policy of Palmerston.* 2 vols., London, 1951.

PANAMA, DECLARATION OF

See Pan-Americanism

PANAMA AND PANAMA CANAL

Located in Central America, between Colombia and Costa Rica and occupying the Isthmus of Panama through which a ship canal connecting the Caribbean Sea to the Pacific Ocean was constructed by the United States (1904–1914). The importance of Panama in U.S. foreign relations has been due not only to the strategic and commercial value of the Panama Canal, but also to the strong political passions the United States presence in Panama has aroused. For some, the Panama Canal has symbolized the "good old days" in U.S. foreign policy, when the United States met great challenges and generally had its way in Latin America. For others, especially Latin Americans, the canal has represented U.S. "imperialism" and "colonialism" in the underdeveloped world. Both perspectives have roots in the history of U.S.-Panamanian relations, and both have shaped the evolution of U.S. policy toward the Panama Canal.

U.S. interest in a transisthmian canal dates back to 1825. Throughout the nineteenth century the United States proclaimed canal doctrine, negotiated canal rights, and sponsored studies of possible routes. In the 1880s the United States threatened war when the builder of the Suez Canal, Ferdinand-Marie de Lesseps, led a French canal project in the Panamanian region of Colombia. Tropical diseases and poor planning drove the French from Panama, with no help from U.S. warships. But the threats reflected a growing political consensus within the United States that no European power should be allowed to build or control a canal across the Central American isthmus.

The consensus grew stronger in the 1890s, as business interests touted a canal as essential to the economic health of the United States. During the Spanish-American-Cuban-Filipino War, the dramatic voyage of the U.S.S. *Oregon* around Cape Horn to join the U.S. Fleet off Cuba convinced many of the military necessity of a transisthmian canal. In 1899, Congress created the Isthmian Canal Commission (ICC), which investigated possible canal routes and recommended a route in Nicaragua. When longtime canal advocate Theodore Roosevelt assumed the presidency in 1901, it seemed certain that the canal finally would be built.

Theodore Roosevelt and the Canal

Political obstacles remained, however. In January 1902 the ICC changed its recommendation when the failed French canal company offered to sell its properties and equipment at the Panama route. The Hepburn Bill, which authorized the Nicaraguan canal, was amended by

Congress to allow the president to negotiate first with Colombia for rights to build the canal in Panama, a province of Colombia at the time. If the president failed to secure an acceptable treaty within a "reasonable time," he was to proceed with the project at the Nicaraguan route. In January 1903 the United States and Colombia signed a treaty generally favorable to the United States, the Hay-Herrán Treaty, which the U.S. Senate ratified in March 1903. On 12 August, however, the Colombian Senate rejected the agreement, citing insufficient monetary incentives and infringements upon that nation's sovereignty.

Roosevelt responded forcefully. When Panamanians angered by Colombia's rejection of the treaty proclaimed their independence in November 1903, marines from the U.S. cruiser *Nashville* prevented Colombian troops from suppressing the revolt. The extent of U.S. involvement in the Panamanian revolution remains a point of dispute among historians. But Roosevelt's role in the revolution led to the treaty that would define the relationship between the United States and Panama for the next seventy-five years: the Hay-Bunau-Varilla Treaty of 1903.

Negotiated and signed within a month of the revolution, the Hay-Bunau-Varilla Treaty provided for U.S. control "in perpetuity" of a canal zone, ten miles wide and forty miles long, across Panama. In return, Panama received $10 million and the promise of an additional $250,000 annually. Negotiated on Panama's behalf by a French adventurer, Phillipe Bunau-Varilla, the treaty also gave the United States the right to intervene in Panama to maintain order and take additional lands needed for the canal's defense. John M. Hay, the U.S. secretary of state, described the agreement as "vastly advantageous" to the United States, and even Roosevelt's political opponents said little against the treaty itself. Senate critics vigorously objected to Roosevelt's methods in obtaining the treaty. But apparently persuaded by Roosevelt's argument that a "failure to ratify the treaty will not undo what has been done," the Senate ratified the agreement, sixty-six to fourteen.

For Theodore Roosevelt, the Panama Canal was to be "one of those great works" of history that would serve not only as a "permanent asset in the nation's material interest," but also as a "standing monument to its constructive ability." During his second term as president, he met continued criticism of his actions in 1903 with a terse reply: "Tell them I am going to make the dirt fly." For Roosevelt the opportunity to build the canal far outweighed any controversy over his methods. In his view, the criticism only hampered the execution of a project "of well-nigh incalculable possibilities for the good of this country and the nations of mankind."

For the first few years, however, the U.S. canal project seemed doomed to repeat the failure of the French. Sani-

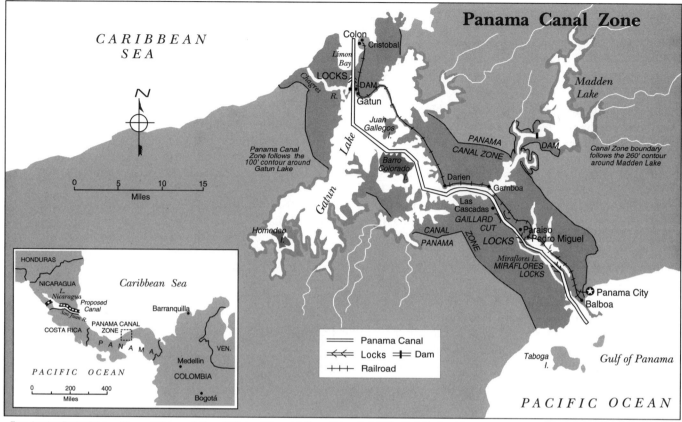

From *American Foreign Relations*, Thomas G. Paterson, J. Garry Clifford, and Kenneth J. Hagan, Volume I. ©1995 by D. C. Heath and Company.
Reprinted with permission of Houghton Mifflin Company

tary conditions on the isthmus appalled the first U.S. canal workers to arrive, and health hazards, insufficient supplies, and a lack of experienced personnel held up the work. Without a clear plan for either a sea level canal or one using a lock system, excavation on the isthmus proceeded in a random fashion, fueling skepticism that the canal would ever be built. Skepticism turned to panic in 1905 with an outbreak of yellow fever. Chief engineer John F. Wallace joined the exodus of workers back to the United States, leaving his replacement, railroad man John F. Stevens, to face "about as discouraging a proposition as was ever presented to a construction engineer."

Stevens turned the situation around by preparing to do the job right. He gave health and sanitation top priority, and he built adequate facilities to house the labor force. Most importantly, Stevens built a railroad, both as a means of supply and to remove excavated material. The rail system alone should have secured for Stevens a prominent place among the heroes of Panama. Yet during the Stevens regime, criticism of the project never let up.

Chief among the critics was journalist Poultney Bigelow, who in January 1906 created a national sensation with a sweeping indictment of the canal project in *The Independent*. In lurid tones Bigelow depicted the sani-

tary conditions on the isthmus as disgraceful, and he charged U.S. officials in the canal zone with corruption and brutality. According to Bigelow, U.S. authorities had even "imported" prostitutes to the isthmus "at the expense of the taxpayer." Called before the Senate Committee on Interoceanic Canals, Bigelow refused to identify his sources, and much was made of the fact that he had spent little more than a day on the isthmus. Yet following a return visit, Bigelow continued to criticize the project, challenging Roosevelt to "learn the truth" by visiting the scene "disguised as a plain man."

Although not going so far as to don a disguise, Roosevelt sailed to Panama aboard the battleship *Louisiana* in November 1906. Splashing through the mud during the worst of the rainy season, Roosevelt toured the isthmus like a commander visiting his troops at the front. Speaking in military metaphors, he praised the "soldiers" of the canal "army," promising them that they someday would "stand exactly as the soldiers of a few, and only a few, of the most famous armies of all the nations stand in history." Upon his return, Roosevelt sent a special message to Congress, the first ever with a photographic supplement and the first and only to employ his "simplified" style. In the message, which was widely circulated throughout the United States and Europe, Roosevelt answered all of Bigelow's charges and branded critics of the project as "slanderers and libelers." "Our fellow-countrymen on the Isthmus are working...in the same spirit and with the same efficiency that men of the Army and Navy work in time of war," Roosevelt declared. "It behooves us...to do all we can to hold up their hands and to aid them in every way to bring their great work to a triumphant conclusion."

Roosevelt's counteroffensive had startling effects. The barrage of critical writings suddenly ceased and U.S. writers began telling a new story of Panama. By 1913 publishing houses and magazines were producing a steady stream of books and articles, all echoing Roosevelt's celebration of the project and his praise for those involved. As the canal neared completion, books telling the story of how this "Eighth Wonder of the World" was built appeared by the dozens, some emphasizing how U.S. health and sanitation forces solved the mystery of mosquito-borne disease, others focusing on the "canal army's" unprecedented achievements in excavation, dam building, or the engineering of locks. All praised the ingenuity and perseverance of everyone involved, from top administrators to laborers. The books created a new generation of heroes, rendering it virtually unpatriotic to speak ill of the project. For many in the United States the new story of Panama became an object lesson in how a great nation ought to conduct itself in international affairs. Animated by the "martial spirit," U.S. citizens had succeeded spectacularly where the French had failed, demonstrating the courage and power of a leader among nations.

Political pressure to revise the 1903 treaty continued to build, nevertheless, both from within and outside the United States. In the context of efforts to improve U.S.-Latin American relations generally, the 1903 treaty became an embarrassment. For many it came to symbolize all that was wrong with the U.S. attitude toward the rest of the world.

Roosevelt himself rekindled controversy over his role in the Panamanian revolution by boasting to an audience in Berkeley, California, on 23 March 1911: "I took the Canal Zone and let the Congress debate, and while the debate goes on, the canal does also." Roosevelt's exact phrasing in the Berkeley speech is a matter of some dispute, but reports of the speech aroused both Roosevelt's political opponents and the Colombian government, which formally protested Roosevelt's "confession." In Congress, Representative Henry T. Rainey headed an investigation of the matter by the House Committee on Foreign Affairs, and in January 1912 the Rainey Committee began hearing testimony implicating Roosevelt in the planning of the revolt. Roosevelt defended himself in the popular press, and little came of the investigation. In

1914, however, the administration of President Woodrow Wilson proposed a treaty with Colombia expressing "sincere regret" and offering $25 million in restitution. As finally ratified more than two years after Roosevelt's death, in April 1921, the Thomson-Urrutia Treaty expressed no "regret" for Roosevelt's actions, but the United States did pay Colombia the $25 million.

Meanwhile, Panamanian nationalists continued to complain about the infringement on their sovereignty implied by the "in perpetuity" clause of the 1903 treaty. Few in the United States paid much attention at first. In 1936, however, the United States agreed to a new treaty, the Hull-Alfaro Treaty, in which the United States abrogated Panama's protectorate status, renounced the right to intervene in Panama to maintain order, promised not to seize additional lands, and granted a number of economic concessions, including an increase in the annuity paid to Panama.

The Cold War Years

Panama and the Panama Canal assumed added importance to the United States in the context of the Cold War. The U.S. military bases in the canal zone were used for a number of operations, including covert ones, as well as for training Latin American military officers. The government of Panama was frequently unstable, with a number of military coups replacing civilian governments, always with at least the tacit support of the United States.

The issue of the Panama Canal Zone continued to sow unrest and to feed Panamanian nationalism. In 1955 the administration of President Dwight D. Eisenhower sympathetically considered Panamanian complaints, negotiating a new Treaty of Mutual Understanding and Cooperation granting additional economic benefits. Yet this treaty still did not repudiate the rights of U.S. sovereignty granted by the 1903 treaty. Nor did it satisfy Panamanian nationalists, as demonstrated by the riots that broke out in 1958–1959 over demands that the Panamanian flag fly in the canal zone.

In the 1960s Panamanian nationalists increased the pressure for recognition of Panamanian sovereignty in the canal zone. Following rioting that left twenty-four people dead and hundreds injured in 1964, President Lyndon B. Johnson's administration negotiated a treaty with Panama that would have terminated the 1903 treaty and recognized Panamanian sovereignty in the canal zone. But vigorous U.S. opposition, along with the military coup that brought General Omar Torrijos Herrera to power in Panama in 1968, prevented the treaty from reaching the floor of the U.S. Senate.

The administrations of Presidents Richard M. Nixon and Gerald Ford renewed talks with the Panamanians on a treaty relinquishing U.S. sovereignty over the canal zone. During negotiations in 1971–1972 the United States agreed to cede jurisdiction over the canal zone to the Panamanians on a fixed date. But Torrijos rejected Nixon's insistence that the United States retain control for some fifty to eighty years as "unthinkable." In February 1974, Secretary of State Henry A. Kissinger visited Panama to sign a joint declaration of eight principles that would govern renewed negotiations. Back home, however, opposition to any new treaty continued to grow. With the distraction of Watergate, little came of the negotiations during the Nixon administration, and President Ford said little about the talks for fear of alienating conservative supporters. After Ronald Reagan, then governor of California, made Panama an issue in the 1976 presidential primaries, both Ford and Democratic candidate Jimmy Carter pledged during their presidential debate to retain U.S. control over the Panama Canal.

As president, Jimmy Carter dramatically reversed his position on the Panama Canal. Resuming negotiations immediately upon taking office, the Carter administration quickly negotiated two new canal treaties, one to govern the canal until the year 2000, the other thereafter. The first, the Panama Canal Treaty, provided for a gradual transition to Panamanian control over the waterway by the year 2000. The second, called the Neutrality Treaty, was to provide for a regime of "neutrality" in the canal zone, even in wartime, after the Panamanians assumed complete control.

The proposed treaties enraged conservatives in the United States. Led by Ronald Reagan, opponents of the treaties spent millions of dollars on campaigns to rally public opinion against the pacts. The Carter administration countered with its own campaign, exploiting the resources of the presidency to get its pro-treaty message across. The Senate then debated for thirty-eight legislative days (the second longest treaty debate in history), finally ratifying the two treaties with but a single vote to spare. Carter had won the first great political battle of his presidency. Yet opinion polls showed widespread opposition to the treaties, even after ratification, and conservative political groups successfully exploited the issue in campaigns against pro-treaty senators in the 1980 elections.

The Noriega Affair

Later events complicated the transition to Panamanian control over the canal by the year 2000. In 1981, Torrijos, who had stepped down as president but still headed the military and held most of the power, died in a plane crash. In 1983, General Manuel Antonio Noriega, the former intelligence chief of the national guard, came to power backed by a reorganized Panamanian Defense Forces (PDF). Initially playing both sides of the fence, Noriega cooperated with U.S. intelligence and military agencies in efforts to topple the Sandinistas in Nicaragua. At the same time, however, he participated in the Contadora group, which sought a negotiated settlement of the Nicaraguan conflict, and cultivated ties with President Fidel Castro of Cuba. Before long, Noriega's brutal suppression of domestic political dissent and reports of his involvement in illegal drug trafficking and money laundering convinced many both in the United States and in Panama that he could not be trusted to oversee the transition to Panamanian control over the canal zone. In 1987 the decapitated body of Noriega's chief political opponent, Dr. Hugo Spadafora, was discovered in neighboring Costa Rica, and the United States suspended millions of dollars in aid to Panama and began pressuring Noriega to step down.

U.S. relations with the Noriega regime deteriorated over the next several years. Condemned by the U.S. Senate and eventually cut off from all U.S. military and economic aid, Noriega clamped down tighter on his domestic opposition and became more defiant toward Washington. When two U.S. grand juries indicted him on drug charges in February 1988, Noriega declared the indictments an act of U.S. "aggression." Yet his continued suppression of political dissent, culminating in attacks on opposition candidates and fraud in the Panamanian elections of May 1989, undermined Noriega's attempts to rally Panamanians to his side. Dissidents within the PDF tried to overthrow Noriega in October 1989, but the coup attempt failed and Noriega grew still more defiant. Thus the stage was set for the U.S. invasion of Panama on 20 December 1989.

The administration of President George Bush officially justified the invasion, dubbed "Operation Just Cause," as necessary to protect U.S. citizens in Panama from Noriega's attacks. In fact, some such incidents had occurred, but it was quite clear that the U.S. objectives were more expansive, including the capture and arrest of Noriega and the dismantling of his corrupt and antidemocratic military force. Besieged for about two weeks, Noriega finally surrendered and was flown to Miami to stand trial on drug-trafficking charges. Noriega's trial was showy and controversial, but in 1992 he finally was convicted and sentenced to forty years in a U.S. prison.

Although Noriega had few supporters among the leaders of other Latin American countries, the Organization of American States nevertheless voted, twenty to one, to denounce the U.S. invasion and called for an immediate U.S. withdrawal. In the United States, however, there was widespread political support for the invasion, both because of its quick success and because Noriega had become such a bête noire. There remained some controversy over whether more Panamanian civilians had died in the fighting than officially had been reported, but the invasion never became a major U.S. political issue. Most

Panamanians also seemed to support the invasion, despite concerns that the United States had exceeded its authority to intervene under the treaties of 1978.

With Noriega gone and Guillermo Endara (the leading opposition candidate in the May elections) installed as the new president of Panama, political violence subsided and economic recovery began. Lasting political stability and economic prosperity proved difficult to achieve, however. U.S. troops were needed to help block a coup attempt in December 1990. Economic problems and drug trafficking continued, contributing to factionalism and declining support for the Endara government.

In May 1994, Ernesto Pérez Balladares, a millionaire businessman who had managed the campaign of Noriega's hand-picked candidate in the 1989 elections, was elected the new president of Panama. Defeating Mireya Moscoso of Endara's Arnulfista Party and five other candidates, Balladares distanced himself from Noriega during the campaign, by invoking memories of his past association with Torrijos. Pledged to honor the canal treaties and opposed to a return to militarism, Balladares brought new hope for a smooth transition to Panamanian control over the Panama Canal by the year 2000.

J. MICHAEL HOGAN

See also Carter, James Earl; Latin America; Noriega, Manuel; Roosevelt, Theodore

FURTHER READING

Abbot, Willis J. *Panama and the Canal in Picture and Prose.* New York, 1913.
Buckley, Kevin. *Panama.* New York, 1991.
Coniff, Michael L. *Panama and the United States.* Athens, Ga., 1992.
DuVal, Miles P., Jr. *Cadiz to Cathay: The Story of the Long Diplomatic Stuggle for the Panama Canal,* rev. ed. Stanford, Calif., 1947.
Hogan, J. Michael. *The Panama Canal in American Politics.* Carbondale, Ill., 1986.
Jorden, William J. *Panama Odyssey.* Austin, Tex., 1984.
LaFeber, Walter. *The Panama Canal,* rev. ed. New York, 1989.
Major, John. *Prize Possession: The United States and the Panama Canal, 1903–1979.* New York, 1993.
McCullough, David. *The Path Between the Seas: The Creation of the Panama Canal, 1870–1914.* New York, 1977.
Mack, Gerstle. *The Land Divided: A History of the Panama Canal and Other Isthmian Canal Projects.* New York, 1944.
Moffett, George D., III. *The Limits of Victory: The Ratification of the Panama Canal Treaties.* Ithaca, N.Y., 1985.

PAN-AMERICANISM

An ideal for political, economic, and cultural cooperation in the Americas espoused at different times by U.S. policymakers, but never a lasting tenet of U.S. foreign policy. As a vision for friendly inter-American exchange, Pan-Americanism had its origins in the Monroe Doctrine and other expressions of anti-European sentiment, as well as in the Congress of Panama (1826), the first international meeting of delegates from the newly independent Latin American republics. In a series of succeeding gatherings Spanish-American countries forged Pan-Americanism, or the Pan-American movement for peaceful exchange in the hemisphere. At times, Latin American exponents of inter-American solidarity criticized the United States for what seemed a U.S. unwillingness to subscribe to a Pan-American ideal. At the Continental Congress of Santiago (1856), for example, Chile, Ecuador, and Peru signed a mutual defense pact directed against the United States in response to William Walker's Nicaragua filibuster (1855–1856). At the Juridical Congress of Lima (1877–1879), the United States would not participate in an inter-American codification of legislation on the grounds that U.S. law was incompatible with that of Latin American states.

Between 1881 and 1938 some U.S. policymakers placed new emphasis on the Pan-American cooperative ideal. Though U.S. leaders advanced themes in cultural, educational, and scientific cooperation, the new Pan-Americanism in U.S. foreign policy was directed primarily at improved and stabilized economic ties in the Americas, and U.S. competitive interests in Latin American business markets. In 1881, Secretary of State James G. Blaine was the first U.S. official to speak of Pan-Americanism as a means of achieving inter-American commercial and cultural cooperation. Blaine proposed a Pan-American conference (the First International Conference of American States), eventually held in 1889–1890. The U.S. invitation to participants mixed the notion of peace and cooperation with the first of many U.S. proposals for the standardization and simplification of inter-American terms of trade. In keeping with earlier suspicions of U.S. motives, Cuban writer José Martí was one of many Latin Americans who viewed Blaine's Pan-Americanism with concern—less focused on hemispheric cooperation than on the expansion of U.S. trade and financial interests.

The most important result of the First International Conference of American States was the formation of the Bureau of American Republics (later, the Pan-American Union) and the creation of a new inter-American system of regular international meetings. At the second (1902) and third (1906) Pan-American meetings, Latin American delegates voiced their dismay over the increasing military interventionism in U.S. policy, at odds with the Pan-American objective of peaceful exchange. Keen on distancing itself from the Dollar Diplomacy of President William Howard Taft, the administration of President Woodrow Wilson revived Blaine's effort to link cultural and commercial cooperation in a Pan-American ideal. Like that of Blaine, however, Wilson's Pan-Americanism was directed primarily at improving economic ties in the

Americas. As such, it differed little from the Dollar Diplomacy of the Republicans. At the First Pan-American Financial Conference in 1915, Secretary of the Treasury William Gibbs McAdoo brought together tens of bankers and diplomats from throughout the hemisphere. Under the banner of Pan-Americanism, those present revived Blaine's project for uniform rules of trade and finance in the region. Once again, many Latin Americans, including the Argentine author Manuel Ugarte, accused U.S. authorities of invoking Pan-Americanism as a cover for their support of U.S. businesses with interests in Latin America.

At the Fifth (1923) and Sixth (1928) International Conferences of American States, Latin American delegates spoke more boldly and directly than they had in the past about U.S. military intervention in the Caribbean basin as a betrayal of the Pan-American ideal. Even so, the United States's Clark Memorandum (1928) and the Good Neighbor Policy of the 1930s highlighted Pan-American values of cooperation and peace; this shift in U.S. policy provided an important impetus for the accomplishments of several Pan-American meetings over the following decade. At the Seventh International Conference of American States (1933), for example, the United States voted for a resolution that denounced the interference by one state in the internal affairs of another. At the Eighth International Conference of American States (1938) delegates affirmed the principle of continental solidarity in the event of war. Ironically, between 1938 and 1945, the growing emphasis on mutual-defense agreements within the Pan-American movement led to the marginalization of Pan-Americanism in the foreign policies of the United States and other states in the hemisphere.

During World War II the inter-American system was decreasingly characterized by a multifaceted Pan-American ideal and increasingly dominated by new military and security alliances. With the creation of the Organization of American States (OAS) at the Ninth International Conference of American States (1948) in the context of Cold War anticommunism, Pan-Americanism declined as an operating principle of U.S. foreign policy. In 1954, at the Tenth International Conference of American States at Caracas, the United States pushed through the Declaration of Caracas condemning "international communism" as incompatible with the inter-American ideal. Thereafter, U.S. and Latin American representatives gathered in special conferences on topics such as technology and international law and in meetings of consultation of ministers of foreign affairs.

DAVID SHEININ

See also Blaine, James Gillespie; Clark Memorandum; Dollar Diplomacy; Good Neighbor Policy; Monroe Doctrine; Organization of American States; Taft, William Howard; Walker, William; Wilson, Thomas Woodrow

CONFERENCE OF AMERICAN STATES (PAN AMERICAN CONFERENCE)

Conference	Date	Location
First	1889-1890	Washington, DC
Second	1901-1902	Mexico City
Third	1906	Rio de Janeiro
Fourth	1910	Buenos Aires
Fifth	1923	Santiago
Sixth	1928	Havana
Seventh	1933	Montevideo
Eighth	1938	Lima
Ninth	1948	Bogotá
Tenth	1954	Caracas

FURTHER READING

Aguilar, Alonso. *Pan-Americanism From Monroe to the Present: A View from the Other Side.* New York, 1965.

Child, Jack. "The 1889–1890 Washington Conference Through Cuban Eyes: José Martí and the First International American Conference." *Inter-American Review of Bibliography* 39 (1989): 443–456.

Gilderhus, Mark T. *Pan American Visions: Woodrow Wilson in the Western Hemisphere, 1913–1921.* Tucson, Ariz., 1986.

Mecham, J. Lloyd. *The United States and the Inter-American System, 1889–1960.* Austin, Tex., 1986.

Perez Triana, Santiago. *The Pan-American Financial Conference of 1915.* London, 1915.

Smith, Gaddis. *The Last Years of the Monroe Doctrine, 1945–1993.* New York, 1994.

Stoetzer, O. Carlos. *The Organization of American States.* Westport, Conn., 1993.

PAN AM FLIGHT 103

A commercial airplane destroyed by a terrorist's bomb on 21 December 1988. The bomb, concealed in a suitcase, exploded on Pan American flight 103 as the plane, bound from London to New York, passed over Lockerbie, Scotland. The blast killed the 243 passengers and sixteen crew members; falling wreckage caused the deaths of eleven townspeople. The tragedy demonstrated the ineffectiveness of military air strikes and economic sanctions as U.S. strategies to combat the spread of terrorism in international affairs..

In November 1991 a joint U.S.-Scottish investigation led to the U.S. indictment of Lamen Khalifa Fhimah and Abdel Basset Ali al-Megrahi, two Libyan intelligence officers. Despite the absence of formal diplomatic relations with Libya or a bilateral extradition treaty, the United States requested that the two Libyan officers be extradited to the United States to stand trial. Libya's leader, Colonel Muammar al-Qaddafi, refused, contending that extradition constituted a violation of Libya's sovereignty. While the United States did not formally charge Libya with culpability in the bombing, unofficial statements suggested that Qaddafi's refusal to extradite the officers implicated Libya. Since the 1970s, Qaddafi had advocated terrorism as a means to achieve the destruction of Israel and to undermine the U.S. presence in the Middle East. Prior to the Pan Am flight 103 explosion, U.S. officials believed that Libyan support for terrorism had subsided after the 1986 U.S. air strike against Tripoli.

On 21 January 1992 the United Nations (UN) Security Council passed Resolution 731, which urged Libya to cooperate in the U.S. investigation. The United States and other Western powers agitated for stronger UN action, and on 31 March 1992, Security Council Resolution 748 imposed economic sanctions against Libya. Although the UN Security Council instituted harsher sanctions against Libya in November 1993, Qaddafi continued to refuse the extradition of Libya's nationals or to claim responsibility for the destruction of Pan Am flight 103.

CHARLES D. McGRAW

See also Libya; Terrorism; United Nations

FURTHER READING

Emerson, Steven, and Brian Duffy. *The Fall of Pan Am 103*. New York, 1990.
Joyner, Christopher C., and Wayne P. Rothbaum. "Libya and the Aerial Incident at Lockerbie." *Michigan Journal of International Law* 14 (Winter 1993): 222–261.
Rubin, Alfred P. "Libya, Lockerbie and the Law." *Diplomacy and Statecraft* 4 (March 1993): 1–19.

PANAY EPISODE

A Japanese-U.S. crisis growing from an attack on 12 December 1937 by Japanese war planes on the U.S. gunboat *Panay* while it was loading U.S. diplomats and residents near Nanjing, China, for evacuation to Shanghai. The boat sank; three U.S. citizens died and several were injured; one of the dead was the captain of a nearby Standard Oil Company vessel. At the time, Japanese soldiers were advancing on the city and the pilots believed that the *Panay*, although flying the U.S. flag, might be carrying Chinese personnel and supplies. They attacked without orders. The incident revived U.S. interest in the East Asian crisis that had begun in 1931 with the Japanese invasion of Manchuria and revealed the failure of U.S. efforts to maintain the post–World War I status quo in Asia.

On 13 December, President Franklin D. Roosevelt conveyed to Tokyo his deep shock, adding that he expected an expression of regret, full compensation, and

guarantees against future similar actions. Secretary of State Cordell Hull believed the attack had been a deliberate provocation by Japanese military leaders in China. Roosevelt asked Treasury Secretary Henry Morgenthau if the U.S. government could legally seize all Japanese assets in the United States as security against payment for damage. Morgenthau replied that a 1933 amendment to the Trading with the Enemy Act gave the president the necessary power. In a cabinet session on 17 December, however, Roosevelt mentioned only the possibility of an export embargo on cotton, oil, and other items. But he also raised the issue of possible naval action. After speaking with the British ambassador, Sir Ronald Lindsay, the president told the cabinet that an U.S.-British blockade seemed feasible and could bring the Japanese to their knees in a year. He assumed that firm action against Japan would prevent a war.

In Congress and the press, the dominant concern was that the incident might lead to a Japanese-U.S. conflict. A strong consensus seemed to form that, while the attack was reprehensible, no vital U.S. interests were involved. The British and French, moreover, soon revealed that they had no intention of taking a hard line in Asia because of the troubles with Germany in Europe. Eager to avoid a worsening of relations with Washington in the midst of their war with China, Tokyo formally apologized before the end of the month and agreed to pay the full amount of indemnity the United States had requested ($2,214,007.36). This reply closed the incident, but the crisis had convinced Roosevelt that war with Japan was a distinct possibility and stimulated him to press Congress for an increase in naval spending.

HUGH D. PHILLIPS

See also China; Japan; Roosevelt, Franklin Delano; Trading with the Enemy Act

FURTHER READING

Iriye, Akira. *The Origins of the Second World War in Asia and the Pacific*. New York, 1987.
Koginos, Manny T. *The Panay Incident*. West Lafayette, Ind., 1967.
Perry, Hamilton. *The Panay Incident*. New York, 1969.

PAPUA NEW GUINEA
See Appendix 2

PARAGUAY

A landlocked republic located in Central South America, bordered by Argentina, Uruguay, Brazil, and Bolivia. The United States opened diplomatic relations with Paraguay in 1861, half a century after its independence from Spain. Prior to this date, a series of dictators who governed the newly independent Paraguay had kept the country insulated from the outside world. The isolation was especially marked during the long rule of José Gaspar Rodríguez de Francia (1814–1840), who called himself "El Supremo" and who imposed autarky by deporting foreigners and severing international communications. When subsequent rulers abandoned these xenophobic policies, however, Paraguay's foreign relations scarcely improved. In 1865, Paraguay fought a territorial war against the Triple Alliance of Argentina, Brazil, and Uruguay, losing in five years about half of its population in war deaths. In 1932, despite efforts by the United States and other countries to resolve Paraguayan conflicts with Bolivia through the Pan American Conference, Paraguay fought another devastating war over the disputed Chaco territory. After three years of war and subsequent international arbitration, Paraguay won most of the disputed territory. During World War II, because of U.S. worries about German influence in Paraguay, the United States sent Lend-Lease assistance and provided loans for Paraguayan public-works projects. Still, the pro-Axis dictatorial regime of Higinio Morínigo did not declare war against Germany until February 1945.

Paraguay's post–World War II relations with the United States gradually deteriorated as the government of General Alfredo Stroessner, who took power in a 1954 military coup and stayed until his regime's overthrow in 1989, became notorious for the activities of military and other senior officials in international trafficking of narcotics and other contraband. Despite Stroessner's record as running a staunchly anticommunist and antiradical government, which included Paraguay's suspension of relations with Nicaragua after former Nicaraguan President Anastasio Somoza was assassinated near Asunci, U.S. officials took an ambivalent attitude toward his successor, General Andrés Rodríguez Pedotti. While they accused him of participation in the international contraband trade, U.S. diplomats praised his government for electoral reforms and commitment to abide by a constitutional prohibition against his reelection to the presidency. U.S. foreign investment was important in Paraguay during the 1960s and 1970s, but Paraguay sought in the 1990s to expand economic relations with its neighbors, joining Uruguay, Brazil, and Argentina in the Southern Cone Common Market.

CHRISTOPHER WELNA

See also Human Rights; Latin America; Nicaragua

FURTHER READING

Miranda, Anibal. *United States-Paraguay Relations: The Eisenhower Years.* Washington, D.C., 1990.

Plate, Carlos F. *Diplomacia y Politica Exterior.* Montevideo, 1988.

PARIS, TREATY OF 1783

See American Revolution

PARIS, TREATY OF 1898

See Spanish-American-Cuban-Filipino War 1898

PARIS PEACE CONFERENCE OF 1919

The meeting of the victors of World War I that drafted the Treaty of Versailles, ending the war with Germany while also launching the League of Nations. Additional peace treaties were subsequently negotiated with Germany's allies (at Saint Germain with Austria and Neuilly with Bulgaria, both in 1919, and the following year with Bulgaria at Trianon and Turkey at Sèvres). Many other territorial issues had to be settled as well, arising from the collapse of the German, Russian, Austro-Hungarian, and Ottoman Empires. In retrospect, the Paris Peace Conference, because it imposed harsh terms on Germany, has often been blamed for planting the seeds of World War II. This negative judgment, however, tends to obscure some of the conference's more positive accomplishments.

Hundreds of delegates from over thirty countries convened at the French capital in time for the formal opening of the conference on 18 January 1919. But (defeated) Germany and (Bolshevik) Russia were excluded. For the first time in U.S. history, an American president traveled to Europe in an official capacity during his term of office. During the next five months Woodrow Wilson would emerge as the leading member of the principal decision-making body of the conference, the Council of Four, which also included British Prime Minister David Lloyd George, French Premier Georges Clemenceau, and Italian premier Vittorio Orlando. He was the chief advocate for the creation (as well as chairman of the commission appointed to draft the charter) of a League of Nations, whose controversial Article X was meant to promote the notion of collective security. The conference, both in its plenary sessions and in smaller committee meetings, provided for pivotal territorial changes in Europe and the Middle East, settled the fate of Germany's former colonies, partly through the introduction of the mandate system, and implicitly recognized Japan as a new world power. In these and other matters, Wilson stood at center stage, claiming for the United States a major influence in the shaping of the postwar world order.

Woodrow Wilson and the Fourteen Points

Wilson's main ideas had been put forward in the famous Fourteen Points speech pronounced before a joint session of Congress on 8 January 1918. Making a case for a just, lasting peace, Wilson called for a new order that would consist of a League of Nations (or "a general association of nations," Point XIV) that would prevent the outbreak of future wars; an end to "secret diplomacy" at the highest levels; and the recognition of the aspirations for self-determination (and thus independence) by the subject peoples of central and eastern Europe. Wilson's lofty tone, and the easily understood subtext of the Fourteen Points, had won for him millions of supporters outside his own country before he ever set foot on European soil.

The Fourteen Points did not fail to make a deep impression on the Germans as well, who were at that point still fighting an energetic two-front war. Wilson's appeal for a "peace without victory" underscored the notion that the United States intended to make no gains, territorial or otherwise, from the war. In the early fall of 1918, German officials sent out peace feelers to Washington, but only when the Kaiser's government in Germany collapsed in late October did Wilson express a serious interest in them. He then dispatched his close friend and confidential adviser, Colonel Edward M. House, to Europe to initiate formal pre-armistice negotiations, which led to the formal armistice agreement signed on 11 November.

Joining Wilson on the American Peace Commission in Paris were Colonel House, General Tasker H. Bliss, Secretary of State Robert Lansing, and Henry White, a veteran diplomat and the sole Republican in Wilson's immediate entourage. To this day, Wilson has been criticized for not including more Republicans, or indeed, any influential senators. On the other hand, the commissioners were accompanied by a fairly large team of territorial and economic "experts," drawn in good measure from the ranks of The Inquiry, a group of mostly academic advisers organized in late 1917 by House to prepare specific analyses and recommendations for all aspects of the postwar settlement.

Without Wilson's presence at Paris, it is inconceivable that the League of Nations covenant would have been successfully negotiated or approved; nor is it likely that the League would have become an integral part of the Versailles Treaty. Ironically, in light of the subsequent senate debate, Wilson's main reason for making the covenant an integral part of the treaty stemmed from his concern that, as a separate issue, the League might be rejected.

Nonetheless, Wilson's lofty ideals did not necessarily reflect popular sentiment back home, and definitely not in the Republican-dominated Congress. To his chagrin, in the 1918 mid-term elections, after Wilson had made his own continuing leadership a key issue, Republicans won a majority in both houses of Congress. Even worse

(for Wilson), the key Senate Foreign Relations Committee would be chaired by Wilson's political adversary, Massachusetts senator Henry Cabot Lodge.

Wilson's desiderata at Paris also differed substantially from the goals and hidden agendas of the British, French, and Italian delegations. All three continental victors had promised their respective electorates that the Germans would have to pay dearly for the war, not least in the form of reparations—including veterans's pensions and civilian damages—in part to help finance the Allies's huge war debt to the United States. In addition, the Italian delegation, led by Premier Orlando, was eager to make good on territorial promises made to Italy through the secret Treaty of London of 1915. The British also intended to maintain their naval supremacy, and were clearly unsympathetic to American interpretations of the "Freedom of the Seas."

The Council of Four represented the "insiders executive club" and a scaling down of the Council of Ten, which had included the four heads of government and their respective foreign ministers, as well as the Japanese delegates. Details of the complicated negotiations over territorial, economic, and other issues were left to the committees of experts appointed by the Council of Ten.

League of Nations

On 14 February, Wilson presented the draft of the League of Nations's covenant to a plenary session. Agreement over the working of the covenant had followed ten days of intense bickering with the delegates of thirteen nations represented on the League of Nations Commission. In a moving speech before the plenary assembly, Wilson set forth the principal actions of the League covenant, which became the first order of business of the conference as a whole and, thanks to Wilson, remained on the top of its agenda until a final draft was worked out a month later.

With this initial victory in hand, Wilson returned to the United States for three weeks to sound out thesenate. Yet the president again misread the public's temper. Opposition to seemingly open-ended U.S. commitments abroad had been mounting not only in Congress, but nationwide. Powerful Republican senators lashed out at the League covenant and especially against Article X, which obligated League members to come to each other's defense. Wilson tried to counter the opposition by inviting more than thirty Republican senators, including Lodge, to a festive meal at the White House. It was perhaps that occasion which led Wilson's wife Edith to note in her memoirs that the president had gained the impression that the senate would accept the League covenant. Throughout the lengthy meal, however, Lodge said nothing. Wilson ignored this ominous signal and only scoffed at opposition to the League. In early March he set sail once more for Paris, having done little to quiet down or persuade his critics. Meanwhile, Senator Lodge initiated a "round robin" letter signed by thirty-seven Republican senators, urging the postponement of the League until peace terms with Germany were finalized, a position Wilson rejected outright.

Back in the French capital, Wilson grew intensely annoyed by what he thought had been Lansing's and House's "disloyal" compromises on League issues during his absence. (The British and French in particular had wanted to scrap the covenant altogether.) In the end, Wilson rescued the covenant by convincing the League Commission to approve certain minor amendments to it: immigration and tariffs would not fall under the League's jurisdiction; the United States could refuse to participate in the mandate system; and in its revised wording the League covenant pointedly restated the validity of the Monroe Doctrine. These moves still did little to alleviate apprehensions back home, even though a full plenary session of the Conference ratified the League of Nations covenant on 28 April. Moreover, in assiduously courting votes among other delegations in pursuit of his League of Nations objective, Wilson was obligated to compromise seriously over other important issues, much to the chagrin of his own advisers, yielding to the Japanese over the Shantung Peninsula, the Italians over the South Tyrol, and the Greeks over western Asia Minor.

One compromise regarding the League covenant that Wilson did not have to make also involved the Japanese delegation. Headed by Prince Kimmochi Saionji, its members had come to Paris ready to proclaim Japan's new status as a world power. The Japanese wanted a special statement inserted in the covenant: a racial equality clause, which the Chinese also strongly supported. This demand embarrassed Wilson (who had a weak record on race relations at home) and promised to antagonize southern senators. The League Commission's ultimate rejection of this clause greatly distressed the Japanese. To mollify them the Big Four not only recognized the Japanese occupation of Shantung, with the Japanese promising that this would be a "temporary" arrangement, but also awarded Japan various former German colonies (the Marshall, Caroline, and Mariana islands) in the South Pacific in the form of "mandates."

With the matter of the League covenant apparently settled, the Conference then turned its full attention to the German peace treaty.

German Peace Treaty and Territorial Changes

In his memoirs of the conference, *The Ordeal of Woodrow Wilson* (1958), future President Herbert Hoover described his horrified reaction (and that of some other observers) to the unnecessarily harsh terms imposed on the Germans. In 1920 the English economist John May-

nard Keynes condemned the treaty even more stridently in his famous book, *The Economic Consequences of the Peace.* These critics were upset by the requirement that the Germans pay huge reparations both in cash (the astronomical sum of $33 billion was finally fixed in April 1921) and in kind (raw materials), and by the unequivocal blame placed on Germany and its allies for starting the war through the treaty's famous "war guilt" clause. To mollify French security concerns, Wilson also agreed to the permanent demilitarization of the German Rhineland and its occupation by Allied troops for fifteen years. Other humiliating conditions imposed on the Germans were the loss of its air force and a severely shrunken army and navy. Germany also lost territory in eastern Prussia, some of which went to the newly independent state of Poland, as well as Alsace and Lorraine, reclaimed by France. German-speaking Austria, now only a rump of its prewar imperial self, was forbidden to unite with Germany. The Versailles Treaty, signed in late June, formally ended the main work of the Paris Peace Conference, although the four additional treaties negotiated with Germany's wartime allies occupied Allied diplomats during the following fourteen months.

The end of World War I spawned many other changes besides the containment of Germany that bedeviled the negotiators at Paris, specifically the territorial adjustments in central and eastern Europe that resulted from the collapse of the German, Russian, and Austro-Hungarian Empires. Many Austrians initially hoped to be allowed to merge with Germany, a hope that was crushed by the Paris negotiators, who feared a resurgent Germany. As victors, the Italians expected the full satisfaction of their territorial claims in Dalmatia and southeastern Anatolia that had been promised them in the secret Treaty of London in 1915. The annexation of Austrian Trentino was simply not enough to placate Italian irredentist ambitions. Wilson, however, strenuously opposed an Italian takeover of the Istrian city of Fiume and its surrounding area, or of part of the northern Dalmatian coast of the new kingdom of Serbs, Croats, and Slovenes. This disappointment so angered the Italians that Orlando withdrew in a huff from the conference, temporarily reducing the Council of Four to Three during late April and early May—a turn of events which also inadvertently facilitated the Big Three's approval of the subsequent disastrous Greek army landings in Smyrna.

Hungary in turn was to lose two-thirds of its former territory, most of it going to Romania and the future Yugoslavia. The French wanted a strong Romania in the east against Bolshevik Russia. For that reason Bessarabia, formerly a part of the Russian Empire, was also annexed to Romania. The conference also carved out a newly independent Poland from lands which, until recently, had been under Austro-Hungarian, Russian, and German control. But in satisfying Paderewski's dreams, large groups of ethnic minorities, especially German-speaking, were consigned to live within Polish borders.

In Bohemia, close to two million "Sudeten" Germans were forced to become part of the new Republic of Czechoslovakia. Less controversially, Finland gained its independence from the Russian Empire, as did Latvia, Lithuania, and Estonia. These nations, along with Czechoslovakia, joined the League of Nations and remained until World War II among the most loyal and active members of that organization.

The collapse of the Turkish Empire raised difficult questions as to the disposition of former Ottoman territories in the Middle East, including Palestine, as well as in North Africa. The "disposal" of the former colonies of the German Empire also loomed large on the conference agenda. These colonies were scattered throughout the Pacific and in Africa. The European Allies and the Japanese both felt they had important strategic and economic stakes in these regions. Thanks to Wilson's firm stand on the matter (Point V of his Fourteen Points had called for a "free, open-minded, and absolutely impartial adjustment of all colonial claims"), many of these former colonies became temporary "mandates," or wards, of the League of Nations; most of them did not become independent until after World War II. Other questions also hovered threateningly behind the scenes at the peace conference, chief among them those that involved Bolshevik Russia, now in the throws of a bloody civil war, and the explosive Irish, post–Ottoman Arab, and Zionist issues, none of which were resolved satisfactorily in Paris. Dozens of delegates from other parts of the world also traveled to France to make their demands heard: Armenians, Albanians, Iraqis, Chinese, Africans, and Indians, all put forward their own nationalist agendas and held their own meetings in Paris, often with the help of sympathetic newsmen. Similarly, African Americans tried to send a delegation of their own under the leadership of William Monroe Trotter, a newspaper editor in Boston and head of the National Equal Rights League. They hoped that the new international order would assure their own equal and just treatment at home. This venture failed when the Department of State refused to issue visas to the delegates. Traveling incognito, Trotter alone made it to Paris but Wilson denied him an audience.

The main work of the conference came to a close with the presentation of the text of the Treaty of Versailles to the German delegation, belatedly invited to the proceedings, on 7 May. Despite their strenuous objections, and under the threat of the renewal of Allied military action, the Germans were forced to sign the treaty in a grand ceremony held in the Hall of Mirrors at the Palace of Versailles on 28 June 1919, five years to the day of the assassination in Sarajevo.

SINA DUBOVOY

See also Versailles Treaty of 1919; World War I

FURTHER READING

Ambrosius, Lloyd E. A. *Woodrow Wilson and the American Diplomatic Tradition: The Treaty Fight in Perspective.* Cambridge, Mass., 1987.

Clements, Kendrick A. *Woodrow Wilson, World Statesman.* Boston, 1987.

Cooper, John Milton. *Pivotal Decades: The United States, 1900–1920.* New York, 1990.

Floto, Inga. *Colonel House in Paris: A Study of American Policy at the Paris Peace Conference 1919.* 1973. Reprint, Princeton, N.J., 1980.

Heckscher, August. *Woodrow Wilson, a Biography.* New York, 1993.

Hoover, Herbert. *The Ordeal of Woodrow Wilson.* 1958. Reprint, Baltimore, Md., 1992.

Lentin, Antony. *Lloyd George, Woodrow Wilson and the Guilt of Germany,* Baton Rouge, La., 1985.

Lewis, David L. *W.E.B. DuBois: Biography of a Race, 1868–1919,* vol. 1. New York, 1993.

Link, Arthur S., ed., *The Papers of Woodrow Wilson,* 68 vols. Princeton, N.J., 1966–1993.

Schulte Nordholt, Jan Willem. *Woodrow Wilson: A Life for World Peace.* Translated by Herbert H. Rowen. Berkeley, Calif., 1991.

Schwabe, Klaus. *Woodrow Wilson, Revolutionary Germany, and Peacemaking, 1918–1919.* Chapel Hill, N.C., 1985.

Sharp, Alan. *The Versailles Settlement: Peacemaking in Paris, 1919.* New York, 1991.

Temperley, H. W. V., ed. *History of the Peace Conference of Paris.* 6 vols. London, 1920–1924.

Trachtenberg, Marc. *Reparation in World Politics: France and European Economic Diplomacy, 1916–1923.* New York, 1980.

Walworth, Arthur. *Wilson and His Peacemakers: American Diplomacy at the Paris Peace Conference, 1919.* Westport, Conn., 1981.

PARKER, PETER

(*b.* 18 June 1804; *d.* 10 January 1888)

Medical missionary and diplomat in China. After earning an M.D. and being ordained a Presbyterian minister, he served in China from 1834 to 1857. He founded the Ophthalmic Canton Hospital and gained international renown as the founder of medical missions. In 1840–1841 he helped persuade the administration of President John Tyler to send a diplomatic mission to China. Then, in his capacity as secretary and interpreter for U.S. commissioner Caleb Cushing in 1844, he persuaded the Chinese to include churches and hospitals in the treaty ports established by the Treaty of Wangxia (Wanghia). As chargé d'affaires ad interim (1846–1848 and 1850–1852) and U.S. commissioner (1855–1857) in China, however, Parker achieved little. He advocated a hard-line policy, including the seizure of Formosa, in order to pressure the Chinese into making such concessions as allowing for the extension of trade throughout China. Ineffective as a diplomat, Parker returned to the United States in 1857. Aside from lobbying Congress to outlaw the inhumane "coolie trade" and serving in such organizations as the Medical Missionary Society, he lived a relatively quiet life in Washington, D.C., until his death.

KENNETH E. SHEWMAKER

See also China; Cushing, Caleb; Missionaries; Wangxia, Treaty of

FURTHER READING

Gulick, Edward V. *Peter Parker and the Opening of China.* Cambridge, Mass., 1973.

Stevens, George B., and W. Fisher Markwick. *The Life, Letters, and Journals of the Rev. and Hon. Peter Parker, M.D.* Boston and Chicago, 1896.

Tong, Te-kong. *United States Diplomacy in China, 1844–60.* Seattle, Wash., 1964.

PASSPORTS AND VISAS

Documents issued by the U.S. Department of State to regulate the movement of people between the United States and other countries. The word "passport" derives from two French words (*passer*, to enter or leave, and *port*, a port) which together mean a permit to leave or enter a port. A "visa" (from the French *vise*) is an endorsement made on a passport usually by consular officials to admit its bearer into their country's territory. The earliest surviving passport issued by U.S. diplomatic officials dates to 1778. Until 1856 the Department of State as well as officials such as governors and mayors issued passports. Because foreign governments did not always honor the nonfederal documents, the department received exclusive authority to issue passports under a law enacted by Congress in 1856. The law also authorized U.S. consular officials abroad to visa a passport for a U.S. citizen at the place of entry into a country whose government required the endorsement.

Until World War I, the United States, like most other countries, did not use the two documents extensively to regulate international travel. During the Civil War the United States required passports only from foreign travelers, but exempted immigrants arriving directly to a seaport. Until World War I, the United States did not require visas from immigrants. Instead, inspectors examined immigrants in New York or other points of arrival to exclude anyone inadmissible under restrictive legislation dating from the Immigration Act of 1875. From time to time, however, the documents became an issue, particularly when countries did not always treat with respect their former nationals who had become naturalized U.S. citizens. Under the treaty made with the United States in 1832, for example, the Russian government tried to exclude from its territory Jews born in Russia who had left to become U.S. citizens. In 1901 the U.S. Department of State mandated that any U.S. citizen entering Russia must bear a passport visaed by an official of that country. After the Russians rejected its demands for the equal treatment of all passport holders, the United States abrogated the treaty as of 1913. When World War I erupted, most Americans in Europe did not have passports.

The war changed passport and visa practices. European governments required U.S. nationals to bear passports which were obtained from U.S. diplomatic and consular officials in Europe. After declaring war against Germany in 1917, the United States used the documents to control the wartime departure or entry of travelers contrary to public security. In May 1918, Congress passed a law requiring visas from immigrants to help identify radicals and anarchists for exclusion. The postwar Red Scare inspired the Immigration Acts of 1921 and 1924, which imposed quotas to limit further the admission of immigrants from particular countries. U.S. consuls issued immigrant visas rather than passenger (visitors') visas to determine who could come under the quotas in cooperation with the U.S. Bureau of Immigration. In 1932 the issue of visas surfaced when the internationally renowned German theoretical physicist Albert Einstein had difficulty in obtaining one because of allegations that he was a communist. Congress and Breckenridge Long of the Department of State later opposed issuing immigrant visas in excess of the quotas to admit political refugees and German Jews from Europe. Advising consuls to be compassionate with refugees who wanted visas during his administration from 1933 to 1945, President Franklin D. Roosevelt permitted others with visitors' visas to extend their stay.

As its relationship worsened with the Soviet Union after World War II, the United States used passports and visas to pursue anticommunist policies at home and abroad. In 1950, Congress passed the McCarran Act, which denied passports to U.S. communists, and two years later it adopted the McCarran-Walter Act, which denied visas to foreign communists. The Department of State withheld visas from politically suspect journalists and scientists who criticized U.S. foreign policies. The department also denied the use of U.S. passports for travel to communist countries such as Cuba and the People's Republic of China in 1950s and 1960s. After the Department of State revoked the passports of Americans such as the famous actor and concert singer Paul Robeson, who rejected a request not to criticize, while visiting Europe, the treatment of African Americans in the United States, the Supreme Court declared in 1958 that the denial of the documents was unconstitutional. Six years later the Court ruled against the provision in the McCarran Act banning passports to U.S. communists. Under the amended Immigration Act of 1965, the Department of State still issues visas admitting preferred immigrants.

Although tensions later subsided somewhat with communist nations and the Immigration Reform and Control Act of 1986 permitted eliminating the use of visas with friendly countries such as Japan, the Supreme Court upheld in 1981 the revoking of the passport of a U.S. citizen for travel in revolutionary Iran. The Department of

State denied visas to both Haitian refugees and Palestine Liberation Organization chairman Yassir Arafat and restricted their granting to AIDS-infected applicants. U.S. immigration officials also have tried to halt the influx of "illegal" aliens without visas. The U.S. government has kept its power to use visas and passports for political and other purposes despite the periodic objections of members of Congress, social activists, and the advocates of civil liberties.

A. WILLIAM HOGLUND

See also Acquired Immune Deficiency Syndrome (AIDS) Pandemic; Arafat, Yassir; Einstein, Albert; Foreign Service; Immigration; State, U.S., Department of

FURTHER READING

Stuart, Graham H. *American Diplomatic and Consular Practice.* New York, 1952.

PEACE CORPS

A U.S. government agency created in 1961 that trains and sends young volunteers abroad to help meet the needs of developing countries. The role of individual citizens of the United States as active participants in the process of foreign relations has taken many forms, ranging from the missionaries of numerous religious denominations, who often preceded official representatives of the young Republic in far regions of the globe, to gunboat diplomats such as Commodore Matthew C. Perry, and more contemporary specialists holding contracts as part of development projects. With the exception of these relatively small groups, direct overseas experience for the average citizen was obtained only through the superficial impressions offered by tourism or as a member of the armed forces. The idea of volunteerism on a substantial scale may be said to have been introduced to the field of foreign relations by President William McKinley in 1901 following the Spanish-American-Cuban-Filipino War. As part of the effort to reshape the newly acquired territory of the Philippines, the federal government called for 1,000 volunteer teachers to staff the Department of Public Education. The concept continued to occupy an acceptable low-level role in foreign affairs through cross-cultural exchange programs such as Operation Crossroads Africa and the Experiment for International Living, but was not formally proposed for government sponsorship until 1959, when Representative Henry Reuss of Wisconsin offered a plan for a "Point Four Youth Corps." Thus, the formal text of Executive Order 10924 of 1 March 1961 issued by President John F. Kennedy calling for the creation of the Peace Corps falls within a framework of established precedent.

The executive order calls for the Peace Corps to "be responsible for the training and service abroad of men

---

TOTAL VOLUNTEERS, LEADING COUNTRIES, 1961-1994
(years of activity in parentheses)

1. Philippines (1961–90, 1992)
2. Colombia (1961–81)
3. Ecuador (1962–)
4. Thailand (1962)
5. Brazil (1961–81)
6. India (1961–76)
7. Malaysia (1962–83)
8. Kenya (1965–)
9. Honduras (1963)
10. Liberia (1962–90)
11. Micronesia (1966–)
12. Sierra Leone (1962–92, 1992–94)
13. Guatemala (1963–)
14. Ghana (1961–)
15. Napal (1962–)
16. South Korea (1966–81)
17. Morocco (1962–91, 1991–)
18. Eastern Caribbean (1961–)
19. Ethiopia (1962–77, 1995)
20. Dominican Republic (1962–)

Source: *Country Status Report,* June 1996. Peace Corps Volunteer Database Management System and the Office of Planning, Policy, and Analysis

---

and women of the United States in new programs of assistance to nations and areas of the world." Kennedy's commitment to the idea of personal involvement in foreign relations as a mechanism to promote world peace and development may be measured by his suggestion at a news conference in Washington on 8 March 1961 that the United Nations should consider forming a similar body of volunteers. His motivations, however, were not merely idealistic. To the extent that the Peace Corps also contributed to development and created a positive image for the United States in the Third World, it also would serve the overall Cold War anticommunist strategy.

The reception of the Peace Corps by the nation was decidedly mixed, as shown by the hearings held on 11 and 15 August 1961 by the Committee of Foreign Affairs of the house of representatives. Coming at a time when Cold War tensions were increasing between the United States and the Soviet Union, the proposal was felt by some critics to be an unwarranted waste of manpower and talent that would be better employed in the more traditional means of ensuring national security. There also were those, such as the Daughters of the American Revolution, who urged that a loyalty oath be required to assure the "patriotism" of all volunteers, and who feared that the egalitarian pay system of the Peace Corps and

REGIONAL SHIFTS IN PEACE CORPS ACTIVITY
(percent of total volunteers, by region)

	1961–1994	1994
Africa	35.0%	39.6%
Latin America	28.5%	25.7%
Asia-Pacific	27.8%	14.4%
Europe, Central Asia, Mediterranean	8.7%	20.3%*

*Principally reflects new programs in the former Soviet Union and Eastern Europe.

Source: *Country Status Report*, June 1996. Peace Corps Volunteer Database Management System and the Office of Planning, Policy, and Analysis

the removal of the volunteers from "the moral and disciplinary influences of their homeland" would create a cadre of socialists. Kennedy, on the other hand, saw the exposure to and experience in foreign lands as one of the benefits for the volunteers. The volunteers would learn from their new countries by living as the majority of the population did, and bring that knowledge home, rather than simply act as paid consultants living in an artificial expatriate community. Kennedy ensured that this thinking was reflected in the formal language of Public Law 87-293, signed on 22 September 1961 and popularly referred to as the Peace Corps Act.

The text of the act begins with a "Declaration of Purpose" setting forth the three goals of the corps. In addition to the obvious aim of assisting host nations in meeting their needs for trained individuals, the second and third goals address the hope of achieving mutual understanding between the citizenry of the United States and the people of the nations served. The act further sets forth the bureaucratic structure needed to support volunteers in the field, similar in form to that of other foreign aid agencies with country program offices run by directors answerable to a headquarters facility in Washington. The Peace Corps presence in each host nation was formally established by treaties signed by designated representatives of the two governments involved. Such agreements commonly set out the fields in which the volunteers would work and specified any legal exemptions to be extended to them for the period of their service. The initial set of invitations for the Peace Corps was obtained by the first director, R. Sargent Shriver, during a lengthy trip in 1961 to Ghana, Nigeria, India, Pakistan, Burma, Malaya, Thailand, and the Philippines. Subsequent host country agreements were handled through conventional diplomatic channels by ambassadorial or consular officials.

The scope of Peace Corps work, while centered principally in education, agriculture, and health care during the first years of the agency's existence, swiftly diversified under pressure both from host nations requesting volunteers with technical expertise and U.S. administrations attempting to adapt Kennedy's vision to altered sociopolitical conditions. While achieving a great deal of its promise, the Peace Corps also ran into problems and controversies in the 1960s. Some of its programs did not succeed as well as others. It also had difficulty at times maintaining its apolitical posture. There were instances in Latin America and elsewhere in which allegations were made that some volunteers were agents or otherwise associated with the Central Intelligence Agency. In other instances host country leaders sought political leverage heretofore absent through the application of sanctions against corps members. These ranged from a formal request that the program be discontinued (as in Gabon) through castigation of the moral, aesthetic, and political behavior of Peace Corps volunteers by President Banda of Malawi, to the summary expulsion of the Peace Corps in Bolivia in 1971.

During the administration of President Richard M. Nixon the Peace Corps was merged with other volunteer programs such as VISTA (Volunteers in Service to America) in a new federal agency called ACTION. This was widely regarded as not just an administrative reorganization but rather as an effort by Nixon, who took a much less positive and at times even hostile view of these programs, to make them less independent and generally weaker. One of the reasons for Nixon's negative view of the Peace Corps was the opposition of many current and former volunteers to the Vietnam War and to other aspects of Nixon's foreign policy, as shown by the criticism of the corps as a tool of imperialism and a 1970 call for its abolition issued by the National Committee of Returned Volunteers.

An evaluation of both programs ordered by President Jimmy Carter early in his term was matched by a determination on the part of corps veterans and their congressional allies to restore the independence and flexibility vital to its survival as an effective presence. Begun with hearings held in September 1977, the process continued for some four years, culminating in the removal of Peace Corps from ACTION in 1981. Changes in the bureaucratic status of the agency were paralleled by amendments to its basic legislation incorporating emerging international aid emphases, examples being the 1978 addition of "women in development" under the influence of the United Nations Decade for Development and the formal inclusion of a statement of the importance of addressing basic human needs. Perhaps the ultimate indication of the agency's solidly established place in foreign assistance came in 1992 when President George Bush announced the opening of Peace Corps programs in response to invitations from the postcommunist governments of Poland, Hungary, and other nations of Eastern Europe. Soon thereafter the first Peace Corps volunteers arrived in Russia and other states of the former Soviet Union. By 1994, some 6,700 volunteers were at sites in ninety-five countries.

The unique impact of the Peace Corps must be measured both in terms of the programs carried out overseas and the contributions former volunteers have continued to make to U.S. foreign relations upon their return. Corps veterans frequently chose to remain in international work through employment in the Foreign Service, the Agency for International Development, universities, foundations, the private sector, nongovernmental and international organizations, and the Peace Corps itself. Some even have been elected to the U.S. Congress. Beyond such activities, the Peace Corps has had the added significance of helping to make a new blend of cultural sensitivity, political pragmatism, and impatience with U.S. provincialism a part of the national consciousness.

ROBERT B. MARKS RIDINGER

See also Cultural Diplomacy; Fulbright Program; Point Four

FURTHER READING

Redmon, Coastes. *Come As You Are: The Peace Corps Story.* San Diego, Calif., 1986.
Reeves, T. Zane. *The Politics of the Peace Corps and VISTA.* University, Ala., 1988.
Rice, Gerard T. *The Bold Experiment: JFK's Peace Corps.* Notre Dame, Ind., 1985.
Schwarz, Karen. *What You Can Do For Your Country: An Oral History of the Peace Corps.* New York, 1991.
Viorst, Milton, ed. *Making A Difference: The Peace Corps At Twenty-five.* New York, 1986.

PEACEFUL COEXISTENCE

See Cold War

PEACE MOVEMENTS AND SOCIETIES TO 1914

Peace movements have been part of life in the United States since the colonial period. Quakers and German Pietists preached pacifist doctrines wherever they went, but it was not until the conclusion of the War of 1812 that societies opposing war appeared that had no formal ties with churches. Opposition to that war had been bitter, especially in New England, and many in the United States decided that not only the War of 1812 but all wars should have their stern disapproval. A Connecticut merchant living in New York, David Low Dodge, and a Massachusetts clergyman, the Reverend Noah Worcester, organized peace societies in 1815. Dodge founded the New York Peace Society in August; Worcester, the Massachusetts Peace Society in December. Approximately fifty similar groups appeared within a few years. In 1828 William Ladd, a Maine farmer whose career as captain of a merchant ship ended with the onset of the War of 1812, organized a federation of peace societies, most of them in the northeastern states, into the American Peace Society. It could claim only about 300 members when the Civil War began.

Through the American Civil War

The pre–Civil War peace movement was divided against itself. Most of its members belonged to Protestant churches and based their opposition to war firmly on the Bible. Some believed that even a war in self-defense was morally wrong and contrary to Christian doctrine, while others believed that such a war was morally justified. Dodge, a strict Calvinist, taught that a Christian should abstain from all war and that there was no real difference between aggressive and defensive wars. He was reluctant to join forces with individuals who thought otherwise, but Worcester, a Congregationalist who became a Unitarian, was less rigid and his group included people who thought war was sometimes necessary. Ladd became a strict pacifist but never sought to restrict membership in the American Peace Society to people who believed as he did.

While most pre–Civil War peace leaders worked through the American Peace Society, the more radical pacifists created other organizations. William Lloyd Garrison, better known as the founder and leader of the abolitionist American Anti-Slavery Society, founded the New England Non-Resistance Society in 1838. In the *Non-Resistant,* published from 1839 to 1842, Garrison and other writers insisted upon the necessity of opposing war in all circumstances. Elihu Burritt, often called the "Learned Blacksmith," was an even more influential radical. A blacksmith who taught himself many languages, Burritt edited the American Peace Society's journal, the *Advocate of Peace,* in 1846, but resigned from the society's executive committee when it described the Mexican War as defensive from the U.S. standpoint. In the United States and in Great Britain Burritt organized the League of Universal Brotherhood, which required its members to renounce all war. Burritt was one of the principal organizers of the numerous international congresses of European and U.S. peace leaders during the 1840s and 1850s.

The American peace movement from the first took particular interest in international organization and international law. Noah Worcester published texts of the Holy Alliance and the manifesto of its founder, the Emperor Alexander I of Russia, believing they offered hope for peace. But U.S. peace leaders became disillusioned by the reactionary course of the Holy Alliance and did not long entertain the idea of U.S. membership in an alliance to maintain peace. They saw more hope in the commissions and arbitral arrangements by which the United States settled differences with Great Britain and Mexico; in the Supreme Court of the United States they saw a model for a court of the world. In 1840 William Ladd published the five best plans for a world organization entered in a contest sponsored by the American Peace Society, together with his own essay, under the title *An Essay on a Congress of Nations for the Adjustment of International Disputes Without Resort to Arms*. Ladd called for a congress of ambassadors to agree upon principles of international law and for a court of nations to arbitrate disputes. Peace workers in the 1840s and 1850s, however, saw more immediate promise in the development of bilateral international arbitration arrangements. A provision in the Treaty of Guadalupe Hidalgo in 1848, in which the United States and Mexico both promised to consider arbitration of future disputes, seemed a hopeful sign.

In 1850 the American Peace Society presented a memorial to Congress urging arbitration treaties. At the same time, peace groups in Great Britain were calling upon British statesmen with similar recommendations, and Prime Minister Lord John Russell proposed a general Anglo-American arbitration treaty. President Zachary Taylor thought the proposal impractical, but in the U.S. senate there was more interest. The secretary of the American Peace Society, George C. Beckwith, prepared a pamphlet in 1851 on what he called "stipulated arbitration" for use of the Senate Foreign Relations Committee. Peace advocates were delighted to find a provision for arbitration of future disputes over U.S. access to British North American fisheries in the 1854 reciprocity treaty concerning U.S.-British North American trade, and they believed Beckwith's efforts had influenced the writing of the treaty. Whatever the truth about Beckwith's role, the idea of treaties promising arbitration—variously called "stipulated," "compulsory," or obligatory" arbitration—had received a strong stimulus.

The Civil War almost ended the peace movement in the United States. The American Peace Society supported the Union war effort, making a distinction between international and civil wars. Some of its members abandoned long-held pacifist ideas and joined the army. Others, while hoping for abolition of slavery and preservation of the Union, remained absolute pacifists and refused to approve the war. Membership declined and remained so small for twenty-five years after the war that the society was rarely able to exercise much influence. There was, moreover, a rival organization. Alfred Love, a Philadelphia wool merchant who had been a conscientious objector, founded the Universal Peace Union in 1866. Love's group existed until his death in 1913, consistently opposing every war and at the same time championing arbitration and the establishment of international courts at every opportunity.

From the American Civil War To World War I

While the peace movement's size and influence during the post-war years were negligible, much was accomplished in international relations which was in accord with its ideas. The treaty of Washington, concluded by the United States and Great Britain in 1871, provided for arbitration of four controversies. Most important was the quarrel over Britain's responsibility for letting the British-built *Alabama* and its sister ships fall into Confederate hands. The treaty established an arbitral tribunal in Geneva, Switzerland, which awarded the United States $15,500,000 for damages sustained as a result of depredations by the Confederate ships. So serious had been U.S. charges, so judicial the conduct of the tribunal, and so large the award that the Geneva arbitration caught the imagination of the peace movement as did no other arbitration. The Geneva tribunal was soon described as a model for a permanent international tribunal. The other three Washington treaty arbitrations were also of importance in the thinking of the nineteenth century. In 1872 the German emperor, William I, as arbitrator, announced a decision favoring the United States that ended a dispute over the international boundary through the San Juan waterway between the United States and Vancouver Island. A mixed commission, consisting of an equal number of British and American members and sitting in Washington, in 1873 awarded Britain $1,929,819 for damages arising from the Civil War. Another mixed commission, meeting in Halifax, awarded Britain $5,500,000 for concessions to the United States in the fisheries off Canada and Newfoundland.

These arbitrations seemed to demonstrate the wisdom of using pacific methods to deal with disputes. On 31 May 1872, before any of the four arbitral decisions had been announced, Senator Charles Sumner of Massachusetts, a leader in the pre–Civil War peace movement, introduced a resolution in the senate that arbitration "should become a substitute for war in reality as well as in name." Henry Richard, a British peace leader, secured passage of a similar resolution by the House of Commons on 8 July 1873. No one better expressed the peace movement's faith in arbitration than did Sumner and Richard, but nearly twenty years passed before there were significant new departures in regard to arbitration in Anglo-American relations.

Peace movements in both the United States and Europe began to demonstrate new vigor during the late 1880s and early 1890s. The year 1889 has been called the *annus mirabilis* of European peace history. The Baroness Bertha von Suttner of Vienna published an emotional antiwar novel, *Die Waffen Nieder* (*Lay Down Your Arms*), which was translated into many languages; almost at once the baroness became one of the world's leading opponents of war. At a meeting of French and British parliamentarians at the Paris Exposition in 1889 the British labor leader, Sir William Randal Cremer, and the French peace leader, Frédéric Passy, founded the Interparliamentary Union. The Union's principal objective was promotion of arbitration. European and U.S. peace leaders also held a meeting in Paris in 1889 to discuss ideas for maintaining peace. It was the first of the Universal Peace Congresses which met annually from 1889 to 1913, excepting 1898 and 1899.

Influences from Europe did much to reinvigorate the peace movement in the United States, but new leadership did more. Robert Treat Paine became president of the American Peace Society in 1891, serving until his death in 1910. A wealthy businessman, Paine frequently went to Washington to urge political leaders to support peace proposals. In 1892 the society appointed as executive secretary Benjamin Trueblood, a Quaker scholar who had taught classical languages and had been president of two Quaker schools, Wilmington College in Ohio and Penn College in Iowa. During his twenty-three years as secretary, the society's membership increased from 400 to over 8,000 and circulation of the *Advocate of Peace*, which he edited, increased from 1,500 to more than 11,000. Trueblood serialized his translation of Immanuel Kant's famous essay, *Perpetual Peace*, and in 1899 published a book inspired by Kant, *The Federation of the World*. Trueblood traveled widely, speaking against war, armaments, and militarism. He gave assistance to Alfred K. Smiley, owner of the Mountain House at Lake Mohonk, New York, when Smiley called a conference at his hotel in 1895 to promote international arbitration. The conference became an annual event. At first fifty people attended; three hundred attended in 1910. Smiley sought as participants people of distinction in peace work, women's organizations, government, diplomacy,

even the army and the navy. He wanted no radical or impractical views. He believed that increased use of arbitration instead of war in settling international disputes was an attainable objective, and hoped that his conferences would spread faith in arbitration among people of power and influence. During the twenty-one years of its existence, the conference listened to accounts of arbitrations, arbitration and conciliation treaties, commissions, and courts.

Throughout the 1890s there was much to alarm and much to encourage peace advocates. The United States energetically pushed naval building, and this decade also saw the stern treatment of Chile in the *Baltimore* affair, the quarrel with Britain over the Venezuela boundary controversy, and the war with Spain. As the United States annexed the Philippines, Guam, and Puerto Rico from Spain, divided Samoa with Germany, and annexed Hawai'i by joint resolution, U.S. behavior in international relations seemed to differ little from that of other imperial powers. U.S. diplomacy, however, had another side. A proposal for a hemispheric arbitration convention at the first Pan American Conference in 1889–1890, reference of the Bering Sea controversy with Great Britain to an arbitral tribunal in 1893, and negotiation with Great Britain of the Olney-Pauncefote arbitration treaty in 1896 were evidence of willingness on the highest levels of the U.S. government to use arbitration. Although they were disappointed by the failure of the Senate to ratify the Olney-Pauncefote treaty, peace leaders were not long discouraged. The First Hague Peace Conference in 1899 made up for many disappointments. Peace leaders were elated by its founding of the Permanent Court of Arbitration and by the fact of the conference itself. If the court could be developed into a tribunal always organized and ready to function, and if a world conference could meet periodically, the ideas of William Ladd and other thinkers about international organization could be realized.

During the fifteen years after the Hague Peace Conference of 1899, diplomacy related to the conference and its successor in 1907 were continuous in U.S. foreign relations. President Theodore Roosevelt's use of the Hague Court in important international controversies, negotiation of arbitration treaties, and proposal for a second conference gave the president and his two secretaries of state, John Hay and Elihu Root, high credentials among peace leaders around the world. When Roosevelt extended good offices to end the Russo-Japanese War and became the first statesman to win the Nobel Peace Prize, U.S. diplomacy seemed to be closer to the ideals of the Hague Conferences and the peace movement than that of any other nation.

The conspicuous role of the United States in the diplomacy of the Hague Conferences was a powerful stimulus to the U.S. peace movement. In the ten years before the outbreak of World War I, forty-five new peace societies appeared in the United States. Benjamin Trueblood, Alfred Smiley, and Alfred Love continued to play important roles, but it was not long before they were overshadowed by such individuals as Andrew Carnegie; Hamilton Holt, the editor of the *Independent*; Edwin Ginn, the Boston publisher; Nicholas Murray Butler, the president of Columbia University; Samuel Train Dutton of Teacher's College at Columbia; James Brown Scott of the Department of State; Secretary of State Elihu Root; and the social reformer and writer on peace, Jane Addams.

When Carnegie gave funds in 1903 to build the Hague Peace Palace, abolition of war became the great philanthropist's preoccupation. Within the next few years he financed construction of the Pan-American Union building in Washington, D.C., and the courthouse of the Central American Court of Justice in Cartago, Costa Rica. He served as president of a new New York Peace Society, subsidized other peace societies, including the American Peace Society, and organized conferences to support peace proposals. In 1910 he gave $10 million to found the Carnegie Endowment for International Peace; four years later he founded the Church Peace Union with $2 million. These foundations, together with the World Peace Foundation founded by Edwin Ginn in 1910 and endowed with almost $1 million upon his death in 1914, made possible publication of innumerable articles and books about peace and international relations.

Carnegie gave the peace movement his money and organizing skill, and encouraged new ideas. He sympathized with traditional proposals for courts, conferences, arbitration treaties, and codes of international law, but believed much more was needed. He called upon the leaders of the great European powers and the United States to create a league of peace which could impose economic sanctions and even use force to counter threats to peace. Several peace spokesmen, among them Hamilton Holt of the *Independent* and Richard Bartholdt, a German-born congressman from Missouri, advanced similar proposals, but Carnegie, Holt, and Bartholdt won little support for these views.

The international lawyers who attended the Mohonk Conferences and joined the American Peace Society regarded schemes for a peace league or a world federation as impractical. Instead, they urged a larger effort to make arbitration more like the proceedings of national courts. So numerous were they and so great their influence after 1905 that the peace movement's historians have set them apart as "legalists." At Mohonk in 1905 several lawyers, among them James Brown Scott and the future secretary of state, Robert Lansing, began organization of the American Society of International Law.

With Root as president and Scott as editor of the *American Journal of International Law*, the new society was from the first a powerful force for development of arbitration and codification of international law. Its work was supplemented by yet another group, the American Society for the Judicial Settlement of International Disputes, organized in 1910 by Scott and a wealthy Baltimorean, Theodore Marburg. President William Howard Taft accepted this group's honorary presidency; Scott became its president. When Root became president of the Carnegie Endowment and Scott secretary of its international law division, the legalists were in firm control of much of the peace movement and its financial resources.

During the years of legalist leadership the peace movement provided support as Root framed proposals for a new world court and as Scott and the head of the U.S. delegation at The Hague in 1907, Joseph H. Choate, secured a draft of a convention for a Court of Arbitral Justice but failed to secure its adoption. The judicial societies and the endowments continued to support Scott when he tried, through almost secret diplomacy, to secure international agreement to found a court before the convening of the Third Hague Peace Conference in 1916. All these efforts came to naught when war began in 1914.

World War I convinced some individuals that periodic conferences, courts, and arbitration treaties were not enough. The world needed an organization with power to maintain peace. Led by Hamilton Holt and William Howard Taft, these people organized the League to Enforce Peace in 1915 and 1916. Holt explained their ideas at the Mohonk Conference in 1915, and Taft presented a full exposition of their program at Mohonk in 1916. They soon had followers, but many men and women who had long spoken forcefully for peace would not entertain ideas about an organization authorized to use force. As President Woodrow Wilson struggled to create a world organization with authority to maintain collective security, he did not find them among his supporters. They continued to proclaim the ideas that had dominated the Mohonk Conferences until 1915, and drew back when Holt, Taft, and Wilson called for new departures. The peace movement was destined to form new societies and to enlist many members after World War I but the Mohonk Conferences never met again and the American Peace Society no longer had a central position in the movement.

CALVIN D. DAVIS

See also Arbitration; Carnegie, Andrew; Carnegie Endowment for International Peace; Hague Peace Conferences; International Law; League to Enforce Peace; Nobel Peace Prize; Peace Movements and Societies, 1914 to Present; Public Opinion

FURTHER READING

Brock, Peter. *Pacifism in the United States: From the Colonial Era to the First World War*. Princeton, N.J., 1968.

Chatfield, Charles. *The American Peace Movements: Ideals and Activism*. New York, 1992.

Curti, Merle. *The American Peace Crusade: 1815-1860*. Durham, N.C., 1929.

———. *Peace or War: The American Struggle 1636-1936*. New York, 1936.

Davis, Calvin D. *The United States and the First Hague Peace Conference*. Ithaca, N.Y., 1962.

———. *The United States and the Second Hague Peace Conference: American Diplomacy and International Organization 1899-1914*. Durham, N.C., 1976.

DeBenedetti, Charles. *The Peace Reform in American History*. Bloomington, Ind., 1980.

Josephson, Harold, ed. *Biographical Dictionary of Modern Peace Leaders*. Westport, Conn., 1985.

Herman, Sondra R. *Eleven Against War: Studies in American Internationalist Thought, 1898-1921*. Stanford, Calif., 1969.

Knock, Thomas J. *To End all Wars: Woodrow Wilson and the Quest for a New World Order*. New York, 1992.

Kuehl, Warren F., ed. *Biographical Dictionary of Internationalists*. Westport, Conn., 1983.

Kuehl, Warren F. *Seeking World Order: The United States and International Organization to 1920*. Nashville, Tenn., 1969.

Marchand, C. Roland. *The American Peace Movement and Social Reform, 1898-1918*. Princeton, N.J., 1972.

Patterson, David S. *Toward a Warless World: The Travail of the American Peace Movement 1887-1914*. Bloomington, Ind., 1976.

Ziegler, Valarie H. *The Advocates of Peace in Antebellum America*. Bloomington, Ind., 1992.

PEACE MOVEMENTS AND SOCIETIES, 1914 TO PRESENT

World War I initiated a transformation in the constituency, organization, and orientation of the U.S. peace movement. Prior to the war, peace advocacy in the United States had become strong among a business and professional elite, people who constituted a well-funded peace establishment and who sought to reform international relations, mainly through understanding, international law, and voluntary arbitration. Thereafter, peace activists ranged from absolute pacifists who rejected all war to liberal internationalists who advocated collective security. They organized not only to defend and promote their points of view, but also to mobilize public support for specific foreign policy positions. They embraced active U.S. leadership in international relations, although they differed among themselves about the specific terms of leadership, and important segments of the movement even challenged national policies based on military intervention.

What appeared to be a series of peace movements was actually the emergence and alignment of peace organizations and public constituencies in relation to changing issues of foreign policy. From 1914 on, the peace movement periodically achieved high visibility in the form of political coalitions for specific campaigns: against intervention in World War I; for various kinds of international commitment in the 1920s; for neutrality in the mid-1930s; for a United Nations organization during World War II; for a ban on nuclear testing from 1957–1963; against the Vietnam War; and in the 1980s for a Nuclear Freeze and Central American solidarity. Those campaigns constituted chapters of what was essentially a continuous story.

World War I: Opposition to War

The pre-1914 peace movement had promoted effectively the principle of obligatory arbitration that was embodied in the arbitration treaties of President William Howard Taft and the "cooling-off" treaties of Secretary of State William Jennings Bryan. The shock of war in Europe had two broad impacts on the movement. Among established internationalists there emerged a core of support for arbitration enforced by sanctions through a formal international organization, while at the same time a new group of leaders arose who campaigned for U.S. peace initiatives but opposed military intervention. They were mainly social workers and activists, feminists, religious leaders, and socialists—all representative of progressive and social gospel attitudes.

On one hand, the war led internationalists like Hamilton Holt (1872–1951), editor of *The Independent* and leader of the League to Enforce Peace (1915), to promote compulsory arbitration backed by sanctions, the kind of international order envisioned by President Woodrow Wilson's concept of a League of Nations. Subsequently, liberal internationalists in the Foreign Policy Association (1921), the League of Nations Non-Partisan Association (LNNPA, 1922), and its successor, the League of Nations Association (LNA, 1929) supported U.S. participation in international organizations including collective security arrangements, while conservative internationalists balked at any constraints on national sovereignty.

On the other hand, the onset of war in Europe generated new peace leaders like the renowned social worker Jane Addams (1860–1935), who brought the social and political activism of the Progressive Era into new peace groups with international connections. The Women's Peace Party (1915), for example, cooperated with European women to promote neutral mediation of the war, an effort that evolved into the Women's International League for Peace and Freedom (WILPF, 1919). The Fellowship of Reconciliation (FOR, 1915) united people who rejected war altogether, mainly on religious grounds. The American Union Against Militarism (AUAM, 1915) fielded a political challenge to Wilson's 1916 military preparedness program and conducted a strong anti-intervention campaign, in cooperation with the Socialist Party of

America (SPA, 1901), which even repudiated the U.S. Declaration of War in April 1917.

Once the nation joined the fighting, most peace advocates supported the "war to end war," hoping for a constructive peace and postwar internationalism. Nevertheless, an antiwar core persisted. Socialists, decrying the war and appealing for liberal peace terms, were viciously persecuted and their ranks were broken. Conscientious objectors (C.O.s) to military service were not well served by federal legislation, and they too faced prison and persecution. The word *pacifist*, which had been coined in 1901 to denote all peace advocates, became a term of derision for those who rejected war altogether. Many of those pacifists found succor in the FOR; some of them organized the American Friends Service Committee (AFSC, 1917) on behalf of Quaker C.O.s; others created the American Civil Liberties Bureau (1917) which later became the American Civil Liberties Union.

Thus, between 1914 and 1919, antiwar pacifism was combined with the progressive emphasis on moral and social reform, problem solving, and accountable government. War was rejected as the antithesis of all those things, and peace was linked to social justice. The value of the state was subordinated to that of transnational humanity. The proponents of these views, who may be called progressive pacifists, established organizations that endured through the rest of the century, notably the FOR, AFSC, and WILPF. Like the liberal internationalists, organized in the LNNPA and later LNA, they acquired international connections and national policy agendas.

The 1920s: Divided Priorities

The peace movement expanded as a public phenomenon, but its various constituencies divided over specific policies. Legalists of the conservative peace establishment supported international law, including some form of outlawry of war, whereas liberal internationalists promoted a Wilsonian order, including the League of Nations and World Court. Progressive pacifists promoted revisionist interpretations of World War I, along with moral and pragmatic repudiation of warfare itself, and they organized an effective political lobby on Capitol Hill. Late in the decade the Kellogg-Briand Pact was endorsed by all factions, but only because it was a minimal statement of their common aspirations.

During the Washington Conference on the Limitation of [naval] Armaments, progressive pacifists organized a press and information service and mobilized expressions of public support for disarmament. This evolved into a permanent peace lobby, the National Council for Prevention of War (NCPW, 1922). Under the dynamic leadership of Frederick Libby (1874–1970), the NCPW reflected the positions of the pacifist leadership in the FOR,

AFSC, and WILPF, especially on military spending and military training in schools, while it acted as both an information service and pressure group on foreign relations for many churches and associations of women, youth, farmers, and labor. Through these constituencies, pacifists promoted a revisionist interpretation of World War I that contributed to public cynicism about the efficacy of warfare. Also seeking alternatives to warfare, pacifists tried to mitigate the differences among nonpacifist internationalists.

On one side there were ranged the supporters of strong international organization. Following the defeat of the League of Nations, they concentrated their efforts on U.S. accession to the Permanent International Court of Justice, or World Court. A coalition led by the WILPF and other women's groups mounted considerable public support, but the effort was frustrated in 1925 by congressional reservations. Other internationalists lined up against any world court having anything more than moral authority, arguing that international law had to be made authoritative before it could be enforced. Republican Senator William Borah of Idaho (1865–1940), exploiting the division among peace advocates in order to keep the country isolated from binding international obligations, deftly promoted the Kellogg-Briand Pact in order to preclude stronger initiatives. Accordingly, public disillusionment with war in the 1920s was not translated into support for an internationalist foreign policy.

The 1930s: Neutrality and Collective Security

Japanese aggression in Manchuria and China, the Spanish Civil War, and threats from German and Italian fascism prompted the formation of a major political coalition of peace activists. Both liberal internationalists and progressive pacifists supported an active U.S. role in international programs for disarmament, political organization, and economic reconstruction. Although at the outset that role appeared to be consonant with U.S. strict neutrality, the peace coalition divided over the issue of neutrality with the onset of war in Europe.

By the mid-1930s progressive pacifists and liberal internationalists were anxious about the rise of violence abroad; given their international connections with the victims of persecution abroad, their concern was intensely personal, not merely abstract. Both wings of the movement agreed that there was an urgent need to stabilize the changing international order, mainly through political and economic reform, and to constrain the economic interests that they held largely responsible for the previous war. For different reasons, both groups also agreed to support legislation that would require an impartial embargo against trade and credit on all belligerents: pacifists hoped that such strict neutrality would preclude

U.S. military intervention; internationalists counted on it to mollify public apprehensions of another war while leaving European powers free to apply their own collective sanctions against an aggressor. With that understanding, it was possible for the peace movement to form a multi-issue coalition.

Pacifists in the NCPW, WILPF (led by lobbyist Dorothy Detzer, 1893–1981), and FOR were instrumental in organizing, servicing, and popularizing the 1934 investigation into the role of the World War I munitions industry by a committee of the Senate headed by Gerald P. Nye (1892–1971), a Republican from North Dakota. The following year they mobilized public support for congressional neutrality legislation and obtained the initiative in a coalition with liberal internationalists, the massive Emergency Peace Campaign (EPC, 1936–1937).

At its peak the EPC operated with twenty area offices, a staff of 150 persons, and active cooperation with labor, farm, business, women's, and student groups. The campaign staff provided information on issues and voting records to its constituencies, from which it channeled popular pressure back to Congress. Its resources were largely exhausted by the fall of 1937, so that its concluding campaign for an international economic conference was run largely by the internationalist wing. In 1938 the coalition was polarized over the Ludlow constitutional amendment for a referendum of war. Led by Clark Eichelberger (1896–1980) of the LNA, liberal internationalists organized a national campaign against the amendment, from which Eichelberger built a coalition for neutrality revision and, after 1939, for intervention "short of war." Following the summer of 1940, the campaign was known as the Committee to Defend America by Aiding the Allies. Meanwhile, progressive pacifists aligned uncomfortably with conservative isolationists to support the Ludlow amendment. For a short time they cooperated with the Keep America Out of War campaign of socialist leader Norman Thomas (1884–1968). By the time that endeavor was subordinated to the right-wing America First Committee (1940), pacifists had largely withdrawn from the political arena to their own communities.

The 1940s: The United Nations Organization

Pacifists were not persecuted during the second world war as they had been in the first one. Nonetheless, they invested a great deal of energy in maintaining the bonds of fellowship and in serving C.O.s in connection with the government's Civilian Public Service program. Beyond that, they publicly protested the saturation bombing of German cities and the forced relocation of Japanese-Americans. The Fellowship of Reconciliation, notably A.J. Muste (1885–1967), also supported experiments

with Gandhian-like nonviolent action on behalf of civil rights and virtually sponsored the Congress of Racial Equality (1943) in its early years. Pacifists also strengthened their transnational orientation and, in that respect, they endorsed the concept of a postwar United Nations organization.

Liberal internationalists associated with the LNA, notably Clark Eichelberger and James T. Shotwell (1874–1965), entered the war with great credibility in the executive branch. They had long worked for the League of Nations and had effectively challenged prewar isolationism. Along with others from the private sector, they were involved in Department of State planning for a successor to the League. Moreover, they were explicitly facilitated by the government to mobilize public support so that the rejection of U.S. participation in the League would not be repeated. Out of a series of organizations, they created the United Nations Association (1943), which absorbed the former LNA in 1944 and waged a massive, bipartisan public campaign. Progressive pacifists in the WILPF and FOR generally supported the goal of a United Nations Organization (UNO, 1945), but voiced reservations about its big-power orientation. In fact, when the UNO was formed in San Francisco, nongovernmental associations were instrumental in strengthening its emphasis on human rights.

Seen in the glaring light of the atomic bomb, the combination of hope and weakness in the UNO led to a flurry of efforts for world federalism. Scientists involved in the Manhattan Project provided a nucleus for the Federation of American Scientists (1946), which campaigned for civilian and international control of atomic energy. By then, several organizations for world federalism had emerged in the wake of the UNO campaign. Most of them merged into the United World Federalists (1947), which grew to 50,000 members by the autumn of 1949, part of an international movement to create a stronger, transnational authority.

Already engulfed in anticommunist controversy by that time, the world federalism movement succumbed to Cold War polarity and collapsed with the outbreak of the Korean War. Increasingly, internationalists endorsed U.S. responsibility to model and ensure world order against the ideological and military threat of the Sino-Soviet bloc.

1957–1963: The Test-Ban Campaign

The nuclear arms race provided the catalyst for the resurgence of the peace movement during the Cold War. Against the atmospheric testing of nuclear weapons there formed a coalition of scientists, liberal internationalists, and progressive pacifists that both fed on grassroots apprehension and fueled it. The minimal demand for a ban on nuclear testing united a broad spectrum of the peace groups and also generated new ones. It appealed to those who wanted to put parameters on the arms race, but it was also a vehicle for those who questioned the Cold War itself. In some measure it contributed to the partial Test Ban Treaty of 1963.

Beginning around 1955, radioactive fallout was protested by scientists and by peace groups like the WILPF, and the issue became especially salient when it was introduced into the 1956 presidential campaign by the losing candidate, Adlai Stevenson. In the spring of the next year a group of peace advocates agreed on a dual approach to the issue: on one hand there would be a traditional campaign for public information and political pressure, while on the other there would be direct action. Out of the first emphasis grew the Committee for a Sane Nuclear Policy (SANE, 1957); from the second came the Committee for Non-Violent Action (CNVA, 1957). Beyond their tactical differences were diverse views of society and a common concern with the nuclear threat.

The CNVA applied Gandhian-like direct action and civil disobedience to the nuclear arms issue at the same time that this approach was being developed in the civil rights movement. As early as 1955 a few pacifists from the Catholic Worker Movement and War Resisters League (WRL, 1923) refused to comply with civil defense drills. That tactic was supplemented by vigils at testing sites, attempts to sail into the Pacific testing zone, picketing of Polaris missile submarines, and public demonstrations such as a "walk" from San Francisco to Moscow. Such actions were seen by CNVA activists as a form of moral witness, and, in the view of some, were not effectively coordinated with political goals.

Meanwhile, SANE tapped grassroots anxiety about testing, if not about the Cold War. Unexpectedly it mushroomed into a membership organization and a campaign of public information and pressure for a comprehensive ban on testing nuclear weapons as a first step toward Cold War disarmament and détente. The movement continued to grow, despite a 1958 U.S.-Soviet moratorium on testing and a divisive controversy over anticommunism within SANE. What is more, new organizations brought in specific constituencies: entertainers, nuclear scientists, Physicians for Social Responsibility (1962), students (Student Peace Union, 1959), and, most dramatically, women (Women Strike for Peace, 1959). The campaign against nuclear testing contributed to the initiation and ratification of the 1963 Limited Nuclear Test Ban Treaty and to public discussion about the terms of Cold War.

The Vietnam War: The Antiwar Movement

The Vietnam War converted the resurgent peace movement of the test-ban coalition into an antiwar movement, to which were added ever more constituencies. Organized opposition to the war came from a shifting, unstable coalition of diverse and often conflicting strands of U.S. social and political culture in the 1960s. The opposition was grounded variously in five assertions about the war: that it was unfeasible, since self-government could not be imposed on Vietnam and since U.S. vital interests did not justify the cost; that it was not wise geopolitics, since it undermined regional stability; that supporting a repressive government violated U.S. ideals and priorities; that the level of destruction to Vietnam was immoral; and that in some respects the effort was imperialistic. The emphasis and tactics of protest varied greatly, and even older, well-established groups like the FOR and AFSC experienced sharp tensions among their leaders, together with deep frustration as the war ground on from 1965 to 1975.

The movement's most visible aspect was its association with political and cultural radicalism. In April 1965 the Students for a Democratic Society (SDS, 1960) sponsored the first major antiwar demonstration, and even though SDS abandoned antiwar leadership, it had attracted the factious Old Left (the Socialist Workers Party, SWP, and the tiny Communist party), together with direct-action pacifists and an amorphous, youthful New Left constituency. These elements became the core of a series of left-wing coalitions, precursors of the National Mobilization Committee (The Mobe, 1967) to which elements of a colorful counterculture became attached. Such a collection of very diverse groups became possible only by subsuming many domestic issues under an antiwar banner. The primary organizing tactics were large-scale demonstrations and draft resistance, but a minority of activists engaged in acts of civil disobedience. Dramatic actions and personalities gained media coverage, so that many people associated the antiwar movement with cultural confrontation. Cresting in 1968–1969, this wing receded thereafter.

Less dramatic was the informal coalition of liberals who were closer to the political center and who focused on the single issue of the war. Active from the beginning of the war, some of them formed the core of the "teach-ins" in the spring of 1965 that gave voice to an informed, authoritative challenge to the government's credibility. In the next two years even more antiwar constituencies were organized, notably by leaders in religion (Clergy and Laymen Concerned, CALC, 1966), labor, health care, sciences, social services, and business. Although they participated in mass demonstrations, these antiwar constituencies stressed continuing programs of public information and debate, petitions, lobbying, and electoral politics.

A key element in the antiwar movement after 1968 was the sharp growth of antiwar veterans groups, especially Vietnam Veterans Against the War (VVAW, 1967), who had enormous credibility without any ideological stamp. Opposition to the war became ever more a part of the political mainstream, especially in the Democratic party as it was refashioned between the 1968 and 1972 presidential campaigns. Antiwar opposition focused on Congress, and public campaigns were targeted at congressional actions: to set a specific date for withdrawal, to cut off funds for the air war, to disengage from the Saigon government, and to cut off aid to it. Meanwhile, the visibility of the antiwar movement decreased almost in proportion to its political effectiveness.

In retrospect, the antiwar movement gave voice to alternative authorities on foreign policy and challenged the credibility of the executive branch. It kept the issue of whether or not the war was morally acceptable or practically viable before the public. It visualized, even exacerbated, popular anxiety, and it mobilized cultural and political opposition to the war. It was, from the first, taken very seriously by the administrations of Presidents Lyndon B. Johnson and Richard M. Nixon, aggravating their obfuscation and duplicity on the war and eliciting extralegal programs of surveillance and harassment. Organized antiwar protest provided a significant check on the government's ability to prosecute the war and helped to redress the congressional role in foreign policy.

The hardening of the Cold War in the final years of the administration of President Jimmy Carter, and the initial Cold War crusade of President Ronald Reagan, combined with technological changes in nuclear arms capability, generated an international campaign that became known in the United States as The Freeze. The public was educated and aroused on a massive basis by a coalition of activists that had a strong grassroots, or local, base. It also had a critical core of support in Congress, where Freeze demands became the leverage by which arms control was revived and institutionalized, even before Reagan shifted to serious disarmament negotiations with the Soviet Union.

During the decade a broad public movement of solidarity with people in Central America emerged to counter the Reagan administration's policy of military support for right-wing military forces in the region. In many respects the solidarity movement appeared to be apolitical, because it put local groups of U.S. professional and community groups into a supportive, even personal relationship with Central American counterparts. In fact, that community base provided political support for a core of congressional supporters who constrained and in some measure reversed the administration's policy.

Peace Movement History

Building on the pioneering work of Merle Curti and a few others, historians from the 1960s on have made the history of peace movements a recognized and prolific field of history. They have undertaken collaborative work with historians of similar movements abroad, and they have been joined by sociologists employing social movement analysis. There is a consensus among these scholars that peace and antiwar campaigns have been important in foreign policy formation, that they have both challenged and reflected prevailing political cultures, and that they have constituted domestic reform movements with transnational connections.

The U.S. peace movement addressed warfare itself as a problem in international relations, and it addressed war in terms of its consequences rather than its ideals. Peace advocates elevated the importance of transnational and humanitarian values, but—especially in the twentieth century—they addressed peace as a process of social change and a condition for accountable power. More specifically, organized peace advocates helped to inform the public at large on foreign policy issues ranging from the conduct of the Spanish-American-Cuban-Filipino or Vietnam Wars to the United Nations or the effects of nuclear testing. They envisioned and promoted many approaches to conflict resolution or management that were subsequently institutionalized by governments. They defended the integrity of the dissenting conscience, and they helped to democratize the process of formulating foreign policy.

CHARLES CHATFIELD

See also Addams, Jane; America First Committee; Arbitration; Atoms for Peace; Cold War; Kellogg-Briand Pact; League of Nations; League to Enforce Peace; Nobel Peace Prize; Nuclear Weapons and Strategy; Nye, Gerald Prentice; Peace Movements and Societies to 1914; Permanent Court of Arbitration (Hague Tribunal); Public Opinion; United Nations; Vietnam War; Women, War, Peace, and Foreign Relations

FURTHER READING

Alonso, Harriet Hyman. *Peace as a Women's Issue: A History of the U.S. Movement for World Peace and Women's Rights.* Syracuse, N. Y., 1993.

Chatfield, Charles. *The American Peace Movement: Ideals and Activism.* New York, 1992.

———. *For Peace and Justice: Pacifism in America, 1914-1941.* Knoxville, Tenn., 1971.

Curti, Merle. *Peace or War.* New York, 1936.

DeBenedetti, Charles and Charles Chatfield. *An American Ordeal: The Antiwar Movement of the Vietnam Era.* Syracuse, N. Y., 1990.

———. *Origins of the Modern American Peace Movement, 1915-1929.* Millwood, N.Y., 1978.

Divine, Robert A. *Second Chance: The Triumph of Internationalism in America during World War II.* New York, 1967.

Howlett, Charles F. *The American Peace Movement: References and Resources.* Boston, 1991.

Johnson, Robert David. *The Peace Progressives and American Foreign Relations.* Cambridge, Mass., 1995.

Kleidman, Robert. *Organizing for Peace: Neutrality, the Test Ban, and the Freeze.* Syracuse, N. Y., 1993.

Wittner, Lawrence S. *Rebels Against War: The American Peace Movement, 1933-1983.* 2nd edition. Philadelphia, Pa., 1984.

———. *One World or None: A History of the World Nuclear Disarmament Movement Through 1953.* Stanford, Calif., 1993.

PEARL HARBOR, ATTACK ON
(1941)

Japanese assault against the U.S. naval base in Hawai'i that brought the United States into World War II as a belligerent. On 7 December 1941 at 7:55 A.M. (Hawai'i time), a day that President Franklin D. Roosevelt said "will live in infamy," a Japanese task force consisting of thirty-two ships—six aircraft carriers, two battleships, two light cruisers, one heavy cruiser, eight destroyers, three submarines, and nine refueling vessels—launched 352 aircraft in two waves against U.S. naval and military forces on the island of Oahu in the then territory of Hawai'i. In less than two hours, a complement of eighteen vessels consisting of eight battleships—*Arizona, Oklahoma, California, Maryland, Tennessee, West Virginia, Nevada*, and *Pennsylvania*—three light cruisers, three destroyers, and four auxiliary craft were sunk, capsized, or heavily damaged. At the same time naval aviation suffered serious loses—thirteen fighters, twenty-one scout bombers, forty-six patrol bombers, three utility craft, two transports, and several fighter planes from the aircraft carrier *Enterprise* that U.S. gunners mistakenly shot down. Army aviation losses were equally heavy—four B17s, twelve B18s, two A20s, thirty-two P40s, twenty P36s, four P26s, two Oa9s, and one O49. In addition, eighty-eight pursuit planes, six reconnaissance aircraft, and thirty-four bombers were damaged. A total of 2,403 Americans were killed; 1,178 were wounded. By comparison the Japanese loses were relatively insignificants: only twenty-nine planes, one large submarine, five midget submarines, and sixty-four men. The two-hour attack ushered the United States into World War II. Republican senator Arthur Vandenberg of Michigan said that the Japanese attack on Hawai'i "ended isolationism for any realist."

Deteriorating U.S.-Japanese Relations

Why did the Japanese attempt such a dangerous feat, and why did the two countries go to war? Even a cursory look at the period from 1850 to 1941 helps explain the evolution of this hostility. After 1853, when Commodore Matthew Perry helped open up Japan to U.S. trade and commerce, the Japanese began to industrialize and build a strong navy and army. Relations between the United States and Japan began to deteriorate in 1895 when the Japanese defeated the Chinese handily in the Sino-Japanese War. Ten years later Japan beat the Russians in the Russo-Japanese War. This victory launched the Japanese on their way to becoming a great power and a challenge to the United States, which had acquired the Philippine Islands in the Spanish-American-Cuban-Filipino War and now considered itself an Asian power. Japan became a major adversary of the United States. In 1905, Japan asked President Theodore Roosevelt to arbitrate a treaty to end the war with Russia. The Japanese were not happy with the results and blamed Roosevelt for not giving them all the fruits of war which they believed they had earned, specifically, more land on the Chinese mainland and more indemnity. During World War I, the Japanese fought on the side of the Allies. For this effort they received mandates over German possessions north of the equator, including the Marshall and Gilbert Islands. The Japanese began to rearm these islands, violating an agreement that they would not do so. Relations were further exacerbated by the fact that through a series of agreements and immigration legislation the United States limited Japanese immigration into this country.

In the 1930s, Japan developed a long list of grievances against the United States, foremost being the recognition of the Jiang Jieshi (Chiang Kai-shek) regime in China and the nonrecognition of Japan's regime in Manchuria (Manchukuo). The very presence in Asia of the United States and European powers was a constant irritation to Japanese pride. The adversarial relationship was further compounded when Japan invaded North China in 1937. Though Japan tried desperately to solve what it euphemistically termed "The China Incident," it began to lose thousands of young men, tons of military equipment, and millions of yen. Japan drove deeper and deeper into the heart of China. In 1939, in pursuit of its self-declared Greater East Asia Co-Prosperity Sphere, Japan turned southward and took over the Hainan Islands off the coast of China. In March of the same year Tokyo laid claim to the Spratly Islands, which offered a potential safe haven for planes and small naval craft in the Saigon, North Borneo, Manila, and Singapore areas. With the fall of France in 1940, Japan stationed troops in north French Indochina, which became its stepping stone to further advancement southward. Impressed by Hitler's military exploits, Japan joined forces with Germany and Italy, signing the Tripartite Pact on 27 September 1940. By this agreement, the three parties agreed to assist one another when one of the three was attacked by a power at present not a belligerent in the European war. Inasmuch as no major power except the Soviet Union and the United States were not belligerents, the target of the treaty stood out.

By 1941 the Japanese were poised to move south. Since all signs pointed to an invasion of the Dutch East Indies as next on their list, the United States had to consider Japan in the context of its Axis alliance, for aid and concessions to Tokyo also meant aid and concessions to Berlin and Rome. Japan grew angry at the embargoes that the United States had slipped on its exports to Japan. The termination on 26 January 1940 of the Treaty of Commerce and Navigation of 1911 removed the obstacle to legal restrictions. Beginning in July 1940, Washington placed all exports of aviation fuel and high-grade scrap iron and steel under federal license and control. In September 1940, after Japanese forces moved into northern Indochina, Roosevelt announced an embargo on scrap iron and steel to Japan, thus hurting the Japanese military machine. By the end of 1940 the United States had cut off all vital war materials except petroleum. Added to the unfavorable immigration policy and the stationing of the U.S. Pacific Fleet at Pearl Harbor, all signs pointed to a collision. Now the U.S. Fleet stood in the way of Japanese plans. The Japanese called this obstacle "Taiheido-no gan" (Cancer of the Pacific).

Japan tried diplomacy to gain U.S. acceptance of its gains in Asia. Tokyo appointed Admiral Kichisaburo Nomura, a former attaché to the United States and a friend of Franklin D. Roosevelt. Nomura generally liked the United States. His counterpart, Ambassador Joseph Grew, liked Japan. Seldom have two countries at loggerheads been represented by such men of good will. But the issues before them increasingly appeared intractable. With the appointment on 18 October 1941 of Hideki Tojo as premier and with U.S. insistence that Japan get out of China, war seemed inevitable.

Japanese Plans and U.S. Intelligence

On January 7, 1941, Admiral Isakoru Yamamoto, Commander-in-Chief, Combined Fleet, began to plan an attack on the Pacific Fleet. He realized that if Japan was to satisfy its needs for territory and new materials imports, the U.S. fleet stood in its way. There was much debate in Japan about Yamamoto's plan and many military leaders, including Yamamoto himself, thought that the Japanese would lose at least half of their aircraft carriers in such an attack on the U.S. fleet and that if the war turned into a protracted one, they would lose the war itself. Nevertheless, Yamamoto threatened to resign if the attack was not pursued. He believed that if Japan wanted to pursue its greater East Asian prosperity policy, it was the only alternative.

The strategy, while naive, was simple: Attack the American fleet, immobilize it for six months, and while the fleet was incapacitated, invade and pick off the riches of Southeast Asia and the Dutch East Indies. After the Japanese had accomplished this task, they would sue for peace. According to their assessment of the U.S. political climate at the time, the Americans did not want war and would either quit soon or not fight at all if given the chance. By reading the American press throughout 1941, the Japanese could gather the impression that the United States had no stomach for war. The U.S. Congress had passed the peacetime draft, after much debate, by only one vote. Charles Lindbergh, the great American aviator and hero, and others advocated staying out of the war and there was strong senatorial support against joining the fray. But the Japanese underestimated the effect of such

an attack on the American people. It united the United States as nothing had ever done before and led to Japan's own doom and eventual devastation.

There were many indications that the Japanese were up to something. Almost one year before the attack, on 27 January 1941, Ricardo Rivera-Schreiber, Peru's veteran minister to Tokyo, heard a rumor that the Japanese were thinking about attacking Pearl Harbor. He passed this information on to Edward S. Crocker, the first secretary to the U.S. embassy, who passed it to Ambassador Grew, who in turn informed Washington. After some fairly close scrutiny by the departments of War, Navy, and State, the official word from Washington was that they placed "no credence" in the rumor. They could not see how the Japanese could possibly sail across the northern Pacific without being detected.

Soon after, on 31 March, a report was prepared for the new commander-in-chief of the Pacific Fleet, Admiral Husband E. Kimmel, by Major General Frederick Martin, commander of the Hawai'i Air Force, and Rear Admiral Patrick Bellinger, chief of naval aviation. The Martin-Bellinger report indicated that the Japanese could attack Pearl Harbor and predicted the route and actions the enemy forces would take, concluding that they would probably attack on a Sunday morning flying in from the northwest. After reading the report, Kimmel filed it away for future reference. On 20 August, Colonel William Farthing, commander of the Fifth Bomb Group at Hickam Field, predicted the same type of attack as did Martin and Bellinger. His report was circulated to the command and filed for reference.

While the United States had not broken the JN 20 code, Japan's military operational code, both the United States and Great Britain had broken the Japanese diplomatic code called Magic. They were monitoring the Japanese code which they dubbed Purple with a machine designated as the Purple Machine. In March 1941 U.S. codebreakers were reading Japanese dispatches with much success. On 24 September, U.S. intelligence officers intercepted a message from Tokyo to its consulate in Honolulu directing its officials there to divide Pearl Harbor up into zones and report the movement of all U.S. ships in and out of these zones. This instruction was the first reference to Pearl Harbor in any Japanese message intercepted by the United States. It became known as "the Bomb Plot Message." It was never passed on to the local U.S. commanders and thus became very controversial during the Pearl Harbor hearings after the war when attempts were made to blame Washington for not notifying its command at Pearl Harbor of an impending assault.

On 16 October the Konoe cabinet fell and Tojo was appointed premier. This change was a strong indication that the Japanese were going to war, because Konoe was purportedly more of a peace advocate, while Tojo was known to be much more war-minded. Soon after Tojo came to power, U.S. intelligence began to decipher other messages indicating that if the United States did not give in to Japan's demands "things were automatically going to happen." Immediately after receiving these messages, on 27 November, Washington notified Kimmel and Short that the Japanese fleet was moving south and that war was imminent. Some believed war would come in the Philippines and Southeast Asia. The commanders in Washington later testified that they believed that after receiving these "war warning" messages the U.S. forces in the Hawai'ian Islands were prepared for a Japanese attack. The Hawai'i commanders, however, took the warnings to mean that the principal danger was sabotage. Hence they lined the planes up side by side to make them easier to defend, but of course simultaneously made them easier to destroy from the air. They worried about sabotage because of the large Japanese population living in Hawai'i.

On 1 December the Japanese changed their codes. This not only made it difficult to read intercepts but was also the second change that month indicating trouble ahead. On 2 December, U.S. intelligence picked up the code message "Climb Mt. Niitaka 1207" (the highest point in the Japanese Empire located in Formosa). While this intercept did not mention Pearl Harbor, it did indicate that Japan was planning an attack somewhere and that it would happen on 7 December. On 3 December another message was intercepted, ordering Japanese embassies all over the world to destroy their coding and deciphering equipment. On 6 December the first thirteen parts of a fourteen-part message were intercepted. The contents were ominous and seemed to indicate imminent war. Early in the morning of 7 December, U.S. intelligence intercepted the last part of the message, which stated that the Japanese would break off relations with the United States at 1:00 P.M. Washington time. Messages so advising were sent to the Pearl Harbor commanders by Western Union because of problems in the military communications facilities. Delivery of the messages was delayed and the commanders received them well after the attack. Ironically, Japanese Ambassadors Nomura and Saburo Kurusu, had scheduled a meeting with Secretary of State Cordell Hull at 1:00 P.M. to deliver the message which would have been approximately 30 minutes before the attack, but because the Japanese envoys' staff tried to type the contents of the message themselves rather than use their American secretary, the message was transcribed very slowly and delivered one hour late. The attack was already under way. Hull met with the ambassadors and dismissed them curtly without telling them that the attack was already taking place. When Yamamoto and other military leaders heard that the message had been delivered late, they became quite upset: in the

Samurai tradition, one always gives the enemy some warning before an attack. This later led to a controversy among politicians and military leaders in Japan as to whether the attack was a sneak attack or a surprise attack. Although to most Americans it was clearly the former, to the Japanese, had the message been delivered on time, it would have been classified as honorable.

Meanwhile, just hours before the attack, the U.S. destroyer *Ward* sank a Japanese submarine in the waters off Pearl Harbor. Information of this action was relayed to headquarters, but by the time Kimmel received the word bombs were already falling on his base.

At 7:10 A.M., Hawai'i time, the Opana radar station picked up a big blip coming from the northwest. The control center, after some deliberation, decided that it had to be U.S. B17s scheduled to arrive from the U.S. mainland on their way to the Philippines even though these planes would be coming from the northeast. As the bombs fell and first word of the attack reached Washington, Secretary of the Navy Frank Knox was reported to have said, "My God, this can't be true, they must mean the Philippines."

The devastating air attack at Pearl Harbor aroused the American people as no other event in history ever had. From coast to coast, from north to south and east to west, came shock, then denial, rage, and finally cries for revenge. "Remember Pearl Harbor" became the slogan and rallying symbol of the war.

Post-Attack Investigations

How could the Japanese have sailed across the Northern Pacific undetected and almost destroy a navy that just the day before Secretary Knox had declared on the front page of the *New York Times* "to be second to none" in the world? How could the Japanese have gotten away with minimum loses? Between 22 December 1941 and July 1946, eight official investigations were held to try to determine what happened and who was to blame.

Although Knox went to Pearl Harbor immediately after the attack to assess the damage, the first investigation was conducted by an eight-man committee chaired by Associate Justice Owen J. Roberts of the Supreme Court. The Roberts Commission met from 22 December 1941 to 23 January 1942. It found that while there were some mitigating and extenuating circumstances, in the final analysis Washington was not to be blamed, but that Admiral Kimmel and Lieutenant General Short, commanders of the Hawai'ian Departments, had been guilty of "dereliction of duty." Basing its conclusions on the Martin-Bellinger report, the Farthing report, the war-warning messages, the sinking of the submarine, and the radar pickup, the commission found that more than enough information had been available to alert the commanders to the upcoming attack.

The findings of the Roberts Commission stirred up much controversy, with many critics calling for the court martial of Admiral Kimmel and General Short. Since there was a question of the statute of limitations in the case of Kimmel, who wanted his day in court, Secretary Knox appointed Admiral Thomas Hart to collect testimony from Navy officers concerning the Pearl Harbor attack, for use in a potential court martial of both Short and Kimmel. Hart's job was just to collect information and not make judgments, but the material that he gathered between from February and June 1944 proved very damaging to both commanders. The Roberts Commission and the Hart inquiry raised more questions than they answered. Soon after Hart's report both the Army and the Navy appointed special boards to determine once and for all what had happened and who bore responsibility.

The Army Board consisted of six members, three of them generals, and was chaired by Lieutenant General George Grunert. The board met 20 July to 20 October 1944. It concluded that while neither Kimmel nor Short had been derelict in their duties they were guilty of errors of judgment, as were their leaders, including Chief of Staff George C. Marshall. The Navy Court of Inquiry, consisting of three admirals and a field grade officer and chaired by Admiral Orin G. Murfin, met at about the same time as the Army Board and concluded that "no offenses had been committed nor serious blame incurred on the part of any person or persons in the naval services."

Both the army and navy inquiries still left questions unanswered. Secretary of the Navy James Forrestal, who had replaced Frank Knox after Knox's death, appointed Vice Admiral Kent Hewitt to make another supplemental inquiry. This inquiry took place between 15 May and 11 July 1945 and produced even more controversy. Major Henry Clausen, who had been a recorder on the Army Board, was appointed to gather additional information for the army as Hewitt had done for the navy. Clausen conducted his investigation from November 1944 to September 1945 and found that Kimmel and Short had both been derelict by failing to disseminate, coordinate, and implement their war plans. While Clausen was conducting his investigation, the army also appointed Colonel Carter W. Clarke to gather yet more information. Clarke held his investigation from 13 July to 4 August 1945; he had previously performed some supplementary inquiries in September 1944.

The U.S. Congress conducted an eighth and final investigation of the Pearl Harbor catastrophe, as questions surrounding responsibility for the attack could have had a great effect on the Roosevelt administration's reputation and held future political implications for both Democrats and Republicans. In addition, information that the United States had broken the Japanese codes could not be released in the earlier investigations. Chaired by Senator, later Vice President, Alvin W. Barkley of Kentucky, the congressional team consisted of ten members—six senators and four representatives. With six Democrats and four Republicans, the committee met from 15 November 1945 to 15 July 1946, reviewing all the available information. While the team's final report was relatively fair it tended toward partisanship. The Republicans fixed the blame more on the Roosevelt administration, the service secretaries, and Chief of Staff Marshall, while the Democrats blamed Commanders Kimmel and Short. The report was useful for its general historical value, the documentation of events, and the recorded testimony of the individuals involved. Like its predecessors, however, it failed to declare who was ultimately responsible. While Kimmel and Short were never court-martialed, they were forced to retire as vice admiral and major general, respectively, one rank below the rank that they had held before the Pearl Harbor attack. Short died in 1948 and Kimmel in 1967. Family and friends of Admiral Kimmel have sought many times to exonerate him posthumously from the blame for the attack and to restore the prior ranks of both men. However, all these attempts have been in vain.

The Revisionists and Debate

It has been said that anyone who was over six years old on 7 December 1941 knew where they were and what they were doing on that day. Pearl Harbor continues to be an inexhaustible source of articles, books, interviews, movies, and television specials. Many of these efforts have centered around fixing blame for the catastrophe, most notably on President Roosevelt but also on others such as Marshall, Kimmel, Short, Secretary of War Henry Stimson, and even Winston Churchill. These authors, scholars, and writers have been dubbed "revisionists." Most of the revisionist claims are built upon second- and third-hand stories, "must haves," "could haves," and assumptions that have never been proved. Some of these writers have relied on letters and messages that cannot be found and interviews that cannot be confirmed. Much of the "new" material released under the Freedom of Information Act is not new at all but has been available for years, published in the massive congressional investigation of 1945–1946 and the multivolume set of Magic intercepts published in the late 1970s.

The legend that Roosevelt had known about the attack beforehand and let it happen began to develop during the last years of World War II. Soon after the war a spate of books were published on the subject. The most reasonable revisionists confined themselves to the criticism of Roosevelt's approach to foreign affairs. William A. Neumann in 1942 wrote that U.S. foreign policy before

World War II was unsound because the Soviet Union was the ultimate winner. Similarly, the major thrust of William H. Chamberlain's book, *America's Second Crusade* (1942), was that if the United States had kept out of the war, communism would have been contained.

Another brand of revisionists believed that Roosevelt deliberately dragged the United States into the war. This school, led by the eminent historian Charles A. Beard, stopped short of claiming that the president schemed to have the Japanese attack Pearl Harbor. In his book *President Roosevelt and the Coming of the War 1941* (1948), Beard depicted Roosevelt as a warmonger who deceived the American people, violated his antiwar campaign of 1940, and maneuvered the Japanese into firing the first shot. Others, such as John T. Flynn in his pamphlet "The Truth About Pearl Harbor" (1944) and Charles Tansill in *Back Door to War* (1952), concurred.

Harry Elmer Barnes was the leading advocate of the thesis that Roosevelt plotted, knew about the attack on Pearl Harbor in advance, and wanted it to happen. To Barnes and others Roosevelt was guilty of a triple conspiracy. First, he wanted the attack to take place because of his campaign promise that Americans would not be sent into war unless the United States was attacked first. Second, to permit such an attack to be unobstructed, he arranged that Kimmel and Short should receive none of the information available in Washington from decoded Japanese messages. Third, Roosevelt conspired to cover up the failure to warn the Hawai'i commanders. Barnes received support from Tansill, who argued that Roosevelt maneuvered the Japanese into firing the first shot because he wanted to get the United States into the war against Germany. This claim has never been proven. Ironically, it was the Germans who declared war on the United States.

A surprising number of naval personnel also concurred with Barnes and Tansill. Rear Admiral Robert A. Theobald's book, *The Final Secret of Pearl Harbor* (1954), suggests that Marshall and Roosevelt left the navy out to dry and made it the scapegoat to achieve their own goals.

Many of the revisionists' claims about Roosevelt have been found to be full of errors, innuendoes, "must have beens," and "might have beens," and were persuasively put to rest by Gordon W. Prange's acclaimed *At Dawn We Slept* (1981). Nonetheless, the thesis that Roosevelt knew about the attack gained renewed attention and instant credibility in 1983 when Pulitzer Prize-winning historian John Toland published his work, *Infamy: Pearl Harbor and Its Aftermath*. Toland claimed that from a listening post in California, Seaman Richard Ogg tracked the Japanese task force across the Pacific and reported it to his superiors, who allegedly told Roosevelt, and that Roosevelt did nothing to warn Pearl Harbor. However, none of these intercepted messages has ever been found and there is no testimony to confirm that Ogg ever delivered the messages or that anyone in Washington saw them.

Donald M. Goldstein and Katherine V. Dillon, in the *Pearl Harbor Papers* (1994), published a series of primary Japanese documents written by the men on the ships that participated in the attack. These documents make it clear that the Japanese maintained the strictest radio silence even to the extent of taking out fuses in the circuits and sealing transmitters so that no messages could be sent. Hence Ogg could not have tracked the task force on its voyage because the Japanese never broke their radio silence.

Although much of the "Roosevelt knew" theory has not been substantiated, two other works have tried to assess responsibility for the attack. *And I Was There* (1983), written by Admiral Edward Layton in collaboration with Roger Pineau and John Costello, lays the blame on jealousy in the navy itself. The villain in this scenario is Admiral Kelly Turner, chief of naval plans, who failed to pass on to Kimmel proper information that Turner was receiving from his codebreakers. This information would have supposedly allowed Kimmel and Short to better assess the Japanese threat and would have made them more aware of a possible attack.

A more recent work by Henry Clausen and Bruce Lee, *Pearl Harbor: Final Judgment* (1992), while it implicates others, lays the blame squarely on Kimmel and Short. The book has been given credence as Clausen had conducted the army investigation in 1944 and was privy to information he claims was never published.

The latest theory, presented by James Rusbridger and Eric Nave in *Betrayal at Pearl Harbor* (1991), is that the British had broken the JN 20 code long before the United States and already were tracking the task force. The British codebreakers allegedly passed this information to Prime Minister Churchill who deliberately withheld it from Roosevelt because he wanted the United States in the war immediately. Because Great Britain, unlike the United States, has not declassified all of its papers pertaining to the war, as of this writing this new thesis has not been confirmed. A similar theory offered by British historian John Costello, in *In Days of Infamy* (1994), asserts that two Russian ships traveling in the same area as the Japanese attack force saw these ships and reported their findings to Soviet Premier Joseph Stalin, who allegedly told Churchill, who then either withheld the information from Roosevelt or told Roosevelt, who then failed to act. The initial report by the two Russian ships has never been verified.

From a military standpoint the Pearl Harbor attack was an excellent example of planning, organizing, coordinating, and execution and demonstrated the application of many of the principles of war, among them surprise, concentration, security, simplicity, economy of force, and offense. Even though all the U.S. ships damaged at Pearl Harbor, except the *Arizona, Utah*, and *Oklahoma*, were eventually repaired and brought back into the war, fewer than 2500 Americans died and every ship in the Japanese task force was eventually sunk, Pearl Harbor stands as a great military victory for Japan.

Because the harbor itself at Pearl Harbor was so shallow, ordinary torpedoes in 1941 would not have been effective. They could not travel in the shallow water and would have stuck in the mud. In order for the attack to succeed the Japanese had to develop a torpedo which would run in shallow water. They accomplished this just months before the attack. The new torpedo was ingenious for its time, made with an adjustable wooden fin which made it effective in less than twenty-five feet of water. Prior to the attack, U.S. forces at Pearl Harbor did not employ torpedo nets, believing that state-of-the-art torpedoes would not be effective in the shallow harbor; hence, the Japanese modification took them by surprise. Early in 1941 the Japanese did not have a bomb capable of penetrating the reinforced decks of many of the U.S. vessels. Through trial and error, by early summer they had developed a bomb that could successfully penetrate the battleship decks. The journey across the Pacific required the refueling of ships in very inclement and harsh weather; through practice and innovation the Japanese also were able to develop refueling techniques that had never before been employed in combat. Finally, the Japanese had to devise better methods of dive-bombing and torpedo tactics, which they did with great success.

Despite their innovations, preparation, and training, the Japanese made errors which would later haunt them. Two of them were particularly important. First, had they bombed the dry docks at Pearl Harbor they could have delayed for months repairs to U.S. vessels in the area, thus preventing deployment of ships and ultimately influencing future naval battles. Second, had the Japanese knocked out the storage tanks the U.S. navy would have been forced to import oil from as far away as San Diego, seriously affecting the training and combat readiness of the fleet. Without the dry-dock facilities and fuel supply, the U.S. navy perhaps would not have performed as effectively as it did later in the successful battles of the Coral Sea and Midway.

Most historians and scholars have regarded Pearl Harbor as a political problem for which blame must be allocated rather than as a military engagement from which military lessons can be learned. People have looked for a simple answer, a single key reason for the debacle, and no doubt they will continue to do so many years from now. But there is no "smoking gun." The real lessons of Pearl Harbor are the appalling damage that can result from underestimating a potential enemy,

from misdirection of attention, from improper use of intelligence, and from failure to pay attention to one's own information, such as the Martin-Bellinger and Farthing Reports, which predicted what could happen with uncanny accuracy and which were totally ignored by those in charge.

In Hawai'i, the *Arizona* Memorial, in which more than 1100 Americans are entombed, is a memorial not only to those who died but to symbolize what can happen when a country is not prepared. The Pearl Harbor Survivors Association, comprised of more than 17,000 men who were present at the attack, is dedicated to the premise "be prepared." Thus, "Pearl Harbor never dies and no living person has seen the end of it," as one of Admiral Kimmel's attorneys wrote some years after the event.

DONALD GOLDSTEIN

See also Japan; Roosevelt, Franklin Delano; World War II

FURTHER READING

Barnes, Harry E., ed. *Perpetual War for Perpetual Peace*. New York, 1969.

Beard, Charles A. *President Roosevelt and the Coming of the War, 1941*. New Haven, Conn., 1948.

Butow, Robert J. C. *Tōjō and the Coming of the War*. Princeton, N.J., 1961.

Clausen, Henry C., and Bruce Lee. *Pearl Harbor: Final Judgment*. New York, 1992.

Conroy, Hilary, and Harry Wray, eds. *Pearl Harbor Reexamined: Prologue to the Pacific War*. Honolulu, 1990.

Costello, John. *Days of Infamy. MacArthur, Roosevelt, Churchill, the Shocking Truth Revealed: How Their Secret Deals and Strategic Blunders Caused Disasters at Pearl Harbor and the Philippines*. New York, 1994.

Farago, Ladislas. *The Broken Seal*. New York, 1967.

Feis, Herbert. *The Road to Pearl Harbor*. Princeton, N.J., 1950.

Flynn, John T. "The Truth About Pearl Harbor." Privately printed pamphlet. New York, 1944.

Goldstein, Donald, and Katherine V. Dillon. *The Pearl Harbor Papers*. Washington, D.C., 1993.

Grew, Joseph C. *Ten Years in Japan*. New York, 1944.

Hull, Cordell. *The Memoirs of Cordell Hull*. New York, 1948.

Iriye, Akira. *The Origins of the Second World War in Asia and the Pacific*. London, 1987.

Kahn, David. *The Codebreakers*. New York, 1967.

Kimmel, Husband E. *Admiral Kimmel's Story*. Chicago, 1955.

Layton, Edwin T., Roger Pineau, and John Costello. *And I Was There*. New York, 1985.

Lewin, Ronald. *The American Magic*. New York, 1962.

Lord, Walter. *Day of Infamy*. New York, 1957.

Melosi, Martin V. *The Shadow of Pearl Harbor: Political Controversy over the Surprise Attack, 1941–1946*. College Station, Tex., 1977.

Millis, Walter. *This Is Pearl! The United States and Japan—1941*. New York, 1947.

Morgenstern, George. *Pearl Harbor: The Story of the Secret War*. New York, 1947.

Morley, James William, ed. *The First Confrontation: Japan's Negotiations with the United States, 1941*. New York, 1995.

Prange, Gordon W., with Donald Goldstein and Katherine Dillon. *At Dawn We Slept: The Untold Story of Pearl Harbor*. New York, 1991.

Prange, Gordon W., with Donald Goldstein and Katherine Dillon. *Pearl Harbor: The Verdict of History.* New York, 1991.

Prange, Gordon W., with Donald Goldstein and Katherine Dillon. *December 7, 1941: The Day the Japanese Attacked Pearl Harbor.* New York, 1984.

Rusbridger, James, and Eric Nave. *Betrayal at Pearl Harbor: How Churchill Lured Roosevelt into World War II.* New York, 1991.

Tansill, Charles C. *Back Door to War.* Chicago, 1952.

Theobald, Rear Admiral, Robert A. *The Final Secret of Pearl Harbor.* New York, 1954.

Toland, John. *Infamy: Pearl Harbor and Its Aftermath.* New York, 1982.

Toland, John. *The Rising Sun: The Decline and Fall of the Japanese Empire, 1936–1945.* New York, 1970.

Wohlstetter, Roberta. *Pearl Harbor, Warning and Decision.* Stanford, Calif., 1962.

Zacharias, Rear Admiral, Ellis M. *Secret Missions.* New York, 1946.

PEARSON, LESTER BOWLES

(*b.* 23 April 1897; *d.* 27 December 1972)

Canada's ambassador to the United States (1945–1946), undersecretary of state for external affairs (1946–1948), secretary of state for external affairs (1948–1957), president of the seventh session of the United Nations General Assembly (1952–1953), and prime minister during two Liberal government administrations between 1963 and 1968. He grew up in Edwardian, Ontario, where British imperial sentiment was strong. After serving in the Royal Flying Corps during World War I, he studied at Oxford, taught history at the University of Toronto, and entered the Canadian Department of External Affairs in 1928. A shrewd negotiator with an engaging personality, Pearson rose quickly in rank. He was stationed in Washington between 1941 and 1946 and played a leading role in shaping postwar international institutions.

Returning to Ottawa in 1946 as undersecretary of state for external affairs, Pearson urged an activist Canadian foreign policy. In 1947 he was chair of the UN Political and Security Committee of the General Assembly and had a major role in the negotiations that led to the partition of Palestine.

One of the architects of the North Atlantic Treaty Organization, Pearson grew disappointed that the alliance did not promote closer economic and cultural ties among its neighbors. After leaving the public service he entered politics in 1948 and immediately became Canada's foreign minister. A strong proponent of NATO and U.S. leadership within the alliance, Pearson nevertheless questioned U.S. policies, especially in Asia. His friendship with U.S. Secretary of State Dean G. Acheson became strained, and his relationship with John Foster Dulles, who succeeded Acheson as secretary of state, was often difficult. When the Suez Crisis caused a grave Anglo-U.S. dispute in 1956, Pearson sought to mend it through the creation of a United Nations Emergency Force, providing the first international peacekeeping force mandated to preserve the truce between two warring parties. He succeeded in convincing others such a force was needed, and his reward was the Nobel Peace Prize in 1957.

The Liberal government fell in 1957. Pearson became the party's leader in opposition and developed a coherent political platform. Although the platform was critical of Canada's enormous dependence on the United States, Pearson emerged as the favorite of President John F. Kennedy's administration, which had come to loathe Conservative Prime Minister John G. Diefenbaker. In 1963, Pearson attacked Diefenbaker's antagonism to the Kennedy administration and his opposition to nuclear weapons for Canadian forces. The Diefenbaker government fell, and Pearson won a minority government in which the total number of opposition members exceeded the number of those in the government, in April 1963.

Pearson's tenure as prime minister was marked by controversy and scandal, but also by remarkable achievements in domestic affairs. He also negotiated the Canadian-U.S. automotive pact, which provided for free trade in automobiles. Pearson's suggestion in April 1965 that the United States halt its bombing of Vietnam offended President Lyndon B. Johnson, and although Pearson tried to avoid public criticism of U.S. foreign policy, he and his government were at odds with Washington. Pearson left office in 1968 when Canadian opposition to Vietnam was intensifying. Pearson was an enthusiastic consumer of U.S. popular culture and believed deeply in U.S. leadership of the noncommunist nations, but he deplored the unwillingness of the United States to consult and work within multilateral organizations.

JOHN ENGLISH

See also Canada; Palestine; United Nations; Vietnam War

FURTHER READING

English, John. *Shadow of Heaven: The Life of Lester Pearson.* Toronto, 1989.

Pearson, Lester B. *Mike: The Memoirs of the Right Honourable Lester B. Pearson,* 3 vols. Toronto, 1972–1975.

Stursberg, Peter. *Lester Pearson and the American Dilemma.* Garden City, N.Y., 1980.

PENTAGON

See Defense, U.S. Department of

PENTAGON PAPERS

A secret study that was conducted by the Department of Defense on the role of the United States in the Vietnam

War. In 1967, Secretary of Defense Robert S. McNamara commissioned the study to examine the history of U.S. involvement in Indochina beginning in 1946. The report, which took about a year and a half to prepare, consisted of forty-seven volumes, over 3,000 pages of narrative, and 4,000 pages of documents. The study became highly controversial for at least two reasons. First, its publication put into motion a Supreme Court case pitting national security interests versus freedom of the press. Second, its revelations revealed dramatic insights into foreign policy decision-making, including glaring discrepancies between stated and actual foreign policy initiatives.

The study was leaked to the *New York Times* (and other newspapers). The *Times* then published a series of articles based upon the study. After the initial article appeared in mid-June 1971, the U.S. attorney general requested that the *Times* cease publication of articles from the study on national security grounds. The newspaper refused, and a suit was filed to halt such publication. The Court of Appeals of the Second District did eventually grant such an injunction. The case then reached the Supreme Court where it ruled in favor of publication (*New York Times* v. *United States*, 1972). The Court held that freedom of the press was a fundamental right in a democracy and should be preserved. The national interest seemed to call for secrecy for some of the documents under review, Justice Potter Stewart wrote in his concurring opinion, but he could not "say that their disclosure...will surely result in direct, immediate, and irreparable damage to our Nation or its people." As such, freedom of the press needed to be affirmed.

The study itself provides a rare in-depth look into U.S. foreign policymaking. The story of U.S. involvement in Indochina is told through official cables and memoranda. The study reveals the depth and length of U.S. involvement in the region and suggests that the United States was engaging in covert actions seemingly at odds with various formal agreements and understandings.

JAMES M. McCORMICK

See also Journalism and Foreign Policy; Vietnam War

FURTHER READING

United States Department of Defense. *United States-Vietnam Relations, 1945–1967*, 12 vols. Washington, D.C., 1971.

New York Times v United States, 403 U.S. 713 (1971).

Shapiro, Martin, ed. *The Pentagon Papers and the Courts: A Study in Foreign Policy-Making and Freedom of the Press*. San Francisco, Calif., 1972.

Sheehan, Neil, et al. *The Pentagon Papers*. New York, 1971.

The Senator Gravel Edition. *The Pentagon Papers: The Department of Defense History of the United States Decision-making on Vietnam*, 5 vols. Boston, 1971.

Smith, Jean E. *The Constitution and American Foreign Policy*. St. Paul, Minn., 1989.

PÉREZ DE CUÉLLAR, JAVIER

(*b*. 19 January 1920)

Fifth secretary-general of the United Nations (1982–1991). Pérez de Cuéllar presided over the transformation of the UN from an institution on the brink of irrelevance to a respected instrument for resolving conflicts and maintaining international stability. During his first term (1982–1986) he faced President Ronald Reagan's hostility to the UN, Israel's invasion of Lebanon, the Falklands/Malvinas War between Great Britain and Argentina, and the Iran-Iraq War, as well as ongoing problems in Cyprus, Namibia, and Afghanistan. The reversal of the Soviet Union's long opposition to UN peacekeeping, the relaxation of superpower tensions, new cooperation among the five permanent members of the Security Council, and the end of the Cold War itself enabled Pérez de Cuéllar in his second term (1987–1991) to play an important role in dealing with several regional conflicts. His "good offices" helped bring an end to the war between Iran and Iraq, and Soviet intervention in Afghanistan; paved the way for the emergence of Namibia as an independent state, the Cambodian peace accords, and the Central American peace process; and led to the freeing of most Western hostages in Lebanon. He oversaw the initiation of nine UN peacekeeping operations between 1988 and 1990 as well as the UN's role in the 1990–1991 Gulf War. He closed his decade as secretary-general in December 1991 by helping the government of El Salvador and its rebel opposition end their twelve-year conflict.

Pérez de Cuéllar served in Peru's diplomatic service before joining the UN in 1975 as Secretary-General Kurt Waldheim's special representative on Cyprus. Much of the UN's success in peacekeeping and peacemaking during the late 1980s can be credited to his quiet, patient, and unassuming diplomatic style as secretary-general. Like Dag Hammarskjöld, he articulated his views on the UN's role in peaceful settlement. He stressed also the responsibility of states, especially the permanent members of the Security Council, to help resolve regional disputes.

Pérez de Cuéllar's lasting legacy is the independence of Namibia, the successful application of collective security in the Gulf War, and the Nobel Peace Prize awarded to UN peacekeepers in 1988. His success in reviving the UN as an instrument for promoting international peace and security helped restore U.S. confidence in the UN as a valuable instrument for furthering U.S. foreign policy interests.

MARGARET P. KARNS

See also Gulf War of 1990–1991; Namibia; United Nations

FURTHER READING

Hume, Cameron R. "Pérez de Cuéllar and the Iran-Iraq War." *Negotiation Journal* 8 (April 1992): 173–184.

Kondracke, Morton, "Javier of the UN" *The New Republic* (August 13, 1990).

Pérez de Cuéllar, Javier. "The Role of the UN Secretary-General." In *United Nations, Divided World*, edited by Adam Roberts and Benedict Kingsbury. Oxford, 1988.

———. "Reflecting on the Past and Contemplating the Future." *Global Governance*, 1:2 (May-August, 1995):149–170.

PERKINS, EDWARD J.

(*b.* 8 June 1928)

First African-American U.S. ambassador to South Africa (1986–1989). Born in Louisiana, Perkins received his B.A. from the University of Maryland (1967) as well as an M.P.A. (1972) and D.P.A. (1978) from the University of Southern California. He joined the Department of State in 1967, working himself up the Department of State ladder during the next fifteen years. In 1985, Perkins received his first ambassadorial appointment, to Liberia. He soon became enmeshed in the controversy surrounding U.S. policy toward South Africa. In order to palliate public opinion and avoid congressional sanctions on South Africa, President Ronald Reagan appointed Perkins, a convinced foe of apartheid, ambassador to Pretoria in 1986. Perkins's appointment did not distract Congress from enacting strong congressional sanctions against South Africa the same year.

Perkins's ability to navigate the many crosscurrents of U.S. diplomacy toward South Africa led to his appointment, in 1992, as the first African-American ambassador to the United Nations. In 1993 he became director-general of the Foreign Service. That same year Perkins was appointed U.S. ambassador to Australia with the title of career minister.

DIANE B. KUNZ

See also South Africa

FURTHER READING

Coker, Christopher. *The United States and South Africa, 1968–1985*. Durham, N.C., 1986

Crocker, Chester. *High Noon in Southern Africa*. New York, 1992.

Shultz, George P. *Turmoil and Triumph: My Years as Secretary of State*. New York, 1993.

PERMANENT COURT OF ARBITRATION (HAGUE TRIBUNAL)

A standing panel of jurists established in 1900 under the 1899 Convention for the Pacific Settlement of International Disputes (revised in 1907). The court, which sits at The Hague, is not really permanent since it convenes only when called upon. An International Bureau and Administrative Council act as registry and handle communications. The arbitration procedure is done by a panel chosen by the disputants. Each party may select up to four arbitrators from the court's appointment list of qualified persons, who serve six-year terms. If the parties fail to agree on the composition of a panel, they may appoint their own arbitrators, only one of which may be a national of each state. The four arbitrators then select an umpire. All types of disputes may be brought before the tribunal, although cases are submitted voluntarily by states. The court's decision is done in private, by majority vote, and is legally binding on the parties. Since 1914, only ten arbitrations have been sponsored by the Permanent Court of Arbitration, and only two since 1945. Among the court's most noteworthy judgments were the *Casablanca* ruling (1909) and the *Dogger Bank* case (1905).

CHRISTOPHER C. JOYNER

See also Permanent Court of International Justice

FURTHER READING

Hudson, Manley O. "The Permanent Court of Arbitration." *American Journal of International Law* 27 (1933): 440–460.

Stuyt, Alexander M., ed. *Survey of International Arbitrations, 1794–1970*. Dobbs Ferry, N.Y., 1972.

PERMANENT COURT OF INTERNATIONAL JUSTICE

The first World Court, established pursuant to Article 14 of the Covenant of the League of Nations. The court was created by a treaty Statute, drafted by an Advisory Commission and approved by the League's Assembly in 1920. The court formally opened on 15 February 1922 and dissolved on 31 January 1946 as the direct predecessor to the United Nations's International Court of Justice. Although not a functional organ of the League, the PCIJ still is regarded as its juridical body. Fifteen judges comprised the court, though no more than one could be a national from any state. Judges were elected by the League Council and Assembly to nine-year terms and could be reelected. Organs of the PCIJ included a president, vice president, the full court, special chambers, and a register. Decisions were deliberated in secret, by majority vote, and judgments were legally binding. During its lifespan the PCIJ handed down thirty-one judgments and twenty-seven advisory opinions. Among the PCIJ's most important decisions were the *Lotus* Case (1927) and the *Eastern Greenland* Case (1933).

CHRISTOPHER C. JOYNER

See also International Law; League of Nations

FURTHER READING

Dunn, Michael. *The United States and the World Court 1920–1935*. New York, 1988.

Hudson, Manley O. *The Permanent Court of International Justice, 1920–1942*. New York, 1943.

Lauterpacht, Hersch. *Development of International Law by the International Court*, rev. ed. London, 1958.

Permanent Court of International Justice. *Judgments and Orders (1922–1930)*, series A; *Advisory Opinions (1922–1930)*, series B; *Judgments, Orders, and Advisory Opinions (1931–1940)*, series A/B.

Canadian Journal of Latin American and Caribbean Studies 7 (1987).

Tulchin, Joseph S. *Argentina and the United States*. Boston, Mass., 1990.

PERÓN, JUAN DOMINGO
(*b*. 8 October 1895; *d*. 31 July 1974)

Career military officer and president of Argentina (1946–1955, 1973–1974) who dominated Argentine political culture during the Cold War period. During 1944 and 1945, while U.S.-Argentine tensions mounted over Argentina's refusal to declare war on the Axis powers, Perón rose to national prominence. As secretary of labor and vice president he implemented corporatist prolabor policies. In 1945 and 1946 he campaigned for the presidency on a platform that opposed foreign influences in his country, particularly that of the United States. During World War II the United States had pressured Argentina to join the Allies in a declaration of war against Germany and Japan. Argentina refused repeatedly, and after 1943 this refusal led to U.S. hostility. U.S. diplomats voiced their suspicions that Perón and other prominent Argentine leaders were Nazi sympathizers. When Perón reviled in the election campaign what he viewed as a U.S. attempt to influence Argentine domestic affairs, the U.S. ambassador to Argentina, Spruille Braden, responded by attempting to publicly discredit Perón's economic nationalism. Perón countered by criticizing Braden's remarks as an escalation of U.S. "influence" in Argentine politics, and he won the presidency.

During the late 1940s Perón maintained a neutral "Third Position" in the Cold War. Perón's anatgonism to foreign investors along with lingering Department of State suspicions of his earlier totalitarian leanings contributed to strained U.S.-Argentine relations through the end of his first presidential term in 1952. During his second term Perón reversed his stand on foreign business, welcoming investments by Kaiser, Standard Oil of New Jersey, and other U.S. firms. U.S.-Argentine relations then improved markedly. Overthrown in 1955 by a military coup d'état, Perón lived in exile until his triumphant return to Argentina in 1973; unable to stave off high inflation and economic stagnation, military authorities finally allowed Perón one last chance at governance. Elected to the presidency for a third time, Perón died before serving out his term.

DAVID SHEININ

See also Argentina; Braden, Spruille; Cold War; World War II

FURTHER READING

Frank, Gary. *Juan Perón vs Spruille Braden*. Lanham, Md., 1980.

Greenberg, Daniel J. "From Confrontation to Alliance: Peronist Argentina's Diplomacy with the United States, 1945–1951."

PERRY, MATTHEW CALBRAITH
(*b*. 10 April 1794; *d*. 4 March 1858)

U.S. naval officer best known for his expeditions to Japan in the early 1850s that were meant to "open" that Asian nation to the West. Perry followed in the footsteps of his older brother Oliver Hazard Perry. The younger Perry enlisted in the U.S. navy in 1809 and attained a rank of commodore in 1841. Although Perry served with distinction in the War of 1812 and the War with Mexico, his greatest achievements came from his activities as a naval diplomatist. In the nineteenth century, because of their ability to combine force with persuasion, naval officers were often authorized to negotiate international agreements, especially with peoples not considered to be "civilized." Perry gained a reputation as a skilled practitioner of so-called gunboat diplomacy. In 1832 he assisted chargé d'affaires John Nelson in obtaining a claims settlement with Naples. As commander of the African squadron (1843–1844), he destroyed several villages of the Fishmen tribe of the Ivory Coast in retaliation for the plunder of the ship *Mary Carver*. Perry then compelled the chiefs to sign compacts promising to protect U.S. citizens and their property. In 1852, Perry calmed a potentially dangerous dispute over U.S. fishing rights in Canadian waters by reaching an agreement with British naval commander Sir George Seymour to restrain the nationals of both sides.

Perry is best known for opening what he called "the hermetic empire" of Japan by signing the Treaty of Kangawa on 31 March 1854. Shortly before his death in 1852, Secretary of State Daniel Webster had granted Perry wide latitude in implementing the instructions for the missions to Japan. Through a combination of deft diplomacy and threats to use the formidable naval force under his command, Perry attained the primary goals set forth in those instructions when he secured coaling stations for U.S. ships in the China trade at the Japanese ports of Hakodate and Shimoda, as well as a promise that shipwrecked U.S. seamen would be treated humanely. Although Perry did not obtain a formal trade agreement, the stipulations allowing the stationing of a resident consul at Shimoda and a most-favored-nation clause laid the foundation for the commercial treaty negotiated by Townsend Harris in 1858. In the Treaty of Naha of 11 July 1854, Perry pressured the authorities of Okinawa into accepting an accord modeled on that with Japan. Although the administration of President Franklin Pierce approved the agreements with Japan and Okinawa, it rejected Perry's recommendation that the United States adopt an imperial strategy by taking possession of the Bonin Islands and establishing a protectorate over Formosa. In opening a Japan that since 1638 had sealed itself from the outside world except for limited contacts with China and Holland, Perry had achieved what he called the "great object" of his life.

KENNETH E. SHEWMAKER

See also Africa; Harris, Townsend; Japan

FURTHER READING

Morison, Samuel Eliot. *"Old Bruin:" Commodore Matthew C. Perry, 1794–1858.* Boston and Toronto, 1967.

Shewmaker, Kenneth E. "Forging the Great Chain: Daniel Webster and the Origins of American Foreign Policy Toward East Asia and the Pacific 1841–1852." *Proceedings of the American Philosophical Society* 129 (September 1985): 225–259.

Wiley, Peter Booth, with Korogi Ichiro. *Yankees in the Land of the Gods: Commodore Perry and the Opening of Japan.* New York, 1990.

PERRY, WILLIAM

(*b.* 11 October 1927)

Secretary of defense (1994–), entrepreneur, scientist, scholar, and high-ranking defense official in two Democratic administrations. Born and raised in western Pennsylvania, he received his undergraduate degree from Stanford and holds a master's degree from Stanford and a Ph.D. in mathematics from Pennsylvania State University. Perry served on active duty with the Army Corps of Engineers for one year between World War II and Korea. He worked for a decade with Sylvania/General Telephone in defense electronics before founding his own company, Electronic Systems Lab (ESL), in 1964. He served as president of ESL until 1977 when President Jimmy Carter appointed him to the third highest position in the Pentagon, undersecretary of defense for research and engineering. In his four years in that post, he was primarily responsible for developing and producing such sophisticated, technologically advanced weapons as cruise missiles, stealth aircraft, and precision guided munitions. During the twelve years of Republican control of the executive branch, Perry worked in investment banking; founded another company (Technology Strategies Alliances); taught at Stanford in the engineering and arms control areas; and served on a number of corporate, government and nonprofit boards, including FMC, United Technologies Corporation, the president's Foreign Intelligence Advisory Board, and the Carnegie Endowment. In March 1993 he returned to the Pentagon as deputy secretary of defense and moved up to secretary in February 1994, after the dismissal of Les

Aspin and the refusal of Admiral Bobby Inman to accept President Bill Clinton's offer. Within a short time, Perry restored a sense of order and discipline to the Pentagon. He successfully managed the military interventions in Haiti and Bosnia, established close relations with Russian and Chinese militaries, enhanced quality of life for military personnel, reformed the Pentagon's acquisition system, and enhanced the nation's defense industrial base.

LAWRENCE J. KORB

See also Bosnia-Herzegovina; Clinton, William Jefferson; Defense, U.S. Department of; Haiti

PERSHING, JOHN

(*b.* 13 September 1860; *d.* 15 July 1948)

Highly decorated U.S. general who led U.S. forces in World War I. He was appointed general of all the armies in 1919, a rare distinction not accorded to any military officer since George Washington. "Black Jack" Pershing, as he was nicknamed after commanding an African-American regiment in Cuba during the Spanish-American-Cuban-Filipino War, was born in Missouri, graduated from West Point in 1886, and served five tours of duty in the U.S. colony, the Philippines, before World War I. During the Russo-Japanese War of 1904–1905, he was sent as an "official observer" to Japan. He married that year, only to lose his wife and three small daughters in a fire ten years later. In 1916 he commanded U.S. troops sent into Mexico to capture rebel Pancho Villa, but Villa remained elusive. Pershing stayed in Mexico until President Woodrow Wilson selected him to be commanding officer of the American Expeditionary Forces in 1917. Until the fall of 1919, Pershing remained field commander of U.S. forces in Europe.

Although Pershing has been criticized for opposing the integration of U.S. forces with Allied troops in Europe, the idea came from Wilson, whom Pershing supported wholeheartedly. Under this meticulous commander, doughboys numbering in the hundreds of thousands began turning the tide of battle against the Germans by the fall of 1918. In late September a half million U.S. troops repelled the German attack at Saint-Mihiel; by 1 November, one million doughboys foiled the last German offensive of the war.

Pershing strongly advocated unconditional German surrender in 1918 and the occupation of Berlin, fearing that the Germans, otherwise, would not consider themselves defeated. This idea was rejected by the Allied leaders, including Wilson, who favored a negotiated peace. (During World War II, in contrast, the Allies were unanimous in their insistence on unconditional

German surrender.) Pershing retired in 1924 and wrote his compelling memoirs, *My Experiences in the War,* which won the Pulitzer Prize in 1931.

SINA DUBOVOY

See also Mexico; Philippines; Villa, Pancho; Wilson, Thomas Woodrow; World War I

FURTHER READING

Goldhurst, Richard. *Pipe Clay and Drill: John J. Pershing, American Soldier.* New York, 1977.
Smythe, Donald. *Pershing, General of the Armies.* Ann Arbor, Mich., 1986.
Vandiver, Frank E. *Black Jack: The Life and Times of John J. Pershing.* 2 vols. College Station, Tex., 1977.

PERSHING II

See Nuclear Weapons and Strategy

PERU

Mountainous republic located in Western South America, bordered by the South Pacific Ocean, Ecuador, Colombia, Brazil, Bolivia, and Chile. The United States has long had an ambiguous relationship with Peru characterized by general respect and friendliness, but tempered occasionally by distrust and outright hostility. Special envoys and consuls were in Peru even before Peru formally won its independence from Spain in 1824. Although trade during the Wars of Independence (1810–1824) along with the whaling industry drew more North Americans to Peru, significant contacts developed only in the middle of the nineteenth century with the guano export boom. The most important U.S. declaration of the era, the Monroe Doctrine (1823), drew little more than curiosity from Peruvians. The Venezuelan Simon Bolívar, the liberator of Peru, distrusted North Americans, as he perceived Yankee intentions to be the spreading of their influence over the entire hemisphere.

When the fertilizing properties of guano were found to help renew depleted tobacco and cotton plantations in the United States, hundreds of North American ships made annual voyages to the Chincha Islands off the west-central coast of Peru from the 1840s through the 1870s to load guano. During the War of the Pacific (1879–1883) the United States favored Peru against Chile. Growing investments in silver and copper mining at the turn of the century, especially by the giant Cerro de Pasco Corporation, reinforced the good diplomatic relations and growing commercial contacts between Peru and the United States. While the International Petroleum Company (a subsidiary of Standard Oil of New Jersey) dominated the Peruvian petroleum business in the twentieth century,

other North American corporations, such as W. R. Grace and Company, developed sea and air transportation and participated in manufacturing across a wide spectrum of products, from cardboard boxes to candies. Indeed, every Peruvian participating in the money economy was touched by the activities of "Casa Grace," demonstrating the impressive presence of that U.S. corporation in the Peruvian economy.

During the regime of President Augusto B. Leguía y Salcedo (1908–1912; 1919–1930), the most pro-U.S. chief executive to govern Peru in the modern era, the high point of good U.S.-Peruvian relations occurred when the United States in 1928 helped successfully arbitrate a long-standing territorial dispute between Peru and Chile. Leguía's affection for the United States was such that he hung a portrait of President James Monroe in the National Palace in Lima, and he encouraged U.S. capital investments.

In the 1920s and 1930s Víctor Raúl Haya de la Torre, founder of Alianza Popular Revolucionaria Americana (APRA), the most successful mass-based political party in Peru, agitated against Leguía and stridently criticized U.S. capitalism and imperialism as contributing to Peru's underdevelopment and poverty. By mid-century, Haya and the Aprista movement had moved to the center and found much to admire in North American life, especially the strengths of democracy and middle class prosperity. The ambiguous relationship between Peru and the United States was well symbolized by Haya de la Torre's long affair with the United States, stormy and critical in the early years, but accommodating as he matured.

Peru's Institutional Revolution of 1968 seriously frayed relations. This intensely nationalistic and socialistic movement nationalized many U.S. corporations and challenged U.S. hegemony in the western hemisphere as Peru sought to carve out a position of leadership in Third World affairs. Numerous arms were purchased from the Soviet Union in the 1970s to symbolize Peru's independence from its traditional suppliers, the United States, France, and Great Britain, but the accompanying debts, exacerbated by a massive expansion of the state in the 1970s, led to staggering economic conditions in the 1980s. This debt brought Peru into direct conflict with the United States, especially after Aprista leader Alan García was elected president in 1985 and repudiated the debt by saying Peru would pay up to only ten percent of its national income to service the debt.

The rise of the narcotics trade and terrorism in the 1970s and 1980s further challenged relations with the United States. Increasing drug abuse in the United States spurred the production of coca in Peru. As the leading producer of coca in the world, Peruvians struggled with a solution. They wished to control it, but were not particularly devoted to its eradication, especially since coca use formed part of the indigenous culture of the highlands. The United States, on the other hand, whose demands for cocaine fueled the illegal trade, sought to eliminate production dramatically. The rise of the most pernicious terrorist movement in late twentieth century Latin America, the Sendero Luminoso (Shining Path), also brought the United States and Peru into conflict. Peruvians viewed this movement, which took more than 20,000 lives between 1980 and 1995, as a direct threat to the very nature of Peru's economic, social, and political institutions, but the United States wanted Peru to put its military and police resources more directly into the eradication and control of coca. Furthermore, the Peruvian military and police establishment, often brutalized by the terrorist tactics, carried the war to extremes, killing widely and irrationally as did the terrorists, and sparking U.S. accusations of human rights abuses.

The 1990 election of Alberto Fujimori, a Japanese Peruvian, to the presidency brought out the ambiguities of the U.S.-Peruvian relationship once more. On the one hand, Fujimori suspended congress in 1992 to enable the military to wage a more effective war against the terrorists and the narco traffickers, thus incurring heavy criticism in the United States for violating the constitution. On the other hand, he began to privatize the Peruvian economy, enforcing tough economic measures to bring Peru's economy (especially a raging inflation and depressed productivity) out of a slump it had been in since the 1970s. While criticizing his high-handed treatment of congress, many in the United States found much to admire in Fujimori's economic policies,

LAWRENCE A. CLAYTON

See also Latin America; Narcotics, International; Terrorism

FURTHER READING

Carey, James C. *Peru and the United States, 1900–1962.* Notre Dame, Ind., 1964.
Clayton, Lawrence A. *The Eagle and the Condor: The United States and Peru.* Athens, Ga., 1997.
Pike, Fredrick B. *The United States and the Andean Republics.* Cambridge, Mass., 1977.
St. John, Ronald Bruce. *The Foreign Policy of Peru.* Boulder, Colo., 1992.

PEURIFOY, JOHN EMIL

(*b.* 9 August 1907; *d.* 12 August 1955)

U.S. diplomat who helped organize a 1954 coup in Guatemala. Born in South Carolina, John (Jack) Peurifoy dropped out of West Point Military Academy in 1928, and in 1938 he became a Department of State clerk. He worked his way up the bureaucratic ladder, becoming deputy undersecretary of state for administration in 1949

under Secretary of State Dean G. Acheson. Confirmed as ambassador to Greece in 1950, he earned a reputation as a staunch anticommunist not at all reticent to intervene in a country's internal affairs. In 1953, under President Dwight D. Eisenhower, Peurifoy was posted to Guatemala, whose President Jacobo Arbenz Guzmán the administration believed had fallen under the Kremlin's spell. At their initial encounter, the outspoken Peurifoy bluntly told Arbenz that his agrarian and labor reforms represented unacceptable behavior. In June 1954 the ambassador helped the Central Intelligence Agency orchestrate Arbenz's overthrow. Peurifoy then negotiated the establishment of a pro-Washington government. His next assignment was ambassador to Thailand, where under mysterious circumstances he was killed in an automobile accident.

RICHARD H. IMMERMAN

See also Central Intelligence Agency; Greece; Guatemala

FURTHER READING

Gleijeses, Piero. *Shattered Hope: The Guatemalan Revolution and the United States, 1944–1954.* Princeton, N.J., 1991.
Immerman, Richard H. *The CIA in Guatemala.* Austin, Tex., 1982.

PHILANTHROPIC FOUNDATIONS, OVERSEAS PROGRAMS OF

The activity of various organizations that have long worked abroad to promote human welfare and which have had both direct involvement in and indirect efforts on U.S. foreign policy. Beginning in the early nineteenth century, U.S. missionaries joined in proselytizing across Africa, Asia, and Latin America. It would be difficult to make the case—a few exceptions to the contrary notwithstanding—that these activities were consciously designed to further U.S. foreign policy interests. The creation early in the twentieth century of such general-purpose foundations as the Carnegie Corporation of New York (1911) and the Rockefeller Foundation (1913) provided the vehicle whereby, after World War II, foreign policy concerns and philanthropy would become inextricably intertwined in the furtherance of U.S. national interests.

The Cold War gave several of the major U.S. foundations their programmatic coherence and strategic direction in advancing U.S. foreign policy objectives. Even before 1945, however, several foundations had initiated overseas programs at least partially intended to enhance U.S. interests. During the 1920s and the 1930s, the Carnegie Corporation and the Phelps-Stokes Fund (1911) collaborated on a number of educational projects in eastern and southern Africa. These activities were facilitated by the British Colonial Office. Foundation staff hoped their programs would encourage Africans to believe that U.S. institutions were more sympathetic to African aspirations than were the British colonial governments.

Even earlier, the Rockefeller Foundation had made a significant commitment to Chinese medical education through the establishment, in 1921, of the Peking Union Medical College. This undertaking was designed to expose Chinese practitioners to the latest Western medical practices, in the hope that these would be emulated at the expense of traditional Chinese approaches. In the 1920s the Rockefeller Foundation launched programs to counter yellow fever in Latin America.

The foundations' overseas activities were possible because language in their charters either specified such involvement or because more general wording did not preclude it. In the case of the Carnegie Corporation, for example, British colonies and dominions were specifically mentioned as areas where the corporation could implement programs. The charter of the Rockefeller Foundation, like that of the Ford Foundation (1952), stipulated that its activities should promote "human betterment" and "well-being." This general language was used to justify the global reach of the foundations' programs, especially after 1945.

It was the Carnegie Corporation and the Ford and Rockefeller Foundations that contributed most to the furtherance of U.S. foreign policy goals. Their support fell into two major, and sometimes overlapping, categories. The first involved underwriting a range of studies and reports that subsequently influenced the shape of foreign policy. A corollary to this was the financing, at a group of major research universities, of many of the nation's first area-studies programs, such as Russian or East Asian studies. The second category involved support for field-based education projects in several developing nations considered to be of geostrategic and economic importance to the United States.

Foundation-Sponsored Reports and Area-Studies Programs

In 1939 the Rockefeller Foundation began its support of the Council on Foreign Relations' War-Peace Studies Project, designed to focus on the long-term problems caused by World War II and, assuming an Allied victory, to shape the peace at war's end. Major recommendations of this study included: the United States must have continued access to strategic raw materials located abroad; U.S. prosperity was dependent on overseas investment and raising the standard of living in Europe and the underdeveloped world; and these goals could only be achieved in a stable, noncommunist world dominated by an international capitalist economy. These recommendations had a major impact on postwar U.S. foreign policy, underpinning U.S. participation in the establishment of

the United Nations, the International Monetary Fund, and the Bretton Woods system. Many of the post-1945 overseas programs of the Carnegie Corporation and the Ford and Rockefeller Foundations were based on rationales similar to those delineated in the War-Peace Studies Project. This is hardly surprising, since numerous officers and trustees of the three foundations had worked in one of the Washington agencies conceptualizing the goals of postwar foreign policy before transferring to foundations positions.

The Rockefeller Foundation helped to create the Russian Institute at Columbia University with a 1945 grant. The Carnegie Corporation soon joined Rockefeller in strengthening the Columbia program and establishing similar ones at Harvard and at several other universities. The Ford Foundation enlisted in this endeavor after 1952; indeed, its efforts soon dwarfed those of the other foundations. By the mid-1960s the three foundations, with Ford contributing the greatest amount by far, had created area-studies and international programs in a handful of research universities from coast to coast.

There was broad agreement among foundation personnel concerning the importance of these programs. The decolonization of much of Africa and Asia after 1945, coupled with the triumph of the communists in China in 1949 and growing instability in Latin America, revealed the paucity of information available to the foreign policy establishment about these areas with which the United States would now have to deal directly, rather than through colonial office intermediaries. Foundation staff noted that the newly minted area specialists would further U.S. foreign policy objectives by sharing with Washington decision-makers their knowledge of these nations, now considered crucial to U.S. security.

Field-Based Projects in the Developing World

The decision by Carnegie, Ford, and Rockefeller personnel to develop programs in a limited number of African, Asian, and Latin American countries after 1945 derived from a number of interrelated concerns. The specter of a well-designed and aggressive Soviet offensive to capture the hearts and minds of Third World peoples resonates throughout foundation planning documents of the period. The Soviets had devised a well-coordinated strategy, the reasoning went, to persuade leaders of these nations that development could best be assured through the institutionalization of a system of state socialism and a foreign policy tilt toward Moscow. A communist-dominated Third World linked to the Soviet Union, coupled with the foreclosing of democratic options, loomed large, according to this analysis.

The corollary to this grim scenario was that communist-dominated governments in the developing nations would deny the United States access to raw materials considered vital to the national interest and sharply curtail opportunities for the investment of U.S. capital abroad. Such actions would restrict the U.S. export market, which in turn would reduce domestic living standards.

Foundation personnel agreed that enhancing the leadership capacities of selected countries was crucial if this disastrous course was to be avoided. Western-educated leaders were certainly in short supply throughout the developing countries in the 1950s and the 1960s. The Soviet Union and its allies were making educational opportunities widely available throughout the developing world, with the predictable result that many future African, Asian, and Latin American leaders would encourage Soviet initiatives while shunning Western influence. It was clear that the democratic alternative needed to be made available without delay.

Foundation officers viewed the extension of a democratically grounded education as crucial to the stability, prosperity, and orderly development of these nations, indeed, as one of the few ways to orient future Third World leaders toward the West and away from their flirtation with state socialism. The foundations were singularly well equipped to undertake this challenge. Their major emphasis since their origins had been support for a well-educated leadership cadre which would give direction to the national polity.

These concerns led the Carnegie Corporation and the Ford and Rockefeller Foundations to launch a series of educational programs in selected Third World nations. At times they worked independently of one another; occasionally they cooperated in their field-based education programs, and at still other times they collaborated with such official agencies of U.S. foreign policy as the Department of State and the Agency for International Development. Their activities sometimes involved them with multilateral aid agencies such as the World Bank. Through their manifold education programs in the developing world, the foundations played an unambiguous role in what Christopher Lasch, cultural and social historian, termed the "cultural Cold War."

The foundations concentrated much effort on improving Third World universities. To this end the Rockefeller Foundation launched its $100 million University Development Program in 1955. This eventually involved universities in Thailand, East Africa, Colombia, the Philippines, Indonesia, and Nigeria. Rockefeller attentions within these institutions focused on biomedical work, administrative reorganization, and the social sciences. The Rockefeller Foundation also continued its long-standing fellowship program that enabled carefully chosen Third World students to study at a handful of elite American universities. These efforts paralleled the foundation's better-known agricultural work in India, the Philippines, and West Africa.

The Ford Foundation focused on a number of universities in various African, Asian, and Latin American nations. Foundation staff concentrated on increasing the quality of instruction in the social and applied sciences and on improving university administrations. They worked as well in the field of agricultural economics. One of the Ford Foundation's singular efforts involved attempts to build up a cadre of public administrators, sometimes within university settings, to staff civil services of developing nations. Their best known program in this area was at the National School of Law and Administration in the Congo, a nation that became a Cold War proxy in the early 1960s, initially over the issue of Katanga's succession. The Ford Foundation's work in the Congo was strongly encouraged by Department of State officials desirous of having a nongovernmental U.S. presence in such a politically unstable and economically important region.

The Carnegie Corporation's work concentrated on raising the quality of teacher education programs, the majority of which were in English-speaking Africa. Beginning in the late 1950s, Carnegie personnel linked a network of teacher-training institutions throughout east, central, and west Africa to Columbia University's Teachers' College. These expanding relationships featured fellowship opportunities enabling Africans to study at Columbia. The field sites were generally overseen by Carnegie-approved staff who served on location for a limited period. They worked with their local counterparts to develop curricula, improve teaching methods, and rationalize expanding teacher-education networks at a time of rapid by increasing school enrollment. The African fellows at Columbia were expected to return home at the completion of their advanced study, at which time they would replace the expatriate staff, thereby ensuring the Africanization of these teacher-education programs.

Foundation personnel envisioned that institutions receiving their support would in turn provide assistance to less-favored Third World universities. This would help to create a network of foundation-influenced universities, staffed and led by indigenous personnel. The foundations would continue to provide financing and guidance, but direct involvement in university development would be noticeably curtailed.

The Foundations and U.S. Foreign Policy

Both the staffs and trustees of the foundations denied that their overseas programs derived from any partisan motives or from a desire to further the foreign policy interests of the United States. Instead, they stressed the humanitarian nature of their involvement, arguing that their programs were undertaken solely to further the development efforts of the selected nations. One way to achieve this desideratum, from the foundation perspective, was to help a group of African, Asian, and Latin American nations expand and upgrade components of their woefully inadequate educational systems.

It is clear that many individuals involved in these efforts had no ulterior motives; they believed that the exclusive purpose driving their programs was to improve the lives of Third World peoples. In numerous instances, the foundation-sponsored programs achieved many of their objectives. This was especially true of the efforts to improve Third World universities.

Disclaimers to the contrary notwithstanding, however, it is also clear that many foundation officers and trustees viewed their programs as logical extensions of U.S. foreign policy. Indeed, it would be surprising if they did otherwise. During the Cold War period the upper ranks of the major foundations read like a chapter drawn from a *Who's Who* of U.S. foreign policy. It simply defies credulity to assume that when individuals like John J. McCloy, Dean Rusk, McGeorge Bundy, or Robert McNamara moved from official foreign policy positions in Washington to leadership roles in the foundations their Weltanschauung changed perceptibly, if at all. As both architects and implementors of various aspects of U.S. Cold War policy, they articulated an unambiguous view of the post-1945 role of the United States in international affairs.

The effort to influence selected Third World nations was part of the United States's cultural offensive. To further this objective, the foundations at times cooperated with more "official" foreign policy agencies, such as the International Cooperation Administration or its successor, the Agency for International Development. Internal foundation documents clearly show the linkage between foreign policy concerns and the direction of their programs.

Even before the end of the Cold War, foundation personnel began to reassess their commitments overseas. They did so partly because some of their efforts were being institutionalized, as was the case when several strategically located universities throughout Africa, Asia, and Latin America were refashioned. At the same time, foundation officers were aware that many local nationals, especially in Latin America, viewed their programs as manifestations of United States cultural imperialism. Moreover, other donor agencies, particularly the World Bank, were becoming more involved in educational projects in developing nations, thereby eclipsing foundation efforts. Lastly, issues at home—urban poverty, for example, or educational reforms—demanded greater attention.

These factors led the foundations to reconsider their international programs by the late-1970s; the result was the refocusing of their efforts in support of U.S. foreign policy objectives. The Carnegie Corporation, for example, increased its support for projects in South Africa, most visibly in the areas of legal education and, with the Ford foun-

dation, the Legal Resources Centre in Johannesburg. The Rockefeller and Ford Foundations shifted their emphasis from broad-based university programs to projects supporting research and evaluation capacities of Third World research centers. The Ford Foundation in particular increased its fellowship funding for foreign nationals studying in the United States, in an effort to develop a coterie of foreign scholars who, upon returning home, would staff the foundation-funded research and evaluation centers.

The halcyon days of foundation international programming had passed by the mid-1980s, notwithstanding their continuing presence in selected developing nations. The relationships linking the Carnegie Corporation and the Ford and Rockefeller foundations with U.S. foreign policy implementation cannot be separated from the larger context of foreign policy formulation in the period from the 1930s to the end of the Cold War. This context necessitates an explication of the almost symbiotic relationship, both financial and personal, linking the foundations to such influential, but unofficial, centers of foreign policy decision-making as the Council of Foreign Relations, and in turn to the official centers foreign policy formulation, the Departments of State and Defense.

The end of the Cold War has brought into clearer relief the efforts of several new foundations that appear determined to influence the direction of U.S. foreign policy. The most visible among these are controlled by financier George Soros. His early activities involved funding for Hungarian political dissidents challenging communist hegemony during the 1980s, and over the last several years Soros's foundations have provided some $250 million for educational programs in Russia and almost as much for a joint university project in Hungary and the Czech Republic. It is premature to say if such efforts will be long-lived or if they will make a lasting impression on the U.S. foreign policy establishment. What is clear, however, is that such efforts represent yet another manifestation of the long-standing relationship linking private philanthropy and U.S. foreign policy.

EDWARD H. BERMAN

See also Agency for International Development; Bundy, McGeorge; Cold War; McCloy, John Jay; McNamara, Robert Strange; Rusk, David Dean; Soros, George

FURTHER READING

Arnove, Robert F., ed. *Philanthropy and Cultural Imperialism: The Foundations at Home and Abroad*. Boston, 1980.

Berman, Edward H. *The Ideology of Philanthropy*. Albany, N.Y., 1983.

Coombs, Philip H. *The Fourth Dimension of Foreign Policy: Education and Cultural Affairs*. New York, 1964.

Cuerto, Marcos, ed. *Missionaries of Science: The Rockefeller Foundation and Latin America*. Bloomington, Ind., 1994.

Curti, Merle. *American Philanthropy Abroad: A History*. New Brunswick, N.J., 1963.

Murphy, E. Jefferson. *Creative Philanthropy: Carnegie Corporation and African Education, 1953–1973*. New York, 1976.

PHILIPPINES

Archipelago of over 7,000 islands located in the south-western Pacific, between Indonesia and China. U.S. relations with the Philippines differ fundamentally from those with other nation-states because the Philippines was, for almost forty years, a formal colony of the United States. Three themes have dominated the history of that relationship. The first is the persistent belief on the part of U.S. policymakers, both in the colonial period and after, that the United States had the capacity to direct the course of Philippine history. The second is the reality that U.S. power and policy initiatives were rarely able to produce the results that policymakers intended. The third is the tendency of U.S. policies throughout the twentieth century to promote the interests of upper-class Filipinos, at the expense of the indigenous lower classes.

The earliest contacts between the United States and the Philippines were economic in nature. In the 1790s commercial vessels from the United States began to trade in the Philippines, then a Spanish colony, selling American and European products and buying sugar, indigo, pepper, rattan, and other goods produced in the archipelago. In the nineteenth century, various foreign nationals, including some from the United States, opened commercial houses in Manila and other ports, and over the course of the century firms such as Peele, Hubbell & Co. and Russell and Sturgis played a prominent role in transforming the archipelago's economy. These firms owned cordage factories and haciendas, served as agents for shipping lines, and, acting as merchant bankers, received funds at interest and made advances to Filipino cultivators. By making those advances, they financed the expansion of cash-cropping in the islands (such as abacá in the Bikol region and sugar on Negros) and, in the process, helped to incorporate the Philippines more fully into the world market economy. Curious though it may seem, the U.S. nationals who probably had the greatest long-term impact on the Philippines were the agents of those commercial houses who worked in the archipelago decades before it became a formal colony of the United States.

Revolution, War, and Conquest

The nature of U.S. relations with the Philippines changed fundamentally at the end of the nineteenth century. In 1896 a revolution, led by members of a secret society intent on ending Spanish rule, broke out in the Tagalog-speaking provinces of central Luzon, in the vicinity of Manila. After scoring a few victories in the province of Cavite, the Filipinos were thrashed by the Spaniards, and in December 1897 their leaders—including the commanding general Emilio Aguinaldo—were exiled to Hong Kong. Sporadic resistance continued in Aguinaldo's absence.

In April 1898, following a protracted dispute turned violent concerning a revolution in another Spanish colony, Cuba, the United States and Spain went to war. Shortly after the declaration of war, Commodore George Dewey's Asiatic squadron eliminated Spain's Pacific fleet, thereby isolating the Spaniards in the Philippines and dealing a crippling blow to Spanish power in the archipelago. In mid-May 1898 Aguinaldo returned to the Philippines and resumed leadership of the revolution. Within a few weeks, his forces defeated or captured most of the Spanish troops on Luzon. Aguinaldo issued a declaration of independence and established a government with himself as president; in the meantime, the revolution began to spread to other parts of the archipelago.

But the revolutionaries' success was to prove short-lived because it soon became apparent that the United States, having made quick work of Spain in the Spanish-American-Cuban-Filipino War, had no intention of leaving the Philippines to the Filipinos. Although President William McKinley appeared to have no fixed designs on the Philippines at the time of Dewey's victory, he gradually warmed to the idea of taking the archipelago from Spain. In October 1898 negotiators from Spain and the United States met in Paris to discuss peace terms; McKinley's instructions to the U.S. delegation required them to demand the Philippines. By the terms of the peace treaty of 10 December 1898, Spain ceded the archipelago. McKinley passed the treaty on to the U.S. Senate for ratification.

As U.S. intentions became clearer, relations deteriorated between Aguinaldo's troops and a U.S. expeditionary force that had been dispatched by McKinley in May 1898. Discussions between representatives of Aguinaldo and Elwell Otis, the U.S. commanding general, solved nothing. Finally, the inevitable collision occurred. On 4 February 1899, two days before the U.S. Senate voted to acquire the Philippines, a U.S. sentry shot and killed a Filipino soldier in the environs of Manila. The Philippine-American War had begun.

The war in the Philippines passed through two distinct stages. From February to November 1899 the elite units of the Philippine Army, concentrated in the northern half of the island of Luzon, fought a conventional war against the United States. One set piece battle followed another, all with similar results—one-sided U.S. victories and heavy casualties for the Filipino forces. A second, unconventional phase of the war began in November 1899, once it became clear to Aguinaldo that his army was incapable of prevailing in conventional encounters. Thereafter, throughout the archipelago, U.S. troops were forced to fight an enemy that engaged in hit-and-run raids on their patrols and on U.S.-occupied towns. Once the guerrilla phase of the war had begun, Aguinaldo's ability to direct the Filipino war effort essentially ceased;

control of military operations passed to a score of local commanders, typically men of wealth and political influence in their communities. Aguinaldo was captured in March 1901, but guerrilla units of considerable size continued to hold out well into 1902, and a few Filipino commanders remained in the field for several years more, occasionally mounting small-scale operations against the U.S. authorities.

U.S. Colonial Rule

Even before the U.S. Army had fully pacified the Philippines, a considerably smaller "army"—this one composed of U.S. civilian administrators—had arrived in the Philippines to begin the task of establishing a colonial government. At the apex of the U.S. colonial administration in the islands was the Philippine Commission, appointed by McKinley, initially consisting of five persons. The commission reached Manila in June 1900. Its president was William Howard Taft.

The period 1900–1913 in the Philippines has often been called the "Taft era," an acknowledgment of the fact that Taft, who later had the title of governor, played the key role in shaping U.S. colonial policy. During those years Taft, the governors who succeeded him, and the other members of the commission, believing that the Philippines was backward and that Filipinos were deficient in many ways, committed themselves to a program of social engineering. Three types of policies were crucial from their point of view: the establishment of a system of mass primary education; "political education" (for example, preparing Filipinos to exercise governmental responsibilities); and the introduction of measures aimed at developing the economy. Taft's long-term objective was to prepare the Filipinos for self-government, but he and his colleagues did not envisage that the Philippines would become independent. The cornerstone of his policy was "indefinite retention."

The U.S. colonial record during the Taft era was mixed. For example, although more than a thousand U.S. teachers were hired to oversee the educational system, the schools could not overcome the problem of maintaining attendance during planting and harvest seasons. Matriculation rates were low and most children received less than two years of schooling. There was not much progress in political education as well, partly due to the commission's own policies. Initially limiting the franchise to adult males with education, wealth, or previous governmental experience, the commission insured that the families that had dominated local politics in the Spanish era would also control local governments in the U.S. period. What emerged was not democracy, but rather a collaborative relationship between Filipino elites and the U.S. administration.

The commission failed to realize its economic objectives as well. Taft aimed to attract U.S. investment in Philippine agriculture by offering investors huge tracts from the public domain. But the U.S. Congress proved uncooperative, allowing the Philippine government to sell no more than 1,024 hectares of public land to corporations. One measure favored by the commission did receive congressional approval and ultimately had an impact: the granting to the Philippines of free trade with the United States. The chief beneficiaries of that legislation were the growers of cash crops—above all, owners of large sugar estates—who now had a guaranteed market for their exports. Once again, U.S. policy had the effect of strengthening the power of indigenous elites.

In retrospect, what is most striking about the U.S. colonial record in the Taft era (and in later years as well) is that, on balance, the United States changed so little in the Philippines. Although critics of U.S. colonialism often charge the United States with exploiting the Philippines and subjecting it to large doses of cultural imperialism, they tend to exaggerate the U.S. influence in this era. Some historical processes already begun may have been accelerated, but extensive social engineering did not occur.

The Taft era also saw the rise to prominence of two Filipino politicians—Sergio Osmeña and Manuel Quezon—who would dominate Philippine politics for the entire colonial period. As part of the policy of political education, the U.S. government had created the Philippine Assembly, an elective body empowered to pass legislation (along with the Commission) for the colony. The first Assembly elections were held in 1907. Osmeña and Quezon, both aligned with the newly formed Nacionalista Party, emerged as the most influential members of the legislature. Osmeña became the speaker of the Assembly; Quezon, initially the floor leader, served between 1909 and 1916 as a resident commissioner in Washington, representing the Assembly in the U.S. Congress.

Both Osmeña and Quezon publicly called for the "immediate independence" of the Philippines; moreover, publicly, both men presented themselves as dogged defenders of Filipino interests. In reality, though, both owed their rise to power to sponsorship by U.S. patrons—Osmeña was a protege of W. Cameron Forbes, a commissioner who later became governor; Quezon, of Harry Bandholtz, a Constabulary officer—and both maintained close relations with the colonial administration. In addition, privately, both expressed reservations about independence (fearing, among other things, that the economy would suffer if the U.S. connection were severed).

The election of President Woodrow Wilson in 1913 seemed to portend major changes in U.S. colonial policy, as the platform of Wilson's Democratic Party called for an immediate declaration that the United States planned to recognize Philippine independence. The subsequent changes, however, were more cosmetic than real. The new governor-general, Francis Burton Harrison, was committed to granting Filipinos more control over their affairs, and a policy of "Filipinization" was introduced, with Filipinos replacing U.S. nationals in important bureaucratic posts. Nevertheless, Philippine independence legislation stalled in the U.S. Congress, and the bill that was finally enacted, the Jones Act of 1916, contained only the vague promise that the United States would recognize Philippine independence when "stable government" could be established. That act also eliminated the commission and established a new bicameral legislature, consisting of an elective Senate and House of Representatives; but it also retained the appointed governor-general, giving that official the power to veto acts passed by the Filipino legislators. The tutelage of the United States continued.

With the return of Republicans to the White House in the 1920s, the tutelage became heavy-handed. Leonard Wood, governor-general from 1921 to 1927, wanted to reassert the authority of his office and came into conflict with Quezon, now president of the Senate. Relations between the two were strained until Wood's death in 1927 and the appointment of a more tactful governor-general, Henry Lewis Stimson. Meanwhile, year after year the Philippine legislature sent missions to Washington, petitioning Congress to grant independence, although, as before, the Nacionalista leadership doubted that the colony was ready for it.

By now, though, the commitment of the United States to the colonial relationship was waning. With the onset of the Great Depression, U.S. sugar, dairy, and cordage interests and organized labor became outspoken in their opposition to Philippine competition, and the U.S. Congress was moved to act. In 1934, concerned primarily with protecting U.S. economic interests, it passed the Tydings-McDuffie Act, providing for a ten-year transition to Philippine independence under a "commonwealth" government. The post of governor-general was eliminated; thereafter, the ranking U.S. official, the high commissioner, was to have limited supervisory authority. The Commonwealth was launched in 1935, with Quezon winning the election for president.

The Commonwealth period, which lasted until the Japanese invasion in 1941, was dominated by Quezon. Manifesting autocratic tendencies, he consolidated his control over the machinery of government and dealt ruthlessly with opponents. His government also showed little concern for the plight of rural Filipinos, whose lot had probably grown worse under U.S. rule, thanks in some measure to U.S. policies that promoted elite interests. When peasants in central Luzon organized to protest against declining conditions, Quezon's response was to call in the constabulary.

Quezon took steps to strengthen the Philippine military as well, hiring Douglas MacArthur, recently chief of staff of the U.S. Army, as military adviser. But MacArthur made limited headway, in part because the Commonwealth government had insufficient funds to do the job correctly and in part because, as time passed, Quezon became convinced that the Philippines was incapable of resisting Japanese aggression. When Japanese troops arrived in December 1941, the combined U.S. and Philippine military units were badly beaten. MacArthur, Quezon, and Osmeña managed to escape.

The liberation of the Philippines from Japanese rule began with the U.S. invasion of Leyte in October 1944. Splashing ashore beside MacArthur was Osemña, who had been elevated in exile to the presidency after Quezon's death earlier that year. Even before the war was over, the United States moved forward with its plans to grant the Philippines formal independence. U.S. sovereignty officially ended on July 4, 1946.

Independence and After

But exactly how independent was this new nation-state? Many scholars who have written about U.S.-Philippine relations in the post-independence period have maintained that the change in flag and status did not appear to be so consequential. In their view, in the aftermath of World War II the United States and a succession of Philippine presidents established a mutually beneficial, cooperative, and neocolonial relationship, one in which the United States exercised inordinate influence over its former colony.

To be sure, the United States was conceded special privileges. Taking advantage of the desperate economic conditions in the Philippines following the Japanese occupation, U.S. officials used the promise of postwar reconstruction aid as leverage to win Filipino approval of the Bell Trade Act of 1946, which gave U.S. nationals valuable trade and investment advantages. Whereas the United States was granted absolute free trade with the Philippines for a period of eight years, the Philippines was not accorded reciprocal privileges: quotas were established for cordage, sugar, and other goods. Furthermore, in the "parity" clause, U.S. nationals were given rights denied by the Philippine Constitution to other foreigners—to own Philippine natural resources and to operate Philippine public utilities. The Laurel-Langley Agreement Act of 1954 somewhat modified those arrangements. Although absolute quotas remained on sugar and cordage, those for some other goods were replaced by "duty-free" quotas: up to a certain point, duties would not be assessed, but beyond that point, they would. On the question of parity, Filipinos were given the same rights in the United States as U.S. nationals had in the Philippines. An agreement in 1947 granted the United States a ninety-nine-year lease of several bases in the Philippines, the largest of which were Clark Air Base and a naval base at Subic Bay.

There can be no doubt that throughout the post-independence era the Central Intelligence Agency (CIA), U.S. embassy, U.S. aid agencies, and, more recently, U.S.-dominated multilateral lending agencies, such as the World Bank and the International Monetary Fund (IMF), heavily influenced many Philippine government policies. To gain a glimpse of the extent of such U.S. involvement, one need merely read the published memoirs of Edward Geary Lansdale and Joseph B. Smith, two CIA operatives assigned to the Philippines, both of whom, if their own accounts are to be believed, played major roles in Philippine presidential politics.

Still, one must beware the tendency to exaggerate both the extent and the pervasiveness of U.S. influence in the Philippines and to underestimate the ability of Filipino leaders to pursue independent policy initiatives. Whereas Manuel Roxas, as president from 1946 to 1948, was inclined to make major concessions to the United States, believing that his country's future depended on continued cooperation with the former colonial power, Roxas's successor, Elpidio Quirino (1948–1953), consistently resisted or circumvented U.S. attempts to dictate to him. Moreover, despite the fact that Lansdale was a close friend and ally of the next Philippine president, Ramon Magsaysay (1953–1957), and even helped to get him elected, Magsaysay, once in office, proved far more interested in promoting the agendas of his domestic allies than in following U.S. orders. Typically depicted as uneducated and easily manipulated, Magsaysay was instead a clever manipulator who used the U.S. connection for his own purposes and whose poor record in improving the plight of rural Filipinos can be explained by his intimate ties to landholding elites and old-guard politicians.

Another case in point relates to the Huk rebellion (1946–1954), an uprising against the newly-independent Philippine government, led by a peasant-based communist-led guerrilla organization, the *Hukbong Mapagpalaya ng Bayan* (HMB). Over the years both defenders and critics of post-independence U.S. policy toward the Philippines have claimed that the defeat of the HMB was due substantially to the assistance provided the Philippine government by the United States. In fact the HMB failed primarily because it self-destructed. Its leaders made serious tactical errors, choosing to engage the government in conventional battles at a time when its military units lacked the resources to succeed. More important, there was a yawning gap between the fairly moderate goals of the peasants who joined the movement—whose major objectives were to get a larger share of the harvest and to end the government's repressive practices—and those of its communist leaders—who wanted to confiscate estates and nationalize the economy.

The limits of U.S. influence in the Philippines were exposed most clearly during the presidency of Ferdinand Marcos (1965–1986). Throughout that period, despite the many changes of leadership in Washington—and despite the fact that different U.S. presidents had different objectives in the Philippines—all of the U.S. administrations essentially followed the same policy of backing Marcos and winking at his deficiencies. In truth, rather than being strong-armed by U.S. officials, Marcos managed, most of the time, to outwit them. By cleverly playing his cards—that is, by emphasizing his opposition to communism and engaging in tough negotiations on the renewal of the military bases agreement—he got what he wanted: military and economic aid, IMF and World Bank loans, and external validation.

Hence, at the height of the Vietnam War, Marcos succeeded in getting a substantial amount of U.S. foreign aid from the administration of President Lyndon B. Johnson in exchange for sending an engineer battalion of Philippine troops to Vietnam. Support for Marcos even increased during Richard Nixon's presidency largely because Marcos presented himself as a dedicated anticommunist. When Marcos, intent on remaining in power, declared martial law in 1972 and imprisoned his political opponents, the Nixon White House was silent. Even the administration of President Jimmy Carter, ostensibly committed to human rights, backed off from criticizing Marcos's abuses because it was more interested in keeping the U.S. bases in the Philippines.

By the early 1980s, however, Marcos's hold on the Philippines had begun to weaken. His health was failing. As a consequence of a slowdown in the world economy following the 1979 oil crisis, the Philippine economy was reeling. Billions of dollars of foreign investments dried up between 1980 and 1983. Then came the assassination in August 1983 of Benigno Aquino, Marcos's chief political opponent, destroying his credibility, damaging the chances for economic recovery, and causing ferment in opposition circles. President Ronald Reagan, a longtime Marcos enthusiast, stood by him, but criticism mounted in the Department of State, in Congress, and even among the Joint Chiefs of Staff, who began to see Marcos's continued rule as more of a threat to, rather than guarantee of, the security of the U.S. bases.

Marcos's fall was a result of major miscalculation on his part. In November 1985, believing that he was still in control and expecting to win, Marcos called for presidential elections. He was outpolled by his opponent Corazon Aquino, the widow of his slain rival, and when he attempted to rig the ballot count, a team of observers led by Republican Senator Richard Lugar, chairman of the Senate Foreign Relations Committee, charged him with fraud. At this point, two of Marcos's longtime allies, Defense Minister Juan Ponce Enrile and General Fidel Ramos, backed by segments of the military, broke with him. They were supported by the Catholic Church and hundreds of thousands of Maneños who flooded the city's major thoroughfare and refused to allow troops loyal to Marcos to reach the headquarters of the rebels. Faced with this dramatic display of "people power," Marcos finally stepped down and went into exile in Honolulu.

While U.S. policymakers and nationals participated in many of the events leading to Marcos's fall from power, the chief actors—the ones who actually toppled him—were Filipinos. Reagan stood by his old ally almost to the end, abandoning him only at the urging of others in his administration when it became apparent that Marcos could remain in power only by using massive force.

U.S. relations with the Philippines have remained generally close in the post-Marcos years. President Corazon Aquino (1986–1992) restored democratic institutions but made little progress in improving economic conditions. Aquino's presidency was also bedeviled by restlessness within the Philippine military. Six attempted coups took place, and one in December 1989 came close to succeeding. Aquino survived that incident largely because at a crucial juncture U.S. aircraft came to her assistance. One final development of consequence during the Aquino years was the end of the U.S. military presence in the Philippines. Several factors combined to doom a new bases agreement: growing Filipino opposition to them; the perception by the U.S. government, in the aftermath of the disintegration of the Soviet Union, that they were no longer so valuable; and the eruption of Mount Pinatubo in June 1991, which covered Clark Air Base with volcanic ash. Negotiations broke down in 1991, after nationalists in the Philippine Senate rejected a proposed treaty, and the bases were soon abandoned.

GLENN ANTHONY MAY

See also Aguinaldo, Emilio; Aquino, Benigno S., and Corazon; MacArthur, Douglas; Marcos, Ferdinand; Overseas Military Bases; Spanish-American-Cuban-Filipino War, 1898; World War II

FURTHER READING

Bonner, Raymond. *Waltzing with a Dictator: The Marcoses and the Making of American Policy.* New York, 1987.
Brands, H. W. *Bound to Empire: The United States and the Philippines.* New York, 1991.
Cullather, Nick. *Illusions of Influence: The Political Economy of United States-Philippines Relations, 1942–1960.* Stanford, Calif., 1994.
Friend, Theodore. *Between Two Empires: The Ordeal of the Philippines, 1929–1946.* New Haven, Conn., 1965.
Karnow, Stanley. *In Our Image: America's Empire in the Philippines.* New York, 1989.
Kerkvliet, Benedict J. *The Huk Rebellion: A Study of Peasant Revolt in the Philippines.* Berkeley, Calif., 1977.
May, Glenn Anthony. *Battle for Batangas: A Philippine Province at War.* New Haven, Conn., 1991.
Paredes, Ruby R., ed. *Philippine Colonial Democracy.* New Haven, Conn., 1988.
Shalom, Stephen Rosskamm. *The United States and the Philippines: A Study of Neocolonialism.* Philadelphia, Pa., 1981.
Stanley, Peter W. *A Nation in the Making: The United States and the Philippines, 1899–1921.* Cambridge, Mass., 1974.

PHILLIPS, WILLIAM
(*b*. 30 May 1878; *d*. 23 February 1968)

A career foreign service officer noted for his failed efforts as ambassador to Italy (1936–1941) to keep Italy from declaring war against the Allies in World War II. William Phillips's diplomatic career bridged two world wars and three continents. Scion of a distinguished Massachusetts family and a 1900 graduate of Harvard University, Phillips served as the chief U.S. envoy to five nations and staffed several important diplomatic missions. Phillips ranks with Sumner Welles and Joseph C. Grew as one of the most capable and distinguished U.S. undersecretaries of state.

Low-level appointments in the U.S. embassies at London and Beijing, China, introduced Phillips to the life of a career diplomat. In 1908 he helped to establish the Department of State's Division of Far Eastern Affairs, and served as its first chief. As assistant secretary of state (1917–1920), Williams negotiated secretly with Mexico's revolutionary government for recognition, an effort which failed. Phillips received appointments as minister to the Netherlands and Luxembourg (1920–1922); undersecretary of state (1922–1924); ambassador to Belgium (1924–1927); and minister to Canada (1927–1929).

President Franklin D. Roosevelt appointed Phillips undersecretary of state (1933–1936) and then gave him his most important assignment—ambassador to Fascist Italy. Seeing in Benito Mussolini "the one influence powerful enough to check Hitler's mad designs," Phillips struggled in vain to prevent Italy's 1940 entry into the war against the Allies.

During the war Phillips served in the newly created Office of Strategic Services before his appointment as Roosevelt's personal emissary to India with the rank of ambassador. Charged with the unenviable task of pressing Great Britain to yield to Indian demands for greater autonomy leading to independence, Phillips succeeded only in prompting a personal tongue-lashing from Prime Minister Winston Churchill.

Phillips retired from the foreign service in 1944, but served as President Harry S. Truman's representative to the Anglo-American Committee on Palestine in 1946, a government-sponsored group that tried and failed to secure a peaceful future for the Middle East because it could not solve Arab-Jewish differences over the status of Palestine. Williams published his memoirs *Ventures in Diplomacy* in 1952.

LEEANNA Y. KEITH

See also Churchill, Winston Leonard Spencer; Grew, Joseph Clark; India; Italy; Mexico; Office of Strategic Services; Welles, Benjamin Sumner; World War II

FURTHER READING

Phillips, William. *Ventures in Diplomacy.* Boston, 1952.
Schmitz, David F. *The United States and Fascist Italy, 1922–1940.* Chapel Hill, N.C., 1988.

PICKERING, TIMOTHY

(*b.* 17 July 1745; *d.* 29 January 1829)

U.S. secretary of state (1795–1800) noted for his intense political partisanship and Francophobia. A native of Salem, Massachusetts, Pickering graduated from Harvard College (1763) and was admitted to the Massachusetts bar (1768). Among the many public offices he held were adjutant general and quartermaster general of the Continental Army during the American Revolution, postmaster general (1791–1795), secretary of war (1795), and Federalist senator from Massachusetts (1803–1811). Becoming the nation's and President George Washington's third secretary of state late in 1795, Pickering's primary goal during his four-and-one-half-year tenure was rapprochement with Great Britain. This objective is understandable only after taking into account his fear, even hatred, of France, the U.S. ally whose revolution in 1789 ushered in political, social, and economic turmoil throughout Europe, sparked two great wars lasting to 1815, and unleashed, at least in Pickering's mind, a dangerous and subversive Gallican faction in the United States. Vilified by this allegedly pro-French faction for his unyielding support of Jay's Treaty (1794), a partnership arrangement between the United States and Great Britain, Pickering lost all objectivity in office. He was generally disposed to overlook all but the most outrageous British actions against the United States (a notable exception occurred when in November 1798, HMS *Carnatic* impressed crewmen off the USS *Baltimore*). He favored war with France during the XYZ crisis, prompted by French seizure of U.S. ships, and opposed negotiations ordered by President John Adams in 1799–1800. As the election of 1800 began, Pickering's activities proved him to be an untrustworthy underling. Adams fired the secretary of state in May 1800.

CLIFFORD L. EGAN

See also Adams, John; Convention of 1800; Federalist Party; French Revolution; Great Britain; Jay's Treaty; Washington, George; XYZ Affair

FURTHER READING

Clarfield, Gerald H. *Timothy Pickering and American Diplomacy, 1795–1800*. Columbia, Mo., 1969.
———. *Timothy Pickering and the American Republic*. Pittsburgh, Pa., 1980.

PIERCE, FRANKLIN

(*b.* 23 November 1804; *d.* 8 October 1869)

Fourteenth president of the United States (1853–1857) who emphasized commercial and territorial expansion. Born in Hillsborough, N.H., he graduated from Bowdoin College; passed the New Hampshire bar; practiced law; served in the New Hampshire legislature, U.S. house of representatives (1833–1837), and the U.S. senate (1837–1842); and participated in the War with Mexico as a volunteer colonel and brigadier general. His administration negotiated the Gadsden Purchase (1853) with Mexico and improved U.S. entrée to Canadian fishing grounds and markets by the Marcy–Elgin Reciprocity Treaty (1854) with Great Britain.

Pierce's policy of encouraging private interests to develop guano deposits on uninhabited islands (especially the Phoenix, Gilbert, Ellice, and Caroline islands) set precedents for the nation's later overseas expansion. The administration actually authorized a U.S. naval vessel to assist private business in ascertaining the guano prospects on New Nantucket (Baker Island) and Jarvis Island, both in the Pacific Ocean. When supposed deposits on the Galápagos Islands could not be confirmed, Secretary of State William L. Marcy did not submit to the Senate for ratification a treaty that had been aggressively sought with Ecuador allowing the United States to collect guano there; however, the secretary backed the interests of the Philadelphia Guano Company on the Aves Islands, 300 miles from the Venezuelan coast. Under a U.S. law dated 18 August 1856, American citizens could claim uninhabited guano islands, and over the next thirty years, U.S. sovereignty was claimed over some seventy of them, including Navassa Island (near Haiti), Christmas Island, and the Midway Islands.

The senate's refusal to ratify the Dallas–Clarendon Convention (1856) as initially drafted thwarted Pierce's effort to get Great Britain to give up its Mosquito Protectorate and Bay Islands colony in Central America. Furthermore, the administration's initiatives to acquire Samaná Bay in the Dominican Republic as a coaling station and to annex the Sandwich Islands (Hawai'i) proved unsuccessful. Pierce used the Spanish seizure of the U.S. steamer *Black Warrior* and its cargo of more than 900 bales of cotton in Havana Harbor on 28 February 1854 as a pretext to pressure Spain into ceding Cuba to the United States. He eventually dropped his aggressive diplomacy with regard to the island because of domestic political opposition to the prospective addition of another slave state, unfavorable publicity about the Ostend Manifesto (a blunt U.S. message to Spain that the United States might seize Cuba from the Spanish empire), and Spanish determination to retain Cuba.

Other incidents demonstrate the assertiveness of Pierce's foreign policy. In his 1853 "dress circular," Marcy insisted that U.S. diplomats substitute the plain suit of a U.S. citizen for European court attire when conducting official duties. The Pierce administration successfully pressured Denmark into revising its policy of imposing duties on ships plying the Danish Sound. It demanded an apology and concessions from New Granada (Colombia), following an anti–U.S. riot in Panama in 1856.

In some instances, the administration restrained its normally expansionist impulses. Pierce issued proclamations against filibusters, and, except for a brief period, withheld recognition from William Walker's regime in Nicaragua. The Pierce administration adopted a policy of neutrality toward the Crimean War, and Pierce and Marcy weathered a crisis with Great Britain over the U.S. naval bombardment of Greytown in Central America.

By declining to assent to the Declaration of Paris (1856), the Pierce administration signaled that the United States adhered to its privateering tradition—a decision that would cause trouble several years later when the United States sought to have European nations outlaw Confederate privateers at the outset of the Civil War.

ROBERT E. MAY

See also Colombia; Cuba; Dominican Republic; Filibusters; Fisheries; Gadsden Purchase; Hawai'i; Marcy, William Learned; Ostend Manifesto; Privateering; Walker, William

FURTHER READING

Gara, Larry. *The Presidency of Franklin Pierce.* Lawrence, Kans., 1991.

May, Robert E. *The Southern Dream of a Caribbean Empire, 1854–1861.* Baton Rouge, La, 1973.

Nichols, Roy F. *Franklin Pierce.* Philadelphia, Pa., 1958.

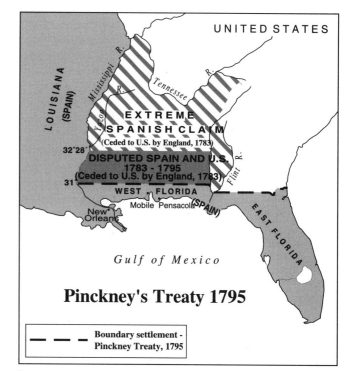

Pinckney's Treaty 1795

– – – Boundary settlement - Pinckney Treaty, 1795

PINCKNEY'S TREATY

An 1795 agreement with Spain named for Thomas Pinckney (1750–1828), soldier, diplomat, and Federalist politician from South Carolina. Pinckney's Treaty is also known as the Treaty of San Lorenzo. While John Jay was in England in 1794 negotiating what became known as Jay's Treaty, other European developments convinced Spain of the need to resolve outstanding differences with the United States involving navigation of the Mississippi River, right of deposit of goods at New Orleans, control of Native Americans along the frontier, and recognition of the U.S. claim since 1783 of the 31st parallel as the southwestern boundary.

Although Spain was an ally of England against France in the wars of the French Revolution, the new Spanish foreign minister, Manuel de Godoy, became concerned about the powerful French Army just across the Pyrenees and withdrew in July 1795 from the alliance with England in favor of peace with France. This step entailed risks, because Great Britain could have engaged in reprisals, and Spain's North American empire lying west and south of the United States might have been vulnerable. With the United States seemingly drawing closer to Great Britain as a result of Jay's Treaty, Spanish officials worried about an Anglo-American attack against its New World territory. American frontier settlers living along the border and with-

in the Spanish Floridas might even have seized the moment to push for secession from the Spanish Empire. To preclude such possibilities, Godoy concluded that concessions to the United States had become necessary.

In the summer of 1794 Spain asked the United States to send an envoy to Madrid to resume previously disrupted negotiations. Almost a year later President George Washington sent Thomas Pinckney, then American minister to Great Britain. Although prepared to make concessions, at first Godoy tried to persuade the United States to accept a triple alliance with Spain and France, in addition to a reciprocal guarantee of Spanish and U.S. territories in the Western Hemisphere. Pinckney, however, refused the offer and stuck to his original instructions, which called for free navigation of the Mississippi River. On learning in July 1795 of the signing of the alliance between France and Spain, Pinckney sensed that his bargaining position had strengthened, although Godoy continued to maneuver for position. When Pinckney finally requested his passport and threatened to leave Spain without an agreement, Godoy acceded to Pinckney's demands on 27 October when the two countries signed the Treaty of San Lorenzo.

Under the treaty's provisions, the United States gained unrestricted navigation of the Mississippi for its citizens, the right of deposit at New Orleans for three years (subject to renewal), settlement of the disputed southwestern boundary with Spain along the 31st parallel north latitude, and a guarantee that the Spaniards would not incite Native Americans to attack settlers. In return, the United States would prevent Native Americans within its territory from raiding Spanish lands.

Americans looked favorably on Pinckney's Treaty and the Senate approved it unanimously on 3 March 1796. A major diplomatic success of the Washington administration, the treaty protected and spurred the economic development of the American northwest, where farmers could now ship their goods down the Mississippi and through the vital port of New Orleans unmolested, and further fueled the expansionist impulse of the United States, which would eventually add a great deal more Spanish territory to its domain in the coming years.

THOM M. ARMSTRONG

See also Continental Expansion; French Revolution; Jay, John; Jay's Treaty; Mississippi River; Spain; Washington, George

FURTHER READING

Bemis, Samuel Flagg. *Pinckney's Treaty: A Study of America's Advantage from Europe's Distress.* Baltimore, Md., 1926.
DeConde, Alexander. *Entangling Alliance: Politics and Diplomacy under George Washington.* Durham, N.C., 1958.
Whitaker, Arthur P. *The Spanish-American Frontier, 1783–1795.* Lincoln, Nebr., 1927.

PINOCHET (UGARTE), AUGUSTO

(*b.* 25 November 1915)

Commander in chief of the Chilean Army when the armed forces of Chile overthrew the leftist government of President Salvador Allende Gossens on 11 September 1973. He headed the governing junta after the coup and in 1974 was named president of the Republic, a position he held until March 1990 when he surrendered power to an elected successor, Patricio Aylwin, the head of the sixteen-party coalition that had defeated him in a plebiscite in 1988.

Pinochet, the son of a customs official, was born in Valparaíso. Entering the Military Academy at an early age, he rose slowly through the ranks, becoming army chief of staff in 1972, a time of increased polarization and violence as the Allende government attempted to push through its radical programs in the face of a hostile congress. Recommended to Allende by his predecessor, who had resigned in the face of anti-Allende pressure by the other generals, Pinochet had already prepared a plan for an Army takeover before becoming commander in chief, but agreed to a coup only at the insistence of the navy and air force two days before it took place.

The U.S. government had tried to prevent Allende's accession to the presidency and was relieved that he had been overthrown. But reports of torture, disappearances, and murder in Chile led Congress to restrict, and in 1976 to cut off, all arms purchases and U.S. military aid to Chile. Additional actions against Chile were taken after the 1976 murder in Washington by Chilean intelligence agents of Allende's former U.S. ambassador, Orlando Letelier, and an American riding in a car with him. The human rights policy of President Jimmy Carter (1977–1981) led to further deterioration in U.S.-Chilean relations, although U.S. conservatives applauded Pinochet's adoption of free-market policies, inspired by the teachings of Milton Friedman of the University of Chicago.

Carter's successor, Ronald Reagan, initially adopted a more favorable policy toward anticommunist authoritarian governments. But in the face of Pinochet's continuing intransigence concerning a return to democracy, and fearing that the Chilean Communist party could benefit, the United States began to use diplomatic and economic pressures to push Pinochet to open the electoral process. In the 1988 plebiscite on Pinochet's continuation in power, the United States spent several million dollars to ensure a fair vote, in effect aiding the anti-Pinochet opposition.

The Aylwin government continued Chile's free-market policies and quickly fulfilled the U.S. conditions for the resumption of military aid. It investigated and publicized, but, with the exception of the Letelier case, did not prosecute most of the human rights violations that had taken place. Pinochet remained as army commander, as the 1980 constitution that had been written under his direction specifically exempted him from its provisions limiting the terms of the military.

PAUL E. SIGMUND

See also Allende (Gossens), Salvador; Chile

FURTHER READING

Arriagada, Genaro. *Pinochet: The Politics of Power,* Boston, 1988.
Constable, Pamela, and Arturo Valenzuela. *A Nation of Enemies: Chile under Pinochet,* New York, 1991.
Sigmund, Paul E. *The United States and Democracy in Chile,* Baltimore, Md., 1993.
Spooner, Mary Helen. *Soldiers in a Narrow Land: The Pinochet Regime in Chile.* Berkeley, Calif., 1994.

PIRACY

Any illegal act of violence or detention perpetrated on the high seas. Such crimes have periodically influenced U.S. foreign relations and defined the global commitments of the U.S. navy, and long preoccupied the United States because of its deep engagement in maritime trade. The Barbary States (Morocco, Algiers, Tunis, and Tripoli) mounted the first major piracy challenge to U.S. shipping in the late-eighteenth century. As a British colony, America had benefited from an arrangement whereby England paid tribute for safe passage along the North African coast. Independence from Great Britain eliminated such protection. The Barbary threat helped support the argument for replacing America's Articles of Confederation with a stronger central government. Consideration of Barbary rapaciousness accompanied the initial debates over what sort of navy, if any, the fledgling U.S. republic should wield. Secretary of State Thomas Jefferson strongly advocated new ship construction to project U.S. power overseas. Meanwhile, negotiations culminated in a 1796 treaty with Algiers that obligated the United States to pay tribute in exchange for the release of captive seamen and an end to further attacks on shipping. Agreements with the other Barbary states soon followed. But continued piracy and demands for additional tribute subsequently spurred Congress to declare a state of war in 1802. The ensuing combat immortalized such mariners as Stephen Decatur and John Rodgers, but the conflict ended inconclusively in 1807. Decatur eventually returned to North Africa with a squadron that subjugated the "Barbary Pirates" and forced peace in 1816.

The dissolution of Spanish hegemony in Latin America engendered a spate of Caribbean piracy beginning in 1810. Congress created a West Indian squadron in 1822 to counter assaults on U.S. merchant vessels. This new force (with some British assistance) effectively eliminated nearly three centuries of pirate dominance in the Caribbean. The threat posed by buccaneers in Malaysian waters and Chinese coastal pirates led to the formation of the U.S. East Indian Squadron in 1835. This unit helped establish a U.S. presence in Asia that culminated in a commercial treaty with Japan in 1856.

The existence of piracy often proved a matter of interpretation. What one state deemed a privateer (private vessel commissioned by a government or revolutionary group) could appear to another as merely a pirate. The Continental Congress authorized privateers to maraud British shipping during the American Revolution, and the War of 1812 witnessed a similar tactic. As the Union navy intensified a blockade of the Confederate coast during the American Civil War, the South increasingly enlisted privateers in an effort to divert Northern warships. By the mid-nineteenth century, improved communications technology and the growth of international trade facilitated greater cooperation against piracy between the United States and various European powers.

JEFFREY D. BASS

See also Articles of Confederation; Barbary States; Freedom of the Seas; Jefferson, Thomas; Morocco; Privateering; War of 1812

FURTHER READING

Hagan, Kenneth J. *This People's Navy: The Making of American Sea Power.* New York, 1991.
———, ed. *In Peace and War: Interpretations of American Naval History, 1775–1984,* 2nd ed. Westport, Conn., 1984.
Williams, Neville. *Captains Outrageous: Seven Centuries of Piracy.* London, 1961.

PITT, WILLIAM

(*b.* 28 May 1759; *d.* 23 January 1806)

British statesman and leading Tory politician, second son of the Earl of Chatham. Pitt the Younger, as he is commonly known, guided Great Britain's policy toward the United States during the quarter century following the Battle of Yorktown (1782). Pitt served as prime minister on three occasions. In early 1783, he briefly headed an interim ministry in the months before the Treaty of Paris, which ended the American Revolution. Late that year, he again became prime minister, a position he retained until his resignation in early 1801. He returned to office in May 1804, remaining there until his death. During this period, Pitt defined not only the British response to American independence, but also British policy toward the French Revolution and Napoleonic Wars.

Most Americans viewed Pitt's policies as hostile to the United States, and although this point is arguable, Pitt certainly concentrated his main efforts on the Irish question, the reduction of the national debt, the reform of Parliament (as well as the East India Company), and eventually the defeat of France. Influenced by the Earl of Sheffield, Pitt adopted commercial policies that excluded U.S. merchants from much of the British Empire, especially the potentially valuable trade with the West Indies. At the same time, Pitt approved the retention of British forts in the American Northwest in order to preserve influence among Native Americans and dominance of the fur trade. Contemptuous of U.S. power and unity, Pitt saw little danger to British interests in such policies.

The years of intense, if intermittent, Anglo-French war after 1793 created additional Anglo-American tensions. By continuing the long-standing British practice of attacking French colonies and commerce rather than committing troops in Europe, Pitt fueled collisions with the United States over maritime issues. Jay's Treaty (1794) eased the conflicts remaining from the 1780s, but failed to resolve the problems resulting from conflicts over neutral rights. When Pitt returned to power in May 1804, he resolved to wage war on France through heightened restrictions on American commerce. In particular, he insisted upon a stricter enforcement of the "Rule of 1756," which declared that any trade that had been closed in peacetime could not be opened in wartime. At the time of his death Anglo-American relations had deteriorated severely.

JAMES E. LEWIS, JR.

See also American Revolution; French Revolution; Great Britain; Jay's Treaty; Napoleonic Wars

FURTHER READING

Ehrman, John. *The Younger Pitt*, 2 vols. New York, 1969.

Reilly, Robin. *William Pitt the Younger, 1759–1806.* London, 1978.

Perkins, Bradford. *The First Rapprochement: England and the United States, 1795–1805.* Philadelphia, Pa., 1955.

PLATT AMENDMENT

(1901)

Amendment to the U.S. army appropriation bill of 1901 that stated the conditions under which the United States agreed to end the military occupation of Cuba (1899–1902), unilaterally imposed binding relations on Cuba, and outlined the formal policy relationship that was to exist between Cuba and the United States. Named after Republican Senator Orville Platt of Connecticut, the Platt Amendment denied the Cuban government authority to enter into any treaties with any foreign power that would "impair or tend to impair the independence of Cuba," to be determined by the United States. Cuba was also obliged to cede to the United States land sufficient to establish a naval station, the territory that eventually was used for the Guantánamo Naval Station. The primary clause was found in Article 3, in which the United States exacted from Cuba the right to intervene for "the maintenance of a government adequate for the protection of life, property and individual liberty." Although the Teller Amendment (1898) had previously proclaimed that Cuba was "of right...free and independent," the Platt Amendment all but eviscerated the substantive attributes of Cuban national sovereignty.

In February 1901 U.S. Military Governor Leonard Wood instructed the Cuban constituent assembly to add the Platt Amendment as an appendix to the new constitution. News of U.S. demands precipitated Cuban protests across the island. Mass demonstrations, marches, and rallies erupted in provincial capitals. Municipal councils, civic associations, and veterans organizations denounced the Platt Amendment and cabled protests and petitions to Wood. Backed by public opinion and encouraged by the press, the constituent assembly balked at the proposed relations. In Washington, the administration of President William McKinley remained adamant and indeed affirmed bluntly that the U.S. military occupation would not end until the Cubans accepted the amendment. Debate in the constituent assembly continued through the spring. In June 1901, faced with the prospect of permanent military occupation or incomplete sovereignty, the constituent assembly acquiesced and agreed to incorporate the Platt Amendment into the constitution of 1901

by a one-vote majority. The Platt Amendment was subsequently incorporated into the Permanent Treaty (1903) between the United States and Cuba.

Under the auspices of the Platt Amendment, the United States exercised sweeping control over Cuban internal affairs, which included three military interventions (1906–1909, 1912, 1917–1922), political meddling, and supervision over Cuban fiscal and budgetary affairs. By the 1930s U.S. officials no longer considered the Platt Amendment a useful policy instrument. On the contrary, it had become a source of political mobilization in Cuba and a powerful catalyst of nationalist sentiment, thereby contributing to the very conditions it sought to contain.

In 1934 all the provisions of the Platt Amendment contained in the Permanent Treaty were abrogated, except the clause sanctioning the U.S. Naval Station at Guantánamo.

LOUIS A. PÉREZ, JR.

See also Cuba; Monroe Doctrine; Teller Amendment

FURTHER READING

Hitchman, James R. "The Platt Amendment Revisited: A Bibliographical Survey." *The Americas* 23 (April 1967): 343–369.

Pérez, Louis A., Jr. *Cuba Under the Platt Amendment, 1902–1934.* Pittsburgh, 1986.

Scott, James B. "The Origin and Purpose of the Platt Amendment." *American Journal of International Law* 3 (July 1914): 585–591.

POINSETT, JOEL ROBERTS

(*b.* 2 March 1779; *d.* 12 December 1851)

Politician and diplomat who served as President Martin Van Buren's secretary of war (1837–1841). Born in South Carolina, Poinsett undertook his first diplomatic service in 1810, when he was appointed special agent to Rio de la Plata and Chile. He spent four years in South America, where he supported and advised the independence movement against Spain. As a member of the U.S. house of representatives (1821–1825) from South Carolina, Poinsett advocated recognition of the new South American republics. Dispatched on a special mission to Mexico from August 1822 to January 1823, Poinsett reported on conditions there (as well as in Cuba). His *Notes on Mexico* appeared in 1824. He became the first U.S. minister to Mexico in March 1825. Poinsett's tenure in Mexico was tumultuous. To counter British influence Poinsett established an Order of York Rite Masons; Great Britain's representative established a competing Order of Scottish Rite Masons. Disaffected by Poinsett's interference in its politics, the Mexican government requested his recall in 1829. Perhaps his most memorable contribution as minister to Mexico was importation of the poinsettia—named for him—to the United States.

As secretary of war during Van Buren's presidency, Poinsett reorganized and increased the size of U.S. military forces. He carried out the policy of Indian removal west of the Mississippi and waged war throughout Van Buren's administration against Florida Seminoles who resisted removal. In 1846 Poinsett warned against underestimating the effort required to win a war against Mexico and urged that Mexico be granted moderate terms at the end of the conflict.

KENNETH R. STEVENS

See also Mexico; Native Americans; Van Buren, Martin

FURTHER READING

Rippy, J. Fred. *Joel R. Poinsett, Versatile American.* Durham, N.C., 1935.
Wriston, Henry M. *Executive Agents in American Foreign Relations.* Gloucester, Mass., 1929.

POINT FOUR

President Harry S. Truman's proposed program of economic aid to developing countries in the form of technical assistance, to be combined with ongoing military assistance, to buttress friendly regimes. The communist threat to Greece and Turkey in 1947 made it clear to Truman that much of the global struggle against communism would take place in the Third World. Truman advocated aid to Third World nations in his 1949 inauguration speech, and the proposal became known as the Point Four program. Funded by the Act for International Development of 1950, it provided some $35 million for United Nations–coordinated technical assistance programs as well as ad hoc bilateral arrangements in which the receiving country paid some of the costs of the technology in question. The legislation gave the executive considerable leeway in choosing the mix of multilateral, regional, bilateral, official, and private methods of assistance, as well as in the type of programs to be funded. In practice, Point Four assistance was placed squarely under the Department of State's Technical Cooperation Administration. In the early years, the program provided primarily "basic needs" assistance, that is, programs to improve food availability, basic health, and housing, rather than to promote private investment.

The Point Four program eventually ran into many obstacles at both the local and global levels. Although isolated projects yielded dramatic results (witness the Green Revolution), they did not generate a sustained improvement in living conditions in many countries. Over time the Point Four program was eclipsed by the microlevel rural community development programs of the Agency for International Development and the Peace Corps on the one hand, and the macrolevel infrastructure development and balance of payments lending of the World Bank and the International Monetary Fund on the other. While technical cooperation continues in various forms, it is no longer a large aspect of developmental aid.

KENDALL W. STILES

See also Agency for International Development; Foreign Aid; Peace Corps; Truman, Harry S.

FURTHER READING

Paterson, Thomas G. "Foreign Aid Under Wraps: The Point Four Program." *Wisconsin Magazine of History* 61 (Winter 1972– 1973): 191–126.
Rondinelli, Dennis. *Development Administration and U.S. Foreign Policy.* Boulder, Colo., 1987.

POLAND

Located in central Europe, and bordered by Germany, the Czech Republic, Slovakia, Ukraine, Belarus, Lithuania, and the Baltic Sea, a country that has undergone dramatic and fundamental changes in the twentieth century and whose relations with the United States have reflected these developments.

The modern Polish state was reconstituted in the wake of World War I. As the result of the Paris Peace Conference of 1919, the three parts of Poland, which had been partitioned in the late-eighteenth century and ruled by Prussia, Austria, and Russia for more than a hundred years, were reunited and Poland became an independent state.

This step, which reflected the activities of Polish nationalist leaders as well as the decisions of the great powers, satisfied the aspirations of most Poles. However, the new Polish state faced many of the same problems as of other new nations in the region. The country had to recover from severe human and material losses. The ensuing war with the Soviet Union in 1920 drained Poland's budget, and high levels of indebtedness put a strain on its economy. The country's new leaders expanded its educational system and attempted to industrialize. However, the success achieved in these areas in the early interwar period was soon followed by the economic devastation created by the Great World Depression of the 1920s. The growing urban working class also suffered from inadequate social services, sanitation, and other facilities in the cities. Political life was complicated by the existence of sizeable Ukrainian, Belorussian, Jewish, and German minorities. Poland's leaders also faced the need to overcome the legacies of the partition and unite the three parts of the country.

Increasing economic and social unrest led many of the country's traditional landowning elites, as well as the military, to support strong leaders who could deal with what many saw as growing political turmoil. The fact that Poland's borders with many of her neighbors continued to be disputed and the impact of Poland's war with the fledgling Soviet Union, which ended with the Treaty of Riga in 1921, fueled these sentiments.

Domestic political factors also contributed to the unstable situation. An electoral system based on proportional representation resulted in a proliferation of political parties and necessitated coalition governments. In part to limit the role of Colonel Jósef Piłsudski, leader of the Polish state after World War I, the political system adopted in 1921 made the presidency largely a symbolic post. The first elected president of the new Polish state, Gabriel Narutowicz, was assassinated in 1922. High military expenditures and hyperinflation also contributed to unrest. The government initiated land reforms and took other steps to improve Poland's economy. However, on 12 May 1926, Piłsudski staged a successful coup. Piłsudski's government at first retained aspects of a parliamentary system but gradually became more authoritarian, particularly as Poland's economic situation worsened as a result of the Depression. After Piłsudski's death in May 1935, Poland was ruled by his protégés until it was partitioned once again by German and Soviet forces in 1939.

President Woodrow Wilson's support for self-determination was one of the forces that aided the creation of an independent Polish state after World War I. The United States recognized the new Polish state in January 1919, and provided food and other humanitarian aid. But although U.S.-Polish relations were cordial throughout the interwar period, they remained at a low level. U.S.-Polish trade accounted for less than one percent of U.S. exports or imports in 1920, for example. In 1922–1924, the United States was the second largest importer from Poland; Poland ranked seventeenth among importers from the United States. Poland received MFN status from the United States in 1931.

Representatives of the approximately four million Polish Americans in the United States often pushed for greater U.S. aid and involvement in Polish affairs. However, U.S. leaders continued to see Poland as marginal to U.S. interests.

Poland relied on alliances with France and Romania to guarantee its borders, although the Treaty of Locarno, signed in October 1925, threatened Polish security by weakening France's commitment to its eastern allies. Poland signed a non-aggression treaty with the Soviet Union in 1932 and a Declaration of Non-Aggression with Germany in 1934. These treaties did not deter Germany or the Soviet Union from invading Poland in September 1939.

World War II and its Aftermath

Poland was one of the countries that experienced the most extensive human and material losses in World War II. Some six million Polish citizens died in the war. Almost all of Poland's sizeable Jewish community perished in the Holocaust. Many ethnic Poles, Ukrainians, and other minorities also died. Some of these losses resulted from the emergence of a strong resistance movement in Poland. Led by the government in exile established in London, the Polish underground organized a wide network of clandestine associations and self-help groups. The Polish Home Army, formed in 1940, engaged in sabotage and otherwise hindered the German military. Approximately 200,000 Poles died in the ill-fated Warsaw Uprising which began in August 1944.

The United States recognized the Polish government in exile in October 1939. Poland was included in the Lend Lease program, and the United States helped to support the Polish underground and its missions abroad. However, U.S.-Polish relations were complicated by consideration of Soviet interests once the USSR joined the Allies. This factor had particularly important implications for Poland as the war's end approached.

Unwilling to antagonize the Soviets over the question of Poland's post-liberation fate, Franklin D. Roosevelt at Tehran and Yalta essentially accepted Soviet proposals concerning Poland's post-war borders and form of government. The efforts of noncommunist Polish leaders in exile, including Stanislaw Mikołajczyk, to prevent such an outcome were unsuccessful.

U.S.-Polish relations after World War II were influenced profoundly by the establishment of a communist government in Poland and by Poland's early subordination of its interests and foreign policies to those of the Soviet Union. In the period between 1944 and 1947, U.S. diplomats supported the right of noncommunist political forces to participate in Polish affairs. The United States protested the manipulation of the January 1947 elections, which gave the Peasant Party, led by Mikołajczyk, far fewer seats than anticipated; but did little to counter the growing influence of the Communist party.

Following the adoption of a new constitution, Communist party leaders began implementing the Soviet model of political organization and economic development in earnest. Steps were taken to ensure the Communist party's political dominance and to discredit its opponents. The flight of Mikołajczyk in October 1947 symbolized the end of openly organized political resistance to the communist system.

Poland's communist leaders nationalized industrial assets and tried to collectivize agriculture. Poland's trade was reoriented toward the Soviet Union and other socialist countries, and ambitious plans were adopted to industrialize the country along Soviet lines. Poland's leaders came to rely increasingly on coercion, including political trials and the subversion of justice, to implement these policies. However, in contrast to many other communist countries, in Poland purged political leaders were subjected to house arrest or imprisonment rather than execution.

As the Cold War intensified, Poland became increasingly isolated from noncommunist Europe and the United States. The United States had provided aid to Polish citizens—through the United Nations Relief and Rehabilitation Administration (UNRRA)—to help repair the devastation caused by World War II, and U.S. officials discussed the possibility of extending loans to Poland. However, U.S. plans to extend the Marshall Plan to central and eastern European countries were opposed by the Soviet Union. As Poland's communist leaders consolidated their Stalinist system, U.S.-Polish relations deteriorated further. Trade declined as the result of the Export Control Act of 1949 and the Mutual Defense Assistance Act (known as the Battle Act) of 1951. Information bureaus were closed, and cultural exchanges ceased. Polish-American groups often protested against the notion of "containment" that came to dominate U.S. policy toward Eastern Europe and sought to keep U.S. interest in Polish issues alive. Closer U.S. ties with Poland, however, would have to await the dramatic changes in the Soviet world of the late 1980s.

De-Stalinization and Workers Unrest: 1956

Perceived by many citizens as a foreign system imposed from without, communism never developed deep roots in Poland. The lack of legitimacy of the Polish regime, coupled with the power of the Catholic Church in Poland and historical antagonism against Russia, left the communist system vulnerable to repeated challenges from within.

The first of these occurred in the wake of Stalin's death. At a middle level of development when Stalinist economic policies were implemented, Poland was one of the first communist countries to experience the negative impact of these policies. By the early 1950s, economic performance lagged far behind the leaders' promises to the population. Because they were thought by many Poles to be puppets of the Soviet Union, Poland's communist leaders were more adversely affected by Moscow's pressure on central and eastern European leaders to remedy some of the worst excesses of the Stalinist system. Allowed somewhat greater leeway, Poland's intellectuals organized independent discussion groups and pushed for greater freedom. Khrushchev's secret speech denouncing Stalin at the Twentieth Party Congress of the CPSU in 1956 set off another, more ambitious round of de-Stalinization in the Soviet Union. Together with growing economic hardship, this provided the catalyst for a massive challenge to communist rule in Poland, seen most visibly in the form of increased intellectual ferment and workers unrest.

In contrast to the situation in Hungary in 1956, where the Soviet Union was able to restore order only by armed intervention, in Poland order was restored largely by relying on the Polish leadership itself. Władysław Gomułka, who was purged from his party positions in 1948 for his efforts to create a form of socialism adapted to conditions in Poland, was brought in to take over the party. Perceived by many Poles as a Polish patriot, Gomułka was also trusted by the Soviets.

The protests of 1956 prompted the leadership to make several important concessions to the population. Collectivization of agriculture was stopped, and agriculture largely reverted to private hands. The regime came to an accommodation with the Catholic Church that included acceptance of the right of the church to use radio to broadcast masses. Poland also received Soviet permission to sell its coal in the West, as well as subsidies to help its ailing economy.

These positive elements were soon outweighed by continued poor economic performance and a turn to more conservative policies on Gomułka's part. Gomułka argued vociferously for suppression of the political reform in Czechoslovakia in 1968. He also presided over a new wave of officially tolerated anti-Semitism in the late 1960s that led to the emigration of many of Poland's remaining Jews. Ironically, Gomułka, who was brought to power as the result of mass workers, protests in 1956, was ousted in 1970 by workers protests sparked by the failure of his government's economic policies.

U.S. policy toward Poland during this period reflected overall U.S. priorities in the region. Rhetorical support for the liberation of central and east European communist countries was coupled with caution and a lack of willingness to become involved in events that would openly antagonize the Soviet Union. U.S. officials expressed interest in the Polish events of 1956 but publicly indicated that the United States would not use force to help the Poles overthrow communism.

U.S.-Polish relations improved under Gomułka, as Polish leaders achieved somewhat greater freedom in the conduct of their country's foreign affairs. As part of the effort to promote change in the region by supporting national communism, the United States began providing economic aid and credits to Poland. Cultural and educational exchanges were also resumed. U.S.-Polish trade increased and, in the late 1950s, accounted for most of U.S. trade with the European communist countries. In 1960 the United States and Poland reached agreement on the compensation of U.S. citizens whose property had been nationalized. In recognition of this fact and of the efforts of Polish leaders to follow policies somewhat independent of the Soviet Union, the United States restored Poland's MFN status the same year. In 1957, Poland joined the GATT and in 1958, the Food and Agricultural Organization of the United Nations.

Polish-U.S. relations continued to improve in the 1960s and 1970s. The United States did not support the plan of Polish Foreign Minister Adam Rapacki in 1958 to create a nuclear free zone in Germany, Poland, and Czechoslovakia. However, the shift in U.S. policy toward the region as a whole to one of peaceful engagement in the early 1960s was reflected in increased contacts with Poland and increased U.S. assistance.

The policy of bridge-building adopted by the Johnson administration saw a further intensification of ties to Poland. Levels of contact and assistance reflected domestic developments in both countries and changes in U.S.-Soviet relations. Poland's MFN status was temporarily suspended in the wake of the Cuban missile crisis of 1962, and U.S. officials began to rethink the benefits of peaceful engagement in light of Gomułka's effort in the mid-1960s to rein in Poland's intellectuals. Trade relations suffered similar variations due to political developments. However, levels of trade between the two nations were far higher by the end of the 1960s than previously. U.S. leaders approved the German-Polish treaty of December 1970 which affirmed the Oder-Neisse line as the German-Polish boundary.

The Gierek Era and the Birth of Solidarity

Shortly thereafter, having been elevated to the top position in the Communist party as the result of workers, protests, Edward Gierek took steps to pacify the workers. Earlier price increases were rolled back, and the leadership promised greater attention to workers' needs. Gierek also presided over a dramatic change in Poland's development strategy. In an effort to modernize Poland's ailing economy, the leadership turned to the West for technology and capital. Poland's hard currency debt soared as Polish leaders sought an infusion of Western equipment and technology to modernize Polish industry. In the first half of the 1970s, this strategy worked relatively well. Industrial output increased, and the population's standard of living improved significantly. However, the positive results of this policy came to an end in the second half of the 1970s, due to a combination of external and domestic factors, including the impact of the world oil crisis.

Polish managers and technicians lacked the skills to make good use of most of the equipment and technology imported from the West. The economy also continued to suffer from the chronic inefficiencies that plagued centrally planned economies.

Efforts to raise prices of basic foodstuffs in 1976 led to new workers' riots and strikes. The government once again rescinded the increases in food prices, but it also imprisoned many of the workers involved in organizing the strikes. In a step that would have important repercussions in 1980, intellectuals organized the Committee for the Defense of the Workers (KOR), to assist the families of those workers who were imprisoned.

The greater opening to the West that began under Gomułka continued and intensified under Gierek. Academic exchanges, which began with the support of the Ford Foundation in April 1957, expanded with the extension of the Fulbright program to Poland and the initiation of university exchanges. Many Poles traveled to the United States as tourists or to visit family members. Economic linkages also increased greatly. The 1971 amendment to the Export-Import Bank Act that once again allowed loans to Poland was followed by extension of new credits and a rapid increase in exports and imports between the two countries. Steps were taken to institutionalize U.S.-Polish economic cooperation by establishing the U.S.-Polish Trade Commission.

Nevertheless, economic performance continued to decline in the late 1970s. Shortages of food and other basic goods became endemic, and citizen dissatisfaction with Gierek and his policies grew. The economy also labored under the burden of high levels of foreign debt. Economic issues were the catalyst for widespread strikes in 1980 that began in the Gdansk shipyards and eventually led to the formation of Solidarity, the first legally recognized free trade union in the communist world. The rapid growth in support for Solidarity, which eventually came to encompass one of every three adults in the country, reflected the clear lack of legitimacy of communism in Poland. The workers' tradition of self-organization, the support provided for independent activists by the Catholic Church, and the inspiration provided by the first Polish pope, John Paul II, also contributed to the rise of Solidarity as did the alliance between workers and intellectuals forged in 1976. Although Lech Walesa, who emerged as the primary spokesperson of Solidarity, and other Solidarity leaders maintained that their organization was only a trade union, Polish and Soviet leaders feared that it was becoming a political force that could challenge the dominance of the Communist party.

Justifying his action as necessary to prevent a Soviet intervention, General Wojciech Jaruzelski declared martial law and outlawed Solidarity in December 1981. Leading Solidarity activists were interned, and Solidarity became an underground organization. However, the tradition of independent organization remained strong. Poland's intellectuals, who supported Solidarity in large numbers, also were able to preserve much of their freedom of maneuver. Martial law was lifted in the summer of 1983.

U.S. policy toward Poland during this period reflected overall trends in U.S. policy toward Eastern Europe. It also reflected the impact of the sizeable U.S. Polish community on U.S. policymakers and the judgment of several successive U.S. administrations that efforts to integrate Poland more fully into the West would be well spent.

The imposition of martial law in December 1981 led to an immediate cooling of U.S.-Polish relations. The U.S. government and many non-governmental organizations, including the trade unions, supported Solidarity and condemned the imposition of martial law and the banning of Solidarity. The U.S. government also imposed sanctions on Poland. High technology imports to Poland were restricted and no new credits for food were granted. In 1982, the United States revoked Poland's MFN status and ended credits for agricultural purchases in response to the passage of the Trade Union Law which abolished Solidarity and other trade unions in Poland. The United States also blocked Poland's entry into the IMF until 1985 and would not negotiate rescheduling Poland's debt. Humanitarian aid was exempt from these restrictions.

The Reagan administration set three conditions for the normalization of relations between the United States and Poland. These included the lifting of martial law, the release of political prisoners, and the institution of a dialogue between the government and Polish society. The United States began to lift economic sanctions against Poland in 1984, in response to the fact that the Polish government had met these criteria, at least at a superficial level. Appeals by Polish dissidents that sanctions be lifted also influenced U.S. actions. After the Polish government declared a general amnesty for political prisoners in 1986, the U.S. government lifted all remaining sanctions. However, the United States retained a cautious attitude toward expanding cooperation with Poland until July 1989. The U.S. government also continued to have contact with the opposition as well as with Polish officials throughout the rest of the communist period.

The Post-Communist Period

In Poland, the end of communist rule was the culmination of a long process of change that had its roots in earlier efforts to change the system. Reformist elements in the Communist party leadership played an important role in negotiating the transfer of power to noncommunist leaders.

As in earlier efforts at change, economic issues provided one of the chief catalysts for the process that eventually led to the unexpected victory of Solidarity candidates in the multiparty elections of June 1989. Continued economic problems led to growing waves of strikes in the late-1980s and, eventually, to the willingness of reformist communist leaders to enter into negotiations with the opposition in early 1989. In the course of these negotiations, the party made a series of concessions, including the agreement to hold multiparty elections for parliament in June 1989. The extent of the electorate's disaffection with communist rule was reflected in the unexpected victory of Solidarity in these elections. Forced to take the reins of power, Solidarity activists presided over the for-

mation of the country's first noncommunist government in forty years in the fall of 1989 and the election of Lech Walesa as Poland's president in the winter of 1990.

Poland's new noncommunist government faced many of the same tasks as its counterparts in other parts of formerly communist central and eastern Europe. In addition to the need to reorient the work of existing political institutions, recruit new political leaders and officials, reshape the country's party system, and create political values and attitudes supportive of democracy, they also faced the urgent need to address Poland's serious economic crisis. Under the leadership of then Finance Minister Leszek Balcerowicz, the leadership adopted what came to be known as "shock therapy" to create a market economy in Poland. Based on strict macroeconomic policies, liberalization of prices, a rapid reorientation of the country's external economic relations to the West, and privatization of state enterprises, this strategy led to the beginning of economic recovery by 1993. However, it also led to considerable economic hardship and uncertainty for large groups of the population as well as to the creation of greater and more visible disparities in wealth.

Coupled with the inability of many of the country's new leaders to cooperate with each other and popular resentment of what many voters perceived to be the growing and inordinate influence of the Catholic Church on political life, these factors led to the fall of several governments in Poland between 1989 and 1993. In the parliamentary elections of 1993, these factors also led to the electoral victory of a coalition comprised of a party that included a successor of the Communist party and the Peasant party that had been allowed to exist during communist rule. The new leadership found its activities constrained by the need to retain the confidence of international financial organizations and lender governments. However, the government did adopt certain policies designed to further the interests of one of its main constituencies, farmers, and its leaders continued to promise to review policies that caused economic hardship for the population.

U.S.-Polish relations since the end of communist rule in 1989 have expanded in all areas. The U.S. government has played an important role in providing assistance to Poland to support the recreation of democracy and the move to a market economy. U.S. officials have emphasized grants and technical assistance rather than export credits, or loans. One of the most important of these efforts has been the Polish-American Enterprise Fund which fostered the development of private businesses, as part of the effort to promote democratization and privatization. In July 1989, President George Bush visited Poland in acknowledgment of the agreement that was reached between Solidarity and the regime. Private sector links between Polish and U.S. enterprises, cultural and educational institutions, and individuals also expanded rapidly after 1989. U.S.-Polish relations continued to be warm after the election of the country's Peasant Party-Democratic Socialist Party coalition in 1993.

As was the case during the communist period, when Poland's relatively independent polices earned it special treatment by the United States, Poland has accounted for the lion's share of U.S. assistance to post-communist Central and Eastern Europe. One of the original beneficiaries, along with Hungary, of the Support for East European Democracy (SEED) Act, Poland had received $123.7 million in direct equity investments and loans to private enterprises through the Polish-American Enterprise Fund by April 1994. Many non-governmental organizations and businesses in the United States also continued to expand their activities in Poland.

Polish leaders have expressed Poland's desire to join the European Union and NATO. A transition agreement between Poland and the European Community went into effect in March 1992. This agreement was replaced by an association treaty in March 1994. On 8 April 1994, Poland officially applied for membership in the European Union (EU). President Walesa was very critical of the Partnership for Peace (PFP), a preliminary military cooperation structure, when U.S. officials first proposed it. After the meetings between President Clinton and the presidents of the Visegrad countries in January 1994, Walesa gave his support for the PFP while remaining adamant about the need for Poland's eventual full membership in NATO. Poland became a signatory for Partnership for Peace on 2 February 1994. Even though Walesa lost the presidency to Alexander Kwasniewski, a former communist, the new government maintained the strong interest in joining NATO. In fact, President Kwasniewski visited NATO headquarters in Brussels in January 1996. U.S. officials have not set out a definite timetable for extending full membership to Poland. However, U.S. policymakers have stated that it is a question of when and not if Poland will become a member.

Since the collapse of the communist system, U.S. investment has exceeded $1 billion and amounts to thirty-five percent of the total foreign investment in Poland. The United States also provided over $36 million in environmental protection related projects. The United States is Poland's third largest creditor.

Poland's trade with the West expanded greatly after 1989. EU countries accounted for the largest share of Poland's trade in the early 1990s. Trade with Germany alone comprised one-third of Polish exports and one-fourth of imports in 1993. U.S.-Polish trade also increased substantially. In 1993, Polish imports from the United States amounted to $18.8 billion; exports to the United States reached $14.1 billion.

SHARON L. WOLCHIK

See also Containment; Eastern Europe; North Atlantic Treaty Organization; Paris Peace Conference of 1919; Russia and the Soviet Union; Walesa, Lech; Warsaw Pact; World War I; World War II

FURTHER READING

Kolankiewicz, George, and Lewis G. Paul. *Poland: Politics, Economics and Society.* London and New York, 1988.

Kovrig, Bennett. *The Myth of Liberation: East-Central Europe in U.S. Diplomacy and Politics Since 1941.* Baltimore, Md., 1973.

Lukas, Richard C. *Bitter Legacy: Polish-American Relations in the Wake of World War II.* Lexington, Ky., 1982.

Meikle, John, and Terry Sarah. *Soviet Policy in Eastern Europe.* New Haven, Conn., 1984.

Ost, David. *Solidarity and the Politics of Anti-Politics: Opposition and Reform in Poland since 1968.* Philadelphia, Pa., 1990.

Wandycz, Piotr S. *The United States and Poland.* Cambridge, Mass., 1980.

POLK, JAMES KNOX

(*b.* 2 November 1795; *d.* 15 June 1849)

Eleventh president of the United States and an expansionist who took the nation to war with Mexico in 1846, settled the Oregon dispute, and added millions of acres of western territory to the United States. Born in North Carolina, reared in Tennessee, and educated at the University of North Carolina, Polk progressed from law practice to state politics and in 1825 entered the U.S. house of representatives in the wake of the rising popularity of his mentor, Andrew Jackson. Polk became speaker of the House in 1935. Four years later he returned to Tennessee and served a term as governor. After failing in 1840 to retain and in 1943 to recapture that office, he was selected in 1844 as a dark horse presidential candidate for the Democratic party.

Polk won the presidency on a platform that promised aggressive westward expansion to "reannex Texas" and "reoccupy Oregon." His extreme, if popular, rhetoric led to serious diplomatic tangles with both Mexico and Great Britain. Polk and Secretary of State James Buchanan spent 1845 attempting to balance U.S. foreign policy between the domestic pressure of "Manifest Destiny" and Mexican and British pressure to contain U.S. expansion.

Ill trained and poorly suited for diplomacy, the obstinate Polk quickly raised British and Mexican hackles. In his inaugural address he asserted that the U.S. claim to Oregon was "clear and unquestionable"—an assertion that offended British national honor and provoked talk of war. He angered an already estranged Mexican government by expressing his determination to establish the Rio Grande as the southern boundary of the prospective state of Texas.

In the summer of 1845, after the British rejected Polk's offer to divide the Oregon territory at the 49th parallel and the Slidell mission failed in an attempt to buy concessions from Mexico—concessions that would give to the United States the disputed Texas territory, New Mexico, and California—impatient and agitated Polk became increasingly determined to fulfill his expansionist goals. He deployed troops into the contested Texas territory and positioned U.S. forces to secure California should war erupt with Mexico; pronounced the so-called Polk Corollary to the Monroe Doctrine in his December 1845 message to Congress that forbade even diplomatic intervention by Europeans in North America; and forced the Oregon issue by calling for Congress to abrogate an existing "joint occupation" arrangement with Britain.

Although a congressional coalition stalled his request until the spring of 1846, when it was granted the arrangement provided the British an opening to renegotiate. Britain accepted a division of the territory at the 49th parallel under the terms of the Oregon Treaty of 1846. Polk had won most of what the United States considered essential in the Pacific Northwest, diminished his culpability in the compromise by drawing the senate into the process at the negotiating stage, and avoided a potential confrontation with Britain at a time of crisis with Mexico. Polk's success warmed relations, allowing the United States to benefit from Britain's recent move toward free trade and encouraging a growing rapprochement between the two Atlantic nations.

Meanwhile, Polk's pressure on Mexico led to a war in which the United States fought to obtain the vast territory that extended from the disputed Texas boundary to the Pacific. Polk rejected Buchanan's suggestion that the administration issue a disclaimer to the British and French stating that the United States did not intend to seize territory from Mexico. He continued to pursue diplomatic avenues that would end the war, but none short of the complete attainment of U.S. goals. When Mexican leader Santa Anna reneged on his promise to end the war after the United States had assisted in his return from exile, Polk dispatched Nicholas Trist to Mexico to negotiate a treaty. Although Trist frustrated Polk by working at cross purposes with the U.S. military command in Mexico, the U.S. agent ignored his recall and negotiated the Treaty of Guadalupe Hidalgo in 1848. A piqued Polk had no alternative but to accept the treaty because it achieved all of his war aims: gaining California, New Mexico, and the Rio Grande boundary.

Polk pursued a set of clear objectives that enlarged the U.S. domain. Yet he rejected a wartime proposition to take all of Mexico and an 1848 bid to seize the Yucatán. As he had promised, he retired after one term and returned to his home in Nashville, where he died within a few months.

DONALD A. RAKESTRAW

See also Buchanan, James; McLane, Louis; Oregon Question; Mexico, War with; Slidell, John; Trist, Nicholas Philip

FURTHER READING

Bergeron, Paul H. *The Presidency of James K. Polk*. Lawrence, Kans., 1987.
Quaife, Milo M. *The Diary of James K. Polk During his Presidency, 1845 to 1849*. Chicago, 1910.
Sellers, Charles G. *James K. Polk, Continentalist, 1843–1856*. Princeton, 1966.

POPULATION POLICY

In 1960 world population passed the three billion mark and was projected to double before the year 2000, having reached 5.5 billion by 1993. There was growing awareness that such rapid growth rates would adversely affect the interests of all nations, not just the poorer or developing nations of the world, where more than ninety percent of the growth was occurring. The first U.S. president to address this issue was Lyndon B. Johnson, who, in his State of the Union message in January 1965, declared: "I will seek new ways to use our knowledge to cope with the

---

WHERE IN THE WORLD DO THEY LIVE?

Of every 100 people in the world in 1991:

21 live in China (mainland)
16 live in India
5 live in the former Soviet Union
5 live in the United States
4 live in Indonesia
3 live in Brazil
2 live in Bangladesh
2 live in Japan
2 live in Mexico
2 live in Nigeria
2 live in Pakistan
1 lives in Egypt
1 lives in France
1 lives in Germany
1 lives in Iran
1 lives it Italy
1 lives in the Philippines
1 lives in Thailand
1 lives in Turkey
1 lives in the United Kingdom
1 lives in Vietnam

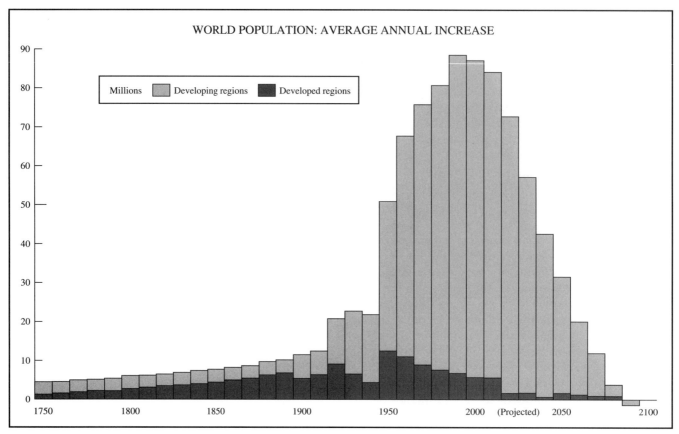

WORLD POPULATION: AVERAGE ANNUAL INCREASE

explosion in world population." A year later he pledged U.S. readiness "to help developing countries deal with the population problem. The U.S. cannot and should not force any country to adopt any particular approach to this problem. It is a matter of individual and national conscience."

Congress was quick and supportive in its response to the president's initiative. Senate hearings launched in 1965 continued on-and-off for nearly three years. They covered every aspect of population growth and family planning. Between 1965 and 1972 annual appropriations for U.S. population assistance programs steadily increased to $130 million. The Agency for International Development (AID) expended these funds as part of its overall development assistance, either through direct bilateral support or through multilateral agencies and private voluntary organizations. Main country recipients were increasingly the larger developing countries of Asia (except China), Africa, and Latin America. U.S. policy emphasized from the outset the principle of voluntarism and informed consent in all family planning programs it supported.

President Richard Nixon saw population pressures adversely affecting living conditions, environment, economic development and even international peace. At the

World Population Conference in Bucharest in August 1974, the United States joined 135 other nations in adopting by consensus the World Population Plan of Action. This plan recognized the basic human right of all couples and individuals "to decide freely and responsibly the number and spacing of their children and to have the information, education, and means to do so." Among its many other provisions, the plan accented the importance of advancing the status and rights of women. In late 1975, the National Security Council (NSC) approved a comprehensive U.S. international population policy. Policy implementation was supervised by an interagency task force, chaired by the Department of State, which reported annually to the NSC on international population program effectiveness and recommended improvements. President Jimmy Carter issued the Global 2000 Report, which included warnings about environmental and other dangers inherent in current world population growth trends.

The administration of President Ronald Reagan ignored both the task force and the Global 2000 Report. At the World Population Conference in Mexico City in September 1984, the U.S. delegation surprised many by

WORLD POPULATION STATISTICS, MID-1996

Characteristic	World	More Developed	Less Developed
Population (millions)	5,771	1,171	4,600
Births per 1,000 pop.	24	12	27
Deaths per 1,000 pop.	9	10	9
Natural increase (annual, %)	1.5	0.1	1.9
Life expectancy at birth	66	74	64
Projected population 2010 (millions)	6,974	1,231	5,743

Source: *World Population Data Sheet.* ©1996 by the Population Reference Bureau. Reprinted with permission of the Population Reference Bureau

depicting population as "a neutral phenomenon" in international development. Moreover, during and after the conference, the United States emphasized its opposition to abortion, which became the new litmus test for international family planning organizations seeking U.S. assistance. This resulted in a decision to end U.S. support for the London-based International Planned Parenthood Federation (IPPF). In 1986 the U.S. ceased supporting the United Nations Population Fund (UNFPA) because of allegations of coercive practices in China's family planning program, which received UNFPA assistance. The administration of President George Bush continued the Reagan administration's

WORLD POPULATION GROWTH

Year	Population (in billions)
1000	0.31
1250	0.40
1500	0.50
1750	0.79
1800	0.98
1850	1.26
1900	1.65
1930	2.07
1960	3.02
1970	3.70
1980	4.45
1990	5.30
2000 (projected)	6.23
2050 (projected)	10.02
2100 (projected)	11.19

Sources: *Historical Estimates of World Population: An Evaluation,* ©1974 by J.D. Durand, University of Pennsylvania, Populations Studies Center, Philadelphia; *The Determinants and Consequences of Populations trends,* Volume I, ©1973 by United Nations, New York; *World Populations Prospects as Assessed in 1963,* ©1966 by United Nations, New York; *World Populations Prospects: The 1994 Revisions,* ©1993 by United Nations, New York; *Long-range World Population Projection: Two Centuries of Population Growth, 1950–2150,* by United Nations, New York

Mexico City Policy (as it came to be known), and Bush vetoed several efforts by Congress to restore funding to the IPPF and UNFPA. With the inauguration of President Bill Clinton in 1993, U.S. policy shifted once again. Already on record as strongly supportive of family planning, Clinton took immediate steps to reverse the Mexico City policy. However, the 1994 congressional elections resulted in Republican majorities in both houses and a Congress which in early 1996, forced through a Continuing Resolution entailing severe cuts in USAID's family planning program.

Overall, the United States has played a leading role from 1965 to the mid-1990s in promoting family planning programs in the developing world, thanks in large measure to the bipartisan supportive role of Congress. During that period the United States has provided about one-third of all donor assistance, and there has been a notable decline in average family size in the developing world, especially in parts of Asia and Latin America.

MARSHALL GREEN

See also Third World; United Nations

FURTHER READING

Green, Marshall. "The Evolution of U.S. International Population Policy, 1965–1992: A Chronological Account." *Population and Development Review* 19 (June 1993).
Piotrow, Phyllis. *World Population Crisis: The United States Response.* New York, 1973.

PORTSMOUTH, TREATY OF
(1905)

Treaty negotiated by diplomats of Russia, Japan, and the United States that ended the Russo-Japanese War (1904–1905). It was signed at Portsmouth, New Hampshire, on 5 September 1905. Motivated by a desire to preserve the Far Eastern balance of power threatened by Japan's surprising advances, President Theodore Roosevelt had repeatedly offered his good offices to the warring nations earlier in the year. Japan held the strategic advantage after its victories at Mukden and Tsushima Strait but, strained under the expense of the conflict, its government finally seized Roosevelt's offer. Czar Nicholas II assented in the hope of attaining an honorable settlement before Japanese forces attacked Russian soil. Contrary to popular assumption, Roosevelt did not personally mediate in the ensuing Portsmouth talks, although he did monitor them and intervened from afar at critical junctures.

No armistice preceded negotiations. The discussions addressed a number of commercial, military, and strategic issues, but the troublesome two were Japan's demands for an indemnity and all of Sakhalin Island, which the Japanese had seized during the summer of 1905. The czar, pressured by revolution at home and influenced in part by U.S. Ambassador George von Lengerke Meyer, instructed his envoys to accept division of Sakhalin between the two combatants. The Japanese government suddenly dropped its demand for an indemnity. The Treaty of Portsmouth ceded the southern half of Sakhalin to the Japanese, and the czar surrendered interests in Manchuria and Korea, including Port Arthur. Roosevelt received wide praise for bringing the belligerents to the peace table. He won the Nobel Peace Prize in 1906 for his role in both the Portsmouth Conference and the Algeciras Conference, which defused tensions between Germany and France over Morocco, but the president's anticipated Far Eastern power balance eluded him as the advantage tilted toward Japan after the Treaty of Portsmouth. Japan blamed Roosevelt for its loss of the indemnity. Relations between Japan and the United States entered a period during which Japanese disregard for the Open Door of equal trade opportunity in its Manchurian domain and restrictive U.S. policies toward Japanese immigrants fueled suspicion and misunderstanding.

PAUL R. GRASS

See also Japan; Roosevelt, Theodore; Russia and the Soviet Union; Russo-Japanese War

FURTHER READING

Esthus, Raymond A. *Double Eagle and Rising Sun: The Russians and Japanese at Portsmouth in 1905*. Durham, N.C., 1988.
Trani, Eugene. *The Treaty of Portsmouth: An Adventure in American Diplomacy*. Lexington, Ky., 1969.

PORTUGAL

A country located at the southwestern tip of the European continent, wedged between Spain and the Atlantic Ocean. Relations between the United States and Portugal have historically been most often defined in geostrategic terms. For much of the Cold War, the United States valued Portugal as an ally primarily because of the geostrategic triangle it formed, along with its possessions in the Atlantic—the Azores and the island of Madeira—that dominated North Atlantic sea routes and approaches to the Mediterranean. This region was also valuable to U.S. strategic interests because air routes to the Middle East and North Africa passed through it. Consequently, in times of war, the United States and other countries have placed a high value on the Portuguese relationship, using the Azores as a mid-Atlantic refueling station for ships and air-based projections of military power.

In the eighteenth century, however, it was Portugal that was interested in the geostrategic value of the United States. Portugal's presence in the Americas actually predates the formation of the United States by more than three hundred years, going back to its "Golden Age" in the early fifteenth century and the period of the discoveries of Madeira (1419), the Azores (1427), and Brazil (1500). Eventually, a vast Portuguese empire encompassed colonies in Latin America (Brazil until its independence in 1822), Africa (Angola, Mozambique, São Tomé and Principe, Guinea Bissau, and the Cape Verde Islands), and outposts in the Far East (Goa, Macau, and East Timor). Throughout its history, Portugal has sought the support of the major maritime nations as a means of guarding against the influence of Spain and as a means of protecting its overseas possessions. Therefore, the Portuguese developed an historic alliance with England in order to counterbalance Spanish hegemony in Iberia, as well as the Americas. For this reason, Portugal's leaders actually took a keen interest in preventing the American War of Independence (1776–1783) for fear that it would detract from Great Britain's ability to come to the defense of Portugal. Despite its centuries-old alliance with Great Britain, Portugal remained formally neutral during the American Revolution. Following the war, the U.S. Congress formally initiated diplomatic relations with Portugal on 21 February 1791, and for the next century and a half, relations between the two countries remained generally friendly.

Portugal in the nineteenth century was a nation in decline. The Napoleonic Wars forced the Portuguese throne to flee to Brazil under the protection of their British patrons, which underscored the feebleness of the monarchy and made elements in Brazil begin to question the desirability of continued dependence on Portugal. King John VI was well aware that his departure, in the wake of the American Revolution and the struggle for independence then going on throughout Spanish America, might result in the loss of Brazil by the Portuguese throne. Before finally leaving for Portugal in 1821, he made a "family compact" with his son, Dom Pedro, who remained in Brazil. If it appeared that independence was inevitable, then Pedro was to preside over the transition in order to save Brazil from "republican adventurers," and to preserve it for the family dynasty. As planned, Pedro declared Brazilian independence on 7 September 1822, proclaiming himself Pedro I, emperor of Brazil. Over the next hundred years, Portugal primarily concerned itself with its own weakening internal situation. The Portuguese monarchy was finally overthrown in 1910, accelerating the country's decline from a world power with a vast maritime empire to one of Europe's most underdeveloped and peripheral states.

Although Great Britain continued to play a crucial intermediary role in Portuguese foreign policy decision-making through the two world wars, the historic alliance with Great Britain was gradually supplanted in the twentieth century by the search for a new patron. The Portuguese government entered the war on the side of the Allies in March 1916, largely in response to a combination of residual faith in England, liberal idealism, and the need to protect its overseas possessions. Once Portugal entered the war, however, its ports became vulnerable to the threat of German U-boat attacks and its domestic defense forces were insufficient to guard against such a threat. At the same time, Great Britain's ability to aid its historic ally in this regard was limited because of other strategic preoccupations of its own. The solution appeared with the entry of the United States into the war in 1917. It was from this period that the historic alliance between Great Britain and Portugal weakened while Portugal's military-strategic relations with the United States grew in importance. The United States received permission to establish a temporary naval base in Ponta Delgada, Azores, in 1917. Although U.S. forces quickly withdrew in 1919, they gained access to an air strip there again near the end of World War II.

During the interwar period, Portugal passed from an unstable democracy into what would become twentieth century Europe's longest lasting dictatorship. The country's first chaotic experience with democratic republican rule (the First Republic, 1910–1928), led to a military coup in 1928 that brought Antonio de Oliveira Salazar into power. Salazar's quasi-fascist dictatorship institutionalized his unique vision of a corporative new state (Estado Novo), a system that lasted until 1974.

Although the Estado Novo had diffuse ideological ties to Benito Mussolini's Fascist Italy, Adolf Hitler's Nazi Germany, and Francisco Franco's Falangist Spain, it was a distinctly Portuguese regime that maintained much better relations with the Western democracies. These relations were strained for a time during the Spanish Civil War (1936–1939) because of Salazar's unofficial support of Franco's nationalists, but officially, Portugal remained neutral during that conflict. The Allies were pleased, however, by Salazar's help in persuading Franco to remain neutral during World War II. U.S.-Portuguese relations often became uneasy during the Salazar regime, but pragmatic cooperation occurred frequently. For example, despite Portuguese neutrality during World War II, tacit cooperation with the Allies occurred after 1943 and U.S. forces were allowed to construct an airstrip in the Azores in November of 1944. Analysts have referred to the Portuguese position during World War II as the belated adoption of a policy of "benevolent neutrality."

Following the war, Salazar's virulent anticommunism found favor in Washington because of the context of the emergence of the Cold War. Dictatorial policies at home were not deemed obstacles to Portugal's membership in the North Atlantic Treaty Organization (NATO), particularly given Portugal's geostrategic value. Thus, Portugal was the only nondemocratic founding member admitted to the Atlantic Alliance in 1949 and NATO in 1950. Portuguese accession to NATO was perceived by U.S. policymakers to be a prerequisite to securing more permanent access to facilities in the Azores. Prior to Portugal's entrance into NATO, the United States had signed two short-term extension agreements with the Salazar regime that broadened access to the Lajes air base on the island of Terceira in the Azores. The first base treaty was signed in 1946 and lasted for eighteen months; the second was signed in 1948 and lasted three years. The third agreement, signed in 1951, set a pattern whereby the United States provided economic or military assistance in return for multiyear base access commitments. In the mid-1990s U.S.-Portuguese relations were moving away from the traditional bases-for-rent formula and toward more bilateral agreements in such areas as educational and scientific cooperation. The base agreement, signed in 1994, maintains approximately 1,800 U.S. troops and their dependents at Lajes, as well as 1,100 local employees.

Although Portugal did not benefit directly from the Marshall Plan because of its neutrality during World War II, its membership in NATO did help pave the way for membership in the European Free Trade Area (EFTA) in 1960 and the Organization for Economic Cooperation and Development (OECD) in 1961. Portugal's role in NATO was never very large, as the regime's primary activities consisted of providing bases and seeking guarantees for the preservation of its crumbling empire in Africa and Asia. Its position eroded even further, from the 1960s onward, as a result of its wars with independence movements in Portugal's African colonies. The nationalist revolt in Angola in 1961, followed by a rebellion three years later in Mozambique, resulted in a full-scale war that drew labor and wealth from what was already one of Western Europe's poorest countries. During the 1960s the Portuguese armed forces represented a proportion per thousand of the population five times the ratio in the United States, and more than forty percent of the national budget was spent on defense. The decolonization issue became a particular source of friction in U.S.-Portuguese relations during the administration of President John F. Kennedy (1961–1963), but when Washington was forced to choose in 1963 between continued U.S. base rights in the Azores and a policy supporting the principle of self-determination for all colonial peoples, strategic concerns prevailed.

Throughout the late 1960s and early 1970s, Portugal's internal politics underwent a period of transition that threatened to alter its relationship with the United States and other Western nations. Salazar suffered a stroke in 1968 and was replaced by Marcello Caetano (1968–1974), who attempted some limited reforms at home but charted what would prove to be an incompatible set of policies based upon evolution without revolution and renewal in continuity. Events in Africa and at home eventually overtook the Caetano regime. Relations between civilian elements of the Estado Novo and the armed forces deteriorated in 1973 and 1974. The final crack in the authoritarian facade occurred on 25 April 1974, when the Armed Forces Movement (MFA) seized power in a relatively bloodless military coup. The leading figures of the old regime were exiled to Brazil, and the MFA initiated a process of political and social revolution that came to be known as the Revolution of Carnations.

The initial U.S. response to the Portuguese revolution of April 1974 was confused, which was the result of at least two factors. First, the United States was in a state of relative retreat from foreign affairs in the aftermath of the resignation of President Richard Nixon and amidst the defeat in Vietnam. Among other things, these helped to produce an overall U.S. policy environment that was reluctant to get involved in another potential international military entanglement. Second, the Portuguese revolution caught the U.S. embassy in Lisbon by surprise, damaging Washington's ability to receive well-informed intelligence on key Portuguese actors during the early stages of the transition to a new regime. This may help explain why Secretary of State Henry Kissinger, who dominated U.S. foreign policy decision-making at the time, misread events in Lisbon as the MFA's revolution increasingly turned leftward in 1975. As the noted U.S.-Portuguese scholar Kenneth Maxwell has observed, "Kissinger abandoned hope for a democratic outcome and toyed with various counterrevolutionary options— some paramilitary, some involving separatism in the Azores." Eventually, the new U.S. ambassador to Portugal, Frank Carlucci, succeeded in convincing Kissinger of the futility of covert military action in Portugal. His perception was that a combination of other less extreme strategies, including CIA funding of Portugal's nonrevolutionary political parties and the mobilization of local anticommunist forces, would succeed in moderating the direction of the revolution. Carlucci's perceptions proved correct. By the time that this fragile process of democratic consolidation was well under way, Washington's preoccupations shifted to the conflict in Angola, an issue that dominated U.S. foreign policy during the presidency of Jimmy Carter.

Several points should be made regarding the enormous discontinuities wrought on Portuguese society by the revolution. First, as a result of a combination of internal and external factors, Portugal went from being one of the oldest right-wing dictatorships in Europe to becoming the first West European nation since the 1940s where a communist government was a real possibility. Second, throughout 1974 and 1975 Portugal teetered very near civil war, as forces from the left and the right struggled to define the direction that the revolution, and the country, would take. Suddenly, Portugal was high on the international agenda as the United States and other foreign countries intervened covertly on behalf of anticommunist forces within Portugal and overtly in its decolonization process in Africa, especially in Angola. By 1976 the perceived threat of a communist government had receded in Portugal, whereas in Angola and Mozambique the Portuguese pullout left a power vacuum that almost immediately led to the continent's most devastating proxy war between the United States and the Soviet Union.

Since 1974 Portugal's identity has been fundamentally altered by the loss of its empire and acceptance into the family of West European parliamentary democracies. Its entry into the European Economic Community (EEC) in January 1986 reinforced the democratization process and strengthened economic and cultural ties to Europe. Furthermore, as a result of Portugal's rapid economic growth since EEC accession (between 1986 and 1992, Portugal's GNP per capita increased in real terms at an average rate of 4.5 percent per year) and the influx of European Union (EU) development funds, the United States has significantly reduced its direct economic and military assistance. In 1985 U.S. military and economic aid totalled $207.5 million, while in 1994 it was reduced to $91 million. Trade relations between the two countries remained significant, however, as the United States was still Portugal's largest trading partner outside of the EU. Cultural ties between the two nations also continued to be strong, due at least in part to the more than 2.5 million Americans who are descendants of Portuguese natives.

The defense and cooperation agreement signed in the fall of 1994 sought to avoid double taxation situations between the two countries, encouraged further direct U.S. investment in Portugal, and improved customs cooperation. This bilateral agreement is indicative of the post–Cold War direction of the U.S.-Portuguese relationship, with less emphasis on traditional military-security issues and more on economic, cultural, scientific, and law-enforcement issues of mutual interest. Besides the EU and NATO, Portugal is also a member of the Council of Europe, Western European Union, Organization Security and Cooperation in Europe, African Development Bank, and African Development Fund.

MICHAEL BAUM

See also Angola; Azores; Brazil; North Atlantic Treaty Organization; Overseas Military Bases

FURTHER READING

Calvet de Magalhães, José, Álvaro de Vasconcelos, and Joaquim Ramos Silva. *Portugal, The Atlantic Paradox: Portuguese-U.S. Relations After the EC Enlargement.* Lisbon, 1990.

MacDonald, Scott B. *European Destiny, Atlantic Transformations: Portuguese Foreign Policy Under the Second Republic 1974–1992.* New Brunswick, N.J., 1993.

Maxwell, Kenneth, ed. "Portuguese Defense and Foreign Policy Since Democratization." *Camões Center Special Report No. 3.* New York, 1991.

POTSDAM CONFERENCE

The third and last of the summit conferences (after Teheran and Yalta) attended by the heads of the American, British, and Soviet governments during World War II. It was held 17 July to 2 August 1945 in Potsdam, a suburb of Berlin, Germany. At the time, Germany had been defeated and the war in the Pacific against Japan was nearing its end. President Harry S. Truman represented the United States. Prime Minister Winston S. Churchill represented Great Britain until 28 July, when he was replaced by Clement R. Attlee, following the Labour Party victory in the British general election. Marshal Joseph V. Stalin represented the Soviet Union. The three heads of state were accompanied by their foreign ministers and large military and civilian staffs. Truman, newly sworn in as president following the death of Franklin D. Roosevelt in April, and inexperienced in diplomacy, hid his nervousness behind a blunt, lets-get-down-to-business manner.

With Germany defeated the three Allies were no longer unified by a common enemy, and the uncertain problems of postwar reconstruction divided them. The conference did establish a Council of Foreign Ministers representing the United States, Great Britain, the Soviet Union, France, and China and instructed the council to proceed with the negotiation of peace terms for Italy, Bulgaria, Finland, Hungary, and Romania—all onetime allies of Germany. The heads of government also confirmed the transfer of a large swath of territory from the eastern part of Germany to Poland (the Oder-Neisse line) and ordered the transfer in "an orderly and humane manner" of German populations from Poland, Hungary, and Czechoslovakia back to Germany.

The Potsdam Conference reaffirmed that Germany would be completely disarmed and demilitarized with the elimination of all industry capable of military production. But Germany was to be treated as "a single economic unit" by the four zones of occupation so that the standard of living of the German people would rise and the economy could reconstruct. The Nazi Party and all of its institutions were ordered destroyed; war criminals were to be brought to trial. After much disagreement and debate, the victors were empowered to take reparations by removing assets from their occupation zones of Germany, and the Soviets, in addition, could have some reparations from the western zones. The amount of reparations to be transferred was not specified, despite Stalin's insistence, because Truman recalled the reparations tangle after World War I and argued that Germany's ability to pay must first be determined. The conferees also debated the political status of Poland, where Truman and Churchill called for free elections clearly meant to forestall a Communist takeover, and Stalin retorted that Great Britain should conduct them in Greece at the time very much in the throes of an anti-leftist "white terror."

On 16 July, the day before the conference opened, the United States successfully tested the first atomic bomb at Alamagordo, New Mexico. President Truman, with studied casualness, informed Marshal Stalin and the latter showed no great interest or surprise. Historians disagree over how important the possession of the bomb was in strengthening Truman's confidence that he could bargain hard with the Soviet Union, but Churchill at the time thought that Truman's knowledge of the bomb "changed" him so that he "bossed" the meeting. On 26 July the U.S., British, and Chinese governments issued the "Potsdam Declaration" calling on Japan to surrender in order to avoid complete destruction of her armed forces and utter devastation of the homeland. The existence of an atomic bomb was not mentioned; nor was Japan told that the institution of the Emperor could be retained. Impatient with protracted negotiations, Truman never attended another summit with Stalin.

GADDIS SMITH

See also Cold War; Germany; Hiroshima and Nagasaki Bombings of 1945; Reparations; Russia and the Soviet Union; Stalin, Joseph; Truman, Harry S.; World War II

FURTHER READING

Alperovitz, Gar. *Atomic Diplomacy: Hiroshima and Potsdam,* 2d ed. New York, 1985.

Feis, Herbert. *Between War and Peace: The Potsdam Conference.* Princeton, N.J., 1960.

Gormly, James L. *From Potsdam to the Cold War.* Wilmington, Del., 1990.

Mee, Charles L., Jr. *Meeting at Potsdam.* New York, 1975.

POWELL, COLIN LUTHER
(*b.* 5 April 1937)

Career military officer who was the youngest U.S. Army General and the first African American to serve as chairman of the Joint Chiefs of Staff (1989–1993). Born in New York City, Powell was the son of working class immigrant parents from Jamaica. Following high school, he enrolled in the City College of New York, where he joined the Reserve Officer Training Corps (ROTC) program. Although an average college student, Powell flourished in ROTC, earning the designation Distinguished Military Graduate and a commission in the regular army as a second lieutenant of infantry. Through the grade of major, Powell's military career followed a pattern not atypical for military officers of his generation. He attended the prescribed military schools (distinguishing himself by graduating second in his class at the U.S. Army Command and General Staff College in 1968). He served overseas in Germany and Vietnam (and would later serve in Korea) and attended graduate school at George Washington University, earning his master's degree in business administration.

The turning point in Powell's career came in 1972 when he was awarded a White House fellowship. The fellowship introduced Powell to the world of high politics and policy and it brought him into contact with senior government officials who formed the basis of an expanding network of influential civilian acquaintances, progressively nearer to the center of power in Washington, D.C. The pattern of Powell's assignments became decidedly irregular. For the last twenty years of his military career, he served only infrequently in the field. In Washington, meanwhile, Powell served in a series of sensitive politico-military positions that earned him rapid promotions and a reputation as a shrewd, hard-working, and extraordinarily well-connected military bureaucrat.

Thus, for example, while assigned as senior military assistant to Deputy Secretary of Defense Charles Duncan during the administration of President Jimmy Carter, Powell was promoted to brigadier general. When Duncan subsequently became secretary of energy, Powell accompanied Duncan to the Energy Department to serve as a key aide. During President Ronald Reagan's first administration (1981–1985), Powell—now a major general—was appointed senior military assistant to Defense Secretary Caspar Weinberger. In June 1986, just promoted to lieutenant general, Powell left the Pentagon to command the U.S. Army's V Corps in Germany. After less than six months, Powell's tour of duty was cut short and he returned to Washington to become White House deputy national security adviser. A year later, in November 1987, Powell succeeded to the position of national security adviser and served in that capacity through the end of President Reagan's second term (1985–1989).

When George Bush succeeded Reagan as president in January 1989, Powell, having received his fourth star, was assigned to command United States Forces Command headquartered in Atlanta. He remained there less than a year before Bush recalled him to Washington to become chairman of the Joint Chiefs of Staff (JCS). Powell's four-year tenure as JCS chairman, beginning in October 1989, coincided with one of the most tumultuous periods in U.S. military history. Powell was the nation's most senior military officer during a period in which the United States invaded Panama to overthrow the dictator Manuel Noriega, in which a massive U.S.-led coalition ousted Iraqi forces from Kuwait in Operation Desert Storm, and in which the Soviet Union, long the arch-foe of the United States, abandoned its competition with the United States and, soon thereafter, collapsed.

As a result of these successes, the prestige of the U.S. military establishment reached extraordinary heights. Each success in turn redounded to Powell's credit as that establishment's most visible representative. By the early 1990s opinion polls ranked him among the most admired and respected citizens of the United States. Powell capitalized on that reputation in several ways. With some restructuring of the U.S. armed forces inevitable in the aftermath of the Cold War, he sought to preempt calls for more radical change by devising a "base force" concept that reduced the military's overall size but preserved the roles and essential structure of each service. Powell also advocated a doctrine of "decisive force" that would restrict the use of the U.S. military to those situations permitting the employment of massive force, offering favorable prospects for rapid decision, in which realistic political objectives were clearly spelled out in advance and in which strong public support was all but guaranteed—precepts that many saw as unduly restrictive in an era in which smaller conflicts were proliferating but in which the likelihood of renewed great power rivalry appeared remote. Powell also led the professional military in its opposition to President Bill Clinton's declared intention of signing an executive order permitting homosexuals to serve in the armed forces. Although this embarrassing showdown raised serious questions about the state of U.S. civil-military relations, it did not dim the luster of Powell's reputation. At the time of his departure from active service in the fall of 1993, Powell's personal popularity was at an all-time high and the general was prominently touted as a prospective candidate for high office. Indeed, many urged Powell to run for the presidency in 1996. Although Powell declined to run in that particular election, he indicated his intention of considering future opportunities for public service.

Powell was the preeminent U.S. soldier-statesman of his generation, wielding significant influence on national security policy during the years when the Soviet-American rivalry drew to a close and the United States began reshaping its policies for the post–Cold War period. Powell exercised that influence not as a warrior in the classic mold but as a political general, adept at bureaucratic maneuver and inside politics, operating comfortably in the realm where military affairs, diplomacy, and partisan issues intersect. He transformed the position of JCS chairman, investing that office with unprecedented power. Within the military, however, Powell was no innovator. Rather, he was a defender of military orthodoxy and traditionalism. His most telling initiative was an attempt to codify a set of strict preconditions that would constrain decisions relating to the use of force.

ANDREW J. BACEVICH

See also Bush, George Herbert Walker; Gulf War of 1990–1991; Joint Chiefs of Staff; Reagan, Ronald Wilson

FURTHER READING

Powell, Colin L., and Joseph E. Persico. *My American Journey.* N.Y., 1995.

Roth, David. *Sacred Honor: A Biography of Colin Powell.* Grand Rapids, Mich., 1993.

PRESIDENCY

The political institution occupied by the principal holder of executive power in the U.S. system of government, the president of the United States. This article deals with the history and evolution of the role and powers of the presidency in U.S. foreign relations and the centrality of presidential leadership to foreign policymaking processes. As such the focus herein is on the constitutional underpinnings and the precedents set in three key areas of presidential foreign policy power: treaties and other international commitments; war powers; and the president's claim to the "doctrine of necessity" as an inherent prerogative in foreign affairs.

Empowered by the vagueness of constitutional grants, judicial interpretation, the acquiescence of Congress, individual personality, institutional advantages, and precedent that would establish tradition, the president's role in determining the general direction of foreign policy has been and continues to be crucial in world affairs. Once the direction of foreign policy has been determined, the president must continue to ensure the effective coordination and implementation of foreign policy in his role as head of the federal bureaucracy. The president is both commander in chief and the nation's chief diplomat. The emergence of the United States as a world power created the context within which the president would become an increasingly important figure both at home and abroad. In the wake of two world wars, of the continuing political, economic, and ideological struggle against the Soviet Union, and of a post–Cold War economic and political matrix, the president's position as leading foreign policy-shaper has become entrenched in both bureaucratic process as well as popular expectation.

Article II of the Constitution reveals how the framers attempted to strike a balance between the two experiences in their own historical context that showed what not to do. On the one hand they continued to fear granting too much power to the presidency lest the president become "a new King George." On the other hand the failure of the Articles of Confederation had shown the dangers of too weak an executive. Indeed, over two hundred years later, for all the theories expounded, political positions taken, and legal briefs filed, the relationship between the presidency and Congress in foreign relations still is best described as by constitutional scholar Edward Corwin as "an invitation to struggle," and as by political scientist Richard Neustadt as not so much a separation of powers as "separated institutions sharing powers."

The Executive Power in Foreign Policy

Before getting into some of the specific provisions of Article II, there are two even more fundamental bases for the presidency's foreign policy powers that need to be discussed.

One is the "doctrine of necessity," or emergency prerogatives, which traces back to John Locke, the seventeenth-century English philosopher whose *Second Treatise of Government* had such influence on the framers. Locke warned that it was impossible for any legislature "to foresee, and so by laws provide for all accidents and necessities," and that therefore in such situations "the laws themselves should…give way to the executive power… to act according to discretion for the public good." Alexander Hamilton called this "the right of self defense which is paramount to all possible forms of government." Even James Madison, generally more wary of executive power, accepted "the impulse of self-preservation." And in 1810 Thomas Jefferson, writing two years after the end of his presidency, stated in a letter his view that "a strict observation of the written laws is doubtless one of the higher duties of a good officer, but it is not the highest. The law of necessity, of self-preservation, of saving our country when in danger, are of higher obligation. To lose our country by a scrupulous adherence to written law would be to lose the law itself, with life, liberty, property…thus sacrificing the end to the means."

Second is the general "executive power" clause of the Constitution. In itself this is a vague and broad mandate that presidents have invoked as the basis for a wide range of actions taken in order to "execute" foreign policy. George Washington was the first president to claim an inherent executive power, and his presence at the Constitutional Convention might imply that the framers anticipated the contingencies under which such claims could be

U.S. PRESIDENTS AND VICE PRESIDENTS

President and Political Party	Born	Died	Age at inauguration	Native of	Elected from	Term of Service	Vice president
George Washington (F)	1732	1799	57	VA	VA	April 30, 1789–March 4, 1793	John Adams
George Washington (F)			61		VA	March 4, 1793–March 4, 1797	John Adams
John Adams (F)	1735	1826	61	MA	MA	March 4, 1797–March 4, 1801	Thomas Jefferson
Thomas Jefferson (DR)	1743	1826	57	VA	VA	March 4, 1801–March 4, 1805	Aaron Burr
Thomas Jefferson (DR)	1743	1826	61		VA	March 4, 1805–March 4, 1809	George Clinton
James Madison (DR)	1751	1836	57	VA	VA	March 4, 1809–March 4, 1813	George Clinton
James Madison (DR)			61			March 4, 1813–March 4, 1817	Elbridge Gerry
James Monroe (DR)	1758	1831	58	VA	VA	March 4, 1817–March 4, 1821	Daniel D. Tompkins
James Monroe (DR)			62			March 4, 1821–March 4, 1825	Daniel D. Tompkins
John Q. Adams (DR)	1767	1848	57	MA	MA	March 4, 1825–March 4, 1829	John C. Calhoun
Andrew Jackson (D)	1767	1845	61	SC	TN	March 4, 1829–March 4, 1833	John C. Calhoun
Andrew Jackson (D)			65			March 4, 1833–March 4, 1837	Martin Van Buren
Martin Van Buren (D)	1782	1862	54	NY	NY	March 4, 1837–March 4, 1841	Richard M. Johnson
W. H. Harrison (W)	1773	1841	68	VA	OH	March 4, 1841–April 4, 1841	John Tyler
John Tyler (W)	1790	1862	51	VA	VA	April 6, 1841–March 4, 1845	
James K. Polk (D)	1795	1849	49	NC	TN	March 4, 1845–March 4, 1849	George M. Dallas
Zachary Taylor (W)	1784	1850	64	VA	LA	March 4, 1849–July 9, 1850	Millard Fillmore
Millard Fillmore (W)	1800	1874	50	NY	NY	July 10, 1850–March 4, 1853	
Franklin Pierce (D)	1804	1869	48	NH	NH	March 4, 1853–March 4, 1857	William R. King
James Buchanan (D)	1791	1868	65	PA	PA	March 4, 1857–March 4, 1861	John C. Breckinridge
Abraham Lincoln (R)	1809	1865	52	KY	IL	March 4, 1861–March 4, 1865	Hannibal Hamlin
Abraham Lincoln (R)			56			March 4, 1865–April 15, 1865	Andrew Johnson
Andrew Johnson (R)	1808	1875	56	NC	TN	April 15, 1865–March 4, 1869	
Ulysses S. Grant (R)	1822	1885	46	OH	IL	March 4, 1869–March 4, 1873	Schuyler Colfax
Ulysses S. Grant (R)			50			March 4, 1873–March 4, 1877	Henry Wilson
Rutherford B. Hayes (R)	1822	1893	54	OH	OH	March 4, 1877–March 4, 1881	William A. Wheeler
James A. Garfield (R)	1831	1881	49	OH	OH	March 4, 1881–Sept. 19, 1881	Chester A. Arthur
Chester A. Arthur (R)	1830	1886	50	VT	NY	Sept. 20, 1881–March 4, 1885	
Grover Cleveland (D)	1837	1908	47	NJ	NY	March 4, 1885–March 4, 1889	Thomas A. Hendricks
Benjamin Harrison (R)	1833	1901	55	OH	IN	March 4, 1889–March 4, 1893	Levi P. Morton
Grover Cleveland (D)			55			March 4, 1893–March 4, 1897	Adlai E. Stevenson
William McKinley (R)	1843	1901	54	OH	OH	March 4, 1897–March 4, 1901	Garret A. Hobart
William McKinley (R)			58			March 4, 1901–Sept. 14, 1901	Theodore Roosevelt

(table continues on next page)

President and Political Party	Born	Died	Age at inauguration	Native of	Elected from	Term of Service	Vice president
Theodore Roosevelt (R)	1858	1919	42	NY	NY	Sept. 14, 1901–March 4, 1905	
Theodore Roosevelt (R)			46		NY	March 4, 1905–March 4, 1909	Charles W. Fairbanks
William H. Taft (R)	1857	1930	51	OH	OH	March 4, 1909–March 4, 1913	James S. Sherman
Woodrow Wilson (D)	1956	1924	56	VA	NJ	March 4, 1913–March 4, 1917	Thomas R. Marshall
Woodrow Wilson (D)			60			March 4, 1917–March 4, 1921	Thomas R. Marshall
Warren G. Harding (R)	1865	1923	55	OH	OH	March 4, 1921–Aug. 2, 1923	Calvin Coolidge
Calvin Coolidge (R)	1872	1933	51	VT	MA	Aug. 3, 1923–March 4, 1925	
Calvin Coolidge (R)			52			March 4, 1925–March 4, 1929	Charles G. Dawes
Herbert Hoover (R)	1874	1964	54	IA	CA	March 4, 1929–March 4, 1933	Charles Curtis
Franklin D. Roosevelt (D)	1882	1945	51	NY	NY	March 4, 1933–Jan. 20, 1937	John N. Garner
Franklin D. Roosevelt (D)			55			Jan. 20, 1937–Jan. 20, 1941	John N. Garner
Franklin D. Roosevelt (D)			59			Jan. 20, 1941–Jan. 20, 1945	Henry A. Wallace
Franklin D. Roosevelt (D)			63			Jan. 20, 1945–April 12, 1945	Harry S. Truman
Harry S. Truman (D)	1884	1972	60	MO	MO	April 12, 1945–Jan. 20, 1949	
Harry S. Truman (D)			64			Jan. 20, 1949–Jan. 20, 1953	Alben W. Barkley
Dwight D. Eisenhower (R)	1890	1969	62	TX	NY	Jan. 20, 1953–Jan. 20, 1957	Richard Nixon
Dwight D. Eisenhower (R)			66		PA	Jan. 20, 1957–Jan. 20, 1961	Richard Nixon
John F. Kennedy (D)	1917	1963	43	MA	MA	Jan. 20, 1961–Nov. 22, 1963	Lyndon B. Johnson
Lyndon B. Johnson (D)	1908	1973	55	TX	TX	Nov. 22, 1963–Jan. 20, 1965	
Lyndon B. Johnson (D)			56			Jan. 20, 1965–Jan. 20, 1969	Herbert H. Humphrey
Richard Nixon (R)	1913	1994	56	CA	NY	Jan. 20, 1969–Jan. 20, 1973	Spiro T. Agnew
Richard Nixon (R)			60		CA	Jan. 20, 1973–Aug. 9, 1974	Spiro T. Agnew / Gerald R. Ford
Gerald R. Ford (R)	1913		61	NE	MI	Aug. 9, 1974–Jan. 20, 1977	Nelson A. Rockefeller
Jimmy Carter (D)	1924		52	GA	GA	Jan. 20, 1977–Jan. 20, 1981	Walter F. Mondale
Ronald Reagan (R)	1911		69	IL	CA	Jan. 20, 1981–Jan. 20, 1985	George Bush
Ronald Reagan (R)			73			Jan. 20, 1985–Jan. 20, 1989	George Bush
George Bush (R)	1924		64	MA	TX	Jan. 20, 1989–Jan. 20, 1993	Dan Quayle
William J. Clinton (D)	1946		46	AR	AR	Jan. 20, 1993–Present	Albert Gore, Jr.

D=Democrat; D-R=Democratic-Republican; F=Federalist; R=Republican; W=Whig;

Source: *Presidential Elections Since 1789*, 4th Edition. ©1991 by Congressional Quarterly, Washington, D.C.

made. When war broke out in Europe on 22 April 1793, Washington issued a proclamation declaring the United States neutral in the British-French war. Washington's decision infuriated pro-French Americans led by Thomas Jefferson and James Madison. On what constitutional grounds was Washington acting? Did the neutrality proclamation infringe on the legislature's right to declare war? How could Congress declare a war if neutrality had been prejudged? This question became the focus of an intriguing political exchange between Hamilton, representing pro-British Americans (using the pseudonym Pacificus), and Madison (writing under the name Helvidius). Hamilton argued that as holder of an executive power the president was justified in issuing a proclamation: "The general doctrine of the Constitution then is, that the executive power of the nation is vested in the President; subject only to the exceptions and qualification, which are expressed in the instrument....It is the province and duty of the executive to preserve to the nation the blessings of peace." When Madison, the father of the Constitutional Convention, took up his pen, he argued that only "foreigners and degenerate citizens among us, who hate our Republican government," could believe that an inherent executive power existed. Such a claim, Madison reasoned, was no different from the dreaded royal prerogatives exercised by the king in England. Moreover, Congress and only Congress, by virtue of its constitutional power to declare war, could make foreign policy. The president was to serve as the executive instrument for Congress's will. The immediate result of the Pacificus-Helvidius exchange was congressional passage of the Neutrality Act, following which Washington admitted he had prejudged the issue.

One of the most explicit formulations of both the doctrine of necessity and a broad construction of the executive power came from President Abraham Lincoln. In a letter to Albert Hodges, Lincoln wrote:

> I did understand, however, that my oath to preserve the Constitution to the best of my ability, imposed upon me the duty of preserving, by every indispensable means, that government— that nation—of which that Constitution was the organic law. Was it possible to lose the nation, and yet preserve the Constitution? By general law, life and limb must be protected; yet often a limb must be amputated to save a life; but a life is never wisely given to save a limb. I felt that measures, otherwise unconstitutional, might become lawful, by becoming indispensable to the preservation of the Constitution, through the preservation of the nation. Right or wrong, I assumed this ground, and now avow it. I could not feel that, to the best of my ability, I have even tried to preserve the Constitution, if, to

save slavery, or any minor matter, I should permit the wreck of government, country, and Constitution altogether.

In 1936, in the case *United States v. Curtiss-Wright Export Corporation*, the Supreme Count furnished an important legal foundation for the theory of inherent powers. That case involved a congressional delegation of power to the president by a joint resolution that prohibited the sale of military equipment to countries in armed conflict. President Franklin D. Roosevelt placed an arms embargo on two such countries, Bolivia and Paraguay. The Curtiss-Wright Export Corporation was indicted for disobeying the president's embargo. The company challenged the constitutional delegation of legislative authority to the executive. The majority opinion written by Justice George Sutherland, who ironically had previously been a U.S. senator and a member of the Senate Foreign Relations Committee, went beyond the specifics of the case to establish broad precedent for an expansive view of presidential powers. First, Sutherland distinguished between foreign and domestic affairs, and the powers apportioned to each.

> The two classes of powers [external and internal] are different, both [as to] their origin and their nature. The broad statement that the federal government can exercise no power except those specifically stated in the Constitution, and such implied powers as are necessary and proper to carry into effect the enumerated powers, is categorically true only in respect to internal affairs.

With respect to external affairs, the grant of power to the president did not depend solely on a constitutional provision, but rather on the sovereignty of the federal government. In essence, "The federal government possessed all power necessary to enable the United States to act in the international arena on equal footing with other sovereign nations." In very sweeping language Sutherland stated:

> In this vast external realm, with its important, complicated, delicate and manifold problems, the president alone has the power to speak or listen as a representative of the nation. He makes treaties with the advice and consent of the Senate; but he alone negotiates. Into the field of negotiation the Senate cannot intrude, and the Congress itself is powerless to invade it.

Sutherland's interpretation of presidential power would later be used to extend the view that the president was government's "sole organ" in the field of international relations.

The 1952 case of *Youngstown Sheet and Tube Co. v. Sawyer* was in many respects the counterpart to *Curtiss-Wright*. In 1952 a divided Supreme Court rejected President Harry Truman's right to seize the nation's steel mills. In December 1951, while the Korean War was going on, United Steel workers were threatening to go on strike. The prospect of an industry so vital to the war effort crippled by a labor stoppage was seen by President Truman as a potential national emergency. Hoping to avert a strike, Truman sent the negotiations between management and union to his administration's Wage Stabilization Board. After repeated attempts to affect a settlement, the union announced it would strike on 9 April 1952. Before the strike could begin, Truman seized the steel mills and put them under the management of the U.S. government, citing "the authority vested in me by the Constitution" as commander-in-chief and the authority to take care that laws (in this case steel contracts with U.S. allies) were executed.

President Truman and his advisers had debated three alternatives. First, he could have invoked an injunction on the strike under conditions of the Taft-Hartley legislation, which had passed the Eightieth Congress in 1948. This was hardly a viable political option since Truman had vetoed Taft-Hartley. Second, Congress had already provided for limited seizure of private property in Section 18 of the Selective Service Act of 1948; Truman could cite this provision as authorization for seizing the steel mills. Third, he could seize the mills under his inherent authority as the chief executive and commander-in-chief "in order to make sure the laws are faithfully executed." The president chose the inherent powers approach, and the Court had to decide whether he could constitutionally seize private property when Congress had already legislated procedures for limited seizures.

The case was first heard in federal district court, where Judge Pyne ruled against the president. While Pyne did not doubt Truman's claim that extraordinary times confronted the nation, he nevertheless considered the claim of authority unjustified:

> I believe that the contemplated strike, if it came, with all its awful results, would be less injurious to the public than the injury which would flow from a timorous judicial recognition that there is some basis for this claim to unlimited and unrestrained executive power....Such recognition would undermine public confidence in the very edifice of government as it is known under the Constitution.

Pyne ruled in favor of the injunction order, and the steel workers called an immediate strike. But an appeals court stayed Judge Pyne's order, returning the mills to private hands. Due to the urgency of the crisis, the Supreme Court took the case on 3 May 1952, and announced its decision on June 2. In a 6-3 decision, the Court ruled that the president's seizure of the steel mills was unconstitutional. Due to the complexity of the issue, the justices wrote seven different opinions. Writing the majority opinion, Justice Hugo Black (with Justice William O. Douglas concurring) proceeded on the theory that the president never has the power to seize private property, even when an emergency exists. In a very strict reading of the Constitution, Black saw no reserve of inherent powers in the presidency. The Constitution clearly authorized Congress to make the laws:

> Even though "theater of war" be an expanding concept, we cannot with faithfulness to our constitutional system hold that the Commander in Chief of the Armed Forces has the ultimate power as such to take possession of private property in order to keep labor disputes from stopping production. This is a job for our Nation's lawmakers [Congress], not its military authorities.

In dissent, Chief Justice Fred Vinson (with Justices Reed and Minton) maintained that the president was within his powers as chief executive and commander in chief to seize the steel mills. Vinson emphasized the impact of the strike on the Korean conflict and mocked the rest of the Court for its "messenger-boy concept" of the presidency:

> The broad executive power granted by Article II to an officer on duty 365 days a year cannot, it is said, be invoked to avert disaster....Under this messenger-boy concept of the Office, the President cannot even act to preserve legislative programs from destruction so the Congress will have something left to act upon....On the contrary, judicial, legislative and executive precedents throughout our history demonstrate that in this case the President acted in full conformity with his duties under the Constitution.

Most influential in a lasting sense has been the concurring opinion written by Justice Robert Jackson. It laid out a threefold "grouping of practical situations." At one end of the spectrum were situations in which a president took action "pursuant to an express or implied authorization of Congress"; that is, exercising powers and authority granted him through a declaration of war, a ratified treaty, a public law, or other congressional action. In such a situation "his [the president's] authority is at its maximum, for it includes all that he possesses in his own right plus all that Congress can delegate." At the other end were situations in which "the president takes measures incompatible with the expressed or implied will of Congress"; that is, actions which run counter to or are otherwise inconsistent with actions taken by Congress whether that action be passing or defeating legislation. In this situation "his [the president's[power is at its lowest ebb, for then he can rely only upon his own Constitutional powers." The *Youngstown Steel* case was deemed to fall in this category. In between was what Justice Jackson called "a zone of twilight" situations in which "the president acts in absence of either a congressional grant or denial of authority." In these situations "he and Congress may have concurrent authority, or...its distribution is uncertain" and thus "any actual test of power is likely to depend on the imperatives of events and contemporary imponderables rather than on abstract theories of law. It was these types of issues that were the most difficult to decide, as to who had what constitutional authority.

Whereas the *Curtiss-Wright* decision took a very expansive view of executive power, the *Youngstown Steel* decision was much more limiting both in its direct striking down of President Truman's seizure of the steel plants and in its more general positing of the "zone of twilight" in which, while stopping well short of asserting congressional pre-eminence, also did not accept presidential pre-eminence. To be sure, over most of the ensuing two decades of "fighting" the Cold War, Congress was quite willing to delegate broad powers to presidents and not challenge the broad claims of executive power. Yet the issue was far from settled, in particular with regard to diplomatic and war powers, as discussed in the next section.

Diplomacy and International Commitments

Article II, Section 2, of the Constitution declares that the president "shall have Power, by and with the Advice and Consent of the Senate, to make Treaties, provided two-thirds of the Senators present concur." However, this power was controversial and, in the first draft of the Constitution sent by the Constitutional Convention to the Committee on Detail, treaty-making authority was included in a general list of legislative functions. Relatively late in the deliberations of the Committee on Detail the motion before the Convention still read: "The Senate of the United States shall have power to make treaties, and to appoint Ambassadors, and judges of the Supreme Court."

It was Alexander Hamilton who suggested that albeit "with the advice of the Senate, the executive be given the power of making all treaties." In his *Federalist Paper No. 75*, Hamilton argued that the executive was the "most fit agent" in the management of foreign negotiations, but that to eliminate the consent of the Senate

would not be proper or safe given human nature and the potential for the misuse of power and position. An elective monarch in particular might be tempted by individual avarice and promises of future economic gain to engage in treaties that might not be of benefit to the nation but could be lucrative to a former private citizen in the role of magistrate. Alternatively, the Senate would be disadvantaged in diplomatic negotiations because it lacked the "benefits of constitutional agency" enjoyed by the president in foreign negotiations. The reasons for excluding the House of Representatives were stated by John Jay in *Federalist No. 64*: "They who wish to commit the [treaty] power...to a popular assembly composed of members constantly coming and going in quick succession, seem not to recollect that such a body must necessarily be inadequate to the attainment of those great objects, which require to be steadily contemplated in all their relations and circumstances." The fact that Senators then were appointed rather than elected and served for six-year terms allowed them to continue in place a sufficient time to become perfectly acquainted with our national concerns and to form and introduce a system for the management of them.

The framers thus attempted to institute a system of consultation between the branches in which executive negotiation would require the Senate's advice. In August 1789, Washington acquiesced to this process, going to Congress for advice regarding an Indian treaty. Washington was delayed for several hours answering tedious questions, many of which had very little to do with the Indian treaty itself. Washington resolved after this experience that his administration would no longer consult the Congress but would continue to abide by requirements for consent.

Since 1789, thousands of treaties have been submitted to the Senate for ratification. Although 150 treaties were withdrawn when defeat seemed likely, only one percent of all treaties submitted to the Senate have been ultimately defeated and three-fourths were approved with no modification. Even those treaties defeated might have met with Senate approval if some compromise had been achieved. A well-known example of presidential intransigence in this regard is President Woodrow Wilson's refusal to compromise on several nonessential issues when the Treaty of Versailles was submitted to the Senate for approval. In this case, the famous personality clash between Senator Henry Cabot Lodge and Wilson left very little room for compromise.

Congress, and especially the Senate, has other ways to influence treaties other than by defeating them. The first part of its "advise and consent" powers provides for some input during the negotiating phase, through legislative committee hearings and private meetings with executive branch officials. It also has been done at various times in history and especially in recent years through official "observer groups" including senators from both political parties who have traveled to places like Geneva to meet with U.S. officials directly involved in treaty negotiations and offer advice while the talks are still going on. This technique was used in both of the two most recent General Agreement on Tariffs and Trade (GATT) trade treaties, the 1970s Tokyo Round and the 1980s–1990s Uruguay Round, as well as in the 1980s U.S.-Soviet arms control negotiations.

The Senate also can change part of the terms of the treaty by amending the text or by attaching a reservation or understanding. Amendments to the text are particularly controversial because they require reopening of negotiations with the other country or countries. Reservations tend to deal with issues related to but not directly part of the treaty, but these too have the potential to be deal-breakers, as almost happened with the "De Concini reservation" to the 1977 Panama Canal Treaties. This provision, named for the senator from Arizona who was its principal sponsor (and who was a Democrat, but a more conservative one than President Jimmy Carter) asserted the continuing right of the United States to intervene militarily if necessary to keep the Panama Canal open, even after the year 2000 when the canal and Canal Zone were to be given back to Panama. This was offensive to Panamanian pride and of questionable legality. But as the smaller, less powerful country, Panama had little choice other than to accept the provision. Indeed, while finally ratifying the Panama Canal treaties, the Senate only did so after having considered over 140 amendments and twenty-six reservations.

On the other hand, presidents also have an array of additional strategies at their disposal. They can abide by an expired treaty, as the Carter administration did when the five-year life of the SALT I arms control treaty had expired yet a deal was struck with the Soviets to stick to its weapons limits. They also can claim to abide by an unratified treaty, as the Ronald Reagan administration did with SALT II in agreeing with the Soviets to "refrain from actions which would undercut" its terms. Presidents also can terminate treaties without Senate approval; the test case here was the Supreme Court's rejection in 1979 of a suit by Senator Barry Goldwater challenging the constitutionality of President Carter's termination of the mutual defense treaty with Taiwan as part of the normalization of relations with the People's Republic of China.

Presidents also have mechanisms other than treaties, such as executive agreements, for making international commitments. The executive agreement is a government-to-government agreement with essentially the same legal force as a treaty. However, it may be concluded entirely without the approval, or even the knowledge, of the Senate. Unlike a treaty, an executive agreement cannot supersede existing law, nor does an agreement reached by one president bind subsequent presidents to comply. Otherwise, executive agreements carry the same force as formally ratified treaties.

The proliferation of executive agreements has been one of the most significant changes in the character of foreign relations. The use of executive agreements does go back to early U.S. history, and included such major commitments as in 1898 for the terms ending the Spanish-American-Cuban-Filipino War. But the ratio of executive agreements to treaties has increased in every historical period from 1:1 for the first century of U.S. foreign policy, to 2:1 for 1890–1932, 10:1 for 1933–1960, 16:1 for 1961–1974, and 22:1 for 1975–1992. Some of the increase can be attributed to the increase in the sheer volume of U.S. international relationships requiring many more agreements of this nature to work out the details. But there also is a pattern of presidents resorting to executive agreements when the prevailing congressional or popular sentiment seems to oppose a presidential initiative. President Roosevelt used an executive agreement in 1940 to assist the British in their war against Nazi Germany with the "destroyers-for-bases" deal at a time when isolationism was still predominant with Congress and the U.S. public. Roosevelt and his successor, Harry Truman, also used executive agreements to reach postwar settlements with the Soviet Union and Great Britain at Yalta and Potsdam. Succeeding presidents made numerous Cold War political and security commitments via the executive agreement route, including agreements with such nations as Spain, Israel, the Philippines, Turkey, Pakistan, Honduras, and El Salvador.

One of the main efforts to restrict the use of executive agreements was a constitutional amendment proposed in 1953 by Senator John Bricker (R-Ohio) requiring congressional approval of all international agreements entered into by the president. After a year of intense debate, the Bricker Amendment fell only one vote short of the needed two-thirds majority in the Senate, 60–31. President Dwight D. Eisenhower's opposition was a key factor holding the line. In 1972 another less intrusive attempt to regain at least a modicum of legislative oversight with regard to executive agreements did pass in 1972. Entitled the Case Act, this legislation was introduced by Senator Clifford Case (a New Jersey Republican) and Representative Clement Zablocki (a Wisconsin Democrat), and included the requirement that the secretary of state give Congress the text of any agreement between the United States and another country, other than a treaty, within sixty days of the time at which that agreement would go into effect. Although its passage did not guarantee Congress a role in making such agreements or the right to alter such agreements once they were made, the act did give Congress greater assurance that no agreement would remain hidden from it.

The Supreme Court has validated the use of executive agreements in cases such as *United States v. Belmont* and *United States v. Pink*, both involving President Roosevelt's recognition of Soviet Russia. In the *Belmont* case Justice Sutherland argued in his majority opinion that executive agreements are legally analogous to treaties even though they do not require the consent of the Senate, and that recognition, assignment, and agreement were within the president's power as "the sole organ of the federal government in international relations." In the *Pink* case Justice Douglas wrote that for the Court to overturn the validity of Roosevelt's executive agreement "would usurp the executive function." More recently, in *Dames and Moore v. Regan* (July 1981) the Court unanimously upheld an executive agreement between President Carter and Iran that arranged for the release of U.S. hostages in return for freeing all Iranian assets in the United States.

It also bears noting that sometimes the most important foreign policy commitments come not from treaties or executive agreements or any other written legal form. They come from speeches and statements by presidents. This was the case, for example, with the Monroe Doctrine, which sprang from a speech by President James Monroe in 1823 to become the bedrock of U.S. foreign policy in the Western Hemisphere. So, too, with the Truman Doctrine (1947) and how its clarion call "to support free peoples who are resisting attempted subjugation by armed minorities or by outside pressures" became a key basis for the containment strategy that Democratic and Republican presidents alike pursued for the next forty to fifty years.

War Powers

The president shall be Commander in Chief of the Army and Navy of the United States...Article II, Section 2. The Congress shall have Power....To declare War....To raise and support Armies....To provide and maintain a Navy; To make Rules for the Government and Regulation of the land and naval Forces....Article I, Section 8.

At the Constitutional Convention limited discussion took place on the power to declare war. The draft presented by the Committee on Detail to the convention gave the legislature the responsibility "to make war." Delegate Charles Pinckney of South Carolina feared the two houses together would be too slow to act, and proposed that the Senate be the organ of government empowered to make war. When another delegate recommended that the executive be vested with the power to make war, Roger Sherman of Connecticut argued that "the executive should be able to repel and not to commence war." Elbridge Gerry

of Massachusetts expressed his astonishment "to hear in a republic a motion to empower the executive alone to declare war." George Mason of Virginia believed the executive could not "safely be trusted with it." He favored "clogging rather than facilitating war." James Madison of Virginia and Gerry then moved to "insert 'declare,' striking out 'make' war; leaving to the executive the power to repel sudden attacks." Rufus King explained that "make" war might be understood to 'conduct' it which was an executive function."

The Constitution assigned Congress the power to declare war, order reprisals, raise and support armies, as well as provide for the common defense. James Wilson, generally recognized as the foremost legal scholar at the convention, provided an insightful summary of his view of these constitutional allocations: "The power of declaring war, and the other powers naturally connected with it, are vested in Congress. To provide and maintain a navy—to make rules for its government—to grant letters of marque and reprisal—to make rules concerning captures—to raise and support armies—to establish rules for their regulation—to provide for organizing...the militia and for calling forth in the service of the Union—all these are powers naturally connected with the power of declaring war. All these powers, therefore, are vested in Congress." There is no record of how the term commander in chief was inserted in the Constitution. Most state constitutions had designated the executive "captain-general and commander in chief"—subject to laws of the legislature.

Yet, notwithstanding the intent of the framers, the history of presidential war powers has been characterized by presidents making wars before Congress declares them. The war powers debate has traditionally centered on one overriding question: who should have the right to commit U.S. forces to combat, and what constitutional restrictions should such a commitment entail?

Historically, presidents who have used their formidable institutional advantages in combination with their constitutional role as commander in chief are virtually insurmountable to a Congress left in a reacting mode. It was Abraham Lincoln who linked the president's commander in chief role with the presidential oath to preserve and protect the Union. Lincoln issued the Emancipation Proclamation "by the power in me vested as commander in chief of the Army" and "warranted by the Constitution upon military necessity." This doctrine of necessity during the Civil War included blockading southern ports, enlarging the army and navy, spending treasury funds without congressional authorization, closing the mails to treasonable correspondence, creating special military tribunals in areas where courts were operating, and suspending habeas corpus. After the violence at Fort Sumter, President Lincoln blockaded southern ports—an act of war according to international law. But could the president carry out an act of war without a formal declaration of war from Congress? Could he, at his own discretion, treat a region of the United States known to be in insurrection, as an enemy country and therefore suspend constitutional rights? The Supreme Court ruled on this question in a number of cases known collectively as the Prize Cases.

The Prize Cases

The government argued that a formal declaration of war was not necessary before the president could exercise his war powers. In the words of government counsel Richard Henry Dana: "War is a state of things, not an act of legislative will." Using the army and navy was an executive function, consistent with the president's pledge "to faithfully execute the laws." In its majority opinion, delivered by Justice Grier, the Court upheld Lincoln's actions:

> If a war be made by invasion of a foreign nation, the President is not only authorized but bound to restrict force by force. He does not initiate the war, but is bound to accept the challenge without waiting for special legislative authority. And whether the hostile part be a foreign invader or a state organized in rebellion, it is none the less a war.

However, because the nation had been at war, the Court did not act until well after Lincoln had acted and after Congress had ratified most of these actions. In the first case in which the Supreme Court was to check one of Lincoln's wartime claims to power, *Ex parte Milligan*, the defense claimed that the proceedings in which one Lambdin Milligan, accused in the state of Indiana of conspiracy against the United States, had been tried and sentenced to hang were unconstitutional. Milligan had been tried and found guilty of treason by a military tribunal. The defense's argument was that constitutionality required Milligan be tried in a court established by Congress and convicted by a jury of his peers. The government argued that the preamble of the Constitution granted powers to the general government that, without express limitation, were lodged in the president, as chief executive and commander in chief.

The Supreme Court declared that the president's power during war was not absolute: martial law could not be declared nor could the writ be suspended in areas remote from actual warfare. Justice David Davis's majority opinion exposed the dangers of the government's view:

> This nation, as experience has proved, cannot always remain at peace, and has no right to expect that it will always have wise and humane rulers, sincerely attached to the principles of the

Constitution. Wicked men, ambitious of power, with hatred of liberty and contempt for law, may fill the place occupied by Washington and Lincoln; and if this right is conceded, and the calamities of war again befall us, the dangers of liberty are frightful to contemplate.

Justice Davis added: "The Constitution of the United States is a law for rules and people, equally in war and in peace, and covers with the shield of its protection all classes of men, at all times, and under all circumstances." Therefore, the arrest and conviction of Milligan, in Indiana, an area not in "the theatre of active military operation," constituted an unlawful violation of citizen rights.

The previous cases provide the foundation within which other presidents utilized the power granted them to defend the country during war. A more controversial example involves Roosevelt who, following the bombing of Pearl Harbor, ordered that 120,000 Japanese-Americans living on the West Coast be evacuated to internment camps. He authorized the secretary of war and the military commanders to designate military areas along the coast and to regulate those areas as they saw fit. The president issued his executive order "by virtue of the authority vested in him as the president and as commander in chief of the Army and Navy." On 21 March 1942, Congress passed a resolution supporting the president's actions. Congress made it a misdemeanor against the United States "to knowingly enter, remain in, or leave prescribed military areas" without authorization. In three different cases between 1942–1944, the Court examined the validity of Executive Order No. 9066 and subsequent orders. In *Hirabayashi v. United States* (1943) the Court upheld the validity of a special curfew program for Japanese-Americans instituted by the president. Although the decision was unanimous, in his concurring opinion Justice Murphy noted that the action "goes to the brink of constitutional power."

Perhaps the most controversial decision in this series was *Korematsu v. United States* (1944), in which the Court held constitutional the executive detention program pursuant to a 1942 act of Congress. Chief Justice Harlan Fisher Stone upheld the legality of the mass evacuation of 112,000 persons by writing that the question "is not one of congressional power to delegate to the president the promulgation of the Executive Order, but whether, acting in cooperation, Congress and the Executive have constitutional...power] to impose the curfew restriction here complained of." In dissent, Justice Murphy argued, "This exclusion of 'all persons of Japanese ancestry, both alien and non-alien,' from the Pacific Coast area on a plea of military necessity in the absence of martial law ought not be approved. Such exclusion goes over 'the very brink of constitutional power' and falls into the abyss of racism."

At the end of World War II the Court again addressed the constitutionality of military tribunals under martial law. *Duncan v. Kahanamoku* involved the arrest and conviction of two civilians by military tribunal of offenses normally handled by civil courts. Two days after the attack on Pearl Harbor and in accord with Hawai'ian Organic Acts, President Roosevelt declared martial law in Hawai'i. Following the declaration, the civil courts were supplanted by military law and provost courts. The Supreme Court ruled the president's order unconstitutional. Justice Hugo Black, writing for the Court, delivered an opinion remarkably similar to the majority in *Ex parte Milligan*. Black found no specific grant giving the president the power, under martial law, to eliminate the civilian courts when they were open and functioning. Since there was no specific authorization, the suspension was unconstitutional. But legal scholar Arthur Miller provided a more revealing explanation for the Court's decision: "As in *Milligan*, judicial bravery became manifest when the rumble of guns had been silenced. One would be ill-advised to rely on *Duncan* as a significant substantive limitation upon presidential power."

World War I

When confronted with the approaching challenge of World War I, Woodrow Wilson exercised broad emergency powers based on congressional enactments. Congress created the Council of National Defense (1916), the Lever Food and Fuel Act (1917), the Trading with the Enemy Act (1917), the War Industries Board (1917), the Selective Service Act (1918), and the Overman Act (1918). Collectively, these enactments gave the commander in chief extraordinary powers. The Lever Food and Fuel Act authorized Wilson to monitor and force compliance on the use of food and fuel during the war; he could seize factories, mines, and private plants to help in the war effort. The Trading with the Enemy Act allowed the president to censor mail, license trade, and regulate business activity with enemy nations. The Overman Act authorized the president to take whatever administrative steps were necessary to mobilize the federal government for national security. The president received discretionary authority to abolish, reorganize, or change the legislative intent of any government office or bureau. The preservation of national security took precedence over constitutional checks and balances.

After World War I, Congress repealed all of these emergency enactments except the Trading with the Enemy Act. This is significant because when Roosevelt assumed office in the midst of a national economic crisis, he declared a bank holiday, basing his action on the 1917 Trading with the Enemy Act (a wartime delegation of authority). Roosevelt also requested broad emergency powers resulting in *New York Times* journalist Arthur

Krock's admonition that Roosevelt "possesses, is seeking and has been offered more absolute power than the sum of the arbitrary authority exercised at various times in history by Generals Washington, Lee, Grant, and Sherman; Presidents Jackson, Lincoln, and Wilson, and all the emperors of the Ming Dynasty. What power has been and will be granted is all technically within the framework of the Constitution. If that document has not been put on the shelf...it has been republished on India Rubber to meet these unusual tests of its flexibility."

World War II

Roosevelt's actions before and during World War II again tested and demonstrated the flexibility of the Constitution. On 8 September 1939 he proclaimed a "limited national emergency." The declaration of a "limited" emergency enabled the president, by executive agreement and without prior Senate knowledge, to transfer fifty over-age destroyers to Great Britain in return for leasing rights to British bases and possessions. This transfer, like the president himself, received broad popular support. Additionally, the attorney general asserted that the transfer was within the president's legal rights.

In 1941 Roosevelt concluded Lend-Lease, which authorized him to supply defense materials to any country "whose defense the president deems vital to the defense of the United States." But Article IV, Section 3 of the Constitution gives Congress responsibility for disposing of U.S. property. Roosevelt's attorney general skirted the issue by arguing that as commander in chief, the president could dispose of property belonging to the armed forces.

Roosevelt also authorized the occupation of Greenland and Iceland in 1941. Before the United States entered World War II later that year, the president issued an order to "shoot at sight" any German vessels threatening to stop U.S. ships from carrying cargo to war-ravaged Great Britain. The order included Roosevelt's own version of constitutional-qua-emergency government. "Whether strictly legal or not [these actions] were ventured upon under what appeared to be a popular demand and a public necessity; trusting then as now that Congress would ratify them." In 1942 the Second War Powers Act authorized the president to allocate defense materials and facilities "in such a manner, upon such conditions and to such extent as he shall deem necessary in the public interest and to promote the national defense."

On 7 September 1942 Roosevelt went to Congress and insisted on a revision of the Emergency Price Control Act. According to legal scholar Miller, the effect of his action was to "suspend the Constitution." But the president knew that the public supported him strongly. In his message to Congress on 7 September 1942 Roosevelt argued that

The responsibilities of the president in wartime to protect the nation are very grave. This total war, with our fighting fronts all over the world, makes the use of executive power far more essential than in previous wars ... The American people can be sure that I will use my powers with a full sense of my responsibility to the Constitution and to the country. The American people can also be sure that I shall not hesitate to use every power vested in me to accomplish the defeat of our enemies in any part of the world where our own safety demands such defeat. When the war is won, the powers under which I act automatically revert to the people—to whom they belong.

Roosevelt's perspective on checks and balances was challenged by Senator Taft, who argued that: "if the president can change the Price law by executive order, he can draft men in violation of the Selective Service Act by executive order and impose taxes by executive order....If this doctrine is sustained in wartime it can easily be stretched to cover the post-war period and a whole series of possible later emergencies until we have a complete one-man dictatorship. Then government by the people will have vanished from America." In this particular crisis, however, Taft's opinion was in the minority and Congress quickly passed the Inflation Control Act, authorizing Roosevelt to stabilize wages and prices.

The Korean War

Roosevelt's comments that "this total war, with our fighting fronts all over the world, makes the use of executive power far more essential" notwithstanding, his successors were no less modest in their use of emergency powers. Harry Truman committed over 250,000 troops to Korea without a formal declaration of war by Congress. Following the surprise invasion of South Korea by communist North Korea, Truman issued a proclamation declaring that, "I, Harry S. Truman, president of the United States of America, do proclaim the existence of a national emergency...." Dean Acheson, in his memoir, *Present at the Creation*, maintains that "there has never...been any serious doubt...of the president's constitutional authority to do what he did. The basis for this conclusion is legal theory and historical precedent." It was Acheson's advice that Truman "should not ask for a resolution of approval, but rest on his constitutional authority as commander-in-chief."

These precedents soon established an acceptable mode for presidential governance. From 1933–1976 Congress passed approximately 470 bills delegating power to the president during national emergencies. However, interpretation of the term "national emergency" was highly context specific. In March 1970, for example,

Richard Nixon declared a state of emergency during a nationwide postal strike; in August 1971 he declared another emergency in order to impose controls during the monetary crisis. In each case, the president's declaration activated a reservoir of reserved powers that at one time were considered the prerogatives of Congress.

In 1976 (in the aftermath of Watergate) Congress took back much of this delegated authority. The National Emergencies Act (Public Law 94-412) terminated as of September 1978 all prior national emergencies and mandated that any new national emergency could be ended by either presidential proclamation or concurrent resolution, which allows no veto by the president. The act stipulates that six months following the declaration of an emergency, Congress reserves the right to review the situation; after one year it can terminate the national emergency.

Vietnam

By 1968 the number of U.S. troops in Vietnam stood at approximately 550,000. No declaration of war was ever issued. How did it happen and where did it begin? President Lyndon Johnson relied upon the loosely worded Tonkin Gulf resolution. On 2 August 1964, the destroyer *Maddox* was returning from an electronic espionage mission when North Vietnamese torpedo boats fired on her. Rather than withdrawing U.S. ships from this danger zone, the president ordered another destroyer, the *C. Turner Joy*, to join the *Maddox* in the Gulf of Tonkin. On August 4, both ships reportedly came under attack. Considerable doubt exists as to whether this second attack ever took place. Although almost certainly North Vietnamese gunboats were operating in the area, weather conditions were so bad and tensions aboard ship so high that Johnson later quipped, "For all I know, our Navy was shooting at whales out there."

On 10 August 1964, Congress passed the Southeast Asia Resolution (P.L. 88–408), which read:

> The Congress approves and supports the determination of the President, as Commander in Chief, to take all necessary measures to repeal any armed attack against the forces of the United States and to prevent further aggression. The United States regards as vital to its national interest and to world peace the maintenance of international peace and security in Southeast Asia...to take all necessary steps, including the use of armed force, to assist any member of protocol states of the Southeast Asia Collective Defense Treaty requesting assistance in defense of its freedom.

For the duration of his administration Johnson maintained that this resolution provided sufficient authority to justify committing troops in the absence of a formal declaration of war by Congress. By 1966, however, a majority of senators, led by J. William Fulbright, felt that Johnson had far exceeded any congressional intent behind the Tonkin Gulf resolution.

When President Nixon took office, with neither the Congress's nor the public's knowledge, he ordered the Vietnam War expanded into Laos and Cambodia, which was then a neutral country. Hundreds of air sortie reports were falsified to make it appear as if the bombings had occurred in South Vietnam, not Cambodia and Laos. On 30 July 1974, the House Judiciary Committee considered the following proposed article of impeachment against Nixon:

> In his conduct of the office of President of the United States, Richard M. Nixon, in violation of his constitutional oath faithfully to execute the office of President of the United States and, to the best of his ability, preserve, protect, and defend the Constitution of the United States, and in disregard of his constitutional duty to take care that the laws be faithfully executed, on and subsequent to March 17, 1969, authorized, ordered, and ratified the concealment from the Congress of the facts and the submission to the Congress of false and misleading statements concerning the existence, scope, and nature of American bombing operations in Cambodia in derogation of the power of the Congress to declare war, to make appropriations and to raise and support armies, and by such conduct warrants impeachment and trial and removal from office.

The House committee concluded the following pertaining to Nixon's actions. On 17 March 1969, after two months in office, the president approved his military advisors' request to begin bombing Cambodia, which began the next day under the code name Menu Operation. The bombing continued until 26 May 1970. Yet the official operational reports falsely stated that these bombing strikes took place in South Vietnam against Vietcong targets. Over fourteen months, 3,695 B-52 sorties dropped 105,837 tons of bombs on Cambodia, at a cost of $150 million. At the president's instructions, the secretaries of defense and state, as well as the joint chiefs of staff, lied to congressional committees falsifying classified records and submitting false reports to Congress based on their records. Not until 16 July 1973 was the truth revealed.

President Nixon defended himself against these accusations by maintaining that he had consulted privately with key members of Congress (which he had). By a vote of 26–12 the Judiciary Committee did not report this article of impeachment to the House. The vote reflected the belief that, as commander in chief, Nixon was carrying out his constitutional duty to protect U.S. troops and that complete congressional consultation and consent, although preferable, was unnecessary.

The War Powers Resolution

It has been argued that the most significant byproduct of the Vietnam period was passage of the War Powers Resolution (P.L. 93–148), over President Nixon's veto. The War Powers Resolution could easily be seen as a response to the war in Vietnam. However, taking a larger and broader view, it can be seen to be the result of ongoing institutional struggle, an attempt by Congress to go back to the intent of the framers by ensuring "the collective judgment of the Congress and the president" on war powers. The War Powers Resolution attempted to restore power and authority to Congress that had "drifted" to the presidency and in so doing recreate the balance of power that the framers sought to establish via the Constitution. A further explanation would include the heightened awareness of the potential for presidential abuse of power that characterized the Watergate era. Perhaps not coincidentally, just four days after Nixon ousted Attorney General Elliot Richardson, Special Prosecutor Archibald Cox, and Deputy Attorney General William Ruckelshaus during the infamous "Saturday Night Massacre" in October 1973, fifteen members of the House reversed their previous opposition to the War Powers Resolution to override Nixon's veto of it.

The president is now required to report to Congress within forty-eight hours after committing U.S. troops to hostile action (if no state of war has been declared). Unless Congress agrees otherwise, the troops must be removed within ninety days. (Actually the troops must be withdrawn after sixty days unless the president requests thirty additional days for ensuring their safety.) The president's fairly unrestricted unilateral action for ninety days is tempered with an encouragement to consult with Congress regarding such action. During debate on the bill, several senators (most prominently New York Republican Senator Jacob Javits) argued that the resolution actually provided a legal basis for sixty days "free" war; and to a degree, this is exactly what has happened. Congress could stop the military commitment by concurrent resolution, which is not subject to the president's veto.

The constitutionality of the concurrent resolution was clouded by the decision in *INS v. Chadha* (1983), in which the Supreme Court ruled that the legislative veto violates the structural provisions of the Constitution. Scholar Louis Fisher argues that in the event that Congress did pass a concurrent resolution to end a presidentially initiated military commitment the president might maintain that "it had no legally binding effect because of *Chadha*....However, such legal reasoning would also publicize the president's determination to keep U.S. forces engaged in hostilities despite the opposition of a majority of both houses of Congress...not a tenable position for the president." After the *Chadha* decision, Senator Robert Byrd offered an alternative method for forcing the removal of troops. He proposed legislation that would require a joint resolution (subject to presidential veto—overridden by two-thirds of both Houses) to force the president to withdraw military units from battle. This legislation did not survive conference committee intact; if it had, the requirement for the joint resolution would, in the event of a presidential veto and override attempt by Congress, allow one-third plus one member in a single House to prevent override and open the door for the president to continue in the pursuit of military objectives to which the majority of both Houses had objected. As of the late 1990s, the concurrent resolution option continued to exist as law despite the fact that it is potentially unenforceable.

The War Powers Resolution (sometimes referred to as irresolution) has had a marginal effect on presidential warmaking, with the size of the margin determined by presidential discretion. Generally presidents have made only token gestures to conform to the resolution's "prior consultation" requirement. The first test of the War Powers Resolution came in May 1975, when the U.S. merchant ship *Mayaguez*, carrying both civilian and military cargo, was seized by Cambodian ships for being in Cambodia's territorial waters. President Gerald Ford reacted quickly, ordering the Marines and the Navy to rescue the *Mayaguez*, without consulting with members of Congress or seeking the body's collective judgment. A White House spokesperson said, "Mr. Ford acted under his constitutional war powers to protect the lives and property of Americans." In his report to Congress, President Ford cited both his inherent executive power and his authority as commander in chief. According to Ford, "When a crisis breaks out, it is impossible to draw the Congress in with the decision-making process in an effective way." He presented a rather stinging critique of the Resolution:

> The Congress has encroached, in my judgment, greatly on the capability of the president to carry out his functions as the chief of the executive branch of the government. This is particularly true in foreign policy....I [also] think that the Congress made a serious mistake in the enactment of the War Powers Resolution. I know this may be controversial but I speak my piece. That's a very serious intrusion on the responsibilities of the president as commander in chief

and the person who formulates and ought to execute foreign policy. The day will come when the Congress will regret that legislation.

A former member of Congress and minority leader, Ford held a different view of checks and balances as president arguing that: "You cannot have 535 commanders in chief. You cannot have 535 secretaries of state....A president ought to maximize his efforts to notify and to consult the Congress, but he cannot give away his responsibility as commander in chief when the lives of American military personnel are involved."

The president's actions may have violated the War Powers Resolution. Congress was not consulted, thirty marines were killed, over fifty were wounded—yet the public increased the president's approval rating by eleven percentage points from 40 percent to 51 percent.

The War Powers Resolution would imply (and many observers agreed) that Congress should have been consulted prior to President Carter's 1980 attempt to militarily rescue the U.S. citizens held hostage in the U.S. embassy in Iran. In his report to Congress, Carter acknowledged that he ordered the operation "pursuant to the president's powers under the Constitution as chief executive and as commander in chief of the United States Armed Forces, expressly recognized in section 8(d)(1) of the *War Powers Resolution*." Carter maintained that as president he had the legal authority to protect and rescue U.S. citizens when the nation where these citizens were located was unable or unwilling to protect them.

In order to protect the highly sensitive and secret mission, Carter chose not to consult with Congress. The chairman of the Senate Foreign Relations Committee believed that "it was stupid on the part of the president not to consult with us." But Senator John Glenn probably represented majority sentiment when he remarked, "If I were on that raid, I wouldn't want it all over Capitol Hill." The rescue attempt also raises the issue of presidential secrecy. When is a president "justified" in withholding information from Congress? Should the judgment of the president alone determine the extent of secrecy as well as define what constitutes hostilities?

In April 1986, for example, President Reagan ordered an air raid against Libya without prior consultation with Congress. Legislative leaders were not briefed until warplanes had already left Great Britain headed for Libya. Reagan's action received widespread support from the general public as well as most members of Congress. Even so, Senator Sam Nunn of Georgia, ranking Democrat on the Armed Services Committee, said: "I don't think there was enough consultation; there should have been more. When the president is examining some of the options, it would be helpful for congressional leaders to look at some of those options, before he decides. That's consultation." However, within days of the air raid, Republicans in both houses of Congress introduced a bill that would authorize the president to respond to foreign terrorism without first consulting Congress.

President Reagan's October 1983 decision to invade Grenada, a small Caribbean island which at the time had a Marxist government, represents another apt example. Reagan ordered 1,900 Marine and Army troops to come ashore in an invasion of Grenada to "protect our own citizens" and "help in the restoration of democratic institutions in Grenada," where a "brutal group of leftist thugs violently seized power." Reagan cited Article 51 of the United Nations (UN) Charter and excluded journalists from covering the military action on the grounds of ensuring their safety and maintaining secrecy. The Reagan administration did not comply with the prior consultation requirements of the War Powers Resolution, merely informing members of Congress that the invasion was taking place. The president also explained that the government of Grenada had requested U.S. support as part of a multinational force and that no declaration of war was needed for a police action.

Section 4(a)(1) of the War Powers Resolution was designed to be activated whenever U.S. troops are introduced into hostilities or imminent hostilities. The president must report under Section 4(a)(1) and it is this report that starts the sixty- to ninety-day clock. As a result, presidents have attempted to avoid reporting under this section and to thereby avoid the deadline that will be established with such a report. President Ford provided his Section 4(a)(1) report of the *Mayaguez* incident only after military involvement had ceased. The War Powers Resolution was invoked for the first time to govern presidential policy when Reagan attempted to skirt the reporting requirement in Lebanon in 1983. U.S. Marines had come under attack on 29 August 1983, resulting in four U.S. casualties. However, Reagan claimed that he did not have to notify Congress that hostilities had started because "isolated or infrequent acts of violence" did not constitute hostilities as defined by the War Powers Resolution. Representative Clement Zablocki responded to Reagan's argument by claiming that it "only reinforces the question of whether there may be imminent hostilities." He likened the situation to a man walking barefoot in a glass factory: "You're bound to get cut." Congress compromised by allowing the Marines to remain for eighteen months in order to complete their peacekeeping mission, but the clock had started with the August 29 hostilities.

In another example of the potential problems associated with a presidential definition of hostility that requires force, President George Bush unilaterally decided to commit U.S. forces to Panama in May of 1989, following fraudulent Panamanian elections of that year. The commitment of troops was required, according to Bush, to protect U.S. lives and treaty rights. Congress was not consulted prior to the troop commitment. Although U.S. troops were ordered not to assist a subsequent coup attempt, in December 1989, U.S. forces invaded Panama and eventually captured and imprisoned its leader, Manuel Noriega, on drug trafficking charges.

Bush did consult Congress regarding the decision to commit troops to the Persian Gulf following the August 1990 Iraqi invasion of Kuwait. After much debate over whether the issue was "the preservation of democracy around the world," or an "exchange of blood for oil," Congress voted in January of 1991 to support the president's decision to send troops to defend the Saudi Arabian border and restore the Kuwaiti government.

Whether the War Powers Resolution has prevented long-term engagements in military conflict is debatable. Long-term engagements similar to Vietnam have been conspicuously absent since 1973; however, that is as attributable to public opinion and political fear as it may be to the War Powers Resolution. The "success" of the War Powers Resolution is difficult to gauge. Although presidents have generally ignored the reporting requirement of the act, they have found ways to inform Congress of the use of military force even if after the fact and, a lively and informal debate did occur in Congress during the Persian Gulf commitment. Ultimately, pathways for negotiation between Congress and the presidency were cleared and the process for limiting the potential for the abuse of presidential power was established.

The Modern Presidency and Foreign Relations

Presidents since Franklin D. Roosevelt have increasingly focused upon foreign policy as the arena in which they seek to establish their historical credentials. Roosevelt's presidency heralded the advent of the "modern presidency": presidencies characterized by stronger and more consistent attempts to influence in legislative affairs, unilateral action, extensive staff support, and unique visibility in the political system. His influence in the creation of the modern presidency resulted from having exercised expansive leadership to successfully resolve the economic crisis of the 1930s, deal with international economic turmoil, and steer the country through involvement in World War II. The centrality and dominance of the presidency that emerged from his extraordinary tenure remains in effect.

Modern presidents have exercised so much power in foreign affairs that political scientist Aaron Wildavsky coined the phrase "the two presidencies," referring to the differing roles, abilities, powers, and success rates inherent in the foreign vs. the domestic presidency. Wildavsky argued that since World War II, presidents were much more likely to meet with legislative success when proposing defense and foreign policy initiatives than they were with domestic initiatives. The ability to utilize emergency powers, negotiate executive agreements, and access the executive bureaucracy have represented crucial tools that, when utilized effectively, are capable of enabling modern presidents to implement decisive and informed foreign policy. Wildavsky wrote that presidents encounter problems in obtaining congressional support for their domestic policies; but in foreign affairs, the president almost always gets support for policies that he believes will protect the nation—the challenge is to find a viable policy. Wildavsky's thesis was based on a world in which the Cold War raged; to wit, he quoted John F. Kennedy as stating that "domestic policy...can only defeat us; foreign policy can kill us." Isolationism had become a deadly game, a game in which a Hitler could move relatively unchecked. In this world the best policy had become the best politics in Wildavsky's terms because incredibly high stakes depoliticized the process. The domestic political theater was populated with political gamesmanship and porkbarrel politics, purposeful ambiguity; while international politics found itself on a stage where life and death, black and white, were the only meaningful terminology.

Presidential success in foreign policy initiatives stood, at the time of Wildavsky's article, at 70 percent. Success with domestic initiatives stood at 40 percent. Since that time, the two presidencies thesis has been revisited and the importance of strong presidential leadership in areas of foreign policy has been questioned. Presidential success rates in areas of foreign and domestic initiatives have narrowed, the Cold War no longer exists, and the increasing importance of international economic policy as well as the interaction effect between domestic policy and foreign policy have all seriously muddled the two presidencies argument. However, the president continues to exert significant powers in foreign affairs. Congress cannot exercise diplomacy nearly to the extent that the president can, nor can it prevent the president from the short-term use of troops. Congress can "frustrate the president's plans" but ultimately, without presidential action, foreign policy would stagnate.

Conclusion

The role of the president in foreign policy negotiation, formation, and implementation has evolved along with the context within which the president attempts to exercise power and leadership. We are currently entering a new and compelling era of the U.S. presidency, an era which proceeds from a fundamental shift in orientation. The post–Cold War orientation is newly developing, characterized by battles that are often economic rather than military and by military intervention that has

become regional rather than international. Within this context the United States must try to determine a foreign-policy course that involves an appropriate balance of commitments and resources, and it must do so within the democratic limits established in the Constitution. Ultimately the primary challenge will be to balance the interests of security and the requirements of democracy.

Today, instead of a well-defined threat to anchor U.S. foreign policy, pervasive uncertainty faces the world's sole remaining superpower as it attempts to anticipate the future foreign-policy environment, establish a new psychological basis for engaging the nation in the world, and develop principles to guide the use of diplomatic, economic, and military tools abroad. For the United States, the post–Cold War world is characterized first and foremost by absence of a known and familiar adversary. The absence of a metaphor like communism representing a clear and defined enemy has created a virtual foreign policy vacuum—perhaps to be replaced by terrorism and the U.S. response to terrorist activities, both international and domestic. Post–Cold War presidents are attempting to fill that vacuum with the creation, articulation, interpretation, communication, and implementation of newer visions. Certainty about the enemy has been supplanted by questions about the identity of future adversaries, their goals and capabilities, and the time frame within which future challenges are likely to arise. Post-Cold War U.S. leaders face a set of novel, diffuse, and unfamiliar foreign-policy problems such as small peripheral states armed with weapons of mass destruction threatening regional and global security, and unconventional challenges posed by narcoterrorists, religious-fundamentalist movements, and ethnic and national violence. Of these, however, none are significant enough, even in the foreseeable future, to replace the strategic bellwether that disappeared along with the Soviet Union.

U.S. leaders must also confront uncertainty regarding alliance and coalition partners in an uncertain political, technological, and ecological environment. The president is instrumental in the determination of future alliance and coalition partners as well as in the nature of those alliances. The absence of a hegemonic challenger has weakened the U.S. commitment to firm alliance arrangements such as the North Atlantic Treaty Organization (NATO); the parameters of future commitments will be in large part determined by presidential initiative. The absence of the Cold War has created unconventional challenges and unconventional challenges do not engender either public concern or political resolve in the way that the Cold War orientation did. However, the president must maintain a practical awareness of ongoing public evaluation, despite the fact that much of it has been characterized by a focus on short-term economic gain and a lack of awareness of both the short- and long-term implications of political, economic, technological, and demographic changes that confront both the modern president and the planet.

LARRY BERMAN
LINDA O. VALENTY

See also articles on individual presidents; Articles of Confederation; Chadha Decision; Congress; Constitution; Curtiss-Wright Case; Executive Agreement; Gulf War of 1990–1991; Supreme Court and the Judiciary; Vietnam War; War Powers Resolution

FURTHER READING

Adler, David Gray, and Larry N. George, eds. *The Constitution and the Conduct of American Foreign Policy.* Lawrence, Kans., 1996.

Corwin, Edward. *The President: Office and Powers, 1787–1984: A History and Analysis of Practice and Opinion.* 5th rev. ed. New York, 1984.

Crabb, Cecil V., Jr., and Pat M. Holt. *Invitation to Struggle: Congress, the President, and Foreign Policy.* Washington, D.C., 1989.

Crovitz, L. Gordon, and Jeremy Rabkin, eds. *The Fettered Presidency.* Washington D.C., 1990.

Ely, John Hart. *War and Responsibility: Constitutional Lessons of Vietnam and Its Aftermath.* Princeton, 1993.

Fisher, Louis. *Presidential War Power.* Lawrence, Kans., 1995.

———. *Constitutional Conflicts Between Congress and the President.* Lawrence, Kans., 1991.

Genovese, Michael A. *The Presidency in an Age of Limits.* Westport, Conn., 1993.

Glennon, Michael J. *Constitutional Diplomacy.* Princeton, 1990.

Henkin, Louis. *Constitutionalism, Democracy, and Foreign Affairs.* New York, 1990.

Mann, Thomas E., ed. *A Question of Balance: The President, Congress, and Foreign Policy.* Washington D.C., 1990.

Neustadt, Richard E. *Presidential Power and the Modern Presidents: The Politics of Leadership from Roosevelt to Reagan.* New York, 1990.

Reveley, W. Taylor, III. *War Powers of the President and Congress.* Charlottesville, 1981.

Schlesinger, Arthur M., Jr. *The Imperial Presidency.* Boston, 1989.

Shull, Steven A., ed. *The Two Presidencies: A Quarter Century Assessment.* Chicago, 1991.

Sutherland, George S. *Constitutional Power and World Affairs.* New York, 1919.

PRESS

See Journalism and Foreign Policy

PREVENTIVE DIPLOMACY

A term coined at the height of the Cold War by United Nations (UN) Secretary-General Dag Hammarskjöld to describe UN mediation and peacekeeping efforts to keep regional conflicts like Suez, Lebanon, and Congo from provoking confrontations between the two super-powers. At its inception, preventive diplomacy thus meant military as well as nonmilitary methods of stopping conflicts. The idea received greater attention at the end of the Cold War, however, when UN Secretary-General Boutros Boutros-Ghali promoted a more expansive andpro-active version in his *Agenda for Peace* (1992). Increased cooperation between the former Soviet bloc and the West did not end all existing wars, and new ones broke out, mostly within states. The difficulties of trying to end these violent conflicts and remedy their humanitarian crises led Boutros-Ghali to advocate earlier international involvement not simply to keep them from spreading but to prevent them from erupting in the first place. He mentioned early-warning, fact-finding, and confidence-building measures between parties to a dispute, preventive deployment of peacekeeping forces, and demilitarized zones; preventive diplomacy could be implemented not only by the UN secretary-general and Security Council, but also by regional multilateral organizations in cooperation with the United Nations.

Other world leaders and observers have echoed the secretary-general's call, including U.S. Presidents George Bush and Bill Clinton; leaders from Great Britain, France, and Germany; and Russian President Boris Yeltsin. The UN General Assembly has discussed preventive diplomacy, international affairs conferences have taken it up, multilateral organizations try new conflict-prevention mechanisms, the United States and other governments have launched initiatives, nongovernmental organizations (NGOs) conduct research and action projects, and plans have been sketched for a coordinated international strategy. Perhaps not since the founding of the United Nations has so much international attention focused on preventing future conflicts.

Definition

Conceptual confusion has arisen as "preventive action" and similar terms such as "crisis prevention" have come into vogue. These terms are often interchanged with other phrases of the day like "peacemaking," "peace-keeping," "conflict management," and "conflict resolution." "Crisis prevention" is waved like a banner over policy agendas as varied as democracy-building, nuclear arms counterproliferation, and sustainable development. Because practical policy cannot proceed from vague slogans, efforts have been made to define preventive diplomacy more precisely. Whether one uses the UN term or a synonym, a clear concept is needed.

In *Agenda for Peace*, preventive diplomacy is "action to prevent disputes from arising between parties, to prevent existing disputes from escalating into conflicts and to limit the spread of the latter when they occur." Boutros-Ghali thus defines preventive diplomacy as acting at several levels of conflict. It treats the basic causes of disputes (dispute prevention), keeps disputes from becoming violent (violence avoidance), and limits escalation of erupted violence (violence containment). But analysts of this subject suggest that identifying preventive diplomacy with actions at virtually any stage in a conflict—from the causes of peaceful disagreements through many possible thresholds of bloodshed—lacks focus. Defining preventive diplomacy as active across the entire life of a conflict, they argue, blurs crucial distinctions between interventions made at different stages, and risks overlooking entry points when action may be the most cost-effective.

Defining preventive diplomacy as keeping disputes from arising, for example, suggests long-term remedies that are expensive and not always effective in stopping violence. Disputes often have roots in deep-seated socioeconomic, political, psychological, and international conditions that are structural in nature: poverty, environmental degradation, lack of education, and leaders' lust for power. But while these conditions may increase the chances disputes will arise, they do not cause the violence itself; more immediate factors must activate actual violent behavior, such as ethnocentric demagoguery. So not all countries experiencing serious structural problems get embroiled in wars.

Therefore, to try to prevent violent conflicts by reducing these structural problems, such as through foreign economic aid, income redistribution, family planning, progressive universal education, disarmament, and psychotherapy, is to address the problem indirectly. Such generalized programs find it difficult to pinpoint when and where particular manifestations of violent conflict will emerge and thus cannot focus on its immediate causes. For example, poor countries like Rwanda received considerable development aid recently, yet they still experienced bloody slaughters. In addition, however worthy long-term structural programs are in their own right, they are costly, and in some cases may be intrusive and controversial. Seeking to prevent conflicts through such ambitious and comprehensive policies would miss the target while at the same time dissipating the limited financing and political support now available for international conflict prevention.

Moreover, correcting structural conditions can help cause rather than prevent violent conflicts. For example, rapid socioeconomic reform, development, or democratization might destroy, rather than transform, the existing ways fragile societies or brittle regimes manage disputes, thus making these countries more susceptible to violence or repression, not less.

Disputes per se do not need prevention; they are a natural outgrowth of clashing interests among groups and nations due to changes in economics, technology, expectations, and so forth. Disputes can be peaceful if pursued through international negotiations, normal national politics, economic competition, and healthy expressions of cultural and religious diversity. Only when disputants try to resolve their differences through armed force or other forms of coercion is conflict prevention required.

The critics also consider the last part of the *Agenda*'s tripartite definition—containment of violent conflicts even after they have escalated—to be problematic. It is reminiscent of Hammarskjöld's notion of keeping regional wars localized. In a loose sense, keeping violence at any level from worsening is "prevention." But thinking of preventive diplomacy as dealing with advanced stages of a violent conflict confuses it with crisis management and stopping wars. To label as preventive diplomacy a hotline between heads of state, cease-fire after a war, or peacekeeping force to implement a peace agreement strains meaningful terminology. This would also include the belated interventions in the middle of the civil wars and humanitarian calamities in the 1990s in Somalia and the former Yugoslavia, whose consequent dangers and costs were the very impetus for many to urge that earlier responses would be less risky and more effective.

The distinction is more than semantic. Much conflict-escalation theory and empirical research on mediation suggest that precrisis and previolence interventions into conflicts can be easier, cheaper, and save more lives than reactive responses to manage, contain, or terminate all-out wars and rebuild war-torn societies. The less violent and enduring conflicts become, it appears, the greater is the ability of mediators to gain access and achieve peaceful solutions. Issues may never be simple, but they are at least less complex and multiple at this early stage; fatalities and thus passions are lower; disputants are less polarized and politically or militarily mobilized behind rigidly opposed causes; communications and institutions may still operate between them; and outside parties are less likely to have joined in on one side or the other.

In sum, rather than defining preventive diplomacy as actions taken all the way from the earliest signs of differences to the advanced stages of all-out wars, a revised view regards the middle part of Boutros-Ghali's definition—preventing peaceful disputes from escalating to tense confrontations or use of armed force—as the most fruitful concept, particularly in the resource-constrained post–Cold War era. Preventive diplomacy operates in between long-term societal and global betterment on the one hand, and short-term crisis management and war mitigation on the other. The most useful definition might read: actions, policies, and institutions used to keep particular states or groups within them from threatening or using organized violence, armed force, or related forms of coercion as the way to settle either interstate or national political disputes, especially where and when the existing means cannot peacefully manage the destabilizing effects of economic, social, political, and international change.

Because its essence lies with the timing of conflict intervention, not this or that method or implementer, preventive diplomacy can use a variety of intercessory (diplomatic), political, military, economic, legal, and other techniques. These could be sponsored by governments, multilateral organizations, nongovernmental organizations (NGOs), and individuals, as well as the disputants themselves.

Policymakers are likely to find that the tools best suited to a given situation depend on the level of hostility and on which sources of possible violence or coercion demand the most attention. Preventive diplomacy thus could range from the positive goals of preconflict peacebuilding to the more negative goals of crisis prevention. For example, even if violence is not imminent, potential national or international disputes may lack any outlets for peaceful resolution. Preventive diplomacy thus could create or strengthen national decision-making bodies such as impartial commissions, or governance structures such as central power-sharing and federalism, to make them functional and legitimate. Or it could initiate interstate negotiations.

Where particular disputes arise and remain unaddressed, deep distrust and past hostile relationships among communities invite renewed intergroup violence that could spiral out of control. Here, "track-two" preventive diplomacy by NGOs at national or grassroots levels might seek to dispel mutual antipathies through nonofficial "problem-solving workshops" and dispute-resolution training. If egregious material needs and social inequities provide tempting pretexts for power-hungry leaders to incite violence; preventive diplomacy could provide politically conditioned economic assistance and target aid to especially aggrieved areas or groups. Media projects could convey messages of reconciliation. Between states, confidence-building measures might allay suspicion and insecurity by increasing transparency between national militaries. To reduce or regulate the weapons that disputants might be inclined to take up, preventive diplomacy could try for arms reductions and nonproliferation agreements backed up by security guarantees.

When intense disagreements have emerged openly among certain parties but remain unresolved, a third party government, the United Nations, regional organizations, or eminent statesmen might actively engage the disputants to find solutions or they might be channeled into the arbitration and adjudication procedures of international tribunals or the International Court of Justice.

Sometimes military confrontation, war, or repression loom just over the horizon. In these cases, preventive diplomacy requires strong measures to deter or block the feared aggressive or repressive acts and protect the physical security of those threatened. This might entail a preventive peacekeeping force, threats of economic and diplomatic sanctions directed at likely belligerents, arms embargoes, activating a war crimes commission (ideally, set up before violations are committed), or nonviolent campaigns by oppressed groups against a repressive regime.

History

Although the post–Cold War period introduced an explicit concept, preventing conflicts is not new. Even before Hammarskjöld came up with the label, city-states, empires, and nation-states used emissaries, treaties, tribunals, and other devices to reduce tensions and avoid wars with potential adversaries. But earlier versions of preventive diplomacy differed considerably from the recent notions, shaped as they were by the major powers and statesmen of past eras and the differing threats they envisioned. A look back at highlights from Western practice since the late eighteenth century shows definite evolution in the "when," the "how," and the "who" of conflict prevention. Preventive diplomacy has shifted increasingly from merely managing crises and containing active wars to earlier involvement to address their causes; from ad hoc unilateral and bilateral acts of prudent self-defense to a priori multilateral arrangements that apply general norms and procedures; and from state-to-state relations to a larger array of nongovernmental as well as governmental tools and implementers. Over this period, the United States emerged from being largely a beneficiary of international conflict prevention to one of its leaders.

Until the late nineteenth century, the United States was weak and marginal in world politics. Its survival as a young nation was due in part, not to isolationism, but to vigilant diplomacy to avoid wars with the more powerful Great Britain, France, and Spain. The United States negotiated crucial treaties to avoid or manage escalating crises with the European powers as early as 1794, when Chief Justice John Jay was sent as an emissary to London after England had seized U.S. vessels bound for its enemy, revolutionary France. The United States also benefited to some extent from the first multilateral agreement among modern nation-states to avoid future wars: the Concert of Europe of 1815. At the Congress of Vienna that year, Napoleon's victorious opponents England, Russia, Austria, and Prussia agreed on certain territorial boundaries, reducing their militaries, security for small states, the use of international tribunals, and periodic consultations among their foreign ministers. Though hardly perfect, the Concert and a less secure Berlin pact of 1871 are regarded as key to maintaining a certain level of peace among the European powers up to August 1914.

By the late nineteenth century, the United States was becoming an industrial and military power, so it took more interest in mediating other nations' disputes and in instituting agreed procedures for preserving international order. Under Nobel Peace Prize–winner President Theodore Roosevelt, the United States mediated the Portsmouth settlement of the Russo-Japanese War in 1905, and helped foster a peaceful settlement of the Moroccan Crisis of 1906 that had pitted Germany against Britain and France.

The United States' first major sponsorship of multilateral institutions to prevent war came with President Woodrow Wilson's efforts in drafting the Treaty of Versailles ending World War I and creating the League of Nations. Wilson failed to win senate ratification of U.S. membership in the League, but the League nevertheless was created. Its covenant was the first to define any war or threat of war as a common threat and to seek limits on arms manufacture. Its provisions for regular meetings of a Council and Assembly, a secretary-general and secretariat, and a permanent court created international organizations to do what in the past the major powers had done in a less institutionalized way, as in the nineteenth-century Concert of Europe. The covenant also provided for the League to call attention to, investigate, and report on threats to international peace, post observer forces, and impose sanctions, revealing its intention to head off crises before they reached the boiling point. It successfully did manage several disputes, especially in the 1920s, such as those involving the Baltic's Aaland Islands, Bulgaria and Greece, and the Saar region.

The League did not have the backing of key players however, lacking the United States and initially excluding Germany and Russia. It could not obtain the wide public support on which energizing its procedures depended. By the 1930s, expedient alliances had displaced the desired multilateral enforcement of mutually accepted rules. The League's unwillingness to oppose Japan's attack on Manchuria in 1931, Mussolini's invasion of Abyssinia in 1935, and Hitler's rearmament violations made it a symbol of failure.

At the end of World War II, when the victorious Allies created the United Nations (1945) to save "succeeding generations from the scourge of war," the United States played the leading role. The UN Charter went further than previous agreements to commit members to uphold, in the words of Article 2, "effective collective measures for the prevention and removal of threats to the peace…and settlement of international disputes of situations which might lead to a breach of the peace." The threat or use of force against any state was now outlawed, except for self-defense and UN peace-enforcement itself. A kind of early-warning procedure allows the members or the secretary-general to bring to the Security Council or General Assembly any "situation which might lead to international friction or give rise to a dispute…to determine whether (it) is likely to endanger the mainte-nance of international peace and security." Technically, this language is not restricted to quarrels between states, but the United Nations' original purview was understood as interstate, not internal, disputes; Article 2(7) ruled out infringement on members' sovereignty.

Chapter VI of the Charter outlines several ways to handle potentially violent disputes peacefully, first by urging the parties themselves to try a menu of procedures, such as binding decision by the International Court at the Hague. The Security Council could investigate threatening situations, assist in mediation, and recommend remedies. If such efforts failed to stem an emerging conflict, Chapter VII authorizes diplomatic sanctions and international military operations. Through its economic and social agencies as well, the United Nations affirmed its continuing philosophy that the weeds of war sprout faster in the soil of material want.

From the late 1940s to the 1970s, however, UN preventive procedures were largely sidelined by the bipolar geopolitical and ideological struggle between East and West. Because Security Council action could be blocked by permanent member veto, UN conflict prevention was largely restricted to situations of relatively marginal superpower interest. Major wars were mainly prevented not by deliberate mutual agreements or multilateral mechanisms, but by the tacit forbearance that arose between the United States and the Soviet Union due to the deterrent effect of their uneasy balance of power. Even so, as argued by Hammarskjöld, the United Nations' good offices, special envoys, and peacekeepers helped fill the power vacuums created by regional conflicts that might otherwise have ignited World War III.

Post–Cold War Developments

Many saw the end of the Cold War as an especially opportune moment for unprecedented collaboration to address potentially violent conflicts before they erupted. Governments became more willing to cooperate through the United Nations and other multilateral channels and were less willing to tolerate unilateral use of force as a foreign-policy tool. The bitter ideological contest between global camps was replaced by wider consensus on goals such as market-oriented economics, democracy, human rights, and rule of law. This new climate advanced international conflict prevention in several ways.

First, more policymakers and citizens accept that, despite sovereignty's prerogatives, national troubles that threaten to erupt into violence or repression and to cause massive refugee flows or other large-scale loss of life and human suffering will greatly burden the international community, and may even threaten its security. Because few interstate conflicts have occurred recently, while the number of ethnic and other national conflicts has remained high, preventive diplomacy no longer means only watching for cross-border aggression. It looks for signs, too, of national crises such as gross violations of human rights, genocide, ethnic cleansing, collapsing states, and military or executive usurpation of established democratic institutions.

Second, regular monitoring for these early warnings of conflict is becoming institutionalized here and there. Boutros-Ghali reorganized the UN Secretariat to create a political affairs branch that is expected to link up with the Secretariat's relief and peacekeeping units to respond earlier to incipient humanitarian crises. University researchers are seeking reliable indicators for potential civil wars, genocide, failing states, and the like. Rapid communications technologies are opening up more nations' affairs to general view, and databases and information-sharing networks are proliferating, as reflected by "Reliefweb," which puts conflict information on-line worldwide.

Third, early warning and preventive diplomacy is not merely more widely advocated, but actual initiatives and procedures are increasing. These involve a wider array of tools and of global and regional actors than simply those of the United Nations. The Organization for Security and Cooperation in Europe (OSCE), the European Union (EU), the Organization of African Unity (OAU), and the Organization of American States (OAS) now employ strategies and mechanisms for conflict avoidance and management. Their special envoys, observer missions, and other tools have been applied with some success in places like Estonia, the former Yugoslav Republic of Macedonia, Congo, and Guatemala. In Asia, the Regional Forum of the Association of Southeast Asian Nations' (ASEAN) is exploring interstate confidence building. Middle East countries are conducting multilateral talks over water disputes, arms control, and regional security. Individual states occasionally take on specific disputes, as seen in the sponsorship by Indonesia and Canada of informal multinational talks regarding control of the South China Sea islands. Though less visible, many NGO projects also carry out nonofficial dialogues and democracy-building programs in areas of high tension such as Macedonia.

Still, these developments have progressed only so far. The notion that national crises are a legitimate international concern is hardly universal. Considerably more has been done in generating early-warning data than in linking it to operating procedures that take preventive actions. Even existing preventive agreements are not always enforced. In late 1994, for example, Russia violated its OSCE commitments regarding major troop movement and human rights protection of civilians when it sought to brutally crush the uprising in the region of Chechnya. Few other OSCE members objected initially. The recent dispersion of preventive activity in the early

to mid-1990s also has the drawback of being highly fragmented institutionally and politically. Perhaps because it was only a "Cold" War, its demise, unlike those of past postwar eras, did not see major powers adopting comprehensive agreements to protect the peace through rules on how to meet future threats. The nearest equivalents to such a treaty are the Paris Charter for a New Europe in 1990, the provisions added by the OSCE's predecessor in 1992, and a symbolic UN summit that year of the heads of state of Security Council members—the meeting that called for preparation of *Agenda for Peace*.

U.S. activity in post–Cold War conflict prevention reveals a mixture of rhetorical backing, effective individual initiatives, and pockets of institutional experimentation. The most visible U.S. preventive initiatives have been predominantly bilateral and interstate and they tend to be promoted with regard to strategically important regional powers such as Russia, Japan, China, North Korea, Iraq, and Iran, such as averting a possible nuclear crisis in the Korean peninsula and another war in the Persian Gulf. A less heralded achievement of this high diplomacy was the negotiation of nuclear arms dismantlement with Ukraine and Russia in 1993. With respect to previolent involvement in possible intrastate crises, however, prevention opportunities were missed at great cost in Somalia, Rwanda, and Chechnya, and the United States deferred to the European Union's ultimately failed effort to avoid the violent breakup of Yugoslavia. But among less-known efforts, a succession of U.S. diplomats has headed the OSCE observer mission in Macedonia since 1992, and about 500 U.S. troops participate there in the United Nations' only preventive peacekeeping mission in a place where no war has occurred in recent decades. U.S. emissaries are also dispatched to head off incipient conflicts or crises when and where the need is seen to arise. Envoys have been sent, for example, into Zaire, Nigeria, and Burundi to coax African leaders resisting the pressures for democratization to turn over the reins of power.

The Clinton administration has been especially vocal about the need for more conflict prevention, with virtually its whole top echelon of foreign-policy officials urging it. The administration's prevention agenda has been dominated, however, by the so-called "global issues," which are long-term in nature: enlarging democracy, opening trade, limiting nuclear arms proliferation, population control, environmentalism, and sustainable development. Less consistent U.S. support has been put behind watching and engaging the key medium-term factors that might provoke violence within global and regional powers, within U.S. partner countries, and in smaller, strategically less important countries. U.S. promotion of UN and regional measures to expand preventive diplomacy has been uneven.

U.S. policymakers have had to contend with domestic opposition to U.S. participation in peacekeeping missions because some U.S. troops have been killed and many in Congress do not believe the recent crises in Somalia, Haiti, Rwanda, and Bosnia affect vital national interests. Nevertheless, as each of these crises unfolded, media coverage of atrocities and accumulating fallout of the wars usually deepened U.S. involvement. Ultimately the United States paid a large portion of the humanitarian, financial, and political costs of these imbroglios. This has stimulated efforts to institutionalize early warning and preventive responses even toward sub-Saharan Africa and other relatively nonstrategic areas. In 1994–1995, the Department of State and Agency for International Development conducted a pilot exercise in rudimentary pre-conflict responses regardless of region which is being developed further by the policy planning staff, and an interagency initiative has sought to improve conflict prevention and food security in the crisis-prone greater Horn of Africa.

In terms of meeting a variety of possible big and small conflicts in the near future, however, the Clinton administration in mid-1996 lacked an overall conflict prevention strategy. With scattered agencies and units looking at different countries and types of possible crises, U.S. preparedness is still patchy and disjointed. Still, absent are government-wide procedures that regularly monitor and systematically assess a range of incipient national or sub-regional political disputes and then link them to decision-making that would assess what is at stake, pose feasible objectives, and consider intervention alternatives based on lessons from past experience. Except in the face of the most compelling global or regional threats, to be crisis preventers U.S. officials and policymakers must work outside established job descriptions, functional program mandates, and bureaucratic routines. U.S. preventive diplomacy has not achieved the status of foreign policy doctrine or standard operating procedure.

Future Prospects

The question remains whether and to what extent deliberate, comprehensive, and effective international preventive diplomacy will advance further. A permanent coordinated worldwide approach to responding to incipient post–Cold War conflicts with appropriate strategies has been proposed. This capacity might build on the current effort in the United Nations, operate through regional organizations or centers, as well as an NGO network, and receive the backing of major states.

One factor that will affect whether such proposals are further realized is how many and what kinds of threats and crises arise as the twentieth century draws to a close. Extant theories see a single feature in future world conflicts, such as widespread "chaos" from collapsing nation-states or the clash of regional cultures. But the potential threats and crises are likely to be more diverse in both type and scale. The list might include troublemaker regimes, some with nuclear weapons; nuclear or conventional interstate wars over borders and natural resources; civil wars over the control of unbending authoritarian states, mounted by ideological movements such as Islamism; the collapse of certain weak national economies and states; conflicts between governments and indigenous ethnic or regional minorities, including major human-rights abuses; and efforts to reverse newly established constitutional democracies.

Only the first three might pose compelling threats to the security of many countries and entire regions; the others are smaller, relatively slow to develop, and highly dispersed. They would erode international order and resources less perceptibly, although significantly over a period of time. It is unclear whether the U.S. and other policymakers, and their attentive publics, would perceive their stake in the latter kinds of conflicts as serious enough to warrant reallocating some resources to prevention and thus away from other foreign policy concerns. The question facing policymakers stated in cost-benefit terms is whether a government's portion of the shared present costs of preventive responses, plus any undesired side effects from them, would exceed the future costs of simply hoping for more favorable scenarios. The equation should factor in not only the human and material costs of possible wars and the price tag for peacekeeping and other attempted remedies, but also the costs of a nation's lost opportunities in trade and investment and the political fallout for leaders who would have to handle a series of quagmires. If preventive diplomacy does not become quietly incorporated into regular foreign policy practices and thus averts more such crises, then each time even a small but bloody war erupts, U.S. and other major powers' leaders would be challenged by questions about putting lives at risk in peacekeeping or peace enforcement operations, even though the prolonging of such wars would damage their countries' interest and values.

A second factor that will affect further progress is whether policymakers are confident that preventive diplomacy actually works. Skeptics say the case is based on hope rather than performance. No one can know exactly when possible conflicts will erupt, or what to do, they say. Since prevention is probably more difficult and costly than its proponents claim, and frequently has unintended consequences, it may not be feasible at a price that appears reasonable enough to engender the needed political will.

This critique is moot if aimed at the many measures that international organizations and governments already have in place to avert troubles they were convinced would otherwise arise in the future, for example, efforts to control the superpowers' nuclear arsenal and to prevent interstate wars in the Americas or Western Europe. The number of wars that still happen do not prove that none of these past efforts have reduced the total that otherwise would have occurred. Indeed, if various mechanisms for conflict prevention were not already operating at many levels—from the remotest village to the UN Plaza—more of the world would be engulfed in the legendary war of all against all. But the special preventive efforts of past eras are today incorporated in the ordinary workings of both national politics and international diplomacy. Because we rarely hear about instances when prevention works, however, while news from the unprevented wars is rife, the case for preventive diplomacy is hampered by its being a victim of its own occasional successes.

The skepticism can pertain, however, to new kinds of conflicts and those in regions that lie outside of current prevention safety nets, as well as to instances when these nets unravel. The turmoil in weak, democratizing African regimes and the security uneasiness among many Asian states may now lie on this frontier. Even in these vulnerable regions, however, prevention efforts are not unknown, and some countries appear to have avoided violent escalations. Thus, the essential question is not whether preventive diplomacy works at all, but what conditions and elements make it effective.

Methodical research has begun to identify the ingredients present in cases of prevention success and absent in failures. Not all conflicts are preventable, especially when highly organized parties are bent on covertly provoking crises or projecting armed force. But preventive diplomacy may make a difference when: a) substantial carrots and sticks are brought to bear before one or more disputant has whipped up a militant political constituency or actually deployed armed force on the ground; b) disputants display give-and-take and avoid unilateral, provocative actions that worsen tensions and discourage compromise; c) international, multitracked strategies address the several sources of potential violence, such as immediate threats to physical security, intercommunal distrust, or the absence of workable processes to engage parties in dispute management; and d) neighboring states and extraregional powers actively support or at least tolerate a peaceful resolution process, rather than undermine it through political or military support to one or other side.

So is further preventive diplomacy likely? Despite recent steps by the United Nations, the OSCE, the United States, and others toward more comprehensive early warning and preventive responses, one strong possibility is that preventive diplomacy in the vulnerable countries and regions will continue to be mostly episodic, decentralized, and half-hearted—except, we may at least hope, for the large-scale dangers. For some time, potentially violent national disputes might still be left largely to particular countries' shaky political institutions, and, initially, most interstate disputes might still be left to whatever bilateral dealings they initiate. Only occasionally and tangentially, where they take a keen interest in specific places, will the major powers respond to most national situations at precrisis stages with concerted preventive initiatives or even support for local, regional, and NGO efforts. Where major international third parties do not respond early, regional powers and other country or nongovernmental efforts may fill in some of the gaps.

It is also possible, however, that significant incremental advances will be made toward institutionalizing wider-ranging, regular monitoring of potential crises, disseminating that information, and mobilizing third-party coalitions or multilateral institutions to respond. Despite the insularizing domestic forces currently shaping the most influential nations' views of their interests, several latent domestic constituencies might be attracted to international conflict prevention "insurance policies" that offer at low cost to keep future disputes from becoming deadly, tragic, costly, and risky imbroglios. These constituencies include budget-conscious military establishments wishing to avoid further peacekeeping burdens, crisis-exhausted private relief and development organizations, financial investors interested in young markets, and politicians and citizens weary of watching moral tragedies and debating military quagmires. Astute statesmen, like their forerunners in past eras, might still discern the gains for their nations of collaborating with other governments and international organizations to address incipient violent conflicts sooner rather than later.

MICHAEL S. LUND

See also Humanitarian Intervention and Relief; Nongovernmental Organizations; United Nations

FURTHER READING

Boudreau, Thomas. *Sheathing the Sword: The UN Secretary General and the Prevention of International Conflict.* New York, 1991.

Chayes, Abram, and Antonia Handler Chayes, eds. *Preventing Conflict in the Post-Communist World: Mobilizing International and Regional Organizations.* Washington, D.C., 1996.

Claude, Inis L., Jr. *Swords into Plowshares: The Problems and Progress of International Organizations,* 4th ed. New York, 1984.

Craig, Gordon, and Alexander George. *Force and Statecraft: Diplomatic Problems of Our Time,* 2nd ed. Oxford, 1990.

Evans, Gareth. *Cooperating for Peace: The Global Agenda for the 90's and Beyond.* New York, 1993.

Lund, Michael. *Preventing Violent Conflicts: A Strategy for Preventive Diplomacy.* Washington D.C., 1996.

Miall, Hugh. *The Peacemakers: Peaceful Settlement of Disputes Since 1945.* New York, 1992.

Munuera, Gabriel. *Preventing Armed Conflict in Europe: Lessons From Recent Experience,* Chaillot Paper 15/16. Paris, 1994.

Rostow, Eugene. *A Breakfast for Bonaparte: US National Security Interests from the Heights of Abraham to the Nuclear Age.* Washington, D.C., 1992.

United Nations, Secretary-General. *Agenda for Peace: Preventive Diplomacy, Peacemaking and Peace-Keeping.* New York, 1992.

United Nations. *Handbook on the Peaceful Settlement of Disputes Between States.* New York, 1992.

PRIVATEERING

The use of privately-owned, civilian-armed vessels commissioned by a government or revolutionary group to capture merchant vessels and warships of an enemy power. Privateering in the age of sail was a favorite recourse of a weak naval power, such as the United States during the American Revolution and War of 1812 with Great Britain. The owners and crews of privateers were not paid by the government, but hoped for and often gained huge profit by dividing the value of captured enemy ships and property. Thus, privateering was naval war by private enterprise. Mariners in the English colonies during the wars with France in the seventeenth and eighteenth centuries engaged frequently and profitably in privateering, especially against merchant vessels in the Caribbean. In turn, however, such privateers often suffered capture by the French. During the American Revolution, American privateers, operating out of French ports, inflicted far more damage on British shipping than did the rudimentary Continental Navy and state navies. Privateers, especially those operating out of Baltimore, became active again in the War of 1812.

The U.S. Constitution recognized privateering in the clause conferring on Congress the power "To declare War, grant Letters of Marque and Reprisal, and make Rules concerning Captures on Land and Water" ("letters of marque and reprisal" being the technical term for commissions to privateers). In order to receive the value of captured property, the owner of a privateer had to submit the "prize" to judicial decision—a federal district court in the United States. Privateering could on occasion blend with piracy, especially during turbulent situations, such as Latin American Wars for Independence, where different groups claimed governmental authority. The crews of privateers, having developed a taste for plunder, were often rather indiscriminate in their targets.

Large naval powers with vulnerable merchant fleets considered privateering an abomination. Accordingly, in the Declaration of Paris of 1856, following the British lead, the European governments banned privateering. The United States rejected the declaration, preferring to retain the right of commissioning privateers as an inexpensive form of warfare. The right, however, was never exercised. In the twentieth century privateering disappeared entirely, although merchant vessels were armed for defense in World Wars I and II.

GADDIS SMITH

See also Piracy

FURTHER READING

Chidsey, Donald B. *The American Privateers.* New York, 1962.
Hepburn, Andrew. *Letter of Marque.* Boston, 1959.
Maclay, Edgar S. *A History of American Privateers.* New York, 1899, 1967.
Stivers, Reuben E. *Privateers and Volunteers: The Men and Women of Our Reserve Naval Forces.* Annapolis, Md., 1975.

PRIZE CASES

See International Law; Supreme Court and Judiciary

PROHIBITION

(1919–1933)

The movement within the United States to prohibit the production, sale, and consumption of intoxicating beverages. The prohibition movement had a long history within the United States and had its roots from a variety of different sources. Religious, economic, social, and political arguments were advanced in favor of establishing prohibition. While a number of social movements, the Prohibition political party, and various groups supported prohibition, the role of the Progressive Movement, the Anti-Saloon League of America, and the Woman's Christian Temperance Union (WCTU) were perhaps the major participants in the effort to enact prohibition into law. Several states had enacted bans on liquor prior to the twentieth century, but prohibition gained its greatest support during the first two decades of the twentieth century. After prolonged pressure from the Anti-Saloon League, a constitutional amendment on prohibition that outlawed "the manufacture, sale, or transportation of intoxicating liquors" within the United States was passed by Congress and submitted to the states by the end of 1917. The proposed constitutional amendment was ultimately rejected by only three states and became the Eighteenth Amendment to the Constitution on 16 January 1920. The Volstead Act, passed in mid-1919, actually put the restrictions of the Eighteenth Amendment into effect throughout the United States.

From the onset of prohibition, resistance occurred and enforcement was spotty. Alcohol was smuggled in from Canada, where national prohibition lasted only from 1917 to 1919, and from Caribbean islands. Once the United States entered World War I, the argument that using grain for producing alcoholic beverages was "unpatriotic" added to support for prohibition. Ultimately, as opposition grew, calls were made for the repeal of prohibition, which was finally accomplished with the passage of the Twenty-first Amendment to the Constitution in 1933 and its ratification by the states within that same year. As a result, prohibition across the nation as a whole was lifted, but the right of states to impose prohibition was retained by this amendment. While some states or portions of states remained "dry," prohibition was eventually abandoned across almost the entire nation.

JAMES M. MCCORMICK

See also Constitution

FURTHER READING

Sinclair, Andrew. *Prohibition: The Era of Excess*. Boston, 1962.
Timberlake, James H. *Prohibition and the Progressive Movement: 1900–1920*. Cambridge, Mass., 1963.

PROPAGANDA

The technique and product of a deliberate effort, usually by a government, to influence domestic or foreign public opinion for special objectives—for example, to instill admiration for one nation or hatred for another. Although the term has pejorative connotations of manipulation, deceit, and lying, propaganda is also the dissemination of truth, generally called information; it can also consist of half-truths and falsehoods, known as disinformation. Propaganda can be overt, or "white," in which case the source is fully identified, or it can be covert, or "black," in which case the source is hidden or falsely ascribed. Moreover, propaganda can rely on censorship of the press as a means to conceal information and thereby influence public opinion.

Because the term "propaganda" has acquired such negative connotations, there are several euphemisms for it. In the United States the foreign policy establishment favors the phrase "public diplomacy" to describe U.S. attempts to influence foreign governments and peoples through such channels as cultural exchanges, academic scholarship programs, and overseas libraries. The U.S. Army abandoned the use of the word "propaganda" as early as World War I, substituting instead "psychological warfare," thereby equating it with economic and military warfare.

Although the use of propaganda is ancient, international propaganda first became widespread in the twentieth century. As the demands of war mobilization increased, greater numbers of people were swept up into a nation's war effort. This necessitated the support of citizens who had formerly been ignored. In World War I governments began conducting propaganda warfare against enemy, neutral, and friendly nations, using posters, leaflets, speakers, and newspaper stories. New technologies, such as the airplane, allowed the military to drop leaflets across enemy lines, while film made its debut as a propaganda tool. By World War II the discovery of the long-distance properties of short-wave radio made it a particularly valuable weapon of psychological warfare.

More recent additions to the arsenal of propaganda include satellite-relayed broadcasting (both television and radio), videocassettes, and the Internet computer network.

The United States launched its first major international propaganda during World War I when President Woodrow Wilson created the Committee on Public Information (CPI). Although most of its efforts were spent on encouraging Americans to support the war at home, an overseas branch sought to influence enemy, allied, and neutral nations. The U.S. Army Military Intelligence Division created a psychological warfare subsection and leafleted German soldiers to undermine enemy combat morale. President Franklin D. Roosevelt authorized first the Office of the Coordinator of Information (COI) and then the Overseas Branch of the Office of War Information (OWI) to communicate with enemy, neutral, and friendly nations. The OWI printed posters, published magazines, filmed movies, created leaflets, organized libraries, wrote newspapers, and, most critically, broadcast over the newly created (1942) government radio station, the Voice of America (VOA). While the OWI generated "white" propaganda, the Office of Strategic Services (OSS) produced "black" propaganda. Nelson Rockefeller oversaw propaganda to Latin America through the Office of the Coordinator of Inter-American Affairs.

At the conclusion of the war, President Harry S. Truman dissolved both the OWI and the OSS, placing the VOA within the Department of State. In 1947 the president created the Central Intelligence Agency (CIA), which took over the job of covert propaganda; six years later President Dwight D. Eisenhower established the United States Information Agency (USIA), with control over the VOA and public diplomacy. In 1949 the CIA, acting through the National Committee for a Free Europe, initiated a broadcasting station directed toward Eastern Europe—Radio Free Europe (RFE). Two years later the CIA-front American Committee for Freedom for the Peoples of the USSR, Inc., created Radio Liberty (RL). Collectively they became known as RFE/RL, or "the radios." Whereas the VOA was chartered to broadcast news of the United States around the world, RFE/RL transmitted news of Eastern Europe or the Soviet Union back into those countries. By the 1980s all three broadcasters had become overt, white propaganda organizations, transmitting news and information to their target areas with an effort to adhere to strict codes of journalism. Thus, the VOA Charter of 1976 required, for example, two independent sources for every news story. In 1985 Congress established Radio Martí, and in 1991 added Television Martí, as broadcasters designed to undermine Fidel Castro's regime in Cuba.

As there has been an extension of technologies that can carry propaganda overseas and of government agencies interested in doing so, there has also been a growth in targeted audiences. In World War I the CPI had offices in friendly and neutral nations as well as enemy countries. All were in Europe. In World War II the OWI directed its propaganda to enemy, Allied, and neutral nations (with the exception of the Soviet Union), and to nations and colonies all over the world.

During the Cold War the issues of propaganda became more complex, as the number of nations targeted by U.S. propaganda expanded. Eisenhower encouraged the growth of the CIA, for which covert propaganda became an integral part in its campaign against global communism. In 1954 the CIA created a covert radio station to advocate the overthrow of Jacobo Arbenz Gúzman in Guatemala. In 1958 the CIA set up a series of black radio stations in the Middle East to counter Egyptian Radio Cairo. During the Bay of Pigs invasion of 1961 the CIA set up a radio station called "Radio Swan" to broadcast disinformation as the Voice of the Revolutionary Council of Cuba, falsely proclaiming that the Cuban army had been routed and calling upon the people of Cuba to rise up and join the "soldiers of the liberation army."

The target audience of each propaganda campaign differs, although over time that audience has grown to encompass most of the world. Nevertheless, U.S. propaganda organizations do not necessarily speak in unison. In the case of the Bay of Pigs, for example, the Voice of America refused to support the CIA and Radio Swan and broadcast the news as honestly as it could. There was no constant definition of key target audiences during the Cold War, as is evidenced by the shifting language services of the Voice of America during the Cold War. (RFE/RL language services remained relatively stable due to their more focused mission). At the end of the 1940s the VOA broadcast in forty-one languages; during the 1950s it broadcast in fifty-four languages. The number diminished in the 1960s and 1970s, and rose again during the 1980s. This increase in languages reflected globalization of the Cold War during the 1950s, and the consequent interest in broadcasting in the 1950s in Gujarati to India, Telegu to the Philippines, and Tatar to central Asia, to name just a few language services that existed during that decade and were then eliminated in the 1960s.

The endurance of RFE/RL and the addition of the special service of Radio and Television Martí for Cuba reflects the core target areas of the Cold War. Congress has repeatedly considered adding a special service to Asia, but to date has not done so. Moreover, attention to audiences in communist nations has not precluded propaganda to friendly countries. During the 1980s the Voice of America established VOA Europe, targeting the youth of Europe. U.S. propaganda changed with the end of the Cold War. In the case of the Gulf War of 1990–1991, the United States had a clear enemy, Iraq, and the goal of military victory. The U.S. military censored the news media to control the flow of news from the battlefront. In this case, the primary goal of censorship was control over domestic opinion, which had the secondary effect of influencing global opinion through the U.S. domestic news media. In earlier examples, the British cut the German transatlantic cable lines during World War I and censored and rewrote all U.S. news reports. The British used censorship as a propaganda tool again in World War II but less effectively. Gulf War news demonstrated, moreover, that the Anglo-American news organizations dominated the international flow of news. The Gulf War also boosted continued support for government-owned-and-operated international broadcasting operations. In 1994 the total U.S. nonmilitary budget for all these operations combined, including construction costs for new transmitters, reached $562,274,000.

The post–Cold War goals and purposes of U.S. propaganda nonetheless reflected a more general confusion over general U.S. foreign policy goals. Coupled with a growing determination to streamline government operations, the end of the Cold War produced some concern over the future of government international broadcasting. At the same time new technologies created new possibilities in the field of propaganda, especially videotapes, as used by the Kuwaitis during the Gulf War, and the Internet, which was only beginning to be explored in the mid-1990s.

Despite all the effort and money expended on propaganda since World War I, there is little agreement about its effectiveness. Scholars continue to debate the ability of externally manipulated symbols to alter deeply held political convictions. As Major Edward Alexander Powell wrote immediately after World War I, evaluating the impact of external propaganda was like assessing artillery fire—it happened on the other side of the line "where visibility was poor."

HOLLY COWAN SHULMAN

See also Central Intelligence Agency; Cold War; Committee on Public Information; Journalism and Foreign Policy; Office of Strategic Services; United States Information Agency; Radio Free Europe and Radio Liberty; Radio Martí; Voice of America; World War I; World War II

FURTHER READING

Lasswell, Harold D. *Propaganda Technique in the World War*. New York, 1927.
Shulman, Holly. *The Voice of America: Propaganda and Democracy, 1941–1945*. Madison, Wisc., 1990.
Taylor, Philip M. *War and Media: Propaganda and Persuasion in the Gulf War*. Manchester, Eng., 1992.
Winkler, Alan. *The Politics of Propaganda: The Office of War Information, 1942–1945*. New Haven, Conn., 1978.

PROTECTIONISM
See Tariffs; Reciprocal Trade Agreements Act

PUBLIC LAW 480
See Food for Peace

PUBLIC OPINION

Term referring, most generally, to the aggregate of individual opinions on issues of public interest. Questions about the sources, nature, and impact of public opinion, however, have given rise to spirited debates among philosophers and statesmen as well as historians and political scientists. Many of these questions are at the center of persisting debates between liberal and realist perspectives on foreign affairs. A long liberal tradition, dating back at least to Immanuel Kant and Jeremy Bentham and through Woodrow Wilson, asserts that democracies are the most peaceful form of government, at least in part because the public can play a constructive role in constraining policymakers. Alternatively, Alexis de Tocqueville and other realists have been intensely skeptical of the public because the effective conduct of diplomacy requires speed, secrecy, flexibility, and other qualities that would be seriously jeopardized were the public, whose preferences are allegedly driven by emotions and short-term considerations, to have a significant role.

The long-standing debate between liberals and realists was intensified by World War I, the first public relations war. President Wilson's hopes for a postwar world order depended significantly on democratizing foreign affairs. Elihu Root, a former secretary of state, summarized the position of those who welcomed an increasing role for the public. "When foreign offices were ruled by autocracies or oligarchies the danger of war was in sinister purpose. When foreign affairs are ruled by democracies the danger of war will be in mistaken beliefs." By more effective international education, "the people themselves will have the means to test misinformation and appeals to prejudice and passion based on error."

Not all observers joined Wilson and Root in applauding the prospect of popular diplomacy. In two trenchant critiques of classical liberalism, the journalist Walter Lippmann argued that the common man is too fully engaged in attending to his everyday needs to have the time or inclination to satisfy the heroic assumptions about the informed and engaged citizen celebrated in democratic theory. Moreover, Lippmann became increasingly skeptical about the ability of his own profession to effectively fill in the gap between the real world and the average citizen's stereotypes. The events of the 1930s and the outbreak of World War II, which seemed to raise serious questions about Wilsonian assumptions while apparently providing compelling confirmation for the realist approach, further tipped the balance of the debate on public opinion and foreign policy in favor of the skeptics.

The Post–World War II Consensus on Public Opinion

The period encompassing World War II and its aftermath coincided with the inception of scientific public opinion polling. The availability of survey data and the assumption of a leadership role in world affairs by the United States stimulated a growth industry in analyses of public opinion. The consensus that developed during the two decades between the end of World War II and the Vietnam escalation centered on three major propositions: (1) public opinion is highly volatile and thus it provides very dubious foundations for a sound foreign policy; (2) public attitudes on foreign affairs are so lacking in structure and coherence that they might best be described as "non-attitudes;" however, (3) at the end of the day, public opinion has a very limited impact on the conduct of foreign policy.

In his pioneering study, *The American People and Foreign Policy* (1950), Gabriel Almond drew on survey data to buttress his concerns about a relapse in the United States into mindless isolationism. He portrayed public opinion as a volatile and mood-driven constraint upon foreign policy: "Perhaps the gravest general problem confronting policy-makers is that of the instability of mass moods, the cyclical fluctuations which stand in the way of policy stability." Lippmann, by the 1950s a widely read columnist, echoed this theme. Depicting the mass public as a powerful and volatile force that constituted a threat to effective foreign policies Lippmann argued "the unhappy truth is that the prevailing public opinion has been destructively wrong at the critical junctures." "Mass opinion has acquired mounting power in this country. It has shown itself to be a dangerous master of decision when the stakes are life and death." Similarly pessimistic conclusions and dire warnings were emerging from other quarters as well, including the respected U.S. diplomatic historian, Thomas A. Bailey; the foremost proponent of a realist approach to international affairs, Hans J. Morgenthau; and George F. Kennan, the diplomat and historian who has often been depicted as the intellectual father of the U.S. policy of containment. Fears of the public led to some proposals to reduce its influence, with Lippmann calling for stronger executive prerogatives in foreign affairs, and Bailey suggesting that it might be necessary for the executive deliberately to mislead the public.

A growing volume of data on public opinion and voting behavior enabled analysts not only to describe aggregate results and trends but also to delve into the structure of political beliefs. In a study based on data from the late

MOST IMPORTANT PROBLEM - SELECTED RECENT TRENDS
What do you think is the most important problem facing this country today?
(Up to three mentions recorded)

	Jan 28–30 1994	Aug 15–16 1994	Jan 16–18 1995	Jul 7–9 1995	Jan 12–15 1996	May 9–12 1996
Economic problems	42%	30%	44%	39%	54%	48%
Unemployment/jobs	17	6	15	12	11	13
Federal budget deficit	8	3	14	11	26	15
Economy in general	17	17	10	9	14	12
Taxes	2	1	5	5	6	7
High cost of living/inflation	1	2	2	1	1	4
Trade relations/deficit	2	1	1	2	1	2
Recession	*	1	0	*	*	*
The budget	-	-	-	-	2	0
Government shutdown	-	-	-	-	2	-
Other specific economic	1	1	3	3	-	3
Non-economic problems	85	86	76	80	79	82
Crime/violence	49	52	27	25	18	25
Health care	31	29	12	7	10	10
Welfare	6	3	12	11	9	10
Poverty/homelessness	9	5	10	9	10	7
Drugs	8	9	6	10	9	10
Ethics/morality/family decline	5	7	6	10	10	14
Dissatisfaction gov't	3	5	5	10	17	12
Education	6	5	5	8	9	13
Youth	-	-	3	2	*	-
International issues/foreign affairs	3	4	2	3	6	4
Foreign aid/focus overseas	1	2	2	3	5	4
Medicare/Social Security	1	1	2	3	8	5
Racism/racial relations	1	1	2	2	4	2
Immigration/illegal aliens	1	2	1	3	1	6
AIDS	1	2	1	1	1	*
Environment	2	1	1	1	2	3
Abortion	-	1	1	1	*	0
National defense	-	-	1	1	1	0
Guns/gun control	3	1	*	1	*	0
Bosnia	-	-	-	-	3	0
Judicial system/lawyers	-	-	-	2	-	-
Other non-economic	11	5	10	8	15	7
No opinion	*	2	2	4	3	7
	189%	169%	161%	168%	204%	195%

*Less than 0.5%

Source: The Gallup Poll News Service

1950s and early 1960s, Philip Converse concluded that the political beliefs of the mass public lack any underlying ideological structure that might provide some coherence to political thinking. Thus mass political beliefs are best described as "non-attitudes." Other voting studies came to similar conclusions about the absence of structure, coherence, or persistence in the political beliefs of the mass public—especially on foreign affairs.

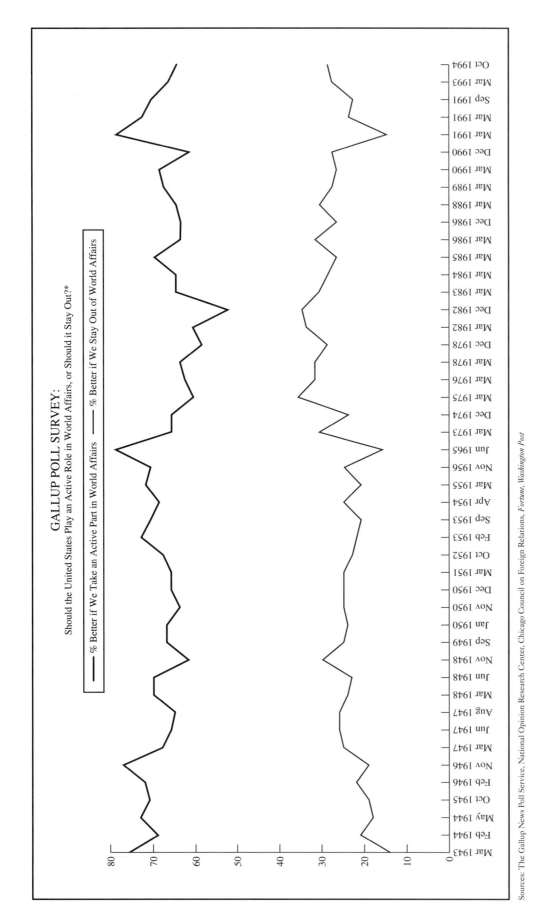

GALLUP POLL SURVEY:

Should the United States Play an Active Role in World Affairs, or Should it Stay Out?*

——— % Better if We Take an Active Part in World Affairs   ——— % Better if We Stay Out of World Affairs

Sources: The Gallup News Poll Service, National Opinion Research Center, Chicago Council on Foreign Relations, *Fortune, Washington Post*

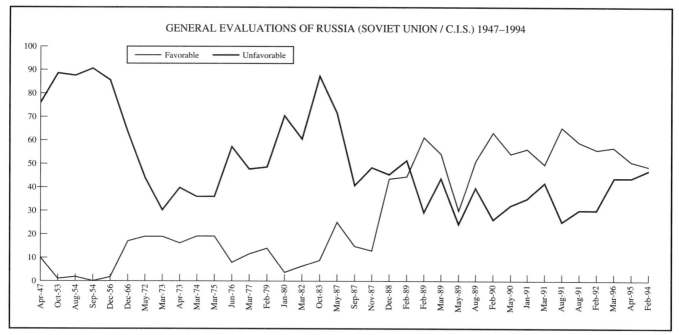

GENERAL EVALUATIONS OF RUSSIA (SOVIET UNION / C.I.S.) 1947–1994

Sources: The Gallup News Poll Service, National Opinion Research Center, General Social Survey, *Los Angeles Times*, *CBS/New York Times*, *ABC/Washington Post*

Impact on Foreign Policy

Interest in public opinion on foreign affairs arises from the assumption that at least some of the time it has an impact, for better or worse, on policy. Indeed, the driving force behind much of the post–World War II attention to public opinion was the fear that an ill-informed and emotional public would serve as a powerful constraint establishing unwise limits on policymakers, creating unrealistic expectations about what was feasible in foreign affairs, and otherwise doing serious mischief to U.S. diplomacy.

By the 1960s a consensus seemed to emerge on a third point: Public opinion has little impact on policy. Or, as one Department of State official put it: "To hell with public opinion....We should lead, and not follow." The weight of evidence cast doubt on the potency of public opinion as a driving force behind, or even a significant constraint upon, foreign policy decisions. An analysis of the public-legislator relationship revealed that constituents' attitudes on foreign policy had less impact on members of Congress than did their views on domestic issues. Another study revealed that Department of State officials had little interest in public opinion, and to the extent that they even thought about the public, it was as an entity to be "educated" rather than a lodestar by which to be guided. The president was widely seen as having "almost a free hand" in the conduct of foreign affairs.

Just as World War II and fears of postwar isolationism gave rise to concern about public opinion and its impact on foreign policy, the Vietnam War stimulated a re-examination of the consensus that had emerged during the previous two decades. Most broadly, many of those who had believed that a strong executive hand on the tiller of public policy, relatively free from the vagaries of public moods, best serves both national interests and global stability, came to re-examine their views in the light of the Vietnam War. At a narrower level, some analysts became increasingly persuaded that existing surveys distorted public attitudes toward the war by posing excessively restrictive and simplistic questions. The conflict in Southeast Asia thus stimulated independent surveys designed specifically to assess foreign policy attitudes in greater depth and breadth. Armed with growing archives of data generated by the major polling organizations, as well as with evidence produced by the independent surveys, analysts have begun to challenge the consensus described above.

John Mueller's study of public opinion during the Korean and Vietnam wars, *War, Presidents and Public Opinion* (1973), posed a major challenge to the thesis of mindless changes in public attitudes. To be sure, public support for the U.S. war effort in both conflicts eventually declined, but it did so in ways that seemed explicable and rational. Increasing public opposition to the conflicts coincided with rising battle deaths, suggesting that the public used an understandable, if simple, guideline to assess U.S. policy.

The most comprehensive challenge to the thesis of public volatility emerged from studies that included more than 6,000 questions that have been posed since the 1930s. In *The Rational Public: Fifty Years of Trends in Americans' Policy Preferences* (1992), Benjamin Page and Robert Shapiro found that public opinion in the aggregate is in fact characterized by a considerable stability on both foreign policy and domestic issues. More importantly, when attitude shifts take place, they appear to be "reasonable, event-driven" reactions to the real world, even if the information upon which they are based is marginally adequate. Virtually all the rapid shifts in public opinion were related to political and economic circumstances or to significant events that sensible citizens would take into account. A variant of the "rational public" thesis stipulated that the public attempted to moderate U.S. behavior toward the USSR by expressing preferences for a conciliatory stance from hawkish administrations, while supporting more assertive policies from dovish ones. This study, by Miroslav Nincic, further challenged the thesis of mindless volatility for it identified the public as a source of moderation and continuity rather than of instability and unpredictability.

None of these challenges to the earlier consensus was based on newly found evidence that the public is in fact well informed about foreign affairs. This gives rise to a puzzle: If a poorly informed mass public does indeed react to international affairs in an events-driven, rational manner, what are the means that permit it to do so?

Although recent research has yet to yield a consensus, there appears to be growing evidence for two general points relating to belief structure. (1) Although the general public may be rather poorly informed, attitudes about foreign affairs are in fact structured in at least moderately coherent ways. Even in the absence of much factual knowledge, members of the mass public use some superordinate beliefs to make some sense of an increasingly complex world. (2) A single isolationist-to-internationalist dimension inadequately describes the main dimensions of public opinion.

The Importance of Public Opinion

Among the most important questions about public opinion are: To what extent, on what kinds of issues, and under what circumstances, if any, does public opinion have an impact on public policy? What are the means by which public attitudes make their impact felt by decision-makers? These are also difficult questions, for the ability to answer them is not materially enhanced by the many technical improvements that have characterized recent public opinion research: better sampling designs, greater attention to construction of questions, and more sophisticated statistical models to analyze the data.

Most post–World War II presidents have followed Theodore Roosevelt in thinking that the White House is a "bully pulpit," whether it is used to "scare the hell out of them" in order gain support for aid to Greece and Turkey in 1947 (Harry Truman), to warn against the dangers of "unwarranted influence, whether sought or unsought, by the military-industrial complex" in 1961

(Dwight Eisenhower), or to drum up support for assistance to the Contras in Nicaragua during the 1980s (Ronald Reagan), or to gain approval of the agreements on the North American Free Trade Agreement (NAFTA) and World Trade Organization. Such efforts have clearly not been equally successful.

The more difficult question concerns influence in the other direction. Did public impatience lead the administration of President Jimmy Carter to embark on the ill-fated effort to free U.S. hostages in Iran, or the administration of President Reagan to withdraw U.S. Marines from Lebanon? Did President John F. Kennedy genuinely believe that he would be impeached should he fail to force removal of Soviet missiles from Cuba, as he told his brother, or was he merely seeking to bolster decisions arrived at that had nothing to do with public opinion? Perhaps a more telling example from the Caribbean confrontation emerges from a crucial White House meeting on the day before the crisis was resolved peacefully. Kennedy was apparently prepared to accept a compromise—withdrawal of the Soviet missiles in exchange for removal of U.S. missiles in Turkey—and he would have done so largely because it would have been hard to explain to the public why such an arrangement had been rejected.

Some other anecdotal evidence may also be suggestive, but it hardly offers irrefutable answers to the question of public influence on policy. Franklin D. Roosevelt was the first president to make extensive use of public opinion data, and all recent administrations have employed public opinion professionals. The detailed accounts written by some of these analysts about how their expertise and data were used suggest that the mass public is not viewed merely as an essentially malleable lump that can readily be molded through public relations activities.

More systematic studies have also challenged the theory that policymakers are relatively free agents on foreign policy because these issues pose few dangers of electoral retribution by voters; elections are largely decided by domestic issues. A study by John Aldrich and his colleagues of presidential campaigns between 1952 and 1984 revealed that foreign policy issues had "large effects" in five of the nine elections. Voting studies have also shown the importance of retrospective evaluations of performance, especially when one of the candidates is an incumbent. Because voters are believed to punish incumbent candidates or parties for foreign policy failures, as in the Iran hostage episode, or reward them for success, as in the invasion of Grenada, decisions by foreign policy leaders may be made in anticipation of public reactions and the probabilities of success or failure.

Finally, two major studies have measured the congruence between changes in public preferences and policy decisions over extended periods. An analysis by Alan Monroe revealed that in almost two-thirds of 222 cases, spanning the years 1960–1974, policy outcomes corresponded to public preferences. The consistency was especially high on foreign policy issues. In their study, Page and Shapiro included 357 significant changes of public preferences between 1935 and 1979. Of the 231 instances of subsequent domestic and foreign policy changes, 153 (sixty-six percent) were congruent with changes in public preferences.

Although correlational analyses can contribute to understanding the relationship between opinion and policy they do not necessarily rule out other explanations. If foreign policy decisions are correlated with public preferences, policymakers might be responding to pressures and constraints from the international system—as realist theorists insist that they should—without any significant attention to public sentiments. Alternatively, the direction of causality might run from policymakers to the public rather than vice versa, as depicted by critics who describe the public as the victims of elite manipulation. This second interpretation loses potency when opinion change precedes policy change. However, we should not rule out still another possibility: the administration manipulates events and the events, now part of the information available to the public, result in opinion change, followed by policy changes that are congruent with opinions. A variant of this sequence is the "rally 'round the president" hypothesis, according to which the executive may manipulate the public indirectly by undertaking external initiatives and responding to events abroad in a manner calculated to increase his popularity with domestic constituents.

Nor is it easy to establish that public opinion is a constraint on action. The Reagan administration undertook a massive public relations campaign of dubious legality during the 1980s to generate public support for assistance to the Contras in Nicaragua, but surveys revealed that a majority of the public consistently opposed U.S. military involvement in Central America. Would the Reagan administration have intervened more directly or massively in Nicaragua or El Salvador in the absence of such attitudes? Solid evidence about contemporary nonevents is rather hard to come by. Even archival evidence may not provide definitive answers. Does an absence of references to public opinion indicate a lack of interest by decision-makers? Alternatively, was attention to public attitudes so deeply ingrained in their working habits that it was unnecessary to make constant references to it? Are frequent references to public opinion an indication of a significant impact on decisions—or of a desire on the part of officials to be "on record" as having paid attention to public sentiments?

Since World War II

It is difficult to summarize briefly the results of hundreds of surveys during the latter half of the twentieth century, but several salient features of public opinion do stand out.

First, fears that the public would turn isolationist after World War II proved unfounded. During the post-Vietnam period there was, to be sure, a diminished enthusiasm for internationalism, but the proportion of those supporting an active U.S. role in world affairs never fell below fifty percent. A further distinction needs to be drawn between two forms of internationalism. "Liberal" or "cooperative" internationalists support such institutions as the United Nations as well as programs designed to deal with international economic, social, and environmental threats. In contrast, "conservative" or "militant" internationalists focus primarily on military threats and support alliances, military aid, and similar security-oriented instruments of policy. During the early years of the Cold War, those who supported one form of internationalism also tended to favor the other, but that has been much less true during the past two decades, both among leaders and among the general public.

Second, military interventions have rarely aroused a great deal of anticipatory public enthusiasm, but once such action is undertaken there is often a short-term increase in support. This was true of the U.S. interventions in Korea in 1950 and in Vietnam during the following decade. Public support for the Korean War eroded as a result of a bloody stalemate near the 38th parallel and rising casualties, but opposition to that conflict did not spill over to other security commitments such as to Japan or the North Atlantic Treaty Organization (NATO). In contrast, as public opposition to the Vietnam War increased, many critics also questioned the premises of all U.S. international commitments. The traumatic Vietnam experience has also tended to dominate the terms of public debates—by means of the so-called "lessons of Vietnam"—on issues that might involve sending armed forces abroad. Opponents of intervention have drawn cautionary parallels between Vietnam and Central America, Angola, Lebanon, Bosnia, and other conflict areas, whereas supporters denounced the "Vietnam syndrome"—that is, blanket opposition to interventions arising from a tendency to view all conflict situations through the lenses of the Vietnam experience—which would prevent the U.S. from protecting its vital interests. The war against Iraq in 1991 was conducted so as to avoid a protracted conflict and large-scale casualties that could be expected to erode public support.

Moreover, survey data do not support charges that the U.S. public is implacably wed to "devil images" of adversaries. Even during the Cold War, periods of thawing relations between Moscow and Washington were usually reflected in moderating attitudes toward the USSR. Well before President Reagan began referring to Mikhail Gorbachev as "my friend" during the late 1980s, there was ample evidence that the general public viewed the Soviet leader in similar terms and the threat of the USSR to U.S. security as rapidly diminishing .

Finally, the public has consistently supported verifiable measures to contain and reverse the arms race. Indeed, the U.S. public has rarely seen an arms control proposal that it did not like, even during such periods as 1979–1982 when it also favored increasing the defense budget. The Second Strategic Arms Limitation Talks and Agreements (SALT II), support for which finally eroded in the face of a powerful public relations campaign against it by the Committee on the Present Danger, appears to be the only exception.

It is customary to distinguish between various strata of the public. Typically a distinction has been drawn between opinion leaders, the informed public, and the mass public. However, before the first of the Chicago Council on Foreign Relations (CCFR) surveys initiated in 1974—followed by similar studies in 1978, 1982, 1986, 1990, and 1994—and the Foreign Policy Leadership Project surveys instituted two years later (1976, 1980, 1984, 1988, 1992, and 1996), systematic information about leadership views on foreign affairs was scarce.

There appear to be similarities in the ways that opinion leaders and the general public structure their political beliefs, despite rather substantial differences in the substance of their opinions. The 1994 CCFR survey illustrates some persistent gaps between opinion leaders and the general public. Leaders overwhelmingly (ninety-eight percent) supported an active U.S. role in world affairs, whereas the general public was more tepid in its enthusiasm (sixty-two percent). Eighty-six percent of the leaders favored economic aid, but only half of the general public did so. When asked to identify the most important foreign policy goals, the top four items for leaders had an overwhelmingly international character: preventing nuclear proliferation, energy security, defending allies, and maintenance of military superiority. The comparable list for the general public included issues with a significant domestic dimension: stopping the flow of illegal drugs into the United States; protecting U.S. jobs; preventing nuclear proliferation; and reducing illegal immigration.

During the early post–World War II years, agreement among prominent leaders of the two major parties contributed to the fact that, among the general public, Democrats and Republicans differed little with respect to internationalist foreign policy undertakings. Since the Vietnam War, sharp partisan differences, reinforced by even deeper ideological cleavages, have characterized the foreign policy beliefs of both opinion leaders and the general public. Ideological-partisan cleavages on domestic issues also tend to reinforce those on foreign policy. A 1948 study found a limited correlation between domestic economic issues and either civil rights or international issues, but during the past two decades the lines of cleavage on domestic and foreign policy issues have increasingly come to overlap, especially among opinion leaders.

The Vietnam War rekindled interest in generational theories of politics. According to some, the war pitted the "Munich generation," which had witnessed the bitter consequences of efforts to appease expansionist dictators, against the "Vietnam generation," which argued that the war was an ill-informed effort to apply the "lessons of Munich" to the jungles of Southeast Asia. This explanation has encountered only mixed support, however. There is some evidence of generational differences within the general public, but among opinion leaders the primary lines of cleavage lie within rather than between generations.

Analysts have also explored the impact of other background factors, including gender, occupation, education, military service, travel abroad, and race, but the mutually reinforcing partisan and ideological cleavages have clearly been dominant in recent years, supporting the conclusion drawn by I. M. Destler, Leslie Gelb, and W. Anthony Lake: "For two decades, the making of American foreign policy has been growing far more political—or more precisely, far more partisan and ideological." Whether the end of the Cold War will soften the partisan-ideological chasm remains to be demonstrated.

Stimulated by the Vietnam War, the consensus of the mid-1960s on the nature, structure, and impact of public opinion has clearly come under vigorous challenge. Because much of the evidence cited above has emerged from a period in which foreign affairs were dominated by the Cold War, a new question arises: Will the end of that confrontation alter or even render obsolete our understanding of public opinion and foreign policy? There has been a sea change in public attitudes toward virtually all of the issues that dominated the Cold War era. Indeed, changing public attitudes preceded rather than followed those at the pinnacles of government on such issues as the appropriate level of defense spending, the primary threats to U.S. national security, Mikhail Gorbachev's goals, and the motivations underlying Soviet foreign policy. Because assessments of the USSR played a key role in organizing foreign policy beliefs, will its disintegration result for many in a loss of structure and consequent disorientation about foreign affairs? Alternatively, are the key concepts that structure beliefs about foreign affairs sufficiently generic that they will survive the dramatic international changes of the past decade?

If we are indeed entering into a period of fewer major power confrontations and greater attention to such nonmilitary issues as trade, immigration, and the environment—as many in the United States believe to be the case—it may also be an era in which public opinion plays a more autonomous role. Even those who do not fully accept the "manipulated public" thesis would acknowledge that crises and confrontations abroad increase the opportunities and temptations for manipulation of the public by leaders. Not only are nonstrategic issues typically resolved over a longer time period—providing greater opportunities for the public, interest groups, the media, and Congress to play a significant role—but they also tend to be more resistant to claims that the needs for secrecy, flexibility, speed of action, and access to classified information make it both necessary and legitimate for the executive to have a relatively free hand. In short, the relationship between public opinion and foreign policy may take on an added rather than diminished significance during the post–Cold War period.

OLE R. HOLSTI

See also Elections and Foreign Policy; Lippmann, Walter; Peace Movements and Societies to 1914; Peace Movements and Societies, 1914 to Present

FURTHER READING

Almond, Gabriel. *The American People and Foreign Policy.* New York, 1950.

Americans Talk Security. Compendium: Results from Twelve Surveys on National Security Issues, 1987-1988. Boston, 1989.

Cohen, Bernard C. *The Public's Impact on Foreign Policy.* Boston, 1973.

Hinckley, Ronald H. *People, Polls, and Policymakers.* New York, 1992.

Holsti, Ole R. *Public Opinion and American Foreign Policy.* Ann Arbor, Mich., 1996.

Mayer, William G. *The Changing American Mind: How and Why American Public Opinion Changed Between 1960 and 1988.* Ann Arbor, Mich., 1992.

Mueller, John E. *Policy and Opinion in the Gulf War.* Chicago, 1994.

———. *War, Presidents and Public Opinion.* New York, 1973.

Page, Benjamin I., and Robert Y. Shapiro. *The Rational Public: Fifty Years of Trends in Americans' Policy Preferences.* Chicago, 1992.

Rielly, John E. *American Public Opinion and Foreign Policy 1975.* Chicago, 1975. Also similar surveys in 1979, 1983, 1987, 1991, and 1995.

Russett, Bruce M. *Controlling the Sword: The Democratic Governance of National Security.* Cambridge, Mass., 1990.

Wittkopf, Eugene R. *Faces of Internationalism: Public Opinion and American Foreign Policy.* Durham, N.C., 1990.

Yankelovich, Daniel. *Coming to Public Judgment.* Syracuse, 1991.

Zaller, John R. *The Nature and Origin of Mass Opinion.* New York, 1992.

PUEBLO INCIDENT

(1968)

The seizure of U.S. intelligence ship *Pueblo* and its eighty-three-man crew by North Korean warships on 23 January 1968 in the Sea of Japan, in the vicinity of North Korea's twelve-mile territorial ocean boundary. North Korea justified the capture by claiming *Pueblo* had violated North Korean territorial waters. President Lyndon Johnson contended that the ship was illegally abducted on the high seas. He later observed that the incident preceded the Tet Offensive of January 30, and that it occurred two days after North Korea tried to assassinate South Korean President Park Chung Hee. Johnson concluded that North Korea had sought to divert U. S. and South Korean forces from Vietnam just prior to Tet.

Fearing an enlarged Asia war, however, the president used diplomacy rather than force to handle the crisis. Johnson urged the United Nations Security Council to pass a resolution condemning North Korea's capture of the *Pueblo* and demanding the safe return of ship and crew. He sought negotiations with North Korea through the Soviet Union and various heads of state, but not until December 1968, after *Pueblo* skipper Lloyd Bucher signed a confession that the United States had spied on North Korea, and chief U.S. negotiator Major General Gilbert H. Woodward conceded as much, did North Korea free the badly mistreated crew and the body of one crewman killed during the ship's capture. Although Johnson succeeded in bringing the *Pueblo* captives home, the prolonged and humiliating nature of the affair led some Americans to view his strategy as a failure because this incident contradicted Johnson's claim that communist forces were losing the Vietnam War; it widened the president's perceived credibility gap and contributed to his decision not to seek reelection in 1968. Johnson's diplomatic resolution of the *Pueblo* crisis contrasts with President Gerald Ford's termination of the *Mayaguez* incident of 1975 through use of force, which many Americans hailed as an example of presidential fortitude. But it resembles President Jimmy Carter's policy during the Iran hostage crisis of 1979–80. Iranian and Korean captors alike released their U.S. prisoners only after prolonged negotiations.

DEBORAH KISATSKY

See also Johnson, Lyndon Baines; Korea, Republic of; Vietnam War

FURTHER READING

Armbrister, Trevor. *A Matter of Accountability: The True Story of the Pueblo Affair.* New York, 1970.

Bucher, Lloyd, and Mark Rascovich. *Bucher: My Story.* New York, 1970.

Murphy, Edward R., Jr. *Second in Command: The Uncensored Account of the Capture of the Spy Ship Pueblo.* New York, 1971.

PUERTO RICO

Former Spanish island colony located in the northern Caribbean Sea between the Dominican Republic and the Virgin Islands, formally annexed by the United States through the Treaty of Paris of 1898. The island is 3,435 square miles (less than half the size of New Jersey). Since 1898, continuing ambivalence has characterized relations between Puerto Rico and the United States, which has defined Puerto Rico as a "commonwealth" and has seldom faced squarely "the colonial question." The 3.5 million inhabitants of Puerto Rico (1990) are U.S. citizens, but they are divided over three status options. As results of the 1993 plebiscite show, Puerto Rico contains at present nearly even numbers of pro-statehood and pro-commonwealth supporters (forty-six percent and forty-eight percent, respectively), as well as a respected pro-independence faction (four percent).

Political and Economic Status: 1898–1930s

During the Spanish-American-Cuban-Filipino War, a U.S. military force seized Puerto Rico in July 1898 after brief Spanish resistance. Although the U.S. Senate had declared that the United States would not annex Cuba, no such self-denying ordinance was applied to Puerto Rico. Formal association with the North American giant appeared attractive to Puerto Ricans in 1898 because of close economic and commercial ties and intense admiration for U.S. political institutions. Although immediate military occupation threatened to curtail the degree of autonomy already obtained from Spain, island political leaders mobilized to influence U.S. policy. They insisted on joining the union as a territory, with a view to self-government, if not statehood. They also expected to receive preferential trade treatment. Thus, as early as 1898, political status and economic security had been identified as the two concepts that would dominate discussion between politicians in the United States and Puerto Rico over the terms of their relationship.

The United States approached the issues equivocally. The Foraker Act in 1900 established a civil government composed of a governor (appointed by the president of the United States) and six department heads, all North "Americans." Puerto Ricans achieved representation, if only nominally, in the legislative branch through a council of state composed of six North Americans (the heads of departments) and five Puerto Ricans and an elected chamber of deputies with thirty-five members. Laws originating on the island required the approval of the council of state. In addition, the U.S. Congress was empowered to veto Puerto Rican laws as well as to legislate for the island. The act also installed a supreme court, made up of five judges selected by the U.S. president. In its economic aspects, the Foraker Act temporarily established a fifteen percent duty on commercial transactions between the island and the U.S. mainland as a way of generating revenue to finance local government. By 1901, however, Puerto Rico was included within the U.S. tariff structure, so that island products entered the United States duty-free and non-U.S. goods imported by Puerto Rico were subject to the same taxes collected in U.S. mainland ports.

The Insular Cases (1901–1922) were a succession of Supreme Court cases that determined the status of U.S. outlying possessions and dependencies. Puerto Rico's status became that of an unincorporated territory. In the most notable of these cases, *Downes* v. *Bidwell* (1901), a U.S. firm sued the federal government over the imposition of duties on oranges it had imported from Puerto Rico in 1900. Because tariffs were supposed to be uniform across the country, the firm held, the taxes collected on the oranges were unconstitutional. The Court ruled that, even though Puerto Rico was clearly not a foreign country, Congress had not stipulated that it was anything more than a possession, a territory that belonged to the United States, without forming a part of it. To Puerto Ricans, the message was that they were neither Puerto Ricans nor Americans—for the purposes of trade, citizenship, protection under the law, and participation in government.

The Jones Act of 1917 confirmed this limbo status. Although it granted Puerto Ricans U.S. citizenship (just in time to be drafted for service in World War I, some critics argued), the degree of autonomy they enjoyed was limited. The president of the United States still chose the governor, although some department heads were now Puerto Ricans. The council of state became a consulting body to the governor, with no legislative powers. A senate and a house of representatives would be elected by direct vote, but the U.S. Congress still had the final say on island legislation. It seemed logical, given the indecision that U.S. actions on the island conveyed and the implicit distrust of Puerto Rican capabilities contained in U.S. policy, that the major Puerto Rican political parties in the 1920s coalesced and realigned in an effort to increase their influence in the United States. The Partido Unionista formed around the objective of autonomy; the Partido Republicano pushed for statehood; and the Partido Socialista sought permanent association with the United States.

Meanwhile, Americans made a deliberate effort to bring Puerto Rico within the cultural and economic orbit of the United States. Public schools, established in accordance with the U.S. model, replaced the Spanish educational system, and basic instruction in English began to reach even remote rural areas. U.S. military personnel improved the island's physical infrastructure, initiated public works projects, and developed public health programs. North American products flooded the island, as did investment in banking, light industry, and agriculture. Women joined the work force in large numbers, mostly in cigar factories and textile workshops. The University of Puerto Rico, which remains the most important learning institution on the island, was founded in 1903 with a broad curriculum.

In the 1930s, however, the threat of economic ruin accompanied the island's political uncertainty. In the early decades of the twentieth century, coffee production virtually disappeared, while the U.S.-dominated sugar industry boomed. By the 1930s huge U.S. companies controlled sixty percent of the more than half a million acres planted in cane; most of the now landless agricultural population were employed in the fields and factories and usually only during the harvest. Unemployment rose even more, food became unavailable, and disease spread during the Great Depression. Labor strikes in the sugar industry and among stevedores threatened U.S. economic interests on the island.

Economic and Political Crises: 1930s–1940s

It took the extraordinary energies of two consummate politicians—Franklin D. Roosevelt and Luis Muñoz Marín—to redirect the unrest that enveloped the island. Muñoz Marín was a young poet, journalist, political activist, and the son of Luis Muñoz Rivera, an influential leader in the early decades of the twentieth century. Although openly favoring Puerto Rico's independence, Muñoz Marín also publicly recognized the urgent need to overcome the economic misery that pervaded the island during the Great Depression. Roosevelt, on his part, had entered the presidency of the United States offering the New Deal—increased government intervention to counteract the economic crisis, and for Latin America he promised to be a "good neighbor." Puerto Rico would be a test case.

Muñoz Marín enjoyed the favor of many in Roosevelt's "brain trust," including Rexford Guy Tugwell, who would later serve as the appointed governor of Puerto Rico (1941–1946). The report of a federal commission headed by Carlos Chardón, the chancellor of the University of Puerto Rico, identified the existence of large landholdings, monoculture, and absentee ownership of land as the basic causes of economic distress. It proposed that the island government buy lands that exceeded the 500-acre limit stipulated by law, establish sugar factories, and distribute land not planted in cane for the cultivation of food crops. Some of the plan's provisions proved impossible to implement, but the Puerto Rico Reconstruction Administration (PRRA), a federal agency charged with providing relief for the population and building economic infrastructure for industry, embraced many of the report's ideas. From 1934 to 1937 PRRA built hydroelectric projects, organized a sugar cooperative, established a cement plant, and ran public health programs.

In the meantime, the Nationalist Party had gathered enormous support under the leadership of Pedro Albizu Campus. A brilliant and fiery advocate of independence, Albizu concentrated his energies on identifying the U.S. presence as the cause of Puerto Rico's problems. He organized a paramilitary organization called the Cadets of the Republic and announced his willingness to use violence to end U.S. domination of the island. When chief of police Francis Riggs was assassinated in 1936, two young nationalist sympathizers were arrested and shot to death, at police headquarters, by authorities. Amidst the ensuing wave of protests, Albizu and seven others were tried and found guilty of conspiring to overthrow the government. Albizu remained in federal prison until 1947.

In the U.S. Congress, Senator Millard E. Tydings tried to force the issue of independence by proposing in 1936 an island referendum, whose only choice was an ill-conceived, economically detrimental separation from the United States. Had the referendum been held, Puerto Ricans would have immediately considered independence, at best, economically disadvantageous. On the island, the "massacre of Ponce," a shoot-out in 1937 between government forces and nationalists who insisted on peacefully demonstrating after the mayor had revoked their permit, left nineteen dead and more than 100 wounded. A subsequent federal investigation held that civil rights violations in the preceding nine months had set the stage for the tragic encounter.

In the following years, Muñoz Marín became convinced that the welfare of the Puerto Rican people could best be achieved through permanent association with the United States. He formed the Popular Democratic Party in 1938 under the slogan "Bread, Land, and Liberty." The party received a majority vote in the 1940 elections. In 1948, when Puerto Ricans were empowered to elect their own governor, Muñoz Marín was elected to the highest island office. His victory symbolized that an overwhelming majority of Puerto Ricans desired increased self-government and economic association with the United States and not independence.

Ambivalent Relationship: 1950s–Present

The promise of political autonomy came in 1950 in the form of Public Law 600, which outlined the nature of relations between the United States and Puerto Rico and paved the way for the approval of a constitution in 1952. For Puerto Ricans, the new relationship, which Muñoz Marín labeled the Estado Libre Asociado (free associated state, or commonwealth) in the constitution, was based on the concept of agreement and on the principle of government by consent. Neither in 1950 when Puerto Ricans voted in favor of Public Law 600 by referendum nor on several occasions thereafter, however, has the U.S. Congress given any indication that it will relinquish what it clearly considers to be its absolute authority over Puerto Rico's political future. One of the most heated points of discussion over the terms of a plebiscite held in 1993 to gauge support for each of the three status options was, therefore, whether (or under what conditions) the United States would abide by the island's decisions.

In an effort to modernize the economy after World War II, Muñoz Marín attracted U.S. industrial firms to the island, offering a cheap labor force, lax environmental laws, generous terms of credit, and tax exemption for a number of years. Operation Bootstrap, as this ambitious plan was called, aimed at stabilizing the island's economy by providing employment in manufacturing enterprises. Beginning in the 1950s, firms producing textiles, electrical equipment, chemical derivatives, and pharmaceuticals established operations on the island. As a result, the predominantly agricultural population changed patterns of work, ways of life, and even domicile in search of more than minimum wages in urban areas during the 1940s and 1950s. At the same time, hundreds of thousands of Puerto Ricans migrated to the U.S. mainland—151,000 in the 1940s, 430,000 in the 1950s, and approximately an additional half million in the next three decades. Many of these and their descendants (close to three million people) remain in the United States (1995), neither fully integrated into mainstream American culture nor recognized as Puerto Rican by their island compatriots.

During the 1950s extreme nationalists continued to demand independence. In 1950 Albizu declared the establishment of a republic in the mountain town of Jayuya. His followers attacked police headquarters in several towns and attempted to kill Governor Muñoz Marín. In Washington, nationalists attempted to assassinate President Harry S. Truman. Government forces in both the United States and Puerto Rico quickly blunted the challenge. Albizu was convicted of attempted murder, illegal use of arms, and subversion and sentenced to prison. His insistence on the morality of his actions inspired another shooting in the U.S. Congress in 1954, as well as continued similar activities by nationalist groups.

These major features of the relationship between the United States and Puerto Rico persisted over the next several decades. Under different names and guises, the forces of statehood, commonwealth, and independence have vied for the public's preferences as well as for Washington's attention. Although they have chosen to represent the island's limited control over its own affairs in a variety of ways, all three major parties agree that Puerto Rico's status is best described as "colonial" and have even brought the issue before the United Nations Decolonization Committee. The island's politicians, however, remain very active in U.S. mainland politics with the expectation of influencing policy, especially immediate economic measures. To cite one example, Section 936 of the Internal Revenue Code, which permits subsidiaries of U.S. companies to repatriate profits without paying federal taxes, has been frequently the subject of intense negotia-tion among island and U.S. mainland politicians. Many in Puerto Rico fear that hundreds of "936 companies" would leave the island should their privileged status change, thus increasing unemployment (officially calculated in 1992 at 16.5 percent) and lowering family incomes.

The United States, which has long considered Puerto Rico a strategic asset because of its location, sometimes yields to the pressure created by the uncomfortable colonial question, most recently when it agreed to a plebiscite on the island's status in 1993 (the previous one was held in 1967). The United States has sidetracked the protests of the inhabitants of Vieques and Culebra, two islands off the coast of Puerto Rico, which claim that U.S. navy exercises with live ammunition disturb their livelihood. More significant, perhaps, has been the astute move on the part of the United States to allow the island to play it both ways. The island's governor, for example, participates in many international meetings as a Latin American head of state, as well as in U.S. governors' conferences; the island attracts tourists by publicizing its "exotic" Caribbean features as well as the more "American" elements Western travelers find comfortable. Puerto Rico has its own Olympic team, while Puerto Rican students apply for financial aid in stateside colleges as U.S. minorities. These contradictory manifestations of the connections between Puerto Rico and the United States confirm the persisting ambivalence of their relationship.

TERESITA MARTÍNEZ VERGNE

See also Good Neighbor Policy; Latin America; Self-Determination; Spanish-American-Cuban-Filipino War, 1898

FURTHER READING

Alegría Ortega, Idsa. *La Comisión del Status de Puerto Rico. Su Historia y su Significacion.* Río Piedras, P.R., 1982.

Carr, Raymond. *Puerto Rico: A Colonial Experiment.* New York, 1984.

Dietz, James L. *Economic History of Puerto Rico: Institutional Change and Capitalist Development.* Princeton, N.J., 1986.

Fernández, Ronald. *The Disenchanted Island: Puerto Rico and the United States in the Twentieth Century.* New York, 1992.

García Passalacqua, Juan M. *Puerto Rico: Equality and Freedom at Issue.* New York, 1984.

———, and Carlos Rivera Lugo. *Puerto Rico y los Estados Unidos: El Proceso de Consulta y Negociación,* 2 vols. Río Piedras, P.R., 1990 and 1991.

Heine, Jorge, ed. *Time for Decision: The United States and Puerto Rico.* Landham, Md., 1983.

Morales Carrión, Arturo. *Puerto Rico: A Political and Cultural History.* New York, 1983.

———. *Memorias, Autobiografía Pública, 1940–1952.* San Juan, P.R., 1992

Silvestrini, Blanca. *Historia de Puerto Rico: Trayectoria de un Pueblo.* San Juan, P.R., 1988.

Q-R

QADDAFI, MUAMMAR AL-
See Libya

QATAR
See Appendix 2

QUADRUPLE ALLIANCE

Alliance formed by Britain, Austria, Prussia, and Russia on 20 November 1815 at the Congress of Vienna, thereby renewing the association among the principal nations that had defeated Emperor Napoleon I of France. The signatory powers vowed to protect Europe against the possibility of further French aggression and, if necessary, each to provide a force of 60,000 men. Most important, Article VI, drafted by British foreign secretary Viscount Castlereagh, created the Congress System, which called for periodic consultations to promote stability and peace.

In 1818 representatives of the member nations convened in Aix-la-Chappelle and agreed to allow France to join the so-called Concert of Europe, thus effectively establishing the Quintuple Alliance. Later conferences at Troppau, Laibach, and Verona signaled serious problems among the members of the alliance—particularly regarding the goal of suppressing revolutions against monarchical or "foreign" rule in Spain, Naples, Piedmont, and the European dominions of the Ottoman Empire. Great Britain, for one, consistently protested against great-power intervention in the internal affairs of other nations as espoused by the Holy Alliance. Castlereagh believed that the Holy Alliance, as envisioned by Czar Alexander I of Russia and Prince Metternich of Austria, would lead those countries, under the pretext of preserving order, to intervene indiscriminately in the internal affairs of other European nations for their own political or economic benefit.

The United States feared that the members of the Quadruple Alliance would intervene in the ongoing revolutions against Spain in the New World. George Canning, who succeeded Castlereagh as British foreign secretary in 1822, also opposed any such intervention. Canning believed that a joint Anglo-American denunciation of any attempts by Spain or France, in particular, to regain control of the Spanish colonies in Latin America would serve his purpose of weakening the Holy Alliance while preserving markets for British goods. Secretary of State John Quincy Adams, however, urged President James Monroe to act alone in warning European powers against any attempts at recolonizing Latin America. Britain's break with the other members of the Quadruple Alliance over the use of French forces in restoring Ferdinand VII to the Spanish throne, as well as London's recognition of the newly independent Latin American republics in 1825, led to the gradual erosion of the Quadruple Alliance.

CAROL A. JACKSON

See also Canning, George; Castlereagh, Robert Stewart; Monroe Doctrine

FURTHER READING
Derry, John W. *Castlereagh*. London, 1976.
Hinde, Wendy. *Castlereagh*. London, 1981.
Kaufmann, William W. *British Policy and the Independence of Latin America, 1804–1828*. New Haven, Conn., 1951.
Webster, Charles. *The Foreign Policy of Castlereagh, 1815–1822: Britain and the European Alliance*. London, 1947.
Weiner, Margery. *The Sovereign Remedy: Europe after Waterloo*. London, 1971.

QUEMOY-MATSU CRISES
See Jinmen-Mazu Crises

QUOTA SYSTEM
See Immigration

RACE AND RACISM

The unscientific idea that presumes to explain variations among different peoples on the basis of observable characteristics, such as skin color, and a doctrine ascribing individual differences of character and capability to race, and asserting the superiority of one race over another or others. Despite its lack of a scientific basis, racial thinking has been pervasive in U.S. history. The expansion of Europe and its settlement of North America coincided with the rise among Europeans of the idea that human beings were divided not only into confessional groupings of Christians and heathens, but also into immutable physical categories or "races." European conquests of territories in Africa, Asia, and the Americas—powered by technological innovations, population pressures, imperial ambitions, and the pursuit of wealth—seemed to indicate that Europeans, or "whites," were the most powerful of these so-called races. The expansion of the British Empire and English influence around the globe nourished the rise of a specific strand of this kind of thinking that emphasized English superiority even among other Europeans. Notions of Anglo-Saxon supremacy traveled westward with English colonists across the Atlantic Ocean.

American foreign relations, from the earliest days of European settlement in what would become the United States, were intimately bound up with the subjugation of peoples of color, as the African slave trade and the expropriation of Native American lands attests. The American Revolution and the Constitution, with the latter's mechanism for amendment, established much of the political and legal groundwork for later movements toward greater racial equality, but their immediate impact was to confirm existing racial hierarchies.

Expansion westward and conflict with Native American nations characterized U.S. foreign relations throughout the nineteenth century. The War with Mexico in 1846–1848, fought with clear racial overtones, brought vast new territories under the U.S. flag. After the interruption of the Civil War, U.S. policymakers renewed the campaign to subdue if not eliminate Native American resistance in the West, culminating in the massacre at Wounded Knee in 1890.

The last decades of the nineteenth century were marked by the outermost expansion of European empires, justified by theories of racial superiority. In those same years, white Americans succeeded, in the aftermath of the abolition of slavery, in recreating a system of racial segregation and often brutal subordination of African Americans in the United States. In the brief war with Spain in 1898, the United States continued its expansion to the south and the west, annexing the lands of other peoples of color in Puerto Rico, Hawai'i, and the Philippines. In the pacification campaign against Filipino insurgents who resisted the new U.S. authorities, the U.S. Army applied the same tactics and racial assumptions that it had used against Apaches and Sioux at home, and "little brown brothers" seeking U.S. guidance became instead savage "goo-goos" deserving of slaughter. The "Far West" of the Indian wars had become the "Far East" of Asia.

U.S. immigration laws made explicit the connection between domestic race relations and foreign policy. From the Chinese exclusion legislation of the 1880s through the nativist quota restrictions of the 1920s on southern and eastern Europeans, white American leaders sought to preserve a predominantly Anglo-Saxon population, even at the cost of alienating other countries such as Japan. Widespread anti-Semitism among the U.S. public and within the government, especially the Department of State, contributed to an unwillingness to change immigration laws in the 1930s so as to assist European Jews seeking to escape from the developing Nazi Holocaust.

In the aftermath of the devastation of World War II came decolonization and the Cold War. The emergence of the Third World transformed international relations into interracial relations, because people of color predominated in the developing nations. Secretary of State John Foster Dulles recognized that traditional U.S. segregation had become a "major international hazard," and he worried during the Little Rock school desegregation crisis of 1957 that racial bigotry was "ruining our foreign policy," especially in Asia and Africa. Competition with the Soviet Union for the loyalty of these people of color, combined with the simultaneous Civil Rights movement at home, encouraged U.S. policymakers to outlaw racial segregation and eliminate racial and ethnic quotas on immigration by the mid-1960s. Examples of explicit racism in the Vietnam War, evident during the My Lai massacre, and racial slurs against Vietnamese as "gooks" seemed to point backwards to the racial fury of the U.S. armed forces fighting Japanese "monkeys" in the early 1940s. But the logic of racial equality continued to work among Americans in the 1970s and 1980s, bringing greater attention to the struggle against apartheid in South Africa as well as to the growing economic prominence of such Asian nations as Japan and China. In a world populated by a majority of people of color and linked by trade and communication, white Americans found that explicit racial discrimination and public statements of prejudice risked losing the United States its influence and goodwill abroad.

Thomas Borstelmann

See also Colonialism; Holocaust; Immigration; Mexico, War with; My Lai Incident; Native Americans; Philippines; Slave Trade and Slavery; South Africa; Vietnam War

FURTHER READING

DeConde, Alexander. *Ethnicity, Race, and American Foreign Policy: A History.* Boston, 1992.

Drinnon, Richard. *Facing West: The Metaphysics of Indian-Hating and Empire-Building.* Minneapolis, 1980.

Hunt, Michael H. *Ideology and U.S. Foreign Policy.* New Haven, Conn., 1987.

Lauren, Paul Gordon. *Power and Prejudice: The Politics and Diplomacy of Racial Discrimination.* Boulder, Colo., 1988.

RADIO FREE EUROPE AND RADIO LIBERTY

Also known as "the radios," these programs began broadcasting during the early years of the Cold War. The Central Intelligence Agency (CIA) initially and secretly funded both broadcasters as part of a larger program of anticommunist operations. Radio Free Europe (RFE) went on the air to Eastern Europe in 1949, Radio Liberty (RL) to the Soviet Union in 1951. Their mission was to undermine communist governments, foster discontent among the people in those areas, and project a positive image of democracy and the United States. Their tactic was surrogate broadcasting—the transmission of domestic news to a target area in the belief that RFE and RL could become the local "free press" of Eastern Europe and the Soviet Union. No other nation has maintained an equivalent radio broadcasting effort.

The structure and goals of "the radios" changed over time. A major turning point came during the Hungarian Revolution of 1956, when RFE was accused of promising U.S. aid and thereby encouraging Hungarian rebels to risk their lives. In the wake of the failed revolt, "the radios" shifted to a policy of supporting liberalization of existing communist governments rather than fomenting revolution against them. After a decade of professionalization of the two broadcasting services, American journalists reported in 1967 that the CIA had long funded both RFE and RL. This revelation led to congressional hearings in the early 1970s. In 1976 the two services were merged into RFE/RL, Inc., openly funded by congressional appropriations. By the 1980s they had come under the management of the Board of International Broadcasting (BIB).

The unraveling of communism in the Soviet Union and Eastern Europe in the late 1980s and early 1990s again changed the political context of RFE/RL and renewed the debate about its mission. Supporters of RFE/RL have claimed that surrogate broadcasting still provided a substitute domestic free press. They have argued that surrogate services should be extended to a "Radio Free Asia." Those who oppose RFE/RL have maintained that all international broadcasting functions as surrogate broadcasting, that every audience seeks quality information and news, and that because RFE/RL's main competitor in Eastern Europe and the former Soviet Union is the Voice of America, RFE/RL performs a duplicate service. In April 1994 Congress passed new legislation placing both the Voice of America and RFE/RL under a board of governors that would oversee all U.S. government sponsored international broadcasting.

HOLLY COWAN SHULMAN

See also Broadcast and Film Companies; Central Intelligence Agency; Eastern Europe; Russia and the Soviet Union; Voice of America

FURTHER READING

Mickelson, Sig. *America's Other Voice: The Story of Radio Free Europe and Radio Liberty*. New York, 1983.
Holt, Robert T. *Radio Free Europe*. Minneapolis, 1958.

RADIO MARTÍ

The U.S.-funded station founded in 1983 to transmit to Cuba propaganda against the regime of Fidel Castro. The United States had initiated plans for the overthrow of the government of Fidel Castro in 1960. After the failure of the U.S.-sponsored Bay of Pigs invasion the following year, and a series of CIA-sponsored attempts to assassinate Castro, Washington turned to less direct efforts to unseat him. As the regime in Havana endured despite the U.S. attempt to undermine it both economically and politically, Cuban exiles and U.S. authorities looked for a sophisticated and effective vehicle for the propaganda aspects of their anti-Castro campaign. In 1985, a powerful station based in southern Florida, and named "Radio Martí," after Jose Martí, the Cuban hero of independence, went on the air.

Radio Martí was supervised and financed by the U.S. government's Voice of America (VOA), which made some effort to assure professional handling of the news, believing that the truth itself would break the regime's news monopoly and undermine its credibility. Analysts agree that many Cubans listened to the broadcasts but differ as to their effect. Some claim that the programs did encourage opposition to the regime, while others hold that they were crudely propagandistic, and that, in any event, they could never match Castro's own brilliant use of the media. Staff members, most of whom have come from the Cuban exile community, quarreled over the purpose of the station: Should it simply stand for a freedom of communication denied Cubans by the Castro regime, or should its role be political, preparing the ground for the return of exile leaders, many of whom had rather conservative agendas, and who attempted to influence programming? The broadcasts became a major obstacle to reducing tensions between the United States and Cuba. Castro retaliated against the opening of the station by suspending the 1984 immigration agreements with Washington. In 1990 Washington raised the stakes by inaugurating "TV Martí." Havana often jammed the TV signal and threatened its own war of the airwaves if Washington did not allow a Cuban station to broadcast its message to the United States.

Despite the end of the Cold War and of efforts by Havana to encourage revolutionary change in Latin America, tensions between the two nations did not subside. As Castro's regime became more openly authoritarian and as its economy all but collapsed with the break up of the Soviet Union and the Warsaw Pact trading bloc to which Cuba was intimately tied, Washington saw an opportunity to bring down the Havana regime. In 1996, when the Cuban air force shot down two exile planes engaged in propaganda overflights of the island, the U.S. Congress passed legislation greatly tightening the thirty-five-year old U.S. economic embargo against the island and increased funding for Radio Martí. As of 1996, the end of the Cold War had not brought an end to the war of words between Cuba and the United States.

JULES R. BENJAMIN

See also Castro, Fidel; Cuba

FURTHER READING

Frederick, Howard H. *Cuban-American Radio Wars: Ideology and International Telecommunications.* Norwood, N.J., 1986.

Cuza Male, Belkis. "Radio Martí: A Cuban Poet's Reflections." *Journal of Contemporary Studies.* 8 (Spring/Summer 1985): 117–127.

Nichols, John Spicer, and Lawrence C. Soley. *Clandestine Radio Broadcasting.* Praeger, 1986.

Warlaumont, Hazel G. "Strategies in International Radio Wars." *Journal of Broadcasting and Electronic Media* 32 (Winter 1988): 43–59.

RAND CORPORATION

See Think Tanks

RANKIN, JEANNETTE

(*b.* 11 June, 1880; *d.* 15 May, 1973)

Suffragist, feminist, pacifist, and member of the House of Representatives (1917–1919, 1941–1943) who voted against U.S. entry into both world wars. Born in Montana, Rankin established her reputation as an advocate of extending the right to vote to women in Montana and eventually became known nationwide for her activism. She won election to the U.S. House of Representatives in 1916 as the first female member of Congress. Rankin argued that women and pacifism were intricately related, especially because only women were truly dedicated to disarmament. Women could educate others about peace, but men would be considered cowards if they did so. She maintained that war would not settle international disputes, and her convictions prompted her to vote against the U.S. declaration of war on Germany on 6 April 1917—a decision that led to her defeat in a bid for the Senate in 1918.

During the interwar period, Rankin participated in peace organizations, including the National Council for the Prevention of War, which fought for neutrality legislation in the mid-1930s. Running successfully on an antiwar platform in 1940, she regained a seat in Congress and, once in office, argued against U.S. aid to the Allies. Rankin believed that President Franklin D. Roosevelt's provocative policies prompted the Japanese attack on Pearl Harbor. Further, in her opinion, military retaliation would not solve any crisis. She cast the lone vote of dis-

sent in Congress on the declaration of war on Japan on 8 December 1941.

She failed to gain reelection in 1942, but Rankin's peace sentiment did not end. Following World War II she traveled to the British colony of India to support nationalism and independence there and to other nations to study pacifist strategies. She criticized U.S. intervention in Korea in the early 1950s and in Vietnam in the 1960s and blamed the military-industrial complex for U.S. foreign policy. She contemplated running for a third congressional term in 1968 to continue her anti-Vietnam stance, but illness prevented her from doing so. Earlier that year, at the age of eighty-seven, she led the Jeannette Rankin Brigade of 5,000 women on a march on Capitol Hill to protest the Vietnam War.

CAROL A. JACKSON

See also Korean War; Neutrality Acts of the 1930s; Peace Movements and Societies, 1914 to Present; Vietnam War; World War I; World War II

FURTHER READING

Chatfield, Charles. *For Peace and Justice: Pacifism in America 1914–1941.* Knoxville, Tenn., 1971.

Hardaway, Roger D. "Jeannette Rankin: The Early Years." *North Dakota Quarterly* (Winter 1980): 29–41.

Josephson, Hannah. *Jeannette Rankin: First Lady in Congress.* Indianapolis, 1974.

Wilson, Joan Hoff. "Jeannette Rankin and American Foreign Policy: The Origins of Her Pacifism." *Montana: The Magazine of Western History* 30 (Winter 1980): 29–41.

———. "Jeannette Rankin and American Foreign Policy: Her Lifework as a Pacifist." *Montana: The Magazine of Western History* 30 (Spring 1980): 39–53.

RAPID DEPLOYMENT FORCE

The Rapid Deployment Joint Task Force (RDJTF) was created by President Jimmy Carter in 1980 to respond to heightened threats to U.S. interests in the Persian Gulf region. Since 1977 the Department of Defense had studied numerous such contingencies. One postulated an Iraqi threat to Kuwait and Saudi Arabia; a second postulated a Soviet invasion in and through Iran, a potential concern since the last years of World War II. The Soviet threat became paramount after the invasion of Afghanistan in December 1979. Simultaneously, U.S.-Iranian relations fell victim to the Islamic Fundamentalist revolution led by Ayatollah Ruhollah Khomeini.

The effort to build the RDJTF and forge a regional strategy was led by Undersecretary of Defense Robert Komer. Related defense programs included maritime prepositioning ships (MPS), which were loaded with equipment for a division-sized marine expeditionary force (MEF); improvement in airlift efficiency; procurement of eight rapid-sealift ships; a vigorous effort to develop port-access arrangements with regional states; regionally oriented exercises such as the Bright Star exercises held with Egypt; and increased naval deployments. The Carter Doctrine made U.S. interests in the region explicit and creation of the RDJTF demonstrated tangible commitment. "Any attempt by an outside force to gain control of the Persian Gulf region," President Carter declared in January 1990, "will be regarded as an assault on the vital interest of the United States of America and such an assault will be repelled by any means, including military force."

These rapid deployment force programs were continued and expanded under President Ronald Reagan-through the procurement of additional C-5 aircraft, serious attention to logistical considerations, and transition of the RDJTF into U.S. Central Command (CENTCOM), which is headed by a four-star general. Through most of the 1980s, planning typically assumed the invasion of Iran by the Soviet Union with a possible defense line at the Zagros Mountains.

Over time, the RDJTF/CENTCOM became a substantial fighting force. In 1989 Secretary of Defense Richard Cheney directed that attention be reoriented on regional threats such as that posed by Iraq. On 2 August 1990, while related plans were still in development, Iraq invaded Kuwait. On 7 August President George Bush ordered General H. Norman Schwarzkopf, CENTCOM commander, to begin deployment of U.S. forces to Saudi Arabia. Operations Desert Shield and Desert Storm were a triumph of defense planning because they demonstrated the importance and effectiveness of a decade's efforts involving three presidents. U.S. rapid deployment forces were superbly equipped and trained for a mission that differed drastically from the Central Region mission on which most attention had been focused for decades. A threat to Kuwait and Saudi Arabia continues to exist and, indeed, in October 1994 some U.S. CENTCOM forces were again deployed to the Persian Gulf in response to Iraqi force movements. This deployment benefited from prepositioning of equipment in Kuwait.

PAUL K. DAVIS

See also Carter Doctrine; Iran; Russia and the Soviet Union

FURTHER READING

Department of Defense. *Conduct of the Persian Gulf War: Final Report to Congress.* Appendix D. Washington D.C., 1992.
McNaugher, Thomas L. *Arms and Oil: U.S. Military Strategy and the Persian Gulf.* Washington D.C., 1985.

REAGAN, RONALD WILSON

(*b.* 6 February 1911)

Fortieth president of the United States (1981–1988) who enlarged military spending, intervened in the Third World, and heated up and then calmed the Cold War. This graduate of Eureka College (Iowa) and former Hollywood actor had little experience in foreign affairs when he won the presidency in 1980. As the two-term Republican governor of California (1967–1975), Reagan had been an outspoken supporter of U.S. intervention in Vietnam and had served on the Rockefeller Commission to investigate the Central Intelligence Agency. Following an unsuccessful bid to win the Republican presidential nomination in 1976, he made his most memorable statement on foreign policy the next year during the debate over the Panama Canal Treaty by claiming that "we bought it [the canal,] we paid for it, and we're going to keep it."

Reagan's Beliefs

Reagan's foreign policies as president reflected beliefs strongly embedded in the U.S. past. First, Reagan and his conservative colleagues subscribed to a devil theory that a powerful, ubiquitous Soviet Union malevolently instigated international instability, stirred up civil wars, aided terrorism, and sought to expand its "evil empire." Soviet leaders, according to Reagan, stood ready "to commit any crime, to lie, to cheat" to achieve communist control of the world. He believed that civil wars in Central America and conflicts elsewhere in the Third World derived from Soviet meddling, not from deep-seated local causes. Having criticized the administration of President Jimmy Carter for abandoning friendly dictators in Iran and Nicaragua, Reagan accepted the distinction Jeane Kirkpatrick, the U.S. ambassador to the United Nations, made between "authoritarian" and "totalitarian" regimes. Authoritarian regimes in such countries as South Africa, Chile, South Korea, and the Philippines nurtured successful capitalist economies and would supposedly respond to U.S. proposals for reform. Communist totalitarian governments imposed rigid state economies, muffled dissent, and were supposedly impervious to change.

Reagan also believed that a major military buildup would thwart Soviet machinations. "Defense is not a budget item," he told officials of the Pentagon. "Spend what you need." The military did, spending approximately $2 trillion and running up record budget deficits. Reagan expanded the navy, pushed the B-1 bomber, augmented special forces for counterinsurgency warfare, and continued the Trident-II submarine, MX, cruise missile, Stealth bomber, and Midgetman mobile missile programs. Somewhat paradoxically, the president also invoked a nuclear abolitionist's faith that U.S. technology could devise an invulnerable space shield that could protect civilian populations from nuclear holocaust. He likened the nuclear arms race to "two Westerners standing in a saloon aiming their guns at each other's heads—permanently. There had to be a better way."

To facilitate public approval for a more militarized foreign policy, Reagan exhorted U.S. citizens to abandon their post-Vietnam "self-doubt" in favor of a "national reawakening." The United States should serve as a model for other nations as it pursued its mission to reform a fractious world. "The world's hopes rest with America's future," he proclaimed. Organizations such as the National Endowment for Democracy used federal and private funds to promote free enterprise and democratic politics abroad. Reagan and his advisers believed that nations must embrace capitalism and "privatize" managed economies; they extolled the "magic of the marketplace." Reagan even quoted Thomas Paine: "We have it in our power to begin the world over again."

He also promulgated the ideas and strategy which became known as the Reagan Doctrine, whereby the Central Intelligence Agency (CIA) openly supported anticommunist "freedom fighters" who fought against Soviet-backed governments in Afghanistan, Nicaragua, Angola, Cambodia, and Ethiopia. The Reagan Doctrine stressed low-intensity conflict instead of direct intervention: military action through allies, proxies, and paramilitary assets. Thus did Reagan promise "no more Vietnams" as elite U.S. forces organized others to fight shadow wars.

The Iran-Contra Affair

"Sometimes our right hand doesn't know what our far-right hand is doing," Reagan once joked. The president's loose management style encouraged bureaucratic bickering among his principal advisers. When Secretary of State Alexander M. Haig resigned in 1982 after failing to become the "vicar" of foreign policy, his successor George P. Shultz often battled for thoughtful conservative solutions against such hard-liners as Ambassador Kirkpatrick, Defense Secretary Caspar W. Weinberger, and CIA Director William J. Casey. The Iran-Contra affair eventually embroiled the White House in part because of Reagan's lax control of the foreign affairs bureaucracy.

Despite strong opposition from Shultz and Weinberger, in 1985 President Reagan ordered the National Security Council staff (NSC) to carry out a covert scheme to trade arms to Iran for the return of U.S. hostages held in Lebanon by Islamic radicals. He had also empowered the NSC to provide secret aid to the Nicaraguan Contras (notwithstanding a ban on such aid by Congress). The two operations eventually intertwined. To ensure secrecy and deniability, NSC advisers Robert C. McFarlane and John M. Poindexter ran both operations in total disregard of Congress and almost completely beyond the purview of the Departments of State and Defense. The action officer in charge of both operations, Marine Lieutenant Colonel Oliver C. North, did not hide his contempt for Congress, traditional bureaucrats, and professional diplomats. "I did not micromanage" North, Poindexter later testified. When North discovered a way to divert profits from arms sales to Iran to the Contras, Poindexter approved, but said he did not tell Reagan because he wanted the president "to have some deniability so that he would be protected."

Although Shultz and Weinberger later claimed that Reagan was misled by his inner circle, available records for all top-level meetings on Iran-Contra show the president speaking more than any of his advisers, passionately steering discussions, and making the basic decisions, whether or not he authorized every operational detail. Reagan subsequently claimed that he "knew Oliver North only slightly," whereupon North rebutted that "the president didn't always know what he knew." An independent federal prosecutor later concluded that Reagan "created the conditions which made possible the crimes committed by others." In 1989 North was found guilty of three felonies (obstructing a congressional inquiry, destroying documents, and receiving illegal gratuities), and in 1990 Poindexter was convicted of five felony charges, including lying to Congress. A federal appeals court later overturned both sets of convictions because Congress had granted immunity for prior testimony.

Soviet-American Relations

Negotiations with Moscow dominated Reagan's first term. The arms build-up as well as loose talk from administration officials about the possibility of winning a nuclear war produced uneasiness at home and abroad. In 1982, 17 senators and 128 House members endorsed a freeze on the production and deployment of nuclear weapons, as did many states, cities, and towns across the country. The president dismissed the freeze as a "very dangerous fraud" that would allegedly perpetuate Soviet nuclear supremacy. To satisfy Western European leaders who wanted U.S. nuclear weapons and to dampen the antinuclear movement in the United States, Reagan proposed to revoke the planned deployment of intermediate-range nuclear missiles in NATO if the Soviets would dismantle its growing arsenal of intermediate range (SS-20, SS-4, and SS-5) missiles aimed at Western Europe. The Soviets initially rejected this "zero option" because it excluded British and French nuclear forces as well as U.S. weapons on submarines and aircraft. When arms negotiator Paul H. Nitze proposed a tentative compromise that fell short of full removal, Reagan said no. After the United States deployed its first Pershing missiles in November 1983, the Russians angrily suspended negotiations at Geneva. Pentagon hard-liners did not complain. Without an agreement, the U.S. arms buildup continued.

Negotiations on strategic nuclear weapons fared no better. Moscow rejected U.S. proposals for deep reductions in ICBMs—precisely those weapons that constituted the heart of Soviet deterrence. Reagan apparently failed to grasp this point, for in 1983 he told stunned members of Congress that he only recently learned that 70 percent of Soviet missiles were land-based. The president's commitment to the Strategic Defense Initiative (SDI), announced in March 1983, also complicated arms talks. Soon dubbed "Star Wars," SDI envisaged an antimissile defense system in outer space—a laser or particle beam shield that could intercept and destroy ballistic missiles before they reentered the atmosphere. Critics argued that SDI would simply not work and that offense could still overwhelm defense; if it ever did succeed, it would undermine the stability of mutual deterrence by eliminating the danger of a Soviet nuclear attack, thus freeing the United States to use nuclear weapons without fear of retaliation. The scheme nonetheless seemed to scare the Soviets and reassure the U.S. public. Strategic arms talks stalled.

Other obstacles hindered serious negotiations. When Poland's communist regime cracked down on the Solidarity labor movement in December 1981, Reagan retaliated by suspending economic agreements with Poland. He also cut back U.S.-Soviet trade and banned Soviet airline flights to the United States. Reagan labeled the destruction of Korean Air Lines Flight 007 by Soviet warplanes in September 1983 "a crime against humanity" and "an act of barbarism." When the Soviets claimed that KAL 007 was on a spy mission for the United States, Washington chose to portray what was probably an unfortunate Soviet mistake as premeditated treachery. Moscow's aging leadership also blocked progress. Not until the accession of Mikhail S. Gorbachev as general secretary in 1985, following the deaths of his predecessors Leonid Ilyide Brezhnev, Yuri Vladimirivich Andropov, and Konstantin Ustinorich Chernenko, did Reagan face a strong Soviet leader with whom he could negotiate.

Gorbachev soon altered the Soviet position on nuclear weapons. In a series of summit meetings with Reagan in Geneva (1985), Helsinki (1986), and Washington (1987), the new Soviet leader agreed to an Intermediate-Range Nuclear Forces (INF) Treaty to eliminate all U.S. and Soviet intermediate missiles and verify their destruction through on-site inspections. What caused the turnaround? Gorbachev had taken the initiative by accepting the "zero option" and urging the United States to respond. Warm personal relations between Gorbachev and Reagan also facilitated negotiations. As well, the most hawkish of Reagan's advisers, including Weinberger, Kirkpatrick, and Casey, resigned during his second term, thus easing the way for substantive agreements. Most important, both superpowers came to regard the treaty as beneficial to their respective national interests. Both faced economic troubles engendered by the protracted

and costly Cold War, and slowing the arms race would permit the shifting of resources to domestic priorities. "How long," Reagan wondered, "can the Russians keep on being so belligerent and spending so much on the arms race when they can't feed their own people?" Many in the United States asked similar questions about themselves, but Reagan countered that the large-scale U.S. military spending and his steadfastness on SDI had forced the Soviets to become more conciliatory.

Gorbachev reduced tensions on other issues as well. In 1988 he signed a United Nations agreement providing for the withdrawal of all Soviet forces from Afghanistan. The Soviet acknowledgement of defeat in Afghanistan was due in no little part to U.S. assistance for the Afghan *mujahedeen* ("holy warriors"), particularly in the form of Stinger anti-aircraft missiles that had wreaked havoc against Soviet helicopter gunships. In December 1988 Gorbachev announced a unilateral reduction of Soviet ground troops by 500,000. Moscow also cut its support for the Sandinista regime in Nicaragua and helped to negotiate the removal of Cuban troops from Angola.

Latin America

Before the happy denouement in U.S.-Soviet relations, the Reagan administration waged the Cold War with relentless intensity in the Third World. The Reagan Doctrine posited that U.S. support for insurgents would add to the costs borne by the Soviet Union in maintaining its empire. Reagan quoted the Truman Doctrine, resuscitated the Domino Theory, and stressed military solutions instead of negotiations. Central America, long a part of Washington's informal empire but bestirred by deep economic, political, and social divisions, became a particular target of Reagan's counterrevolutionary crusade. A "Moscow-Havana axis" allegedly had used Fidel Castro's Cuba to foment revolution, train insurgents, and spawn new "Cuba-model states" that would "provide platforms for subversion, compromise vital sea lanes, and pose a direct military threat at or near our borders." To avoid "another Cuba," Reagan officials vowed to suppress leftist rebels in El Salvador, to overthrow the Sandinista regime in Nicaragua, and to bring Honduras and Guatemala into a tight military network designed to promote counterrevolution.

In El Salvador the Reagan administration saw "a textbook case of indirect armed aggression by communist powers." It also seemed a place where the United States "could win one for a change," as one senator put it. Despite spending some $4.5 billion in El Salvador during the 1980s, victory in the bloody civil war still eluded Reagan when he left office. Right-wing "death squads" and government security forces battled against the radical Farabundo Martí Front for National Liberation (FMLN). According to the United Nations Truth Commission, 85 percent of the 75,000 people killed in the Salvadoran civil war died at the hands of government forces or death squads. Indeed, U.S. military advisers trained some of the units responsible for the killings. Ambassador William Walker cited "management control problems," as U.S. officials failed to investigate atrocities. When national guard troops raped and killed four American churchwomen in 1980, the Salvadoran government refused to prosecute the officers who ordered the murders. Ambassador Kirkpatrick seemed to justify the slayings by saying "the nuns were not just nuns," but "political activists" for the FMLN.

Reagan blamed much of the Salvadoran turmoil on Cuba and Nicaragua, which sent small supplies of arms to the insurgents. Secretary of State Haig claimed that the Soviets had a "hit list" of Central American states, with Nicaragua first, El Salvador next. When the Sandinista government postponed free elections, refused to sever ties with Cuba, moved to one-party rule, and used Cuban advisers and Soviet weapons to build a strong military, the Reagan administration targeted Nicaragua as a Soviet satellite. In November 1981, he ordered the CIA to train and arm the anti-Sandinista Contras. Comprised mostly of followers of the former dictator Anastasio Somoza Debayle, the Contras grew into a mercenary army of some 15,000 to 20,000 virtually dependent upon U.S. support. When Congress in 1982 prohibited the use of funds to overthrow the Nicaraguan government, Reagan officials ignored the restriction by having the CIA work with Contra commandos in early 1984 to mine Nicaraguan ports. The Sandinista regime charged the United States before the World Court with violating international law, but Washington refused to recognize the Court's jurisdiction, just as it later ignored the Court's ruling that the United States had violated international law and should pay an indemnity to Nicaragua.

In order to evade congressional restrictions under the Boland Amendment's ban on government aid to the Contras, the CIA, Pentagon, and NSC worked with private right-wing U.S. groups to channel millions of dollars of supplies to anti-Sandinista forces. Retired general John K. Singlaub, retired major general Richard V. Secord, and Cuban Americans in Miami helped Colonel North coordinate a network of planes and ships and construct a large airstrip in Costa Rica—all without informing Congress. Reagan, who personally authorized the illegal aid effort, told his advisers that if the "story gets out, we'll all be hanging by our thumbs in front of the White House." In 1985–1986, North diverted profits from secret arms sales to Iran to the Contras by utilizing Israeli intermediaries and a clandestine Swiss bank account. Nevertheless, even after Congress reversed itself and approved $100 million in military aid to the Contras in 1986, the anti-Sandinista war fared poorly. The Contras feuded

among themselves, attracted little support within Nicaragua, failed to seize and hold towns, and succeeded only in forcing the Sandinistas to shift funds from social programs to defense and to repress internal dissent.

The weaknesses of the Contras notwithstanding, Reagan still insisted that the Sandinistas should cry "uncle" and rejected all negotiations for a political settlement. When the Contadora group, consisting of Mexico, Venezuela, Panama, and Colombia, proposed in 1983 that the five Central American states agree to limit foreign advisers, reduce armaments, and promote democratic pluralism, Washington opposed the plan because of Nicaragua's alleged failure to hold early democratic elections. Notwithstanding the subsequent exposure and embarrassment of the Iran-Contra scandal, Reagan officials rejected a similar plan in 1987 by Costa Rican President Oscar Arias Sanchez calling for a cease-fire and national reconciliation. Only after Reagan had left office, after more than 20,000 had died in the Contra war and the Nicaraguan economy lay in ruin, did the administration of President George Bush acquiesce in a peace process and eventual elections in Nicaragua in 1990. Critics charged that Reagan had brought only more instability to Nicaragua, but he countered that the ultimate defeat of the Sandinistas in the elections demonstrated U.S. success.

For Reagan administration officials, Cuba instigated much of the turmoil in Nicaragua and El Salvador. Secretary of State Haig wanted to "go to the source." "Give me the word," he bragged, "and I'll make that island a —— —— parking lot." Reagan rejected such advice but banned business and tourist travel to Cuba, denied Cubans visas, stopped Cuban newspapers and magazines from entering the United States, and kept up a steady drumbeat of anti-Castro propaganda. Reagan demanded that Cuba renounce Soviet assistance and cease support for Third World revolutions; Cuba insisted on an end to the U.S. economic embargo. Regarding Central America, Castro accepted the Contadora process, urged the Sandinistas and Salvadoran rebels to negotiate, and welcomed a ban on foreign weapons and foreign advisers. Washington denounced such Cuban offers as fraudulent. Havana and Washington did, however, sign an accord in late 1984 that would have made it easier for the families of Cuban exiles to emigrate to the United States. When Washington started up Radio Martí to broadcast anti-Castro propaganda into Cuba, Castro furiously abrogated the agreement. Isolated Cuba remained dependent on Soviet military and economic aid and defiant of the United States.

The U.S. invasion of Grenada in October 1983 sent a warning to Castro. Taking advantage of political violence between factions in the Grenadian government, the United States landed 6,000 troops on the small Caribbean island to topple a Marxist regime with close ties to Cuba. More than one hundred people died in the fighting, including some twenty-five Cubans helping to build an airstrip. Reagan charged that the airfield was meant to service the Cuban and Soviet militaries, although British engineers explained that its purpose was to expand Grenada's tourist industry. The president also justified the invasion in order to rescue one thousand U.S. citizens, mostly medical students, reportedly threatened by the Marxist regime. After closing the Soviet embassy and deporting all remaining Cubans from the island, U.S. forces left Grenada within two months. When the United Nations Security Council condemned this latest example of gunboat diplomacy, the United States vetoed the resolution. The Organization of American States protested a violation of its charter. Most in the United States, however, cheered such a swift and relatively bloodless victory, especially as it followed a terrorist attack that had killed 241 U.S. soldiers in Lebanon only a few days earlier.

The Middle East

Israel invaded Lebanon in June 1982 to eliminate forces of the Palestine Liberation Organization operating out of that country. Israeli troops quickly drove all the way to Beirut. Appalled at the bloodshed, Reagan protested to Israeli prime minister Menachem Begin about the "holocaust." "Mr. President," Begin replied, "I think I know what a holocaust is." U.S. officials arranged for the evacuation of Israeli and PLO troops and the introduction of peace-keeping forces that included French, Italian, and U.S. troops. U.S. citizens soon became targets because the United States was viewed as siding with Christian Lebanese factions in a smoldering civil war against Shi'ite Muslims and Druse military forces backed by the Syrian army. In April 1983 terrorist bombs hit the U.S. Embassy in Beirut, killing sixty-three persons. When the battleship *New Jersey*, steaming off the Lebanese coast, retaliated by shelling Shi'ite and Druse positions, another terrorist in October drove a truck loaded with explosives into the U.S. Marine barracks near Beirut, killing 241. Even though Reagan insisted that retaining Marines in Lebanon was "central to our credibility on a global scale," he quietly withdrew all U.S. forces from Lebanon in February 1984. The president later admitted that he "didn't appreciate fully enough the depth of hatred and complexity of the problems that make the Middle East such a jungle."

Lebanon seemed to exemplify what CIA Director William Casey called an "undeclared war" waged by international terrorists. In 1985, for example, more than 800 terrorist incidents throughout the world claimed some 900 lives, including twenty-three U.S. citizens. Passengers on commercial jets became targets for hijacking and murder. That year U.S. warplanes forced down an Egyptian airliner carrying four Palestinians who had earlier killed a U.S. passenger on the Italian cruise vessel *Achille Lauro*. "You can run but you can't hide," Reagan warned. The president particularly blamed Libya's radical ruler Moammar Gadhafi for much of the terrorism in the Middle East. Reagan called the flamboyant Libyan a "mad clown" and charged that Libyan assassins had been sent to the United States to kill him. Washington broke diplomatic relations with Libya in 1981, imposed an embargo on Libyan oil imports the next year, and banned all trade in 1986. After a series of terrorist attacks at busy European airports, Reagan officials claimed Libyan responsibility and sent U.S. warships into the Gulf of Sidra, which Libya regarded as territorial waters. When Libyan jets and patrol vessels came out to challenge, Reagan authorized retaliation and hot pursuit. After Libyan agents were implicated in the bombing of a West Berlin discotheque in April 1986, Reagan ordered an air attack on Tripoli, and specifically against Gadhafi's headquarters. The raid missed Gadhafi but killed his adopted daughter and wounded two of his sons.

The Iran-Iraq War also engaged Reagan's attention in the Middle East. Approximately two million died in this bloody war (1980–1988) for deep water ports and regional influence. Although Washington opposed both the expansionist ambitions of Iraqi leader Saddam Hussein, a long-time Soviet client, and the Islamic fundamentalism espoused by Iran's Ayatollah Ruhollah Khomeini, the Reagan administration played a double game by giving secret aid and military intelligence to both sides. Hoping to create a stalemate that would prevent the domination of the oil-rich Persian Gulf by either power, Reagan officials generally worked with Israel in the early 1980s to sell several billion dollars worth of U.S. military equipment to Iran. When Iran seemed close to victory in 1987, however, Washington quickly expanded aid to the Iraqis. After Iran began sinking oil tankers carrying Iraqi cargoes in the Persian Gulf, Reagan vowed to keep the Gulf open to international trade and beefed up the U.S. naval presence in the region. Kuwaiti oil tankers were "reflagged" as U.S. vessels to increase their protection. In May 1987 Iraqi missiles hit the U.S. frigate *Stark*, killing thirty-seven members of the crew. Iraq promptly apologized. A year later, in July, the cruiser *Vincennes*, thinking itself under attack despite sophisticated equipment that should have indicated otherwise, shot down an Iranian airliner killing all 290 aboard. The United States admitted the error, while covering up the fact that the *Vincennes*, in violation of international law, was inside Iranian territorial waters at the time of the incident.

Although Iran and Iraq agreed to end their costly war in August 1988, Reagan's tilt toward Iraq left an ominous legacy. Not only had Reagan officials, in violation of the law, approved off-the-books arms transfers to Iraq but both the Reagan and Bush administrations encouraged Iraqi grain purchases from the United States on generous terms and were blind to illegal private bank loans that facilitated Saddam Hussein's burgeoning nuclear, chemical, and biological weapons program. The Iraqi dictator's use of poison gas against Iran as well as against domestic rebels should have dispelled thoughts of using Iraq as a geopolitical client. Instead, such aid probably fed Saddam Hussein's megalomaniacal ambitions, allowing him to believe he could bully regional neighbors like Kuwait with impunity.

Africa and Asia

Reagan also had to deal with intransigent, long-term problems in Africa. Deadly famine, as in the Sudan in the mid-1980s, civil strife in Angola and Ethiopia, where Soviet and Cuban troops assisted ruling Marxist regimes and CIA aid buttressed insurgents, the status of Namibia, and especially the racist policy of apartheid in South Africa demanded Washington's attention. Viewing Africa within the framework of Reagan's basic goal of stopping Soviet expansionism, the administration first adopted a policy of "constructive engagement" toward white-ruled South Africa. Rationalizing that the United States lacked the leverage to coerce South Africa to end its oppression of its black majority, Reagan officials decided to disapprove apartheid but avoid overt pressure (like economic sanctions) and urge gradual reform instead.

"Constructive engagement" did not work. The Pretoria government balked at serious reform and black South Africans protested and died for their freedom, demanding that the world support their cause. World opinion grew highly critical of U.S. policy for seeming to tolerate racism. As violence rocked South Africa and black moderates flirted with radical measures, Reagan also worried that the Soviets and communists would take advantage of the chaos. Protests in the United States pushed the issue higher on the political agenda. Members of Congress, as well as church, labor, and academic leaders, picketed the South African embassy in Washington, even inviting arrest to publicize the moral issue. The 1984 recipient of the Nobel Peace Prize, South African bishop Desmond M. Tutu, appealed to the United States to levy economic sanctions against his government. Cities and states passed divestiture laws requiring the sale of stocks from U.S. firms doing business in South Africa. Anti-apartheid groups also pressed U.S. corporations and universities to divest. Some companies pulled out. By late 1985, U.S. investment in South Africa had dropped to $1.3 billion from $2 billion in 1981.

To dampen protest in the United States and to rein in Congress, Reagan tried minor sanctions in September 1985. In addition to the long-standing UN ban on arms exports, Reagan restricted nuclear and computer sales and banned private U.S. bank loans to the South African government. The next month, however, a strong bipartisan consensus in Congress passed much stiffer economic sanctions over Reagan's veto, banning new U.S. investments and oil exports to South Africa and prohibiting imports of uranium, steel, and agricultural products from South Africa. Such economic pressure eventually helped to bring about the dismantling of apartheid in the next decade. Elsewhere in southern Africa, the new U.S.-Soviet deténte made possible a Washington-mediated settlement in 1988 in which Angola, Cuba, and South Africa agreed to black majority rule in Namibia and the withdrawal of Cuban troops from Angola.

In Asia, troubles with the Philippines beset the Reagan administration. Since becoming president in 1965, Ferdinand Marcos had established a dictatorship notorious for its corruption, military rule, and conspicuous personal aggrandizement. By the 1980s the Philippines staggered under high unemployment, a foreign debt of more than $20 billion, and continuing economic paralysis. Business leaders, the Catholic Church, intellectuals, and professional groups agitated for reform. A communist New People's Army and the Moro National Liberation Front of Muslims led separate insurgencies. The discontent against Marcos exploded in August 1983 when assassins gunned down the anti-Marcos leader Benigno S. Aquino on his return to Manila from exile in the United States. All evidence indicated a military plot connived by Marcos. When Cardinal Jaime Sin, the Catholic prelate in Manila, visited Washington in 1984 and told Reagan that Marcos had to step down, the President still feared that the alternative to Marcos would be communism.

At stake for the United States were private investments of $2 billion, commercial transactions of equal value, outstanding debts owed to U.S. banks, and two important U.S. military bases: Subic Bay Naval Station and Clark Air Base. "There is no hope for my naval base with that guy as president," commented Admiral William Crowe after a tour of the Philippines. "Choose between Marcos and that base." Even though Reagan vowed not to treat Marcos "as shabbily as our country had treated another former ally, the shah of Iran," he abandoned the Filipino dictator in February 1986 after Marcos stole an election from Benigno Aquino's widow, Corazon Aquino. After riots in Manila forced Marcos to seek sanctuary, U.S. Air Force planes flew him and his family into exile in Hawai'i. U.S. aid soon flowed to the new Aquino government.

A growing trade deficit became the focus of U.S.-Japanese relations during Reagan's presidency. A long-time strategic ally providing bases for the U.S. military and foreign aid to such countries as South Korea and Pakistan, Japan had become an economic rival, flooding U.S. markets with inexpensive, high-quality products. By 1985 the U.S. trade deficit with Japan had reached $50 billion—out of an all-time high total trade deficit of $148.5 billion. Much of the deficit resulted from a strong dollar abroad—making U.S. exports more expensive abroad and foreign goods cheaper in the United States—and growing Third World indebtedness, which meant fewer purchases of U.S. products overseas. Many in the United States, however, believed that Japan's tariff barriers, quotas, and subsidies blocked U.S. access to Japanese markets. Protectionists urged retaliatory tariffs on Japanese goods so that U.S. industries could compete and U.S. workers keep their jobs. Although the Japanese agreed to place quotas on automobile and carbon-steel exports to the United States, Congress demanded more than tokenism. Reagan imposed some restrictions on Japanese products in 1987, and the following year the Omnibus Trade and Competitiveness Act authorized economic retaliation against countries refusing to lower trade barriers.

The Reagan Legacy

Any fair assessment of the Reagan diplomatic record must recognize the achievements, especially at the end of his presidency: the cease-fire and transition to independence in Namibia, the Intermediate-Range Nuclear Forces Treaty, progress in strategic arms talks, the departure of dictators in the Philippines (Marcos) and Haiti (Jean-Claude Duvalier), the end of the Iran-Iraq War, and the evacuation of Cuban troops from Africa. Over the course of his two terms, Reagan seemed to have grown less ideological and more pragmatic. Deténte with the Soviet Union presaged the imminent demise of the Cold War, as Gorbachev ended the war in Afghanistan and relaxed Soviet domination of Eastern Europe. Conservative analysts claimed that the Reagan military buildup had forced the Soviets to make concessions; others pointed out that huge U.S. defense expenditures actually delayed détente by undermining Soviet moderates in their debates with Kremlin hard-liners. In the long run, moreover, Reagan may have caused the decline of U.S. power by running up the largest deficits in history and failing to repair the economy and reform the U.S. educational system, so that the United States could remain competitive.

Reagan's legacy also included the Iran-Contra affair, which subverted democratic procedures and might have led to the impeachment of a less popular president. In Central America, Reagan's policies contributed to high death tolls, ongoing insurgencies, ravaged economies, declining literacy rates, and misplaced support for the Contras. Regarding South Africa, Congress pushed the executive to take serious measures against apartheid. Reagan's reassuring rhetoric, moreover, could not obscure the fact that the national debt tripled to $2.8 trillion, that the United States had become a debtor nation.

Reagan's administration defied ideological opponents, built up massive military forces, financed counterrevolution, and defended global interests. In his confident assumption that the United States could make a flawed world perfect, he reaffirmed U.S. exceptionalism. Reagan's exuberant valedictory address claimed that "America is respected again in the world, and looked to for leadership." He departed Washington with the highest approval rating of any modern president.

Since leaving the White House, Reagan has written his memoirs, *An American Life* (1990), overseen the building of the Reagan Library in California, and received lucrative fees for speeches and lectures on public policy issues. He was diagnosed in 1994 as suffering from Alzheimer's Disease.

J. GARRY CLIFFORD

See also Afghanistan; Africa; Bush, George Herbert Walker; Cold War; Contras; Cuba; El Salvador; Gorbachev, Mikhail Sergeevich; Grenada; Grenada Invasion; Haig, Alexander Meigs, Jr.; Haiti; Intermediate-Range Nuclear Forces Treaty; International Trade and Commerce; Iran-Contra Affair; Iran-Iraq War; Israel; Japan; KAL-007 Incident; Lebanon; Marcos, Ferdinand; National Endowment for Democracy; Nicaragua; Nitze, Paul Henry; North, Oliver Lawrence; Nuclear Weapons and Strategy; Panama and Panama Canal; Philippines; Presidency; Race and Racism; Radio Martí; Reagan Doctrine; Russia and the Soviet Union; Shultz, George Pratt; South Africa; Strategic Defense Initiative; Terrorism

FURTHER READING

Cannon, Lou. *President Reagan: The Role of a Lifetime.* New York, 1991.

Carothers, Thomas H. *In the Name of Democracy: U.S. Policy Toward Latin America in the Reagan Years.* Berkeley, Calif., 1991.

Oye, Kenneth, Robert J. Lieby, and Donald Rothchild, eds. *Eagle Defiant: U.S. Foreign Policy in the 1980s.* Boston, Mass., 1983.

———, *Eagle Resurgent: The Reagan Era in U.S. Foeign Policy.* Boston, 1987.

Reagan, Ronald. *An American Life.* New York, 1990.

Schaller, Michael. *Reckoning with Reagan.* New York, 1992.

Shultz, George P. *Turmoil and Triumph: My Years as Secretary of State.* New York, 1993.

Vaughn, Stephen. *Ronald Reagan in Hollywood: Movies and Politics.* Cambridge, Mass., 1994.

REAGAN DOCTRINE

The idea, advanced by President Ronald Reagan and some of his principal foreign policy advisers, that the United States should assist insurgent groups opposing communist or communist-supported governments and groups in the Third World. In 1985, in a statement which some journalists referred to as the "Reagan Doctrine," the president declared: "Our mission is to nourish and defend freedom and democracy." To this end, the United States would support those "on every continent, from Afghanistan to Nicaragua to defy Soviet-supported aggression and [to] secure rights which have been ours from birth." U.S. "support for freedom fighters," he explained, "is self-defense."

In its fundamental strategy of not just containing communism but pushing it back, the Reagan Doctrine resembled the "rollback" concept espoused by Secretary of State John Foster Dulles in the 1950s. The difference, however, was that whereas Dulles did little to move beyond the rhetoric of rollback, the Reagan administration most definitely did. Indeed, even before the 1985 speech, U.S. military and intelligence capabilities for what became known as "low intensity conflicts" (LICs) were being increased and enhanced. Such operations had the virtue of being relatively cheap and unlikely to provoke direct conflict with the Soviet Union, while still threatening Soviet interests.

The Reagan Doctrine also reflected ideas voiced in 1979 by Jeane Kirkpatrick (whom Reagan named ambassador to the United Nations) in a widely circulated article published in *Commentary*. Kirkpatrick accused the administration of President Jimmy Carter of destabilizing friendly "right-wing autocracies" by foolishly criticizing alleged human-rights violations. When such regimes collapsed, she said, they would likely be replaced by pro-Soviet, anti-U.S. radicals.

William Casey, Reagan's director of the Central Intelligence Agency believed that the Soviet Union was "tremendously overextended and vulnerable." If the United States challenged the Soviets everywhere and defeated them in even one place, "that will shatter the mythology...and it will all start to unravel." Casey said: "Nicaragua is that place."

Between 1981 and 1989, the United States trained, supplied, and paid for anticommunist insurgencies in Angola, Mozambique, Kampuchea (Cambodia), and Afghanistan, as well as Nicaragua. In El Salvador, Washington supported government forces engaged in a brutal civil war against left-wing guerrillas.

President Reagan himself traced the idea of a Reagan Doctrine back to a speech he delivered in March 1982 at his alma mater, Eureka College. At that time, he renewed an offer to Moscow to negotiate strategic arms reductions, but warned then and in related speeches that the United States stood ready to retaliate against Soviet expansion. Reagan later explained that he wanted Kremlin leader Leonid Brezhnev to understand that "we knew what the Soviets were up to and that we weren't going to stand by and do nothing while they sought world domination." The president hoped to "send out a signal that the United States intended to support people fighting for their freedom against communism wherever they were."

The Reagan Doctrine's record was mixed. Its main successes were in Afghanistan and Kampuchea, where the U.S.-supported guerrillas ultimately helped force the Soviet and Vietnamese armies, respectively, to withdraw. In Afghanistan, however, the extreme violence and instability that ensued have led some observers to question the consequences and the costs of this operation, which armed Islamic guerrillas to fight Soviet forces. In Angola, the Union for the Total Independence of Angola (UNITA) faction of Jonas Savimbi kept fighting even after the United States cut off its support and in spite of elections being held and a United Nations peacekeeping mission being sent. The issue of Nicaragua and whether the Reagan policy was part of the solution or part of the problem were intensely debated in the United States both during the Contra war and since February 1990, when free elections were finally held in Nicaragua and the Sandinistas were voted out of office.

MICHAEL SCHALLER

See also Afghanistan; Angola; Carter, James Earl; Casey, William Joseph; Containment; Contras; Dulles, John Foster; El Salvador; Nicaragua; Reagan, Ronald Wilson; Rollback and Liberation

FURTHER READING

LaFeber, Walter. *America, Russia and the Cold War, 1945–1992.*, 7th ed. New York, 1993.
Schaller, Michael. *Reckoning with Reagan: America and Its President in the 1980s.* New York, 1992.
Scott, James M. *Deciding to Intervene: The Reagan Doctrine and American Foreign Policy.* Durham, N.C., 1996.

REALISM

A philosophical position that has both a general and a specific definition. Realist thought can be found in all civilizations; it is identifiable as a skeptical or somber attitude toward the human condition and prospects for moral progress. The Greek historian Thucydides, the Indian thinker Kautilya, and Arab philosopher Ibn Khaldun, and most notably the British philosopher Thomas Hobbes, all shared this attitude toward politics as an unremitting struggle for power and survival in an anarchic, hostile world. Realism (with a capital "R") is a specific political doctrine that first arose in early modern Europe. In this form, Realism is a tradition of systematic speculation and scholarship regarding the nature and conduct of international affairs. Both defenders and critics of this latter conception of realism acknowledge it to be the predominant "theory" of international affairs.

The Doctrine of Classical Realism

The renaissance "advice to princes' tradition," and particularly the sixteenth-century writings of Italian philosopher Niccolò Machiavelli, provide the intellectual origins of realism. Living at a time when the European state system was taking shape and beginning to transform the political map of the continent, Machiavelli formulated the conceptual basis of modern statecraft. Political behavior, he argued, ought to be based on the realities of political life and not on the moral precepts of Christian doctrine. Students of politics should understand how politicians actually behave rather than how they ought to behave as good Christians. Advocating a "civic religion" as a means to unify his fractious fellow Italians, Machiavelli argued for what is today called "nationalism" as embodying the highest loyalty of human beings. Machiavelli's secularization of political thought bequeathed to his fellow Europeans the conception of political affairs as an autonomous realm of action and scholarly analysis and thus laid the intellectual foundations of modern Realist doctrine. The Thirty Years War (1618–1648) and the Treaty of Westphallia (1648), ending the bloody internecine struggles in Europe, were the formative events in the European Realist conception of statecraft. After three decades of religious slaughter, the statesmen who gathered at Westphallia agreed that thenceforth religious and other domestic matters were not to be considered legitimate concerns for international relations. In order to limit conflict, they decreed that international politics should be concerned only with the interests of states, and states should not intervene in the internal affairs of other states. Thus, the doctrine of national sovereignty and the principle of nonintervention became the principal foundations of the European conception of international statecraft.

During the following century, additional elements were added to the classical Realist theory of international politics. Foremost among these components of Realist thought was the primacy of the state in international affairs. Strongly influenced by the new Newtonian mechanics, Realist thinkers and statesmen regarded the state essentially as a closed structure embedded in a system of impersonal forces of contending interests and power balances. The objective of the state and its foreign policy was to defend its national interest, defined mainly in terms of territorial security. The principal means of pursuing the national interest was the use of military power. Both power and interest, like physical forces, were regarded as measurable quantities that could serve as an objective basis for political calculation and policy formulation.

Over time, and on the basis of this mechanistic model of the international system, Realist thought and practice reinforced one another: Realist thinkers drew from the behavior of states and Realist ideas helped guide the actions of statesmen. Together, Realist writers and practitioners made three very important contributions to international statecraft. The first innovation that emerged from this joining of theory and practice was the Grotian (after Dutch jurist Hugo Grotius) conception of European statecraft; Europe was regarded as "a society of states" whose members were bound by international law with respect to such matters as diplomatic behavior and the conduct of war. The second innovation was the concept and practice of the balance of power as a system of international governance; the Europeans created a novel set of devices and institutions, such as permanent diplomacy and multilateral treaties, to preserve the power balance among the great powers and thereby prevent the domination of the continent. The third innovation was the equally novel concept of war as an instrument of national policy; war was transformed from an unlimited clash of societies to a limited means by which to achieve specific political objectives. While these three innovations became less relevant to the vastly changed world at the end of the twentieth century, they were still a lasting contribution to modern statecraft.

American Realist Thought

Although the founders of the United States, as George Kennan wrote, were adherents of European Realism, the Realist conception of statecraft faded as American exceptionalism triumphed. The United States turned its back on European statecraft with its emphasis on the role of power and struggle in international affairs. The United States entered World War I reluctantly, and President Woodrow Wilson envisioned a postwar international order that would reject Realism and would be based on such liberal principles as the concept of collective security and the self-determination of all peoples. Despite the trenchant criticism of Wilsonianism by E. H. Carr in the late 1930s, the victorious democracies following World War II once again anticipated the triumph of liberal values. The unanticipated advent of the Cold War and the confrontation with the Soviet Union ran directly counter to this revival of the Wilsonian dream and gave rise to the great debate in the early 1950s between American liberalism and European Realism.

While American Realists, such as Kennan, Walter Lippmann, and Reinhold Niebuhr were important contributors to this debate, European expatriates were especially important in the effort to transplant Realist ideas to the unreceptive American liberal soil. The task of domesticating European Realism and making it more palatable to liberal America was carried out principally by Hans Morgenthau in his highly influential *Politics Among Nations*. For the early postwar era, *Politics* became the basic text of American Realism. A refugee from Nazi Germany, Morgenthau wrote against the background of the failure of the liberal democracies to understand the evil of German "universal nationalism" and his belief that the democracies were again threatened as a result of Soviet expansion.

Morgenthau sought to reconcile American liberalism and social science with the Realist "advice to princes" tradition. Realism, he declared, was an objective science based on the universal principle of statecraft that states pursue their national interests defined in terms of power. Morgenthau cautioned, however, that Realism was not a license for the amoral behavior of an Adolf Hitler or a Joseph Stalin. Therefore, he advised American "princes" to act prudently and moderately in the pursuit of American national interests.

The successor generation of American realists accepted Morgenthau's emphasis on the state, national interest, and power; as they developed what became known as neo-Realism, however, they rejected his simplistic conception of social science, his unsuccessful attempt to reconcile realism with liberal morality, and the narrow scope of his Realism. While neo-Realism is as intellectually diverse as classical Realism, it should be noted that neo-Realist scholars drew heavily on the theories of contemporary social science and generally eschew the "advice to princes" tradition. They also tend to place more emphasis on the effect of the international system on foreign policy. Kenneth Waltz, in his highly influential *Theory of International Politics* (1979), could in fact be labeled a "structural realist" because, for him, the structure of the international system with its distribution of power between or among "poles" (e.g., bipolar, multipolar) largely determines state behavior; other neo-Realist writers, such as Robert Gilpin, on the other hand, acknowledge the important role of domestic factors in foreign policy. Finally, whereas Morgenthau, for example, had almost no interest in economic matters, neo-Realism has had a significant role in the development of new critiques of the international political economy. Despite these changes, however, American neo-Realism is very much an offshoot of the classical Realist tradition.

Both American Realists and neo-Realists supported the major objective of postwar U.S. foreign policy, that is, containment of Soviet expansion. It was Kennan who set forth what became known as the Containment Doctrine, and throughout the postwar years, leading Realist thinkers frequently disagreed with important aspects of U.S. policy. Walter Lippmann and other Realists, for example, strongly dissented from the transformation of the Containment Doctrine into a global ideological struggle between communism and democracy. Realists also believed that the United States had no quarrel with Communist China. Further, they argued that the United States had few national interests at stake in the Third World, and they therefore objected to U.S. intervention there, especially if the objective was the ideological one of defeating communism or promoting human rights. It is noteworthy that many leading Realists strongly opposed the Vietnam War; Vietnam, they reasoned, lay outside the sphere of U.S. interests, and U.S. intervention would inevitably lead to a conflict with China. The policy prescriptions of Realists such as Kennan, Morgenthau, and Henry Kissinger were all intended to contain the Soviet Union while also supporting a concentrated effort to reach specific arms control and other diplomatic settlements so that the Cold War would not escalate into a hot war, which neither side wanted; the goal was not to win an ideological victory. In brief, the foreign policy agenda of the Realists was a narrow but important one based on what they perceived to be the national interests of the United States. Realist ideas, however, did not match American liberal attitudes, and these ideas seldom received the hearing desired by realists.

Critiques of "Realpolitik"

Critics have long condemned Realism (or as they prefer, Realpolitik) as immoral. From Friedrich Meinecke's attack on Machiavellianism to more recent assaults on Realists as apologists for U.S. imperialism, detractors have charged that Realism has rationalized the evil practices of states. This charge does indeed raise a troubling problem, because, despite Morgenthau's principles of prudent diplomacy, Realism lacks an adequate moral foundation to counterbalance Thucydides's assertion that "the powerful do what they can and the poor suffer what they must." As Alexander George and Gordon Craig have argued, however, this distorted interpretation of Realism should be distinguished from the Realism whose central purpose has been in fact to moderate state behavior. The concept of national interest, for example, was introduced to limit the arbitrary and contentious behavior of absolute monarchs. The state was conceived by early Realists as the embodiment of the people and not as the ruler's personal fiefdom; foreign policy should be in the interests of the whole society rather than in the narrow dynastic interests of the ruler. The crucial idea that if each nation were to pursue its self-interest and were to respect the interests of others, the result would be a moderation of international politics that has underlaid this conception of statecraft.

Late twentieth-century critics also emphasized the limitations of Realism's assumptions. Whatever relevance Realism may have had in the past, they argue, its assumptions are increasingly unrealistic. In the contemporary world, they point out, multinational corporations and other powerful nonstate actors compete with the state; further, the state is constrained by transnational forces. The goals of statecraft are also alleged to have been transformed; some argue that domestic welfare, environmental protection, and other nonsecurity goals have become of equal or greater importance than the traditional national security concerns emphasized by Realists. Lastly, the spread of democracy, critics argue, is making societies more peaceful. Moreover, many assert, the advent of nuclear weapons has made war an anachronism. Contemporary developments are thus alleged to have outmoded Realist doctrine.

The Realism attacked by most critics is a highly oversimplified one. Realists have always recognized that the state has had to share the stage with other powerful actors; for example, the Dutch East India Company, which had its own army, conducted a foreign policy, and managed a global empire, makes late twentieth-century multinational corporations pale in comparison. In general, Realists have not denied the importance of welfare and nonsecurity goals in human affairs; they have been fully aware, to paraphrase Thucydides, that human beings are motivated by honor, economic interests, and fear. Fear or the desire for security, however, has always been the most fundamental human motive. With respect to the effects of the spread of democracy and the utility of war in the nuclear age, there is not yet compelling evidence that nations, including democratic ones, have given up reliance on military power; military strength continues to be built and nuclear weapons proliferate throughout the world. Despite important islands of peace and cooperation, one does not need to be reminded that international politics continues to be a struggle for national survival.

Realism as a philosophical disposition—that is, realism with a small "r"—toward political affairs will probably never disappear. Based on a conception of human nature as being corrupt and self-centered, realism assumes, in the words of Morgenthau, that mankind is corrupt and is driven by an insatiable "lust for power" that manifests itself in all ages and under all conditions. Realism as a specific doctrine of statecraft based on the primacy of the state, however, may one day be superseded. Realism with a capital "R" originated in a particular economic, technological, and political environment; it has been embraced because it has addressed perceived needs of the time. As historical circumstances change and new challenges arise, Realism may not retain its relevance for human affairs, but for this transformation to occur there would have to be a significant shift in human loyalties away from the state or ethnic group to some larger, more inclusive political entity.

ROBERT G. GILPIN, JR.

See also Kennan, George Frost; Lippmann, Walter; Kissinger, Henry Alfred; Morgenthau, Hans

FURTHER READING

Bull, Hedley. *The Anarchical Society*. New York, 1977.
Craig, Gordon A., and Alexander L. George. *Force and Statecraft: Diplomatic Problems of Our Time*. New York, 1990.
Kennan, George F. *American Diplomacy, 1900–1950*. Chicago, 1951.
Keohane, Robert, ed. *Neo-Realism and Its Critics*. New York, 1986.

Meinecke, Friedrich. *The Doctrine of Raison d'État and Its Place in Modern History*. Boulder, Colo., 1984.
Waltz, Kenneth. *Theory of International Politics*. Reading, Mass., 1979.

RECIPROCAL TRADE AGREEMENT ACT
(1934)

Congressional legislation, which amended the Smoot-Hawley Tariff of 1930, that gave the president the power to make foreign trade agreements with other countries about the reduction of duties without the approval of Congress. The legislation produced a serious backlash for U.S. economic interests. Rather than allowing U.S. firms to regain a competitive edge by excluding cheap imports, the high tariffs of President Herbert Hoover's administration led to retaliation by U.S. trading partners, including the generally cooperative Latin American nations. World trade contracted sharply, and U.S. imports fell from $5.4 billion in 1929 to $2.1 billion in 1933. President Franklin D. Roosevelt was initially ambivalent about the merits of opening the U.S. market at a time of depression, but after the failed London Conference of 1933, he was persuaded by Secretary of State Cordell Hull to take the risk. Hull drafted the Reciprocal Trade Agreement Act (RTAA)—technically an amendment to the Smoot-Hawley legislation—and pushed it through Congress in 1934. The act gave the president temporary authority to negotiate up to 50 percent cuts in tariffs on a bilateral basis. The negotiations were based on reciprocity and most-favored-nation principles, although trade agreements tended to focus on products in which the negotiating parties were dominant suppliers.

The RTAA represented an intellectual and political breakthrough, with the result that U.S. tariffs fell progressively, following periodic renewals of the president's negotiating authority, from roughly 50 percent overall in 1933 to close to 5 percent by 1950. Not only did the RTAA help propel a modest recovery in world trade in the mid-1930s, but it became the legal and philosophical foundation for the General Agreement on Tariffs and Trade (GATT) negotiations through the early 1960s. These negotiations brought an end to tariff barriers as a major obstacle to international trade and saw an unprecedented expansion of economic vitality and exchange of goods.

KENDALL W. STILES

See also General Agreement on Tariffs and Trade; Hull, Cordell; International Trade and Commerce

FURTHER READING

Donnelly, William, ed. *American Economic Growth: The Historic Challenge*. New York, 1973.
Kindleberger, Charles. *The World in Depression, 1929–1939*. Berkeley, Calif., 1975.

RECIPROCITY

See Reciprocal Trade Agreement Act

RECOGNITION

The practice of sovereign, independent nations to recognize the authority and legitimacy of each other's governments. The act of recognition can be a formal declaration or implicit in the addressing of a communication to another government. Recognition among large- and middle-sized countries normally is accompanied by the exchange of ambassadors or other envoys and the establishment of diplomatic offices in the capital cities of the other. Recognition, however, can stand alone without the institutions of active relations. Non-recognition can mean denial of the legitimate statehood of a country; for example, the United States did not recognize Manchukuo, the puppet entity of Japan in Manchuria in the 1930s. More frequently, non-recognition applies only to a particular regime, such as the military regime of Haiti in the early 1990s.

Governments sometimes break diplomatic relations to express extreme disapproval of another government—in time of war, for example—but a break in relations does not necessarily mean the end of recognition. Nations can also have diplomatic relations without formal recognition. Between 1972 and 1979 the United States and the People's Republic of China maintained "liaison offices" in each other's capitals. In this case, not until full "normalization" and the exchange of ambassadors were full diplomatic relations and recognition achieved. Similarly, in 1994, the United States and Vietnam opened liaison offices, but did not establish full diplomatic relations. Another device by which two countries with less than friendly relations can maintain contact after a break in diplomatic relations is through the "interest section"—an office run by a friendly third country out of its own diplomatic premises. Thus, after the United States and Cuba broke diplomatic relations in 1961, Switzerland provided an interest section for the United States in Havana and Czechoslovakia did the same for the Cubans in the United States. In 1977 Americans and Cubans staffed the respective interest sections in the opposite capitals. Representatives of the two countries could thus negotiate agreements without having official diplomatic relations.

Recognition ordinarily expresses no approval, but is a simple necessity of communication. In theory the nature of the government to be recognized is irrelevant as long as it is in effective control of the country. In 1793, following the violent overthrow of the French monarchy by a revolutionary regime, Secretary of State Thomas Jefferson enunciated the classic American position: "We surely cannot deny to any Nation that right whereon our own government is founded, that everyone may govern itself according to whatever form it pleases; and change these forms at its own will; and that it may transact its business with foreign nations through whatever organ it thinks proper, whether King, Convention, Assembly, Committee, President or anything else it may choose, the will of the nation is the only thing essential to be regarded." U.S. diplomatic relations with France continued unbroken. Or as Winston Churchill put it in 1949 while advocating recognition of the new People's Republic of China by Great Britain: "One has to recognize lots of things and people in this world of sin and woe that one does not like. The reason for having diplomatic relations is not to confer a compliment, but to secure a convenience."

The United States held to the classic position through the nineteenth century, adding the provision that to be recognized a government must show respect for its international obligations. But in 1913 President Woodrow Wilson, in dealing with governments of Latin America, introduced a new principle: the government must have been established through constitutional procedures respecting the will of the people. He put it this way: "Cooperation is possible only when supported at every turn by the orderly processes of just government…[and] just government rests always upon the consent of the governed." Wilson used the withholding of recognition as a weapon against those who did not meet his standards, most notably the military regime of General Victoriano Huerta in Mexico. Under political, military, and economic pressure, Huerta resigned. Similar arguments were used by Wilson and subsequent administrations in withholding diplomatic recognition from the Soviet Union for sixteen years.

The administrations of Franklin D. Roosevelt and Harry S. Truman made a limited attempt to return to the Jeffersonian position. Roosevelt recognized the government of the Soviet Union and the two countries established diplomatic relations in 1934. Roosevelt also recognized and maintained diplomatic relations with the Vichy government of France established in 1940 after the German conquest in spite of Vichy's fascist taint and dependant relationship with Nazi Germany. This pragmatic policy was heavily criticized by liberals as providing support for evil. When American troops landed in North Africa in 1942, the United States broke relations with Vichy. The Truman administration tried to return to a pre-Wilson policy toward Latin America and explicitly rejected the argument that only democratic governments should receive recognition. Secretary of State Dean Acheson in 1949 declared: "We maintain diplomatic relations with other countries primarily because we are all on the same planet and must do business with each other. We do not establish an embassy or legation in a foreign country to show approval of its government." However, less than a week after Acheson's statement the People's

Republic of China was proclaimed in Beijing (1 October 1949) and the Truman administration refused to recognize the new Communist government.

During and after the Cold War the United States decided issues of recognition on a case-by-case basis in response to perceived national interests and domestic political pressure. The Reagan administration maintained diplomatic relations with the Sandinista regime of Nicaragua during the 1980s even while covertly seeking its overthrow. The Bush administration did not favor the precipitous breakup of the Soviet Union or of Yugoslavia and was slower than Western European governments to extend recognition and establish relations with the independent successor states. No U.S. administration dared, largely for domestic political reasons, to reestablish formal relations with Fidel Castro's Cuba after they were broken in 1961. The Bush and Clinton administrations recognized Jean-Bertrand Aristide as president of Haiti for years after he was ousted in a military coup in September 1991 and not only refused recognition but in 1994, through military invasion, removed the military regime in Port-au-Prince. The classic Jeffersonian position was all but dead.

GADDIS SMITH

See also Acheson, Dean Gooderham; Ambassadors and Embassies; China; Cuba; Diplomatic Method; France; Huerta, Victoriano; Jefferson, Thomas; Vietnam; Wilson, Thomas Woodrow

FURTHER READING

Whiteman, Marjorie M. *Digest of International Law*, vol 2. Washington, D.C., 1963.

REFUGEES

U.S. refugee policy, like many other aspects of U.S. foreign policy, blends three different elements: first, U.S. idealism; second, the U.S. national interest; third, U.S. domestic politics. As in other aspects of U.S. policy, the precise mix that may prevail at any given moment is difficult to predict. It will often change over time. Much depends on whether domestic or international considerations are primarily at stake, as well as on the intensity of competing pressures. Each of the three elements motivating U.S. policy has a particular relevance to refugee matters. U.S. idealism about helping refugees arises out of a deep awareness that the United States was largely peopled by refugees, by those who had to flee their home countries to find freedom and a better life in the United States. The U.S. national interest also becomes powerfully involved because the United States wants to help friendly countries that are bearing the burdens of a refugee inflow; it also will often use refugees to underline the illegitimacy of the regime from which the refugees are fleeing. Finally, U.S. domestic opinion is an essential part of refugee matters because Americans often support their preferred refugee groups with private donations as well as through the government; domestic opinion comes into play even more when refugees come to the United States in large numbers.

Despite these different and sometimes mutually contradictory elements shaping U.S. refugee policy, the broad trend of that policy has been consistent since the middle of the twentieth century. Since World War II, the United States has been at the center of the global system for protecting, assisting, and resettling refugees. The U.S. government has been the principal financial supporter of every major international refugee organization as well as of most separate programs. The United States has also accepted more refugees for resettlement than any other country, and those refugees have for the most part been quickly integrated into their new communities. The operations of U.S. voluntary agencies span the globe, helping refugees on virtually every continent with private as well as public support.

The Interwar Period

The U.S. commitment to refugees was not, however, always as strong as it was to become. The United States played only a very small role in helping the millions of European refugees who were created by the redrawing of European borders after World War I and the simultaneous dissolution of several European multinational empires. The U.S. government, hobbled by widespread isolationist sentiment and preoccupied with the postwar recession, was not disposed to become involved in solving what most saw as a European problem. President Woodrow Wilson asked Herbert Hoover, who had headed the Belgian Relief Commission, to assume charge of a U.S. relief operation that ultimately provided almost $1 billion in assistance in over twenty countries, but the United States did not become substantially involved in the refugee relief and resettlement operations conducted by the League of Nations. Great Britain and France, along with smaller European governments and especially the Scandinavian states, provided the bulk of the assistance and personnel for refugee relief and rehabilitation.

After its involvement in World War I, the United States increasingly withdrew into its own concerns as the 1920s advanced and did even more so after the onset of the Great Depression. Entry to the United States was governed by the U.S. immigration laws of 1921 and 1924 which had promulgated a quota system favoring groups already strongly represented in the U.S. population. Such an arrangement sharply limited entry of refugees. In addition, the United States kept out persons "likely to become a public charge," a category that clearly encompassed most of the penniless refugees.

By the late 1920s and early 1930s, immigration to the United States had sunk to the lowest peace-time levels in decades and the United States continued to remain aloof from relief operations to help refugees stranded in Europe. U.S. political and public opinion were also deeply suspicious about the motivation of refugees, especially those who might want to come to the United States. There was widespread fear that the virulently revolutionary regime in the Soviet Union would try to use refugees to infiltrate the United States for sabotage, subversion, and propaganda. That fear applied with at least equal force to the Fascist and Nazi regimes in Italy and Germany. The U.S. government shifted the Immigration and Naturalization Service (INS) from the Department of Labor to the Department of Justice to permit closer security surveillance of refugees as well as other applicants. But the principal concern raised by the Nazi regime was its determined persecution of Jews in Germany and German-occupied countries. The Nazis, whose first anti-Jewish policy was expulsion, began to flood Europe with refugees. More and more Jews tried to flee to neutral European states and then to the United States. President Franklin D. Roosevelt, the Department of State, and many influential U.S. political and intellectual groups had deep reservations about permitting large numbers of Jewish refugees to settle in the United States. Roosevelt was reluctant to single out Jewish groups for special entry although he involved himself in some individual cases (such as that of Sigmund Freud) and arranged for some relaxation of consular requirements for documentation. Roosevelt became alarmed, however, when the Nazi annexation of Austria in March 1938 suddenly produced a new and massive wave of refugees. He called for an international forum on refugees in 1938. But that forum, held in the French resort city of Evian-les-Bains, showed no inclination by any state to accept large numbers of Jewish refugees. Roosevelt's initiative at the Evian forum led to the formation of the Inter-Governmental Committee on Refugees (IGCR). That committee was given two tasks: first, to negotiate with Germany on the orderly departure of refugees, permitting persons to take at least some of their possessions and avoiding the kind of overwhelming and unanticipated floods of refugees that swamped any hopes for relief and resettlement; second, to locate resettlement opportunities. The committee was unable to achieve either because the Nazis refused to permit orderly departures and the Western states were unwilling to commit to fixed immigration pledges. Negotiations were broken off after the German invasion of Poland in September 1939. The U.S. Department of State and the U.S. Congress, like European authorities, were resistant to permitting entry of Jewish refugees. The German annual immigration quota of 23,370 was not filled during most of the 1930s, with annual totals running between 4,000 and 10,000 (most of them Jewish). By 1939 and 1940, as the European crisis deepened, refugees filled almost all of the German quota, but Congress refused to permit refugee entries above the quota. As World War II continued, however, and as the U.S. government began receiving ever more explicit reports about the Nazi extermination camps and Jewish groups were becoming ever more insistent, the U.S. government acted to ease the requirements for entry of Jewish refugees. The creation of the War Refugee Board in January 1944 stimulated both easier refugee entry and a more active U.S. international role. The Department of State asked European governments to refuse to repatriate Jews to Germany. These interventions were effective in many countries, such as Spain, where many refugees from Nazism had fled. But they proved to be too little and too late. Stung by its failure to act swiftly and generously, the U.S. government undertook more steps toward international coordination and increasingly began to take the lead in refugee matters. President Roosevelt invited the allies to another conference on refugees, this one held in Bermuda in April 1943. The allies agreed that the IGCR should expand its functions to help all refugees created by the war. The IGCR also helped to support the underground escape routes used by refugees from the Nazis. It continued to play a coordinating role among the Western states during and after World War II. In 1946, it established an internationally recognized travel document for refugees and began resettlement operations. The organization that Roosevelt had created thus proved able to help refugees in a variety of ways even if it fell short of accomplishing its original mandate.

The Years After World War II

After World War II, the United States assumed a much more important role in refugee matters than it had assumed after World War I. It became a driving force behind a new and much-expanded European refugee effort as France and Great Britain had exhausted their own resources. It took the lead in offering aid as well as resettlement opportunities to refugees. The U.S. government's active role was strongly supported and even spurred on by a host of U.S. voluntary agencies financed by private contributions. It was also endorsed by its allies, who provided important legal and political support to refugee protection and assistance efforts even if they lacked U.S. financial resources. The United States was the largest contributor to the United Nations Relief and Rehabilitation Agency (UNRRA) that attempted to repatriate refugees throughout Europe until 1947. It then also became the most important contributor to the International Refugee Organization (IRO), which succeeded the IGCR and which concentrated on the resettlement of refugees in third countries, after it had become clear that many refugees and prisoners of war did not want to return to countries in Eastern Europe and especially to the Soviet Union. The United States contributed more than one-half of the IRO's $400,000 budget. In a dramatic reversal of its prewar policies, it accepted more than a third of the million European refugees who were resettled outside their home countries.

The United States and its major allies did not wish to have the IRO under the United Nations (UN) itself, although the IRO had been created by the UN General Assembly, for they thought that the tasks of the IRO would be primarily humanitarian and social. The United States and its allies also agreed that the IRO mandate should be limited in time (to four-and-a-half years) because refugees were to be considered a temporary and not a permanent international phenomenon. But refugee questions could not remain purely humanitarian, for decisions by refugees and about refugees were often made on a political basis. And the political problems associated with repatriation and resettlement became increasingly evident as the United Nations began deliberating refugee issues. The Soviet Union insisted that all Soviet and East European citizens should be immediately repatriated to their home countries, if necessary by force. Through the efforts of Eleanor Roosevelt, the late president's widow, the United States led the counterargument for free choice. The argument with the Soviet Union about refugee policy helped persuade the U.S. government that the conflict between Western and Soviet attitudes could prevent cooperation even on supposedly nonpolitical matters. By 1949, it had become clear that persistent Soviet demands for forcible repatriation could be a real threat to refugees if it was followed up by Soviet diplomatic pressure against states where refugees had found asylum. The Western allies decided that a person and an organization with a clear mandate to safeguard refugee rights was needed after the IRO's term had expired.

At Western urging, the UN General Assembly established the office of United Nations High Commissioner for Refugees (UNHCR) and gave the new high commissioner the responsibility for protecting refugees. The United States wanted to give the high commissioner the authority of the United Nations mantle in order to help protect refugees, but it did not wish the high commissioner to be subject to political guidance or to be deterred by a veto in the Security Council. The high commissioner was to act on a humanitarian basis. Like the IRO, however, the mandate of the high commissioner was limited in time (three years beginning in 1951). The General Assembly accepted the U.S. and Western view. The United States also urged creation of another organization, the Inter-Governmental Committee for European Migration (ICEM) to assume the operational functions of the IRO even as the UNHCR assumed the protection functions. The United States also led in financing the ICEM. (Since its foundation, the ICEM has had several name changes as its functions have expanded, and it is now known as the International Organization for Migration, the IOM.) The United States and its allies also gained widespread international approval of a document spelling out refugee rights, the UN Refugee Convention of 1951. That convention defined a refugee as a person who, "...owing to well-founded fear of being persecuted for reasons of race, religion, nationality, membership in a particular social group or political opinion, is outside the country of his nationality and is unable or, owing to such fear, is unwilling to avail himself of the protection of that country...." That original definition, regarded as temporary like other postwar actions regarding refugees, was extended indefinitely and globally by a 1967 protocol. The definition therefore now covers refugees everywhere. Because the UN Convention and the high commissioner's responsibilities were originally confined to Europe, another organization was needed to support Palestinian refugees after the creation of the state of Israel in 1948. The United States helped to establish the United Nations Relief and Work Agency (UNRWA) in 1949 and became the organization's principal single donor. The United States also made special arrangements to help refugees in and from Korea and China.

The Cold War Years

By 1947, the Cold War had begun in earnest. The Berlin blockade of 1948–1949 had convinced the U.S. government and U.S. public opinion that the Soviet Union was a threat to U.S. interests in Europe as well as to the freedom of Western Europe itself. The Soviet coup in Czechoslovakia in 1948 had shown that Moscow would not tolerate democracy. The North Korean attack against South Korea in 1950 had suggested that the Soviet Union and its allies would use military force when it suited their interests. The combination was widely interpreted as a sign that the United States and its allies confronted the same kind of militaristic and potentially aggressive totalitarian dictator in Stalin that they had earlier confronted in Hitler. And all U.S. policy, including U.S. attitudes toward refugees, began to be shaped by this analysis and by the Cold War itself. Because Soviet totalitarianism, like Nazi totalitarianism, would not tolerate dissent, refugees were legitimized as victims of repression who were seeking liberty. They were often termed "freedom fighters" and seen as heroes. As the U.S. government and its allies moved with increasing vigor to protect and assist refugees in Europe and elsewhere, U.S. officials wanted to offer refugees the opportunity to resettle in the United States outside the limitations of the U.S. immigration laws. President Harry S. Truman issued an Executive Order on 22 December 1945, permitting voluntary agencies to issue guarantees that a refugee would not become a public charge. This facilitated entry of refugees, who could normally not be sponsored by family members like regular immigrants. Truman then urged Congress to pass the 1946 Displaced Persons Act which ultimately permitted the entry of over 400,000 refugees into the United States. For the first time in U.S. history, refugees were placed outside the regular immigration stream. Religious, ethnic, and welfare groups could coordinate with private voluntary agencies to assist entry and resettlement of refugees outside the quota system.

The U.S. Congress continued to give special consideration to refugee entry. In 1952, after it had passed the restrictive McCarran-Walter Immigration Act, it approved the Refugee Relief Act which allowed over 200,000 refugees from communist-controlled countries in Europe to enter outside the immigration quotas. The act also permitted entry of refugees from China, a departure from the longstanding U.S. immigration practice of excluding Asians. In 1957, in response to the Hungarian uprising, Congress further liberalized entry of refugees. In 1960, under the Fair Share Law, Congress offered the first permanent U.S. refugee legislation. It authorized the admission to the United States of 25 percent of refugees that were admitted for resettlement in other countries. Congress also authorized entry of refugees from Cuba. Despite the best efforts of many nations, the refugee problem in Europe was not eliminated even ten years after World War II. Although the number of refugees had been gradually whittled down, over 100,000 remained as burdens for the countries of asylum and the agencies supporting them. It became clear that major funds would be needed to solve the problem. The UN high commissioner asked the Ford Foundation in New York for a grant to help provide for assistance and resettlement, which the Ford Foundation provided in 1953 and 1954. Thus, the high commissioner began to assume the function of assisting refugees as well as the function of protecting them. To permit the high commissioner to continue in that new role, governments agreed to help fund a UNHCR assistance program. In short order, the United States and other Western states established the Executive Committee of the High Commissioner's Program to assume the responsibilities for broad management of the aid funds even though the high commissioner retained the protection function. The need for assistance funds exploded with the Hungarian uprising in 1956, as over 200,000 refugees poured into Austria and Yugoslavia. They needed not only protection but shelter, food, medicine, and other services that the local governments and voluntary agencies could not provide. The high commissioner's program began to reflect those needs, rising to

$12 million by 1958. Of those funds, the United States contributed $5.1 million, beginning the practice of having the U.S. government be the largest donor to the UNHCR.

The Globalization of Refugee Problems

With its response to Hungarian refugees, the United Nations—with strong U.S. support—had put into place the basic structure of the international refugee regime. The UN high commissioner was at the center, not only insuring protection but increasingly providing assistance, while other international organizations played roles as necessary. Voluntary agencies served as operating instruments, using their own funds and those provided by national governments through the UNHCR. The West European and North American states, with help from Japan, Australia, New Zealand, and some others, provided the funding and the resettlement places. They also provided the public and political support needed to make certain that the system would be maintained. The United States was also bringing its domestic legislation into line with the new international realities. President John F. Kennedy prompted the enactment in 1962 of the Migration and Refugee Assistance Act, granting permanent authorization of U.S. funding for such multilateral organizations as UNHCR and ICEM and also instituting a contingency fund to support refugee assistance and resettlement in emergency situations. President Lyndon Johnson continued Kennedy's tradition of generosity toward refugees, putting refugee admissions on a more structured basis. At his urging, Congress passed the Immigration and Nationality Act of 1965 which for the first time inserted a permanent refugee section into U.S. immigration law. It permitted the reservation of visas for persons who had fled from communist or communist-dominated countries or areas as well as from the general area of the Middle East. But the refugee problem did not remain confined to Europe and to the Middle East. Instead, it spread to almost all parts of the world. As it spread, the number of worldwide refugees continued to grow almost every year. So did the demand for U.S. resources to support refugees and for U.S. resettlement spots to accept those refugees who wanted and needed to come to the United States.

Most of the new refugee flows during the 1960s and 1970s were in places where the United States had no national interest and where there had been very little if any U.S. involvement before the new states had become independent and before the refugee crises. Some refugees, as from Biafra, Uganda, Zaire, Rwanda, and Burundi, were created by colonial conflicts, by postcolonial ethnic wars, and by the actions of dictators within new African states. Others, as in the creation of Bangladesh (formerly East Pakistan), resulted from a mixture of ethnic and political factors. Whatever the reasons, U.S. resources were needed and had to be shifted from earlier areas of concentration. It also proved increasingly necessary to offer assistance to refugees in asylum countries who could not offer protection without such aid. By the mid-1960s, the U.S. government was contributing more funds to rapidly expanding UNHCR operations in Africa than to the shrinking needs of European refugees. But some problems involved U.S. interests very directly. The rising surge of refugees from Fidel Castro's Cuba raised a consistent demand for direct asylum in the United States during the 1960s and 1970s, with a total of more than half a million Cuban refugees coming to the United States by the end of the 1970s. There was also a growing U.S. concern during the late 1960s and during the 1970s about refugee flows created by Soviet involvement in such newly independent African states as Mozambique and Somalia. As these crises unfolded, U.S. political and humanitarian interests began to coincide in developing countries as they had earlier coincided in Europe, and the United States dedicated itself to supporting international operations not only to help refugees but also to help protect the states that neighbored on the new allies of the Soviet Union.

U.S. interest also focused increasingly on Indochina and especially on Vietnam. After the French defeat at Dien Bien Phu in 1954 and the creation of separate North and South Vietnamese states, the United States had helped South Vietnam to accept and integrate the million refugees that came from North Vietnam. After 1975, when the United States was itself defeated in Vietnam, the U.S. Congress approved asylum for 150,000 refugees from South Vietnam. About 130,000 came during 1975, and other smaller numbers arrived during 1976 and 1977. By the end of the 1970s, the refugee problem had become a crisis for the United States and for the world as a whole. In Vietnam, the communist government in 1978 began a thorough and brutal campaign against any private property. This campaign included collectivization of agriculture and nationalization of commerce. Property holders at any level were subject to harsh and immediate punishment. Almost simultaneously, Vietnamese forces invaded Cambodia. Within weeks, the South China Sea was filled with what became known as the "boat people," desperate refugees trying to go to any country that would grant them asylum. Such Southeast Asian states as Thailand or Malaysia were prepared to grant first asylum to these refugees only if the United States and other Western nations would agree to accept them for permanent resettlement. The following year, crises erupted in the Caribbean, as Fidel Castro chose to permit Cubans who wanted to emigrate to the United States to be picked up at the Cuban port of Mariel by any boats ready to carry them. That flow of refugees was matched by thousands from Haiti. The United States reluctantly became a country of first asylum, as Haitians and Cubans clogged the waters around Florida. But it soon became clear that Castro was not only permitting refugees to leave but was also sending inmates of his prisons and psychiatric clinics to the United States. At the same time, war broke out between Somalia and Ethiopia as Somalia tried to seize parts of Ethiopia where ethnic Somalis lived. With Soviet support, Ethiopia won a decisive victory and over a million Somali ethnics who had lived in Ethiopia fled toward Somalia. The Ethiopian government also launched campaigns against ethnic minorities in its northern provinces, compelling half a million members of those minorities to flee to Sudan. In 1979, the Soviet Union invaded Afghanistan in support of a regime that it had installed in a coup d'etat in 1978. Over five million refugees fled, with more than three million going to Pakistan and the remainder to Iran. They became the world's largest group of refugees. They also needed the most support because they settled in desolate areas where almost every essential for existence had to be supplied from outside.

The combination of these crises vastly expanded U.S. involvement in global refugee affairs and brought them very close to home. It also provided a powerful political impetus for refugee support, for the new major groups of refugees had fled from communist and Soviet-supported regimes. President Jimmy Carter established a new office, the U.S. Coordinator for Refugee Affairs, to try to provide coherent leadership in a crisis that involved not only vast new overseas expenditures but that also included new inflows of refugees to the United States from the Caribbean and from the countries of first asylum in Southeast Asia. The U.S. Congress agreed to admit 14,000 refugees a month from Southeast Asia. It also permitted the president to grant asylum to Cubans and Haitians, but the president and Congress made clear that they would not permit the Mariel boat flow to continue. The United States, as in the past, wanted some control over the persons it would admit. Engulfed by the crises and recognizing that refugees had become a global phenomenon driven by many different kinds of circumstances, the United States in the 1980 Refugee and Migration Act for the first time in U.S. legislation used the global UN definition of a refugee instead of the earlier definition that had been based upon flight from communist and communist-dominated states and initially concentrated on Europe. The Refugee Act also initially allowed a specific quota of 50,000 refugee admissions per year. It permitted higher numbers under special circumstances, and the numbers have been higher than 50,000 in every year since the passage of the act largely because of refugees from Indochina.

During the 1980s, the United States, other states, the UNHCR, and the international voluntary agencies concentrated their combined efforts on trying to sustain the new refugee populations and, wherever possible, either to resettle them in other states or to encourage some form of local settlement. Immediate refugee needs could be met but few refugees could permanently escape from camp life except for those Indochinese chosen for resettlement in the West. The UNHCR annual budget remained at one-half billion dollars during much of the decade, with the U.S. contribution at about $150 million. The number of Vietnamese and Cambodian refugees in Southeast Asia was slowly reduced, largely because the United States accepted three-quarters of a million dollars for resettlement. As the Ethiopian government lost its ideological absolutism and made peace with ethnic groups, most of the refugees in Sudan and Somalia were able to return home. The Soviets left Afghanistan in 1988 but only limited numbers of refugees returned until the regime that Moscow had installed was defeated in 1992. The collapse of communism at the end of the 1980s led many U.S. government officials and international refugee offices to hope that the global refugee crisis was over. As events developed, those hopes proved ill-founded.

New crises erupted. The ethnic wars in Yugoslavia, further upheavals in Somalia, a civil war in Rwanda, and other upsurges of refugees combined to demand urgent U.S. attention and resources. Ethnic minorities in Iraq were being persecuted by the central government in Baghdad, even after that government had been defeated by U.S. and other forces in the Gulf War. By 1994, the UNHCR budget had risen to over $1.5 billion and the U.S. refugee budget to almost half a billion dollars. The United States also found itself faced with the threat of more refugees from Haiti and even with a resumption of boat people coming from Cuba with Castro's encouragement. The United States also had to contemplate a further expansion of the refugee mandate. Whereas in the past it had always been assumed that persons could only be considered refugees if they were forced to flee their home country, the new ethnic wars created refugees who might still be theoretically within the protection of their government but who were actually under severe political and even military threat. Bosnian Muslims within the borders of Bosnia were driven from their homes by Bosnian Serbs. Hutus and Tutsis in Rwanda were decimating each other within their common borders as central authority evaporated. Refugees had to be assisted and protected, sometimes by U.S. military forces, even within what was theoretically their home country. And they were being attacked not by communist-led forces or even by forces from another country but by their fellow citizens. This raised new problems for U.S. refugee policy. The

guiding principle of anticommunism that had initially led to U.S. support of refugees during the 1940s and 1950s and that had animated much of U.S. refugee policy during the Cold War had lost its pertinence. Instead, new groups of refugees were being driven by local considerations that mattered little to most U.S. citizens and that were often far removed from the U.S. national interest. Yet the United States was more engaged than ever. U.S. forces, U.S. aid personnel, and U.S. resources were committed in refugee areas in Europe and Africa and were on guard in Iraq. In Rwanda, the U.S. military tried to facilitate relief operations and to make sure that supplies could reach refugees. In Bosnia, the U.S. Air Force and Navy bombed Bosnian Serb forces in order to block Serb military operations that could generate additional refugee flows. In the post–Cold War world in which the United States was the world's only superpower, U.S. forces found themselves not only protecting refugees in place but also trying to prevent others from having to flee. As the Cold War ended, the United States was trying to develop a coherent refugee policy that would serve humanitarian objectives, coincide with the national interest, generate public and Congressional support, and remain within the tight U.S. budget.

Current U.S. Policies

The United States, a nation of immigrants and refugees, has done more than any other state to support refugees worldwide. U.S. contributions to international refugee organizations have consistently been the highest of any nation on a total basis although not on a per capita basis (an honor held by the Scandinavians). The United States has generally contributed about one-third of the funds going to UNHCR, although the share has slipped below a third from time to time, and it has also been highest in contributions to UNRWA and IOM. In 1993, U.S. contributions amounted to over $500 million, far above that of any other state. Because of the U.S. role in funding, as well as because of the large U.S. interest in refugee matters across the board, the deputy positions in both UNHCR and UNRWA have usually been held by U.S. citizens. At IOM, a more operational and less politically sensitive agency, a U.S. citizen has usually been the director. The United States has not only been the principal contributor to UNHCR and to other international refugee agencies, but it has also consistently accepted the largest number of refugees for permanent resettlement. The number of refugees resettled per year reached a peak in 1980, when over 200,000 came to the United States—most of them from Indochina. It then leveled off between 60,000 and 80,000 for several years, but in the early 1990s again rose to over 100,000 per year. As most of the refugees coming to the United States come from warmer climates, relatively few have resettled in New

England or in the Northern Plains States such as the Dakotas. Most resettled in warm climates in California, Texas, and Florida.

The United States has taken account of political as well as humanitarian factors in its support for refugees as well as in the resettlement opportunities it offers. Although the 1980 Refugee and Migration Act had adopted the global UN definition of a refugee, refugees from communist countries such as Vietnam or the former Soviet Union were much more likely to be admitted to the United States than refugees from an African dictatorship. The U.S. government and U.S. courts were more likely to grant asylum to refugees from Fidel Castro in Cuba or from the Sandinista regime in Nicaragua than to refugees from Central American military dictatorships. During the spill of refugees over much of the Middle East after the Gulf War of 1990–1991, the United States provided only very limited aid to refugees in Iran, a state that the United States regarded as unfriendly, but provided considerable aid to Turkey, a U.S. ally. These and other U.S. actions have long led to complaints that U.S. refugee policy was guided more by political than by humanitarian considerations. Those complaints had some merit, as U.S. aid for refugees from communism served U.S. political as well as humanitarian purposes. On the other hand, because of U.S. support of UNHCR general programs, U.S. dollars often went to persons who had fled from governments friendly to the United States—and whom those governments regarded as terrorists or guerrillas. Generally, U.S. political preferences showed themselves more in U.S. admissions policies than in U.S. assistance policies, largely because admissions policies are under direct national control whereas decisions about assistance are usually made by international organizations carrying out a global mandate. Some African-American groups have complained that U.S. admissions and resettlement policies militate against black refugees, as the United States has not only rejected most Haitian requests for asylum but has rarely taken more than several thousand African refugees for resettlement in any given year. To this, the U.S. government has replied that those Africans who would be most likely to find resettlement places in the United States are precisely those that are most needed at home, and that bringing them to the United States would constitute a brain drain. It has thus been reluctant to resettle persons that had any chance of going home. Moreover, most African states—unlike the states of Southeast Asia—were prepared to offer protection to refugees without resettlement provisions. African refugees wanted to return home, and were expected to do so as soon as possible, rather than to move to the West.

The United States, as if to make up for its neglect of Jewish refugees from Hitler, as well as at the urging of Jewish opinion leaders, has helped to further the emigration of Jews to Israel from several areas. Washington played a key role in urging the Soviet Union to release Russian Jews. Jewish emigration was a constant theme for U.S. negotiators with Soviet officials from the 1960s through the 1980s. Many of the Russian Jews later chose to go to the United States instead of going to Israel. The United States also discreetly supported the emigration of Falasha Jews to Israel from Ethiopia, often arranging airlifts to bring large groups out of Ethiopia on an emergency basis while persuading Ethiopian authorities to look the other way. The U.S. government has favored voluntary repatriation of refugees whenever and wherever possible, even on occasion to areas of communist control such as Vietnam. It has given special financial support to UNHCR programs which served that purpose and has tried to help arrange voluntary repatriation programs wherever they seemed compatible with refugee interests. As a second preference, it has favored local settlement of refugees in the country of first asylum or nearby. It has especially favored that option in Africa, where many refugees fled for ethnic rather than political reasons and could establish themselves with some support in neighboring countries governed by compatible ethnic groups.

The United States has never wanted to be a country of first asylum. Like other states, it wants to keep its borders inviolable and it wants to select those persons it permits to enter. This attitude was especially reflected during the 1970s and 1990s with respect to refugees from Haiti and Cuba. The United States was also determined not to grant permanent asylum to most refugees from Central America who had entered the United States. Because U.S. courts have been more generous than the U.S. government toward some groups of refugees, and because a good immigration lawyer could generally prolong a proceeding for several years until asylum applicants had fully established themselves in the United States or had melted into the general population, the U.S. government has tried hard to stop entrants at its borders. It has also tried to conduct refugee processing at places like Guantanamo Naval Base in Cuba, where the asylum applicants and alleged refugees were not fully on U.S. soil. Wherever possible, the U.S. government has tried to avoid having refugees take to boats or go to a first asylum country in the first place. It has, wherever possible, tried to make arrangements under which potential refugees could apply for entry to the United States even before they had left their home states. This was especially important in Vietnam, where the United States wanted to facilitate entry for persons who had helped U.S. forces and had been punished in prison or re-education camps. U.S. negotiations were finally successful in the late 1980s, and by the early 1990s almost half the refugees coming to the United States from Vietnam were coming directly through the

Orderly Departure Program instead of first having to go to first asylum countries as boat people.

As the record of U.S. policy toward refugees shows, the U.S. government is continually called upon to make decisions regarding refugee protection, assistance, admissions, and resettlement. It must also decide what support to offer refugees after they have arrived in the United States. Most of those decisions can be made on a humanitarian basis but they can be complicated by political considerations. All have political consequences, intentional or not, because they affect not only large numbers of persons but also many states. They also involve significant amounts of relief and resettlement funds. Because many refugee groups are linked to segments of the U.S. population, decisions on refugee affairs receive close domestic as well as international scrutiny. Many U.S. agencies become involved in the decision process. In the White House, the National Security Council (NSC) as well as the Office of Management and Budget can play key roles in deciding who is to be supported, who is to be admitted, and what funding levels will be forwarded to the U.S. Congress. The issues are sensitive enough that the president may have to decide them himself, and he must do so if U.S. armed forces or the Coast Guard are to be deployed.

The Department of State, through the Bureau for Refugee Programs (RP), is the principal agency for supporting refugee protection measures and for deciding among various relief and resettlement programs. It maintains contact with international agencies and foreign governments interested in refugee matters. It has specially assigned specialists in refugee affairs at embassies in major refugee areas—as in Thailand, Sudan, or Honduras—as well as in missions to international refugee organizations. The director of RP prepares the annual statement to Congress proposing the numbers of refugees to be resettled in the United States, but the statement will normally be presented at the cabinet or subcabinet level. The Department of Justice, through the INS, makes the final determination about what specific persons are to be admitted or rejected for entry to the United States. It also decides which asylum applicants already in the United States may remain, a decision that is often subject to challenge in the courts. The Department of Health and Human Services, through the Office of Refugee Resettlement (ORR), finances federal government assistance programs for refugees. The U.S. Congress, through its control over the budget, ultimately decides refugee programs as well as the numbers and groups of refugees to be resettled. Several Senate and House committees become involved, and Congress as a whole follows refugee policy closely. Individual members of Congress may also concentrate great attention on refugee matters because of their own or their constituents' interest.

Because of countless disputes among the agencies regarding levels of refugee assistance and numbers of refugees to be resettled, President Jimmy Carter in 1979 established the position of U.S. Coordinator for Refugee Affairs to facilitate a common policy. But the office never functioned as intended, in part because it was physically located in the Department of State instead of at the White House and thus did not carry the authority of being on the president's immediate staff. After several incumbents failed to carry out the original mandate, the office was left vacant after 1993. The Department of State attached the RP bureau to the new office of Undersecretary of State for Global Affairs who is to coordinate refugee policy with other worldwide U.S. actions abroad. Outside the U.S. government itself, other organizations also play a role in U.S. refugee policy. The separate states have an intense interest in resettlement levels because they must pay for many services for refugees—such as schools, infrastructure, and some aid programs. The major voluntary agencies, most of which are active in the United States as well as internationally, not only receive government funding to support their refugee services but contribute funds of their own as well as their members' freely volunteered time. Many of them have a broad humanitarian purpose but some have special interests in one or another group of refugees for ethnic or religious reasons.

U.S. refugee policy reflects this mix of sometimes cooperative and sometimes conflicting interests, groups, and personalities. It also reflects both humanitarian and political attitudes. Out of the complex process, the United States has emerged as the world's largest provider and supporter of refugee protection, assistance, and resettlement.

W. R. SMYSER

See also Cuba; Haiti; Immigration; Vietnam War

FURTHER READING

Breitman, Richard, and Alan M. Kraut. *American Refugee Policy and European Jewry 1933–1945.* Bloomington, Ind., 1987.
Gallagher, Dennis, ed. "Refugees: Issues and Directions." Special issue of *International Migration Review,* 20 (Summer 1986).
Goodwin-Gill, Guy S. *The Refugee in International Law.* Oxford, 1988.
Gorman, Robert F. *Mitigating Misery.* Lanham, Md., 1993.
Holborn, Louise W. *Refugees: A Problem of Our Time,* 2 vols. Metuchen, N.J., 1975.
Kritz, Mary M. *U.S. Immigration and Refugee Policy.* Lexington, Mass., 1983.
Loescher, Gil. *Beyond Charity.* New York, 1993.
Marrus, Michael R. *The Unwanted: European Refugees in the Twentieth Century.* New York, 1985.
Rogers, Rosemarie, and Emily Copeland. *Forced Migration: Policy Issues in the Post–Cold War World.* Medford, Mass., 1993.
Smyser, W. R. *Refugees.* New York, 1987.